W9-BYU-734

ENCYCLOPEDIA OF
URBAN CULTURES

ENCYCLOPEDIA OF
URBAN CULTURES

Editors

Melvin Ember • President, Human Relations Area Files
Yale University

Carol R. Ember • Executive Director, Human Relations Area Files
Yale University

Advisory Board

Sandra T. Barnes • University of Pennsylvania
Theodore C. Bestor • Harvard University
D. Douglas Caulkins • Grinnell College
Dean Forbes • Flinders University
Josef Gugler • University of Connecticut
Karen Tranberg Hansen • Northwestern University
Robert V. Kemper • Southern Methodist University
Owen M. Lynch • New York University
Gary McDonogh • Bryn Mawr College
Sharon Nagy • DePaul University
Peter Nas • Leiden University
Deborah Pellow • Syracuse University
Antonius C. Robben • Utrecht University
Robert Rotenberg • DePaul University
David Satterthwaite • International Institute for Environment and Development
Norman E. Whitten, Jr. • University of Illinois, Urbana-Champaign

ENCYCLOPEDIA OF URBAN CULTURES

CITIES AND CULTURES AROUND THE WORLD

PUBLISHED UNDER THE AUSPICES OF THE
HUMAN RELATIONS AREA FILES AT YALE UNIVERSITY

EDITED BY
MELVIN EMBER AND CAROL R. EMBER

Volume 3

A Scholastic Company
Danbury, Connecticut

WINGATE UNIVERSITY LIBRARY

Copyright © 2002 by Human Relations Area Files, Inc.

This work was prepared under the auspices and with the support of the Human Relations Area Files, Inc. (HRAF) at Yale University. The foremost international research organization in the field of cultural anthropology, HRAF is a not-for-profit consortium of 19 Sponsoring Member institutions and more than 400 active and inactive Associate Member institutions in nearly 40 countries. The mission of HRAF is to provide information that facilitates the cross-cultural study of human behavior, society, and culture. The HRAF Collection of Ethnography, which has been building since 1949, contains nearly 1 million pages of information, indexed according to more than 700 subject categories, on the cultures of the world. An increasing portion of the Collection of Ethnography, which now covers more than 365 cultures, is accessible via the World Wide Web to member institutions. The HRAF Collection of Archaeology, the first installment of which appeared in 1999, also is accessible on the Web to those member institutions opting to receive it.

All rights reserved. No part of this book may be reproduced or transmitted in any form or by any means—graphic, electronic, or mechanical, including photocopying, taping, or information storage and retrieval systems—without prior written permission of the publisher.

Published by Grolier Publishing Co., Inc., 90 Sherman Turnpike, Danbury, CT 06816.

Library of Congress Cataloging-in-Publication Data

Encyclopedia of urban cultures: cities and cultures around the world/edited by Melvin Ember and Carol R. Ember.
p. cm.
Includes bibliographical references and index.
ISBN 0-7172-5698-7 (lib. bdg. : alk. paper)
1. Cities and towns--Encyclopedias. 2. Sociology, Urban--Encyclopedias. I. Title: Urban cultures. II. Ember, Melvin. III. Ember, Carol R.

HT108.5 .E53 2002
307.76'03--dc21

Printed and Manufactured in the
United States of America

1 3 5 4 2

ENCYCLOPEDIA OF
URBAN CULTURES

La Paz

Bolivia

ORIENTATION

Name of City. La Paz—or Chukiyawu as it is known to thousands of indigenous Aymara residents—is the administrative capital of Bolivia, a South American nation of some 8 million inhabitants. Founded by the Spanish conquistadores, the city was christened La Ciudad de Nuestra Señora de La Paz (City of Our Lady of Peace) in 1548.

Location. The city is located at 16°30′ south latitude and 68°9′ west longitude. At 3,650 meters (11,975 feet) above sea level, La Paz is the highest capital city in the world.

Distinctive and Unique Features. The city center nestles on the side of a steep canyon below a vast expanse of treeless plain called the *altiplano,* or high plateau, which surrounds La Paz on the west and south. The canyon protects city dwellers from the cold winds that sweep off the Andes Mountains, and it is dominated by the snowcapped Mount Illimani, a majestic 6,458-meter (21,188-foot) peak that looms over La Paz's eastern flank. Temperatures in the city center range from average highs of 15°C (59°F) in the dry winter months (May–October) to 22°C (72°F) in the summer rainy season (November–April), but they vary considerably with altitude.

Population. The population of La Paz is approximately 500,000; as it is difficult to get accurate census information in Bolivia, all numbers are estimates. The influence of indigenous peoples, especially the Aymara, is felt more strongly in La Paz than in any other capital city of the Americas. The Aymara have shaped a vibrant urban culture that is best symbolized by the elegant *chola paceña,* an urban Aymara woman noted for her wide pleated skirts (*pollera*), bowler hat, elegant shawl, and long braided hair. On the sidewalks of the city center, these women mingle with briefcase-toting businessmen, fashionably coiffed ladies in high heels, foreign tourists, students, politicians, and rural peasants. They also dominate the commercial activity in many of La Paz's marketplaces, where city residents purchase a wide variety of fruits, vegetables, meats, dairy products, and household goods.

HISTORY

The Origin of the City. La Paz was strategically located in one of the most densely settled Indian areas of the Andes, and it served as a center from which the Spaniards controlled the labor of indigenous peoples and the agricultural resources of the surrounding hinterland. The Spaniards tore the fabric of indigenous social life by forcing Indian laborers to work in agricultural activities, textile mills, silver mines, and urban households. The social ruptures dramatically reconfigured Andean society and created continual strife between native Andeans and the Spanish overlords. Simmering tensions erupted into a major indigenous rebellion against Spanish rule in 1781, when Indian rebels, led by Tupac Catari, encircled La Paz and besieged the city for several months. The Spaniards eventually put down the uprising and executed Catari, but despite the defeat of the insurgents, the revolt remained an important point of reference for both indigenous and nonindigenous peoples, who continue to interpret its significance in different ways today.

By the early 19th century, La Paz was the largest city in the colonial district of Upper Peru, and its Creole elite had begun to chafe at the restrictive trade policies imposed by the Spanish crown. In 1809 rebels led by Pedro Domingo Murillo took control of the local government and declared independence from Spain. Their actions represented the first declaration of independence by a Spanish colony, and they prompted a long series of independence wars in the Americas that lasted from 1809 to 1825. Bolivia emerged as an independent nation in 1825, and the southern city of Sucre became the first Bolivian capital.

Migration: Past and Present. La Paz displaced Sucre at the end of the 19th century, when the emergent tin-mining industry placed it at the center of Bolivia's economic and social life, and La Paz remained the preeminent Bolivian city throughout the 20th century. It grew from a mere 178,000 inhabitants in 1950 to a burgeoning metropolis of more than 1 million people at the turn of the millennium. Rural-to-urban migration accounted for the majority of this growth. Steadily eroding rural living conditions prompted an average of 10,000 men and women to migrate to La Paz every year between 1965 and 1975. Many peasants had received small parcels of land after a 1953 agrarian reform broke up large estates and redistributed the land to former estate workers and indigenous communities. In subsequent years, however, inheritance fragmented these landholdings, and subsistence agriculture became increasingly unsustainable on diminishing parcels of land. A series of civilian and military governments further aggravated the plight of peasant families by ignoring their needs for technical assistance, loans, and price supports. Government officials directed federal assistance and international loans to large-scale agroindustrial producers of cotton, sugarcane, cattle, and soybeans in the eastern lowlands, where large estates remained untouched by the land reform. Not surprisingly, the flood of immigrants that flowed to La Paz during the 1960s and 1970s did not abate, and La Paz continued to grow at an annual rate that hovered around 5%.

INFRASTRUCTURE

The physical expansion of La Paz took place in two directions: upward and downward. During the 1960s and 1970s rural immigrants constructed new neighborhoods on the steep canyon walls above the city center. Neighborhoods such as Alto Chijini, Munaypata, and Villa Dolores sprouted up at elevations above 3,658 meters (12,000 feet), and some became thriving commercial entrepôts. The growing urban population eventually burst out of the canyon that had contained La Paz for centuries. New settlements developed on the altiplano in an area called El Alto, which by the 1980s was receiving the vast majority of new immigrants. On this cold plateau located more than 3,962 meters (13,000 feet) above sea level, nighttime temperatures in the winter months frequently dipped below freezing, and the rarefied air

© OWEN FRANKEN/CORBIS

Two women in traditional dress walk down a street in La Paz, Bolivia.

and cold winds frequently neutralized the warmth of the intense daytime sunshine.

As in many other Latin American cities, the municipal government ignored the burgeoning immigrant population. The residents of El Alto had significantly less access to social services than many of their counterparts in La Paz, but as they began to flex their political muscles in the 1980s, municipal officials increasingly perceived them as a threat to social stability and feared their potential impact on urban politics. They granted autonomous status to El Alto in 1989, and La Paz's impoverished sibling became a city in its own right. El Alto, with a population of 551,528 people, was the fourth-largest city in Bolivia by the start of the 21st century, and some inhabitants referred to it as the "Aymara capital of the world." It was also Bolivia's poorest city. The 1990 census classified 73% of El Alto households as poor, while 45% of La Paz households were so designated.

CULTURAL AND SOCIAL LIFE

Ethnic, Class, and Religious Diversity. As impoverished Aymara immigrants created new neighborhoods in the upper elevations of La Paz and El Alto, high-ranking government bureaucrats, prosperous businesspeople, and professionals moved out of the city center and constructed exclusive neighborhoods in the warmer, lower parts of the canyon. A number of North Americans and Europeans associated with embassies and international-development agencies joined them. Obrajes, a textile center in the colonial period; San Miguel; and Calacoto became exclusive redoubts of the upper class in the 1970s, but they were surpassed in subsequent decades by newer, and frequently more ostentatious, suburbs that penetrated ever lower into the canyon. Residents invariably surrounded their large, spacious homes with high walls that, in many cases, were built with shards of broken glass embedded along the tops. In the 1990s one of these exclusive enclaves, Valle de Aranjuez, became the city's first gated community. Following trends in other Latin American cities, residents posted security guards at the entrance to the neighborhood and limited access to homeowners and those with special permission.

Wealth and poverty, then, are inversely correlated with altitude in La Paz. So, too, is ethnicity. In the city's lowest reaches, the wealthiest inhabitants speak Spanish and define themselves as *blanco* (white) or *criollo*, a term that denotes European ancestry. In the city's highest neighborhoods, the poorest residents are either rural-born Aymara speakers, who speak Spanish as a second language, or they are second- and third-generation urban dwellers. Affluent residents of the city refer to immigrants as *indios* (Indians) or *cholos*. *Indio* is a derogatory term that denotes racial inferiority. It refers to rural dwellers who cultivate the land, speak an indigenous language, and labor for others. *Cholo* is a much more complex category. It denotes people of mixed racial and cultural heritage who speak some Spanish and wear Western-style clothing, and it represents a vaguely defined cultural and social frontier between the racial divisions of *indios* and *blancos*. Although many whites struggle to uphold the power and privilege upon which this classificatory schema is based, the boundaries that separate *indios, cholos,* and *blancos* are constantly contested, as people struggle in their daily lives over access to resources and cultural symbols.

The shifting terrain of urban ethnic politics is aptly illustrated by the city's rich and diverse religious life. Although Catholicism is the dominant religion in La Paz, as in the rest of Bolivia and Latin America, it is not practiced and understood the same way by everyone. The annual festival that commemorates the patron saint of Gran Poder (May–June) displays a dynamic form of folk Catholicism associated with an upwardly mobile, self-consciously Aymara group of entrepreneurs. These businesspeople are meat sellers, transporters, and wholesalers of all types of household appliances who immigrated to La Paz and established the neighborhood of Gran Poder in the 1960s. They have since acquired significant wealth and a measure of political power, but, because of their immigrant backgrounds, they are spurned by white society and excluded from its most prestigious institutions. Sponsorship of the various festivities that honor Gran Poder's patron saint, however, is one way that these individuals demonstrate their newly accumulated wealth, garner the respect of others like themselves, and demonstrate their commitment to an urban Aymara version of popular culture.

A lavish parade featuring musicians and colorful native-dance groups highlights the celebration. The participants include devil dancers performing the *diablada*, whip-wielding slave drivers dancing the *caporales*, young women clad in mini-*polleras*, and musicians pounding on drums and blasting away on tubas. The performers are generally urban-born or longtime city residents and not recent arrivals from the countryside. They practice for weeks before the parade. Their elaborate costumes crafted by local artisans are extremely expensive, and each dance group therefore needs at least one sponsor.

The parade was for years strictly a neighborhood attraction. It followed a circuitous route through the steep, narrow streets of Gran Poder and contained a relatively small number of participants. In the mid-1970s, however, the parade underwent a major transformation that coincided with the consolidation of the economic power of Gran Poder's aspiring Aymara residents. The number of dance groups burgeoned, and the parade penetrated the heart of white-ruled La Paz, where it flowed for hours along the Prado Boulevard through the central business district, until finally dispersing at the Plaza del Estudiante. Municipal authorities, politicians, and non-Aymara business leaders took notice of the event and tried to use it for personal and political gain. By the 1990s the parade had also become a major tourist attraction.

This highly visual, flamboyant, and expensive display of urban Aymara culture is inaccessible to the vast majority of rural immigrants, who, unlike their wealthier counterparts, lack the means to craft such a costly and highly public version of urban Aymara ethnicity. The economic situation of most immigrants fails to improve in the city, and "Aymara-ness" remains associated with rural poverty, backwardness, and being "Indian." As immigrants, who are nominally Catholic, search for solutions to their social and economic problems, and as established institutions fail to adequately address their suffering, many find temporary relief in a variety of Christian fundamentalist churches that have sprouted up in the poor neighborhoods.

The churches include the Baptists, the Jehovah's Witnesses, and the Seventh-Day Adventists, but Pentecostals are by far the most numerous. Sometimes the churches operate from converted garages or storefronts, but in the case of the Seventh-Day Adventists, they occupy more-elaborate premises. The growth of these congregations is due less to the displacement of Catholic churches than to the expansion of newer chruches into areas where the Catholic Church has had little presence. Nowadays it is easy to walk through an immigrant neighborhood in the evening or on Sunday morning and hear the strains of guitar music and prayer emanating from a variety of diverse religious gatherings.

Pentecostal *cultos,* or worship services, are the most common forms of worship. They are ecstatic events characterized by music, singing, and praying, and they are intensely participatory occasions that bring together groups of 20 to 100 people several times a week. Congregants receive the healing power of the Holy Spirit by testifying and collectively cleansing themselves of sin. The *cultos* provide residents—particularly new immigrants and women—with an institutional setting in which to build and reaffirm new social relationships. Unlike folk Catholicism, which encourages the worship of saints and sanctions fiestas in their honor, Pentecostalism discourages the worship of intermediaries and encourages believers to establish a direct relationship with God through self-sacrifice and upright living. Those who have encountered God testify about their experience in highly emotional accounts. Yet the effects of these religious encounters often fade with time. People may move on to another church with a slightly different message, and there is considerable religious mobility in La Paz as people struggle to find meaning in their lives and to define a place for themselves in the city. Yet affiliating with different religious groups has not provided impoverished urban dwellers with solutions to their severe economic problems, and La Paz is currently balkanized into pockets of wealth and vast areas of poverty.

A deep depression in the 1980s aggravated class differentiation, and the free-market policies of successive governments since 1985 further accentuated class differences. These policies froze wages, pushed more women into the workforce, and obliged people to work longer hours to satisfy their basic necessities. They also eliminated many state-sponsored social services, such as food and transportation subsidies, and privatized others, such as health care, telecommunications, sanitation, and mining. The result was that many people no longer had access to basic social services, while others, who could afford the expense, paid higher rates for services that in many cases remained inadequate. At the same time, lower tariff barriers on imported goods generated an influx of cheap imports that undercut local producers and drove more people deeper into poverty. The most dramatic result of the free-market revolution, however, was a spectacular influx of impoverished, Quechua-speaking miners to La Paz, after the government closed state-operated tin mines and forced thousands of people out of work.

Impoverished immigrants scrape together a living through a variety of low-paid, insecure forms of work. Men labor as part-time construction workers, cargo carriers, night watchmen, street vendors, gardeners, and so forth. Women face fewer options; the vast majority occupy themselves in street vending and domestic service. Street vending has become so common that during rush hour, the sidewalks in the city center are completely clogged with vendors. The number of sellers who participate in officially sanctioned urban street fairs has also burgeoned. The huge biweekly fair in El Alto's Villa 16 de Julio, for example, contains more than 10,000 registered participants. Most of the vendors sell small quantities of fruits, vegetables, and used clothing. They have little chance of acquiring more stable, highly paid employment in the city's small manufacturing sector, because many local factories went bankrupt after the government's turn to free-market policies.

QUALITY OF LIFE

To alleviate the city's deepening poverty, a number of nominally private, internationally financed nongovernmental organizations (NGOs) have sprouted up in La Paz and have partially filled the void left by retreating state social-service agencies. A veritable explosion of NGOs took place in La Paz and El Alto during the 1980s. Although assessing the actual numbers of NGOs is difficult, there were, according to conservative estimates, 40 in El Alto by the mid-1990s, and many more were based in La Paz. Some operated small-scale projects in a variety of locations around the country; others focused their services specifically on La Paz and El Alto. All targeted small groups of individuals in poor neighborhoods or rural communities, and typically provided a range of different services that, in urban areas, included basic health care, adult literacy classes, small loans, and business development. The NGOs argued that, because of their experience with small-scale, local-level development, they were more in touch with the poor and more administratively agile than bureaucratic state agencies. Critics claimed, however, that NGOs could address the needs of only a limited number of people, and that they were therefore a poor substitute for a democratically managed citywide development initiative. In addition, critics charged that the NGOs controlled huge amounts of international-development funds and implemented projects with no local or national accountability. By the end of the 1990s, however, NGOs had replaced state agencies as the principal vehicles through which urban poverty was addressed, and they had become an important source of employment for middle-class professionals.

Yet despite the best efforts of nongovernmental organizations, La Paz, and especially El Alto, remain examples of what is problematic with the global economy. Fiscal-austerity measures have not only made social and economic life more precarious for the city's poor majority, they have also left public schools to deteriorate, and made affordable, quality health care even less available than in the past. The brief reappearance, in 1991, of cholera—a 19th-century plague that was once thought to have been eliminated—is not surprising, given that there are only two doctors in El Alto for every thousand residents.

With the deregulation of the public-transportation system in the early 1990s, a flood of minibuses replaced large, lumbering buses, or *colectivos,* as the primary means of urban transportation. Although nowadays one can easily hail a minibus in the city center, where a number of routes converge, getting hold of a minibus in the more distant immigrant communities is not so straightforward. Fewer routes service these areas, and when a minibus arrives, it is frequently full. There is also no system of bus transfers, which means that riders must frequently pay twice, and lax fare regulation and fierce competition between drivers gives rise to quixotic rate fluctuations in certain parts of the city.

Mind-numbing traffic jams have also become a serious problem in La Paz over the past 15 years, and they have made air pollution a growing issue. Severe traffic congestion wastes people's time and considerably lengthens their workdays. For example, a gardener traveling from a new immigrant neighborhood in El Alto to a job in the wealthy suburbs of lower La Paz can easily spend 90 minutes to two hours in transit. Affluent residents must also contend with long traffic delays, although they usually travel shorter distances to jobs in the city center. A fleet of taxis and *truffis*—collective taxis that follow a fixed route—in addition to the ubiquitous minibuses, service the needs of these individuals.

As in many large Latin American cities, there is a widespread perception in La Paz that crime is getting worse. People are dissatisfied with the police force, and complaints of police ineffectiveness are widespread. City dwellers from all social backgrounds believe that police officers are less interested in protecting citizens than in separating them from their money through fines and the extraction of bribes. Yet compared to other large cities in North and South America, violent crime is not widespread in La Paz and El Alto. This is because few people own guns. The homicide rate is therefore very low, and the urban police do not regularly use deadly force against criminal suspects.

The government, however, is often quick to criminalize people who demonstrate against its highly unpopular policies, and it frequently deploys the police and the military to contain popular discontentment. Indeed, street demonstrations against the wave of privatizations and government cutbacks have became almost a daily affair in La Paz, and because La Paz is the seat of government, contentious national issues are played out in the city as well. Peasant coca growers from the Chapare region of Cochabamba department, for example, have repeatedly marched on La Paz to express their displeasure with government initiatives to eradicate coca cultivation, which is their primary source of income.

Bolivian demonstrators find themselves on the cutting edge of a growing worldwide movement against the ravages of what is widely referred to as globalization, a euphemism for unfettered capitalism. Unlike the U.S. demonstrators who closed down the Seattle meeting of the World Trade Organization in November 1999, these impoverished people have not captured international headlines. Yet they are the ones who experience most intensely the depredations of the new global society. The future of La Paz will depend to a considerable extent upon the ways in which their grievances and problems are addressed.

BIBLIOGRAPHY

Albó, Xavier, et al., *Chukiyawu: La Cara Aymara de La Paz: El Paso a la Ciudad, Cuaderno de Investigación,* 1, no. 20 (Centro de Investigación y Promoción del Campesino 1981).

Albó, Xavier, et al., *Chukiyawu: La Cara Aymara de La Paz: Una Odisea: Buscar Pega, Cuaderno de Investigación,* 2, no. 22 (Centro de Investigación y Promoción del Campesino 1982).

Albó, Xavier, et al., *Chukiyawu: La Cara Aymara de La Paz: Cabalgando Entre dos Mundos, Cuaderno de Investigación,* 3, no. 24 (Centro de Investigación y Promoción del Campesino 1983).

Albó, Xavier, et al., *Chukiyawu: La Cara Aymara de La Paz: Nuevos Lazos con el Campo, Cuaderno de Investigación,* 4, no. 29 (Centro de Investigación y Promoción del Campesino 1987).

Albó, Xavier, and Matías Preiswerk, *Los Señores del Gran Poder* (Centro de Teología Popular 1986).

Buechler, Hans C., and Judith-Marie Buechler, *Manufacturing Against the Odds: Small-Scale Producers in an Andean City* (Westview Press 1992).

Buechler, Hans C., and Judith-Marie Buechler, *The World of Sofia Velasquez: The Autobiography of a Bolivian Market Vendor* (Columbia University Press 1996).

Gill, Lesley, *Precarious Dependencies: Gender, Class and Domestic Service in Bolivia* (Columbia University Press 1994).

Gill, Lesley, *Teetering on the Rim: Global Restructuring, Daily Life and the Armed Retreat of the Bolivian State* (Columbia University Press 2000).

Klein, Herbert S., *Bolivia: The Evolution of a Multi-Ethnic Society,* 2d ed. (Oxford University Press 1992).

LESLEY GILL

Lagos
Nigeria

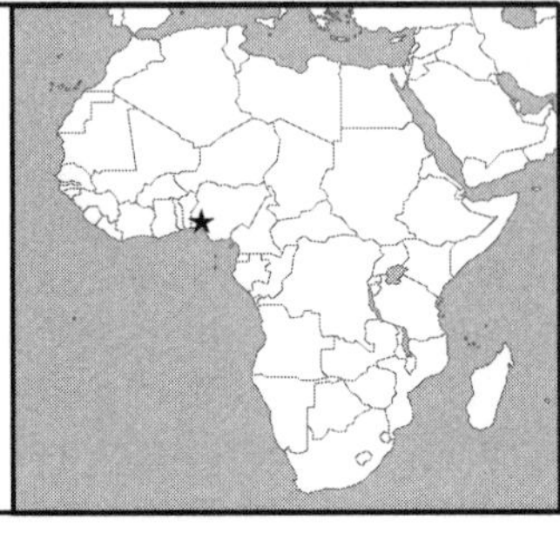

ORIENTATION

Name of City. The city was named by explorers from Portugal in the 15th century. Lagos in Portuguese means "lagoons" and "lakes," of which it has an abundance.

Location. The city of Lagos is located at approximately 6°26′ north latitude and 3°23′ east longitude, on the Atlantic coastline in the southwestern corner of Nigeria. It fronts that stretch of West Africa's coast known as the Bight of Benin in the Gulf of Guinea, and occupies several islands—Lagos, Iddo, Ikoyi, and Victoria—that are connected by bridges to the mainland, where most of the metropolitan Lagos population resides.

The climate is hot and humid, with little variation in temperature between seasons. The dry season is November to March, and the wet season is April to October. Annual rainfall averages 1,836 millimeters (72.3 inches). The mean temperature is 27.8°C (82.5°F) and the range is 20° to 32°C (68° to 91°F).

Lagos is situated midway in a series of lagoons and creeks that form an almost unbroken 644-kilometer (400-mile) corridor from the Volta to the Niger rivers and run parallel to the Atlantic shoreline. The city is surrounded by swamps, marshes, and waterways that were once considered some of the richest inland fishing grounds in West Africa. Much of the city is only a few feet above sea level. Of the 1,183 square kilometers (457 square miles) of territory in the metropolitan area, only 728 square kilometers (281 square miles) is dry land.

Population. Lagos is the largest city in Nigeria and one of the largest in sub-Saharan Africa. In a census taken in 1991, the population was roughly 6 million, but because many residents returned to their villages in fear of being counted, experts revised the actual population estimate. It is now believed that there were nearly 11 million people in 1996, and that in 2000 the population reached 13 million. The United Nations estimates that the population will be 20 million by 2010.

The growth of Lagos has been dramatic. The first census, taken in 1866 shortly after it became a British colony, counted 25,083 people. Barely a century later, in 1952, the population had increased more than tenfold—to 267,407, with 3,838 people per square kilometer (1,481 per square mile). Another near-tenfold jump took place only 22 years later, when the 1974 population reached 2,437,335 people, and the square-kilometer density—indicating the high degree of crowding—increased to 13,665 per square kilometer (5,275 per square mile). The Lagos state government estimated in 2001 that there were residential areas where the population density had reached 20,000 people per square kilometer (7,720 per square mile).

The most significant population increases took place in the decades following World War II. At times, the annual growth rate varied, so that the island averaged 10% growth, whereas suburban growth ranged from 18% to 43%. In either instance, this far exceeded the 2.8%-per-annum growth rate of the country as a whole, which meant that some 75% of the metropolitan area's increase was the result of migration. Young men were more likely than women to migrate in search of jobs, education, vocational training, or more exciting opportunities than rural life could offer. In 1991 this led to a ratio of 53% men to 47% women. The age structure showed a preponderance of people under 30 and very few over 60 years—78% versus 1.8%, with 3.4% being the national average for the latter.

Distinctive and Unique Features. For 500 years, Lagos was known to foreign traders. Europeans first glimpsed the Lagos area in the 1470s, and found that it was in a propitious location because Lagos offered one of only two openings from the sea into the inland waterways between the Volta and Niger rivers, and therefore it possessed greater opportunities for engaging in trade. Passage into the harbor was difficult, however, because of dangerous surf and a shifting sandbar at the entrance, and small craft were used to transport people and goods from the city to ships anchored 3 kilometers (2 miles) offshore. Lagos became a major center in the Atlantic slave trade in the late 18th century, despite the hazards of coastal landing and the loss of many lives to rough water. As part of an effort to stop the slave trade and take advantage of legitimate commerce in palm oil and other valuable products, Lagos was made a British colony in 1861. Early in the 20th century, the sandbanks at the harbor entrance were dredged to allow large seagoing vessels to pass through and engage in greater amounts of trade.

Lagos became the main port, communications, commercial, industrial, and transportation center of the colony, and remains so to the present. It has also been a national and state capital. It first became the capital of the colony of Nigeria, continued to be its capital after independence in 1960, and remained so until 1991, when the inland town of Abuja became the country's capital. Many federal-government offices are still in Lagos. The capital of Lagos state—Nigeria's smallest state—is concentrated in the metropolitan area at Ikeja.

Major Languages. Nearly 80% of Lagos residents are Yoruba-speaking, although there are many dialects of this large language group. The Yoruba dialect in Lagos, known as Eko, has emerged from centuries of migration from and exposure to neighboring language groups, including Edo to the east and Egun to the west. Eko has considerable prestige, and other Yoruba dialects tend to shift in its direction. There are also large numbers of Hausa, Ibo, Ibibio, and Ijaw speakers in Lagos. The lingua francas are English—used in government, business, and education—and a form of street pidgin, used primarily in communicating across ethnic-group boundaries. Many residents are bilingual or multilingual.

HISTORY

The Origin of the City. There was virtually no activity in the Lagos region when it was observed in the late 15th century by a Portuguese trader. By the second half of the 16th century, however, the area was developing as a military and trading center. The original settlement at the northwestern tip of Lagos Island was a small fishing community whose leader, Aromire ("lover of water"), gave a piece of land to Benin warriors to establish a camp as part of their kingdom's westward expansion along the coast. Other predecessors of the Benin warriors are believed to have settled on Iddo Island, situated in the lagoon between Lagos Island and the mainland. Origin myths claim that the Iddo residents were hunters of the Awori subgroup of Yoruba-speaking peoples who had fled southward to avoid warfare in their homeland. They and the descendants of Aromire still live on their original site, as do the descendants of the original Benin warriors. From the arrival of the Benin warriors in the area to the early 19th century, the people of Lagos were linked to Benin through tribute payments and through their local rulers, who could not take office until they were confirmed by the king of Benin. Throughout this time, Lagos was known by many names: Benin called the town Eko; Itsekiri neighbors called it Ikurami; the French, Oni or Onim; but the one that lasted was the Portuguese name of Lagos.

A close relationship with Benin was documented in 1603, when a German surgeon aboard a Dutch merchant ship visited Lagos and found it under the suzerainty of Benin and inhabited by soldiers and four military commanders who ran the town in what the surgeon described as a stately manner. The town was attracting many traders who came by water and land to sell goods such as cloth, ivory, elephant tails, and pepper. Food was plentiful, and included fish, wild fowl, meat, fruits, and yams. Later, in the 1680s, a Dutch visitor wrote that Lagos had the best laws and policies of the towns he had visited along the coast. Still under Benin, it was well protected, with double palisades, sentry boxes, and guards at each of its gates. The historical record was then silent until about 1760–1790, when the center of coastal trade shifted from Porto Novo, Cotonou, and Badagry eastward, and Lagos assumed the role of chief port for trade with Europeans. In addition to slaves, the merchants in the city exported large quantities of handwoven cotton cloth, most of which came to them via interior trade networks. When Lagos became the hub of the lucrative Atlantic trade, political power in the city was hotly contested, and various neighboring kingdoms sought either the favor of Lagos's rulers or their overthrow—whichever gave the neighbors greater advantage. This meant that Lagos was infiltrated by an ever-more-diverse number of ethnic and linguistic groups from all directions. At various times, it came into conflict with the great kingdoms of Oyo, Dahomey, and Ijebu—but Lagos, while paying tribute to Benin, managed to retain its local autonomy in everyday affairs despite a series of internal disputes and civil uprisings. The city also grew larger. By 1800 Lagos had 5,000 inhabitants and was surrounded by a large number of villages and markets scattered from east to west along the nearby lagoons and creeks.

Missionaries moved into the city in the mid-19th century and were joined by numerous liberated Africans from Sierra Leone, Cuba, and Brazil; by refugees fleeing warfare that ravaged Yoruba communities north of the city; and by an increasing number of Europeans, including British, who were seeking legitimate trade opportunities. The British were attempting to stop the slave trade, but, in response, civil war broke out among Lagos's ruling factions—for and against the trade—and the British bombarded the city in 1851 in a successful attempt to bring opponents of the slave trade to power. Ten years later, Britain imposed a colonial regime. Once the treaty ceding Lagos to the British was signed, immigration into the city increased. Some of the growth was attributed to Lagos's becoming a free colony where escaped slaves could be liberated, and some to the expanding opportunities that a new European demand for palm oil and other local produce was providing.

In 1906 Lagos colony was joined with the British protectorate of Southern Nigeria, and in 1914, when Southern and Northern Nigeria were amalgamated, it became the administrative heart of the nation-state we know today as Nigeria. From the time Nigeria came into being, Lagos was a center of the Nigerian nationalist movement. As the heart of learning and development, it attracted a highly educated and articulate group of people who used newspaper ownership, legal avenues, and whatever professional expertise they could command to bring about independence in 1960. Soon thereafter, the discovery of and export of petroleum brought considerable wealth to Nigeria, much of it concentrated in Lagos. This, too, accounted for a sharp increase in population.

Three circumstances in Nigeria's postcolonial years have had a strong effect on the development of Lagos. First, the country has been fraught with internal political conflict between people of the northern regions, who are dominated by Islam, and those from the south, where Christianity prevails. The first military coup, in 1966, precipitated civil war between the southeast and other regions of the country from 1967 to 1969. From that time, control of local governance reeled from one form of local government to another, and from one set of community leaders to another, as regimes shifted from military to civilian and back again—with the military in power most of the time. Each shift in the federal government affected the way Lagos was administered. In civilian regimes, there were locally elected representatives on city and suburban town councils. The military appointed local officials—sometimes an entire local council, and sometimes only a sole administrator. An elected regime returned in 1999 with a civilian regime, and now consists of elected representatives. A second shift since independence has been in the economy of the city. At the end of the colonial era, Lagos's workers relied primarily on civil-service employment and small-product manufacturing. The oil boom of the 1970s changed the emphasis to industry and manufacturing. A third circumstance is that work on improving the city's infrastructure moved increasingly slowly. Government was unable to keep up with the population growth, and residents were in need of many city services and resources.

INFRASTRUCTURE

Public Buildings, Public Works, and Residences. The island of Lagos is the center of the city's cultural, political, and economic life. It contains an architectural history of the city, including old and new indigenous structures, Portuguese, mission, colonial, and modern styles. Contemporary structures—skyscrapers, international business houses, and government offices—stand only a few blocks from the ancient compounds of Lagos's first settlers. The oldest sector of the city, known as Isale Eko, houses the palace of the *oba* known as the Iga Idunganran and numerous smaller palaces of the city's hereditary chiefs; the ornate two- and three-story houses of Brazilians and Cubans who returned to the city in the 19th century and decorated them with ornate plaster facades and decorative moldings; the Gothic-style churches of some Christian denominations; and mosques constructed by the Islamic faithful following Middle Eastern aesthetics that call for elaborately molded arches and minarets. Most public buildings are done in postwar modernist style, including the University of Lagos, City Hall, banks, hotels, government buildings around Tafawa Balewa Square and its colonially-inspired racecourse, and some upper-income apartment buildings.

Some precolonial-style housing, especially the houses of notables, was influenced by the ancient kingdom of Benin. This kind of housing consists of compounds with connected rooms surrounding an atrium. More recent indigenous architecture consists of long, rectangular buildings with two rows of rooms, lined front to back, and bisected by a single corridor. Older houses had mud-block walls and thatch roofs, whereas newer houses are made of concrete blocks and are covered with corrugated-metal roofing.

Mainland neighborhoods house most of the city's industrial and manufacturing concerns. The main port, Apapa Quay, is on the mainland to the west of Lagos Island. Otherwise, mainland and suburban areas are primarily residential. The large suburban community of Mushin is filled with multifamily dwellings intended for tenants and owners and their families. An average house has 45 residents living in 13 rooms, of which 11 are rented out. Throughout the metropolitan area, the average density is 3.5 people per room. High-cost housing is found mostly on Ikoyi and Victoria islands and mainland Apapa. An absence of zoning laws means that all areas are inhabited by mixed-income groups and integrate business and residential use.

There are only a few squatter settlements, and they are located on the periphery of the metropolitan area. Their structures are identifiable by their makeshift walls of boards or iron sheeting.

Politics and City Services. The metropolitan area is divided into eight local-government authorities. The number grows as the population grows. Local government is administered primarily by the Lagos state government's Office of Local Government Affairs. Each local government has an elected chairman and councillors who are vested with the tasks of overseeing the affairs of the local council and civil-servant staff. Local government oversees numerous services, including economic development and planning; traditional chieftaincy affairs; food distribution and preparation (markets, slaughterhouses, kiosks, and restaurants); licensing and fee collecting, including property tax; statistical record keeping (birth, death, and marriage); construction and maintenance of roads, streets, lighting, drains, parking lots, and open spaces; sewage and refuse disposal; and financial affairs (loans and grants).

Emphasis on these tasks varies from one administration to another. The first military period, starting in 1966, had four priorities: environmental services (such as water, sewage, drainage), general administration, public transportation, and education. The 1979–1983 civilian government focused on roads and housing. In the second military period, which lasted up to 1998, some roadways were maintained, but housing, public transport, water, electricity, and sewage removal deteriorated. The current civilian regime is emphasizing public health and transportation.

Educational System. The government operates free primary schools, teacher-training facilities, technical and vocational schools, and a university. Numerous private schools and Christian and Islamic educational institutions also function in the city. In 1993 about 1.3 million Lagos children attended primary (63%) and secondary (35.4%) schools; attendance is high despite the fact that many children are too poor or too valuable as a source of income to attend school regularly. The adult literacy rate in the entire country was 34% in the 1980s. Institutions of higher education had roughly 20,000 students in 1993.

Transportation System. Lagos is the transportation and communications nexus of the country. It serves as the southwestern terminus for road and rail transportation and has both international and domestic airports. Ships from around the world berth at Apapa and at Tin Can Island, the main ports. Public transportation is an issue because of the deterioration of the city's fleet of buses, minibuses, taxicabs, and cars for hire. In 1988 more than 100,000 public vehicles were counted. Traffic congestion is a severe problem, and a series of overpasses have been constructed to relieve rush-hour problems, known as "go slows."

CULTURAL AND SOCIAL LIFE

Ethnic, Class, and Religious Diversity. Religion plays a significant role in the lives of Lagos's inhabitants. At least 50% are Christian, who belong to congregations such as those associated with the World Council of Churches, or to one of the many independent, separatist churches. In the 1990s a large

© DANIEL LAINE/CORBIS

Adeyinka Oyekan II is the *Oba* (hereditary chief) of Lagos, Nigeria.

number turned to evangelical, born-again Christian groups. Indigenous religions are recognized by about 10% of the populace. The remainder are Muslim. Islam was more pervasive in early colonial years, but Christian migrants have tended to outnumber them. Fundamentalist Islam, although prevalent in northern Nigeria, has found little favor in Lagos. Religion does not influence residential patterns, although ethnicity does in some cases.

Lagos has been ethnically diverse since its founding. Today, almost all 250 ethnolinguistic groups of Nigeria are represented. The dominant group in the city is Yoruba-speaking, but there are many subgroups within this rubric—Ijebu, Egba, Ibadan, Oyo, Ife, Ilesha, Ondo, Awori, and Egbado, to name only a few. Some dialects of Yoruba are mutually unintelligible; some social and cultural practices vary significantly; yet a standard version of the language is recognized in schools, and a pan-Yoruba identity has emerged, especially in the national political arena. Historically, the city contained large settlements of Edo-speaking peoples from the easterly kingdom of Benin, Egun- or Gu-speaking peoples from the west (today's Republic of Benin); and Nupe- and Hausa-speaking peoples from the north. In more-recent times, large numbers of Igbo, Hausa, Tiv, Igbibio, and Kanuri have settled in the city. Non-Nigerians include people from Benin, Togo, Ghana, Lebanon, India, Europe, and the United States.

The class structure differs markedly from that found in Europe or North America. Elites are educated largely in the western tradition, and include political, military, intellectual, professional, business, and people in the arts. The income of high-level civil servants may be 30 times greater than that of clerical workers. Rather than a large middle class, as in the West, there is a very large low-income sector and only a small middle- and high-income sector. Thus, there is a great problem with poverty—with two-thirds of the population living below the poverty line, and an unemployment rate of roughly 40%. The per capita gross national product (GNP) in Nigeria in 1997, according to the World Bank, was $260; that of Lagos, however, is thought to be about 30% higher than that of Nigeria as a whole. The average for other sub-Saharan African nations was $500; for low-income countries, it was $350.

Family and Other Social Support Systems. The government plays its greatest role in providing social support through education and health. Metropolitan Lagos has 55 hospitals, public and private, including an orthopedic hospital, tuberculosis sanitariums, a teaching hospital attached to the University of Lagos, and numerous traditional medical practitioners. In addition to government health services, there are many small private clinics and doctors, but the patient-to-doctor ratio is 5,000 to 1, and there is one hospital bed per 900 residents. Health problems are mainly malaria, pneumonia, dysentery, an undetermined HIV/AIDS (human immunodeficiency virus/acquired immune deficiency syndrome) population, and a high accident rate. About 85% of Lagos's children have some immunizations.

Government provides a limited amount of public welfare. There are a few facilities in Lagos for the aged and destitute, but they reach only a small number of people. This means that the family is a central part of the social-security system, and that household income is more relevant to understanding the basics of survival than is individual income. Young people support elderly parents and relatives. Orphans are fostered by extended-family members. New migrants live with relatives until they are settled. The lack of institutionalized support places stress on households as they try to accommodate needy relatives. For the most unfortunate, it leads to malaise and crime. There are several safety nets, however. Ties to hometown relatives can be reactivated by urban residents when they wish to return. In the city, some religious organizations and hometown associations offer support to members when they are in need.

Work and Commerce. By the year 2000 Lagos accounted for 62% of Nigeria's GNP. About half of the country's commercial and merchant banks have head offices in Lagos, and the rest have branch offices there. This has led to 40% of the country's currency circulating in Lagos alone. Of five development-finance institutions, four have head offices in the city, and of the country's insurance firms, 68% have main offices there. Nigeria's stock exchange is located in Lagos, and 90% of the companies quoted on it are headquartered in metropolitan Lagos. The city also serves as headquarters for most European companies and banks that do business in Nigeria.

In 1984, 1,000 industries were located in the metropolitan area, about a quarter of the nation's total, and 53% of Nigeria's manufacturing employment was there. About 45% of Nigeria's industrial workforce was employed in metropolitan Lagos, which meant that the bulk of the country's skilled and semi-skilled workers were employed in Lagos. This concentration is strengthened by the city's leading role in transportation and communications, and the development of industrial estates in the metropolitan area as early as the 1950s. There are now 18 industrial estates in the metropolitan region; they include steel, auto and radio assembly, plastics, chemicals, and the manufacture of metal products, electronics, textiles, chemicals, pharmaceuticals, soap, and furniture. Small business focuses on foods, beverages, paints, soaps, cosmetics, pharmaceuticals, textiles, provision of services, and fishing. It is the headquarters for Federal Radio Corporation of Nigeria and the Nigerian television authority.

Employment has two sectors: formal and informal. The formal sector consists of most wage-paid occupations, especially in industrial or civil-service capacities, of whom 25% are in public administration, and 20% in other services. The informal, which is the main form, includes casual labor, fishing, domestic service, and petty trade; the latter constitutes 25% of the workforce and is mainly women. Between 50% and 70% of the population rely on informal undertakings for their income. Much unemployment or underemployment is rationalized as informal work.

Arts and Recreation. Cultural life in Lagos centers on numerous institutions, including museums, galleries, the national theater, libraries, and institutions of higher education. The University of Lagos began in 1962, the College of Technology in 1948, and the National Museum in 1957. The museum houses superb collections of ancient and more-recent art from throughout the country. There also is a large sports stadium, a racecourse, and an amphitheater where public parades and displays are held.

Lagos is an important crucible for the development of contemporary art. Artists of all types congregate in the city, including creators of sculpture, painting, cartoons, textiles, and prints. There is an outpouring of popular dance and music, with recording studios and performing centers and clubs that cater to audiences of all levels and tastes, from local to international styles. Well-known musicians include King Sunny Ade, Ebenezer Obey, and the late Fela Anikulapo (Ransome) Kuti. Musicians compose music for the world market as well as traditional songs that are frequently performed at the city's popular ceremonies and rites of passage.

Many authors are prolific in their writings about and in Lagos. They include Chinua Achebe, Flora Nwapa, and Cyprian Ekwensi. There is a large literary community, and many of the country's 3,000 periodicals are produced in the city. Other popular arts range from hair styles, clothing, and sign painting to television sitcoms, film, and photography.

QUALITY OF LIFE

Lagos Island is overcrowded. Its southwestern shore houses most of the commercial, financial, and international business establishments. Its northwestern tip still contains compounds and palaces of the city's first settlers and nobility. By contrast, Iddo, Ikoyi, and Victoria islands and parts of mainland Apapa house upper-income groups and tend to be less crowded. Some of the business and residential areas in these places are planned, and tend to have water and sanitation services for most residences. Only high-cost-housing areas have underground sewers, while the sewers in most of the metropolitan area are open.

Residential patterns are unusual in that lower-income areas tend to concentrate in the suburbs, and higher-income housing is closer to the city center. Even then, it can be difficult to find homogeneous, class-based neighborhoods except in the most expensive housing areas, since high-income residential areas will have civil servants at the bottom of the pay scale living next to the highest-income people of the city. Elsewhere, there can be large, high-quality houses next to tenements inhabited by lower-income residents. One of the few ways to differentiate among income groups is in the size and quality of a building.

There also is a dual-population pattern in that indigenous residents occupy old sectors of the city, which tend to be overcrowded and have poor infrastructural services, whereas new sectors are inhabited by migrants. The old sector is a section of the city where high-, middle-, and low-income residents live side by side in a crowded but tightly knit, highly interactive community.

There are vocal demands for improvements in the urban infrastructure: greater road capacity to decrease long-standing traffic problems; more provision of basic services such as sanitation, communications, public transportation, and improved housing opportunities. Some of the most deeply felt concerns are for improvements in the supply of water and electricity. Only 30% of the residents have access to running water in their houses. Electricity is pervasive, but subject to frequent outages.

FUTURE OF THE CITY

Growth is expected to take the city to more than 24 million residents by 2015, and make it one of the largest metropolitan areas of the world. Rapid urbanization has led to unplanned and uncontrolled urban expansion, and therefore to a paucity of the kinds of services that are necessary for the health and well-being of the people of Lagos. The hardest hit are the poorest residents, and they constitute the greatest challenge to Nigeria's leaders.

BIBLIOGRAPHY

Abiodun, Josephine Olu, "The Challenges of Growth and Development in Metropolitan Lagos," *The Urban Challenge in Africa: Growth and Management of Its Large Cities,* ed. by C. Rakodi (United Nations University Press 1997): 192–222.

Aderibigbe, A. B. ed., *Lagos: The Development of an African City* (Longman 1975).

Barnes, Sandra T., *Patrons and Power: Creating a Political Community in Metropolitan Lagos* (Manchester University Press for International African Institute/Indiana University Press 1986).

Cole, Patrick, *Modern and Traditional Elites in the Politics of Lagos* (Cambridge University Press 1975).

Olowu, Dele, *Lagos State: Governance, Society & Economy* (Malthouse Press 1990).

Peil, Margaret, *Lagos: The City is the People* (G. K. Hall 1991).

SANDRA T. BARNES

Lahore

Pakistan

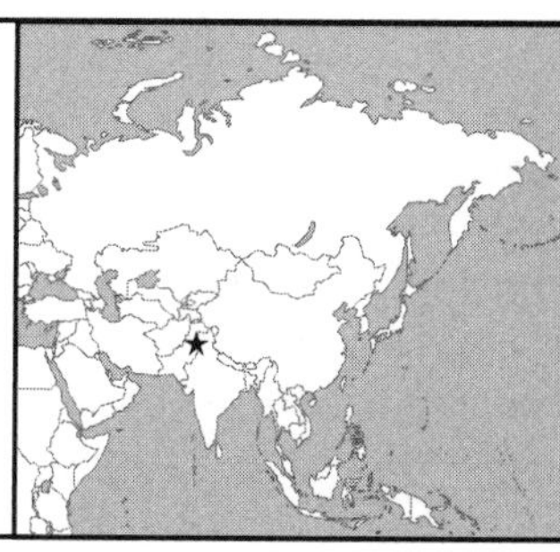

ORIENTATION

Name of City. Lahore, once known as "the Paris of the subcontinent," is the name of the city. The city's residents are called Lahoris (la hôr ee) in local parlance.

Location. Lahore is located in the Islamic Republic of Pakistan at 31°35′ north latitude and 74°13′ east longitude. The city is situated approximately 25 kilometers (16 miles) from Pakistan's border with India, on the eastern edge of Pakistan's Punjab province. Pakistan is one of seven countries making up the South Asian region (along with Bangladesh, Bhutan, India, the Maldives, Nepal, and Sri Lanka).

Population. Results from a 1998 national census in Pakistan have yet to be fully compiled and made public. In the most recent published census (1981), Lahore's population was 2,952,689.

More-recent projections suggest that the city's population was around 6.7 million in 2001, reflecting an estimated average annual growth rate (since 1981) of approximately 4.5%.

Distinctive and Unique Features. Lahore is situated on the right bank of the Ravi River in a gently undulating alluvial plain prone to recurring seasonal floods. The area's dynamic riverine setting and long history of human occupation and agricultural cultivation have made the silt-rich soils around Lahore remarkably fertile, a feature common to much of Punjab province. The fertile soils and year-round availability of water have long made this region of the Indian subcontinent a rich source of agricultural produce, most notably wheat, pulses, tree fruits, and vegetables. The red clays in Lahore's soil have also lent their color and substance to the city's architecture for hundreds of years, as nearly all buildings, whether modern or historic, are built with locally manufactured bricks. Calcite nodules that form naturally at shallow depths in the soil surrounding the city are used in the manufacture of Lahore's famously durable mortars and pristine white plasters. The latter were used as surface finishes on many of Lahore's most significant historic buildings.

From the air, Lahore appears as a dense, irregular network of low-rise buildings spread out across a large, sparsely vegetated plain approximately 500 square kilometers (about 300 square miles) in area. The city is constrained to the north by the floodplain of the Ravi River and to the east by Pakistan's border with India. Recent urban expansion has taken place largely to the south and west of the original city. On closer inspection, a number of different spatial patterns become evident in the city, each deriving from the particular circumstances under which it was established. The oldest district of the city, called simply "the Old City" by local residents, lies close to the Ravi River at the northern edge of town. This is a densely-settled irregular polygon nearly 5 kilometers (about 3 miles) in circumference, separated from the surrounding area by thick masonry walls. The street layout in this part of Lahore derives largely from medieval precedent, and is characterized by narrow, winding lanes interspersed with wider, straighter market (bazaar) streets.

To the south of the Old City, in an area sometimes referred to as the "civil station," building density decreases, and roads are generally longer, wider, and straighter than elsewhere in the city. Roads in the civil station link the major commercial and institutional buildings of Lahore to one another in loosely axial relationships. Still farther out, in the zones surrounding Lahore's civil station, suburban developments planned and settled since the 1960s abut one another according to principles that are often more incidental than systematic. Unplanned and unregulated settlements occupy the interstices of this suburban framework, and make up a large percentage of built space in the city. Streets and buildings in these interstitial areas take shape according to a variety of circumstances, some seemingly haphazard. In contrast, to the southwest of the city (in a several-square-mile area now well within the municipal limits of Lahore), a residential settlement called "Model Town" evokes the regular geometry of Ebenezar Howard's late-19th-century "Garden City" proposal. Howard's circular layout and radial transportation system was indeed replicated by the local residents who planned and built Model Town during the 1920s and 1930s.

Though building densities across the city are high, Lahore has long been known as a "city of gardens," a reference to the many open green spaces, both formally and informally planned, scattered throughout the city. The most popular of these include the Jinnah Bagh (garden) and Zoo, in the heart of the civil station; Nasser Bagh, near the Provincial Secretariat campus; Iqbal Park, to the north of the Old City; and Shalimar Gardens, a well-restored Mughal (Mogul) garden complex located a few miles east of the city. Developed over time in a piecemeal fashion, Lahore's complex mosaic of streets and neighborhoods, and the many abrupt transitions between older and newer urban spaces one encounters there, characterize much that is familiar and identifiable about the city to its local inhabitants.

Attractions of the City. Lahore is Pakistan's second-largest city, and enjoys a reputation as the center of arts and cultural activity in the country. As the capital of Punjab, the wealthiest and most populous province in Pakistan, Lahore is also an important nexus of regional government, education, industry, and finance. While most of the city's economy is geared toward domestic (largely local) consumption, a garment-manufacturing industry has developed during the past several years, with links to consumer markets in Europe and North America. Lahore also provides business opportunities for small- and medium-scale wholesale manufacturers of cloth, shoes, and machine parts, among other items, and for retailers of food, clothing, furniture, and other durable consumer goods.

Foreign tourists visit Lahore in relatively small numbers. In 1992 the total number of foreign visitors to Lahore from all countries was estimated by the Lahore Chamber of Commerce and Industry to be only about 70,000. The majority of foreign tourists come to Lahore from the United Kingdom, the United States, India, Afghanistan, and western Europe, in descending order of frequency. Domestic tourists, on the other hand, visit Lahore in far greater numbers. These tourists come predominantly from smaller cities in Punjab province, the majority staying with friends or relatives in the city rather than in hotels. As the region's primary metropolis and home to a thriving commercial-film industry (centered around an area in the city fondly referred to as "Lollywood"), Lahore has long been a favorite destination for short-term visits by Punjab's rural or small-town residents in search of an evening's entertainment.

Despite its poorly developed tourism industry, Lahore is home to a number of important historical monuments that attract a small but steady stream of visitors. Many of these buildings derive from the Mughal (Mogul, Moghul) period (circa. 1526–1857), when Lahore was occasionally the capital city of the Mughal Empire. Lahore's Mughal-era fort (begun 1584), the tombs of Emperor Jehangir and his wife, Nur Jehan (circa 1630), the Mosque of Wazir Khan (1634), and Aurangzeb's Badshahi Mosque (1673) are among the finest specimens of Mughal architecture to be found anywhere in the world. In addition to these monuments, a 1980s survey of buildings in Lahore's Old City identified more than 1,400 buildings of historical importance. The latter include numerous ornate houses (some dating from the 17th century); several important Hindu and Sikh temples and *samadhs* (cenotaphs); and a number of Muslim

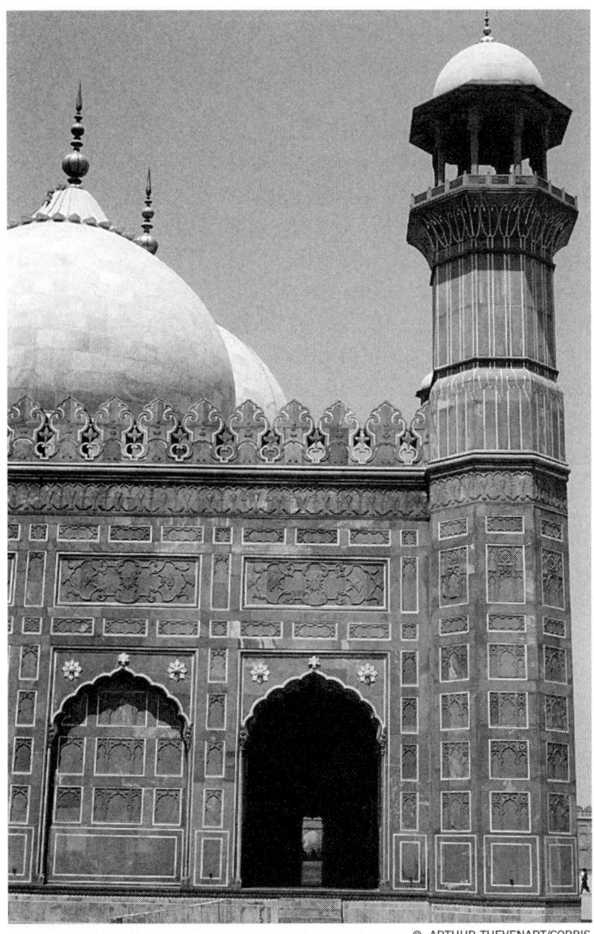

© ARTHUR THEVENART/CORBIS

The Badshahi Mosque is one of many Muslim places of worship in Lahore, Pakistan.

shrines, tombs and mosques, including the diminutive Mosque of Saleh Kamboh (1659), one of the city's finest and oldest. The Gurdwara of Arjun Dev (the fifth of Sikhism's ten holy gurus) and the cenotaph of Lahore's 19th-century Sikh ruler Maharaja Ranjit Singh (d. 1839) are located near the Lahore Fort in a single complex; both holy sites are visited annually by Sikh pilgrims from India on the anniversary of the guru's death. Important British colonial monuments in Lahore include the Lawerence and Montgomery halls (1862 and 1866, respectively), Lahore Railway Station (1857), Punjab Chief Court (1889), Lahore Museum (1890), and Town Hall (1890). While many of Lahore's older monuments enjoy legal protection from destruction or removal, much of the city's 19th-century urban fabric is disappearing at a rapid pace.

Relationships Between the City and the Outside. Over the course of the past century, many of Lahore's residents have moved away from the older central-city districts and out into the city's suburbs. The Old City, though still home to around 200,000 people, has increasingly become a district of small industrial workshops and warehouses interspersed among decaying lower-income residences. Most of the city's upper-class elites occupy exclusive single-family compounds in developments on the outskirts of town, while a majority of middle-income and lower-middle-income residents inhabit the far-less-exclusive suburbs that have grown up around Lahore's peripheral industrial estates.

For the residents of small towns and villages in Punjab province, Lahore has long served the function of providing an urban foothold for families who send (invariably) male members there to earn income from nonagricultural labor. In addition, as the center of learning in the province, Lahore is the destination of choice for young people seeking to enhance the economic and social standing of their families by pursuing higher education.

Prior to the partition of British India into the independent states of Pakistan and India, Lahore's population was divided among followers of the Christian, Hindu, Muslim, and Sikh faiths. At the time of partition, in 1947, most of the city's Hindu and Sikh residents left their homes and were forced to resettle in India. Because of this, many Indian citizens with historical family ties to the city hold Lahore in their memories with a combination of nostalgic fondness and sensate loss. For many Indians and Pakistanis alike, however, Lahore evokes the twin images of faded grandeur and sophisticated, cozy, cosmopolitanism. A favorite proverb, cited by schoolchildren and elders alike, sums up much of this broadly shared sentiment: "Those who have not seen Lahore have not yet been born."

Major Languages. While the official language of Pakistan is Urdu, a majority of Lahore's residents speak Punjabi as their first language. Urdu and English are the languages of instruction in the city's schools, and educated middle-class residents are often fluent in the former and competent in the latter, regardless of their mother tongue. The upper classes in Lahore, as elsewhere in Pakistan, prefer English as their medium of discourse. For a broad segment of Lahore's population, however, Punjabi is the only language in use.

HISTORY

The Origin of the City. Legend attributes the foundation of Lahore to Loh, one of the two sons of Rama, who figures prominently in the Hindu epic

Ramayana. This epic, formulated during the first few centuries of the present era, narrates events thought to have taken place around 900 B.C. Archaeological evidence suggests, however, that human settlement in the oldest part of Lahore, on a slight mound at the northern edge of the Old City, dates to no earlier than the 1st century A.D. The Chinese traveler Hiuen Tsang was perhaps the first person to record mention of Lahore in a written document; the city appears in his travel chronicle dated 630 A.D. At the time of the first Muslim conquests in Punjab (ca. 10th century A.D.), Lahore was known as the seat of an important Hindu principality, a role it continued to serve until the end of the 10th century A.D. In 1021 the Muslim ruler Mahmud of Ghazni established control over Lahore, effectively ending Hindu sovereignty. Lahore would henceforward remain an important city within a succession of Muslim dynasties, including those of the Ghauris, Khiljis, Tughlaqs, Sayyids, Lodhis, and Mughals.

Following the death of Aurangzeb (1707), the last of the "great" Mughal emperors, Lahore was repeatedly captured and lost by a succession of Muslim and Sikh leaders. In 1759 Afghan Shah Durrani finally established lasting control over Lahore, ruling the city for 40 years. In 1799, following a successful battle led by Maharaja Ranjit Singh, Lahore became the seat of a large Sikh empire. At the time of his death in 1839, Ranjit Singh ruled over the last large territory in India to remain free from British occupation. This was a situation, however, that would not last very long.

Capitalizing on the disarray surrounding succession struggles after Ranjit Singh's death, and only partially diminished by a war fought against the Sikhs on their eastern frontier, British troops rode into Lahore in February 1846 and garrisoned troops in the citadel. Two unstable years later, the British were drawn into a second war with the Sikhs. After a series of closely fought battles, the Sikh army was finally defeated at Gujrat, 100 kilometers (62 miles) north of Lahore. In March of 1848, following the British victory, Ranjit Singh's son and heir to the throne, Dalip Singh, was formally deposed in Lahore. Within a year, Punjab was formally annexed to the British Empire, and Lahore was made the provincial capital.

British rule over the city lasted until 1947, when the independent states of Pakistan and India were carved out from the former British Empire. During the roughly 100 years of British sovereignty, Lahore expanded considerably in population and geographic extent. The plains outside the older walled city were built up; a large military cantonment was constructed at Mian Mir, 8 kilometers (5 miles) east of the civil station; and the city was connected to the rest of India by rail, telegraph, and, later, telephone services.

Migration: Past and Present. Under the British, Lahore became an important destination for Indians from other provinces seeking employment in the colonial government. The historian Kenneth Jones has written that by the late 1880s Lahore was a "city of strangers," recording a higher percentage of citizens born outside its own district than any other north Indian city. Another group of migrants to the city during this time were the British civilians and government officials themselves, for whom Lahore was considered a desirable posting. Though never more than a few hundred in number, white European residents were a conspicuous feature of Lahore's 19th- and 20th-century social landscape.

At the time of partition in 1947, Lahore's population had reached around 700,000. Four years later, according to Pakistan's first official census, the city had grown by nearly 150,000, mostly as a result of in-migration by Muslims from India. It has been estimated that 8 million Muslim refugees entered Pakistan from India at partition, and 6 million Hindus and Sikhs left Pakistan. Lahore was one of the first ports of entry for refugees who participated in this violent historical event of epic proportions.

Since 1947 Lahore's population has increased roughly tenfold through a combination of regional in-migration and natural population expansion. Most of the city's newer immigrants have come from outlying districts in Pakistan's Punjab province. A small number of educated professionals arrive in the city each year from other large cities in Pakistan to take up managerial positions in Lahore's business and industrial firms.

INFRASTRUCTURE

Public Buildings, Public Works, and Residences. As a provincial capital city, Lahore is home to a large number of public governmental institutions. These include, among others, the Punjab Legislative Assembly building, High Court complex, District Courts, General Post Office, district commissioner's office, Public Works Department complex, and Punjab Civil Secretariat, a large campus housing most of the administrative offices of the provincial government.

The Public Works Department (PWD) administers Lahore's roads and bridges and, in addition, the several canals that bring water for irrigation and human-consumption purposes into the city. Most parts of the city are supplied with electricity and phone connections, though service in many areas is frequently interrupted or irregular. Responsibility for Lahore's water and electricity supply lies with the Water and Power Development Authority of Pakistan (WAPDA).

Residences in the city span a range of different types. In the older districts of Lahore, two- or three-story attached row houses predominate, while detached single-family structures are common in newer suburbs. Makeshift residences that are constructed with a variety of new and recycled materials characterize housing in Lahore's numerous squatter settlements. A small segment of the city's population live in residential dormitories or hotels, low-rise apartment complexes, and, more recently, luxury high-rise condominiums.

Politics and City Services. The Lahore municipality is governed by the Lahore Municipal Corporation (LMC), a body consisting of both elected officials (corporators) and appointed managers and technicians. The LMC is presided over by an elected chairman who is the figurative head of the city.

In the perception of most residents, the municipality of Lahore lacks both the resources and institutional stability to provide an adequate level of city services to its burgeoning population. In response, a number of private and semiprivate philanthropic organizations operate in the city to provide health care, education, and other social services to the city's poor. The Gunga Ram Charitable Trust hospital in Lahore's civil station and the Karachi-based Edhi Ambulance are exemplary of the latter types of institutions.

Lahore plays an important role in Pakistan's national political system, both substantively and symbolically. Because Lahore is the capital city of the country's wealthiest and most populous province, no politician aspiring to national office can afford to neglect the concerns of its residents. Historically, many of Pakistan's leading political families have long-standing ties to the city and province, and at least one of Pakistan's recent prime ministers (Mian Nawaz Sharif) is a native of the city. In addition, many of the senior officers in Pakistan's politically powerful army are natives of the region, as are a majority of lower-ranking officers and troops.

On a more symbolic level, the shrine of an 11th-century saintly scholar buried in Lahore, Abul Hasan Ali (better known as Data Ganj Baksh), has long been used as a rallying place by Pakistani politicians and leaders embarking on national political campaigns. Another symbolic site in the city, the tomb of Allama Iqbal (1873–1938) near the Lahore Fort, commemorates the final resting place of the nationalist scholar who first enunciated the "two-nation theory," commonly thought of as the political and philosophical underpinning of a Muslim homeland (Pakistan) in the Indian subcontinent.

Educational System. The present system of education in Lahore is largely an inheritance of the colonial period. The normal sequence of public instruction includes primary, secondary, and post-secondary institutions linked to one another through the medium of nationally administered exams. Secondary education begins in eighth standard (or "grade"), and extends to a "matriculation" exam at the end of the tenth standard. After matriculation, secondary education is complete once a student has passed the "intermediary" exam at the end of the 12th year. The bachelor of arts degree (B.A.) is awarded after successful completion of two years in an accredited postsecondary college. Private institutions based on compatibility with the British and American systems are also popular in Lahore, though most are prohibitively expensive for all but the middle and upper-middle classes.

Postsecondary liberal-arts and professional education are offered at a number of colleges and universities in the city, all of which offer baccalaureate degrees. The University of the Punjab and the University of Engineering and Technology offer post-graduate programs of study leading to master's and doctorate degrees as well. Many of Pakistan's medical doctors received their training at the prestigious King Edward Medical College in Lahore. The National College of Arts in Lahore (NCA) is Pakistan's premier fine-arts institution. In addition to offering bachelor's degrees in fine arts, design, and architecture, the NCA has recently begun offering a master's of fine arts degree program.

Religious education organized in the more traditional *madressa* (Islamic school) system exists alongside the public-school system in Lahore. Students in *madressas* are trained in the corpus of Islamic pedagogy, including instruction in the Arabic language, interpretation of the Koran, and Islamic jurisprudence (or *fiqh*). While *madressas* train a small minority of students in the city, most families in Lahore arrange for private instruction in reading the Koran for their school-aged children. Those who cannot afford private lessons may send their children to attend classes at neighborhood mosques.

Private preschools have become popular among middle-class and upper-middle-class residents in recent years, reflecting increased competition for admissions into Lahore's private primary and secondary schools. There is a widely shared sentiment in the city that a good education is a necessary preparation for success in the contemporary economy. Private colleges offering degree courses in business management and computer-based information technology have proliferated in Lahore in recent years.

Transportation System. Lahore's location at one terminus of the newly completed, ultramodern, multilane Pakistan Motorway (complete with its own separate police force) belies the otherwise-prosaic nature of its internal surface-road network. While major road intersections across the city are provided with traffic signals, most of Lahore's smaller roads and lanes are still largely unregulated. Vehicular traffic in the city travels in the left lane, a custom begun while Lahore was still part of the British Empire. Cars, trucks, buses, motor rickshas, bicycles, and motorbikes share space with a variety of animal-driven vehicles on most of Lahore's city streets. Horse-drawn carts are still the conveyance of choice for people and goods traveling between Lahore's railway station and Old City, and small vans (or "wagons") and municipal buses ply the streets of most parts of the city. An area to the north of the Old City, along the floodplain of the Ravi, serves as a bustling regional depot for trucks and buses transporting goods and people across the country. Here, and at a few other locations in the city, private companies sell passenger tickets on buses bound for nearly anywhere imaginable within Pakistan.

Lahore has an international airport at the eastern edge of the city, with nonstop service to a range of national and international destinations, including London. Trains travel between Lahore and most other cities in Pakistan, and have a reputation for being highly reliable. Train and bus connections are available to India from Lahore, and both pass through the border post at nearby Wagah.

CULTURAL AND SOCIAL LIFE

Distinctive Features of the City's Cultures. Lahore is perhaps distinctive among other large South Asian cities for the degree to which both men and women favor wearing the national dress. For both men and women, this is a two-piece ensemble consisting of a knee-length tunic (*kamiz*) worn over

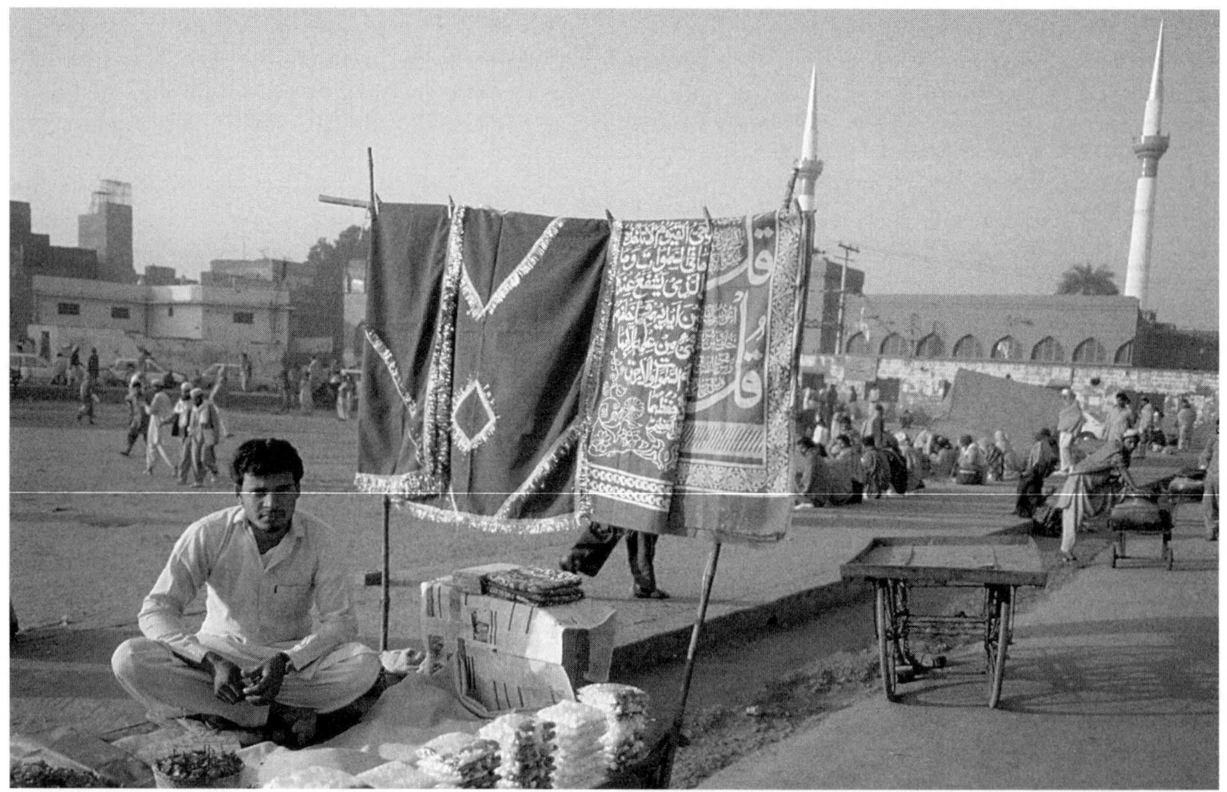

© NIK WHEELER/CORBIS

A Pakistani street vendor displays his goods at the Data Ganj Baksh (also known as Abdul Hasan Ali) shrine in Lahore.

loose pajamas (*shalwar*). Nearly all women wear a version of this outfit in Lahore, and all but a small minority of men do so as well. The latter favor Western-style shirts and trousers for business and leisure attire. While this group is concentrated mostly among the city's middle-class and upper-middle-class males, no hard-and-fast rules seem to govern the choice of attire. At weddings and other formal events, women sometimes prefer to wear saris, a type of wrapped clothing worn more often by women in neighboring India. Most residents place great emphasis on the cleanliness and repair of their clothing and shoes whenever appearing in public.

Visitors to Lahore will encounter that city's reputation for unstinting hospitality as both a source of local pride and as an actually realized set of social practices. Lahori generosity and warmth of expression are well-deserved stereotypes used by many to characterize the city's inhabitants. A commonly held belief that people of virtue comport themselves with deference and dignity is an inseparable component of this reputation. Concomitant with this idea is the notion that women are responsible for upholding, in their personal demeanor, the esteem and reputation of the family. While the practice of secluding women in public and in the home (*purdah*) is observed by many in Lahore, there seems to be no broad consensus as to the desirability of following this practice strictly. Outside of market areas specializing in women's clothing and accessories, however, public space in Lahore is dominated by men.

Cuisine. A few stores in Lahore's upscale shopping districts carry imported foods and drinks, but the vast majority of Lahore's households serve regional dishes made from locally grown foods. A rich variety of seasonal vegetables and grains are consumed on a daily basis, and a serving of meat (chicken, fish, beef, or mutton) should ideally accompany the evening meal. Lahore has acquired extralocal prestige for its unleavened breads (*naan, kulcha*), yogurt-based drinks (*lassi*), and rich variety of sweets, among other delicacies. Tea drinking is a national pastime inherited from the British, and most locals prefer their tea prepared with thick cream and lots of sugar. While the consumption of alcohol is officially prohibited in Pakistan, a hemp-based drink preparation (*bhang*) with comparable effects is consumed by some for pleasure.

Ethnic, Class, and Religious Diversity. The majority of Lahore's residents, both rich and poor, trace their ethnic roots to Punjab province. Since partition, however, a growing minority population in the city derives from areas outside Punjab. This is especially true of the descendants of refugees from other provinces in north India. Perhaps the most distinctive difference between the former group and the latter is linguistic—the Punjabi language is favored by the province's indigenous residents, while most others converse more comfortably in Urdu. While ethnic tension between these two groups is not unheard of, divisions between people over religious matters are far more common.

A small minority of Lahore's residents practice the Christian faith, both Protestant and Catholic. Hindus form an even smaller minority in the city, and few practice their religion openly. The vast majority of residents in Lahore, as in Pakistan generally, are Muslims. Among them, the Shi'ah and Sunni sects predominate, though Lahore has a small number of Khoja and Ismaili Muslims as well. Political and religious conflict in the city exists primarily between the Sunni and numerically smaller Shi'ah groups.

No one ethnic group in Lahore can be said to predominate among the upper classes. Members of the few non-Muslim communities, however, are statistically more likely to be poor. Recent estimates suggest that as many as one-third of Lahore's households live below Pakistan's official poverty level. In contrast, less than 2% of households are estimated to earn more than a middle-class income.

Family and Other Social Support Systems. The majority of Lahore's households are organized into extended or joint families. Familial connections are important for securing a range of social goods, including admission to schools, opportunities for employment, securing finance for new business ventures, and even receiving proper health care when hospitalized. In addition, great value is placed on marriages for sons and daughters arranged within the extended-family network. At some point in their lives, most men and women in Lahore will consider marrying and having children to be, among everything else, a social necessity. There are few, if any, other institutions in Lahore able to function as well as the family does in providing necessary social-support networks.

Work and Commerce. A list of occupations practiced by Lahore's residents would be long and diverse. People employed within the "organized," formal-sector economy would make up only part of such a list, as informal economic activity in the city is widespread. The average size of firms in Lahore's commercial and service sectors is typically small, though larger organizations offer employment in the provincial-government, transport, and industrial-manufacturing sectors. In the recent past, a family's workplace and residence were often combined in a single building, and particular trades in the city were associated with ethnic or kin-based groups clustered together in a single locality. At present, and with the exception of unpaid female labor, the typical workplace in Lahore is located outside of the home. Commuting to work requires walking, bicycling, driving, or hiring a conveyance, sometimes over considerable distances. Most of the city's neighborhoods are serviced with small markets and shops that provide all daily essentials. It is still common practice in Lahore for vendors of vegetables, fruits, and milk to call on, and deliver their goods to, households in person.

Arts and Recreation. Lahore has been home to several historically renowned painters, dancers, musicians, and writers. Dedicated and accomplished practitioners of each of these arts continue to live in Lahore today. Every spring, Lahore plays host to an all-Pakistan music festival, and to an international puppet and dramatic-arts festival, both of which are well attended. There is a small but popular community of actors in the city who perform stage plays in the Urdu and Punjabi languages. Oral performances drawn from a more traditional corpus of folk romances are also popular in the city.

The residents of Lahore appear in all their diversity most fully during the city's many annual fairs and celebrations. Major celebrations include those held on each of the Muslim religious holidays, on the occasions of the death anniversary of revered Muslim saints buried in the city, and on Pakistan's national Independence Day (August 14). In late January or February of each year, Lahoris celebrate Basant, a festival that marks the passing of winter into spring. This is the city's most colorful and playful festival, featuring kite-flying tournaments, singing, and the fashionable display of yellow clothing.

QUALITY OF LIFE

In recent decades, Lahore has become a congested and heavily polluted city. Lahore's drainage, water, and sewage systems are inadequate in all but the most exclusive suburbs of the city. Every year, hundreds of Lahore's residents die from illnesses caused by poor sanitation or exposure to industrial toxins. Heavy traffic in the city also accounts for a large number of fatal accidents every year.

Violent crime in Lahore is far less common than in most comparably large cities in the West, but petty crimes such as theft and fraud are notoriously common. A wide gulf separates the quality of life between Lahore's tiny elite minority and the majority of people in the city, who live at or near the poverty level.

BIBLIOGRAPHY

Aijazuddin, F. S., *Lahore: Illustrated Views of the 19th Century* (Granta 1991).

Jones, Kenneth W., *Arya Dharm: Hindu Consciousness in 19th Century Punjab* (University of California Press 1976) [while not focused exclusively on Lahore, this work provides important historical documentation of the non-Muslim social groups active in the city during the last decades of the 19th century].

Latif, Syad Muhammad, *Lahore: Its History, Architectural Remains and Antiquities* (Sang-e-Meel Publications 1892; 1994).

Qadeer, M. A., *Lahore: Urban Development in the Third World* (Vanguard 1983).

WILLIAM J. GLOVER

Lilongwe
Malawi

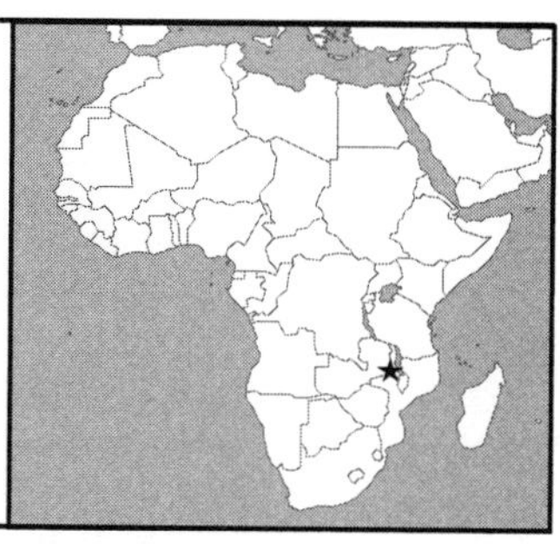

ORIENTATION

Name of City. The national capital of Malawi since 1975, Lilongwe was given the same name as a nearby river.

Location. Lilongwe is located at 13°97′ south latitude and 33°82′ east longitude. The city is situated in the fertile agricultural plains of central Malawi.

Population. According to the 1998 census by the Malawi National Statistical Office, the city of Lilongwe had a population of 435,964 people, of which 228,940 were male and 207,024 were female and 48% of the total population was below age 17 years. Since its inception in 1975, the city has grown dramatically. While in 1966 there were roughly 19,000 people residing in Lilongwe, a decade later that number had risen to 102,000. Between 1975 and 1985 the city experienced an astounding growth rate of 15.8% per annum, and by 1991 the population had reached 234,000. Recent estimates indicate that the city's population is currently increasing at a rate of 9% per annum, although this growth is expected to decline further to about 5% per annum in the near future. While most of this growth is due to the move of the capital from Zomba, in the Southern region, to Lilongwe, it must also be kept in mind that the area of Lilongwe was redrawn to include a larger expanse of 350 square kilometers (135 square miles) incorporating villages that surrounded the old Lilongwe. Amid many environmental and social problems, Lilongwe has proved to be an engine of development for the transformation of the Central and Northern regions.

Distinctive and Unique Features. Lilongwe was declared the future capital in 1966 by the late Dr. Hastings Kamuzu Banda, the first president of Malawi after the end of British colonial rule. With most government functions moving to Lilongwe in 1975, the city took the place of Zomba, the former colonial capital of the country, as the new capital of the postindependence government. Using funds borrowed mainly from South Africa, impressive infrastructure such as government buildings and roads were built. However, the parliament continued to operate from Zomba until 1994, when it moved to Lilongwe with the inauguration of the nation's second president, Bakili Muluzi. The president, however, continues to reside in Blantyre, the commercial hub of the country, which is located in southern Malawi.

Geographically, the city is extensive, covering a large territory of 565 square kilometers (218 square miles) built around two centers, the old city, which functions as a service and distribution center, and the new City Center, also called the Garden City or Capital Hill, 5 kilometers (3 miles) away, which houses the new government buildings, embassies, banks, and other businesses. Major projects that came with the development of the new city during the 1970s and 1980s included Lilongwe International Airport, rail connections to the Malawian district of Salima to the east and the Zambian border to the west, industrial areas in the northern part of the city, and a development program for the fertile tobacco lands of the Central region watered by the Lilongwe, Bua, and Dwangwa rivers. The city itself lies on a plateau west of the Great Rift Valley of eastern Africa at an altitude of about 1,067 meters (3,501 feet). Temperatures range throughout the year from moderate to warm, although from October through December it can be hot. Lilongwe and its environs benefit from adequate rainfall for agricultural production. On average Lilongwe receives 750 millimeters (30 inches) of rain annually, most of which falls between November and April.

Lilongwe has often been characterized as a difficult city to live in because of its poor layout. The city was designed by a South African team at the heyday of apartheid and as such mirrors an apartheid layout, with the rich closer to the main places of work and the poor farther out on the margins of the city. The layout gives Lilongwe its unique and bewildering, intangible atmosphere, which affords a sense of large distances: it has been described as a city that isn't. The new part of the city is spread over a large hilly area, and the natural drainage lines and seeps that run off the high ground are still quite wooded. These have been left undeveloped, which means that even in the new City Center there is the feeling of being out in the bush. For example, at night one is likely to hear spotted hyenas whooping it up as they stroll through the moonlit City Center. During the day these scavengers live in the little local nature reserve close to the City Center, but at night they roam freely, self-appointed, unpaid members of the city refuse-collection department.

Boasting only a couple of skyscrapers, the City Center is thus dominated by local trees and bushes. For most of the postindependence area (1964–1995) this spacious layout, seemingly incorporating the extremely modern idea of wildlife corridors, made it very difficult to get around if one did not have an automobile—which many people in Malawi, the world's seventh-poorest nation, do not. Many of the local residents therefore had to walk long distances to work and continue to do so even today. However, with the coming of the Muluzi government in 1964 and the opening of trade with several gulf states such as Dubai, there has been a proliferation of secondhand minibuses throughout the city. Nevertheless, many people prefer to walk to work, as minibuses are often involved in fatal accidents and are deemed to be unsafe. These difficulties aside, Lilongwe is very beautiful, with distant mountains and hills dotting the landscape around the city and offering breathtaking panoramic views. In the City Center itself modern architecture is complemented by carefully tended public gardens that incorporate a wide array of brilliantly colored tropical blooms and plants. During March and April rows of dazzling yellow acacia trees line the city streets, and in winter bright red poinsettia add splashes of color to the landscape, soon followed by the lilac of jacarandas in bloom.

Around the City Center are high-income residential areas with modern houses in spacious gardens. However, the majority of the residents live in what is known as "traditional housing" in high-density, low-income areas. Houses in these sectors are generally made of wattle and daub, but most have corrugated-iron roofing. Urban agriculture is another distinctive feature of the city. The poor supplement their diets by growing their own vegetables and corn, the main staples, in undeveloped plots throughout the city.

The old city, which is divided from the City Center by the Lilongwe Nature Sanctuary, is the most vibrant part of Lilongwe. It is the main business and shopping area on both sides of Kamuzu Procession Road. Along this road from north to south are the Lilongwe Hotel, branches of the national and commercial banks, the main post office, the largest branches of the Kandodo and PTC supermarkets, and several other important offices and businesses. Just before crossing the Lilongwe River, Kamuzu Procession Road makes a roundabout with Sir Glyn Jones Road. On the other side of the river, one finds the old Indian trading complex. Here Kamuzu Procession Road intersects Malangalanga Road, on which are located the busy old walled market, the bus station, bars, and rest houses.

Attractions of the City. Although Lilongwe is by no means a tourist mecca, the Lilongwe Nature Sanctuary is a worthwhile destination. Several hours of treading through its many trails will yield a rewarding view of small and large mammals, birds, and reptiles. Among the animals in the sanctuary are the spotted hyena, otter, porcupine, bushpig, gray duiker, and bushback and vervet monkeys. There are also a few crocodiles along the Lingadzi River,

© MARTIN B. WITHERS; FRANK LANE PICTURE AGENCY/CORBIS

Rows of hoes are displayed for prospective buyers at a marketplace in Lilongwe, Malawi.

which passes through the preserve. The reserve also offers excellent birding. Birds such as brown eagles, kingfishers, Hueglin's robins, weavers, finches, and the colorful Schalow's turaco hop from tree to tree. A walk along the nature sanctuary's trails offers a glimpse of Lilongwe as it used to be.

In so far as tourism is concerned, Lilongwe should be seen as a taking-off point to the many attractions within a day's drive to the north and to the east. There are many forest and game reserves around Lilongwe, such as Mchinji, Kasungu, and Dedza districts. The beaches of beautiful Lake Malawi are also within a day's drive in Salima, to the east.

Lilongwe also offers many business opportunities and involvement in the global economy. Indeed, many of the commercial and industrial businesses headquartered in Blantyre have moved some of their operations to Lilongwe. Investment opportunities in the growth of the nation's capital abound in all sectors of the economy. However, given that Lilongwe was initially financed by South Africa, most of the businesses are South African–owned, orienting the city toward that country's interests.

Relationships Between the City and the Outside. Lilongwe was selected as the new capital of Malawi because of its central location in order to counterbalance the city of Blantyre in southern Malawi, which dominated the urban hierarchy during the colonial era, a circumstance that resulted in lopsided development of the country wherein the Southern region enjoyed prosperity while the Central and Northern regions lagged behind. Since its inception Lilongwe has grown tremendously to challenge Blantyre's leading position. The new City Center is surrounded by modern residential neighborhoods whose inhabitants work in the new government offices. Occupants of the traditional-housing areas of Kawale and Area 25 commute to work in the City Center via Lilongwe's many minibuses. The buses run back and forth between the old town and the new capital city, as well as throughout the city itself, on a very regular basis. There are also plenty of taxicabs in Lilongwe and fares are cheap by international standards. However, local Malawians find the fares to be expensive owing to inflation and the constant devaluation of the kwacha, which has put the Malawian economy in crisis. At the international level Lilongwe is host to many Malawian and foreign companies, largely from South Africa. It has also proved to be a collection hub for produce from the Central and Northern regions, particularly tobacco. Thus the city offers employment to the local people, and it is a strong challenge to Blantyre, tipping development northward. Lilongwe has succeeded not only in its objective of balancing development but also in its mission of connecting Malawi to the international community via its road, rail, and air links.

Major Languages. While Chichewa is the national language, other languages such as Chitumbuka, Chiyao, and Chisena are spoken for unofficial communication in Lilongwe. The majority of the residents in the city and elsewhere can speak, read, and write Chichewa. English is the language for official communication in government and business.

HISTORY

The Origin of the City. Lilongwe's origins can be traced back to the era of British colonial rule in the Nyasaland Protectorate (later, Malawi). Lilongwe initially became the site of a *boma* (a colonial outpost) in 1902, after a request made by Chief Njewa. Located in an area called Bwaila, the new *boma* took the name of the nearby river, Lilongwe. In 1904 it was made an administrative center for Lilongwe district, and shortly thereafter it was designated a provincial headquarters for the newly created region know as Central Angoniland. The choice of Lilongwe as a new administrative center by early colonial officers was dictated by its centrality in the new province. It is estimated that by 1905 the population of this new settlement was no more than 130 people. By 1920 the settlement had grown considerably and boasted a few buildings that included a small post office, a police station, a prison building, and the resident's office. The resident was the person responsible for the day-to-day administration of the settlement. His tasks were multipurpose, serving as judge, tax collector, administrator, and so forth. In 1930 the status of Lilongwe was raised to that of a sanitary area since the presence of a Sanitary Board was synonymous with a town council. The chairman of this board was the resident, and soon his title was changed to that of district commissioner. This board was responsible for public health, planning, and raising of revenue for the development of the *boma*, that is, the district headquarters.

By the 1950s Lilongwe was a flourishing administrative outpost in central Nyasaland. A number of factors played a crucial role in the historical growth of Lilongwe during the colonial era. Among these was the emergence of Lilongwe as a communications center in the protectorate's central region. The

African Trans-Continental Telegraph company's line reached this region in the early years of the establishment of Lilongwe. Roads connecting Lilongwe to other administrative centers in central Nyasaland were also built, which facilitated the task of administration and commerce. In the 1920s tobacco emerged as the main cash crop in the Lilongwe environs, and the colonial government was quick to promote the growing of tobacco by small farmers as a means of generating revenue for the colonial government. Lilongwe became this new industry's central collection point. Soon trading companies such as the Imperial Tobacco Company, the African Lakes Corporation, the Blantyre Supply Company (Kandodo), and the Kabula Stores Limited opened branches in Lilongwe to take advantage of the wealth generated from tobacco growing by both large-scale agricultural estates and farmers with small holdings. The tobacco industry in turn fueled the building of roads linking Lilongwe to many of the tobacco-producing areas in central Nyasaland. The booming commerce in Lilongwe created an atmosphere in which hawking and commercial trading of other commodities such as foodstuffs, cattle, and fish from Lake Nyasa (later, Lake Malawi) became a daily routine of urban life.

As Lilongwe grew, the physical layout of the town mirrored the colonial mindset of imperialism and racial segregation. In colonial Lilongwe all potential urban inhabitants were not ministered to on an equal basis. Local indigenes were frequently allowed to live only in certain areas of the city, commonly under inadequate, degrading, and tightly regulated conditions. In most colonial settings, physical space was invariably used to promote the separation of social space. In 1924 colonial Lilongwe was thus divided into sectors, one part for the native people on the eastern bank of the Lilongwe River and the other for the residences of the district commissioner and his fellow colonial officers and other Europeans on the river's western bank. Thus while the initial city was founded on the western bank of the river, all indigenes were ordered to move to the eastern bank in 1924. The Asians, mostly Indians who came to Malawi at the turn of the 20th century as indentured laborers, were allocated the southeastern portion of the city on the same side as the indigenous people. It should be noted that the area on the western bank of the river was on higher ground and hence was thought to pose a smaller risk of malaria, cholera, and other diseases—prime ground for European settlement.

The term Asian is often used in eastern and southern Africa to denote south Asians of mostly Indian, Pakistani, and Bangladeshi origin. During the 19th and early 20th centuries as Britain began colonizing Indian and African peoples, Indians were brought to eastern and southern Africa to provide support for exploration and colonization. After the British Imperial East African Company was granted its royal charter in 1888, it encouraged Indian immigration to parts of eastern and southern Africa, primarily to provide indentured labor for railway construction and sugarcane plantations. Most laborers were poor younger sons from middle castes, or peasants released from land debts in their home villages. Many came from the agricultural areas of the Indian regions of Uttar Pradesh, Bihar, and Madras. Others, mostly Hindus, Muslims, Sikhs, and Christians, came primarily from Gujarati- and Punjabi-speaking areas, as well as from Konkani-speaking Goa. A few of these found their way to the emerging settlement of Lilongwe around 1900.

As soon as the town of Lilongwe began to grow, Asians began to occupy the middle level of a three-tiered hierarchy in British colonial Malawi, below white settlers and above Africans. In general, Indians enjoyed fewer restrictions on property ownership than Africans and better access to the resources needed for commercial enterprises, such as bank credit. Consequently, greater numbers of Indians were able to establish themselves as shop owners, hoteliers, commercial farmers, and export merchants. Although the economic mobility available to this group did not immediately foster anti-Indian sentiment, during Banda's rule, Asians' land was confiscated, noncitizens were deported, and Asians were forcibly removed from rural areas to the three urban centers of Lilongwe, Blantyre, and Zomba. They could conduct their commerce only in these three areas. Today Asians are involved in commercial enterprises such as retail shops and banks and control most of the economy in Malawi. At the time when Asians were being persecuted by the Banda regime, their numbers dropped from a high of 15,000 to 5,000. Most Asians decided to return to India and Great Britain as well as to other parts of the world. Today the Asian populations is estimated to be 10,000 strong, 2,500 of whom reside in the City of Lilongwe.

Despite the social and physical distances between the races, Lilongwe continued to grow and boundaries were adjusted as the city expanded outward. Lilongwe's fortunes changed significantly in 1930 when the Lilongwe Sanitary Board was established, which meant that Lilongwe would soon graduate to a township with a town council. The board had powers similar to those of a town council with regard to public health and planning albeit with limited revenue-collection powers. It consisted of the district commissioner, district medical officer, the engineer, two Europeans, and two unofficial Asian members. By 1947 the status of Lilongwe had been raised to full-fledged township. The segregated layout of the old part of Lilongwe can be traced to the zoning activities of the Sanitary Board and later the Lilongwe Town Council. Indeed, many of the problems facing Lilongwe today can be traced to the philosophy of segregation that was instituted during the colonial era.

Lilongwe's fortunes came to a pinnacle with the end of colonial rule and the ascendancy to power of Dr. Hastings Banda in 1964. Upon independence in 1964, Banda announced that his Gwelo Plan No. 2 was to begin: a lakeshore road was to be built, the University of Malawi created, and the capital moved from Zomba to Lilongwe. Legend has it that while Banda was languishing in a colonial jail at Gwelo in Rhodesia (later, Zimbabwe), he dreamt of initiating various projects in Malawi, including the transfer of the capital to Lilongwe, a more centrally located position given the elongated shape of the country. The justification for the move was cleverly couched in economic rather than politically expedient terms. In a speech given to parliament by Banda, then prime minister of newly independent Malawi, he voiced the need, first, to improve the efficiency of government by concentrating central government administration in one city and, second, to stimulate development in the Central and Northern regions by establishing a major growth point near the center of the country. When the British government refused to fund the new capital plan, the Malawian government turned to the apartheid-era South African government for the loans that made Lilongwe a reality.

Migration: Past and Present. Central Malawi has a long history of human settlement. When the first Europeans such as David Livingstone in the mid-1860s and early Portuguese explorers in 1811 passed through the present-day Lilongwe area, they found thriving communities led by powerful Chewa chiefs such as Tambala, Malambo, Chimphango, and Thope. Simple and complex rock paintings dating back to about 200 B.C. have been discovered in the hills to the south of Lilongwe. These paintings are thought to have been the work of the Batwa, a group of hunter-gatherers who inhabited the Lilongwe plains during the "Later Stone Age" between 8,000 and 200 B.C. Other artifacts from this period have been unearthed on the site of the new City Center itself. Pottery and metal finds in this region also seem to indicate the arrival of Bantu speakers who brought with them the knowledge and art of iron smelting and farming in about 300 A.D. These new immigrants slowly displaced the original Batwa inhabitants. By the end of the 15th century, the Chewa of central Malawi, a Bantu group, had established a powerful kingdom known as the Maravi empire, from which present-day Malawi derived its name. Although Lilongwe was not the headquarters of this kingdom, most of the chiefs in this area were subchiefs of the Maravi empire.

Current census data indicate that Lilongwe is attracting people from all over the country. Both formal and informal sector employment offer appealing opportunities to young people. One remarkable feature of the new city is the proliferation of numerous stalls set up alongside major roads by small vendors in the informal economy. These stalls, made of cardboard materials and scavenged iron sheets, would not have been tolerated during the Banda era on the grounds that they were an eyesore. Indeed, the Muluzi government and the Lilongwe Town Council contemplated removing the vendors but backed down owing to fear of the riots that might erupt in the process. The informal sector has thus become one of the few survival mechanisms for the new migrants to the city.

INFRASTRUCTURE

Public Buildings and Public Works. The new development north of the Lingadzi River boasts a number of notable buildings. There are large administrative and commercial buildings of modern, striking design, often set among huge, landscaped compounds. Among a few of these buildings are the headquarters of the Malawi Congress Party, which ruled the country for more than 30 years, until 1994. Across the road is the spectacular Reserve Bank Building, top-heavy and shaped like a traditional basket, in which the wealth of the country accumulates. The City Center boasts several skyscrapers and shopping emporiums such as the Hyperstore. Government offices are located north of the center on Capital Hill. The imposing former State House (now the new parliament) is situated at the end of Presidential Way. On the other hand, the old town, as noted earlier, is livelier, home to vendors, Indian shops, and the walled market. It offers a fresh atmosphere in comparison to the sterile and formal City Center. Some of Lilongwe's roads are in good shape, although the majority have potholes and are in need of repair, particularly in residential areas.

Politics and City Services. In present-day Lilongwe, city governance is modeled along a city council led by an elected mayor and councillors. The original Lilongwe Town Council was elevated to Lilongwe City Council in 1975 when the capital moved from Zomba to Lilongwe. The Lilongwe City Council is responsible for the health and environmental well-being of the city. It is supposed to provide many services to the residents, such as refuse collection and landscaping. However, with increasing economic hardships, city programs and services are virtually nonexistent and funding from the government to run the City Council's programs is at the verge of drying up.

Throughout Malawi, street vendors have taken over the narrow and dirty streets of the nation's main urban centers such as Lilongwe, Blantyre in the south, and Mzuzu in the north as hordes of people with no formal employment battle to make a living. These people sell their wares on the streets, causing congestion and litter. Internationally imposed economic reforms, a weak currency, high inflation, and rampant unemployment are all lined up against the suffering public, forcing them to engage in the informal sector to make survival incomes. In Lilongwe, for example, the drainage system around the walled market in the old town, which originally consisted of open drains and canals, has disappeared, having been filled with dirt and refuse. These new landfills now host the stalls and kiosks of vendors flanking Malangalanga Street to the bus depot, who sell items ranging from secondhand clothing to roasting meat. Tea drinking is one of the popular activities currently taking place in the missing drain. Lacking the necessary funds and will, the City Council has failed to dislodge the ubiquitous vendors throughout the city. Despite the difficulties Lilongwe is facing, it plays a major role in national politics as the capital of Malawi, with most of the government functions and political parties based here.

Educational System. In Lilongwe, and in Malawi in general, two major systems of education exist: informal and formal. Informal education, which is still very much a part of rural society, is encouraged by the government on the basis that it instills respect for tradition and culture. The formal education system is the most common in the city and is patterned along the British system, which consists of three tiers: primary, secondary, and tertiary. At the end of eight years of primary education, students take the Primary School Leaving Certificate Examination and the few who are successful are admitted to a four-year secondary school program. After two years in secondary school there is a weeding process wherein students are required to write Junior Certificate Examinations. The successful students continue on to the last two years of secondary school, at the end of which they sit for the Malawi Certificate Examination. Students who do extremely well in the latter (and these are few in number) are then selected to the five constituent colleges of the University of Malawi. Some join technical, professional, or teacher-training colleges.

As a capital city, Lilongwe has a fair share of primary schools, secondary schools, and tertiary institutions of learning, both private and public. For example, Kamuzu College of Nursing, a constituent college of the University of Malawi, is located in Lilongwe, and Bunda College of Agriculture situated on the outskirts of the city.

Transportation System. Lilongwe is a well-connected city by road, air, and rail. Lilongwe International Airport links Malawi to the surrounding countries and the rest of the world by air. Buses provide access to the agriculturally rich hinterland. There is a railway that goes from the city to the border with Zambia to the west and to Salima in the east for the transportation of freight to the rest of the world via the port of Nacala or Beira in Mozambique. Locally, minibuses run back and forth between the old town and the new City Center as well as throughout the city itself on a very regular basis. There are also plenty of taxicabs in Lilongwe, and fares are cheap by international standards.

CULTURAL AND SOCIAL LIFE

Distinctive Features of the City's Cultures. In urban areas women usually wear a skirt and blouse or a modern colorful dress. Men are clad in pants, shirts, shorts, and occasionally a suit. Middle-income professionals are always nicely dressed in western-style suits. During Dr. Hastings Banda's dictatorial rule, there was a strict dress code: women could not wear slacks, shorts, or miniskirts and men could not let their hair grow long. This dress code was repealed in 1994 under the democratically elected government of Bakili Muluzu. Malawi does not have a traditional dress, although Muslim men will often wear a traditional white cassock; women, a head cover.

Cuisine. The diet for the majority of residents in Lilongwe consists mainly of *nsima* (thick porridge) made from maize flour that is rich in carbohydrates and poor in protein. To compensate for the lack of protein in maize flour, *nsima* is eaten with a side dish called *ndiwo* made from a variety of leafy vegetables, beans, poultry, eggs, game, meat from livestock, fish, insects, as so forth. For high-income professionals, rice can substitute for *nsima*. For the tourist not used to Malawian dishes, there are several good restaurants that serve food ranging from hamburgers, curries, stews, steaks, chicken and chips, and baked potatoes to ice cream. Among the notable eateries in the city are Annie's Coffee Pot, the Gazebo Restaurant, the Sunshine Restaurant, the Summer Park Ice Cream Parlour, Southern Fried Chicken, and Modit's Restaurant. The major hotels in town, such as Lilongwe Hotel and the Capital Hotel, have their own restaurants, which offer high-quality food. For the daring tourist wanting to try Malawian cuisine, the best place to go to is a series of local restaurants located around the walled market and the bus station in the old town, where chicken with *nsima* or rice might cost as little as $1.

Ethnic, Class, and Religious Diversity. Lilongwe is a meeting place of various Malawian ethnic groups such as the Tumbuka, the Chewa, the Yao, the Sena, the Lomwe, and the Ngonde. In total, Malawi boasts more than 15 ethnic groups, none of which can be said to be in the majority. However, ethnicity per se is not the cause of any conflicts, but residents do tend to ally themselves based on the region from which they hail. Politically, northerners prefer to stick with northerners and they have their own national political party, Alliance for Democracy (AFORD). The people from the Central region rally around the Malawi Congress Party, and those from the south, irrespective of ethnicity, support the United Democratic Front, which first came to power in 1994.

To unify the country at the time of independence in 1964, Dr. Hastings Banda decreed Chichewa and English the national languages. Although there is a multiplicity of ethnic groups, most Lilongweans speak Chichewa in addition to their own languages and English. During the colonial era, as the city grew, the British colonial officers separated it into three units: one for the local Malawians without regard to their different cultural backgrounds, the second for the Indians who were involved in commerce, and the third for the European residents. This pattern continued into the postindependence era, with the European quarters being taken over by upper-class or high-income Malawians. At the end of colonial rule in 1964 and the departure of the British, the city was stratified by income or class. Thus the city is now divided into high-income residential sections such as Areas 3, 10, and 12; middle-income residential sectors such as Areas 15 and 18; and low-income residential enclaves such as Kawale, Biwi, and Area 25. With the continuing economic crisis, the gap between rich and poor has grown wider and manifests a high degree of inequality.

Family and Other Social Support Systems. Rural in-migration has helped the growth of Lilongwe greatly. Driven from the hinterland because of poverty, the new migrants keep in touch with their rural families, periodically sending remittances back home. In time, other family members follow to stay with the new migrants in the city. It is not unusual for residents to keep in their home several members of their extended family who are newly arrived from the countryside. As such, extended kinship and other community networks are important in surviving the strange ways of the city of Lilongwe.

Work and Commerce. As noted earlier, traveling through the city of Lilongwe, one cannot help but notice the proliferation of numerous stalls set up alongside major roads by small vendors in the informal economy. The majority of people in the city make their survival incomes through the informal sector. The urban informal sector, defined as untaxable small-scale enterprises such as petty trading, has tried to alleviate urban unemployment and the blow dealt to the majority of the people by economic restructuring. Informal activities are easy to enter, unregulated, predominantly family-owned, and labor-intensive and rely on indigenous resources. The scarcity of formal-sector jobs to accommodate both in-migrants and the general urban populace seems to have resulted in an increase in informal-sector jobs. In a random survey taken in Lilongwe in 1991, about 300 households (30% of the sample) indicated that they were involved in at least one small business or income-generating activity. Selling goods or services was found to be the single most important survival mechanism, and a significant proportion of households in all income categories reported that for at least a portion of the year they were obliged to become involved in some form of small business in order to make ends meet. Other coping mechanisms in times of economic turbulence have included borrowing from friends and relatives and from small businesses, or selling products on an irregular basis or engaging in urban agriculture. There also appears to be an increase in the more negative aspects of the informal economy, such as smuggling, black marketing, and prostitution.

The business of smuggling goods to and from the surrounding countries of Mozambique, Zambia, and Tanzania is vibrant. *Katangale,* or black marketeering, ranges from petty thieving to a complex networking system that involves selling stolen goods. Crime and violence by unemployed youths in urban areas seem to be on the increase as well. For some women it has become necessary to work as "bar girls" in order to buy food and other essentials. In the process these women, some as young as 14, turn to one form of prostitution or another in order to make ends meet. The rise in prostitution is more serious today in light of the high possibility of contracting and/or transmitting HIV (human immunodeficiency virus, the virus that causes AIDS, or acquired immune deficiency syndrome). Data from Malawian urban centers indicate that Malawian cities are among the hardest hit by the AIDS epidemic.

Armed robbery, murders, and rape are on the increase, and the national government is finding it increasingly difficult to stem the tide of crime. Corruption at the highest level of government is also a source of great concern.

While this dark side of Lilongwe is a reality, there are also formal-sector jobs—albeit a limited number of them—particularly in civil service, banks, shops, light industries, and other professions. Modern neighborhoods surround the new City Center and Capital Hill. Most of the professionals need drive only a short distance to work. However, the majority of the poor who live in substandard housing far out of the areas of employment have to either walk, ride a bicycle, or catch a minibus. Unfortunately, the formal sector employs only a quarter of the population of Lilongwe.

Arts and Recreation. As Malawi is a former British colony, soccer is the main sport throughout the country but more so in the urban areas of Lilongwe, Mzuzu, Zomba, and Blantyre. The Malawian national team is quite a force in southern Africa's soccer competitions and has on occasion won a number of regional championships. Soccer clubs such as the Limbe Leaf Wanderers, Bata Bullets, MDC, and Telecom Wanderers compete for a number of prized trophies throughout the year. Every Saturday and Sunday, thousands of people converge at Civo Stadium in Lilongwe to watch various clubs play skillful soccer.

In terms of entertainment and other recreational activities, young professionals in urban areas flock to Western-style clubs and bars. During presidential political rallies, people may perform traditional and modern dances to entertain the political dignitaries and other spectators. Television has only recently been introduced into the four major urban centers of Malawi, including Lilongwe, but offers just one channel and for only a couple of hours a day. However, upper- and middle-income families may own a television, a VCR (videocassette recorder), and a satellite dish and thus may be able to treat themselves to a rental movie or a movie via satellite. As far as art is concerned, one tends to find a rich variety of wooden carvings, oil paintings, and other beautiful works of art depicting various indigenous village scenes and daily ways of living for sale to tourists.

QUALITY OF LIFE

While there is little access in rural areas of Malawi to modern services such as health-care facilities, schools, and electricity, these are readily available in the city of Lilongwe. However, availability does not imply accessibility, as many residents of Lilongwe are poor and cannot afford expensive amenities and private health care. Government facilities such as the Lilongwe Central Hospital are experiencing difficulties in providing quality care to the city's residents because of the economic difficulties the government is facing. Among the major debilitating diseases are malaria during the rainy season, schistomiasis and other intestinal worm infections, tuberculosis, measles, and, recently, the proliferation of the HIV/AIDS pandemic. The general health of the population is poor, and the time spent being sick, attending curative services, looking after the sick, or attending funerals is enormous for most of the people. Malnutrition of all forms and anemia are also quite common. The result of the poor state of health is manifested in the high rates of early childhood mortality. In 1995 the under-5 mortality rate stood at 234 deaths per 1,000 children, and the infant mortality rate was estimated at 134 per 1,000 live births. Life expectancy is low—46 years for men and 48 years for women—and these figures are expected to decline as AIDS takes its toll. Data from the 1998 census indicate that life expectancy may have declined to 38 years on average, owing to the devastating effects of the HIV/AIDS epidemic.

Because the financially strapped city government of Lilongwe is no longer able to meet its service obligations, environmental problems such as uncollected refuse and dirty streets and drainage systems are quite common. The supposed "Garden City" of Lilongwe is slowly disappearing. Housing is also in short supply, and the majority of people are forced to live in shantytowns and other low-income areas. Crime is on the increase, necessitating serious security arrangements for the residences of the rich. Despite these difficulties, Lilongwe is still a vibrant city and Malawi's gateway to the international community.

FUTURE OF THE CITY

As noted previously, as the new capital city Lilongwe was developed to act as a countervailing national center to the dominance of Blantyre in Malawi's urban hierarchy, as a means of spreading development northward. In addition, Lilongwe was "planned" to develop into a sustainable modern city that would effectively cater to the needs of its residents. At the turn of the 21st century, an assessment of these dual functions indicated mixed results. While at the national level Lilongwe has grown remarkably into a formidable intervening opportunity rival to Blantyre's commercial primacy, the spatial morphology of the city itself has created problems for most of the inhabitants, particularly the very poor.

At the national level, Lilongwe in the seat of most of the country's administrative functions and a small set of economic and social institutions. Examples of these include headquarters of government ministries, the parliament, the police, the army, banks, the international airport, tobacco auction floors, the Kamuzu College of Nursing, and the national grain silos. Locally, Lilongwe seems to have failed to provide the growing population with adequate infrastructure. This is a direct result of the way the city was spatially planned, with four nodes separated by large distances and empty spaces as buffer zones. The allocation of the poor to the most northerly sectors of the city, which still remain undeveloped, has exacerbated their precarious position. The much talked about propulsive effect of the international airport in the northern part of Lilongwe has also fizzled out. The airport was supposed to stimulate the nearby industrial area at Lumbadzi, attracting raw materials by air and offering a gateway to the international market for light-industrial products. However, this did not materialize and most industries that started locating in this sector of the town have closed owing to the economic crisis the country is currently going through. Only a few regional flights to South Africa, Zamiba, and Zimbabwe fly out of and into the airport, and there is a once-a-week British Airways flight to and from London. The residents of Lumbadzi and northern sections such as Areas 25, 55, and 53 have no recourse but to commute daily to the old city to engage in informal-sector activities, a less-than-satisfactory survival alternative. Others are retiring back to the countryside as the economic situation becomes unbearable. While this study is an indictment of the spatially unsound design of the city of Lilongwe, it also calls for a rethinking of Lilongwe's future. Policymakers need to revise the master plan in favor of a more realistic model that could rationalize the currently planned land-use pattern into a more compact city. A less ambitious and more spatially compact layout would make it easier for the provision of infrastructure and the growth of industries in close proximity to the place of residence for the majority.

BIBLIOGRAPHY

Bandawe, C. R., "Aspects of Urban Society in Lilongwe: 1939–1959," *History Seminar 1988/89,* Paper no. 8 (Department of History, Chancellor College, University of Malawi 1989).

Briggs, P., *Guide to Malawi* (Bradt Publications 1996).

Carter, Judy, *Day Outings from Lilongwe* (Wildlife Society of Malawi 1991).

Chakufa, C. A., and M. S. Polela, "Population Growth and Provision of Housing in Malawi," Paper presented at the National Seminar on Population and Development in Malawi, Chancellor College, Zomba, Malawi, June 5–9, 1989.

Chilowa, W., *Food Insecurity and Coping Strategies Among the Low-Income Urban Households in Malawi* (Department of Social Science and Development, Chr. Michelsen Institute 1991).

Cole-King, P. A., *Lilongwe: A Historical Study* (Government Press 1971).

Coleman, G., "International Labour Migration from Malawi," *Malawi Journal of Social Science* 2 (1973): 31–46.

Conell, J., "Lilongwe: Another New Capital for Africa," *East African Geographical Review* 10 (1972): 90–98.

Du Mhango, G. L., "Traditional Housing Areas (Site and Services Schemes) in Malawi," Paper presented at the Annual Conference of the Association of Local Government Authorities in Malawi, Salima, Malawi 1984.

Gerke, W. J. C., and C. J. Viljoen, *Master Plan for Lilongwe: The Capital City of Malawi* (Purnell 1968).

Kalipeni, E., "Contained Urban Growth in Post-Independence Malawi," *East African Geographical Review* 19, 2 (1997): 49–66.

Kalipeni, E., "The Spatial Context of Lilongwe's Growth and Development in Malawi," *Sacred Spaces and Public Quarrels: African Economic and Cultural Landscapes,* ed.

by E. Kalipeni and Paul Tiyambe Zeleza (Africa World Press 1999): 73–108.

Malawi Government, *Lilongwe Outline Zoning Scheme* (Office of the President and Cabinet, Town and Country Planning Department 1986).

Malawi National Statistical Office, *Malawi Population Census 1966: Final Report* (Government Printer 1969).

Malawi National Statistical Office, *Malawi Population Census 1977: Final Report* (Government Printer 1980).

Malawi National Statistical Office, *Malawi Population and Housing Census 1987: Analytical Report,* vol. II (1994).

Malawi National Statistical Office, *Malawi Population and Housing Census 1987: Summary and Results* (Government Printer 1991).

Mathews, A., et al., *Lilongwe and the Central Region of Malawi: An Official Guide* (Central Africana Ltd. 1991).

Matope, J. J., "Lilongwe: New Capital City of Malawi," Paper presented at the Workshop on New Capital Cities in the Developing Countries: A Critical Examination of Experiences, Abuja, Nigeria, March 4–9, 1984.

Matope, J. J., "Spacial Aspects of Population and Development: Spatial Development Policy and Strategy," Paper presented at the National Seminar on Population and Development in Malawi, Chancellor college, Zomba, Malawi, June 5–9, 1989.

Mjojo, B. K. M., "Urban Development: The Case of Lilongwe: 1920–1964," *History Seminar 1988/89,* Paper No. 12 (Department of History, Chancellor College, University of Malawi 1989).

Mlia, J. R. N., "Malawi's New Capital City: A Regional Planning Perspective," *Pan African Journal,* vol. III, no. 4 (1975): 388–401.

Mlia, J. R. N., "Spatial Dimension of Development in Malawi," Paper presented at the National Seminar on Population and Development in Malawi, Chancellor college, Zomba, Malawi, June 5–9, 1989.

Mlia, J. R. N., and E. Kalipeni, "Population Growth and National Development in Malawi," *Malaysian Journal of Tropical Geography* 15 (1987): 39–48.

Potts, Deborah, "Capital Relocation in Africa: The Case of Lilongwe in Malawi," *Geographical Journal* 151 (1985): 182–96.

Richards, G., *From Vision to Reality: The Story of Malawi's New Capital* (Lorton Publications 1974).

Roe, Gillian, *Beyond the City Limits: Anatomy of an Unplanned Housing Settlement in Lilongwe, Malawi* (Center for Social Research, University of Malawi 1992).

Stuart-Mogg, David, *A Guide to Malawi* (Central Africana Ltd. 1994).

Yashini, Patrick A., "Urban Project Implementation and Lilongwe—New Capital City Project Implementation," Master's thesis, Department of Urban and Regional Planning, University of Nairobi, Kenya 1984).

Useful Web Site

www.africana.com/Articles/tt_313.htm [Agular, Marian, "Indian Communities in Africa," 2000: 1–5].

EZEKIEL KALIPENI

Lima

Peru

ORIENTATION

Name of City. Peru's metropolis of Lima is the national capital and the fifth-largest city in Latin America.

Location. Lima is situated on the desert coast of western South America at 12°03′ south latitude and 77°03′ west longitude, 1,300 kilometers (800 miles) south of the equator. Its location in the Rimac River valley is delimited on both south and north by rocky hills encompassed within the sandy coastal desert, which lack any vegetation. To the east, the arid land rises abruptly to the formidable peaks of the high Andes, reaching altitudes of over 5,000 meters (16,400 feet) only 80 kilometers (50 miles) from the city. The Andean ranges and high plateaus separate Lima from the heavily populated highland valleys as well as from the vast Amazonian hinterland of the continent.

Population. Although founded in 1535 as the seat of Spain's largest viceregal colony in the New

World, Lima's growth to a population of approximately 7.35 million by the year in 2000 resulted almost exclusively from its rapid expansion in the 20th century. The first census in 1614 showed a population of only about 26,000. Until 1836, well over 50% of Lima's people (Limeños) were African slaves brought to Peru to replace the native population, which quickly succumbed to Old World diseases. The rest of Lima's people were Spaniards and a fast-growing population of mestizos (children of American Indian and European parents). In 1836, some 300 years after the city's founding, the population was only 55,600; but by 1876 it had reached 100,000. That year, Lima's mestizo inhabitants then represented 56% of its people; Afro-Peruvians, 18%; Indians, 13%; Europeans, 10%; and Chinese, 2%. Indentured Chinese laborers had been carried to Peru after 1849 to work on coastal plantations and later to build the Andean railroads.

From 120,000 inhabitants in 1900, the population mushroomed, reaching an annual growth of 9% in 1950. By 1999 this had dropped to a modest 2.1% per year. Lima's ethnic composition is now overwhelmingly mestizo in character, but with about 12% of European origins (Italian, German, English, Spanish) and less than 5% of African, Chinese, or Japanese backgrounds. Included within the mestizo population are a large, but under-censused number of Quechua and Aymara Indians.

Distinctive and Unique Features. As one of the largest and most productive of the 52 such "oases" found along the Pacific coast, the Rimac River valley was an attractive city location because it offered ample food and fuel and a large native population available for service in the Spanish colony. Setting the city back 12 kilometers (7.5 miles) from the coast to protect it from attacks, Lima's founders availed themselves of the port they established at Callao, from which political and commercial contact with Spain developed.

The adjacent Pachacamac Valley had been the most important religious center in the Andean region for at least 2,000 years, and the Rimac Valley itself also held imposing temple structures of similar antiquity. Since one of the goals of conquest was the conversion of the native peoples to Christianity, this location was propitious. At 150 meters (500 feet) above sea level—in contrast to the first site chosen for the capital, Jauja, at an altitude of about 3,400 meters (11,250 feet)—the Europeans suffered less from *seroche* (hypoxia) and the cold. In the Southern Hemisphere summer of January 1535, Lima's temperatures of 26°C (80°F) were attractive.

The coast is swept by the cold Humboldt (Pacific, or Peru) Current, whose fish-laden waters make it one of the world's premier fishing grounds, but this was unimportant to the conquerors. The Spanish discovered that the cold waters created a low cloud cap and thermal inversion during long winters, making for cool 15°C (59°F) temperatures and often 90% humidity from June to September. These conditions produce frequent mists—called *garúa*—besprinkling one's eyeglasses and dampening shoulders, although normally it never rains. This pattern changes with the periodic arrival every 15–20 years of the El Niño phenomenon, which can cause heavy rains in winter and hotter summers.

Similarly, the Spaniards were not aware of Lima's special vulnerability to severe earthquakes caused by the geologic mobility of the Nazca Plate under the deep trench just offshore, which thrusts into the continental landmass, forcing the Andes upward. Since the first earthquake recorded in 1568, 39 significant quakes (one every 12 years) have struck Lima. Some were accompanied by tidal waves, which swept over Callao's port area.

The original city was 13 blocks long and 9 wide, with one side abutting the Rimac River. Across the river to the north, the barrio of Rimac developed as a settlement for the laborers, artisans, and slaves, in an area still known as "beneath the bridge." The city was platted in the grid pattern used by Spain in founding all of its New World towns, with important buildings located around a central square (Plaza de Armas): the municipal hall and seat of government, ecclesiastical offices, cathedral, and homes of the "first" citizens. A protective city wall around the oldest section was begun in 1685 in response to pirate attacks, and the enclosed area became known as the Cercado (walled place). In 1872 the infamous American contractor Henry Meiggs, the "Yankee Pizarro," was hired to tear down the wall to "modernize" the city.

The outlying settlements also followed the grid pattern, but not in alignment with the old Cercado. Thus Lima is a collection of grids at odd angles to each other across the broad, flat valley. Fitting together with its Pacific point at Callao, the metropolitan area is roughly triangular in shape. By 2000, Lima covered more than 2,700 square kilometers (1,042 square miles), with an average density of 2,722 persons per square kilometer (1,051 per square mile).

Attractions of the City. Lima reflects the evidence of its colonial foundations, its turbulent 19th-century history, and the impact of its explosive 20th-century growth. It is a primatial city, the cosmopolitan hub of the nation, the center of all major governmental decision making, and the locus of the most important educational, cultural, and intellectual activity. Its attractiveness stems from this concentration of resources, power, and socioeconomic opportunity. For visitor and citizen alike, Lima is where Peru begins. Although historically and culturally interesting, Lima's landscape is no longer as visually beautiful as it was during the first decades of the 20th century. During the second half of the century more than 5 million people arrived from provincial regions, stressing Lima's resources and infrastructure.

In the 1980s, tourism declined for a decade as a result of poor economic conditions and the violent, unsuccessful revolution attempted by the Shining Path movement (an offshoot of the Peruvian Communist Party). Regaining its former stability, Lima attracted 480,000 foreigners in 1998, more tourists than ever before. Apart from the quaint *rincones criollos* (Creole corners) of Lima, there are several museums with outstanding archaeological collections, among them the National Museum, the Anthropology and Archeology Museum, Gold Museum, and Rafael Larco Herrera Museum. At the outskirts are the immense ruins of the temples of Pachacamac and the house of the Inca lord at Puruchucu.

The tourist center has shifted from the Cercado to the district of Miraflores near the ocean, where the newest hotels, restaurants, and shopping areas await visitors. There are large markets specializing in Andean crafts, pottery, leather, and alpaca and woolen weavings. Automated teller machines (ATMs) offer easy exchange from foreign currencies to the Peruvian "Nuevo Sol" (New Sun) emblematic of the Inca empire, and with the widespread acceptance of credit cards, traveler's checks are difficult to cash and almost obsolete. On July 28 and 29 each year, celebrations marking national independence start an official two-week national holiday with civic and military parades and the president's report on administration activity. The best time to visit Lima, however, is during the spring and summer, from October through April, when most public fairs and fiestas take place.

Relationships Between the City and the Outside. Since Lima's founding, its culture and society have been oriented toward Europe, and during the past century, increasingly toward the United States, to which over 450,000 Peruvians have now emigrated. For all Peru's migrants, Lima is the steppingstone. At the beginning of the 20th century, Lima could be reached only by steamship after an arduous and often weeks-long trip from other continents, but today numerous international airlines from Europe, Asia, and the Americas fly into Jorge Chavez International Airport. The port of Callao continues to be the main maritime connection for the country, and Lima is the hub of Peru's highway system, which connects the metropolis with the Andean hinterlands, and internationally to Ecuador and Chile via the coastal Pan American Highway.

As Peru's core city, wherein virtually everything of societal value is concentrated—power, wealth, knowledge, well-being, and even respect—Lima's national role exceeds its demographic dominance. Greater Lima has in excess of 80% of all of the nation's banks and 98% of private investment; consumes 70% of the country's energy; produces 69% of the national product; is home to 54% of all teachers and 50% of students in higher education, as well as 50% of Peru's employers and 73% of its physicians, whose patients use 53% of all hospital beds; and enjoys the use of 76% of all of the country's telephones. The pattern extends to every area of socioeconomic development. Every important aspect of governmental, judicial, and administrative activity is concentrated in Lima, as are all foreign embassies and international agencies, and the headquarters—the "little Pentagon"—of the joint chiefs of the armed forces. Major bases are also here: the air force command and airport at Chorillos, the main naval base at Callao, and the army's armored division in Rimac.

Major Languages. Spanish is the dominant language amongst Lima's inhabitants, but as thousands of migrants from the Andean highlands entered the city, Quechua (the principal language of the Inca empire and the Spanish colony outside of Lima during much of the colonial period) was increasingly heard. Today, Lima's residents speak primarily Spanish; in business, academic, or tourist contexts, English is widely used and to lesser degrees French, German, and Japanese. As evidence of foreign influence, the Italian word for goodbye, *ciao* (in Peru, spelled *chau*), has entirely replaced the Spanish *adios* in everyday usage. Although Quechua is spoken by 30%–40% of Lima's population, with about 4% speaking Aymara, the other major native language, these are used largely in domestic contexts. In the early 1970s both were recognized as official languages, much to the distress of the traditionalists in Lima. The *provincianos* (persons born outside of Lima) had indeed captured the city from its native peoples.

HISTORY

The Origin of the City. Officially founded on February 18, 1535, by Francisco Pizarro, the Spanish conqueror of the Inca empire, Lima became known as the "City of the Kings" because of that date's proximity to the Catholic celebration of Epiphany, the visit of the Three Kings to the infant Christ. Pizarro was engaged in a contest with rivals to establish a viable colony, control the huge native population, capture the wealth of the Inca empire, and survive the rigors of a strange environment. Communication, trade, and political support from Spain were critical and Lima's location best suited the conquerors' purposes. Lima's establishment on the coast with its "back" to the rest of the country constituted an abrupt change from the demographic and political organization of the Inca empire, whose center was in the southern Andes at Cuzco.

The disastrous War of the Pacific with Chile (1879–1883) produced significant changes in Lima for the first time since fully realizing independence from Spain (1825). Chilean forces occupied Lima and Callao, leaving them with serious recovery problems, which led to realignments of political and economic interests. Lima passed through a period of poverty and social and political confusion to one of growth after 1895.

Migration: Past and Present. Urban migration is the most striking feature of Peru's demography as provincial natives move to the largest cities, and especially to metropolitan Lima. Because things of cultural and institutional value are concentrated there, Lima obliges socially mobile individuals and families to migrate there. Coming largely from Andean villages and cities, the *provincianos* continue the capital's metamorphosis, to the regret of "traditional" Limeños. Formerly looked down upon by them, highland migrants now dominate Lima's politics and commerce and the middle and lower classes of the city. In the 20th century Lima changed from a small, elitist center with about 4% of the national population to a sprawling core city with almost 30% of all Peruvians. Migrant demands for services and economic and political domains reinforce the government's proclivity to favor the metropolitan area in its budgets and programs, although attempts to develop better regional distributions of resources are made.

A victim of urbanization was the highly productive irrigation agriculture of the Rimac Valley. The 4,000-year-old canals are now filled in or submerged beneath pavement, sometimes reemerging to provide water for a park. Indeed, the National Agrarian University at La Molina is now surrounded by urban development, its experimental fields slowly encroached upon.

INFRASTRUCTURE

Public Buildings, Public Works, and Residences. Colonial Lima was built by African artisans who then constituted the skilled labor force in the craft and construction trades. But Lima's bursts of growth during the past 120 years under the influence of various urbanization policies and budgetary constraints yielded an architectural jumble of styles ranging from baroque and Moorish to monolithic high-rises of concrete, steel, and glass. Neocolonial mansions and Victorian residences stand in contrast to bamboo squatter huts, and 250-year-old constructions are juxtaposed with nondescript concrete-block structures. Huge government-sponsored apartment complexes cover many blocks, and in the "better" sections, impressive private condominiums create an urban skyline. Offsetting family-built squatter houses are housing projects with squadrons of identical, single-family concrete homes arranged in long rows over the peripheral desert landscape.

The upper-middle-class or upper-class houses in erstwhile "residential areas" are sometimes ostentatious in ways that Limeños would call *huachafo* (stylistic overkill). These areas are at times juxtaposed with concatenations of shacks. Throughout the city, such impoverished sectors (*tugurios*) fill the interstices disguised by tall portals that block them from street view: these are the infamous "alleys with one spigot" immortalized in a classic *criollo* song with that title.

Several colonial churches in the Cercado area date from the late 16th or the 17th century having survived several earthquakes. The "Palace of Government" or "House of Pizarro" on the Plaza de Armas has gone through numerous revisions and is the official home of the president, executive offices, and ceremonial areas. Its broad patio faces the plaza, where palace guards dressed in Napoleonic splendor parade daily for tourists. Other landmarks include the large Spanish fort of San Felipe, which guards Callao harbor, and the Acho bullring in

Rimac. Elsewhere are various "Creole corners" consisting of the remaining colonial and early-19th-century mansions, adorned by ornate, Moorish-style balconies. The Cercado, with its famous shopping promenade, Jirón de la Union, connecting the Plaza de Armas and Plaza San Martín, remains interesting for the visitor. Although ravaged by temblors and poor maintenance, the area was refurbished in the last years of the 20th century.

Politics and City Services. Despite the magnitude of Lima's expansion, the political structure of the city has remained essentially the same since independence. Peru is divided into departments, within which are provinces and their districts. Lima's metropolitan area comprises virtually all of the province of Lima, with 43 political districts, and the province of Callao, with 6 districts. All provinces and districts have elected mayors and councils. The 49 district governments of Lima manage their municipal affairs independently, with some overall coordination by the provincial mayors, but there are few visible indications of any boundaries separating one district from another. The complexity of this arrangement is illustrated by the district of Lima, which includes the old Cercado, 54 squatter settlements (*pueblos jovenes*, or "young towns"), planned urban-development areas, enormous apartment complexes, and 2 urban barrios, each having a different name and organization.

There are great discrepancies in resources among the districts, and significant differences in managerial effectiveness between them as well. At the end of the 20th century the manicured streets of San Isidro (estimated population 63,000) contrasted sharply with the badly paved (or unpaved) roads of Villa El Salvador (estimated population 254,000), typical of the sprawling settlements that engulf the core of Lima and its old "suburbs."

The squatter settlements established by migrants beginning in the 1940s and continuing to the present hold more than two-thirds of Lima's population. Their incorporation into Lima has been a conflictive—even violent—process, with authorities dispatching the police or occasionally sending the army to suppress land invasions or to forcibly relocate the well-organized settlers. These actions uniformly fail to halt "spontaneous" or "clandestine" urbanizations.

© GALEN ROWELL/CORBIS

An apartment building in Lima, Peru.

Lima's periphery consists of a dusty regimen of bamboo shacks, partially constructed brick houses, and rectangular two- or three-story concrete buildings stretching for dozens of square kilometers into the waterless desert encroaching upon the Andean foothills.

All of the more than 800 recognized *pueblos jovenes* began with aggressive grassroots organizations seeking official recognition within the urban political system. Recognition permitted access to municipal services such as water and electricity and a legitimate political voice. Since 1950, the creation of 21 new districts in the newly urbanized areas formalized openings for political participation for the new Limeños within the constitutional system and access to national budgets.

Since the 1980s, local interests and personalities rather than formal political parties have dominated politics within the city. Several factors, including the impact of the Shining Path movement, ineffective government programs, corruption, and the poor performance of the existing parties, led to this situation. Ripple effects of the cocaine trade also filtered downward to municipal levels, and financial dilemmas affecting the nation as a whole accompanied the collapse of foreign development-assistance programs, exacerbating management problems. Lima's municipalities struggle to overcome these quandaries with varied success.

Educational System. There are two educational systems in Lima, one public, the other private. Public schools are funded by the ministry of education, which certifies and pays teachers, manages school districts, and prescribes classroom content. Primary and secondary schools are found in all of the city's political districts but vary in quality, maintenance, and performance. The private schools constitute one-fourth of all of the city's schools and appeal to diverse interests, ranging from religious preference and intellectual approach to ethnic orientation. Roman Catholic and Protestant schools are common; other schools offer instruction in languages such as English, French, German, Chinese, Japanese, and Italian. Some of the private-school curriculum is also mandated by national policy, and all public and most private schools require school uniforms.

The National Autonomous University of San Marcos, founded in 1551, is the oldest university in the Americas, and with about 50,000 students (as of 1999) is the largest university in Peru, but it has suffered from political and economic woes for several decades. Nevertheless, Lima has 13 other universities that enroll well over 200,000 students. These include the national institutions Universidad Agraria La Molina, Nacional de Ingeniera, and Federico Villareal; and private ones such as the Pontifícia Universidad Católica, San Martín de Porres, Cayetano Heredia, and the Universidad de Lima.

Transportation System. Lima's streets for the most part enclose rectangular blocks of various sizes, with few thoroughfares crosscutting the city to facilitate vehicular needs. The urban area has no subway, although a lengthy monorail system has been under construction since the mid-1980s; in 1996–1997 it began to provide some service, with the promise that it eventually will connect the southern periphery to the city center. Most public transport is provided by private and municipal bus lines, collective minivans (*combis*), and taxicabs plying the streets in competition for passengers going to any part of greater Lima.

Since 1975, the number of vehicles of all types on Lima's streets has enormously increased, producing massive traffic congestion in the older areas of the city and in all market areas. This is partially relieved by the cross-city freeway, the Paseo de la República (called the *zanjón*, or "ditch"), which runs from the edge of the Cercado 13 kilometers (8 miles) to the district of Chorillos. Other recent highways bypass some congested areas en route to the international airport in Callao or the central highway leading east to the mountain city of Huancayo and south or north to the Pan American Highway, which runs along the coast. Vital to the city's social and commercial life are the numerous, but uncoordinated, terminals from which the dozens of interprovincial bus lines and trucking firms operate, connecting Lima to the interior.

CULTURAL AND SOCIAL LIFE

Distinctive Features of the City's Cultures. The traditional culture of Lima is described as *criollo* in character. In the jargon of Lima, the *criollo* way is a sense of being and behaving, a style, a set of preferences, a sphere of knowing, and a sense of identity that typifies a real Limeño in contrast to provincial—especially highland mestizo and indigenous—culture and persons. Even in the viceregal era, the *criollo* culture and society distinguished itself from the rest of the nation in dress, architecture, culinary preferences, music, language, and its social origins in the old world. Although Spanish influences were powerfully felt, they became mixed with elements of African culture. Subsequently the amalgam represented in highland mestizo culture was added to the mix.

The *criollo* character of Lima is understood to be in tune with the fast pace of life, yet spontaneous to the point of occasional unreliability. *Criollo* cultural behavior is considered as being quick-witted, ready to take advantage of opportunities for good or ill, fascinated with the nuances of personal relationships, romantic, and given to poetic expression. Thus traditional Limeños feel that they have a certain style, grace, and comportment and certain ways of walking, thinking, and interacting. As newcomers adjust to Lima, they are seen to become *acriollado* (creolized), and it is sometimes said that there is no one more capricious or clever than a *gringo acriollado*—an American or European who has become *criollo*.

After the Chilean war, Lima culture became associated with Victorian characteristics, mediated through strong British influences because of commercial and mining interests. Thus *futbol* (soccer), golf, and tennis entered Lima life, with sports and recreation clubs inviting membership in an urban milieu with new avenues for social mobility. Generally, highland migrants were not socially welcome in Lima, and by the 1890s many were organizing their own associations with such names as "The Progressive Union of Sons of Machahuay District." People from the same district or town (*paisanos*) socialized but also served as self-appointed mediators between the metropolitan center and their home communities. The regional clubs published newspapers, raised funds for hometown projects, and served as lobbyists for their communities.

By 1950 there were hundreds of migrant associations, and 50 years later there were an estimated 8,000 representing virtually every hamlet and district outside of Lima. In this respect, Lima is one of the most unusual cities in the world. The clubs are a response to Lima's primacy and serve as a method to capture resources for provincial interests from the pull of the urban vortex. They provide, moreover, an important subcontext to city life, as migrants retain their natal ties by observing festivals and other hometown social events. This same pattern is found among Peru's international migrants in the United States, Europe, Australia, and Japan.

Cuisine. Anyone born in Lima can be referred to as a *masamorrero*, one who eats the traditional purple corn pudding associated with the October fiestas. Lima is known for its excellent seafood dishes, such as *cebiche de corvina* (lime-cured sea bass) or oven-baked scallops on the half shell. Chicken dishes such as *aji de gallina* (chicken with hot yellow peppers) or *carapulcra* (a combination of potatoes, chicken, olives, and other ingredients) are common menu items. Many *criollo* dishes utilize the native hot peppers called *aji* and *rocoto*. Rice and pasta are the major staples, although the native potato remains important.

The most popular of the traditional foods are *anticuchos*, small pieces of marinated beef heart skewered and broiled over charcoal. These are commonly sold by women vendors (*anticucheras*), who roll their carts to "their" corners ready to cook to order in the late afternoons and evenings. Throughout the city are hundreds of Chinese-Peruvian restaurants, called *chifas*, probably the most common eateries, which range from the most elegant to commonplace. So popular is this *criollo* affection that cooking classes in *chifa* cuisine are widely offered. Finally, the delicious national cocktail known as the *pisco* sour, a blend of Peruvian grape brandy (*pisco*), lime juice, sugar, and egg whites, is characteristic of Limeño social events.

Ethnic, Class, and Religious Diversity. Social classes, like the city itself, have been transformed since the mid-20th century. Gone is the era when a relative handful of prominent families governed Lima's society, politics, and economy. It remains true that virtually all who are part of a national elite live in greater Lima, but they are not so easily identified. The national upper class has not been homogeneous since the 1850s, when the English, Italians, Austrians, and Germans arrived and began integrating themselves into the upper ranks of society through marriage and economic alliances. Although family name remains an important credential, its entitlements are uncertain in contemporary society.

Issues of race and class frequently underlie social relationships and interaction in Lima. Persons are commonly identified by their physical appearance and referred to in terms of classic stereotypes that foreigners may find discomforting. The terms *cholo* and *indio* are applied to persons thought to be of indigenous backgrounds; Afro-Peruvians are designated *zambos, negros*, or *morenos*. The generic term *chinito* (little China man) is used for all Asians, and Europeans and North Americans are collectively called and referred to as *gringos*. Such terms may or may not have negative meanings, depending on who uses them and how.

The burgeoning middle class of entrepreneurs, managers, professionals, teachers, and corporate and government employees pushes hard against the erstwhile upper echelons of society. The origins of this diverse group are largely provincial, representing migrants who came from the small Andean cities and towns. Coming from the Andean mestizo culture, with its indigenous roots, many retain their property and maintain social and kin ties with their provincial *patria chica* (little fatherland). Others of the metropolitan middle classes come from coastal cities and are already identified with *criollo* culture. Middle- and upper-class persons evince strong international interests and often pursue careers that link Lima with global affairs.

The vast majority of Lima's poor are highland migrants who are of mestizo and *cholo* (a term used to refer to bilingual indigenous persons acculturating to a mestizo lifestyle) cultural backgrounds. Some, however, are of old *criollo* ancestry, Afro-Peruvians and mestizos with deep roots in Lima, living in *tugurios* in the oldest neighborhoods and districts. Most lower-class persons prefer to live in the *pueblos jovenes,* where they come to own their homes. All of these people engage in labor-intensive work in construction, in domestic service, as street venders, in the lowest levels of municipal employment, and in a multitude of part-time activities. In economic terms they fall well below Peru's statistical poverty line and form the poorest 50% of Lima's inhabitants, concentrating on their daily work and survival in a highly competitive and unforgiving environment. In striving for social mobility, they hold education in high esteem, although their average schooling is three to four years of primary education. These migrants see their prospects for socioeconomic betterment as being achieved through their children.

Roman Catholicism is the official faith, and Lima's annual Independence Day celebrations feature High Mass led by the cardinal, with all major government officials in attendance, at the cathedral on the Plaza de Armas. Lima's principal religious practices spring from the colonial experience and follow the veneration of its own sacred personages: the internationally known Saint Martin of Porres and Saint Rose of Lima ("Patroness of the Americas"). However, the Señor de los Milagros (Our Lord of Miracles, or "the Nazarene") generates the greatest religious interest. Painted by an unknown artist in 1651, the crucifixion scene on a chapel wall survived the major earthquake of 1655 although other churches were destroyed. African slaves who used the chapel attributed miraculous powers to the painting and began to venerate it, and within 20 years the observances had become a major religious occasion and the church itself a mecca.

October is now known as the "purple month" in honor of the Señor, and devotees wear purple ties, capes, dresses, and religious ornaments during that month. During several days of processions, 100,000 persons regularly participate, effectively paralyzing central Lima. The cult of the Señor de los Milagros is widely diffused throughout Peru through the influences of the provincial migrants. In addition, the cult's Brotherhood has acquired numerous properties in Lima and remains closely associated with Afro-Peruvians. October is also the major bullfighting season, with *toreros* brought from Spain and Mexico to enhance events surrounding religious celebrations. These activities at the onset of Lima's spring mark a festive atmosphere as sunshine reappears through the dissipating cloud cap.

Apart from the strong expression of Catholicism, Lima also has witnessed the steady growth of Protestant Christian denominations resulting from foreign missionary activity, especially the Adventists, Mormons, and various evangelical faiths. These are particularly active in the *pueblos jovenes* and among the lower-class highland immigrants and now have about 250,000 members.

Family and Other Social Support Systems. The extended family is of major importance to Limeños of all social groups, with relationships regularly activated through birthday, baptism, and wedding celebrations and by frequent visiting and daily telephone calls. An inclusive kin network is regarded as essential to a normal social life, and activities in relation to this can take precedence over other events. Family roles broadly follow Hispanic patriarchal traditions, although women have increasingly enlarged their range of activities since the last decades of the 20th century in Lima, where women's employment outside the home is vital to family interests. Women head over 20% of households.

Limeños actively use the Catholic institution of godparenthood to expand the circle of extrafamilial relationships. Named for baptisms, marriages, confirmations, and some secular events, one's godparents often assist in gaining employment and in financial or social support. Similarly, the friendships made during one's high school and university studies form a cohort of age-mates upon whom one can rely. For migrants, the regional social clubs made up of one's *paisanos* are often important in maintaining effective relationships as well as economic and political ties with one's hometown. Those involved

© NIK WHEELER/CORBIS

Relatives place flowers on graves in a multistory cemetery in Lima, Peru.

in the formation of *pueblos jovenes*, housing cooperatives, and the like also develop very strong political and social ties within their residential areas that serve to defend their property interests as well as advance their general well-being. Despite the often chaotic appearance of the *pueblos jovenes*, or the seemingly uncoordinated nature of the urban social landscape, Lima is a city brimming with a wide variety of voluntary and official organizations.

Work and Commerce. The industrial, service, marketing, and managerial importance of Lima in the national economy is overwhelming. In 1835 when Charles Darwin visited Peru, travel between Callao and Lima was uncomfortable and dangerous owing to bandits and general disorder in the city. Today those avenues between the two places are lined with factories and streets now made precarious because of heavy traffic. Industrial development follows the highways leading north and east to the central highlands, and trucks carrying agricultural produce pour into Lima's huge central wholesale market.

The streets of most districts—except the wealthiest—are the busy scenes of Lima's "informal" economy, where open-air markets and vendors dominate commerce, occupying an estimated 350,000 persons daily. While waiting for traffic lights to change, one can buy Chilean or Peruvian wine, a set of Chinese pliers, fresh fruit, German kerosene stoves, newspapers, toilet paper from a neatly stacked pyramid, or even a book about Lima's informal economy. The formal commercial picture has dramatically changed as several internationally based wholesale merchandisers and malls have opened, bankrupting prominent old establishments. The array of products casually at hand throughout the city is testimony to Lima's multifaceted connections to global interests through the major national port or Jorge Chavez International Airport, both of which are in Callao.

Average income per capita in Lima as of 1998 was more than double that of people in highland areas, amounting to about U.S.$3,500 yearly, but annual income was much more for those in the middle and upper socioeconomic classes and much less for the poor. Despite conditions in many of the *pueblos jovenes* and their often ramshackle appearance, people find them preferable to their hometowns because of the opportunities that Lima offers.

Building construction employs an army of poorly equipped workers, who scramble up ladders in sandals with buckets of cement, brick, and steel rods to earn $3 to $4 daily and who receive few if any fringe benefits. Over 30% of migrant women and 10% of the men work as domestic servants at some point during their integration into Lima life. The overwhelming majority of Lima's working women are occupied as either servants or street vendors.

The "work ethic" of Lima's lower class is a strong one, and people are highly entrepreneurial. In the *pueblos jovenes*, there are thousands of unregistered, non-tax-paying ("clandestine") businesses ranging from shoe repair shops to small factories making household items, clothing, automobile parts, and a myriad of other products. Industrial workers and other manual laborers employed by registered businesses are entitled to various state services such as hospital and health care, but many thousands in the informal sector are often excluded or largely unprotected by labor laws. Lima is the nation's most industrialized place and factory jobs are greatly coveted.

Lima is renowned for its bureaucracy, which is the domain of the city's middle classes and their principal employment. Known as *empleados*, white-collar workers control operations of the governmental bureaucracy and private-sector managerial tasks.

The classification *empleado* (a salaried employee) traditionally entitles one to greater benefits under the nation's social security programs, including separate hospital facilities, pensions, and other perquisites. Because of this, and the fact that manual labor is customarily less respected, *empleado* status within the workplace is highly prized, in many cases despite poor salaries.

Arts and Recreation. Lima's public spaces and recreational facilities are heavily used. Streets, plazas, and parks are filled with people engaged in vending, sleeping, exercising, romancing, reading, playing *futbol,* or conversing. The *malecón,* a promenade at the edge of the ocean bluff in Miraflores district, features open-air concerts at the base of an amusing statue of two lovers, a place visited on weekends by brides and grooms to lay flowers by the monument. In Pueblo Libre district nearer the center of Lima, the *Parque de las Leyendas* (Fairytale Park) is a delightful children's playground and zoo, which surrounds an enormous preconquest temple mound (*huaca*). The national stadium hosts major athletic encounters between Lima's professional soccer teams such as Alianza Lima and Sporting Cristal or foreign competitors. There are several private clubs and recreational centers, including the popular Hippodrome racetrack in the district of Monterico. The beaches lining Lima's south coast attract thousands during the summer despite the cool Pacific waters and are also an international surfing Mecca.

Limeños are well known for their fiestas, which rarely begin before 9 P.M. and are attended by members of the extended family and friends. Copious amounts of food and drink accompany the dancing, in which everyone participates. At home or in the numerous clubs and restaurants, fiestas typically feature Lima's poetic music, the *vals criollo* (Creole waltz), performed by both men and women singers accompanied by guitars and a box drum as the audience claps in syncopation. The classic *vals criollo* is nostalgic and romantic, frequently eulogizing Lima traditions. Other musical forms associated with Lima include the often picaresque *marinera,* and Afro-Peruvian *festejos,* in which the verse is followed by a repetitive chorus of several voices to accompany innovative dancing.

Always alert to international fads, Limeños are quick to accept new musical styles just as they keep up with trends of all sorts. Rock and roll, hip-hop, and rap emanate from any number of Lima's 70 radio stations, alternating with *salsa, cumbias,* and *merengues.* Limeños have become more accepting of the native *huaynos,* the Andean country music brought to the city by highland migrants whose performers sing in Quechua or Aymara as well as Spanish.

Although radio remains very important, Lima's busy television networks carry a battery of *telenovelas* (soap operas) beamed nationwide. Most of these, however, are made elsewhere—in Mexico, Argentina, Brazil, or Venezuela—and portray themes of amorous intrigue, villainous behavior, or social comedy. Game shows, talk and discussion panels, and news and sports presentations follow the broadcast patterns found throughout the Americas.

QUALITY OF LIFE

While millions of persons are attracted to Lima with hopes of improving their lives, it is the perverse result of this growth that has caused a decline in many aspects of the city's original attractiveness. Vehicles plying the streets, and particularly the picturesque older ones, produce significant quantities of greenhouse gases and thus contribute to the very high levels of air pollution found throughout Lima. This is especially bad in winter months when the cloud cap entraps the particle-laden air and desert dust. Although people in Lima enjoy far greater access to medical facilities than do other Peruvians, they also suffer extensively from eye and respiratory illnesses.

Vast disparities exist in the availability of health resources throughout the city, ranging from the most modern to the nonexistent. The dusty squatter settlements offer residents only basic clinics and have few medical professionals to serve them. Elsewhere in Lima, some of these services are on a par with those found in the wealthiest nations. The adequacy of the water supply is another serious problem, since Lima is entirely dependent on the Rimac headwaters for its potable water and these sources are directly impacted by droughts. Lima also experiences serious waste-disposal problems as refuse collects and sewage sometimes befouls its beach areas and the Rimac River. Such environmental limitations sharply call into question the sustainability of Lima's uncontrolled growth, quite apart from the administrative and financial issues that plague the city's management.

FUTURE OF THE CITY

Lima remains a magnet for the rest of Peru. Its primacy in all features of national life continues to make it the preferred place of residence and work. As the city expands it is ironic that both upper-class subdivisions and *pueblos jovenes* vie for more livable space at the fringes of the city. Lima maintains its prominence as the core city by devouring the nation's resources in disproportionate levels even though its rate of growth has subsided and urban birthrates have fallen. It seems likely that both these trends will continue.

More important will be the policies that govern the ways in which national resources, employment, and other opportunities are made available outside the metropolis. Success in this regard would reduce Lima's primacy, lessening its appeal to migrants. On the other hand, it will be essential for Lima to become less dependent on its informal economy and service sectors, which exploit the migrant stream for cheap labor. The development of more capitalized, productive enterprises that can sustain a productive urban system without the necessity of devouring the national budget will be essential. Whether Lima will be able to pay for itself remains to be seen.

BIBLIOGRAPHY

Bunster, Ximena, and Elsa M. Chaney, *Sellers and Servants: Working Women in Lima, Peru* (Praeger 1985).

Deitz, Henry A., *Urban Poverty, Political Participation, and the State: Lima, 1970–1990* (University of Pittsburgh Press 1998).

De Soto, Hernando, *The Other Path: The Invisible Revolution in the Third World* (Harper & Row 1989).

Dobyns, Henry F., and Paul L. Doughty, *Peru: A Cultural History* (Oxford University Press 1976).

Doering, Juan Günther, and Guillermo Lohman Villena, *Lima* (Collecciones Mapfre 1992).

Doughty, Paul L., "Life Goes On: Revisiting Lima's Migrant Associations," *Migrants, Regional Identities and Latin American Cities,* ed. by Teófilo Altamirano and Lane Ryo Hirabayashi (Society for Latin American Anthropology 1997) 13: 67–96.

Hudson, Rex, ed., *Peru: A Country Study* (Federal Research Division, Library of Congress 1993).

Klarén, Peter Flindell, *Peru: Society and Nationhood in the Andes* (Oxford University Press 2000).

Lloyd, Peter, *The "Young Towns" of Lima* (Cambridge University Press 1980).

Paerregaard, Karsten, *Linking Separate Worlds: Urban Migrants and Rural Lives in Peru* (Oxford Berg 1997).

Varillas Montenegro, Alberto, and Patricia Mostajo de Muente, *La Situación Poblacional Peruana* (Instituto de Estudios en Población y Desarrollo 1990).

Webb, Richard, and Graciela Fernandez Baca, *Perú en Números: 1991 Anuario Estadístico* (Cuánto 1991).

Webb, Richard C., *Una Economia Muy Peruana: Ensayos Sobre Economia y Sociedad* (Ediciones del Congreso de la República, 1999).

Useful Web Site

www.lanic.utexas.edu [Latin Americana Network Information Center (LANIC)].

PAUL L. DOUGHTY

Lisbon

Portugal

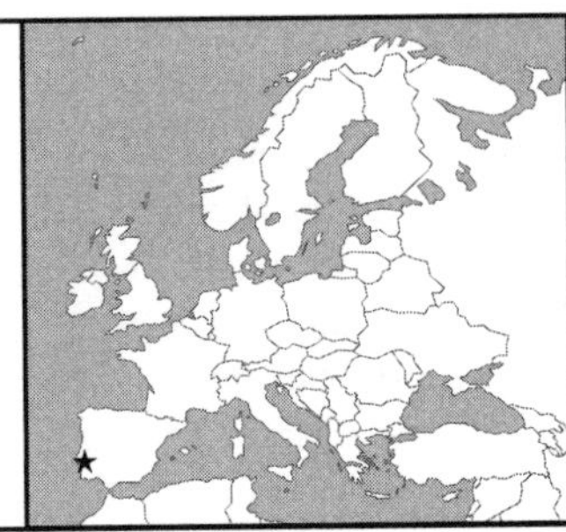

ORIENTATION

Name of City. Contemporary names include Lisboa (Portuguese and Spanish), Lisbon (English), Lisbona (Italian), Lisbonne (French), and Lissabon (German); ancient names include Olisipo (Roman) and Al Uxbûna or Luxbûna (medieval Moorish). Locally, a resident is a Lisboeta (plural: Lisboetas).

Location. The city is located at 38°42′ north latitude and 9° west longitude. Situated on the western Iberian Peninsula, at the extreme western edge of the province of Estremadura, in south-central Portugal, Lisbon is located 20 kilometers (12 miles) inland from the Atlantic Ocean, extending for 15 kilometers (9 miles) along the north bank of the broad Tagus River, which is southern Europe's largest estuary. The city's area is approximately 83.4 square kilometers (32.2 square miles). The area of the metropolitan region is 3,128 square kilometers (1,207 square miles).

Population. The population of Lisbon city is 660,000 (1991); that of the metropolitan area is 2.5 million (1991), or approximately 25% of the nation's population of 10.5 million. The broader metropolitan area is sometimes referred to as Lisboa-Setúbal.

Distinctive and Unique Features. A major Atlantic port city for more than 2,000 years—and still the westernmost major port in Europe—Lisbon is located near the juncture of the Mediterranean and the Atlantic, an important maritime trade link between the Mediterranean and northern Europe, Europe and the Americas, and Europe and coastal Africa. The city has been the political and administrative capital of Portugal, including its expansive past colonial empire, for almost eight centuries. Today, it is a primary city within Portugal: the largest city, home to a quarter of the country's population, and the national economic and cultural center. Today's commercial and naval port facilities are concentrated in the eastern part of the city, and recreational and cruise-line boating facilities in the west. Lisbon's business districts and residential neighborhoods are scattered over a series of low hills, traditionally numbered at seven, stepping back from the Tagus to the north. Building construction is generally low-rise, with no real skyscrapers in evidence, and few other tall buildings. The city is known for its mild, sunny climate that mixes Mediterranean and Atlantic influences, and the warm, pastel colors of its buildings.

Residents and visitors have long enjoyed Lisbon's cityscapes; its hilly topography offers continual vistas, especially from Lisbon's 35 parks specifically designed for viewing the city—the *miradouros* (belvederes). The most famous, in the historic center, are São Pedro da Alcântara in Bairro Alto, Santa Luzia and Largo das Portas do Sol in Alfama, and Nossa Senhora do Monte in Graça.

At the center of the successive Phoenician, Roman, Arab, and Portuguese medieval cities, the Castelo hill contains historic structures and remnants from all these eras, although St. George's Castle has been extensively reconstructed twice in this century, after being mostly destroyed by the Great Earthquake in the 18th century. Inside the castle walls lies the small, medieval Santa Cruz neighborhood. On the south side of the hill lies Alfama, developed during the city's Moorish period, which still retains its Moorish street plan intact, despite many reconstructions and occupations. Most streets—especially the narrow *travessas* and *becos*, which can be as little as 2 meters (6.6 feet) wide—are constructed for pedestrian use only. Once the abode of Lisbon's nobility, in recent centuries Alfama has been a fishing community of humbler folk. Castelo and Alfama constituted the entire city for the first two millennia of Lisbon's existence, until the 12th century. Mouraria, on the north side of Castelo hill, also retains a Casbah-like street plan, but housing there is in a state of severe decrepitude, with much poverty among its residents.

Lisbon's "downtown," called the Baixa, is located to the west of the old city along the riverfront, was developed in the 13th century, and continues as Lisbon's major commercial center. The city's northward development since the 18th century has also been on radii extending outward in all directions from the Baixa as a hub. The Baixa district's rectangular street grid extends between the two major squares of Rossio on the north and the river-facing Praça do Comércio on the south. The elegant Rossio dates from medieval times, and was the location of the city's active House of Inquisition. North of Rossio lies the wide Avenida da Liberdade, copied from Paris's Champs Élysées in the late 19th century, and newer 19th- and 20th-century urban zones beyond. In the Baixa's south, the Praça do Comércio is a handsome arcaded square with a neoclassic design based loosely on Rome's St. Peter's. The square lies open to the Tagus River and was built on the site of the Terreiro do Paço, the old royal-palace grounds from 1585 to 1755. Many locals still refer to it by this older name.

Today, an estimated 1,600 shops line the Baixa's streets. Banks, bookstores, and prestigious cafés, and the offices of many government ministries are found there as well. The Baixa is the city zone most frequented by tourists. During the city's reconstruction after the 1755 earthquake, the Baixa's streets took names of the earlier medieval trade and craft guilds, such as Rua dos Correiros (saddlers), Rua dos Sapateiros (shoemakers), and Rua dos Prata (silversmiths), names that remain today. Adjacent on the west is the prestigious shopping, arts, theater, and café district of Chiado, mostly reconstructed after a disastrous August 1988 fire that consumed more than three blocks of historic buildings.

Bairro Alto ("the high neighborhood," on a hill to the northwest of the downtown) has been the center of Lisbon's 20th-century nightlife until recently, when it has had to share the spotlight with several new zones of clubs, bars, and restaurants. These are mostly in redeveloping waterfront districts, such as the *docas* ("docks") in Alcântara; the 24th of July Avenue in Santos; and the Parque das Nações, the modern minicity in the eastern part of the city that was the site of the 1998 Lisbon world exposition, and which contains several new state-of-the-art performance spaces.

The city offers a cornucopia of architectural styles, though most pre-18th-century structures were destroyed in the 1755 Great Earthquake. Lisbon's Roman Catholic cathedral, dating from 1150, has Roman, Visigoth, and Arab foundations; a Romanesque structural form and exterior with Gothic vaults; and baroque altars, art, and decoration inside. Rich Gothic, mannerist, baroque, and neoclassic styles are evident in buildings throughout the city, and are especially well preserved in Lisbon's 102 Roman Catholic churches, dating mostly from the 13th to the 18th centuries. Perhaps owing to isolation during the mid-20th-century dictatorship, and the lack of corporate economic development in much of the 20th century, the city seems to have largely skipped boxy, modernist, international styles of architecture. Newer construction, such as Tomás Taveira's Amoreiras commercial center, and structures such as the Alváro Siza Vieira's Portuguese Pavilion at the Parque das Nações, tend to exhibit postmodern styles. Portugal's arguably most revered architectural treasure is located in Lisbon's Belém section—the Monastery of Jerónimos, and the associated Santa Maria Church (both usually referred to simply as Jerónimos). The complex is the premier example of Manueline architecture, a uniquely Portuguese, highly elaborated late-Gothic style that features exuberant decorative motifs related to the Portuguese "Discoveries."

Within the city, today's residential concentration is mostly in the newer neighborhoods away from the historic center, especially toward the north, on the east and west sides of the Saldanha-Campo Grande nexus in the so-called "new avenues." This area is also a major site for the proliferation of newer office buildings linked to contemporary business development.

Most of those who work in the city, and three-quarters of the metropolitan area's population, live outside Lisbon's limits to the north and west in a ring of newly suburbanized towns, in vast complexes of high-rise apartment buildings. These metropolitan communities include Oeiras to the west; Amadora and Loures to the north; Vila Franca de Xira to the east; and the towns of Montijo, Barreiro, Almada, Seixal, and Setúbal on the south side of the Tagus (typically referred to as the *outra banda*—"the other side"). The south bank of the Tagus is today the chief industrial and manufacturing zone for the capital, and is linked to the city by two bridges, a train line, and an extensive series of river ferries. Even farther outward are the affluent suburbs of Estoril and Cascais in the west, where expatriate American and British communities are mostly concentrated, and Sintra to the north. In all, 18 smaller adjacent towns (*conselhos*) join with Lisbon to form its metropolitan area.

The 20th century especially witnessed an intense interregional rivalry for national influence between Lisbon and the country's second major metropolitan area, Oporto (Porto in Portuguese) to the north. Oporto is the center of the nation's heaviest industrial area, with its own major port, Leixões, 8 kilometers (5 miles) from the city. Oporto's population—at 302,000, with a metropolitan area of 1 million—draws mostly migrants from nearby central and northern rural Portuguese regions, but has few international migrants. While the city has always had strong business ties with the United Kingdom, especially evident in its famous port-wine trade, it is not as strong a center of global business and tourism as Lisbon.

Attractions of the City. A global, cosmopolitan city for at least 500 years, Lisbon attracts considerable domestic and international tourism—more than 4 million visitors per year on average in the 1990s. Almost two-thirds are foreigners, mostly from Europe (especially Spain, Germany, Italy, France, and the United Kingdom), Brazil, and North America. Since Portugal's entry into the European Union (EU), foreign investment and international business travelers have continued to increase dramatically. Many foreign and multinational companies now have offices, stores, and other facilities in the city. Lisbon's hosting of its 1998 world's fair, on the theme of the "Oceans, Heritage of Humankind," gave increased international visibility to the city. Outsiders find Lisbon unique within Europe, a city that offers unusual and even exotic mixes of old and new, traditional and modern, European and "developing nation"—reflecting, as some Portuguese scholars have recently put it, the nation's "incomplete modernity."

Major Languages. Portuguese ("continental" dialect) is the major language. The second language preference—evident in public signage, foreign-language instruction in schools, and many bilingual publications—is English. Educated Lisboetas of older generations, but not many younger people, are likely to know French, which was widely taught as a second language in schools until the mid-1970s. The most common immigrant language is Cape Verdean–

Guinean creole, or *crioulo* (a mixture of Portuguese and various West African languages).

HISTORY

The Origin of the City. Legend has it that the city was founded by Ulysses, but Phoenicians were the first recorded inhabitants (circa 1200 B.C.), followed by Greeks, Carthaginians, and finally Romans, who arrived in 205 B.C. and developed the city into a *municipium* under Julius Caesar in the 3rd century B.C., as Felicitas Julia Olisipo (usually shortened to Olisipo), the western capital of Greater Hispania. Overrun by Alans, Suebi, and finally Visigoths in the 5th century A.D., Lisbon was conquered by Moors from North Africa in 714, remaining an Arab-dominated city for the next four and one-half centuries. In 1147, today regarded as the contemporary city's official birth, it was recaptured by Portuguese Christian king Alfonso Henriques and his army, with help from Anglo-Norman forces on their way to the 2nd Crusade. The Portuguese court moved to Lisbon from Coimbra in 1256, and Lisbon has remained national capital since. Its university was established in 1290.

The Roman, Arab, and early-medieval Christian cities all occupied the summit and slopes of an easily defensible promontory looking over the Tagus basin, now called Castle Hill (Castelo), site of today's St. George's Castle and below it, the Arab-constructed, Casbah-like Alfama and, later, Mouraria quarters. After what Portuguese refer to as the (Christian) "Reconquest" of the city, Lisbon's remaining Moors were restricted to Mouraria, and Jews as well were ghettoized in the lower Alfama and in the Baixa, until both were expelled from Portugal in 1496. Although Arab influence remains palpable today in the language, music, place-names, and architecture of the city, the first mosque since the 1147 "reconquest" was opened only in 1985. As of 2000 the city still had no synagogue.

In the old city, each cultural occupation was placed over the previous one. Today's St. George's Castle displays the remains of the Christian castle, built over the demolished Moorish one, which replaced Roman fortifications. Lisbon's cathedral, as well, was built over the site of the city's grand mosque, which in its own turn had replaced a major Roman temple.

In the 14th century, Lisbon's port began to grow through increased mercantile trade with England, Flanders, and the Italian city-states, and King Fernando extended the reach of the city's walls from the older Cerca Moura (Moorish wall) to encompass an area six times larger, which would come to include the new 14th- and 15th-century districts of Graça and Bairro Alto, as well as the Baixa. As a result of the Portuguese "Discoveries," and as a center of a growing global mercantile empire beginning in the 15th century and extending into the 16th, reaching to Africa, India, Japan, and Brazil, the city enjoyed great wealth and expanded even farther, to the west and east along the Tagus River, while hugging closely to the shoreline. The Indian Ocean spice trade, especially in cinnamon, pepper, and cloves, brought great wealth to the crown. At the turn of the 17th century, Brazilian gold enriched the capital further for another century. This 15th- to 17th-century era has always been—and is still—commemorated in Portuguese literature, culture, and history as the country's, and the city's, golden age.

On the morning of November 1, 1755, while the city's populace was in church celebrating Mass on All Saints' Day, Lisbon's most formative event from a planning perspective took place. The Great Earthquake brought two major tremors, a large tidal wave, and widespread fire that destroyed the major part of the city, especially the Baixa area, and killed—by some estimates—up to 40,000 people. Under the direction of the king's prime minister, the marquess de Pombal, the city's downtown was rebuilt in a regular, grid-patterned, neoclassic design, still intact as today's Baixa.

Industrial development began in the late 19th century in the city's eastern waterfront zone, until that time an area of agriculture and isolated convents and estates. The city's first suburban rail developments occurred at this time, toward Sintra and Cascais, expanding Lisbon's metropolitan reach. Lisbon also grew in size by annexing the towns of Belém in the west and Olivais in the east. More-modern, 20th-century industry and manufacturing are concentrated in the municipalities south of the Tagus, especially in nearby Setúbal.

As national capital, Lisbon has been the site of most Portuguese political upheavals and struggles. Portugal's bloodless "Carnation Revolution" of April 25, 1975, took place there, ending the 48-year-old, right-wing isolationist regime begun by dictator Antonio Salazar (referred to today simply as *a dítadura,* or "the dictatorship"), opening up the country to a new era of parliamentary democracy and broad cultural and artistic freedoms that have turned Lisbon into a dynamic center for all kinds of artistic endeavor.

Portugal and Lisbon have always been geographically isolated, with extremely poor highway and rail linkages to the rest of Europe (for example, the train to Paris takes 24 hours), and historically focused on external, seaborne links through the Atlantic to the Portuguese empire abroad. Since the 1975 revolution, however, and especially since the country's 1986 integration with the EU, Lisbon and Portugal have finally turned their face more toward Europe. The city was the site of the presidency of the EU during 1992, and again in 2000.

Migration: Past and Present. Either because of needs of empire in the early modern period, or because of relative lack of economic development more recently, Portugal and Lisbon have long been distinct places of out-migration (emigration) rather than immigration, until the 1990s. The 19th century especially saw large flows to Brazil; the 20th century, flows to Europe (especially France and Germany). Lisbon's 20th-century growth came mostly from internal rural migration from all regions of the country, and from a large wave of Portuguese settlers and officials—the *retornados,* or "returnees," who arrived after Portugal gave up its African colonies after the 1975 revolution. Lisbon city and the northern suburbs have drawn mostly internal migration from northern and central regions of the country; the *outra banda* of southern suburban towns tends to draw from southern regions such as Alentejo and the Algarve. Since 1975 the city has also attracted many immigrants, both legal and clandestine, from the former colonies—Cape Verde, Guinea-Bissau, São Tome and Príncipe, Angola, Mozambique in Africa, Goa and Macao in Asia—and, more recently, Brazilians, mostly of the middle class.

INFRASTRUCTURE

Public Buildings, Public Works, and Residences. Important sites linked to government include the neoclassic Palace of São Bento in São Bento, which houses the national parliament (the Assembly of the Republic); the National Palace of Belém—formerly the royal palace, and now official residence of the president of the republic; and Town Hall, the ceremonial and executive city hall in Municipal Place in the Baixa, the mayor's office. Another unusual structure is the Aqueduct of Free Waters, first built in 1748, whose prominent elevated arches rise to 65 meters (213 feet) as they cut across the Alcântara Valley, the endpoint of the earlier municipal-transport system that delivered water to residents from 58 kilometers (36 miles) outside Lisbon. Other prominent structures already described include the Sé (cathedral), dating from 1150; the Castle of St. George, of 8th-century Moorish origins; Jerónimos Monastery in Belém, begun in 1502; and the nearby Manueline Tower of Belém (1515), which used to guard the river entrance to Lisbon. More-modern notable monumental structures and developments include the fascist-era Monument to the Discoveries in Belém (1960); the Cultural Center of Belém ("CCB" to natives), the city's major arts-and-performance complex, built in 1992; and the avant-garde minicity, the 1998 Parque das Nações, former site of the city's Expo '98 world's fair. Adjacent to the Parque is Lisbon's new, visually dramatic intermodal train station, the Gare do Oriente, as well as the city's second bridge across the Tagus, the Vasco da Gama Bridge, Europe's longest.

Lisboetan private housing is usually a multiple-dwelling *casa* ("home")—typically designating an apartment, either rented or owned, except for the upper-middle and upper classes, who sometimes live in one- or two-family *vivendas* or *palacetes*. Rents in older housing in central zones have been frozen for tenants since 1975, prompting disinvestment in and degradation of the older housing stock in the historic center. The city's historic center also has an aging and increasingly diminishing population, though the beginnings of gentrification are evident in some zones, especially Alfama, Graça, and Bairro Alto. Neighborhoods in the until-recently mostly industrial eastern riverfront of the city (such as Beato, Marvila, and Madre de Deus) are mostly working class, and in the western areas (in quarters such as Lapa, Belém, and Restelo), traditionally upper-middle-class and upper-class.

High-rise public ("social") housing projects are very heavily concentrated in the Chelas and Olivais districts in the northeast. Many residents of these projects are relocatees from squatter settlements demolished by the city. From 5% to 10% of the metropolitan population, and from 3% to 5% of Lisbon's population, live in squatter settlements, locally termed *bairros da lata* ("tin neighborhoods") or *barracas,* located mostly in peripheral neighborhoods such as Charneca and Carnide, numbering more than 130 in the early 1990s. Their residents are principally ethnic minorities, especially Rom (*ciganos*), Africans (mostly Cape Verdeans), or people of Indian origin, often migrants from Portuguese East Africa. The city of Lisbon and the adjacent municipality of Loures both have aggressive programs for eradicating squatter settlements and for relocating their residents into public housing. There is a small amount of homelessness in the city.

Politics and City Services. Lisbon's city government, the Câmara Municipal de Lisboa (CML), is governed by a municipal parliament, called the Assembly of the Municipality, which is elected from the city's 53 local administrative districts, or *freguesias*, every four years. Elections are for party-based slates, reflecting national party lines, rather than for individuals; the winning party's leader becomes mayor, or "presidente," of the Câmara Municipal. Most city services are managed directly by offices within a large, permanent municipal bureaucracy, directed by *vereadores*, or managers, drawn from the municipal parliament and ruling parties. Through the 1990s Lisbon was governed by a coalition of the Socialist and Communist parties, with a Socialist mayor, until the 2001 elections, when power passed to a new municipal government controlled by the Social Democrats. Each of the city's 53 *freguesia* districts also has its own smaller district "assembly," directed by an executive council, or *junta*, and headed by a president. Beginning in the late 1990s the city's government began experimenting with devolving to the local districts more budgetary and management powers over services and planning in their areas.

Educational System. All education in Portugal is under the supervision of the national Ministry of Education. Lisbon and its broader metropolitan area fall under the administration of the ministry's Regional Administration for Lisbon and the Tagus Valley; the city government has little or no involvement in educational issues.

Nine years of school attendance—four of primary school, two of preparatory school, and three of secondary school—are compulsory, and many students leave school at 15. Early school leaving before 15 is a serious problem among poor children. Beyond the mandatory nine years, three more years of "complementary" education are necessary to qualify for university admittance.

Because of the aging of Lisbon's population in the city center, schools are underenrolled—whereas in peripheral and suburban neighborhoods, where most families live, overcrowding is the problem. As the city's middle classes grow, they are joining the upper class in enrolling their children in the city's many private schools, or *colegios*, some secular and some Catholic. Among the city's expatriate communities, the Americans, British, French, and Germans all run their own "international" schools. Nursery school and kindergarten are an increasingly common experience for all children, mostly privately financed, with subsidies available for lower-income families.

Lisbon is home to more than a dozen universities, the two public ones being the most prestigious—the University of Lisbon and the New University of Lisbon. For many years, Catholic University was the city's only private university, but in the 1990s it was joined by many newer, less-selective private universities. Portugal is unique among all European countries in that women students in higher education outnumber men almost two to one.

Levels of educational attainment, like social status in general, vary widely and depend on generation. In the mid-1990s only 27% of the overall city's population had completed 12 years of schooling, and only 12% had attended university. Forty-two percent of the population had attended school six years or less. These numbers, however, are dramatically reversed among younger age groups. For example, among those aged 15–20 in 1994, the number of secondary school graduates was 52.1%, as compared to figures of only 14.1% for those aged 30–44 and 4.1% for those aged 45–65.

Transportation System. The city is well served by the extensive four-line Metropolitan underground-rail system (the Metro), dating from the 1960s and still under development, and an efficient, extensive network of bus routes. Several tram lines operate, with three funiculars (*elevadores*) on some of the steepest hills. Taxicabs are relatively inexpensive and plentiful. Two major surface-rail commuter lines travel to the west—including *a linha* ('the "Line"), with one terminus in Cascais at the mouth of the Tagus, and another going north to Sintra. Intercity trains leave from Santa Apolónia Station to Oporto (4 hours) and Madrid (12 hours). Ferries follow six water-transit routes to the south side of the Tagus, from Lisbon's Cais da Alfândega and the Cais de Sodre, as well as from Belém. A small but recently modernized international airport on the city's outskirts at Portela links Lisbon by air to all the world's major cities.

CULTURAL AND SOCIAL LIFE

Distinctive Features of the City's Cultures. Dress of the city's residents follows contemporary European and Mediterranean styles, although among recent immigrants, African and South Asian traditional costumes are common. Rom in Lisbon, especially men, usually dress in black.

In personal etiquette, Lisboetas are fairly formal and reserved in social interaction and in public behavior, though more relaxed and informal in private settings. Educational and professional titles are widely used, significant social markers, and are carefully observed in conduct and speech, including honorifics: Portuguese distinguishes three different levels of formality in addressing others, and Lisboetas routinely use all of them.

As national political, cultural, and religious capital, Lisbon is widely associated with public celebration, commemoration, and holidays—a reputation often critically observed in Portugal's more serious, industrial north. Lisbon is a deeply Catholic city, and most holidays center on the religious calendar. The city's two patron saints are Saint Vincent and Saint Anthony. The more popular of the two is Saint Anthony, who was born in Lisbon in 1195 and lived there until adulthood before going to Padua, Italy. Saint Anthony's *festa* on June 12–13 is the city's major festival, intensely celebrated in Alfama and other historic central neighborhoods and the first of three "popular saints" days in June, along with those of Saint John and Saint Peter. During Saint Anthony's *festa*, the city's older neighborhoods also publicly stage the competitive *marchas populares* ("popular marches"), with always-changing costumes, props, dance and march routines, and song lyrics that celebrate the heritage of their neighborhoods.

© GAEL CORNIER/AP/WIDE WORLD PHOTOS

A butcher delivers meat to a restaurant by bicycle in Lisbon, Portugal, in September 2000. The city was observing a car-free day.

The city government also sponsors an extensive series of free music and arts events through the month of June, called the Lisbon Celebrations (*Festas da Lisboa*). During June, many *freguesias* (local neighborhood districts) also host their own *arraial*, a one- or two-week-long public celebration with outdoor dining, music, and dancing. June 10 is also the "Day of Portugal and the Communities," celebrating the birthday of the national poet, Camões, and the uniting of Portuguese-speaking emigrant communities around the world.

Other popular holidays include the pre-Lenten Carnival and a variety of secular political holidays mostly celebrating important political anniversaries or victories in Portuguese history, such as "the 25th of April" (commemorating the 1975 revolution), Republic Day on October 5, and Independence Day on the 1st of December. Most official holidays stress religious and political unity within the state and nation, though a growing trend in official cultural and arts programming, especially during recent summer "Lisbon Celebrations" and the 1998 world's fair, is to stress the global, multicultural character of Lusophone cultural expression.

Cuisine. The city's quite varied cuisine reflects Lisbon's cosmopolitan character. Typical dishes served in homes and restaurants reflect all of the country's different regional traditions that migrants have brought with them to the city. Much of the city's—as well as the country's—food shows general North Atlantic influences, based on different preparations of cod and potatoes. The most common food, in fact, is salted codfish, or *bacalhau*—as a rule imported, since no cod fisheries exist in Portuguese waters—which is prepared using hundreds of different recipes. Fish and seafood of all kinds are readily available from nearby coastal areas, and the Portuguese (and Lisboetas) eat the highest per-capita amount of fish of all European nationalities. Lamb, beef, chicken, and especially pork are other common protein sources. Some foods are seasonal, such as summer grilled sardines. Many Mediterranean-style rice dishes also exist, especially seafood-based. Many regional varieties of cheeses are available, principally made from sheep and goat's milk rather than cow's milk. Vegetables and fruits are present but are not major parts of the diet. The city is famous for its pastry shops and extensive offerings of baked sweets, which accompany most meals.

As is common throughout the Mediterranean, foods are divided into "sweet" and "salty" categories that are never mixed in the same course, or even in the same small meal. The city has hundreds, if not thousands, of cafés, and coffee drinking is a highly developed art, with an elaborate taxonomy of types of coffee preparations known to all. The most common coffee in Lisbon is the simple small cup of espresso, called a *bica,* or simply *café.*

A variety of dishes and foods from the former colonies, such as the African chicken piri-piri and Indian *chamusas* (or samosas in English; meat or vegetable turnovers), are widely known and eaten. Though internally diverse, Portuguese cuisine has an integrity of its own and is highly esteemed, and few other national cuisines—especially other European ones—are publicly supported in restaurants or grocery stores. "Ethnic" restaurants are limited to occasional Asian restaurants—mainly Chinese, and some Indian, mostly Goan dishes—and a few African restaurants. Franchised "fast food" is still relatively rare, and tends to be popular only among the young.

Ethnic, Class, and Religious Diversity. Lisbon's population has always been, relative to Portugal as a whole, cosmopolitan and diverse. As the seat of the Portuguese empire, it was always the commercial and political center for far-flung colonies and possessions, with frequent visits from foreign merchants, diplomats, and tourists. As always, of course, the city's population has been predominantly Portuguese (now more than 90%).

The city and its metropolitan region grew rapidly in the mid- and late 20th century, owing largely to internal rural migration resulting from concentration and mechanization of the country's agricultural sector, displacing especially small landholders and farmworkers. Historically, Lisbon has been the only one of Portugal's cities to have drawn population in this manner from the entire nation—north, central, and south. In the 20th century, rural migrants were so numerous that those born in the city with some generations of Lisbon roots merited a special designation, *alfacinha* (literally "little lettuce"), a name also applied to a series of older, working-class neighborhoods oriented mostly toward fishing and maritime trades, such as Alfama and Marvila. Many, if not most, urban families of all classes maintain close ties to their *terra,* or ancestral rural homeplaces, often returning home to gather with extended kin. Some participate in revivalist regional folkloric dance and music groups that perform in the city.

Within Portugal, Lisbon is a magnet for migrants from Portugal's former colonies. A large number of these ethnic minorities are Portuguese nationals. Except for some all-African squatter settlements, which evince racial residential segregation, racial integration is the pattern at all income levels and in all neighborhoods, and the contemporary city has no ethnic neighborhoods, quarters, or ghettos. Modest levels of anti-immigrant tensions and interracial violence do exist, but they are very low in comparison with usual European levels.

The city is deeply Catholic, with estimates running as high as 97% of the population, even though considerably smaller numbers are actually observant. Another 2%, mostly foreigners, are Protestant, and the remainder mostly Muslims and Hindus.

In the mid-1990s, about 17% of the population classified themselves as upper-class or upper-middle-class, 25% as middle-class, 28% as lower-middle-class, and 30% as lower-class. Since the 1980s the city and metropolitan region have seen an enormous growth of the middle classes (though they are still small by European standards), as postrevolution education levels have risen and the service economy has provided for more managerial, technical, and professional positions. Increased consumerism is a widely recognized trend, fueled by increasing availability of consumer credit for auto, housing, and other purchases.

Family and other Social Support Systems. Lisboetas as well as other Portuguese are strongly family-centered. Most residents live near extended kin, and even if they have migrated to the city, the country's small size makes regular family visits possible. There is no organized practice of non-kin "baby-sitters," and child care is usually left to extended-family members or handled directly by parents. Fertility rates have been dropping considerably in recent decades, and most young families now have only one or two children. Young adults generally live with their families until marriage and remain close to their parents, socializing frequently with them and other older relatives. Grandparents often support younger working families by providing child care. Large-group socializing is common among young people, who join school or work colleagues for outings in the city. As do other Portuguese, Lisboetas consciously value their collective social ties, and often contrast themselves with social trends toward stronger individualism—trends that, they believe, characterize North America and northern Europe.

Work and Commerce. The city's economy is increasingly based in the service sector, with an estimated more than 60% of all metropolitan employment—including administrative and business services; social services; food services and hospitality; transport and communications; and finance, insurance, and real estate. The vast majority of the entire nation's jobs in these areas are located in the Lisbon area.

In families of all income groups, women typically are part of the workforce. Among the poor and working class, a high proportion of women work as maids for business or commercial establishments, as well as in private households. Men in these groups tend to be concentrated in unskilled or semiskilled construction labor. For some immigrants, this labor is clandestine. Most industrial jobs, estimated at one-quarter of all metropolitan employment, are located on the south side of the Tagus, especially in the Setúbal area. Petroleum refining and cement, steel, and consumer-goods manufacturing (textiles, soap, foodstuffs) are the major industries. Because of Portugal's low labor costs relative to the rest of Europe (about one-third the EU average), manufacturing continues to grow modestly in Lisbon, even while the general urban economy hurtles in a postindustrial direction.

Lisbon is known for its proliferation of thousands of small, family-owned and -operated retail businesses. Only in recent years have shopping centers (*centros comerciais*) and megastores (*hipermercados*) appeared in any large numbers; these are mostly on the metropolitan fringe, rather than in the center. Lisbon's two largest shopping centers are now *Colombo* and *Amoreiras*. Current laws offer considerable protection for small-scale commerce. Informal street commerce is modestly evident on Lisbon's streets, especially in the city's center.

Arts and Recreation. A major Portuguese, mostly urban, folk tradition, dramatically evident on building exteriors as well as interiors, is that of *azulejos*, or decorative tiles, originally a 14th-century Arab tradition brought to Iberia from North Africa. The coordinated sets of multicolored tiles have been used to cover facades and to provide decorative interiors in many buildings, especially as part of the 1755 earthquake reconstruction. The city's National Museum of Azulejos in Madre de Deus offers a stunning review of five centuries of this popular art form. Contemporary artists continue to create new designs, making this a still-vital and evolving medium.

Lisbon has an elegant, late-19th-century neo-moorish bullfighting ring in Campo Pequeno. The traditions and personnel of Portuguese bullfights (*touradas*) differ from those of the Spanish, especially in the types of weaponry, the use of horses, and the fact that the bull is not killed. The Ribatejo region adjacent to Lisbon, especially nearby Vila Franca da Xira, is the heart of the country's bullfighting tradition.

Fado is a distinctively urban song tradition, at first disreputable, that developed in Lisbon's working-class neighborhoods and taverns in the early 19th century. The 20th century saw its rehabilitation into an immensely popular and heavily touristy performance art. Fado song lyrics touch especially on themes of love for Lisbon and the Tagus, and of love, loss, and betrayal in romantic and family relationships, and tend to evince the uniquely Portuguese sensibility of *saudade* (longing or nostalgia). Typically a solo singer, either male or female, is accompanied by two instrumentalists playing a Portuguese *guitarra* and a Spanish-style viola. Fado is sung in professional fado houses serving mostly tourists, or in smaller neighborhood restaurants where staff and patrons spontaneously sing *fado vadio* ("casual fado") as amateurs.

Fado is only one of several important modern popular Portuguese musical traditions, including *música popular portuguesa* (contemporary urban folk music, inspired by the 1960s and 1970s Latin American "new song" movement), that address contemporary social, cultural, and political themes. Fado and other types of popular music contain many songs whose lyrics praise the beauties and mysteries of the city of Lisbon, which is usually gendered and spoken of as female. Because of the influx of musicians from the former colonies, especially Africa, Lisbon also hosts a dynamic "world music" scene as well, as European, Asian, Latin American, and African musicians search to create new Lusophone fusions that also mark Lisbon's status as capital of the Lusophone world. A small but sophisticated jazz tradition also exists, centered on the 50-year-old "Hot Clube" club and school, as well as a lively and distinctively Portuguese rock-music scene, also centered in Lisbon.

There are thousands of small cafés, bars, pastry shops, ice-cream parlors, and restaurants located throughout the city, on almost every block in every neighborhood. For all classes, it is common to "go out" to these locales, which are gathering places for families and neighbors throughout the day and at night.

QUALITY OF LIFE

While Lisbon is viewed by many foreign visitors as poorer and less developed, and physically more degraded, than most other European capitals, its outstanding quality of life and humane pace are widely recognized as virtues. Its natural beauty, active arts scene, cuisine, and lively nightlife are attractions for others. For visitors as well as for many residents, good food, lodging, and transportation are available at reasonable cost, by European standards. The city is pollution-free, and Portugal has one of the lowest crime rates in all of Europe.

BIBLIOGRAPHY

Berger, Francisco Gentil, et al., eds., *Guia de Arquitectura Lisboa 1994* (Guide to Lisbon Architecture) (Associacao dos Arquitectos Portugueses 1994) [bilingual Portuguese-English guide to all the city's significant architectural features].

Boulton, Susie, et al., *Lisbon* (Dorling Kindersley 1997) [another excellent English-language visitor's guide to the city].

Cordeiro, Graça Índias, *Um Lugar na Cidade: Quotidiano, Memória e Representação no Bairro da Bica* (A place in the city everyday life, memory and representation in the Bica neighborhood) (Dom Quixote 1997) [the groundbreaking first and only anthropologically informed community ethnography yet completed of one of Lisbon's neighborhoods].

Ferreira, Vítor Matias, *A Cidade de Lisboa: De Capital do Imperio a Centro da Metropole* (The city of Lisbon: from capital of the empire to metropolitan center) (Dom Quixote 1987) [the seminal late-20th-century sociological treatment of Lisbon's historical development and current transformations].

Ferreira, Vítor Matias, "Lisboa," *Urban Landscape Dynamaics*, Urban Europe Series, ed. by A. Montanari, et al. (Avebury 1993) [brief summary account of Lisbon's social and economic development, focused heavily on current trends].

Ferreira, Vítor Matias, and Francesco Indovina, eds., *A Cidade da Expo '98* (The City of Expo '98) (Bizâncio 1998) [a book reporting the results of a series of studies conducted on contemporary urban change, especially in the area of waterfront redevelopment, as a result of Lisbon's 1998 world's fair].

Ferreira, Vítor Matias, et al., *Lisboa, a Metrópole e o Rio* (Lisbon, the metropole and the river) (Bizâncio 1997) [reporting the results of studies of the Center for Territorial Studies research projects on Lisbon's waterfront redevelopment in the context of late-20th-century economic history and urban planning].

Gurriarán, José Antonio, *Lisbon, an Unforgettable City* (Límite 1997) [excellent English-language translation of the most substantial general visitor's guide to Lisbon, originally published in Spanish as *Lisboa, Una Ciudad Inolvidable*].

Laidlar, John, *Lisbon*, vol. 199 of the *World Bibliographical Series* (Clio Press 1997) [an outstanding English-language annotated bibliography on all aspects of Lisbon history, economy, culture, and politics].

Jacinto, Jorge M. Laureano, ed., *Lisboa Always, Bilingual Edition* (Produce Edições 1994) [an outstanding picture book with ample thoughtful textual interpretation, which treats Lisbon's special qualities, distinctive customs, and aesthetic particularities].

Pais, José Machado, et al., eds., *Práticas Culturais dos Lisboetas* (Cultural practices of the Lisbonites) (Edições do Instituto de Ciências Sociais da Universidade de Lisboa 1995) [a review of social characteristics, everyday practices, and attitudes of Lisbon residents, as measured by a series of sociological surveys completed in the early 1990s].

Pais de Brito, Joachim, ed., *Fado, Voices and Shadows* (Museu Nacional de Etnologia 1995) [an English-language museum catalog, with cultural and historical interpretive articles, of a mid-1990s exhibit on fado at the National Museum of Ethnology].

Soares, Luís Bruno, et al., eds., "Dossier: Lisboa: Que Futuro?," (Lisbon: what future?), *Sociedade e Território* 10–11 (1988): 1–152 [now a social-science classic, a special issue of the major urban sociology journal in Portugal that focuses on a broad range of planning, development, and rehabilitation issues in contemporary Lisbon].

Santana, Francisco, and Eduardo Sucena, eds., *Dicionário da História de Lisboa* (Carlos Quintas & Associates 1994) [an outstandingly complete, 1,000-page, one-volume encyclopedia of Lisbon history, especially thorough on issues of space, place, and architecture].

R. TIMOTHY SIEBER

Ljubljana

Slovenia

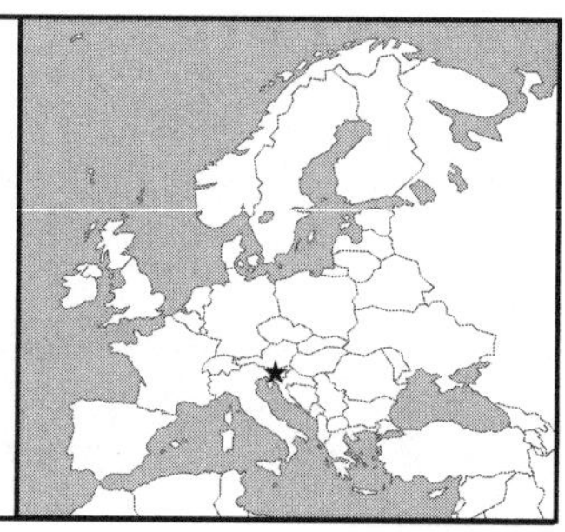

ORIENTATION

Name of City. Ljubljana (*ljoo'blyä.nä*) is the Slovene name of the city known as Laibach in German and Lubiana in Italian. The German name is first mentioned in written sources in 1114, followed two years later by the Slovene name. The etymology of the name has not been clarified yet, but the most likely explanation is that it derives from a Slavic description of the narrow gap between the river and the settlement clinging (*pri-ljubljeno*) to the hillside.

Location. The city is located at 46° north latitude and 14° east longitude at the junction of the Eastern Alps and the Dinaric Alps, at an elevation of 298 meters (978 feet). It is situated in the southern area of the Ljubljana Basin, at the 1.5-kilometer- (0.9-mile-) wide "Ljubljana Gate," the only lowland passage between the Alps and the Adriatic Sea. The average annual temperature is 9.7°C (49.5°F)—with January's average temperature −1.1°C (30°F), and July's average temperature 19.6°C (67.3°F). From the last Ice Age until the Bronze Age a lake extended south of the city. Despite artificial draining the area has remained a flood plain to the present day and is sparsely settled. Owing to its location in a basin, Ljubljana is often affected by temperature inversions in winter, causing fog throughout the day.

Population. In the early 19th century the city had approximately 10,000 inhabitants, a number that doubled by mid-century. The city then continued to spread and incorporate the nearby settlements, a process that is still reflected by the structure of the development as well as by the names of the city's individual areas. In 1935 "Great Ljubljana" was established, with a population of 80,000 in an area of 65 square kilometers (25 square miles). The fastest population growth occurred after World War II, when Ljubljana became the capital of the northernmost republic of Yugoslavia. During the 1948–1993 period, the population increased by 123% as a result of migrations from the immediate hinterland, the rest of Slovenia, and from all over Yugoslavia. The growth rate settled after 1981 and has stagnated in recent years. The city proper as of the last census in 1991 had about 270,000 inhabitants, but the entire metropolitan area had more than 500,000 people. Owing to suburbanization processes, the population of the central city had already started to decrease in the late 1970s. This explains why, out of 157,000 people working in the city, more than one-third are commuters. It is estimated that this trend will continue, and that it will even be enhanced by the completion of the modern highway network that is now under construction.

Distinctive and Unique Features. Ljubljana's most outstanding feature is its location between the Alps and the Adriatic Sea. The northern background of the city consists of a 25-kilometer- (16-mile-) distant Alpine mountain range, while the Mediterranean is just 70 kilometers (43 miles) linear distance away and Venice to the southwest a mere 180 kilometers (112 miles). Because Ljubljana has spread predominantly along its five access roads, and thus obtained the distinct shape of a star, the sections between the arms of the star consist of relatively large areas of undeveloped natural spaces, and the city thus has many natural recreation areas in its vicinity. Tivoli, the largest park, connects the center with the areas on the periphery; but any hiker who advances beyond it will soon encounter warning signs that he or she is entering bear territory. In short, besides being a relatively small metropolis, the spatial development of the city was such that the inhabitants of downtown Ljubljana still have easy access to the natural environment.

Attractions of the City. The city's most prominent sight is Ljubljana Castle, located on the steep castle hill that rises above the oldest part of Ljubljana. The castle was first mentioned in connection with the city in 1141. It was rebuilt and enlarged several times, and the last renovation is still under way. The castle's tower provides the best possible panoramic view of the entire city. In the late 16th century, the Jesuits left their mark on the city with baroque architecture, after which major buildings were modeled in later periods. Although it is much smaller, Ljubljana is compared to Prague in this respect. The older part of the city is still dominated by baroque buildings: the Franciscan Church, the Cathedral (started in 1701), the Palace of the Carniolan Estates (which today houses the Slovene Academy of Sciences and Arts), the Ursuline Church (erected in 1726), and the fountain of the Carniolan rivers.

Most public buildings, dating from the 19th century, belong to the historicist style (for example, the National Museum, the Opera, and the Slovene Philharmonic Hall), while the late 19th century is noted for Secession architecture, the Viennese version of art nouveau. Between the two world wars, Slovenia's most famous architect, Jože Plečnik (who has been called the Slovenian Gaudi) was responsible for urban planning and many new buildings: the National and University Library, a number of churches, the regulation of the Ljubljanica River, and so on. His most remarkable contribution was the arrangement of Prešernov trg (Prešeren Square), which is today the attractive and lively heart of the city. Another interesting contribution is that of the architect Vladimir Šubic, who, inspired by American models, built in 1933 the city's first "skyscraper," at that time the tallest building in this region of Europe. Interesting architecture from the latter half of the 20th century includes the modernist Trg Republike (Square of the Republic), featuring a big cultural and congress center, and some other similarly modernist complexes of buildings in the northern area of the city, which make this relatively small urban agglomeration comparable to cities that are much larger.

© BOJAN BRECELJ/CORBIS

Apartment buildings line the river in Ljubljana, Slovenia.

Relationships Between the City and the Outside. Since 1991, when Ljubljana became the capital of the most developed of the former socialist countries of eastern Europe, its international, political, and economic influence has been growing. The city is the cultural, economic, and political center of Slovenia, and it is becoming an important transport and commerce center as well as a window to southeastern Europe. The city is also developing as an international cultural and tourist center.

Major Languages. The official and common language is Slovene (Slovenian), but nearly everybody also speaks at least one foreign language: most members of the middle and younger generations speak English, the older generation German or Italian, and most of the adults can communicate in Croatian or Serbian.

HISTORY

The Origin of the City. According to one of many legends, the first town at this location was founded by Jason and his Argonauts. Finds from the Ljubljana Marsh confirm settlement prior to the 2d millennium B.C. The Roman settlement at the site of present-day Ljubljana was called Emona. In the 7th century A.D., the Slavs settled the area in considerable numbers, and in the Middle Ages the city came under the rule of the Habsburgs. The end of the Middle Ages was marked by the upheavals of the Reformation and the Counter-Reformation, the latter resulting in major demographic changes caused by the expulsion of Protestants. In 1809 Ljubljana was made the capital of the short-lived French Illyrian Provinces, which extended as far as Dubrovnik in the southern Adriatic Sea. In 1821 Ljubljana was the venue of the Congress of the Holy Alliance, the union of monarchies that had defeated Napoleon. After the violent 1895 earthquake, the baroque city underwent major changes, and its infrastructure was modernized.

After World War I, Ljubljana became the capital of the northernmost province of Yugoslavia. During World War II, the city was occupied successively by the Italians and the Germans. The fierce resistance of the population led the Italians to gird the city with a barbed-wire fence in 1942, transforming it into a virtual concentration camp. The resistance movement liberated the city on May 9, 1945, and Ljubljana became the capital of the Socialist Republic of Slovenia in Yugoslavia. Finally, on June 26, 1991, it became the capital of the new independent state of Slovenia.

Migration: Past and Present. The central area of Ljubljana was inhabited as early as the Paleolithic. Permanent settlement started with the pile-dwelling culture of the end of the late Stone Age. In the 12th century B.C., the Ljubljana Basin was settled by an Illyrian people. The Romans established a permanent settlement in the area of present-day Ljubljana in the 1st century B.C., and remained there until the invasion of the Huns in 452, when the city was destroyed. Little is known of later migrations, but since the city lies on the shortest route between the plains of Pannonia and the north Italian lowland (Po Valley), it is quite likely that there were intensive migrations, especially from the east to the west. What is known is that for a short time in the 6th century, the area of the city was settled by Langobards, and that soon afterward Slavs started to invade the region. The oldest evidence of Slavic settlement dates from the 9th century. Until the end of the Middle Ages, the city also had a Jewish community; the majority of the population was, however, of Slovene origin. In the early 17th century, the city saw major demographic changes as a result of the persecution of the Protestants. The inflow of migrants from the other Habsburg lands started with industrialization. On the eve of World War I, Ljubljana had a substantial German community.

The latest migration wave occurred after World War II, and consisted almost exclusively of migrants from the former Yugoslavia. Most of the immigrants were from neighboring Croatia and from nearby Bosnia and Herzegovina. Immigration peaked in the 1975–1982 period. In the course of the 1990s immigration was completely stopped, but Ljubljana, as well as the rest of Slovenia, became a transition target for illegal migrants from more-remote countries such as Albania, Turkey, and Iran and from Africa.

INFRASTRUCTURE

Public Buildings, Public Works, and Residences. Most of the public buildings are concentrated in the area of the city that was developed in the interwar period or after World War II. Nearly all government and cultural buildings and most commercial buildings are located there. After Slovenia gained independence in 1991, the "citification" process intensified, and this was one of the reasons why the population in the center of the city decreased. During the period of Ljubljana's fastest growth—in the 1970s and early 1980s—large housing estates were developed in the northwestern, northern, and eastern areas of the city, creating small satellite towns. During the first period, which lasted until around 1979, public housing prevailed, but even before the political system was changed in the early 1990s, the share of privately owned housing facilities was higher than that of public housing. After the housing system was reformed in 1994, mass denationalization and privatization was carried out, and today more than 80% of the housing resources are in private ownership.

Politics and City Services. Especially in the period following World War II, the political and administrative organization of the city changed quite often. The last major change occurred in 1994. Until then, Ljubljana consisted of five municipalities, which included a major part of the rural hinterland. The reform of the municipal system throughout the country led to the urban areas of these five municipalities being merged into a single Municipality of Ljubljana (MOL). The city is governed by a 45-member City Council and the Mayor's Office, which has a well-structured city administration with no fewer than 13 departments.

Educational System. The first high-schools date back to the first half of the 17th century, and in 1810 the Écoles Centrales, a short-lived French university, was established. The present University of Ljubljana was founded in 1919—after the disintegration of the Austro-Hungarian Empire. Today, it is the biggest Slovene university, with 23 faculties and with more than 30,000 undergraduates and about 3,000 postgraduate students enrolled in 1998–1999. In 1997, 177 research organizations with 6,312 researchers and technical staff existed. The 55 elementary schools had 24,243 pupils in 1998–1999, and the 34 secondary schools had 27,192 students from all over Slovenia. Schooling is free and compulsory up to age 16.

Transportation System. The railway, which was to connect Vienna and Trieste, reached Ljubljana as early as 1849, but road traffic is nowadays more important and much more developed. A new highway already connects Ljubljana with Italy to the southwest, and the highways extending to the northwest (Austria), northeast (Austria, Hungary), and southeast (Croatia) are being rapidly completed. Owing to the heavy increase of motor traffic and poor public transportation, congestion in the innercity, caused by traffic and especially illegal parking, is a major problem. In recent years, several multistory parking lots have been constructed, but it has become obvious that radical systemic interventions are required to solve the problem.

CULTURAL AND SOCIAL LIFE

Distinctive Features of the City's Cultures. To the inhabitants of Slovenia, Ljubljana is a big city, being the largest in the country. To most visitors from abroad, however, it appears to be a little town, which strives to appear—and occasionally succeeds in appearing—bigger than it actually is. The same can be said about life in the city. Some areas are still predominantly rural in appearance, while other views create the impression of a modern commercial center, which, owing to the lack of space, continues to grow up rather than out. Arriving in Ljubljana by train and getting off at the venerable, but outdated and neglected, railway station, a visitor will get the impression, despite improvements dating from the 1990s, that he or she has come to a hardly definable, chaotic urban space. Driving a car to the center may be a more rewarding experience, but only on a Saturday afternoon or Sunday morning, when the city is almost deserted. The best impression is that provided from the air, which enables the visitor to view the city together with its environs.

Some areas of Ljubljana show Mediterranean influences, in others strictly continental features prevail, and some feature a Balkan variety of the Orient. The city offers to the visitor some uniquely designed spaces, but also monotonous "socialist realism" and pretentious modernist design. Ljubljana's cultural scene is very diversified, and ranges from opera and concerts of classical music to productions of alternative and experimental music and populist cultural, entertainment, and recreation events. Perhaps the most pleasant way to experience the city's pulse is to visit the open-air food market with its amiable crowds; consisting of a wide variety of people, they may even include Slovenia's president and other prominent people of public life.

This small metropolis thus offers its inhabitants and visitors substantially more than might be expected based on its size. Ljubljana indeed provides arguments for and against the famous slogan: "Small is beautiful."

Cuisine. In the 1990s the gastronomic scene of Ljubljana saw major improvements and diversification. In addition to the traditional domestic (Slovene) cuisine—which, in all honesty, differs only slightly from the central European traditions—the city now has many restaurants with a variety of cuisines. The choice of restaurants increasingly illustrates the city's location at the junction of the Alpine, Mediterranean, and Balkan worlds. At the turn of the century, the Mediterranean (Italian, Spanish) cuisines seem to be prevailing. And quite astonishingly, Chinese restaurants have popped up everywhere in no time. A considerable number of good restaurants are situated on the fringes of Ljubljana or in the small towns and villages in its immediate vicinity, a circumstance that adequately meets the leisure habits of the Ljubljanians, consisting of short recreation trips in the city's natural environs, followed by a meal in a pleasant restaurant.

Ethnic, Class, and Religious Diversity. The 1991 census showed that the population of Ljubljana consisted of 78% Slovenes, 6.2% Serbs, 4% Croats, 2.9% Bosnians, and less than 1% Albanians, Montenegrins, and Macedonians. The rest of the population is ethnically undefined, but the majority emigrated from the territory of the former Yugoslavia. Owing to the social and political changes in the 1990s, social stratification has increased in general, but this process has not yet led to a distinctive spatial segregation. There are, however, some problematic areas with very low housing standards. One of the biggest concerns for city planners in Ljubljana is the existence of numerous illegally constructed houses with very poor public-utility services in locations quite close to the city center. This is a longstanding problem, which originated at the time of the most intense immigration from 1975 to 1982. The increased degree of social segregation in the 1990s is also confirmed by the increased number of beggars, who previously were not much in evidence. Another major problem is the big differences in housing standards generated by the existing housing system. The inadequate reforms of the housing system

© BOJAN BRECELJ/CORBIS

Snow does not deter shoppers at an outdoor market in Ljubljana, Slovenia.

have put young low-income families into a very hard position owing to the shortages of low-priced housing.

The religious diversity of the city more or less corresponds to the ethnic structure. Besides the predominant Catholics and a very limited number of Protestants (Slovenes and Croats), there are also members of the Orthodox Church (Serbs). Although there is a quite substantial number of Muslims (mostly from Bosnia), the city does not have a single mosque.

Family and Other Social Support Systems. In 1984 nearly 19,000 children attended a total of 135 nursery schools. Later, the falling birth rate and employment rate substantially decreased the number of children in nursery schools, and in 1998 only 12,234 children attended a total of 108 nursery schools. On the other hand, the need for care of the elderly is constantly increasing, because, as in most other European countries, the population is aging fast. The health system, too, has seen major changes since the 1990s. The introduction of private health care has additionally increased social differentiation. Nevertheless, the basic health services continue to be acceptable and are universally accessible. The city has 70 general-medicine offices with 150 doctors and 168 other staff members. The city's hospitals have approximately 4,000 hospital beds and employ about 700 doctors. These capacities are, however, also used for patients from other areas of Slovenia.

Work and Commerce. Industry, previously the most propulsive economic branch, has been in decline since the 1980s. In the early 1990s a World Trade Center was built in the north of the city, and at the eastern fringe the biggest shopping mall in Central Europe was developed. With a share of 40%, the service sector (transportation and communication, trade, tourism, crafts, and community services) is the major employer. The second-most-important sector is industry, with a share of 32.8%. The metalworking industry, the electrical-goods industry, and construction continue to be the leading branches. Strong positions are also occupied by the food and chemical industries. The more-or-less chaotic transition to a market economy and general globalization effects are expected to cut down employment in these branches. Now that Ljubljana has become the capital of a new independent state, the significance of financial and business activities, education, health, social work, and public administration, which now have a 26.4% share in employment, is expected to increase. The development of small service companies, especially software-oriented ones, on the other hand, is promising. And the city is also increasingly attractive as a destination for tourists. After the huge drop in the number of foreign visitors in the turbulent early 1990s, when the former Yugoslavia started to disintegrate, the number of tourists has been increasing, but has yet to reach the pre-1990 figures. There are 3,748 hotel beds in various facilities, in private guest houses, and on camping sites.

Arts and Recreation. Considering its size, the city has an eminently diversified cultural life. The Ljubljana Philharmonic Society was founded in 1794, and even preceded the Viennese Musikverein. Its most prominent member was undoubtedly Gustav Mahler. The city has three professional symphonic orchestras. The Ljubljana Jazz Festival is the oldest in this part of Europe, and the musical scene of the city has included rock concerts for several decades. Ljubljana has several professional theaters and a range of other performance venues. The city is a world-famous center of the graphic arts, and is growing into a center for modern eastern European visual arts. In 1997 Ljubljana hosted the European month of culture, which in fact lasted 50 days and presented more than 200 different cultural events. Ljubljana also organized Manifesta 2000, the second Exhibition of Modern East European Art. The most prominent cultural institution in the city is Cankarjev dom, a cultural congress center. In addition to the permanent (classical) cultural institutions such as the opera, theaters, ballet, and concerts, the variety is enriched by festivals and music events—for example, jazz and alternative music, a film festival (LIF), numerous experimental theater and dance groups, and two alternative cultural centers ("Metelkova" and the France Prešeren Arts & Cultural Center).

Ljubljana has quite abundant and diverse recreation and sports facilities, which, together with the nearby natural environment, meet the requirements of an increasing number of people taking up active recreation and sport. Since the 1960s Ljubljana has organized quite a number of major sports events: world and European championships in table tennis, basketball, gymnastics, ice hockey, weight lifting, figure skating, and so on. Together with the adjacent provinces of Carinthia (Austria) and Friuli-Venezia Giulia (Italy), Ljubljana (Slovenia) is making a joint bid for the 2010 Winter Olympic Games.

QUALITY OF LIFE

The city's rich cultural and economic life and its charming environs provide for a relatively high quality of life, which is reflected in the high prices of real estate. The proximity of the Alpine landscape to the north and the pleasant warmth of the Mediterranean to the south lure away many of Ljubljana's inhabitants during the weekends and make the city appear rather dreary on Saturdays and Sundays. The quality of life is, however, affected by the dense traffic, which is disproportionately anarchic considering the city's modest size. The city administration also faces major difficulties in solving some environmental issues. Excessive air pollution, caused in part by increasing traffic, is exacerbated by geographic conditions that make the problem difficult to address. In addition, the city has not yet succeeded in finding an adequate solution for the increasing quantities of waste and is still without an operating wastewater-treatment plant.

FUTURE OF THE CITY

In the 1990s the city became the metropolis of a new state, augmenting Ljubljana's significance and enhancing its specific identity in the central European region. New traffic and political connections as well as the globalization processes will allow Ljubljana to make even better use of its geographic location. The major real threat to the city is that the spreading suburbanization will affect precisely its major advantage—its charming natural environment. Ljubljana has yet to find effective means to prevent extensive development and put a stop to the "urban sprawl" in its immediate environs.

BIBLIOGRAPHY

Adamič, Perko, Kladinik, *Priročni krajevni leksikon Slovenije (Handbook of Slovenian towns)* (DZS 1996).

Gabrovec, Matej, Oražen Adamič, *Ljubljana—geografija mesta (Ljubljana—Geography of the town)* (ZRC-SAZU 2000).

Hrausky, Koželj, Prelovšek, *Plečnikova Ljubljana (Plečnik's Ljubljana)* (DESSA 1996).

Leskovar, Malečkar, ed., *Ljubljana mesto kulture (Ljubljana, city of culture)* (Mestna občina Ljubljana 1997).

Mandič, Srna, *Stanovanje in država (Housing and the state)* (ZPS 1996).

Mihelič, Breda, "From Provincial to National Center: Ljubljana," *Shaping the Great City,* ed. by R. Blau, et al. (DZS 1999).

Mihelič, Breda, *Ljubljana City Guide* (DZS 1990).

Statistični letopis Ljubljane (Ljubljana Statistical yearbook (Mestna občina Ljubljana 1999).

DRAGO KOS

Lomé

Togo

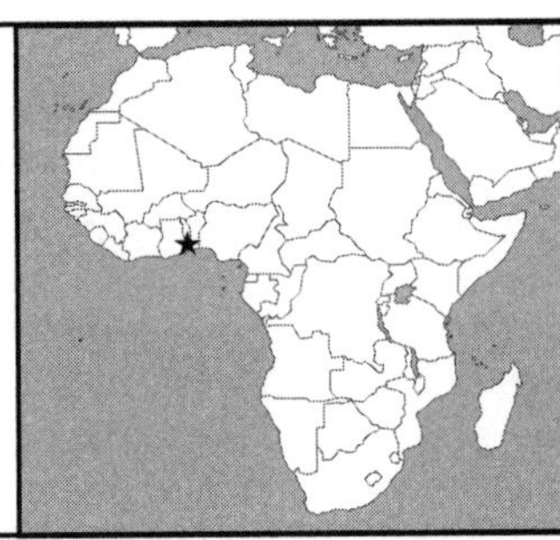

ORIENTATION

Name of City. The name Lomé comes from the Ewe (pronounced Ev'hé) word *alo* or *aloti,* a small shrub of the Anacardiacea family (the same as the kola tree), which produces edible fruits, and which once grew wild where the town is situated.

Location. The capital of Togo, West Africa, Lomé is situated on the border of Ghana and Togo, along part of the marshy lagoon that links the Volta (in Ghana) and the Mono rivers. The city is located 6°10′ north latitude and 1°10′ east longitude.

Population. The population of the city, including the outlying semirural regions, is currently estimated to be 1 million. The most recent government census dates from 1981. Growth is estimated at 3.5% per annum for the whole country, with a higher figure for the capital.

Distinctive and Unique Features. Lomé is in the unique position of being the only world capital located on an international border, which gives rise to a tense political climate and a large informal economic sector. The original German plan for the city, that of a semicircle divided into administrative and economic halves, has bequeathed the city an order and uniformity uncommon for an African metropolis. Lomé is a melting pot of the 30 or more ethnic groups that make up the population in Togo, and an attempt in 1995 to rename the streets of the city to represent all the regions of Togo reflects this heterogeneity. According to one scholar, though, it is from a class and wealth perspective that the city displays its unique feature—that of complete integration of rich, middle-income, poor, and very poor in the same urban environment.

Attractions of the City. Lomé is currently a very unappealing site for either business or tourism, although it was not always so. Both the deep port and the no-questions banking sector caused a business boom. During the 1970s and 1980s numerous five-star hotels were frequented by vacationers with Club Med, and cruise ships docked in the port. The fetish market, the beautiful beaches, the casinos, and the famous nightclub circuit were drawing cards.

Political violence and deadlock, the withdrawal of international donor agencies, and the renovation of commercial facilities in Cotonou and Lagos have all contributed to the current malaise. In 2002 Air France remained the only international carrier to provide services to the unprofitable Lomé-Tokoin International Airport.

Relationships Between the City and the Outside. Lomé is the largest city in Togo, and home to one-fifth of the population. On the West African coast, Lomé is one of the smallest capital cities, but it serves as an entrepôt to much of the Sahel region, via its international port and free-trade zone. From a national perspective, Lomé is the headquarters of the Union of the Communes of Togo, and the mayor of Lomé serves as its president. The commune of the city of Lomé is part of an international organization dedicated to decentralizing government, in such cities as Duisburg, Germany; Bay City, Michigan; Marseilles and Nice, France; Dakar, Senegal; Ougadougou, Burkina Faso; Kinshasa, Democratic Republic of the Congo; and Shenzhen, People's Republic of China. The commune is a member of many international bodies, including Les Cités Unies and the Union des Villes Africaines. In 1988 Lomé was designated Messenger of Peace by the United Nations, and in 2000 was host to the summit of the Organization of African Unity (OAU).

Major Languages. French is the official language of government, but both Ewe of the Kwa and Kabye of the Gur language families have official status. Ewe has a much wider use than its ethnic boundaries, partly as a consequence of German colonial education policies (1904–1914), which mandated the use of German in schools. Mina—a constantly evolving derivative of Ewe mixed with French, English, and other languages—is the lingua franca of Lomé, the coastal zone, and of commerce in general.

HISTORY

The Origin of the City. Lomé has been the capital of Togo since the German colonial administration moved their headquarters from Zébé, part of modern-day Anécho, to the coastal beachfront in 1897. It became the nexus for the extensive railway and road network inaugurated by the Germans. Lomé remained the German colonial capital until the end of German rule (1884–1914). In 1914 Togo was occupied by French and British forces, who invaded from the neighboring Gold Coast colony and Dahomey, and Lomé and its hinterland came under British control. From 1919 until 1960 Lomé, along with the greater part of the former German colony, was placed under the League of Nations mandate, and later the United Nations trusteeship, of France.

The city continued to grow slowly during the colonial period—with many immigrants from Keta in the former Gold Coast—maintaining the original German planning divisions, but with small changes. Much of commerce remained in the hands of the so-called Brazilian families (mixed-race descendants of returned slaves from Brazil) although land ownership always remained democratic and affordable. The French created new *quartiers* with various incentives, including the opportunity to obtain a freehold, and a system of arrondissements and the *commune mixte* (a municipal council elected with limited suffrage) in 1932. The city spread beyond the lagoon to the north and joined the villages of Bê, Kodjoviakope, and Aflao (in present-day Ghana) prior to independence.

After independence, the city grew more rapidly and with less control. Migration from all regions of the country swelled the population of the commune of Lomé. A new international port was added in 1967. On April 1, 1971, the extent of the city was delimited by Decree No. 71/76, to the north by the Groupement Togolais d'Assurance (GTA), the Ghana-Togo frontier to the west, and the gasoline refinery to the east.

As the city surpasses its original administrative division, the new *quartiers* are governed partly by the Prefecture du Golfe and partly by the commune. *Quartiers* are informal titles given to regions in the city, and the names may have historical significance (for example, Amoutivé, a traditional, chiefly *quartier*), religious (Forêt Sacrée or "Sacred Forest"), or geographic (Ramco-Solidarité, named after the Indian-run Ram and Company).

Migration: Past and Present. From its very beginnings, Lomé was a city of migrants. Although a planned town, it was neither a colonial nor a typical African city, but very much a product of the commercial bourgeoisie. Many Brazilian families, living in Anécho and in Dahomey, occupied the early commercial settlements along the coast, while large numbers emigrated from Keta in the Gold Coast colony. During the 1940s at least 45% of families traced their origins to Keta. At the same time, large numbers of Ouatchi also migrated to the city. As Lomé grew in size and influence, migration from central and north Togo increased. The French government forcibly resettled large numbers of Kabye people in the south, some of whom eventually found their way to Lomé.

Postindependence, Lomé continued to expand largely from migration, much of it from the north. Refugees from the political turmoil in Ghana, economic migrants from the north and the Sahel states, and military men relocating their families all contributed to its growth. During the early 1990s political strife led to more than one-third of the population of the city leaving for neighboring Ghana and Benin, although most have returned. Their return has been coupled with large numbers of Liberians and Yoruba fleeing ethnic tension in their respective countries.

INFRASTRUCTURE

Public Buildings, Public Works, and Residences. The city of Lomé and the coastal region have been deeply influenced by the architectural programs of the successive colonial regimes. Vestiges of the German administrative buildings, several cathedrals, and many churches are key sites in the capital. The British period featured no architectural innovation, but more than 40 years of French administration left its mark, most prominently in the work of Georges Coustère. The works of this French national are to be found throughout the country and include the national-independence monument, a number of administrative buildings, the residence of the French ambassador, and the international airport (built in 1944).

During the prosperous 1960s and 1970s, various presidents oversaw an extravagant building program, lavishing upon Lomé and elsewhere five-star hotels, a new port, and sports and government buildings. The skyline is broken by four enormous skyscrapers, most prominently the five-star Hotel Deux Février (newly renovated for the 2000 summit of the OAU), the local headquarters of the Organization for the Economic Cooperation of West African States (ECOWAS/CEDEAO), and several private banks. Since the economic decline and indebtedness of the 1980s, few new projects have succeeded. In 2000, however, the Chinese government built a 30,000-seat stadium in a northeast section of the capital.

In private housing and building, Lomé architecture offers startling originality. Scholars have focused on the importance of the family home, and the outside markers imprinted on the enclosure that signify the family name, history, and origins. In many cases, housing forms a square, each side occupied by different branches of the same extended family, with an open center space for communal activity and animals. In the current dire economic climate, private Togolese citizens invest their small incomes in private building, usually constructed with homemade concrete bricks. Land title, however, remains the subject of intense litigation, which takes place in the civil courts. Warnings are often written in red on the walls of land parcels to deter sale or deception.

Politics and City Services. Lomé remained the capital under the French administration. It became a *commune mixte* on November 20, 1932, after a French decree to that effect of November 6, 1929, which called for the creation of institutions that would permit "the sufficient development and disposal of necessary resources accounting for a balanced budget and the growth of the city for its residents." This law was modeled on that of April 5, 1884, which instituted the municipal administration in France. At the beginning, the nonelected mayoralty consisted of the office of mayor-administrator, assisted by an appointed commission of four French nationals and four Togolese. During the first 15 years, the officers met in the former Elder Dempster building, currently the Ministry of Justice.

The first Lomé mayor (and later first president) was Sylvanus Olympio (1958–1959), and from then to the present day the free election of the mayor has posed a significant threat to an oftentimes undemocratic national government. Laws enacted in 1981 provide for the accountability and financial and administrative independence of the commune. The commune is immediately responsible to the minister of the interior and security. It consists of two elected organs: the Municipal Council, the legislative body, is elected for a term of five years by universal suffrage, and among themselves the council members elect a mayor, the executor of legislation. A decree of 1984 created five arrondissements in the city of Lomé, each with a deputy mayor and a council of nine members. The arrondissements have no financial responsibilities. The 45 members of the council meet twice yearly, in March and September, and at any time at the convocation of the minister of the interior, the mayor, or a two-thirds majority of the council's members. Extraordinary sessions must not exceed 48 hours. All meetings are open to the public. At the commencement of each five-year term, six special commissions and one ad hoc commission are constituted to discuss matters and to promulgate solutions relating to the administration of the city. They are: the Commission for Public Finances, Budget, Police and Civil Security; the Commission for Culture, Leisure and Social Affairs; the Commission for Public Works and Transport; the Commission for Public Markets; the Commission for Civic, Demographic and Electoral Affairs; and the Commission for the Environment, Public Health, and Hygiene.

The mayor is assisted by six deputy mayors and the five from the arrondissements. Beneath the mayor is the General Secretariat, with its secretary appointed by the mayor. The secretary-general coordinates the day-to-day running of the city's services, including administrative, commercial, and technical—everything from personnel and pensions to taxation and public events. With a budget of approximately CFA 1,000 (U.S.$1.40) per capita in 1999, however, services are skeletal at best.

Educational System. Until the age of 5, children remain at home. Initiation ceremonies occur from this age and throughout adolescence, though these are decreasing in importance in Lomé. After the age of 5, all children can commence school, providing they pay a nominal school fee and purchase the school uniform. On average, boys are three times more likely to complete primary schooling than are girls. This discrepancy increases into secondary schooling, and is most marked among the poorer sectors of the city's population.

Secondary schooling is more common in Lomé than elsewhere in Togo, and numerous private and public schools offer the French baccalaureate system. In 1981 one-quarter of the city's population attended school. Many families send their children to school in Aflao or Denu in Ghana, because the students there are instructed in English and are more likely to complete a full year of schooling. Often children are sent abroad during strikes. No new public schools or colleges have been built since about 1980, which partly accounts for the rapid rise in the popularity of private schooling. Togo has one university, located in Lomé, and it offers first- and second-level degrees in the arts and sciences, as well as in medicine and law.

There is little government support for the physical and social sciences in Togo, beyond the existence of a Ministry for Scientific Research and Education. Private organizations and nongovernmental organizations (NGOs) provide various services, and a private academy of social sciences was formed in the late 1990s.

Transportation System. The Togolese capital is without an organized, publicly owned transit system, but rather, operates on a privately owned system of taxicabs, consisting of both automobiles and motorcycles. Essentially, to travel from any point A to B in Lomé, an individual has three choices. He or she may *louer* (rent) a car for a minimum of 500 CFA (less than U.S.$1 in 1999), take a motorbike or *zemidjan* and pay for the distance, or attempt to negotiate the complex system of *taxis-routes* that crisscross the city. The latter operate along set routes, pick up and deposit at designated spots, and charge a minimum of 100 CFA (U.S.$.20), with 25-CFA increments. To enter or leave the city, you take a taxi to the appropriate *gare routière,* depending on your destination.

Lomé is the hub of the nation's very limited railways and national highways. Trains are not used for public transport, only for commercial needs beyond the city.

CULTURAL AND SOCIAL LIFE

Distinctive Features of the City's Cultures. Cultural and social activities in Lomé are a mélange of many ethnic, linguistic, and foreign elements. Unlike Accra and other West African cities, Lomé is less westernized in dress, social behavior, food, employment, and religion. Public displays of affection are rare. Men and boys hold hands, but boys and girls do not. In the city, old people and *quartier* elders are highly esteemed, though the climate of political fear, caused by repeated annulment of elections and the imprisonment of opposition activists and journalists, has resulted in the increasing influence of youths as they become more cognizant of national political currents. Women and men are often separated at social gatherings, and women often dine after men. When guests arrive, water is offered, and the traditional greeting, asking of the family members and their health, ensues.

Organized religions maintain a strong hold over much of the population. Funerals are a major event in Lomé; wildly extravagant (by western standards) funeral celebrations are a daily occurrence. Marching bands, choirs, football tournaments, banquets, and stately services are as fundamental as an expensively decorated coffin. Funerals often take place over a month or more, and families not infrequently sell or mortgage land or homes to pay for the funeral of a beloved and elderly relative. Wealthy Loméens may be buried at the Cimetière de la Plage, but for the poor it is often the cemetery of the airport.

Cuisine. Loméens usually have two or three meals per day, each consisting largely of a starch product, such as cassava, sorghum, maize, millet, yams, or plantains. A Loméen's diet is more flexible and diverse than that of many other African cities. A hot, spicy sauce is served with midday or evening meals, consisting of a protein—for example, fish, goat, beans, or beef—and often rich in palm (red) oil or peanut paste. Fruits and vegetables, though readily available, are eaten more by the bourgeoisie. Traditional French staples, such as baguettes and other products, are mainstream.

Food and alcohol (beer, gin, or *sodabi,* a distilled palm wine with a high alcohol content) are all important ceremonial items. For city dwellers from the north, food, beer, and sacrificed animals are offered to spirits and consumed by those in attendance. For southerners, alcohol is often the key ingredient. Among wealthy middle-class Togolese, the usual French three or four course meals are always served at functions. Eating is done most often with the right hand, although among the bourgeoisie, the use of flatware is prevalent.

Ethnic, Class, and Religious Diversity. Until the dictatorship of Gnassingbé Eyadema (1963; officially president from 1967), the southern Ewe culture predominated in all realms of life and was second only to the influence of French. After 1967, however, the president deigned to redress the southern bias in Togolese cultural, political, and social life, and to this end created *authenticité,* modeled on the same program of the Zaire dictator Mobutu. This movement attempted to highlight the many and diverse cultures of Togo, especially within the Ewe-dominated Lomé, via various methods, including the recent renaming of all the streets in the city.

Ethnic tensions are minimal, despite the persistent murmurings of certain politicians. Political strife in the country came to a head in 1991–1994, and did result in violence between north and south, with its concomitant refugees and resettlement, but Togo's 30 ethnic groups continue to mix and intermarry throughout the country.

Lomé is home to a large migrant community, including many Yoruba from Nigeria, Hausa/Fulani from the Sahel states, and, more recently, small numbers of Arabic, Indian, and Chinese immigrants attracted by commercial opportunities. The city is also home to a large community of French expatriates, and smaller numbers of Germans, Americans, and others.

Class divisions in Lomé are usually based on wealth and family background. At one point, several large Brazilian families controlled much of the land outside the city and the commercial sector within. Elements of their descendants and other purely Ewe and non-Ewe families remain a veritable plutocracy in Lomé, though their influence is waning. The Togolese middle class is small and restricted largely to the capital. The urban poor can be found throughout. There are no slums per se, but large sections of the capital are run-down and without sanitation.

Since the inception of the League of Nations mandate, freedom of religious worship has been protected by law. The French interpreted this to include animistic African religions, and this perhaps partly accounts for the popularity of traditional voodoo

© CAROLINE PENN/CORBIS

Two women attend a voodoo trance ceremony in Lomé, Togo.

cults and rituals. Throughout the country, many different forms of Christianity and Islam are practiced. Roman Catholicism is the most prevalent form of Christianity, but various American Baptist sects, the Assembly of God, Mormons, Jehovah's Witnesses, and Eckankar have been making headway among the urban population. Islam was brought to Lomé from the north, and while the French decreed that mosques be built in the *quartiers* specially designated for Muslims, the Zongos, a Muslim presence can now be found throughout the city.

Family and Other Social Support Systems. Traditional systems of social organization are significant in the daily lives of Lomé residents. Kinship systems provide networks for support and are visible during all major life-cycle ceremonies. Marriage practices vary among Togo's ethnic groups, although organized religions and the state have altered the ceremonies of even the most traditional. Social disapproval of ethnic exogamy is lessening, though government unofficially discourages it. Marriage law follows French legal statutes and requires an appearance before a magistrate for all state apparatuses to be in effect. Customary marriage, without state sanction, is still widespread. A dowry remains important throughout Togo, but less so in the capital. Polygyny is officially decreasing, though unofficial relationships uphold its role. Frequently, men do not propose marriage in Lomé until they can provide a home for children, and as rents are high, this partly accounts for the increasing incidence of children born out of wedlock.

The basic family structure is extended, although nuclear-family units (four-to-six members) are increasingly commonplace, particularly among the middle class. Traditionally, the man is the supreme head of the household. In the absence of the husband, the wife's senior brother holds sway. Statistics (circa 1990) indicate, however, that one-third of women over 40 years of age seek a divorce, and 25% of households now have a woman as head. The extended family has a redistributive economic base. Inheritance laws follow French legal statutes in the case of a legal marriage. In the event of a customary marriage only, customary inheritance laws are enforced. Most ethnic groups are patrilineal by tradition or have become so as a consequence of colonization. In Lomé, patriarchy is omnipresent.

Infants are cared for by the mother and female members of the household, including servants. Most Lomé families—even the poorest—have one or more servants, who are often poor village relatives. Among some ethnic groups, often infants are not exposed to the father until eight days after birth, but this practice and others are slowly disappearing in the capital. Vaccination against all childhood diseases is strongly encouraged by the government, and health workers may occasionally visit domestic homes.

Health services are ostensibly available to all residents of Lomé, and, as with other developing tropical nations, Togo's population is challenged by numerous health problems—including parasitic, intestinal, nutritional, venereal, and respiratory diseases. Malaria is endemic to Lomé, and it is especially severe among children, the elderly, and people with compromised immune systems. Other common diseases include schistosomiasis, meningitis, tuberculosis, and pneumonia. The incidence of leprosy is declining, and poliomyelitis has been eradicated from Lomé.

The government's expenditure on health continues to fall, and most foreign-contracted specialists quit Togo by mid-1999 because salaries were unpaid. The two main government hospitals in Lomé are understaffed and undersupplied, and there are no emergency facilities. Frequently, products from international donors, unavailable in hospitals, are for sale in local markets. Public-health problems are further exacerbated by inadequate waste disposal, sewerage, drinking water, and food storage.

The HIV/AIDS (human immunodeficiency virus/acquired immune deficiency syndrome) is taking its toll on Lomé's population. By 1996 up to 200,000 Togolese were infected with the HIV virus, representing 5% of the total population. The presumed percentage for the capital is much higher. There is one national testing and counseling facility based in Lomé.

Traditional healing methods and preparations continue to be the most widely used form of health care in Lomé. Herbalists abound, and one market in Lomé specializes in the sale of medicinal herbs. Frequently, medical treatments are coupled with visits to the local voodoo house or fetish priest, many of which can be found throughout the city.

Work and Commerce. Agricultural and manufactured products are sold both retail and wholesale in shops and markets. The informal economy is significant, and the most important market is the Assigamé (Grand Marché). There is little major industry in Lomé—or, for that matter, anywhere in Togo. The 1990s saw most government industries privatized. The mining of phosphates, run as a monopoly just outside the capital, remains Togo's largest industry. Electricity production is a distant second. Lomé's once highly favored banking sector is declining, and tourism is insignificant. A small oil refinery, telecommunications, and information technology are growth industries in Lomé. The roads and rail infrastructure are rapidly declining, however, despite the launching of Lomé's Free Trade Zone in 1989. In 2001 unemployment was very high in Lomé, with some estimates placing it at 35–40% of the city's adult population. Travel to work is by means of the previously described transportation system or privately owned vehicles.

Customary divisions of labor generally do not still hold in Lomé, although men do most heavy construction work. Women perform almost all other manual labor and control small-market commerce. One interesting phenomenon is that of the Mama/Nana Benz, a group of entrepreneurial women so named after their fabulous wealth accrued from marketing and their penchant for Mercedes-Benz. They shut down the government in the early 1990s after the president attempted to tax them.

Child labor is ubiquitous, and in 1996 and 1998 several incidents of child slavery were exposed. Traffic usually occurs across the Ghana border, or via the lagoon that virtually encircles the city. In much of Togo, girls are more likely to work than go to school.

Professional positions are usually occupied by individuals who have had postsecondary-school education. Successful businesspeople may or may not have formal education, but often have relatives, friends, or patrons who helped finance their establishment.

Women, although having attained legal equality, remain unequal in all walks of life. Women and men are kept apart in most social gatherings. Discrimination against women in employment is common practice and widespread. Women have little place in political life and less in government programs, although there is a ministry allocated to women's and family affairs. Only women descended from ruling tribal families, successful businesswomen, or women politicians enjoy privileges equal to those of men, more often won than granted.

Arts and Recreation. There is little government support for the arts in Togo, beyond the rudimentary presence of a Ministry of Culture and the poorly funded departments of the university. Private organizations include the Centre Culturel Français, the American Cultural Center, and the Goethe Institut.

Privately, traditional and modern music, voodoo ceremonies, and funerals serve as the main forms of artistic and recreational activity. Sports are popular, especially soccer. On the weekends, bathers congregate at Ramattou, just on the eastern edge of Lomé, and often picnic and dance. The National Lottery (LONATO), betting on races, the numerous bars and once-famous nightlife, and the regular Sunday-afternoon beach party outside the Hotel Palm Beach are other popular diversions.

QUALITY OF LIFE

Compared with that of many other African capital cities, the quality of life in Lomé is relatively good. On an international scale, however, the Human Development Indicators published by the United Nations are very unfavorable, placing Togo 145th out of 172 in 1999 (and 29th out of 53 among African states). Average life expectancy in 1998 was 51 years, although this is declining steeply with the onset of the AIDS epidemic. The per-capita income for Togo in 1993 was U.S.$250 and falling, although it is higher for Lomé residents. Housing remains affordable to most, and occupancy is very high. Among the wealthy, cellular telephones and Internet use are common.

Sanitation and sewage systems are rudimentary at best in most parts of the city, and flooding occurs in many sectors during the rainy season. Pollution has not reached serious levels, although car use and the increasing number of taxi-motos without catalytic converters is diminishing the air quality. Water quality is poor, and water treatment is irregular. Water pressure is unreliable, and there are frequent power outages. Violent crime is on the increase, including a number of carjackings and murders, largely as a consequence of poverty. Homelessness is an unassessable problem and remains largely ignored by the government, as does poverty alleviation. Overfishing by international fishing trawlers along the coast has significantly reduced the catch of Lomé fishers, and the decrease in protein consumption by the poorer sectors of society is visible. Malnourished children are commonplace in many of the poorer parts of the capital.

FUTURE OF THE CITY

As the city grows, it can extend only east toward Anécho and Benin, and northeast toward Kpalimé. The Ghana border prohibits western expansion.

It is difficult to be very optimistic about the future of Lomé despite the fanfare heralding the OAU summit in July 2000. The roads and houses were painted, the homeless were bused out of town, and millions of dollars diverted from needier causes for the renovation of hotels for dignitaries and heads of state. But, like the preparations for the visit of French president Jacques Chirac in 1999, all of this was cosmetic change masking very serious urban and social malaise. It is difficult to envision a positive course for the city and the nation until the political stalemate regarding elections and the succession to Eyadéma's presidency is resolved. In the meantime, the city faces an uncontrollable AIDS epidemic and fatigued public-health and -education systems.

From a private perspective, there is significant building and development. The number of Arabic and Chinese businesses continues to grow. Many poorer marketeers are being forced off their traditional holdings near the beach by businesspeople anxious to build enterprises in the center of town. To the north of the capital, too, sharecroppers have been evicted without compensation, in order to build housing, ostensibly for the OAU summit. Accordingly, rents are rising rapidly—for the poorest sectors, a sum of CFA 5,000 (U.S.$7.00) per month in 1999 (with an impossible deposit of three months' to one year's rent) is very common for a room in a house. The division between rich and poor is increasing dramatically in all sectors of public and private life, with all its concomitant social and political problems.

BIBLIOGRAPHY

Bouraima, Nouridine, and Yves Marguerat, *La Population du Togo en 1981: Premières Observations sur les Résultats Provisoires du Recensement de Novembre 1981* (République Togolaise, Ministère du Plan, de l'Industrie et de la Réforme Administrative, Direction de la Statistique 1983).

Cornevin, Robert, *Histoire du Togo,* 3d ed. (Berger-Levrault 1969).

Decalo, Samuel, *Historical Dictionary of Togo,* 3d ed. (Scarecrow Press 1996).

Gayibor, Nicoué Lodjou, et al., *Le Centenaire de Lomé, Capitale du Togo, Collection "Patrinoines" n° 7* (Université du Benin à Lomé 1998).

Gérard, Bernard, *Lomé: Capital du Togo* (Delroisse 1975).

Lawrance, Benjamin Nicholas, "Most Obedient Servants: The Politics of Language in German Colonial Togo," *Cahiers d'Études Africaines* 159 (2000).

Marguerat, Yves, *Dynamique Urbaine, Jeunesse et Histoire au Togo: Atricles et Documents, 1984–1993* (Presses de l'Université du Bénin 1993).

Marguerat, Yves, *La Naissance du Togo: Selon les Documents de l'Époque/Documents Traduits et Présentés par Yves Marguerat* (Editions Haho, Karthala 1993).

Marguerat, Yves, ed., *Lomé—Capitale du Togo* (Université du Bénin à Lomé 1997).

Marguerat, Yves, *Lomé, les Étapes de la Croissance: Une Bréve Histoire de la Capitale du Togo* (Editions Haho, Karthala, 1992).

Marguerat, Yves, *Lomé, un Siécle d'Images, 1884–1990, Vol. I: Lomé entre la Terre et la Mer* (Presses de l'Université du Bénin 1993).

Marguerat, Yves, *Lomé, un Siécle d'Images, 1890–1990, vol. II: Lomé, Fille du Commerce* (Presses de l'Université du Bénin 1996).

Marguerat, Yves, *"Si Lomé m'Etait Contée . . . ": Dialogues avec les Vieux Lom . . . ens,* 3 vols. (Université du Bénin à Lomé/ORSTOM 1993–1996).

Marguerat, Yves, *Trésors Cachés du Vieux Lomé: L'Architecture Populaire Ancienne de la Capitale du Togo* (Editions Haho 1993).

Sebald, Peter, *Togo 1884–1914: Eine Geschichte der Deutschen "Musterkolonie" auf der Grundlage Amtlicher Quellen* (Akademie-Verlag 1987).

BENJAMIN NICHOLAS LAWRANCE

London

United Kingdom

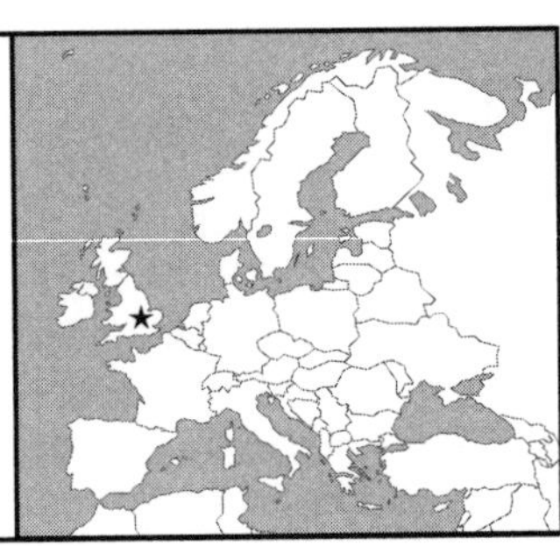

ORIENTATION

Name of City. London is the name that is universally used by English speakers.

Location. London is the capital and largest city of the United Kingdom of Great Britain and Northern Ireland. Central London is located at 51°30′ north latitude and 0°5′ west longitude. The Royal Observatory in the London suburb of Greenwich sits astride the prime meridian, 0° longitude, and is the starting point for determining every longitude in the world. Politically, London and the British Isles are integrated into the European Union, but Londoners consider themselves distinct from Europe, which they see as starting on the French side of the English Channel.

Population. The population of Greater London—a 1,580-square-kilometer (610-square-mile) area built largely before the outbreak of World War II in 1939—was 6.9 million according to the 1991 census, and 7.2 million according to a 1998 government estimate. Inner London—a 324-square-kilometer (125-square-mile) area built largely before 1900—had a population of 2.6 million in 1991, and an estimated 2.7 million in 1998. The South East region of England surrounding Greater London had a population of 7.8 million in 1991, and an estimated 8 million in 1998. Many residents of the South East region had strong ties to Greater London (London's Gatwick Airport was in the South East region rather than inside Greater London), but the majority identified more closely with the South East region's self-sufficient cities, such as Brighton, Oxford, and Reading.

Distinctive and Unique Features. The layout of London is influenced primarily by the generally west-to-east flow of the River Thames, which divides the city into north and south banks. The original settlement was built north of the river, and development has always been much more extensive on that side. The south bank grew much more slowly because London had only one bridge across the Thames—a succession of spans named "London Bridge"—for nearly 2,000 years, until Westminster Bridge provided a second crossing in 1750.

A second distinctive feature of London's geography is a strong split between the East End and West End. The East End, dominated by port facilities, has been home to London's working class, poor, and recent immigrants. The West End, dominated by royal palaces, has been home to London's aristocrats and merchants.

The east-west and north-south divides are complicated by a third distinctive feature of London's topography. Cutting through both the north and south banks are deep, wide north-south valleys formed by tributaries of the Thames. Industry and poorer-quality housing have clustered in these valleys on both sides of the Thames. Well-to-do families moved to the hills, especially those to the west of the two north-south valleys.

Attractions of the City. Along with New York and Tokyo, London ranks as one of the world's three most important centers of international banking, finance, insurance, securities exchange, and currency trading. Key to London's preeminent position was deregulation of the capital and securities markets during the 1980s, which the British called the "Big Bang." London has also become the most important center for trade within Europe, in part because the United Kingdom's economic policies are only partially integrated with those of other European Union countries.

London also ranks as one of the world's most popular tourist destinations. Principal attractions are shopping, cultural facilities, and places associated with royalty.

Relationships Between the City and the Outside. Foreigners may consider London an attractive destination for business or pleasure, but Britons have traditionally regarded their capital city with suspicion. Literary references to London abound, rarely favorable. From William Blake, a prominent

19th-century British poet: "I behold London, a human awful wonder of God!" Around the same time, the British journalist and reformer William Cobbett called London "the Great Wen," using a now-obsolete word that meant "spot," "blemish," or "stain." The perception that London was spreading out of control, staining the British landscape, was widely held in Britain, and led to national legislation in the 1940s to guide and limit its growth.

Major Languages. English is the language of communication in London. Most of London's immigrants were born in English-speaking countries.

HISTORY

The Origin of the City. The Romans established a settlement on the north side of the Thames called Londinium around 43 A.D.. Still visible today are remains of the wall built by the Romans around 200 A.D. to protect the north, or land, side of the settlement. Celts probably occupied the site at an earlier date, but left behind no visible trace. The Romans abandoned Londinium in the 5th century, but a few yards upstream (west), the Saxons built a new settlement called Lundenwic, which was an important trading center by the 7th century. Danish invaders controlled the city for much of the 9th and 11th centuries.

After the Norman Conquest of England in 1066, the city, now known as London, grew with few interruptions for 900 years. From about 15,000 at the time of the Norman invasion, London's population increased to 30,000 in 1200, 80,000 in 1300, and 200,000 in 1600.

Within a few years of the Conquest, William I built his palace and government center at Westminster, 3.2 kilometers (2 miles) upstream from the City of London. A portion of William's original palace was incorporated into the present-day Houses of Parliament. The pattern put in place by William the Conqueror in the 11th century has essentially survived into the 21st century. The City of London has remained the center of commerce, whereas the City of Westminster has remained the center of government. By the 17th century, "London" was generally regarded as encompassing both the City and Westminster.

A handful of 17th-century aristocrats—including the Earl of Bedford, Lord Portman, and Sir Thomas Grosvenor—converted their estates situated between the two centers into handsome residential areas for the growing middle-class merchants of the City and public officials of Westminster. Estates west and

© BOB KRIST/CORBIS

The famous Tower Bridge stretches across the River Thames in London, England.

north of Westminster soon followed. Thus, as the population of London continued to increase, beginning in the 17th century, so did the land area.

By 1800 London had become the first city to indisputably exceed 1 million inhabitants, and it grew to about 5 million in 1900. From less than 26 square kilometers (10 square miles) in 1800, the built area considered part of "London" exceeded 130 square kilometers (50 square miles) in 1900. London's extensive suburbs to the northwest, west, and southwest became known as "Metroland," because their growth depended on an extensive network of rail links to Central London built beginning in the 1860s by the Metropolitan Railway and the Metropolitan District Railway, now part of the London Transport Underground (subway) system's Metropolitan and District lines.

Meanwhile, the share of London's population housed in the 2.6-square-kilometer (1-square-mile) City of London declined from nearly three-fourths in 1600 to one-fourth in 1700 and one-tenth in 1800. During the 20th century, the City's population declined rapidly in absolute terms as well, from 100,000 in 1900 to 5,000 in 1970.

At the outbreak of World War II in 1939, the Greater London region had a population of 8.6 million, its historic peak. Since then, government policies to reduce the region's population have had the desired effect, so London has dropped from the ranks of the world's most populous cities.

London's 1,000-year history of growth was severely tested twice, during the 1660s and 1940s. During the 1660s, 70,000 Londoners—one-fifth of the population—died from plague in 1664 and 1665, then five-sixths of the City burned in the Great Fire of 1666. Many of the contemporary City's most prominent structures, including the current St. Paul's Cathedral, were built soon after the Great Fire, from designs of Sir Christopher Wren.

During World War II, about 30,000 Londoners died, and another 50,000 were injured in German air attacks. Property damage was widespread, especially in the City and the docklands to the east. Miraculously, the City's most important building, St. Paul's Cathedral, escaped unscathed even though every building surrounding it was destroyed. The City was once again rapidly rebuilt, and within a decade, few signs of the Blitz remained. However, the heavily damaged East End was rebuilt at a much lower population density.

Migration: Past and Present. London has always been a magnet for immigrants. Historically, most immigrants came from the British countryside. The British government encouraged migration from rural to urban areas between 1750 and 1850 through the Enclosure Movement, which consolidated small farms into larger holdings that could be farmed more efficiently. People forced from their farms found jobs in London's factories and shops and used their wages to buy food supplied by the more efficient farms. Most rural immigrants came from counties surrounding London, although some originated in Ireland, Scotland, and Wales.

Immigrants from outside the United Kingdom arrived in London in large numbers beginning in the late 19th century. Through the first half of the 20th century, these immigrants were mostly Italians, French, and other Western Europeans, as well as Russian Jews and Chinese. The principal source of immigrants switched to former colonies of the British Empire during the 1950s and 1960s. The transition to independence brought many immigrants who preferred to keep British passports, as well as citizens of the former colonies who received preferential treatment in the years immediately following independence. Former colonies in the Caribbean and South Asia were the leading sources of immigrants to London.

INFRASTRUCTURE

Public Buildings, Public Works, and Residences. The skyline of Central London is dominated by church towers, palaces, and other public structures, rather than by high-rise office buildings. British monarchs were responsible for much of the construction. The Palace of Westminster, now containing the Houses of Parliament, was the residence of the kings and queens of England between the 11th and 16th centuries. A portion of the palace dates to 1097, but the rest is a 19th-century structure, built after the old palace burned in 1834. The single most important symbol in London—and arguably the entire country—is the clock tower on the north end of the palace universally known as Big Ben (actually the name of the bells inside the clock that toll the hour).

Buckingham Palace, the London residence of the monarch since the 19th century, occupies a prominent location, adjacent to several royal parks that are open to the public and give London a more green and open feeling than other very large cities. Tourists congregate outside the gates of Buckingham Palace to witness the Changing of the Guard.

The Tower of London, at the eastern edge of the City, a portion of which was constructed by William I in the 11th century, served as a royal palace until the 17th century. After a succession of fortifications and towers were added by William's successors, the tower became a notorious fortress and prison.

London's most important religious structure, St. Paul's Cathedral, was built around 600. The current cathedral was completed in 1710 to replace one that burned in the Great Fire of 1666. Westminster Abbey, across the street from the Palace of Westminster, has been the site of the coronation of every British monarch (with two exceptions) and the place of burial for many of the country's most prominent leaders and artists. An abbey was first built on the site in the 8th century, and the current building dates from the 13th century.

Most Londoners live in so-called terrace housing, long rows of identical-looking two- or three-story buildings. High-rise apartment towers and detached houses surrounded by land yards are relatively rare. Density is lower in London than in other cities of comparable population, and the difference in density between Central London and suburbs is less extreme. Lower density means that London is more spread out than other cities of comparable population. Tourists quickly learn that the major sites of Central London are not within walking distance of each other.

Politics and City Services. Administratively, "London" refers to two entities. The 2.6 -square-kilometer (1-square-mile) financial district is known as "the City of London," and is governed by the City Corporation led by the lord mayor. When most Londoners lived inside the City of London, the corporation and lord mayor wielded considerable authority, but with the area now making up only a tiny percentage of London's population and land area, their power is largely symbolic.

The Greater London Authority (GLA) offers some governmental services for a 1,580-square-kilometer (610-square-mile) area encompassing Inner London and older suburban areas, although not the outer ring of suburbs. The GLA came into existence only in 2000, with powers limited to a few areas of authority, including environment, transportation, and planning. London had a regional government called the Greater London Council (GLC) beginning in 1963, but the national government abolished the GLC in 1986 because Prime Minister Margaret Thatcher disagreed with its leaders' policies.

Most day-to-day administrative responsibility in Greater London is fragmented into 32 boroughs (plus the City of London). During the decade and a half between abolition of the GLC and creation of the GLA, the boroughs were the only local governments operating in Greater London, hence few services were offered citywide. Londoners think of themselves as living in a neighborhood or postal-code district, rather than in a place called "London," and assigning local-government authority to the boroughs strongly reinforces this identification.

Educational System. Consistent with London's fragmented local government, each of the 32 boroughs runs its own school system. Schooling is free and universal, but because separate systems are operated by each of the boroughs, quality varies widely through the London metropolitan area and becomes a factor for parents in considering where to live. The percentage of Londoners who have completed high school is relatively low compared to other world cities, reflecting both traditionally high dropout rates in working-class families and the city's large population of recent immigrants. About 10% of London children, primarily those of wealthy families, attend private schools (called "public" schools).

The city's major institution of higher education, the University of London, is actually a federation of several dozen institutions, some obscure and highly specialized. University College, Imperial College, King's College, and the London School of Economics are internationally prominent units of the University of London that operate with a very high degree of autonomy.

Transportation System. London's public-transportation system has a reputation for cleanliness, safety, and ease of operation in comparison to those of other large metropolitan areas. London Transport operates the subway system known as the Underground, as well as several hundred bus routes. In addition, a dense network of rail lines converge on Central London from all directions, bringing commuters along with long-distance travelers.

The first Underground, an 8-kilometer (5-mile) line constructed by the Metropolitan Railway and opened in 1863, still operates as part of the Metropolitan Line. Londoners refer to several of the Underground lines as "tubes," because tracks were placed in tubes, deep below the surface, in contrast to the earliest lines, which were built close to the surface by tearing up the street. The various lines were consolidated into one operating authority in 1933. The London Underground opened three entirely new lines in the late 20th century and extended several existing lines.

An extensive network of commuter rail lines also converge on Central London. A ring of terminals was constructed around Central London during the 19th century. Few Underground lines were constructed south of the Thames, so commuters from southern suburbs depend primarily on rail service to reach Central London.

Surface travel is less easy. Central London's contemporary street pattern is a legacy of the Roman Empire and medieval British royalty. Not even the widespread destruction of the Great Fire of 1666 or the Nazi blitz of the 1940s provided sufficient impetus for constructing a modern road network. Only one-sixth of commuters into Central London drive private cars.

Motor-vehicle usage is much higher in London's suburbs. Limited-access highways, known as motorways, have been built in suburban London in recent years. Several long-distance radials connect London with other regions of the country, but they have not been extended into Central London. The heavily congested M25 motorway forms a complete circle around London at a radius of about 24 kilometers (15 miles) to accommodate the growing demand for intersuburban travel.

© INGE YSPEERT/CORBIS

Red double-decker buses transport Londoner around the city.

London's fleet of black taxicabs is especially distinctive. Rather than adapting ordinary cars, as elsewhere in the world, London taxis are special-purpose-built to be rugged, comfortable, and easy to maneuver through narrow streets. Obtaining a license to drive a taxi requires expensive and time-consuming training, culminating in a requirement to pass a detailed examination covering London's geography.

CULTURAL AND SOCIAL LIFE

Distinctive Features of the City's Cultures. London's cultural habits are dominated by extremes of reserve and raucousness. On the one hand, Londoners are widely viewed as notably polite. They are well known for willingness to stand in lines (queues) to board buses and pay cashiers. Londoners apologize ("sorry," rather than "excuse me" or "pardon me") not only when they are causing an inconvenience, but just as often when they are on the receiving end. A strong criticism is to judge something or someone as "awkward."

Business and social dress is much more formal in London than in other cities: dresses, skirts, and suits for women, not trousers (never called "pants," a term that refers to underpants); black pin-striped suits and long-sleeved shirts with stiff collars for men, accompanied by long umbrellas tightly folded into thin rods.

At the same time, the center of social life in London—as in the rest of Britain—has since the Middle Ages been in public houses ("pubs" for short). Pubs dot virtually every street corner of London. They have long served as centers for socialization. A typical pub is divided into a public bar, frequented primarily by men, and a saloon bar for women as well as for men willing to pay slightly higher prices for more-comfortable seats. Most are owned by a handful of large national breweries.

Cuisine. London's cuisine until recently could be described as plain at best and often grim. The handful of top restaurants typically featured roast beef with Yorkshire pudding (eggs, flour, and milk baked in the meat droppings), accompanied by several kinds of potatoes and vegetables. Well-to-do families consumed similar meals on Sundays at home after church. More typical of London's cuisine was tough beef, mushy vegetables, sausages filled with animal by-products, and greasy deep-fried fish-and-chips (french fries) wrapped in newspaper.

Pub food was even worse—moldy cheese and stale bread ("ploughman's lunch"), hard-boiled egg caked in sausage and deep-fried ("Scotch egg"), chunks of gristly meat and kidneys underneath a piecrust ("steak and kidney pie").

London's late-20th-century culinary "revolution" was fueled by two factors. First was the introduction of "foreign" foods by immigrants, especially curry from South Asia in the 1950s and 1960s. Second was the "rediscovery" of the high level of quality of rural Britain's animal and vegetable products, which are handled and prepared sensitively in many London restaurants, as well as by many home cooks. Organic and "whole" foods are now widely available in local markets, and vegetarianism is widespread. Even many pubs serve well-prepared meats and salads made with high-quality ingredients.

Ethnic, Class, and Religious Diversity. The principal cultural divide among Londoners has traditionally been along social class lines. Middle-class and working-class Londoners lived in different neighborhoods and led lives that rarely intersected except when performing a service. Higher-class residential areas developed west of the City of London in Mayfair and Westminster, following the lead of the royal family. East Enders—often called "cockneys"—are said to be the only true Londoners, because they are born and reared within the sound of Bow Bells in the Church of St. Mary-le-Bow.

As London expanded in the 19th century, middle-class families pushed up the hills to the northwest, whereas working-class families pushed east and south near the docks and factories. Immigrants settled in the slums of the East End, immediately east of the City.

Social-class areas within London are identified by name or postal code. For example, "SW1" refers to the politically powerful residents of Westminster who live near the Houses of Parliament, and "NW3" refers to the intellectual and cultural residents of the hilltop neighborhood of Hampstead. London is divided into postal-code districts according to eight compass directions—N, E, SE, SW, W, and NW, plus WC and EC (west and east central).

Large-scale immigration from former British colonies during the second half of the 20th century has turned London into a multiethnic city. One-fourth of Londoners were ethnic minorities, according to a 1998 government estimate, divided about evenly between Asians (primarily Chinese, Pakistani, and Indian) and "blacks" (primarily from Caribbean and African countries).

The settlement pattern of ethnic minorities within Greater London is complex—London does not have one extensive, inner-city, minority-dominated residential area. Two-thirds of London's Caribbean and African immigrants live in several Inner London neighborhoods, especially south and east of Central London. On the other hand, two-thirds of ethnic Asians are located in several Outer London neighborhoods, primarily to the northwest and northeast. Ethnic minorities make up less than 10% of the population in 7 of the 20 Outer London boroughs, primarily those in the southwest and southeast.

At the scale of specific streets, the ethnic pattern is even more complex and dynamic—groups constantly shift locations, and neighborhoods frequently change ethnic character. Boundaries among ethnic groups are blurred, as segregation by skin color is much less common in London than in American cities.

National-planning policies blurred the east-west divide during the second half of the 20 century. Large complexes of publicly owned high-rise apartment buildings (called "council housing estates") were built in the suburbs, primarily for low-income families displaced from homes demolished or destroyed by German bombs in the East End. The landmark Town and Country Planning Act of 1947 set aside an 8-kilometer- (5-mile-) wide "Green Belt" of permanent open space around London, severely limiting construction of American-style suburban housing.

Family and Other Social Support Systems. London's West End has long been inhabited by merchants, aristocrats, and officials with the means to purchase services. Extended-family relations traditionally dominated the social structure of London's East End, where several generations would crowd into slum housing. Kinship is still important in the East End, but government policies severely reduced its importance, especially after World War II.

Two government policies were especially critical in changing social relations in London's East End. First was a government decision not to reconstruct most of the homes in the East End destroyed in the Blitz. Indeed, the government even demolished many of the East End houses that German bombs missed. Many East End families were resettled in suburban housing, or in entirely New Towns outside London. East End families gained better-quality housing, but lost proximity to their informal social-service network provided by friends and relatives.

The second government policy that broke the East End's traditional reliance on informal-kinship networks was the creation of a National Health Service in the United Kingdom in 1947, guaranteeing essentially free and universal access to health care. A wide variety of other social-service and public-assistance programs transferred care of sick, poor, elderly, and other dependents from families to the state.

Work and Commerce. London's contemporary economy is based on the same two pillars that have defined the city for 1,000 years—trade and government. The City of London has solidified its position as the world's largest employment center for financial and business services. National government ministries occupy most of the office space in the City of Westminster.

London was a major manufacturing center of consumer products prior to the Industrial Revolution, taking advantage of proximity to one of the world's largest and wealthiest markets, as well as port facilities. The manufacture of furniture, armor, and clothing in the Middle Ages gave way to publishing, electronics, and motor vehicles. London's long tradition of manufacturing largely disappeared during the second half of the 20th century. Greater London lost more than 1 million industrial jobs between 1960 and 2000, leaving only 10% of the region's workforce in that sector.

Replacing London's lost manufacturing employment are jobs in retailing, tourism, and other consumer services. Large department stores and specialized shops, clustered in the West End and Kensington areas of Central London, are the region's dominant retailing core. Strong government controls have restricted the number of suburban shopping malls.

Arts and Recreation. London stakes a claim as the world's foremost center of Western (European/North American) culture. Especially notable elements of London's cultural scene are the performing arts and museums.

London's principal theater district is the West End nestled between the City and Westminster, near Piccadilly Circus, Leicester Square, and Covent Garden. About 50 live-performance theaters are clustered in a 1.3-square-kilometer (0.5-square-mile) area of the West End; and another 50, known as the "fringe," are scattered elsewhere in the metropolitan area. The Globe Theatre, where most of Shakespeare's plays were first performed beginning in 1599 until it burned in 1613, has been faithfully reconstructed, including a standing-room area for the audience around an open-air stage.

Five major symphony orchestras are based in London, including the BBC Symphony Orchestra, London Philharmonic Orchestra, London Symphony Orchestra, Philharmonia Orchestra, and Royal Philharmonic Orchestra. The orchestras perform during the winter in two major concert halls—Royal Festival Hall and the Barbican Centre. Chamber concerts are also performed at Wigmore Hall.

Royal Albert Hall—built as a memorial to Queen Victoria's husband, Prince Albert—is the venue of London's principal summer concert series, the Promenade, or "Proms" for short. Closing night of the Proms is one of Britain's most visible patriotic occasions, as thousands of concertgoers wave Union Jack flags and join in the singing of the country's principal patriotic songs, including "Land of Hope and Glory," "Rule Britannia," and "God Save the Queen."

London's popular music is invigorated by integrating styles indigenous to the Caribbean and South Asia with British tradition. Theater, clothing, and other popular arts have also been infused by ethnic diversity.

The British Museum, founded in 1753, contains some of the Western world's most important antiquities, including the Rosetta Stone (instrumental in deciphering ancient Egypt's hieroglyphic writing) and the Elgin Marbles (sculptures and friezes removed from the Parthenon in Athens by Lord Elgin in the early 19th century). Also in the British Museum are two of four existing copies of the Magna Carta, signed in 1215 by King John, the foundation of the guarantee of civil liberties to Britons. The British Museum Library—the world's largest, with 12 million volumes—relocated from the British Museum to a new building in 1997.

The National Gallery in Trafalgar Square contains the country's most important collection of historical paintings, especially Europe's Old Masters. The Courtauld Institute Galleries house a major collection of French Impressionist and Postimpressionist paintings.

The Tate Gallery has the country's most important collection of 20th-century art, as well as a large percentage of the works of Britain's greatest 19th-century painter, J. M. W. Turner. In addition to its main building north of the Thames, the Tate operates a museum in a recently converted power plant on the South Bank of the Thames, as well as a museum in Liverpool.

A complex of museums in the South Kensington area, built on the site of the Great Exhibition of 1851, include the Victoria and Albert and the Natural History. The Victoria and Albert has a very large collection of non-Western and medieval art, as well as furniture, musical instruments, and other decorative arts.

The most popular spectator sport in London is football (soccer). Half a dozen of England's top two dozen teams play in London, including Arsenal, Chelsea, and Tottenham Hotspur. The country's most venerable cricket ground, Lord's, is located in the north London neighborhood of St. John's Wood. The All England Lawn Tennis and Croquet Club hosts one of the world's most important tennis tournaments, popularly known as Wimbledon, the suburb where the club is located.

QUALITY OF LIFE

Among world cities, London long enjoyed a reputation of offering a high quality of life. Crime rates and cost of living were low. Health care was good, thanks to universal access to the National Health Service, as well as the clustering of specialists along Harley Street. Housing densities were low, and public transportation efficient by world standards.

London's quality of life traditionally suffered from two major blemishes. First was the city's extremes of wealth and poverty, known as "Upstairs, Downstairs." The comfort of wealthy Londoners living "upstairs" was made possible by large numbers of servants toiling "downstairs," in the basement kitchens and cleaning rooms.

London also suffered in the past from high levels of air and water pollution. London was the first major city to experience smog—a combination of fog and smoke—thanks to widespread burning of coal in homes, factories, and power plants. The Thames was subject to destructive flooding, and fish died from industrial discharges.

London's air quality has improved substantially in recent years following strict emissions controls and the closing of many "smokestack" industries. Elaborate flood-control barriers have been erected on the Thames, and the water is clean enough for fish to survive again. Private household service has been replaced by a service economy in offices and shops.

At the same time, London has experienced a deterioration of its traditional strengths. The cost of living has soared faster than in other cities, especially for housing and transportation. London's traffic congestion ranks among the world's worst, and public transport is less clean, safe, and reliable than in the past. Violent crime against individuals remains low, but random terrorist acts, especially by the Irish Republican Army, have plagued the city. Homelessness and poverty are much lower than in most other eras of London's long history, but they have not been eradicated.

BIBLIOGRAPHY

Allen, Rick, *The Moving Pageant: A Literary Sourcebook on London Street-life, 1700–1914* (Routledge 1998).

Arnold, Dana, *The Metropolis and Its Image: Constructing Identities for London, c. 1750–1950* (Blackwell Publishers 1999).

Bailey, Paul, ed., *The Oxford Book of London* (Oxford University Press 1995).

Barker, Felix, and Peter Jackson, *The History of London in Maps* (Barrie & Jenkins 1990).

Barker, T. C., and Michael Robbins, *A History of London Transport: Passenger Travel and the Development of the Metropolis* (Allen & Unwin 1963).

Clout, Hugh, ed., *The Times London History Atlas* (HarperCollins 1991).

Creaton, Heather, *London* (Clio Press 1996).

Cullingworth, J. B., and Vincent Nadin, *Town and Country Planning in the U.K.* (Routledge 2001).

Donnison, David, and David Eversley, eds., *London: Urban Patterns, Problems, and Policies* (Sage Publications 1973).

Hall, Peter, *London 2001* (Unwin Hyman 1989).

Hancock, David, *Citizens of the World: London Merchants and the Integration of the British Atlantic Community, 1735–1785* (Cambridge University Press 1995).

Hardingham, Samantha, *London: A Guide to Recent Architecture* (Artemis 1993).

Jones, Edward, and Christopher Woodward, *A Guide to the Architecture of London* (Thames & Hudson 1992).

Kynaston, David, *The City of London* (Chatto & Windus 1994).

Lee, Trevor R., *Race and Residence: The Concentration and Dispersal of Immigrants in London* (Clarendon Press 1977).

Manley, Lawrence, *Literature and Culture in Early Modern London* (Cambridge University Press 1995).

McKellar, Elizabeth, *The Birth of Modern London: The Development and Design of the City 1660–1720* (Manchester University Press 1999).

Ogborn, Miles, *Spaces of Modernity: London's Geographies, 1680–1780* (Guilford Press 1998).

Palmer, Alan W., *The East End: Four Centuries of London Life* (Rutgers University Press 2000).

Powell, Kenneth, ed., *World Cities: London* (Academy Editions 1993).

Rutherfurd, Edward, *London* (Crown 1997).
Schofield, John, *The Building of London: From the Conquest to the Great Fire,* 3d ed. (Sutton 1999).
Shepherd, John, et al., *A Social Atlas of London* (Clarendon Press 1974).
Sheppard, F. H. W., *London: A History* (Oxford University Press 1998).
Twyning, John, *London Dispossessed: Literature and Social Space in the Early Modern City* (St. Martin's Press 1998).
Wilson, A. N., ed., *The Norton Book of London* (Norton 1995).
Winter, James, *London's Teeming Streets: 1830–1914* (Routledge 1993).
Wolfreys, Julian, *Writing London: The Trace of the Urban Text from Blake to Dickens* (St. Martin's Press 1998).

JAMES M. RUBENSTEIN

Los Angeles

United States

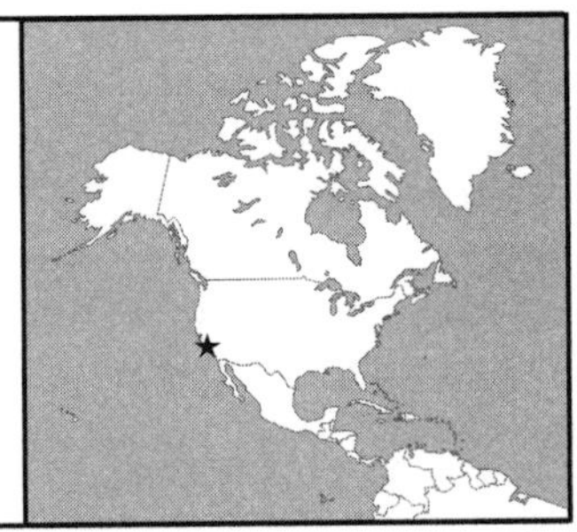

ORIENTATION

Name of City. Los Angeles is, by 1990 population figures, the second-largest city in the United States. The city's original Spanish name, *Nuestra Señora Reina de Los Angeles,* is translated as "Our Lady Queen of the Angels." The shortening of the name to *Los Angeles* was done during and after the U.S. occupation and subsequent ceding, in 1848, of the territory of California to the United States following the Mexican War and is used generally by the Anglo population in Los Angeles and the outside world. The abbreviated *L.A.* is more often used in common vernacular when referring to the city. Either nomenclature is also applied to the sprawling metropolitan region that includes five counties in southern California.

Location. Los Angeles is located on the western coast of the United States in the southwestern portion of California. The city is situated at 34°03′ north latitude and 118°14′ west longitude.

Population. According to the 1990 U.S. census, the city of Los Angeles is home to approximately 4 million people. The larger metropolitan area comprises the counties of Ventura, Los Angeles, Orange, San Bernardino, and Riverside and has a population of about 14 million people. Los Angeles has one of the most diverse populations in the United States, scattered in a loosely knit community extending from Ventura to San Bernardino and from Malibu to Balboa.

Distinctive and Unique Features. The Los Angeles metropolis consists of a composite of terrain. It encompasses a group of inland valleys and a coastal plain separated by low but steep mountains with many passes, all lying between an arc of high rugged mountains and the dual crescents of Santa Monica and San Pedro bays.

The central city lies within the coastal plain that creates the Los Angeles basin, the high mountain wall surrounding the basin that can be easily observed from an airplane approaching the city. A prominent geographical feature is the San Fernando Valley, which is a fertile valley located northwest of central Los Angeles. First visited by Spanish explorers in 1769, it forms an important part of the city of Los Angeles.

Northwest to the Pacific lies a complex knot of mountains known as the Santa Susanas. Directly north of the city are the San Gabriels, extending for some 95 kilometers (60 miles) of Cajon Pass and ranging in height from 900 to 3,000 meters (3,000 to 10,000 feet). The highest peak is Mount Old Baldy (Mount San Antonio), with an elevation of 3,068 meters (10,064 feet) above sea level. Eastward of Cajon Pass are the San Bernardino Mountains, also about 95 kilometers long. Mount San Gorgonio, their dominant peak, at 3,506 meters (11,502 feet), is the highest in southern California. Finally, the San Jancinto Mountains angle southward into Mexico, with their tallest peak taking its name from the mountains and rising 3,293 meters (10,804 feet) into the sky. The Spaniards called these encircling ranges the

"Sierra Madre," source of their water of life and literally the mother of the region.

The mountains provide a visible wall, a comfortable enclosure, and separate the Los Angeles metropolis from its hinterland, often inhospitable stretches of desert climate. This geographic feature insulates the city from the intense summer heat and winter cold found in the interior. The significance of this topographic arrangement is that whereas the Sierra Madre is highest behind the Los Angeles region, the Santa Monica–Santa Ana range is very low in the section that crosses the region, allowing the sea breeze to penetrate to some extent into the valleys, while the storms break against the Sierra Madre in the rear. It is this peculiar circumstance that has been responsible in large part for the building of the region and for its favorable conditions for human occupation. Yet it is this same topographic feature that creates an air inversion that traps pollutants in the air within the basin plain of Los Angeles, resulting in the smog for which Los Angeles has become notoriously famous. The Los Angeles plain, lying in front of the Santa Monica–Santa Ana range, has been built in recent geologic time by the eroded material carried through the mountains by three rivers: the Los Angeles, the San Gabriel, and the Santa Ana.

The San Andreas Fault, which is a major zone of fractures in the earth's crust, extends along the California coastline and passes through the northern part of the city of Los Angeles as it makes its way to the Gulf of California. In California, two great plates are sliding past each other along the San Andreas Fault. The narrow western plate is moving northwest, while to the east, the North America plate is moving southeasterly. The San Andreas and its associated faults in southern California are visible results of the motion, and the uplift of the San Gabriel Mountains and the opening of the Gulf of California are products of deformation along the boundary between the two plates. Thus in metropolitan Los Angeles, earthquakes are inevitable.

In most metropolitan areas, the only thing of value under the ground is gravel. But in Los Angeles two subsurface products—water and petroleum—have been significant. Water is the first essential, and the arrangement of mountain and plain has created a number of basins of porous alluvium, ideal for the storage of water. Petroleum deposits were found first just north of downtown Los Angeles and then in a variety of locations. Fortuitously, the major oil fields were discovered in the early 1920s, just when great demand for gasoline for automobiles was emerging. The presence of oil fields has had a notable effect on the establishment of neighborhoods, blighting some spots for a time and delaying their development until the resource was exhausted, at which time large blocks of land, formerly bypassed, became available. As a result, entire communities were designed as a unit, such as the La Brea apartment complex and Century City.

The 770 square kilometers (2,000 square miles) of generally flat lowlands are the most densely settled and the heart of the metropolis. The lowlands are not as picturesque as the mountains or as romantic as the seashore, but it is on these prosaic areas that the "action" was, is now, and, in all likelihood, will be in the future.

It was the lowlands, watered by the mountain streams, that attracted the first settlers. These regions provided the pastures for the cattle ranches; they were the scene of the great agricultural developments of the American irrigator and orchardist. The lowlands could be easily crossed by the railroads and interurban rail systems, thus bringing the mountains and the seacoast within range of the urban settler. The subdivider, too, lured by to the lowlands, where roads and other improvements could be built at a reasonable cost. And it is on the lowlands today where the vast majority of Angelenos live, where manufacturing plants have been built and shopping centers erected, and where a new Angeleno skyline has risen up.

Attractions of the City. The Los Angeles urban region is today one of the largest industrial metropolises in the world, having in the 1990s passed Greater New York in manufacturing employment and total industrial production. Employment and production in high-technology industries have expanded to make metropolitan Los Angeles perhaps the world's biggest "technopolis," with more engineers, scientists, technical specialists, and security-cleared workers than any other urban region. Moreover, metropolitan Los Angeles has grown to become a world city, the gateway to Asian markets and to the economies of the Pacific Rim. There has been tremendous growth in the financial, banking, and both corporate- and public-management sectors, making Los Angeles the financial hub of the western part of the United States and with Tokyo the "capital" of financial markets in the Pacific Rim.

Today the ports of Los Angeles and Long Beach, which is about 35 kilometers (20 miles) to the south, form one of the great harbor complexes of the nation. Although divided by a municipal boundary and with quite different histories, they constitute a single geographic and economic terminal and are often called the Twin Ports. Together, they are among the largest and fastest growing in the world in terms of exports and imports, handling nearly half of the trans-Pacific trade of North America.

The entertainment industry has made Los Angeles its home since the beginning of the 20th century. *Hollywood* has become synonymous with the city, earning Los Angeles the nickname "tinsel town" owing to the creativity and dominance of the entertainment industry in this urban region. Metropolitan Los Angeles was among the first urban areas in which theme parks for the enjoyment of the public and tourists were conceived. Perhaps the most famous of these is Disneyland and the Magic Kingdom, which has become the icon that strongly connects Los Angeles with fantasy and the future.

Major Languages. English is the primary language spoken by the metropolis's 14 million residents, but several other languages are spoken daily throughout the Angeleno landscape. Spanish is the predominant non-English language, but Korean; Vietnamese; the various dialects of Chinese, Japanese, Thai, Hindi, Arabic, African, and Native American languages; and European languages are all heard on the streets of Los Angeles—evidence of its status as a world city.

HISTORY

The Los Angeles metropolis is one of the newest urban areas in the United States in terms of sizable growth, but if one considers origins, Los Angeles itself is one of the nation's older cities. Further, the heritage of the past is still visible and important in the area despite the municipality's imposing modern veneer.

The Origin of the City. A distinct tribe of Indians occupied the Los Angeles area when the Spanish explorer Gaspar de Portolá arrived in 1769. The name of the tribe has been obscured by history. As a result, its members have been called the Gabrielinos, after their attachment to Mission San Gabriel Arcángel, an event that came late in their history. Anthropologists estimate that in 1770 the Native American population was about 5,000. This is a conservative estimate. Their territory extended from a point between Topanga and Malibu to Aliso Creek in Orange county. Their northern limit was the San Gabriel Mountains and adjacent ranges. In addition, the language spoken on Santa Catalina, and probably on San Clemente Island was Gabrielino. The tribe lived in villages, small collections of round, symmetrical huts made of tules over a frame of willow branches. The exact number of settlements is unknown, although one source estimates 40, and they tended to be clustered along the coast.

The original Native Americans have long since disappeared, apparently not leaving a single survivor. What of their long occupancy appears in the modern city? Not much directly. Some of their trails were used by the Spaniards and have been of service ever since. For example, Portolá apparently followed a well-marked trail leading from the Native American village of Yanga (perhaps the present location of the intersection of Los Angeles and Commercial streets) directly west to the Brea Pits, today's Wilshire Boulevard. Moreover, some Native American place-names survive in Spanish spellings of the original sounds: Topanga, Cahuenga (Place of the Mountain), Cucamonga, Azusa, and, a bit farther out, Malibu (Place Where Mountains Run Out to the Sea), Simi, and Sespe. Today, however, Los Angeles boasts having the largest concentration of Native Americans in the United States, who represent 500 tribes.

Nevertheless, to realize how Portolá came to the Gabrielinos' land, one must return to the discovery and Spanish conquest of California itself.

The year was 1542. Only 50 years before, Christopher Columbus had sailed the Atlantic and encountered the New World. Nearly 30 years had passed since Vasco Núñez de Balboa first saw the Pacific Ocean from the peak of Darién. Hernán Cortés had captured the Aztec capital at Mexico City some 20 years prior. Francisco Pizarro had captured the Inca capital of Cuzco in Peru almost a decade before. Thus in 1542 Juan Rodríguez Cabrillo was given two vessels to explore the still-unknown Pacific side of New Spain. He was instructed to sail northward to look for "Cathay" (*Cathay* is the ancient name for China) and to search for the "Strait of Anian," the supposed water route to the Atlantic. What Cabrillo found was California. A summary of his journal exists and it records the first European impression of the southern California landscape. His ships explored what is now San Diego Bay up to beyond present-day Santa Barbara.

The Spanish place-names owe their christening to Sebastián Vizcaíno, who sailed northward, surveying the Pacific shore of New Spain from Acapulco to Oregon in 1602–1603. On November 29, 1602, he entered a bay that he named San Pedro, and near the shore he found an idol upon which he placed the Christian cross. Both Cabrillo and Vizcaíno had described the California coast in optimistic terms to their sovereigns. Even so, it was forces outside the region—exaggerated reports of Russian and perhaps English activity in the North Pacific—that moved Spanish authorities to action, rather than the intrinsic attractions of southern California. The Council of War convened in 1768 and ordered an expedition to occupy the port of Monterey and to secure it for the Spanish crown through the founding of a presidio (a fortified military post) and mission. Two parties traveling overland up the rugged Baja California peninsula set out under Captain Gaspar de Portolá from San Diego determined to reach Monterey in 1769. Portolá's band camped in what is today Los Angeles along the Los Angeles River, and they pioneered a trail up the California coast that was to form the broad outline of El Camino Real (The Royal Road). A chain of 21 missions was created along the Camino Real. Mission San Gabriel Arcángel, near Los Angeles, was founded on September 8, 1771. Missions San Fernando and San Buenaventura were late editions founded in, respectively, 1797 and 1782.

Nuestra Señora Reina de Los Angeles was founded as a pueblo (village) by Governor Felipe de Neve on September 4, 1781. Families from Sonora and Sinaloa were recruited for the settlement on the Porciúncula River (Los Angeles River). Spanish sovereignty, dating from the 18th century, produced four types of landholdings, which were modified somewhat under the 26 years of Mexican rule (1822–1848). The Spanish founded missions, of which two were in the Los Angeles area. Pueblos were organized, including the Pueblo of Nuestra Señora Reina de Los Angeles, and presidios were established, but not in the Los Angeles area. Some other lands were given to army veterans as ranchos. The Mexicans, when in control, secularized the missions, recovered the mission land, and expanded the rancho holdings 20-fold. The rancho period began in earnest and reached a peak in the 1830s and 1840s under Mexican control, when there were 55 ranchos in the Los Angeles area. The rancho boundaries have remained significant as boundaries of private holdings, and as the boundaries of counties and cities.

Migration: Past and Present. Under U.S. sovereignty, the rancho landholdings were broken up and developed into smaller private parcels. By 1870, immigrants from the Midwest and east coast began to arrive in droves, creating new markets for agricultural produce. And in 1876 the Southern Pacific Railroad extended its line west to Los Angeles. All of these events stimulated urban growth. The first large real estate boom occurred during the 1880s. The force behind the initial wave of population expansion and subsequent urbanization was a search for better health. Many people with lung problems, after living years in the dirty industrial cities back east, found that they could be helped by rest and the sunshine and clean air of the southern California climate. Many after living hectic lives in the East lived the simple life in their new home, hiking and hunting in the canyons. Los Angeles claimed to be the "Capital of the Sanatorium Belt," and its hotels and boardinghouses did host many of these health seekers.

Another factor that facilitated the boom of the 1880s was the completion of a second rail line, the Santa Fe Railroad, into the city in 1885. Now the existence of two lines made rate competition a given, and fares were slashed dramatically. Not only did the railroads bring in even more migrants, but the location of their lines influenced the alignment and provided the focus of many of the new subdivisions: more than 100 towns were platted from 1884 to 1888 in Los Angeles county (62 of which no longer exist).

By the turn of the 20th century the impetus for Los Angeles's growth shifted to agricultural development: wheat in the San Fernando Valley, oranges and other citrus crops in Orange county. The agricultural age created a large number of towns dependent on farming. As the region became urbanized this system of settlements became an integral part of the Los Angeles metropolis. For example, a line of orange-belt towns were established on the north slope of the San Gabriel Valley—Pasadena, Arcadia, Sierra Madre, Duarte, Azusa, Glendora, and Covina. To the south and west, Pomona, Claremont, Upland, Ontario, Redlands, Riverside, and Corona were also citrus towns.

The development of the Angeleno metropolis, however, really occurred in the 20th century. New industries began to spring up in metropolitan Los Angeles. Among these was tourism. With its roots in the developments of the 1880s, tourism increased considerably in the early 1900s. This was the era of railroad travel, when tourists came by Pullman car and winter was the tourist season. The typical tourists were wealthy easterners free to flee the rigors of the grim northern winter. Pasadena emerged as the prototype of the burgeoning tourist industry.

The oil was discovered in the 1920s that sparked an oil boom for the city. From 1920 to 1924 there were sensational oil developments in the Los Angeles region. Seven major fields were discovered during this period. Huntington Beach (1920), Santa Fe Springs (1921), and Signal Hill (1921) alone pumped a total of 650,000 barrels a day. By the end of the century the Wilmington field (1932) had produced a total of more than 1.6 billion barrels, reaching a peak in 1970. Its 2,300 wells still give it the lead over all other California fields in annual production. Petroleum meant more to Los Angeles than just a local source of energy: in the 1920s it constituted a large part of the area's nonagricultural exports. Closely related to the industry is the manufacture of oil-well tools and equipment, a branch of manufacturing in which the Los Angeles area ranks second in the nation.

Motion pictures, a development as unexpected as the discovery of oil, were to help transform the area in the 20th century. The industry required no raw materials, and its finished products were so light that they could be shipped from anywhere—the apparent isolation of Los Angeles didn't matter. The small community of Hollywood—a mixture of citrus groves, wooden bungalows, and open fields—soon became the favorite location, and early clusters of studios appeared on Sunset Boulevard and on Melrose Avenue. As the industry grew and prospered, so did the community; land values rose, and as early as 1915, studios were being built in other locations. Soon they were widely scattered—MGM in Culver City (1915), Universal in Universal City (1915), Warner Brothers in Burbank (1928), Republic in Studio City, Disney in Burbank, and Fox in Westwood. However, despite the early dispersal of the studios, *Hollywood* continued to be used by writers to refer to the movie-production community regardless of geographic location. Radio and television became spin-offs to form part of the larger, growing entertainment industry for which Los Angeles is known worldwide.

The mushrooming of the aircraft-aerospace industry also contributed to Los Angeles's evolution. Early aviation depended on clear skies, light winds, and mild winters, and the Los Angeles climate fit the bill. The region's assets for year-round flying were on exhibit in January 1910, when it was host of the nation's first air meet. The aircraft industry expanded phenomenally during World War II. Soon after the war, it added electronics to its capabilities, but after 1958 the emphasis on the "space race" revolutionized the old aircraft firms and new organizations emerged. The complexity of missile and space projects necessitated an increased emphasis on research and a change in the nature of the workforce. The Los Angeles aircraft industry is now reputed to have assembled the greatest concentration of mathematicians, scientists, engineers, and skilled technicians in the United States. For almost three decades after World War II, the aerospace industry—the aircraft-missile-electronics complex—functioned as the foundation of the regional economy. At its peak in 1967, it furnished employment for about half a million people, nearly 43% of the total manufacturing employment. The industry has, however, subsequently declined in importance.

Since 1970, there has been a rapid increase in jobs in the service sector as well as in wholesale and retail trade. Finance, insurance, and real estate have had a spectacular boom. High-technology industries have expanded in Los Angeles since the 1980s. The growth of the garment industry reflects another dramatic change in the regional labor market and economy. Not only has the high-technocracy settled in extraordinary numbers in Los Angeles, but so too has what is probably the largest pool of low-wage, weakly organized, easily exploited immigrant labor in the country.

Los Angeles at the dawn of the 21st century is positioned increasingly toward the ranks of the three other centers of global capital: New York, London, and Tokyo. The emergence of a skyline locating downtown Los Angeles symbolizes the corporate-financial citadel of central Los Angeles, which is keeping pace with the accelerated centralization, concentration, and internationalization of industrial and financial capital that have marked contemporary restructuring of the world economy.

INFRASTRUCTURE

The visual environment of Los Angeles is one of mountains, parks, and other public lands that provide opportunities for development and conservation. Approximately 400 square kilometers (150 square miles) of hills and mountains lie within the city of Los Angeles. The Santa Monica mountains alone account for 246 square kilometers (92 square miles), an area larger than the city of San Francisco. Since they are largely undeveloped, the hills and mountains represent a tremendous land resource for recreation as well as for housing. Further, they provide a welcome visual contrast to the lowlands. Griffith Park, one of the largest urban parks in the United States, is found within the city of Los Angeles, affording views of the San Fernando Valley on the eastern slopes and of the Pacific Ocean on the western slopes. Open lands used for public-utility purposes such as flood-control channels and basins, water reservoirs, and power-line rights-of-way, as well as freeway interchanges, have great potential for both regional and local open-space and recreational use.

Infrastructure dedicated to tourism has become an important part of the Angeleno contemporary landscape. The economic impact of the tourist industry is impressive in particular in the growth of international tourism. In 1999 the Los Angeles Economic Development Corporation ranked tourism as the third-largest industry in Los Angeles county, supporting approximately 272,000 jobs there in 1999. In that year alone, the total economic impact of the visitor industry in the county was more than $28.2 billion, including $6.3 billion in household income (wages and salaries); direct spending by overnight visitors contributed $12.3 billion, up 3.3% from $11.9 billion in 1998.

Politics and City Services. The political geography of the metropolitan area of Los Angeles is confusing because it is fragmented. The region includes five county governments and more than 60 independent municipalities and unincorporated areas. Cooperation among the various political entities is thus a challenge. The Southern California Association of Governments (SCAG) has evolved as the largest of nearly 700 councils of government in the United States. It functions as the metropolitan planning organization for six counties: Los Angeles, Orange, San Bernardino, Riverside, Ventura (Los Angeles metropolitan area) and Imperial. This larger region encompasses a population exceeding 15 million persons in an area of more than 98,000 square kilometers (38,000 square miles). As the designated metropolitan planning organization, SCAG is mandated by the federal government to research and draw up plans for transportation, growth management, hazardous-waste management, and air-quality management.

Transportation. Transportation within the metropolitan area has been negatively stereotyped with scenes of freeway gridlock. However, public transportation has expanded since the 1980s. The Southern California Rapid Transit District was reorganized in the 1990s to consolidate the largest public-transit system in the nation. The Metropolitan Transit Authority oversees rail service, light rail service, and buses throughout the metropolitan region. Los Angeles's once dominant extensive public-transit rail system was dismantled in favor of buses during the 1950s. But by the late 1990s, the city was reconstructing a new public-transit rail system connecting communities to entertainment centers.

CULTURAL AND SOCIAL LIFE

Unlike New York City, Los Angeles is new to its present-day role as an immigrant mecca. While the comparatively late advent of immigration is not a uniquely Los Angeles phenomenon, the metropolis has experienced immigration differently from almost all other major urban regions. Contemporary Los Angeles is home to a far larger share of today's foreign-born U.S. population than the immigrant New York of old. Large as it is, Los Angeles contains roughly the same portion of the nation's total population as did New York in the early 1900s. Consequently, immigrants were far more overrepresented in the Los Angeles of 2000 than they were in the New York of 1910.

Distinctive Features of the City's Cultures. Los Angeles has been stereotyped as 101 suburbs looking for the center. The distinctive feature about Los Angeles is its physical expansion and seeming lack of a central place. Unlike other world cities, such

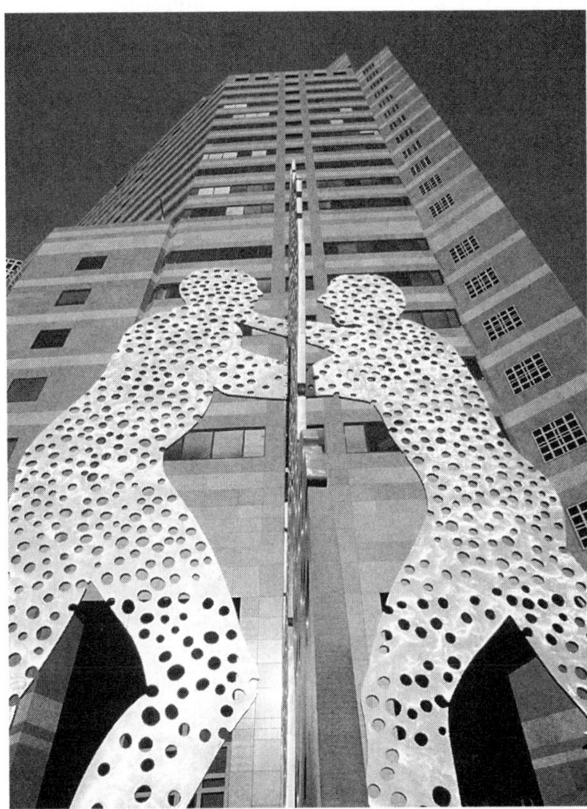

© RICHARD CUMMINS/CORBIS

A sculpture called *Molecule Man* stands at the Federal Building in Los Angeles, California.

as New York or London, in which the city envelopes you the moment you set foot in Times Square or Picadilly Circus, one must go out and find Los Angeles. The lack of a core has resulted in the creation of several nuclei throughout the southland. In essence Los Angeles is many cities, each with its own tangible character: the architectural style and heart of Venice differ from the "feel" of the village of Westwood, the affluence of Pacific Palisades, historic Hollywood, gentrifying Silverlake, and Latino Echo Park and Alvarado Street in Pico Union. Thus the myriad city cultures are hidden within the glare and opulence of "tinsel town." The cultural diversity of past and present migrations has created distinct cultural realms within the Angeleno landscape. The culture of tolerance and the "laid-back atmosphere" are the result of visible colliding with the invisible cities found within Los Angeles.

Cuisine. The Los Angeles metropolis is home to a variety of ethnic foods. Cuisine indigenous to Los Angeles has been forgotten along with the original peoples from this region of the world. However, what has come to be known as "indigenous" is a distinctive Mexican influence in the Angeleno cuisine. This provides the basis for innovative fusions with other Latin American cuisines from the Caribbean and from Central and South America. Asian communities have added to the flavor of Los Angeles, offering regional foods from throughout China, Korea, Japan, and Thailand. Southeast Asia has contributed its own touch to the menu. African American specialties have also expanded the Angeleno palate, as have European foods from France, Germany, Russia, and Italy. The diverse ethnic cuisine is fused to create a cuisine that is truly Angeleno . . . for where else can one get a kosher, teriyaki burrito!

Ethnic, Class, and Religious Diversity. Within Los Angeles county, ethnic diversity is quite evident. Between 1960 and 1990, the Latino population jumped from 11% to 36% and the Asian population from 2% to 11%. If the greater undernumeration of Latinos could be taken into account, it would be clear that by 1990 there were almost as many Latinos as non-Latino whites in the county. Outside the Los Angeles core, Anglos made up two-thirds of the population in the four suburban counties in 1990. Although Anglos are still the majority in the suburbs, there has been a noticeable falloff from the peak levels of Anglo predominance recorded in 1960. Other groups have made substantial gains: African Americans rapidly suburbanized, and Latinos and Asians, their numbers swollen by immigration, moved to the suburbs in even larger numbers than did African Americans.

Los Angeles has become a city of fragmented pockets of affluence and Third World urban misery. The downtown Los Angeles core is indicative of this socio-spatial trend. New upscale condominiums tower next to the World Trade Center, the Bonaventure Hotel, and the newly revamped Convention Center and Staple Center Sports Complex in close proximity to poor immigrant residences of Chinatown and Pico Union. Skid Row, just east of City Hall, has the largest homeless population in the nation. The suburbs also reflect this spatial segregation by class. The western, affluent San Fernando Valley contrasts sharply with impoverished eastern San Fernando. Pockets of low-income areas have emerged in the once all-affluent Orange county. Santa Ana, the county seat, is home to the greatest concentration of poor Latino immigrants in the county. Westminster has the largest Southeast Asian population, which neighbors affluent Costa Mesa along the coast of Orange county.

Los Angeles is as diverse religiously as it is in terms of ethnicity and class. The largest Buddhist temple in North America is in the southland. Hindu

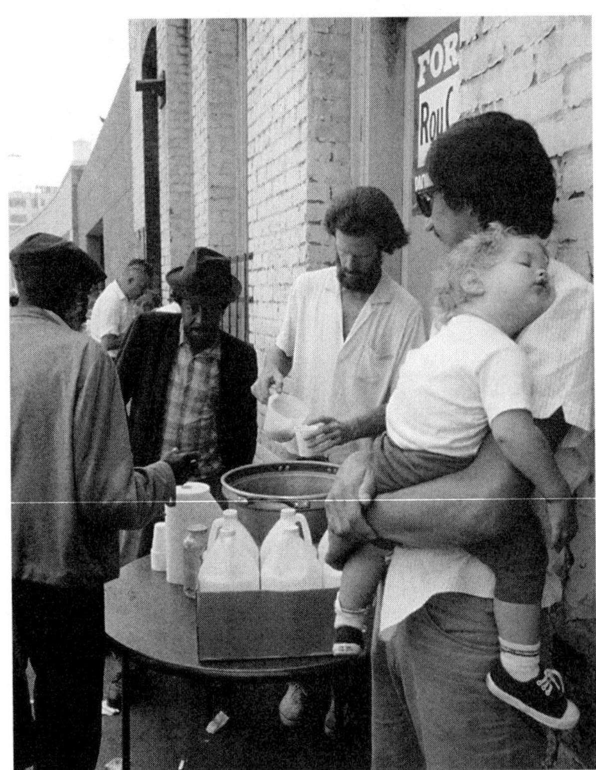
© VINCE STREANO/CORBIS

Homeless and poor people line up for free food in Los Angeles, California.

temples are in evidence from the coast in Malibu to Temple City northeast of downtown Los Angeles. Jewish temples are found in the San Fernando Valley and the Fairfax district in the Los Angeles core. The Muslim community is concentrated in West Los Angeles, with affluent Westwood home to a large Iranian population and less affluent Palms and Culver City home to Pakistani, Arabic, and Indian Muslims. A myriad of Christian churches dot the Angeleno landscape, from Gothic cathedrals (such as St. Basil's in downtown Los Angeles) to a high-tech cathedral (Crystal Cathedral, in Orange county) to storefront churches in Hollywood and South-Central Los Angeles.

Arts and Recreation. In addition to the recreational opportunities afforded by its natural areas and theme parks, the arts and café culture abound in the metropolitan region. The Los Angeles County Museum of Art is the premier visual-arts institution in the western United States. Its holdings include more than 150,000 works spanning the history of art from ancient times to the present. The museum celebrates the ethnic and cultural diversity of Los Angeles by promoting local artists and exhibiting works representative of that diversity. The newly expanded J. Paul Getty Museum in the Santa Monica mountains overlooking Westwood is an international cultural and philanthropic institution devoted to the visual arts and the humanities that includes an art museum as well as programs for education, scholarship, and conservation. Small community theaters from Silver Lake to Venice are supported by a café culture that promotes theater and the arts. Along with the cafés, independent bookstores that sponsor poetry readings and the theatrical art are emerging.

FUTURE OF THE CITY

Los Angeles has been designated by some urbanologists as the prototype of the postmodern city. The emergence of a Los Angeles School that would overtake the Chicago School in urban studies has been written about in the academic literature. Los Angeles has evolved from its simple roots as a pueblo, and later a mecca for midwesterners, to a bustling world city that rivals New York or London in terms of commercial and financial trade internationally. Poised near the border with Mexico and at the gateway to Asia, Los Angeles is undergoing a metamorphosis that reflects the changing economic, demographic, and cultural processes in cities of the 21st century.

BIBLIOGRAPHY

Baldassare, Mark, ed., *The Los Angeles Riots: Lessons for the Urban Future* (Westview Press 1994).

Berry, Sandra H., *Los Angeles Today and Tomorrow: Results of the Los Angeles 2000 Community Survey* (Rand 1988).

Davis, Mike, *City of Quartz: Excavating the Future in Los Angeles* (Verso Press 1990).

Gumprecht, Blake, *The Los Angeles River: Its Life, Death and Possible Rebirth,* (Johns Hopkins Press 1999).

Karlstrom, Paul J., *Turning the Tide: Early Los Angeles Modernists, 1920–1956* (Santa Barbara Museum of Art 1990).

Soja, Edward, *Postmodern Geographies: The Reassertion of Space in Critical Social Theory* (Verso Press 1989).

Waldinger, Roger, and Mehdi Bozorgehr, eds., *Ethnic Los Angeles* (Russell Sage Foundation 1996).

Marcelo Cruz

Lusaka
Zambia

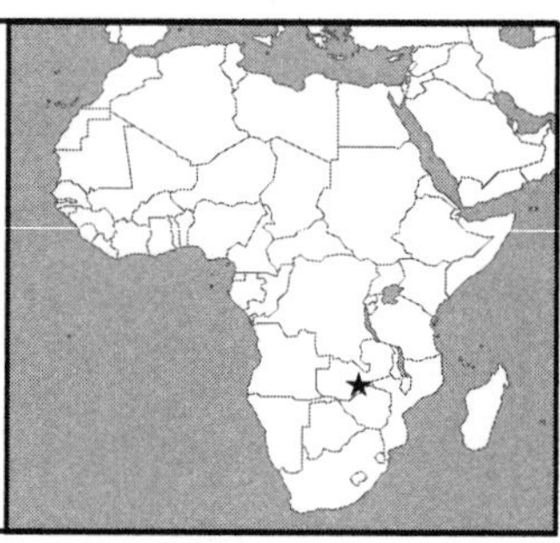

ORIENTATION

Name of City. Lusaka, Zambia's capital, takes its name from a local chief or headman, Lusaaka, which, in the Lenje language, means "thornbush."

Location. Lusaka is situated south of the equator on the Central African Plateau, some 1,300 meters (4,300 feet) above sea level. The city is located at 15° south latitude and 28° east longitude. The high altitude relieves the city of the extreme heat and humidity often associated with tropical climates. Even during the hottest months, October and November, the nights are always cool. The capital stands almost equidistant from Livingstone in the extreme south and the mining towns on the Copperbelt in the north.

Population. Between 1963 and 1990 the population of Lusaka grew from 123,146 to close to 1 million. At the outset of the 21st century, the population of Lusaka was estimated to be more than 2 million.

Distinctive and Unique Features. The legacy of colonial urban planning with its racially segregated residential areas is still evident on the urban landscape, although the relevant distinctions today are based on class and not race.

Attractions of the City. The capital was planned as a garden city—with housing on large plots, and wide streets and avenues with small parks and lots of trees in-between. Many roads are lined with flowering trees. The lanes of major streets and avenues are divided by islands in the middle where bushes and flowering trees add seasonally changing colors to the cityscape.

Relationships Between the City and the Outside. Lusaka has functioned as a port of entry for migration, especially from the rural areas of the Eastern Province. As the nation's capital, Lusaka hosts numerous foreign embassies and headquarters of major foreign firms, especially from South Africa, and it provides a temporary home to representatives of many nongovernmental organizations (NGOs), both secular and religious, from across the world, including North America, Europe, Japan, and Australia. Zambia's capital harbored major liberation groups in exile during the freedom struggles for Namibia, Zimbabwe, and South Africa from the 1970s until 1994, when South Africa came under black majority rule.

Major Languages. English is the official language of Zambia. The language most commonly used in Lusaka is Nyanja, which is spoken in the Eastern Province, the area from which the majority of the city's population originates. In recent years, the Bemba language has been spoken increasingly in Lusaka, reflecting in-migration to Lusaka from the economically depressed Copperbelt region, where Bemba is the major language.

HISTORY

The Origin of the City. The origin of Lusaka dates to back 1905 during the early British colonial period, when it was established as a siding along the railway line that was being built to connect Cape Town in South Africa with the copper-mining areas of the Belgian Congo (formerly Zaire, now the Democratic Republic of the Congo). The small town grew slowly—serving as a transportation center for the railway, and supplying a small community of white immigrant farmers, mainly of South African background. Some stores owned by Jewish and Greek immigrants, hotels, a school, a church, and a clinic developed to serve the needs of the town's white population. The quarrying of limestone, the most common rock underlying the town, was one of the earliest industries. Migrant Africans, mainly men, from near and far labored as domestic workers and farmworkers.

Lusaka became the capital of Northern Rhodesia, as Zambia was called during the colonial period, in 1935, when the administration decided to move the site of the capital from Livingstone on the Zambezi River to a healthier and more central location. In anticipation of this move, British-inspired town-planning principles were applied for the first time to Lusaka. Neighborhoods for whites were laid out with large building plots and wide-open spaces adorned with greenery. Government buildings were located on a hilly area with pleasant views 5 to 6 kilometers (3 to 4 miles) from the city center. Housing for Africans was situated on the outskirts of the city. But plans for the capital's development were curtailed—first by the Great Depression, and later by World War II. Lusaka's status as the capital declined further during the Central African Federation, 1953–1963, when the government functions of Northern Rhodesia, Nyasaland (now Malawi), and Southern Rhodesia (now Zimbabwe) were jointly administered from Salisbury, Southern Rhodesia (now Harare, the capital of Zimbabwe).

Throughout the colonial period, Lusaka maintained the general structure of a racially segregated city. The white residential areas varied in physical beauty and housed different income groups. Most of the Asiatic population, predominantly traders from different parts of the Indian subcontinent, lived on their business premises in an area allotted to their use. Lusaka's African residents, the majority of the city's population, lived in simply constructed housing on Lusaka's outskirts or in shacks on their employers' premises.

© PAUL ALMASY/CORBIS

This monument in Lusaka, Zambia, commemorates a meeting there of nonaligned nations.

From the earliest years of Lusaka's existence, unauthorized housing shot up. Here lived Africans—self-employed workers and women and children—who found no employer-provided housing. In such settlements, people took up residence without holding legal rights of tenure. Locally referred to as squatter settlements, these areas have remained part of Lusaka's physical geography ever since the early colonial period.

Independence from British colonial rule in 1964 triggered substantial growth of all of Zambia's urban areas, but most spectacularly of Lusaka. The new nation's capital was an attractive destination for a growing number of migrants who anticipated increased work and housing opportunities in the wake of independence. Some new housing areas were built, but never on a sufficient scale to accommodate the capital's growing number of residents. A sharp economic decline since the mid-1970s has reduced the building of government-supported housing, and the private sector has not considered the low-income-housing market to be profitable. The exception is the squatter areas that have continued to grow as more and more urban residents turn to self-built housing as their only option for accommodation. Owing to the general shortage of housing, a housing market is developing in these areas where poor households and individuals are renting rooms from homeowners and absentee landlords.

Migration: Past and Present. Among all the nations of sub-Saharan Africa, Zambia has experienced one of the highest, and most rapid, urbanization rates. Informed estimates suggest that half of Zambia's total population of some 8 million today is urban. A long history of rural-to-urban migration, foreign immigration, and, more recently, high annual population growth rates accounts for Zambia's high urbanization rate. The local migrants come from all of Zambia's different ethnic groups—which, according to an official handbook, number 73. The majority of these migrants are from the Eastern Province, followed by the Southern Province, and, in recent years, the Copperbelt and the Northern Province.

Extensive rural out-migration was set into motion by British colonial policy, which forced men to leave their villages in order to earn money to pay taxes. For a long time, the colonial government attempted to restrict African migration to men who were provided with housing by their employers and were expected to return to their home villages once they had completed their work contracts. This policy was abolished after World War II, when whole families commonly settled in the towns. In addition to a population of white immigrants engaged in farming, commerce, and copper mining, the settlement of people with Indian background also took place, focusing on trade with Africans. The population of white settlers decreased considerably prior to independence.

In the postcolonial period, Lusaka has been the temporary base for expatriates from many different countries who are working for international development agencies and NGOs. Professionals from the Indian subcontinent, both Hindu and Muslim, have diversified the existing settlement of Indian traders. A substantial number of Chinese and Cuban doctors work in the capital as well. In the wake of economic reforms aimed at opening up the economy in the early 1990s, a trading community with Lebanese background and experience from elsewhere in Africa has established itself in the capital, as have a number of white South African retail firms.

INFRASTRUCTURE

Public Buildings, Public Works, and Residences. Administrative offices, ministries, and court buildings constructed during the colonial period and shortly after independence remain concentrated in the location where they first were built, most of them in dire need of renovation. An exception is the National Assembly, Mulungushi Hall, originally constructed in 1970 in a high-income residential area as a conference center for a meeting of the Non-Aligned Nations.

Zambia produces and exports hydroelectric power. The capital's electricity provision functions reasonably well except in crisis situations. Several private residences have electric generators for backup.

Lusaka's water system is insufficient for the city's size, and several residential areas experience water shortages during the dry season. Many private residences have their own wells on the grounds.

The waste-disposal system is unsatisfactory, and waste is not collected from most of the low-income residential areas. Several civic groups are working on increasing environmental awareness in campaigns to keep Lusaka clean.

Today, Lusaka's residential areas are differentiated in terms of socioeconomic standards rather than race, as was the case during the colonial period. The most attractive residential areas house expatriates on contracts and Zambians in professional jobs in the private sector. The least desirable areas continue to be inhabited by the poorest segment of the urban population and are located on the outskirts of towns, with access to very limited services.

Politics and City Services. In administrative terms, Lusaka's status has shifted from being a city council to a district. At present, Lusaka has an elected city council, headed by a mayor. The council conducts its activities through a number of standing committees, and operates special departments to address issues concerning housing, public health, and fire, among others. The shift from a one-party political system to a multiparty government in 1991 has introduced more openness in and criticism of the city council's management, especially concerning issues of street vending, sanitation, and public health in general.

Educational System. Schooling is not compulsory in Lusaka, and although most residential areas have public fee-paying schools that take students through the first seven grades, some do not have secondary schools. As a result, students attending public secondary schools walk long distances, go by public transportation or private car to attend school, or board in sex-segregated secondary schools elsewhere in the country. Christian missions still run many schools, with government support. The number of private fee-paying schools has grown in recent years, but school enrollment rates have declined because of growing poverty and the inability of parents to pay school fees. There is an international school that graduates students with international baccalaureates rather than the British O and A levels, as do the regular schools. A great number of privately run training institutions offer computer training.

Several institutions of higher learning are based in Lusaka, among them the Great East Road Campus of the University of Zambia, which opened in its present location in 1968. The Ridgeway Campus houses the School of Medicine, conveniently located near the University Teaching Hospital. The Evelyne

Hone College offers vocational training in journalism, arts, design, and the hotel industry.

Transportation System. The name of the north-south Cairo Road, the main thoroughfare in Lusaka, is a legacy of colonial aspirations of connecting two ends of Africa under British imperial presence. Cairo Road continues into the Great North Road (leading from the south to the Democratic Republic of the Congo and Tanzania), and is joined by the Great East Road (connecting to Malawi and Mozambique). A number of smaller feeder roads cut across them. This major road junction in the city center causes great congestion during the early-morning and late-afternoon rush hour and at lunchtime—which, in this part of Africa, still sees many people leaving city offices to go home to eat, and then return to the city.

The capital's built environment is scattered across a wide area and was planned with private automotive transport in view. The majority of the population, however, cannot afford private cars. They rely instead on privately supplied mass transportation largely in the form of minibuses and private (illegal) taxicabs. A fleet of minibuses connect the city center with residential areas on the outskirts of the capital. There is one electric-rail line to one of the townships, and long-distance buses, most of them privately owned, transport people and goods between Lusaka and most regions of the country. The north-south train that travels all the way to Dar es Salaam in Tanzania is a transportation option, but not one that is used as first choice because of frequent delays and poor rail service and maintenance. This railway line was built by the Chinese in the late 1960s. Lusaka's international airport, opened in 1967, is provided with local and international services by major airlines and a number of private-charter companies that serve the tourist industry.

CULTURAL AND SOCIAL LIFE

Distinctive Features of the City's Cultures. Postcolonial Lusaka is the permanent and temporary home to numerous local ethnic groups, to several resident groups of different national and racial backgrounds, as well as to expatriate communities from across the world. National holidays, trade fairs, and religious observations celebrate the achievement of independence and the country's multicultural heritage. Specific cultural events tend to have a religious focus.

Cuisine. The standard meal in Zambia consists of a stiff, starch-based porridge often prepared from maize meal, called *nshima,* and a relish consisting of fried onions, tomatoes, some greens, and perhaps beans. If household means allow it, beef, chicken, or fish is added to the relish. White bread with margarine or jam, and tea with milk and sugar have been parts of the standard diet since the colonial period. Few spices or herbs are added to cooked meals, save on special occasion when pounded groundnuts or a few chili peppers may enhance the sauce. The long-term presence of an Indian residential community has hardly affected everyday food-consumption practices in Zambia. While members of the local elite and upper class frequently will enjoy examples of European cuisines in restaurants, there is little culinary variety in the home diet. Hotels and restaurants today present a range of foods—from Chinese, Mexican, and Creole to Italian and French, not to mention standard British cooking.

Ethnic, Class, and Religious Diversity. In nominal terms, Zambia is a Christian country, and the majority of the population claim membership of a Christian church. A number of Protestant denominations have joined the United Church of Zambia. The growth of Pentecostal churches and fundamentalist Christianity were particularly noticeable during the 1990s, when the president declared Zambia a Christian nation. The Hindu and Islamic religious communities are by and large of Asian background. Islam has attracted African followers and converts in recent years, with most conversion efforts funded by Saudi Arabia. Lusaka's Indian trading area closes at lunchtime on Fridays for Muslim prayers in a nearby mosque. There is also a Hindu hall and a Sikh temple that serve both religious and secular functions. The Anglican cathedral often serves as a concert venue.

Ethnicity is not a great dividing factor in Zambia. In Lusaka the residential areas are ethnically heterogeneous, and there are few public occasions when ethnic distinctions are expressed.

Family and Other Social Support Systems. The basic social-support system for people in need in Lusaka is provided by relatives and NGOs that seek to relieve crisis situations caused by declining formal employment and the spread of HIV/AIDS (human immunodeficiency virus/acquired immunodeficiency syndrome). For example, NGOs are seeking to relieve the problems of the growing number of street children who either have no homes or leave their homes for lack of support. The support that orphans might expect from extended-family members has come under pressure because of the declining economy and increasingly tight budgets within households. As a result, child-headed households are emerging, and with them, new power relations as youth are sustaining entire families. The Lusaka YWCA (Young Women's Christian Association) has a shelter program for battered women. Its courses include gender-sensitivity training of police in an effort to improve intervention in cases of domestic upheaval.

Work and Commerce. At the outset of the 21st century, Zambia's capital is an administrative headquarters and transportation hub. The economic significance of its light industry is overshadowed by commerce and distribution in retail trade of largely imported commodities. Lusaka hosts an annual agricultural and commercial and trade show attracting local and regional exhibitors and featuring public entertainment. The show grounds were built during the colonial period, when the annual show was an important venue that brought together white residents and African spectators.

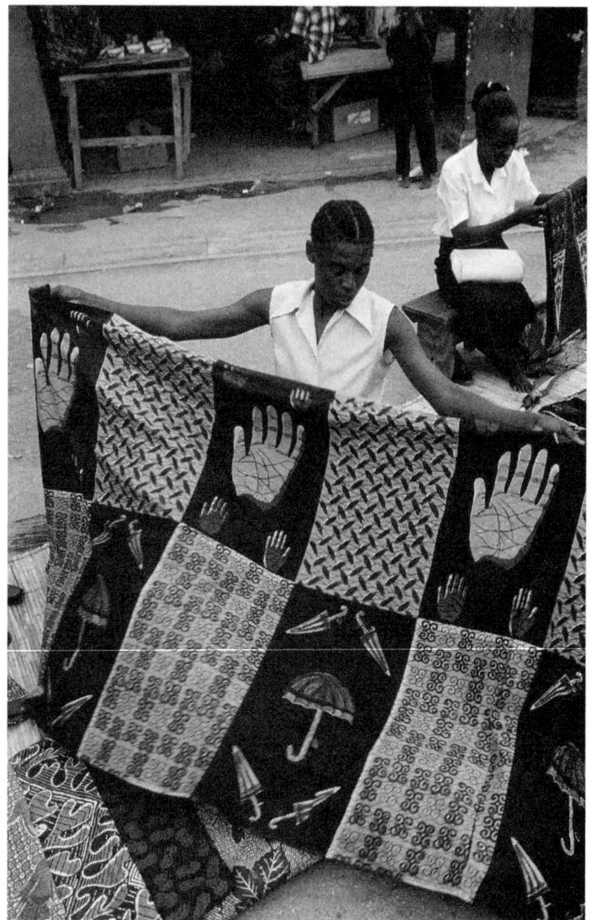

© CAROLINE PENN/CORBIS

A woman examines textiles for sale at Bamba market in Lusaka, Zambia.

The capital plays a role in the broader regional tourist network as a staging point for overlanders, backpackers, and visitors to the country's magnificent game parks and tourist resorts, including Victoria Falls on the Zambezi River. Several hotels of international standard cater to this trade and to the needs of traveling development consultants.

Arts and Recreation. The National Museum opened in the mid-1990s in a building originally planned to house the party headquarters under construction by the Chinese government but never completed. The museum is the home of an impressive collection of contemporary Zambian visual arts, a collection of ethnographic artifacts from across the country, and a political exhibit that celebrates the struggle for independence. At the Kabwata Cultural Village in one of the old low-income settlements, artisans produce tourist curios, and traditional dances are performed on Sundays. Craft shops come and go in the major hotels. The city's many markets also sell handicrafts and colorfully printed woven fabrics, called *chitenge,* that appeal to visitors.

Major hotels offer music entertainment at night, and Lusaka possesses several discotheques and popular nightspots where the local jet set and expatriates meet. There are numerous bars and drinking places in all residential areas of the city regardless of income. Movie theaters tend to be located in dangerous areas, and attract mainly a daytime audience for B-rated movies, among which martial-arts films are particularly popular with young Zambians. The Lusaka Theatre draws a small audience for its performances, many of which feature local talent both as authors and actors.

Sports are popular across all walks of life. While football (soccer) is the most popular sport and attracts large audiences in Lusaka's two stadiums, there is more limited participation in tennis, golf, polo, and cricket. There is a racecourse and a polo field as well.

QUALITY OF LIFE

The design of spacious gardens and lush greenery that were part of the garden-city plan when Lusaka was opened as the new capital in 1935 has today been largely hidden from view by tall stone or metal wall-fences topped with razor wire or broken glass. Many residents in high-income housing areas make use of around-the-clock security services, including watchmen and electric alarms. Burglaries and armed robberies in daylight are so common that the United States Department of State regularly issues warnings to travelers and tourists not to move around in the city after sunset.

The health of the public is seriously at risk in Lusaka at the outset of the 21st century due to the combined effects of overcrowding, declining infrastructure, and insufficient services. Every rainy season during the 1990s has sadly seen the return of cholera in Lusaka and other towns. A major cause of death is tuberculosis, an effect of HIV/AIDS that is carried by a large proportion of the urban population.

The lifestyle of the majority of Lusaka's population, the more than 50% who live in squatter areas, is wanting in respect to quality-of-life factors—as indicated by substandard housing, insufficient infrastructure and services, and lack of employment options.

FUTURE OF THE CITY

Lusaka's future hinges on making the capital sustainable in terms of environmental and basic infrastructure, economic growth, and improvements in the life chances of the majority population. The development scenario demands economic growth along with equitable distribution. The challenge to create housing for all will become ever more urgent in the 21st century. This challenge involves a rethinking of conventional housing options to expand the provision of basic rental units rather than owner-occupied housing for the capital's growing poor population.

BIBLIOGRAPHY

Ellison, Gabriel, *They Came to Build: Early Lusaka and 50 Years of Anderson + Anderson, 1906–1998* (Anderson + Anderson 1998).

Hansen, Karen Tranberg, *Keeping House in Lusaka* (Columbia University Press 1997).

Hobson, Richard, *Showtime: A History of the Zambia Agricultural and Commercial Society, 1914–76* (Agricultural and Commercial Society of Zambia 1979).

Sampson, Richard, *So This Was Lusaakas: The Story of the Capital of Zambia to 1964* (Multimedia Publications 1982).

Williams Geoffrey W., ed., *Lusaka and its Environs* (Zambia Geographical Association 1986).

Williams, Geoffrey J., *The Peugeot Guide to Lusaka* (Zambia Geographical Association 1984).

KAREN TRANBERG HANSEN

Macau

China

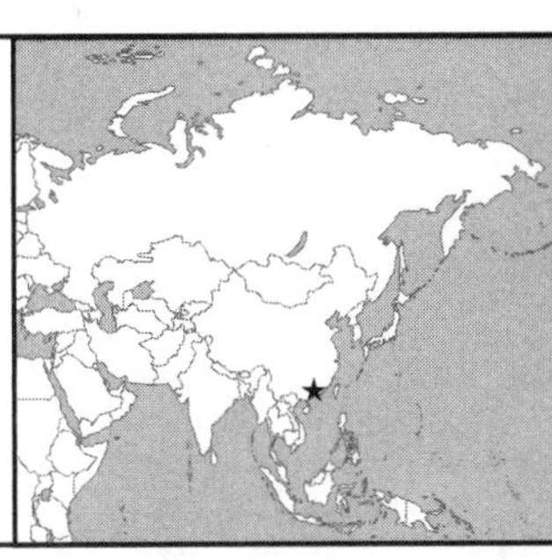

ORIENTATION

Name of City. Among Cantonese speakers, Macau (Macao) is known as Ou-Mun ("Gate of the Bay"). Putonghua (Mandarin) speakers pronounce the same two Chinese characters as *Ao-Men*. The name *Macau* was given to the territory by the Portuguese when they settled there in the 1550s. Tradition has it that the name derives from A-Ma-Gau, which, when translated, literally means "Bay of A-Ma." It was so-named in honor of A-Ma, the protectress of seafarers, to whom one of the oldest temples in the territory is dedicated. Until the handover to China on December 20, 1999, Macau's full name was City of God of Macau, there is no Other more Loyal.

Location. Macau is in southeast China, in the Pearl River Delta. It is located at 22°14′ north latitude and 113°35′ east longitude. The local time is seven hours ahead of the Greenwich meridian. Macau's climate is subtropical to temperate, with two major seasons—a humid and rainy spring and summer, and a drier autumn and winter. The average temperature is about 23°C (73°F). The typhoon season lasts from May to October.

Population. Macau's estimated population as of March 2000 was 434,700 inhabitants, out of whom more than half were females. About 97% were ethnically Chinese. About a quarter of them were of Portuguese descent. The rest were Macanese, Portuguese, Filipinos, and others. In addition, 23.2% of the population were under 15, 69.1% were between 15 and 64, and 7.7% were 65 and over. Both the census of 1991 and the by-census of 1996 indicated that Macau had a relatively high "floating population" (13.7% and 9.7%, respectively), referring to people who are not Macau residents but who remain temporarily in the city for a variety of reasons, such as tourism, family visits, or business, reflecting Macau's status as a tourism- and service-oriented city.

Macau is one of the three cities in a dynamic triangle, along with Hong Kong, 60 kilometers (37 miles) to the northeast on the left bank of the Pearl River, and Guangzhou, 145 kilometers (90 miles) to the north. Macau's immediate neighbor is the Zhuhai Special Economic Zone.

Distinctive and Unique Features. The territory of Macau consists of one peninsula, Macau—7.8 square kilometers (3 square miles), originally 3.4 square kilometers (1.3 square miles); and two islands, Taipa—6.2 square kilometers (2.4 square miles), formerly 2.3 square kilometers (0.9 square mile), and Coloane, 7.6 square kilometers (2.9 square miles), originally 5.9 square kilometers (2.3 square miles). Another 2.2 square kilometers (0.8 square mile) of land has been reclaimed in between Taipa and Coloane—called Cotai, resulting in a total area of 23.8 square kilometers (9.2 square miles). Since the beginning of the 20th century, the overall area of Macau has continuously been expanded by progressive land reclamation from the sea, since the tiny enclave had no other possibility to expand in order to accommodate its growing population. The peninsula of Macau is one of the most heavily populated areas of the world. Until 2000, when a second border crossing opened on Cotai, there was only one access and exit by land, located near the historical China Gate; there are two access ways by sea, through the Inner Harbour and the Outer Harbour; and since 1995 one can arrive and depart from the Macau International Airport.

From Macau's founding until the early 1840s, the Portuguese were the only foreign nationals tolerated on Chinese soil. To defend the city from European contenders, the Portuguese began to erect a chain of fortresses in the first half of the 17th century, which they placed on the highest hills and along two major waterfronts. Together with the churches and convents, some of whose origins date back to Macau's primordial days, the city's skyline resembled that of an old European town far into the 20th century. Thus, Macau was not only a bastion of commerce, but of faith, too. The highest elevation on the peninsula, at 90 meters (295 feet), Guia Hill is the location of the oldest lighthouse (1865) still in operation on the China coast. Beginning in the 1970s, the pressing need for space resulted in the loss of buildings, that today would have been included on the list of protected properties and sites. Structures of great cultural interest had to make way for cheap, modern architecture erected with little regard for urban planning or coordinated styles.

Nowadays Macau is better known as the Monte Carlo of the East. It is the only place in China where gambling is legal, and it annually attracts about 20 times the city's local population.

Attractions of the City. For many people tourism in Macau is synonymous with gambling. Despite China's aversion to the activity and its perceived adverse effects on social and cultural mores, gambling remains Macau's main attraction, centering on the Lisboa Hotel, the mainstay of Macau's casino industry. The Sociedade de Turismo e Diversões de Macau (STDM, Society for Tourism and Entertainment of Macau), founded by the tycoon Stanley Ho in 1962, is Macau's biggest private employer. More than 40% of the city government's income derives from gambling. STDM operates all casinos under government franchise, which expired in 2001 and had to be renegotiated. The casinos serve mainly the domestic tourism market from neighboring Hong Kong, mainland China, and Taiwan. By the end of 2000 Macau had the tenth-highest tower in the world—338 meters (1,109 feet)—together with a huge entertainment center at its foot, both built by STDM.

The other major attraction in Macau is the remains from its colonial past, in the form of fortresses, churches, and other structures, among which figure prominently the ruins of St. Paul's and the adjacent Monte Fort. The official list of monuments, buildings of architectural interest, classified areas, and sites, published by the local Cultural Institute, provides many examples of the conservation priorities that have been realized through restoration projects aimed at preserving key public buildings and residences built for both the Chinese and Portuguese communities over almost four and a half centuries of settlement. Interesting solutions have been found for some of these monuments, such as their conversion into hotels, museums, libraries, or public departments.

Through closer cooperation with planners and stakeholders involved with the development of the Pearl River Delta region, tourism continues to be emphasized as the main attraction for investment in such sectors as hotels, shopping outlets, transportation, entertainment, and leisure and recreational facilities. The government is keen to develop alternative forms of tourism such as cultural and family-oriented attractions—for example, through the meetings, incentives, conferences, and exhibitions (MICE) market—in order to enhance the international business profile of Macau and to diversify the tourism industry. The government also hopes to attract local and foreign investment to make Macau a key player in the global economy, especially since China's commitment to joining the World Trade Organization (WTO). This strategy must be balanced with the priority of encouraging more entrepreneurial initiatives among the local populace, since the policy of localizing employment opportunities is a key element in economic and social progress following the 1999 handover. The territory's only drawing card is a pool of educated and trained personnel, since it is so dependent on the mainland for other resources.

Relationships Between the City and the Outside. Through its historical and current relationship with Portugal, Macau has European links in economic, scientific, cultural, and educational spheres. It has independent memberships in the WTO and Asia-Pacific Economic Cooperation (APEC). The perception of the city from outside is that it continues to be a bridge between East and West and a gateway to China. The international community in Macau consists mainly of Portuguese civil servants and professionals who remained after the handover of sovereignty to assist in the administration of the territory as it establishes its new identity as a Special Administrative Region (SAR) of China. Others have established their own private companies. Individuals from all over the world are employed in foreign companies located in Macau, as well as in teaching and in the health sector. Overseas workers from mainland China and the Philippines occupy many, mainly low-level, positions in the service sector, while others are engaged on construction projects.

Major Languages. There are two official languages in Macau, Chinese and Portuguese, although Portuguese is rarely spoken outside the administration. The two main spoken languages are Cantonese and, increasingly, Mandarin. English is used extensively for education, for international and even local business transactions, as well as for communications between the Chinese and the Portuguese.

HISTORY

The Origin of the City. When the Portuguese reached China in 1513, they found a "closed" empire owing to China's temporary policy of isolationism, which included the prohibition of foreign trade, both regarding Chinese who wanted to do business abroad and foreigners who wanted to do business with China. But since business opportunities were very promising (silk, spices, precious metals), the Portuguese could not be deterred from returning to China year after year, and increasingly so after their exploration of Japan in December 1542 or January 1543. Although the Chinese regularly destroyed Portuguese settlements, in 1557 the Portuguese made one more attempt to gain a foothold in China and settled down on the peninsula of Macau. Because of trade with Japan, which saw the Portuguese as carriers of Chinese silk to Japan and of Japanese silver to China, the city grew and prospered very fast. In 1639, however, the Japanese put an abrupt end to this trade for internal political reasons. This was the most important in a series of unfortunate events for the Portuguese in Asia, which left Macau an isolated territory in the 1640s. Without further prospects of trade, the city seemed doomed.

Apart from Macau's great economic importance, its role as religious hub, sending Catholic missionaries all over the Far East, must not be forgotten. The missionaries were not only converting the "heathen," but were active agents of intercultural exchange between East (mainly China) and West in fields as varied as architecture, art, literature, philosophy, geography, astronomy, mathematics, and so on. In 1594 the Jesuits established there the first European-style university in the Far East, the College of St. Paul, with a degree course in theology and arts subjects from 1597 onward.

Macau's economic situation started to improve slightly in the first half of the 18th century, when there was a growing demand for Chinese products in Europe, mainly silk and tea. Since Canton, the only Chinese city open to foreign trade, was off-limits for foreign women, the traders' families used to settle in nearby Macau, which gave the city a unique cosmopolitan flair and brought new wealth to its inhabitants. This situation lasted until the 1840s, when the Chinese had to agree to the opening of the so-called treaty ports following the Opium War. In addition, the British had settled in Hong Kong since 1839, and very soon Hong Kong would overshadow and overtake Macau. Consequently, Macau lost its importance as the only gateway to China.

In 1887, after a century-old dispute with the Chinese about their territorial rights over Macau, the Portuguese managed to become the rightful owners of Macau through the Treaty of Tianjin (Tientsin). Although the Chinese soon challenged the validity of this treaty, they never went beyond rhetorical attacks to change the status quo. In the wake of the Portuguese Revolution of April 25, 1974, Portugal voluntarily gave up all claims to its former overseas territories and colonies. Yet at the time, because of the problems created internally by the Cultural Revolution, China was not prepared to reclaim Macau. In April 1987 both countries signed the *Joint Declaration of the Government of the Republic of Portugal and of the Government of the People's Republic of China on the Question of Macau,* which inaugurated Macau's "transitional period," and was decisive for its social and economic development in the years to follow. The handover to China took place on December 19, 1999; the next day China assumed full authority over Macau.

Migration: Past and Present. Migration into and out of Macau must always be seen in the wider context of the political and economic situation in both Macau and China. Traditionally, in times of great internal upheaval in China—such as the Taiping Rebellion (1850–1864), the Japanese occupation of Hong Kong (1941–1945) during World War II, and the Cultural Revolution (1966–1974)—Macau was flooded with refugees. Many temporary immigrants tried to stay on in Macau even after the situation had improved in China. Some brought capital and skills with them, giving an important boost to the local economy.

From 1851 until 1873 Macau was one of the major ports shipping tens of thousands of cheap Chinese laborers, called "coolies," from surrounding Chinese provinces to overseas destinations such as California, Cuba, Peru, and Australia. Today Chinese from Macau emigrate mainly for reasons of education and better employment prospects. One favorite destination for work and study is Taiwan, while the People's Republic of China is chosen by many to further their studies.

The relatively strong imbalance in the sex ratio, which became more marked in the 1990s, can be explained by the effect of increased female migration to Macau. They are predominantly young women from mainland China, who work in Macau's light industry (textiles) and the service sector (tourism and related activities). A comparatively small number of Portuguese expatriates was present until the late 1980s, consisting mainly of civil servants. After the signing of the Sino-Portuguese Joint Declaration in 1987, hundreds of individuals were called in the fields of administrative affairs, law, education, engineering, and health. This was a temporary phenomenon, however, because most of them have returned to Portugal owing to the localization policy, which determined that the region's administration be filled with locals who, for the most part, are Chinese.

INFRASTRUCTURE

Public Buildings, Public Works, and Residences. One of the earliest major improvements in Macau's infrastructure was the construction of the first bridge connecting Macau and Taipa (1974), which allowed the development of the islands and gave the territory a sense of unity. But only after the signing of the Joint Declaration in 1987 were further projects launched and completed. This significantly improved Macau's accessibility and the quality of life of its residents. Among the most important "hard projects" were the new jetfoil terminal in the Outer Harbour, the Ka Ho container harbor, the second Macau-Taipa bridge, the Macau International Airport, the new border gate, three wastewater-treatment plants, the incineration plant, the new buildings of the Legislative Assembly and the Supreme Court, and a bridge linking Macau with the Zhuhai Special Economic Zone. Two hospitals—a public one practicing Western medicine and a private one practicing traditional Chinese medicine—are located on the peninsula. Since the connecting bridges to the city are kept closed during severe typhoons, a new hospital is needed on the islands to care for their growing population. Macau has a state-of-the-art telecommunications system. In general, it can be considered a city with a modern infrastructure.

Civic pride in the unique cultural heritage of Macau is manifested in a variety of museums and exhibition centers, such as the Macau Museum, the Maritime Museum, a wine museum, and the Grand Prix Museum, devoted to the annual Grand Prix automobile race. The demand for more leisure facilities has accelerated the construction of complexes such as the Cultural Centre on reclaimed land in the Outer Harbour area, a sports stadium on Taipa, a marine-sports activities youth center on Coloane,

© MACDUFF EVERTON/CORBIS

Cars cross a modern bridge from Taipa Island to Macau in this photograph from 1995.

and an Olympic-size swimming pool on Taipa. Following the handover of administration by the Portuguese government, both their diplomatic presence and the official residence of the consul are located in historic buildings, the latter in the magnificently restored former Hotel Bela Vista.

Macau's most important investments in the territory's human capital, or "soft projects," were the founding of the University of Macau (1988), the Macau Polytechnic Institute (1991), and other institutions of tertiary education. Macau has been chosen as the location of the United Nations Software Institute.

Politics and City Services. Since December 20, 1999, Macau has been an SAR of China, and has been governed by a Basic Law, similar in content to that of Hong Kong, which also reverted to China on July 1, 1997. In the eyes of the People's Republic of China, both territories serve as living proof of the viability of the "one country, two systems" concept, devised by Deng Xiaoping in 1982. According to the Basic Law, the present order, or status quo, in the territory—namely Macau's socioeconomic system and lifestyle—will continue to exist for another 50 years. During that time, Macau will be governed by Macau residents and is granted a high degree of autonomy, except in foreign affairs and defense matters. As established under the Portuguese colonial administration, Macau has an executive-led government, in which the chief executive, who is appointed and dismissed by the central government in Beijing, has much wider powers than the heads of government in democratic systems. The chief executive is supported in the exercise of his functions by five secretaries and the Executive Council. The Legislative Assembly, which represents local interests, is composed of 23 members with tenure of four years. Only eight of them are elected directly by universal suffrage; another eight are elected indirectly by local interest groups, and seven are appointed directly by the chief executive. In the future the number of members in the Legislative Assembly is going to increase, first to 27 and later to 29. The Macau SAR has its own flag, composed of a white lotus flower on green ground, topped by five yellow stars.

Macau is divided into two administrative municipalities: the Provisional Municipal Council of Macau and the Provisional Municipal Council of the Islands. The former substitutes the Loyal Senate of Macau, the foundation of which dates back to 1583. Until the middle of the 19th century, it was also the seat of power, when it was definitively demoted to a municipal council. Its president has traditionally been a Macanese. As the word *provisional* indicates, there is uncertainty about the future of both municipal councils because, according to Macau's Basic Law, some of the more political functions exercised by the councils must disappear.

Educational System. Before the signing of the Sino-Portuguese Joint Declaration in 1987, the Portuguese administration of Macau had adopted a noninterventionist stance toward education and did not attribute many resources to it. The main providers of education were the Catholic Church, some social-service organizations, and private individuals. Consequently, Macau has never had a unified educational system. The different systems supplied themselves in terms of structure, curriculum, teaching personnel, and textbooks from various sources—namely, the People's Republic of China, Taiwan, Hong Kong, and Portugal. This has resulted in a visible disparity regarding the qualifications and knowledge of the students. Therefore, the University of Macau and polytechnic institutions usually submit secondary-school graduates to entrance examinations.

In the 1990s, however, education was one of the big priorities of the Macau government; each year more than 10% of the public expenditure was consumed by it. Yet the unequal distribution of funding has benefited mainly a small number of government schools, leaving the private schools with a very unfavorable teacher to student ratio, with all its negative consequences. On the other hand, in 1995–1996 a law for free basic education was implemented, which was also subscribed to by many private schools. The law mandates free education during the first seven to ten years of schooling.

About one-quarter of Macau's population is enrolled in the various teaching establishments of the territory, ranging from kindergarten to tertiary levels. The language of instruction is overwhelmingly Cantonese, but there are also institutions offering education from preschool to secondary school in either Portuguese or English. All institutions of tertiary education try to attract students from mainland China in order to increase the number of students and to enhance the spirit of competition among local students. An increasing number of individuals participate in programs of adult education.

Transportation System. Considerable improvements in the provision of public transport were made in the 1990s, but the increasing number of private vehicles placed great strains on the infrastructure in the city. Local buses, taxis, commercial vans, and tourist coaches vie with private cars for road use. In recent years, there has been a proliferation of motor scooters, adding to the traffic problems. However, there are no restrictions (yet) regarding the use of private cars, as there are in Hong Kong or Singapore. Sea transport is a vital component of the economy, providing links with the region. Owing to the sediment load carried by the Pearl River, Macau's shallow waters have to be dredged continuously. For inbound and outbound passenger traffic, a jetfoil service is in operation to Hong Kong and China. The Macau International Airport allows residents and visitors to travel between several destinations in the region. A helicopter service also operates routes to Hong Kong and China.

CULTURAL AND SOCIAL LIFE

Distinctive Features of the City's Cultures. Macau can serve as a laboratory for experimenting with one's intercultural fitness and ability to deal with two cultures as different as the Portuguese and the Chinese. Besides the language barrier, their respective cultural differences increase the difficulty of effective communication. Good places to observe or experience these problems are Portuguese (and other Western) restaurants frequented by Chinese, and vice versa, mainly when members of both cultures share a common meal.

Another interesting feature of Macau is that the street names, which are written in both Portuguese and Chinese on white Portuguese-style tiles with blue writing, generally have a different meaning in each language. Taxi drivers usually react only to the Chinese designation of a place. Therefore, one can argue that the same city has a very different meaning for its Portuguese, Macanese, and Chinese inhabitants. In addition, every building in Macau has its own house name, reminiscent of a time long gone by when all streets were not yet named.

Macau has a small community of residents engaged in fishing, who live on boats in the Inner Harbour. Traditionally, this group has occupied the lowest level in South China's social-strata. Intermarriage with outsiders is very rare, which creates a caste-like system. A part of the population in Coloane village still lives in houses on piles, and there are also four shipbuilding yards engaged mainly in the construction of wooden boats. Their workmanship is well known in the surrounding regions.

Cuisine. Macau provides a good opportunity to savor three distinct cuisines. There is the local Cantonese cuisine, which is proverbial in China because of its immense variety and excellent flavors, from the simplest to the most elaborate dish. Then there is Portuguese cuisine, whose essential ingredients are imported from Portugal—such as dried codfish and special types of sausages, olive oil, and wines. Portuguese chefs regularly train local chefs to maintain standards and keep up with new trends. A third cuisine, with its own distinctive traditions, is Macanese food. Its ingredients, modes of preparation, and even the designations for a variety of dishes reflect the places through which the Portuguese had passed before their arrival in Macau, mainly India (Goa) and Malacca (Malaysia), and where they found their first wives. Macanese cuisine is a family matter, full of individual interpretations and preferences, and recipes for the same dish may vary from cookbook to cookbook.

Ethnic, Class, and Religious Diversity. The overwhelming percentage of the population of Macau is ethnically Chinese. However, the varieties of dialects that can be heard reveal that not all of them are locally born Cantonese. From among the seven major groups of Chinese dialects, four can be heard in Macau. The great majority of Chinese are Yue (Cantonese) speakers, which has become the common language of the Macau Chinese as a whole. Another important dialect throughout Macau's history has been the Fujianese, or Min, dialect, which is maintained by immigrants from Fujian province. Another, later group of immigrants from Jiangsu and Zhejiang provinces are Wu dialect speakers. In addition, Mandarin, or Beifang, is on the rise. Although the dialects may be very different phonologically, all Chinese dialects share the same writing system.

Although Portuguese was the only official language during most of Macau's history, this language is spoken by only a small group of Chinese, usually those who entered the civil service. By December 19, 1999, Chinese was the mother tongue of 87.6% of Macau's civil servants; Portuguese, of 11.3% (out of whom only 2.5% were born in Portugal); and other languages (including English), of 1.1%. The gradual increase in Cantonese speakers among public servants, compared to previous years, can be explained through the localization policy.

The Macanese (Macaenses), or Sons of Macau, as they call themselves, are a small community consisting of only a few thousand individuals. They are the result of centuries of coexistence between the Chinese and Portuguese cultures. The Macanese have been defined according to three main vectors—race (a mixture of Portuguese and Asian, not necessarily Chinese, blood), language (they master Portuguese written and spoken, and Cantonese spoken), and religion (Catholicism)—although the three vectors do not have to be present in an individual at the same time. Traditionally more oriented toward Portugal and Portuguese culture, the certainty of the handover to China stirred up many questions regarding Macanese identity. During the 1990s, some Macanese moved closer to the Chinese culture, resulting in a sinicizing trend, which is visible, for example, in a readier acceptance of intermarriage with Chinese or in the study of written Chinese. Their traditional language, Patois or Patoá—a Creole based on Portuguese and Cantonese, with Malaysian, Indian (Goa), and English sprinklings—is not spoken anymore, but survives in literature, songs, and drama. The emigration of Macanese started in the 1840s, first to Hong Kong and to Shanghai, then to other regions in the world, mainly in search of education and employment. Although living abroad for several generations, many Macanese have never lost touch with the city of their ancestors. They have organized themselves in associations called *Casa de Macau* (literally "Macau House"), where memories are kept alive and traditions continued. They exist in Canada, the United States, Brazil, Portugal, South Africa, and Australia, the most typical destinations for emigrants.

Apart from these three characteristic, although numerically very different, groups of Macau residents, there are relatively large communities of Filipinos and overseas Chinese from Myanmar (Burma), Cambodia, Indonesia, and other countries in the region.

There is freedom of religion in Macau, as can be seen in the Catholic churches, Buddhist and Taoist temples, and even a mosque, scattered all over the territory. The major religions are Taoism and Mahayana Buddhism, which are practiced, often concomitantly, by the Chinese population, although a large number of people do not follow any religion. The Portuguese introduced Catholicism in the second half of the 16th century, but today the majority of the Catholic community of Macau is ethically Chinese. Many of Macau's public holidays are based on religious festivities of one or the other religious community.

Family and Other Social Support Systems. The Confucian heritage is visible in the overall importance attributed to the family in general, but the younger generation's pattern of family structure moves away from the traditional extended family toward a preference for the nuclear family. Although the one-child policy practiced in mainland China does not apply in Macau, young couples tend not to have more than two children. Owing to the growing participation of young women in the labor market, the socialization of children shifts from the nuclear family to other institutions or relatives at a very early age.

Beyond family social-support systems, there are 24 neighborhood associations, *kaifong*, representing the so-called common people and the myriads of problems resulting from living in overcrowded conditions. Traditionally the *kaifong* have been the link between individuals or groups of Chinese and the Portuguese administration, a role that they continue to exercise under the Chinese administration. Largely pro-Communist in their outlook, the *kaifong* also possess the power of mass mobilization, which could be observed during some of the handover activities.

The Institute for Social Action is the government's answer to dealing with social problems, from providing cheap housing to family counseling and running homes for the elderly. Other important institutions of social support are the Catholic Church through Caritas and the Holy House of Mercy (established in 1569), and the Red Cross. Wealthy individuals, families, or businesses support a great variety of charitable organizations, often in a way that may seem paternalistic to Western eyes, but they are important in order to compensate for the lack of social assistance provided by the government.

Work and Commerce. Although there has been a decline in manufacturing business conducted in the city, small enterprises provide the main source of employment alongside those factories, which still recruit local workers. As of 2001, Macau had one of the largest Asian textile-industry export quotas to the United States and Europe. However, many entrepreneurs have moved their operations over the border to nearby Zhuhai, or to other locations in the Pearl River Delta. Apart from small workshops offering tailor-made goods and repair services, business is focused on the retail sector supplied by goods from the hinterland, and the majority of enterprises specialize in exporting, with liberal quotas gained from trade agreements with Europe and North America.

The tourist trade is catered to by an abundance of restaurants offering both Chinese and various of foreign cuisines. Antique and furniture shops compete for customers with ubiquitous gold and jewelry outlets. Fashion boutiques are popular enterprises and are quite profitable owing to the lack of large department stores or malls, which are common elsewhere in East and Southeast Asia. Since many of the central-market and shopping precincts now provide access for pedestrians only, the image of Macau as a shopping destination has improved. Retail stores in other locations, however, suffer a lack of business because of heavy traffic and a shortage of parking spaces.

Arts and Recreation. The visual and performing arts are well represented in Macau at both professional and amateur levels. Undergraduate studies are offered at the Macau Polytechnic in fine arts and graphic communication, but as yet there is no equivalent for the performing arts. Chinese calligraphy and landscape painting are ardently followed forms of expression alongside artists using more-Western approaches to fine arts and graphic design. Cantonese opera draws large audiences for performances in temporary structures in various locations in the territory. Traditional and contemporary ballet and dance are popular attractions, especially those performed in the more permanent Cultural Centre. The International Youth Dance Festival held every year is enthusiastically supported by the local community, while the International Music Festival provides a program featuring both Chinese and Western classical musicians. The popularity of traditional Chinese martial arts and related activities is evident in the existence of more than 40 Kung Fu and Lion Dance associations. Artists from Hong Kong, Taiwan, Japan, and the mainland influence popular music, although mainly in the form of karaoke renditions in hotels or private clubs. Jazz is popular with the Portuguese and Macanese community, but there are few local exponents performing in public.

QUALITY OF LIFE

There is a great income disparity between the public and private sectors, owing to the elevated salaries favored by the administration since the 1980s, used to attract qualified personnel from Portugal for the improvement of Macau's infrastructures. The inequality between the two sectors is further exacerbated by additional benefits for public servants, such as free health care and a pension plan, which do not exist in most private companies. The gap between rich and poor appears to be widening, especially since the opportunities for full-time employment are increasingly limited because of a lack of enterprise development in the private sector.

Among the major problems related to the quality of life are noise pollution, the excessive waste produced by the growing population, and air and water pollution caused by industrial development and construction projects, both within Macau's borders and mainly on neighboring sites in China. Conservation and recycling are not supported in a society that still believes that the old must be disposed of to make way for the new. The incineration of waste encourages this attitude, while reclamation seems to offer a solution to the problem of space for yet more real estate development, despite the plethora of empty dwellings forcing property prices and rentals even lower.

Crimes such as money laundering, organized prostitution, and loan-sharking, are generally related to the gambling business. They occur in a very restricted milieu and rarely involve outsiders. The shootings that occasionally made international headlines seemed to have been restricted to the period from 1997 until the handover. Despite the problems pointed out, Macau would count among the places with high human development according to the Human Development Index, although the territory is not (yet) listed by the United Nations. For instance, the life expectancy at birth (77 years) and the infant mortality rate (4.1 deaths per 1,000 live births under 1 year old) are among the most favorable in Asia.

FUTURE OF THE CITY

The members of Macau's different ethnic communities have different concerns and visions regarding the city's future. The Portuguese and Macanese would like to see the preservation and promotion of some of their cultural relics and traditions, because they perceive them as a valuable asset for Macau's future development, and as the "small" difference that makes Macau distinct and unique from the tens of thousands of Chinese cities on the mainland. They also imagine Macau as China's spearhead and platform regarding the relations between China and the European Community on the one hand, and some of the former Portuguese colonies, such as Brazil, Angola, and Mozambique, on the other hand.

However, for the majority of the local Chinese, half of whom were not even born in Macau, Portugal and the Portuguese are part of Macau's colonial past and are better off forgotten. For them, Macau is a Chinese city, one that should strive for greater integration with the Chinese hinterland. Yet numerous members of the local Chinese elite, many of whom received Western education either in Macau, Hong Kong, or in the West, understand that Macau's main asset is exactly the difference that it can maintain from any other Chinese city, and the usefulness that this may have for mainland China. In fact, Macau does not have much to offer to the motherland in terms of location or humanpower, since both are generally cheaper in China—except its international links and international community, its status as a free port, a stable financial system, and low tax rates. All will depend on the balance between integration and differentiation that the new government will be able to implement. This is certainly no easy task, at a time when the economic future of Macau appears to be the major challenge of the moment.

BIBLIOGRAPHY

Boxer, Charles R., *The Great Ship from Amacon* (Instituto Cultural de Macau 1988).

Coates, Austin, *Macao and the British, 1637 to 1842: Prelude to Hongkong* (Oxford University Press 1989).

Coates, Austin, *A Macau Narrative,* 3d ed. (Oxford University Press 1993).

Cremer, Ralph D., ed., *Macau—City of Commerce and Culture,* 2d ed. (API Press 1991).

Direcção dos Serviços de Estatística e Censos (Statistics and Census Department), *Macau in Figures* (2000).

Forjaz, Jorge, *Famílias Macaenses,* 3 vols. (Fundação Oriente, Instituto Cultural de Macau, Instituto Português do Oriente 1996).

Gunn, Geoffrey, *Encountering Macau: A Portuguese City-State on the Periphery of China, 1557–199* (Westview Press 1996).

Lam, Lai Sing, *Generational Changes in the Cultural Attitudes and Activities of the People of Macau* (Instituto Cultural de Macau 1997).

Lamas, Rosmarie Wank-Nolasco, *History of Macau: A Student's Manual,* 2d ed. (Institute of Tourism Education 1999).

Ljungstedt, Anders, *An Historical Sketch of the Portuguese Settlements in China and of the Roman Catholic Church and Mission in China & Description of the City of Canton* (Viking Hong Kong Publications 1992).

Lo, Shiu Hing, *Political Development in Macau* (Chinese University Press 1995).

Montalto de Jesus, C. A., *Historic Macau: International Traits in China Old and New,* 2d ed. (Salesian Printing Press 1926).

Pittis, Donald, and Susan J. Henders, eds., *Macao: Mysterious Decay and Romance* (Oxford University Press 1997).

Porter, Jonathan, *Macau: The Imaginary City: Culture and Society, 1557 to Present* (Westview Press 1996).

Ramos, Rufino, et al., eds., *Macau and its Neighbors toward the 21st Century* (University of Macau and Macau Foundation 1998).

ROSMARIE WANK-NOLASCO LAMAS
and ROBERT IAN CHAPLIN

Madrid

Spain

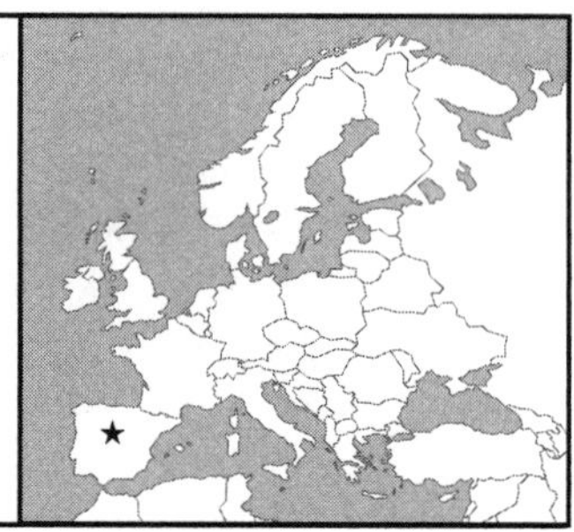

ORIENTATION

Name of City. The origin of the name *Madrid* is blurred by controversy. According to philologist and Arabist, Federico Corriente, Madrid's first name was the Romance word *Matricê,* which means Matrix, or Mother of Water, later transformed into the Arabic Mayrarit.

Location. Madrid is located along the Manzanares River at the heart of the Iberian Peninsula's central plateau. The city is located at 40°24′ north latitude and 3°41′ west longitude.

Population. According to the 1991 national census, Madrid city had 3,084,673 people. By 1998 the municipal census registered a lower population figure, 2,881,506, although the metropolitan region had increased in the same census to 5,091,336 inhabitants.

Distinctive and Unique Features. Madrid is Spain's biggest city—ranked eighth largest among European metropolitan regions. It is one of the highest capitals of Europe—650 meters (2,133 feet) average altitude above sea level. It is situated almost in the center of the Iberian Peninsula on a plateau (the Meseta). To the north lies the Central System Range, with some peaks that rise more than 2,000 meters (6,562 feet), which are partly responsible for a continental climate of crisp winters and hot summers. Average temperatures range between 5°C (41°F) and 24°C (75°F), and can reach 40°C (104°F). Spring and autumn are temperate and less dry (there are between 80 and 90 rainy days a year, mainly in those seasons).

Madrid is a city composed as a puzzle of different areas, street grids, and styles. From its beginning around the Alcazar, where today the Royal Palace stands, a grid of Arab origin spreads south and southeast. That area's main streets, those connecting with the settlement gates and main roads, have influenced all its later evolution and have a funnel shape widening outward (Calle Mayor, Calle de Alcalá, Calle de Toledo). Among these and the existing quarters, new urban pieces have been added, and reflect different structures, functions, styles, and representations in a city that is court driven. The Morería (Moorish), Judería (Jewish) or Habsburg (Austrian) quarters are still recognized by Madrilenians—that is, Madrid's inhabitants—although just part of the grid and a few extant buildings of those eras remain. Despite its capital role, Madrid is not a city of outstanding monuments. During the 19th and 20th centuries, Madrid grew in a star-shaped fashion along its six radial roads connecting the city with the rest of Spain. There are, though, some limits to this growth by the old hunting grounds, now public areas, of the Casa de Campo and Monte del Pardo to the west and northwest, respectively. New bits, stripes, and pieces of urban development appeared during the past two centuries. Distinctive neighborhoods (such as Argüelles's and Salamanca's quarters) in the city enlargements could be mentioned along with the University City, as well as the city main axis: the Gran Vía and Alcala (both running east-west) or Paseo del Prado-Recoletos and Castellana (south-north).

On the main streets, Calle de Alcalá, Gran Vía, or in squares such as the Puerta del Sol or Plaza de España, may be found the distinctive array of Madrid styles. There is the old, austere, rural, and inward-looking (toward patios and quiet gardens) architecture of the 16th century. There are the baroque facades of buildings and churches (such as Churrigera's current Museo Municipal) and the 18th-century neoclassical Royal Palace, San Fernando Fine Arts Royal Academy, and Museo del Prado. The Bank of Spain, National Library, Ministerio de Agricultura, and the old Atocha Railway Station date from the 19th century. Examples of 20th-century architecture include the Gran Vía buildings and Saénz de Oiza's Banco Bilbao Vizcaya. To the east of the Paseo del Prado lie the Buen Retiro Gardens. Farther east are some of Madrid's landmarks, the Plaza de Toros Monumental (Monumental Bullfighting Ring) and two soccer stadiums (Santiago Bernabeu's Real Madrid and Vicente Calderon's Atletico de Madrid).

Attractions of the City. Madrid has gained its strength as a service and financial center from its role as capital of the state and its function as an administrative city. The city houses the main Spanish Stock Exchange and a great deal of bank and finance and insurance institutions of Spain as well as many corporate headquarters. Since the late 1970s, Madrid's involvement in the global economy has accelerated the concentration process responsible for a dramatic increase in real estate and a growing suburbanization of its citizenship. The city has other relative strengths: 11 universities (6 public and 5 private), as well as research centers (such as the Spanish Council for Scientific Research, and other public and private institutions) that concentrate one-third of scientific and humanistic research in Madrid. The collateral advantage of this unusual concentration of learning activity is a highly skilled population.

Services related to the capital role also benefit from an extensive network of hospitals (3.7 beds per inhabitant), and the city's museums and cultural offerings allows for important tourism activity (more than 1 million visitors a year). One of the most attractive tourism areas is the "cultural triangle," which stretches along the 18th-century Paseo del Prado. This area includes the Museo del Prado, the Thyssen-Bornemisza Museum, and the Centro de Arte Reina Sofía National Museum. However, one of Madrid's greatest appeals is the city itself. A great deal of Madrid's everyday life happens in the public space, although the ongoing internationalization and globalization process has restricted this way of life. Characterized as a city "that never sleeps," Madrid has a widespread and active nightlife, with its bars, taverns, pubs, and restaurants offering a wide variety of entertainment supplemented by theaters, concerts, and cinemas.

Major Languages. Castilian Spanish is the official language of Madrid. Although other languages of Spain—Catalan, Galician, and Basque or Euskera—are also spoken, they are not official outside their regional or national territories. A growing number of other European languages, as well as Arabic and Romany, can be heard in the city.

HISTORY

The Origin of the City. Madrid's origin is clouded by the scarcity of extant documentation as well as by the first chronicles written on the history of the city by Christian scholars shortly after its nomination as capital of the Spanish kingdoms of Spain. Although the Madrid area has been inhabited since Paleolithic times, Madrid was founded by Muhammad I in 854 as a Muslim castle and citadel (Alcazar and Almudayna). During the medieval era Madrid's original function as a node of the border defensive system—first against the Christian lords, later against the Muslims—shaped its development. The town's high rate of cavaliers and soldiers accounted for the slow crafts and market growth of Madrid in spite of its excellent location and adequate site. Madrid was also a religiously diverse city until the expulsion of the Jews dictated by the Catholic kings in 1492 and by the Muslims in 1610.

In 1561 Philip II nominated Madrid as the permanent capital of his empire. Added to his lack of a strong nobility and church hierarchy, the king's decision seemed influenced by the healthy site and abundance of water, as well as by the proximity to the royal hunting grounds of El Pardo. Since its designation as the empire's capital. Madrid's maze of narrow and crooked streets did not fit properly with the assumed greatness an opulence of an "empire where the sun never sets." The old and reformed Alcazar became the king's seat. However, during the first decades the king's greater building emphasis would be set in the surrounding areas of Madrid: El Escorial Monastery and Palace or the Aranjuez Palace and Gardens.

The baroque world of Philip III and Philip IV would begin a two-centuries-long shaping process of transforming Madrid into an adequate setting of the Spanish monarchy. First it was necessary to built a public space adequate to stage the crown and public ceremonies: the Plaza Mayor (1616–1619); second, to the east of the city a new palace, Buen Retiro Palace, was devised as a leisure and arts space adequate to the king's magnificence. To the south, along Toledo Street, the Imperial College (1625) of the Jesuit order educated the court elite.

During the second half of the 18th century, Madrid was an increasingly complex imperial city, with court-driven economic development—the church presence was then a major economic feature of the city. The king's foundations of Royal Manufactories and the Friends of the Country Royal Society (to promote enlightened modernization and industries), as well as the major economic and financial activity of Madrid's five main guilds, helped diversify the city's social structure and enrich its cultural dimension. Madrid was a macrocephalic city that needed a huge area to keep itself fed, housed, and clothed; it was also a magnet for population. The growing importance of market and economic development in the city and its regional countryside tended, according to David Ringrose, to soften the regulatory and political grip of the capital over Castile by the end of the 18th century and the whole of the 19th. The city itself was transforming into a less imperial city—that is, the predominance of the court as the major element in the city decreased while the state bureaucratic organization grew along with market, financial, and industrial activities. Society evolved correspondingly, although the new bourgeoisie would slowly consolidate during the next century. The political dominance of the aristocracy was not only restricting bourgeois growth but also, and more important, the elevated transport costs and relative isolation of Madrid promoted just the economic activity able to be absorbed by the city market. Nevertheless, its size and trend toward consumption instead of production isolated the capital more from the most industrialized and dynamic areas of Spain.

As impressive as this growth may have been, the city still lagged behind other European capitals in urban design and magnificence. However, the second half of the 18th century witnessed major transformations in Madrid. The most remarkable urban and building activity was led by the so called Major-King, Charles III, who not only promoted the erection of monuments and great buildings, but also a whole urban renewal of the city based on regulation and public works: sanitation, lighting, and building regulations (Instrucción para el saneamiento de la ciudad, 1761). A new main street was set, the Paseo del Prado, which was designed originally as a relaxing and enlightening public space. Many of the scientific institutions promoted by the king would be located in this same space.

Hampered by the destruction inflicted on the city by the Independence War fought against the Napoleonic armies, 19th-century Madrid began a slow-paced transformation process that was limited by the colliding interests of the old-regime elite and the new, liberal bourgeoisie. The latter would eventually impose its interest over the rest of the population. However, the first transforming momentum proceeded from a political decision: the process of *desamortizaciones* (the disentailment and sale of church and municipal land) eventually sold to wealthy citizens who progressively transformed Madrid´s old-regime landscape into an oligarchy and a bourgeois city. Land not only enhanced the rising classes (so willing to connect with the aristocracy), but also was itself transformed from an entailment of privilege (Ancient Regime) to a valued commodity in the market.

Immigration and the growing productive economic activity, in part owing to an improving road and railroad system, enabled a progressively increased pace of growth. The most important transformations of 19th-century Madrid were made possible during the two relatively more politically stable periods. During the first (1833–1858), Madrid's already-existent grid was reconfigured not only by the new bourgeois buildings but also by the old city grid streets' transformation. A new public gas-lighting system (1830), extended to the homes in 1848, was inaugurated, as was the construction of the first sanitation system (1850) and public watering system (Canal de Isabel II, 1858). These improvements modernized the city and gave Madrid the chance to attract industries, but also helped to widen social and economic differences. The second phase, which began in 1860, was dominated by the enlargement plans of the city. A first, though limited, plan of city expansion (Proyecto de Castro) of square-shaped neighborhoods was designed. Many of the most notable buildings of the Paseo del Prado and Recoletos were built: the National Library, the Stock Exchange, the Spanish Royal Academy, Museum of Anthropology, the Bank of Spain, and the Ministry of Fomento (today´s Agriculture). Trams or streetcars began to run, pulled by animals, and the global urban space was clearly divided into interior, enlargement, and outliers. The speculative activity increased, including many illegally constructed new modest spaces of single-family buildings in land strips not designed for such purposes.

Madrid at the beginning of the 20th century, was a city overcrowded (539,835 inhabitants) by strong rural immigration currents from all over Spain. The city suffered from labor and political unrest, and a very high rate of mortality owing to a lack of planning. Madrid was becoming a dynamic city with no urban-planning vision. Yet some impressive French-style buildings (la Unión y el Fenix, Hotels Ritz and Palace) were erected, and the distinctive Gran Vía was designed and built between 1910 and 1930.

The Second Republic (1931–1936) period was one of mixed results. The new authorities were trapped between long-term planning and the short-term urgency to help the poorest people. The most outstanding legacy of this period was the great increase in public-education buildings and the devised—but not developed—urban plans dating back to the 1920s.

© ABILIO LOPE/CORBIS

La Bolsa is the Stock Exchange in Madrid, Spain.

Paradoxically, these plans were partially applied shrouded in Falangist and Franco's rhetoric.

Once the Spanish Civil War was finished and some reconstruction done, a new city plan was devised to develop a center devoted to the administrative and services sectors, along with an industrial surrounding area buffeted by a greenbelt from the suburbs. Unfortunately the council did not effectively enforce the plan, nor did the great immigration numbers allow a well-balanced growth. One of the most outstanding features of those years was the public-housing policy. The booming slums and shantytowns spread mainly around the south and southeast of the city—in precisely the areas the plan intended to preserve green. These areas eventually were transformed into a cramped maze of modest neighborhoods. The other distinctive feature of the period was Franco´s interest in developing a strong industrial and financial base to balance Catalonian and Basque economic development.

The 1960s and the first half of the 1970s were dominated by a technocratic political stance and an accelerated industrialization development, with little care for the city's old heritage. The increased value of the city's central spaces expelled citizens from the better-located quarters and drastically increased the number of automobiles and traffic jams, prompting a council policy destined to build new subterranean parking spaces and causing the disappearance of the old boulevards. The spatial social-segregation process was accentuated by economic development, and the upper and middle classes fled to the north and northwest of the city, out of the urban area, toward a suburban lifestyle that spread a car- and mall-oriented way of life. These processes put a great strain on the already existent infrastructures, which will take a heavy toll on future planning and development.

The implementation of a coordinated metropolitan planning policy lagged behind the more pressing necessities of political decentralization sought by the transition to democracy that began after Franco's death in 1975. However, an urban policy more sensitive to the citizens' needs and wishes was developed, as well as a policy of building rehabilitation instead of demolition. Finally, in the 1980s a new metropolitan region was defined. Today a new era of coordinating and planning strategies is developing the city and the metropolitan region of Madrid.

Migration: Past and Present. Following its designation as capital of the empire by Philip II in

1561, Madrid's growth was shaped by its capability to concentrate political and administrative power. During the second half of the 19th century, the increased productivity of the country surrounding Madrid, and the shrinking of its productive hinterland, induced a strong migration to the city. In 1920, 40% of Madrid's population consisted of rural immigrants.

After the Spanish Civil War (1936–1939), Madrid suffered a wave of immigration without precedent. During the 1950s the city's inhabitants increased from 1,500,000 to 2,177,123, while in the 1960s the number escalated to 3,120,941. In 1975 Madrid reached its peak: 3,228,059. Then a slow decrease began, with 2,881,506 inhabitants by 1998 (city census). Yet these figures may be misleading because Madrid city could not be isolated from the metropolitan area, which added 1 million people from 1970 to 1980. What actually happened was a process of decentralizing that first reached the expanded 1963 metropolitan area and, since the 1980s, the whole autonomous community of Madrid, now defined as a metropolitan region (1981 population, 4,686,895; 1990 population, 4,845,851; and the estimate of 1998, 5,091,336).

From 1975 the immigration pattern changed, from huge numbers of arrivals from the Spanish regions to a reduced number of foreign immigrants from Latin America, Morocco, and other African (mainly Muslim-majority) nations, Europeans, and Asians (a majority of them Filipinos). Madrid's 1998 census registered only 69,166 foreigners. Although later estimates doubled the amount of nonregistered or illegal immigrants, the rate still was quite low compared with other European Union members and capital cities. With these immigration changes, Madrid´s attitude toward its arrived inhabitants has changed, and a city that prides itself on being open is becoming more suspicious of non-European immigrants (the main targets of this xenophobia are Muslims).

INFRASTRUCTURE

Politics and City Services. Madrid is ruled by a democratically elected City Council composed of 52 council members. These members elect a mayor, who appoints among the councillors the ruling officials of the City Council administrative departments (circulation, urbanism, and so on). Each of the 21 districts has its own subordinate administration. The city revenues come from two main sources: municipal taxes and the allocation of state and regional revenues.

Madrid's metropolitan nature places some of its most pressing and administrative matters outside the reach of the City Council. The regional government, also with a democratically elected assembly, has a major role in planning the development of the city and the metropolitan region.

Madrid's role as capital of the state shapes its main administrative function and services, as well as making it a privileged location of business and culture, and an area of special concern for the state government.

Educational System. Madrid's public and private educational systems are administered by the regional government. An extended public education, which also supports private schools complying with the public curricula, is maintained by the regional government. Primary and secondary education on these premises is free. Private schools not complying with the regional education regulations and curricula do exist, and are maintained by their pupils. In addition to the public educational institutions, the Catholic Church rules a majority of the primary and secondary schools. However, those schools supported by public funds are be open to a lay education, offering classes in ethics instead of Catholic religion.

Madrid also has 11 universities—6 public (Complutense and Polytechnic, located mainly in the Universit City, Autonomous, Alcalá, Charles III, and King Juan Carlos I) and 5 private (Pontificia Comillas, San Pablo-CEU, Alfonso X el Sabio, Europea Madrid-CEES, and Antonio de Nebrija). There are some research institutions and foundations devoted to research (the biggest state-sponsored research institution, the Spanish Council for Scientific Research, is located in Madrid).

Transportation System. Although automobile use has increased in Madrid, public transit is well developed. There is a public bus service run by the Municipal Transport Company (Empresa Municipal de Transportes, or EMT), and an extensive subway system (164 stations serving 176 kilometers (109 miles). In addition, expanded public and privately operated parking systems try to ameliorate traffic congestion.

The suburbs and the metropolitan region are linked to the city by ten radial commuter rail lines, private buses, roads, and highways. Public city, private metropolitan, and commuter rail lines are integrated into the Regional Transport Authority, which coordinates the whole system.

CULTURAL AND SOCIAL LIFE

Distinctive Features of the City's Cultures. Most of the people living in Madrid were not born in the city, and residents remain linked to their hometowns. A well-known Madrilenian expression is: "I am going to my town" when they return to vacation in their hometowns. The great majority of the old immigration comes from the Extremadura and Andalusian regions, although important contingents of Galicians, Castilians, and Basques inhabit the city. While nationally diverse, Madrid has acted as a Spanish melting pot, and its cultural mix is a rural, outspoken, friendly way of behavior, prone to bar and street socializing. Actually Madrid's typical character was clearly influenced by late-19th-century and early-20th-century Zarzuelas set in Madrid (light opera or Spanish operettas depicting popular figures). Madrid's dress, behavior, and etiquette tend to be casual.

Open public spaces such as the Retiro Park in the middle of the city are reinvigorated examples of public space where citizens and visitors alike walk, sport, rest, or amuse themselves with amateur spectacles, music, or any kind of activity. Although some economic activities demand formal dress during business hours, this seems to be quickly disappearing from the city landscape and is regarded by some as a "sign of show off" or "rural origins."

The Madrilenian "flavor" was induced and promoted by the first democratically elected City Council. Verbenas (fiestas held in a quarter in honor of its patron saint—the whole city's patron saint is Sain Isidro Labrador, whose verbena is held in mid-May) and open-street amusements boosted a sense of belonging. At the same time, Madrid boomed with a bottom-up cultural movement called *movida* ("in movement"), characterized by its reaction to any kind of ideological strictures, creativity, and the explosion of a sensual way of life, whose most famous internationally known product was filmmaker Pedro Almodóvar. Cafeterias and bars or taverns are numerous and traditional meeting places. Some old cafés still house *tertulias* (informal conversational gatherings dealing mainly with politics and culture where, in the past, famous intellectuals, artists, and politicians met with common citizens).

Cuisine. Madrid's cuisine is not the most elaborate of Spain. One of the city's distinctive features is the traditional tapas (different kinds of prepared little snacks) consumed in bars and taverns all day long, with wine, beer, or soft drinks. A great variety of restaurants with a wide range of prices covers all the Spanish cuisines. International or ethnic restaurants, however, are not as widespread as in other European capital cities. *Cocido madileño* (a boiled mix of meat, poultry, peas, potatoes, and other vegetables served in two dishes) and *callos a la Madrileña* (pork tripe) are its two most recognized specialties. Madrilenians are very fond of fresh fish and seafood.

Ethnic, Class, and Religious Diversity. Added to the variety of Spanish origins of Madrilenians is a new group of immigrants from North and sub-Saharan Africa, Latin America, and Asia that accounts for less than 7% of the city's total population, but is nonetheless a visible ethnic presence in Madrid. Though they do not tend to wear their traditional dress (except some Muslim women), these immigrants can be easily identified by the rest of the population. These later groups have no clear public spaces, although they do congregate in some squares, as well as some pubs and discotheques. In addition, Spanish regional identity is articulated through regional houses that promote culture, language, and holiday-specific social events, and that maintain meeting spaces. European and American foreign communities also exist, although they are less visible.

The great majority of the population is nominally Catholic by tradition (and by Franco's enforcement). There is a growing Muslim community of immigrants and native-born Spaniards who meet in the mosques and the Islamic Cultural Center, and there are also some Jews and Protestant groups such as the Jehovah's Witnesses.

Madrid is a city of increasing social and economic diversity as well, and this diversity tends to be more spatially segregated. This trend adds to the traditional division of Madrid or Madriles, denoting the city's low (owing to both class and lower topographical location) and high quarters. "Low" quarters tend to be to the south and southeast of the city, just where the industrial belt of Madrid is located. Meanwhile, the north and northwest are predominately middle- and upper-class suburbs, and more car-oriented, like the American way of life. Old-city quarters have followed different paths, with the best located to the north and tending to concentrate around corporate and financial headquarters. Old popular areas are diversifying through immigration, and residential and commercial middle- to upper-class neighborhoods are becoming populated with the elderly.

Family and Other Social Support Systems. Madrid has few civic or neighborhood organizations.

Besides public and private health care, the principal social-support system is the family, which complements the retirement institutions, kindergartens, and day-care centers. The nuclear family resides together, although the extended family (particularly grandparents and aunts) helps take care of the children.

Work and Commerce. The Madrid metropolitan region accounts for one-eighth of the population of Spain, and 17.7% of business firms and 17.3% of the country's workers. Compared with the rest of Spain, the region surpasses the national average sector activity only in services, 73.15% to 61.56%; and lags behind in agriculture, 1.05% to 8.03%; industry, 17.48% to 20.51%; and construction, 8.32% to 9.90%, respectively. The concentration of services in Madrid (national and regional administrations, finance, insurance, bank, consulting) has focused population movement and commutation toward the center. Commerce, shopping, and industry, however, tend to cluster in different areas of the metropolitan region, yet the old-city traditional shopping areas maintain their ascendancy over the inhabitants. Progressive opening hours, deregulation, and the growing influence of great shopping centers and malls is a controversial issue in a city embracing economic and globalization trends.

Arts and Recreation. Madrid's size and function as capital allow it to have a wide spectrum of arts and recreation. So-called high culture is well represented. The Paseo del Prado ("Avenue of Arts") houses three museums with an most important collection of European paintings, as well as many other museums and heritage centers. Television broadcasting networks have their headquarters in the city as well. Along with exhibitions, theaters, cinemas, opera, and classical music, the city shares its space with popular culture, sports, and flamenco dancing and music. Soccer is the favorite sport, and the bullfighting season is one of the best in the world. But one of the most enticing features of life in Madrid is its busy nightlife. Eating, having a drink and tapas with friends, and enjoying fiestas are popular activities after work. During the weekends, many Madrileneans leave the city to stay in the surrounding countryside or, if time allows, flee to beaches that are 300 to 400 kilometers (186 to 248 miles) away.

QUALITY OF LIFE

The quality of life in Madrid is generally good, although in a number of aspects it is not very promising. According to the United Nations Development Programme, life expectancy, literacy, and unemployment in Madrid compare less favorably with other cities in developed countries. For example, life expectancy in Madrid is 77.6 years (81.6 for females and 73.8 for males), compared to 79 in Hong Kong (Spain is ranked 20th in the world life-expectancy statistics). Madrid ranks 50th in the world for literacy. Publicly held educational and health services are supported by taxes. Madrid reflects this situation, though unemployment levels are reaching the 9% level. There is a marked increase in economic differences between the poor and rich classes: 6.4% of the households are poor (three points below the national average).

Housing and food account for the majority of household expenses. With relatively more-expensive utilities than in the rest of the European Union, the inhabitants of Madrid are prone to consumption outdoors (restaurants, bars, cafeterias, and celebrations). This gives the city its "never sleeps" image. Crime, a main concern of the citizens, is moving from petty offenses to more violent and major crimes. Drug dealers and organized crime are increasing. Pollution is high, and Spain's problem of desertification means lower water resources in the city. In spite of

© ELKE STOLZENBERG/CORBIS

Christina Hoyos is a flamenco dancer in Madrid, Spain.

such disturbing aspects, Madrid still retains some of its charms.

FUTURE OF THE CITY

Since the 1980s Madrid's character has been transforming. The globalization of its economic activity and the impact of foreign immigration into the city (particularly the Muslims and black Africans) have aroused, first, a more international way of life (exemplified in a change of eating schedules and suburbanization), and second, and more important, the rise of a increasingly open xenophobic and racist attitude. Some traditional neighborhoods now have a visible presence of citizens from developing nations, as in Lavapies and some modest suburban areas. Occasional conflicts have their impact on everyday life in a setting unable to develop a multicultural stance.

Madrid's future is connected with Spain's development. The increasing internationalization of Madrid's finance and economic activity resulting from its role as a national political center will influence its growth as a European city regaining some of its past global significance. From a social and cultural point of view, Madrid will need to accommodate the various groups that are now established there with the economic progress and transformation the city is currently undergoing.

BIBLIOGRAPHY

Brown, Jonathan, and John H. Elliott, *A Palace of a King: The Buen Retiro and the Court of Philip IV* (Yale University Press 1980).

Fernandez Garcia, A., ed., *Historia de Madrid* (Editorial Complutense 1993).

Marin, Francisco J., and Rafael Mas, "Madrid," *Atlas Historico de Ciudades Europeas: Peninsula Iberica, I,* ed. by Manuel Guardia, et al. (Centre de Cultura Contemporania de Barcelona, Salvat 1994).

Otero Carvajal, Luis E., and Angel Bahamonde, eds., *Madrid en la Sociedad del Siglo XIX,* 2 vols. (Comunidad de Madrid 1986).

Ringrose, David, "The Impact of a New Capital City Madrid, Toledo, and New Castile, 1550–1600," *Journal of Economic History,* 33 (1973): 761–91.

Ringrose, David, *Madrid and the Spanish Economy, 1560–1850* (University of California Press 1983).

Ringrose, David, *Spain, Europe, and the "Spanish Miracle," 1700–1900* (Cambridge University Press 1996).

Segura, Cristina, et al., *Madrid: Historia de una Capital* (Alianza/Fundacion Caja Madrid 1994).

FERNANDO MONGE

Makassar

Indonesia

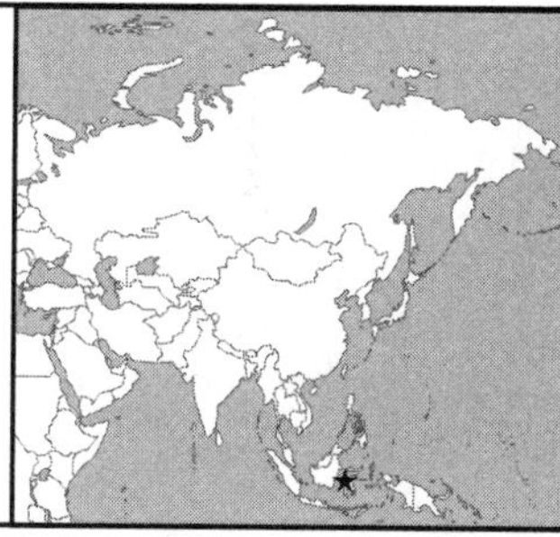

ORIENTATION

Name of City. The official name of the city since late 1999 has been Makassar. This is the name best known internationally; however, in the literature various names and spellings are used for Makassar, including Ujung Pandang, Ujungpandang, Makassar or Makasar. Makassar (Mangkasara in Makassarese language) was the name of a kingdom at least since the 14th century, and it became associated with the city in the 16th century. In 1972 Mayor H. M. Daeng Patompo renamed the city Ujung Pandang, the name customarily used by the Buginese and Makassarese people of the interior, but it was officially renamed again in 1999.

Location. Makassar is in the southwestern part of the island of Celebes (Sulawesi), Indonesia, in Southeast Asia. The city is located at 5° south latitude and 119° east longitude.

Population. Makassar had 1,107,267 people in 1996, according to official data. By 2000 there were an estimated 1.3 million inhabitants. Precise numbers are not easy to obtain, owing to the fact that thousands of ricksha drivers and small vendors live for months every year—or even permanently—in the city without being registered. The population increase in recent decades was 5.5% (1971–1980), 1.5% (1980–1984); and 2.9% (1980–1990). The area of Makassar is 19 square kilometers (7 square miles);

that of the *Kotamadya* (municipality) Makassar, 175.8 square kilometers (67.9 square miles).

Distinctive and Unique Features. Makassar has always been a city of historic importance and regional as well as international relevance. Furthermore, the city is known to be the center of the Makassarese and the Buginese, prominent ethnic groups in Indonesia. Makassar is a center of trade, business, and education. For centuries, Makassar has been a truly multiethnic city—with intra- and interethnic rivalry, but a comparatively low rate of violent communal conflicts. Makassar does not easily fit into urban typologies. It is still a city dominated by bureaucracies and trade. Within Indonesia, this city could functionally be categorized as a secondary city and as a regional metropolis. Makassar has always been physically situated in the Indonesian periphery (Outer Islands), but it is the largest commercial center east of Surabaya (in eastern Java).

The outline of the streets, even in the old parts of the city, shows a grid pattern seldom found elsewhere in Indonesia. This was established in colonial times to meet administrative needs and especially to control the people by arranging separate ethnic quarters in an ordered fashion. Government, concentrated in regional and urban administration, is one of Makassar's biggest employers, and industrialization has been part of the city only since the 1990s. The ethnic or family relation between the actors involved in economic transactions is paramount in the city. Such is the case with the staff of local government agencies, who often are selected informally following ethnic lines. The market in real estate—apart from bigger housing developments—is also person-oriented. There are few ads in the newspapers and few real-estate agents, because most people seeking land, houses, or apartments want personal advice. The prices on the land market are influenced by noneconomic factors. Modern culture and modern patterns of consumption are framed in traditional-family norms, localized concepts, and clientele relations. This form of "peripheral urbanization" is typical of southern and Southeast Asian countries, but can be found in Western countries as well—for example, in earlier periods in Madrid and Rome, and today in Athens.

Attractions of the City. The city is known more for its people and relaxed atmosphere than as a locus of business opportunities or famous tourist sites. Guidebooks for tourists portray Makassar as a charming city with an unhurried atmosphere and a relaxed rhythm, particularly compared to Jakarta.

© CHRISTOPHER ANTWEILER

Supplies are loaded onto schooners in Paotere harbor at Makassar, Indonesia.

Tourists stroll on the long esplanade along the waterfront (Pantai Losari), known for its sunsets and hundreds of small restaurants. One might have a beer in one of the bars, gazing out at the old harbor (Paotere) with its famous Buginese schooners (*pinisi*). A few historic buildings, such as the colonial Fort Rotterdam and Chinese temples, attract some foreign tourists and a growing number of domestic ones. In 1999 a small "Museum Makassar" opened, displaying artifacts and manuscripts documenting the city's vibrant history.

Many travelers, however, experience Makassar as a typical "modern," somewhat boring, administrative city, and most often the city is passed only as the "Gateway to Toraja." The average tourist usually arrives via Jakarta or Bali and spends a night in town just to take the bus to the area of the Toraja people (Tanah Toraja), some nine hours farther north. For migrants from eastern Indonesia and visitors from the province's rural areas, however, the city is very attractive. Makassar is positively perceived by them as being *ramai*—that is, crowded, noisy, and filled with energetic life. Among domestic tourists, Makassar is well known as the center of a pronounced Islamic region and as the place of the grave of Diponegoro (1755–1855), a Javanese resistance fighter in the "Java War" (1825–1830) against the Dutch and a national hero.

Relationships Between the City and the Outside. Makassar is the capital of the province of South Celebes (Propinsi Sulawesi Selatan). In economic terms, Makassar has established itself as the regional primary city for the province of South Celebes. Its inhabitants as of 2000 were only 9% of the population of the province, but made up about 65% of the province's urban population (up from 57% in 1971). Makassar is the location of the centers of the army and navy command. Furthermore, Makassar is the bureaucratic, economic, and education center for the neighboring province of Southeast Sulawesi. The region of South Celebes is one of the centers of Islam in Indonesia and has a comparatively low settlement density. The province's agriculture is based mainly on rice, as well as cocoa, fishing, and shrimp farming. There is also a slowly growing industrial sector and the development of international as well as domestic tourism. The urban economy is based on the harbor, political administration, and facilities for higher education. As a center of in- and out-migration and due to its regional functions, the city can be characterized as a "peripheral metropolis." Many of the inhabitants come from eastern Indonesia. A lot of former residents, especially members of the footloose Buginese, have migrated permanently to other parts of Sulawesi and other islands. Most often they are deeply immersed in local economies and even integrated into local cultures. Despite having only a scant inclination to resettle, some of these people were pressed to return to the city by recent communal riots in Eastern Indonesia. The principal ethnic groups that are represented in the city—Makassarese, Buginese, Mandarese, and Toraja—all have their roots in the province. The region surrounding the city was only lately integrated into the Indonesian nation politically, but it has remained a historic and "hot" region, well known for isolationist or secessionist tendencies.

There is a growing sense of a regional belonging and province-related collective identity in the city and parts of the province. Everyday discourse as well as official propaganda speak of "South Celebes people" (*orang Sulawesi Selatan,* or *orang Sulsel* for short), and mention a unified culture of the prov-ince, the "Culture of South Celebes" (*kebudayaan Sulawesi Selatan*). More and more people speak of "South Celebes dances" and "South Celebes houses." This regional concept gives an orientation transcending ethnic boundaries. Going beyond Islam, it is capable of integrating the mainly Christian Toraja. The core of this conception is heavily biased toward the four principal ethnic groups of the province (Buginese, Makassarese, Mandarese, and Toraja). These four groups are usually differentiated from another in the first instance. But they have such close historical ties and similarities in their cultural makeup that the remaining ethnic groups are almost forgotten.

The image of the city among people from outside Indonesia is formed by its eminent role in the history of the whole archipelago, and by its two well-known ethnic groups, Buginese and Makassarese. Both have a strong profile within Indonesia as adventurous, status-oriented, and proud people. Makassar's strategic position in the regional trading and communication network for 500 years has earned it such glorious labels as "Gateway to the Eastern Islands," "Eastern Emporium," "Door to the Spice Islands," and "Mercantile Turntable." Naturalist Alfred Russel Wallace and novelist Joseph Conrad described late colonial Makassar as a clean and vibrant city. Within today's Indonesia, Makassar is well known as the home region of the ethnic group of the Makassarese, feared as a hotheaded people with a penchant for defending their honor (*siri*). The Buginese are known for their wandering spirit and their economic skill as retail traders and in the transportation business. Due to their wide distribution throughout the Indonesian archipelago, many people have experiences with Buginese settlers.

Major Languages. The main language used in offices, in public exchange, and in everyday life in the households is Indonesian (Bahasa Indonesia). Long-established and intensive interaction has resulted in a distinctive Ujung Pandang slang. Most older people also use ethnic languages—mainly Makassarese, Buginese, Mandarese, Torajanese, and some Chinese dialects. English is not commonly spoken.

HISTORY

The Origin of the City. As far back as the 14th century, Makassar was already a collecting point and trading place for pearls, rattan, wood, and copra from eastern Indonesia. During the 16th century, the maritime trading state of Makassar with its port became the major power within the politically unstable region of Sulawesi. This was due to the rise of the two kingdoms of Gowa and Talloq. Makassar developed as a trading city located between the centers of these two petty states and the maritime-oriented Bajau Laut people who lived on small islands (Spermonde archipelago) within reach of the city. Makassar was armed by several forts. The city grew rapidly between 1600 and 1630, and had about 100,000 people. The coastal extent was about 12 kilometers (7.5 miles) and the city became a great entrepôt for trade within Southeast Asia as well as international trade.

The main Dutch motive for engagement in the Indonesian archipelago was to control the regional trade in spices (nutmeg, pepper, clove, and mace) from the Molucca Islands. After several unsuccessful attempts, the kingdom of Makassar, the leading regional power, was defeated by combined Dutch and Buginese forces in 1667. Ujung Pandang, one of the main forts, was surrendered, renamed Fort Rotterdam, and completely reconstructed into a well-fortified Dutch castle. As a result of the defeat, and as the entrepôt function was severely diminished, many traders wanted to escape the Dutch, and left the region for other islands. This was the first of several waves of out-migration, especially of Buginese people from South Celebes. The new part of the city was a small one, with 5,000 people in 1730, half of them slaves.

Makassar had a peripheral position within the Dutch power structure, being a colonial backwater compared to Batavia (today Jakarta). It was situated in a region only partially controlled by the Dutch. Socially, it was a typical company town of the Vereenigte Indische Compagnie (VOC), characterized by hierarchies and ethnic pluralism. People were divided into clear-cut categories according to their status as free or slave, their ethnic alignment, religion, and (at least implicitly) race. Company officials and soldiers lodged in the fort, whereas other European, Christian, and the Chinese people lived in a small walled city (Vlaardingen). This area remained the city's commercial center until the early 1950s. The larger of the other social segments (mardijkers and burghers) lived in specific quarters, and the big trading communities, such as Buginese and Malays, had their own named settlements (Kampung Wajo, Kampung Melayu). The Malays had come in the 1550s, and were the largest community in 1730, with close to 1,000 people. Despite the residential segregation, interethnic exchange was even more pronounced than in Batavia. Familial relations and interethnic ties were an important social capital. Cultural contacts thus were not established between whole groups, but through specific personal connections relevant for production and trade.

During the 17th and 18th centuries, the economy and social life were based largely on the colonial fort and slave work. The trade in slaves was organized by, among others, members of the colonial staff intensively linked with the Buginese and Makassarese aristocracy in the countryside. The slaves made up the only flourishing export during the 18th century. With the abolition of the slave trade and the upcoming competition by the port of Singapore, this slave-oriented economy came to an end. The city's function returned to its earlier role as an entrepôt.

Migration: Past and Present. During the booming economy in the 19th century, the population of the city grew from 15,000 in the early 19th century to about 40,000 in 1915. The population in 1930 was about 85,000. The 17th-century population size of 100,000 thus was not surpassed until the 20th century. This quick growth of Makassar as well as the specific interethnic dynamics were linked with migration processes. South Celebes was a region with heavy rates of intraprovincial migration and out-migration from the province. In the beginning of the 20th century, the city grew mainly through migration from the countryside. Makassar become a municipality (*gemeente*) in 1906, and many immigrants to the city were moved by the Dutch expansion from Makassar into its hinterland beginning in 1910. Economic possibilities in the city were a further motivation. The city became politically important in 1938 as the capital of the proposed huge Dutch province of all of eastern Indonesia (De Groote Oost, "The Great East"). Between 1942 and 1945 the Japanese ruled a large area, including Kalimantan, from Makassar. The residence of the presidency of the state of Eastern Indonesia was in Makassar from 1947 to 1950. The city grew in the 1950s owing to many migrants coming as refugees escaping the insecure life in large parts of the interior of South Celebes where there was regional rebellion against the national government. The fighters were led by Kahar Muazakkar, and used terrorist measures to force the rural people to take sides.

Most migrants came between 1957 and 1960; after that, the city grew mainly due to natural increase. Problems arose, as most of the migrants were poor and uneducated, and there were few jobs. Immigrants had no resources to build dwellings, and the city lacked money to build water pipes and streets or to organize the removal of refuse. Immigrants seeking to establish themselves had to face the problem of securing land for building their homes. They could either attempt to enter the market for property, or sidestep the issue by becoming squatters. The development of land tenure in Makassar has thus led to squatters having legitimate rights to land, and to the emergence of a land-tenure situation very different from that prevailing in most Western cities. Individual adaptations and uncoordinated actions by certain groups prevented any effective urban planning.

INFRASTRUCTURE

Public Buildings, Public Works, and Residences. Being modern in many ways, Makassar city shows a somewhat rural character in its dwellings and lifestyle. Large areas of the city were settled lacking an adequate infrastructure and without establishing a legally clear land tenure. The rural building structure (*kampung* housing consisting of one-story wooden huts) dominates this city; people cannot afford better housing because so many are (at least seasonally) unemployed. Modern multistory houses are found almost exclusively on the street fronts, whereas the inner areas of blocks and generally the poorer parts of the city are characterized by urban *kampung*—with narrow lanes, small huts, and low houses. Even recently erected dwellings are often made from wood, and many are constructed on stilts.

Today, the city is still characterized by too few working positions in the formal economy. Furthermore, there are severe gaps in the infrastructure and many unsolved issues concerning land tenure. Large parts of the old town, including Chinatown, are severely run-down. One main Chinese temple demolished during ethnic riots in 1997 still had not been renovated in 2000. Modern Makassar is represented by big office, bank, and hotel buildings, and mostly two-story shophouses combining dwelling space with economic functions.

Politics and City Services. During Mayor Patompos's term of office in the 1970s, the planning of the city followed Western conceptions and an American master plan. The eastward expansion of the city was planned, and the area was increased by legislation in 1971. Streets were widened, and one central street was proudly declared a "shopping area." Central parts of the city were rebuilt, and a Chinese cemetery was relocated to make room for administrative buildings and a new central market. The realization of these modernistic plans, however, is far from complete. There are parts of the modern city with run-down houses or lacking infrastructure, and there are illegally used spaces and land tracts with unsolved tenure status.

After a period of tremendous growth ending in the 1970s, the late 1990s again brought severe changes, a general modernization, and even some signs of postmodern development, despite the still-somewhat-provincial character of this city. There are now many supermarkets, whereas ten years ago there were only two. The shopping center at Pasar Baru was demolished, and a new four-story center was built. In 1999 a shopping mall similar to those in Jakarta opened its doors. There are several new luxury hotels partially financed with money from Jakarta and Singapore. The hotels, seldom used by tourists, are used mainly by higher government officials during visits to the city; they also may be used for land speculation. The central post office was modernized in 2000, and throughout the city there are computerized telephone booths (*warung telpon, Wartel*). Not only in the central business district, but throughout the city, there are an increasing number of Chinese-style multistory shophouses (*rumah toko, Ruko*) combining dwelling and business functions.

Many houses facing the seaside had to make way for the harbor, which was modernized and extended. A new toll road to this harbor was recently finished. On the road to the Hasanuddin Airport near the town of Maros north of the city, new office buildings and industrial estates abound. Large areas of the city's outskirts now are scattered with planned residential settlements, including shops and supermarkets. They are for the upwardly mobile, mostly Chinese and Buginese. They include elements of Western urbanism (guards, cul-de-sac streets, and Spanish-style bungalows), with local adaptations as well (Indonesian-style guest rooms and bathrooms). The names of these settlements convey modernistic and romantic ideas (for example, Panakkukang Emas, "Golden Panakkukang"). A huge area in the southern part of the town, facing the sea (Tanjung Bunga), was designed as a site for business and recreation to be developed according to an ultramodern master plan. It is still nearly a rural area, but is being built up slowly. The main urban administrative functions were moved from the former colonial area near Fort Amsterdam (Benteng) to various arteries on the outskirts of the city.

Educational System. Makassar fulfills an important role in providing possibilities for higher education for students from the eastern part of Indonesia. Many students from Timor and the Moluccas study at the high schools and at the hundreds of small private or religious institutions of higher education called universities. There is an important pedagogical high school: Institut Keguruan dan Ilmu Pendidikan (IKIP, recently renamed Universitas Negeri Makassar, "State University of Makassar"). The largest university (Universitas Hasanuddin, UNHAS) is located at Tamalanrea on the outskirts of the city and now has more than 10,000 students. It was founded in 1956, and was the first university outside Java to offer graduate studies (since 1986). Schooling is compulsory and free for all children, but school books and uniforms are too costly for the poor, and not all children are able to attend school regularly.

Transportation System. Peddlers on bicycles deliver everyday goods and fresh food, while local small food stalls (*warung*) sell small meals. Three-wheeled bicycle pedicab rickshas (*becak*) are important for the local transport and bring children to their schools. There were several unsuccessful attempts to restrict the bicycle rickshas from certain parts of the city. The official explanation was that the restrictions would prevent traffic jams, but satisfying the ideals of a prosperous and modern city were most likely behind these measures. Public transport is dominated by privately run Japanese minibuses locally known as *pete pete,* and by ordinary buses. Traffic has increased considerably within the past few years. In 2001 there were more than 1,200 taxicabs, whereas in 1991 there were only 200. Traffic jams are a normal experience; there are now some traffic lights, and most big roads are now one-way.

There are age-old links between Makassar and East Kalimantan (today the province of Kalimantan Timor, Kaltim). Since the 1980s East Kalimantan has been the main aim of people migrating out from Sulawesi in search for work. Together with the ports of Tanjung Priok (in Jakarta) and Tanjung Perak (in Surabaya), Makassar today is a main node of the Indonesian interisland passenger network (operated by Pelayaran Nasional Indonesia, PELNI), which was reorganized in the 1980s. Makassar Harbor is the door to the eastern part of the archipelago and Australia. Since the 1970s the province of Irian Jaya, for example, has received almost all consumer goods, canned food, and beer via Makassar or Surabaya. But this position is now being contested. Direct lines from Jakarta to Ambon, Irian Jaya, Kendari, Palu, and Manado have been established, thus diminishing the port's importance. The competitive relation of Makassar to its rival Surabaya, as well as the subdominant position to "the center"—that is, Jakarta—are a cultural theme of this city, especially among local politicians. The Hasanuddin Airport is now an international airport, with direct links to Singapore several times a week.

CULTURAL AND SOCIAL LIFE

Distinctive Features of the City's Cultures. Even among the generally multiethnic cities of Indonesia, Makassar stands out in cultural diversity. Everyday life is characterized by an intense interaction among the many ethnic groups originating in the province and migrants from elsewhere, especially eastern Indonesia. Makassar is dominated by the four main ethnic groups of South Celebes: Buginese, Makassarese, Mandarese, and Toraja. But Makassar is not simply a "city of minorities," like Medan in Sumatra. The city is situated in an area of the former Makassarese kingdom of Gowa and near the border to the traditional Buginese area. Thus, Buginese and Makassarese, together more than 90% of the inhabitants, are prominent in the city's life and urban politics. Apart from these, Toraja and Chinese are important ethnic groups. Toraja have come from their home area, Tanah Toraja, since the 1930s, and are generally regarded as part-time urban dwellers. The Chinese, today speaking mostly the Makassarese language, dwell mainly in the dense and congested old urban center and on big streets in the outskirts. The city has come to be known as a "microcosm of the eastern seas." People from many places in eastern Indonesia, especially from Flores and Timor, live long periods in Makassar as students or traders. Life in Makassar is like a step from the village into the world for many Indonesians from the eastern part of the archipelago. In recent years, there have also been refugees fleeing communal struggles in the Moluccas (Maluku). Situated in a region of a growing sense of regional consciousness and cultural processes transcending ethnic boundaries today, Makassar remains a city dominated by Makassarese and Buginese.

Cuisine. Cuisine in small restaurants is quite basic and consists principally of soups, rice, fish, and some vegetables. There are many sorts of fish and fresh marine products, and the sheer variety and sophistication of fish dishes are worthy of mention. For those who like seafood, Makassar is a paradise.

The most popular local fishes are *baronang* (like flounder) and *bolu.* Local specialties are *ikan baker* (fish) and *udang baker* (prawns), both grilled quickly over hot charcoal. The prawns are good and often of enormous size, and lobsters are cheap, as they are not preferred by most local people. Among locals soups are very popular, especially one (*coto Makassar*) made of buffalo leftovers, including lungs, intestines, tripe, and liver, which is eaten as a meal with patties of rice by many citizens. Chinese restaurants in the city provide good ethnic dishes in a clean atmosphere.

Ethnic, Class, and Religious Diversity. Members of many different ethnic groups interact in Makassar—not only at the workplace, but also in everyday life. Thus, contrary to other Indonesian cities, Makassar is not to be regarded simply as a "plural city." All groups (except a part of the Chinese community) intermingle. Since colonial times, close interethnic economic relations and interethnic marriages have been established among members of the elite of the respective cultural groups. Today, such exchange is found in all social strata. Social differentiation and rank, being a central cultural theme in South Celebes, is based mainly on socioeconomic, not ethnic, factors. Residential ethnic segregation is low. There are quarters where one ethnic group has the majority, and some neighborhoods maintain their ethnic names, but only a few quarters have more than 50% of one group. The highest dominance of any one ethnic group in the urban quarters was about 80% in the 1980s.

The dominance of South Celebes regional ethnic groups in the city has implications for the specific interethnic relations in Makassar. Here, the traditional norms and values (*adat*) of the Makassarese and Buginese are not only relevant for these two groups, but for all others as well. This is in contrast to other Indonesian cities, such as Medan, where the majority come from another island. Current norms and values guiding life in Makassar are a result of a combination of parts of the *adat* shared by members of the four South Sulawesian groups, rules of interaction established through centuries, and an orientation on values of modern nationalized Indonesian urban culture.

The dominance of the Buginese and Makassarese presents a specific social environment different from that of other Indonesian cities. Most urbanites in Indonesia can be regarded as being bicultural. They follow their regional culture (*kebudayaan daerah*) and a so-called "Indonesian culture" (*kebudayaan Indonesia*). In Makassar, people of the nondominant group must know Buginese-Makassarese patterns as a third culture. Only sporadically are there communal conflicts. Usually involving minor issues, such as conflicts between young people of different blocks, they are quickly framed in ethnic terms.

The city's economy, especially the informal sector, is partially segregated following ethnic and regional lines. Average Makassarese are working in the informal sector—for example, as ricksha drivers. In the intermonsoon months, there are about 10,000 people working as ricksha drivers in town. They are mostly ethnic Makassarese coming from the drier area around the town of Jeneponto in the southern part of South Celebes. The Buginese and Chinese work as traders or are shop owners; the Toraja most often are carpenters, teachers, cobblers, or they work in the services sector. The economy is still more segregated according to emic views. Makassarese are seen mostly as being poor workers, and Chinese are uniformly regarded as being *orang kaya* (rich people).

Family and Other Social Support Systems. Families and extended-kinship networks are very important, especially in case of illness or economic problems. People in the city are regularly visited by relatives from the countryside or other islands in the archipelago, often bringing goods. These "visitors" often seek work or higher education in the city, and thus stay longer periods, but fulfill work tasks in their relatives' households. In recent years, Buginese originating in the city returned as refugees from the turmoil in the Molucca Islands. They were housed by relatives living in Makassar, who often used their networks to provide a new economic basis for them.

Work and Commerce. Makassar is a center of a 7-million-person province with low population density and an economy that, thanks to healthy exports, is relatively vibrant compared with that of Java. Makassar itself is characterized economically by a strong services sector, especially administration. Until recent years, there was only a scant development of industries. Petty trade was important, as it allowed workers to maintain links to relatives living in the countryside and to work seasonally on the paddy fields. Basic livelihood and consumption patterns are still heavily dominated by the informal sector. The regional economy—for example, in rice, cocoa, and cloves—is important for the city's economy because many households have intensive links to relatives in the countryside.

Until the early 1970s there were only about 100,000 salaried positions. Of these, 75% were in the services sector, and only 8% in the refining industry. Thus, graduates of local higher schools and migrants from the countryside found jobs mainly in the service sector or in the informal economy. Most people in the formal economy now work for government offices. The position as a government clerk (*pegawai negeri*) and office work in general (*kerja kantor*) are the main work ideals for young people.

Arts and Recreation. Urban popular culture consists mostly of the loud and vibrant everyday life on the streets. The Makassar and Buginese are well known for specific dances and wedding feasts. Dances are regularly performed at the Cultural Center situated in Fort Rotterdam. There is one big recreation park and some smaller ones that are rundown, but heavily visited by the public at weekends. Many young people are fans of the local soccer club, PSM Makassar. People like to stroll through the supermarkets without buying anything or browse in the recently opened shopping mall. Members of the upper class like to use the pools of the big hotels. Some of the islands in Makassar's anchorage attract local visitors (Pulau Kayangan) and foreign tourists (Pulau Samalona). The Spermonde archipelago—more than 16,000 square kilometers (more than 6,000 square miles)—has 150 coral reefs within over 80 kilometers (50 miles) of the town. It ranks high in biodiversity, and some diving sites are among the world's best. Well-known caves with paintings (Leang Leang); a tremendous waterfall at Bantimurong, near the town of Maros; and the hill resort of Malino, some 70 kilometers (43 miles) from the city, are the main attractions in the nearby countryside.

Some of the recreation and tourist facilities attract a limited number of visitors, but have important political implications. A huge cultural park (Minatur Sulsel), 7 kilometers (4 miles) from the city's center, shows many wooden stilt houses of members of the elites of the principal groups and regions of the province. The general outline is in line with Indonesian cultural and tourist policies. In its treatment of folklore and its reduction of cultural diversity, the park mirrors the "archipelago concept" (one island/province, one culture) used in Jakarta's cultural park, Taman Miniatur Indonesia Indah. But Minatur Sulsel shows a self-conscious regional profile and a bias toward certain groups and subregions. The park is one of the arenas where struggles of provincial autonomy as well as ethnic dominance are acted out. Politicians, local anthropologists, historians, and elite members of the respected groups are engaged.

A linked arena of dispute is the growing tourism in the area of the province that is still dominated by Tanah Toraja. The Toraja are portrayed in tourism brochures and schoolbooks as "the people of South Celebes." Torajan items are even displayed in ordinary homes of Makassarese, Buginese, and Mandarese people. The Buginese and Makassarese who are concentrated in the southern parts of the province and in Makassar are now trying to get their share of tourism, but infrastructure and services outside the city are still poor.

QUALITY OF LIFE

Makassar is a city where basic life items are affordable. Western goods, however, imported mainly from Australia—for example, cheese, and alcohol—are quite expensive. House rents are extremely high for foreigners. The former colonial parts of the inner city still have many trees, creating a relaxed atmosphere. Other parts of the inner city—especially the old parts with many Chinese inhabitants—are poor, run-down, and congested. Despite the image of the Makassarese as aggressive, there are few criminal offenses involving violence.

FUTURE OF THE CITY

Makassar historically was a city of regional and even international economic importance, but it had a peripheral position within the colonial hierarchy. Today, its role as a primary city for the island is uncontested, and the harbor is still important for eastern Indonesia. The city's larger role within Indonesia is open to debate. The future will depend on policies of development (*pembangunan*, "awakening" or "building up") not yet determined after the demise of former president Suharto. In terms of regional development in Indonesia, Makassar—together with Jakarta, Surabaya, Medan, and Ambon—is considered a center of a "special development region." Potential functions of the city in the future might include the leading position in eastern Indonesia (versus the currently still-dominant Surabaya) and as the tourist center of the entire island of Celebes (competing with Tana Toraja in the north of South Celebes, and with the city of Manado in North Celebes). Regional rivalries as well as ethnic and religious issues are involved within these competitions.

There are several recent trends in the city's evolution that bear relevance for Makassar's future in national, regional, and ethnic terms. Predominant is a recent strengthening of the Islamic character of the city, a certain makassarization/buginization, and the rivalry between Buginese and Makassarese. A new bombastic monument (Monumen Mandala), similar to the Monumen Nasional in Jakarta, celebrates the "liberation" of Irian Jaya. A huge mosque (Mesjid Al Markaz Al Islami), in Saudi Arabian style and financed partly with Saudi money was erected on the former campus of the university.

New Buginese/Makassarese-style buildings were added to the airport, thus reducing the former Torajan symbolic dominance. Torajan houses (*tongkonan*) are still used as the tourist symbol of the province, but Buginese-Makassarese *pinisi* schooners are more prominent than ever as the cultural icon of the city. The sailing of a wooden boat from Makassar to Madagascar, built in the traditional style and with traditional navigation, provided one of the main topics of public discourse in recent years. The dispute centered around "traditional navigation," "authentic ships," and "suitable crews." The real issue involved was about the historical primacy of Makassarese versus Buginese.

Changes are also to be found in many new denominations in the public realm, including the names of schools, colleges, and streets. And in 1999—symbolically most important and following intensive discussions in recent years—the city's name reverted from Ujung Pandang to its old name: Makassar.

BIBLIOGRAPHY

Adams, Kathleen Marie, "Touting Touristic 'Primadonas': Tourism, Ethnicity, and National Integration in Sulawesi, Indonesia," *Tourism, Ethnicity, and the State in Asian and Pacific Societies,* ed. by Michel Picard and Robert Everett Wood (University of Hawaii Press 1997): 155–80 [on debated issues in tourism and regional policies].

Antweiler, Christoph, *Urbane Rationalität: Eine Stadtethnologische Studie zu Ujung Pandang (Makassar), Indonesien,* Kölner Ethnologische Mitteilungen, vol. 12 (Kietrich Reimer Verlag 2000) [on local knowledge and decision making exemplified in intraurban residential mobility].

Conkling, Robert, "Bureaucracy in Makassar, Indonesia: The Political Anthropology of a Complex Organization," Ph.D. dissertation, Department of Anthropology, University of Chicago 1975 [ethnographic study of an office in Makassar].

Forbes, Dean Keith, "The Pedlars of Ujung Pandang," Working papers, 17, Monash University Centre of Southeast Asian Studies 1979 [on the informal-sector economy].

Kotamadya Ujung Pandang Dalam Angka, Statistik Tahunan, Ujung Pandang (Bappeda dan Kantor Statistik Kotamadya Daerah TK, II Ujung Pandang [yearly statistics, basic official data].

Mangemba, Hamzah Daeng, *Kota Makassar Dalam Lintasan Sejarah* (Universitas Hasanuddin, Fakultas Sastra, Lembaga Sejarah 1972) [on the history of the town].

Mattulada, *Menyusuri Jejak Kehadiran Makassar Dalam Sejarah (1510–1700)* (Hasanuddin University Press 1991) [on an important phase in the city's history].

McTaggart, W. Donald, "Urban Policies in an Indonesian City: The Case of Ujung Pandang, South Sulawesi," *Town Planning Review* 47, no. 1 (1976): 56–81.

Reid, Anthony, "The Rise of Makassar," *Review of Indonesian and Malaysian Affairs* (1983): 117–60 [on recent cultural politics exemplified in a cultural park].

Reid, Helen, and Anthony Reid, *South Sulawesi* (Periplus 1988) [Periplus Adventure Guides—very good guidebook, but a bit dated; pp. 27–53 on Ujung Pandang–Makassar].

Robinson, Kathy, "History, Houses, and Regional Identities," *Australian Journal of Anthropology* 8, no. 1 (1997): 71–88 [on recent cultural politics exemplified in a cultural park].

Sutherland, Heather, "Eastern Emporium and Company Town: Trade and Society in Eighteenth Century Makassar," *Bridges of the Sea: Port Cities of Asia from the 16th to 20th Centuries,* Comparative Studies in Asian History and Society, ed. by Frank J. A. Broeze (New South Wales University Press 1989): 97–128.

Sutton, R. Anderson, "Performing Arts and Cultural Politics in South Sulawesi," *Bijdragen tot de Taal-, Land- en Volkenkunde* 151, no. 4 (1995): 672–99 [on some contested cultural themes and trends in the city and its hinterland].

Ujung Pandang, Periplus Travel Maps, Regional Maps, Indonesia (Ujung Pandang 1:20,000, Central Ujung Pandang 1:12,500 (Periplus Editions circa 1997) [a map that is reliable for the central parts of Makassar and dated for the outskirts].

Villiers, John, "Makassar: The Rise and Fall of an East Indonesian Maritime Trading State, 1512–1669," *The Southeast Asian Port and Polity: Rise and Demise,* ed. by J. Kathirithambi-Wells and John Villiers (Singapore University Press 1990): 143–59.

Walinono, Hasan, et al., *Peta Sosiologis Kota Madya Ujung Pandang* (Suata survey) (Universitas Hasanuddin, Lembaga Penetilian Sosial Politik 1974) [social analysis of Makassar based on survey data].

CHRISTOPH ANTWEILER

Malta

Malta

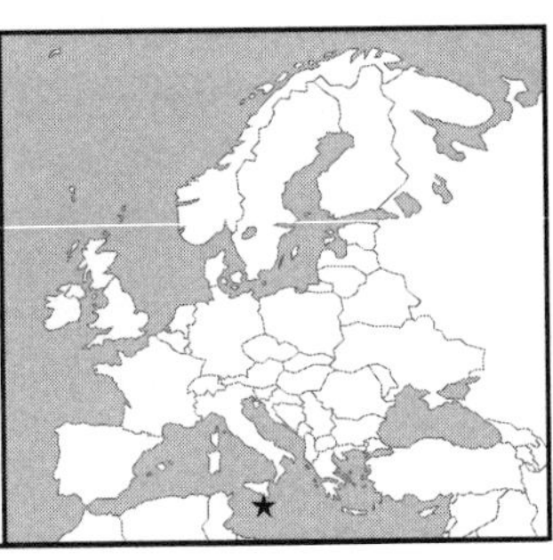

ORIENTATION

Name of City. Malta is the name of an island nation located in the Mediterranean Sea. It is considered here to be an urban area owing to its small size and dense population. As an urban area, Malta, for definitional purposes, can be compared to New York City; although made up of five distinct boroughs, people living in these diverse areas all consider themselves "New Yorkers."

Such is the same for Malta. It is made up of two main islands: Malta and Gozo. There is also a third, very small island called Comino. It is made up of what the Maltese call not boroughs but villages, towns, or cities. In Malta there are major cities such as Valletta, Birkirkara, Naxxar, Mosta, Mdina, Rabat, and others of smaller size. There are also towns or villages, such as Dingli, Marsaskala, Kercem, Mgarr, Santa Lucia, Ramla, and Marsalforn. Some specific cities, towns, or villages will be mentioned to highlight aspects of Malta as an urban area.

Location. Malta is located in the Mediterranean Sea, approximately 97 kilometers (60 miles) south of Sicily. Libya to the south and Tunisia to the west are each about 322 kilometers (200 miles) away. Malta lies at 35°50′ north latitude and 14°35′ east longitude. The total land base amounts to about 311 square kilometers (120 square miles), about the size of Washington, D.C.

Population. Currently one of the most densely populated urban areas in the world, Malta was estimated in January 2000 to have 375,000 people. This calculates to an average density of about 1,158 people per square kilometer (3,000 people per square mile). The inhabitants are referred to as Maltese. Gozo, situated a few miles to the northwest of Malta, is about 70 square kilometers (27 square miles) in size. The roughly 25,000 inhabitants of Gozo refer to themselves as Gozitans. The third and smallest island, Comino, is 2.6 square kilometers (1 square mile) in size, and is located midway between Malta and Gozo. There are only a few permanent Maltese residents on Comino.

Distinctive and Unique Features. Although each section of Malta may be said to have a distinctiveness of its own, all inhabitants are clearly part of the larger Maltese culture in terms of history, body and verbal language, economics, family, politics, education, work, and religion. People from Malta might disagree in this assessment. Gozitans are clearly viewed as different—perhaps more rural one could politely say—by the mainland Maltese.

Malta was most probably viewed in ancient times as a place of barren rocks. Unlike the hostile terrain, the Maltese people, however, are considered to be friendly and affable to tourists and newcomers alike. The weather of Malta is mild to hot during the summer months, with a mild-to-temperate winter period. The rainy season begins in late September and continues until mid- to late February. The temperature in Malta during a typical summer day averages between 28° and 35°C (82° and 95°F), with the nighttime temperature averaging some 6° to 8°C (10° to 15°F) lower. Humidity in the summer is mostly high. Winter daytime temperatures range from a high of 15°C (60°F) to a low of 10°C (50°F).

Attractions of the City. Tourism in Malta is high during the summer months, generally swelling the population to nearly 1 million. The population of Gozo sometimes grows threefold to 75,000 on a summer's day. Most visitors to Gozo are day tourists returning to Malta at the end of a guided tour. Overnight guests to Gozo are usually Maltese from the main island who visit Gozo on the weekends. Foreign tourists who are on vacation more often stay overnight on Malta. However, with new hotel construction, Gozo is becoming a more-sought-after overnight attraction for foreigners.

Tourists go to Malta to see life as it may have been lived hundreds of years ago contrasted with the new businesses of the 21st century. Thus, a tourist may see a cathedral built around 1600 close to a

Burger King restaurant. Many of the buildings that survived the devastation and destruction of the bombings of World War II maintain the dignity of the era in which they were built. Mixing the history of Malta's buildings with modern-day commerce offers the tourist a glimpse of the ability of the Maltese to maintain the entrepreneurial spirit of their ancestors without losing perspective.

That there is a large population of entrepreneurs in Malta seems to indicate, among other things, that Malta values its free-spiritedness. The unique application of natural resources, by both government and individuals alike—such as the use of land and water and efficient use of limited space for housing—is characteristic of the innovative Maltese. At the start of the 21st century the Maltese are considered to have higher income levels than residents of other European urban areas, although during the late 1990s the economy the nation was challenged by the reverberations of the events in Eastern Europe and the former Soviet Union.

Relationships Between the City and the Outside. Malta had been a colonial base for various European interests from about 1500 until 1964. From about 800 to 1500, Malta was heavily dominated by the Arabs and prior to that by the Greeks and Romans. Saint Paul is said to have landed on Malta in 60 A.D. and introduced the people of Malta to Christianity. To this day, the inhabitants of Malta are virtually 99% Catholic. Roman Catholicism is considered the official religion of the country.

Malta is strategically located in the Mediterranean Sea, a convenient spot for resting sailors and for repair of ships from seafaring nations. As far back as the time of the Phoenicians and Carthaginians, Malta was an important port of call for ship repair and settlements. During World War II, Malta was a major strategic location for the Allied forces. This fact was not lost on the Axis powers of Germany and Italy, for Malta was severely damaged by Axis air power and was subject to bombing raids almost daily during critical periods of the war. The residents of Malta received the King George Cross for their tenaciousness in doing all they could to survive the ravages of war. Malta never surrendered and, to this day, that survival is a source of pride to Maltese all around the world.

Major Languages. The Maltese maintain two official languages: Maltese and English. Maltese is a Semitic language, spoken by only about 1 million people worldwide—presumably all of Maltese heritage. It is a beautiful, poetic language, and has been influenced by Arabic, Italian, and English, as well as other European and North African tongues. In Malta, British-style English, the other official language, is taught in the schools.

Industries that are newly significant in Malta—such as tourist-related businesses, offshore banking for European and American companies, and electronics—now require that employees have a higher level of formal educational training than before and that they be fluent in English and other European languages. This requirement pertains also to store clerks and tradespeople—such as carpenters, plumbers, and builders—who deal with foreigners.

A sign of the ever-growing importance of English as a spoken and written language in Malta may be the fact that during the summer of 1992, a new English-language newspaper, the *Malta Independent*, began publishing as a competitor to the already-existing, half-century-old *Times of Malta*. And eight new radio stations, programming mostly in English, have been on the air since October 1991.

HISTORY

The Origin of the City. Malta's interesting archaeological, historical, and social factors span thousands of years: the prehistory of Malta dates to before 10,000 B.C. Many buildings—ranging from Neolithic temples and early Christian sites to the 16th- to 18th-century secular and religious architecture of the Knights of the Order of Saint John—survive today. There are numerous edifices and castle-like structures that double as tourist attractions, including Arab-style buildings and many churches (more than 300) and cathedrals. These add to Malta's list of historical buildings containing art for tourists and everyday Maltese alike to enjoy. One major archaeological attraction is the prehistoric temple at Ggantjia, on Gozo. The temple is considered the oldest known human-made structure on earth, built around 4,000 B.C.

Malta obtained independence in 1964 from the British, who had ruled since 1801, after having taken control from France. The French, under Napoleon, occupied Malta for only a few years, from 1798 to 1801. Those years under French domination were considered a dark and destructive period for all Maltese. This and other aspects of Malta's past have been ingrained in the memories of the local population. During the period of French rule, the churches of Malta were plundered of virtually all their gold, silver, and artworks, which were taken to France, never to return. Prior to French control, Malta was overseen for more than 200 years by the Knights of The Order of Saint John—or, as they are more commonly known, the Knights of Malta.

Malta is the product of a long, rich, and complex history, its history and people a collage of Mediterranean ethnic groups: Arab, Sicilian, Norman, Spanish, Italian, and British. Malta's history has been one of tremendous suffering and exploitation by most of its former rulers, either in practice or perception. For example, Gozo was virtually depopulated by the Turks in about 1551, when its citizens were either taken as slaves or slaughtered. A learned Maltese described that historic incident as "the devastation of Gozo." It was soon after this depopulation that the knights moved to Malta to defend the Maltese people; however, the knights also had their own interests.

Aspects of modern Malta are by-products of British influence from the early 1800s to 1964, when Malta gained independence. Where the earlier influence of the Romans, Italians, Sicilians, and Arabs gave the Maltese a Latin and Arabic flair and contributions to their language, the British brought, among other things, systematic statistical computation, educational guidelines, bureaucracy, and driving on the left side of the road.

Migration: Past and Present. Malta has experienced outward migration, mostly to Australia and Canada. However, Maltese have also settled in the United States near Detroit, New York City, and San Francisco. Some of those who left Malta owing to economic hardship are now finding it desirable to return home. This immigration is generating concern about the need for a new social policy that will maintain the general population as well as the returnees, many of whom are elderly. Although the numbers in themselves are not large, the pattern is enough to destabilize existing policy, for the population of Malta seems to be already overextending existing provisions, considering its small size.

INFRASTRUCTURE

Public Buildings, Public Works, and Residences. Malta's many historical public buildings are in themselves monuments to time and the survival instincts of the Maltese. Many buildings date to the period from 1565 to 1798, when the knights were overseers of Malta. Mdina is the ancient capital of Malta and has its own uniqueness. The walls of the original fortress of Mdina contain influences of the Romans, Byzantines, Arabs, and Normans. Also called the "Silent City," Mdina is located near the center of Malta and is a major stop for tourists, both foreign and local. Mdina lost the title of capital after the knights arrived and Valletta was built, during the late 1500s and early 1600s. Some newer buildings in Valletta date to the 1700s and beyond.

The city is located at the north end of Malta near its center and overlooks the Grand Harbor. Valletta contains many tourist attractions and shops as well as churches, business, and public offices. It is also the home of the famous Saint John's Co-Cathedral, which is the burial location for many Grand Masters of Malta, and the beautiful, world-renowned masterpiece, *The Beheading of St. John,* painted in 1608 by Caravaggio. Beautiful buildings and many offices are located in Floriana, adjacent to Valletta.

On Gozo, in Victoria, is The Citadel, a beautiful fortress that once was responsible for the security of Gozo's population. Built in the late 1500s, the Citadel contains both public offices and commercial businesses as well as a cathedral constructed in the late 1600s.

Mixed among the churches and businesses are the homes of the Maltese. The outside of a residential home usually appears modest. From a simple entranceway, one passes through the front door and often finds a palatial home, perhaps with gardens and marbled floors. Cleanliness is the rule of the typical Maltese household. Maltese families pride themselves on having conveniences such as air-conditioning and satellite or cable television. These modern accommodations serve dual purposes: first, to maintain a sense of comfort, and second, to let visitors know the true status of the homeowner or occupant.

Politics and City Services. Malta, which became a republic in 1974, is governed under the rules of a parliamentary democracy. There are two main political parties. The Nationalist Party, seemingly the more conservative, tends to favor business; the Maltese Labor Party is seen as more favorable toward labor. Towns, villages, and cities now have elected mayors, whose political influence overshadows the previous influence of the parish priests. Politics in Malta is a lively topic of discussion, and election time often sees tensions rise among the voting population.

Health care is free to the citizenry, and is considered modern by most standards. Direct social policy is important to the Maltese, as it is the concern of most politicians that the increase of known dysfunctional families has had a serious effect on the welfare of women and children in particular, and on the stability of the traditional Maltese way of life. The Catholic religion is still a major influence in the activities of the population. Family life and its decline, birth control, and drug and alcohol abuse are topics of discussion and concern. Educational policy has been to prepare students for employment as adults and to provide higher education to as many of the populace as possible.

Educational System. Maltese children are educated on the British model, although influences of Catholicism are still dominant. It can be said, however, that the influence of religion on education is significantly less than in the past. Compulsory schooling for a child beginning at age five consists of six years of primary education and five years of secondary education.

In Malta today, formal education is one of the most significant of the identifying factors of an individual's status. The tourism industry and the application of Malta for entry into the European Union (EU) are two important reasons for the increasing further education. Foreign—mainly European—tourists have many vacation options available. To meet the competitive demand, the Maltese government has made a commitment to educating its population in a formal manner through special academic programs designed to prepare young people, and those older people who choose to go back to school, in subjects dealing with the tourism industry. The University of Malta, which originated in the mid-1500s, is a well respected European university and helps educate and prepare Malta's youth for today's demands. Its enrollment in 2000 was approximately 7,000, including foreign students. Popular subjects, considered necessary in order for Malta to better compete in the international market, are business administration, hotel management, travel, medicine, and law, as well as the social sciences and applied sciences, all of which are taught by a highly qualified staff. Computer science is also gaining as an important field of study. Formal education for all Maltese is understood to be a primary solution to the problems of how to better prepare to compete in world markets, to serve the local economy, to solidify marriages strained by world influences, and to service the many industries that feed into tourism—agriculture, small crafts, beverages, hotels, auto rentals, clothing, jewelry, services, restaurants, and transportation.

Transportation System. There is a public-transportation system that operates buses throughout Malta, providing transportation to those Maltese and tourists alike who either cannot drive at all or are unable to navigate narrow Maltese roads. There is also a public ferry service, operated by the government, to and from Gozo. Tourists arrive mainly by way of the newly refurbished Maltese International Airport. Most workers live close to their jobs and commute mostly via automobile—on a clear, windless day the smog over Malta can be heavy due to the exhaust of many cars. Mass transit—usually state-owned buses—although better than ever, is still developing. Tourists generally use these buses more than rental cars, although with newly built roads and some recent redirecting of traffic on existing roadways, Malta is becoming more navigable by car for tourists and foreigners.

CULTURAL AND SOCIAL LIFE

Distinctive Features of the City's Cultures. Upon arriving in Malta, either at the airport or by ship, one notices the distinctiveness of the buildings of European and North African style. Each Maltese city, town, or village resembles a British town, with a center tower, a church, and tiny roadways for small cars, usually leading to the center circle or square. Homes seem to be hidden behind facades. Each section of Malta has a distinctiveness that is unique, and native Maltese can identify a fellow citizen's area of origin from his or her use of the Maltese language.

Contemporary social life encompasses family gatherings and meetings at social clubs. The social clubs are traditionally tied to each of the two main political parties: the Nationalist Party and the Maltese Labor Party. These clubs are an integral part of Maltese daily life. However, during summer months, attendance at a *festa* is a principal method of an individual's or family's reconnecting with neighbors and friends. A Maltese *festa* is an annual celebration to the patron saint of a city, village, or town. *Festas* are deeply rooted in Maltese tradition and are the basis for many a new friendship and the reestablishment of solid bonds between extended families and friends, and are still a primary event for young singles preparing for the dating-and-marriage ritual. Many future marriages begin with meetings made between men and women at *festa* time. Often quiet business issues are tended to during these times as well, and it is common for a family to attend many or all the *festas* in order to get caught up with neighbors, friends, politics, or business. Friendly rivalries are frequently played out via the honors offered to the village, town, or city's patron saint by, for example, the two main political parties. It is during these *festas*, which occur weekly, each at a different village, town, or city, primarily during the summer months—that fireworks are displayed, parades are held, special masses are said, meetings take place, almost as if New Year's Eve were being celebrated weekly rather than annually, as it traditionally is on December 31. Actually, a *festa* is a sort of New Year's celebration, a new beginning, usually tied to an important date in the village, city, or town's history: a date such as some saint's birthday, for example; or a celebration of some special event in a saint's life such as the feast of the Assumption of the Virgin Mary (August 15), when it is said she was raised to heaven by God.

Nowadays, dress at these and most functions in Malta resembles that in the rest of modern-day Europe or the United States. Casual dress for men may be khakis or blue jeans and polo shirts or silk shirts, especially during the hot summer months. During winter, sport jackets and suits may be appropriate for some, but the manner of dress varies little from summer to winter. For women, fashion—usually from Italy or elsewhere on the continent—plays a major role in influencing their choice of clothing.

AP/WIDE WORLD PHOTOS

These two women on Malta are wearing the traditional veil called the faldetta.

An interesting aspect of Maltese ways is the smile turned upon visitors, tourists, and locals alike. That Maltese smile wins hearts, perhaps dating from the time when the Maltese were subservient to the many rulers of its past: the Arabs, the Turks, the knights, the French, the British. Although Malta is now an independent nation, the gentle and polite Maltese smile, and the sense of peace it confers, continues.

Cuisine. The diet of the Maltese includes dishes with Sicilian, North African, and Turkish influences and includes pasta, fruits, vegetables, and herbs and spices as well as meat and fish. A favorite treat of the Maltese is a pastry named *pastizzi*: a small, flat, flaky dough, about the size of a fist, with pitalike pockets filled with ricotta, peas, or beef that make wonderful daytime treats or nighttime snacks. To read about Maltese food does it no good service: a taste of it tells all. Soups and peppered goat cheeses are favorites for natives and expatriates alike. Sundays are traditionally family-gathering and eating days. *Festas,* too, are a time for special meals to be prepared and shared among close family members.

Ethnic, Class, and Religious Diversity. Malta is fairly homogeneous regarding ethnicity, social class, and income distribution. There may seem to be distinctiveness internally among some older Maltese—a carryover from the past traditions of nobility prior to World War II. Yet the majority of the population of Malta today is part of its very wide middle class; nobility is a thing of the past. Higher social class and distinctiveness and upward mobility may be achieved through formal education in medicine, the law, or education and is not necessarily tied to wealth, such as that gained through business. It is common for the wealthier to live among those less fortunate, for the outside of one's home doesn't often speak of its occupant's wealth or social class.

With regard to ethnicity and its variety within the Maltese culture, language is a clear marker of a true Maltese; Maltese is the predominantly spoken language for locals. The ability to speak Maltese, and how one speaks the language, identifies the speaker as a member within a privileged group. Maltese students must pass rigorous Maltese and English language examinations. The dialect and use of Maltese varies from village to village, town to town, and city to city. Some older Maltese can tell which specific area of Malta a speaker is from. To the untrained ear, however, the language may sound the same from person to person. Gozitans are said to speak a local variation of Maltese, and sophisticated listeners' ears can distinguish between spoken Gozitan Maltese and mainland Maltese.

Nearly all Maltese are baptized Catholics. Religion still plays a major role in the decisions of the populace in daily matters, although its influence, particularly in politics, is less pronounced than it was in the 1980s. This deeply rooted religious tradition that enmeshed politics and religion and family life goes back to Saint Paul's conversion of the population. The Maltese may privately have differences of opinion about Roman Catholicism, but, almost to a person, the people live and love their religion. Catholicism grounds their behavior.

Family and Other Social Support Systems. To the Maltese, family is the most important aspect of the social fabric. Extended is also very important, particularly for business purposes, and ties are often reestablished during *festa* time. By law, divorce is still not allowed, but legal separations are on the rise. Social support through governmental agencies may be compared with a form of paternalistic governance, as it can be said that most Maltese are part of the same family. There is concern in political areas these days that the unraveling of the fabric of the family, exemplified by the increase in the breakup of marriages, may have far-reaching social implications for Maltese life in the 21st century.

Work and Commerce. Tourism is a major industry of Malta. Within the framework of the economy, however, there are many major industries, some tourist related. Although the economy is currently running below full potential, there is optimism that it will continue to grow when and if Malta becomes a full member of the EU.

Employment increases have been mainly in the private-market service sector, as Malta's economy transitions from government-run services such as banking and communications to privately held enterprises. Job growth has come from insurance, banking, real estate, private services, property income, public utilities, and public administration.

Arts and Recreation. Arts and recreation activities for the Maltese naturally vary according to gender and age. Younger Maltese enjoy popular cultural activities such as dancing and movies, as well as taking advantage of the beaches during the summer. Older Maltese enjoy sports as activities both to participate in and to watch. Football (soccer) is a most popular sport in Malta, and there are also several basketball clubs. There is also a thriving artistic community on Malta. Artistic activity in Malta is complex and rich in historical roots, dating back thousands of years. The modern art era in Malta began in 1952 with the establishment of the Modern Art Circle. The Ministry of Education is attempting to encourage artists to remain in Malta, rather than going abroad for training, but the island does not yet have a museum dedicated to its modern artists.

Although the *festas* still are major events in the life of the Maltese, for young and old alike, such places as gyms and discotheques and the university are becoming influential in effecting changes in dating and mating patterns. Older Maltese still find conventional Maltese social outlets for arts and entertainment—such as extended-family gatherings and political clubs as well as the summertime *festas*—to be useful methods of diversion from work and other stressful activities.

QUALITY OF LIFE

Since the mid-1990s the Maltese government has embarked on a growing program of reform and social policy to enhance the quality of services, and subsequent quality of life, for both the indigent and the average Maltese citizen. Health care is provided by the government. Socialized medicine enables the Maltese people to feel secure that they will be taken care of in time of medical crisis. Additionally, new social programs have been instituted to assist the individual and family in crisis. This shift has come about partly owing to the acceptance of these issues as having a real impact on Maltese daily life, both socially and economically.

Crime, although on the increase statistically, is relatively insignificant. It might be safe to say there is neither homelessness nor poverty in Malta. However, it is evident that some Maltese do in fact live better than others.

FUTURE OF THE CITY

With its long history and with its tradition of surviving most crises, Malta has growing promise as a developed nation in the new millennium. The Maltese people were destitute, after the Axis bombing during World War II. Today, education is on the rise, and it is evident that the impact of formal education on the population will only continue to better conditions for the population. Much can be learned from the Maltese and their approach to problem solving.

The cultural changes as a result of increased tourism and access to satellite/cable television and the

Internet will demonstrably affect the very core nature of the Maltese. However, the integration of the positive aspects of these international cultural influences may only make Maltese core culture stronger. Malta is, and always has been, a collage of cultures—from the Mediterranean, from Europe, both Western and Eastern, and from the many countries of the tourists who visit the island.

The Maltese people are friendly, sociable, and educated. Their resilience, persistence, and historical conditioning of survival, as well as the profound influences of their religion, are reasons for anyone interested in social development, history, or exciting archaeological finds to visit Malta.

BIBLIOGRAPHY

Blouet, Brian, *The Story of Malta* (Faber and Faber 1979).

Boissevain, Jeremy, *Saints and Fireworks: Religion and Politics in Rural Malta* (1965; Progress Press 1993).

Boissevain, Jeremy, *A Village in Malta* (1969; Rinehart, Winston 1980).

Caruana, Claudia M., *Taste of Malta* (Hippocrene Books 1998).

Clews, Hilary B., *Malta Year Book* (DeLaSalle Brothers 1990).

Elliot, Peter, *The Cross and The Ensign* (Naval Institute Press 1980).

Luttrell, Anthony T., *Medieval Malta* (British School at Rome 1975).

Sultana, Ronald, and Godfrey Baldacchino, *Maltese Society: A Sociological Inquiry* (Mireva Publications 1994).

Vassallo, Mario, *From Lordship to Stewardship* (Mouton Publishers 1979).

Useful Web Sites

www.searchmalta.com [Maltese portal linking Maltese all over the world, with local news, headlines, entertainment information, chat rooms, and more].

www.aboutmalta.com [online guide to information about the Maltese Islands provided by an expatriate Maltese living in the United States].

ROBERT J. LAFAYETTE

Manchester

United Kingdom

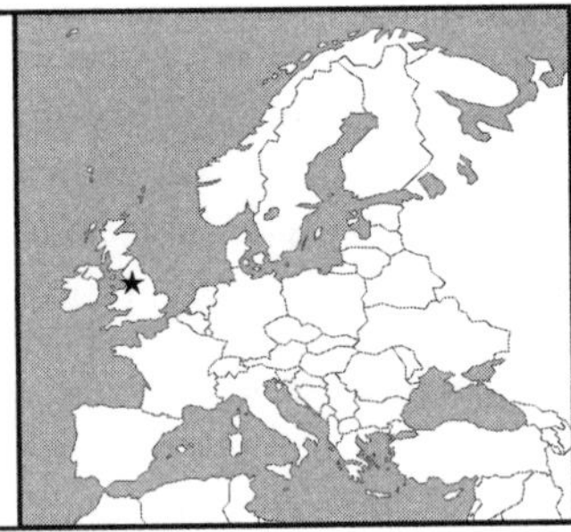

ORIENTATION

Name of City. Manchester, the city's modern name, came into general use in the 16th century as an English version of earlier place-names. The initial (1st century A.D.) Roman fort was called either Mamucium or Mancunium and the later Anglo-Saxon Chronicle of circa 923 A.D. called the settlement Mameceaster.

Location. Manchester is located at 53°29′ north latitude and 2°14′ west longitude, on the western flanks of the Pennine Hills in England's North West. The city has grown around the confluence of three small rivers—the Irwell, the Irk, and the Medlock—that flow to the sea, 64 kilometers (40 miles) to the west, through the estuary of the River Mersey. Manchester lies in a belt of dense urban settlement from Liverpool in the west to Leeds and Sheffield in the east.

Population. The city is the core of the broader urban area of Greater Manchester, which formally comprises ten administrative districts (Manchester, Bolton, Bury, Oldham, Rochdale, Salford, Stockport, Tameside, Trafford, and Wigan). In 1999 Greater Manchester had a population of 2,577,000; Manchester itself had a population of 438,500.

Distinctive and Unique Features. Manchester can claim to be the world's first industrial city. Its development of large-scale factory-based textile manufacturing had begun, by the end of the 18th century, to replace earlier rural-based manufacturing. During the 19th century, it developed as a major entrepôt for trade in cottons. Much of this industrial heritage is still evident in its legacy of Victorian buildings—cotton warehouses and mills, marts and markets, municipal buildings, and 19th-century terraced houses—and of infrastructure associated with early canals and railways. But, equally, the city can claim to be the first to have reinvented itself as a postindustrial city.

Attractions of the City. Tourists visit Manchester in large numbers. It provides an excellent center for touring a region of great natural beauty, with the English Lake District and the Pennine Hills in close proximity. Within the urban area, well-trained guides take visitors on planned walks through old and new Manchester. The Museum of Science and Industry, which incorporates the world's first passenger-railway station, is just one of a range of exciting venues. Among its wealth of leisure and cultural facilities, some have impressive architectural features—such as the new Lowry Centre, the Bridgewater Hall, and the restored Royal Exchange.

Relationships Between the City and the Outside. Manchester plays both regional and international roles. It is the principal fulcrum of England's North West. Its labor catchment spreads widely: Cheshire in the south; southern Lancashire to the north; the Peak District to the east; and even its sister city, Liverpool, to the west. Manchester's shopping and entertainment facilities draw on an even wider catchment across the north of England. The city's major airport has helped to ensure that its international role continues to be an important one. Manchester has developed a strong network across other European cities, playing a lead role in such formal urban networks as the European Union's (EU's) Eurocities. Its multinational population and strong trading ties have ensured continuing links with the Far East.

The city lies at the junction of key transport lines—north-south on the motorway and rail lines between Scotland and southern England, and east-west on the trans-Pennine links between the ports of Merseyside and the Humber. Improvement of links on this east-west corridor has positioned Manchester as a key node in the links between the burgeoning economy of Ireland and the opening up of the European economy in eastern Europe.

Major Languages. English is the principal and official language, although the multiethnic composition of the population means that a variety of Asian and European languages are used by subgroups on an everyday basis. This is reflected in many of the official documents of the City Council, which are customarily printed with versions in Chinese, Urdu, Bengali, Arabic, and other languages.

HISTORY

The Origin of the City. Manchester originated with a Roman fort at the confluence of the Irwell and Medlock rivers, on the line of a Roman road linking the key garrison towns of Chester and York. This site, now known as Castlefield, was largely built over with canals and railway junctions during the 18th and 19th century, but sections of the original walls of the fort have been excavated and reconstructed. The medieval core of Manchester developed to the north of this site at the junction of the Irwell and Irk rivers. Here, a parish church, a market, and a college (now an internationally famous music school with one of the country's few preserved medieval libraries with chained books) formed the core of a small town described in 1542 by Leland as "the fairest, best builded, quickest and most populous town of all Lancastershire." While it had already become an important center for the production of linen and wool, Manchester's industrial explosion in the late 18th and 19th centuries could hardly then have been guessed at. The growth of the factory system, the development of cotton manufacture, and the international trade in cotton goods drew in a huge migration of population and made Manchester "the shock city" of the 19th century—a place to which visitors came to be both excited and appalled by the vitality and the squalor of what was a new phenomenon, the industrial city. Manchester's growth was fueled by technical innovations in textile machines and transport. The duke of Bridgewater's canal opened in 1761, the first of a sequence of canals built to link the city to raw materials and provide cheap access for bulk goods to national and international markets. The railway age was ushered in with the opening in 1830 of the Liverpool-Manchester line.

The city gradually developed more as a trading center than as a site of manufacture of textiles, and some of its principal buildings reflect that trading rationale—a major cotton exchange and corn exchange, warehouses, banks, and financial services. The trading links are best symbolized in the ceiling of the Great Hall of Manchester's Victorian Town Hall, which flaunts the shields of the numerous countries and cities around the world with which Manchester did business.

One of the key achievements in linking the city to the outside world was the construction of the Manchester Ship Canal, which gave direct access to seaborne trade. Opened by Queen Victoria in 1894, it brought ships of up to 13,000 tons into the heart of the urban area at Manchester Docks. For 39 of the 55 years between 1904 and 1964, this inland Port of Manchester ranked third or fourth among the most important of the U.K. ports in terms of the value of imports and exports.

Cotton manufacturing was accompanied by the growth of heavy engineering, both in the east of the city and in Trafford Park Estate, built adjacent to Manchester Docks. The Tafford development, the world's first industrial project, was designed to capitalize on the presence of the Ship Canal by attracting firms in engineering, textiles, food production, and oil and chemicals. The British Westinghouse Electric Company (subsidiary of the American parent) built the largest U.K. engineering works there and employed 12,000 workers by 1903, introducing American production methods and foremen. By the early 1930s more than 200 American firms operated in Trafford Park, among which the Ford Motor Company (in 1910) and Kellogg's European factory (in 1938) were notable. They joined a variety of indigenous companies, such as the flour mills of Co-Operative Wholesale Society and of Hovis.

The growth of industry and trade in the center of Manchester fundamentally altered the nature of the city. The impact was most evident in the residential ecology of Manchester. Central residential areas that had been home to many professional households were invaded by commerce and industry and by the headlong expansion of small terraced houses for factory workers. Professional households began to desert the center from as early as the first half of the 19th century. The earliest and most dramatic example of such suburbanization was Victoria Park, which developed in the south of the city from 1834. Its prosperous residents built villas in an enclave protected by tollgates that were not finally abolished until 1954.

Migration: Past and Present. The 19th-century growth was fueled largely by in-migration, drawn from across England and internationally. During the 19th century, significant migrant streams came from Ireland (especially during the recurring famines in that country) and from central Europe (with significant streams of Jewish refugees from eastern and central Europe). German industrialists played a key role in the early years of the city's history. Friederich Engels, for example, was based in his father's cotton mills and offices in Manchester for 20 months, and this experience fed directly into his *Condition of the Working Class in England in 1844*.

In the 20th century, international migration continued, with workers from southern and central Europe and, in the postwar years, from countries in the former British Empire. This has created a rich international tradition in the city, and has helped link Manchester more firmly to the outside world. For example, the fifth Pan-African Congress was held in Manchester in 1945, and included later notables such as Jomo Kenyatta, Hastings Kamuzu Banda, and Kwame Nkrumah. Likewise, the now-sizable Chinese community has strengthened links with Hong Kong and mainland China.

Net migration is now predominantly outward. For Greater Manchester, between 1996 and 2001 there were 511,000 in-migrants and 546,000 out-migrants. For Manchester itself, there was a net outward flow of more than 12,000, and all bar one of the ten districts had net outward flows. Much of this is a decentralizing process, with population moving to the outskirts and to ever-more-distant locations beyond the administrative boundaries—north Cheshire, the Peak District, and elsewhere. But even though there is net out-migration, large absolute numbers flow into the city; from 1996 to 2001, for example, 166,000 people moved into the city.

INFRASTRUCTURE

Public Buildings, Public Works, and Residences. The legacy of Victorian buildings is a significant feature of the city's townscape. Many of its 19th-century warehouses and commercial buildings are jewels of Victorian Gothic architecture. Manchester's most grandiloquent public building is its Town Hall, designed by Alfred Waterhouse and opened in 1877. It was built to symbolize the success and to reflect the confidence of the merchants of a thriving provincial city. The Gothic corridors and magnificently ornate public rooms of the Town Hall capture the self-importance of a city that saw itself without equal elsewhere in the world. Many of the city's most notable buildings reflect the combination of florid grandeur and philanthropy that characterized Victorian Britain, the John Rylands Library being a good example.

That is all past legacy, however. In the 20th century, Manchester was generally ill-served by architects. There are exceptions, such as some 1930s housing developments that embody the principles of the garden-city movement—most notably the huge public-sector Wythenshawe development in the south of the city, designed by the internationally renowned planner Barry Parker. Most of the postwar architecture, however, parachuted uninspired concrete high-rise housing onto a townscape that had previously consisted of low-rise domestic terraced streets.

More recently, the city has rediscovered a local vernacular style that has begun to reinvent a Manchester image. The city's Design Guide tries to stamp a form to new development by advocating relatively dense "urban" design, prominent street corners, and designed-in public spaces. Its cadre of local architects have begun to develop a distinctive "Manchester" style and have produced distinguished additions to the city's built form.

Ironically, the greatest opportunity for Manchester to re-create its physical form came in the aftermath of one of its greatest traumas—the bombing of the city center by the Irish Republican Army in 1996. The bomb destroyed a significant part of the central shopping area, but for a city that prides itself on its can-do attitude, this provided an opportunity to reconfigure its very heart. The old medieval core has now been reincorporated into the street pattern of the shopping center, creating a new Exchange Square, a transport interchange, and a lively new shopping center well placed to defy the challenge posed by the large out-of-town shopping complex at the Trafford Centre.

The speed and success of the rebuilding of the bombed area betokens Manchester's ability to work in partnership mode. The task force established to oversee the work was led by the council, and drew on powerful private- and public-sector stakeholders. This style of collaboration to develop strategy and oversee the delivery of regeneration has been one of Manchester's hallmarks.

Politics and City Services. The urban area is divided into ten boroughs, each of which is a "single-tier" authority with responsibility across the range of local services. All ten are controlled by Labour administrations (or have "hung" councils with no overall political control) consisting of local councillors elected for each ward. Manchester itself has 33 wards, each with three councillors. In 2001 the overall council had 78 Labour and 21 Liberal Democrat councillors. Since 1999 the council has operated with a small core executive together with five "overview and scrutiny committees" that advise the executive. Increasingly, the council has devolved functions to a more local level, and now has ward plans on which residents are invited to comment.

Like other British cities, only a minority of local finance depends on the local taxation base, which is levied on households through a property tax. Most of Manchester's financial resources come through grants from central government. These are allocated through a Standard Spending Assessment formula that aims to provide services at a common standard across the country, and therefore takes account of the balance of local needs and resources. Needs are calculated through a variety of indicators of poverty and deprivation.

Central government also provides specific targeted financial assistance to areas with severe deprivation. Most of the boroughs in the urban area have numerous such programs. Within Manchester, one example is East Manchester, an area decimated by the loss of 20,000 jobs between 1971 and 1985 through the disappearance of the engineering and other industries that had once made this the industrial powerhouse of the city. The area has unemployment levels twice those of the city, low educational levels, severe problems of crime, and extensive areas of derelict and abandoned land and housing. Whole streets of houses are virtually unsalable or unrentable. The area now has an array of regeneration plans, many of which are supported through central-government programs—for example, New Deal for Communities, Educational Action Zone, and an Urban Regeneration Company. Given the social and economic problems faced by many of the areas in the doughnut area around the city center, it is not surprising that Manchester has benefited from almost every government regeneration initiative.

Educational System. The city's public-education system comprises a comprehensive system of primary (5- to 11-year-olds) schools and secondary schools, most of which offer schooling for 11- to 16-year-olds, complemented by a small number of sixth-form colleges that provide post-16 education. Within Manchester, there are two principal "further-education" colleges. There are numerous "private" schools that charge fees for most pupils—most notable among which are Withington High School and Manchester Grammar School, both of which regularly rank among the highest-performing schools in the country.

There are no fewer than five universities in Greater Manchester. Three (Manchester University, Manchester Institute of Science and Technology, and Manchester Metropolitan University) sit cheek by jowl in a large campus south of the city center. Manchester University can claim some striking scientific-research achievements: the invention of the world's first computer in 1949 and the radio telescope at Joddrell Bank being two of the most notable. The student population numbers more than 80,000, and this represents a significant asset—in the international contacts that students bring; in the high-quality labor force that they represent; and, more prosaically, in the market that they represent as consumers of goods and leisure activities and their impacts on the housing market.

Transportation System. Greater Manchester has excellent motorway provision—with a now-complete motorway that circles the urban area, and links to the main north-south M6 motorway between Scotland and London and the east-west M62 between Liverpool and Hull. Despite car-ownership levels being lower than the national average, there is congestion in the city core, and considerable effort is being expended on providing more-extensive and -effective public transport. A new on-street light-rail metro system was opened in 1992, and plans are in progress to extend the system to cover more of the city.

Mainline rail services to London run hourly, and there is a 20-minute east-west service on the trans-Pennine corridor. Suburban rail services provide a small but important element of local-commuting flows.

The most distinctive element of Manchester's transportation system is the role of Manchester Airport. This provides international services worldwide as well as charter services. The growth in the number of passengers has exceeded that of almost all other British airports, and in 2000 annual trips exceeded 15 million. The airport plays a significant role in attracting investment into Manchester and puts the city firmly on the international map. It also generates substantial finances for the city, since the airport is jointly owned by the ten boroughs, with Manchester itself having a majority stakeholding.

CULTURAL AND SOCIAL LIFE

Distinctive Features of the City's Cultures. Manchester can boast a spectrum of cultural activities—from the "high" culture of theater, opera, and orchestral music to the "low" culture of pop music and sport. As a fun city, it has consciously cultivated an image of youth culture.

Cuisine. Given its history of immigration, it is not surprising that Manchester offers the widest possible variety of styles of eating. The traditional "working-class" fare of fish-and-chips, offered through street-corner shops, has been partly replaced by takeout food from around the world—Chinese stir-fry, Indian curries, Greek and Cypriot kabobs, North American filled potatoes. The same variety is seen in the array of formal restaurants, with French cuisine joining that of English, Japanese, Thai, Chinese, Indian, and many more. Restaurants of all types, national and international chains, jostle for customers. A mile-long stretch of one road in south Manchester is popularly known as "the curry mile" because of the concentration of Indian restaurants; and the extensive Chinatown in the heart of the city offers not only world-class Cantonese and other Chinese cuisine, but an array of Chinese supermarkets. The growth of specialized coffee bars has been one of the more recent innovations in the city.

Ethnic, Class, and Religious Diversity. The 1991 population census (now outdated, but the only accurate estimate) shows something of the ethnic diversity of Manchester. For Greater Manchester, only 5% of the population were of black or Asian origin. The city itself was much more diverse, with more than 12% nonwhite population: Indian subcontinent origins representing 5.3% (with the largest group being Pakistani); and African-Caribbean origins representing 3.4%. The majority of ethnic minority groups are relatively concentrated geographically, with strong nodes in Longsight and Hulme/Moss Side in the south and in Cheetham in the north. The Chinese population has grown significantly in the 1990s. The census suggested that it had risen by more than 3,000 in Manchester, but, like all the ethnic groups, this is probably an underestimate. Certainly, since 1991 their population has increased substantially. Residentially, they differ from other groups in being widely dispersed across the urban area, partly as a reflection of the wide distribution of Chinese takeout restaurants. However, Chinatown, located in the center of the city, represents a social as well as a commercial nexus, and on Sundays draws large numbers of Chinese families from across the whole of northern England to socialize and attend Chinese schools.

The bald census figures do not reflect the essentially multicultural feel of the city. Its long history of in-migration has produced significant Irish, Italian, Polish, and other European communities, as well as groups largely from Commonwealth countries in Africa and Asia. Overseas students add to the lively international feel of the city.

"Indigenous" Christian religions have been augmented by numerous others, and there are many mosques, temples, and synagogues in the city. Polish Catholic churches, Greek Orthodox churches, and

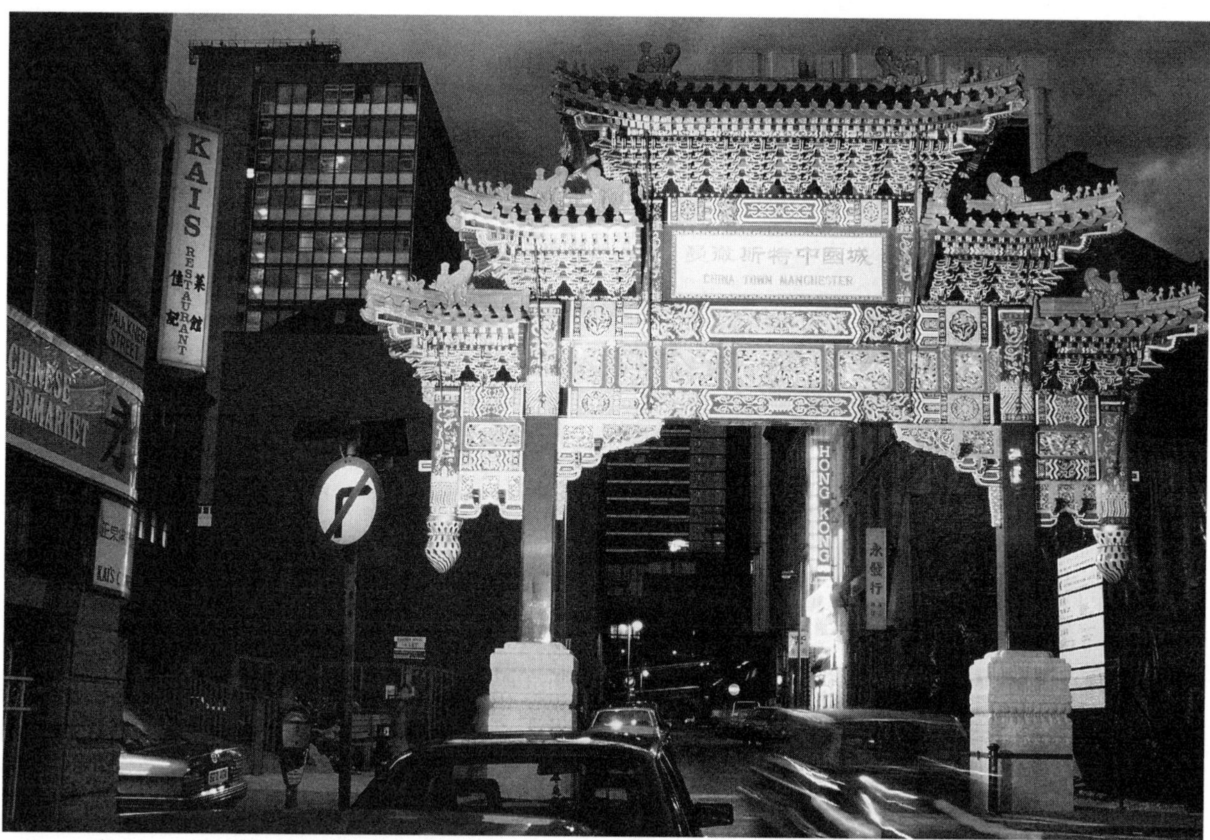

© MARTYN GODDARD/CORBIS

An ornate, illuminated archway is the entrance to Chinatown in Manchester, England.

Welsh Presbyterian chapels reflect the intersection between ethnicity and religion. The Jewish community, whose numbers grew significantly in the 19th century, continues to play a highly significant role in the business and cultural life of Manchester, with both Orthodox and Reform movements well represented.

Family and Other Social Support Systems. Support for deprived families and individuals comes through the national welfare-state system, which offers financial support such as unemployment benefits, sickness and disability benefits, and assistance to working families who are in a low-income bracket. Health provision is free through the National Health Service. The local-authority Social Services department provides social workers and other forms of assistance to help poor families, in particular children and the elderly.

In addition to such statutory provision, the city has a large and very active array of nonstatutory, voluntary-sector agencies working partly alongside and partly independent of statutory bodies. Some specialize in aiding particular groups (the elderly, ethnic groups, children); some operate geographically as tenant groups or community centers.

Work and Commerce. The city is no longer dominated by manufacturing. As recently as 1971 at least 46% of the workforce were in manufacturing; but by 1998 employment in manufacturing in Greater Manchester had fallen to less than 20%. This represents a loss of some 323,000 jobs in the manufacturing sector. Growth has been in professional and public-service jobs, and in leisure-related areas such as hotels and catering. These changes have seen significant shifts in the gender composition of the workforce, with marked growth in female (and part-time) employment.

Arts and Recreation. Manchester probably has the liveliest cultural scene of any British city outside London. It has 12 major live theaters that cover the whole gamut from popular to classical as well as experimental and youth-centered work. One example is the Royal Exchange Theatre, whose principal venue is a stage built on the floor of the old Cotton Exchange, and whose productions "in the round" offer great theatrical scope to well-known and enterprising directors. The recently built Lowry Centre offers a home to ballet, opera, and music. The latter is a strong element of Manchester's cultural life. Classical music, for example, is offered through three resident orchestras based in the new Bridgewater Hall, which replaced the earlier Free Trade Hall as the home of the city's Halle Orchestra. The Halle, whose conductors have included the legendary Sir John Barbirolli and the Japanese American Kent Nagano, was established in the 19th century, and still provides an internationally renowned repertoire. Popular music has a huge venue in the Manchester Evening News Arena, which is regularly filled by fans wanting to hear the latest popular-music idols. Much of the success of British popular music was built on Manchester's thriving club scene, where venues such as the Hacienda carved out a new brand of popular entertainment for young people, earning the city the nickname of "Madchester."

One of Manchester's particular claims to fame is its "Gay Village" and its support for homosexual lifestyles. This development initially met with some opposition but has now merged into the life of a city marked by its tolerant and cosmopolitan outlook.

Over and above its claims as the entertainment center of the north, however, is Manchester's unparalleled impact in sport. The unexpected success of British cyclists at the Sydney Olympics of 2000 was attributed to their training at the Velodrome, a recently built international-standard cycling arena. Manchester now has a new international swimming pool, which, it is hoped, will have the same impact in breeding a new generation of swimmers. This, together with the Velodrome and a new football-cum-athletics stadium in East Manchester, is part of the facilities that will be used in the 2002 Commonwealth Games, to be hosted in Manchester.

The 2002 Games follow the city's unsuccessful attempts to host the Olympic Games and reflect its determination to stamp a mark as a major center of sport. Nowhere is this more evident than in the city's football (soccer) teams. Manchester United is perhaps the world's most successful football "company," both in the success of its team (which boasts having won the Treble—European Cup, English League, and English Cup—in 1999) and in the commercial impact of its trading activities. The team has avid followers from around the world; match days bring a galaxy of powerful politicians and celebrities to the city; and the name of Manchester is probably associated as much with its football as with any other attribute of the city. And beyond the Theatre of Dreams at Old Trafford are other well-established football teams of the region—as well as rugby union, rugby league, and the new up-and-coming basketball teams.

QUALITY OF LIFE

Manchester has extremes of wealth and poverty. Most of the prosperous "comfortable" areas are in the suburbs, especially in the south of the urban area (in Trafford and Stockport) and in the commuting belt outside the urban area (such as Alderley Edge and Knutsford in Cheshire). A quite new phenomenon—central-city living—has begun to change this pattern. Since the 19th century, with the exception of London, no big industrial cities in Britain have had professional households living in central areas. However, over the course of the past decade, Manchester has seen a growing number of residential developments right at its heart. Most are conversions of Victorian warehouses: some are newly built developments. Many have capitalized on the attractions of canal-side frontages, and all have been marketed on the basis of access to the entertainments as well as the jobs in the city center. In 2000 the city center's first £1 million flat was sold; in 2001 its first

© TEMPSPORT/CORBIS

The Manchester United soccer team competed against Everton in the 1995 Football Association Cup Final in Manchester, England.

£2 million penthouse was marketed. Most of the people who have moved to the center are young, small, childless professional households; most work in the city center itself.

For both the suburban and professional city-center dwellers, the quality of life is high. Services are excellent, pressures of congestion are less than in London, access to airport and train services is good, and wonderful countryside is cheek by jowl with the city. Only the much-maligned (and greatly exaggerated) wet weather dims the silver lining.

For the families outside these areas, however, life can be very different. Most socioeconomic indicators show the extent of deprivation in much of Manchester. The contrast between the million-pound apartments of the center and the deprivation in the doughnut areas immediately adjacent could hardly be more stark. Life expectancy in Manchester is half the British average. Educational performance is below average. Unemployment is currently over 8%—more than twice the national average—and in many wards, unemployment is more than 20%. As many as 20% of households receive Income Support from the state (suggesting low levels of family income). Crime hot spots exist in many areas in the doughnut zones. Many such areas have now lost their industrial base and suffer significant outflows of people, with whole streets of houses empty and abandoned. While the national-average house price is over £100,000, more than 10% of houses in Manchester sell for less than £20,000. Many households in poor areas are trapped in the spiral of "negative equity"—with houses that may have cost £40,000 now selling for as little as £10,000. Manchester's relatively low level of GDP per capita (compared to London and the South East) reflects, on one hand, the extent of the contraction of the economic base of the city and the degree of poverty amongst many of its inhabitants; but, on the other, for those with regular jobs and high incomes, it implies a higher standard of living than they would find in southern parts of England.

FUTURE OF THE CITY

The city's two greatest challenges are to strengthen its economic base and to link the fortunes of the deprived areas with the prosperity of its core. Economic growth is partly tied to national policy and partly in the hands of the city itself. Britain is a highly centralized economy, with overheating in the South East and under-investment in the North. In 1999 London and the South East had a GDP per capita of £16,000 whereas the North West's was £11,300. The fortunes of Manchester depend partly on the success of devolution and the role of the Regional Development Agencies (RDAs) established by the government to tackle regional disparities. The North West RDA has as one of its priorities the welfare of Manchester and Liverpool, the two big cities in the region. This could be helped both by further investment in transportation in the east-west trans-Pennine corridor, not least as the EU spreads farther east. It could be helped by conscious investment in research and development in Manchester. However, part of the city's economic future is in the hands of local stakeholders. The airport and the universities are enormous strengths on which Manchester can build. So, too, is the leisure-sport and cultural potential of the city. Professional services (in law, banking, and finance) continue to be well represented in the city. There is great scope to develop the economic synergies across the wider complex of big cities in the region (Liverpool, Leeds, and Sheffield alongside Manchester) as a global gateway that could act as a countermagnet to London.

The problem of social exclusion is a long-term issue. Targeted-training programs, improvements to local educational provision, and initiatives to link the deprived to the new jobs in the center are clearly important elements of any program to enhance social inclusion. Many such plans are now in place, although their outcomes may not be evident for some years.

Manchester's great promise lies in the record of its ability to respond to change, to innovate, to adopt a can-do attitude, and to work collaboratively across the public and private sectors. These are the strengths that should stand the city in good stead in the face of economic and social change. It is Manchester's success in reinventing itself—with new buildings and by creating for itself a new image of sport, leisure, youth culture, and science far removed from the industrial images of smoking chimneys and blackened buildings—that gives substance to its claim to be able to build on its success as a postindustrial city.

BIBLIOGRAPHY

Archer, John H. G., ed., *Art and Architecture in Victorian Manchester: Ten Illustrations of Patronage and Practice* (Manchester University Press 1985).

Bamford, Phill, *Manchester: 50 Years of Change* (HMSO 1995).

Briggs, Asa, *Victorian Cities* (Odhams Press 1963).

City Pride Management Team, *City Pride 2: Partnerships for a Successful Future* (Manchester City Council 1997).

Cochrane, Alan, et al., "Manchester Plays Games: Exploring the Local Politics of Globalisation," *Urban Studies* 33 (1995): 1319–36.

Farnie, D. A., *The Manchester Ship Canal and the Rise of the Port of Manchester, 1894–1975* (Manchester University Press 1980).

Frangopulo, N. J., *Tradition in Action: The Historical Evolution of the Greater Manchester County* (E. P. Publishing 1977).

Greater Manchester Research and Information Planning Unit [monthly and annual series of research and information papers that provide invaluable statistical information on aspects of the economy, demography, and physical development of the ten districts of Greater Manchester].

Griffiths, Steve, *A Profile of Poverty and Health in Manchester* (Manchester Health Authority and Manchester City Council 1998).

Hulme City Challenge, *Rebuilding the City: A Guide to Development* (Hulme Regeneration 1994).

Kargon, Robert H., *Science in Victorian Manchester: Enterprise and Expertise* (Manchester University Press 1977).

Loftman, P., and B. Nevin, "Going for Growth: Prestige Projects in Three British Cities," *Urban Studies* 33 (1996): 991–1019.

Marcus, Steven, *Engels, Manchester, and the Working Class* (Weidenfeld & Nicolson 1974).

Messinger, Gary, *Manchester in the Victorian Age: The Half-Known City* (Manchester University Press 1985).

Parkinson-Bailey, John J., *Manchester: An Architectural History* (Manchester University Press 2000).

Peck, Jamie, and Adam Tickell, "Business Goes Local: Dissecting the 'Business Agenda' in Manchester," *International Journal of Urban and Regional Research* 19 (1995): 55–77.

Peck, Jamie, and Kevin Ward, eds., *City of Revolution: Restructuring Manchester* (Manchester University Press 2001).

Quilley, Steven, "Manchester First: From Municipal Socialism to the Entrepreneurial City," *International Journal of Urban and Regional Research* 22 (1998).

Redhead, Brian, *Manchester: A Celebration* (Andre Deutsch 1993).

Spiers, Maurice, *Victoria Park Manchester: A Nineteenth-Century Suburb in Its Social and Administrative Context* (Cheetham Society 1976).

Williams, Bill, *The Making of Manchester Jewry, 1740–1875* (Manchester University Press 1976).

Williams, Gwyndaf, "Rebuilding the Entrepreneurial City: The Master Planning Response to the Bombing of Manchester City Center," *Environment and Planning* 27 (2000).

Williams, Mike, with D. A. Farnie, *Cotton Mills in Greater Manchester* (Carnegie Publishing 1992).

Useful Web Site

www.manchesterupdate.org.uk [*Update Manchester: The Bulletin of Economic and Development Issues,* Manchester City Council, provides statistics and details of current developments in the city].

BRIAN ROBSON

Mandalay

Myanmar

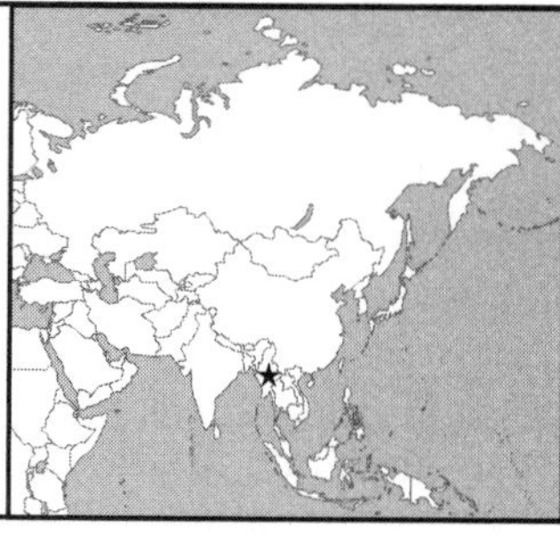

ORIENTATION

Name of City. Mandalay is named after Mandalay Hill, which is situated in the northeast of the city. The city was founded officially in 1857, and in 1861 King Mindon Min moved his capital from Amarapura to Mandalay. Unlike many locales in Burma, its name has not been changed in recent years.

Location. The city is located at 21°57′ north latitude and 96°.04′ east longitude, more or less in the middle of Burma on the eastern bank of the Irrawaddy River. Mandalay lies some 700 kilometers (435 miles) north of Rangoon, in the center of what is known as the dry zone.

Population. The present population of Mandalay is approximately 800,000, although some estimates place it as low as 600,000.

Distinctive and Unique Features. In recent years Mandalay has been most famous as a center of commerce related to three commodities: rubies, jadeite, and heroin. The trade in these items is known as the red, green, and white lines. About 200 kilometers (124 miles) north of Mandalay lies the famed ruby (and sapphire) mining town of Mogok, which has been a source of fine gems for perhaps a thousand years. The best Mogok rubies are widely regarded as the finest in the world. Burma is also the source of most of the world's gem-quality jadeite. The "jade tract," *Kyaukseinmyo* in Burmese, lies some 400 kilometers (248 miles) north of Mandalay along the Uru River, west of the town of Mogaung in the state of Kachin. As for heroin, it is produced mainly in the state of Shan, to the east of Mandalay. While much of Burma's rubies, jadeite, and heroin flow directly across the border into Thailand and China, a considerable amount also passes through Mandalay, and the wealth generated by them plays a significant role in Mandalay's economy.

Attractions of the City. Mandalay has been treated rather harshly by foreign writers over the years. In the early 20th century B. Talbot Kelly was moved to comment: "Never were preconceived ideas so completely shattered as were my own with regard to Mandalay! I had expected to find a handsome city of Oriental character, instead of which it proved to be as mean as its river approach." Arriving by air in 1951, Norman Lewis was no kinder: "Mandalay! In the name there was a euphony which beckoned to the imagination, yet this was the bitter, withered reality. Through the suburbs mile followed mile of miserable shacks; a squalid gipsy encampment, coated with a bone-white dust which floated everywhere, like a noxious condensation of the heat-haze itself. Pigmy pagodas sprouted like pustules . . . "

As one might surmise, Mandalay is not a particularly impressive city, but it is not without attractions. The center of the city is dominated by Mandalay Fort, within which is the former royal palace. The fort occupies about 2.6 square kilometers (1 square mile), and its walls are surrounded by a moat that is about 30 meters (100 feet) wide and 3.7 meters (12 feet) deep. The moat served in the past as the main source of drinking water in the town. The fort was occupied by the British in 1885 and renamed Fort Dufferin. Fierce fighting near the end of World War II severely damaged the fort. In particular, the former royal palace, which was built of wood, caught fire, and was largely burned. The fort and palace are currently undergoing reconstruction. The city also boasts a number of noteworthy Buddhist religious structures. Several of these are located in the vicinity of Mandalay Hill. These include Kyauktawgyi Paya, with its large marble Buddha image, and Kuthodaw Paya, with 729 marble slabs on which are inscribed the entire text of the Buddhist canon (*Tripitaka*). In the southwest of the town is Mahamuni Paya, which was built in 1784, prior to the founding of Mandalay. It houses a highly venerated Buddha image (the "Manamuni"), which was brought from Arakan and is believed to have been made almost 2,000 years ago.

There are a number of important attractions located relatively close to Mandalay. These include the ancient cities of Amarapura, Ava (Inwa), Sagaing, and Mingun. The first three of these at various times served as the Burmese capital prior to the founding of Mandalay. In addition to ruins they have a number of important Buddhist religious structures. Today, Sagaing functions as a particularly important Buddhist center. About 70 kilometers (43 miles) to the east of Mandalay is the famous hill station of Maymyo (Pyin U Lwin).

Relationships Between the City and the Outside. Mandalay is connected to other parts of the country by road, rail, river, and air. There are no direct international air connections. Mandalay is a major tourist destination within Burma. It is also an important hub of cross-border trade with China and, as noted above, in general serves as a center for international commerce in gems and narcotics. The main Chinese border crossing lies to the northeast of Mandalay: the town of Ruili lies on the Chinese side, and Mu-se on the Burmese side. It can be reached from Mandalay by road via Lashio. This is the Burma Road of World War II fame (later known as Highway 3).

Major Languages. The major language of Mandalay is Burmese. The city has small but significant Indian and Chinese minorities who also speak their own languages in addition to Burmese. Various dialects of Chinese are spoken in Burma, with, according to J. George Scott, "the Yünnanese . . . mostly found in Upper Burma, and in greatest numbers in Mandalay and Bhamo. Yünnanese is a dialect of Western Mandarin." By and large, this is still the case, although the Chinese population today is perhaps a little more mixed than it was in the past.

HISTORY

The Origin of the City. The core area of initial settlement in the lowlands of Burma for the Burmese ethnic majority lies in the relatively arid middle of the country adjacent to the Irrawaddy River. Their first great capital lies to the southwest of Mandalay at Pagan (Bagan). Pagan was officially founded in 849, but in fact the settlement is older than this; it lost power in the late 1200s. Subsequently, the center of Burmese political power moved north to the vicinity of Mandalay. Sagaing, located about 19 kilometers (12 miles) to the southwest of Mandalay, became the capital of a Burmese kingdom in 1315 (the kingdom is erroneously attributed to the Tai-speaking Shan in many histories. In 1364 King Thado Minbya, the grandson of the kingdom's founder, moved the capital a short distance to the north to Ava (Inwa). The mid-1500s saw the rise of the Burmese rulers of Taungoo, who eventually became the rulers of Ava, which continued to serve as the capital of a unified Burmese kingdom off and on over the next few centuries. Burmese political power went into decline in the 1700s, and the rival Mon kingdom captured Ava in 1752. Burmese power was soon restored under the strong leadership of King Alaungpaya (who became king in 1752, with his capital initially located in Shwebo, to the north of Ava). In 1765 Ava once again became the Burmese capital, but in 1783 King Bodawpaya decided to move his capital to the newly founded city of Amarapura (Amayapôya) "Abode of the Immortals," located a few miles to the north of Ava. The capital was moved back to Ava in 1823. However, in 1841 Amarapura once again was made the capital.

Following their defeat in the first Anglo-Burmese War in the 1820s, the Burmese were forced to cede territory to the British in the south of their empire. After their defeat in the second Anglo-Burmese war in 1852, the Burmese empire was effectively split into two: British-ruled Lower Burma, with its new capital at Rangoon; and Burmese-ruled Upper Burma, with Mandalay as its capital. The extremely unpopular King Bagan Min, who had led his country into the disastrous war with the British, was deposed by Mindon Min in 1853. Mindon Min established peace with the British and was widely viewed as a rather progressive ruler.

Soon after ascending to the throne, Mindon Min decided to build a new capital a short distance to the north of Ava. Mandalay was officially founded in 1857. Scott and J. P. Hardiman give the following account of the decision to move the capital to Mandalay:

> King Mindon wished to change the site of the capital from Amarapura, which had always been unhealthy, so he called together the chief *Sayadaws,* the Crown Prince, the Ministers, and astrologers and consulted them. The King suggested the neighbourhood of Mandalay Hill and this was unanimously approved. The hill had long been noted as a pleasant and well-ornamented place, and the wise men now declared that, if the King built a new city there, he would meet with all kinds of success . . . and peace and tranquillity would be insured.

According to tradition, "while he was still a Prince, Mindôn Min had many dreams, all of which pointed to Mandalay Hill." The area around Mandalay previously had been occupied by a few important Buddhist religious structures. There is a legend that the Buddha himself, along with his disciple Ananda, visited Mandalay Hill and prophesied that a great city would be founded below the hill. The precise auspicious date on which to commence construction of the city was determined to be February 13, 1857. Using Mandalay Hill as a starting point, the new city was mapped out. A new royal palace was built from the wood of the palace at Ava, and King Mindon Min moved his capital from Amarapura to Mandalay.

In addition to the fort and palace, King Mindon had a variety of other structures built within as well as outside the compound. In 1870 four large buildings were completed within the palace to house the public works, police, agricultural, and financial departments. Those outside the palace included a number of hospitals or almshouses. In 1876 the public-works department began embanking the Irrawaddy River to prevent the flooding that had occurred almost every year and also set about digging new canals. Several of the most important Buddhist religious structures in the city date from King Mindon's reign, as do some of the Christian structures.

The city grew quickly, but in April 1866 a large part of it was consumed by fire. It is estimated that as many as 3,800 houses were destroyed. A couple of months later, in June, there was a revolt against the king, led by two of his nephews. After a good deal of fighting, during which the king's brother was murdered, the rebels fled south on a commandeered steamer and eventually reached British territory, where they were interned. Another fire broke out in the city the next April, but this time it was contained before doing too much damage.

King Mindon Min died in 1878 and was succeeded (thanks in large part to the machinations of his mother) by Thibaw Min. Thibaw's rule began with the massacre of a large number of his kinsmen (something of a tradition among Burmese rulers), and conditions within the kingdom quickly degenerated. In addition to the ongoing purges and occasional fires, the population of Mandalay also suffered from an outbreak of smallpox. A dispute with the British in 1885 escalated into the third Anglo-Burmese war. The British sent troops and gunboats to Mandalay. They met only minor resistance, but their occupation led to very unsettled conditions in the city. According to Scott and Hardiman, "under the Royal Government the population of the city and much of the population of the town consisted of officials, hangers-on of the Court, and soldiers. The great majority of them were thrown out of employment by the change in the form of administration." The following April and May (the hot months) there were a number of fires, some set on purpose and others accidental. Scott and Hardiman further note that such fires were common in Mandalay, "which was not surprising in a town almost entirely built of mat-houses with thatch roofs." This time, "800 houses out of a total of 5,800 within the city walls were burnt . . . and between 2,000 and 2,500 out of a total of 24,000 in the town outside."

Over the next few years peace was gradually restored as the British established control over the region around Mandalay and much of the rest of Upper Burma. The British made Rangoon the capital of the now-unified Burma, and Mandalay was reduced to the status of a provincial town that served as a minor regional administrative and commercial center.

Migration: Past and Present. Mandalay is located in the heart of traditional ethnic Burmese territory, and from its founding it has been predominantly an ethnically Burmese city. As the Burmese capital between 1857 and 1885, its population consisted primarily of Burmese government officials and employees who lived in and around the fort and palace complex. It also served as an important center for the Buddhist religion and attracted a large number of Buddhist monks and nuns. As a commercial center it had a small but economically active migrant population, mostly Indian and Chinese. There was also a small contingent of European officials and merchants.

Under British rule the European population grew a little, but it never became as significant as was the case in Rangoon (in 1900 there were only 12,491 Europeans in the entire country, including about 4,000 troops). Under British rule there were many migrants from India, but the majority of them settled in the southern part of the country. It has been noted, for example, that while Lower Burma received 130,000 migrants during the late 19th and first few years of the 20th century (mainly from India), only 22,000 migrants went to Upper Burma during the same period. Some of the latter settled in Mandalay, but many also went to the hinterland, often to work in the teak and mining industries. The arrival of these Indian migrants led to the emergence of a mixed population of "half Madrassi, half Bengali, half Burman" that lived mostly in the towns. Again, most of these lived in Rangoon, but some were also found in Mandalay.

The Chinese population in northern Burma began to grow during the latter part of the reign of the Chinese emperor Ch'ien-lung (1736 to 1796), following the ending of hostilities between China and Burma in 1769. Of particular importance was the trade in jadeite, which began to be exported from the jadeite-mining area in Kachin state to China in the 1780s. Many of the Chinese who engaged in the potentially rewarding but dangerous jade-mining trade lost their lives. During the British colonial period there was also a small but commercially significant Chinese population in Burma (in the 1901 census the total Chinese population in Burma was only 47,444). Many of these Chinese lived in the north of

© OWEN FRANKEN/CORBIS

A group of monks carrying sunshades was photographed on a rural street in Mandalay in 1996.

the country, where the gem-mining industry grew considerably under British rule.

Following the outbreak of World War II, Mandalay was occupied by the Japanese in 1942. When Allied troops reentered the city in March 1945, they met stiff resistance from the Japanese. In the course of the fighting, the city suffered considerable damage. A good deal of the fort was destroyed, and the palace (which was made of wood) was burned. Norman Lewis described the scene when he visited the fort in 1951: "Beyond the walls stretched a desolation of tumbled bricks and weeds. . . . Nothing had survived the citadel's devastation but a few antique canons." The city was rebuilt, but for several years progress was slowed by the unsettled conditions in and around Mandalay.

Economic reforms in Burma that were initiated in the 1990s led to something of a boom in Mandalay in later years. Especially important was a growing Chinese presence in the city (in terms of people, money, and consumer goods). Since the early 1990s the population of the city has grown from around 500,000 to between 600,000, and 800,000. As it has grown the city has changed in appearance to some extent. In the city center new hotels, restaurants, office buildings, and department stores have sprung up. Parts of the riverfront have developed into centers of gambling, prostitution, and drug dealing. The government forced many people to move out of the center of the city as part of its modernization initiative, and they have now settled in new townships that surround the city.

INFRASTRUCTURE

Public Buildings, Public Works, and Residences. Talbot Kelly described Mandalay as "Climbing the high bund which protects the low-lying city from inundation, a drive of two miles or more, through streets lined with huts as poor as any I had seen in the country, brought me to the 'fort,' in the heart of which is the only part of the city which can boast of any architectural pretension, though even here hovels lie between 'pukha' . . . built shops of the bungalows of residents." Outside of the commercial district, the town has been described as an enlarged Burmese village, "dilapidated but picturesque." There are, however, some nice religious structures. The new, largely restored fort and palace still dominate the center of the city, with several of the larger Buddhist structures—such as those around Mandalay Hill and Manamuni Paya to the south—among Mandalay's most important architectural features. The city also has a central market (*zeigyo*) that occupies two large buildings surrounded by numerous street vendors.

Educational System. Since the 19th century Mandalay has been an important center of Buddhist and secular education. Tertiary institutions in the city include Mandalay Arts and Sciences University; the School of Fine Arts, Music, and Drama; and Mandalay Institute of Technology. These were closed in 1996, but Mandalay Institute of Technology has since been allowed to operate some programs. There are also a number of small, private business, computer-science, and foreign-language schools in the city.

Transportation System. Public buses serve the main areas of Mandalay. Economic reform and the subsequent boom have resulted in there being a relatively large number of private taxicabs in the city. These include a variety of three- and four-wheel vehicles. There are also trishaws. In the past, horse carts were an important means of transportation within the city and to outlying areas, but these are relatively rare now and are encountered mainly in the outer parts of the city.

CULTURAL AND SOCIAL LIFE

Distinctive Features of the City's Cultures. Despite its recent changes, Mandalay remains in many ways a very Burmese city. At the heart of this lies the Buddhist religion and its Burmese folk elements. Mandalay and the surrounding area not only boast many Buddhist religious structures and institutions, but are also reputed to be the home of more than half of the country's 250,000 monks. The importance of Buddhism is manifest in various festivals. The middle of April is the time of the Burmese New Year, which is marked by a water festival (*thingyan*), perhaps the best known of Burma's religious festivals. The Burmese believe that during this time the king of the spirits (*nats*) visits the human world to make an accounting of the good and bad deeds of humans. Homes and temples are decorated to welcome the spirit, and his departure after three days is believed to mark the beginning of the new year. On the ceremonial side, young people wash the hair of their elders, and Buddha images are washed. Prior to British rule the event was marked by the ceremonial washing of the heads of the king and chief queen, followed by their giving alms to a number of elderly poor people and a state feast. Today *thingyan* is viewed largely as a time for festivities and raucous behavior—in particular, young people throw buckets of water on passing people and vehicles. The event is celebrated throughout Burma, but the celebration is especially noteworthy in Mandalay. Not only is it a time for festivities by the city's inhabitants, but it is common for many people from the region to visit the city to celebrate as well.

Cuisine. The city's cuisine reflects its major ethnic groups: Burmese, Chinese, Indian, as well as Shan (also known as Tai Yai). Like all Burmese towns, Mandalay has many tea shops, which function as popular gathering places. The number of restaurants in the city grew considerably at the end of the 20th century. Mandalay has long had numerous Chinese restaurants; not only are there many more of them now, but a number of them are upscale, reflecting the flood of Chinese money into Mandalay's economy. Western-style ice cream has long been popular, and it is served in small establishments that also sell other sweets. The city still has relatively few Western-style restaurants.

Ethnic, Class, and Religious Diversity. Mandalay has been characterized as "a Burmese city built for Burmans, and, excepting for a few of the commercial streets, almost solely occupied by them." The city is, in fact, overwhelmingly Burmese, with small minorities of Indians and Chinese who play a major role in local commerce. Compared to Rangoon the Indian population in Mandalay is relatively small. In Mandalay it is the Chinese more than the Indian minority that is especially important in commerce. This became even more apparent in later years as the city as a whole came under increased Chinese economic influence as a result of its status as a northern gateway to the increasingly important China trade: Mandalay's unofficial Chinatown grew over the past decade.

There are also members of northern minority groups living in the city (for example, Shan, Palaung, Jingpho, and so forth), but their numbers are small. Late 20th-century political regimes forced some of them to resettle in Mandalay, away from areas where insurgents had been active in the past. Others went voluntarily because of employment or perceived economic opportunities. Taking members of conquered minorities, especially those with artisanal skills, to live in Mandalay and the older capitals is a relatively long-standing tradition in Burma. Members of northern ethnic minorities, especially Shan from the east, visit Mandalay in relatively large numbers during festivals.

Essentially, the city has two elites. By far the more powerful one is Burmese of relatively high status within the regime, who form the city's political elite. Because of the regime's involvement in commerce, members of this group often are comparatively wealthy, but their wealth is often derived from siphoning money from those more directly engaged in commerce. There is also a small commercial elite that includes—in particular—a number of Chinese. There is a middle class in the city consisting largely of Burmese professionals, government employees, and Burmese, Chinese, and Indians involved in business. The lower classes of the city include members of all three of these ethnic groups.

The population of the city is overwhelmingly Buddhist. Its Chinese and Indian minorities include Moslems, Hindus, Sikhs, and Christians. There are several mosques and Hindu temples as well as a Sikh temple. French Catholic and American Baptist missionaries were very active among northern Burma's minority peoples and also established a presence among the lowland Indian and Chinese minorities. There are two Catholic churches in Mandalay. Their congregations are mainly Indian and Chinese. There is also the Judson Baptist Church, which is named after a famous American missionary.

Family and Other Social Support Systems. Family is very important to Burmese, including those living in Mandalay, and is the most important institution that provides social support. The Burmese reckon descent bilaterally. Upon marriage, a newly wed couple may reside with the parents of one partner for a time (often with the parents of the wife), but usually they soon establish their own household. The nuclear family is the core of the domestic unit, but it is common for it to include extended-family members as well, such as unmarried siblings, widowed parents, or a variety of distant unmarried or widowed male and female relatives. The husband is the nominal head of the household, but the wife retains considerable authority as well.

Beyond the family, the most important source of social support for most people comes from religious institutions. Throughout Mandalay, religious centers are popular gathering places—not only for worship, but also to socialize, to seek advice, and to find assistance in time of need. Especially for those closely associated with the regime, the government also provides many forms of support. This is particularly evident for those in the military, whose families have access to many special services and facilities.

Work and Commerce. The government, including the military, is an important employer in Rangoon, but the majority of people in the city today are employed in the private sector. Private enterprise was suppressed in Burma for decades, but since the early 1990s has been allowed to grow. There is relatively little industry in the city. What processing and manufacturing there is in Burma tends to be concentrated in Rangoon. One of the oldest industries in the city is Mandalay Brewery, which was founded in 1886. Mandalay is also an important center of handicraft production.

In the past much of the gem trade in Mandalay was not conducted in public. The regime banned private exploration and mining for gems and sought to control gem trading, largely through the gems, jade, and pearls emporium held in Rangoon. In 1995 the regime once again allowed private citizens to trade in gems, which are now widely sold in public in Mandalay. Burma's largest private jade market is found along Mandalay's 86th Street. Two nearby villages located south of 86th Street, Kyawzu and Minthazu, specialize in cutting, polishing, and carving jade.

The tourist industry has been an important part of Mandalay's economic boom. A good deal of the "new" money in the city has been invested in hotels. As of 1999 there were 63 hotels in Mandalay (with 1,873 rooms). A few of these are state-owned, but most are privately owned. Among Mandalay's three largest and most expensive hotels, one is a joint venture between the Burmese government and a Singaporean company, and another is the international Novatel Mandalay.

Arts and Recreation. Mandalay is the cultural heart of Burma and is the home of many forms of artistic expression. *Pwe* is a form of entertainment that includes traditional dramas as well as more-modern skits (which include comedy and sometimes social commentary), music, and dance. There are many *pwe* troupes in Mandalay that perform at festivals locally and elsewhere in the country. Mandalay is also a center for traditional marionette performances. The Mandalay Marionettes and Culture Show has its own theater, and its performances include marionette shows as well as traditional music and dancing. Marionette performances are based on the Buddhist *jataka* and the Indian epic the *Ramayana*.

Under the Kon-baung dynasty, which ruled Burma from Mandalay and the older capitals to the south, Mandalay and the nearby towns developed as centers for a wide variety of artisanal crafts. Artists and artisans served the court as well as the wider public. Buddha images were made of bronze and marble (for example, the large marble Buddha in Kyauk-taw-gyi Paya, which was dedicated in 1865). Wood carving was also a highly developed art form. Examples of this type of art are to be seen at the famous Shwe-nan-daw monastery, which was originally a royal apartment in the palace and was moved to its present site in 1880 and made into a monastery. The Tampawadi district in Mandalay is a center for carpenters, wood-carvers, and for casting brass and bronze. During the 19th century Mandalay was also a leading center of making gilded lacquerware (a technique learned from Thailand).

Mandalay and nearby communities are also important centers for weaving. Two types of textiles stand out in this regard. One is a distinctive style of handwoven silk cloth known as *acheik.* The technique employed in making *acheik* appears to have been introduced by captured weavers from Manipur in India (who were resettled near Amarapura in the 18th century) but the motifs are Burmese. The second type of textile is known as *kalaga,* a Sanskrit word meaning "foreign curtain." These are tapestries that are lavishly decorated with embroidery, appliqué, and other techniques using gold and silver thread, colored yarn, sequins, and even sometimes gems and glass beads. The images on the tapestries traditionally depicted scenes derived from the *jataka* and *Ramayana.* Later, many other images were incorporated, including some of European derivation, which probably grew out of textile traditions of such peoples as the Shan. The earliest *kalaga* appear to have been made during the reign of King Alaung-hpaya (1752-60). King Mindon Min brought Shan artisans to Mandalay to make *kalaga* to decorate his palace. *Kalaga* were also made by artisans in Mandalay for wealthy commoners and monks. The making of both *acheik* and *kalaga* declined during the British period. Pursuing a policy of self-reliance, after 1962 the socialist government in Burma sought to promote hand-weaving, which included the revival of *acheik* weaving in Amarapura. In the 1980s there was a revival of *kalaga* making as well. The new *kalaga* tend to be relatively small, and are made primarily for the tourist market (they are also made in Chiang Mai, Thailand, and in Rangoon).

QUALITY OF LIFE

Economic growth in Mandalay at the end of the 20th century improved the standard of living for many of its inhabitants. Nevertheless, Burma remains one of the world's poorest countries and, while they are better off perhaps than many people living in the countryside, most people in Mandalay are still very poor. The city has a small elite that lives very well, and a growing middle class whose economic situation remains precarious at best. Burma is also ruled by one of the world's most oppressive regimes, and this has an impact on people's lives in many ways. People are subject to arbitrary arrest, and detainees are often tortured. Residents on occasion have been forcibly relocated at the whim of government authorities. Periodically, they may also be pressed into service as laborers for civic projects. They also must live with censorship and with limited educational opportunities, since most of the city's institutions of higher education remain closed.

FUTURE OF THE CITY

Continued strong international demand for heroin and Burmese gems, and economic growth in adjacent regions of China mean that Mandalay's spate of economic growth probably will persist into the 21st century and that Chinese influence will keep expanding as well. What this actually means for the city and its inhabitants, however—beyond more hotels, karaoke lounges, and traffic—is difficult to predict.

BIBLIOGRAPHY

Aung-Thwin, Michael A., *Myth and History in the Historiography of Early Burma* (Ohio University Center for International Studies, Institute of Southeast Asian Studies 1998).

Fraser-Lu, Sylvia, *Burmese Crafts Past and Present* (Oxford University Press 1994).

Hertz, W. A., *Burma Gazetteer: Myitkyina District: Volume A* (Superintendant, Government Printing and Stationery Office 1912).

Kelly, B. Talbot, *Burma: The Land and the People* (J. B. Millet 1910).

Lewis, Norman, *Golden Earth: Travels in Burma* (Charles Scribner's Sons 1952).

Scott, J. George, *Burma: A Handbook of Practical Information* (Alexander Moring 1911).

Scott, J. George, and J. P. Hardiman, *Gazetteer of Upper Burma and the Shan States,* Part I, Vol. I (Superintendant, Government Printing, Burma 1900).

Scott O'Connor, V. C., *Mandalay and Other Cities of the Past in Burma* (1907; White Lotus Press 1996).

Stanislaw, Mary Anne, *Kalagas: The Wall Hangings of Southeast Asia* (Ainslie's 1987).

MICHAEL C. HOWARD

Manila

Philippines

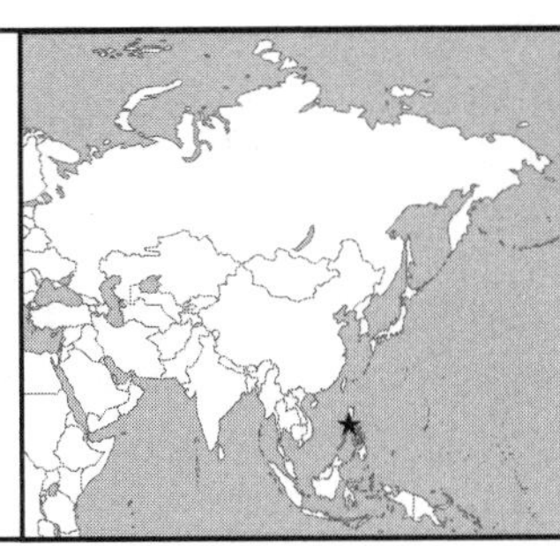

ORIENTATION

Name of City. Manila derives its name from the Tagalog phrase *may-nilad,* which is commonly thought to refer to the location of the *nilad* plant, a flowering shrub that grew along the banks of the Pasig River.

Location. Manila is located along the eastern shore of Manila Bay at 14°37′ north latitude and 121° east longitude on the island of Luzon in the Republic of the Philippines.

Population. The population of the metropolitan Manila region was 9.4 million persons according to the 1999 census; later estimates ranged from some 10.5 to 12 million. With a total area of 636 square kilometers (248 square miles), the population density is in excess of 16,500 persons per square kilometer (42,300 persons per square mile).

Distinctive and Unique Features. Metropolitan Manila stretches some 32 kilometers (20 miles) along the eastern shore of Manila Bay, a landlocked harbor 56 kilometers (35 miles) wide and extending inland 63 kilometers (39 miles). Manila is the chief port, major trade center, leading manufacturing area, financial center, and focus of political and cultural activity of the Republic of the Philippines. The official national capital is located in Quezon City, the northeastern suburb of Manila. To the north of the city is Mt. Arayat, a sacred mountain to the original Malay settlers; to the west are the Mariveles Mountains, and to the east is a large lake called Laguna de Bay.

The metropolitan Manila area includes the chartered cities of Manila, Pasay City, Quezon City, and 12 other municipalities. The Pasig River flows through the city, dividing it into two sections, with Intramuros (the old Spanish walled city) on the south and newer sections on the north. Before World War II, Intramuros contained examples of 17th-century Spanish architecture, but all of the buildings except the St. Augustin Church (1606) were destroyed in the fighting. Burnham Green and Rizal Park lie south of the Intramuros and port areas, and Roxas Boulevard and Taft Avenue lead southward along the bay through older residential neighborhoods. Opposite Intramuros are Binando, the Chinese district, and Tondo, the slum district. Malacanang Palace, the presidential palace, is one the most imposing structures in the city. The original port area is located south of the Pasig River, with docks and warehouses built by the United States. While many of the businesses and government offices dealing with shipping services remain in the port area, larger facilities have been built along the bay north of the city. Urban subdivisions extend across Rizal province into what had been rural towns and villages. Local names are applied to districts that are not formal political units (such as Diliman, where the University of the Philippines is located).

Attractions of the City. The climate of Manila is similar to that of other lowland areas along the west coast of the Philippines, with two pronounced seasonal variations in rainfall; the first, from January through April, is normally dry, with the second (particularly June through October) marked by heavy rains. There is little temperature variation across the seasons, with a mean of 28°C (83°F) in May, and 24°C (76°F) in February. The annual total of 159 days of rain produces an average of more than 203 centimeters (80 inches) of rain each year, although there is substantial variation from year to year.

Many government buildings and larger tourist hotels are located on Roxas Boulevard, which runs the length of the city along Manila Bay. The Manila Yacht Club, Manila Zoological and Botanical Gardens, Philippine Cultural Center, Folk Arts Theater, and Philippine International Convention Center are all located within two blocks of Roxas Boulevard. Intramuros, Malacang Palace, and other major tourist sites are located along the Pasig River. Newer suburbs include Quezon, Pasig, and Makati. Quezon City, now the official capital of the republic has new government buildings and medical centers. Makati is the commercial center of the metropolitan Manila region, with the Philippine Stock Exchange, international corporations and banks, hotels, and exclusive residential subdivisions, including Forbes Park and Bel Air Village.

Relationships Between the City and the Outside. Manila was the colonial administrative center for Spanish and later American colonial interests. It developed as a primate city, forming the point of first contact between the Philippines and the outside world. As the economic, cultural, and political center of the Philippines, it continues to dominate other areas of the country: Filipinos everywhere are made aware of economic, cultural, and political events in Manila. Large numbers of persons move to Manila in search of economic and other opportunities; more than half of the population was born elsewhere. The Philippines has an average of 1.8 million tourists a year, bringing average annual receipts of some $2.5 billion, with much of the tourist traffic focused on Manila.

Major Languages. Language issues have figured prominently in debates over Filipino culture and identity. The compulsory study of Spanish was not abolished until 1987. In 1990 President Corazon Aquino ordered all government offices to use Pilipino (or Tagalog, which is the indigenous language of central Luzon) as the official language of communication. Tagalog is spoken in 93% of the city's households, but English remains the major language of instruction in public and private schools, and most Filipinos speak both English and Tagalog (the national language). Recent migrants to the city will also speak the local dialect of their province, these include Cebuano, Ilocano, Hiligaynon or Ilonggo, Bicol, Waray, Pampango, and Pangasinense. The dialects belong to the Malay-Polynesian language family and are related to Indonesian and Malay, although no two are mutually comprehensible. In the large ethnic Chinese community, various dialects of Chinese area also spoken.

HISTORY

The Origin of the City. Chinese and Arab traders made use of the area around Manila Bay for trade and commerce as far back as the 9th century, and in the 12th century a seaport named Maynilad was established at the mouth of Pasig River, which controlled access to the inland Laguna de Bay. In 1570 the port was captured by the Spanish. Miguel Lopez de Legaspi established the fortified colony that became the official capital of the Spanish Felipinas. The islands were placed under the authority of the viceroy of New Spain in Mexico City, and official communication (and later trade) between the two areas was maintained by a galleon that annually traveled between Acapulco and Manila. The region was developed by Spanish missionaries. The Franciscans were the first to arrive in 1577, followed by Dominicans, Jesuits, and Augustinian Recollects. These orders founded convents, churches, and schools, and became very powerful in local government. The diocese established an *audienca* (supreme court) in 1583 that would function until the end of the Spanish colonial period; Spanish civil code was not in force in the islands until 1889.

Discontent with Spanish rule among urban Filipinos increased in the latter half of the 19th century, inflamed by the execution in 1872 of three Filipino priests charged with leading a military mutiny at an arsenal near Manila. The execution by Spanish authorities of José Rizal y Mercado, a popular nationalist leader, on December 30, 1896, resulted in armed uprisings. The defeat of the Spanish fleet at Manila Bay in 1896 was one of the major battles of the Spanish-American War, resulting in the ceding of the islands to American military control. A period of general unrest followed, as Filipino nationalists insisted that they had been promised independence once the Spanish had left. Several hundred thousand U.S. troops were required to suppress the Filipino uprisings that followed, with much of the fighting focused in the areas around Manila (such as the siege of Caloocan, now one of the northern municipalities). It was not until 1901 that a new civil government under U.S. control was definitely established.

Much of the later history of the Philippines was focused on events in and around Manila. Early in World War II, Manila was heavily bombed by the Japanese, although it had been declared an open city. It was occupied by Japanese forces from 1942 to 1945, and during the final Japanese retreat from the city, extensive residential areas were destroyed and thousands of Filipinos were killed. Quezon City was made the capital in 1948, when new government buildings were constructed. The period of democratic rule following independence was short-lived, with the military dictatorship of Ferdinand Marcos ruling the city and countryside by martial law while siphoning off millions (if not billions) of dollars of international aid in what would become known as crony capitalism. On August 21, 1983, opposition leader Benigno Aquino was assassinated after returning to Manila. The Marcos era was brought to an end with the People Power Revolution, which played out on the streets of Manila in 1986, and Aquino's widow, Corazon Aquino, was elected president. During the Aquino presidency, there were six unsuccessful coup attempts in the capital, the most serious occurring in December 1989.

Migration: Past and Present. At the time of Independence (1946), the population of Manila reflected the colonial history of the nation and included a mix of the original Malay population, a larger mestiza (mixed Spanish and Malay) population, a strong ethnic Chinese community, along with Spanish and American and other nationals. Since that time population growth in metropolitan Manila has included an expanding international business community, but has been most heavily influenced by a large migration of people from rural areas of Luzon and from cities and rural areas of other islands. While some of these people are attracted to the city because it is the center of business and educational opportunities in the Philippines, others come to the city as a last resort, looking for employment in whatever jobs might be available. Efforts to decentralize education and other services, and to promote economic development in other regions to stem this migration have not been successful.

INFRASTRUCTURE

Public Buildings, Public Works, and Residences. Major public buildings in Manila include structures from Spanish colonial times, the period of American administration, and from the later period of independence. Much of the Spanish walled city of Intramurus containing 15 churches and 6 monasteries was destroyed in fighting during World War II. The church and monastery of St. Augustin is one of the few structures remaining intact. Malacanan Palace, built as the residence of the Spanish governor, was also the residence of the Philippine president until the fall of the Marcos regime, when it was turned into a public museum. The Executive Office Building (now housing the Senate of the Republic, the National Museum of the Philippines, and other government offices), the Treasury Building, and other offices from the American period are located along Roxas Boulevard and Taft Avenue. Public buildings from the period of independence following World War II are located in the Makati and Diliman districts, including the Ayala Museum of Philippine History, and in newly developed areas along Manila Bay, such as the Cultural Center of the Philippines (which includes a theater, art gallery, and museum).

Major public-works projects were planned and developed by Spanish engineers in the last years of Spanish control. Planning for a system of freshwater supply was begun in 1867, and in 1882 the first public fountain was opened, providing fresh water to city inhabitants for the first time. The General Plan for Railways, including a network of some 1,700 kilometers (1,056 miles) of track on the central island, was created in 1876. Regular service between Manila and Dagupan began in 1892, and included a major bridge over the Pampanga River and construction of the Tutuban Station in the Tondo district of Manila. A public-transportation network of 5 tramway lines to connect the city with the rapidly growing suburbs was planned as early as 1878.

Major infrastructure projects for the metropolitan Manila region and for the country as a whole are outlined in the Medium-term Philippine Development Plan for 1994. These include the planning, construction, and maintenance of infrastructure (such as roads and bridges, major flood-control systems, and water-resource projects). The provision of fresh water to the rapidly growing outer districts of Manila remains a major problem. Only 69% of the metropolitan Manila area is covered by piped-water connection, and there six times as many persons per connection as in Singapore and Kuala Lumpur. A 1996 study by the International Development Research Centre estimated that 60% of the water produced by the Metropolitan Waterworks and Sewerage System (MWSS) is lost to illegal connections and leakages. Many persons living in lower-income neighborhood do not have service from the MWSS.

Residential areas within metropolitan Manila include older districts within the city as well as new subdivisions and squatter communities on the outskirts. New housing in the suburban districts often combine a generic Spanish colonial design (stucco walls with red tile roofs) with native elements. But these newer areas are often surrounded by squatter settlements, with structures built from discarded building materials to provide basic shelter from the elements. Despite government programs to provide housing and remove squatter settlements, particularly along the Pasig river, these areas continue to grow.

Politics and City Services. Manila was the administrative center for the province of the same name, and for the remainder of the islands, during the period of Spanish colonization. After three years of military rule, on July 1, 1901, Manila became the first of the Philippine chartered cities, and other municipalities of the old Spanish province of Manila became part of the new Rizal province. The administrative code of 1917, amended in 1921, provided for a mayor appointed by the U.S. governor-general (later by the Commonwealth president) and confirmed by the Senate, and a municipal board of ten members elected at large, each serving a three-year term. Following independence in 1946 the office of mayor in all chartered cities was made elective. Because the seat of the national government is in Manila and Quezon City, none of the cities and municipalities in the metropolitan Manila region operates with complete autonomy.

The framework for planned development in Manila was prepared in 1905 by the architect and urban planner Daniel Burnham. The Burnham plan called for the construction of boulevards, a park system, and a new civic center, with a focus on development in the area along Manila Bay and south of the Pasig, since the older areas north of the river were already congested with narrow streets, small property holdings, and dense population. The war almost completely destroyed the city, particularly the area south of the Pasig River. In 1945 the National Urban Planning Commission (NUPC) designed a new street system of eight radial and four circumferential routes "laid out in the form of a spider's web." Trolley lines that had existed before the war were abandoned in favor of automobile traffic. A new master plan for Manila was drawn up in 1954, with a focus on the development of subdivisions and roads in suburban municipalities. In 1959 the local autonomy law transferred planning jurisdiction from the NUPC to local governments.

Aside from the plan prepared by Burnham in 1905 for Manila and the postwar capital city plan for Quezon City, there have been no comprehensive plans for the growth and development of metropolitan Manila. The result of this lack of planning has been mixed land uses, urban sprawl, substandard buildings and slums, traffic snarls, fires and flooding, and real-estate speculation. The homepage of the Metropolitan Manila Development Authority (MMDA) includes the following vision statement: "Metropolitan Manila shall become a human, world-class metropolis known for its livability, economic vitality, and sociocultural exuberance. It shall be the center of a growth polygon, which will influence the creation of socioeconomic opportunities for areas beyond metropolitan areas."

Yet the question of how to achieve these goals has been on the public agenda for several decades. In 1973 a special Inter-Agency Committee recommended the creation of a Metropolitan Manila Authority to oversee coordination of health and hospital services. In 1974 the Metropolitan Mayors Coordinating Council (MMCC) recommended the creation of a Metropolitan Manila Commission to enact metro ordinances, integrate services, undertake development planning, and promote cooperation among local governments. Another plan called for the creation of a National Capital Region covering a radius of 50 kilometers (31 miles) around Manila, with a general manager appointed by the president. The MMDA, which traces its roots to the Metropolitan Manila Commission, or MMC, has jurisdiction over the 12 cities and 5 municipalities comprising metropolitan Manila but acts in a coordinating capacity and lacks ultimate political authority to make binding policy or enforce decisions.

Educational System. Public education is available without charge to all children across the metropolitan Manila region. School participation rates for the country as a whole are 97% for the elementary grades, 65% for secondary school, and 24% for postsecondary education. A literacy rate of 95% is reported for persons in Manila. One of the more serious problems confronting the Philippines is the large number of trained professionals who are unable find employment equal to their educational skills; many have left for jobs in the United States and elsewhere, while many of those left behind found themselves out of work or forced to take jobs that did not make use of their educational training.

Early colleges and universities were founded by religious orders during the period of Spanish colonization. These include the University of Santo Tomas (1619) and the Collegio de San Juan de Letran (1640) founded by the Dominicans, and the Collegio de San Jose (1601) and the Escuela Municipal (later the Ateneo de Manila, 1859) founded by the Jesuits. The Ellinwood Seminary, a union theological school, was established for the training of Protestant ministers. The Far Eastern University was the largest university in greater Manila for much of the 20th century. The Philippine Normal College, Philippine College of Arts and Sciences, Philippine College of Commerce, and the University of the Philippines are major national public institutions.

Transportation System. While the city is well-connected with the outside world by an international airport and extensive dock facilities, transportation within and across metropolitan Manila became an ever-increasing problem in the years of growth and expansion following World War II. Highway construction around the city completed in the 1960s linked the outer municipalities and older arterial highways, but did little to relieve the congestion of traffic on local highways. Manila is served by a comprehensive bus system, but service is marred by choking traffic. Other major modes of transportation include taxicabs, pedicabs, horse-drawn carriages, and the inexpensive and ever-present *jeepneys* (brightly-colored jeeps often outfitted with tassels and decorative horns and mirrors, which transport about one-third of the city's commuter traffic). A light-rail transit system known as Metrorail (MRT) was opened in Manila in 1985 to reduce the traffic congestion. Approximately 250,000 passengers are served daily by Metrorail, but it has not solved the problem; the traffic jams across metropolitan Manila have grown to almost legendary proportions.

CULTURAL AND SOCIAL LIFE

Distinctive Features of the City's Cultures. Manila is one of the most cosmopolitan cities in Asia. There are many daily newspapers and periodicals, numerous radio and television stations, a symphony orchestra, and more than 20 universities and colleges. Manila has long served as the cultural center for the country, and because of the many years of colonial rule, it has served as the port of entry for cultural ideas and social change from abroad. Many Filipinos view themselves as having a cultural heritage that is European, not Asian, and this is especially true in the capital city.

Cuisine. Manila is the cosmopolitan center for a country of diverse ethnic, religious, and language groups; the cuisine is both "local" in character as well as "cosmopolitan." The typical Filipino diet of rice, chicken, and fish supplemented by a wide range of tropical fruits is common across the metro region. Ethnic as well as regional differences in foods are found among groups that have moved from rural areas and from other islands, and among those of Chinese ancestry. In addition to the indigenous or local cuisine, there was, in the late 20th century, a growth of fast-food franchises. Because Manila is a major tourist and business destination, a large number of fashionable restaurants serve an international cuisine.

Ethnic, Class, and Religious Diversity. More than half of all Filipino households have incomes below the poverty line; the differences between the prosperous Filipino upper class and other groups may be even more evident in Manila than in other urban centers. Many of the significant elites in Philippine society—the higher civil servants, manufacturing entrepreneurs, and legislators—are Manilenos (persons born in or educated in or around Manila), who have college and university degrees, most often in law or business. The three classes of elites are connected through personal ties and political connections and have become important agents of change and nation-building. They have created an upper-class lifestyle, including membership in exclusive clubs and organizations (the Lions' Club or Rotary), large and modern houses in the suburbs, a summer home in Baguio or other resorts, and education at private academies for their children.

The contrast with the vast number of poor families in the capital is striking The major social division is between those who have a regular source of income and those who make up the informal sector of the economy. Those in the informal sector earn a living by salvaging material from garbage dumps, begging, occasional paid labor, and peddling. Although this may provide an income above subsistence level, they have no claim to any type of protection or social insurance.

Almost all of Manila's population is Roman Catholic, and the majority is ethnic Filipino (this includes the ethnic Malay population as well as a large mestiza population). The largest ethnic population is Chinese, most of whom trace their Filipino roots back many generations.

© CATHERINE KARNOW/CORBIS

Two men eat a quick meal at an outdoor noodle stand in Manila, Philippines.

Family and Other Social Support Systems. Philippine society is characterized by strong religious faith, respect for authority, and a high regard for *amor proprio* ("self-esteem") and smooth interpersonal relationships. Personal alliance systems are anchored by kinship, beginning with the nuclear family, and intensified and extended by bonds of ritual kinship established on ceremonial occasions—baptism, confirmation, and marriage. Interpersonal ties within one's group of friends are an important factor in the development of personal alliance systems. Even in modern urban settings such as Manila, social organization continues to be marked primarily by personal alliance systems, groupings of kin networks, friends, and partners in commercial exchange.

A large number of nongovernmental organizations (NGOs) have developed to provide programs and services to households and individuals who may not be able to make use of kinship networks and personal alliances. In the case of squatters, these groups have demanded land titles, an end to forced evictions, and construction of new housing for displaced households; other groups (syndicates) have occasionally acted as informal governments in some areas, levying fees that have been used to build roads and sidewalks, provide water and electricity, and other services. Other voluntary groups and support services are based on hometown associations (with membership based on the home province or city), and there is a growing number of women's groups and support services.

Work and Commerce. Metropolitan Manila has long been the dominant manufacturing and trade center in the Philippine islands. Rapid growth in the post–World War II period solidified Manila's position as the primate city, with more than a third of all the country's manufacturing employment and production activity. The expansion of a highway system around the city in the 1960s greatly expanded residential as well as industrial and commercial areas. Manufacturing employment in the city includes textiles and clothing, food and beverage processing, lumber and plywood production, chemical and drug processing, metal fabrication, and shipbuilding. It also is the heart of service facilities for the islands, including finance, education, and medicine. It is estimated that one-half of all professional persons in the country are employed in the metropolitan Manila region.

Arts and Recreation. The rich historical and cultural heritage of the Philippines can be seen at many museums. The Ayala Museum in Makati has dioramas depicting scenes from Philippine history, the Cultural Center of the Philippines Museum includes archaeological finds and ethnological exhibits as well as contemporary artworks, and the Metropolitan Museum of Manila mounts exhibits of classical and modern masters. There are also private galleries and specialized museums, such as Casa Manila, the model turn-of-the-century Spanish house at Intramuros; the Rizal Shrine in Fort Santiago; the Ecclesiastical Art Collection of the San Agustin Church; and the Museo de Malacanang at the Presidential Palace. Ballet companies, symphony orchestras, theater guilds, and pop artists perform regularly, and many hotels and restaurants feature nightly performances of band music, folk and jazz singers, and ethnic dance troupes. Open-air concerts and performances entertain weekend crowds at Paco Park, Puerta Real Gardens and Luneta Park.

QUALITY OF LIFE

Health conditions in urban centers in the Philippines are comparable to those of other Southeast Asian cities. While life expectancy increased to 71.9 years for women and 66.6 years for men, infant mortality was 52.6 per 100,000. The ratio of physicians and hospitals in the total population is considerably below that of European countries. This is in part a result of the continuing out-migration ("brain drain") of dentists, nurses, physicians, and other medical personnel to the United States and other countries that began in the 1970s. Malnutrition remains a perennial concern of local government and health-care professionals, with some 20% of preschool children suffering from second- or third-degree malnutrition, a consequence of the extraordinary high level of poverty (estimated at more than 40% of all households for the country as a whole). Air pollution is widely considered the number one environmental problem in metropolitan Manila because of its negative effects on people's health and on the social and economic condition of the region.

It was estimated that as many as one in four metropolitan Manila residents in the 1980s was a squatter; this number may well be an accurate estimate for the present time, evidence of overpopulation, lack of employment opportunities, and a continuing and virtually uncontrolled rural to urban migration. Manila is estimated to have more than 500,000 squatters and Quezon City another 370,000. Many squatters have found their living by peddling, day work, and hundreds if not thousands have been reduced to prostitution and salvaging food and other materials from garbage dumps. Extensive poverty, the spread of communicable diseases, malnutrition, and other public health problems are greatly exacerbated by the extensive squatter communities.

FUTURE OF THE CITY

Manila confronts a number of serious problems as it enters the 21st century. These include the continuing in-migration of persons from rural areas, a lack of adequate housing and services for the growing population, and high levels of unemployment and poverty. Many of these problems stem from the poor economic performance of the Philippine economy (by many measures, the worst of the Southeast Asian countries over the last decade of the 20th century). The transition from the crony capitalism of the Marcos era to a period of democratic reform has not resulted in economic growth. Without substantial improvement in the national economy, urban problems are likely to mount in the capital, there will not be adequate resources to deal with them at the metropolitan level, and increased civil unrest may follow.

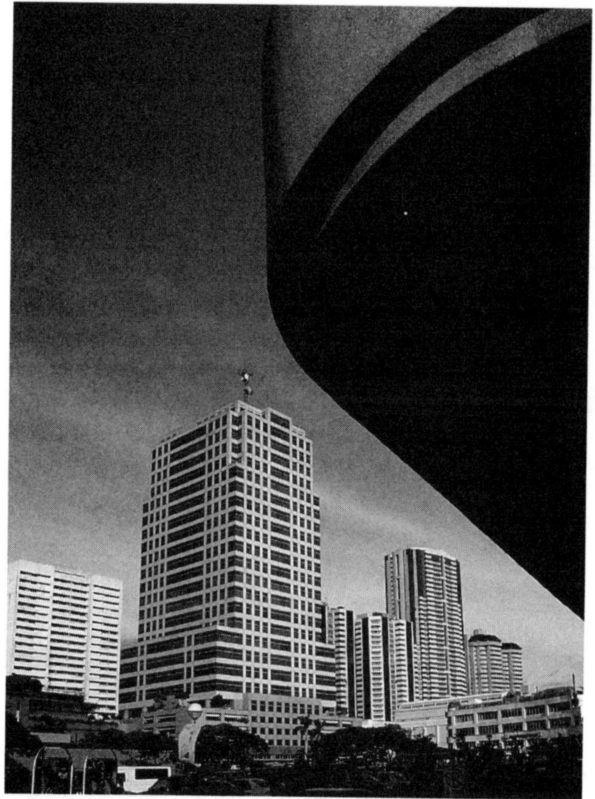

© PAUL A. SOUDERS/CORBIS

Modern office buildings and apartments crowd downtown Manila, Philippines.

For several decades the Philippines followed a policy of encouraging growth in secondary cities in other regions of the country. This policy had little effect in taking population pressures off the capital city. There was much speculation that the increased globalization of capital would increase growth pressures on the world cities, making national policies of decentralization less effective. But there was evidence that Manila has simply been left out of the emerging global markets in Southeast Asia, making economic recovery even more difficult.

While differences between wealth and poverty often are more visible in urban areas, this is especially true of metropolitan Manila, where extensive squatter settlements and slums exist in the shadow of the modern office towers of Makati. The future of the capital of this "Pearl of the Orient" will depend on the as yet unpredictable consequences of the globalization of capital and the as yet unproven ability of the national economy to produce jobs and incomes sufficient for the urban population.

BIBLIOGRAPHY

Background notes, Philippines (U.S. Department of State, Bureau of Public Affairs, Office of Public Communication 1998).

Costello, Michael A., et al., *Mobility and Employment in Urban Southeast Asia: Examples from Indonesia and the Philippines* (Westview Press 1987).

Doeppers, Daniel F., *Manila, 1900–1941: Social Change in a Late Colonial Metropolis* (Yale University Press 1984).

Hollnsteiner, Mary R., "Becoming an Urbanite: The Neighborhood as a Learning Environment," *The City as a Centre of Change in Asia,* ed. by D. J. Dwyer (Hong Kong University Press 1972).

Laquian, Aprodicio A., "Manila," *Great Cities of the World: Their Government, Politics, and Planning,* ed. by William Robson and D. E. Regan (Sage Publications 1972).

Mercado, Monina Allarey, ed., *People Power: An Eyewitness History. The Philippine Revolution of 1986* (Writers & Readers Publishing, Inc. 1986).

Mercado, Monina Allarey, ed., *Metro Manila—A Gateway to the Philippines,* part one and two (National Coordination Statistical Board 1998).

Rodan, Garry, et al., eds., *The Political Economy of Southeast Asia* (Oxford University Press 1997).

Viloria, Leandro A., "The Manilenos: Significant Elites in Urban Development and Nation Building in the Philippines," *The City as a Centre of Change in Asia,* ed. by D. J. Dwyer (Hong Kong University Press 1972).

RAY HUTCHISON

Maputo
Mozambique

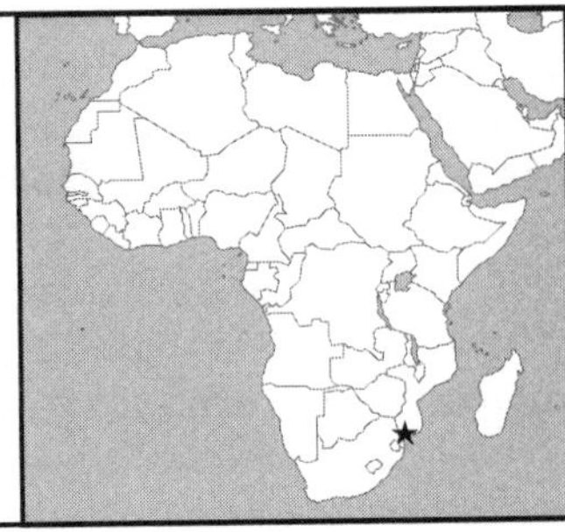

ORIENTATION

Name of City. The capital of and largest city in the Republic of Mozambique, Maputo was previously known (before 1975) in the Portuguese colonial era as Lourenço Marques (named for a Portuguese navigator), and the latter name is still used by some Portuguese and Portuguese-descendant groups in Mozambique and South Africa.

Location. Maputo is located at 25°58′ south latitude and 32°35′ east longitude, on the southeast coast of southern Africa. It lies on the north bank of Espírito Santo Estuary in Delagoa Bay, a large inlet on the Indian Ocean.

Population. In 1991 estimate of Maputo's population was estimated at roughly 1,098,000, with that of the larger metropolitan area approximately 2 million people.

Distinctive and Unique Features. The city contains a large harbor that serves as Mozambique's primary port. Perched on a point that juts into Delagoa Bay, Maputo is surrounded by the quiet waters of the bay on three sides, with several rivers entering the ocean in its vicinity. The city comprises three general parts. The "baixa," or physically lower part of the city near the port, is the older, original city and consists primarily of colonial Portuguese buildings. This is also the downtown or center of the city.

The baixa sits at the foot of a large bluff on which a good deal of the newer parts of the city are situated, together with the diplomatic quarter, the more modern hotels, and a large variety of Portuguese-era residences. Toward the outskirts of the newer part of the city is the large informal "reed city," which consists of densely packed, traditional African huts where many of Maputo's new arrivals live.

The city has a skyline of tall buildings and is well known for its colonial Portuguese architecture—much of it now, however, in crumbling disrepair. There is an impressive promenade along the city's waterfront, as well as numerous indications that Maputo was once a carefully engineered city constructed for gardenlike beauty. One of the more important features of the city is the Nossa Senhora da Conceiao (Our Lady of Conception) fort, which was the center of the original settlement by the Portuguese. The Polana Hotel is a recently restored, five-star colonial-era hotel that the rich and famous frequent and where much international business and diplomatic activity are conducted. North of the city along a strip of beach is a tall, multistory, partially completed concrete building that was under construction at the time of the Portuguese departure from Maputo in 1976. Apparently disgruntled at their imminent exit, workers reportedly poured concrete down the elevator shaft, rendering the building useless.

Much of the formal city is laid out in two general grids situated at different angles: one, a tighter grid in the older baixa part of the city, and the other, a more ample grid in the upper or newer part of the city that contains numerous broad avenues. Many of these avenues are named for former socialist leaders from Africa and elsewhere, as well as to honor important Mozambican leaders and to commemorate key events in the nation's history. The informal part of the city is more a jumble of roads and pathways.

Lourenço Marques was at one time among the most beautiful cities in Africa. However, major changes came to the city in the late 1970s subsequent to the 23-year war between the colonial government and the Front for the Liberation of Mozambique (FRELIMO)—and the departure of most of the Portuguese population. After independence in 1975 there was a very large influx of rural people into the city. Rural immigrants crowded into apartment buildings and former colonial mansions: municipal electric and water services were largely nonfunctioning. A 16-year postindependence war between the FRELIMO government and insurgents of the Mozambique National Resistance (RENAMO) further caused widespread dislocations in the interior and migrations into Maputo, resulting in a large growth of the informal city. The city is now slowly recovering some of its former glory, and certain parts are being impressively rehabilitated. Recent international donor activity in the city has contributed this resurgence, and Maputo now enjoys growing tourism from South Africa and Europe.

Attractions of the City. From the unenviable position of the capital of the economically poorest country in the world in the latter part of the 1990s, a nation whose primary relationship with the international community for some time has been as recipient of foreign aid, Maputo has achieved significant growth and recovery from the country's long wars. Peace, policy reform, and donor activity have created a much improved business climate in many domains. Agribusiness, transport, tourism, and road construction are some of the more important growing business opportunities in and about the city. More and more, Maputo is becoming involved in the global economy as the port is rehabilitated and is increasingly serving parts of western South Africa as well as the southern half of Mozambique, and as markets, transport, and associational and organizational life continue to recover. The market economy was just beginning to emerge in Mozambique as of 2000, with the service sector being one of the more promising. Economic reforms instituted in the late 1980s have resulted in the privatization of more than 900 state-owned enterprises, including the entire banking system and a number of state manufacturing firms. By 2000 such reforms had made the country the fastest-growing nation on the African continent. Such promising economic indications have led to considerable increases in foreign direct investment. Investments are focusing on communications, power facilities, agriculture, the steel industry, mineral resources, and tourism projects. On the other hand, the international business community is quite aware of the very low purchasing power of the majority of Mozambique's population, and the very low levels of education and job experience that are found nationwide act as deterrents for many potential commercial venture.

There are considerable opportunities for tourism in and around Maputo, primarily associated with the long beach that stretches north of the city and is popular with mainly South African tourists and local city inhabitants. A growing number of tourist hotels in Maputo are intended to cater to the high-quality, low-volume tourist strategy of the government. Nearby, Inhaca island is accessible from Maputo by speedboat and offers much in the way of holiday tourism. A continuously operating fair in the baixa, called the Fere de Populare, has circus rides and dozens of bars and discoteques that are quite lively and operate well into the night.

Relationships Between the City and the Outside. Much of the periphery of the city is occupied by the jumble of informal suburbs made up principally of traditional African huts constructed out of locally available materials. As well, there is a thriving "green zone" in parts of the peri-urban area, especially to the north of the city, in which significant intensive agriculture is attempted. There are also a considerable number of larger houses under construction on the northern edge of the city along the beach.

Maputo serves as the administrative, financial, and service capital of the country. However, in some ways the city's location at the extreme southern end of a long north-south–oriented country has proved problematic. For reasons connected to colonial history, the primary direction of most long-distance transport roads in Mozambique is east-west, facilitating extraction of agricultural and natural resources. As a result, transport from the interior to the Maputo harbor in the south of the country is difficult. Nevertheless, the link between Maputo's harbor and the eastern portions of South Africa, and specifically with Witbank, South Africa, is an important one for both nations, providing imports and exports.

Although Maputo is the jumping-off place for tourism and international businesses looking for vacation and investment opportunities in the interior of the country, roadways that connect the city with the countryside have suffered enormous destruction during the long years of war in Mozambique, severely hindering access to and from the interior. As well, the communications infrastructure linking the interior with the city had been targeted during the RENAMO-FRELIMO war and was largely destroyed. Government and donor programs have been working to rebuild much of this infrastructure.

The current character of the city varies between splendor and squalor. The rehabilitated and new hotels and resorts are often world-class and take advantage of Maputo's spectacular location overlooking the Indian Ocean. The diplomatic quarter and associated residences are situated along wide and manicured boulevards. Elsewhere the city is dominated by a more African character, which is both informal and vibrant. With Maputo's continued recovery from decades of war and economic malaise, the perception of the capital is changing and the city is once again coming into its own with regard to tourism and many other opportunities. For many immigrants from rural areas, though, Maputo can be a disappointment, contradicting their perceptions and expectations of greater opportunity and a higher quality of life in the city.

Major Languages. Portuguese is the official language of Maputo, and of Mozambique. However, because the country is surrounded by English-speaking states that belong to the British Commonwealth of Nations (which Mozambique joined in 1995), and with increasing English-speaking representation among the international business and donor communities, English is now widely spoken in the city. As a result, much in the way of official communication now takes place in both Portuguese and English. However, official communication at Maputo's Eduardo Mondlane University, the national university, continues to be Portuguese.

Unofficial communication in the city takes place in some 30 indigenous and regional languages: Chopi, Chwabo, Koti, Kunda, Lomwe, Makhuwa, Makonde, Makwe, Manyika, Marendje, Mazaro, Mwani, Ndau, Ngoni, Nsenga, Nyanja, Nyungwe, Podzo, Ronga, Saka, Sakaji, Sena, Shona, Swahili, Swati, Tonga, Tsonga, Tswa, Yao, and Zulu.

HISTORY

The Origin of the City. Vasco da Gama arrived at the Mozambican coast in 1498 with the idea of establishing supply depots for the Portuguese sea routes to India. This led to a Portuguese occupation in what became Mozambique for nearly 500 years prior to being dislodged by the FRELIMO liberation movement in 1975. During the colonial era Portuguese interests developed into the gold and ivory trade, and then the slave trade.

Maputo was founded as Lourenço Marques in the late 18th century at the site of the Nossa Senhora da Conceiao fort. Central authority for the country was initially located on Mozambique Island, approximately 3 kilometers (2 miles) from the northern part of the mainland; it was transferred to Lourenço Marques in 1898, which became the capital of Portuguese East Africa. The city subsequently functioned as a center for trade and industry; it was also utilized as a port to serve the gold fields of South Africa. The renamed city then continued as the capital of the country when Mozambique won its independence in 1975.

Migration: Past and Present. Significant migrations into the city, which had been almost the exclusive domain of Europeans, began with the great exodus of Portuguese citizens in 1975 and 1976, heralding the end of the colonial era and initiating the African occupation of the city. Vast numbers of rural migrants poured into the city during the subsequent RENAMO-FRELIMO war as a result of the widespread dislocations occurring in the countryside. The end of this civil war in 1992 was capped by a severe drought. This devastating condition led to still more rural migrations into Maputo by those looking for a means of survival.

Subsequent to 1992, resettlement in the city took on a smaller scale as limited economic opportunities and extreme poverty continued to prevail in the countryside. In 2000, large-scale flooding in southern Mozambique caused a resurgence of mass migration into the city.

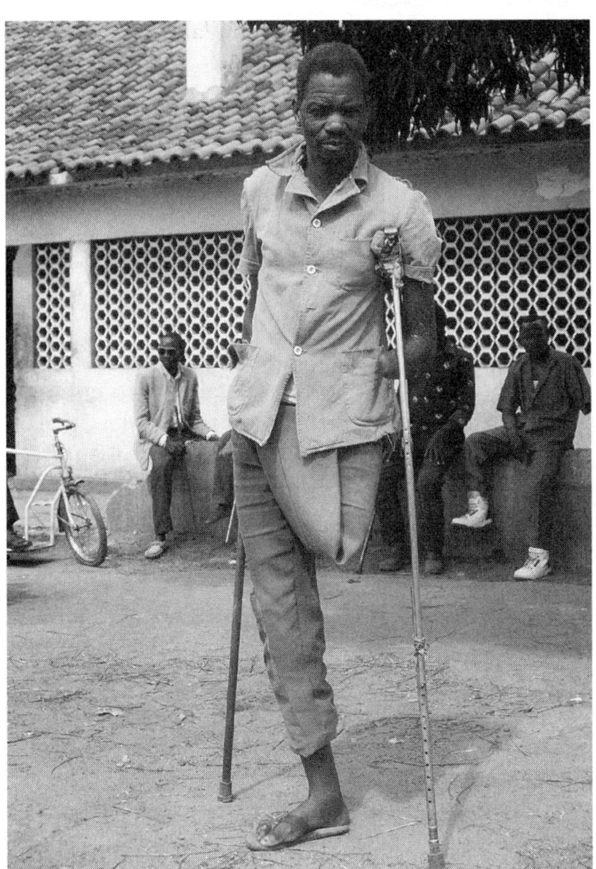

© GARY TROTTER; EYE UPIQUITOUS/CORBIS

A man who lost his leg in a mine explosion stands outside the central hospital in Maputo, Mozambique.

INFRASTRUCTURE

Public Buildings, Public Works, and Residences. Several public buildings are of note in Maputo. The central market in the baixa is large, colorful, and boisterous and is abundantly stocked with a wide variety of seafood, local vegetables, meats, animal products, household products, and local crafts. The Central Railway Station, also located in the baixa, is very ornate, contains several restaurants, and serves as a point of departure for rail transport to South Africa and Zimbabwe. As well, Maputo offers a museum that contains paintings and sculptures by local artists, several soccer stadiums, and numerous parks and recreation areas. However, much of the city's infrastructure, including public buildings, public works, and colonial-era residences, has crumbled into disrepair during the long years of war and policy miscalculation, which resulted in significant neglect and occupation by squatters.

The port, railway, and international airport in Maputo are the primary public works in the city. While these are presently regarded as inadequate for the city, roadway and bridge reconstruction is under way as Maputo recovers from prolonged war and poverty.

Many of the upscale residences are in or near the diplomatic quarter near the Polana Hotel. However, much of the housing in Maputo is severely overcrowded and lacks sufficient sanitation services, consisting either of apartments built during the colonial era in the city's core or of grass huts and other informal housing in the outskirts. The need for adequate housing in the city far exceeds availability, and housing policy and its implementation remain significantly problematic.

Politics and City Services. There are two types of municipal bodies in Maputo: "representative" bodies such as councils, which are elected positions, and "executive" bodies and officials, including administrators and mayors, who are "designated." The electability or designation of mayors is the subject of some debate and interpretation of the nation's constitution.

City programs and services are limited and rudimentary and are supported primarily by the international donor community. City sanitation continues to be a large problem, especially in the informal part of city that houses most of the migrants from elsewhere in the country. However, the government is strongly committed to development in this regard, and this situation may change in the future. Much of the service infrastructure in the city was neglected during the protracted civil war: while the war itself never actually reached the city, the conflict did require much in the way of city and national resources.

During the colonial era the Portuguese made no attempt at social investment in Mozambique. The few schools and hospitals in existence were concentrated in Maputo and other cities and were reserved for the Portuguese, other whites, and *assimilados* (Africans who had assimilated to the Portuguese culture and who could speak the language). In the aftermath of the RENAMO war, education and health services are slowly recovering, financed by the donor community and international and national nongovernmental organizations (NGOs). Government support for these services has increased, targeted mainly at improving the primary school enrollment rate and the coverage for key vaccinations.

A national monopoly provides telecommunications services to the city, where telephone use is the highest in the country. Internet services are considered to be good in the capital.

Educational System. The educational challenge that Maputo and Mozambique face is considerable. At independence the illiteracy rate for the country was 97%, thought to be the highest in the world, with most of those who were literate residing in Maputo. The city's illiteracy rate at that time was 28.5%. Since independence the Mozambican government has made considerable strides toward reducing illiteracy, which in the mid-1990s stood at 32.9% nationally, as compared with the African average of 40.8%. The educational infrastructure of the city suffered considerably during the civil war, with many schools becoming inoperable. But other problems factored in, including the low relevance of the curriculum, teaching methodologies that were too formal, calendars and timetables that were too strict, and exclusive use of the Portuguese language.

The current overall government strategy regarding education is to reduce the rate of illiteracy as fast as possible, and there are programs of adult education with this objective in mind. The ministry of education, which oversees Maputo's 85 schools, places priority on increasing primary education in rural areas and targeting women in the city and elsewhere, as education for women is thought to have the biggest social impact. It is estimated that only about 40% of children of primary-school age are enrolled in schools nationwide, although this figure is most likely considerably higher in Maputo. While primary education is free, community-level contributions are often needed. Secondary education is not free and parents pay according to their means. Textbooks are shipped from India, financed by donors and distributed free by the government. Donors finance approximately 50% of the educational system of the country, with the main priorities being the construction and rehabilitation of educational institutions, accommodation of the many students who attend boarding school, and technical assistance, as well as expanding institutional capacity. There is generally a weak performance of children who do not continue their education.

There are limited opportunities in Maputo for professional, technical, or university education. Eduardo Mondlane University, located in the city, is the only national institution of higher education in the country, with approximately 4,000 students enrolled in and about 600 graduates per year. The university is run with significant aid from Portugal, but it is hampered by aging and inadequate facilities and an antiquated curriculum. Of the few other, smaller universities in Maputo, some have religious orientations, including the Pedagogic University and the One World University.

Demand for higher education far exceeds capacity. As well, a vast number of those who do graduate find that there is no suitable place for them in the nation's labor market. There is no tradition of internship; however, there is the beginning of private-sector education, and the first polytechnic school in the country was opened in 1996, the Instituto Superior Polytechnico e Universitario.

Because there is a tendency among primary school graduates to join the ranks of the urban unemployed, the government has taken steps to strengthen basic vocational education, thus attempting to ready young people for growing labor markets. At present, technical education exists at three levels. The elementary 3-year level teaches basic skills such as carpentry; the second 3-year level covers topics such as agriculture, mechanics, and electrical engineering; and the third 3-year level covers more advanced technical aspects of agriculture, chemistry, and other such fields. The working and learning environment of the schools is limited, with libraries and laboratories barely available. Of the nation's two second-level facilities, one is in Maputo and the other is in the central city of Beira. The government has reopened a business administration college.

A core problem with the Mozambican educational system generally is the shortage of schools and teachers. This dearth is thought to be the principal reason for the extreme scarcity of human resources in the city and country.

Transportation System. Like other infrastructures in Maputo that suffered during the RENAMO-FRELIMO war, transportation in the capital can only improve. Many primary streets in the city have not seen repair for some time. Outside investment in the transportation system drives much of the road construction and improvements in the city as well as those roadways connecting Maputo to other parts of Mozambique and to other countries. Paved roadways in Maputo are laid out on a system of grids, while the dirt roads in the informal part of the city are laid out on an ad-hoc and as-needed approach.

Maputo harbors the central installations for the nation's rail, port, and air services. The national airline, Lineas Areas de Moçambique (LAM), operates regular flights to capital cities in neighboring countries, several European capitals, Rio de Janeiro, and the larger cities and towns in the country. Various charters fly from Maputo to airstrips in smaller towns in the country on an irregular basis; the development of these charter air services occurred as a result of rural insecurity over long-distance ground travel. Maputo is also linked by rail to Swaziland, South Africa, and Zimbabwe, and there is ferry service from the city to a number of locations across and along Delagoa Bay.

Public transportation facilities in the city are quite limited and there are very few buses. It is common for people to be packed into trucks for intraurban transport. However, for those with adequate finances, taxicabs and rental cars are available.

The Maputo Development Corridor Initiative, between the city and initially Witbank, South Africa, is a major transportation development project between the Mozambican and South African governments. This corridor is meant to improve transportation in road and rail to and from the port at Maputo, which is considered one of the best in Africa. Due to be completed in 2005, it is expected to add significantly to Maputo's urban renewal, as well as the Mozambican economy, and at the same time give South Africa access to the Maputo port.

CULTURAL AND SOCIAL LIFE

Distinctive Features of the City's Cultures. Virtually all Mozambican ethnic groups are represented in the city. However ethnic and cultural distinctions are not readily apparent on the street by dress or other visual means, with common dress for all groups that inhabit Maputo primarily Western and casual. In addition to Mozambique's indigenous groups in the city, there are populations of Europeans, Euro-Africans, and Indians.

Apart from distinctive animist religions and religious practices, approximately 30% of the populace of Maputo are Christian, and 20% are Muslim. There are numerous churches and relatively fewer mosques, with some of the latter, especially in the baixa, being quite old.

A peculiarity of Portuguese colonialism is the idea and identity of *assimilados*. Portuguese colonialism pursued the notion of socioeconomic class based on proximity to Portuguese culture, such that Africans of mixed Portuguese descent or who were culturally assimilated were given prestige and privilege well beyond other Africans. This legacy can still be seen in Maputo today, where a significant group of elites cling to the notion of Portuguese culture as a socioeconomic position.

Numerous public spaces in Maputo encourage the informal gatherings that go on virtually all day and well into the night. As a Portuguese city, Lourenço Marques was built with numerous parks and public spaces, most of which show signs of considerable deterioration but nevertheless still serve as public spaces. In these locations men (primarily) gather to broker, chat over the news of the day, or offer services ranging from alcohol sales to car washing and money changing. In the baixa there are several public areas frequented by artists and craftspeople, who display the unique sculpture and batik artwork of Mozambique. Some of the city's parks, including prominent ones, are occupied by migrants and those dislocated from elsewhere in the country, making these essentially into encampments of displaced persons.

While many public spaces in the city generally conform to Western notions in terms of use of urban space, in other parts of Maputo it is culturally acceptable to engage public spaces for purposes that would more closely resemble the use of rural tracts by those more familiar with rural life, including for water, land, building materials, soil, trash disposal, cooking, sleeping, and sitting.

Cuisine. Food continues to be Mozambique's and Maputo's largest import by value. Nevertheless, Maputo is more fortunate than most of the country with its proximity to the sea, rivers, fertile land, and South Africa. As a result, the most impressive cuisine of Maputo is the abundance and variety of seafood. From prawns and shellfish to shark and squid, the seafood is widely and consistently available in the city's markets. And restaurants in the city are quite adept at a variety of delicious seafood dishes.

Indo-Portuguese cuisine is popular as well in many Mozambican restaurants. Specialties include *piri-piri* (spiced) chicken and *matapa,* which is largely a sauce of cassava leaves, ground peanuts, and maize porridge. In the poorer sections of the city the food is more likely to tend toward maize, cassava, tubers, sorghum, and rice cooked in various basic dishes.

Ethnic, Class, and Religious Diversity. Ethic diversity in Maputo is highest in the informal city, where members of ethnic groups from all over the country reside. Indigenous languages generally fall out along ethnic-group lines, the dominant ethnic-linguistic groups being Shangaan, Manyika, Chokwe, Sena, and Makua, as well as a number of smaller groups noted earlier in the section on languages.

Socioeconomic class differentiation in Maputo is considerable, as is the degree of inequality. At one end of the continuum are the expatriate personnel of foreign embassies and the local Mozambican government and business elite, and at the other end are the recently arrived migrants who come to Maputo from elsewhere in the country, frequently destitute and seeking opportunity.

Family and Other Social Support Systems. Although family and extended-kinship relations are extremely important to Mozambicans, for much of the country, and Maputo especially, these have been considerably disrupted by the years of war, droughts, floods, and destitution. Dislocation from social support systems has led to massive migration to Maputo. As a result, Maputo very likely hosts one of the larger concentrations of people in the country without significant family and social support systems, which no doubt contributes considerably to their continued destitution.

For the most part the state and the city lack the resources to provide alternative, workable social support systems. Some of this need is taken up by local and international church groups and NGOs.

Work and Commerce. Portuguese colonial policy excluded most Mozambicans from skilled and management employment, and this legacy lingers in Maputo and poses one of the most pressing problems in the city. Although statistics regarding unemployment in the city are difficult to gather and error is high, unemployment is visibly apparent throughout the city. Much employment takes the form of seasonal migration from Maputo and southern Mozambique to South Africa to work in mines. The state bureaucracies hire large numbers of people in a wide variety of positions, and the abundance of unskilled labor and lack of everything from industrial to household machinery and products means that considerable unskilled wage labor is needed to support the lifestyles of the higher socioeconomic strata. Day and otherwise temporary labor is common in Maputo, as is vending of household and personal manufactured goods. Many in the city, however, attempt to survive by a combination of odd jobs, reciprocal favors, and other activities that seek to take advantage of lineage-based social networks. Urban agriculture is quite common, as many city inhabitants try to grow at least some of their own food.

Transportation in and about the city is so limited that it is frequently provided for by employers, who move workers around on trucks. The few buses that are available in the city are extremely overcrowded, and workers often crowd into informal taxis and trucks. For those better off, there are formal taxis and individual vehicles. Most inhabitants in the capital have no opportunity to purchase vehicles, owing to low wages, the temporary nature of work opportunities, and the very high price of personal vehicles, which must all be imported. A great many city inhabitants simply walk to work.

Access to markets and shops is relatively easy, and the number and location of these compensates to a significant degree for the lack of transportation means. Of course, the densest concentration of shops is found downtown in the city, but these establishments tend to cater to those for whom transportation is less of a problem.

Arts and Recreation. Mozambican art is varied and very distinctive, and it clearly explores directions that are unburdened by Western traditions. In Maputo there are numerous galleries and other locations that display the work of the nation's many artists. Sculpture, paintings, and batiks are widely available. Much of the local art seems to express the past agony of Mozambican life in war, famine, and colonialism. However, while much, if not most of the population of the city has no access to such art, compared with that found in other African cities Maputo's art scene is significantly developed. Foreign embassies and NGOs often support artistic activities in the city.

Since the end of the civil war in 1992, and especially since 1994 when peace became a widespread reality, people began to circulate much more freely outside their homes, and recreational activities increased greatly. Cafés, bars, and discotheques sprang up in all parts of the city. Much of recreational life in Maputo revolves around the many bars and discotheques, which offer both Mozambican and European music and dancing. The number of these clubs in the informal city is quite large, and one is usually within walking distance of at least a couple of such locations. The beach and associated activities are also a major recreation draw in Maputo, with the resorts that dot the beach north of the city frequented by the city's elite and expatriates.

For those who can afford it, sea fishing, sailing, sail surfing, canoeing, and scuba diving are available in Maputo Bay, and golf, horseback riding, and tennis are popular. There are several historic sites, frequented primarily by foreign tourists, which include old forts, the railway station, the botanical garden, the French Cultural Center, and museums of natural history, revolution, and geology.

QUALITY OF LIFE

The need to import virtually all manufactured products means that life in Maputo can be costly. Unless one's own social support networks are able to provide food and shelter, or one has the means or employment, life in Maputo can be quite difficult in the face of unpredictably rising prices.

Health and disease concerns in Maputo are considerable, and medical facilities are extremely limited and medicines are in short supply. Doctors frequently require payment up front for services. Common diseases include dengue fever, filariasis, leishmaniasis, AIDS (acquired immune deficiency syndrome), malaria, plague, relapsing fever, trypanosomiasis, typhus, bilharzia (schistosomiasis), polio, cholera, hepatitis, rabies, diphtheria, and meningitis. Statistics are difficult to come by, but it is estimated that countrywide about one child in five dies before the age of 5. Tap water is unsafe to drink, rivers and lakes can be unsafe to swim in because of waterborne disease, and insect-borne diseases are significant causes of illness. In the informal part of Maputo, crowded housing, poor sanitation, and pools of standing water contribute to outbreaks of infectious diseases was well. Foreign aid agencies handle many health projects.

Crime is a significant problem in Maputo, and violent carjackings, kidnappings, armed robberies, and home invasions are common, with foreigners often targeted.

Poverty is a very large problem in Maputo and is abundantly visible throughout the city. In the late 1990s Mozambique economically was the poorest country in the world according to World Bank indicators, and Maputo, especially the informal part of the city, was the urban illustration of this. Major international donors have instituted extensive poverty-reduction programs with the government in the city and throughout the country. Much of the state's own development priorities are geared toward the same goal. With the very large number of impoverished migrants having arrived in the city, poverty in Maputo is perhaps the city's primary problem. Crowded temporary housing, together with unsanitary conditions, makes homelessness, health concerns, and crime a significant combination in Maputo.

BIBLIOGRAPHY

de Araújo, Manuel, "A cidade de Maputo: crescimento demográfico e transformações sociais (The City of Maputo: Demographic Growth, and Social Transformations)," *Gazeta Demográfica,* (Demographic Gazette), 11 (1997): 2–16.

Hewlett, M., *A History of Mozambique* (Oxford University Press 1995).

Kyle, S., "Economic Reform and Armed Conflict in Mozambique," *World Development* 19 (1991): 637–49.

Poverty Alleviation Unit, *Mozambique—Rural Poverty Profile* (Maputo Ministry of Planning and Finance 1996).

Raimundo, I. M., "Que urbanização existe em Moçambique (Urbanization of Mozambique)," *Gazeta Demográfica,* (Demographic Gazette) 8 (1995): 22–7.

Vines, A., *Renamo: From Terrorism to Democracy in Mozambique?* (Center for Southern African Studies, University of York).

Willet, S., "Ostriches, Wise Old Elephants and Economic Reconstruction in Mozambique," *International Peacekeeping* 2 (1995): 34–55.

Ximane, A., "Para uma reflexão sobre o sector informal citadino (A Review of the Informal Sector of the City)," *Gazeta Demográfica,* (Demographic Gazette) no. 5/6 (June 1990): 51–67.

Jon D. Unruh

Marseilles

France

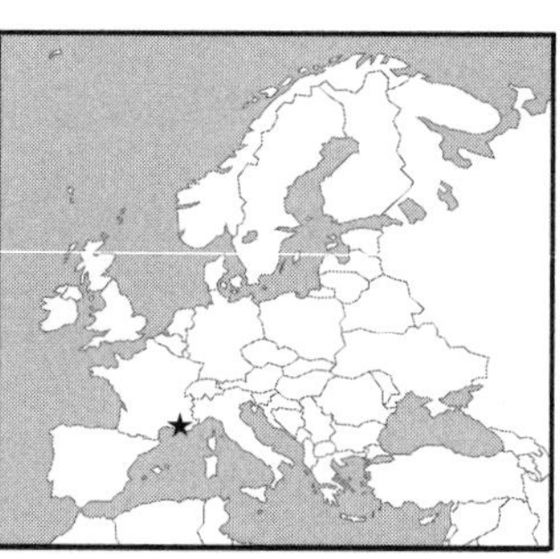

ORIENTATION

Name of City. Marseilles, the most ancient town in France, was founded in 600 B.C. by the Phocaeans. When invaded, it was named Massilia; a few centuries later it was renamed Marseilles (Marseille in French).

Location. France's second-largest city—with an area of 240 square kilometers (93 square miles)—and first trading port, Marseilles is the great metropolis of the South of France. The city is located at 43°18′ north latitude and 5°22′ east longitude. On the east coast of the Rhône delta, in the Bouches-du-Rhône *departement*, Provence region, Marseilles lies between the Mediterranean Sea and surrounding hills, and covers an area that is twice as large as Paris.

Population. The city of Marseilles has a population of 800,500 residents, with 1,231,000 in the Greater Marseilles area. More than 25% of the residents are less than 20 years of age.

Distinctive and Unique Features. The 57 kilometers (35 miles) of coastline constitute an outstanding asset, the main advantages of which are the 50 beaches. The Prado beaches alone have 3 kilometers (1.9 miles) of developed seafront, around which lie 45 hectares (99 acres) of parkland (the beaches are the regular meeting spot for kite fliers, windsurfers, and roller skaters, and are among the finest seaside resorts in Europe).

Marseilles has a mild Mediterranean climate. Generally, winters are mild and sunny and summers are hot and dry. Summer temperatures range from 22°C to 30°C (72°F to 86°F); in winter, temperatures are generally 8°C (46°F) and higher. Rainfall is less than 800 millimeters (31 inches) per year, and there are fewer than 50 days of rain. Marseilles has more than 300 sunny days a year. The mistral (a local wind) brings on the sun and chases depressions, and Marseillais custom says that the mistral gives the sky its purity and guarantees the exceptional luminosity of the landscapes.

The vegetation is varied: Aleppo pines, umbrella pines, holm oaks, and the *garrigue* (wastelands with thistles, gorses, and aromatic plants). Many fruit trees also adorn the landscape. Running along the beach, the land of Marseilles begins at the Estaque on one side and goes until the Calanques on the other side, with an area of 24,000 hectares (59,000 acres) and 57 kilometers (35 miles) of littoral.

L'Estaque, situated north of Marseilles, is a very famous place. From 1860 to 1920 dozens of well-known artists including Cézanne, Renoir, Derain, Braque, Dufy, Marquet, Othon Friesz, and others visited Estaque because of the concentration and abundance of motifs and colors in a limited area. Estaque is associated with three pictorial movements: impressionism, fauvism, and cubism (Braque painted his first cubist picture there). Today, Estaque remains a popular district not much different from the one the artists knew.

From Estaque, when driving along the Marseilles coast, one reaches the former docks (which have been restored) and the Vieux Port (Old Port) at the heart of the city. Continuing this route, leaving the Vieux Port by La Criée (Marseilles national theater) and the Fort Saint-Nicolas, the road goes along the seaside from the Catalans beach. All along the Corniche, below the viaducts, one can see other beaches and little fishing ports such as le Vallon des Auffes, Endoumes, Malmousque, and Maldorné. Opposite Frioul Island, the road reaches the seaside park of Le Prado (a vast expanse of greenery and beaches). A copy of Michelangelo's masterpiece *David* stands at this traffic circle. The seaside road continues toward the beaches and Pointe Rouge harbor. There is a succession of small creeks as far as Les Goudes, which goes until the Calanques massif.

The Calanques (sea inlets) are a preserved site of 4,000 hectares (about 9,900 acres), almost 20 kilometers (12 miles) long by 4 kilometers (2.5 miles) wide in Marseilles (from Marseilles to Cassis communes). The limestone range drops abruptly into the deep-blue sea. This Mediterranean fjord landscape is unique in Europe. Rare species of flora and fauna are also attractions of this site, including Bonelli's eagles, peregrine falcons, and eagle owls. Caves below sea level—inhabited during the Neolithic period—and freshwater springs abound.

Relationships Between the City and the Outside. Its coastal location makes the city open to North Africa and to other countries. *Chef-lieu,* (administrative center) of the region, Marseilles has an important role in all of the South of France. It is also a congress city (convention center). More than 140,000 congress days (conventions) are organized per year, and the number of congresses and congress days is increasing every year (65,000 in 1995; 122,000 in 1998; 131,000 in 1999).

Marseilles is also a tourist city that receives French people (80%) and foreigners (20%). Marseilles has more than 5,250 hotel rooms. A large part of the city—near the Old Port or Estaque, for example, lives with the commercial accommodations or tourist shopping.

Major Languages. The residents of the city are called the Marseillais and Marseillaise. The major language is French.

HISTORY

The Origin of the City. The oldest town in France dates back 26 centuries to when it was first established by the Greeks, later by the Romans. Greek sailors (from Phocaea, a Greek port in Asia minor—later known as Foça in Turkey) arrived in the Lacydon Calanque—later to become the Vieux Port—and founded Massilia. These seagoing people were also skilled farmers, improving wheat- and wine-growing methods in Massilia and introducing olive production. Later, the city was closely linked with the Saracens and was subsequently destroyed on two occasions: in 736 by Charles Martel (a powerful Frankish leader) and in 739 by the Catalonians.

Involved in the Crusades, and besieged by the Aragonese, Marseilles was attached to the sovereignty of France only in 1482. These political problems had few repercussions for the fortunes of the city, which knew great periods of prosperity. It was in Marseilles that the first chamber of commerce was created in France (in August 1599). Marseilles lived through a succession of wars and plagues (40,000 deceased in 1720), and fought a long time for its independence.

During the 17th century the city rode a switchback, alternating between economic strength and depression. Still less than obedient to the central power, Marseilles was occupied in 1660 by soldiers of the king. Louis XIV invested in constructing a port with two forts at the city's entrance and an arsenal—enabling the development of its commerce and riches.

During the French Revolution, Marseilles, the "rebel," took sides against the royalty and became (in 1792) the first city to demand the abolition of the monarchy. The famous battalion of the volunteers of Marseilles, formed to march on Paris, supported the revolution, making famous "the battle hymn of the army of the Rhône"—which later became the national anthem, "La Marseillaise."

Under Napoleon the wars brought the English blockade, which asphyxiated the port and ruined the commerce. Marseilles recovered with colonial expansions and the construction of the Suez Canal, leading to a rapid growth of its port and a vigorous urbanization (boulevards, public monuments, cathedral, Pharo, Notre-Dame-de-la-Garde, stock exchange, Longchamp, and so on).

The completion of the Suez Canal in 1869 allowed the development of new trading routes, and the port required a further expansion. It was under the Third republic that the industrialization of Marseilles gathered speed. Refineries, ship repairing, and mechanical-engineering industries developed, and the port area continued to enlarge.

World War II hit the city hard. As a "free zone" early in the war, Marseilles provided refuge to and helped fleeing German democrats, Jewish refugees, and others from Eastern Europe. But the Nazis withdrew the free-zone status and occupied the Mediterranean coastline. Twenty thousand Marseillais were forced to leave their homes; some were deported, and 1,980 buildings were razed. In May 1944 an Anglo-American bombing raid targeting strategic sites in the city overflowed into civilian areas, causing considerable damage. The war ended in Marseilles on August 15, 1944.

Marseilles recovered by looking for new strengths and qualities, creating a port extension and new industries with the enormous developments at Fos-sur-Mer, to the west of the Bay of Marseilles.

Migration: Past and Present. The first great migrations into Marseilles started at the end of the 18th century. One out of two Marseillais was not native to the city, but came from Italy or Spain. The town with its port was a crossroads city that experienced great European expansionism. At the end of the 19th century, foreign workers were dominant in the city, and represented the overwhelming majority of laborers in a few industrial sectors. At the end of the 19th century, and continuing into the middle of the 20th century, the Latin population formed the most important immigrant group in Marseilles, and Spaniards and Italians represented almost 40% of the city's population. In the middle of the 20th century, the first Maghrebi (mostly Kabyles) began to reach Marseilles. World War I brought Italians, Spaniards, Armenians (escaping genocide), and Africans. Just before and during World War II, Marseilles experienced an influx of migrants from Italy (because of Mussolini) and from Spain (because of Franco).

In the 1960s, with decolonization and industrialization, more people from North Africa arrived. Thus, the Latin and Christian populations in Marseilles were joined by a Mediterranean Oriental, Arab, and Islamic population. These groups represent the majority of the population in some districts. Since 1975 the census has indicated that only about 10% of the population of Marseilles is not French. Approximately 20% of the population of Marseilles is formed by people who came from the north of France.

INFRASTRUCTURE

Public Buildings, Public Works, and Residences. Marseilles is an urban city with very concentrated residences and a population density of more than 300 people per square kilometer (116 per square mile). Typical in the Calanques zone are *cabanons* (seaside houses). People come to this area with its "small cabanon, no larger than a pocket handkerchief," according to an old song, to relax, to find a cool atmosphere during the summer, to enjoy the benefits of the sea, and to lunch *sous la tonnelle* ("outdoors under the vine bower").

On the other side of the city are the *bastides* (*cabanons* for the wealthy). They look like little châteaux, with noble classical facades and formal French gardens. Other than these traditional constructions, Marseilles is a modern city with tall buildings and towers.

Land and buildings in the city are divided among a variety of owners: The public sector owns the largest share; the French state is the second-largest landowner; and a smaller portion of the land in Marseilles is privately owned.

Politics and City Services. Marseilles is the most important city of the department of Bouches-du-Rhône and of the region of Provence. As previously noted, the public sector owns a large part of the city and has a large role in all the services to the population.

Educational System. Marseilles has become an important center for higher-education research and high technology, and is second only to Paris for research. The city has more than 3,000 research institutes and more than 90,000 students in three universities and 15 *grandes écoles* (high level tertiary education).

All areas of scientific application are represented in the universities—immunology, cardiology, neuroscience, genetics, ocean engineering, numerical modeling, agrochemistry, and nuclear research. Notable achievements include the first heart-transplant operation in France and the creation of the computer language Prolog.

Transportation System. Marseilles Provence metropolis, at the heart of the big markets of south-

© KEVIN FLEMING/CORBIS

A worker sprays paint on the side of a huge tanker in dry dock in Marseilles, France.

ern Europe, possesses a land, air, and maritime infrastructure network of exceptional complexity, with its port open to the whole Mediterranean basin. Marseilles is the largest Mediterranean port, the largest port in France, and the third-largest port in Europe. The international airport—situated in Marignane, 22 kilometers (14 miles) from Marseilles—is the second-largest freight airport and the third-largest passenger airport in France.

Marseilles also has a road system that is complex but well adapted: it opens up the region to southern Europe (Spain, Italy, Portugal) as well as to the northern European capitals. In 1970 the construction of the A6-A7 (*l'autoroute du soleil*—"the motorway of the sun") motorways linked Marseilles and Paris. Moreover, a new railway system (TGV Mediterranean) shortens Paris-to-Marseilles travel time to three hours.

CULTURAL AND SOCIAL LIFE

Distinctive Features of the City's Cultures. The Vieux Port area and the Rue Canebière along the harbor are popular and active areas after dark. La Canebière was grand during the second and third empires (1852–1940), when the fine old buildings lining the avenue were built, and an intense intellectual and business activity was omnipresent in the cafés, high-class hotels, and shops. Now, most of that luster is gone, although the bustle and activity in some areas are reminiscent of the older Canebière.

There are some other attractions and places unique in the city. The Ferry-boat (known by the English name, but pronounced "Ferrybôite") goes from the southern Rive-Neuve quay to the other side, Le Cours d'Etienne d'Orves.

Another popular attraction is Le Château d'If (the If Castle). In 1524 François I had a fortress built on the island of If (a 20-minute crossing from Marseilles). It became legendary for its prisoners—both real and imaginary, such as the count of Monte Cristo. The well-preserved environment and building make the Château d'If one of the Mediterranean's most outstanding sites.

The archaeological vestiges of the Phocaean time, which were excavated in 1967, can be seen near the Old Port. The "horn" of the ancient port can still be viewed, as the sea used to come up to that point. The historical museum located there exhibits collections related to the founding of the Phocaean city and the Greek town.

Christianity took root in Provence between the 3d and 5th centuries, and the first monastery appeared in 415 in Marseilles (the Saint-Victor). The statue of Our Lady of the Guard (La Bonne Mère) is one of the highest points in the city. She belongs to all the inhabitants of Marseilles, and pays particular attention to the people on the sea: she looks out to sea and the port entrance.

Romanesque art gave birth to Old Major, an austere, mid-11th-century cathedral, which was built on the site of a former construction adjoining a vast baptistery. Today, only a large nave and an octagonal dome remain, following alterations and mutilations during the building of the present cathedral. Nearby is the Roman St.-Laurent Church (17th-century bell tower). Across the Old Port stands the imposing silhouette of St. Victor Abbey with its crenellated towers—one of the most complex monuments in the Bouches-du-Rhône. The 13th-century crypts include the ruin of the 5th-century construction built by Cassian; they form a series of chapels decorated with stelae and sculptures from the 4th to the 12th century. Dating back to the golden age of the 11th century is the Isarn Porch. The stark, late-13th-century church is a fine example of Provençal Romanesque style, despite its late construction. The fortifications are from the 14th century.

Cuisine. Marseilles has some specific specialities, such as bouillabaisse, whose origins are humble. It was, at first, a dish made with unsold or cheap fish, and eaten by the fishermen. Later, after many variations, it became more "aristocratic." Bouillabaisse is a speciality whose basic ingredients are such rockfish as red hogfish, red gurnet, sea devil, whiting, pageot, mackerel, stingfish, saran, muraena, and girella. However, the recipe varies with the seasons and the catch. Another specialty is *pastis*, a traditional drink, made from aniseed liqueur, which is drunk with icewater. With a dash of orgeat, it becomes a *mauresque*—very famous in all Marseillaise terraces.

There are some foods eaten in Marseilles (and the Provençal region) during specific celebrations. The Christmas supper offers the "13 Christmas desserts" featuring *fougasse* ("girdle cake"); white nougat with hazelnuts or pine nuts; black nougat with honey; grapes; dry figs; almonds; walnuts; pears; crystallized citrons; and newly picked fruit such as apples, oranges, dates, and tangerines. During *La Chandeleur* (Candlemas) in Marseilles on February 2, the congregation follows in procession the Vierge Noire (Black Virgin) in St. Victor Abbey, illuminated by traditional green-wax candles. The typical food of this festivity is the *navette*, an orange-flavored biscuit whose boat shape is reminiscent of the legendary Saintes-Maries (Sainte Marie Jacobe; Sainte Marie Salome; and Sara, the Gypsy Black Virgin, who lived in Camargues after leaving Palestine).

Ethnic, Class, and Religious Diversity. As a port that opens out into the world, Marseilles has an extremely diverse and mixed population. Its location as the first port of call after the Maghreb has, over the centuries, brought a variety of people of different nationalities to its shores—including large proportions of immigrants from northern Africa, but also Italians, Spaniards, Turks, and Portuguese. Immigrants represent 10% of the total population of Marseilles, but because the newcomers live in specific districts of the city, some people think that Marseilles has become a city of foreigners. For example, the north district of Marseilles is between 50% and 70% Maghrebi. The center of the city is the wealthiest district, but a large portion of the suburbs (except the Calanques and other famous places) are home to the poorest classes, frequently the immigrants.

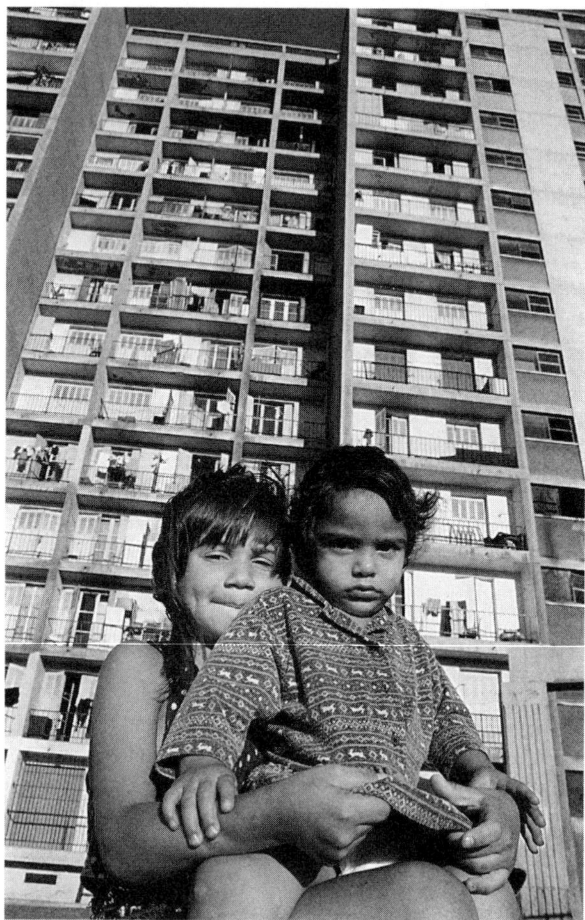

© DAVID TURNLEY/CORBIS

Immigrant children pose outside an apartment house in Marseilles, France.

Family and Other Social Support Systems. As in Latin tradition, the family is very important in the Marseillais way of life. Familial mutual aid remains important even if many traditions are changing as a result of modernization.

Work and Commerce. A large part of the industry in Marseilles is related to the port. At the end of the 19th century, the city saw rapid development, which, among other things, resulted in a reorganization of the distribution circuits for perishable foodstuffs. It became necessary to adjust supply and demand. The Marseilles MIN (Marché d'Intérêt National) network was created in 1953 to bring together buyers and sellers.

In 1995 the port handled 92 million metric tons of goods. Boats up to 400,000 metric tons can be accommodated in the port with its 30 kilometer (18.6 mile) quays and 220 commercial berths. The port's ship- and steel-repairing facilities represent 80% of the national production.

With its leading high-tech firms, Marseilles is decidedly future oriented. Its thriving port was the foundation of the city's prosperity. The Marseilles-Fos triangle is famous because of its import-export, phytosanitary sector, heavy metallurgy (4 million tons of iron and steel per year), refineries (four refineries and two steam crackers), and aeronautics. Data processing, electronics, biotechnology, and other high-technology industries have also put Marseilles on the map. The city boasts some world-famous industry leaders—such as Comex (deep-sea diving), Gemplus (magnetic cards), and nearby Eurocopter (helicopters).

Marseilles has the highest rate of new-business creations outside the Paris region, and a rich network of innovative small and medium-size businesses. Marseilles population includes office workers, manufacturing workers, and those involved in intermediary professions. There are 48,000 enterprises in the city (90% with fewer than ten employees). The service-industry sector is the most important and innovative, and it represents 81% of employment.

The Marseilles-Fos industrial-port complex is only a partial success, because the ultramodern steelworks have been affected by the crisis in this industry. Modern industrial seaport activities create few jobs. In the 1980s the ship-repairing industry declined. However, petrochemical activities succeeded, and soon Marseilles became the second-busiest port in Europe in that business. Marseilles produces 32% of France's petrochemicals.

Local products such as *savon de Marseille* and *santons* (clay figures dressed in traditional Provençal costume, displayed in Nativity scenes) are typical of the region. *Le savon de Marseille*—the Marseilles soap (72% oil content), duly marked—is an impossible challenge to imitators. Sold in big cubes, it is still manufactured in a half-dozen soap factories in nearby Salon-de-Provence and in Marseilles.

Arts and Recreation. There are 25 theaters (two national), 10 concert locations, one opera, and one national ballet in Marseilles. The city also boasts some popular music groups.

Marseilles is also a museum city, with 22 museums specializing in such varied topics as Mediterranean archaeology, African arts, fashion, faience (hand-painted pottery), Egyptology, contemporary arts, and so on. The city also has resources for a variety of sports activities, including hiking (on the hill trails of the coves), sailing, kayaking, sea fishing, scuba diving, golfing, beach volleyball, and soccer (the city's renowned team, Olympic Marseilles, with its blue and white colors, makes its home in the 60,000-seat Velodrome stadium).

Marseilles also has old traditions and activities. At Christmas Marseilles and all of Provence exhibit their traditions most intensely. The Nativity is celebrated by many events. Midnight Mass welcomes the *tambourinaires* (timbrel players), the shepherds descending from the hills in procession for the presentation of the lamb, the *pastrage* ceremony, La Pastorale Morel (combining the secular with the sacred, the pastorale is a theatrical Nativity play in Provençal language; it was created by Antoine Maurel in 1842).

Lagnel, the first *santon* maker, created the Nativity characters in clay as early as the 18th century. *Santons* are made of fine clay from Aubagne or Marseilles. Cast in plaster, each *santon* is hand-finished, its face precisely modeled, and the completed figure is delicately painted. Their traditional costumes are made from the famous Provençal printed fabrics. *Santons* represent the Holy Family, the three Wise Men, the donkey, and the ox—but also the angel hanging from the stable's vaulted ceiling, the *ravi*, the *pistachie*, and many other characters from a typical Provençal village: the fisherman, the hunter, the lavender picker, the baker, the knife grinder, the *Boumian* (Gypsy).

Also well known in Marseilles is *la pétanque*, a game of *boules* (similar to lawn bowling) that is played from a stationary position with the feet together. Originating in La Ciotat (near Marseilles) in 1910, this game is actually known throughout the world—but the most passionate games are played in the shady provençal squares. *Les joutes Provençales*—nautical jousts—is a tradition that carries its 2,000 years lightly on the 57 kilometers (35 miles) of littoral all around Marseilles. The game uses two boats—one being a white and blue boat and the other a red and white one. Each boat has six rowers and a jouster, who stands steadily on the *tintaine* (fore platform) with a lance and shield. When the boats are jousting, the jouster who stays on the *tintaine* wins the game.

QUALITY OF LIFE

With its rich cultural mosaic, Marseille is without comparison in its quality of life and deeply rooted traditions. To wander around Marseilles is to discover more than a hundred different villages (111 bell towers!) grouped around a former Phocaean port and a very typical population and traditions.

According to Martin O'Brien (*Time*, June 15, 1998), "In true Mediterranean style, Marseilles is a city of brisk, business-like mornings and long sultry afternoons, when it basks in what the writer Flaubert called its 'oriental indolence.'" But there is much more to say. From Estaque to the Goudes, walking in the old Panier district and the Catalans, the many villages have preserved their identity and specificity even if they have some regional characteristics. The quality of life is generally good in Marseilles.

There are also some negative features. Like any port, Marseilles has always been a rough town, with its fair share of villainy. Just as O'Brien said, "When law enforcement agents set out to crack the French Connection in the early '70s, [Marseilles] was exposed as a center for drug-trafficking, prostitution, and racketeering." The Marseilles Mafia was as notorious as the Sicilian one. Continuing, O'Brien noted that "Marseilles has also suffered a succession of financial scandals and rigged elections, not to mention undue camaraderie between the forces of law and disorder. Corruption spread to soccer in 1993, when the home team, Olympic Marseilles, was banned from competition for a year for alleged match fixing, and the team's flamboyant owner, Bernard Tapie, was convicted of bribery, embezzlement, and tax evasion."

"Added to all this," O'Brien continued, "Marseilles endures the racial tensions of a city with one of the highest levels of immigration [mostly from the Maghreb] in the country—and a flock of far-right extremists are ready to exploit that fact." They have not won in Marseilles, but the extremists have won in some nearby cities (such as Vitrolles, Marignane, and Toulon).

FUTURE OF THE CITY

At the dawn of the 21st century, with the relative decline of the ship-repairing industry, Marseilles is struggling against an unemployment rate above the national average. Notwithstanding—and despite the poverty that affects a third of the city's population, and the scale of the recent immigration—Marseilles has been relatively less affected by urban violence than have other French cities.

Two large urban-development projects have been studied and initiated. The first is the "Great Urban Project," which is an operation of deep renewal of the northern sector of Marseilles (on a social and economic-development level), focusing on reinvigorating the south of the city. The second is the Euro-Mediterranean Project. This last is very important. The town-planning project involves 300 hectares (more than 700 acres) of the city center. It is an economic movement focusing on Marseilles as a metropolis of European dimensions, but at the same time, it is intended to harmonize with the city's existing historical urban structure. The project skillfully combines residential and office buildings, which presents many advantages in terms of urban renewal and construction while providing large, open-air public areas.

BIBLIOGRAPHY

Baratier, Edouard, *Histoire de Marseille* (1973; Privat 1988).

Bertrand, Regis, *Le Vieux Port de Marseille* (Jeanne Laffitte 1998).

Bonillo, Jean-Lucien, et al., *Marseille, Ville et Port* (Parenthèses 1992).

Duchêne, Roger, and Jean Contrucci, *Marseille, 2600 Ans d'Histoire* (Fayard 1998).

Guiral, Pierre, and Félix Reynaud, *Les Marseillais dans l'Histoire* (Privat 1998).

Jasmin, C., *Marseille au XIXéme: Rêves et Triomphes* (Musées de Marseille 1991).

Rambert, Gaston, *Marseille, la Formation d'une Grande Cité Moderne,* 2d ed., 7 vols. (1934; reprint Plon 1966).

Urbain, Pascal, *Architectures Historiques à Marseille: Éléments de L'Habitat Ancien* (Edisud 1987).

Zalio, Pierre-Paul, *Grandes Familles de Marseille au XXéme Siécle: Enquête sur L'Identité Économique d'un Territoire Portuaire* (Belin 1999).

SYLVIE CHIOUSSE

Mecca

Saudi Arabia

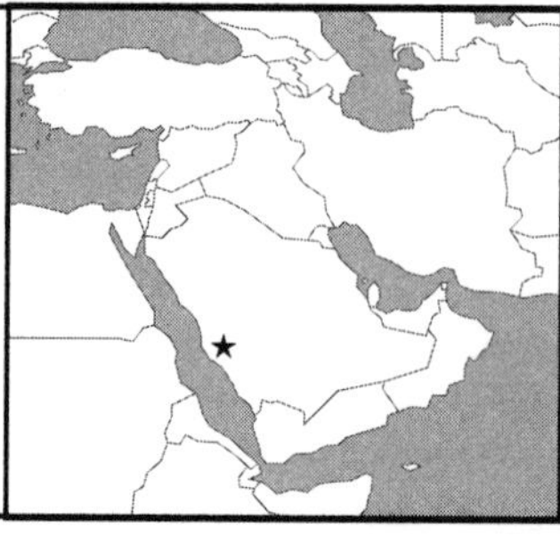

ORIENTATION

Name of City. In Arabic the name of the city known to the West as *Mecca* is *Makkah,* or more commonly, *Makkah-al-Mukarramah* ("Mecca the Revered"). Mecca is often associated with the city named by Ptolemy as *Macoraba,* but this identification has been challenged.

Location. Mecca is situated at approximately 39° east latitude and 21° north longitude and is now in the Kingdom of Saudi Arabia on the Arabian peninsula. The capital of the Hejaz province, Mecca lies about 72 kilometers (45 miles) east of Jeddah (Jidda), its port on the Red Sea, and about 480 kilometers (300 miles) to the south of Medina. Mecca is located in the sandy, narrow valley of the Wadi Ibrahim and is surrounded by hills from 60 to 150 meters (200 to 500 feet) high. The 915-meter- (3,000-foot-) high Jabal Khandama rises nearby. Because it occupies a sort of corridor between two ranges of hills, Mecca, despite its arid location, has been prone to periodic flooding. The climate is extremely dry, with very occasional but heavy rain (hence the floods), and the area cannot support any significant agriculture. The wells were very important for the town's water supply, and one of the roles of the early political groups in the area was to oversee and safeguard those supplies.

Population. Mecca's population at the start of 2002 was almost 1 million. In recent years it has often risen by another 2 million during the annual pilgrimage. As has Saudi Arabia as a whole, Mecca has experienced rapid population growth in recent years. The Kingdom both discourages immigration and encourages residence by religious Muslims from elsewhere in the Islamic world who will influence government policies back in their homelands. Some Muslims do choose to move to Mecca to retire.

Relationships Between the City and the Outside. Whatever Mecca's origins, there are few if any cities in the world so marked by religious significance. Even before the arrival of Islam, as the Qur'ān confirms, Mecca was regarded as a sacred site. This sacred nature of the city has played a huge role in defining both its appearance and activities. The main commercial activities are servicing the pilgrims and maintaining the institutions that are needed to accommodate such a large number of visitors. The visitors are exclusively Muslim, non-Muslims not being permitted to visit the holy sites (nor even to fly over them). Although Mecca is often represented in Islamic iconography, it is not an important political or economic center in Saudi Arabia, its status being largely limited by its religious role.

Mecca is defined by its physical difficulties. It is in a barren region and can produce no food of its own. This led to early dependence on food imports, initially from Egypt, and on water from the *zamzam* well outside the city and from elsewhere. The name *zamzam* means "wait wait," referring to Hagar's desperate search for water for her son Ishmael while running between the mountains Safa and Marwa; hajjis today recapitulate this journey.

Water supply has been a continual problem; although many large projects have been carried out to solve it, most have failed. Even when adequate supplies have been established, the local bedouin often interfered with the supply for financial reasons. During the hajj, water often become a crucial issue, and it sometimes was sold to the hajjis at exorbitant rates. The Meccans provided food, drink, and accommodation to the pilgrims; they also provided animals to be sacrificed, barbers to shave the pilgrims, and all the facilities required for the visitors to perform the necessary rites in accordance with Islamic law. It is hardly surprising that in the Islamic world, Meccans are often regarded as having as their main motive the fleecing of the pilgrims, and there is a long tradition of their purchasing goods and services for eventual resale to pilgrims at a substantial profit. On the other hand, it must be recognized that Meccans have only a short period—only a few weeks a year—to earn what is in effect their annual income, so their shrewdness is a matter of necessity. Nevertheless, many hajjis profess to be shocked by the rapacity of the Meccans, who are, after all, their coreligionists and who are fortunate to live permanently in the holy city.

Major Languages. The language of Mecca is Arabic, the language of the Qur'ān itself and of Saudi Arabia. The significant tourist industry in the city has ensured that a wide variety of languages are spoken by the guides and those providing services to the pilgrims—in particular, of course, the languages of the Islamic world.

HISTORY

The Origin of the City. Mecca is a very ancient city, and its origins are the subject of historical controversy. According to many historians, the city's position was initially favorable for trade, since a good deal of traffic passed through the area going north to Syria, west to the Red Sea port of Jeddah, northeast to Iraq, and south to Yemen. There is taken to be evidence that Mecca attracted much of the trade passing through Syria and the Mediterranean, and between southern Arabia and the Indian Ocean, especially when there was conflict between the Persians and the Byzantines in the pre-Islamic period. The lack of physical resources in Mecca was compensated for by the apparent sophistication of the city as a service center, and, in particular, as a commercial force in the region, both financing and investing in enterprises along the trade routes that went through the town. This standard view of Mecca's early importance has recently been challenged by historians who point to the absence of any solid evidence to support such a view of the city.

The issue of the origins of the city are highly controversial. Of great significance is the fact that the Prophet Muhammad was born in Mecca in about 570. The Qur'ān is scathing on the subject of the merchant culture of Mecca, and it calls on Meccans to embrace the one God and abandon their overwhelming materialism. Initially the message fell on stony ground, and in 622 Muhammad left for Yathrib (Medina), a far more sympathetic environment for him. Over the next few years, there was continual struggle between the Muslim forces of Medina and the Meccan authorities. In the end the Muslims overcame the Meccans, and the *ka'ba*, (Kaaba), the central religious shrine in Mecca, was cleansed of its association with idols and became the *qibla,* or direction of prayer, for Muslims. Of particular importance was the area around the *ka'ba,* which soon became surrounded by a mosque, the *masjid al-haram,* thus formalizing a holy area.

Migration: Past and Present. Over the next few centuries, Mecca frequently suffered invasion and destruction by different religious and tribal groups. The pilgrimage was often disrupted or rendered impossible, and the Meccans sometimes flirted with a degree of independence under the sharif (literally "noble"; linked with being a descendent of the Prophet) clan. The political struggle over the rule of the sharifs came to a head early in the 20th century, when the Ottoman Empire became embroiled in World War I and could not adequately defend the holy places. Another local power, the family of Sa'ud, who came from the Nejd, to the east of the Mecca and Medina region, overcame the Husseins of the sharif clan and brought Mecca and Medina under their authority. The Sa'uds brought a Wahhabi (orthodox and puritanical) Sunni orientation to the city, and this has had a long-lasting effect on its cultural and physical life. The authority of the less strict and rigid sharifs now disintegrated, and businesspeople, *mutawwifun* (guides), and religious teachers (*ulema*) came to the fore.

The *ka 'ba* is said to have been built by God for Adam and to be modeled on the divine residence itself. Abraham is supposed to have rebuilt it after its destruction during the Flood. Today it is considerably larger than it was originally, when it is said to have been made up of loose stones and to be not that much taller than an average human being. It is made of black meteoric stone and is covered with a large cloth, quite simply decorated with writing and embroidery. The *ka'ba* today stands in the midst of an open courtyard, the *haram al-sharif* ("noble sanctuary"). A cubical, flat-roofed building 15 meters (50 feet) high, it rises from a narrow marble base on mortared bases of a local blue-gray stone. The entire *ka'ba* structure is draped with a black silk covering, called a kiswa, upon which passages from the Qur'ān are embroidered in gold. Opposite the northwestern wall of the *ka'ba* is an area of special sanctity called the hijr, which Muslim tradition identifies as the burial place of Hagar and Ishmael. In Muhammad's time the *hijr* was a place used for discussion, prayer and, significantly, for sleep and visions. The *ka'ba,* the *zamzam* well, the *hijr,* and the hills of Safa and Marwa are now all enclosed in a vast structure called the *masjid al-haram* ("noble mosque"). Ringed by 7 towering minarets and 64 gates, this truly monumental building has 133,800 square meters (160,000 square yards) of floor space and is capable of holding more than 1.2 million pilgrims at the same time.

In Islam the hajj pilgrimage is a fundamental obligation to be performed at least once by all male and female adults whose health and finances permit it. The pilgrimage takes place each year between the 8th and 13th days of Dhu al-Hijjah, the 12th month of the Islamic lunar calendar. When the pilgrim is about 11 kilometers (7 miles) from Mecca he or she enters the state of holiness and purity known as ihram and dons special garments consisting of two white, seamless sheets that are wrapped around the body. Entering the great mosque in Mecca, the pilgrim first walks seven times around the *ka'ba* shrine in a counterclockwise direction; this ritual is called *tawaf,* or turning.

Next, entering into the shrine, the pilgrim kisses the sacred stone. The stone is mounted in a silver frame in the wall, 1.3 meters (4 feet) above the ground, in the southeast corner of the shrine. It is oval in shape, about 30 centimeters (12 inches) in diameter, composed of seven small stones (possibly basalt) of different sizes and shapes, joined together with cement. During the next few days, the pilgrim walks a ritualized route to other sacred places in the Mecca vicinity (Mina, Muzdalifah, Arafat, the Mount of Mercy, and Mount Namira) and returns to the *ka'ba* on the final day. Once a believer has made the pilgrimage to Mecca, the title *al-hajji* may be added to his or her name. Pilgrims use a variety of signs to indicate they have made the hajj. These include pictures of the *ka'ba* painted on the walls of their homes; there is a good deal of iconography involving the *ka'ba* and the mosque surrounding it in Muslim homes.

The history of Mecca has been tempestuous. The different factions in the Islamic world fought each other for control of Mecca, often in Mecca itself. The city was often invaded; the population frequently suffered at the hands of the invaders. On the other hand, Mecca was generally far distant from the main centers of power and authority and so, perhaps, was less affected by political and military upheaval than other important regional cities such as Damascus, Cairo, and Baghdad. As a means of securing religious legitimation of their policies in general, Muslim politicians often would seek influence in Mecca by financing supporters within the city, which, not unnaturally, greatly increased the wealth of Mecca's leading families. Since the different political factions each would have their own representatives in the city, a good deal of wealth circulated.

At some stage around the 10th century, walls were constructed around the city, and they lasted for a few centuries. The city's area is said to have been approximately 16 hectares (40 acres) in 661, extended to 142 hectares (350 acres) in 1924, and is well over 810 hectares (2,000 acres) today. The intimate nature of the old city has certainly been substantially diminished. Serious attention to other buildings—such as the houses of Khadija, the Prophet's first wife, or of his Companions—is discouraged; certainly those sites are not treated as focal points of the city.

Mecca, and indeed, the Hejaz as a whole, was declared open only to Muslims during the caliphate of 'Umar (634–644). Jeddah remained open to non-Muslims and was an important commercial center, but the exclusion from Mecca did presumably leave the commerce lined with the hajj in the hands of the local Muslims. On the other hand, it further limited the ability of Mecca to diversify outside of its sacred role, since any wider commercial undertaking would necessarily no longer be parochial and might involve those of other faiths. This was a significant issue even before globalization.

As a sacred city Mecca suffered several serious problems. The religious endowments (*waqf*) on which the colleges and mosques relied for their operating expenses frequently collapsed owing to the distance of the city from the centers of power and hence the ease with which such funding could be curtailed. In any case, *waqf* finance is always rather uncertain, relying as it does on using the income produced by one enterprise to finance another, and the records suggest that although considerable funds often were directed to Mecca, in many instances far less actually arrived. Expenditure was often on prestige projects, those with religious relevance, and so did not add to the ability of Mecca to generate income by itself. The distance between donor and beneficiary meant that there was little control of how the money was spent, and the returns in Mecca itself were often feeble. The city's wadi location resulted in frequent floods, and the flimsily constructed original buildings could not survive the regular periods of flooding and destruction. The religious significance of the city invited attack by those seeking to impose their views on the Islamic world, and the pilgrimage trains to and from the city were far from secure.

Finally, the various rulers of the city have sought to copy the Prophet in restoring what they have taken to be the appropriate rituals. According to Islamic tradition, Abraham initially set up the *ka'ba* to worship God, but it was subsequently used by polytheists to worship false gods. Muhammad instituted Muslim pilgrimages, the annual hajj and the minor *'umra,* which can take place at any time, to replace pagan pilgrimages. Subsequent rulers have all changed the city physically in order to make it accord better with their own conception of its sacred status. Few were as radical as the Qarmatians, who, in 929, massacred many of the inhabitants and removed the *ka'ba* stone to Bahrain! Throughout all the changes in policy, however, there do not appear to have been any radical changes to the *ka'ba* itself, which is now much as it was when the Prophet's tribe, the Quraysh, constructed the building in 605. Yet the buildings around the *ka'ba* have been continually altered; often they have just fallen down. Different rulers put up palaces near the shrine and financed religious institutions as ways of projecting their authority. Changes in regime would frequently lead to change in the buildings and what went on within them, and the new projects must have injected considerable funds into the city. They also must have seriously strained communications, since virtually all building materials had to be imported over difficult terrain and lengthy distances. Again, it can only be assumed that the effect this had on the local economy was to boost it, renewing the reputation of Mecca as a dynamic service center well able to absorb and benefit from large-scale public and private works.

INFRASTRUCTURE

Public Buildings, Public Works, and Residences. Since World War II, Saudi Arabia's great oil wealth has radically changed the city. The mosque at the center of the city itself has been greatly enlarged.

One of the major influences of the Saudi regime on Mecca has had to do the secondary sites, those associated with the life of the Prophet Muhammad rather than with the *ka'ba* itself. From pre-Islamic times there apparently had been many holy sites in the vicinity of Mecca, and the Prophet's tribe, the Quraysh, had control over some of these and over the provision of water. One of their motivations for hostility to Muhammad was their fear of losing this valuable monopoly, since they thought that the pilgrimage trade might be destroyed by the new religion of Islam. As it turns out, the pilgrimages were only strengthened by Islam, and the various groups and families who controlled different parts of the holy city and its environs benefited greatly over the centuries—although, of course, the groups who actually enjoyed this power changed over time. The secondary sites were particularly popular with Muslims who stayed on in Mecca after either the hajj or the *'umra* pilgrimage, captivated as they were by the holiness of the environment. There have been fewer such sojourners recently owing to the Saudi disinterest in the secondary sites and their increased policing of those in the country on pilgrimage visas.

Politics and City Services. As the guardians of the two holy cities, Mecca and Medina, the Saudis have a difficult task in facilitating the safe arrival and departure of so many pilgrims over such a comparatively brief period. In recent decades the majority of pilgrims have arrived by air, further altering the nature of the hajj from its previous status as a physically strenuous activity even before one arrived in the city. As throughout its long history, however, Mecca has continued to flourish as a service center, attracting banks and hotels through its role in the hajj while itself producing little in terms of goods. It is worth pointing out that although the hajj brings in considerable funds, it also requires considerable expenditure. Nevertheless, the changing of money and the provision of animals for sacrifice, and simply the annual incursion of up to 2 million people from every corner of the Islamic world, has an effect on Mecca that is difficult to quantify. Undoubtedly, much of the city lives for the hajj, existing through the rest of the year off the income generated in the pilgrimage period. Some major facilities, such as hospitals, lie virtually idle for most of the year, really being used only during the hajj.

There are no elections in Saudi Arabia, and the city government is appointed centrally.

Educational System. Mecca's numerous educational colleges for the teaching of the Islamic sciences are busy throughout the year. The city has a university, Umm al-Qara. Of the considerable influx of Muslims from all over the world, some stay on to study. There is extensive provision of free schooling for young people, who make up a large proportion of the city's population. After the age of 6, the sexes are segregated in school.

Transportation System. Many plazas have been constructed near the central mosque, roads have been built and widened, and much attention has been paid to parking and other facilities, such as tunnels for pedestrians between the different areas that are part of the hajj itinerary. Buildings have often been demolished and reconstructed on a grander scale, inevitably with loss of charm, and the widespread introduction of electricity has made the city yet another modern place. Preservation is not regarded as a serious issue by the Saudis, although there is now sometimes mild criticism of the widespread destruction of old buildings.

CULTURAL AND SOCIAL LIFE

Distinctive Features of the City's Cultures. The local inhabitants wear what is regarded in Saudi Arabia as Islamic dress, the men often wearing long robes and the women veils and all-encompassing clothes in public. In private a great deal of informality is possible.

Cuisine. Saudi cuisine is a version of Middle Eastern Arab cooking. No pork is eaten, and the typical diet includes stews, salads, bread, rice, and coffee with cardamom. The hajj leads to consumption of lamb in considerable quantities, although much of it is also given away as charity.

Ethnic, Class, and Religious Diversity. Although only Muslims live in or even visit Mecca, there are considerable distinctions of nationality and, of course, wealth in the city.

Family and Other Social Support Systems. The family is the main site of social control in Mecca, with kinship links determining career, education, and housing. Although women have little public role,

© ADREES LATIF/REUTERS/TIMEPIX

Muslims praying at Islam's holiest site, the *ka'ba* in Mecca.

they play a crucial part in influencing marriage, and so in the development of kinship relations. In this way they play a large part in what is the key to Saudi society, the structure of the family. Yet there are severe restrictions on their movement and on their participation in life outside of the family and home.

Work and Commerce. Servicing the hajj is the main occupation of the local inhabitants. During the rest of the year, the city both recovers from the last hajj and prepares for the next one. Given the very large numbers of pilgrims, such preparations are, obviously, both protracted and essential.

Arts and Recreation. Within Mecca itself, poetry and to a certain extent music are acceptable art forms, as are the bedouin handicrafts, such as jewelry- and textile-making, although the latter is in steep decline. Calligraphy is the art form that receives the highest degree of official approval. Although the hajjis often represent the *ka'ba* pictorially on their return home, within Mecca itself representational art is not encouraged. Wahhabi interpretations of Islam frown on representation, especially of human beings and holy places, and the religious police try to ensure that in Mecca, of all places, the aesthetic rules of respectability are strictly observed.

QUALITY OF LIFE

Mecca is a wealthy city, with an adequate provision of public spaces and health and educational facilities. Petty crime is considerably reduced by a draconian punishment system, which is often criticized for being particularly severe on aliens. The educational attainments of women necessarily fall significantly behind those of men.

The rapid development of the city has greatly improved the quality of life of the average Meccan, since the expansion has been accompanied by heavy governmental investment in housing, transportation, and health. The heavy buildup of population during the hajj inevitably brings with it pollution and overcrowding problems, but these are only temporary. The environmental issues surrounding the large-scale slaughter of sacrificial animals are formidable, and for a period there are unpleasant smells in the area. Nevertheless, the general organization of the hajj is efficient and has managed to obviate any permanent environmental problems. Inevitably, however, with the rapid growth of the city, a great deal of its charm has disappeared forever.

BIBLIOGRAPHY

Bogary, Hamza, *The Sheltered Quarter: A Tale of a Boyhood in Mecca,* tr. by Olive Kenny and Jeremy Reed (Center for Middle Eastern Studies, University of Texas at Austin 1991) [translated from the Saudi Arabia novel *Saqifat al-Safā*].

Burton, Richard, *Personal Narrative of a Pilgrimage to Al Madinah and Meccah,* 2 vols., ed. by Isabel Burton (1893; reprint, Dover 1964) [reprint of the "Memorial Edition"].

Crone, Patricia, *Meccan Trade and the Rise of Islam* (Princeton University Press 1987).

Esin, Emel, *Mecca, the Blessed: Madinah, the Radiant* (Crown Publishers 1963).

Ibrahim, Mahmood, *Merchant Capital and Islam* (University of Texas Press 1990).

Peters, F. E., *The Hajj: The Muslim Pilgrimage to Mecca and the Holy Places* (Princeton University Press 1994).

Peters, F. E., *Jerusalem and Mecca: The Typology of the Holy City in the Near East* (New York University Press 1986).

Al-Sarīf, Ahmad Ibrāhīm, *Makkah wa-al-Madīnah fī al-jahilīyah wa-'hd al-Rasūl* "Mecca and Medina in Pre-Islamic Times and in the Time of the Prophet" (Dar al-fikr al-'arabi 1965).

Watt, W. Montgomery, *Muhammad's Mecca: History in the Qur'ān* (Edinburgh University Press 1988).

Wolfe, Michael, ed., *One Thousand Roads to Mecca: Ten Centuries of Travelers Writing About the Muslim Pilgrimage* (Grove Press 1977).

OLIVER LEAMAN

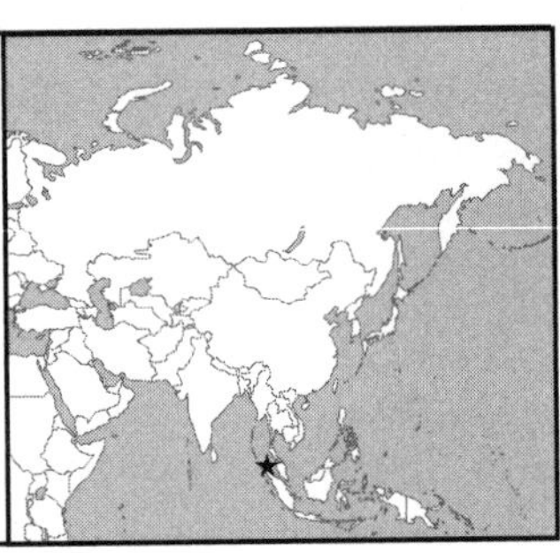

Medan

Indonesia

ORIENTATION

Name of City. The name *Medan* is said to be from the Malay language, meaning "a gathering place," since Medan has been a center of trade and plantation from its beginnings. Some believe the name may be from the Portuguese word *medina,* which is the origin of the Indonesian word *medan,* meaning "arena" or "field."

Location. The city is located at 3°30′ to 3°43′ north latitude and 98°35′ to 98°44′ east longitude. Medan ranges in elevation from 2.5 to 37.5 meters (8.2 to 123 feet) above sea level. The city is in the province of North Sumatra, on the island of Sumatra, Indonesia, in Southeast Asia.

Population. In 1998 the population was 2,008,753. The area of Medan city is about 265 square kilometers (102 square miles), with a population density of 7,447 people per square kilometer (2,875 per square mile). The metropolitan area includes Binjai and part of Deli Serdang, which give the metropolitan area a population of 3.1 million (1997) and an area of 1,634 square kilometers (631 square miles).

POPULATION (1823–1998)

Year	Population	Note
1823	200	Recorded by John Anderson, British trader
1860	3,500	
1906	14,000	Combined population of the Dutch authorities area of Medan plus the area of the sultanate of Deli
1920	45,000	
1935	76,000	
1942	93,000	Japanese occupation era; includes refugees who came to Medan
1950	160,000	East Sumatra declared an independent country
1957	330,000	Includes migrants from West Sumatra, Tapanuli, and Aceh
1960	465,000	Medan made the capital of the North Sumatra province
1965	705,000	Medan made a municipality
1971	630,000	Census for the General Election
1978	1,500,000	Census for Bureau of Statistics
1998	2,008,753	Census for Bureau of Statistics

Distinctive and Unique Features. Medan is the third-largest city in Indonesia. It is the western gateway of the country, with the Belawan seaport in the north and the Polonia Airport in the center of the city. Medan is the center of trade, industry, government, and cultural activities for the north of Sumatra. Many consular offices are located in the city.

Medan has been a multiethnic city since its beginning as a plantation center during the Dutch colonial period in the 1860s. Plantation companies from Holland, England, Belgium, and elsewhere brought in Chinese immigrants from Singapore and Malaysia and Javanese laborers from Java to work their plantation concessions. Europeans, Chinese, and Indians moved to Medan to take advantage of trading opportunities, as did people from local ethnic groups in Sumatra, such as the Batak, Malays, Nias, Acehnese, Mandailing, and Minangkabau.

During the colonial period Medan was divided by the Dutch into four main areas:

(1) The Government area was subdivided into blocks without residential buildings.

(2) The European residential area, or Polonia area, was designed based on garden-city concepts.

(3) The commercial area was subdivided into commercial plots that were taken up mainly by the Chinese immigrants.

(4) The Sultan Deli area, belonging to the former sultan of Deli, consisted of the Sultan's Palace, Sultan's Mosque, the Sultan's court, the Madrasah (Islamic school), and the Royal Park and residential areas provided for the noble families of the sultanate.

The urban development of Medan developed with segregation of the various racial and ethnic groups. The Europeans, the smallest in numbers, showed their dominance by occupying the largest part of the city core with a low-density neighborhood. The Indian neighborhood grew up adjacent to the European district within walking distance from the Sri Mariaman temple, which was first built before 1884. Their area, then known as Kampung Madras (later Kampung Keling), referred to Madras in India, where they came from. The Chinese neighborhood grew up close by the market and trading areas. They occupied most of the city in the west and also the east, building densely populated areas. In their district, streets were named after Chinese places—for example, Peking Street, Hong Kong Street, Kanton Street. The Arabs lived in the center of the city in Kampung Arab, near the oldest mosque in Medan, called Mesjid Bengkok. Their population was quite small but exclusive; they formed a merchant area similar to the Chinese district. A small number of Indonesians, white-collar workers for the Dutch, lived in areas set up by the municipal government adjoining the European settlement areas. Other native ethnic groups—such as Malays, Mandailing, and Minangkabau—settled in the outskirts of the city under the rule of the sultan. The Javanese who worked for the plantations lived in barracks outside the original city; however, over time the city expanded to include some of these areas.

After the 1950s Medan developed rapidly, but the basic pattern of the city did not change. The history of Medan can be seen through its buildings—with colonial buildings in the former Government and Polonia areas, shophouses in the Chinese quarters, and Malay houses close by the Maimoon Palace and the Sultan's Mosque. The Kesawan area in the center of Medan is famous for its display of architectural styles, including classical, neoclassic, Chinese, art deco, and postmodern. One of the most distinctive buildings there is the Tjong A Fie Mansion, built by a Chinese millionaire named Tjong A Fie, who was very influential and flamboyant in the early 1900s. One can easily see the influences of the British colonial architecture in Medan, brought over by the planter community. They were strongly focused on the nearby island of Penang, off the Malay Peninsula, and on the city of Singapore, both of which were British colonies.

The basic change in Medan at the start of the 21st century was its role as the center of the larger metropolitan area called Mebidang, consisting of the cities of Medan and of Binjai and of the adjoining parts of Deli Serdang regency. This expansion influenced policies of development in general, requiring additional roads and public facilities such as malls, superstores, and bus terminals. In addition, the increase in traffic caused congestion in some parts of the city. The number of motor vehicles in Medan, although relatively small (about 700,000 cars in 1998—or one car per three people), increased faster than road capacity and was responsible for increased air pollution.

The development of the city also demands new functions for some areas. Thus, main streets, such as Diponegoro Street, in high-class residential areas are gradually changing to become commercial areas with banks and offices. Old shophouses in the Kesawan Area, with its continuous arcades, are demolished and replaced by new high-story shophouses, without consideration given to their surroundings. In most cases, new buildings in Medan have been built in modern international architectural styles, replacing old buildings that had character and charm. The local government has issued regulations to maintain the character of the old areas, but their implementation through law enforcement needs to be strengthened.

Attractions of the City. Medan is attractive both as a place of business and for living. It offers the following features:

(1) It is a center of government administration, industry, trade, and finance, with economic resources such as plantations, farming, fishing, and tourism.
(2) The city is the western gate of Indonesia, with international ports for export-import facilities, which make Medan Indonesia's third-largest contributor to international trade.
(3) Medan is Indonesia's gateway city for the Indonesia-Malaysia-Thailand Growth Triangle, located close to Singapore, the center of trade and business in Southeast Asia.
(4) Medan covers an area of 265 square kilometers (102 square miles) with a population of more than 2 million. The rate of education is higher than the national average.
(5) There are three public universities (University of North Sumatra, State University of Medan, and State Islamic Institute of Medan), plus more than a dozen private universities and colleges.
(6) Medan has seven industrial areas, including the Medan Industrial Area (Kawasan Industri Medan, or KIM), which covers 505 hectares (1,248 acres).
(7) Medan is a base for consular offices in Sumatra, and also has three sister cities—Penang (Malaysia), Ichikawa (Japan), and Kwangju (Korea)—which opens possibilities for international relations.
(8) There are institutional infrastructures for business and international communities, such as

the Chamber of Commerce and Industry, foreign banks, and the Medan International School.

(9) Medan offers diverse tourist attractions: multiethnic culture and cuisine; a rich architectural heritage; natural attractions such as Lake Toba, the largest lake in Southeast Asia; and orangutans and national parks.

Relationships Between the City and the Outside. Since the Dutch planter Jacob Nienhuys founded the Deli tobacco industry in 1863, Medan has been a center of the international tobacco trade as well as a trade center for other plantation products from the east coast of Sumatra. The role as a trade center continues, and is not limited to plantation products.

Diplomats early noticed the importance of Medan and opened representative offices in the city to serve their business and interest in Sumatra. The United States opened its consulate in Medan on April 29, 1919; its first consul was Algar E. Carleton. By late 2000 there were 13 consulates in Medan. In addition, cooperation with sister cities is actively maintained. These cities have exchanged trade missions, exhibitions, and cultural performances regularly. The same is true with respect to Medan's participation in the Indonesia-Malaysia-Thailand Growth Triangle (IMT-GT), particularly in the tourism sector. For example, Medan passport holders may travel without paying an exit tax to Penang (Malaysia) and the southern part of Thailand. Medan is also the home of the Leuser Development Programme (LDP), a project to save the Leuser National Park (Taman Nasional Gunung Leuser, or TNGL), which is jointly funded by the Indonesian government and the European Union. The Leuser is undoubtedly the most diverse of all conservation areas in Southeast Asia between India and the Philippines, ranging from coastal mangrove and riparian areas to tropical mountain areas. The boundary of TNGL is only 50 kilometers (31 miles) from Medan; a TNGL recreation center and an Orang Utan Rehabilitation Centre are located 80 kilometers (50 miles) northwest of Medan at Bukit Lawang.

Major Languages. Bahasa Indonesia is the principal language spoken in Medan. However, various ethnic groups speak their own native languages, including Batak, Javanese, Hindi, and Chinese (Hokkien).

HISTORY

The Origin of the City. The beginnings of Medan are traced from the kingdom of Aru in Deli Tua, close to the current Medan. In the early 16th century, the Aru were led by a queen, in legend named the Green Princess. With the kingdom's abundant natural resources, the Aru had a lively trade with the British, mainly for pepper. The Deli area was rapidly developed only after a Dutch planter named Jacob Nienhuys started a tobacco plantation in 1863. Since then, the high quality of Deli tobacco has given it an international reputation. Deli was also famous for other plantation products, such as coffee, tea, rubber, and palm oil. Nienhuys was given his plantation lands by a concession from the Deli sultan, Mahmoed Perkasa Alam. At the end of the 19th century, there were several European and American plantation companies in and around Medan; the largest and most influential was the Deli Maatschappij. Its headquarters were in Labuan Deli, which functioned also as the center of government and trade. In 1869 the Deli Maatschappij moved its administration center to a village called Medan, using as its port a seaport, Belawan.

Medan was about 10 kilometers (6 miles) from Labuan Deli, located between the Babura River and the Deli River, and had 200 inhabitants in 1863. In a short time, the village was transformed into the center of the plantation business for the east coast of Sumatra. Deli Maatschappij developed most of its infrastructure—such as the railway between Medan and Labuan Deli, Elizabeth Hospital (1885), the telephone company (1886), the water supply company Ajer Beresih (1905), and Polonia Airport (1928). Following the move of the region's commercial center to Medan, the Deli sultanate took the same initiative to move to Medan, and in 1887 built Maimoon Palace. The palace was designed by the Italian architect Ferrari, and was situated on the west side of the Deli River. Two years later the government of the Dutch Indies acknowledged the importance of Medan by naming an assistant resident for Medan. Then, in 1906 the Dutch installed a city council, Afdeelingsraad van Deli, but abolished it three years later when Medan became an independent municipality.

The main buildings in the core city of Medan were built in the early 19th century; designed by Dutch architects, they created a distinctive image of Medan as a colonial city. The old Town Hall was built by C. Boon, and Chinese captain Tjong A Fie endowed the Town Hall with a clock tower in 1913.

Eduard Cuypers designed the Javasche Bank building, which became the representative of the Central Bank in Medan. The main post office on the Esplanade was designed by J. Snuyf and was said to be the first example of innovation in architecture in Medan. Harrisons and Crossfield—a British trading, rubber-plantation, and export company—erected an office building in 1914 on the western corner of the Esplanade. The gracious environment of the Esplanade (later called Merdeka Square) was created in the 1930s. Meanwhile, the Kesawan area was transformed into a modern (western-style) shopping street with continuous facades in different architectural styles.

Migration: Past and Present. When Nienhuys started the first tobacco plantation in 1863, he recruited Chinese workers from Singapore. During the colonial era, 300,000 Chinese workers arrived in Belawan seaport for work on the east coast of Sumatra; only one-third of them went back to their place of origin when their contracts were finished. The British government in the Malay Peninsula objected to the recruitment of Chinese workers from Singapore, so it was stopped. Then Nienhuys recruited Chinese workers directly from China, together with large numbers of workers from Java.

In 1905 Medan showed the dominance of the Chinese—with a population that consisted of 6,397 Chinese, 3,705 other Asiatics, 3,195 Indonesians, and 954 Europeans. But in the next 25 years (1930), the composition of the population changed to become 37,096 Indonesians, 27,180 Chinese, 4,292 Europeans, and 3,408 Arabs or other Asiatics. The unique nature of Medan as a melting pot of different ethnic groups and nationalities continues. (See the table on page 158, showing the development of the population in Medan.)

INFRASTRUCTURE

Public Buildings, Public Works and Residences. Development in Medan is planned according to five Regional Development Areas (RDA):

(1) RDA A covers the three northern coastal subdistricts of Medan Belawan, Medan Marelan, and Medan Labuan with Belawan as the development center. These areas are used for seaport activities, industry, housing, marine recreation, and associated facilities.

(2) RDA B covers one subdistrict of Medan Deli, with Tanjung Mulia as the development center. This area is for offices, trading, housing, and indoor recreation.

(3) RDA C includes the six eastern subdistricts of Medan Timur, Medan Perjuangan, Medan Tembung, Medan Area, Medan Denai, and Medan Amplas, with Aksara as the development center. These subdistricts are for housing, trade, recreation, and associated activities, including small industry.

(4) RDA D includes the five central and southern subdistricts of Medan Johor, Medan Baru, Medan Kota, Medan Maimoon, and Medan Polonia, with the core city, Medan Kota, as the development center. These subdistricts are for business- and government-office activities, plus education, housing, and associated activities.

(5) RDA E includes the six western subdistricts of Medan Barat, Medan Helvetia, Medan Petisah, Medan Sunggal, Medan Selayang, and Medan Tuntungan, with Sei Sekambing as the development center. They are to be used mainly for business and housing, with associated development; however, there are many small industries plus government and educational establishments in these areas.

According to the regional plan, the development of Medan will be directed to the northern, eastern, and western parts of the city, since the northern part of Medan has vast vacant areas and is flood-free. The southern areas are reserved for conservation or as greenbelt districts, as well as for water catchment and filtration.

Housing and settlement sectors have priority in the development of Medan, and involve the public as well as the private sector. The public sector took the following initiatives:

(1) It developed a housing complex for fishers in the Sei Mati village, consisting of 1,086 units of various types.

(2) It provided financial assistance to improve housing conditions in poor villages.

(3) It developed apartment housing in Sukaramai for vendors and low-income residents.

(4) It developed affordable public housing in Martubung for middle- and lower-income people.

(5) Through the Kampung Improvement Project it improved the environmental facilities and infrastructures of densely populated residences—providing pathways, neighborhood roads, clean-water supplies, public bathrooms, and rainwater sewerage.

The city of Medan launched a campaign called Medan Bestari, which loosely translated means clean, healthy, well-managed, safe, and beautiful Medan. The campaign was set as a solution to the production of garbage that totaled about 1,135,000 tons per day in 1998. It also worked to improve open space of about 38 hectares (94 acres) for sports areas, gardens, city parks, and boulevards.

Public facilities were developed to support Medan, including hotels (159 units in 1998), hospitals (two public hospitals and several private hospitals), telecommunications, electricity (distribution increase of 9.9% per annum), and water supply (serving 71% of the total population).

Politics and City Services. Since independence in 1945, Medan has had 13 mayors. The mayor has a secretary for governance and municipal affairs, a works department, and a planning department.

Educational System. All children in Medan are entitled to primary and secondary education. Because Medan has a mature population, the numbers of such school-age children are actually declining. Since 1995 the number of primary students decreased by 7.2% per annum, and the number of junior-high students decreased by 1.0% per annum. Senior-high-school buildings decreased by 3% per annum.

The government's North Sumatra University is the oldest university in North Sumatra. It is supported by two other state universities and numerous private universities. There are also many vocational schools and colleges providing nonformal education.

Transportation System. Land-transportation development in Medan aims to expand downtown and intercity bus services and to improve the main road system. In 1998 there were 1,607 kilometers (998 miles) of state, provincial, and city roads in Medan. The growth in the number of vehicles, especially private-use automobiles, has been faster than the city's capacity to construct and maintain new roads. Consequently, many roads are becoming congested, resulting in traffic jams and accidents.

Most of the railways and trains in Medan have been in use longer than they were originally designed to last. From 1994–1998 the number of rail passengers and rail-freight volume increased by 3% per annum.

The port of Belawan, 26 kilometers (16 miles) from the city center, plays an important role in the city's economy. About 87,500 domestic passengers passed through the port in 1998, a decrease in its use compared with previous years. However, Belawan remains a major port for export-import activities.

Medan has had an international airport, Polonia, since 1928 (named for the plantation of a Polish planter). There are direct flights to Penang and Kuala Lumpur (Malaysia), and to Singapore.

CULTURAL AND SOCIAL LIFE

Distinctive Features of the City's Cultures. Medan's richness as a multiethnic city offers many traditions and cultures. Ethnic groups keep their traditions alive through ceremonies and celebrations on a near-daily basis, particularly in rituals surrounding marriages and deaths. Batak especially continue to observe their traditions; their weddings are typically held in large public halls, and a series of ceremonies are held over several days following the death of a family member. In addition, when someone dies red paper flags are displayed in front of the house and at the end of the street. If the deceased is a grandparent or parent, there will be a traditional music performance for the public.

Numerous traditions are related to religious teachings through festivals and national holidays. There are many cultural organizations from every ethnic group, all of whom preserve their cultures with regular performances. Performers can be hired for ceremonies and celebrations. Medan also has such modern outlets for entertainment as pubs, discotheques, and karaoke bars. Music performances, especially showcasing popular artists, are presented on a regular basis, especially on campuses. Other forms of entertainment are cinemas and video rentals. Medan has several radio stations offering different types of music, as well as talk shows. Taman Budaya, the city's "culture park," is where performances are held on a regular basis and where Medan's artists gather. For painting and sculpture, regular art exhibitions are held at the Simpassri building and in several other galleries.

Cuisine. Medan is famous for Padang food, which usually includes very spicy meat and fish dishes. In a Padang restaurant, a bowl of rice and a variety of different dishes of food are placed on the table. "Eat what you like; pay for only what you eat" is the protocol.

Chinese food and seafood are also popular in Medan. There are many Chinese restaurants, some open on early Sunday mornings for dim sum breakfasts. Well-known Chinese-food areas are Selat Panjang Food Park and Semarang Food Park, two narrow streets with many small restaurants and open food stalls. The atmosphere is cozy and original, the prices reasonable. They are good places to enjoy

Medan in the evening. Indian, Javanese, Japanese, and Western food are all found in Medan in small food stalls, restaurants, hotels, and international franchise outlets. For nostalgia, the famous Tip Top Restaurant, located in the old part of the city, provides a Dutch colonial atmosphere with Western and local cuisine. For local ambience, there is also the members-only Medan Club.

There are many popular dishes to be found in Medan, but nothing is more popular than *bika ambon*, a sweet yellow cake made from eggs, flour, and coconut milk. Majapahit Street is full of *bika ambon* shops; some shops welcome guests directly into their kitchens. Visitors to Medan buy this cake as an *oleh-oleh* (souvenir to take home), along with *markisa* juice (fresh passionfruit juice) and *teri* fish (small white fish).

Ethnic, Class, and Religious Diversity. Located between India and China, Medan became a transit point for many different religious beliefs. Merchants from China brought Buddhism; Indians practiced Hinduism; Arabs introduced Islam; Europeans spread Christianity. The diversity of religions can be seen from the places of worship around the city. These include the big Chinese temple, Vihara Gunung Timur; the historic Sultan's Mosque; the Hindu Sri Mariaman Temple in Kampung Keling; and the various Christian cathedrals and churches.

Family and Other Social Support Systems. As the third-largest city in Indonesia, Medan provides all the facilities needed by a family. There are schools for all student levels, as well as an international school, the Medan International School. There are health services (traditional and modern), sports facilities, many training institutes, banking facilities, telecommunications, and so on.

Most families in Medan still enjoy an extended-family system that is very supportive for parents of young children when both wife and husband work. There are always family members (grandparents, aunts, in-laws) to look after the children. Wealthy families have several household helpers, including maids, a cook, a driver, and a gardener.

Work and Commerce. The Chamber of Commerce and Industry in Medan actively promotes business opportunities through its weekly columns in local newspapers. Skilled personnel, especially those with computer skills and ability in Chinese and/or English, are in demand by the private sector. Chinese is needed mostly by private companies that are dominated by Chinese businesspeople, while English is needed by foreign companies and also by local companies involved in international trade. Medan has adequate infrastructure for foreign investment, with banking, telecommunications, and transportation facilities.

The informal sector has grown, especially since a monetary crisis in 1997 when many employees lost their jobs, many of whom became entrepreneurs, starting small, home-based businesses such as restaurants, souvenir shops, and so on. There is also a "cottage industry" in Medan selling secondhand clothing, bags, and rugs. These businesses were first located on Mongonsidi Street, giving the business its name, Monza, meaning Mongonsidi Plaza—although, in fact, there is no plaza there at all. Since 1998 these secondhand businesses have spread rapidly and now often occupy space in shopping plazas. Secondhand clothing of many kinds is imported through neighboring countries, especially Malaysia and Singapore, and sold in bales in lump-sum transactions. The clothing is then resold by the piece for a profit.

Arts and Recreation. Many people now spend their leisure time in the malls and plazas that are replacing the traditional shopping areas. The malls are very crowded on weekends, especially with teenagers, many of whom go to the malls to socialize with friends.

Medan has great potential as a center for "back-to-nature" recreation. Brastagi and Bukit Lawang are two very popular weekend destinations. Brastagi, a favorite with Medan residents, is a cool mountain area that is known for its fruits and vegetables (Brastagi oranges are famous in Medan). Bukit Lawang is known for its Orang Utan Rehabilitation Center. The rivers around Bukit Lawang are attractive for white-water rafting, although one must exercise caution. Medan has a zoo with traditional shows on Sundays. There is also a privately run wild-animal museum. Other attractions include a crocodile farm, Asam Kumbang, where one can see crocodiles in various sizes in the swamps and rearing tanks.

For sports, Medan offers activities from horseback riding to golf. There are numerous swimming pools and several golf courses that are open to the public. Early-morning walking, jogging, and exercising are popular, especially on Sundays. Groups meet regularly for morning walks around Merdeka Square in the center of town.

Indonesia has become well known for the unpleasant custom of corruption. Indonesians them-

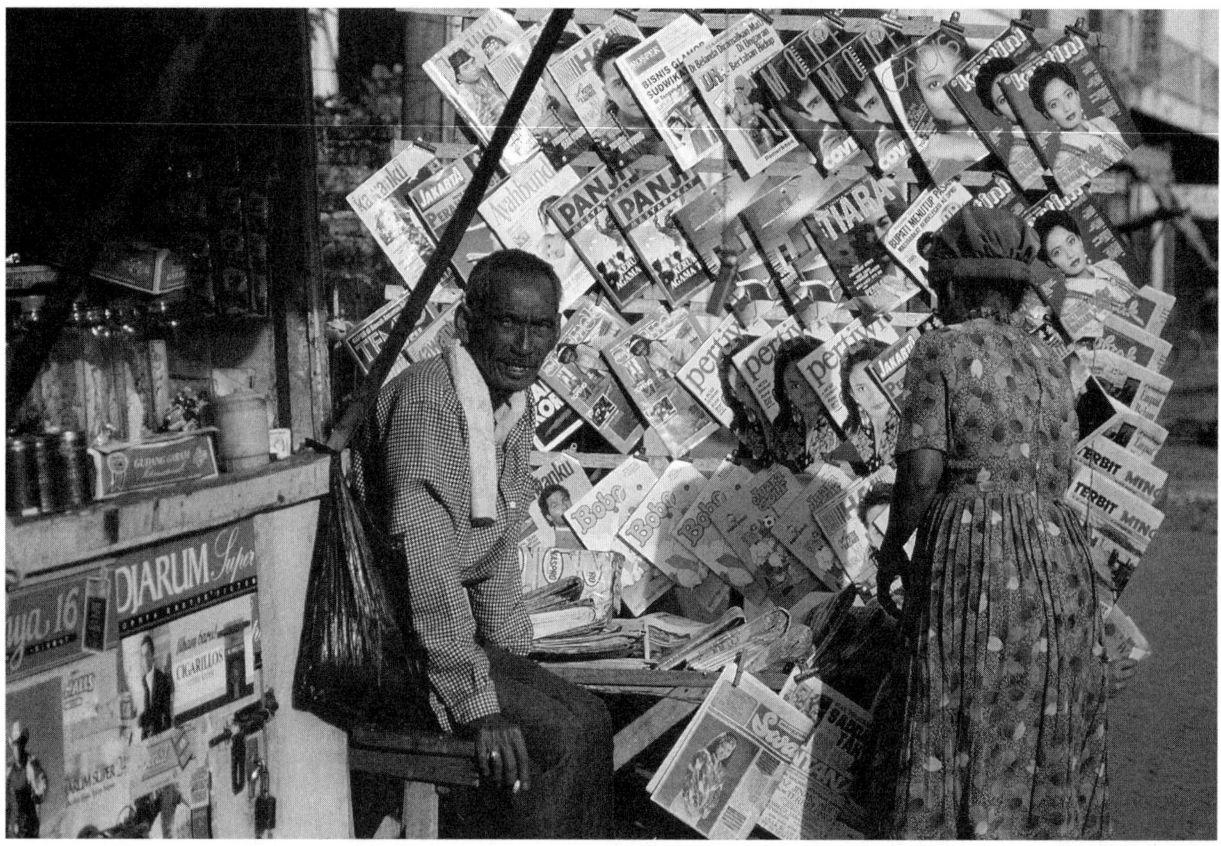

© NIK WHEELER/CORBIS

A woman selects a magazine at a newsstand in Medan, Sumatra, Indonesia.

selves are trying to deal with this problem, and visitors are encouraged to respect the efforts to eliminate corruption. People in low-paid positions appreciate small tips or other token gifts; officials or businesspeople who insist on larger, payments know full-well that it is wrong; if there is resistance, they will usually cease their demands.

QUALITY OF LIFE

Medan is a pleasant residential city. What are considered the elite residential areas are the most attractive parts of the city, with trees and adequate infrastructure. These areas are occupied mostly by high-ranking government officers, foreigners, and wealthy Chinese.

However, the pressures of a growing population and new development are creating traffic congestion, pollution, excess garbage, illegal settlement, and crime. Medan is a city where every main area is dominated by a group of local bullies known as *preman*. They earn income through the concessions they hold to collect parking fees, usually targeting business areas.

FUTURE OF THE CITY

The development of Medan as a metropolitan area will put more pressure on city government to enforce laws and maintain a better quality of public service. There are several urgent problems in the city that require immediate attention: traffic control, waste management, and enforcement of zoning regulations. Zoning has become an issue as businesses have relocated to the more upscale neighborhoods, bringing with them a host of problems.

Medan also must encourage its many ethnic communities to preserve their traditions and legacies. In addition, the city administration needs to focus on a conservation plan for historical buildings, the center-city area, and the older downtown areas, to safeguard its cultural vibrancy for all members of the community. If Medan fails to maintain and develop its special character, it risks not reaching its potential, and it threatens to become a city without memories.

BIBLIOGRAPHY

Chopra, Reeta, ed., *Living in Sumatra,* 3d ed. (Medan International School P.T.A. 1994).

Ellisa, Evawani, et al., *A Historical Study of the Urban Area Composition and Character of Medan Town during the End of Colonial Age* (Faculty of Engineering, Osaka University 1995).

Oey, Eric M., ed., *Sumatra, Indonesia,* 2d ed. (Periplus Editions 1996).

Sinar, Tegku Luckman, *The History of Medan: In the Olden Times* (Satgas MABMI 1996).

Siregar, Timbus, *Sejarah Kota Medan* (1980).

HASTI TAREKAT

Medellín

Colombia

ORIENTATION

Name of City. The capital of the department of Antioquia, Colombia, Medellín was originally named Villa de Nuestra Señora de la Candelaria de Medellín. The city is now referred to by locals and outsiders simply as Medellín.

Location. Medellín is located at 6°25′ north latitude and 76° west longitude, in the northwestern corner of South America.

Population. In 2000 the population of the metropolitan area was approximately 3.24 million, distributed in the ten municipalities of Caldas, La Estrella, Sabaneta, Itagüí, Envigado, Medellín, Bello, Copacabana, Girardota, and Barbosa. Of these, 2.02 million live in Medellín.

Distinctive and Unique Features. Medellín lies in the Aburrá Valley, an elongated depression with an area of 1,152 square kilometers (445 square miles) and an altitude that ranges between 1,400 and 1,800 meters (4,600 and 5,900 feet). The valley is surrounded by mountains about 1,000 meters (3,280 feet) higher, with the highest points reaching an altitude above 3,000 meters (9,800 feet). Outside of the valley, northeast of the city, is a region of high-altitude hills and plains known as the Oriente. Rionegro is the largest town in this region. Oriente is an important producer of agricultural goods for Medellín. The ten municipalities that form the metropolitan area are located along the Medellín River, which runs through the valley. The waters of the Iguana and the Santa Elena streams feed the Medellín River in the central part of the valley. The three hills of El Salvador, El Volador, and El Cerro Nutibara provide spectacular views of the valley. With an average temperature of 22°C (72°F) and highest and lowest temperatures of 29° and 16°C (84° and 60°F) respectively, the city has a very comfortable climate and is referred to as the City of Eternal Spring.

The Aburrá Valley is situated on the highlands of the Cordillera Central, one of the three Andean mountain ranges that traverse Colombia. This location has resulted in the city's access to a wide range of resources from the various climatic and topographic zones that surround it. To the west is the valley of the Cauca River and to the east is the valley of the Magdalena River. These valleys and the slopes of Cordillera Central provide the city with a great diversity of resources that have stimulated and supported its growth. The exploitation of these resources has depended on the development of transportation networks to link the mountain-locked city with other regions.

Attractions of the City. Despite its natural landscapes and many urban attractions, Medellín has traditionally drawn few tourists. Churches are the oldest structures standing in the city. La Veracruz and San Benito churches, built in the late 17th century, are among the oldest. The two largest churches today are La Candelaria, completed in 1776, and the Metropolitan Cathedral, finished in 1930. The latter is regarded as the largest sun-dried-brick church in South America. Among the major attractions of the city are the floral varieties found in the region and in the city's botanical garden, which houses Medellín's renown orchids. The Cerro Nutibara is an important attraction not only for the view of the city the hill provides but also because it has a replica of a typical Antioquian town and the Park of Sculptures, in which are displayed works by South American artists. The city's museums exhibit the works of new local artists as well as that of nationally and internationally established ones such as Debora Arango, Pedro Nel Gómez, Rodrigo Arenas Betancur, Eladio Velez, and Fernando Botero. Many of these artists' murals and sculptures can be appreciated in the city's plazas, public buildings, and universities. After being destroyed by a bomb, the remains of *El Pãjaro* (*The Bird,* subsequently referred to as *The Dove of Peace*) one of Botero's sculptures, stand in the piece's original location in the Plazuela San Antonio, across from the police headquarters, as witness to the violent processes that have shaped the city's recent past.

Relationships Between the City and the Outside. The land of the Aburrá Valley was increasingly transformed into pastureland during the colonial period, and by the early 20th century, families had begun to cultivate coffee to supplement household income. In the 20th century the processes of urbanization and industrialization account for inmigration to, and further transformation of, the valley. A major implication of these processes is that the bulk of what is consumed in Medellín today comes from outside of the valley, mostly from the Magdalena and Cauca valleys and the agricultural lands of the slopes of the Cordillera Central. The region surrounding Aburrá is a primary source of hydroelectric power for the city. These elements suggest the close ecological connections between Medellín and the larger mountainous territory of the department. In addition, the city's elites and working class turned Medellín into a center of industrial and commercial activity that has been linked to global trade networks of products such as gold, coffee, and cocaine.

Major Languages. Spanish is the nation's official language and is the principal language spoken in Medellín.

HISTORY

The Origin of the City. Northeastern Antioquia was one of the main sources of gold for the Spanish empire during the early colonial period. Santa Fe de Antioquia was founded as the province's capital and a center of colonial administration, which was dominated by a slave-owning elite. At this time, the Aburrá Valley attracted only a few settlers and was used as pastureland by the wealthy from Santa Fe de Antioquia. The valley did not have the large numbers of indigenous peoples as a potential labor force that attracted settlers elsewhere. During the first quarter of the 17th century, gold production in northeastern Antioquia ceased, while new sources were discovered in the streams and rivers of the central region of Antioquia near the Aburrá Valley. In 1675, the settlers attracted to the valley by this new gold boom founded the town of Nuestra Señora de la Candelaria de Medellín.

Colonial Period. This new era was characterized by the widespread mining of riverbeds, which made it difficult for a few individuals to control gold sources. Rather than a powerful mining aristocracy, Medellín saw the rise of a merchant class that supplied a dispersed class of miners and bought their gold dust. Its mountain-locked location favored the control of importation and commercialization of goods in mining districts by city residents rather than outsiders. The risks involved in mining operations and in long-distance trade extended the miner-merchant nexus to include a large set of social exchanges. The well-being of merchants and the flourishing commercial of activity in the city rested on the gold dust extracted by small groups of slaves and independent miners. Most city residents had access to land and were self-sufficient in foodstuffs. Powerful landowners owned vast extensions of land throughout the province.

This pattern of mining and access to land inhibited the emergence of one small dominant elite. Merchants did figure as the most prosperous and better off sector of the population, followed by miners and farmers. Whites of Spanish descent constituted the wealthiest sector, having exploited the labor of black slaves, indigenous peoples, and poor mestizos, or people of mixed Spanish and indigenous descent.

19th and 20th Centuries. During the 19th century Medellín merchants invested in export booms of several agricultural products, but their most successful enterprise was coffee production. Medellín served as the base for expansion of the coffee frontier and as its main point of commercialization. Throughout Antioquia and south of the department, pioneering families cleared the forest and opened farms dedicated primarily to coffee production. As market opportunities opened up in Europe and North America, Antioquia consolidated as the principal coffee exporter during the first decades of the 20th century. A familiar pattern emerged wherein small coffee farms were integrated into global trade networks through the role of Medellín merchants in advancing resources to settlers and purchasing and exporting the coffee they produced. Merchants did not constitute a specialized class. The elite that emerged diversified its investment in commerce, agriculture, and industrial production. Capital from coffee exports subsidized the early industrialization of the city. During the first two decades of the 20th century, Medellín investors accomplished the task of introducing mechanical looms to the highlands of the Aburrá Valley. At the same time, location of the valley helped industrial elites to protect the local market for industrial products from foreign competitors. Throughout most of the 20th century, Medellín was Colombia's leading industrial city and one of Latin America's leaders in textile production. Northeastern Antioquia continues to be a major source of gold: about 70% of the nation's gold originates in Antioquia.

Migration: Past and Present. During the first decades of the 20th century, with the growth of the coffee-export economy and the consolidation of the city as a center of industrial production, immigration from rural regions of the department was the main factor behind demographic growth. In 1905 the valley had a population of 105,305 inhabitants, 59,815 of whom resided in Medellín. The first generations of textile workers were predominately women who were often recruited in rural areas. During the period known as La Violencia, from the late 1940s to the late 1950s, immigration to the city intensified as a result of political violence in the countryside in which 200,000 people (by conservative estimates) were killed. With the demographic and industrial growth of the 1950s and 1960s, Medellín consolidated as the center of a large metropolitan area. By 1964, the population of the Aburrá Valley was 1,084,660 inhabitants, of which 772,887 lived in Medellín. While the first waves of migrants originated in the mountainous territory of the department, during the second half of the century migrants originated both in highland and lowland territories. Violence in the countryside continues to be a major force for migration. During 1998, 5,000 families fled to the city to escape violence in the countryside. This is only a fraction of the calculated 300,000 people displaced from their homes that year. Humanitarian aid organizations estimate that the number of displaced persons had reached 1.5 million by 2000.

People from Medellín have led waves of migration to other countries. During the 1970s, Venezuela was the principal destination. The east coast of the United States quickly replaced it. Miami, Chicago, and New York City are today the main destinations for migrants from Medellín and other parts of the country.

INFRASTRUCTURE

Public Buildings, Public Works, and Residences. The enclosure of the valley by high mountains put a limit to the access to flat land for the horizontal expansion of the city. Urban sprawl marked the city's growth during the second half of the 20th century, when people displaced by violence from the countryside occupied the hills on the outskirts of Medellín. This resulted in irregular settlements with substandard housing and without access to some of the basic public services. The highest buildings are located in the central part of the city. They consist mainly of official and private office buildings. Resembling a needle, the 35-floor Coltejer building is the tallest structure in the city. It is the headquarters of the Compañia Colombiana de Tejidos, a leader in the industrialization of the city and in textile production in Latin America. Large official buildings such as the Palacio Nacional, Palacio Municipal, and Gobernación served until recently as the administrative and political centers of local, departmental, and national governments. Preserving their architectural styles, these edifices were recently renovated and function now as commercial centers or as cultural and educational institutions. All government offices are now located in the Centro Administrativo La Alpujarra, a recently constructed multiblock area. This complex was built at the site of the historic Medellín railroad station, which connected the city with the Magdalena Valley and which during the first half of the 20th century was the exclusive means of transportation and linkage with international markets.

The local government has played a central role in the development of public services. By 1918, public services were administered directly by the local government. The negative impact of political conflicts on the administration of public services during the 1930s and 1940s favored a movement toward a more decentralized system that culminated with the creation of the Empresas Públicas de Medellín in 1958. This was conceived as an autonomous and decentralized company that could be free from the contingencies of a public administration dependent on the patronage system of local politics. The Empresas Publicas de Medellín brought together four companies that provided electricity, water, sewage, and telephones. Of this, the Empresa de Energía Electrica was the most important and the chief support of the Empresas Publicas de Medellín. The latter has remained in Latin America an example of an efficiently run public company and a main source of revenues for the city's government. The infrastructure for the aqueduct was installed in the 1940s. Until the early 1960s there was no centralized system for the recollection and processing of sewage, which was for the most part dumped into the rivers. Electric energy and telephones are the most developed public works. Since the early 20th century the city has enjoyed a relatively regular and stable flow of electric energy. An automated telephone system has existed since the 1940s. Recent projects by the Empresas Públicas de Medellín include the replacement of copper conductors with fiber optic cables in the communication network and the expansion of the domestic use of natural gas. According to official figures, Medellín's need for electric energy is met 100%; water, 99.2%; sewers, 95%; and telephones 87%.

Housing throughout the metropolitan area has consisted principally of one- and two-story constructions. Since the mid-1980s, apartment buildings have mushroomed through the valley. Many of these are being created in the form of exclusive apartment complexes.

Politics and City Services. The country's political system rests on a two-party system dominated by the Liberal and Conservative parties. Medellín and the region of Antioquia have traditionally been Conservative Party strongholds. The clientelistic and patronage bases of the political system mean that access to resources and social services is often mediated by political contacts. Opposition parties have had a minimal impact on this structure, but peace negotiations with several guerrilla groups culminated in the writing of a new national constitution in 1991. This constitution established the direct election of mayors, who until then had been appointed officials. The mayor and the Concejo Municipal govern each municipality. The council members who are also elected officials make up the Concejo Municipal.

The national political system has been characterized by the concentration of political power in Bogotá, the country's capital. But a process of decentralization that includes municipal autonomy in designing local development has been taking place since 1990. Discussions about development in Medellín take the notion of human rights as a starting point. These include the basic socioeconomic needs of the population as well as those related to the protection of the noncombatant population in the current armed conflict, of which Antioquia is one of the main arenas. The state, right-wing paramilitary organizations, primarily the United Self-Defense Forces of Colombia (AUC), and the leftist guerrilla Army of National Liberation (ELN) and the Revolutionary Armed Forces of Colombia (FARC) are the central armed parties to this conflict. Most of Antioquia is engulfed in this conflict, and the future of the city and of the country will likely be determined by the outcome of the current efforts to find a political solution to this conflict.

Educational System. The educational system is organized in three levels. The basic primary level starts at age 6 and consists of five years of schooling. It is followed by four years at the basic secondary level and two years at the intermediate level, in which emphasis is placed on technical education. In 1999 the number of children who did not make it into the educational system was 32,608, or 13.58%; 24,709, or 15.8%; and 12,514, or 20%, for each level respectively. The city has eight major universities offering bachelor's, master's, and a growing number of doctoral programs. The University of Antioquia occupies a central role in the region's education and has served as the springboard for the emergence of private universities such as the Universidad Pontificia Bolivariana (founded in 1936), which has a Catholic orientation, and the Universidad de Medellín (founded in 1950), with a liberal orientation. These developments reflected changes in the political orientation of the university as well as in the composition of the student body. The University of Antioquia has from its origins educated the region's elites and become one of the largest public universities in the nation, offering members of the middle and lower classes a professional education.

Transportation System. In November 1995 the first metro system in Colombia was inaugurated in Medellín. It consists of one main, 23-kilometer- (14-mile-) long surface line running between the south end and the north end of the Aburrá Valley. The 5-kilometer- (3-mile-) long section in the center of the city runs on an elevated viaduct. A second 6-kilometer- (3.7-mile-) long line connects the western side of Medellín to the center of the city and to the main metro line. Privately operated bus and minibus companies that link the municipalities of the valley and Medellín's neighborhoods with the center of the city complement this system. With the construction of the metro there has been a reorganization in the flow of traffic and the pedestrianization of the central part of the city. Two bus terminals at both ends of the city provide service to Antioquia's municipalities and major Colombian cities. A railroad line built in the early 20th century provides service toward the Magdalena River valley. National and international flights use the José María Córdoba Airport, built in 1985, in Rionegro. Its construction left the Olaya Herrera airport, located in the center of the Aburrá Valley, for the use of only non-jet aircraft, mainly for departmental flights.

CULTURAL AND SOCIAL LIFE

Distinctive Features of the City's Cultures. Medellín is often perceived as having a traditional and parochial social and cultural life owing to its mountain-locked location, strong Catholic tradition, and feelings of self-sufficiency, which have at times stimulated a federalist sentiment. The close relationship between city and countryside resulted in a sense of identity that emphasizes the region rather than the city. Families trace their roots to particular towns in Antioquia, and rural traditions shape the culture of the city. In fact, inhabitants of the city do not perceive themselves as possessing a unique and separate cultural identity but instead see themselves as part of the larger cultural complex of the region. Rather than using the term *Medellínense,* they use *Antioqueño* or *paisa* to define themselves. *Antioqueño* refers to the inhabitants of the department, while *paisa* is a more inclusive concept that extends to the coffee-producing region of the Cordillera Central. These concepts emphasize hardworking and entrepreneurial characteristics assigned to *paisa* culture.

Cuisine. While the city enjoys access to a rich variety of fruits, vegetables, roots, and meats, most people's diet consists of a basic combination of beans and carbohydrates. Middle- and upper-class residents find an increasing number of restaurants in upscale neighborhoods that offer all kinds of international dishes. *Arepa* (corn bread) and *sancocho* (meat-and-potato stew), are the most typical elements of *paisa* cuisine. A significant part of social life takes place around *tintos,* small cups of black coffee. A *tinto* is offered to visiting friends or relatives or during business occasions, or is consumed in cafés where people gather to socialize.

Ethnic, Class, and Religious Diversity. Although there are a growing number of people converting to Protestant religions, most of the city's residents ascribe to the more traditional values of the Roman Catholic Church. The great majority of the city's inhabitants derive their ethnicity from the physical and cultural fusion of Spanish, indigenous, and African traditions. However, Antioquia is regarded as one of the departments with a greater percentage of whites. These religious and ethnic elements combine to form an ideology about the superiority of a *paisa* race. This ideology emphasizes a *paisa* work ethic and entrepreneurial spirit, church-sanctioned marriages, and white Hispanic values. It de-emphasizes indigenous and African traditions. This ideology is also used to distinguish the *paisa* race from people in other parts of the country and especially from the provinces' frontiers in the lowlands where indigenous, African, and non-Catholic values have greater acceptance.

Socioeconomic differences are more evident in housing and patterns of occupation of the valley. Three distinctions can be made. First, while historically the wealthiest families lived in the center of the city, more recently upscale neighborhoods, such as El Poblado, a high-market residential area with the best hotels and restaurants in the city, sprung up away from the city's center. Second, the majority of immigrants of the turn of the 20th century who became the working class of the textile industries occupied and transformed the villages of the valley into bustling industrial centers. Bello in the north and Itagüi in the south became the largest working-class municipalities in the metropolitan area. Third, the immigrants of the second half of the 20th century who settled in the irregular settlements on the unstable ground of the hill slopes around the city gave rise to large, poor neighborhoods known as *comunas.* A stark contrast exists between the *comunas* and the rest of the city. While their streets may be paved and their houses may have drinking water and electricity, *comuna* residents are politically, socially, and culturally disenfranchised. These neighborhoods have become recruiting grounds for organizations involved in drug trafficking, as well as the focus of state repression.

Family and Other Social Support Systems. In meeting the needs of daily life and long-term goals, extended families and kinship networks have been the most important resources. These networks typically connect people from the city and the countryside and are used to exchange goods, information, and help in times of crisis and as a resource to meet employment or educational goals. In addition to immediate relatives, households frequently include distant relatives and married siblings and their children. Children are not expected to establish independent households once they reach maturity. It is more often the case that single adult children remain in the household.

Neighborhood associations are also a crucial source of support. Promoted by the national government, the Acción Comunal usually serves as an intermediary between local communities and municipal resources. Commonly these associations recruit voluntary labor and the local government supplies the materials or additional labor for works to improve the neighborhood. They provide a series of social services for the community and often serve as stepping-stones into local politics.

Many of the city's poor typically meet their needs with the assistance furnished by the Catholic church and benevolent organizations. In fact, in order to offset a discourse of class struggle, the church and industrial elites have historically promoted a paternalistic relationship with the working classes in which elites cultivated an image of themselves as benevolent and philanthropic. The Sociedad San Vicente de Paul plays a major role in providing educational and health services to the poor, as have various orders of nuns.

Work and Commerce. Manufacturing represents the largest sector of the city's economy: 80% of the textiles produced nationally are produced in Medellín, representing half of the industrial activity of the city. The other main industries of the city are the production of plastics, leather, bricks, food, metals, and chemicals. As a result of the negative impact of the neoliberal reforms of the late 20th century on local industries, principally the textile industry, unemployment rates have steadily risen. These reforms have greatly undermined the achievements of organized labor. Job stability is today one of the major issues for workers in the industrial sector, as well as for professional employees. Temporary contracts without basic benefits are the principal form of employment.

The informal economic sector provides employment and subsistence for a large segment of the population. This includes petty commerce in foods and goods in street stands and in small and medium-size stores and markets functioning out of people's homes. More formalized retail businesses constitute a substantial sector of the city's commercial activity. In addition to major store chains and financial institutions, in Medellín and all the municipalities of the metropolitan area a great number of retail businesses can be found. Contraband trade fuels a significant number of these, especially those dealing in electronic products. More recently, giant home-furnishing stores selling unassembled furniture and large shopping malls have been become part of the city's commercial landscape.

Arts and Recreation. Medellín has a vibrant artistic and cultural life. In addition to several major theaters that offer international and national artistic performances, the city has a large number of movie theaters offering commercial and artistic film productions. It also has many local theater companies. While these activities are predominant among the city's middle class, student population, and intellectuals, a significant number of festivals and public events attempt to bring the arts to a wider audience. One example is the International Poetry Festival, which was founded in 1991 and conceived as an alternative to the intolerance and violence present in the city. Its first version in 1991 had the

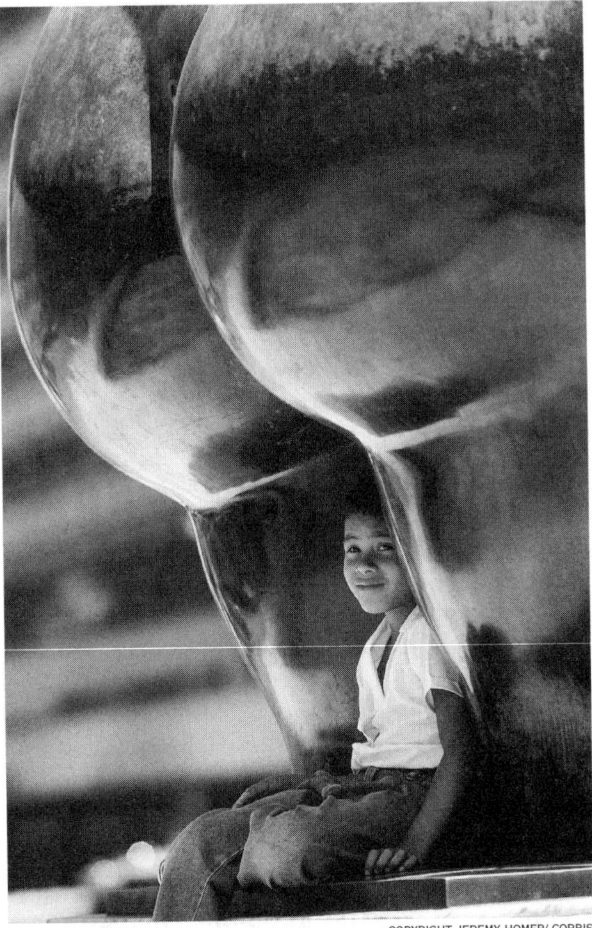

COPYRIGHT JEREMY HOMER/ CORBIS

A boy sits inside a sculpture by Fernando Botero in the Colombian city of Medellín, Antioquia.

participation of 13 poets from Colombia and a combined audience of 1,500 people. The 11th festival in 2001 had the participation of 101 poets from 69 countries representing the five continents, recitals in several towns of Antioquia and other cities of the country, and a combined audience well beyond 100,000 people. The Desfile de Silleteros parade, the main event of the one-week-long Feria de las Flores ("Flower Festival"), is one of the most traditional public events of the city. Families in the colder plains in the east grow flowers that are used to create large designs in mounted frames that participants carry on their backs during the parade through the city's main streets.

Traditionally, Mexican bullfights and Argentine tango music have been a dominant part of popular culture in Medellín. The death of Argentinean Carlos Gardel, tango's most prominent interpreter, in Medellín in 1935 is a significant popular memory, and the city is today known as the Capital of Tango. But soccer is the chief form of popular recreation, especially among the male population. Weekend trips to the towns outside of the valley and especially to the Oriente region is a main form of recreation, particularly for the city's middle class.

QUALITY OF LIFE

Although Medellín continues to enjoy the reputation as the City of Eternal Spring, it faces growing problems of air pollution and contamination of waters resulting from car exhaust and industrial waste. In fact, respiratory infections are a leading health issue. Most important, however, are the social dislocations produced by economic inequalities. Although the city has outstanding medical centers where pioneering surgical procedures have been conducted, the poorest sectors of the population have no access to health services, live in substandard and crowded housing units, and have minimal educational services. Of the 21% of children under age five suffering from malnutrition in Angioquia, 2.2% reside in the Aburrá Valley. Even the formally employed working classes with access to health benefits find these services threatened by the current process of privatization of medicine.

Violence has been a major factor affecting quality of life in the city. The cocaine economy and the violence generated by the Medellín cartel served as a catalyst for various forms of preexisting organized crime, stimulated the spread of vigilante groups as the means for the solution of interpersonal and social conflicts, and undermined the culture of paternalism and deference toward upper classes. In the poor neighborhoods surrounding the city, the new generations of youth with few social alternatives became stigmatized as the carriers of violence and disorder in the city. Many of them organized in bands and joined the opportunities offered by the Medellín cartel as paid killers, bodyguards, or drug carriers. But, most significantly, entry to the underground economy seemingly afforded these generations the means to achieve the cultural expectations of the *paisa* ethos: entrepreneurship, economic improvement, and the ability to gain dignity by providing basic resources to their families. Members of these organized bands were in fact notorious for their religiosity and devotion to the Virgin Mary.

An open confrontation between state forces and the Medellín cartel created a state of war during the late 1980s and early 1990s. The weak state presence in the poorest neighborhoods of the city, and the state's inability to regulate social relations or to punish criminal activity, have facilitated the operation of death squads that in numerous massacres claimed the lives of mainly young males in Medellín's poor neighborhoods. Combined with the assassination of political and civic leaders and repression of popular social movements, this created what came to be known as a culture of fear. It also reinforced the belief in the existence of violence as an inevitable phenomenon as well as its tolerance in daily life. The death of Pablo Escobar, the Medellín cartel's leader, in December 1993 and disarmament agreements with these bands in 1994, some of which had taken a more social and political projection, led to a decline in violent confrontations. At the same time, the destruction of the Medellí cartel gave rise to a large number of dispersed armed organizations.

Another major result of the cocaine economy has been the increase in the value of real estate. People associated with the drug trade become prolific spenders who indicate their achievement through conspicuous consumption. One main area of investment has been real estate, which has had the impact of making housing less affordable for the majority of the population.

FUTURE OF THE CITY

The demise of the Medellín cartel did not end the cocaine economy. There is no doubt that the future of the city, and of the country, will be greatly shaped by the issues concerning the drug trade. But the future of the city has to be considered also in the context of the armed political conflicts taking place in Colombia today and the basic socioeconomic conditions of the population. The battles between guerrilla organizations, right-wing paramilitary forces, and the national army for control of the rural areas of Antioquia department causes the internal displacement of thousands of people who then view Medellín as a haven. The expansion of this war toward the Aburrá Valley, the disruption of transportation and productive and extractive industries in rural areas, and waves of internal refugees make the future of this conflict a central theme for the city. This situation is aggravated by reforms that undermine stable employment and seek the privatization of basic social services: in just a decade alone, official unemployment rates in Medellín increased almost 70%, from 12.4% in 1990 to 20.8% in June 2000. The latter translates to a figure of some 280,577 economically active but unemployed people.

The city also faces many other challenges. The 20th century was marked by a process of rapid population growth in the Aburrá Valley. Growth in the 21st century will need to seek a balance between demographic growth and the likely environmental degradation to occur. Pollution, contamination of waters, deforestation, and levels of noise and congestion will undoubtedly become more salient issues in the future. Many local governments are already discussing the need to put limits on the vertical growth of their cities. Pronounced industrial and demographic expansion is likely to take place in the Oriente region. The construction of rapid means of transportation, such as tunnels, between this region and Medellín are already under discussion and will probably become major infrastructural projects of future governments.

BIBLIOGRAPHY

Abad Gomez, Hector, "Public Health Problems in Medellín," *Cities in Crisis: The Urban Challenge in the Americas,* ed. by Matthew Edel and Ronald G. Hellman (Bildner Center for Western Hemisphere Studies 1989).

Farnsworth-Alvear, Ann, *Dulcinea in the Factory: Myths, Morals, Men, and Women in Colombia's Industrial Experiment, 1905–1960* (Duke University Press 2000).

Melo, Jorge Orlando, ed., *Historia de Medellín,* 2 vols. (Compañia Suramericana de Seguros 1996).

Roldan, Mary, "Colombia: Cocaine and the 'Miracle' of Modernity in Medellín," *Cocaine. Global Histories,* ed. by Paul Gootenber (Routledge 1999).

Salazar, Alonso J., *Born to Die in Medellín,* tr. by Nick Caistor (Latin America Bureau 1992).

Twinam, Ann, *Miners, Merchants, and Farmers in Colonial Colombia* (University of Texas Press 1982).

León Arredondo

Melbourne

Australia

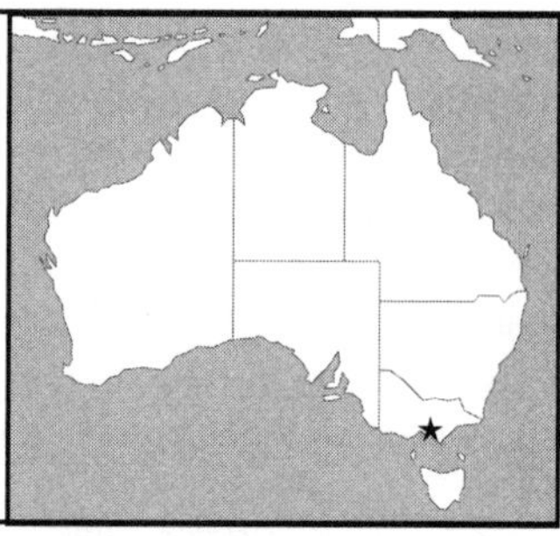

ORIENTATION

Name of City. Melbourne is the name that British settlers in Australia gave to the village they established in 1835 on the banks of the Yarra River, at the head of Port Phillip Bay (so-named by European explorers in 1802), on the southeastern tip of mainland Australia. It became the hub for settlement of what eventually became the state of Victoria. Melbourne took its name from the British prime minister at the time of its foundation, William Lamb, 2nd Viscount Melbourne. The name was chosen in 1837 by the governor of New South Wales, of which the new settlement was then a part. These British names overlay others that had been used by the aboriginal Kulin people for thousands of years. The Woiworung tribes called the Yarra River the Birrarang, and the European town site had been used by the Kulin for generations as an interclan meeting place.

Location. The city is located at 37°49′ south latitude and 144°58′ east longitude, on the southeastern edge of mainland Australia. It has a temperate climate with four distinct seasons. Melbourne comprises a metropolitan field of some 7,800 square kilometers (3,000 square miles), which extends for over 40 kilometers (19 miles) along the bay to the south, ripples against the picturesque Dandenong Ranges

30 kilometers (19 miles) to the east, and spreads another 25 kilometers (15 miles) to the north and 30 kilometers across the flat plain lands to the west.

Population. The Australian Bureau of Statistics estimated the population of metropolitan Melbourne in June 1999 as 3.4 million people. About 187,000 of these inhabitants live within a 5-kilometer (3-mile) radius of the General Post Office, but the overwhelming majority of Melburnians live in sprawling, low-density suburbs. Melbourne is the capital of Victoria, and contains a remarkable 73% of the state's total population. The city has the lowest proportion of Aboriginal residents of any Australian capital city but is a mecca for immigrants. Almost 1 million Melburnians were born overseas, and the city is home to the highest proportion of southern European migrants—especially Italians and Greeks—in Australia.

Distinctive and Unique Features. Melbourne sprawls across a wide basin at the apex of one of the world's largest bays, Port Phillip Bay. Yet it is Melbourne's cultural landscape that gives the city its distinctiveness. Melbourne encapsulates the historical processes of European expansionism that created a global network of "instant cities" in the core regions of New World European settlement during the 19th century. Melbourne's significant place within this trend was recognized by the British historian Asa Briggs, who devoted a chapter to the city (his only non-British case study) in his seminal book *Victorian Cities.*

The cultural landscape of Melbourne contains many diverse elements, but three deserve special mention. First, there are the landscape and architectural survivals of 19th-century city building. This historical landscape has a cohesion anchored in a symmetrical rectangular grid of land allotments, delineated by wide streets and softened by an abundance of parks and gardens. The grid plan of central Melbourne, formulated by government surveyor Robert Hoddle in 1837, has become famous in the history of town planning. The second distinctive element of Melbourne's cultural landscape is suburban sprawl, which found early expression in an extravagant house-building boom during the 1880s and was reinforced by what historians have called the spread of the "cream brick frontier" during the 20th century. Melbourne is, appropriately, the setting for the long-running and internationally popular television drama series *Neighbours,* and the original kitchen set is preserved in Museum Victoria as an icon of Australian suburbia. The *Australian* newspaper recently commented that Melbourne "is the city where the great Australian dream of owning your own home is at its healthiest." This dream—of a detached, owner-occupied house on a suburban "quarter-acre block"—continues strongly into the 21st century, with the fastest population growth (at a national as well as a local level) occurring on Melbourne's fringe. The third element has its origins in the late 20th century: Melbourne has begun to turn itself outside in. The middle-lying suburbs of the cream brick frontier that boomed during the third quarter of the 20th century have lost population since the 1990s, whereas the inner suburbs and the city center—which had lost population for generations—are now gaining population at a rapid rate.

Attractions of the City. The Victorian State Government and the City of Melbourne ambitiously seek to make Melbourne the business center of the southern hemisphere. The city enjoys an excellent strategic location in the Asia-Pacific region, its port

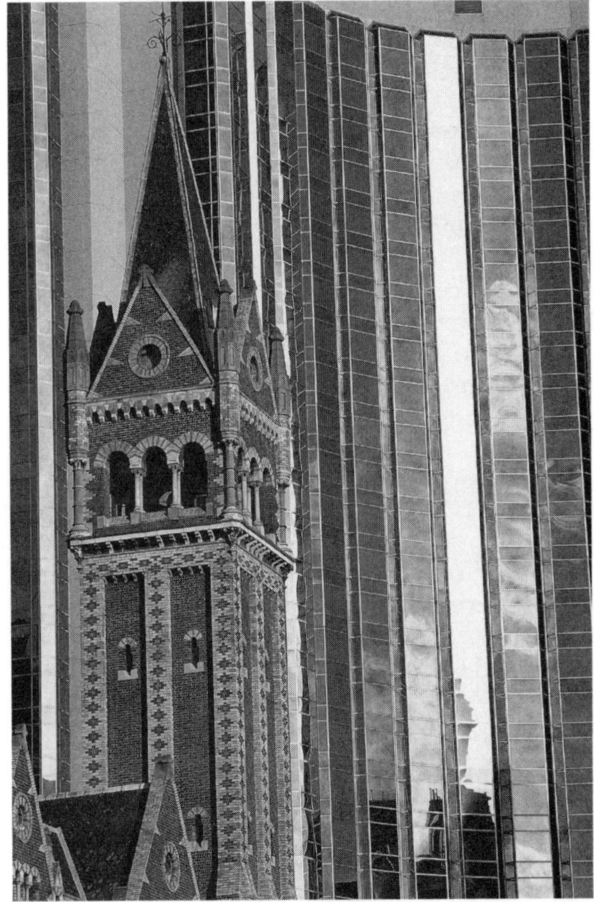

© PAUL A. SOUDERS/CORBIS

Modern Hyatt hotel tower stands in contrast to Victorian-style building, Melbourne, Australia.

is the largest in the nation, and it boasts a sophisticated industry base and a skilled workforce. Using indicators such as business costs, crime rates, infrastructure, research investment, and cultural life, international surveys have identified Melbourne as one of the best places to live in Southeast Asia.

Tourists visiting Melbourne, and Melburnians themselves, relish other features of the city. The whole is a cultural heritage artifact, with a rich assemblage of historical structures that range from tiny 19th-century workers' cottages to the majestic 1880 Royal Exhibition Building. Tree-lined boulevards such as St. Kilda Road and Royal Parade, products of garden-city planning early in the 20th century, and a multiplicity of parks and gardens—the highlight among which is the Royal Botanic Gardens—balance the built environment. Melbourne regards itself as Australia's center for the arts, gastronomy, and sport. It hosts the Melbourne International Festival of the Arts and the International Comedy Festival as well as major sports events such as the Australian Open tennis championships, the Australian Formula 1 Grand Prix, the Australian Football League Grand Final, and the Melbourne Cup horse race.

Relationships Between the City and the Outside. Melbourne dominates its region and is well anchored in international networks in terms of trade and immigration. Australia's foremost city in the 19th century, it lost that position to Sydney early in the 20th century, and it has ever afterward competed vigorously to regain the lead. The rivalry between these two cities is intense. Many observers, however, reviewing demographic, social, and economic trends since the late 1990s, have concluded that Melbourne's challenge has failed and that Sydney has consolidated itself as Australia's one truly global city.

Major Languages. English is the official language. Nevertheless, Melbourne is home to over 140 ethnic groups, and community languages are actively supported by all tiers of government.

HISTORY

The Origin of the City. When Europeans first explored Port Phillip Bay, the surrounding region was occupied by a constellation of Aboriginal tribes comprising the Kulin peoples. Two tribes, the Woiworung and the Bunurong, had custodianship of the lands where central Melbourne now stands, and the Woiworung clan group called the Wurundjeri occupied the site where European settlement began.

The first British settlement at Port Phillip Bay (on its southeast, near present-day Sorrento) was authorized by the British government in 1803. It was a failure. The second attempted settlement, in 1835, was illegal. It was undertaken by adventurers from Van Diemen's Land (Tasmania), across Bass Strait, in search of new grazing lands. This was the beginning of present-day Melbourne. The new settlement's legitimacy was grudgingly conceded by the colonial authorities in Sydney in 1836. Fewer than 200 people then lived in the infant township. Melbourne prospered as the gateway through which sheep farmers and cattlemen settled the interior, and by 1851, when Melbourne became the capital of the autonomous colony of Victoria, it had grown into a substantial town of 20,000–30,000 inhabitants.

Migration: Past and Present. The discovery of gold in Victoria in 1851 transformed Melbourne from a town to a metropolis. Over half a million immigrants from around the world came to Victoria during the 1850s. Most arrived via Melbourne, and many settled there. By 1861 its population had swollen to over 123,000 people, making it the largest city in Australia. Only three decades later, in 1891, its population was nudging the half-million mark. Mass migration had transformed a township into the 22d-largest city in the world: larger than Madras; larger than Boston; larger than old European cities such as Madrid, Brussels, or Naples; larger than Birmingham, the third-most-populous city in England. Known as "Marvellous Melbourne" (a sobriquet coined by the visiting English writer George Augustus Sala in 1885), Melbourne became Australia's national capital on Federation in 1901. It remained so until the seat of government was transferred to the purpose-built capital city of Canberra in 1927.

After the shadow of world depression and war, Melbourne—which by 1947 numbered 1.25 million people—was transformed by a new immigration wave. Nearly 5 million immigrants settled permanently in Australia between 1947 and 1982. Melbourne was the destination for many. A million and a half people lived in Melbourne by the time of the 1956 Melbourne Olympic Games. Twenty years later another million inhabitants had been added to Melbourne's population. A third immigrant wave, this time from Indo-China, was then beginning; it endures to the present day.

Alongside this metahistory of immigration change, internal migration within the Melbourne region dramatically altered the demographic contours of the metropolis. Until the 1880s, 70% of Melburnians lived within the city center and inner ring of suburbs. Melburnians thereafter migrated outward, aided by the development of an extensive cable-tram network from the mid 1880s. By 1901 barely half of metropolitan Melbourne lived within the inner region, and by World War II this proportion had declined to only 10%. From 1947 until 1995, the inner region experienced an absolute decline in population as the outer suburbs continued to boom. Significantly, in 1960, the private car overtook public transport as Melbourne's main transport mode, and in the same year the massive car-centered suburban Chadstone shopping center (Australia's largest) opened for business.

International and intrametropolitan migration converge in Melbourne's recent inner-suburban neighborhood history. Population drift from inner Melbourne had provided a context, during the period 1937–1970, for a slum-clearance program (the largest in Australia) that displaced over 10,000 people from supposed slums in the inner region. Migrant settlement (mostly Italian and Greek) in this low-cost housing area during the 1950s and 1960s introduced a lively cosmopolitan character, contradicting the slum stereotypes on which "renewal" projects were based. As one observer noted in 1963, the "city's traditionally cold heart is . . . [now] surrounded by the ebb and flow of Mediterranean life." By that time, more Italians lived in Melbourne than in some major Italian cities, such as Parma. Australians flocked to live alongside them. The inner suburbs were reborn, and in 1969–1970 grassroots mobilization among inner-suburban residents defeated the state government's "urban renewal" plans. A crucial victory had been won.

INFRASTRUCTURE

Public Buildings, Public Works, and Residences. Melbourne retains an impressive variety of historic public buildings within its high-rise central business district. These include Parliament House, the Treasury Building, Town Hall, General Post Office, Public Library, Queen Victoria Market, and a necklace of fine churches and two cathedrals. St. Patrick's Cathedral is the largest Roman Catholic cathedral in Australia. Constructed in 1863–1939, it is one of the finest examples of the Gothic Revival style in the world. St. Paul's Anglican Cathedral was built between 1880 and 1891, with its impressive tall spires added between 1926 and 1931. Also surviving are important public works that highlight the massive infrastructure developments underpinning metropolitan development from the late 19th century into the 20th. Two of the most remarkable are the Spotswood Pumping Station (now part of Museum Victoria), which operated Melbourne's sewerage system from 1897 until 1964, and Victoria Dock, opened in 1893 as the hub of Melbourne's port facilities. Today the latter is the centerpiece of the chic new Melbourne Docklands redevelopment precinct.

Ambitious public works continue to transform the city. The Docklands project, for example, which covers 220 hectares (544 acres) of old docks, has already absorbed approximately A$2.6 billion (U.S.$1.3 billion) of development investment. The A$300-million (U.S.$153-million) Melbourne Museum (center of the multivenue Museum Victoria) also opened in 2000. It is a modernist architectural gem, in happy juxtaposition with the historic Royal Exhibition Building, and contains exhibition spaces designed to be daringly experiential and interactive. Revitalization of the Yarra River embankments is well advanced, with obsolete railway yards replaced by new parks and walkways, the old Customs House refurbished as an immigration museum, the Melbourne Aquarium opened, the National Gallery of Victoria extended, and the adjoining Southgate precinct (comprising residential, retail and office space, and a casino) completed. The culmination of these projects is Federation Square—built to commemorate the centenary of Australian Federation—which includes a vast new museum of Australian art.

Although since the 1970s many affluent residents have been tempted back into the central city and inner suburbs by the restoration of 19th-century terrace rows and, since the easing of zoning restrictions in 1993, by the construction of high-rise luxury apartments and townhouses, two-thirds of Melbourne's population lives in the southeastern suburbs. The City of Melbourne now has one of the fastest rates of population growth of any local government authority in Australia, but 60%–75% of new metropolitan growth is still occurring around the outer fringe, in areas such as Berwick, Narre Warren, and Cranbourne in the southeast and Melton and Werribee in the west.

Politics and City Services. All Melbourne residents 18 years and over participate at three levels of government: local, state, and federal. The City of Melbourne—an area of 36.5 square kilometers (14 square miles)—is administered by the Melbourne City Council. Local government amalgamations across the broader metropolitan area during the mid-1990s generated resentment at the erosion of grass-roots democracy. One symptom of this mood is the Save Our Suburbs movement, which began in 1998 as local residents—mostly in middle-class areas—spoke out against what they saw as overdevelopment and poor design standards.

Educational System. Melbourne enjoys a strong education and training system. An excellent public school system is run by the state government, and it is complemented by a network of private schools. Some of these schools—their uniforms and architecture echoing the old world—have historically formed the pillars of Melbourne's social elite. Nevertheless, there are some state schools (such as Melbourne and MacRobertson high schools) with histories as long and academic results as distinguished as their expensive private counterparts. The metropolis hosts eight major public universities (although no major private ones), including the prestigious University of Melbourne, the second-oldest in Australia, founded in 1853. The higher-education sector attracts many students from overseas.

Transportation System. Melbourne is a car-centered metropolis, with an extensive roadway system that includes the new multibillion-dollar, privately operated City Link tollway network. Rapid suburban growth in the outer metropolitan areas has placed huge pressures on the ancillary road system. Although residents of these growth areas have shunned public transport, Melbourne has an extensive and efficient system of trains, trams, and buses. Melburnians' beloved tramway system—unique in Australia—has its origins in the 19th century, when the city's cable tram network was the largest unified urban-transit system in the world. The system was almost scrapped during the 1950s and 1960s as private car sales boomed, but it has instead been expanded and modernized (including, sadly, the introduction of computerized swipe tickets and elimination of conductors—"connies"—in 1998). The system still runs some of the historic green-and-yellow "W-class" trams built from the 1920s to the 1950s (others have been sold in recent years to North American cities as tourist attractions for a quarter of a million Australian dollars [U.S.$127,000] each). A scattering of modern trams have been transformed by artists and advertisers into eye-catching collages of color and humorous display. Melburnians are rediscovering the bicycle, and over 500 kilometers (310 miles) of bike paths crisscross the metropolis.

© PAUL A. SOUDERS/CORBIS

Passengers wait for a commuter train on platform, Melbourne, Australia.

CULTURAL AND SOCIAL LIFE

Distinctive Features of the City's Cultures. Melbourne is a kaleidoscope of neighborhood cultures. Some are explicit and are given clear focus by being bracketed with a particular street. Brunswick Street in inner-suburban Fitzroy is a reference point for youth cultures; Lygon Street in nearby Carlton is a center of Italian ambience; Little Bourke Street in the city center is the hub of Chinatown; Acland Street in bayside St. Kilda is infused with Jewish character; and in inner-suburban Richmond, the shop signs along Bridge Road are in Vietnamese rather than English. These places are well known, but many others, more subtle and diffuse, are spread throughout the metropolitan region.

There is a renewed vibrancy in the inner-city region. The around-the-clock bustle of the city is the drawing card. As the Melbourne *Age* newspaper commented, "Like pioneers on a new frontier, the young and trendy have discovered the promised land that is Melbourne's inner city. It's now hip to reside within walking distance of the GPO." Old office buildings and warehouses are being recycled as apartments, and new apartment blocks are being built. Supermarkets have reopened in the central business district, and restaurants, late night cafés, bars, theaters, and downtown cinemas are booming.

Cuisine. Melburnian cuisine is an eclectic mix of national traditions. Chinese influence is long established, and Vietnamese, Thai, Malaysian, and Indian cuisines have emerged as major influences over the past 30 years. European cooking traditions have been consolidated by post-1945 immigration, and Italian and Greek styles are especially evident. Turkish and Lebanese foods have become enormously popular as a result of immigration flows from these countries since the 1970s.

The city is regarded as the gastronomic capital of Australia. According to 1998 data, there were over 500 cafés and restaurants in the central business district alone. Notwithstanding the ubiquitous supermarket chains, many Melburnians still visit the produce markets. The best-known of these is the historic Queen Victoria Market ("Viccy Market") in the city center, where stallholders offer a huge selection of fresh fruit, vegetables, fish, meat, and delicatessen items.

Ethnic, Class, and Religious Diversity. Melbourne is a multicultural metropolis. About one-third of Melburnians were born overseas, and they collectively represent over 140 countries. Italians in Melbourne make up the most numerous group from a non-English-speaking background. Melbourne is the largest Greek-speaking city outside Greece. Since the 1970s Vietnamese and Chinese immigrants have greatly outnumbered those from Europe. This ethnic pluralism is mirrored in religious diversity and toleration.

Notwithstanding Australia's reputation as an egalitarian society, class differences are clearly expressed in Melbourne's geography. More highly paid and educated Melburnians are concentrated in the eastern, southern, and inner suburbs. Lower-income families are concentrated around the metropolitan fringe and also persist in "ungentrified" parts of inner suburbs such as Collingwood, Carlton, North Melbourne, Flemington, and Kensington. In some middle-ring suburbs, such as those around Footscray in the west and Heidelberg West in the northeast, low incomes, nonfluency in English, and unemployment overlap.

Family and Other Social Support Systems. Immigrant settlement in Melbourne has been sustained by what may be described as chain migration from particular places overseas. Strong kin networks and grassroots community organization persist in the receiving society. In Melbourne as a whole, however, the traditional family model of two parents with children has eroded since the 1960s. Fertility rates are declining, and the size of families is shrinking. Households comprising childless couples or singles now constitute the largest and fastest-growing household types.

Work and Commerce. From a low point of recession during the early 1990s, Melbourne has experienced continuous and rapid economic growth. Victoria is Australia's manufacturing center. Melbourne is the hub for these activities, and it is the headquarters for the majority of Australia's largest businesses. The city is also the busiest port in Australia and is serviced by more than 40 shipping lines connecting it to over 200 direct-call ports. Melbourne is the center of medical research in Australia, and also of research development in key industries such as biotechnology, telecommunications, food, paper, chemicals, petroleum, transport, and electrical equipment.

Arts and Recreation. Melbourne has long been recognized as a center for the arts. On two occasions, in the 1890s and the 1940s, it decisively influenced Australian painting. During the 1890s the Heidelberg School of artists—including Arthur Streeton, Tom Roberts, Charles Conder, and Frederick McCubbin—created a new style of Australian landscape painted that consolidated national self-identity on the eve of Federation. During the 1940s another radical trend in Australian art—this time associated with Sidney Nolan, Albert Tucker, John Perceval, and Arthur Boyd—developed in Melbourne. Both of these traditions are highlighted at the National Gallery of Victoria, and the Heide Museum of Modern Art.

Music, ballet, theater, and creative writing flourish. A distinctive Australian style of academic history was developed there, associated with Manning Clark and Geoffrey Blainey (both historians of Australia) and Greg Dening, Rhys Issac, and Inga Clendinnen, who together created the internationally acclaimed Melbourne Group of ethnographic history. Melbourne also prides itself on being Australia's sporting capital, the high temple of which is the Melbourne Cricket Ground. Begun in 1853, it served as the main arena for the 1956 Olympic Games.

QUALITY OF LIFE

International surveys during the late 1990s rated Melbourne as one of world's most livable cities. It is an efficient workplace, and the "Melbourne style" of life is judged second to none. The place offers the exciting diversity of a large city without the negatives often associated with metropolitan scale. The 2001 Melbourne Prosperity Index (regarded as a credible instrument) showed Melburnians to be materially better off than ever before. Yet the index also confirmed a worrying trend identified earlier by the Australian Bureau of Statistics and the National Centre for Social and Economic Modelling (using 1996 census data): a widening gap between rich and poor. Although the proportion of Melburnians living below the poverty line has remained roughly the same for 30 years, social mobility is less widespread and the number of long-term poor has grown. This socioeconomic divide is most evident in the housing market. Although Melbourne has the highest rate of home ownership in Australia, lower-income households are experiencing greater difficulties in finding affordable housing. The waiting list for public housing has grown to over 50,000.

FUTURE OF THE CITY

Melbourne's population is expected to reach 4 million people by 2020. Its size and prosperity will be determined by global trends in advanced manufacturing and shipping. Rapid outer-suburban growth is set to continue in the new century, but the future of the middle ring of "baby-boomer" suburbs is at the crossroads. If rapid population growth continues in the city core and inner suburbs, a reversal of Melbourne's history is in store, with the wealthy returning to the center and the poor moving to the fringe.

BIBLIOGRAPHY

Briggs, Asa, *Victorian Cities* (1963; reprint, Penguin 1990).

Brown-May, Andrew, ed., *The Encyclopedia of Melbourne* (forthcoming, Oxford University Press).

Cannon, Michael, *Old Melbourne Town before the Gold Rush* (Loch Haven Books 1991).

Cannon, Michael, *Melbourne after the Gold Rush* (Loch Haven Books 1993).

Davison, Graeme, *The Rise and Fall of Marvellous Melbourne* (Melbourne University Press 1978).

Frost, Lionel, *The New Urban Frontier: Urbanization and City-Building in Australasia and the American West (New South Wales University Press 1991).*

Grant, James, and Geoffrey Serle, eds., *The Melbourne Scene, 1803–1956* (Melbourne University Press 1957).

Lewis, Miles, et al., *Melbourne: The City's History and Development* (City of Melbourne 1994).

McLoughlin, John B., *Shaping Melbourne's Future? Town Planning, the State, and Civil Society* (Cambridge University Press 1992).

Presland, Gary, *Aboriginal Melbourne: The Lost Land of the Kulin People* (McPhee Gribble 1994).

Shaw, A. G. L., *A History of the Port Phillip District: Victoria Before Separation* (Melbourne University Press 1996).

Useful Web Sites

www.abs.gov.au [Australian Bureau of Statistics].
www.melbourne.vic.gov.au [City of Melbourne].
www.museum.vic.gov.au/ [Museum Victoria].
www.slv.vic.gov.au/ [State Library of Victoria].
www.visitvictoria.com.au/ [TourismVictoria].

ALAN MAYNE

Mendoza
Argentina

ORIENTATION

Name of City. The city of Mendoza is one of the oldest settlements in Argentina. It was named in 1561 for the Chilean governor García Hurtado de Mendoza. The name *Mendoza* is used by both natives and the outside world.

Location. Mendoza is situated in the western part of Argentina and is the capital of Mendoza province. To the north, Mendoza province borders on the province of San Juan; to the east, on the province of San Luis; southeast, on the province of La Pampa; south, on the province of Neuquén; and west, on Chile. Mendoza province is located between 31°59′ and 37°35′ south latitude and between 66°30′ and 70°35′ west longitude. It has an area of 150,839 square kilometers (58,224 square miles), constituting 4% of the territory of Argentina. Although the area of Mendoza province comprising urban, rural, and uninhabited subarid zones takes up 16,692 square kilometers (6,443 square miles), the urban settlement covers just 160 square kilometers (62 square miles).

The city of Mendoza is located in the north of the province. Far removed from Buenos Aires, the capital of Argentina (1,085 kilometers, or 674 miles, to the east), it is much closer to the Chilean capital, Santiago (380 kilometers, or 236 miles, to the west). The geographical location of the city is 32°50′ south latitude and 68°50′ west longitude. It lies at an elevation of 750–800 meters (2,460–2,625 feet).

Population. According to the most recent national census in 1991, the city of Mendoza had a population of some 770,000, although current estimates put the number of people now living in Mendoza at about 900,000. It is the fourth-largest city in Argentina and is home to more than 60% of the province's inhabitants (1991 estimated provincial population 1.5 million).

Most Mendozaneans have Italian and Spanish roots; a smaller segment of the population is descended from German and French immigrants. During the past few years, a growing number of people have immigrated from Chile, Bolivia, and Peru. Nowadays immigrants also arrive from Southeast Asia.

The mean population growth per year of Mendoza province is 1.4%, slightly above the national average of 1.3% (1990–1997).

Distinctive and Unique Features. The city of Mendoza is situated in a subarid zone at the foot of the Andes mountains in a piedmont area. The piedmont lies between the pre-cordillera and the plains, with slopes of between 1° and 5° to the east. It is a glacial region that is subject to constant erosion by the water draining away along dry riverbeds after sporadic heavy precipitation, transporting large amounts of sediment to the lower areas. This is a very dangerous phenomenon that has caused some intensive alluviums in the past, endangering the city. Consequently, a series of anti-alluvial constructions have been erected, such as drainage canals.

Because of the city's "isolated" location in a subarid zone, the settled area is known as an oasis. Life in the oasis depends on the water from the Mendoza River, which is charged by meltwater from the high mountains. The river provides the city with drinking water and supplies irrigation for agriculture.

About 200 kilometers (125 miles) away from Mendoza on the highway to Chile, the Aconcagua (the highest mountain of the Andes, with a height of 6,959 meters, or 22,832 feet) can be seen. Mendoza is therefore a popular starting point for tourist trips, especially for mountaineering but also for rafting, skiing, and other activities.

Mendoza's climate is very comfortable. Summer temperatures generally range between 20° and 24°C (68° and 75°F), but sometimes exceed 40°C (105°F). During winter, a temperature of between 7° and 10°C (45° and 50°F) prevails. The temperature rarely falls below freezing. Average rainfall per year is nearly 200 millimeters (8 inches). Distribution over the year is quite uneven, and in some years 80% of the annual precipitation may fall within just a few days.

The soil is very fertile owing to the presence of volcanic stones and can be used for agriculture when irrigated. The main crops are grapes, fruits, and vegetables. The Mendoza region is the largest wine-producing area in South America, and about 75% of all Argentine wines come from Mendoza. Of merely regional significance until the second half of the 19th century, the winemaking industry boomed on the eve of the 20th century as a result of the construction of the railway line to Buenos Aires, opening up a much larger market, and the immigration of numerous winegrowers from southeast Europe.

Mendoza province's natural resources include uranium, oil, and minerals. On the outskirts of the city is a Spanish-owned refinery. Marble is quarried locally for use in housing construction.

To promote economic development, in 1991 Brazil, Argentina, Uruguay, and Paraguay set up MERCOSUR (the Southern Common Market) in an effort to gradually eliminate all tariff barriers and to harmonize the member states' macroeconomic policies; Chile and Bolivia are associate members. The improvement of transport links between Mendoza and Santiago, in the sense of renovation and extension of the highway to Chile, is geared toward supporting the aims of MERCOSUR and strengthening Mendoza's economic position. A new venture recently undertaken with the assistance of the provincial government is the construction of a dam for a hydroelectric project on the Mendoza River near Portrerillos.

Attractions of the City. In 1861 the city of Mendoza was totally destroyed by a severe earthquake, and therefore architectural reminders of the colonial epoch are rare. Nevertheless, the city was rebuilt to plans that took the latent earthquake risks into account—for example, by including much more open space, allowing residents to seek refuge and affording the city a certain verdant charm. A large square, the Placa Independencia, containing greenery and fountains was laid out in the city center. Nearby are four more pleasant squares, one in each direction: Plaza Espana, Plaza Italia, Plaza San Martín, and Plaza Chile. Each square is uniquely decorated with palms and other trees, fountains, monuments, and colored paving, creating a relaxing atmosphere.

The streets are arranged in a grid. Low buildings dominate in the residential areas. The sidewalks in front of the buildings are paved with colorful stone. Between the sidewalk and the street are small canals that provide the big trees, mainly plane trees, with water. Mendoza's residents have always kept the sidewalks clean in front of their homes and they also water nearby trees—an activity that enhances the city's green image, one indicator of the high quality of life in Mendoza compared with that found in other Argentine cities.

In 1926 the first high-rise building was erected in Mendoza. As it survived the 1927 earthquake unscathed, many other high-rise buildings were soon constructed using reliable building strategies. As a result, the city suffered only minor damage during the last earthquake in 1986.

For the tourist, the city offers numerous amenities and services, and four new hotels are currently being built in the city center. An ideal conference venue, Mendoza enjoys good road and rail links and an airport for international air traffic.

© HUBERT STADLER/CORBIS

A large tilework depicting fruit and flowers adorns the Plaza Espana in Mendoza, Argentina.

One principal attraction is General San Martín Park, which covers 420 hectares (1,040 acres) and contains numerous plants and foreign trees, playgrounds, sports clubs, and an artificial lake 1 kilometer (0.6 mile) long. Not far away is the Cerro de Gloria—a hill offering a splendid view over the city, where a large monument commemorating General José de San Martín, the early-19th-century liberator of Chile and Peru, stands. Other highlights include the archaeological museum and the ruins of the San Francisco Church.

The tourist information offices are in the city center, including one in the town hall. Visitors to the town hall should use the opportunity to go up onto the roof terrace, which provides a view of both city life and the Andes.

In addition, tourists can visit wineries and taste the different types of wine that are produced. Every year from January until March, Mendozaneans and their guests celebrate the Fiesta de la Vendimia—a major festival with a host of cultural and artistic highlights, which starts off with grape-harvesting celebrations. Following a number of rituals, the high point of the fiesta is the coronation of the wine queen. This popular festival is attended every year by thousands of visitors from elsewhere in Argentina and all over the world.

Major Languages. The official language in the city is Spanish, and it has much in common with the Spanish spoken in Chile. As may be expected from the population's roots, the other main languages spoken are Italian and German.

HISTORY

The Origin of the City. Before the arrival of the Spanish conquerors, the area was inhabited by the Huarpe Indian tribe. They cultivated the land to grow cereals and built the first artificial irrigation system.

The city of Mendoza was founded on March 2, 1561, by the Chilean Pedro del Castillo at the foot of Mount Tupungato. In 1562 the city was relocated to the banks of the Mendoza River following an attack by Indians. Agricultural irrigation was continued by the Spanish immigrants—one reason being the necessity of maintaining a supply point for caravans on their way to Chile via the Andes.

Until 1776 the city of Mendoza belonged to Chile. Control of the region then passed to the viceroyalty of the Río de la Plata. Mendoza became part of the Federal Republic of Argentina following the country's foundation in 1853.

Domingo Faustino, the president of Argentina from 1868 to 1874, did much for the development of the city and Mendoza province. In particular, he supported the construction of railway lines, paving the way for the intensification of economic exchange with the eastern parts of Argentina, especially Buenos Aires. The resulting economic upswing in Mendoza was largely on account of wine production.

During its history dating back more than 400 years, Mendoza has suffered numerous earthquakes. The worst one occurred in March 1861 when Mendoza was at the epicenter of a seismic shock. Most of the 25 blocks constituting the old city were destroyed and 4,000 inhabitants (a third of the population) were killed. This catastrophe virtually wiped out colonial Mendoza. Reconstruction of the city started in 1862, headed by the French architect Julio Balloffet, who developed new guidelines for urban planning that took into consideration the risk of earthquakes.

Migration: Past and Present. Initially, most of Mendoza's immigrants came from Chile. They also settled throughout the whole of the Cuyo (the name given to the area comprising the provinces of Mendoza, San Juan, and San Luis). In 1869 the population of the Cuyo consisted of 93.3% Argentines and 6.7% foreigners. More than 90% of the foreigners came from neighboring countries.

In 1895 a wave of immigration from European countries began, with the biggest influx being recorded in 1914 in response to the economic and social crisis in Europe. Numerous immigrants from Spain and Italy arrived in the Cuyo, along with a smaller group from France. In 1914 the share of foreigners in the Cuyo was 26.4%. Some 86% of this group came from Europe, with the rest arriving from neighboring countries. The advent of these European immigrants heralded economic changes. Cereal production was reduced in favor of wine production, a switch that spawned an economic upturn.

Internal population changes attributed to migration can be described on the basis of the 1960 census. Most of the migration tendencies at that time were movements within the Cuyo. The present situation is characterized by the immigration of the rural population from the province to the city.

INFRASTRUCTURE

Politics. Mendoza province is divided into 18 districts or *departamentos*. The city of Mendoza itself includes 6 independent *departamentos* with their own local authorities: Capital, Guaymalien, Godoy Cruz,

Las Heras, Maipu, and Lujan. The urban parts of the *departamentos* form an agglomeration with no visible borders known as Gran Mendoza.

Educational System. The Argentine educational system is divided into four levels: preschool or kindergarten; primary; secondary; and higher. Preschool attendance is not compulsory; primary education is. State-financed schools are free of charge, unlike the private schools. The pupils wear uniforms, the younger ones dark blue and the older ones white. In 1999 a number of changes were made to the school system, such as the integration of the primary and secondary levels.

In 1939 the main state national university, Universidad Nacional de Cuyo, was founded in the city. There are also some private universities, such as the University of Mendoza.

Transportation System. Local transport consists of taxicabs, trolleybuses run by the local authorities, and privately operated diesel buses. The national rail network is managed by a few private companies. There are routes connecting Mendoza to Buenos Aires, Santiago, and other destinations.

CULTURAL AND SOCIAL LIFE

Distinctive Features of the City's Cultures. Mendozaneans like walking through the city, strolling through its parks and shopping boulevards. They often sit outside cafés and restaurants, enjoying a meal or a coffee and meeting friends or relatives. The traditional greeting for friends is a kiss on both cheeks. Performances of music and street theater are a common sight outside various buildings. Mendozaneans take pains to ensure a well-dressed, smart appearance.

The center of the city is divided into districts, each with its own dominating function. For example, the area around Plaza San Martín is the banking center, while the San Martín street and the neighboring streets are popular shopping boulevards, which also contain plenty of restaurants and bars. The Sarmiento street is a pedestrian street (*la peatonal sarmiento*) and a favorite meeting place for young people in particular.

Outside the city center, new shopping centers have been constructed during recent years, while in the east a shopping center built in 1991 has now been expanded to create a hybrid complex that also houses entertainment outlets. Surveys indicate that residents approve of the combination of shopping and leisure facilities. The southern part of the city contains the *barrio civico,* the political and administrative center.

Cuisine. Like most Argentines, Mendozaneans enjoy beef. However, chicken, lamb, goat, and pork are also served. Meat is mainly fried or grilled, and served with vegetables (such as tomatoes and a green salad) as well as with bread. A typical fixture in any Mendozanean kitchen is the *asado,* or spit roast, which is an indispensable part of the much-loved barbecue parties. Pasta and pizza are also very popular owing to the Italian roots of many inhabitants.

The main meal of the day is dinner, which is rarely served before 10:00 P.M. Breakfast normally consists of tea or coffee and some pastries. A specialty only available locally is Mendoza jam made from fruit known as "alcallota." Snacks are often eaten during the day, with many people opting for a full lunch.

Religious Diversity. More than 90% of the population of Mendoza are Catholic. In the poor quarters (*villas miserias*), various sects are also known to burgeon.

Family and Other Social Support Systems. The extended family forms the main basis for stability and survival. On average, each family has two or three children. The number of single households is presently on the increase, but it is still far from the level prevailing in Europe.

Work and Commerce. According to the 1991 census figures for Mendoza province, 54% of the population aged 14–60 years was involved in the economic sector. One-quarter of those economically active currently work in the primary sector, chiefly in agriculture. A second quarter are employed in the secondary sector, in industry. About half work in the service sector. Since many jobs are very poorly paid, moonlighting and "black-economy" activities (short-term jobs in the informal economy) are common.

QUALITY OF LIFE

The city of Mendoza is known for its high quality of life. Both the climate and the economy are better than what is found in many other places in Argentina. Nevertheless, living conditions vary depending on the area of the city. The socioeconomic division of society is resulting in an increasing contrast between high-income districts and the poverty-stricken *villas miserias*.

Health-care standards are high in Mendoza, and there are both state-financed and private hospitals. People choose their medical service depending on their income.

Environmental Problems. Aside from the risk of earthquakes, another problem that Mendoza suffers is sporadic heavy precipitation, which causes flooding. This is a serious danger for the western residential districts of the city and especially for the squatter settlements located in dried-up riverbeds. Very poor families are able to live here as agricultural usage is impossible and ownership is unclaimed.

The bulk of the air pollution in Mendoza is caused by buses, cars, and factories not fitted with pollution-control equipment. The situation is exacerbated by limited fresh-air exchange due to the specific conditions of the location and the low wind speed.

Another serious problem is water pollution. Wastewater from industrial plants, wineries, slaughterhouses, and tanneries is discharged into the large Canal Pescara. The filthy water is used untreated to irrigate agricultural fields at the end of the canal.

Crime. During the past few years, the crime rate in the city has risen sharply, with mainly robberies and muggings on the increase. This is detrimental to the quality of life for the local population, who prize being able to walk through parks and streets (including at night) without fear. The social division between rich denizens and masses of very poor people is assumed to be the principal reason for this development.

In 1994, about 77 *villas miserias,* with an estimated 33,000 residents, were registered in the Mendoza agglomeration. The shelters are poorly built, offering insufficient protection against extreme heat during the summer and torrential downpours, and there are no sanitary facilities. An acute, clearly noticeable problem is children begging for money on pedestrian walkways and even at traffic lights on very busy streets.

FUTURE OF THE CITY

The future development of the city will be characterized by sustained population growth. The main reason is the ongoing immigration of people from less developed regions in the province and the rest of the country seeking to improve their living conditions.

The differentiation between the rich and the poor, who heavily outnumber them, is increasing. One clear indication of this is the erection of a number of gated compounds for the very wealthy where they live independently of the surroundings with their own services, facilities, and security forces—something that is quite new for what, by Latin American standards, is considered to be a medium-size city.

The many construction sites in the city center are another indicator of economic prosperity, and the city will be well prepared for its future tasks as MERCOSUR expands. Nevertheless, only part of the population profits from this development. Masses of poor people have to live in growing *villas miserias,* feeling socially stigmatized despite the success of the consolidation efforts in parts of their settlement.

The city of Mendoza still offers an attractive cityscape and a relatively high quality of life compared with that of other Latin American cities. To maintain these values, it is essential that its environmental quality (especially the greenery) be preserved and that environmental problems such as air and water pollution be dealt with.

BIBLIOGRAPHY

Ayero, Javier, "'This Is a Lot Like the Bronx, Isn't It?' Lived Experiences of Marginality in an Argentine Slum," *International Journal of Urban and Regional Research,* vol. 23 (1999).

Baratta von, Mario, *Der Fischer Weltalmanach* (Fischer Taschenbuch Verlag 1999).

Bühnsdorf, Jürgen, *Argentinien* (Klett-Verlag 1992).

Cortellezzi, Mónica, et al., *Geografía de Mendoza* (Libro de edificion Argentina 1999).

Endlicher, Wilfried, and Barbara Zahnen, "Weather Types, Local Winds, and Air Pollution Problems in Mendoza, Argentina," *Conference of Latin Americanist Geographers Yearbook 25* (1999).

Lipp, Uli, *Argentinien* (Schettler, Hattdorf 1995).

Nolte, Detlef, and Nikolaus Werz, *Argentinien: Politik, Wirtschaft, Kultur und Außenbeziehungen* (Vervuert 1996).

Trifiró, Maria Cristina, and Lidia Arboit, *Evolución zy Características de la Población en las Provincias de Mendoyza yund San Juan* (Tintar editorial 2000).

SIGRUN KABISCH

Mexico City

Mexico

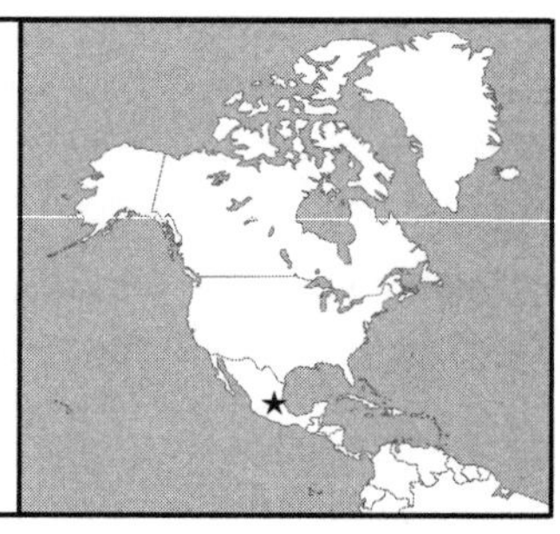

ORIENTATION

Name of City. Capital of the nation of Mexico, Mexico City is known as La Ciudad de México in Spanish, the nation's principal language, although often it is referred to as México; México, D.F.; or D.F. (Distrito Federal in Spanish; Federal District in English). The name of the city derives from the Nahuatl-speaking people called the Mexica, more widely known as the Aztecs, and results from the combination of their terms for "moon" (*meztli*), "belly button" (*xictli*), and "place" (*co*). This place, symbolizing the moon's belly button, served as the focus of Aztec life before the arrival of the Spaniards in 1519 and, five centuries later, continues to be the central place of the Mexican people.

Location. Within the Mexican nation, all roads literally begin from Mexico City, since the geographic marker for the "zero point" is at the city's main square, known as the Zócalo. Mexico City is located at 19°26′ north latitude and 99°9′ west longitude, in south-central Mexico, at an altitude of 2,240 meters (7,349 feet) above sea level. Mexico City proper covers an area of 1,479 square kilometers (571 square miles) while the Distrito Federal is slightly larger, at 1,546 square kilometers (597 square miles). The metropolitan area has extended in recent decades well beyond these limits and now occupies most of the Valley of Mexico (a basin about 100 kilometers [62 miles] long by 50 kilometers [31 miles] surrounded by mountains on the northwest, west, south, and southeast). Because the mountains frequently cause thermal inversions, the entire valley is subject to serious air-pollution problems, mitigated only when the spring winds blow or the summer rains fall.

Population. In 1900 the population of Mexico City was 345,000; in 1950 the metropolitan population had reached 3.1 million. This grew rapidly to around 9 million by 1970, and many experts in the 1970s were projecting that the area's population might surpass 30 million by the year 2000. Fortunately, the natural growth rate has slowed in recent decades, and the impact of cityward migration has declined considerably, especially in the wake of the specific damage suffered by the capital in the 1985 earthquake and the general chaos caused by the economic crisis of the 1980s. Despite these setbacks, the metropolitan area currently ranks among the largest in the world, with its estimated population of between 18 million and 20 million people. Only the Tokyo urban area is larger, at 28 million. Mexico City's population is on a par with that of Bombay, São Paulo, Shanghai, and New York City; and ahead of that of Beijing, Jakarta, Lagos, and Los Angeles. After Toyko (21%), Mexico City (20%) has the highest share of national population of any of the world's great cities. Metropolitan New York City, with about the same population as metropolitan Mexico City, is home to only 6% of the U.S. population. And among the world's great cities, Mexico City is the only one located on the ruins of an indigenous civilization subjected to European conquest and subsequent assimilation.

Preliminary results for the year 2000 Mexican government census for the Mexico City metropolitan area counted 17,437,634 people—8,591,309 in the Distrito Federal, plus the populations of 23 adjacent *municipios* administratively affiliated with the state of Mexico.

Distinctive and Unique Features. Mexico City concentrates an extraordinary proportion of its nation's population, governmental infrastructure, economic resources, educational facilities, media, and cultural activities. It is a "primate city"—that is, a capital whose size is disproportionately large when compared to other cities in the nation. This enormous population concentration is all the more unusual because of Mexico City's high altitude and great distance from water-based transportation found at other world-class cities. On the other hand, the climate of Mexico City is generally mild, given its unique combination of high altitude and tropical latitude. The average annual temperature is 16°C (61°F). Temperatures in May range from 11°C (52°F) to 26°C (80°F); those in December, from 6°C (43°F) to 20°C (69°F). With regard to rainfall, about 80% of the year's average of 762 millimeters (30 inches) falls from June through October.

Attractions of the City. Mexico City is full of attractions for tourists as well as for residents. What is unusual is that so many of its attractions are public, rather than privately owned. It has no Disney World, no "Six Flags Over Mexico," no Universal Studios to draw visitors' pesos. Instead, Mexico City offers museum after museum, monument upon monument, architectural and historical delights beyond one's imagination. Stroll on a Sunday afternoon from the Zócalo—with its Metropolitan Cathedral, National Palace, Templo Mayor, and other grand colonial-era buildings—westward past the Plaza Garibaldi and its strolling mariachi bands—to the Alameda Park. Passing the Fine Arts Palace and the Franz Mayer Museum, continue southwest along the Avenida de la Reforma, past the monuments to the Revolution, to Columbus, to Cuauhtémoc, to Independence, and to Diana the Huntress before arriving at Chapultepec Park to see the monument to the Niños Héroes, the military-school cadets who gave their lives defending the hill of the Chapultepec Castle (where the National History Museum now is located) against the U.S. troops who had invaded Mexico in 1848. Then, after catching your breath in the thin, polluted air, continue walking westward along the Reforma past the Modern Art Museum, the Rufino Tamayo Museum, and the National Anthropology Museum, until reaching the National Auditorium. Following that, one might board one of the Route 100 buses (the most-traveled bus line in the world!) and travel northeast, ar-

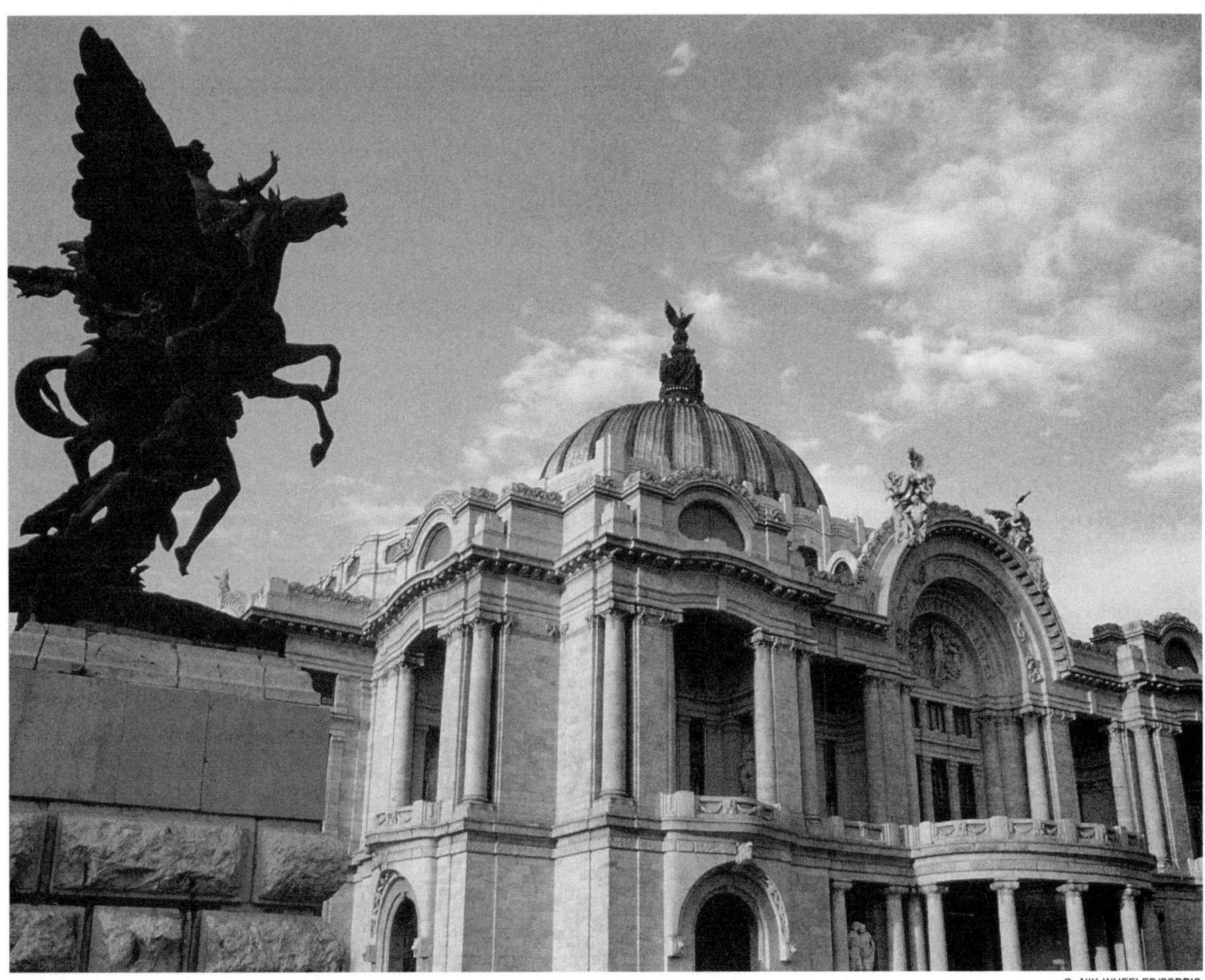

© NIK WHEELER/CORBIS

The imposing Palacio de Bellas Artes houses cultural events in Mexico City, Mexico.

riving at the Basilica of Guadalupe at Tepeyac in time for evening Mass. And on a Sunday afternoon, when museum admissions are free, all this costs very few pesos!

Relationships Between the City and the Outside. The reason for Mexico City being where it is derives from the decision of Hernán Cortés to build a Spanish colonial administrative center on the ruins of the capital of the far-flung Aztec empire. His choice has dictated that Mexico City has always been a place both dominant and dependent with regard to its hinterland. From the beginning, the city's leaders have had to find ways to provide water, food, building supplies, and even people—in effect, all of the stuff that any city requires—from considerable distances, even from across the oceans. Over five centuries, as the urban area has grown 100-fold from about 15 square kilometers (6 square miles) to about 1,500 square kilometers (579 square miles), its inhabitants and those who live in its ever-lengthening shadow have had ambivalent views of the capital's place in the world.

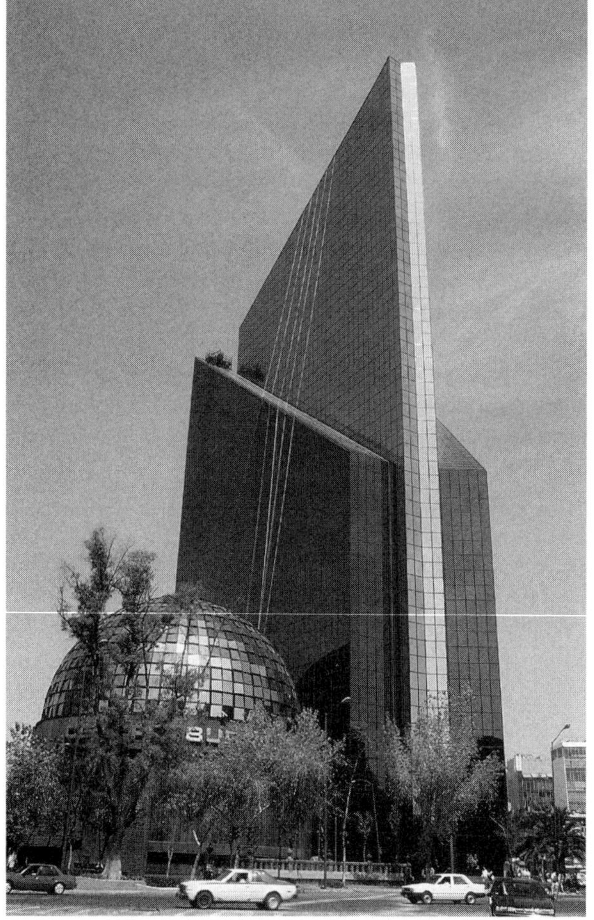

© THE PURCELL TEAM/CORBIS

Modern skyscrapers grace the Federal District in Mexico City.

Major cities in the central highlands—Querétaro, Tlaxcala, Toluca, Pachuca, Puebla, and Cuernavaca—and the smaller communities in their own hinterlands are part of the capital's zone of influence on a daily basis. Characterized as "leviathan," "megalopolis," and "mega-city," Mexico City is overwhelming in its complexity, a nightmare for urban planners who endeavor to take it all into account. In 1978 the federal government began the process of developing a National Urban Development Plan, the focus of which was better understanding and planning for the National Urban System and the place of the ever-expanding capital within this national context. A critical element of this plan was a governmental commitment to decentralization—that is, to encourage and even to require that government agencies and private-sector corporations abandon the Mexico City metropolitan region in favor of other urban areas. Despite the government's good intentions, few significant changes took place until the 1985 earthquake brought down dozens of buildings in Mexico City. For example, with its main buildings in ruins, the National Institute of Statistics, Geography, and Information was moved to the midsize city of Aguascalientes, in the state of the same name. Indeed, since 1985 fear of another earthquake has probably done more to reduce the demographic and economic growth of Mexico City than any actions taken by the government! In 2000 the eruptions of the volcano Popocatepetl added to concerns about the future of life in the entire Valley of Mexico.

Mexico City also operates as a global metropolis. As Mexico has expanded its political and economic policies in recent years, especially with the creation of the North American Free Trade Agreement (NAFTA) in 1994 and similar multilateral and bilateral agreements with Central American and South American nations, the capital increasingly has become involved in international affairs. Entering the 21st century, Mexico City's reach may once again approach what it was in the 18th century.

Major Languages. Spanish is the language of Mexico City, although in recent years English has become the city's second-most-spoken language. More surprising is the fact that more than 200,000 city residents are speakers of indigenous languages. The most numerous group are the speakers of Nahuatl (the language of the Aztecs), followed by speakers of Otomí, Mixteco (Mixtec), Zapoteco (Zapotec), and Mazahua, but another 40 native languages may be heard in the streets on any given day. European and Asian languages also are used by those who have immigrated to Mexico City or have come to work there as representatives of multinational corporations. Latin used to be heard in Roman Catholic masses but Spanish has replaced it in nearly all urban parishes, and Hebrew is used in Jewish synagogues located in affluent neighborhoods such as Polanco.

HISTORY

The Origin of the City. Although the site now occupied by Mexico City was settled by different populations as far back as 20,000 B.C., the beginnings of its urban development are not ancient by world historical standards. According to legend, in 1325 A.D. a fierce nomadic group known as the Culhua Mexica came from the north into the Valley of Mexico. When their priests saw an eagle with a snake in its beak perched on a cactus, they knew to build a temple to the sun god. This new place, known as Tenochtitlán, was built on a small island in Lake Texcoco and was connected by long causeways to the land beyond the lake. Ceremonial, administrative, economic, and military center of what became a vast empire in less than 200 years, the city and its hinterlands around the lake basin may have had a population (estimated at 300,000 inhabitants) larger than that of any European city of the time.

The fall of Tenochtitlán between 1519–1522 to Hernán Cortés and his small army of Spanish soldiers and native allies marked the end of one era and the beginning of another. The conquering Spaniards converted the Aztec empire into a colonial system subvervient to the king of Spain and his Council of the Indies. Mexico City—as Tenochtitlán came to be called—continued in its role as hegemonic center of a colonial space (called the Viceroyalty of New Spain) extending from Central America in the south to northern California and the Philippines to the far west. Even when the administrative changes known as the Bourbon Reforms were imposed by Charles III in the second half of the 18th century, Mexico City continued its central role in colonial life. In fact, by the late 1700s Mexico City had become the largest and most important city in the Americas. According to Kandel, it had "over 130,000 inhabitants and an architectural inventory that included 150 ecclesiastical buildings, a dozen hospitals, an Academy of Art, the most advanced school of mining, and one of the great universities of the world." The exploitative, dependent character of Mexican urbanization during the colonial era reflected the economic, political, religious, and social institutions responsible for building and maintaining the hierarchy of places dominated by Mexico City's elite.

Independence from Spain in 1821 did not usher in an era of rapid urban growth. On the contrary, the grand estates—which Eric Wolf has called "the ramparts of power in the countryside"—assumed a central place in the economic and political struggles between the liberal and conservative forces in the new nation of Mexico. Mexico's urban system changed very little between 1821 and 1860, a period whose close may be marked by the Reform Laws in Mexico. Although the political and cultural hegemony of Mexico City (with an 1862 population of 210,000) was unchallenged, the effects of the Reform Laws, especially the disentailment of the holdings of large civil and religious corporations after 1859, coincided with the emergence of Mexico City as a "primate city." By 1884 Mexico City had 300,000 inhabitants, while the next three largest cities—Guadalajara, Puebla, and Monterrey—had 80,000, 75,000, and 42,000, respectively. The disparity increased by 1910, the year in which the Mexican Revolution broke out. Mexico City had grown to 471,000, but the other cities had reached only 119,000, 96,000, and 79,000. There is great irony in the fact that the repressive dictatorship of Porfirio Díaz (1877–1910) marked a period of considerable urban development for the capital. Many magnificent public buildings (including the Post Office and the Palace of Fine Arts) were constructed in modern steel and concrete so that Mexico City would take on the flavor of a European capital.

The 1910 Revolution brought a temporary halt to urban development while turning Mexico City into a place of refuge for both peasants and elites fleeing violence in the countryside. The capital captured 60% of the urban growth between 1910 and 1921, and nearly half the urban growth between 1921 and 1940. In 1921 the metropolitan population reached 662,000, in 1930 it topped 1 million, and by 1940 it had jumped to 1.5 million. With the bureaucratic and institutional developments of the postrevolutionary period, Mexico City diversified and strengthened its social, economic, and cultural functions in the national system. The city also expanded toward the peripheries of the Federal District. Large upper-class subdivisions (for example, Polanco and Lomas de Chapultepec in the west) were developed as many elite families moved out of their old homes in the increasingly crowded central-city zone. This shift in elite population opened the way for the creation of central-city slums where rent control and small *vecindad* ("place of neighbors") apartment houses were the forerunners of the *ciudades perdidas* ("lost cities") of the 1960s and 1970s. The other effect of the city's spatial expansion was the creation of the Department of the Federal District in 1929 to cope with urban problems beyond the narrow jurisdiction of Mexico City per se. Despite these changes in the capital's spatial structure, urban life was still focused inwardly, toward the Zócalo, and differed relatively little from that of the late 19th century.

With the 1940s came Mexico City's urban and industrial "explosion." Governmental policies of import-substitution industrialization emphasized the locational advantages of the capital. Its centrality in the transportation network, its relatively well-skilled workforce, and its larger consumer population made inevitable the concentration of urban growth in the metropolitan area at the expense of other cities in the nation. This implicit centralization policy involved not only industry but also all other aspects of social and political life—from services to insurance companies, banks, labor unions, and institutions of higher learning. As the Valley of Mexico was being industrialized, its urban infrastructure and services were being improved, more water and electrical power were brought in from distant regions, more upper- and middle-class subdivisions were built, and more peripheral squatter settlements were established. The combination of public and private investment in the capital was so high that intensive centripetal forces were generated.

The escalation of oil prices in the late 1970s fueled a sense of euphoria among urban planners in Mexico, but declining prices in the 1980s brought on a serious economic crisis from which Mexico City and the nation at large have, perhaps, still not recovered. The 1985 earthquake also awakened citizens to the possibilities of living and working elsewhere than the capital. From 1985 to 1990 the Federal District lost more than a million people. During the 1990s the capital continued to lose its own younger residents and failed to attract as many young migrants as it had in earlier decades.

Despite governmental efforts to decentralize the capital's urban economy, Mexico City still contains far too large a share of the nation's industry, service-sector businesses, and commerce, and it is still the single largest employment market in Mexico. The metropolitan area actually contributes more to the government's revenues than it extracts in expenditures. Clearly, present and future initiatives by the government and by the private sector must take into account these problems of urban concentration in the Mexico City metropolitan area.

Migration: Past and Present. Mexico City has been a migratory magnet throughout its history—first attracting Spaniards during the colonial period of restricted population movement between the Old World and New Spain, and later attracting a wider range of international immigrants after independence in 1821. Fearful rural dwellers swelled the city's population during the revolutionary period from 1910–1921, and the Civil War in Spain during the 1930s brought thousands of expatriate Spaniards to the capital, including a corps of intellectuals whose scholarly endeavors formed the basis of what later would become the prestigious Colegio de México.

The post–World War II industrial boom brought tens of thousands of new arrivals to the capital every day. It was during the early phase of this industrial expansion that the anthropologist Oscar Lewis followed migrants from the village of Tepoztlán (in nearby Morelos state) to Mexico City. His concept of "urbanization without breakdown" showed that these peasants adapted well to life in the capital—contrary to the expectations of U.S.-based sociological theories. Subsequent research documented the important role of migrants in urban growth during the post–World War II period.

Mexico City proved a fertile field for developing and testing ideas about rural-urban migration. Lewis's work on the "culture of poverty" continued his studies among the Tepoztecans in the capital's inner-city slums. The work of Lewis's student, Douglas Butterworth, replicated his mentor's work among migrants from Tilantongo (Oaxaca). These early studies of migrant adaptation were followed by others that also emphasized the positive features of the migrants' experiences as individuals and households in Mexico City.

By the late 1970s research shifted away from migrant adaptation and individual decision making toward their "marginal" and "informal" economic status in the urban setting. Lomnitz found that social networks allowed even very poor migrants to survive in Mexico City. The positive features of their social organization—including kinship, *compadrazgo* (co-godparenthood), and *cuatismo* ("being good buddies")—provided survival mechanisms built on *respeto* ("respect") and *confianza* ("trust"). Rather than decrying the social disorganization of the poor, scholars celebrated their ability to cope with the extreme structural inequalities of life in the capital, thus providing an important corrective to Lewis's earlier "culture of poverty" concept, which had led many observers to focus on the negative qualities of urban life.

Migration was also associated with ethnicity, especially among diverse Indian groups who came to the capital to escape the poverty of the countryside. For example, Arizpe's study of migration among the Mazahuas in Mexico City demonstrated that the linkages between their communities of origin in the state of Mexico and their circumstances in the capital were consequences of changing relationships within the broader political economy. Migration came to be seen as an issue of labor and "cultural capital" rather than of individual choice.

By the 1990s investigators were paying less attention to migration per se, and more to the urban culture in which migrants participated, especially the populist movements that arose in response to the economic crisis of the 1980s and the ecological crisis of the 1990s. The role of women in these movements brought a heightened interest in gender issues and urban processes, including migration. Local initiatives in community building also were examined as transformation of urban power structures. As a result, at a time when migration to the capital was in relative decline, migration was seen as a consequence of broader urban processes rather than as an independent force for urban growth.

INFRASTRUCTURE

Public Buildings, Public Works, and Residences. The Zócalo, the popular name of the Plaza de la Constitución, is the heart of the city and its chief ceremonial center. Ever since Aztec times, festivals and public announcements have been celebrated here, and in recent centuries the Zócalo also has been the site of demonstrations to protest governmental actions—for here, on the eastern side of this great square, sits the National Palace, the seat of the national government, while on the south side are the offices of the Federal District, and on the north side is the great metropolitan cathedral. On the northeast corner of the Zócalo, residents and tourists can see, since its partial excavation since the 1970s, the impressive stone remains of the Aztecs Templo Mayor ("Great Temple"). On the northwest corner of the square is the Nacional Monte de Piedad ("pawnshop"), which has served the needs of the people since the 17th century.

The Centro Histórico covers some 9 square kilometers (3.5 square miles) in the area immediately north and east of the Zócalo, and includes in the designated zone some 1,436 buildings that date from the 16th to the 19th century. Since 1980 citizens and governmental agencies have been working together to restore hundreds of buildings, ranging from churches, schools, and hospitals to former residences of the colonial nobility. In 1987 the Centro Histórico was added to the World Heritage list of cultural properties that were sponsored by the United Nations Educational, Scientific and Cultural Organization (UNESCO).

To the west of the Zócalo is the Alameda, an area containing a large park (laid out in 1592), the Palace of Fine Arts (famous for its Tiffany glass curtain and the Ballet Folklórico), several colonial-era churches, and the outstanding Franz Mayer Museum. Unfortunately, the 1985 earthquake destroyed several important buildings along the Alameda, and now only empty lots remain in their places. Between the Alameda and the Zócalo, at the intersection of Francisco Madero Avenue and Lázaro Cárdenas Avenue, stands the 44-floor Latin American Tower—the tallest building in Latin America when it was constructed in 1956—where, on the rare clear day, one can view the entire city from its observation deck. Across the street from the tower is the Casa de los Azulejos ("House of Tiles"), built in 1596 as the residence of the noble Orizaba family, but currently the anchor of the very successful Sanborn's chain of "restaurant-cum-pharmacy and gift shops."

Politics and City Services. Political power within the nation is concentrated in Mexico City. The head of the Federal District formerly was appointed by the president, but since 1997 has been elected by popular vote of the city's residents. In 1997 Cuauhtémoc Cárdenas of the Partido de la Revolución Democrtica (PRD) won the first popular election as head of the Federal District, and Andrés Manuel López Obrador (also of the PRD) won the post in 2000. The city is governed by "delegates," one in charge of each of the 16 "delegations," and by a local Assembly of Representatives. The Federal District also is represented in the national Senate and Chamber of Deputies.

The Federal District—created in 1928—is directly dependent on the federal budget for its resources. Since 1970 the Federal District has been organized into 16 "delegations." These delegations and the *municipios* surrounding the Federal District have been cooperating in planning and public administration for the metropolitan area since the mid-1970s, especially for the development of the Metro; the expansion of the streets and highways through the region;

the provision of water, sewage, and sanitary services; and efforts to deal with air and ground pollution throughout the Valley of Mexico.

Local-level political decision making is not only carried out by bureaucrats, but often is influenced by citizens' groups at the "*colonia*" and block levels. In the metropolitan area, more than 1,800 *colonias* compete for scarce urban services and resources. For several decades, local-level politics has been dominated by issues related to the lack of housing for the rapidly growing urban population. The administration's attitude toward illegal and quasilegal housing developments has varied from violent repression to passive acceptance to active endorsement. Some squatter settlements have been bulldozed, while others have been ignored, and still others provided with "sites and services" infrastructure. Title to individual properties is difficult to obtain. It may take more than a decade of bureaucratic problems before a family can obtain legal documentation of their claim to a specific lot in a formerly illegal subdivision or to a house in an inner-city slum.

Grassroots movements have been especially important since the 1985 earthquake devastated much of the older, central section of Mexico City. The inaction of the local government and the dominant political party, the Partido Revolucionario Institucional (PRI), led to disaffection with the old political order. As a result, many citizens voted for opposition-party candidates in the 1988, 1994, and 2000 elections. The challenges to the newly elected administration of President Vicente Fox are measured by the daily tensions of political action in the metropolis. Success will be measured by transforming a "culture of resistance" into a spirit of cooperation in the struggle to deal with Mexico City's manifold problems.

In the 1990s Mexico City has become a much more dangerous place in which to work and live than it was in earlier times. For the rich and for the poor, violence has replaced tranquility. Robbery, assault, kidnapping, and murder have become commonplace, even in broad daylight in crowded public places. The traditional corruption of the metropolitan police forces has been augmented by the impact of drugs and drug money on all forms of authority in Mexican society.

Educational System. On a typical day, more than 3 million children, adolescents, young adults, and adults attend schools in metropolitan Mexico City. The search for educational opportunities has been a major component in the growth of the metropolis since the middle of the 20th century. Millions of people have come to the capital so that they or their children might pursue studies in public or private schools. Despite spending more on education than on any other budget domain, the Federal District still suffers with many inadequate, overcrowded schools staffed by teachers whose real salaries have fallen dramatically in recent years. For decades, the public schools have offered double (morning and afternoon) sessions for children and then reopened in the evening to provide educational opportunities for adults. Many parents, especially those in working- or middle-class households, spend a significant share of their incomes to send their children to school. Aspirations for educating the coming generation are much higher than the real possibilities; current estimates suggest that more than 2 million adolescents are likely to be frustrated in their efforts to attend university.

Among the most important universities in the capital are the Universidad Nacional Autónoma de México (established in 1551 and given autonomy in 1929), the Instituto Politécnico Nacional (1937), the Colegio de México (1940), the Universidad Iberoamericana (1943), the Instituto Tecnológico Autónomo de México (1946), the Universidad Anáhuac (1964), the Universidad Autónoma Metropolitana (1973), the Universidad Pedagógica Nacional (1978), and the branch campus of the Instituto Tecnológico de Monterrey (1943). These and other colleges and universities enroll more than 250,000 students at the bachelor's-degree level alone.

The Universidad Nacional Autónoma de Mexico (UNAM) always has been the nation's preeminent university. Since 1954 its principal campus has been located in the architecturally and artistically acclaimed University City in the southern sector of the capital. UNAM enrolls some 142,000 bachelor's-level students and a total of 270,000 students. The faculty numbers some 30,000, of whom almost 5,000 are full-time. Even more significant is that UNAM performs 50% of all university-based research projects and enrolls 55% of all doctoral students in Mexico.

University students, and UNAM students in particular, have been the locus of political activism and strikes since the 1960s, including the 1968 student movement that resulted in the infamous Tlatelolco Massacre on October 2, 1968. Although it now costs a mere 20 centavos (2 cents U.S.) for a year's tuition at UNAM, the university administration has been stopped by protests each time it has tried to raise tuition fees. Not surprisingly, demand for admission has overwhelmed the university's capacity. For the 152,000 applicants in a typical year, only 40,000 places are available; of these, 32,000 are reserved for graduates from UNAM's own high-school system. In 1999 many of the "excluded" students took over the university's main administration building and closed down UNAM for several months to alert the public to their plight.

Transportation System. Even though it has some of the great boulevards—such as the French-inspired Avenida de la Reforma—typical of any world-class city, transportation (and its associated air contamination) remains one of Mexico City's greatest challenges. Continuing work on the extensive grid of one-way axial roads, the Interior Circuit, and the Periférico ring road has provided only modest improvements in what are, day in and day out, some of the world's worst traffic bottlenecks. Now that the government is selling off so many assets, a joke has begun to circulate. Question: "Which company should buy the city's road system?" Answer: "Coca-Cola—because they already are experts in making bottles."

Traffic had become so burdensome by 1989 that the city government imposed a system called *Hoy No Circula* ("Don't Drive Today"). Each car is restricted from being driven in the city one day during the Monday–Friday workweek. Although initially this system reduced traffic, gas consumption, and air pollution, soon the city's residents began to purchase second cars for their families to beat the system—and car sales and gasoline consumption surpassed previous levels!

Mexico City not only has a very large fleet of cars, trucks, buses, taxicabs, shared-ride shuttles, motorbikes, bicycles, and even pedicabs, it also moves some 5 million riders daily on its Metro, one of the world's busiest subway systems. The capital also is the center of bus, truck, and railway systems that daily transport enormous quantities of cargo and passengers into and out of the city in all directions. The national bus system departs from and arrives at four separate regionally focused stations (the TAPO serves the east and southeast, Taxqueña the south, Observatorio the west, and the north terminal serves all routes connecting to the U.S.-border cities). Rail lines from all points of the nation converge on the Buenavista station, located just north of the downtown business district.

The Benito Juárez International Airport, located about 6 kilometers (3.7 miles) east of the Zócalo, is continually being renovated as the federal government and some 35 airlines work to maintain domestic and international service to this, the only commercial airport in the metropolitan area. Once isolated on the city's eastern edge, the airport now creates noise and pollution that threaten the peace and health of the several million people living or working within a kilometer or so of its security perimeter.

CULTURAL AND SOCIAL LIFE

Distinctive Features of the City's Cultures. For Mexicans, Mexico City is referred to simply as México. In a sense, the capital does encompass *all* of the nation. It is the macrocosm that mirrors the transformations of the Mexican people through the centuries, from two centuries of the Aztec empire through three centuries of Spanish colonial domination to two centuries of independent statehood. But a deep ambivalence persists between those who live in Mexico City and all other places, collectively known as *la provincia* ("the provinces"). There is an old saying, *"Fuera de México, todo es Cuautitlán"* ("Compared to Mexico City, anyplace else might as well be the village of Cuautitlán"). The folks from the "provinces" respond by labeling all of the capital's residents as "know-it-alls," and use the colloquial term *chilango* for this purpose, as in the phrase "*¡Como son neuróticos los chilangos!*" ("Those know-it-all Mexico City residents are so crazy!").

Mexico City is the home to the nation's media. Some 30 newspapers (for example, *Excélsior, La Reforma,* and *Uno más Uno*) and dozens of magazines (such as *Nexos, Proceso,* and *El Tiempo*) vie for the attention of readers in a marketplace with the highest literacy rate (90%) in the country. The privatization of telecommunications has increased the number of television and radio stations and has made cable and satellite television available in many middle- and upper-class neighborhoods. No longer can the government dominate the news coverage as in early decades, when access to newsprint and official advertising was tightly controlled by the government, and editors were beholden to bureaucrats.

The capital is the largest center for book publishing in Latin America. The Fondo de Cultura Económica has translated thousands of foreign-language titles into Spanish and assured their diffusion throughout Mexico and Latin America. Many commercial presses (for example, Siglo Veintiuno) focus on contemporary issues, and several university presses (especially UNAM and El Colegio de México) and governmental agencies (such as INAH and SEP) pour forth a torrent of new titles every year. The annual weeklong Book Fair, held in a renovated colonial-era palace, draws tens of thousands of eager book buyers. Specialized book expositions (such as the annual anthropology book fair at the National Anthropology Museum) are long-running successes. Bookstores can be found in almost every neighborhood in the capital, and the best (for example, the Librería Gandhi in Coyoacán) carry selections rivaling those of the best bookstores anywhere in the world.

Cuisine. In every neighborhood of the metropolitan area, restaurants large and small, elegant and economical, endeavor to satisfy millions of unending appetites. From a rooftop patio restaurant overlooking the Zócalo to the elegant colonial San Angel Inn in southwestern Mexico City, from the Metro's subterranean vegetarian cafés to the *cocinas económicas* serving *comida corrida* ("home-style café with a set three-course meal") in the northwestern industrial zone of Naucalpan—Mexico City's inhabitants are never more than a moment away from a place to eat. If the saying attributed to Balzac is true—"Tell me what you eat and I will tell you who you are"—then getting to know Mexico City is a never-ending delight.

Literally thousands of restaurants, cafés, and food stalls dot the urban landscape. People walk down the street with taco and drink in hand. Sidewalks are overrun by restaurant tables topped with umbrellas to protect patrons from sun or rain. Vendors walk up and down the streets offering baked goods, gelatins, or corn on the cob with *picante* sauce and heavy cream. Little children run about holding tight a plastic bag, filled with a carbonated drink, sucking it out through a straw. Families go out at night to restaurants specializing in *pozole,* a stew with grains of corn, meat, and old and new spices. Mexico City's residents crave *antojitos,* the traditional tacos, quesadillas, tamales, and similar tidbits made from corn with fillings of meats, cheeses, or vegetables.

The cuisine in Mexico City is not only cosmopolitan and international, but also includes regional cuisines from the states of Yucatán, Veracruz, Puebla, Oaxaca, Michoacán, and beyond. Mexico City currently is enjoying a renaissance in its traditional cuisine. Going beyond classical French and continental dishes, chefs are utilizing ingredients from prehistoric and colonial times in new and exciting combinations. Exotic ingredients—*huitlacoche,* a black fungus that grows on corn; *nopales,* the fleshy pads of catcus; *cajeta,* a sweet caramel flavoring made from goat's milk—supplement the ancient triad of corn, beans, and squash. The chocolate-peanut-based sauce known as *mole* (said to have been invented in the kitchens of a convent in Puebla in the 16th century) is produced in a tongue-boggling variety of flavors, usually served over chicken or turkey on holidays, birthdays, saints' days, or other special occasions. And much of the local cuisine depends on the dozens of varieties of chilies (capsicum) produced in the provinces, brought to the capital's wholesale markets, and then redistributed to restaurants, stores, and weekly neighborhood marketplaces for the gustatory delight of the capital's consumers. This new Mexican cuisine is even being exported to the United States and elsewhere.

Mexico City is a serious consumer of beverages—ancient and modern, hard and soft. *Pulque, mezcal, aguardiente de caña* (*chirguirito*), and tequila are high-proof alcoholic drinks with long lineages that compete with local and imported beers, wines, and spirits to quench a thirsty public. Mineral waters, national and international soft-drink brands, carbonated drinks, and blended fruit drinks are available everywhere. And because the local drinking water is not always safe from contamination, many families use bottled water for cooking and drinking.

New foods in new combinations appear every day: Coca-Cola is already a staple; hamburgers and hot dogs are everywhere; fast-food franchises (for example, McDonald's, Dunkin' Donuts, KFC, Domino's Pizza) open every day, but with a twist: hamburgers can be ordered with chilies and Mexican sauces rather than cheese and ketchup, and pizzas can include mole and other local flavors. The increased modernization and internationalization of the food system in Mexico City has potentially serious consequences, especially in the face of the inequitable distribution of basic foodstuffs. The government maintains fixed prices on a basket of basic consumer goods (such as milk, tortillas, and beans), and operates stores in low-income neighborhoods to facilitate the distribution of necessities. In many areas beyond the gaze of tourists or the local elite, women and children line up in the predawn hours to get milk at subsidized prices. Nutritious foods seem to be giving way to highly processed foods full of empty calories. Obesity is a growing problem in affluent sectors of the city, at the same time that millions of children and adults in the slums lack adequate daily caloric intake and suffer from diet-related and waterborne illnesses.

Ethnic, Class, and Religious Diversity. In Mexico City, ethnicity is an "invisible" dimension of urban life. The indigenous groups are rarely visible in daily life in sufficient numbers to be recognized as significant actors in the urban setting. "Aztec"-style dancers perform at the Basilica of Our Lady of Guadalupe, while women and children dressed in "native" garb sit on sidewalks, where they offer their artisanal goods for sale or put out a hand to beg from passersby. Such images of the indigenous population have so mesmerized the public that the tens of thousands of other indigenous people in the capital go unnoticed.

Foreigners are not counted as "ethnic" residents in official Mexican census data, merely being listed according to country and continent of origin rather than by ethnicity. During the past 100 years, the Federal District has received between 16% and 37% of all foreign immigrants. The lowest numbers go back to 1895, when the census reported 9,505 foreigners (of a national total of 54,737 immigrants) in the Federal District. The peak was in 1960, when 83,076 (out of 223,468) were reported in the Federal District. The census data for 1990 recorded only 55,412 foreigners (out of 340,824) in the capital, as many foreign companies dispersed their operations away from Mexico City, either because of the 1985 earthquake or in response to governmental incentives to decentralize.

Class represents the great watershed in the metropolis. The poor are everywhere to be seen in the slums of the inner city and in the squatter settlements on the urban periphery. In between, the working and middle classes struggle to achieve a stable existence in the face of recent decades of economic crisis. Meanwhile, the elite goes on to new heights of consumption. The gap never seems to close, only to grow ever wider. In the folklore of the capital, the "Marías" (women of indigenous appearance who beg on the sidewalks outside tourist hotels, museums, and churches) characterize the suffering of the poorest; the "juniors" (children of high government officials and corporate leaders) epitomize the excesses of the political and economic elite.

During the 1980s and 1990s, when many middle-class families faced mounting consumer debts, organizations such as El Barzón came into existence to protest foreclosures and bankruptcies. Originating in Mexico City and other metropolitan areas, these groups have spread across the land, so that even small-town residents can find support in resisting banks that would take away property for nonpayment of loans originally made at high rates of interest—loans that are now incapable of being repaid, as the peso has continued to be devalued for more than a decade.

The city's religious institutions have been dominated by the Roman Catholic Church ever since Cortés arrived, accompanied by priests, in 1519. The Archbishopric of New Spain was established at Mexico City in 1546, with the cathedral intentionally constructed over the ruins of the Great Temple of Tenochtitlán. Even more important was the development of the cult honoring the Virgin of Guadalupe, who appeared in a vision to an Indian peasant named Juan Diego in 1531 on a hill at Tepayac (in northeastern Mexico City), which had been a place of honor for Tonantzin, an Aztec goddess. By the middle of the 17th century, the Virgin had emerged as the key symbol of Mexican identity. In 1754 Our Lady of Guadalupe was proclaimed by the Roman Catholic Church as Patroness of Mexico.

The end of the official relationship between the state and the Roman Catholic Church came in 1858 during the Juárez presidency—with the disentailment of the church's property—and has extended to the present day. This separation of church and state also permitted the entry of Protestant missionaries and evangelists into Mexico in the latter half of the 19th century, and their influence has been felt in the establishment of numerous Mexico City–based denominations and seminaries. As Mexico City moves into the 21st century, the Roman Catholic Church is still the most dominant religious force, but Protestant groups are gaining followers in significant numbers. Pilgrimages to the Basilica of Guadalupe on December 12 continue as always, but evangelical and Pentecostal churches are growing rapidly in the working-class neighborhoods throughout the metropolitan area.

All but a handful of Mexico's some 40,000 Jews live in Mexico City. The original Spanish (Sephardic) Jews were totally integrated into the general population, and lost their Jewish identity. Today, the community is primarily Ashkenazi. The modern-day Jewish community has remained ethnically distinct and separate, despite its 450 years of history in Mexico.

Family and Other Social Support Systems. Isolated individuals have a difficult time making a life in Mexico City. Nearly everyone draws upon an extensive bank of social resources, ranging from immediate families to neighbors and companions at work or in school. Membership in formal organizations is less important than establishing and sustaining personal social ties beyond one's household. The presence of powerful social networks among even the poorest of the poor provides a way to survive in an unforgiving urban environment. And, at the other end of the power pyramid, social networks ensure that political and economic control are maintained among a relatively small number of elite families with the "right" connections within governmental and corporate circles.

The heart of social life in Mexico City lies in *confianza*, a cultural construct that, according to Carlos Vélez-Ibañez, "designates generosity and intimacy as well as a personal investment in others; it also indicates a willingness to establish such generosity and intimacy." *Confianza* is critical to building and maintaining social relationships beyond the immediate family, including *compadrazgo* (co-godparenthood), *amistad* or *cuatismo* (friendship or palship), *padrino político* (political godfather), *asesor* or *coyote* (consultant or broker), and *cacique* (political power broker). Reciprocity is the operating principle for relationships of *confianza*. These relationships operate at all levels of society in Mexico City and provide the social cement that bonds together people of different socioeconomic statuses, in different neighborhoods, and in different institutional settings.

Voluntary associations, especially those attaching city residents to their communities of origin, provide valuable social networks to millions of residents. For example, migrants from a Mixtec community in Oaxaca have established the Allende Society to provide a mechanism for helping their hometown, and Zapotec migrants from other Oaxaca towns sustain their identity at both informal and formal levels through mutual-aid associations.

Thousands of *tandas* (small-scale rotating credit associations) operate informally outside regular financial channels to provide individuals with a mechanism to purchase consumer goods that otherwise would be beyond their means. For example, women representing 12 different households might agree to buy 12 televisions, one each month, from a local store. Each woman would pay in a monthly contribution (equivalent to one-twelfth the cost of a television), and would receive her television on a schedule determined by drawing lots.

Myths and stereotypes about gender roles in Mexican families abound in popular novels and in the social-science literature. The reality is much more complex. In recent years, a reevaluation of family structures and processes has occurred, especially in light of the rise of feminist studies in Mexico City's intellectual circles. A long-standing awareness of the "survival strategies" of poor families has been extended to issues facing families in the middle and upper classes during the economic crisis of the 1980s and 1990s. The role of women in sustaining domestic units through time has received considerable attention; at the same time, stereotypical views of male machismo have been reinterpreted. And beyond the household, women have played crucial roles in organizing the poor and middle classes to deal with neighborhood problems that affect their families, homes, and children. As Matthew Gutmann has argued, "Grassroots activities and cultural creativity on the part of women who over men's objections have expressed their desire to work for money, as well as on the part of women involved in popular urban movements, certainly constitute part of women's initiative to make men change. . . . For many, the most radical aspect of their politics is revealed in their determination not to be forced to adapt to the system but rather to be included in it on their own terms."

Work and Commerce. Mexico City is the dominant economic power in the nation. As the nation's largest source of production, focus of the national distribution system, and home of the greatest concentration of consumers the capital would rank as the world's 35th-largest economy if it were a freestanding country. It is the site of the national bank and the stock exchange, and home to major corporations and financial enterprises. The economic crisis of the 1980s resulted in a dramatic decline in the availability of industrial jobs in the metropolitan area, although the services sector continued to expand. The trilateral NAFTA treaty among Canada, the United States, and Mexico has heightened awareness of the capital's role in production, distribution, and consumption. International corporations are attracted to Mexico City because of its potential consumer and labor markets, even while the government is determined to encourage decentralization of economic activities.

Perhaps the greatest economic challenge to Mexico City is the growing gap between earnings and the cost of living at the family level. The number of minimum-wage jobs needed to sustain a typical family has grown beyond the labor capacity of many households. High rates of "self-employment" disguise the real unemployment and underemployment rates in the metropolis. A survey carried out in 1995 revealed that basic costs of living continued to rise faster (around 10%) than the increase in the minimum wage (about 7%). Years and years of such imbalances have placed many middle- and working-class families in jeopardy of homelessness and bankruptcy.

In such circumstances, many families pursue multiple economic strategies in order to survive. Ideally, one family member will have a steady job with a government agency so that all of the family is covered by the government's medical plan and so that a modest pension can be expected upon retirement. Meanwhile, other family members look for work in the private sector or pursue opportunities in entrepreneurial self-employment—for example, running a small store from a front room of the house. This combination of steady work and entrepreneurship provides a better hedge against economic failure than either strategy taken alone.

Arts and Recreation. Mexico City has a wide spectrum of arts and recreation opportunities available to residents and tourists. On the western side of the city, Chapultepec Park (the oldest natural park in North America) contains several important museums—including the world-class National Museum of Anthropology, the National History Museum, the Natural History Museum, the Modern Art Museum, and the Rufino Tamayo Museum—as well as extensive recreational spaces and facilities where, on any given Sunday, tens of thousands of families come to picnic, to row boats in the lake, to stroll through the zoo and nearby botanical garden, to play friendly soccer games, to visit the Children's Museum (and see shows at the IMAX theater), to ride the roller coaster known as La Montaña Rusa ("The Russian Mountain") in the amusement park, and to hear rock concerts at the 18,000-seat National Auditorium. On the eastern side of the city, the San Juan de Aragón Park contains a zoo and extensive recreation fields, and other, smaller parks dot the metropolitan area. Many families travel on weekends to Xochimilco, an ancient but "at-risk" ecological zone in southeastern Mexico City where extensive canals and *chinampas* ("floating gardens") are traversed by hundreds of canoes adorned with arcs of multicolored flowers. In 1987 Xochimilco was added to the World Heritage list of properties sponsored by UNESCO.

In the south-central section of the capital, the Plaza México—the largest bullring in the world, with seats for 50,000 people—provides the best bullfighting in the republic. Other professional sports include soccer, baseball, jai alai, horse racing, auto racing, and wrestling. Every weekend witnesses hundreds of local amateur-league soccer matches as well as a growing number of American-football games at high schools and colleges throughout the metropolitan area. In addition to physical activities, almost everyone plays the lottery, run by the government for the benefit of public-welfare programs.

Mexico City is home to several excellent classical-music groups, including the National Symphony Orchestra, the National Opera, the Mexico City Philharmonic, and the State of Mexico Symphony. Theaters and cinemas are found throughout the city and its suburbs, with fine-art and foreign films shown at the Cineteca Nacional in the southern part of the city. Several areas—especially La Zona Rosa ("Pink Zone"), San Angel, Coyoacán, Polanco, and Lomas de Chapultepec—feature fine-art galleries and bookstores.

QUALITY OF LIFE

Life in Mexico City offers many attractions for its residents. The overall quality of housing is higher than in the rest of the nation's towns and cities. Educational opportunities abound for qualified students, including more than 1 million matriculated in 35 universities. Health-care and medical-research facilities are concentrated in the capital. Every week offers hundreds of cultural events, ranging from concerts to art exhibits to the theater. The world's largest wholesale food market supplies more than 40,000 restaurants offering every flavor of international and Mexican regional cuisines. More than 50 radio stations, 27 daily newspapers, and more than 100 weekly magazines compete with numerous television stations for the public's attention. And more than 100,000 stores offer goods from every part of the world.

But the constant movement of life in Mexico City is very stressful. Every day, people comment on the hectic pace of urban life and the need for peace and quiet to offset the city's rapid heartbeat. Many workers and students get up at 5:00 A.M. to get a spot on a microbus that takes them to the nearest Metro station. Then they are jammed into the cars—men separated from the women and children during rush hours—to make their way across the city before climbing aboard another bus or *pesero* (shared taxi) to get close to their final destinations. Then several million workers and students repeat the process going home at the end of the day.

So, when the air pollution is especially severe, the garbage has not been picked up on schedule, or the "Popo" volcano is threatening another eruption, moving away from the capital to the provinces or going northward to the United States seem like attractive alternatives. But Mexico City goes on, with eager migrants replacing those who abandon hope of succeeding in the metropolis. The people who carry on, day after day and year after year, are amazingly tolerant and resilient as they cope with the best and the worst that their country has to offer.

FUTURE OF THE CITY

In a recent political campaign, the slogan of the winning candidate was "*Una ciudad para todos*" ("A city for everyone"). But which Mexico City? The megalopolis filled with unmanageable urban problems? Or the city of a thousand neighborhoods where people survive and even prosper in the face of the endless problems and stress of residing in a place of impossible dreams? The end of the 20th century brought with it the predictable commentaries on the challenges of urban planning for Mexico City in the new millennium.

García Canclini has suggested that it is useful to recognize four great periods in the development of contemporary Mexico City: (a) that of its historical and territorial concentration of the nation's demographic and economic resources into the Federal District, during a long process lasting until the late 20th century; (b) that of industrialization and metropolitan growth, which in recent decades led to spinning off urban elements from the capital's core into the adjacent areas in the state of Mexico; (c) that of the global city, which has assumed a major role in services and communication systems reaching throughout Latin America and North America; and (d) that of multiculturalism and democratization, which has not displaced the three other features of Mexico City but has brought them into new relief.

Going into the 21st century, the people of Mexico City are more aware than ever before in their history that heterogeneity and multiculturalism are the norm of their lives together. Mexico City is becoming what García Canclini calls a "hybrid city," an urban space in which local demands for fairness, equality, and diversity are expressed in the context of powerful forces for globalization. As he points out, the neighborhood organizations dedicated to renovating and sustaining the Centro Histórico zone in downtown Mexico City connect their efforts to international ecological movements and preservationist agreements. Protest marches to the Zócalo, the great square in front of the National Palace and the cathedral, bring together people of every class in their efforts to urge the government's leaders to transform today's urban problems into tomorrow's achievements.

BIBLIOGRAPHY

Arizpe, Lourdes, *Indigenas en la Ciudad: El Caso de las "Marías"* (SepSetentas No. 182 1975).

Arizpe, Lourdes, *Migración, Etnicismo y Cambio Económico (un Estudio Sobre Migrantes Campesinos a la Ciudad de México)* (El Colegio de México 1978).

Butterworth, Douglas, "A Study of the Urbanization Process among Mixtec Migrants from Tilantongo in Mexico City," *América Indígena* 22, no. 3 (1962): 257–74.

Cornelius, Wayne, *Politics and the Migrant Poor in Mexico City* (Stanford University Press 1975).

Davis, Diane E., *Urban Leviathan: Mexico City in the Twentieth Century* (Temple University Press 1994).

Eckstein, Susan, "Poor People versus the State and Capital: Anatomy of a Successful Community Mobilization for Housing in Mexico City," *International Journal of Urban and Regional Research* 4, no. 2 (1990): 274–296

Eckstein, Susan, *The Poverty of Revolution: The State and the Urban Poor in Mexico* (Princeton University Press 1977).

García Canclini, Néstor, "Introducción: las Cuatro Ciudades de México," *Cultura y Comunicación en la Ciudad de México,* ed. by Néstor García Canclini (Universidad Autónoma Metropolitana, Iztapalapa, and Editorial Grijalbo 1998): 19–39.

Gilbert, Alan, *In Search of a Home: Rental and Shared Housing in Latin America* (University of Arizona Press 1993).

Gutmann, Matthew C., *The Meanings of Macho: Being a Man in Mexico City* (University of California Press 1996).

Hirabayashi, Lane Ryo, *Cultural Capital: Mountain Zapotec Migrant Associations in Mexico City* (University of Arizona Press 1993).

Kandel, Jonathan, *La Capital: The Biography of Mexico City* (Random House 1988).

Kemper, Robert V., "Desarrollo de los Estudios Antropológicos Sobre la Migración Mexicana," *La Heterodoxia Recuperada, en Torno a Angel Palerm,* ed. by Susana Glantz (Fondo de Cultura Económica 1987): 477–99.

Kemper, Robert V., "Migración y Transformación de la Cultura Mexicana: 1519–1992," *Tradición e Identidad en la Cultura Mexicana,* ed. by Agustín Jacinto Zavala and Alvaro Ochoa Serrano (El Colegio de Michoacán y Consejo Nacional de Ciencia y Tecnología 1995): 533–47.

Kemper, Robert V., *Migration and Adaptation: Tzintzuntzan Peasants in Mexico City* (Sage Publications 1977).

Lara Ramos, Luís Fernando, *Diccionario del Español Usual en México* (El Colegio de México 1996).

Lewis, Oscar, *Five Families: Mexican Case Studies in the Culture of Poverty* (Basic Books 1959).

Lewis, Oscar, "Urbanization without Breakdown: A Case Study," *The Scientific Monthly* 75 (1952): 31–41.

Lomnitz, Larissa Adler de, *Networks and Marginality: Life in a Mexican Shantytown* (Academic Press 1977).

Messmacher, Miguel, *México: Megalópolis* (Secretaría de Educación Pública, Foro 2000 1987).

Mora Vázquez, Teresa, *Nduandiki y la Sociedad de Allende en México: un Caso de Migración Rural-Urbana* (Instituto Nacional de Antropología e Historia 1996).

Schteingart, Martha, "Mexico City," *Mega-Cities,* vol. 2 of *The Metropolis Era,* ed. by Mattei Dogan and John D. Kasarda (Sage Publications 1988): 268–93.

Scott, Ian, *Urban and Spatial Development in Mexico* (Johns Hopkins University Press and the World Bank 1982).

Selby, Henry, et al., *The Mexican Urban Household: Organizing for Self-Defense* (University of Texas Press 1990).

Unikel, Luís, et al., *El Desarrollo Urbano de México: Diagnóstico e Implicaciones Futuras* (El Colegio de México 1976).

Vargas, Luís Alberto, "Diet and Foodways in Mexico City," *Ecology of Food and Nutrition* 27 (1992): 235–47.

Vélez-Ibañez, Carlos G., *Bonds of Mutual Trust: The Cultural Systems of Rotating Credit Associations among Urban Mexicans and Chicanos* (Rutgers University Press 1983).

Vélez-Ibañez, Carlos G., *Rituals of Marginality: Politics, Process, and Culture Change in Central Urban Mexico, 1969–1974* (University of California Press 1983).

Ward, Peter M., *Mexico City,* rev. 2d ed. (John Wiley & Sons 1998).

Wolf, Eric, *Sons of the Shaking Earth* (University of Chicago Press 1959).

ROBERT V. KEMPER

Miami

United States

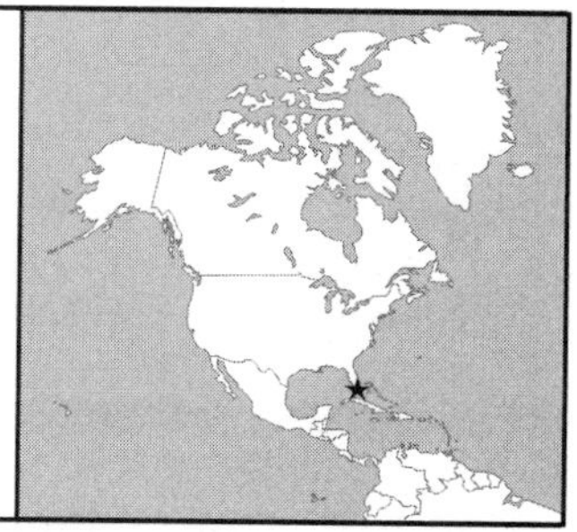

ORIENTATION

Miami is a relatively new city, barely more than 100 years old. During this period of time, Miami has been able to achieve a level of development that has taken many other cities hundreds of years. Today Miami has the sophistication of some of the largest metropolitan cities in the United States and the world.

Name of City. Perhaps the oldest nickname given to Miami is the "Magic City," which is the most preferred by its residents and perhaps the expression that has been around the longest. There are many people who claim that Miami has the ability to always bounce back, just like "magic," whether the problems to be overcome are natural disasters such as hurricanes, political disagreements, or citizen unrest.

Miami's geographic location has made it a convenient place to seek refuge in times of problems. Traditionally, Miami has been a haven for people seeking political sanctuary and economic opportunities. Many political leaders from Caribbean countries have made Miami their home at times of political unrest at home. This has resulted in Miami's being called the "Casablanca of the Caribbean."

In recent years, Miami has been referred as the "City of the Future." This last name reflects the changes of the city and its multicultural flavor. This cultural pluralism has been the result of mass immigration from Latin American and Caribbean countries. These newcomers, speaking a different language and with different cultures, have created an excellent environment for trade and commerce with Latin America.

Location. The city of Miami is located at 25°8′ north latitude and 80°3′ west longitude, in the state of Florida, county of Miami-Dade, in the United States. The city is located on the southeast tip of the Florida peninsula. The boundaries of the city are the Atlantic Ocean and Biscayne Bay to the east, the Everglades National Park to the west, and the Florida Keys to the south. Broward county is located to the north.

The city of Miami is the largest of the incorporated cities that form the county of Miami-Dade. When talking about Miami, people are referring to the whole metropolitan area without realizing that there are other municipalities within that area. It would be hard for outsiders—and often for some residents of Miami-Dade county—to know when they cross city boundaries.

The connection of all of these municipalities and other unincorporated areas prompted a name change for the county of Dade. In 1997 the original name of the county was changed by voters from Metro Dade county to Miami-Dade county. For the purpose of this article, Miami refers to the entire metropolitan area—that is, what the residents of the county refer to as Miami. This is also the way that the U.S. Census Bureau defines the area.

Population. The city of Miami has a population of 362,470 (2000 census), and an area of approximately 114 square kilometers (44 square miles). When the municipalities and areas identified as Miami are included, the population of the county is 2,253,362, with an area of more than 5,180 square kilometers (2,000 square miles). There are 30 other municipalities in Miami-Dade county, each one a little different, with lifestyles reflecting the ethnic composition of each community's residents. According to statistical data from the U.S. Census Bureau, in 2000 the population of Miami was approximately 57% Hispanic, 24% non-Hispanic white, and 20% African American.

Distinctive and Unique Features. The location of the city of Miami, at the very tip of the Florida peninsula, is in itself a unique feature. This location puts the city very close to the Caribbean countries and Latin America, and in a unique way, removed from the U.S. mainland. It is common to hear many people comment that being in Miami is like being in another country. These comments are sometimes made with resentment, and sometimes in awe of the distinctive and unique differences of the area.

If there were only one word to describe today's city, it would be diversity. As Alejandro Portes has pointed out, "What makes Miami so unique is not the number of immigrants arriving into the city, but the rupture of an established cultural outlook and a unified social hierarchy in which every group of newcomers takes its preordained place."

Attractions of the City. There are countless attractions in the Miami area, but prime among them are the beaches and year-round subtropical climate. This subtropical climate, with an annual average temperature of 24°C (75°F), allows for outdoor activities all year. The rainy season occurs during the summer months. Many residents claim that there are only two seasons in Miami: warm or warmer. For the most part, this is true; however, close proximity to the ocean allows sea breezes to make summer weather more tolerable.

CORBIS-BETTMANN

A sailboat lies on its side near the Miami waterfront as the 145-kilometer-per-hour (90-mile-per-hour) winds of Hurricane Diana hammer the city in September 1960.

Owing to its proximity to the Caribbean islands, the port of Miami has become a destination point for thousands of tourists boarding cruise ships to many different countries. This has given Miami another nickname, the "cruise capital of the world." The mild weather and the abundance of moderately priced hotels, deep-sea fishing, and countless restaurants have made Miami an attractive tourist destination all year-round.

Relationships Between the City and the Outside. Owing to the geographic location of the city and the influence of a large Latin population, the bond with Latin America is very strong. This relationship goes back to a time, before the city was chartered, when Bahamian and Cuban fishermen visited the coast of Florida. Many of these fishermen traveled frequently between their countries and the coast of Florida, establishing temporary settlements.

Years later the aviation industry became another factor in the relationship of Miami with the outside world. Miami was home to Pan American Airways, a pioneer in the aviation industry. Pan American's first flight to Havana, Cuba, in 1927 established a strong relationship between the two cities. By 1935 Pan American Airways had more than 35 flights connecting Miami to Central and South America. Eastern Airlines, another pioneer in the aviation history, connected Miami with New York, Chicago, and other eastern cities.

All of these factors were crucial in developing a strong relationship with countries abroad as well as with the rest of the United States. Eventually these early interactions with other cities and countries helped Miami in its development as a major banking and commercial center for Latin America and Caribbean countries.

The close relationship with Caribbean and Latin American countries has been very influential for the economic development of Miami, but has also created social problems. Drug traffickers, taking advantage of Miami's unique location, have made it a drop-off point for their illegal activities. This has in turn resulted in an increase in drug-related crimes.

Major Languages. Although English is the official language of the state, many other languages can be heard around the city. Among these, Haitian Creole is widely used for the unofficial communication of the increasing Haitian population. Spanish is the predominant language used in Miami. In many parts of the city, it would be hard for the non–Spanish speaker to get by. The ability to speak Spanish and English is desirable and very often a requirement to obtain employment. This has caused some friction between the native and immigrant populations of Miami.

Friction with the Anglo population intensified during the 1970s, and in 1980 an amendment to the Florida constitution was introduced. The Citizens United of Dade County, a grassroots organization, was successful in introducing an amendment prohibiting the use of county funds for the promotion of any language and/or culture other than English; 84% of the voters ratified the amendment.

The friction between immigrants and natives continued, resulting in a displacement of Anglos to other counties, in particular Broward County. As stated by Alejandro Portes, "The white Anglo population feeling a loss of cultural hegemony, has led to a massive white flight, not only out of the city, but out of Dade county [the Miami metropolitan area] altogether." It has been estimated that the metropolitan area lost approximately one-third of its native population as a result of this white migration. A decline in Miami's total population was prevented only by the arrival of thousands of immigrants.

HISTORY

The Origin of the City. The development of Miami is relatively new when compared with that of other American cities. Although temporary settlements of Bahamian and Cuban fishermen were established on the tip of the Florida peninsula, they were not lasting. These first settlements came from the outside—that is, the Caribbean islands,—establishing early on a pattern of migration that would eventually grow into a steady flow.

The Spaniards were the first to establish a settlement on the banks of the Miami River. In 1566 Pedro Martinez de Avila and a Jesuit priest named Francisco Villareal established the first community in what later would be the city of Miami. It was not until the early 1800s that the first European settlers arrived in the area.

Hundred of years before that, Tequesta Indians inhabited small villages around the banks of the Miami River. These small bands of peaceful hunters and gatherers were the natives that the Spanish found, but their days would be numbered. Diseases unknown to them and brought by Europeans decimated the native population almost to total extinction.

Other Indians from Georgia, Alabama, and South Carolina started to enter the state of Florida, settling on the lands formerly occupied by the Tequestas. These Indians, coming from a variety of tribes, were escaping the advancement of colonization. Collectively, they were called Seminoles—from the word *Simi-in-oli*, meaning "wild." These Indians were later joined by runaway African slaves.

Colonization from within the mainland United States was slow at first. One of the reasons was that Florida was a Spanish territory, but another reason was the inhospitable conditions of the terrain. Impenetrable swamps, insects, and hostile Indians kept settlers out of the area until the 1800s. In 1821, after 200 years of Spanish domination, Florida was sold to the United States for $5 million.

Colonization of the new territory continued to be slow, as the colonists encountered the ongoing hostility of the Seminole Indians. Conflict with the American government, which was trying to relocate the Seminoles to reservations to the northwest, set the stage for the longest Indian wars in American history. The three Seminole Indian wars covered a period of time between 1818 and 1858, with some periods of relative peace in between.

The city of Miami was incorporated in 1896. Many historical events have contributed to the development of the city as we know it today: a city with an international flavor. Some of these events were the building of the Florida Railroad, the development of tourism, and the expansion of the aviation industry. Of these important factors, most historians agree that the one single event that changed the city forever was the Cuban Revolution.

This event took place approximately 400 kilometers (250 miles) to the south of the city, on the island nation of Cuba. The revolution displaced thousands of Cuban refugees seeking political asylum. Unlike many other immigrants, who come seeking economic opportunities, this first wave of middle- and upper-class immigrants brought with them education, skills, and money, and they were able to transform the monocultural aspect of the city to one of pluralistic flavor. The first wave of Cuban immigrants consisted mainly of doctors, attorneys, teachers, and business professionals. Collectively, they possessed the drive and the means to change the city. Owing to their social status, they were well received by the United States, and in a few years they were able to gain a strong foothold in Miami, economically as well as politically.

This first group also felt that their displacement to Miami would not be a permanent one. This is one of the reasons for the tenacity with which they kept their language and customs intact. The Cubans refused to be absorbed into the culture of the United States. With a very strong sense of cultural identity, they adapted to their new country without changing their ethnic identity.

One of the ways in which they were able to maintain their cultural identity was through their language. Very often the inability of a group to speak English well is associated with poverty or developing-nation status. This was not the case with the Cubans. They continued to speak Spanish and to teach their children Spanish. English was reserved for activities outside the home, but at home, Spanish was the language spoken. This has resulted in a bilingual young population that continues to carry on the traditions of their culture.

As time passed, the Spanish language would be heard more and more all over the city. Relatively soon, the Spanish language was no longer reserved for the home only, but became a part of everyday life. As author Joan Didion comments, "What was so unusual about Spanish in Miami was not that it was so often spoken, but that it was so often heard." The author is referring to the prevalence of the Spanish language in the everyday activities of the city. Didion also states that "Unlike other places in the United States where Spanish becomes a barely audible noise, spoken by the people that wash the cars, trim the trees or clear tables in restaurants, in Miami, Spanish is spoken by those that eat in the restaurants and own the cars and the trees." This is true: the Spanish language is as common in the Miami area as English would be in the heartland of America. In Miami, the inability to speak Spanish makes it very difficult and sometimes impossible to conduct business. This has created some tensions in the city, and it is cited as one of the reasons why many Anglos have opted to move out of the metropolitan area.

Anglos were not the only ones to feel threatened by the changes caused by mass migration. African American residents felt that they were being displaced by the Cubans. They also perceived that the arriving Hispanics were taking jobs away from them. Without the economic means to leave the city, blacks had to stay and see themselves once again left out of economic opportunities that would improve their way of life.

In 1980 a violent and costly racial riot erupted in Miami. The reason for the unrest was the not-guilty verdict for four members of the Public Safety Department (now called the Miami-Dade Police Department) accused of beating to death a black insurance agent, Arthur McDuffie. Owing to a charged political atmosphere, where blacks felt disenfranchised and persecuted, the trial had been moved to the city of Tampa on the west coast of Florida. Nevertheless, when the officers were found not guilty, riots, causing more than $80 million in property damages, broke out in Miami. Many people were killed or injured during the three days of rioting. Three other race riots have taken place in Miami (1968, 1982, 1989), the only city in the United States where four racially motivated riots have occurred.

Migration: Past and Present. The history of South Florida shows the constant arrival of new people, from within the United States as well as from other parts of the world. The most significant pattern of migration started with the first wave of approximately 248,000 Cuban immigrants arriving in Miami in the late 1950s and early 1960s. In 1965 an additional 5,000 Cuban refugees were allowed to leave through the port of Camarioca. After that, the freedom flights added another 340,000 refugees. It is estimated that the steady flow of Cuban immigrants gradually added approximately 600,000 immigrants to the Miami area.

In 1980 another large group of Cuban refugees arrived in Miami. The "Mariel Boat Lift," as it is called, added approximately 125,000 refugees to Miami in less than six months. This group of Cubans, unlike previous ones, lacked skills and education. Many of them were criminals released from Cuban prisons and mental hospitals. The large number of refugees and their criminal pasts put a strain on Miami's resources and increased the tensions in the community.

During this time, hundreds of Haitian refugees were also arriving on Florida's coast. The "black boat people," as they were often called, had a hard time claiming the right to stay in Miami. This group of refugees lacked the political clout of the Cuban immigrants.

The events that led to the Cuban exodus of the early 1960s had an effect on the migration patterns of other Hispanic groups. Immigrants from Colombia, Peru, Ecuador, and other Latin American countries were diverted to Miami instead of New York. Nicaraguans escaping the left-wing Sandinista government also came to Miami. That pattern of migration is likely to continue into the 21st century, reshaping the city as well as the native population.

INFRASTRUCTURE

Public Buildings, Public Works, and Residences. The architecture of Miami reflects the diversity of the city as well as its past. The first city skyscraper was built in 1924 on Biscayne Boulevard, close to the downtown area. This building, first owned by the *Miami News* (a newspaper no longer in circulation), became a processing center for early Cuban refugees seeking political asylum. The building, called the Freedom Tower, has become a symbol for thousands of Cuban refugees who left the island in the early 1960s. Other interesting buildings in the downtown area are the Guzman Center for the Performing Arts, the Gesu Catholic Church, and the Miami-Dade Cultural Center, which hosts one of the largest libraries in the southeastern United States.

The city of Miami Beach offers an excellent example of art deco architecture. This type of architecture has its roots in French art nouveaux and is characterized by pastel colors and linear forms. Approximately 800 buildings constructed during the 1920s and 1930s can be found in this famous art deco district. Many areas in the city, in particular Coral Gables, offer good examples of Mediterranean-style architecture. The city of Miami Springs, north of Miami International Airport, offers many examples of Pueblo-style architecture. Pueblo-style architecture is a style of construction that uses adobe bricks and is found mainly in the southwestern states.

Politics and City Services. Miami-Dade county is governed by an executive mayor and a board of county commissioners. The system of government is two-tiered and consists of a large unincorporated area and 30 incorporated areas or municipalities. The board of commissioners, as the legislative branch of the government, oversees police and fire services for both the unincorporated and the incorporated areas of the county. This board is also responsible for the enforcement of building codes, zoning, and the collection of garbage and trash.

The other municipalities, of which the city of Miami is the largest, have their own government, providing the same type of city services such as police and fire. The intertwining of some of these municipalities is such that those not familiar with political divisions would not know that they are in a

© ALAN DIAZ/AP/WIDE WORLD PHOTOS

Miami election officials study a challenged ballot during the controversial presidential election of 2000.

different city. Many citizens comment that the only way they can tell one apart from the other is by the name written on the police cruisers patrolling the different areas of Miami-Dade county.

The large parks and recreation division of Miami-Dade county and other municipalities offers a variety of cultural and recreational activities. Within a short distance from the bustle of the city, a vast number of nature parks and historical tours are available. Among these parks, the Everglades National Park is the largest. This park covers over a million and a half acres and is the only subtropical preserve in North America. Everglades means "river of grass," and consists of a system of rivers flowing from the middle of the state toward the ocean.

Educational System. As part of the Miami-Dade school system, the city of Miami offers many educational opportunities for students. Miami-Dade is the 4th-largest public school system in the nation, with an enrollment of over 300,000 students in kindergarten through 12th grade. As part of this system students can choose from charter schools, which are recognized as public schools, and magnet schools, specialized programs in such areas as foreign languages or art that also provide multicultural interaction among students. Students in Miami-Dade are required to pass a Florida Comprehensive Assessment Test (FCAT) in order to graduate from high school. The test has been extremely controversial, with a number of schools failing to achieve the required mark. (This has been attributed to the large number of immigrant students.) In 2001 none of the public schools received failing marks on their annual accountability report; however, 63% of 10th graders taking the test failed the math portion and 54% failed the reading portion.

The city has an excellent higher-educational system, with a variety of colleges, universities, and vocational schools. Miami Dade Community College, one of the largest community colleges in the country, offers a variety of academic and vocational programs. It has five campuses located in different parts of the county.

The main campus of the college, located in the north end of the county, houses the School of Justice and the School of Fire and Environmental Sciences. The School of Justice provides professional training for police and corrections officers. The School of Fire and Environmental Sciences offers training in fire fighting, hazardous-waste-site operations, and other environmental issues. Police and fire departments in the Miami-Dade county area use this facility to train their forces, as well as for their career-development courses.

Miami is also home to the University of Miami. The School of Law and the School of Medicine of this private university are nationally recognized as among the best in the country. Florida International University, a state-supported institution, has become a truly international university, attracting students from all over the country and the world. Other private universities in Miami are Barry, St. Thomas, and Florida Memorial College. In addition, several other universities offer their programs in Miami. One of these, the Johnson and Wales University from Rhode Island, offers associate and bachelor's degrees in culinary arts and hospitality management.

Transportation System. As with most big cities, Miami traffic could be intimidating to some. In spite of frequent road improvement, the rapid growth of the city has made rush-hour traffic a nightmare. Roadways are often congested, and unpredictable accidents can add much time to commuting.

Most of the city residents have learned to cope with traffic problems as well as find ways to avoid it. Although automobile transportation is the preferred choice for most of the city residents, a mass-transit system is available. Buses of this system connect commuters with the metro-rail system and the metro-mover serving the downtown area.

One of the major highways that crisscross Miami-Dade county is the Palmetto Expressway, which runs east to west from the Golden Glades interchange in the northern part of the county and then turns to north and south. The Dolphin Expressway, or State Road 836, is another highway that connects the southern part of the county with the airport and downtown areas. For commuters from other counties, the tri-rail system is usually the best choice. This is a light-rail system that links Dade, Broward, and Palm Beach counties.

Many good roads connect Miami with the rest of the state and country. On the eastern shore, Interstate 95 and U.S. 1 connect the city with the northern part of the state. When traveling to destinations in the center of the state—such as Orlando, the home of Disney World—a toll road, the Florida Turnpike, is the best choice. On the west side of the state, Interstate 75 connects Miami with cities on the west coast, such as Tampa–St. Petersburg. Other roads that run north are Highway 27 and Highway 441. These last two are older roads and are less used by travelers. Using these older roads can take travelers through some picturesque towns in the state, thus giving the traveler the opportunity to see what rural Florida looks like. To the south of Miami-Dade county, a causeway connects Miami to the Florida Keys.

CULTURAL AND SOCIAL LIFE

Distinctive Features of the City's Cultures. There are many cultural groups living in the Miami-Dade county area. One of the best ways to explore the traditions of these groups is at the museum folklife program of the Historical Museum of Southern Florida, which has identified more than 60 cultural groups in the area. These groups have adapted well to the American way of life, while retaining their individual characteristics.

Of the different cultures represented in Miami, the Cubans have been the most significant. According to Guillermo Grenier, "Nowhere else in America, or even in American history, have first-generation immigrants so quickly, so thoroughly appropriated political power." This group of Cuban immigrants was able to establish the best example in the United States of an ethnic enclave. As described by Portes, "An ethnic enclave is a distinctive economic formation characterized by the spatial concentration of immigrants who organize a variety of enterprises to serve their own ethnic market and the general population." Their businesses, churches, and schools provided cohesiveness and social networks among the immigrants. Establishment of this enclave was crucial for the preservation of cultural traits as well as independence from the host country. It is possible for Cubans to work, conduct business, and maintain a social life without leaving their ethnic community.

Other Hispanic groups attracted by this enclave have also made Miami their home. A large community of Nicaraguan immigrants occupies a large section to the northwest of Miami, a section known as "Little Managua."

Haitian immigrants are another significant group adding to Miami's diversity. Concentrated in the area formerly called Lemon City, they have established businesses, churches, and extensive social networks, adding to Miami's diversity. This section, located north of the downtown area, is called "Little Haiti."

Cuisine. The cuisine of Miami is as diverse as its population. The city is dotted with regional and international restaurants, making dining a truly cultural experience. Cultural diffusion, or the movement of cultural traits among different groups, is very evident in Miami's cuisine. With the arrival of thousands of Cuban refugees, Cuban food has become an integral part of Miami's cuisine. Small coffee shops offering cups of Cuban coffee are seen all over the city. The Cuban tradition of *cafecito* (a small shot of strong Cuban coffee) has been adopted by most of Miami's population. Many other ethnic groups are present in the area, and Caribbean restaurants abound. Of these others, Haitian food has become increasingly popular in Miami, and many good Haitian restaurants can be found in the area.

Ethnic, Class, and Religious Diversity. Religious diversity is well represented in Miami. The variety of churches of all different denominations is evidence of this diversity. Most ethnic groups tend to adhere to one predominant religious affiliation. For example, a great majority of Cubans are Catholic. Other nontraditional religious organizations are represented within these ethnic groups. An example of this would be the Santeria religion, a mixture of Catholicism and African religion. This Afro-Cuban cult was introduced in Miami during the 1980s by the more recent wave of Cuban immigrants. The Santeria religion has become more acceptable today, but it remains a practice primarily of the lower classes. Many Haitians practice Catholicism, but some also practice voodoo, also a mixture of Catholicism and African religion. Both of these less traditional religions were first adopted by African slaves trying to conform to the indoctrination of the Catholic Church. In the case of Santeria, Catholic saints were given the name of African deities and were worshiped in the African tradition.

Jews are well represented in Miami. The Jewish Museum of Florida offers programs illustrating their long presence in Miami and their contributions to the development of the city.

Family and Other Social Support Systems. One tradition common to most of the recently arrived cultural groups is family cohesiveness. Within the Haitian community, family support systems lend help to kin and friends. Their informal economy makes it possible for them to adapt and survive. Churches as support systems play an important role in the Haitian community.

Hispanics tend to live in extended-family settings. This type of living arrangement provides emotional support and enables the whole family to participate in the formal economy of the county. Cuban women in particular have a very high rate of participation in the labor force.

Work and Commerce. The Miami economy is based primarily on tourism. Other activities that contribute to the economic growth of the city are trade and commerce. Film production is expanding, and manufacturing and agriculture also provide employment in the area.

Arts and Recreation. Miami-Dade has made advances in the art scene. Numerous nonprofit cultural organizations have been working to promote the expansion of the arts. The Miami Art Museum and the Historical Museum of Southern Florida, located in downtown Miami, offer exhibitions from museums around the world. The Florida Philharmonic Orchestra, the New World Symphony, and the Miami City Ballet also contribute to the art scene in Miami. The visual arts, although not as well represented as the others, are beginning to grow. Many art galleries are beginning to be seen in Miami Beach, Coconut Grove, and other parts of the city.

Miami is also home to four major teams in some of the most popular sports: the Miami Dolphins of the National Football League, the Miami Heat of the National Basketball Association, the Florida Panthers of the National Hockey League, and, in major-league baseball, the Florida Marlins.

QUALITY OF LIFE

Miami offers a good quality of life for those that embrace diversity and the fast pace of a large metropolitan city. An adequate transportation system, good medical facilities, and an excellent school system add to the benefits of the city. A low unemployment rate and a growing economy play an important role in the quality of life.

FUTURE OF THE CITY

As Miami enters the 21st century, it seems that migration will continue to be a major factor in population growth. As with any large city experiencing rapid growth, the cost of living and the scarcity of affordable housing will be issues of concern.

BIBLIOGRAPHY

Didion, Joan, *Miami* (Simon & Schuster 1987).

Grenier, Guillermo, and Alex Stepick III, *Miami Now* (University Press of Florida 1992).

Parks, Arva Moore, *Miami Memoirs* (Arva Parks 1987).

Peters, Thelma, *Lemon City* (Banyan Books 1976).

Porter, Bruce, and Marvin Dunn, *The Miami Riot of 1980* (Lexington Books 1982).

Portes, Alejandro, and Alex Stepick III, *City on the Edge: The Transformation of Miami* (University of California Press 1993).

Stoneman-Douglas, Marjorie, *The Everglades: River of Grass* (Pineapple Press 1997).

GRACE FERNANDEZ-MATTHEWS

Milan

Italy

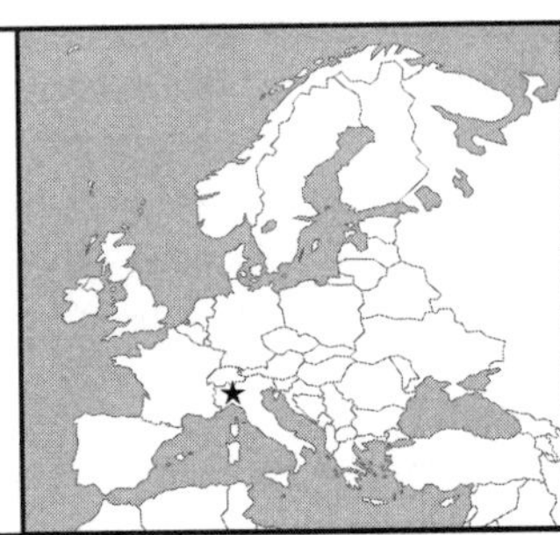

ORIENTATION

Name of City. Milan (Milano) is the capital of the province that bears its name, as well as of the region of Lombardy in northern Italy. Although it was not the birthplace of Italian unification, many Milanese as well as other Italians believe that Milan should have become the capital of Italy. It is the most prominent modern city in Italy. Its place in world history is secured through its contributions to the development of the Renaissance, its world-class musical heritage, and its role in industry, finance, and fashion. It is the most modern city in Italy.

Location. Milan is located at 45°28′ north latitude and 9°12′ east longitude. It is situated on the Lombard Plain in northern Italy and in the Po River basin. The city lies at the intersection of major transportation routes, a geographic factor that has made it a major commercial, industrial, and financial center since medieval times. It is Italy's second-largest city (Rome is the largest) and its leading financial and industrial center. Milan has Italy's highest per-capita income.

Population. Milan's population, as of the 1991 census, was 1,369,231.

Attractions of the City. Milan has numerous attractions to draw and dazzle both foreign and Italian visitors. The city is one of the international capitals of luxury goods, fashion, business and finance, and design. Businesspeople, buyers, editors, journalists, and students from around the globe flock to the city for major trade and fashion shows featuring the latest styles in everything from clothing to furniture to jewelry to industrial design. Milan is home to some of the world's leading fashion houses (Armani, Prada, Versace), and shops and boutiques throughout the city present the newest trends and products from top designers.

The city's abundant cultural offerings include restaurants, theaters, dance companies, museums, opera (in particular the renowned 18th-century Teatro alla Scala, considered the premier opera house in the world), and universities. Its gracious promenades, including the Corso Vittorio Emanuele, Montenapo, and Via Spiga, are lined with magnificent historic buildings, and with cafés, restaurants, and specialty shops.

Among the many masterpieces housed in Milan's churches, cathedrals, palaces, and museums is Leonardo da Vinci's most famous fresco, *The Last Supper,* located in the refectory of the Church of Santa Maria delle Grazie. The Palazzo di Brera contains works by such Italian masters as Bernardino Luini, Gentile and Giovanni Bellini, Tintoretto, Veronese, and Titian.

The Basilica of Sant' Ambrogio (archbishop of Milan), dates from the 4th century and is known for its magnificent architecture. Other attractions in the city include the Ambrosian Library, the Church of Sant' Eustorgio (9th century), the Leonardo da Vinci Museum of Science and Technology, the gallery of modern art, and the Poldi Pezzoli Museum, whose collection includes works by such famous Italian artists as Boticelli, Pollaiuolo, Mantegna, and Piero della Francesca.

Italians love to say, "for every church in Rome, there is a bank in Milan." However, Milan has many magnificent churches of its own. Its white marble Gothic cathedral (Duomo), is in the center of the city on the Piazza del Duomo. Built between 1386 and 1913, the lengthy period of its construction is reflected in the cathedral's various architectural styles. The Duomo is 146 meters (480 feet) long and 85 meters (280 feet) wide. It features 52 sequoia pillars, more than 200 statues, and 135 marble spires. A statue of the Madonna adorns the cathedral's tallest spire.

Relationships Between the City and the Outside. Milan is the most significant commercial and industrial city in Europe. Moreover, it exerts strong political and cultural influences. Milan's economic sector, for example, is a dynamic one. It combines the industriousness of its people with an entrepreneurial character. Milan features both large industrial plants and small manufacturing industries. Its products include those from engineering, steel, chemical, textile, printing, and woodworking industries. Not surprisingly, Milan employs about 60% of its population in services such as banking, insurance, the Italian stock exchange (Borsa Italiana), and other pursuits befitting a major international commercial center. Cultural, as well as industrial and commercial, events link Milan with the outside world. The Carnevale Ambrosiano (Ambrosian Carnival), the Fiera Campionaria (the April Trade Fair), the La Scala Opera season, and the Festa dei Navigli in June are major cultural events.

Major Languages. Italian is the predominant language of Milan. However, English is virtually a second language, and other world languages are freely spoken as a result of Milan's commercial, artistic, intellectual, financial, and fashion activities.

HISTORY

The Origin of the City. The Gauls, a Celtic people, founded Milan around 600 B.C. Known as Mediolanum, it became the capital of the Insubres. An important trade center, in 222 B.C., it was conquered by Rome.

© KAREN TWEEDY-HOLMES/CORBIS

A gargoyle protrudes from a cornice of the Duomo, the famous cathedral of Milan, Italy.

It became capital of the Western Roman Empire in 305 A.D. and remained its capital until 402. In 313 the emperor Constantine granted religious toleration in the Edict of Milan. Saint Ambrose, renowned for his eloquence and the liturgy he founded, was bishop from 374 to 379. Ambrose played a major role in the conversion of Saint Augustine, the future bishop of Hippo and an influential theologian. By that time, church and state were united, so Milan was also the center of religious rule in the area. Sacked by Attila the Hun in 452 and destroyed by the Goths in 539, by the latter 10th century Milan had once again become a powerful city. Under Charlemagne—who incorporated Milan into his kingdom—and his descendants, the city had revived. Around 1000 Milan's archbishop assumed political power. This marked the origin of the city's medieval greatness.

By the 12th century, Milan was a free commune and ruled the other cities of Lombardy. However, during the period from the 11th to the 13th century, Milan underwent a period of civil war involving various competing groups—such as rich versus poor, those who supported the pope versus supporters of the emperor, as well as wars with rival cities—which helped Emperor Frederick I in destroying the city in 1163. Nevertheless, Milan and its Lombard League obtained revenge in helping defeat Frederick I at Legnano in 1176. The Peace of Constance in 1183 acknowledged Milan's independence.

In the 13th century, however, Milan lost its republican liberties when the Torrianis and then the Viscontis (1277) took control as its rulers. In 1395 Galeazzo Visconti formally received the title of duke from the emperor. Under Visconti's rule, Milan became the leading city in its area, and one of the more important in all of Italy. In 1447, when the last Visconti died, the Sforzas assumed leadership of Milan. In 1553, however, the city came under Spanish rule as a result of its involvement in the Italian Wars.

Under the Sforzas, Milan became a major artistic center. Around 1480 Leonardo da Vinci went to Milan as guest of Ludovicao Sforza and remained for 16 years. In Milan, Leonardo completed a number of major works, including his *Essay on Painting,* as well his notebooks. As part of his job as court artist, Leonardo was responsible for organizing festivals, and even in this somewhat mundane pursuit he displayed genius. The plagues of 1484 and 1485 directed his curiosity to town planning and sanitation. Additionally, Leonardo was concerned with architecture during this period in Milan, as his drawing demonstrates. His interests were quite practical, and Leonardo became a consulting engineer while also working on various churches and cathedrals. In 1483 he painted the *Madonna of the Rocks*. Leonardo began his *Last Supper* in 1495, and completed it three years later. Ludovico Sforza commissioned Leonardo to work on a monument to Francesco Sforza, his father. As with so much of his work, it was never completed, and the model was destroyed in 1499 when the French invaded Milan.

In 1535 the reigning duke of Milan died suddenly, and Charles V, the Hapsburg emperor, took control of Milan. In 1540 he gave the city to his son, the future King Philip II of Spain. Spanish sovereignty lasted until 1706. It was a period of political, economic, and artistic decline for Milan. The plague of 1630 formed an integral part of the Milanese author Alessandro Manzoni's (1785–1873) *I promessi sposi* (The Betrothed). This historical novel is not only a masterpiece of European literary art, it was also a key factor in the Risorgimento, the movement for Italian independence. The end of the dreary period of Spanish rule came with the War of the Spanish Succession, 1701–1706. This war began with the death of Charles II of Spain. In September 1706 Austria assumed rule over Milan.

Under Austrian rule (1713 to 1796), Milan gradually began to experience economic, political, and artistic growth. Intellectual growth was marked by the works of people such as Cesare Beccaria, the founder of criminology and a noted economist, and Pietro Verri, the gifted administrator and man of letters. Beccaria and Verri were among the members of the Società dei Pugni, which accepted the innovations of the leaders of the French Revolution.

Milan became part of Napoleon Bonaparte's Italian kingdom (1797–1814). In 1815 Napoleon was defeated and Austria resumed its rule over Milan. Milan resisted Austrian rule and became a major center of the Risorgimento. In 1848 the city joined the general revolts against Austria's reactionary system of rule and participated in the various liberation movements of the period. In fact, the Milanese managed to expel the Austrians. Nevertheless, the rulers soon returned, remaining until Milan joined the kingdom of Sardinia.

Napoleon III aided Italy in what Italians refer to as the second War of Italian Independence. Following the behind-the-scenes manipulations of the Count de Cavour, the premier of the kingdom of Sardinia, Milan had joined France in a war against Austria. The Battle of Magenta (June 4, 1859) ended Austrian rule over Milan. Victor Emmanuel II of Sardinia and Napoleon III rode in triumph into the city.

Milan was already part of the industrial revolution and a wealthy center of trade and intellectual ferment. In 1861 Milan became part of the new kingdom of Italy and was a major industrial center.

After World War I, Milan was a center of the right-wing Fascist movement, founded there on March 23, 1919, by Benito Mussolini. During World War II Milan, which suffered tremendous damage from air raids, became the headquarters of the anti-Fascist underground Committee of National Liberation for Upper Italy. Although much of the city was rebuilt, some of its historic buildings were damaged beyond repair. On April 25, 1945, the Allied powers liberated Milan from German rule. Intense efforts at reconstruction helped to heal the wounds of World War II, and Milan has since regained and expanded its economic and artistic leadership in Italy. The city's economic stability has provided support to a strong Communist Party.

Migration: Past and Present. Milan's prosperity has attracted a large migration from the impoverished south, increasing the city's population. Slums and shantytowns have grown apace with this immigration—8% of all Milan's residents are immigrants, compared with an Italian average of 2%.

INFRASTRUCTURE

Politics and City Services. Milan has played a major role in Italian politics since at least the Risorgimento. It was a center of fascist development after World War I. Since the end of World War II, it has been a focus for both communist and right-wing organizations. Currently, Milan is central to Italian politics as the neonationalist Northern League struggles to control the political scene in modern Italy.

Educational System. Milan's general educational system follows that of the Italian republic. Schooling is compulsory, beginning at age 6. Primary education lasts for five years, until age 11. Primary schools can be either state-owned and -operated or privately run. The school week varies from 27 hours to 40. Class size ranges between 10 and 25 students. Students study the Italian language, a foreign language, mathematics, science, history, geography, social studies, art, sound and music, physical education, and religion. Religion is an optional subject, and the student's family must choose to include it.

Upon completing five years of school, a primary school graduation examination is taken (*esami di licenza elementare*). Successful completion of the examination permits students to move on to three years in the lower-secondary school (*scuola media*). The *scuola media* is compulsory.

The upper-secondary program, revised after 1998, includes the classic lycées scientific lycées, art college, technical schools, and vocational institutes. These courses last from three to five years but are compulsory only for the first year. When finished with their upper-secondary education, students are able to either continue to higher education or get a job at a middle-management level or pursue a career as a skilled worker.

Additionally, Milan has special schools for gifted children, schools for those who are learning-disabled, and other specialized schools. The city is home to five major universities. They are descended from various divisions of the University of Milan, begun in the 1920s, and offer specializations across the spectrum of knowledge. Milan's Bocconi University has one of the leading graduate business schools in Europe.

Transportation System. Milan is a center of Italy's transportation. It has a modern subway system, with directions that are easily available on the Internet. Excellent train service is also readily available. However, the city has serious ground-traffic and air-traffic problems, and traffic jams have become a regular part of life. Many Milanese have simply decided to drive in the middle of the road with their hazard lights flashing. The police appear to have stopped caring and have gone along with the plan. Increasing traffic has led to terrible air quality. Sometimes traffic is banned on Sundays, providing the Milanese with great fun and a cause for a holiday.

The air-traffic problem is on its way to a hoped-for solution. Linate Airport Milan is overcrowded, and traffic has been shifted to Malpensa Airport, about 48 kilometers (30 miles) from Milan. Although some foreign airlines complained about the move because Alitalia, the Italian airline, would continue to use Linate Airport, the Italian government proceeded with its plans.

CULTURAL AND SOCIAL LIFE

Cuisine. The Milanese style of cooking is lighter than that of southern Italy. In the general division of Italian cooking, butter versus oil, Milan favors butter. A typical dish is *risotto all Milanese,* made with butter, chopped beef marrow, onions, rice, white wine, chicken bouillon, salt, pepper, and Parmesan cheese. In common with other northern Italian cooking, Milanese cooking uses a lot of veal and greens. Its sauces tend to be lighter than those of the south. Much of the "northern Italian" cooking so prominent in upscale restaurants is really Milanese cooking.

Because of its pace of life, Milan has become famous in Italy as a fast-food city. Fast food in Milan, however, means fast service with inexpensive wine. Delicatessens and cafeterias allow for fast but good food, other than hamburgers. Gelato (a rich and intensely flavored ice cream) is found throughout the city, and offers a portable dessert to Milan's busy workers.

Ethnic, Class, and Religious Diversity. From about 1980 onward, Milan has seen an influx of workers from the Common Market countries, Africa, and Asia, as well as from the former Soviet bloc. Many people from the former Yugoslavia, as well as Albanians, for example, have sought better conditions in Milan and other northern industrial cities. Ethnic groups have become increasingly important in Milan's life. The new immigrants are moving into proletarian jobs, while former blue-collar workers are moving into more-clerical-style employment. There are various conflicts, but these appear to be less prevalent in Milan than in Turin or Florence, for example. The influx of people of different areas has revitalized Milan's economy, and prosperity seems to diminish ethnic rivalries.

Family and Other Social Support Systems. In the midst of change and increasing globalization and modernization, the Italian family has maintained its strength. They still celebrate traditional holidays, Sunday dinners, birthdays, and religious feast days. Family ties and background count for a great deal in Milanese society, where old established families command respect. Young people live with their families until they can strike out on their own. Families are expected to support their kin, protect them from the outside world, and provide money as well as psychological support.

Work and Commerce. Growth is evidenced predominantly in mechanical industries—the production of automobiles, airplanes, motorcycles, major electric appliances, railroad materials, and other metalworking. Textile manufacturing in cotton, hemp, silk, and artificial fibers is also important. Milan's clothing industry is legendary. Additionally, the city produces chemicals, medical products, dyes, soaps, and acids. Milan is a graphic-arts and publishing center, and is noted as well for food, wood, paper, and rubber products. Recently, the city has become the electronic-media center of Italy, specializing in high-tech products.

Arts and Recreation. Milan is a major center of opera, theater, and dance. The city's vibrant nightlife matches that of Rome. It hosts a major soccer team and promotes the sport through various youth programs. The city does lack sufficient park space, but features lovely small parks and elegant promenades. It is often called the modern city with a Gothic heart, for its beautiful Gothic-style buildings, especially the Duomo.

FUTURE OF THE CITY

Milan's past offers great hope for its future. The city has been able to revive itself after barbarian invasions, civil wars, foreign occupations, and world wars. Each time, it has built upon its past glories to proceed forward into the future. Milan has been able to move to the vanguard of Italian political, social, and economic life. Its culture is the forefront of Italian achievement. By the start of the 21st century, the city was the leader in industry, fashion, and commerce. Milan continues to expand at a time when many world cities are facing stagnation.

BIBLIOGRAPHY

Allievi, S., ed., *Milano Plurale: L'Immigrazione fra Passato, Presente e Futuro* (Comune di Milano-IREF 1997).

Fiora, Maria Teresa, *Bernardino Luini and Renaissance Painting in Lombardy: The Frescoes of San Maurizio Al Monastero Maggiore in Milan* (Skira 2000).

Hodges, Richard, and William Bowden, eds., *The Sixth Century: Production, Distribution and Demand,* Transformation of the Roman World, vol. 3 (Brill 1998).

Jannsen, Johannes, *Opera* (Barron's Education Series 2000).

Morris, Jonathan, *The Political Economy of Shopkeeping in Milan, 1886–1922* (Cambridge University Press 1993).

Pagdan, Anthony, *Spanish Imperialism and the Political Imagination* (Yale University Press 1990).

Petsimeris, Petros, "Urban Decline and the New Social and Ethnic Divisions in the Core Cities of the Italian Industrial Triangle," *Urban Studies* 35 (March 1998): 449–65.

Verzotti, Giorgio, "It's Academic (Contemporary Art in Milan, Italy)," *Xinhua News Agency,* May 3, 1999.

Frank A. Salamone

Minsk
Belarus

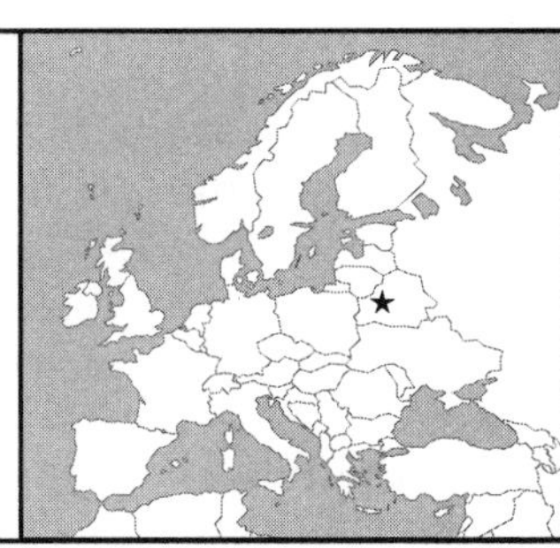

ORIENTATION

Name of City. Since January 1, 1919, Minsk was the capital of the Byelorussian Soviet Socialist Republic, which was a constituent of the former Soviet Union. After the collapse of the Soviet Union on December 8, 1991, Minsk became the capital of the independent state of the republic of Belarus.

Location. Minsk is located in the west of the eastern European plain on the Minsk Upland in the Svisloch River valley (Dnieper Basin). The city is located at 53°5′ north latitude and 27°5′ east longitude. Minsk covers a total area of 255.8 square kilometers (98.7 square miles); parks account for 15% of the city's area. The maximum elevation within the city limits is 280.4 meters (920 feet) above sea level; minimum elevation is 184.1 meters (604 feet) above sea level.

Population. By the end of 1999 the Minsk population was 1,729,000, accounting for 16% of the population of the republic of Belarus. Minsk is a multinational city. Belarusians account for the largest share of the urban population (81.2%), followed by Russians. Poles, Jews, Tatars, Lithuanians, Latvians, and others also reside in the city.

Distinctive and Unique Features. Although the age of the city is 934 years, very few material monuments reminding of its ancient history remain in Minsk. Located on the crossroads between West and East, Minsk more than once was raided by invaders and razed to the ground. During World War II, 80% of the city's buildings were destroyed, and the population size reduced by 75%. However, due to the diligence and persistence of the townspeople, the city revived from ash and ruins. The present-day Minsk that survived the tragedy of numerous wars and invasions is a beautiful, modern city with broad streets, in the center of which rises the Victory Obelisk to commemorate all known and unknown heroes who sacrificed their lives for the freedom and independence of Belarus. This monument also reminds that the city has survived despite all ordeals.

Relationships Between the City and the Outside. As in past centuries, modern Minsk is located on the transit roads connecting Russia with eastern and western European states—Ukraine, Moldova, Lithuania, Latvia, Estonia, and northwestern Russia. For many entities in the Commonwealth of Independent States (CIS), Minsk is some kind of a "window to Europe," specifically for Russia, since using Minsk as a large railway and automobile hub is of critical importance to Russia.

Inasmuch as Minsk features some economic and geographic advantages, it officially hosted coordinating bodies of the CIS—formed by Azerbaijan, Armenia, Belarus, Georgia, Kazakstan, Kyrgyzstan, Moldova, Russia, Tajikistan, Turkmenistan, Uzbekistan, and Ukraine after the USSR collapsed in 1991. In 1998 the Minsk free economic zone (FEZ) was established for a period of 30 years.

Notwithstanding the fact that Minsk is not regarded as a large tourist center, the historical part of the city is rather interesting and attracts tourists. This area is split into three historical and archaeological zones: an old, or Upper City zone, where 17th- to early-19th-century buildings remain; a Troitskoe and Rakovskoe suburb zone; and an old castle area—Minsk Castle, an archaeological sanctuary. Architectural monuments also include a number of monasteries, Roman Catholic churches, and Orthodox churches—in particular, Peter and Paul's Church (1612–1620) and the Jesuit Roman Catholic church and monastery (1654).

Major Languages. Despite the fact that Belarusian is the national language, the majority of city dwellers use Russian as the main means of communication. Due to this, the 1995 referendum made a decision to assign national-language status to Russian.

HISTORY

The Origin of the City. The city of Minsk is mentioned as Mensk in the Old Slavic chronicle *Narratives of Years of Time* in 1067 in relation to the description of events in the Kiev Rus. Archaeological excavations provide evidence of an ancient settlement of the 12th century located on the Nemiga River, the territory of which is encompassed by the modern Minsk territory. The location of ancient Minsk was conditioned by one of the so-called waterways "from Varangians to Greeks," through which merchants could pass on their ancient vessels from the Baltic to the Black Sea by rivers.

In the 12th century, Minsk turned into a center of an Old Slavic appanage principality. In the 13th century, it became a constituent of the great duchy of Lithuania. In 1499 the city was endowed with a self-governing right provided by the Magdeburg Law. At that time, in addition to trade, the town's economic activity encompassed 20 types of craftsmanship that included pottery, blacksmithing, goldsmithing, tailoring, and joinery.

In 1565–1566 Minsk was the center of the largest Minsk *voivodeship* in Belarus, which included 60 towns and other settlements. As a result of division of the Rzeczpospolity (Poland) in 1793, Minsk was assigned to the Russian empire and became the administrative center of the Minsk province. After the February and October revolutions of 1917, which led to the fall of the Russian empire and brought Bolsheviks to power, Minsk was within the Russian federation until the BSSR (Byelorussian Soviet Socialist Republic) was established in 1919 to become its capital.

Horrible ordeals befell Minsk during World War II. Hitler's invaders established an occupation regime in the city and set up nine death camps with branches and affiliates, as well as the Jewish ghetto to accommodate more than 100,000 residents. During the occupation, more than 400,000 people were killed in Minsk and its suburbs, and 80% of the city was destroyed.

After Minsk was liberated from German and fascist invaders, it was restored from ruins and turned into one of the largest industrial cities in the former Soviet Union and then in the CIS as well. In 1993 Minsk hosted the First World Congress of Belarusians and, a year later, the World Congress of Belarusian Youth.

Migration: Past and Present. Migration processes involve substantial changes in the city's population size. Over the past five years, average annual population migration growth has amounted to 11,000 people. Until the 1960s, migrations from Russia, Kazakstan, Latvia, Lithuania, and Estonia prevailed. In 1990–1998 the inflow of immigrants to Minsk increased from other republics of the former Soviet Union. At the same time, emigration increased in the late 1980s to the early 1990s, with the majority of people being of Jewish nationality. Over recent years, emigration was reduced, but national composition and geography were extended. Minsk remains a major center of the migration attraction in the republic, both for the rural population and for other residents of Chernobyl-disaster-affected areas.

INFRASTRUCTURE

Public Buildings, Public Works, and Residences. Minsk covers an area of 255.8 square kilometers (98.7 square miles). The city's territory is not densely populated (the population density is 82 residents per square kilometer, or 32 per square mile). Minsk is divided into nine administrative and economic districts. Each of them has its own administration to oversee economic and cultural activity. All districts—Zavodskoi, Leninsky, Moscovsky, Oktyabrsky, Partizansky, Pervomaisky, Sovetsky, Frunzensky, and Centralny—are networked with thoroughfares. The main one is Skorina Avenue, the development of which began early in the 19th century. The streets, which in turn are the thoroughfares of districts, branch off and exit the city to connect to the main highways. Skorina Avenue, measuring about 9 kilometers (5.6 miles) in length, constructively influenced the city's architecture and development. Currently, it is crossed by major transport thoroughfares connecting the city's downtown with all nine districts. The oldest is Minsk Independence Square, accommodating the House of Government, located at the very beginning of Skorina Avenue.

Architectural compositions, located on the highest elevations along the Svisloch riverbank, define the skyline of the city in its central part: the Opera Theatre; administrative building with an expressive classical colonnade; open-worked, spirelike towers of the temple on Freedom Square; District House of Officers; and the residence building of the president of the republic of Belarus. Victory Square, with the Victory Obelisk and eternal fire, is located in the center of Skorina Avenue. City dwellers taking a stroll along the avenue are offered an opportunity to taste national cuisine by numerous restaurants, and also may familiarize themselves with Belarusian folk art and works of artists and sculptors.

Differences in the terrain relief were efficiently used for the layout of dwellings and public buildings on Masherov Avenue, being the component of the second urban diameter. The left-hand side of this avenue is built-up with dwelling blocks, while the right-hand side features serpentlike curves and the granite embankment of the Svisloch River, on the bank of which rises the Palace of Sport. Vostok, a dwelling borough that is a sort of Minsk gate, as the Moscow highway enters the city, is located at the end of Skorina Avenue. The past five years saw an intensive development of new dwelling boroughs, funded both by citizens' savings and public loans, since the problem of providing high-quality housing for all who need it has yet to be solved. According to the urban-development plan, the housing area is projected to increase by up to 25 square meters (44 square feet) per person over the next ten years.

In addition to numerous parks and public gardens, the urban development also efficiently incorporates natural forest areas within the boundary of Chelyuskintsev Park, and also those of dwelling boroughs Zeleny Lug and Vostok. Painting dwelling and public buildings yellow, green, and dark red in combination with contrasting white shades of architectural and decorative elements gives a unique picturesque color to them.

Politics and City Services. The Minsk Municipal Council, a representative body formed for a period of four years through election by direct vote, is an authority through which citizens administer the city. Its powers include approving the city's economic- and social-development programs, approving the local budget and reports on its execution, fixing local taxes and dues, and setting the dates of local referenda. The city's mayor is appointed to, and dismissed from, that post by the president of the republic of Belarus and is approved in that post by the Minsk Municipal Council. The city's executive body is the Minsk Municipal Executive Committee. In addition, each of nine city districts is governed by a District Executive Committee and a District Administration head.

Educational System. The city's educational system includes preschool, secondary, vocational and technical, secondary-special and higher education, training of scientific and scientific/pedagogical personnel, and follow-up and retraining of personnel. The education policy is based on a number of principles, the major one being accessibility to all types of education, providing conditions for choosing the education form, orientation at world standards, and compulsory secondary education (ten-year training period). There are 33 higher-educational establishments (21 public and 12 private), about 250 secondary schools, and more than 20 gymnasiums and lycées.

© AFP/CORBIS

Young cadets at the Suvorov military school in Minsk, Belarus, practice marching in 1998.

Transportation System. Minsk is characterized by an extensively developed public-transport network. Daily, hundreds of thousands of Minskovites and visitors of the city are serviced by trolleybuses, buses, trams, taxis, electric trains, and subway trains. For example, more than 1 million passengers are transported daily by buses only, and the length of the transport network is more than 33,000 kilometers (about 20,500 miles). A tram is one of the oldest modes of the public transport. The first tram service was launched in Minsk in 1929, and currently the length of the tram-service network is 48 kilometers (30 miles).

Every five years, the Minsk Municipal Council of People's Deputies approves the plan of developing the itinerary network of the municipal passenger transport providing for the development of the main street network and aimed at improving the transport service of peripheral dwelling boroughs with the city's downtown, as well as scheduled service on urban itineraries. Minsk also operates two airports: Minsk-1 and Minsk-2.

CULTURAL AND SOCIAL LIFE

Distinctive Features of the City's Cultures. Abandoning a socialist system characterized by evening individuals and collectivistic approaches to public life gradually forms new specific features of the urban culture. This is manifested, first of all, in the altered city's appearance, changeover from architectural simplification and uniformity to individual creativeness and use of historical architectural images. The city seems to be trying to find its image at the boundary between Slavic and western cultures. Construction of religious temples is being revived, with specific historical features of various confessions being preserved. Thus, an Orthodox church, a Roman Catholic church, and a synagogue may be located in proximity to each other due to a tolerant attitude of Belarusians to alien religion, culture, and traditions.

Transition to the market-oriented economy, abandonment of the system guaranteeing a high degree of social protection, improvement of competition, and pressure of daily life have led to a substantial reluctance of the city dwellers to be involved in public life. It seems that an open and broad Slavic nature conflicts with the pragmatism and individualism brought by the industrially developed society and market.

Cuisine. The national Belarusian cuisine offers, first and foremost, potato dishes. More than 100 different dishes are cooked from that product. Various pancakes, being an essential component of the Belarusian cuisine, may be tasted in Minsk. In addition, numerous city restaurants and cafés offer a great variety of world cuisine, ranging from French to Chinese to Latin American.

Ethnic, Class, and Religious Diversity. The city's composition is rather homogeneous. Belarusians account for 81.2% of the population, with the largest ethnic groups being Russians, Poles, and Ukrainians.

The USSR-collapse-induced break of economic links resulted in the deterioration of the living standards of the majority of the population. A transition from the socialist to the market-oriented economy has led to social stratification. Yet this tendency is not explicit, since the Gini factor has not exceeded 0.254–0.261 over the past five years.

Well-to-do city dwellers prefer to have residences in the city's center. Until recently, the apartments in buildings of the 1950s–1960s, Stalin's era, were extremely popular. However, currently, Minsk residents prefer to purchase apartments in new elite houses or to build their own cottages in the suburbs. As a rule, medium- and low-income citizens build housing in the new, so-called "sleeping" microboroughs. The state provides assistance to the needy categories of the population in procuring housing by granting long-term and low-interest loans.

Family and Other Social Support Systems. Transition to the market-oriented economy affected primarily the low-income families, as the support from the government dwindled. This resulted in an increased number of needy families, while the number of families receiving government benefits was reduced. The birthrate is still decreasing, and the number of marriages decreasing, while the number of divorces goes up. For example, since 1995 the birthrate has declined by almost one-third.

Despite the social-protection guarantees provided for by the legislation, their real value is far from being sufficient to meet the needs of the city dwellers. The older-generation problems still persist and are most difficult to address. The pensioners account for about 30% of the total city population. The ratio of the average annual pension to the average annual wage is 43%. The reduction in the working population (by 10% over the past five years), with the number of pensioners increasing by 8%, adversely affects the capacity to provide an adequate pension. The city's authorities also developed the program of supporting elderly and disabled people.

The public-social-insurance system is responsible for paying pensions and benefits. Although unemployment is not a pressing problem in the city—with its level being only 1.4%, and the number of unemployed 12,900—the unemployment fund is used to finance retraining of the unemployed and to grant credits for self-employment.

Work and Commerce. Minsk is the largest industrial center of Belarus. More than 300 large and medium-sized industrial enterprises operate in the city. These enterprises produce 22.9% of the total output of the republic. Leading sectors of the economy include automobile and machine building, metalworking, instrument making, radio electronics , and light industries. Minsk is the sole producer of all tractors, motorcycles, and bicycles in the republic; more than 73% of the nation's color television sets and 90% of the watches are produced in the capital. The largest industrial enterprises include the Minsk Tractor Works and Automobile Plant, and Scientific and Production Association "Integral." Minsk-brand products are exported to 109 countries of the world. About 70% of the products turned out in the city are sold outside the republic of Belarus.

In recent years, the share of the private sector, which accounted for 43.2% of the total employed population in 1999, has been developing at a high rate—45% of the private enterprises of the republic operate in the city. Minsk is also a large scientific center—164 research-and-development institutions and the National Academy of Sciences of Belarus, incorporating 33 research institutions, are located there. The National Bank of Belarus and 28 commercial banks, 11 of them with a foreign-capital share, are involved in the banking sphere in Minsk. The average monthly wage of a city dweller is U.S.$70; in the industrial sector, it is slightly higher.

Arts and Recreation. The city's museum collections—in particular expositions of the National Museum of History and Culture of Belarus, State Picture Gallery, Museum of History of the Great Patriotic War, and some others—are of great interest. The Belarusian culture is also represented by 11 theaters, including the National Academic Theater of Opera and Ballet, the productions of which have been awarded international prizes. For example, the ballet performance based on the national historical theme "Passions" received a prestigious prize of the International Choreographers Association, "Benoua de la Dance" (France) for the best choreography in world ballet art.

Minsk is also a cinematography center. Belarusfilm is a studio that provides its production facilities not only to national film directors but also to moviemakers from the CIS countries, Poland, the United States, and elsewhere. It also accommodates the animated-cartoon-film studio.

The city dwellers enjoy recreation in numerous public gardens and parks that operate a wide range of sideshows for children and adults; the show facilities serve to stage theatrical performances. Visitors to the Central Botanical Garden may admire the collection of plants, the number of species and forms of which exceed 9,000. A picturesque lake is located in the center of the garden to provide habitat for swans. Numerous cafés and restaurants welcome Minskovites and Minsk guests to taste both national dishes and European, American, and Oriental cuisine, as well as to dance and listen to music.

QUALITY OF LIFE

The quality of life in Minsk was one of the highest in the former Soviet Union; however, even at that time, it substantially lagged behind the quality of life found in the industrially developed countries. Transition to a market-oriented economy and aggravation of the situation in the social sphere resulted in a significant decrease in the living standard of some categories of city dwellers. This, for example, resulted in the reduction in such an indicator as life expectancy—being 69.4 years in 1999, while it was 72 years in 1990. An infant death rate of 8.9 per 1,000 infants is rather high. This is conditioned by a number of factors, including the reduction in incomes of households and those of pensioners in particular, thus impairing the nutrition pattern, eroding funds for procuring medicines, reducing funds allocated for the public health, and so on. In addition, introduction of new values, the need to adapt to new realities, and a keen competition in everyday life are perceived rather painfully (with difficulty), especially by people of the older generation. This has resulted in a higher disease rate, including mental, and also higher mortality, specifically in the elder age groups. For example, mortality has almost doubled in all age groups from 25 to 70 years of age over the period from 1990. It should be noted

© VICTOR DRACHEV/AFP/CORBIS

An ice swimmer takes a frigid dip in Minsk, Belarus.

that such a situation is characteristic not of only Minsk; such processes are observed in many economies in transition.

Despite the fact that Minsk is a rather safe city in terms of crime, over the past few years, the crime rate has significantly increased. Of specific concern is a sixfold increase in drug-related crimes. One of the reasons is that after the fall of the iron curtain and the lifting of restrictions on trips abroad for Belarusians, Minsk appeared to be a convenient transit terminal for trafficking drugs from East to West.

FUTURE OF THE CITY

An objective reality of the Minsk geopolitical position predetermines that it has to be integrated economically and politically both into the system of the Commonwealth of Independent States and the European Community. The Minsk Municipal Executive Committee is involved in designing the strategic Minsk development plan. This document emphasizes that the city needs to have a tool allowing it to adequately respond to the requirements of globalization of the economy and international markets. That is why the plan has to be drawn up. In this respect, the World Bank is involved in negotiations regarding granting loans to fund a number of the city's programs, in particular public-transport development. Reaching a competitive edge is of special concern—to attain this goal, internal and external investments need to be attracted into the city's economy. For this purpose, the Minsk FEZ as well as a number of industrial parks were established in the city in 1998. The Minsk FEZ operated over two and a half years, and went beyond the framework of an economic experiment—since the output of its residents is estimated in tens of millions of U.S. dollars, and half of its products are exported. The major lines of business are machine building, construction, and energy conservation. The Minsk FEZ provided a formidable impetus for developing the Shabany industrial zone. The FEZ administration plans to establish customs terminals at which the residents may resort to services of the airport customs office, available infrastructure, facilities, and warehouses. Implementing this project will allow the Minsk-2 Airport's capacities to be used more efficiently, thereby providing an impetus to airport business development as a whole.

BIBLIOGRAPHY

Brovka, Peter V., and Dmitrieva, Tatiana T., eds., *Minsk: City-Hero* (Belarussian Encyclopedia 1986).

Glushakov, Vladimir S., and Gennadi P. Pashkov, *Republic of Belarus* (Belarussian Encyclopedia 2000).

Golovanov, Valentin S., ed., *Minsk: The Capital of the Republic of Belarus* (Pangraph 1998).

Kylagin, Alexander K., ed., *Minsk, Outlines* (University Press 1994).

Minsk and Minsk Province, *Minsk Gorispolkom Report* (Printcorp 1999) [publication that provides information about city's economic and social life].

Minsk Statistical Yearbook (Ministry of Statistics and Analyses of Belarus 2000) [excellent source of basic statistics].

Monuments of History and Culture of Belarus (Belarussian Encyclopedia 1988).

Otrovski, Vasil S., *Town-planning of Minsk* (Belfact Press 1999).

Shamov, Valeri P., *Minsk Monuments* (Polimya Press 1991).

Shamyakin, Ivan ed., *Minsk: Encyclopedic Reference Book* (Belarussian Encyclopedia 1983).

Shibeka, Zakhar, and Sophya Shibeka, *Minsk: Pages of Ancient City Life* (Belarus University Press 1994).

Voitekhovski, Adam I., ed., *City Planning in Minsk* (Belgeodezia 1995).

Zagogulski, Eduard M., *Origin of Minsk* (Science and Technology Press 1982).

Irina Tochitskaya

Mogadishu

Somalia

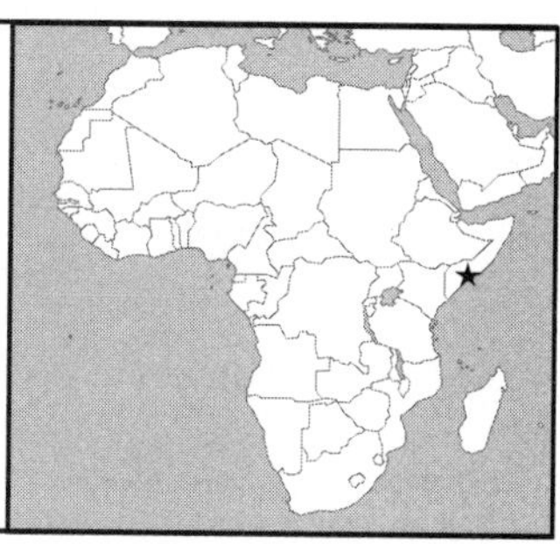

ORIENTATION

Name of City. Mogadishu is the capital of and largest city in Somalia. The city's name is spelled in a variety of ways that attempt to reproduce a similar phonetic pronunciation, including *Muqdishu, Mugdisho, Maqdishaw, Makdishu, Maqdashaw,* and *Mogadiscio*. The original, now older part of the city is known as Xamar Weyne by both local inhabitants and longtime residents.

There is uncertainty regarding the meaning of the city's name. There is some indication that *Mogadishu* is a Somali version of the Arabic *maqad shah,* meaning "imperial seat of the shah," perhaps alluding to Persia's role in the origin of the city. As well there is evidence that *Mogadishu* is a mispronunciation of the Swahili *mwyu wa,* meaning "the last northern city," which raises the possibility of Mogadishu being the northernmost of a chain of Swahili cities strung along the East African coast.

Location. Mogadishu lies along the southeastern coast of Somalia on the Horn of Africa, a region that occupies the extreme northeast corner of the continent. Somalia is bounded on the north by the Gulf of Aden and on the east and south by the Indian Ocean and shares its western border with Kenya, Ethiopia, and Djibouti. As of 2001 the self-declared states of Somaliland (1991) and Puntland (1998) occupied what was once the northern part of Somalia. The geographical location of the city is 1°30′ north latitude and 46° east longitude.

Population. Population estimates for Mogadishu have been difficult to come by owing to the lack of adequate data, the mobile lifestyle of the nomadic population, and refugee movements into and out of the city. The latest (1995) estimate for metropolitan Mogadishu put the city's population at approximately 982,000. However, in 1992 the population was estimated at roughly 2 million, swelled by large numbers of refugee arrivals. The national population is about 7 million. But again, with the population primarily nomadic, and ethnic Somali areas existing in neighboring Djibouti, Ethiopia, and Kenya, a precise estimate of who is a citizen of these states is difficult.

Distinctive and Unique Features. Mogadishu sits on coastal sand dunes in an extremely arid, desert environment. The long beach north and south of the city is used heavily by the city's occupants and visitors from the interior for temporary encampments and as a travel route. The topography of the city is generally level; however, drainage during infrequent wet-season storms is something of a problem, occasionally sweeping away portions of the informal city and depositing a significant amount of sewage through the city, with subsequent disease problems.

The city is laid out in five distinct sectors, which illustrate different stages of its history, from its founding to the present day. The original city, Xamar Weyne, is thought to have been settled by Arabs in about the year 900 and is located on a small spit of land in the Indian Ocean. This portion of the city is constructed from locally available coral blocks, bleached white, and is built in the traditional Arab architectural style, with archways, latticework, and ornate wooden doors and shutters. The streets are narrow and mazelike, sandy or made of block, and suitable only for walking. The buildings are several stories tall, and the interconnected passageways, doorways, and walls make navigating Xamar very difficult for the nonresident. The occasional open spaces within Xamar are used for different kinds of markets and commerce. Another nearby section of the city, just to the north, called Shangani, also features a similar arrangement in terms of street irregularity and structure. Numerous mosques of varying age, size, and elaborateness dot this section of the city.

Abutting Xamar Weyne is the portion of the city constructed between 1900 and 1934, during the Italian colonial administration. This sector of the city contains colonial architecture, wide streets made for vehicular traffic, intersections, sidewalks, planted palm trees, and spaces for ornamental vegetation in medians and in other sidewalk spaces. It is laid out in an angled grid, with paved crumbling streets and several central thoroughfares converging to form traffic circles at different points. Many of the buildings have inner spaces walled off from the street outside. A few remnants of the Portuguese interest in Mogadishu are found near this sector of the city, including a lighthouse tower.

The majority of the built commercial city outside of the colonial area and Xamar (surrounding these on the land side) comprises drab Soviet-style block buildings erected during the postcolonial socialist era, which began soon after independence from Italy in 1960. Many of these buildings are several stories high, designed with parking spaces in front that are frequently dumpsites for litter. This area of the city is also laid out on a general grid with paved but crumbling roads. Along the mainly sandy roads off the paved roads are a number of imposing residences of general Arab or block architecture, with walled compounds. Several socialist-era monuments are scattered through this sector of the city, commemorating various national heroes or movements. This portion of the city also includes the newer, post-socialist-era constructions as well as several large mosques, some quite ornate. Many government buildings are likewise found in this sector, erected during or subsequent to colonialism. To the south of the city is the international airport and the modern deepwater port facilities.

Toward the outskirts of the city are two kinds of informal urban settlements, which in one form or another have probably existed for some time. One is fashioned from materials not intended to be mobile and comprises a jumble of residences and shops made from local materials, wood, and metal roofing. Streets are entirely sand, and travel is primarily by foot. This sphere of the city is where a good portion of the migrant communities and other local inhabitants reside. The other informal settlement is made up largely of nomads visiting Mogadishu for various periods of time. This area is marked by mobile nomad huts, thorn fences, and livestock. The layout is uncoordinated, and the size of this settlement varies significantly.

At the turn of the 21st century, large expanses of these different sections of the city were in a state of rubble and abandonment as a consequence of the urban warfare in the 1990s. Residents scavenge construction material from damaged structures, and building debris and rusted and twisted metal are strewn along the streets such that scarred and vacant buildings are currently among Mogadishu's primary features, along with the enormous piles of garbage that dot the city. The desert appears to be creeping into and retaking the city, with sand covering main roads and highways, and the now small urban population to a significant degree leads a rural lifestyle in the midst of the devastated city.

Many of the city's commercial buildings and industries remain closed and damaged. The airport and port are typically closed, operating sporadically as shipments of aid arrive and businesspeople attempt varying forms of commercial enterprise.

Attractions of the City. By the 1990s there were no attractions for tourists in Mogadishu. From the time of the implosion of the Somali state early in that decade until the election of President Abdul Kasim Salat Hassan in August 2000 there was no central national government, and the city was subjected to urban warfare involving clan-based factions and military units from the United Nations (UN) and the United States. There is little involvement of the city in the global economy, as most of the world keeps its distance from a city and a country that made international news in the 1990s as a debacle for the United Nations and the United States. Kidnappings of aid workers, killings, battles involving significant firepower, carjackings, and banditry are common in the city and serve to keep away all but the internally connected and most intrepid entrepreneurs.

Relationships Between the City and the Outside. Prior to the chaos of the 1990s, Mogadishu was the diplomatic, commercial, manufacturing, and economic center of Somalia, and the country's chief seaport. Most of the international community administering the many development programs were located in the city, along with embassy personnel. The city was the principal point of arrival and departure for those entering and leaving the country by air.

Currently the primary relationship between Mogadishu and the countryside is as a destination for those dislocated by war and famine, and as an obstacle to recovery as continued warfare in the city prevents substantial recovery for the surrounding areas. For much of the nomadic population in the interior of Somalia, there is little relationship or connection to Mogadishu, as this population is largely dependent on livestock mobility to take advantage of the temporally and spatially variable grazing and watering opportunities. The various clan-based factions that vie for control of the city have an important link with the parts of the country that are their ethnic homelands.

The food and health assistance provided by the international community to the city, and use of the city as a staging area for aid deliveries to the nation's interior, are essentially the only involvement that Mogadishu presently has with the outside world.

Major Languages. Somali currently serves as the primary language of Mogadishu. Somali itself exists as several dialects that are to a significant degree mutually intelligible. The Somali language belongs to a set of languages known as the lowland Eastern Cushitic stock. The various dialects include Common Somali, Coastal Somali, and Central Somali.

Other languages used less in the city are Arabic, Italian, English, and Swahili. During the colonial era Italian was the official language of government in Mogadishu. After independence until 1973, both English and Italian were officially used as the languages of administration and instruction in schools, and Somali was the most widespread and unofficial language. The establishment of the Somali script in 1973 brought the language into official use. Arabic, or a heavily Arabized version of Somali, has been widely used in various cultural and commercial domains in the city, and the Islamic Koranic schools and religious courts operate in this form of Arabic.

HISTORY

The Origin of the City. Mogadishu was one of the earliest Arab settlements on the East African coast and was initially founded and settled by Persian and Arab traders in the early 900s for reasons of facilitating trade. By the 12th century the city had become a significant center for trade. Mogadishu was at its height of prosperity in 1331 when Ibn Batuta, a well-known Arab traveler, arrived in the city. Ibn Batuta noted that "Maqdashu" was "an exceedingly large city" that exported cloth to the Middle East and elsewhere.

A substantial period of decline started in the 16th century, and then in 1871 the city fell under the control of the sultan of Zanzibar. The Italians first leased the city's port in 1892 and then purchased the city in 1905, making it the capital of Italian Somaliland. During World War II Mogadishu was occupied by the British, and the city became the capital of independent Somalia in 1960.

In 1991 and 1992 Mogadishu was the scene of intense interclan warfare that devastated much of it. The city became the focus of a U.S. and then a UN peacekeeping and food relief operation from 1992 until 1995, which was intended to ease the countrywide famine and restore a central government. During this period even more of the city's buildings were damaged in the fighting between clans and between Somali groups and the UN troops. The UN operation ceased in 1995, being unable to end the interclan warfare and reestablish a government. Clan warfare continued in the city after the United Nations' departure and continues at the time of writing.

A considerable number of the city's industries and commercial activities are currently closed, while others more suitable to the fluid physical and economic environment (such as telecommunications and currency trading) have flourished. Mogadishu's port functions intermittently, and some local entrepreneurs have opened some shops. Private generators provide limited electricity to some locations within the city. A peace conference in Djibouti in 2000 has produced the most hopeful prospects for a central government. A broad coalition has been formed with the intention of including different clan groupings and women's groups. The government was installed but as of early 2002 ruled little more than Mogadishu, with even this being contested by different militia leaders. Significant opposition to the new government exists in various large parts of the country as well.

In late 2001 and early 2002 Somalia became the focus of significant international interest with regard to the potential for accommodating terrorists in its fluid social environment on the heels of the attack on the United States and subsequent American intervention in Afghanistan. The new government in Mogadishu has responded by hosting international visits with the intention of proving that those fleeing Afghanistan were not arriving in Somalia.

Migration: Past and Present. Arab and Persian migration in the course of developing trading networks first occurred in Mogadishu in the 900s, serving to establish it along with other cities along the Somali coast, including Merca, Brava, and Kismayo. Throughout the centuries nomads have migrated to and from Mogadishu as part of their both regular and irregular migrations.

More recently, migration into Mogadishu is a strategy for agricultural and nomadic households attempting to flee drought, famine, and warfare.

Wars with and in neighboring countries have accounted for large refugee migrations into the city over the past decades. The most dramatic of these followed the fall of the regime of Mohamed Siad Barre in January 1991. The subsequent civil war resulted in influxes of thousands of refugees from the interior of the country. Informal camps of displaced persons in the city have increased since 1991, and most of the small dome-shaped huts that house the displaced, which are modeled after the mobile nomad hut, are made from sticks, paper, and trash scavenged from the city's rubbish.

INFRASTRUCTURE

Public Buildings, Public Works, and Residences. By the year 2000 very little existed in the way of functional public buildings and public works as a result of almost a decade of war in the city. Marketplaces are now virtually the only public areas, and the majority of these are open-air. The better residential areas likewise have been largely damaged—many reduced to rubble. Residences that are still standing are inhabited by squatters, or by those able to protect such property. Many residences in the city exist in, or are made from, rubble.

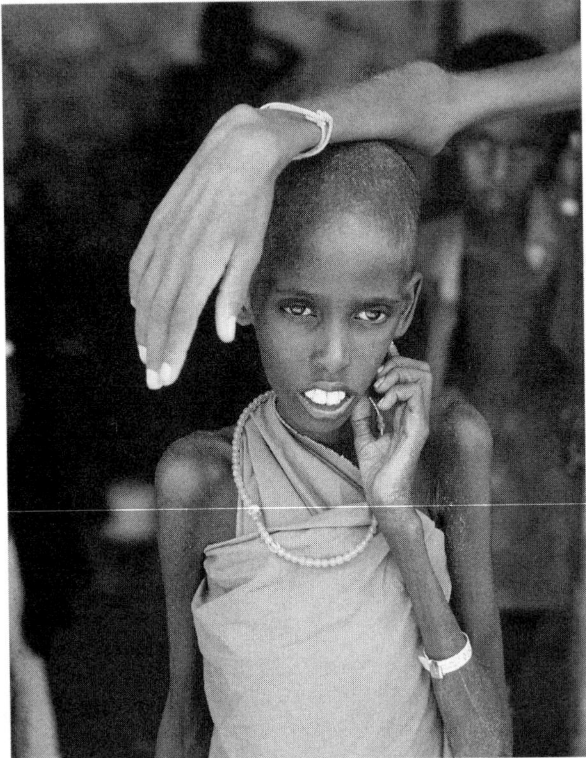

© PETER TURNLEY/CORBIS

Civil war in Somalia resulted in a national famine. This young boy, photographed in Mogadishu in 1992, was one of the victims.

Politics and City Services. City services are nonexistent and much of the infrastructure for these has been destroyed as the city's inhabitants dismantle the infrastructure for other uses. However, private business interests do operate an impressive set of cell-telephone services in the city. The result of the total lack of services has left the city with extremely poor sanitation and security and a grossly inadequate water supply and educational system. In Benadir Hospital, in south Mogadishu, only a small number of volunteer nurses tend to cholera patients lying on floors and in abandoned wards. A doctor at the hospital performs a limited number of mostly emergency surgeries, and patients or relatives must obtain all needed medical materials and be able to pay the doctor a fee.

Islamic organizations do provide some assistance to the displaced in the city, primarily during the Muslim festivals. These organizations tend to focus on orphanages, the funding of Koranic schools, or business ventures. The primary Islamic organizations include the International Islamic Relief Organization; Al Haramayn, Al-Islah Charity; Monazamat Al-da'wa, the African Muslim Agency; and Muslim Aid UK. There are also a few Western humanitarian organizations that maintain a small presence in the city, including the International Committee for the Red Cross, Doctors without Borders—Spain, Action Internationale Contra la Fame, Peace and Life (Sweden), and Daily Bread (Germany). As well, the United Nations maintains offices for representatives from the United Nations Development Programme, the Food and Agriculture Organization, the United Nations High Commissioner for Refugees, the World Food Programme, and the World Health Organization. The humanitarian representations have no permanent expatriate presence and instead depend on a small group of local staff. A local Somali humanitarian organization, Somali Refugee Agency (SORA), has been able to work to some degree among camps of dislocated persons. SORA has recorded over 130 such camps in north and south Mogadishu. Another nongovernmental organization, Action Against Hunger, estimates that by 2000, more than 230,000 displaced persons were living in some 200 camps in the city.

Politics in Mogadishu is extremely complicated. A number of clan-based factions control different areas of the city. The more prominent parts of the city are the northern and southern sections, and these are ruled very differently. Hussein Aideed, the U.S.-educated son of Mohamed Fara Aideed, a former warlord, controls southern Mogadishu militias that largely do as they please. South Mogadishu is extremely dangerous, and only the gun provides any form of power or order. The streets are deserted and dark at night. In northern Mogadishu, guns are less visible, there is a bustle to the streets, the streets are lit at night, and a few police can be seen. North Mogadishu is controlled by Ali Mahdi and a leading Islamic cleric, Sheikh Alidheri. It remains to be seen how or if Mogadishu will resolve the issue of governance in the future.

Since the 1990s, numerous outside interests have attempted to propose, fund, and implement various approaches to end the fighting in Mogadishu. Entities such as the states of Djibouti, Kenya, and Egypt; the League of Arab States; the Organization of African Unity; the Islamic Conference; and the United Nations have all made numerous unsuccessful attempts to end the clan warfare in the city.

Educational System. The educational endeavor in Mogadishu is confined mainly to the occasional Koranic school, which only small children attend. Koranic instruction focuses on learning passages from the Koran by repetition and provides minimal literacy and mathematics. No state educational system has been in place since the primary, secondary, and university education systems all collapsed in the early 1990s.

Transportation System. Likewise, no transportation system currently exists in the city. Most of the Mogadishu's inhabitants walk amidst the city's rubble to get to their destinations, and vehicles are often owned and operated by one of the militias active in the city.

CULTURAL AND SOCIAL LIFE

Distinctive Features of the City's Cultures. The city is inhabited almost exclusively by ethnic Somalis of various clans, together with a relatively small number of residents of Arab extraction. The dress of Somali males consists of the northeastern African version of the sarong, called a *ma'awiss,* which is worn with a Western-style, buttoned, long-sleeved shirt and frequently with an additional piece of fine cloth over the shoulder. Many men adopt variations of the turban, or the Muslim skullcap. As well, Western trousers are worn, particularly during the workday. Women tend to prefer a colorful dress or skirt with several long, colorful, light cloth wraps, wound around the upper body and the head.

The city and country are Muslim, and Muslim cultural features prevail among the people and their daily activities. Many aspects of Somali nomadic life are likewise visible in the city, such as mobility, a lack of attachment by many inhabitants to a single place, and hence minimal investment in permanent structures.

Within Somali society the clan system is the predominant cultural feature. Clans segment Somalis into groups that themselves are further segmented into various subclans. The political machinations between clans and subclans are what constitute Somali political life, with this particularly concentrated and problematic in Mogadishu.

Cuisine. The cuisine of Mogadishu has been heavily influenced by the Italian colonial era. Pasta is virtually a staple, as are bananas from the nearby Shalambood irrigated area south of the city just inland from the coastal town of Merca. Rice is also a common staple. Goat is perhaps the most easily obtainable meat, with chicken, lamb, and beef also available. It is customary for boiled lamb or goat to be served with either pasta or rice. Occasionally vegetables are consumed, and spiced sauces are widely used. There are few functioning restaurants in the Western sense in Mogadishu. The problems currently afflicting Mogadishu have affected what the city can offer in terms of cuisine for local inhabitants. Many city dwellers simply attempt to survive by obtaining what little they can in terms of food. Food aid in the form of wheat, maize, and beans can also be found in the city, provided by the international community. As in many Muslim societies, alcohol is not widely available. However qat, or chat (*Catha edulis*), a bushy plant that provides a mild stimulant (cathin) when the young twigs and leaves are chewed, is frequently imported from the eastern highlands of Ethiopia and is used by many on a daily basis, usually in the afternoon.

Ethnic, Class, and Religious Diversity. Virtually all inhabitants of Mogadishu are ethnic Somalis and Muslim. There are some shopkeepers and traders of Arab descent, although they are in most ways culturally Somali. Considerable socioeconomic class differentiation exists in the city, from the wealthy businesspeople and leaders of various militias, to the sizable destitute populations that have migrated to the city seeking food. There is also differentiation among city inhabitants with regard to the degree of westernization. While a significant portion of the city's population live in traditional ways, which include seasonal migration with livestock to different grazing and watering areas, there are many in the city who are more urban and have for various reasons less of a relationship with the nomadic lifestyles of the interior. These include those who are descendants of city dwellers, with personal histories as merchants and traders, and those dislocated from a traditional pastoral lifestyle. Various clan militias operate in the city, and membership in or connection to a militia may offer certain advantages not available to others arriving in the city searching for food and water.

Family and Other Social Support Systems. As a result of the breakdown of the Somali state and much of wider Somali society, family and clan support systems have taken primary importance in the individual's functioning in city society and survival. Such family and especially clan systems can be very extensive and involve long-standing and wide-ranging support systems designed for the sharing of food, livestock, and other assistance, such as protection and retribution, and access to grazing and watering resources. However, for the urban disenfranchised and the destitute migrants, such support systems can be significantly compromised, with little else available in the city to replace them. The various militia groups may also provide some support to members or those connected to such militias. But clan, subclan, and militia rivalries also cause much in the way of damage to each other's family and clan support systems.

Work and Commerce. Commerce in Mogadishu revolves around both large central neighborhood markets offering food and a variety of other miscellany of urban life. As well, weapons and ammunition commerce is common in the city, as is the provision of communications facilities, such as cellular telephones. The commercial life of the city generally has been much reduced owing to the destruction of the urban infrastructure and ongoing security problems. Western notions of employment and unemployment are difficult to apply to the inhabitants of Mogadishu; however, most of the city's inhabitants must be considered unemployed, with relevant statistics largely nonexistent. Many people in the city make their living through their connections to family and clan, which facilitate the process of mutual obligation and redistribution of resources. Most further survive by pursuing odd jobs and multiple minor commercial opportunities. Access to shops is problematic for the vast numbers of destitute who have arrived dislocated from the interior, and somewhat better for those with the knowledge and connections to negotiate the city.

Arts and Recreation. Art forms in Mogadishu are difficult to come by in the current situation, but in any case a developed art culture involving tangible articles is not an important feature of Somali culture. However, Somalis are renowned for their oral poetry, an art form practiced widely, and highly respected among the male members of the population. Such poetry revolves around all aspects of nomadic and political life and has a very rich traditional and historical texture, with fables, sayings, and morals tied into poetic speechmaking. While some Somali poetry exists in written form, for the most part the outside world has very little entry into this important Somali art form.

For the adult males of the city, one of the most prevalent forms of recreation is the daily chewing of qat (noted earlier), with the men gathering in groups to participate during afternoons and evenings. In addition, gatherings in local tea shops and in private residences provide significant male recreation. Most female recreation goes on in and around market activities, primarily involving women's groups engaged in trading, marriage, and other social plans, and chatting on the topic of the day. For male children and young adults, soccer (international football) is a popular recreational outlet.

QUALITY OF LIFE

Quality of life in Mogadishu is universally quite low. While a provisional government is in place, the lack of social services, physical security, adequate food and water supplies, and sanitation, and the destruction of many of the city's buildings, has made the quality of life easily one of the lowest in the world. Health and disease problems go largely unattended beyond what one's immediate family is able to do, and crime is difficult to control. Homelessness and poverty are widespread, and there are no city services in place to deal with these.

FUTURE OF THE CITY

The future of the city is quite uncertain. Numerous attempts at peace for Mogadishu and Somalia have been made since the early 1990s, culminating with a conference in Djibouti that has successfully derived a coalition government. In early 2002 this government was making headway in attempting to bring some form of recovery to the city. Reports indicate that efforts at reestablishing a police force was under way, with significant legal assistance to the government provided by parishioners of Islamic Shari'a law. It remains to be seen if the city and country can successfully move forward with nation-building.

BIBLIOGRAPHY

Besteman Catherine, and Lee V. Cassanelli, *The Struggle for Land in Southern Somalia: The War Behind the War* (Westview Press 1996).

Biles, P., "Somalia, Starting from Scratch," *Africa Report,* 36, no. 3, May–June 1991: 55–59.

Bongartz, M., *The Civil War in Somalia: Its Genesis and Dynamics* (Scandinavian Institute of African Affairs 1991).

Cassanelli, Lee, *The Shaping of Somali Society: Reconstructing the History of a Pastoral People, 1600–1900* (University of Pennsylvania Press 1982).

Laitin, David, and Said Samatar, *Somalia: Nation in Search of a State* (Westview Press 1987).

Lewis, I. M., *A Modern History of Somalia: Nation and State in the Horn of Africa,* rev. ed. (Westview Press 1988).

Metz, H. C., *Somalia: A Country Study* (Federal Research Division, Library of Congress 1993).

Simons, A., *Networks of Dissolution: Somalia Undone* (Westview Press 1995).

JON D. UNRUH

Mombasa

Kenya

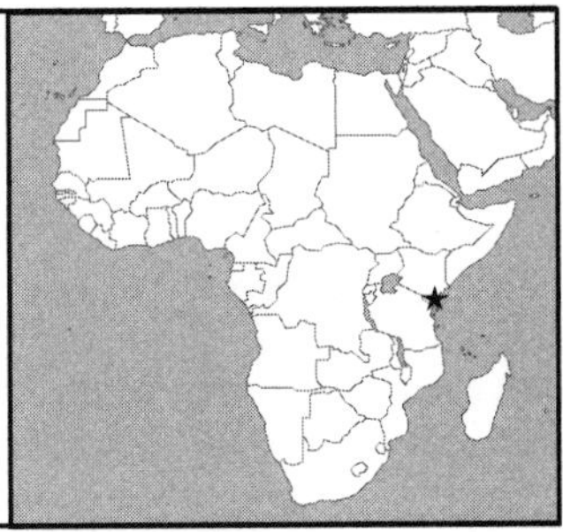

ORIENTATION

Name of City. Mombasa is the name of both a city and the island on which the bulk of that city lies. The island has also in the past been known as Mvita, and although some of the populace still use this term, it is not common practice.

Location. Mombasa is located at 4° south latitude and 39°40′ east longitude, in the republic of Kenya, in East Africa. The island itself is only 21 square kilometers (8 square miles) in extent; the modern city boundaries include approximately 260 square kilometers (100 square miles) of the mainland around the island.

Population. In 1989 (the last year for which figures are currently available), the population of Mombasa as a city was 461,753. The population of the island itself was 127,720, this being the most densely populated part of the city. Of the remainder of the population, the bulk were living in the three relatively small mainland areas of Likoni (to the south), Changamwe (to the west), and Kisauni-Bamburi (to the north).

Attractions of the City. The island of Mombasa is neatly embayed in the coast, with the mainland lying close on the west, south, and north of the island. There are anchorages on the north and south of the island; that to the south is larger, but more difficult for sailing vessels to access, and for that reason the north anchorage was preferred until the 20th century. In the west, the island is almost joined to the mainland at Makupa, and the narrow strip of water has in the 20th century been crossed by a causeway. Several creeks, largely lined with mangroves, run inland for some miles from Mombasa; these have in the past played an important role in a very local transport system that allowed food grain to be brought to the island on small boats.

The island itself is largely of coral, and the rag of the island and of the adjoining coast has provided ready building material for many centuries. Much of this older architecture has now disappeared; there are some 18th- and 19th-century buildings in Mombasa—notably in the Old Town, on the north of the island—but most of the buildings in the city are from the 20th century. The area around Treasury Square has a small number of buildings of early-20th-century colonial style. Generally, only recent commercial and administrative buildings are built to any grand scale; the notable exception is the large 16th-century Portuguese-built stronghold of Fort Jesus, at the entrance to the north anchorage. This, having served as residence for precolonial rulers and then as a colonial prison, is now a museum, and is one of the island's main tourist attractions.

Mombasa Island itself is composed largely of old coral; so, too, is a strip along the shoreline of the mainland to north and south. Coral rag has also long been burned to produce lime for cement; this is now done on an industrial scale in a quarry and factory at Bamburi, on the north mainland, which produces much of the region's cement. The sea that produced this coral also provides Mombasa with its two other economic mainstays: Mombasa is the region's most important port; and the still-living coral reef that lies just underwater, and the attractive mainland beaches south and north of the island, have made this a center for Kenya's tourism industry. Mombasa has long been a port, but its regional predominance, and its very considerable commercial and industrial role, are all 20th-century phenomena.

Relationships Between the City and the Outside. Mombasa, as well as the coast in general, occupies a distinctive place in Kenyan society and economy. Long contact with the Indian Ocean world meant that Islam came to the coastal settlements more than a thousand years ago, and while not all coastal peoples were or are Muslims, the culture of coastal urban settlements such as Mombasa was overwhelmingly Muslim by the 19th century, whereas society in the rest of what was to become Kenya was nonurban and neither Muslim nor Christian.

The coast was linked into the trading economy of the Indian Ocean, and in the 19th century, it was through the coast and its people that commercial and political changes of extraordinary significance reached the rest of what was to be Kenya. Caravans from the coast brought firearms, cloth, and other trade goods to exchange for ivory, slaves, and other products. Societies in this area did not suffer from slaving to anything like the extent that other parts of Africa did, as caravan routes largely passed to the south; but coast people came to be associated with commercial exchange and material goods. "Swahili," an ethnic label applied to certain coast peoples before 1900, has in the 20th century become

© EYE UBIQUITOUS/CORBIS

Giant tusks arch across Moi Avenue in Mombasa, Kenya.

also a general term for urban people involved in commerce—often Muslims—and for those who are perceived to have abandoned the practices of rural society.

Despite this association between the coast and what might be called "modernity," it is also the case that the Kenya coast in general lost much of its economic importance during the 20th century. Attempts to develop a colonial plantation economy foundered, and the political and economic focus of Kenya moved inexorably inland to the fertile and well-populated highland of central and western Kenya. Because of its importance as a port for this up-country economy, Mombasa fared better than the rest of the coast, but in this city—as elsewhere on the coast—there is a feeling that the coast has lost out, and there is no little resentment against the up-country people (mostly Christians) who dominate the politics and economy of Kenya. Mombasa itself is a most cosmopolitan city, however—a character derived from its history and present position as a major port, and from its role in the tourism industry.

Major Languages. The official languages of Kenya are English and Swahili; both are widely spoken all over the country. In Mombasa there is a very large community that speaks Swahili as a first language, and this language is used here with greater fluency and elegance than it is in much of the rest of the country. Migration to Mombasa has produced sizeable communities in the city who speak other languages, notably Somali and other Kenyan languages such as Dholuo or Luhyia. However, it is very generally the case that English will suffice for most official and unofficial purposes.

HISTORY

The Origin of the City. Mombasa first appears in the historical record in the 12th century, when it was one of a number of port towns along the East African coast that were known to, and regularly visited by, traders from Arabia and the Red Sea. At that time, the town was reported to have a king; it is not clear what the religion of the populace was. By the 14th century, when Ibn Battuta wrote an account of the town, it evidently had a considerable—and politically dominant—Muslim population, and was exporting a limited range of luxury items, presumably obtained from the hinterland. Like other settlements of the coast, Mombasa was quite culturally distinct, in terms of religion and lifestyle; yet there was evidently very close contact and population exchange with the nonurban, non-Muslim population of the local hinterland, who supplied trade goods and food grains. Mombasa was only one of several such settlements at this time, and the town covered only a small part of the island, along the edge of the northern harbor. There was also a smaller, distinct settlement on the southern anchorage, Kilindini.

In the 16th century, Mombasa began a steady rise to local prominence, owing partly to the natural advantage of good anchorages and partly to the combined effect of Portuguese colonial rule and a period of intense conflict in the hinterland. Vasco da Gama visited Mombasa first in 1498 and (by his account) narrowly avoided falling into a trap laid by the ruler of the town. The Portuguese sacked Mombasa several times in the 16th century, but this did not diminish the importance of the town, which in 1505 had been reported as a busy port with 10,000 inhabitants. At the end of the 16th century, Mombasa was chosen as the principal Portuguese base north of Mozambique. A grand fortress was constructed there, which was called Fort Jesus; and the ruler of another town, who had shown himself to be an ally of the Portuguese, was settled in Mombasa as the founder of what was intended to be a new dynasty.

The Portuguese controlled Mombasa for most of the 17th century. Their hold was always rather shaky, and an uprising in 1631 led to the massacre of the Portuguese population, after which there was never any significant presence of Portuguese settlers or traders. At the end of the 17th century, the Portuguese were finally expelled—after an epic siege of the fort, from 1696 to 1698, largely as a result of the intervention of Omani forces. This established a link with Oman that was to affect the coast of East Africa for the next three centuries. The Portuguese-installed "ruling family" had lasted only until the 1634 uprising, and, in the 18th and early 19th centuries, Mombasa became the subject of political contention; during the course of these struggles, settlement came to be concentrated almost entirely on the north side of the island. The rulers of Oman sought to exercise political dominance against their own appointed governors—the Mazrui family, who were of independent mind—and against the populace, notably the "Twelve Tribes" of the Mombasa Swahili, as a whole. As the Mazrui sought allies and protectors, Mombasa briefly became a British protectorate, from 1824 to 1826; but the British government declined to maintain this arrangement, and by the late 1830s the Busaidi rulers of Oman had effectively established political control. The struggle had taken its toll: by 1847 the population was estimated to have fallen to 3,000.

In the period from 1850 to 1880 Mombasa temporarily lost its political importance and its economic centrality. The Omani state was divided in 1856, and a new Busaidi sultanate was formed in East Africa, based on the island of Zanzibar. This shifted the political and economic focus south, away from Mombasa, and the major caravan routes ran inland from ports nearer to Zanzibar from the 1850s to the 1880s. But despite this relative decline, Mombasa's absolute prosperity and population probably did grow from around 1850, with the rapid overall expansion in Indian Ocean commerce. In the late 19th century, much of the island was given over to coconut-palm gardens and bush, but the settlement was expanding. Grain had long been grown on the immediately adjacent mainland, and these grain gardens expanded from the 1850s with the widespread use of slave labor.

The return of British rule at the end of the 19th century further revived Mombasa's fortunes. Both the Imperial British East Africa Company—which "ruled" from 1887 to 1895, and the British East Africa protectorate, established in 1895, made Mombasa their headquarters. In 1907 the capital of the protectorate moved inland to Nairobi, but by then the building of a railway had confirmed Mombasa's importance to the economy of the region. The Uganda Railway, as it was first known, was started from Mombasa in 1896 and reached Lake Victoria in 1901. This investment ensured that Mombasa would be the main harbor of the region; through the port came all the commerce of the British East Africa protectorate (which was renamed Kenya colony in 1920), the Uganda protectorate, and the northern parts of German East Africa—which became Tanganyika territory after World War I.

The city grew enormously as a result of the development of the port. By 1913 the population of the island was estimated at 19,600; by 1931 it was 41,000. During the first decades of the 20th century, much of the island was covered by buildings. Much of this was low-cost, private-enterprise building to house a rapidly growing African population, but a considerable portion of the island—most of the southeastern part—was taken over for the housing and recreational needs of the European population. This Southern Residential Area was exclusively white until the late 1930s; and it was there that the golf course and other sports facilities were located. Early on in the colonial period, the northern anchorage ceased to be the principal harbor: all new investment in facilities was concentrated on the deeper southern anchorage of Kilindini, where several deep-water berths were constructed in the 1920s. Buildings associated with the docks came to take up much of the southern part of the island. With the island increasingly built over, residential areas were being established on the mainland, especially after the completion of road-bridge links to the west (in 1926) and to the north (in 1931).

Also in the 1920s there was an attempt to replan the rapidly growing African parts of the town; areas were cleared to create what is still the main shopping street and commercial area. From the 1940s to the 1960s—when there was a determined effort to create a new, "stabilized" urban labor force—areas in the northwest of the island and on the southern and western mainland were built as municipal-housing developments. Since the 1960s there has been considerable, largely uncoordinated expansion of housing provision, largely on the mainland around the island. The quality of this housing varies widely, some of it being in planned estates with services provided, but with much of it opportunistic and unplanned.

Since Kenya became independent in 1963 Mombasa has continued to serve as the major port of the country and of the wider region. Much transit traffic for Uganda, Rwanda, and the eastern part of the Democratic Republic of the Congo passes through this port, which was adapted in the 1970s to deal with containerized cargo. The city has, however, lost its claim to be the "Gateway to Kenya," despite its role in the tourist industry, as most air traffic arrives at Nairobi. Like other major Kenyan cities, Mombasa has suffered from chronic problems with the financing, efficiency, and reliability of local government since the 1980s; in Mombasa the sense that Kenya's political center is far distant has compounded popular dissatisfaction over these problems, as leaders from the coast have remained largely marginal to national politics. In recent years there have been several outbreaks of popular violence directed at immigrants from elsewhere in Kenya, and to some extent at the government as a whole. Not unsurprisingly, there was considerable resentment when it was announced in 2001 that Kisumu, on Lake Victoria, was to be recognized as a city before Mombasa was awarded with that status.

Migration: Past and Present. Mombasa has long attracted migrants: in the 16th century the Portuguese found Indian merchants living in the city, and there is ample evidence of a steady immigration from the Gulf and Red Sea that has gone on for more than a thousand years. During the early colonial period, immigration from the Indian subcontinent increased for a time, but the bulk of 20th-century immigration has come from areas within Kenya. A long-established pattern of population exchange with the local hinterland—in which the city was probably a net gainer over time—was superseded from the 1890s by immigration from farther up-country as the vastly increased demand for labor encouraged immigration.

By the 1950s something like three-quarters of Mombasa's wage-labor force came from highland Kenya or other parts of East Africa. Some came as contracted laborers, who would work out their "ticket" and then return to their rural homes. But more were attracted by the relatively well-paid casual employment at the docks, which offered workers a degree of control over their own time that was unusual within the colonial economy. A large informal sector developed to service this casual-labor force, providing economic opportunities for a growing number of women and men who stayed in the town for long periods, creating a new, informally employed urban populace.

From the 1940s, employment practices at the docks were changed in an attempt to foster a permanent urban population in formal employment. Migration to Mombasa continued in the period after independence. Increasingly, immigrants were drawn by opportunities in the tourist sector rather than at the docks, and casual and informal employment has continued to be the destination of many migrants. The rate of migration to Mombasa slowed in the 1980s, however; the city's population grew by only 3% a year in the period 1979–1989, slightly below the overall national average for the period, while Nairobi's population was growing by 4.7% each year. Growth figures for 1989–1999 are not yet available. This 20th-century immigration has transformed the religious profile of Mombasa; it was in 1900 an overwhelmingly Muslim society, but by the end of the century, the city—while remaining overtly Muslim and coastal in culture—had a substantial Christian population.

© THE PURCELL TEAM/CORBIS

Laundry dries on a balcony in Mombasa, Kenya.

INFRASTRUCTURE

Public Buildings, Public Works, and Residences. Mombasa is a district and provincial headquarters; it houses provincial postal and telecommunications facilities and is the base for the Kenya navy. Treasury Square, by Fort Jesus, was the center of colonial administration and is still the site for the offices of the municipality and the colonial-period buildings that house the district administration; a rather larger and more modern building, some way along the coastal road, houses the provincial administration. The president's official residence at the coast is on Mombasa Island.

Fort Jesus itself is now a popular museum, under the control of the Kenya Museums Service; as well as the fortress itself there is a permanent exhibition on coastal history and archaeology. Next to the fort stands the elegant early-20th-century building that formerly housed the High Court; this is also now in the care of the Kenya Museums Service. Other places of interest include the old harbor of Mombasa town, now used largely by small coasting and fishing vessels; and the fruit and vegetable market known as Mackinnon Market, built in the early 20th century. On the former Kilindini Road (now Moi Avenue) stand two pairs of metal tusks, erected in 1952 on the occasion of the royal visit of Queen Elizabeth. There are a number of religious buildings: an Anglican cathedral of some architectural interest; a Catholic cathedral; a Jain temple and a very substantial number of mosques, old and new. The Basheikh mosque, with its distinctive rounded minaret, may be some 700 years old; the Mandhry mosque is reliably dated to the 16th century.

The older sports facilities toward the southern end of the island—golf course and sports grounds—were supplemented in the 1960s by a municipal stadium at Tononoka, in the northeast, which is the main venue for public football matches.

Politics and City Services. Mombasa has an elected Municipal Council. Like other local-government bodies in Kenya, the council suffers chronic financial difficulties and provides minimal services, despite an apparently large payroll. Rubbish collection, water supply, and urban roads are all council responsibilities, and the council has a range of regulatory and planning powers. The city returns five members to the Kenya National Assembly, the country's legislative body, which sits in Nairobi.

Educational System. Mombasa, like the rest of Kenya, has an eight-four-four educational system—eight years of primary education, four years of secondary education, and four years of university. Public education at primary level is notionally free but practically conditional upon payment of all kinds of costs and fees. Schools tend to be underfunded, with teachers poorly motivated. A great many children who have completed primary education are unable to afford, or find places in, secondary education. There are a number of private secondary schools in Mombasa—as elsewhere in the country—that are better resourced than are public secondary schools. There is as yet no university in Mombasa or anywhere at the coast, although it has been announced that one will soon be established. Generally speaking, educational achievement at the coast—as measured by examination results—lags behind that found elsewhere in the country.

Transportation System. Within the city and its immediate suburbs, public transport is provided largely by a great number of minivans, most of them owned by quite-small-scale entrepreneurs who keep such vehicles as one of a diversified range of economic activities. These are the *matatus,* notorious for being undisciplined and noisy, with a degree of disregard for their customers. Several private bus companies, operating larger vehicles, run bus services to the immediate hinterland, and along long-distance routes up and down the coast or to Nairobi.

Mombasa occupies a nodal point in the transport system. It is the start of the railway, which operates passenger and freight services up-country; and it lies at the junction of the only all-weather road that runs up and down the coast and the only all-weather road that links the coast and the highlands. A bridge connects Mombasa to the north mainland; a road causeway and railway bridge link it to the west; and there is a ferry (across the harbor mouth) carrying road and passenger traffic from the island to the south mainland. The city also has an international airport (on the mainland west of the island) that handles regional and intercontinental traffic, most of it related to the tourism industry.

CULTURAL AND SOCIAL LIFE

Distinctive Features of the City's Cultures. Several parts of Mombasa—notably the Old Town, around the north harbor, but also much of the Majengo settlements in the center and west of the island—are very evidently Muslim in culture. Many women wear black robes and veils to go out, and men wear long white gowns, particularly on Friday. There is a considerable emphasis on the importance of respectful behavior in such areas. Other parts of Mombasa are, however, much more cosmopolitan, and in places these cultural zones lie surprisingly close together, with nightclubs full of sailors and prostitutes within shouting distance of tranquil mosques. This proximity causes occasional frictions, notably in the few public spaces that Mombasa possesses, such as Makadara Gardens, where strident Christian evangelists make their pitch along the edge of an overwhelmingly Muslim residential area.

Cuisine. Coastal "Swahili" cuisine is distinctive. Characterized by an imaginative use of spices and coconut milk, it draws on both Arabic and Indian traditions of cooking. Popular local dishes are *biriani* and *pilau* (rice cooked with meat and sauces); and various fried pastries such as *hamri* (plural *mahamri*) and the rice-flour *kitumbua* (plural *vitumbua*), often taken with pigeon peas cooked in coconut sauce (*mbaazi*).

Ethnic, Class, and Religious Diversity. Mombasa's cosmopolitan nature has already been noted: this is a city with two cathedrals, several temples, and dozens of mosques. The bulk of the Muslim population are Sunni, of the Shafi' *medhheb*; there are, however, some Omani Ibadhis and a considerable body of Ithnaasheri and other Shi'ite groups. There are chronic debates within coastal Islam over the propriety of certain innovations in religious practice, such as the playing of music in mosques. The Christian population is similarly characterized by diversity; the cathedrals are Anglican and Catholic, but more people pray at Pentecostal or charismatic churches.

Religious and ethnic differences are partly revealed in settlement patterns on the island. Old Town and Majengo are predominantly Muslim, Tononoka and Tudor more Christian. In the mainland suburbs, religions are more mixed. Distinctions of wealth are very stark in Mombasa, as they are elsewhere in Kenya, and are clearly revealed in settlement. The wealthy, of all races, live at Nyali, on the north mainland, or in the old Southern Residential Area on the island.

Family and Other Social Support Systems. Kinship continues to be of great importance for many people in Mombasa. Weaknesses of state provision in health and education, the unpredictability of bureaucratic processes, and the widespread feeling that access to many resources is dependent on "knowing someone" mean that people are constantly turning to kin for assistance and support. Ethnicity may also be an important mobilizing social factor, for the same reasons. These networks of support and alliance tend to be much more robust than those built around such institutions as churches—membership of which can be volatile—and trade unions, which are largely moribund at present.

Work and Commerce. Tourism is a major employer on the coast, as is the related security sector. A sense of the inadequacies of the police system has led to the widespread use of private guards. There are also a number of industrial employers in and around Mombasa: the cement works, a vehicle-assembly plant, aluminium-extrusion works, and others. Horticulture, the most dynamic sector of Kenya's economy at present, is insignificant at the coast, as climatic conditions do not favor it.

The commercial area on Mombasa Island provides the city's principal shopping facilities; here, there are bookshops, clothing shops, hardware shops, and the like. These now compete with a large supermarket on the south of the island, near the ferry. There are fish and produce markets on the island and a large produce market on the north mainland. Small retail outlets are ubiquitous. These mostly take the form of kiosks, the majority of which sell the same basic range of items: soap, bread, matches, batteries, aspirins, soft drinks, sugar, tea leaves, and margarine. There are also—especially in the mainland residential areas—even-more-basic stalls, often consisting of no more than an upturned crate, from which sellers—usually women or small children—sell vegetables, fruit, and cooked foods. In Nyali and Bamburi, there are also shopping facilities for tourists, stocking a range of more-expensive items.

Arts and Recreation. There are a number of public manifestations of Muslim urban culture—notably the evening festivities during the month of Ramadan, but also including occasional wedding processions. There are fewer large-scale events for followers of other religions; occasional mass-prayer meetings are the most obvious. Football (soccer) matches provide another regular occasion for gatherings. Places of worship generally provide one social focus for many of the populace; drinking places (many of them technically illegal palm-wine dens) provide another. For the young, inexpensive "video cinemas" are a popular amusement. The tourism industry has created its own particular culture of entertainment, which revolves around nightclubs, restaurants, and bars. The higher end of this is so expensive as to exclude all but an affluent few of the local populace; however, there are cheaper bars and discotheques, on the fringes of the main hotel area, which are more affordable for a youthful group who aspire to involvement in this culture.

QUALITY OF LIFE

As a tourist destination, Mombasa offers multiple attractions: sunshine, warmth, beaches, and coral reefs. People from elsewhere in Kenya often think of Mombasa an easygoing place, and some aspire to retire there. However, the quality of life of a considerable number of residents is poor. Malaria is endemic, and there are chronic problems with both the quantity and the quality of water supplied. Many people have to buy water from water peddlers, either because they have no access to a tap or because their taps have no water in them. Like other parts of Kenya, Mombasa suffers at present from a chronic deficit of electricity, which periodically becomes a crisis, with prolonged power cuts (even for those who are lucky enough to have power connected to their houses). Food tends to cost more in Mombasa than it does in the highlands—since so much has to be brought to the coast—and land prices in desirable locations, particularly near to the shoreline, are very high.

Access to land is a major issue in Mombasa, as the wealthy or well-connected have taken control of many prime sites. While Mombasa is largely spared large-scale pollution, the "grabbing" of land and the development of ecologically fragile seashore areas have raised serious environmental issues. Disputes over access to land highlight a major concern—extreme and growing inequalities of wealth, which are related to a serious problem of crime. Theft and robbery are common, and while tourists are generally protected by the extensive investment in private-security systems, many ordinary Mombasans are not so fortunate. Inequality and the general sense of insecurity have in the recent past led to the eruption of serious violence, directed at migrants from up-country.

BIBLIOGRAPHY

Berg, F., "The Swahili Community of Mombasa, 1500–1900," *Journal of African History* 9 (1968).

Cooper, F., *On the African Waterfront: Urban Disorder and the Transformation of Work in Colonial Mombasa* (Yale University Press 1987).

Cooper, F., *Plantation Labour on the East African Coast* (Yale University Press 1977).

Freeman-Grenville, G., *The East Africa Coast: Select Documents from the First to the Early Nineteenth Century* (Clarendon Press 1962).

Gray, J., *The British in Mombasa, 1824–26* (Macmillan 1957).

Kenya Population Census, 1989 (Government of Kenya 1994).

Salim, A., *Swahili-Speaking Peoples of Kenya's Coast* (East African Publishing House 1973).

Willis, J., *Mombasa, the Swahili, and the Making of the Mijikenda* (Clarendon Press 1993).

JUSTIN WILLIS

Monrovia

Liberia

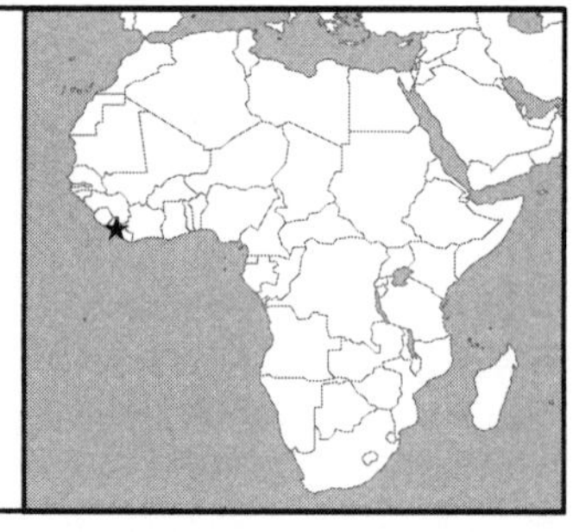

ORIENTATION

Name of City. Monrovia is the capital city of Liberia, Africa's oldest independent republic. After their initial struggles to establish a settlement, the African American settlers who founded the city laid out a town they called Christopolis. Renamed in 1824 on the advice of the American Colonization Society (ACS), the town became known as Monrovia, honoring U.S. president James Monroe.

Location. The city is located on a peninsula on the West African coast, at 6°18′ north latitude and 10°48′ west longitude, where the St. Paul and Mesurado rivers meet the Atlantic Ocean. The first few buildings and a street layout were established on a rocky outcrop that forms a promontory on the peninsula, looking down on indigenous settlements closer to the water's edge. The promontory eventually became the central business district and administrative center of the city, with several six- to eight-story buildings adding to the city's distinctive profile as viewed from the sea.

Immediately to the north of the peninsula, across the mouth of the Mesurado, the city extends onto Bushrod Island, which hugs the coastline (separated from the mainland on the east by a small creek) for a distance of 3 kilometers (2 miles). The island is bordered on the north by the St. Paul River lagoon, Monrovia's northern limit. From its few early indigenous settlements, Bushrod Island grew into the city's principal industrial area, including the Free Port of Monrovia, as well as several high-density neighborhoods. Southeast from the town center, Monrovia extends about 2.4 kilometers (1.5 miles) through many different retail commercial, and residential areas. These two geographic axes of the city, extending north and southeast from the city center, anchor the two principal highways that connect Monrovia to the rest of Liberia.

Population. In the mid-1970s a national census placed the population of Liberia at 1.5 million and of Monrovia at about 204,000. Government population estimates in the mid-1980s placed the national population at about 2 million, with Monrovia at 400 thousand. The city's residents represented the full range of ethnic and socioeconomic diversity in the country and included substantial numbers of immigrants from other West African countries.

Monrovia is Liberia's largest city. Along with the descendants of its 19th-century African American settlers, it has attracted migrants from all the rural areas in the country. Among the many indigenous groups in the urban population at the census were large numbers of Kru-speaking peoples from the southeast, Kpelle and Loma peoples from the northeast regions, and Vai peoples from the northern coast. Although the urban population resides in ethnically mixed neighborhoods, throughout the 1970s and

1980s a number of distinctive ethnically based areas of the city survived, including New Krutown and Vai Town, on Bushrod Island, and Loma Quarter south of the city center.

The city's West African immigrants include persons from Nigeria, Guinea, Sierra Leone, and the Ivory Coast. During the 1970s the Liberian government maintained an "open door" policy designed to stimulate entrepreneurship and investment in the country. As a result, Liberia was an attractive location for West African migrants. And from early in its history, the Monrovian population has included Lebanese and other Middle Eastern populations, historically active in the retail economic sector throughout all of West Africa.

Distinctive and Unique Features. The architecture of Monrovia reflects the country's diverse history. As they built their homes and churches, many of the early African American settlers adopted the architectural styles of the 19th century American South. These early homes, mostly wood (and later brick or corrugated metal), were built on top of cement or brick columns to adapt to the tropical climate. While later settler generations abandoned these homes for new residential areas to the southeast of the city center, many of these structures remain, nestled among Western-style office buildings, schools, and churches. The city's architecture is an interesting mix of the new and the old.

By the 1980s the city center had grown to include modern government and commercial buildings. Broad Street, the main thoroughfare in the city center, contained Lebanese-owned shops, upscale restaurants, and jewelry and clothing stores occupying the ground floors of buildings, with offices and apartments in the floors above. Metal structures between the more substantial buildings housed cookshops, tailors, and craft sellers. West of Broad Street bars, nightclubs, and dance clubs formed a small entertainment district. Still further west, on land gradually approaching the seacoast, were located several ethnic neighborhoods, a city cemetery, and schools. East of Broad Street the roads more abruptly descended from the promontory down to the Mesurado River lagoon. Along that waterfront the city's main marketplace, Waterside, grew—a crowded assemblage of shops, outdoor stalls, and export establishments. North of the promontory, below its rocky cliffs, was West Point, reportedly the most densely populated and poorest neighborhood in the city.

Southeast of the city center lie the executive mansion and the National Legislature and Supreme Court buildings, along with the small, Spriggs-Payne Airfield. The southeastern suburbs, particularly one known as Sinkor, formerly included many foreign delegations and homes of wealthy Liberians. Bushrod Island, to the north, contains several densely populated ethnic neighborhoods as well as much of the city's heavy industry, including mining depots for the railroad, a power-generation plant, and food processing and manufacturing firms.

Attractions of the City. Liberia has rich natural resources, including iron and diamond deposits, and in the past the economic policies of the country have encouraged foreign investment and drawn foreign technicians and other visitors. Thus, the city center, particularly in the 1970s and 1980s, maintained an air of cosmopolitanism. European and American foods, entertainment, and fashions were readily available in Monrovia. Arts from the entire West African region were on sale. It was not unusual to see elite families from neighboring West African countries visiting Monrovia on extended shopping trips. In 1979 Liberia hosted the Organization of African Unity, having constructed a new international luxury hotel and conference center just north of Monrovia across the St. Paul River. This facility became a major tourist attraction and resort. Until the civil war of 1989–1996 Monrovia was a bustling center attractive to Liberians and expatriate populations alike.

Relationships Between the City and the Outside. Monrovia is a primate city; no other Liberian city approaches it in size. The highly centralized Liberian government system based in the city prompts rural peoples to travel to Monrovia to consult legislators on local political issues just as frequently as they pursue those issues in the rural areas themselves. The highest-quality medical services, manufactured goods, entertainment venues, and institutions of higher education have been established in Monrovia; these attract many rural visitors. The city's economic sector has been the most vital in the country, aside from several mining and rubber concessions in the rural areas. Hence, the city is a magnet for rural residents seeking new jobs and an improved standard of living.

Major Languages. Given the city's ethnic diversity, all indigenous Liberian languages are represented in the population, including the Kru language group (Kru, Bassa, Grebo, and Krahn), Kpelle, Loma,

Vai, and Kissi. All of these languages fall within the greater Niger-Congo linguistic grouping, which is the largest of sub-Saharan Africa. English was introduced along the Liberian coast by British traders in the 18th century. Some early forms of pidgin English developed by the British and indigenous coastal Africans were already present in the region when the African American settlers arrived in 1822. Most of these settlers were English speakers, having been born in the United States, representing both Northern and Southern regional American English dialects. As a result of settler dominance in Liberian politics and economics, English became Liberia's official language, and it is widely spoken in Monrovia. English is closely associated with Western education; the concentration of secondary and postsecondary education in Monrovia, and the abundance of government and service-sector jobs, creates an urban environment that fosters the use and prestige of English.

HISTORY

Liberia's history was abruptly reoriented through political events that took place in the last two decades of the 20th century, beginning with a coup in 1980 and lasting through the civil war. Monrovia was substantially affected by these events.

The Origins of the City. The early inhabitants of the city site were indigenous Dei peoples, along with a small settlement of Kru-speaking peoples who, from the 17th century, had migrated west along the coast to take advantage of growing European trade. In 1822 a group of African Americans financed by the ACS arrived at the mouth of the Mesurado River and were allowed to settle on the mainland on a promontory overlooking the indigenous villages of the area. The ACS had been founded in the United States in the early 1800s as a philanthropic association dedicated to the repatriation of free persons of African descent to Africa. After several false starts the group of African American settlers who disembarked at the mouth of the Mesurado River established an ACS "colony." These settlers, who called themselves "Americo-Liberians," were charged by the sponsoring society not simply to build constructive and fulfilling lives for themselves in Africa but to serve as beacons of Christianity and civilization for the rest of the continent. The establishment of a geographically separate settlement of Americo-Liberian homes on the promontory—rather than adjacent to the existing indigenous villages—reflected marked differences between the newcomers and the indigenous groups with regard to dress, food, conduct, and faith. Until the 1980s the descendants of Americo-Liberian settlers, although no more than 2% of the national population, monopolized most of the political positions and economic resources in the country.

The Americo-Liberian settlers were inspired by the U.S. ideal as they set about establishing their settlement. By the 1840s the settlers chafed at the supervision of the colony by the ACS. In 1847 they declared themselves an independent republic, Liberia: a beacon of freedom for any black person who could make his or her way to its shores. Their constitution was written by two Harvard political scientists, and it established a national system based on the U.S. model of executive, judicial, and legislative branches. A national flag was designed with thirteen alternating red and white horizontal stripes and a field of blue with one lone star.

For most of its history Liberia retained a cordial relationship with the United States, nurtured by common political ideals and increasingly interdependent economic connections. The difficulty experienced by the United States during World War I in obtaining sufficient rubber supplies led Harvey Firestone to establish major rubber plantations and processing plants in Liberia in the 1920s. During World War II military facilities were built outside of Monrovia to facilitate the transport of troops and supplies to the North African campaign. Until the Liberian civil war, U.S. paper currency was used in the country. Moreover, throughout the 1960s and 1970s, the largest Peace Corps contingent in sub-Saharan Africa was stationed in Liberia, based in Monrovia.

By the late 1970s, under the presidency of William R. Tolbert, Jr., the Liberian economy was experiencing severe difficulties in its principal export sectors. The prices of basic commodities had increased significantly, particularly for food in Monrovia and other urban areas. In April 1979 riots erupted in Monrovia when the government raised the price of rice, a staple of the Liberian diet. The riots did not solve the economic problem, but the refusal of the national army and police to open fire on citizens demonstrated to many the weakness of the national government. One year later a successful military coup was staged by Master-Sergeant Samuel K. Doe and a small group of enlisted men. President Tolbert was killed, and a military government was established. Americo-Liberians were removed from office and replaced with descendants of indigenous Liberians. By the mid-1980s the Doe government had gained the confidence and support of the Liberian population. Monrovia residents saw neighborhood roads paved and new clinics and marketplaces established. Throughout the country the population was engaged in the development of a new constitution. However, this process culminated in a national election in 1985 that a majority viewed as fraudulent. Doe, now in a suit instead of a military uniform, was elected president.

For the next five years corruption and economic difficulties plagued the Doe administration. On Christmas Eve, 1989, Charles Taylor, an Americo-Liberian who had received military training in Libya, launched a campaign in the rural areas to remove the Doe government. This began a six-year civil war in which Monrovia was very much the target.

During 1990 Taylor's National Patriotic Front of Liberia (NPFL) was supported by popular discontent with Doe. Taylor's forces included a small number of trained, disciplined soldiers, including many with previous experience in the Liberian national army. Increasingly, however, his "citizen's army" included untrained men, women, and children, who were given weapons with a promise of rewards after a successful campaign.

Taylor gained control over nearly the entire country, with the exception of Monrovia. His campaign was made more complex by the emergence of several breakaway factions from within the NPFL (one of which succeeded in September 1990 in luring President Doe to the Free Port of Monrovia, where he was executed). Taylor's efforts were further marred by the behavior of his largely undisciplined forces. Terror and looting became the hallmarks of the advance on Monrovia. With Liberia on the verge of chaos, a group of West African nations, members of the Economic Community of West African States (ECOWAS), created a joint military force to intervene in the Liberian civil war. This cease-fire monitoring force, the ECOWAS Cease-fire Monitoring Group, or ECOMOG, entered Monrovia in August 1990 to prevent Taylor's forces from taking the city. Under their supervision an Interim Government of National Unity (IGNU) was installed in Monrovia. By the end of 1990 "Greater Liberia" was under Taylor's control, while Monrovia was protected by the IGNU, with ECOMOG support.

The efforts of ECOWAS were not simply military. They organized several conferences to attempt a negotiated end to the civil war. Taylor, however, refused to recognize the interim government. By the mid 1990s a new agreement was fashioned to replace IGNU with a transitional government in which all warring factions would be represented. Initially, this effort was not successful, and Taylor's forces attacked Monrovia once again, although they again failed to take the city. Following another agreement, however, a second transitional government was established in 1996. The success of this effort resulted from Taylor's recognition that he would not be able to take Monrovia by force; instead, he would advance his objectives through cooperative participation in the transitional government. Thus, in 1996 Taylor entered Monrovia with no gunshots, as part of a transitional government preparing for a national election. In July 1997 presidential elections were held, and Taylor won more than 75% of the vote. The Taylor civilian government took office in August 1997 and allowed ECOMOG to move freely outside Monrovia to help disarm combatants throughout the country. By mid-1999, ECOMOG forces had withdrawn from the country. Unrest continued, however, especially in Lofa county on Liberia's border with Guinea.

Migration: Past and Present. Population statistics for Monrovia and Liberia are not extensive. However, while the city experienced substantial growth in the first half of the 20th century, the civil unrest beginning in 1979 led to unprecedented increases in migration.

After the military coup of 1980, Monrovia experienced an initial population gain that dissipated as many persons, fearing for their safety, returned to their rural areas. But, during the 1989–1996 civil war, as Taylor's forces moved throughout the countryside, thousands of Liberians sought to reach Monrovia for safety—particularly after ECOMOG forces established themselves in the city. Estimates suggest that Monrovia's population swelled to over 1.5 million, having increased by at least one-half million after the civil war began. Death rates in the city were high during this period. During Taylor's sieges of the city, many citizens were killed. But even during other periods, the swelling population strained deteriorating city services. Food and medicine were in short supply, and neighborhoods became severely overpopulated. The very young and the aged fell as victims to disease and starvation. No reliable numbers for these casualties are available.

In 1996 an estimated 800,000 internally displaced persons (IDPs) were located in and around Monrovia. By 1999 about 75,000 IDPs were living in 36 displacement centers in the city. The government urged these people to return to the rural areas, and estimates show that only about 10,000 persons remain. But the IDPs in official displacement centers do not reflect the total number of unrecorded displaced persons living with relatives and others in crowded Monrovia neighborhoods.

INFRASTRUCTURE

Public Buildings, Public Works, and Residences. The civil war destroyed much of Monrovia's infrastructure, and little was rebuilt in the years following. Prior to the civil war Monrovia had a number of landmark buildings, located mostly in the city center, including the National Legislature, the Executive Mansion, the Department of State, other government ministries, a national museum, the national archives and the John F. Kennedy Medical Center (the two latter located in Sinkor), as well as the campus of the University of Liberia. Many of these structures suffered damaged during the civil war and are only partially in use today.

Urban residences are in a state of acute damage and disrepair. During the sieges of the city, firewood and cooking coals were in short supply. Buildings were looted of wooden window frames and doors, not to mention furnishings, to use as fuel. Palm trees were used for fuel, significantly degrading the natural landscape of the city. Today, many urban structures provide only walls and roofs for their inhabitants.

Politics and City Services. Historically the national government has directly or indirectly run the city of Monrovia. That situation has not changed as a result of the civil war.

The war destroyed the country's major hydroelectric plant, located outside of Monrovia. No part of the city has electricity for 24 hours each day, and some parts of the city remain entirely without electricity. Most of the city does not have running water, although some progress has been made in the 1990s in digging new bore holes on the eastern side of Monrovia to augment what remains of the city water system. For some time after 1996, the government trucked water into Monrovia neighborhoods daily; now private companies sell this service. No city sewage system has operated for years.

In 1916 Kru residents of the city, historically among the oldest inhabitants of the site, were granted special administrative autonomy through an act of the Liberian National Legislature. Until the 1990s their Kru Corporation provided governance for a large neighborhood on Bushrod Island, as well as a framework to ensure the mutual wellbeing of all Monrovia Kru, regardless of neighborhood of residence

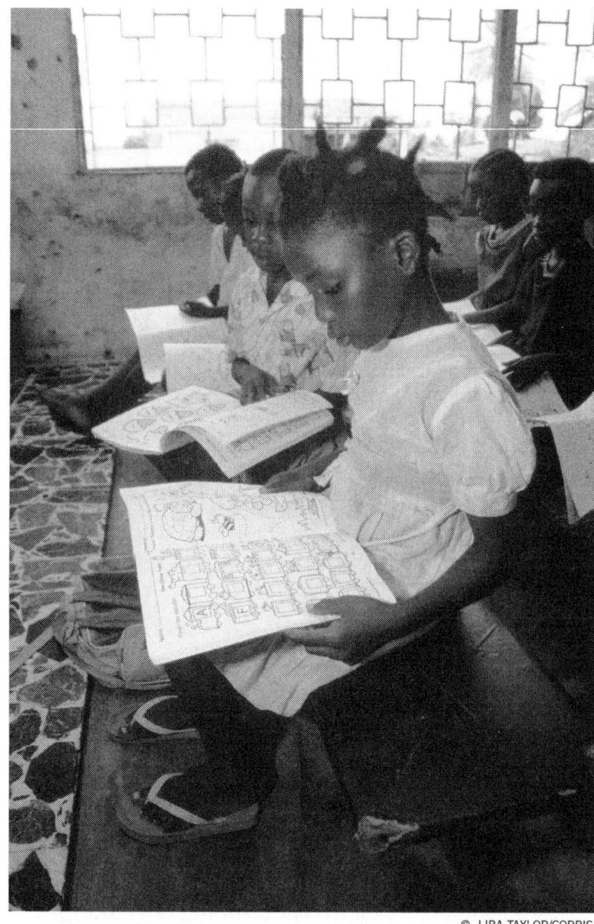

© LIBA TAYLOR/CORBIS

Children left parentless by the war in Sierra Leone and Liberia read books in an orphanage in Monrovia, Liberia, in 1993.

Educational System. Prior to the civil war the Monrovia Consolidated School System ran public elementary and secondary schools. In addition, there were a great number of church-sponsored and other private schools. Some public schools are now open, and many private schools survived the civil war. But the number of young children out of school has increased. Many families cannot afford school fees, and there are many urban street children who do not have the means to attend.

The University of Liberia functioned for much of the civil war, although its campus was badly damaged. However, the university was closed indefinitely in 1999, and its future remains uncertain.

Transportation System. Until civil disturbances began in the 1980s, an inexpensive urban bus system and ubiquitous taxicabs facilitated frequent and easy transportation throughout all areas of the city. The war and the attacks on the city nearly destroyed the transportation system. City roads are in serious disrepair.

Public transportation has not yet been fully reestablished. Following his election in 1996 President Taylor had all the taxicabs painted with a fresh coat of yellow. But public transportation remains expensive and unreliable.

CULTURAL AND SOCIAL LIFE

Family and Other Social Support Systems. Even in the most prosperous times prior to the civil war, limited social services were available to Monrovia's population. Family, kinship, and ethnic ties provided a framework for most urban residents that facilitated their initial migration as well as their personal welfare once established in the city. Many indigenous ethnic groups recognized urban "chiefs" or clan officials to help ensure mutual well being and social order.

During the war various grassroots self-help organizations arose to facilitate the distribution of food and medical supplies. Many of these groups worked together with numerous churches throughout the city to ensure—as best they could—the survival of the Monrovia population during times of armed attack. At the same time these networks tended to weaken the role of ethnic administrations in city neighborhoods.

Work and Commerce. Prior to the war the urban occupational structure included a growing sector of professional, technical, and administrative and managerial positions, alongside a large sector of manual labor. As in many other sub-Saharan African cities, unemployment in Monrovia was high (it was estimated at 16% for males and 25% for females in the mid-1970s). By the late 1980s male unemployment in Monrovia had increased to nearly 35%; female unemployment decreased slightly as more women entered the informal economy by taking up food vending. The extent to which the civil war destroyed the urban occupational structure is not fully documented, but it is clear that unemployment has become more significant than ever in Monrovia's day-to-day life.

FUTURE OF THE CITY

By the 1980s Monrovia was a thriving capital of modern buildings and attractive Western-style residences alongside bustling, densely settled neighborhoods of indigenous persons—with increasing ethnic diversity resulting from the in-migration of many more of Liberia's indigenous ethnic groups. While that population diversity remains, the city continues to slowly recover from the massive destruction of its infrastructure, services, and amenities resulting from its civil war.

Monrovia's future is inextricably bound up with the reconstruction and redevelopment of post–civil war Liberia. The political situation in the country is not yet viewed as stable, however, and economic recovery remains in its initial phase. Reestablishing basic city services such as electricity and running water will require international financing well beyond the current level of assistance. Regional instability (for example, warfare in neighboring Sierra Leone) continues to complicate the situation. Family and kinship ties remain strong, however, and are likely to continue to play a central role in the survival of Monrovia's population for the foreseeable future.

BIBLIOGRAPHY

Breitborde, Lawrence B., "Structural Continuity in the Development of an Urban Kru Neighborhood," *Urban Anthropology* 8 (1979): 111–30.

Ellis, Stephen, *The Mask of Anarchy: The Destruction of Liberia and the Religious Dimension of an African Civil War* (New York University Press 1999).

Fraenkel, Merran, *Tribe and Class in Monrovia* (Oxford University Press 1964).

Tanner, Victor, "Liberia: Railroading Peace," *Review of African Political Economy* 25 (1998): 133–47.

LAWRENCE B. BREITBORDE

Monterrey

Mexico

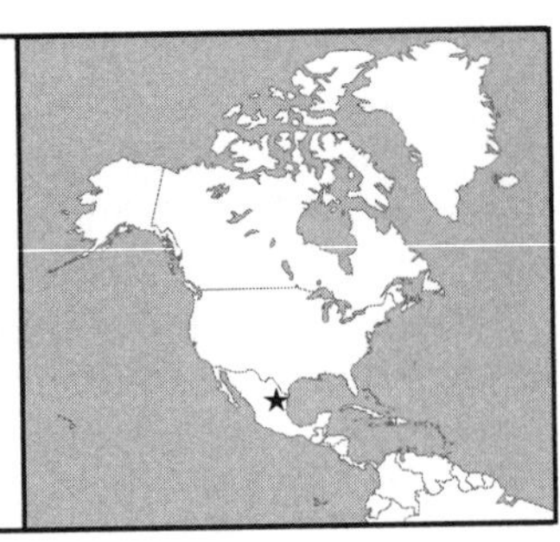

ORIENTATION

The industrial city of Monterrey, Mexico, stands as a tangible and metaphorical transition between the rich north and the poor south—the United States and Latin America—and, located 224 kilometers (139 miles) south of the U.S. border, is a "borderland" on the border.

Name of City. Modestly named "La Ciudad Metropolitana de Nuestra Señora de Monterrey" when founded in 1596, today the city is referred to simply as Monterrey. The people of Monterrey are *regiomontanos*, or *regios* for short. Monterrey has acquired a number of appellations and nicknames, including "la Reina del Norte" and "la Sultana del Norte" (respectively, "Queen of the North" and "Sultaness of the North"), as well as comparative ones such as "the Chicago of Mexico" and "Mexico's Pittsburgh." Two preeminent symbols of Monterrey are Cerro de la Silla (Saddleback Mountain) and the city's industry.

Location. Monterrey, the capital of the state of Nuevo León, is located in northeastern México at 25°40′ north latitude and 100°18′ west longitude and at 534 meters (1,752 feet) above sea level. Nuevo León is bordered by the Mexican states of Tamaulipas, San Luis Potosí, Zacatecas, and Coahuila and the U.S. state of Texas.

Population. In 1990 the population of the city was 1,069,238 and the population of the metropolitan area was 2,558,494, with Monterrey thus retaining its position as third-largest among Mexico's cities and metropolitan areas, after Mexico City and Guadalajara. Estimates for 1995 placed the metropolitan area population at 2,936,613, an increase of 14.8%. The metropolitan region comprises the *municipios* of Monterrey, Apodaca, General Escobedo, Guadalupe, San Nicolás de los Garza, San Pedro Garza García, and Santa Catarina and small sections of García and Juárez. The total area is nearly 43,000 hectares (107,000 acres). Population density for Monterrey alone in 1990 was 3,163 per square kilometer (1,221 per square mile).

Distinctive and Unique Features. Monterrey is located in a valley near the eastern edge of the Sierra Madre Oriental and flanked on the northwest by Cerro de las Mitras, on the north by Cerro del Topo Chico, on the southeast by Cerro de la Silla, and to the south by the Sierra Madre. The Monterrey Valley was formed by the Río Santa Catarina, which still intermittently flows through the city south of its center. Climatically, Monterrey's metropolitan area straddles the subhumid extratropical lowlands, the tropical highlands of the Sierra Madre, the semiarid steppe lands of the Mesa del Norte, and the humid subtropical Gulf Coastal Plain.

Monterrey is well known for its extremes in temperatures: hot to very hot in the summer, with maximums of 35° to 40°C (95° to 105°F), to cold in the winter, with lows of 0°C (32°F) common. Monterrey has more available water than the bulk of the surrounding region, although most of it is underground and not sufficient for the needs of the metropolis.

The initial layout of the city followed the Spanish grid pattern employed throughout most of Latin America, with a central plaza (*plaza major*) and closely spaced houses along narrow streets. Major religious, governmental, and commercial structures were situated around the main plaza, with the homes of upper-class citizens located around this central core. Until the late 19th century Monterrey's appearance was essentially that of an elongated, compact town along the north bank of the Río Santa Catarina.

The basic grid pattern still remains in *el centro* ("downtown"), although recent developments have altered much of the original layout and dimensions. Today the Gran Plaza, or "Macroplaza," dominates central Monterrey. This project absorbed the original *plaza major* of Zaragoza along with much of the surrounding city blocks but incorporated several older structures with many new features and structures.

The terrain of the metropolis's immediate environs and the great expanse of generally flat lands to the north and east have allowed urban growth to spread horizontally. Buildings of more than 10 stories did not appear until the 1950s, and there are still few buildings of more than 20 to 25 stories.

Attractions of the City. Monterrey is the principal industrial, manufacturing, and commercial center in northern Mexico. It is second only to metropolitan Mexico City in gross domestic product and in terms of importance in banking, finance, and transportation. Major industries include cement, glass, brewing, petrochemicals, plastics, and steel. Monterrey is also important in retailing and franchising. The metropolitan area has two international airports and is also serviced by excellent highway, railroad, and communications systems. These connections have proved to be extremely vital under the North American Free Trade Agreement (NAFTA) for across-the-border trade networks to south Texas, San Antonio, Houston, and Dallas–Fort Worth, strengthening links to the north, along what is often called the "San Antonio–Monterrey corridor."

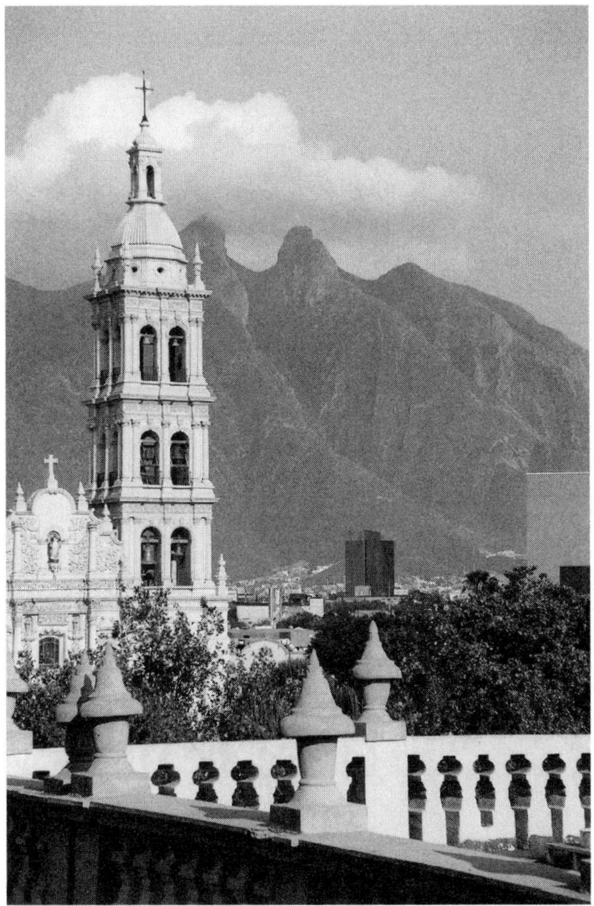

© JAMES F. HOPGOOD

Cerro de la Silla (Saddleback Mountain) is seen in the distance in this photograph of the cathedral at Monterrey, Mexico.

Monterrey is the home of a number of major industrial groups, often referred to collectively as *el grupo Monterrey* (the Monterrey Group). Among these companies are several that provided the basis for Monterrey's industrialization in the early 20th century. Today these and their descendant companies, such as Grupo Alfa, Vitro, and Cemex, are among some of Mexico's largest multinationals and conglomerates, having many diverse ventures in Mexico and in various countries.

Signs of globalization are common in metropolitan Monterrey: Japanese electronics and cars, American franchises and computers, German medical technology, clothing from France and Italy, and so on. Numerous efforts and incentives exist to encourage foreign firms to locate operations in the Monterrey area, including several public and private industrial parks, deregulation measures, and tax breaks.

Monterrey is a major destination for thousands of travelers, tourists, and businesspersons each year. In 1996 approximately 2,024,000 visitors to the city were recorded, based on hotel stays. Most visitors are businesspeople, with only about 25% being tourists. The vast majority of visitors were Mexican, with only 17.4% being foreigners. Hotel accommodations in the metropolitan region range from "grand tourism" and five-star hotels to the very basic among the 51 hotels in the area in 1991. Monterrey's new convention center, the Cintermex, with an area of 6.5 hectares (16 acres), is Latin America's largest.

The metropolis offers many diversions for visitor and tourist. The Gran Plaza, marked by a 70-meter- (230-foot-) high, red-orange monolith-like structure, the Faro del Comercio, has a number of attractions. These include several museums, Monterrey's cathedral, City Theatre, Casino Monterrey (a recreational club), the central library, and several government buildings. The Gran Plaza also contains several smaller plazas, fountains, gardens, scenic walks, and other diversions. In the recently renovated and restored Barrio Antiguo, just east of the cathedral, there are many 19th-century structures and several museums and galleries. Barrio Antiguo also offers live entertainment, bars, dining, and discotheques, providing, along with Monterrey's downtown Zona Rosa (Pink Zone), ample opportunities for a lively evening.

Away from the immediate downtown area, there are numerous other sights and places of interest in the city. Particularly notable is the Museo Regional de Historia, or "Museo del Obispado," located in the former Bishop's Palace. It is of considerable historical merit as Monterrey's first bishopric, as the only remaining example of colonial architecture, and also as a hotly contested battleground between U.S. and Mexican forces in 1846.

Outside the metropolitan area, but nearby, there are many popular attractive destinations frequented by local people and tourists. The section of the Sierra Madre known as Chipinque overlooks the city from a height of approximately 1,500 meters (5,000 feet) and is part of a large national ecological preserve. It is a popular venue for picnics and outings, and with its hotel, restaurant, and meeting facilities it is often the site for business conferences.

For shopping there are formats to suit all tastes and incomes. Numerous upscale shops and stores can be found downtown and in wealthy suburbs. Downtown several streets have been converted for foot traffic only to better accommodate shoppers. In the suburbs there are many shopping malls and centers built on U.S. models, and convenience stores now dot the urban landscape. More economical shopping is available near downtown Monterrey and in districts near traditional *mercados* (markets) in the metropolitan area. A giant open market is held on weekends in a large reclaimed section of the Río Santa Catarina.

Relationships Between the City and the Outside. One stereotype of *regiomontanos* has them as industrious, hardworking, and maybe a little too much like *gringos*. Another has the *regiomontano* as *codo*, or stingy. Monterrey and its people are viewed in both positive and negative ways by people in other parts of Mexico, but a consistent motif is the city's role as a leading industrial center and as a municipality that has remained, in many ways, a "frontier" and a bit "provincial."

© NEIL BEER/CORBIS

Metal grilles cover the windows and doorways of homes in an old quarter of Monterrey, Mexico.

Monterrey has long had a special relationship with the United States, and with Texas in particular. There is a regular flow of *regiomontanos* who travel north to Texas, either to the border or on to San Antonio, Houston, Dallas, or Chicago to visit family and friends and to make purchases before returning home. The city's elites send their children to English-speaking schools in Monterrey and later to universities in the United States and Europe. Adding to the international climate of the city are small colonies of Americans, Germans, Lebanese, Palestinians, Spanish, Japanese, Chinese, and Ashkenazi Jews, as well as other Latin Americans.

Monterrey has long dominated Nuevo León, as its capital and chief economic center. With about 82% of the state's population and the major concentration of its wealth, industry, and cultural facilities, metropolitan Monterrey is clearly the social, political, economic, and cultural center for the state and for northeast Mexico.

Major Languages. Spanish is the official language. In many of the city's larger businesses, command of English, either spoken or written, or both, is a requirement. Speakers of indigenous languages, such as Nahuatl, Huasteco, and Mixtec, in the Monterrey area are recent migrants from elsewhere in Mexico. The indigenous Native Americans who inhabited the Monterrey area at the time of the Spanish conquest are extinct.

HISTORY

The Origin of the City. The successful founding of Monterrey in 1596 by Diego de Montemayor was the third attempt by Spanish conquistadors. Montemayor led a small group of Spaniards, mestizos (people of both indigenous and Spanish descent), mulattos, and Native Americans to locate a settlement near natural water springs, now occupied by downtown Monterrey. In the early years, Monterrey served mainly as a way station between Saltillo and the mines in northern Nuevo León. The first *regiomontanos* had to adapt to poor soils, famine, epidemics, floods, limited resources, and continuous hostilities from the surrounding nomadic bands of Native Americans. Thirty years later, in 1626, the settlement numbered 48 persons, not counting children and Native Americans. By the middle of the 17th century, Nuevo León was a principal center for sheep raising. Some *haciendas* (plantations) developed based on wheat farming in the vicinity of Monterrey and were needed primarily to supply the small mines north of the city.

Development was slow throughout the colonial period, but in the late 18th and early 19th century the opening of seaports on the northeast Gulf coast increased Monterrey's role as a distribution center for imports and exports in northern Mexico. During the War for Independence (1810–1821), Monterrey became the focal point for migration from the central region owing to its relative peacefulness, resulting in a population of 12,282 by 1824. Following the Mexican War (1846–1848), Monterrey functioned as a commercial and industrial center, and during the American Civil War, as a commercial intermediary for trade between the Confederacy and Europe. Capital and experience gained during those periods were important for the city's pristine industrialization in the 1890s and early 1900s. Railroads made trade much swifter and safer, and by 1891 Monterrey was connected to Laredo, Texas; Mexico City; Tampico; and other points, making the city an important hub. The startup of several new industries, however, propelled Monterrey into the forefront of industrial development in Mexico. The Cervecería Cuauhtémoc (1890), the Compañía Fundidora de Fierro y Acero (1900), Cementos Hidalgo (1907), and Vidriera Monterrey (1909) brought beer, steel, cement, and glass production to Monterrey. By 1900 Monterrey was Mexico's fourth-largest city in population.

In the 1940s favorable national laws and governmental policies encouraged further industrialization, and World War II provided additional stimuli. The inability to acquire U.S. and European products stimulated internal production of goods, and U.S. demand for iron and steel increased Mexico's market considerably. This was a boom time for Monterrey, as it was the country's only significant producer of iron and steel at the time. And, by 1940, as already indicated, Monterrey was second only to Mexico City in industrial and commercial standing.

Migration: Past and Present. Until Monterrey's steps into industrialization, the city's attraction for migrants from other parts of Mexico was largely limited to its location away from major wars and disturbances. Monterrey registered significant gains in population between 1940 and 1960, with annual increases of about 6.2%. Between 1960 and 1990 annual increases of 4.3% for the metropolitan area were recorded. Much of this growth was due to in-migration. In 1960, 32.9% and in 1990, 25.5% of the metropolitan region's population had been born outside of Nuevo León. Most migrants to Monterrey come from rural areas of Nuevo León and the surrounding states of San Luis Potosí, Coahuila, Tamaulipas, and Zacatecas. While not all migrants have relocated from rural settings, most do and many others come from small towns, rather than cities.

INFRASTRUCTURE

Public Buildings, Public Works, and Residences. Monterrey's new Gran Plaza, covering some 40 hectares (100 acres), is promoted as one of the largest plazas in the world. Built between 1981 and 1984 (although additional expansion is possible), the plaza is Monterrey's grandest public work and meant to move it into the ranks of "world-class cities." The plaza provides the setting for many new and older public structures, together with fountains and a host of monuments. The principal governmental buildings include the state capital building, state congress, state supreme court, federal building, post office, and Monterrey's municipal building. The plaza also provides for underground public parking, shopping, and connections with Monterrey's subway system. The offices of many other municipal, state, and federal agencies are located in various parts of the city and metropolitan area.

Residences in Monterrey's metropolitan region range from the palatial homes of the wealthy of Colonia Del Valle to the shacks (*jacales*) of poor squatters. Most, however, are between the two extremes and are constructed of concrete, block, or brick, and over 95% have electricity, piped water, and drainage. Today the distribution of residential *colonias* (neighborhoods) in the area is very mixed, exhibiting no clear or simple spatial pattern.

Residences for workers and the lower middle class have taken a variety of forms. Some of the first purpose-built housing for workers was constructed by the leading factories such as the Cervecería Cuauhtémoc and the Fundidora. These residential *colonias* were built north and east of downtown in the 1920s and 1930s and generally consisted of one-story block or concrete houses with most utilities supplied.

Housing programs for the lowest income groups began in earnest in the mid- and late 1970s after many years of unmanaged, illegal settlement by squatters on public and private lands and the eventual organizing of squatters as a political front that city, state, and federal officials could not ignore. Early small, uncoordinated efforts with "sites and services," and self-help housing, gave way to a major effort called Fomerrey (Fomento Metropolitano de Monterrey). This, and other programs, attempted to halt illegal invasions of land by providing house lots, basic services, and assistance to families in building their houses in planned settlements. The organized political drive by squatters of the 1970s and 1980s was effectively blunted, and by the 1990s there were several hundred Fomerrey settlements in the metropolitan area, with a total population of over 400,000 persons. Despite these programs there was an estimated deficit in 1988 of 69,000 housing units and another 176,000 units constructed of inadequate materials in metropolitan Monterrey.

Politics and City Services. The primary unit of governance of Monterrey, as throughout Mexico, is the *municipio,* a combined city-county government organized under a set of regulations called the "Reglamentación Ayuntamiento" (municipal regulations). Each *municipio* has a *cabildo* (municipal council) and a municipal president. Every three years voters elect *regidores* (aldermen) and *síndicos* (trustees) to the *cabildo,* as well as its president. For 2002, the Cabildo de Monterrey had 25 *regidores* (including 6 women) and 2 *síndicos*. No immediate reelection of the president is permitted.

Services for the metropolitan region are provided by a vast array of agencies at the municipal, state, and federal levels. The *municipios* of metropolitan Monterrey furnish a range of public services, including public lighting, electricity, water, sanitation, sewerage, drainage, natural gas, parks and recreational facilities, security and judiciary, transportation (buses and, in the city, a subway system), construction and maintenance of streets and of sidewalks and pedestrian bridges, assorted health and educational services and programs, clinics, markets, slaughterhouses, and cemeteries. Additional services are also provided by state or federal agencies, sometimes in conjunction with municipal agencies.

Monterrey has long seen political struggles between state and federal governments and Monterrey's local elites. The Partido Revolucionario Institucional (PRI), Mexico's de facto ruling party for over 70 years, and its various sectors have often been at odds with the *regiomontano* attitude of independence and conservative politics. Since the late 1930s Monterrey's leading industrialists have supported Mexico's main opposition party, the Partido Acción National (PAN) and its more conservative, church- and private-enterprise-oriented policies. Throughout most of its history PAN has been unsuccessful electing candidates except at the local level. The Cabildo de Monterrey, for example, had 6 PAN *regidores* to the PRI's 19 for 1992–1994. However, beginning in the 1980s PAN started winning more state- and federal-level elections in the northern states, and in the 1990s PAN showed renewed strengths in gaining 17.7% of the vote in the national elections of 1991. With the national elections of 2000, PAN not only saw their presidential candidate, Vicente Fox, elected but continued to make inroads into traditional PRI territory. In Nuevo León and Monterrey, PAN candidates were successful in winning both the governorship and the municipal presidency for the first time in 1997, gains they held onto in 2000. Also in 2000, PAN increased its control in the Cabildo de Monterrey with 17 *regidores* to PRI's 5, and 2 for the Partido del Trabajo.

Educational System. The city and metropolitan region have a full range of public and private schools, from preschools to universities, totaling 2,863 institutions in 1992–1993. Most students attend public schools, with about 15% enrolled in private schools. The 1990 literacy rate of 96% for metropolitan Monterrey was one of the highest in Mexico. The best schools are found in Monterrey proper and in the wealthy *municipio* of San Pedro Garza García. However, within any of the *municipios,* understaffed and underequipped public schools running two shifts can be found serving the *colonias* of workers and the poor.

In regard to institutions of higher learning, there are over 30 colleges and universities located in four *municipios* of metropolitan Monterrey. The main campus of the state's autonomous university, the Universidad Autónoma de Nuevo León (founded in 1933), straddles the *municipios* of Monterrey and San Nicolás de los Garza and serves more than 115,000 students. The best-known institution of higher learning in Monterrey is the Instituto Tecnológico y de Estudios Superiores de Monterrey (ITESM), or simply the "Tec." It was founded in 1943 by Eugenio Garza Sada, a graduate of the Massachusetts Institute of Technology and one of Monterrey's leading industrialists. Often referred to as "the M.I.T. of Mexico," the Tec has long been esteemed as Mexico's best school for engineering, applied sciences, economics, and business administration and enrolls over 14,000 students. Among other colleges and universities of note are the Universidad de Monterrey, the Universidad Regiomontana, and the Universidad Mexicana del Noreste.

Transportation System. Monterrey is well connected by highways, rail, and air to all points in Mexico and international destinations. Within the metropolitan area, the primary features of the transportation system include an urban bus system with approximately 147 routes and a subway (the Metrorrey). The subway is currently limited to two lines connecting San Bernabé in the northwest and Guadalupe in the east via downtown and serves approximately 137,000 persons daily. Additionally, some 15,000 taxicabs cruise the area, most commonly the small white-and-green "Ecotaxis" that have displaced most of the once common *peseras* ("peso cabs").

CULTURAL AND SOCIAL LIFE

Distinctive Features of the City's Cultures. Monterrey is located in a region of Mexico dominated by mestizo- and European-derived culture. At the time of Spanish intrusion native peoples were nomadic, hunting-and-gathering groups, globally referred to as "Chichimecas." None of these groups survived contact and no local indigenous trace or local mestizo culture resulted. Instead, it would come largely from central Mexico with the population movements over the course of the region's and Monterrey's development. Today this regional variant of Mexico's mestizo culture is referred to as *norteño,* or "northerner," and geographically includes not only Nuevo León but the neighboring northern states. The image of the *norteño* is much like that of the cowboy of the American West, and like that counterpart, it carries a mix of negative and positive connotations: a *fronterizo* (frontiersman), a bit wild and daring, but strong with *coraje* or *ánimo* (valor or courage); a *ranchero* (rancher) and a bit of a "hick" and a heavy drinker given to blatant exhibitions of machismo.

In Monterrey the *norteño* is only one of several cultural threads that include the *campesino* (peasant), the *charro* (cowboy), and the *pocho* ("gringoized" Mexican-American). However, many *regiomontanos* would not want to be so characterized because for them the terms *negocios* (business) and *movimiento* (busyness) best describe themselves and the nature of their city. Local elites are participants in a global culture.

Cuisine. Cuisine varies according to social and economic class, age, and occasion. Most foods eaten elsewhere in Mexico are also to found in Monterrey. If international fare is preferred, Monterrey offers French, German, Chinese, Japanese, Argentine, Spanish, Italian, and many other national cuisines. A "traditional" diet built around beans, tortillas, and chiles remains at the core of meals for many *regiomontanos.* Among the poorest people (*la gente humilde*), little else may be consumed at times. Most, however, consume a wide variety of foods. Frequent additions to meals are *sopas* (a stew or soup) of some kind, rice, fruits, squashes, eggs, and chicken. The regional dishes of *cabrito* (roast kid), *cabrito al pastor* (barbecued kid), and *menudo* (tripe) are eaten, if at all, on special occasions, as are dishes containing *mole* (a special sauce). Coffee is a standard, especially with milk or cream (*café con leche*). Although soft drinks have displaced it in many families, coffee continues to be preferred with the morning meal. Dishes of beef are very popular in Monterrey and several types of *carne asada* (grilled beef filet) are local favorites. Perennial Mexican standards such as tacos, enchiladas, and quesadillas of many varieties are everywhere and part of the popular cuisine. The Mexican version of the sandwich, the *torta,* is losing ground to the *hambürguesa* (hamburger). In Monterrey, beer is the alcoholic drink of choice. With ever increasing frequency, *regiomontanos* are choosing a fast-food franchise like McDonald's, White Castle, Kentucky Fried Chicken, Pizza Hut, or Carl's Jr. for many meals. These places are also popular with children and teenagers, along with packaged snacks and soft drinks while on the go.

Ethnic, Class, and Religious Diversity. Monterrey is characterized by relatively high ethnic homogeneity owing to the lack of an extant indigenous population and the absence of any sizable international immigration. Although there are small numbers of North Americans, Germans, Italians, Lebanese, Ashkenazi Jews, and Chinese, among others, their presence has not led to the development of an ethnically heterogeneous city, nor are there distinctive ethnic neighborhoods. From the beginning, most immigrants came from Spain and most migrants were mestizos from northern and central Mexico.

There are notable social and economic class differences in Monterrey that are reflected in place of residence, education, income, and wealth. Geographically, the wealthiest families live in such Monterrey neighborhoods as Colonia Vista Hermosa to the west of downtown and San Pedro Garza García (for instance, Colonia Del Valle) to the southwest. Upper-middle-income families are clustered to the south and southeast of downtown in *colonias* such as Contry, Ciudad Satélite, and Las Brisas and to the east in Colonia Linda Vista. Lower-middle-income homes are found mainly in the center and to the north and northeast of downtown. Lower-income families live in some of the older popular *colonias,* such as Independencia, near the factories to the north and east, and in former squatter settlements regularized by government programs. Many are also located in the newer *asentamientos* (settlements) built to accommodate some of the poorest of families. These settlements are scattered throughout the metropolitan area but generally from the northwest to the northeast in peripheral and out-of-the-way locations. While there are few ethnic group differences, skin tone and "racial" features are good predictors of social and economic status in Monterrey. Lighter skin tones and European features are seen among people of the higher socioeconomic groups; darker skin tones and more Native American features, among persons of lower socioeconomic status.

For Mexico overall, income distribution is skewed greatly in favor of the top decile, which garnered over 42% of the total income in 1992. The lowest decile received 1.3%. Moreover, between 1984 and 1992 the top decile increased its share by more than 16%, while all other deciles experienced decreases of up to 18.8%. The type of concentration of wealth indicated by these figures, while typical of the country as a whole, also approximates the case for Monterrey. Some of Mexico's wealthiest people and families live in Monterrey. Many are related, or have ties, to the elite families of the Monterrey Group of industrialists, which include the Garza, Sada, Elizondo, Zambrano, Lagüera, and other families. Members of these families are often listed among the richest in Mexico and Latin America.

In the Monterrey metropolitan region, income distribution can be approximated by means of monthly salary data. In 1990, for employed persons, 12.6% received less than the minimum daily wage; 42.8% from one to two times the minimum; 27.3% from over two to five times the minimum; and 3.6 percent more than five times the minimum (with 0.9% reporting no salary and 3.6% not specifying salary). The average minimum daily wage for metropolitan Monterrey during 1990 was the equivalent of about U.S. $3.60.

Most people in Monterrey are Roman Catholic, although often "nominally Catholic" and steeped in folk beliefs. The Virgin of Guadalupe, as elsewhere in Mexico, is the most venerated of saints. Protestants, especially Pentecostals, have made considerable gains in recent years, most notably among the lower economic sector. In the 1990 census, nearly 6% of the population 5 years of age and older were reported as being Protestant.

Family and Other Social Support Systems. Regardless of socioeconomic position, *la familia* is the most important institution in the life of the people of Monterrey. The term *familia* may refer to either the nuclear family or to some parts of the bilateral extended family. Households frequently contain other relatives beyond the nuclear unit and sometimes nonrelatives. It is also common to find related families living next door or in the same neighborhood. Kinship is bilateral, but there is a patrilineal bias in naming and in postmarital residence.

Fictive-kin relations are forged through the *compadrazgo* (co-parenthood) system. Formal relations of *compadrazgo* are ritually established by the Roman Catholic Church on the occasion of the baptism, confirmation, or marriage of a child in order to provide *padrinos* (godparents) for the child. The *padrinos* assume certain responsibilities for the *ahijado* (godchild), but the major existential relationship is that created between the parents and co-parents (*compadres*). Extrafamilial ties may also be secured using patron-client dyadic relationships (the *patrón* system). These reciprocal ties are important throughout much of Mexican society, and in Monterrey they are often established between employee and boss as a way of rising in the organization and establishing loyalty. In a political context, such paternalistic ties continue to fill important positions in much of the bureaucracy, as well as building a cadre and network of followers for the politician. Ties are commonly employed as a *palanca* ("lever") to gain favors and to "oil" the bureaucratic machinery.

Numerous types of organizations exist at all levels and for all age groups of *regiomontano* society. From the exclusive country and golf clubs of Del Valle, to sports clubs in many *colonias* and places of work, to Boy Scouts, to youth gangs and street-corner groups (*pandillas* and *palomillas*), there are many options for socializing and doing business. Fraternal organizations such as the Club de Leones (Lion's Club), Rotary International, and many others afford a conduit for philanthropic work by middle- and upper-income persons. Churches, Catholic and Protestant, provide various avenues of association for religious, social, and charitable purposes. At the level of the *colonia* or neighborhood, *juntas de mejoras* (neighborhood betterment associations) exist for a variety of purposes, including maintaining external political ties, acquiring services and neighborhood improvements, lending assistance for members in need, and socializing.

Work and Commerce. Employment rates for metropolitan Monterrey during 1990 averaged 96.6% of the economically active population age 12 and older. The ratio for employed men to women was about 7 to 3. Most *regiomontanos* work in the services and informational sector (roughly 60%), followed by the manufacturing and crafts sector (approximately 38%). Less than 1% are engaged in the husbandry, fishery, and extractive sector in the rural areas of recently urbanized *municipios*. In terms of branch of work, most are in manufacturing (28%) and commerce (21%). The services area, including the financial, educational, health, and governmental arenas, make up about 13%. The category "other services" constitutes about 25% and includes much of the unskilled and semiskilled workers such as gardeners, car washers, janitors, street vendors, cooks, and domestic helpers. Those working in construction account for some 7%.

In 1990, travel within the metropolitan region was primarily by bus (59%), followed by motor vehicles (35%) and foot or bicycle (5%). These figures do not include Monterrey's new subway, which placed its first line into operation in April 1991.

Arts and Recreation. Many forms and styles of urban recreation are found in Monterrey. Much entertainment is oriented to traditional music forms such as *norteño, ranchero, tejano,* and *huapango*. Live concerts and televised events are very popular in Monterrey. The 60 or so radio stations in the metropolitan area broadcast the latest groups and versions of traditional and contemporary music.

The city's youth, especially of the middle- and upper-income groups, are attracted to the latest forms of music and dance from the United States and Europe. There are many *discotecas,* video bars, and other nightlife establishments that provide fare geared toward young people concerned with *la onda* ("style"). Video arcades are found throughout much of the area and have become a favorite pastime for the youth of Monterrey. Mexican-produced comic books, once extremely popular nationwide, are all but extinct today, the victim of both television and the video arcade.

There are nine television stations operating in Monterrey, and most broadcast both locally and nationally produced programs during the week and popular variety shows on weekends. *Telenovelas* (soap operas) are the mainstay of Mexican daytime television. While Mexican television offers much Mexican fare, cable television and the satellite dish bring predominantly American-produced programs, including many in English.

The traditional Sunday evening courtship *paseo* can still be seen in many of Monterrey's plazas, as young men and women "pass" each other in opposite directions. There are some contemporary modifications, as when the "passing," glancing, and even staring is done from cars and on just about any evening. Attending one of the city's dozens of movie theaters and discoteques is another venue for carrying out courtship activities, as are frequenting dances and fiestas, public and private.

Religious fiestas for patron saints of the several municipal centers are held annually. Most are not well attended and often go unnoticed. A major exception is the fiesta for the Virgin of Guadalupe on December 12. For several weeks in anticipation of her day, dozens and dozens of organized pilgrim groups led by costumed *matachine* dancers make the trip to her basilica in Colonia Independencia. Thousands of individual pilgrims and the curious also make the journey. In the vicinity of the basilica, a variety of temporary amusements and concessions are set up for the pilgrims and casual visitor. Other fiestas and fairs are held in the metropolitan area in association with national holidays and special events of local significance. One such observance, the annual Alfonso Reyes International Festival, is a month-long series of cultural events held at locations throughout the region to honor a local man of international status in literature.

There is something for all cultural tastes in Monterrey. For those with European-style fare in mind, there are live theater, opera, ballet, symphonic orchestra concerts, art shows and exhibitions, book fairs, and poetry readings. These events involve local organizations, such as the Monterrey Opera Company, as well as visiting groups and performers from around the globe.

For recreational sports, possibilities abound, from contact to spectator sports. *Fútbol* (soccer) is the favorite of all ages and is pursued from the early ages through the school years, with many opportunities to participate. Boxing, baseball, and soccer matches draw *regiomontanos* of all classes. Bullfights at Monterrey's Plaza de Toros are also popular among all classes. For the wealthy, golf, tennis, equestrian events, and the *charrería* (Mexican rodeo), among other exclusive diversions, offer relaxation and sociality for both participants and observers.

It is customary during *semana santa* (Holy Week) to take a holiday. This may be a day trip to nearby recreational and scenic locations away from the city, or for those who can afford it, an extended trip to Acapulco, Oaxaca, Houston, New York, or even Europe.

QUALITY OF LIFE

Nuevo León and its capital, Monterrey, rank among the best regions in Mexico in terms of quality of life, well-being, and human development criteria. In terms of literacy rates, levels of education, consumption of goods and services, and low crime rates, Nuevo León falls in the top 25% of Mexican states and often ranks first or second. In Human Development Index terms used by the United Nations (for example, political liberties, basic education, life expectancy, and health), Nuevo León's level is close to that of Portugal and Singapore and among the highest in Mexico.

By measures of mortality, health, and housing for 1990, Nuevo León presented a generally positive picture, except in the area of mortality, the statistics for which were mixed. The infant mortality rate of 17.33 placed the state eighth among all Mexican states, and the annual mortality figure of 4.24 put it sixth. Regarding leading causes of death, Nuevo León ranks high in mortality rates from cardiovascular and respiratory diseases and from cancer and comes in above the mean for Mexico in all three. Trauma and diseases related to nutritional, metabolic, endocrine, and immunity factors were lower in Nuevo León than the mean for the country as a whole.

According to 1995 figures for Nuevo León, more than 74% of households had at least one member with health-care coverage, with most (85%) receiving service from the Mexican Social Security Institute (IMSS), underscoring the overriding importance of the national social security system. Persons lacking health-care coverage must turn to the ministry of health (SSA) or private charities. In metropolitan Monterrey, about 24% of the population was not covered in 1990 by either a public or private medical plan. Of the 29 public and private hospitals in the area in 1990, 23 were in Monterrey, and the largest percentages of all medical facilities and professionals were also located in Monterrey.

By measures of crowding in housing, the state ranked third least crowded in the nation for 1995 and, with an average of 4.47 persons per housing unit. If one measures quality of housing by the number of households with potable water, electricity, and toilets, the standards found in Nuevo León are among the highest in the nation.

FUTURE OF THE CITY

Monterrey's prospects for the future are tied to several local, regional, national, and global circumstances. Population projections for the Monterrey metropolitan area ranged from 3.15 to 3.47 million for 2000 and are estimated at 3.53 to 4.22 million by 2010. In all cases, the metropolis is viewed as continuing its spatial expansion in a large arc across the north from west to southeast. Meeting future needs, as well as addressing continuing deficits, in housing, potable water, drainage, domestic and industrial sewage treatment and disposal, power, and transportation are the key challenges faced by public and private concerns alike. Consequently, the role of urban planning for the metropolitan area and the state will become increasingly critical in attempts to manage available resources. The perennial and often crucial issue of maintaining adequate supplies of water, always precarious for Monterrey, will continue to challenge the region's best planners and tax the resource base. A range of ecological and environmental considerations have become of growing concern for many citizens and will likely increase as industrial and urban expansion places additional pressure on the local environment. Attaining and directing the resources needed to meet demands from its citizens for future services in the infrastructure domain, housing, and other areas in this burgeoning metropolitan region, are dependent on a stable political scene and an expanding economy, locally and globally.

BIBLIOGRAPHY

Balán, Jorge, et al., *Men in a Developing Society: Geographic and Social Mobility in Monterrey, Mexico,* Latin American Monographs, No. 30 (University of Texas Press 1973) [landmark study of men and work in Monterrey including coverage of the social, economic, and geographical origins of migrants].

Cerutti, Mario, *Burgesía, Captiales e Industria en el Norte de México: Monterrey y su Ámbito Regional, 1850–1910* (Editorial Patria, S. A. 1992) [fundamental work addressing the origins of capital formation in northern Mexico with a focus on Monterrey's major industrialists and placed in the context of national and international events].

Garza Villarreal, Gustavo, coordinator, *Atlas de Monterrey* (Universidad Autónoma de Nuevo León 1995) [volume covering the Monterrey metropolitan area in considerable detail by exploring all major geographical, historical, economic, political, and urban-related topics].

Hibino, Barbara, "Cervecería Cuauhtémoc: A Case Study of Technological and Industrial Development in Mexico," *Mexican Studies/Estudios Mexicanos,* vol. 8, no.1 (Winter 1992): 23–43 [a fine-grained study of one of Monterrey's major industries, the Cuauhtémoc Brewery, and how it and its many vertically integrated subsidiaries have developed new technologies and goods for export].

Hopgood, James F., *Settlers of Bajavista: Social and Economic Adaptation in a Mexican Squatter Settlement,* Papers in International Studies, Latin America Series No. 7 (Ohio University 1979) [an ethnographic study of one Monterrey squatter settlement and its environs, focusing on in-migration, intra-urban migration, work, family and extrafamilial organization, and internal social and political organization].

INEGI (Instituto National de Estadística, Geografía e Informática), *Anuario Estadístico del Estado de Nuevo León,* Edición 1992 (1993); INEGI, *Monterrey, Estado de Nuevo León, Cuaderno Estadístico Municipal,* Edición 1993 (1994); INEGI, *Nuevo León: Conteo de Poplacíon y Vivienda 1995, Resultados Definitivos, Tabulados Básicos* (1996); INEGI, *Perspectiva Estadñstica de Nuevo León* (1997) [basic sources for national- and state-level data].

Megee, Mary C., *Monterrey, Mexico: Internal Patterns and External Connections,* Department of Geography, Research Paper No. 59 (University of Chicago Press 1959) [an early study (in English) of the origin and development of Monterrey up to the mid-1950s].

Montemayor Hernández, Andrés, *Historia de Monterrey* (Asociación de Editores y Libreros de Monterrey, A.C. 1971) [a standard reference on the city's historical and economic development and supplies good detail on urban developments].

Pick, James B., and Edgar W. Butler, *The Mexico Handbook: Economic and Demographic Maps and Statistics* (Westview Press 1994) [an excellent reference and source on statistical data on many aspects of Mexico, with data presented by states on most characteristics].

Pozas, María de los Angeles, *Industrial Restructuring in Mexico: Corporate Adaptation, Technological Innovation, and Changing Patterns of Industrial Relations in Monterrey,* Monograph Series, 38, Center for U.S.-Mexican Studies, tr. by Aníbal Yáñez (University of California at San Diego 1993) [investigation of the relationship of the state and the Monterrey Group of corporate industrialists, offering an analysis of the group's restructuring and adaptation to changing national and international economic circumstances following the crisis of 1982].

Saragoza, Alex. M., *The Monterrey Elite and the Mexican State, 1880–1940* (University of Texas Press 1988) [excellent detail on the history and workings of the several families of Monterrey's industrial elite, their involvement in local and national politics, and their worldview].

Vizcaya Canales, Isidro, *Los Orígenes de la Industrialización de Monterrey: Una Historia Económica y Social Desde la Caida del Segundo Imperio Hasta el Fin de la Revolución (1867–1920),* 2d ed. (Librería Tecnológico, S. A. 1971) [a classic, "Monterrey-centric" view of the development of the city's industrial groups, up to about 1920].

James F. Hopgood

Montreal

Canada

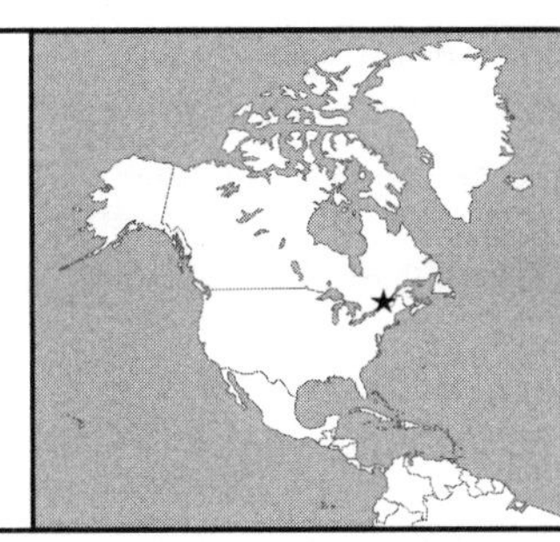

ORIENTATION

Name of City. The appellation *Montreal* refers to any in a series of concentric regions: the city of Montreal is located on the Island of Montreal with almost 30 other municipalities. These municipalities are part of the Montreal Urban Community (MUC), an intermunicipal organization providing various services for Montreal and the suburbs on the island. The MUC is found in the Greater Montreal area, a region with over 100 municipalities, on and off the island.

The original French settlement on the island was called Ville Marie; how and why it became Montreal remains conjecture. A plaque atop Mount Royal, the hill around which the city developed, claims that in 1535 the explorer Jacques Cartier climbed the mountain with local native guides and was so impressed with the view that he named the hill Mount

Royal. From there, it is said, comes the name Montreal. Not all historians are in accord with this account.

Location. Montreal is in the southwestern part of the Canadian province of Quebec, less than a day's drive from the major cities in northeastern North America. Montreal is 550 kilometers (342 miles) east of Toronto and 250 kilometers (155 miles) west of the Quebec capital, Quebec City. It is located at 45° north latitude (the same latitude as Geneva, Switzerland) and 74° west longitude. Montreal is situated on the St. Lawrence River 1,500 kilometers (932 miles) from the Atlantic Ocean.

Population. Montreal is the second largest metropolitan center in Canada and the largest French-speaking city outside France. According to the last census in 1996, 1,016,000 people live in the city of Montreal, 1.8 million live in the Montreal Urban Community, and upwards of 3.4 million in the greater Montreal area, which is nearly half of the province's population.

Distinctive and Unique Features. Montreal is built on a series of terraces that step up from the St. Lawrence River west to Mount Royal. At the river shore is the port, with Old Montreal near the riverfront on the lowest terrace. Farther up is the newer modern town with skyscrapers and a commercial downtown.

Montreal is the only city in North America built around a mountain. Mount Royal, referred to locally as the Mountain, is a 234-meter- (768-foot-) high hill found in the heart of the city. In 1876 it was designed as a nature reserve by Frederick Law Olmsted, the landscape architect who designed Central Park in New York City. Local lore contends that the mountain is an ancient volcano, but this is scientifically refuted.

Montreal is located in an area rich in natural resources. This abundance allowed the region to develop as the center of the North American fur trade in the 1700s. When fur trading declined, shipping became the region's chief industry. Montreal, located between the Great Lakes and the Atlantic Ocean, has the world's largest inland seaport. Also useful, the waterways around the island provide a sizable amount of hydroelectric power. Montreal is in the most fertile and productive agricultural region of Quebec, making the city a food-processing center.

The urban morphology of the island follows the style common to French colonization. The nucleus of the original village, Old Montreal, follows a clustered dwelling model, whereas the interior of the island was laid out along the French *côte* system, an orthogonal grid of roads that followed the lay of the land and divided surveyed from unsurveyed district strip developments. The roads were called *côtes* and have since become the major traffic arteries on the island. The districts formed by these *côtes* were substantial in size, equivalent to villages in themselves. Many continue to make up the city's neighborhoods, of which Côte-des-Neiges is one of the oldest.

Montreal's buildings reflect three main architectural periods: the French period, the Victorian era, and the modern age. Few traces of New France remain in the architecture of the city, since many structures were built of wood and burned in various fires. In Old Montreal, stone buildings line cobblestone streets and stately monuments remind all of its Victorian history, with only a few structures predating British influence. Juxtaposed with the Victorian old town are the modernist structures of the new town that made Montreal into a corporate city.

A unique feature of Montreal is the inordinate number of churches that grace the city's skyline, many noted for their Gothic style. As Mark Twain said, "you can't throw a stone without breaking a church window" in Montreal.

Most of the houses in Montreal are located in the West End, including a number of mansions on the slopes of Mount Royal. Most of the apartments are in the East End, where one will find the most rundown dwellings. The domestic landscape in the city is dominated by 'plexes, Montreal's most distinctive form of urban architecture. This form of architecture developed to suit the needs and incomes of the working population, the majority of whom were tenants. Constructed chiefly during the 1920s and 1930s, these rows of duplexes and triplexes are usually of brick or the less modest greystone. The majority of 'plexes have an exterior front staircase leading to the second floor, designed to make maximum use of inside space and said to be the most enduring mass architectural feature in the city.

Another unique feature of Montreal's architecture is found underground: the downtown area includes the world's largest network of underground walkways, called the Underground City. The 30 kilometers (19 miles) of underground pedestrian walkways link office buildings, subway stations, major hotels, apartments, restaurants, boutiques, movie theaters, universities, bus stations, train stations, and colleges. With winter windchill dipping below –30°C

(–22°F), the Underground City is a well appreciated feature of downtown.

Attractions of the City. It was predicted by an economic think tank that Montreal would lead Canadian cities in economic growth from 2001 to 2004; housing starts were up, commercial and industrial construction was increasing, a program to improve the transportation system was on the books, and the vibrant aerospace, telecommunications, and pharmaceutical industries and the multimedia sector and the old-economy textile industry were doing well. That said, high provincial taxes continued to put the city at an economic disadvantage, and the underfunding of educational institutions in the region was threatening to take its toll.

Montreal is a major center for finance, industry, and trade, ranking second only to Toronto within Canada. It has the largest bilingual, multicultural labor force in the country, a labor force that is stable, educated, and highly qualified. The city's location at the entrance to the St. Lawrence River contributes to its economic importance; its port handles highly diversified cargo year-round and links North America's industrial heartland with Europe and the Mediterranean. This location also allowed Montreal to develop as the railroad center of Canada, although that position has declined somewhat in recent years.

© KELLY-MOONEY PHOTOGRAPHY/CORBIS
A young couple relaxes at Place d'Armes, a former market square, in Old Montreal, Quebec.

The provincial language laws require all companies in Quebec with 50 or more employees to conduct business in French. Some international companies are unwilling or unable to adapt to this requirement; however, legal loopholes and exemptions allow certain businesses to continue working primarily in their native languages.

In its heyday in the early-to-mid-20th century, there was no question of Montreal's role as an international metropolis. By the start of the 21st century, however, Montreal had lost much of its "empire," and many would argue that Montreal will never again compete with the likes of Toronto, New York, or Hong Kong in terms of global political economy. Montreal is more of a regional center with a strong role to play in the Quebec nationalist project. That said, there are still many consulates, foreign banks, and international organizations in the city, and Montreal remains one of the most popular places for international conventions on the continent.

There is plenty for the tourist in Montreal, a city with some of the country's tallest skyscrapers, largest department stores, and finest restaurants and hotels, including the Queen Elizabeth Hotel where John Lennon and Yoko Ono held their famous "Bed-In" in 1969. Millions of tourists visit the Montreal area yearly, making it Canada's second most popular tourist destination after Toronto. While the foreign visitor may find taxes high (tax and tip on a restaurant meal can add 30% to the bill), generally low prices and favorable exchange rates for Americans make it an attractive destination.

Montreal has become known as the City of Festivals. Summers seem like one long cultural event as festivals line up back-to-back. There are more than 40 festivals and major international events each year, including the International Jazz Festival, the World Film Festival, the Formula One Grand Prix, the International Fireworks Competition, and the Tour de l'Île, when 45,000 cyclists take over the streets for what is said to be the largest noncompetitive sporting event in the world. Montreal is also home to many historic sites and world-class galleries and museums.

Relationships Between the City and the Outside. Montreal tends to have a tense relationship with its suburbs. Because the metropolitan area is one of relatively little tax-base sharing, and because Montreal relies so heavily on property tax for its revenue, the city is intent on keeping its citizens from moving to the suburbs, and keen on annexing neighboring suburbs into the city of Montreal. Many suburbs want to keep local autonomy, however, and do not trust annexation.

Montreal is a major university destination for youth from across the country; the city has a compelling pull for this age group. Many older Canadians, however, some who fondly remember a time when English was dominant in Montreal, avoid the city, afraid of hostility toward Anglophones. They resent the Québécois, feel threatened by Quebec's political insistence on being a "distinct society," and fear the power of a provincial referendum to divide "their" country. The little things that make Montreal unique (for example, the fact that one cannot make a right turn on a red signal; the cavalier pedestrians who move in herds ignoring traffic signals; the way people queue for the bus; the fact that traffic signs are marked with a 24-hour clock) are held up by some as an example of Montreal's flagrant refusal of "all things Canadian."

For those without this consternation and cynicism, these differences give Montreal its exotic "Paris of the North" or "Paris without jetlag" reputation. This is especially true outside Canada where people do not have as much to lose by a secession mandate. In this light Montreal is seen as a city with history and flair, where espresso is served any hour of the day and baguettes abound. This is a city where anything goes: nightlife starts at 11 o'clock (even when the temperature is below freezing) and goes well into the wee hours; there is a large, social gay and lesbian village; beer and wine are sold in corner stores; strip clubs are not zoned and are found everywhere—even right in the middle of shopping districts; fashion is the bottom line; and smoking is still considered "cool."

Relations with members of the "First Nations" have long been contentious. When the religious settlement on the island of Montreal was first established, one of its key directives was to convert the "savages" to Christianity. There remained tense relations between local Aboriginal communities and the non-Aboriginal citizens. The Oka Crisis in 1990, an armed standoff northwest of the island between the local Mohawks, the provincial police force, and the Canadian Army, was a major reminder of this tension. A Mohawk community south of Montreal erected a sympathy barricade on a commuter bridge during the standoff, making it a long, hot political summer.

Major Languages. French is the official language in Montreal as decreed in a provincial French Language Charter known locally as Bill 101. Bill 101, passed in 1977, restricts the language of work, business, and public signs and restricts access to English schools for new immigrants. In greater Montreal, as of 1996, 68.6% of the population was native French-speaking, while 13.3% was English-speaking, and 18.1% was *Allophone,* the official term for a person whose mother tongue is neither English nor French. However, half of Montrealers spoke both languages, and only 4% spoke neither of the two. One-fifth of the city was fluent in three languages. This stands in comparison to the rest of the province, which is much more homogeneously Francophone.

HISTORY

The Origin of the City. When Cartier first arrived on the island of Montreal, he was the first European in a territory Amerindians had inhabited for thousands of years. At the time of contact there were approximately 1,500 Iroquois living on the island in a village called Hochelaga. This village had disappeared by the time Samuel de Champlain arrived in 1603; the reasons for this disappearance, as well as the exact location of the village, remain open for debate.

Originally called Ville Marie, Montreal was founded as a French missionary colony in 1642. It had a population of about 3,500 in 1710, and it was the commercial heart of France's North American empire, thanks to its location at the confluence of the St. Lawrence and Ottawa rivers. This location made it an important center of trade for European goods on their way to the North American West and provided a gateway to the valuable supply of furs in Canada's interior and to the abundant forests of the northwest.

Montreal was surrendered to British troops in 1760, and the Treaty of Paris in 1763 made Canada a British colony. American forces briefly occupied Montreal during the American Revolutionary War, but in 1776 Britain regained the city; it has never been surrendered since.

Migration: Past and Present. Montreal has experienced great changes in its cultural demographics since its inception. Under French and early British control, Montreal was a homogeneous city with very minimal immigration. With the American War of Independence came an increase in the black population as loyalists came over the border to safety in the British empire. Soon after taking control, Britain encouraged the immigration of British stock to assist the governing of their French Catholic subjects. Traders were the first group to move into the area, developing a lucrative business as middlemen, shipping raw materials to the motherland and bringing manufactured goods back to the colony. This class of families went on to build the mansions of the Golden Square Mile on the slopes of Mount Royal.

Montreal expanded across the island from the late 1700s to the 1800s. English-speaking merchants established businesses and gradually gained control of the town's economy. By 1800 Montreal's population had reached 9,000, and immigration from the British Isles continued; large numbers of immigrants fleeing the Napoleonic wars, the potato famines in Ireland, and the Industrial Revolution came to the region.

By the middle of the 18th century, the city had an anglophone majority, a large proportion of which was Irish. The Irish tended to settle in southwestern neighborhoods where they mingled with French-Canadians, religion and poverty bringing the groups together. The importance of the Irish in the city's history continues to be acknowledged; the shamrock is still on the city flag, and the St. Patrick's Day parade is the largest in the city.

Railways were built linking Montreal to the Eastern Seaboard and areas west, and many industries developed along the Lachine Canal, built in 1825. Thousands of British immigrants and French Canadian migrants went to find jobs in the new factories as Montreal became a major industrial and port city. Montreal's port grew to rival that of New York's by the latter part of the 19th century, and by the turn of the 20th century, the mercantile and industrial bourgeoisie in the city held the majority of Canada's wealth.

While immigration from the British Isles eventually slowed, French-Canadian numbers continued to increase between 1850 and 1900; as opportunities grew in the Montreal area, out-migration to the textile mills in New England and opportunities in the Canadian West became less attractive. In the city the French tended to settle in the East End where light industry was growing, whereas the British were in the central, southern, and northern parts. This increasing French migration, coupled with the high French-Canadian birth rates, reestablished a Francophone majority in the city.

By 1871 the population of Montreal was over 100,000. The final wave of British immigration in the early 20th century was mostly skilled workers arriving to fill steel, locomotive, and shipyard positions and women sought as servants for the Westmount bourgeoisie. Thus, at the turn of the century, the city had a very Victorian appearance, but a strong French majority (over 60%), making it less cosmopolitan than other North American cities of the time. English speakers continued to gravitate to mixed neighborhoods in the southwest, and upward social mobility in the 1920s took them even further from the Francophone majority as they moved to newer suburbs in the west and northwest, and eventually to the West Island and across the river to the South Shore.

While a minority, the British elite continued to dominate the political and economic scene in the city and Montreal remained the center of Anglophone Canada, with English business and money controlling the urban environment. Until the 1970s immigrants generally studied English when they arrived, believing that it would provide richer promise for jobs and mobility. Because of this ethnic interest in English, the category "Anglophone" started to make more sense as a linguistic marker than as a cultural category signaling only those from the British Isles.

By 1911, over one-tenth of the population was "ethnic," each group forming cores around which future waves of immigrants would settle. With the two World Wars and the Great Depression came a much more ethnically diverse flow of immigrants. For example, the Jewish population on the island, which had been well integrated into the British elite, became more widely diversified with waves of Ashkenazi Jews from eastern Europe and then Jews from northern Africa. Large numbers of Jews, Italians, Greeks, Portuguese, Haitians, Caribbean Islanders, and Chinese arrived, each immigrant group generally carving out a specific niche in the local economy. Workers usually settled near their workplace, creating a linguistic geography on the island.

For example, the black community was tiny but consolidated in what is now called Little Burgundy, and grew as new migrants and immigrants arrived from other parts of Canada, America, and then the West Indies. The immigration of blacks was originally encouraged to provide domestic workers and train attendants. Racism limited their movement into other professions, and immigration quotas limited their numbers. It was not until 1962 that racial quotas were removed, after which time West Indian immigration increased substantially. Groups of Haitian professionals began arriving in the 1960s, increasing in the 1970s. But, because of their French language, they tended to settle in the francophone East End.

Chinese immigration was also influenced by railway development and workforce needs. Half of those who came between 1890 and 1920 returned home, however, because restrictive immigration policy denied them rights to bring family members; meanwhile, a parallel policy encouraged Italian families to immigrate. A second wave of Chinese landed in the 1960s, and by 2000 there were about 85,000 Chinese in the area. A vibrant Chinatown developed where cultural events and festivals took place. The Chinese Garden at the Botanical Gardens is the largest of its kind outside China.

Until 1970 the majority of the new immigrants were Europeans. The first wave between 1880 and 1930 included Jews, Germans, Poles, Hungarians, Ukrainians, and Italians. After World War II, immigrants from all over central, eastern, and southern Europe arrived. Generally, immigrants arrived at the port and made their way up "the Main" (Boulevard Saint-Laurent) to settle in neighborhoods east and north of the city core. Over time the Main took them further north to settle in middle-class neighborhoods in what became known as the immigrant corridor, and from there to the suburbs in the west, north, and northeast.

Until the 1960s the English language reigned in the city; this changed drastically with what became knows as the Quiet Revolution. In 1960 the Assembly for National Independence was founded in Montreal, and the Front de Liberation du Quebec (FLQ), a terrorist organization, formed shortly thereafter. Between 1963 and 1970 over 200 bombs exploded in the region, culminating in the October Crisis of 1970, when members of the FLQ kidnapped a British trade commissioner and the Quebec labor minister, the latter of whom was eventually murdered. In 1976 the Parti Québécois, a political party dedicated to the separation of Quebec from Canada, was voted into power, spurring thousands of Anglophones (mostly of British ancestry) to leave Quebec. Language became a hotly politicized issue, and public policy shifted radically to a nationalist agenda.

In the "new" Montreal that developed, Anglophones of British ancestry became just another ethnic group among many in a multicultural city. This new Montreal was now proud to be a French-speaking city, and the use of English in public was restricted. This depopulation of the Anglophone community has been called an exodus; while perhaps an extreme descriptor, there was a great shift in demographics, a shift that drastically changed Montreal. The number of Anglophones has continued to decrease, with numbers dipping below the percentage of Allophones counted in the 1996 census. This decline has not been only because of out-migration, but also because of a decrease in the number of English-speaking Canadians arriving from other provinces, coupled with a decrease in the number of Francophones leaving the area.

Shifting demographics required changes to immigration policy. In the late 1970s the Quebec birth rate had sunk below replacement levels, the population was aging, and many immigrants had left for other provinces. The provincial government, concerned about this decreasing population, opened the door to a larger number of immigrants. At this time immigrants were mostly from Asia, the Middle East, and Latin America, and the government insisted that their children be schooled in French.

Economically Toronto had eclipsed Montreal as the Canadian industrial center and financial capital. The reasons for this change were many, including the growing importance of the United States as a Canadian trading partner, the opening of the St. Lawrence Seaway (allowing ships to bypass the port of Montreal), and the economic development of the western provinces. The political situation that allowed this economic shift was complicated. Did the English lose their stronghold on Montreal because the French gained popular control, or did the French gain control only because the English money had already begun shifting to Toronto? Could Montreal have remained a national center without strong English elites? Whatever the case, many would argue that Montreal was definitely no longer a Canadian metropolis, but had become a metropole for a "nation" of Québécois, a people who no longer self-identified as French-Canadians.

Two provincial referenda (1980 and 1995) saw only slight majorities vote against the separation of Quebec from Canada. Few Anglo-Montrealers are confident in their future in the city, and many will leave if talk of another referendum heats up. There is still a critical mass of Anglophones that ensures enclaves where services (health, education) and cultural and social spaces (theaters, tourism) exist in English. If Quebec did become sovereign, many would leave if the existence of these cultural institutions was at stake.

By the beginning of the 21st century, immigration needs and concerns were layered and complex in Quebec. Quebec still had the lowest birth rate in the country and needed a larger proportion of immigrants to support its aging population and to support an economy where skilled workers were needed to fill jobs in the rapidly expanding information technology, aerospace, and biotechnology industries. Some sovereignists claimed immigrants were also needed to keep alive the Francophone presence in North America; others were worried that Quebec did not have the ability to absorb the influx, and especially not the Greater Montreal area where 90% of immigrants settled. Key immigrant issues revolved around what skills the immigrants could bring, what languages they spoke, and how they could be convinced to stay in Quebec after they arrived.

INFRASTRUCTURE

Public Works, Public Buildings, and Residences. By the early 1950s Montreal's population had topped 1 million, and by the end of the decade, the city had entered a period of great economic growth. A program to enlarge the harbor and the opening of the St. Lawrence Seaway attracted hundreds of industries. Further, the construction boom in the 1960s gave the city a new downtown skyline; old buildings were replaced with banks, hotels, and skyscrapers. A trade mart and a major cultural center were built, and the underground city network, new highways, and a subway system were begun.

A major symbol of the shift from Anglophone to Francophone control in Quebec at the time was the "nationalization" of electricity. Hydro Quebec was created in 1962 at a time when the Quebec state structure was being consolidated and centralized, reducing Anglophone control over education, health, and social service. While separate parallel Anglophone services continued (hospitals and school boards, for example), the autonomy of the Anglophone services was greatly diminished as the Francophone population took the helm of the state bureaucracy.

The economic boom carried Montreal successfully onto the world's stage: Expo 67, the World's Fair, was held in 1967 attracting 50 million people; in 1975 a new international airport opened; and in 1976 Montreal hosted the Summer Olympic Games and built the Olympic Stadium. After Expo and the Olympics, however, followed a moribund period in Montreal's economy as the reputation for political instability and hostility towards non-Francophones grew. The economy was successfully revived in the 1980s with several construction projects and investments for the 350th Anniversary of Montreal in 1992. Two new museums were built and the riverfront was redeveloped as a public promenade for family entertainment.

The availability and quality of housing in or near the downtown sets Montreal apart from other major North American cities. In 2000 there were more than 50,000 people living around the business district. Montreal is a city of tenants with a lower proportion of single-family houses and a higher proportion of apartment buildings than any other Canadian city. Almost three-quarters of city households rent out their dwellings, compared with 58% in Vancouver and 53% in Toronto. About 8% of housing stock in Montreal is social housing, a number congruent with other large urban centers.

Politics and City Services. Montreal has a mayor-council form of government with elected four-year terms. The mayor is the administrative head of the city government, supervising the various departments. An executive committee appointed by council members prepares the city budget, proposes new laws, and chooses directors of city departments.

The city of Montreal gets many government services from the Montreal Urban Community Council (MUC), created by the provincial legislature in 1969. The MUC administers such services as public security, transportation, environmental quality, territorial development, economical planning, public health, traffic control, and water supply. The metropolitan government of the MUC is a fairly weak governing body since it only includes the island municipalities and not the surrounding communities. This, therefore, hinders regional consolidation and competitiveness.

A large portion of Montreal's revenue comes from property taxes, and especially from the residential sector as heavy industry declines in the area. Thus, housing has become a major part of the city's economic development strategy. The rest of the funds come from taxes on sales, businesses, water, and amusements and from aid given by the province. As in most large cities, the rising costs of government services is a major problem for Montreal, and the government is presently struggling to find funding to build more low-cost housing, to provide higher pay for city employees, and to maintain public services and facilities.

Educational System. The public school system in Montreal used to be based on religion as required by the Canadian Constitution, with no linguistic guarantees; generally however, Catholic schools were French, while Protestant schools were English. The Protestant schools traditionally accepted non-Christian immigrants as well, whereas the French were more homogeneously Catholic.

Because immigration has created English and French populations in Montreal that no longer divide so exactly along religious lines, provincial legislation now bases public schooling on language (English or French). Enrollment in English-language public schools has dropped substantially because legislation narrows access to these schools: enrollment in English schools is limited to children of Canadian citizens who were themselves educated in English at the primary level in Canada. Immigrants and the French-speaking population of the province are required to enroll their children in French-language schools.

Because of the sovereignist focus on building a strong Francophone middle class, young Montrealers tend to be highly educated. All students who plan to attend university or to get technical qualifications must attend Cégep after high school, a public community college with academic and professional programs in English or French. There are four universities (two English, two French) in Montreal, with a total enrollment of nearly 150,000 students, giving Montreal more university students per capita than any other city in North America, including many international students (especially American). Since the 1990s Montreal's McGill University has been ranked the top university in Canada.

Transportation System. The MUC transit commission (STCUM) serves the island of Montreal, operating the subway system (the Métro) with four subway lines and a fleet of 1,600 city buses. The Métro is one of the world's quietest subways because of its rubber tires, and also one of the safest. It has been called "the largest underground art gallery in the world" because of the vibrant mosaic decorations in its stations.

Municipalities to the west and northwest of the city are linked to downtown by three commuter trains, integrated into the bus and Métro system. More than ten major highways serve Montreal, including the Trans-Canada Highway, and nearly 20 railroad and highway bridges and one tunnel connect the island with the city of Laval in the north and the South Shore. Regular rail service is available to eastern and western Canada and across the border to the United States, and Montreal has two international airports, one for regular scheduled flights and one for charter air traffic and cargo.

CULTURAL AND SOCIAL LIFE

Distinctive Features of the City's Cultures. Montreal is a place to be seen, with appearance and body language very important social markers. Dress code in Montreal is generally slim, black, and stylish. As a city of extreme temperatures, Montrealers generally pile it all on in the winter, albeit stylishly, and take a good part of it off in the summer, again with style. Montreal is considered the fur capital of the country: fur clothing is very popular in the winter for those who can afford it and agree to wear it. For those who will not or cannot wear fur, there is a particular homegrown line of winter wear, the insignia of which immediately pegs the wearer as a tried-and-true Montrealer.

Greeting a Montrealer can be confusing for outsiders. The customary way to greet friends or ac-

© DAVE G. HOUSER/CORBIS

Illuminated Crowd, a sculpture by Raymond Mason, stands in front of the National Bank of Paris in Montreal, Quebec.

quaintances is to kiss them on both cheeks starting with the right, a much more intimate expression than a simple handshake. Newcomers to Montreal often get confused, invariably going for the wrong cheek. A local English-language daily advertises their paper as being "as Montreal as a two-cheek kiss."

Direct eye contact is particular to Montreal, even between strangers. This characteristic, plus the intimate two-kiss greeting, helps give the city its reputation as a "sexy city," one with less social inhibition than the more "uptight" cities such as "Toronto the Good." At least, this is what many Montrealers would claim, fueling the ongoing rivalry between the two cities: Montreal the fun center, Toronto the financial center.

Virtually every Montrealer has at least halting command of the two major languages, and signs and menus tend to be in both French and English, as do many personal and commercial answering machine greetings. Generally in the tourist sector, nobody seems to mind communicating in English, especially if the visitor makes an effort with at least a traveler's vocabulary. In the more homogeneous East End, unilingual Anglophones might run into negative attitudes about their lack of French, but generally hostilities have abated since the Quiet Revolution.

Montreal is a very livable city, and public spaces are generally clean and safe. This fact, in tandem with a growing cosmopolitanism, has ensured that its reputation as a tourist destination is strengthened. During the International Jazz Festival, for example, free outdoor shows with crowds of thousands safely take over the downtown, all ages and all cultures dancing in the streets until midnight.

Contrary to trends in most North American cities, smoking is still popular in Montreal, and it is accepted in many public places. Little-by-little, policies are requiring office buildings and shopping malls to be smoke-free; however the public is a long way from the antismoking attitudes found in such cities as Vancouver.

Summer—starting on the first warm day of spring—makes Montreal's winter bearable. After a long, cold, dark winter, Montrealers come out of the woodwork into public, ready to drink sangria on patios and worship the sun. A lot of skin is exposed in public places in the summer, especially in the parts of town where tattoos, body piercings, and bellybuttons are all on display. A balcony is a much coveted possession, extending living space into public display in the summer; similarly, bistros and cafés sprawl out onto sidewalks in nice weather.

Montreal has a self-propelling street life not found in other Canadian cities. There is a spirit that comes with 24-hour bagel stores, bars that stay open until 3 o'clock A.M., and an abundance of summer street fairs. There are many traditions throughout the year that keep the city ticking: in the summer, the *Tam-Tams* bongo-fest spontaneously erupts every warm Sunday afternoon at the eastern base of Mount Royal, where hundreds of people of all ages and persuasions dance and play Frisbee until the sun goes down. In the winter, parents and grandparents, with children in tow, line the streets of St. Catherine to watch the Christmas display in a local department store window, a store tradition dating back to 1947.

The symbols, if not necessarily the beliefs, of the Catholic legacy in Montreal are still a major part of urban culture. For example, French swearing tends to draw on religious icons, and there is a 30-meter-(98-foot-) high illuminated cross on the eastern peak of Mount Royal overlooking Plateau-Mont-Royal, erected in 1924 in remembrance of a flood that threatened the original French colony. A new lighting system was installed for the 350th anniversary of Montreal, and the lights can appear in four colors. White is generally used, and local lore contends that purple is reserved for the death of the Pope.

Montreal is also a city where vibrant community groups celebrate cultural activities in public spaces. For example, each year the urban Aboriginal community holds a public powwow; the gay-pride parade draws half a million spectators following a week-long celebration of alternative lifestyles; the Portuguese community has street celebrations in their neighborhoods . . . the list goes on and on.

While generally there is an appreciation of multiculturalism in Montreal, the *Two Solitudes* metaphor (the title of a 1945 novel by Hugh MacLennan) continues to describe the division of the Anglophone and Francophone communities. While the hostility of the October Crisis is no more, the two groups still tend to move and live in parallel universes. This phenomenon is perhaps best exemplified by comparing two "national" holidays: the Québécois holiday, Saint-Jean-Baptiste Day, is celebrated at the end of June and very popular in Francophone districts. Canada Day, a countrywide celebration on July 1, is more popular in the western parts of the island in Anglophone neighborhoods. July 1 is actually the official moving day in Montreal, so for many it is a day of work instead of being the celebration of Canada's birth.

Cuisine. Fine food is a popular delight in Montreal. The average household spends 13% of its income on food, compared to 12% for the rest of North America. Montreal is famous for its smoked meat, bagels, and *poutine* (a gooey combination of fried potatoes, gravy, and cheese curds). Montreal bagels are distinctive in that they are made with eggs and baked in a wood-burning oven.

With thousands of restaurants serving the cuisine of some 80 countries, Montreal provides an international mosaic of gastronomy, in a variety of settings (many bring-your-own-bottle) with a variety of price scales. When it comes to alcohol, Montreal is European in style: beer and wine are sold in convenience stores, whereas in the rest of Canada such sales are forbidden; the legal drinking age in Québec is 18, whereas it is 19 in most of Canada; Montreal is a place where ales are preferred over lagers, while in Toronto it is the reverse. A willingness to experience new tastes has meant that the selection of imported beers in the city is broad, and the interest in fine beers has resulted in a renaissance in brewing in the surrounding area.

Ethnic, Class, and Religious Diversity. Language became a hotly politicized issue in Montreal during the Quiet Revolution in a way foreign to other North American cities where multiculturalism is more a fact of life than an issue for open debate. The French spoken in Quebec is different from that spoken in France in many turns of phrase and in accent. The Office de la Lanque Française ("office of the French Language") regulates new words, and tries desperately to keep Anglicisms from creeping into Québécois French. But, on a Friday afternoon you are sure to hear *bon weekend*! wishes as workers leave the office, and, in the name of tourism, English words such as smoked meat often appear in French advertising.

In addition to French, more than 100 languages and dialects are spoken in the greater Montreal area, the most common of which are English, Italian, Spanish, Greek, Arabic, Chinese, Portuguese, and Vietnamese (in that order). People of French ancestry account for over 60% of the population, and people of British and of Italian descent each make up about 7%. Other groups, in order of size, include Jews, Arabs, Greeks, blacks, Chinese, and Portuguese. The most common countries of immigration are, in order, Haiti, Lebanon, France, China, Romania, Sri Lanka, Philippines, India, Vietnam, and Morocco.

While there are up to 30 different religions in Montreal, Roman Catholics make up about four-fifths of the population. The majority of Roman Catholics are of French descent, whereas English-speaking Montrealers tend to be Protestants. Jews form the third-largest religious group, about 3% of the population.

As mentioned above, a linguistic geography originally defined Montreal: the English lived in the west, the French in the east, with Allophones somewhere in between. Today, the East End is still predominantly French; however, as Anglophone numbers decline the western suburbs are seeing more Francophones move in. Immigrants have tended to settle in homogeneous clusters, with their neighborhoods then taking on the cultural characteristics and institutions of their cultural group. Some such neighborhoods are well established, such as the Italian community in Little Italy, or the Jewish Hasidim in Outremont and Mile End. Other areas, such as Côte-des-Neiges, have a mobile, multiethnic population, with low rents attracting new immigrants who will then move to the more established neighborhoods if and when their social standing improves. Because of increasing international immigration, many neighborhoods—both low-income and more established ones—are becoming more and more heterogeneously multiethnic.

Many immigrants believe that Montreal does not provide equal opportunities for newcomers, complaining that they feel unwelcome in Quebec. Many feel torn trying to reconcile their new Canadian identity with the sovereignist one required of the nationalist policies of Quebec. Indeed, in a referendum on separation at the end of the 20th century, the provincial premier bitterly blamed "money and the ethnic vote" for the separatists' narrow defeat. His remark was seen by many as a racist scapegoating of minorities, and an assault on the English business establishment. Similarly, tensions exist between visible minorities and the predominantly white police force in the city.

Family and Other Social Support Systems. In the last decades of the 20th century, French Canadians went from being renowned for their huge families to a situation where birth rates were below replacement levels. Once devout Catholics, the French-Canadian population has the lowest marriage rates and the highest proportion of common-law families in Canada. The large households have broken down into nuclear family units, with an aging population in the inner city and families with children in suburbs where housing prices are lower and green space is more abundant. Similarly, inner-city immigrant neighborhoods have more children than the upwardly mobile districts where young urban professionals start families later in life, ultimately having fewer children. Housing and city services have yet to adjust to suit the needs of the aging population.

Community organizations are important to Montrealers, with social, political, and economical roles to play in the city. They range from cultural organizations (the Native Friendship Centre) to environmental (Friends of the Mountain) to economic (Community Loan Circles) to residential (housing cooperatives) to heritage concerns (Heritage Montreal). An umbrella charity funds hundreds of charitable and community groups and projects in the greater Montreal area.

Work and Commerce. Manufacturing is a leading source of employment in greater Montreal. The more than 7,000 factories in the area employ about a fourth of its workers. These plants produce about $25 billion worth of goods yearly and account for about two-thirds of Quebec's industrial production.

Leading industries in Montreal include aerospace, information technology, and pharmaceuticals. Montreal has the highest concentration of high-tech jobs in Canada, accounting for 7% of all jobs in the city. Nearly half of the Canadian pharmaceutical industry is located in the Montreal area and the city has the highest concentration of biomedical research institutes in Canada.

Food processing (beer, canned goods, and sugar) is also a major industry, and petroleum refineries in Montreal produce about a tenth of Canada's gasoline. Greater Montreal is also one of Canada's major centers for the manufacture of chemicals, clothing, and tobacco products. The area also leads Quebec in the production of electrical machinery and electronic equipment.

Half of the Canadian fashion industry is based in Montreal. The North American Fur and Fashion Exposition in Montreal is the largest trade show of its kind on the continent. The downtown has the highest concentration of stores in Canada as well as the largest collection of fashion boutiques and shops.

A large portion of Montreal's economy is also rooted in the service industry and the financial sector. The cultural industry accounts for a sizable portion of employment: for example, Montreal is Cirque du Soleil's international headquarters, employing 500 people to create and produce the internationally renowned dance performances.

Commuting in Montreal can be a nightmare as it is in many urban environments, and only more so when one adds snow and freezing rain, making buses full and highways slippery. The commuter bridges leading onto the island operate beyond capacity.

Arts and Recreation. Montreal is one of North America's leading cultural cities, and Place des Arts is one of the finest centers for the performing arts. Montreal has outstanding dance, drama, and musical groups: the Montreal Symphony Orchestra, the Montreal Metropolitan Orchestra, the Montreal Opera, Les Grands Ballets Canadiens, as well as jazz dance companies and French and English theater groups (including the National Theatre School of Canada). It also has art galleries, science centers, and museums that rank among the top in Canada.

Montreal is also a city for sports, both professional and amateur. Montreal often ranks number one as the "best cycling city" in North America, with 750 kilometers (466 miles) of bicycle paths in the area. Furthermore, within 100 kilometers (62 miles) of the city there are many downhill ski runs, golf courses, and marinas. The city is also known for its well-planned parks, which include playgrounds, indoor and outdoor pools, and skating rinks.

QUALITY OF LIFE

Montreal is faced with problems characteristic of large urban centers: unemployment, poverty, homelessness, declining quality of public services and facilities, and an ever-changing demographic. Yet, Montreal has been called "a livable city with a vibrant core," and it ranks high on the United Nation's Human Development Index. Gardens, parks, and green spaces cover more than 10% of the Montreal area, with one tree per two inhabitants; Plateau-Mont-Royal is one of North America's "hippest neighborhoods" according to the *Utne Reader* magazine; and a study reported that Montrealers are generally contented workers with optimistic attitudes.

Housing costs in Montreal are considerably lower than in Toronto (41%) or Vancouver (15%); similarly, renting in Montreal is much more affordable. However, 1996 statistics reported that almost half of Montrealers were paying over 30% of their gross income on rent, signaling financial problems. The average after-tax income in Montreal was lower than the Canadian average, as was the city's gross domestic product (GDP) per capita. Income taxes are the highest in North America, and provincial debt of the highest in Canada.

Poverty is a problem in Montreal: in the 1991 census, the Montreal area had the highest percentage of low-income persons in a Canadian city. Nearly one out of three in the City of Montreal lived in poverty, with the elderly having the highest rates. The climate in Montreal is extreme, and homeless shelters fill beyond capacity every winter.

As in the rest of Canada, health-care reform is on the agenda in Montreal, given the inadequacies and financial problems in the existing system. Two super-hospital complexes, one for each major language, have been proposed for the city; however public opinion is concerned that long-term care should be more of a priority and that the present social system is giving way to privatized care.

Overall, as compared to other North American cities, Montreal is a very safe, clean city, making for great street festivals and student life. The homicide rate in Montreal is 8 times lower than New York and 13 times lower than Atlanta. The crime rate in the MUC dropped in the 1990s: in 1998 crime was down almost 29% from 1991. A revitalized inner core was surely partly responsible for this improvement. That said, drug trafficking and biker gang wars increased violence and fear in the East End, and calls for new antigang laws were fresh in the ears of politicians. Further, Montreal has a highly lucrative car-theft trade.

FUTURE OF THE CITY

There is a plan on the provincial agenda for municipal reform in Quebec. For Montreal, this could mean dissolving the current MUC and replacing it with the Montreal Metropolitan Community, an island-wide megacity with taxation rights that spread across 28 new boroughs. Many municipalities on the island are fighting strongly against this "one island, one city" legislation, their key concerns relating to taxation and service delivery. Bilingual municipalities are especially worried about loss of Anglophone rights and are resisting the legislation.

BIBLIOGRAPHY

Cardinal, Claudette, *The History of Quebec: A Bibliography of Works in English* (Concordia University Press 1981).

Demchinsky, Bryan, ed., *Grassroots, Greystones, and Glass Towers: Montreal Urban Issues and Architecture* (Véhicule Press 1989).

Dodge, William, ed., *Boundaries of Identity: A Quebec Reader* (Lester Publishing 1992).

Germain, Annick, and Damaris Rose, *Montreal: The Quest for a Metropolis* (Wiley 2000).

Jenkins, Kathleen, *Montreal, Island City of the St. Lawrence* (Doubleday 1966).

Levine, Marc, *The Reconquest of Montreal: Language Policy and Social Change in a Bilingual City* (Temple University Press 1990).

Linteau, Paul André, *Histoire de Montreal depuis la Confédération (History of Montreal since confederation)* (Boréal 1992).

Locher, Uli, *Les anglophones de Montreal: émigration et évolution des attitudes, 1978–1983 (The anglophones of Montreal: Emigration and evolution of attitudes, 1978–1983)* (Québec: Gouvernement du Québec, Conseil de la langue française 1988).

Marsan, Jean-Claude, *Montreal in Evolution: Historical Analysis of the Development of Montreal's Architecture and Urban Environment* (McGill-Queen's University Press 1981).

Pendergast, James F., and Bruce G. Trigger, *Cartier's Hochelaga and the Dawson Site* (McGill-Queen's University Press 1972).

Prévost, Robert, *Montreal: A History,* tr. by Elizabeth Mueller and Robert Chodos (McClelland & Stewart 1993).

Radice, Martha, *Feeling Comfortable? The Urban Experience of Anglo-Montrealers* (Les Presses de L'Université Laval 2000).

Rudin, Ronald, *The Forgotten Quebecers: A History of English-Speaking Quebec, 1759–1980* (IQRC 1985).

Trigger, Bruce G., *The Children of Aataentsic: A History of the Huron People to 1660* (McGill-Queen's University Press 1976).

Trigger, Bruce G., *Natives and Newcomers: Canada's "Heroic Age" Reconsidered* (McGill-Queen's University Press 1985).

Westley, Margaret, *Remembrance of Grandeur: The Anglo-Protestant Elite of Montreal, 1900–1950* (Libre Expression 1990).

York, Geoffrey, and Loreen Pindera, *People of the Pines: The Warriors and the Legacy of Oka* (Little, Brown 1991).

MARY ELLEN MACDONALD

Moroni

Comoros

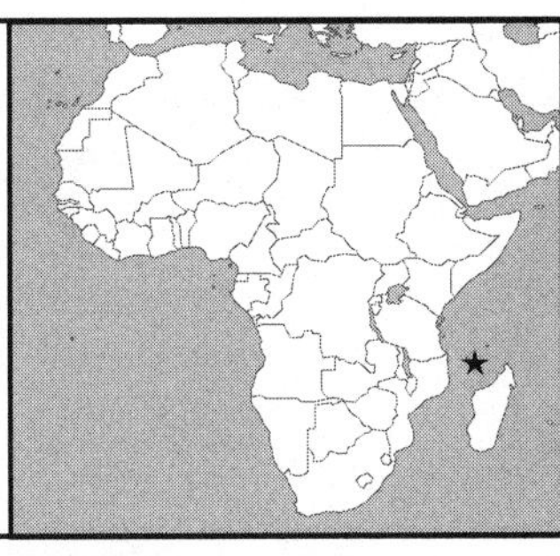

ORIENTATION

Name of City. Moroni, the capital of the Federal Islamic Republic of the Comoros (RFIC), was originally named *Undroni,* meaning "to be in good condition." Peoples moving in from East Africa changed it to *Moroni,* which means "in a river" or, possibly, "in the fire." The former may refer to a small stream in the city (there is no large river); the latter may refer to the volcano Karthala.

Location. The Comoros Islands are located between 11° and 13° south latitude and between 43° and 46° east longitude, in the Mozambique Channel of the Indian Ocean, off Africa's east coast. Grouped together, the Comoros Islands would be about the size of Delaware (2,171 square kilometers, or 838 square miles). The capital city, Moroni, lies on the west coast of the main island, Grande Comore. The other islands of the Comoros are, from west to east, Moheli, Anjouan, and Mayotte (claimed by France).

Population. In 1993 the population of Moroni was 25,600. The surrounding area—villages that have grown out from the city as suburbs—has another 15,000 residents; beyond the suburban villages are open hinterlands. The population of the Comoros is 548,000 (1998).

The city of Moroni is home to many sorts of people, from wealthy families to very poor ones. The richest elite, and most foreign residents, live outside the city in large compounds. Functionaries, merchants, teachers, students, fishers, and the unemployed all live in Moroni; many maintain a subsistence farming plot outside the city.

Distinctive and Unique Features. Initially, Moroni appears nearly unchanged from a century ago. The one exception is the newly built harbor, which serves traditional Arab-style dhows as well as modern cargo ships. The most distinctive feature of Moroni is its proximity to the volcano Karthala; the city lies at the base of Karthala's slope, spread out against the shores of the Indian Ocean. The first thing one sees approaching Moroni from the sea is the large, white Friday Mosque, which sits next to the port.

Attractions of the City. For a capital city, Moroni is small and has few modern features. There are hotels and restaurants that cater to tourists and elite residents, yet the majority of tourists eschew Moroni for the more modern resorts in northern Grande Comore or other islands. The Coulée is the coastal road, with some cafés offering views of the harbor and beaches. Itsandra beach, at the north edge of the city, is very popular among tourists and locals alike.

The major export houses for the country's spice trade (mostly family-controlled), which are also the major importers of retail merchandise, are located in Moroni. It is very expensive to import to the Comoros, mainly because of high insurance costs.

Relationships Between the City and the Outside. As the capital city of the Comoros, Moroni contains all major governmental offices, business headquarters, and foreign missions. The country's only international airport is at Hahaya, just north of Moroni, so most international travelers pass through the city. Because of its status as the capital, Moroni is home to a number of different people who originate from all parts of the country, yet it is a distinctly Grand Comorian city. The city maintains an uneasy relationship with its outer-island inhabitants as well as with the rest of the country it administers, especially in light of the political events of the 1990s.

The casual observer may find it difficult to distinguish Moroni proper from the surrounding villages. The capital has grown significantly since independence from its origins as a small town. Nevertheless, many of the upper-class functionaries, businesspeople, and expatriates live in large compounds in villages outside of the city. A vast number of Comorians live and work in France, especially

© RODRIQUE NGOWI/AP/WIDE WORLD PHOTOS

Wooden sailing dhows are anchored in front of an old mosque in Moroni, capital of the Comoros.

in Marseille. Therefore, there is a constant flow of people back and forth between Moroni and France, particularly during the season of the "Grand Marriage."

Major Languages. The official languages of the Comoros are French and Arabic. The indigenous language on Grande Comore is Shingazidja, a Bantu language related to Swahili. The Comorian languages are mutually intelligible to native speakers and are written in either the Arabic or Roman alphabet. Arabic is studied by all youngsters in the Koranic schools but is spoken by few adults. Most Moroni residents are conversant in French. Because the language of instruction in schools is French, anyone who has had some secondary education will read and write French. All official business is conducted in French. English is studied as a school subject, but is not widely spoken. Workers in the large hotels, airports, and important agencies in Moroni speak some English.

HISTORY

The Origin of the City. As the capital city of a small developing nation, Moroni has a history inalienable from the history of the country as a whole, and especially from that of the island of Grande Comore (Ngazidja).

Evidence discovered in Mohoro, south of Moroni, suggests that the first inhabitants of Grande Comore may have been Persian, or Shirazi, immigrants of the late 800s. Sakalava and Merina settlers from Madagascar moved into the archipelago over several centuries; in the 18th century these settled communities were raided by Europeans for slaves. Arab slavers moved into Grande Comore in the same period. Otherwise Europeans paid no special attention to the archipelago, with the exception of the pirates who frequented the trade routes around Madagascar.

During the "scramble for Africa," the French, having occupied Madagascar, became interested in the Comoros as a counter to British presence in East Africa and the Seychelles. Up to the 19th century, the Comoros were divided into seven sultanates (one of which was based in Moroni). Sultan Said Ali bin Said Omar of Grande Comore struck a deal with the French in the 1870s, and by 1886 the entire archipelago was a proclaimed French protectorate, administered from Madagascar.

In 1958, while the islands were still a French overseas territory (TOM), Saïd Mohammed Cheik became the Comoros's first popularly elected president. Between 1962 and 1964 Cheik moved the capital from Dzaoudzi, on Mayotte, to Moroni. Following the decolonization charter of the United Nations, a global referendum was held on December 22, 1974, in which 94% of the total population voted for independence. However, of those who voted on Mayotte, 64% elected to remain under French control. On July 6, 1975, the Federal Islamic Republic of the Comoros was declared independent. Nevertheless, the French maintained control over Mayotte, ignoring the universal nature of the initial independence referendum. The history of Mayotte is marked by much more Malagasy and European influence than was experienced by the other islands, and Mayotte also has a larger non-Muslim population. A large French naval base, which is located on Mayotte, affords control of the strategic Mozambique Channel. The Organization of African Unity (OAU) and the United Nations support Comorian claims to the island, and the issue has continued to be pivotal in Comorian politics.

Independent Comoros's first president, Ahmed Abdallah, was overthrown after only a few months in office by a socialist visionary named Ali Soilih. Soilih was assisted by European mercenaries led by the infamous French mercenary Bob Denard. Soilih began a strict program of agricultural and educational reform, leading to increased agricultural production and educational opportunity. Domestically, Soilih's austerity programs were unpopular, as was his increasing reliance on youth brigades charged with enforcing the implementation of his programs. Moreover, Soilih became unpopular among Muslim nations by denouncing several Islamic traditions, such as the veiling of women. At the same time, his economic policies were not appreciated by Western aid donors, so Soilih's foreign support quickly waned. In 1977 Abdallah overthrew Soilih—with the aid of Denard. Abdallah successfully led the country away from a socialist economy and, with the constant assistance of Bob Denard, managed to maintain order. But Comorian resentment of the mercenary cadre grew, and by 1989 Abdallah was planning to oust Denard with the aid of the French and South African governments. In November 1989 Abdallah was shot and killed at his Moroni residence, and Denard took control for several weeks before being persuaded to leave by Paris and Pretoria. The head of the Supreme Court, Saïd Mohammed Djohar, was elected president in March of 1990, and he held office for six years.

In October 1995 Bob Denard returned to Moroni to assist a military rebel group led by an Anjouanais captain named *Combo*. For several days, Denard and Combo held power in the capital, until French paratroopers landed and forced Denard to leave. Djohar, however, by that time had lost all political credibility. He died of a heart attack soon thereafter. On March 16, 1996, a new president was elected, Mohammed Taki. Taki became less and less popular as stories of his vast personal spending and constant travels abroad became well known. As opposition to Taki grew, the feelings of marginalization in Anjouan grew as well.

In 1997 the island of Anjouan declared its independence. Anjouan cited Taki's neglect of the island's needs and the lack of Anjouanais representation and influence in the republic's government. Moroni sent federal troops in to put down the secessionists, but they were not prepared for the well-organized reception they received. Anjouanais fighters repelled the federal troops, who never succeeded in gaining control over the island. Anjouan initially claimed that it wanted to be recolonized by France. This surprising demand arose from the frustration many Comorians experienced on witnessing the relative prosperity of French-held Mayotte. France refused to recolonize Anjouan, and soon a president of the island was named and a new government took control of Anjouan's affairs.

President Taki's spending and neglect of the Comorian economy lost him all support of the World Bank and the International Monetary Fund, and thus other potential donors. Taki died in November of 1998. The new president, Tadjidine Ben Saïd, was considered to have a much more conciliatory view toward the separatists, and hopes for an end to the crisis were high. Yet, by December of 1998 the separatist crisis was obviously not dissipating, and the UN and OAU were scrambling to find a peaceful solution to what was becoming an increasingly violent situation. In January of 1999 South Africa hosted a regional ministerial meeting in an attempt to address the constitutional concerns of all of the parties involved, but there was no concrete outcome. The following month the former French prime minister Michel Rocard visited the Comoros in his capacity as president of the Commission on Cooperation and Development of the European Parliament. Rocard stated his support for a form of federalist union of states in a new Comorian federation. This angered the OAU, which had refused to recognize

Anjouan's independence and vehemently supported the integrity of the RFIC from the beginning of the crisis.

In April 1999 the OAU sponsored a conference in Madagascar, and France promised 20 million French francs (U.S.$4 million) in aid if the situation could be resolved. Unfortunately, while a peace agreement was drafted, only Moheli and Grande Comore signed; Anjouan refused. Anjouan's blocking of a peace agreement led immediately to an outpouring of anti-Anjouanais sentiment on the main island, and many Anjouanais families resident in Grande Comore reported being harassed, even beaten, by bands of Grande Comorians shouting at them to leave. This unrest prompted Colonel Azali Hassounani to take military control of the government on April 30, 1999. Azali stated that he intended to remain in power only until the Comoros became stable and elections could be held. In September 2000, Azali and Anjouan separatist leader Lieutenant Colonel Said Abeid Abderemanein signed an agreement to restructure the nation and replace the constitution, the flag, even the country's name. The overhaul was planned to take place over a period of 18 months.

In December 2001 some 70% of the Comorian population voted in a referendum to accept a new constitution granting greater autonomy to each island. Azali agreed to step down for an elected president, and elections were scheduled for March 2002.

Migration: Past and Present. While other islands received many Malagasy migrants, Moroni (and Grande Comore in general) have a stronger Swahili influence originating from the mainland African coast. The northern part of the island still is home to families of Zanzibari background, and Swahili and English are often heard spoken there. In addition to this East African orientation, the northern area was strongly influenced by 19th-century French settlers, and descendants of early French settlers maintain a certain status today. A large number of Moroni's residents have spent time living in France, primarily in Marseille.

INFRASTRUCTURE

Public Buildings, Public Works, and Residences. The area of town known as "Building" has two structures that house several federal ministries. The national radio station (Radio Comores), the National Institute of Education (INE), National Research Center and Museum (CNRS), and National Assembly make up the major public buildings in Moroni. The Central Post Office has facilities for international mail, telephone, and fax transmission and is located next to the main offices of the main bank. A parastatal corporation operates all electricity services in the city, and sanitation services are contracted out. There is no home delivery of mail or garbage pickup. Residences are spread out in all areas of town.

Politics and City Services. Moroni is of central importance in the political life of the Comoros. All political and governmental actions (legal and illegal) take place in Moroni. Laws are passed and governments are overthrown, all in Moroni. There are opposition newspapers and radio stations operating out of Moroni, as well as the core of support for the ruling party.

Educational System. The educational system is based on the French model, with *école primaire* (elementary school), *collège* (junior high school) and *lycée* (high school) leading up to a national matriculation exam, the baccalaureate. These are all free and coeducational, and the language of instruction is French. Those wishing to continue with further studies must travel abroad, and there are many Comorians at universities in France, Madagascar, Morocco, and Senegal, as well as in Quebec and some in the United States.

Children attend Koranic school from about age 4 or 5, so most Comorians can read the Arabic alphabet. The adult literacy rate is 57%, but it is much higher among those of student age today. Comorians traditionally read their own language in Arabic script, but recent efforts have promoted Comorian in the Roman alphabet. Compared to other developing countries, the Comorian schools have a high percentage of female students. Many Comorian youths take up an apprenticeship with a craftsman (fundi) in lieu of an academic education. A large percentage of children attend school through *collège,* and *lycée* attendance is high compared to other African nations. Few students, however, pass their baccalaureate exam; French is a second or third language for Comorian students, and the exam, in French, is designed to be taken by students in France. There are a large number of expatriate teachers at the *lycées,* as well as other positions in the Ministry of Education. The country faces a difficult challenge in keeping its educated professionals and intellectuals at home.

Transportation System. Most villages on all the islands are connected by a system of bush taxis (*taxi-brousse*) that are privately owned and unregulated. City taxis in Moroni are cheap and plentiful.

There are few roads, but nearly all are paved. One international airport, at Hahaya, 19 kilometers (12 miles) north of Moroni, serves the country. International airlines fly in from Europe via East African cities such as Nairobi and Dar es Salaam. Flight connections can be made to the other Comoros Islands as well as to Madagascar, Mauritius, and Réunion. There are several boats that make passenger and freight trips among the islands.

CULTURAL AND SOCIAL LIFE

Distinctive Features of the City's Cultures. Moroni is divided into neighborhoods, each with a tradition and personality like that of a separate village. The center of town has the oldest neighborhood, Badjanani. Here the old buildings are packed close together, and a mazelike web makes up the Arab-style medina. Next to Badjanani is the city's main mosque, the Friday Mosque. Other major areas in Moroni are Itsandra, the beach to the north; the main market, at Volo-Volo; and the government offices in the area known as "Building."

The neighborhoods of Moroni, like the exterior villages, each have their own *place publique*, or public square. Usually situated near an important mosque, these squares serve as general meeting places, debate forums, celebration venues, and marriage arenas, and they represent the heart of their particular neighborhood.

The most conspicuous aspect of the Comorian cultural landscape is the Grand Marriage (*Anda*). Any man who wants to participate fully in his community must marry off his eldest daughter (and other daughters if he can afford it) in a Grand Marriage ceremony that lasts more than a week and is extremely expensive. Maternal uncles (*Mdjomba*) can also give a Grand Marriage for their nieces. Money is saved specifically for the Grand Marriage. The family will host their entire neighborhood for dances and meals that are held on specific days during the week, and the guests will offer expensive gifts as well. All gifts are recorded, as future reciprocity obliges. The marriage is traditionally arranged between members of the same social class, but it is becoming increasingly common for the bride and groom to choose one another. The father will have built a house for his daughter in which the couple will live, and he can then be a full-fledged member of the community's group of elders, or Notables (*Wana Wamdji*). The Grand Marriage began as a simply celebratory event, but in recent years it has acquired great social importance. Furthermore, it has become competitive; each ceremony must outdo the previous one in that neighborhood. The implications are great, since some families suffer financially in order to save all their money for the wedding, and they may spend little on more-basic needs. Financial obligation may be passed to future generations. People can marry without a Grand Marriage, and they are considered fully wed, only not into the Notable social class.

Cuisine. Comorian cuisine is an exciting mélange of the Indian, East African, Arab, Malagasy, and French culinary traditions. The afternoon meal in a home will be a starchy vegetable such as cassava, or manioc root (*mhogo*) or plantains (*ndrovi*), along with some meat (*nyama*), usually grilled or boiled with gravy (*mtuzi*). A hot pepper sauce called *putu* is always served alongside a meal and is eaten with all types of food. Dinner in a home is usually a rice dish, and it is the big meal of the day. Some people eat their rice dish in the middle of the day, especially in the capital at one of the many small restaurants. In a more affluent home, meals are served at a table with utensils and are eaten in a Western fashion. Other families will eat on a mat on the floor, everyone sitting cross-legged around several shared plates of food. Comorians eat with their right hands only, and wash in a dish of water before and after eating. Utensils are not uncommon, however, and will usually be offered to a guest. All meals are prefaced with the short blessing *Bism'illah* ("in the name of God"). Comorians often serve food to any visitors who are present around mealtimes. Any guests will usually be served with the men of the household, while the women will cook and serve. In the absence of guests, the whole family eats together.

Restaurants follow the same Western traditions as in France, and a tip of 15–20% is expected. There are several local restaurants, however, that serve basic dishes to Comorians who are single or do not live with their families. Comorians eat a lot of rice, all of which is imported, creating a great strain on the economy. Fish is a main source of protein, and local fish is plentiful and delicious. Most commonly found in the markets are tuna, barracuda, wahoo, and red snapper. Cassava is very common, and is eaten fried, boiled, or grilled. Taro, green bananas, breadfruit, and potatoes (both white and sweet) are often served. Goat meat is more commonly eaten than fresh beef (though imported beef is widely sold), and chicken is popular. In the cities one can find imported meats of all kinds. Pork is not eaten, as it is forbidden by Islam. Coconut is used in Comorian cooking, and a sauce with coconut and chicken or fish is served over rice. Another coconut dish is *madaba,* which is a paste of cassava leaves and coconut milk, also served over rice. In the markets, one can find most common vegetables—such as tomatoes, onions, cucumbers, and green beans. Fruits such as oranges, bananas, pineapples, papaya, mangoes, passion fruit, and litchi are available seasonally. Several indigenous spices are used—for example, cloves, cinnamon, saffron, and cardamom. Water, tea, or fruit juice is taken with meals. Most towns have bakeries that offer French bread. Alcoholic beverages are available in restaurants and hotels, but are rare in homes.

Ethnic, Class, and Religious Diversity. The backgrounds of the peoples from each island differ, but they have more similarities than differences. Loyalties are first to one's family, then to neighborhood and village, and finally to nation. Most people in Moroni are descendants of both Arab slavers and African mainlanders brought in as slaves (WaShenzi) to be shipped north to the Arabian Peninsula and Nile basin. Those with more Arab blood often enjoy a higher social status than darker-skinned Comorians. There are some families with Malagasy or Asian ethnic backgrounds, yet there is very little ethnic diversity among the indigenous population. There are many groups of foreigners resident in Moroni, as in any other national capital. The largest of these groups is French.

There is great class diversity in Moroni. The wealthy elite lives in large mansions next door to poor families in small, thatched huts. The economy of the city, as well as of the country, is small and slow. Most families in Moroni maintain a plot of land outside the city in which they cultivate foods on a subsistence level. The small middle class has emerged based on remittances from family members working abroad. The few people in Moroni who earn a paycheck are usually forced to support an extended family on their meager earnings. The wealthy families derive their resources from long-owned land, the earnings of the major import/export firms, or political connections.

Nearly 100% of Comorians are Sunni Muslim. The country is officially the Federal Islamic Republic of the Comoros (RFIC), although Sharia, Islamic law, is not standard. Islamic traditions and holidays play a great role in the country's government and daily life. Muslims believe that the Koran is the final word of God, (Allah), as revealed to his prophet, Muhammad. Muhammad is the last in a long line of prophets holy to Islam, from Adam and Abraham to Moses and Jesus. Devout Muslims pray five times daily, and the call to prayer can be heard regularly from the mosques in all areas of Moroni. The holy day is Friday, when all men go to the Friday Mosque for communal prayer at noon. Not all Moronians regularly observe these practices, but most attend the Friday prayers. There is little sympathy for Islamic fundamentalism. Some remnants of traditional non-Islamic beliefs persist (such as the spirit ceremonies of Malagasy origin), but most have been incorporated somehow into Islamic practices. Other religions are tolerated; the majority of foreigners are Roman Catholics, with some Protestants as well. Moroni has both a Catholic church and Protestant churches.

Family and Other Social Support Systems. Comorian families are large and extended; there is little concept of a "nuclear family." Polygamy is common, so the extended family can be vast. The society is patriarchal in the public sphere. Women don't work outside of the home except in the urban areas. Men are in charge of the families' finances and property. Women are, however, masters of the domestic arena. Traditional Comorian society is matrilocal, meaning that after marriage a couple will live with the woman's family. As a part of the Grand Marriage ceremony, a man builds a house for his marrying daughter. The newlyweds live in this house, and should any problems occur between the couple, the man must leave and the woman keeps the house. Moroni women are not submissive, and they are proud of their traditional role.

The tradition of names in the Comoros is very interesting. A child will be given a first name by his or her parents (and grandparents), and will use his or her father's first name as the last name. At approximately the age of 18, sons usually build themselves a *paillotte,* or thatched hut, somewhere near the family home. They still eat at home and take part in family activities, but they sleep and entertain guests at their *paillotte.* Daughters live at home until they marry. Small children are cared for by older sisters, and elders are well cared for and live with their descendants once they are no longer able to live alone. Men do very little domestic work but farm or fish for their subsistence.

In Moroni, most families live in concrete buildings of varying sizes, though many live in thatched *paillotes.* There is very little open "dating" in the Comoros Islands; opposite-sex relationships are kept very discreet. Many community organizations are localized around particular neighborhoods. These organizations conduct fund-raising activities to help their members toward working abroad, and they also carry out local development and humanitarian projects.

Work and Commerce. Businesses are open from about 8:00 A.M. to about 6:00 P.M., closing for at least two hours for lunch. Stores are closed on Friday afternoons and Sundays. In Moroni several stores offer all kinds of foods and supplies. As in much of East Africa, Asian (Pakistani and Indian) merchants operate on a large commercial scale, with much economic influence. At the same time, there are many street-side vendors who sell common items. All fresh produce and meat is bought in the markets, which run every day from dawn to dusk. Prices are not negotiable in stores and are generally the same everywhere. Bargaining on the street or in the markets is common. Cash is paid for everything; bartering with payment in kind is rare. Credit cards and checks are accepted at only a few elite hotels and restaurants. Business may be conducted in the home, but only between people who are well enough acquainted to do so. Wage earners work from about 7:30 A.M. to 2:00 or 3:00 P.M. Only a small percentage of the population could be considered wage earners, and 80% of those employed are members of the civil service.

The Comorian economy is based upon the export of exotic spices, such as vanilla, cinnamon, and cloves. The ylang-ylang flower is also extremely important, because its oil is used as a base for many fine French perfumes. These products are rare, and ylang-ylang is unique to the Indian Ocean islands. The revenues from these exports do not nearly make up for imports to the country. France is the largest trading partner, but there is also limited trade with Madagascar, South Africa, and the United States. There are no factories or other production industries in Moroni, and the Comoros consistently run an enormous trade deficit. Individual families maintain subsistence plots of fruits and vegetables, as well as a few goats and cows; 53.6% of households take their main income from agriculture.

Families also augment their incomes with remittances from the thousands of Comorians who work abroad, mostly in France. The country is heavily dependent upon foreign aid, largely from France, the European Union, and the United Nations Development Programme. The Comoros use the CFA Franc, the same as found in many West African Francophone countries. In 1990 the per-capita income was $U.S.480. In 1995 the Human Development Index (a measure used by the United Nations Development Programme) for the Comoros was 0.411 out of 1, indicating relatively poor access for the average person to income, education, and health care. Tourism is a growing area of the economy but still quite small. Political instability, inconvenient travel access, and relatively high prices have prevented the Comoros from rivaling other regional tourist destinations.

Arts and Recreation. There are several local night spots in Moroni that cater to all classes and tastes. Comorians enjoy dancing to African pop music in a nightclub atmosphere, and expatriates and tourists also frequent the popular clubs. There is a small but very talented community of local musicians in Moroni, and they play a distinctly Comorian style of pop music, much of which is derived from traditional Grand Marriage rhythms. At Mitsoudjé, 11 kilometers (7 miles) south of Moroni, is a small wood-carving industry, although it is neither as strong nor as well established as that of Domoni, on the island of Anjouan. There is no other distinctive handicraft tradition, and dramatic performances are rare.

QUALITY OF LIFE

The quality of life in Moroni is poor, according to all major development indices. The economy is stagnant, and the difficult political situation has prevented strong foreign investment. The land around Moroni is volcanic tuff, making it difficult to grow many sorts of crops. Most retail items are imported and prohibitively expensive. Health care is poor and likewise expensive; the Al-Marouf Hospital in Moroni is chronically short of supplies and staff. Malaria is endemic, and poor sanitation encourages other types of diseases. Most Moronians are poor and work very hard to make ends meet. Despite this situation, the people of Moroni have a surprisingly upbeat outlook. Violent crime, though rising, is very low compared with its incidence in other African capitals. Most families produce enough food on their plots to eat substantial daily meals, and fish and fruit are plentiful. Families are ashamed to see relatives begging, so homelessness is nearly nonexistent.

FUTURE OF THE CITY

The future of Moroni depends on the resolution of the separatist crisis and the achievement of political stability. The average resident of Moroni is worse off today than at independence. Once Moroni is recognized as a safe environment for development, investment, and tourism, people will begin to prosper. Such stability is a tall order, and unlikely to come about in the short term.

BIBLIOGRAPHY

Fasquel, Jean, *Mayotte, les Comores et la France* (L'Harmattan 1991).

Guebourg, Jean-Louis, *La Grande Comore: Des sultans aux mercenaires* (L'Harmattan 1994).

Middleton, John, *The World of the Swahili* (Yale University Press 1992).

Ottenheimer, Martin, *Historical Dictionary of the Comoro Islands* (Scarecrow Press 1994).

Shepherd, G., "Two Marriage Forms in the Comoro Islands," *Africa* 47, no. 4 (1977): 344–58.

Useful Web Site

www.comores-online.com

MATTHEW B. DWYER

Moscow

Russia

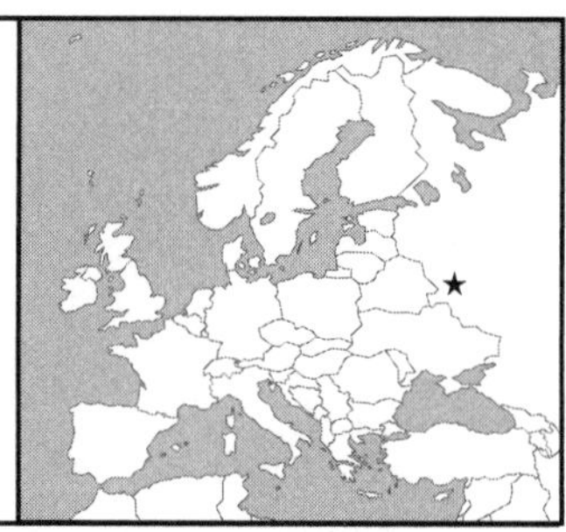

ORIENTATION

Name of City. The capital of the Russian Federation, Moscow is know as Moskva in Russian.

Location. Moscow is located at 55°45′ north latitude and 37°42′ east longitude, in the east European plain in a zone of mixed forests.

Population. As of January 1, 1998, the population of Moscow city was 8,537,200. The population of Moscow Oblast (province), excluding the city of Moscow, was 6,517,200.

Distinctive and Unique Features. The origins of the city date back 1,000 years. In the 10th and 11th centuries, the ancestral Slavic populations pushed north and east into the forests that afforded safety from nomadic populations of the southern steppes. The city of Moscow was a fortified outpost of the Prince of Suzdal, first mentioned in 1147 when the Prince Yuri Dolgorukii of Suzdal is recorded as having invited an ally to "Moskov." Starting as a minor fortified town—with a population of a few hundred people—the settlement grew, over time becoming a principality and an empire. Though Moscow was abandoned as capital for more than two centuries, the city continued to grow, and in the 19th century emerged as a major industrial center before becoming the capital once more after the Bolshevik Revolution. At present, it remains a major metropolis changed by 70 years of communism, though preserving the legacy of its history. Though the city's primary ethnic group is Russian (more than 90% of the permanent population), Moscow has always been a cosmopolitan city. For example, Moscow has a historical German quarter that dates back to the reign of Ivan IV (1533–1584), housing migrants invited to Russia. Modern Moscow, a metropolis of well over 8 million people, is home to a great diversity of peoples that continue to contribute to the development and cultural life of the city.

Attractions of the City. Perhaps the most well known attraction of the city is the Kremlin, a self-contained medieval city with a multitude of palaces, armories, and churches. A popular tourist spot, it is also the seat of presidential power in the modern Russian Federation, with the Senate serving as the official presidential residence. It was under the reign of Ivan III (known as "the Great," ruling from 1462 to 1505) that Moscow's Kremlin took its present appearance. Ivan had the old *kreml'*—fortress or citadel—demolished in order to build a new one in its place. Moscow is not the only city with a *kreml'* but its fortress, or the Kremlin, is best known to foreigners. Rising above the banks of the Moskva River, the Kremlin dominates Moscow's core. Central to the Kremlin are the ornate cathedrals that are a testament to the power of the city. Ivan called upon architects from Renaissance Italy to come to Moscow and aid in the construction of the new Kremlin. Using the Vladimir Cathedral as inspiration and model, Assumption Cathedral was built in four years (1475–1479) under the direction of Alberti Fioraventi, an architect from Bologna. In the following 50 years, the Kremlin was transformed. What had been a center dominated by ramshackle wooden buildings and walls was replaced with heavy brick fortifications and numerous stone churches, cathedrals, and other edifices.

Red Square also dates back to Ivan the Great, when, in 1493, he ordered the mass of houses, stalls, and other buildings that lined the walls of the Kremlin to be dismantled. Though its original purpose was to prevent the spread of fires that continually threatened the wooden fortifications and buildings, Red Square for most of its history served as an open-air market lined with stalls. The square was never "red," with the term *krasnaya* used in the past to signify beauty. St. Basil's Cathedral now dominates the beautiful square, or *krasnaya ploschad*. Though a wooden church predated the present structure, St. Basil's was rebuilt in 1555–1560 to honor Ivan IV's victory over the Tatars at Kazan. With its multicolored "onion-shaped" domes, this cathedral has become an icon of Moscow's distinctive style of architecture, fusing building techniques from the Renaissance and more-traditional styles that were part of the landscape of earlier Kievan *Rus'*.

Red Square is flanked by the State Department Store (GUM). The department store has been thoroughly revamped in recent years. Inside, foreign stores dominate, selling a variety of prestige consumer goods. Facing GUM are the Kremlin walls and Lenin's Mausoleum. The lines waiting to pay homage to Lenin lying in this low-lying marble structure have disappeared, but questions still remain as to what to do with this structure and Lenin's corpse. Behind the mausoleum, along the Kremlin walls, a number of Soviet notables were buried, including Stalin.

Alexander Gardens are located along the walls of the Kremlin. This treed park provides some shade. At its north end can be found the Tomb of the Unknown Soldier, erected in memory of those who died in World War II, known in Russia as the Great Patriotic War.

The history of the Cathedral of Christ the Savior serves as a bellwether for the changing politics of Russia. The cornerstone of the cathedral was laid in 1839, but it took more than four decades before the completed cathedral was dedicated in 1883 in memory of the defeat of Napoleon 70 years earlier. The final building, about 400 meters (a quarter of a mile) from the Kremlin, towered over central Moscow. Stalin ordered the building dynamited in 1931, and the site was to serve as the Palace of the Soviets. A majestic statue of Lenin 91 meters (300 feet) in height was to grace the Moscow skyline, standing on the palace that was to be the tallest edifice in the world, an estimated 366 meters (1,200 feet) in height—more than 6 meters (20 feet) higher than the Empire State Building. The project was initiated, but the thousands of tons of concrete poured could not provide a stable foundation in the damp soil beside the Moskva River. In its place the world's largest heated, open-air swimming pool was built. With the collapse of the Soviet Union, Moscow's mayor took it upon himself to rebuild the cathedral. The reconstruction was completed in 1997 in time to celebrate the 850th anniversary of the first historical mention of Moscow. The cathedral, 103 meters (338 feet) in height, with its gold cupolas once more dominates the cityscape.

As Moscow is the religious center of the Russian Orthodox Church and home to the Russian patriarch, numerous churches and monasteries dot the landscape. As is the case with the Kremlin, high defensive walls surround the exquisite monastery buildings. Central to Russian religious and family ties are the cemeteries: Russians will frequently visit the graves of family members and will equally visit the graves of famous Russians. One exquisite convent located within Moscow is the Novodevichiy Convent and Cemetery. Founded in 1524, the cemetery holds the remains of some of Russia's greatest authors and artists, including Nikolai Gogol and Anton Chekhov. More-recent burials include that of Nikita Khrushchev, the only Soviet leader not buried along the Kremlin walls behind Lenin's Mausoleum.

The "Big" Theater, the Bolshoi, is located in the Theater Square (*Teatral'naya Ploschad*). The "Small" Theater (*Maly* Theater) is located just to the south of the Bolshoi. This section of the city had to be rebuilt after the invasion of Napoleon and the great fire that destroyed much of the city in 1812. As was the case in Red Square, older buildings were cleared to make way for more open and planned spaces. The Bolshoi thus replaced the older Petrov Theater that had been gutted by the burning of the city. The Bolshoi is world renowned for its ballet and opera productions.

Old and New Arbat are two of the best-known streets in Moscow. The Old (*Stary*) Arbat Street is closed to traffic. During the day, vendors sell a variety of souvenirs, and the street features a number of stores and restaurants. The New (*Novy*) Arbat Street is lined with various stores and bars. These include one of Moscow's largest bookstores, Dom Knigi, or "house of books."

As the capital and largest city, Moscow has several hundred museums and art galleries covering every topic imaginable. Premier art museums include the Pushkin Museum of Fine Arts, which houses a respectable collection of European Renaissance, Egyptian, and Classic Art. The Tretyakov Art Gallery holds a large collection of some of the most important Russian works of art, including paintings, sculptures, and icons. Given the high esteem with which most Russians hold the literary greats, a number of museums are dedicated to such authors as Aleksandr Pushkin, Gogol, Chekhov and Fedor Dostoevsky.

The gleaming white marble facade of the State Duma Building is one of the central features of Moscow's modern landscape. The State Duma, Russia's "White House," houses the Russian Federation's 450-member State Duma, or lower legislative assembly.

One of the most monumental, and possibly one of the most controversial, projects undertaken in Moscow since the fall of the Soviet Union is the Victory Park (*Park Pobedy*). Located in the western outskirts of Moscow, this war memorial complex was built to commemorate the 50th anniversary of victory on *Poklonnaia Gora* (Bowing Hill, a name derived from an old tradition in which travelers coming to Moscow bowed to the Russian capital). The Victory Park is within a short distance of the Russian "Arc de Triomphe," commemorating the Russian victory over Napoleon in the First Great Patriotic War.

During the Stalin era in the early 1950s, the Moscow skyline was transformed with the construction of seven neoclassic skyscrapers referred to as the "seven sisters." These "wedding-cake" buildings house, among other things, the Moscow State University tower on the Lenin Hills; the Ukraine Hotel overlooking the Russian parliament building; and the Foreign Ministry headquarters, near the Old Arbat. Constructed of masonry, the ornate exteriors of Stalin's skyscrapers recall Gothic cathedrals.

Moscow features a large selection of parks and green spaces covering almost one-third of the city, including Gorky Park, an amusement park located on the shores of Moskva River. Although not located in Moscow proper, a number of historical cities are found within a few hundred kilometers of Moscow, including Vladimir, Suzdal, and Yaroslavl among others. These cities surrounding Moscow, the "Golden Ring," provide some of the best examples of Kievan *Rus'* and early-medieval Russian architecture.

© MORTON BEEBE/CORBIS

These buildings along the Moskva River in Moscow were built in the "wedding-cake" style popular during the Stalinist era.

Relationships Between the City and the Outside. Russia is still a dominant regional power trying to maintain a sphere of influence over what it considers its "near abroad," generally the former republics of the Soviet Union. Moscow still has a great power of attraction: as the capital and economic hub of Russia, it offers a wealth of business and employment opportunities that are not available elsewhere. Russia, however, has maintained the tsarist and Soviet system of residence permits, the *propiska*. In both Moscow and St. Petersburg, Russians living outside of these cities cannot legally reside and work there without obtaining a local residency permit.

Major Languages. Russian is the lingua franca of the Russian Federation, spoken by virtually all

Muscovites. However, given the economic and political importance of the capital, the city has attracted migrants from across the Soviet Union. As a consequence, dozens of other languages—from Armenian to Uzbek—are spoken in the city.

HISTORY

The Origin of the City. Although Moscow recently celebrated its 850th anniversary, the origin of the city predates 1147, the date when medieval chroniclers first mentioned Moscow. The city's origins are modest. It was merely a village, dwarfed in economic, political, and historical importance by neighboring cities of Kievan *Rus'*. By the 10th century, Kiev had emerged as the capital of a large principality (*Rus'*) that consisted of more than 300 towns under the control of the prince and a council of boyars and wardens. Even though the first rulers of Kiev were of Scandinavian origin and they adopted the Orthodox Christian faith of Greek-speaking Byzantium, Kiev is seen as the birthplace of three Eastern Slavic peoples: Russians, Ukrainians, and Belorussians.

The rise of Muscovy begins with the fall of Kiev. As was the case in the early Western feudal period, the death of a prince often led to internal conflict. By 1100, Kievan *Rus'* had disintegrated into a number of feuding principalities, besieged by raiding nomads. Divided among a number of warring princes, between 1237 and 1240, the Mongol hordes led by Genghis Khan conquered the lands of *Rus'*. Only the cities of Novgorod and Pskov remained unconquered, while the rest of *Rus'* remained under the tutelage of the khan and his descendants, with the principalities of *Rus'* obliged to pay tribute to the Mongols, also known as the Tatars (Tartars). Although the Mongol invasions did ensure that the lands of *Rus'* would never be politically or ethnically unified in the future, it did allow for the rise of Muscovy.

The lineage of Moscow princes was founded by Daniel (1263–1303), the youngest son of Alexander Nevsky of Novgorod, legendary leader—later Russian Orthodox Saint—who had defeated the German Teutonic Knights on the ice of Lake Peipus (Chudskoe in Russian). Daniel and his successors, by using their role as tax collectors for the Mongol Tatars, continued to expand the power, influence, and territory of Moscow over lesser principalities. Located close to the headwaters of a number of rivers, Moscow was ideally situated for expansion both north and south: with a series of short portages, it is possible to sail from England to the Mediterranean via central Russia.

The rise of Moscow as the center of a new empire began in the 15th century. Under the rule of Ivan III (the Great), Moscow stopped paying tribute to the Mongols. Though the Mongol Tatars had gathered for an attack on Moscow, they hastily retreated in 1480 without engaging in battle. By 1502 the Mongol Horde ceased to exist as a unified political or military force, having fractured into numerous smaller khanates. Over time, these would be absorbed into the growing Russian Empire.

By 1505 Moscow ruled over much of Eastern *Rus'*, having brutally invaded and conquered Novgorod and other Russian lands. In 1572 Ivan IV (the Terrible, as known in English—though perhaps more appropriately the "formidable" or "threatening" as he is known in Russian) married Sophia Paleologue, niece of the last Byzantine emperor. Based on the marriage of Ivan IV and Sophia, the princes of Moscow took the title of tsar, or "Caesar," and claimed Moscow as the "Third Rome." Though perhaps presumptuous, in the early 16th century Moscow was the new capital of a growing empire that was soon to cross the Ural Mountains and spread across Siberia in search of sable furs for trade with Europe. Later the Russian Empire would push south into the Caucasus and west into what are now Poland, Ukraine, and the Baltic States.

With the death of Ivan IV in 1584, Muscovy was faced with a great period of unrest referred to by historians as the Time of Troubles. Having killed his eldest son in a fit of rage, Ivan IV was succeeded by his son Fyodor, who died at an early age in 1598 without leaving an heir. Muscovy was beset by 15 years of chaos as a succession of tsars, pretenders to the throne, and foreign powers grappled for power. The lands of Muscovy almost came to be ruled by the Polish crown. In 1612 a militia was formed under the leadership of Cosmo Minin, a butcher and merchant, and Prince Dmitri Pozharsky to drive the Poles out of Moscow. Following the expulsion of the Poles from Moscow, a council of all the land (*zemskii sobor*) was convened to elect a new tsar. Five hundred or so delegates—boyars, service nobles, clergy, merchants, Cossacks, townspeople, free peasants—on February 7, 1613, elected 16-year-old Mikhail Romanov as the new tsar. The Romanov family would rule over Muscovy and the Russian Empire for more than three centuries, until the Russian Revolution.

Moscow, though central to the rise of the Russian Empire, was abandoned in the early 18th century as the political capital, for more than two centuries. In 1703 Peter the Great undertook the construction of St. Petersburg. Built at the cost of thousands of lives in the latest architectural style, St. Petersburg was to be a modern capital fit for a tsar who was set on "modernizing" the Russian Empire. Moscow subsisted in the 18th century as the center of small-scale trade and manufacturing by artisans. The population continued to grow, but quite slowly. In 1701 it numbered roughly 200,000. Close to 150 years later, in 1848, it had grown to 377,000. However, in the second half of the 19th century, Moscow's population soared as the city began to be a major center of industry and trade. By the 1890s Moscow's population numbered approximately 900,000 people, and by the end of the 19th century, it would surpass 1 million. With the freeing of the serfs, increasing numbers could leave their homes in the countryside to seek jobs in the city. Even though the Russian Empire had two of world's most populous cities, city planning lagged behind other large urban centers. Moscow remained a city of churches interspersed with factories, workshops, and open-air bazaars.

The Revolution restored Moscow as the capital of Russia in 1918, and of the Soviet Union in 1922. The inhabitants of the city did not escape the ravages of the Revolution and the Civil War. By 1918 Moscow's population had reached 1.7 million. The numbers declined by several hundred thousand as people fled to the countryside in 1919 and 1920, but Moscow quickly began to grow once more, with central planning shaping the city. As the new capital, various government ministries were opened in Moscow. Then, with rapid industrialization in the 1930s, the city grew in economic importance as an important industrial center. The marking moment of the 1940s was the Nazi invasion of the Soviet Union, with the German army coming within view of Moscow.

Following World War II, Moscow continued to change. Skyscrapers were constructed, and increasing numbers of apartment buildings were erected in the periphery of the city. Many old architectural features—notably churches, cathedrals, and monasteries—were destroyed. However, Moscow did retain many of the features of the older medieval city: The Kremlin and surrounding buildings remained largely untouched. In the 1950s much of the construction was still concentrated within the Garden Ring. During this period the dominant architectural style was the five- to nine-story brick apartment building. In the 1960s Moscow witnessed the growth of its "suburbs." These new neighborhoods were dominated by a series of similar high-rise apartment buildings constructed out of prefabricated concrete slabs that were hurriedly assembled to build apartments for the burgeoning population. Outside of Moscow are a number of smaller cities, some of which were integrated into the Moscow city administration in the 1960s and 1970s. Surrounding Moscow is a greenbelt, a popular site for dachas—summer cottages—which are prized by Muscovites and provide space for gardens to grow potatoes, cabbage, and other produce.

Migration: Past and Present. From inconspicuous origins, Moscow grew to be one of Europe's largest cities. In 1560 Moscow was estimated to have been home to more than 150,000 people, a population slightly larger than London's at that time. The city grew by adding fortification in concentric rings—first the Kremlin walls, then those of Kitai-Gorod (walled city), and finally those that came to define the Garden Ring, the border of the old city.

Following the freeing of the serfs in 1861, Moscow began to grow once more at an unprecedented pace. From the 1860s to the Revolution in 1918, the city's population more than quadrupled to 1.7 million people. One of the problems engendered by this large-scale migration to Moscow was the chronic shortage of apartment space. The Bolsheviks tried to solve this problem with the creation of communal apartments. The population declined with the Civil War after the Revolution, but Moscow quickly recovered, and by 1940 the numbers had more than doubled to almost 4.5 million inhabitants. By 1959 the population had tripled to 6 million and though the growth of the city slowed, the population peaked in 1989 at 9 million. This growth can be attributed to two factors: the overall increase in residents and the shift in population from countryside to the city. In 1926 less than one-fifth of the citizens lived in urban areas, whereas in 1991 almost three-quarters of the population of Russia was urban. At present, Moscow—the largest and richest city in Russia and the former republics of the Soviet Union—continues to attract migrants from the regions and the "near abroad." With the fall of the Soviet Union and the economic and social disruptions that plague Russia, more people are now dying in Moscow than are being born, and since 1991 Moscow's population has declined by 300,000 people. In fact, the life expectancy has been dropping throughout Russia, especially for men. This is owing to a number of factors, notably the inadequate level of medical care, the high rate of work-related injuries, high rates of alcohol abuse, pollution, and the increasing crime rate. The situation may get worse owing to social and economic instability, which favors the spread of various infectious diseases, such as HIV/AIDS (human immunodeficiency virus/acquired immune deficiency syndrome) and forms of tuberculosis resistant to antibiotics.

INFRASTRUCTURE

Public Works, Public Buildings, and Residences. The modern Russian metropolis has been shaped by one man: the charismatic and populist mayor of Moscow, Yuri Luzhkov. Since the late 1990s, Luzhkov has remade Moscow and marked it with a number of grandiose—though controversial—monuments.

The pivotal moment was the city's 850th anniversary—not of the founding, but of the first mention of the city—in 1997. Luzhkov organized a massive celebration and invested in cleaning, refurbishing, and aggrandizing the city. The momentum that began did not end. Since the collapse of the Soviet Union, the city administration has been continually working on upgrading the city's infrastructure. Examples include new highways and upgraded streets. The already extensive Metro (subway) continues to expand by adding new stations. Much effort has been put into cleaning and repainting the city, notably in the central core. Additionally, new monuments have been built or, in some cases, rebuilt.

The renovations undertaken are part of the city's new development plan adopted in 1998. The plan called for, among other things, the reconstruction of the city center, and to date 120 historical and cultural monuments and features have been restored including the historical Kazan Cathedral housing the *Virgin of Kazan* icon that in the early 17th century is reputed to have miraculously routed the Poles from Holy Russia, thus ensuring the survival of Orthodox Russia. As part of Stalin's war against religion, it was completely demolished in 1936. The rebuilt cathedral is now open to the public. The plan also is guiding the renovations and reconstructions in several important cultural and historical zones including Theater Square (where the Bolshoi Theater is located) and the Kremlin and neighboring zones. In addition to the reconstruction, new features were added including a three-story underground shopping center located at the Manezh Square. As is the case with the renovated GUM, this shopping center features a number of quite expensive boutiques selling foreign goods to Moscow's wealthy and visiting tourists.

One of the largest projects undertaken was the rebuilding of the Christ the Savior Cathedral. Another large project undertaken at this period was the vast memorial complex at Victory Park. Built on the spot where in popular legend Napoleon waited to enter victoriously into Moscow, the site now hosts a massive complex with the Museum of the Great Patriot War (World War II) and a 141-meter- (462-foot-) tall obelisk. At the base is a statue of St. George on a steed with a spear and with what can be best described as a sliced dragon. The location is a popular site for the various holidays commemorating the war and in the summer is now a prized location for taking wedding photos. Also, with its miles of sidewalk and many plazas, it was a popular location for young inline skaters in the late 1990s.

Moscow's Victory Park highlights the increased prominence of religion in the Russian Federation, as it now includes the Church of St. George the Victorious, a synagogue, and a mosque. The site features a number of other monuments designed by the highly controversial Georgian sculptor Zurab Tsereteli whose designs are described as "infantile," "cartoon-like," or simply "kitsch," and who was patroned by Luzhkov. Other projects undertaken by Tsereteli include a huge statue devoted to Peter the Great on the banks of the Moscow River.

The Moscow landscape was radically changed not only by the new public monuments but also by the new private businesses and ventures that now cover the city. After the fall of communism, Moscow went through a period of wild capitalism with much of the city's business being conducted in massive open-air markets and in small tarp "tents" lining streets that sold every good imaginable. Such enterprises still exist, but are becoming increasingly rare. This was evident in the early years of the millennium: new buildings were being constructed throughout the city to house a variety of businesses. Whereas Muscovites had to line up for Big Macs in the 1980s, McDonalds and various other foreign businesses and franchises now dot the urban landscape. Local business has moved from the small tents to more permanent kiosks that now cater to a variety of consumers. Also, larger corporations and government monopolies such as GAZPROM have built a variety of office towers to house their headquarters.

The spate of building and renovating is not limited to government and business. In the city, since the turn of the millennium, a number of luxury apartment towers have been built to cater to the city's wealthy. However, the growing—though fragile—middle classes equally dream of upgrading their living accommodations. The goal of most Muscovites is the "evroremont" or the apartment renovated according to Western standards and furnished with a European flair. A number of local businesses were established to meet the need, and the international giant IKEA set up shop in a massive outlet in the outskirts of the city.

The general development plan of the city calls for the gradual reconstruction of the bedroom neighborhoods that house most of the city's population. Though many of the apartments have been privatized, the city is still responsible for the upkeep of the structures, and much work will be required to maintain these structures built in the period of rapid expansion following World War II.

Politics and City Services. The Moscow City Duma passed in 1995 a law reorganizing the city's administration. The city is now divided into ten districts (*okrug*) that are in turn composed of 125 neighborhood municipalities (*raion*). Moscow is governed by an elected mayor, an elected duma consisting of 35 elected councillors representing individual city districts, in addition to elected officials at the *okrug* and *raion* level. The mayor is responsible for every branch of the city's administration, although the Moscow City Duma does have its own chair. The Moscow Duma is responsible for local legal regulations, for approving the city's budget, and for setting city taxes, although the mayor does have certain powers of veto. In addition to the city administration, the Moscow Oblast has an elected governor with the administrative offices and the regional duma being located in Moscow City. Moscow, however, does not fall under the regional authority; instead, the mayor reports directly to the Russian federal government.

Educational System. Nine years of education are compulsory, though students must now complete 11 years before being admitted to college. Moscow schools tend to offer specialized programs of instruction in music, the humanities, physics and mathematics, foreign languages, and a number of other disciplines. There is much competition for admittance into the most prestigious institutes and universities, of which there are more than 75 in Moscow. The M. V. Lomonosov Moscow State University (MGU) crowns the city's postsecondary education system.

Transportation System. Moscow has a well-developed transportation system. An international airport serves the city, with Aeroflot and foreign airlines connecting Moscow to the world. Travel by train is still a major form of transportation within Russia and eastern Europe. A series of train stations serve as railway hubs, connecting Moscow to all of Russia, central Asia, China, and eastern Europe. The Metro subway system, inaugurated in 1935, is always growing, with each stop designed to be unique, featuring sculpture, mosaics, and other artworks. It serves as the major transportation artery for the majority of Muscovites. Tramways and buses collect passengers and feed them into the Metro, which radiates out from the center of the city. Moscow is faced with a growing number of automobiles. In the late 1990s many Muscovites could afford to purchase automobiles made locally or imported from Europe and America. As a consequence, the city roadways have been overwhelmed with large numbers of vehicles that the city had not been designed to accommodate.

CULTURAL AND SOCIAL LIFE

Distinctive Features of the City's Cultures. Moscow, as much as Eastern Europe, underwent a traumatic period with the collapse of communism, the shock transition to a form of capitalism, and the collapse in value of the national currency, the ruble. In spite of the radical declines in living standards and the uncertainty, the city and the country never descended into chaos. This is in part due to the importance that is placed upon order and being "cultured."

Over the years, countless Muscovites went without pay or were paid very little for months at a time, yet the city continued to function. Even though the outskirts of the city can be seen as grimy and rundown, a lot of patient effort is put into maintaining neighborhoods and preserving a certain order and cleanliness: the floors continue to be mopped and garbage is collected.

The guardians of social order are nonetheless the "babushkas" or "grandmothers." These elderly women will never hesitate to voice their opinions as to inappropriate conduct and will not hesitate to publicly scold those who do not conform to the expected social etiquette. In Moscow, it is still imperative to give one's seat on the Metro or bus to an elderly person or a pregnant woman. Such etiquette is valued and maintained.

Muscovites, however, do exhibit two distinct personae. The public persona is clearly aloof and, if encountered as a government employee, can be downright rude. Should this individual, however, greet you in their home, he or she would spend a week's wages to offer you a meal with caviar and "Soviet champagne." It is thought to be a feature of the Russian national soul: Russians see themselves as naturally kind, good-natured, and hospitable. Others equally claim to be more hospitable than the Russians, whether they be Armenian or Georgian or any of the countless other groups.

Cuisine. Moscow's cuisine is characterized by its simplicity. The peasantry's basic staples influenced Russian cuisine: potatoes, cabbage, cucumbers for pickling and salads, beets, and carrots. These are combined to make a variety of soups—notably borscht—and salads to be eaten with Russia's dark rye bread. *Blini,* or Russian crepes, are a popular meal often eaten with red caviar or a thick, sweet condensed milk. Muscovites and others are particularly fond of gathering wild mushrooms. In addition to ethnic Russian cuisine, Moscow has a number of Georgian and Armenian restaurants. These cuisines are renowned for *shashlik*—barbecued shish kebab. Unlike Russian traditional foods, the cuisine from the Caucasus region tends to make more liberal use of spices.

Ethnic, Class, and Religious Diversity. Even though the last census (1998) reported "140 different nationalities" living within the city, Moscow is more ethnically Russian than is the Russian Federation as a whole. In 1994 slightly more than 90% of the city's population was Russian by nationality, with the largest minorities being Ukrainians (2.4%), Jews (1.5%), Tatars (1.9%), Belorussians (0.7%), and Armenians (0.7%)—to name but the largest groups. It should be noted that "nationality," in Soviet times and continuing to the present, is usually selected based on the "official" nationality of one or both parents, and is not necessarily indicative of culture, language, or even self-identification. These statistics do not include all the people of the city, only the permanent residents. It is estimated that there are roughly 500,000 people that live in the city as "visitors"—refugees, short-term migrants, and illegal immigrants. This population includes many individuals from the Caucasus and migrants from central Asia and the other former Soviet republics.

The Russian Federation does not have an official religion, but the Russian Orthodox Church has gained in stature since the collapse of the Soviet Union. Close to 95% of Moscow's population is Russian Orthodox by practice or by ancestry. The second religion in terms of numerical importance is Islam (2.5%), followed by Judaism (2.0%) and small percentages of Roman Catholicism, Lutheranism, Buddhism, and shamanism.

© MARC GARANGER/CORBIS

Russian Orthodox Patriarch Alexy II blesses worshipers during his birthday mass at a Moscow cathedral in 1991.

Family and Other Social Support Systems. The nuclear and extended family is one of the primary social safety nets of the Russians, whether they live in Moscow or elsewhere. During the years of persecution and repression, close family members were those that could (in most circumstances) be trusted. Likewise, goods were often hoarded and bartered with close kin, and family members used their connections to get into good universities and obtain positions. Such tendencies remain: contacts facilitate upward mobility and family members can provide money or goods in times of need. This is especially helpful when salaries are not being paid or the salary received is not sufficient. Likewise, it is expected that elderly parents will move in with their children: it would be considered inhumane to send one's parents to a public retirement home. Family quite often ensures survival in chaotic times.

Work and Commerce. Moscow is a major industrial and financial center, and this is reflected in the distribution of jobs in the city. Even though the number of people working in industrial jobs has decreased since the 1960s, close to 20% of Muscovites still work in factories. Growing numbers of people are working in sales and services, almost 15% of the working population in 1994. Construction has picked up, giving jobs to more than 13% of the workforce. Finally, close to one-fifth of the population is still employed in research, teaching, or the arts.

Arts and Recreation. As in most large cities, Muscovites can choose from a variety of arts and entertainment. In addition to the hundreds of museums, theaters, movie cinemas, opera houses, and other arts venues, the Moscow Circus is a perennial favorite. Football (soccer) and hockey are favorite sports. The city has not only sports arenas but also various sports complexes for its population to use. A traditional place of relaxation for Muscovites and Russians is the sauna (*banya*), and Moscow features a number of bathhouses and saunas.

QUALITY OF LIFE

If one considers the political, economic, and ecological climate in which the people of Moscow live, much has improved since the Soviet period. The majority of Muscovites can now live their lives in a relatively democratic society that has made major inroads in protecting individual human rights. One of the major problems faced by city residents, however, is the rampant corruption that plagues all levels of government and administration.

Although Muscovites faced another economic crisis with the devaluation of the ruble in 1998, the inhabitants of the city were economically favored compared with those living in the more distant regions of Russia. Though the post-Soviet period saw the emergence of the New Russians—a class of very wealthy individuals who accumulated their riches largely through their political influence and former positions of power in the Soviet Union—Moscow was beginning to see the emergence of a small middle class. These were mainly professionals employed in the new industries of Russia, such as banking and retail commerce. A lot of money was in circulation, making Moscow one of the world's most expensive cities, though the average salary was never much more than U.S.$500 per month.

Finally, Moscow is beset by a problem common to many of the world's largest cities: pollution. The pollution comes from a number of sources, including the large numbers of industrial plants located within the boundaries of the city, the electricity-generating plants, and the increasing numbers of cars, often older models without pollution-reducing catalytic converters. The result is severe air pollution. One of the challenges of improving air quality is finding the necessary capital for industry to upgrade its equipment and reduce pollution emissions into the environment. However, the biggest offenders when it comes to air quality are private vehicles. At the turn of the century there are well over 2 million vehicles in Moscow, more than three times the number that were on city streets a little over a decade ago. The underground aquifers have been polluted by chemical and biological contaminants leaching through the soil, thus leading to pollution of the city's water. Recognizing the danger of pollution, the Russian state adopted new legislation in the 1990s to deal with the problem.

FUTURE OF THE CITY

Since 1991, Moscow has faced one of the most difficult periods of its long history. The collapse of the Soviet Union left the city with a series of economic, social, and environmental problems that continue to plague Moscow and its inhabitants. However, given its status as the capital city and main economic center of the Russian Federation, Moscow has been reinventing itself. It may not be the "Third Rome," but Muscovites hope their city will soon rival other metropolises such as Paris, New York, and London in importance and stature. Given its rise from obscurity close to 1,000 years ago to one of the world's major cities, Moscow should never be discounted.

BIBLIOGRAPHY

Berton, Kathleen, *Moscow: An Architectural History* (St. Martin's Press 1977).

Bradley, Joseph, *Muzhik and Muscovite: Urbanization in Late Imperial Russia* (University of California Press 1985).

Brower, Daniel R., *The Russian City Between Tradition and Modernity, 1850–1900* (University of California Press 1990).

Hamm, Michael F., ed., *The City in Russian History* (University of Kentucky Press 1976).

Hosking, Geoffrey, *Russia: People and Empire, 1552–1917* (FontanaPress 1998).

Pares, Bernard, *A History of Russia,* definitive ed., with a new introduction by Richard Pares (Dorset Press 1991).

Rozman, Gilbert, *Urban Networks in Russia, 1750–1800, and Premodern Periodization* (Princeton University Press 1976).

Schmidt, Albert J., *The Architecture and Planning of Classical Moscow: A Cultural History* (American Philosophical Society 1989).

MICHEL BOUCHARD

Munich

Germany

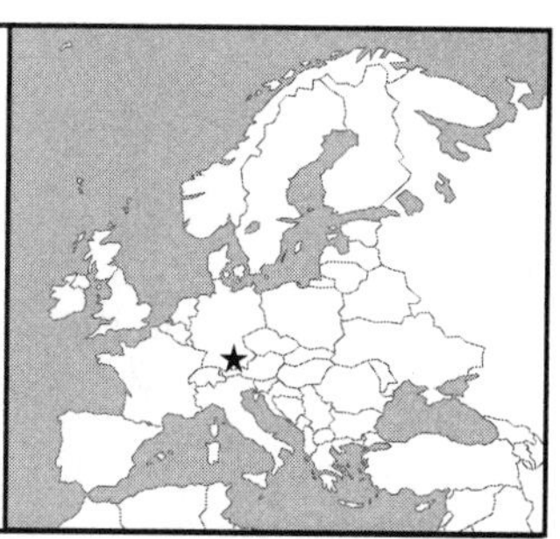

ORIENTATION

Munich is the state capital of the Freistaat Bayern (Bavaria) and has a population of 1.29 million. Greater Munich is composed of the city itself and eight neighboring counties, with a total population of 2.4 million inhabitants.

Name of City. The name *Munich* (German, *München*), derives from the fact that the early community was associated with an abbey of Benedictine monks (*Munichen*).

Location. Munich is situated at 48°08′ north latitude and 11°34′ east longitude, in southern Germany. It is 586 kilometers (364 miles) south of Berlin, 140 kilometers (87 miles) northwest of Salzburg, and 222 kilometers (138 miles) southeast of Stuttgart. In the regional hierarchy, Munich is an urban center of "highest centricity" (*Grosszentrum*)—that is, it is one of Germany's most important cities in terms of size, economic importance, and other measures—with an immediate hinterland that covers much of southeastern Bavaria.

Munich lies some 60 kilometers (37 miles) north of the Alps on the largely level Swabian-Bavarian plateau, which slopes gently toward the north. Forests and lakes in the south give way to mossy regions and moors in the north. A mixture of maritime and continental climate prevails, with hot spells during the summer and periods of below-freezing temperatures in winter. Inversions of hot and cold air can cause smog buildup, and the occasional foehn (*Föhn*) from the Alps brings warm winds, clear views, and high pressure. The elevation of the city averages 530 meters (1,740 feet). The Isar River, with its headwaters in the Alps, bisects Munich south to north as it flows northward toward the Danube. Except for some natural gas and oil deposits to the east of Munich, the area is not rich in mineral resources. Gravel, especially from pits just to the north of the city, is important to the construction industry, while the Isar River serves as a source of energy and recreation; historically the river was used to transport lumber on rafts from the Alps.

Distinctive and Unique Features. The city covers an area of 310 square kilometers (120 square miles)—26 kilometers, or 16 miles, from east to west; 21 kilometers, or 13 miles, from north to south. The 91 hectare (225 acre) semicircular Altstadt (old city center) is bounded to the east and southeast by the Isar River, to the north by the Englisher Garten (Munich's premier city park), and to the west by the main train station. The Altstadtring (bypass route) runs along much of the city's former defensive wall, with only four gates remaining from the original ramparts. The core of the Altstadt is formed by the central square, the Marienplatz, which is adjoined by the Viktualienmarkt (produce market) to the southeast. This area is the eastern end of a pedestrian zone, which runs some 800 meters (2,625 feet) westward to the Karlstor and to the Odeonsplatz to the north. In the northeastern quarter of the Altstadt is the Residenz (palace) of Bavaria's former rulers. To the south and north of the Altstadt, two of Munich's partially tree-lined grand avenues, Maximilian- and Prinzregentenstrassen, lead eastward over the Isar. Another grand avenue, the Ludwiggtrasse, runs from the Odeonsplatz near the Residenz into the northern suburbs.

The street pattern in the inner neighborhoods surrounding the old city center, in contrast to the more uneven network in the Altstadt, tends to be gridlike, interspersed by the occasional roundabout. In this zone are found the main train station, Hauptbahnhof to the west, with the large Theresienswiese (Theresa's meadow) where the annual Oktoberfest takes place, to the south. Beyond the Altstadtring, the city's inner neighborhoods are bounded by the Mittlerer Ring, a circular traffic bypass at a radius of about 3 kilometers (2 miles) from the city square. On its northwestern edge is the Olympiapark (site of the 1972 Olympic Games), and just beyond the Ring to the west is the Schloss Nymphenburg (royal summer residence) and its adjoining garden and park. Several Autobahnen (freeways) connect to the Mittlerer Ring. Most of the partially completed Autobahnring around Munich is beyond the city borders. Industry is strung along the railroad axis east and west of the Altstadt. Additional industrial areas are found in the southeast and especially the north between the Mittlerer Ring and the Autobahnring. A number of planned satellite towns exist in these outlying districts. Upscale residential areas are located near the banks of the Isar to the east and south of the old center and near Nymphenburg to the west.

Bombing during World War II destroyed about half of the built-up area of the city, 90% in the Altstadt. While the street pattern and property lines were largely retained after the war, much of the prewar architecture was replaced with buildings in a more contemporary style. The city, however, was exemplary in reconstructing most of the historical structures in their original form. The medieval ambience of steeply gabled, half-timbered, overhanging buildings along narrow alleyways can now be found in Munich's Altstadt. This is because the city was a royal residence for centuries during which burgher houses were replaced with princely representative structures and churches. The early Gothic and subsequently Renaissance styles of these structures were, in the 17th and 18th centuries, replaced by baroque-style architecture. It was the 19th-century monumental neoclassical form, however, that influenced Munich's Altstadt and immediate surroundings perhaps more than any other style: an architectural expression of the new Bavarian monarchy. The Jugendstil (art deco style) of the early 20th century was especially notable in the artistic district of Schwabing north of the Altstadt. Since World War II, height limits have been enforced in and near the city center, with three to four levels being the norm. High-rises have appeared in more outlying districts, chiefly in satellite towns, as residential and commercial blocks interspersed with communal green areas. More contemporary architecture is represented by the Olympiapark, which features opaque, tent-like roofs spanning several stadiums, and by the nearby Bayerische Motoren Werke AG (BMW) administration building designed around four piston-shaped towers. Since the 1970s, new suburban housing developments emphasize single- and double-occupancy homes (two to three levels) that include small private gardens.

Attractions of the City. Munich is one of the largest industrial centers in Germany in terms of numbers of employed and of total industrial sales annually. Its strength lies especially in the transportation industry (BMW) and in microelectronics (Compaq Computer Corporation, Intel Corporation, and Microsoft Corporation). Also, giant Siemens AG is headquartered in the city. Munich is a publishing center, a main locale for Germany's television and film industry (Bavaria-Film), and important in financial and insurance services (Bayerische Hypo und Vereinsbank Aktiengesellschaft, Allianz AG). The city's international importance is indicated by the fact that approximately 46% of Munich's DM61-billion (U.S.$36-billion) industrial production is exported, that over 60 countries maintain consulates in the city, and that its trade-fair exhibits annually serve 2 million visitors. It is also the headquarters of the large European and German patent offices. Munich's location in the center of Europe is of great advantage to business, although Berlin has become increasingly prominent following German reunification. Munich's transportation infrastructure is excellent, maintained by one of the highest infrastructural investment rates in Germany (17% of the city budget). Its educational facilities, including two major universities and several technical colleges, assure a highly skilled work force. Of three hundred economic zones in Europe, the region of Oberbayern, with Munich at the center, is considered to be the most attractive for business.

Munich is one of the major tourist destinations among German cities. In 1999 3.5 million visitors, 1.4 million of them from outside of Germany, visited the city. Munich's Bavarian ambiance and the artistic scene in Schwabing and Haidhausen (east of the Isar) combine with outstanding cultural facilities. Munich is home to a wide range of museums and the charming Marienplatz, with its famous chimes and dancing figures in the neo-Gothic Neues Rathaus belfry (1908), is a center for tourists, as is the adjacent pedestrian zone. The imposing Residenz in the Altstadt and Nymphenburg to the west are also favorite tourist destinations, as are the Englischer Garten and the Olympiapark. Tourists also flock to Munich's Oktoberfest in the fall. The city's location near the Alps further undergirds its status as tourist center. To the south and southwest are the pleasant lakes of Ammersee and the Starnberger See. The Alps are an easy day trip away, including Mittenwald, Garmish-Partenkirchen, and the fairy-tale-like castle Neuschwanstein, near Füssen. Now a museum and exhibit area, the town of Dachau to the northwest of Munich was the site of the Nazi's first concentration camp.

Relationships Between the City and the Outside. The Altstadt of Munich is considered by residents to be the heart of the city, where its historical origins and identity lie. Until they were incorporated beginning in the mid-19th century, the outlying districts were independent villages and towns; some of them have retained their distinct nature and identity. Relations between the city center and these districts tend to be good. Residents near the city's northern border, however, believe that they receive the brunt of environmentally damaging industrial investments. Business investments from Munich (especially in the west, north, and east, beyond its borders) support neighboring economies, while in the south recreational visitors from Munich stimulate local commerce. Munich is part of two interregional planning organizations. The Regionale Planungsverband München coordinates the regional development of Munich and eight surrounding counties in south-central Bavaria. Munich also belongs to the larger Wirschaftsraum Südbayern (Munich, Augsburg, and Ingolstadt), which encourages the balanced development of southern Bavaria in the competitive context of Bavaria, Germany, and the European Union (EU). Competition is more marked between Munich and the second-largest urban-commercial center of Bavaria, Nuremberg, 150 kilometers (93 miles) north in Franconia. As the seat of Bavaria, one of the wealthiest states in Germany, Munich is important in national and international affairs.

Major Languages. In education, government, and commerce, High German is the standard language for Munich residents. Variations of the Bavarian dialect are common in informal settings, a practice that crosses class lines. Dialects are widely used in folk-theater performances, and they have their own literary traditions. Munich shares these dialects with the larger Bavarian region south of Franconia.

HISTORY

For most of its history Munich was the seat of the Bavarian court. This has left a heavy mark on the city's built environment and its cultural characteristics.

The Origin of the City. The east-west salt and grain trade across the Isar River was important in the early history of Munich. In 1156, when Emperor Frederick Barbarossa gave the duchy of Bavaria to Henry the Lion, the latter decided to shift the lucrative salt trade between Reichshall and Augsburg to a crossing over the Isar near Munich that he controlled. The first ring of walls around this early settlement covered only 17 hectares (42 acres). In 1180, Barbarossa handed over Bavaria to Otto von Wittelsbach, whose family held on to the throne of Bavaria until the end of World War I. Munich became the ducal seat of the Wittelsbach family in 1255, with its first residence in the Alter Hof near the central city square (today's Marienplatz). In the 14th century the city's defensive walls were extended to include 91 hectares (225 acres).

During the burgher period in Munich (the 14th and 15th centuries) the commercial importance of the city expanded. Long-distance trade included storage rights of salt and grains, as well as of goods brought to the city on rafts via the Isar from the south.

At the end of this period, the domicile of the duke was relocated to a fortress where the Residenz is now located. Commercial activities were concentrated in the southern half of the Altstadt, while the northern half was increasingly taken over by cloisters, churches, and royalty.

From the 16th to the 19th century, Munich was transformed from mainly a burgher city to a residence for royalty such as the dukes and eventually the kings of the Wittelsbach dynasty. Because of its strong Counter-Reformation stance in the 16th century, Munich became known as Germany's Rome. Although allied with the Hapsburgs during the Thirty Years War, the city was able to buy its freedom from the Swedish leader Gustav August in 1632. In the mid-18th century, the Enlightenment brought to the city public education and the establishment of the Bavarian Academy of Science (1759). To gain more space, the city walls were razed beginning in 1792. With the help of the American-born British social reformer Count Rumford, the former royal hunting grounds along the west bank of the Isar were transformed into an English-style public park, the 373 hectare (922 acre) Englisher Garten.

Owing to the Napoleonic intrusion, Bavaria was elevated to a kingdom in 1806 and Maximilian I was crowned its first king. During this period of upheaval, many of the city's cloisters and churches were secularized. Property and civil law were improved, some civil rights were introduced, and Protestants and Jews were allowed to live in the city. Bavaria received a constitution with a *Landtag* (provincial legislature) headquartered in the city. Under Ludwig I (1825–1848) Munich became an artistic and royal administrative center of the neoclassical architectural style. The population of the city grew from

40,500 in 1800 to about 100,000 in 1850, in an urban area that had expanded from the original 91 hectares (225 acres) to 1,652 hectares (4,082 acres) in 1850, including several newly planned suburbs next to the Altstadt.

The revolutionary year of 1848 did not have a long-lasting effect on Munich. Maximilian II (1848–1864) continued the building boom initiated by Ludwig. To accommodate the need for additional space, the Munich administration in 1854 took the first step to expand the city area by incorporating neighboring villages. Owing to these acquisitions and the influx of immigrants attracted by industry, the population grew from 170,000 in 1871 to 350,000 in 1890. The threat of annual flooding from the Isar began to be solved by means of spillways, dikes, and by straightening the riverbed. In 1864 Maximilian II was succeeded by his mentally unstable son, Ludwig II, whose grandiose building projects, many of them outside of Munich, caused great distress to the state treasury. Following his mysterious drowning in the Starnberger See in 1886, Ludwig was succeeded by Luitpold (1886–1912). Bavaria became a state of the newly unified Germany in 1871, and the subsequent Gründerzeit period (the last third of the 19th century) witnessed an industrial boom in Munich. With additional territorial incorporations and immigration, the city population nearly doubled between 1881 and 1912, to 600,000, turning the city into the third largest in the country. A lively artistic and bohemian scene in the northern suburb of Schwabing added a cosmopolitan flavor to the otherwise rather provincial atmosphere of Munich. Among the individuals active in the city at the time were Thomas Mann, Paul Klee, Franz von Lenbach, and Lion Feuchtwanger.

Political instability in Germany and Bavaria after World War I had an impact on Munich. Late in 1918 Bavaria was declared a republic, and in the resulting power vacuum, a Soviet-style government was established in the city, only to be suppressed a few months later by government troops. In August 1919 Bavaria became part of the Weimar Republic as a parliamentary state with its seat in Munich. Partly owing to the economic difficulties in the inflationary years of the early 1920s and of the Great Depression of the 1930s, right-wing influence grew in Munich at the expense of the more liberal and artistic climate of the previous decades.

Adolf Hitler and others tried to take over Munich's political power (the Beer Hall Putsch in 1923, which was stopped in front of the Feldherrnhalle, or Odeonsplatz). In the 1920s and 1930s, industrial and residential ribbon developments spread along the rail and road networks, extending suburbanization beyond the immediate vicinity of the old city center. Territorial acquisitions continued, and by 1942 the city's area had grown to 310 square kilometers (120 square miles) with a population of nearly 800,000. The Nazis received a majority of the city vote in 1933, and the Dachau prison camp was opened a few months later (it processed 200,000 prisoners until 1945, of whom 32,000 were murdered). In 1935 Munich was declared the *Hauptstadt der Bewegung* (capital of the movement), and in 1938 it was the site of the Munich Agreement, in which the British agreed to Germany's occupation of Czechoslovakia. The first allied air raids took place in 1942, eventually destroying about half of the city's buildings and killing 6,000. The student opposition group Weisse Rose called for resistance at the main university in 1943, only to be captured and executed. On April 30, 1945, U.S. forces entered the city, which by then had a population of only 470,000. Of the 10,000 Jews who had lived in the city in 1933, only 84 remained.

Bavaria became a state of the newly formed Federal Republic of Germany in 1948. A year later Munich had regained its prewar population of 800,000. In the 1950s and 1960s, Germany's economic miracle spilled over into Munich, with such giant companies as Siemens, MAN Aktienqesellschaft (trucks), and MTU (Motoren- und Turbinen-Union) headquartered in the city. Munich became a center for the film industry ("Hollywood on the Isar") and of publishing (prestigious Süddeutsche Zeitung). By 1957 Munich had a million residents, and a year later it celebrated its 800th anniversary. By then, much of the postwar reconstruction had been completed, and efforts shifted to providing new housing to the growing population with the construction of large residential high-rise complexes in outlying districts. For a period in the 1960s, the city administration followed a car-friendly urban policy when it constructed the Altstadtring and Mittlerer Ring around the city center. With the coming of the Olympics in 1972, the city's administration reconsidered its development strategy and began to incorporate the needs of pedestrians and public transportation in its planning. The Olympic Games, while elevating Munich into the league of world metropolitan centers, were marked by tragedy when nine Israeli participants were murdered by Palestinian terrorists. By 1985 Munich had become Germany's largest center of microelectronics, known as Silicon Bavaria. The city's airport was relocated from the district of

Riem in 1992 to a site 30 kilometers (19 miles) to the northeast, near Freising.

Migration: Past and Present. Munich has always attracted immigrants. For most of its history, more than half of the city's residents had been born elsewhere, primarily coming from surrounding areas of Bavaria. Early in the 19th century, Protestants and Jews settled in the city, becoming dynamic contributors to its administration and economy. The attraction of Munich for the surrounding rural population increased with industrialization, a trend reinforced by a series of territorial incorporations undertaken between 1854 and 1942. It has been estimated that during this period, 70% of the city's population growth—from about 100,000 to 800,000—was the result of such territorial acquisitions and in-migration. Immigration (fostered by the economic boom years of the 1950s and 1960s) and natural growth lifted the population to 1.33 million in 1972. Since then, it has ranged between 1.3 and 1.2 million. Beginning in the 1960s with the guest-worker program, the city experienced an increase in the number of foreigners, a trend that continued until recently with the coming of asylum seekers during the 1980s and 1990s. While in 1979, 17% of the population was foreign, by 2000 20% of the population was foreign-born.

Approximately 230,000 residents relocate each year within the city. Since the 1960s there has been a tendency for residents to move away from the city center to the growing number of large satellite towns, or to the increasingly accessible neighboring communities outside Munich's borders. Continuing to serve as the primary business and administrative center of the city, the Altstadt and the inner neighborhoods within the Mittlerer Ring are subject to a large stream of daily in- and out-bound commuters.

INFRASTRUCTURE

Public Buildings, Public Works, and Residences. As the longstanding governing center of Bavaria, Munich is filled with historical and contemporary public buildings. Many of the public structures in and near the Altstadt were built in the 19th century according to neoclassical, neo-Gothic, and neobaroque designs. Among these representative, in some cases massive, buildings are the Alte Pinakothek and Glyptothek (art museums) northwest of the Altstadt, the Justizpalast at the Karlsplatz, the university complex and the Bavarian Staatsbibliothek along the Ludwigstrasse, the monumental Maximilianeum east of the Isar (seat of the Bavarian Landtag), the Neues Rathaus on the Marienplatz, and many more. Belonging to the same genre are the more symbolic structures, such as the Ruhmeshalle (hall of fame) adjoining the Theresienwiese, the Siegestor (victory arch) at the end of the Ludwigstrasse, and the Feldherrnhalle dominating the Odeonsplatz. The long, neoclassical Haus der Kunst on the Prinzregentenstrasse also belongs to this group, although it was built much later during the Nazi period. The Altes Rathaus (old town hall) on the central square with its bell turrets and steep gables, while a rebuilt version, represents an earlier era (15th century) in the town center. Among downtown churches, especially noteworthy is the graceful, 13th century Gothic (with Renaissance-era modifications) Peterskirche next to the Marienplatz. The late-Gothic, majestic Frauenkirche (1488) to the west dominates the downtown skyline with two onion-tipped spires. There are also the baroque Theatinerkirche (17th to 18th century) opposite the Residenz, the large Renaissance Michaelskirche (late 16th century) adjacent to the pedestrian zone, and the rococo Asamkirche in the southern part of the Altstadt (1733). The two impressive royal residences define Munich's center (Residenz) and its extension into the western suburbs (Nymphenburg).

The Deutsches Museum, on an island in the Isar, is an early functionally designed public edifice in Munich. Nearby, on the western banks of the Isar, are the overpowering, contemporary tower blocks of the Deutsches- and EU-Patentamt. Newer are the sun-roofed, postmodern Neue Pinakothek (museum of 19th century art), the large and contemporary Siemens Forum (a corporate museum) near the Karlsplatz, and the Bayerische Staatskanzlei (chancellery) in the old Army Museum next to the garden of the Residenz. Several cultural centers opened in later years, some located in former factory buildings (Kulturzentrum Ost), others in structures built for them; the most important of the latter is the imposing brick-framed Gasteig Kulturzentrum in Haidhausen, home to the Münchner Philharmoniker (Munich Philharmonic). The Ostbahnhof east of the Isar, and the large hall of the Hauptbahnhof to the west, define the east-west rail axis by way of the Südbahnhof (south of which are the city's extensive wholesale market buildings) around the Altstadt. One of Munich's major public-works projects in the 19th century was the taming of the Isar to prevent flooding; in the late 20th century the construction of the commuter rail system was of equivalent significance. Further from the city center are the futuristic facilities in the

Olympiapark, together with a 298-meter (978-foot) television tower and rotating restaurant. The main trade-fair grounds are located at Riem, to the east, while the airport (Franz-Joseph-Strauss Flughafen) operates out of a prize-winning terminal northeast of the city.

Politics and City Services. The city government is headed by a Stadtrat (city council) composed of 80 elected members, including a head mayor (Oberbürgermeister). The Stadtrat has two functions: first, it executes laws defined by the federal and state governments; second, it is responsible for the city budget, traffic, planning, special education, cultural programs, welfare, housing, and other affairs directly involving local concerns. With a separate mandate the Oberbürgermeister has considerable leeway to maneuver, which is helpful given that the council tends to be roughly evenly divided between the conservative Christian Social Union and the liberal Social Democratic party (usually the mayor belongs to the latter party). About 20% of the council members are affiliated with minority parties. The council includes 10 professional members to lend expertise to the 17 working committees formed by councilors. These committees give direction to the administrative counterparts in the city bureaucracy. Fifty percent of the DM9.435-billion (U.S.$4.3-billion) city budget in the year 2001 was derived from city taxes (mainly business taxes and license fees), the rest comes from federal and state subsidies. Since 1985 the city council has had an office of women's affairs to assure equal rights to women both within and outside of the administration. To encourage local empowerment Munich is divided into 25 districts, each of which is represented by district representatives according to the population size. Representatives' responsibilities range from weekly markets and social services to cultural programs and local urban planning. Munich is the seat of the Bezirksregierung Oberbayern. This intermediate administrative unit covers much of south and southeastern Bavaria and serves as a coordinating entity between the community and the Bavarian state in matters of supervision. Besides being represented on the federal level by Bavaria, Munich also has a voice through membership in the Bayerischer Städtetag, an association of Bavarian cities and towns. Membership in the general assembly is selected from elected councilors of each city, town, and municipality, with voting power proportionate to the population of each community. One of the main functions of the association is to assure that members are given adequate financial resources by the state and federal governments through taxation and subsidies.

Educational System. Secondary public education in Munich is divided into three levels: *Hauptschulen* (leading to apprenticeship in industry and crafts), *Realschulen* (for middle-level professional training), *and Gymnasiums* (in preparation for higher education). Munich has 182 elementary schools and *Hauptschulen*. The 30 *Realschulen* are attended by approximately 11,000 students, and about 34,000 attend the 48 *Gymnasiums*. Munich's 191 vocational schools serve about 63,000 students, and the city also offers adult education to around 12,000 individuals. Free public higher education is mainly provided by the Ludwig-Maximilians-Universität and the Technische Universität München. The former, founded in 1472, was moved to Munich in 1826. Later the university, with its main campus along the Ludwigstrasse in Schwabing, serves about 65,000 students (56% female and 12% foreign) in 12 departments (among the strongest are medicine and economics). The Technische Universität was founded in 1833, and continues to be the only technical university in Bavaria. It emphasizes the engineering sciences and is attended by approximately 22,000 students, with its main campus next to the Alte Pinakothek. Other institutions of higher learning include the Akademie der Bildenden Künste, Hochschule für Philosophie, Hochschule für Politik, and the Universität der Bundeswehr (armed forces). Thirty percent of Munich's youth attend *Gymnasiums* and 25% universities. Altogether, 30% of university students in Munich specialize in the natural and applied sciences. A number of public research institutes are located in the Munich region, most prominent among them are the headquarters and five institutes of the Max-Planck Gesellschaft. Also private concerns maintain research facilities in the city, such as Siemens, International Business Machines Corp. (IBM), BMW, DaimlerChrysler Aerospace, and MAN-Technologie. Of the 24 libraries and archives in Munich, the Bayerische Staatsbibliothek and the Bibliothek des Deutschen Museums stand out as internationally known collections.

Transportation System. Although they enjoy an excellent public transportation system, Munich residents do like their automobiles. The city has about 800,000 registered vehicles, of which almost 700,000 are passenger cars. Added to this must be about 200,000 vehicles that enter Munich daily on the *Autobahnen*. The city, through the Münchner Verkehrs- und Tarifverbund, has a wide-reaching integrated public transportation system. It includes 510 kilometers (317 miles) of S-Bahn (city train), 137 kilometers (85 miles) of subway, 94 kilometers (58 miles) of tram, and 656 kilometers (407 miles) of bus lines. Its major west–east commuter train axis runs underground parallel to the main pedestrian zone in the Altstadt. The system reaches far into Munich's hinterland in a spokelike manner, covering a radius of about 30 to 40 kilometers (19 to 25 miles). Improved connections among the spokes, especially by means of bus and tram services, are being expanded. Munich is connected to Germany's *Autobahn* grid through seven freeways, the major ones leading to Augsburg and Stuttgart, Nuremberg and Berlin, and Innsbruck and Salzburg. High-speed intercity rail service passes through Munich's Hauptbahnhof to Hamburg, Berlin, Vienna, Zurich, Frankfurt, and other centers. With the relocation in 1992 of the airport to a new location, Munich now has an air terminal of international size and quality, which handles more than 20 million passengers per year. It is the second-busiest airport in the country.

CULTURAL AND SOCIAL LIFE

Since 1980 various district and community organizations, supported by the *Kulturreferat* (the department of cultural affairs), have attempted to rediscover the folk traditions of the Munich area. Today there are 50 associations furthering local traditions and 55 folk-dress clubs. Folk costume is not uncommon in Munich; women frequently wear *Dirndl,* and men sport *Lederhosen,* knee-length leather pants, hunters' jackets, and green, pointed hats. The *Lederhosen* tradition was not common for men in pre-1830s Munich; instead, they typically wore top hats, long coats, and cloth pants. Rather, the *Lederhosen* style was a late import from the Alps to the south. Wearing the traditional costume of Munich at formal oc-

© ADAM WOOLFITT/CORBIS

Two men in traditional *lederhosen* walk toward a McDonald's restaurant in Munich, Germany.

casions has become acceptable again. Among the upper class it is considered fashionable for women and men to wear a refined form of the Alpine *Tracht* (costume), in which *Loden* (a sturdy woolen cloth), stylishly tailored into jackets or capes, plays an important part.

As a metropolis (some say it is the most Paris-like of all German cities in its pace and atmosphere) Munich exhibits a variety of cultural characteristics. Residents of Munich generally share with Bavarians a tendency to be fun-loving and hedonistic. However, as an urban variant of this mainly small-town Bavarian quality, the "real" Munich native (by reputation) also grumbles and complains a lot—about crowds at the *Oktoberfest*, about the Föhn—doing so in a loud, yet *gemütlich* (easy-going) manner. Munich's excellent beer, wonderful music, top-of-the-line car manufacturing, outstanding sports facilities, and champion football teams contribute to the self-confidence and pride that characterize the city's natives. Yet, Munich natives are frequently critical of themselves and their surroundings. Munich's humor tends to be scornful of self and others, and is tinged with melancholy. Class differences are expressed through three major cultural themes: Closest to the Munich native core are the rough, unsophisticated, dog-loving families whom one encounters in beer gardens and cellars—the *Lederhosen* and *Dirndl* crowd. Next are the upper-crust and culturally sophisticated, who frequent the opera and boutiques along the Maximilianstrasse. Stylishly self-confident, some of them wear the casual, yet expensive *Loden Tracht* (costume) to symbolize their association with upper-class Bavarian society. Finally, there is the bohemian contingent. The bohemian scene used to be concentrated in Schwabing where it continues in cafés and street art displays, but it has expanded to Haidhausen, east of the Isar. This café crowd, Munich's cultural *avant garde,* has a youthful and vibrant quality to it.

Cuisine. Munich's food is decidedly southern Bavarian in character, emphasizing pork, beef, potatoes, cabbage, and bread. Favorite dishes include *Schweinshaxe* (pork knuckles), *Kalbshaxe* (veal shanks in pickle sauce), and *Schweinebraten* (pork roast). These are served with *Knödel* (dumplings, either potato or bread), cabbage in various forms, mixed green salad, and buns or pretzels. Fish including carp, pike, and trout, is served in place of meat, particularly for religious reasons in Roman Catholic communities. *Wurstteller* (sausage plates) are served with various garnishes, usually in the evenings. Snacks include *Leberkäs* (a spicy meat loaf), *Strudel* (stuffed rolls of thin pastry), and *Steckerlfisch* (grilled mackerel or herring on a stick). *Dampfnudeln* (yeast dumplings with vanilla sauce) are a favorite dessert. Late morning is the traditional time for Munich's most famous type of sausage, the *Weisswürste* (peeled veal sausages that are eaten with sweet mustard).

An entire culture has evolved around beer. Among the main types of beer, all brewed according to the Purity Law of 1516, are *Bockbier* (strong, served in the spring); *Dunkles* (dark beer); *Pils* (bitter, less malty than other types); and the most popular, *Helles* (pale ale), which is served in half– or full–liter mugs. Another favorite is *Weissbier*, an oxygen-rich, smoky brew that is made from wheat malt and is served in tall gasses, often with *Weisswürste,* at mid-morning.

A wide variety of international foods are readily available in Munich, especially Italian. Many traditional Munich restaurants and inns have been converted to serve foreign fare, prompting Munich's cultural affairs office to encourage the *Münchner Wirtshaustradition*. Out of nearly two thousand drinking and eating establishments, about one hundred are designated as conforming to the Munich tradition. Modern fast foods have made inroads in Munich, both in the Altstadt and the outlying districts.

Ethnic, Class, and Religious Diversity. Since the early 1990s the foreign-born among Munich's population have totaled about 20%. By far the largest group, about 30%, are from the former Yugoslavia region, followed by Turks (17%). Greeks, Italians, and Austrians make up the third-largest groups, about 7% each. Many foreigners live near the Altstadt's inner neighborhoods and in satellite towns to the north and southeast. Occasionally tensions flare between foreigners and locals, particularly when local right-wing elements are involved (including the Munich variety of "skinheads"). In most cases, however, relations are cordial, even if not intimate. Foreigner-born citizens of EU countries may participate in citywide and district elections even if they are not German citizens, and the range of city and state services provided to foreign-born residents is quite extensive. The city administration has an office representing foreign residents that reports directly to the mayor, and an ombudsman offers legal advice to foreigners. Since 1998 both offices have been integrated into an office of intercultural cooperation, in which the positive aspects of cultural diversity are stressed. Nearly 200 private and church-based associations, many affiliated with a specific nationality, help foreigners with legal matters and with securing housing and employment. A number of cultural organizations, such as the Deutsche-Türkische Gesellschaft and the Italienisches Kulturinstitut, try to bridge the ethnic divide.

Munich's elite (less than 1% of the population) is socially somewhat removed from the rest of the society, even though it is mostly a working elite that is active in politics, the commercial sector, and in entertainment and fashion. Its parochial nuance is the result of an adherence by some members to a Bavarian sophistication in speech and dress, known as the *Lodenmantelschickeria.* Residential enclaves of the elite can be found in villa estates to the east, south, and west of the Altstadt. Private- and public-sector white-collar workers make up the largest class (30%); this group ranges from professionals, high-level business managers, and public-service administrators to the middle class. Similar in its socioeconomic status is the *Mittelstand* (the middle- and upper-middle-class entrepreneurial group), which makes up about 10% of the population. These large groups are widely distributed among Munich's residential areas. They are found in condominiums near the city center, in new duplex and single-housing neighborhoods, in satellite towns to the northeast and southwest, and, in some cases, in villa neighborhoods. About 35% of the population are blue-collar workers, including supervisors, and skilled and unskilled workers. They often live in areas not far from the industries in which they are employed. Lower-level service workers, such as waiters in restaurants and sales personnel in stores, make up about 12% of the population. With the movement of the of the middle-class from entrepreneurial employment to service-sector employment since World War II, reaching the middle class has become more possible for lower and lower-middle class workers. Mobility has also been encouraged by increasingly broad educational opportunities. Many of the poor, about 12% of the population (25% of whom are foreign-born), reside in economically depressed inner-city neighborhoods to the east, south, and west of the Altstadt, and in subsidized housing in some of the more economically disadvantaged satellite towns in northern and western districts.

A center of the counter-Reformation, Munich remained exclusively Roman Catholic until the Napoleonic interlude, when Protestants and Jews were admitted to the city. While the Jewish community never numbered above around 11,000 members, the proportion of Protestants in the city reached 16% in 1919 (around 104,000 members); by 2000 it was 17%. From the beginning Protestants tended to belong to the upwardly mobile sector of the population, and continue to be over-represented in Munich's wealthier residential areas. The city, however, remains a predominantly Catholic community. Not only are 46% of the population Catholic, but the officially recognized religious calendar suggests a strong Catholic identity. Although church attendance among both Roman Catholics and Protestants is quite low, the churches are very active in charities; contributions come from a 5% church tax members are obliged to pay. Muslims are the next-largest religious group, represented mainly by the Turkish population. Also, denominations of the Eastern Orthodox Church are active in Munich. Munich was the first city in Germany in which a new synagogue was established after World War II (1947). The city's Jewish community by 2000 had about 3,000 members.

Family and Other Social Support Systems. The national trend toward smaller families, increased age at first marriage, and decrease in marriage rate also exists in Munich. In 1999, 45% of adults were single, 41% were married, 7% were divorced, 6% were widowed, and 1% were married but lived separately. Women average 31 years old before the birth of their first child, while about one-third of women never have children despite Germany's good record in providing child support and paid maternity leave. The average age at first marriage for females is 31 and 33 for males. Seventy-eight percent of the 726,000 households in Munich are one to two person units, 22% have three or more persons.

Up to World War II, the male-dominated nuclear family was the standard household type in Munich. A multiplicity of domestic forms has appeared since then. Today, 53% of all households are single-person units; these include not only widowed and divorced individuals, but also unmarried singles. Households formed between unmarried couples have increased in number. It is estimated that about 80% of recently married couples first live for years in such *Lebensgemeinschaft* (life partnership) households. Close to 20% of domestic units are single-parent households, most of them females with one child. Close to 60% of married woman under 35 with children are in the work force. For them the 38,000 places provided in *Kindergärten* by the city, churches, and other support groups are very important. On the other end of the age scale, the city and state maintain close to 13,000 places for care of the elderly in 68 institutions for those without a supporting family or an adequate pension. In contrast to foreigners from southern and eastern Europe, the significance of extra-family kin among Germans tends to be less important. Friendship networks based on work, neighborhood, and hobby are at least as important, as are the social-welfare services extended by the government through mandatory public health insurance, old age pension schemes, and youth assistance programs. There also exists a large network of church-sponsored charities.

Work and Commerce. Of the 665,000 civilians employed in Munich, 15% are self-employed, which illustrates the entrepreneurial climate found in Munich. Over the years there was a shift in Munich's labor market toward the service sector. Whereas in 1974, 58% were employed in that sector, in 1999 the ratio stood at 74%. Between 1990 and 1999 employment expansion was especially strong in business services, health care, education and publishing, and insurance. In the manufacturing sector most find employment in machine building and vehicle assembly (38%), and in the information technology sectors (40%). Women make up 44% of the workforce, ranging from 20% in industry to 50% in trade. Foreigners are concentrated in the building trades (27%). Working conditions are relatively good in all sectors; they are negotiated and maintained by industry-wide agreements between unions and management. Seven to eight working hours per day, five days a week are standard. Wages in Munich also follow industry-wide norms, with an average of DM5,000 (U.S.$2,500) per month for a mid-level industrial worker. Compared to the rest of Germany, Munich has a low unemployment rate, only 5.5%. Forty-four percent of the unemployed are women and a disproportionately high 28% are foreigners. Unemployment insurance—mandatory for all full-time employees—and subsidized retraining programs reduce the problems accompanying unemployment. With commercial and residential areas widely dispersed in Munich, many employees find it possible to live near their place of work.

The Altstadt, especially its pedestrian zone, is the premier retail core of the city. In the later decades of the 20th century a number of retail centers appeared in the city's outskirts. Department stores, hypermarkets, discount warehouses, and malls draw customers, usually by automobile, from throughout the region. Each district has several strings or clusters of restaurants, fast-food outlets, small supermarkets, and specialty stores to serve neighboring residents. Shops are generally open from 9:00 A.M. to 8:00 P.M. during the week and from 10:00 A.M. to 4:00 P.M. on Saturdays. Most businesses are closed on Sundays, the official day of rest. Munich residents also have access to public markets. The largest and most popular of these is the Viktualienmarkt near the Marienplatz, the center of the downtown produce retail trade. When in the 1960s and 1970s large housing developments and satellite towns were constructed in the outskirts, they were often undersupplied with shopping facilities. Since 1968 specialty markets, such as farmers' markets (produce) and *Öko-Märkte* (organic foods), are available in Munich. Flea and antique markets are also very popular. The most traditional of these, the Auer Dult, takes place in April, July, and October near the eastern banks of the Isar. Four weeks before Christmas a number of Christkindlmärkte operate in Munich, with the largest one on the Marienplatz. There toys, carved figures, and other seasonal goods can be bought while sipping mulled wine.

Arts and Recreation. Munich is the cultural center of Bavaria. With 59 theaters in the city, stage plays are widely available to the public. The Staatschaulspiel and the Münchner Kammerspiele theaters specialize in serious drama, and the latter also features *avant-garde* pieces. Comedy is enjoyed at the Komödie am Bayerischen Hof. There are scores of smaller stages that present experimental pieces, local folk comedies, and satire. It is the opera, however, that is considered the epitome of high culture in Munich. The prestigious Bayerische Staatsoper performs at the Nationaltheater near the Residenz. The upper end of the classical music repertoire is presented by the Münchner Philharmoniker at the Kulturzentrum Gasteig east of the Isar. There are 300 singing clubs and choirs, 150 amateur theater groups, and more than 250 folk music and dancing associations.

A number of cultural centers exist outside of the Altstadt. Among the best known of these is the Kulturzentrum Gasteig, located in a massive new building. Not far from it, on the grounds of a former factory, is the Kunstpark Ost. With 60,000 square meters (646,000 square feet) of space and 300,000 visitors a month it is the largest entertainment center in Germany. It includes 35 clubs, bars, and restaurants, and numerous discos and cinemas. Large rock concerts are usually performed at the Olympiapark. Disco, club, and jazz venues are concentrated in Schwabing, where (together with Haidhausen) the café and bistro crowd can be found. Munich's 84 cinemas are attended by 5 million viewers a year.

Although most of Munich's museums are mainly visited by tourists, especially popular among local residents are the Deutsches Museum, Alte Pinakothek, the BMW-Museum, Siemens Forum, and the Museum Mensch and Natur (natural history) at Nymphenburg. The Englisher Garten and adjoining Isar area are favorites for informal outdoor recreation. Despite efforts by the city and neighboring communities to increase the recreational attraction of the northern fringe areas of the city, the region south of Munich, with its lakes and the Alps, continues to be the main destination for residents on weekends and short vacations. Rafting along the Isar from the south to Munich is enjoyed by many. The Tierpark Hellabrunn, the largest zoo in Europe, is visited by many, and so is the Bavaria-Filmstadt at Munich's southern border.

Munich has a yearly cycle of events in which locals participate. It begins in January and February with a series of *Fasching* (carnival) balls and shows, and continues in April and May with a spring festival on the Theresienwiese. June and July are the months of the Tollwood Festival at the Olympiapark (a world cultural event with music and food), the Corpus Christi Procession in the Altstadt, and of the Christopher Street Day centered on the Marienplatz, which is one of the largest gay and lesbian events in Germany. At the end of this period a *Sommerfest*of live bands and outdoor sports takes place at the Olympiapark. From September to the beginning of October is the time of Munich's premier event, the Oktoberfest on the Theresienwiese. This affair includes costume parades, music, dance, and many rides. It is considered the largest folk-festival in the world, annually drawing some 6 million visitors who consume 5 million liters (1 million gallons) of beer. In November a six-day bicycle race at the Olympiahalle is accompanied by entertainment and food. The year ends with the Christkindlmärkte on the Marienplatz and elsewhere in the city.

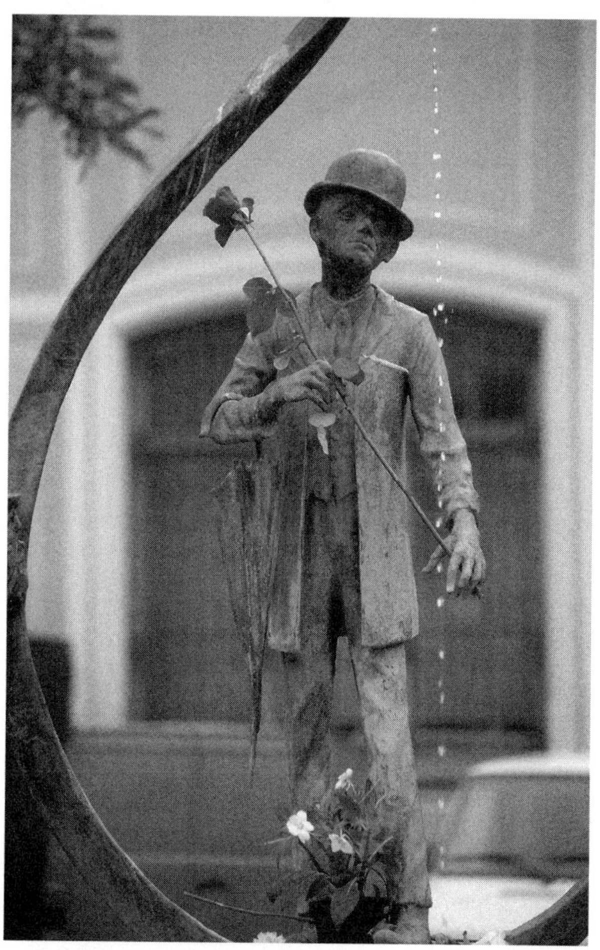

© ADAM WOOLFITT/CORBIS

A rose adorns a sculpture on a street in Munich, Germany.

Among the most popular informal recreational activities are hiking in parks and nearby forests, strolling on city streets to window shop (especially during Christmas time), meeting friends, and visiting beer gardens, restaurants, and cafés. Also popular is participation in sports. Altogether, Munich has 655 sports clubs with 350,000 members. With its Olympiapark München, the city has the largest sports and recreational complex in Europe, stretching over an area of 850,000 square meters (9 million square feet). Most spectator sports in Munich are carried out there. Munich's main football (soccer) clubs, TSV 1860 and FC Bayern München, play in the Olympiastadium, which can seat 72,000.

QUALITY OF LIFE

Munich's dynamic economy, favorable location, and rich cultural and recreational facilities make it one of the most pleasant cities in Germany. The quality of life is good. But Munich is also an expensive city. Next to Berlin, Munich has the highest rental rates for properties in Germany, and only in Düsseldorf and Frankfurt is the cost of owning an apartment or home higher. For the poorer sector of the population, this situation is only partially alleviated through public housing assistance. Close to 10% of all houses and apartments are social-welfare residences (65,000 units). Urban renewal efforts by the city, and modernization programs in and near the Altstadt, have improved the living conditions and the physical quality of the built environment, but they also have encouraged gentrification. The city administration is concerned about the increasing tendency of residential real estate to be converted to commercial use. A law regulating this process was implemented in 1972, and today 130,000 homes (most of them centrally located), within which 230,000 persons live, are subject to restrictions on use conversions.

Munich's population is relatively healthy, an enviable condition that comes with middle-class urban life in Germany. The average age of death is 71 for males and 79 for females, with the main cause of death (50%) being cardiovascular disorders. The overall good health of the population is maintained by subsidized public health insurance and services. The city has 56 hospitals with 13,000 beds.

Only 14% of Munich's urban area is green. Much of this open space, however, exists in high-quality and centrally located zones, such as the Englischer Garten, the Nymphenburger Park, and the Isar meadows. These park areas are key to the city's relatively good environment; they also provide recreational outlets for Munich's citizens. There are extensive forest areas beyond the city borders to the southwest, south, and east and wetlands along the upper reaches of the Isar, to the north. Munich's most pressing environmental concerns are air and noise pollution. The city is prone to inversions of hot and cold air masses, which, combined with a dense vehicular population and some dirty industry in the north, make smog a problem. Some improvements have been made. Sulfur-dioxide levels (especially damaging to forests) have been reduced to one-fifth of what they were in the 1960s. Lead pollution is down since the introduction of lead-free gasoline in 1975–1976, and carbon-monoxide levels have been reduced with emission-control devices in cars. However, some of these improvements have been offset by increasing traffic density. The goal of the city to reduce carbon monoxide levels by 50% in a decade will be a challenge. Traffic noise is one of the main complaints among citizens; some of the worst areas are along the Mittlerer Ring, the freeways feeding into the city, and the railroad shunting yards in the north. The city has a program to assist affected citizens, which installs noise-abating windows and builds noise barriers along speedways and rail lines. The quality of the city's drinking water is good. Because of the mountain-stream character of the Isar, and owing to restrictions on untreated water entering the stream, the pollution level of Munich's waters is considered moderate. Efforts are being made to renaturalize the river and meadowy banks without increasing the threat of floods.

About 150,000 (12%) of Munich's population are poor. In addition to church and other private groups, city and state welfare programs help this group. Public subsidy for general living costs is extended to 54,000 individuals, while unemployment assistance is given to 49,000 persons (in each case, about 4% of the population). Approximately 12,000 children receive regular public support of various kinds. Munich has some 5,000 homeless (0.4%). Most of them are offered accommodations in city-owned shelters and in other subsidized housing.

Of the 110,000 punishable offenses committed in 1999, 45% involved theft; there were 50 murders committed in that same year. Given the size and social diversity of Munich's population, and the fact that it is visited each year by millions, these numbers suggest that crime is not a major problem. Some districts do experience elevated crime rates. These include housing developments in northern, southeastern, and western areas. As is the case in so many of Germany's cities, crime near the *Hauptbahnhof* (railroad station) is also a problem. That is one of the reasons why the city administration plans to redevelop 150 hectares (371 acres) along the western rail track leading to the *Hauptbahnhof,* which will include a park, commercial space that will provide 11,000 new jobs, and housing for 17,000 residents.

BIBLIOGRAPHY

Ardagh, John, *Germany and the Germans. An Anatomy of Society Today* (Harper 1987) [entertaining survey of contemporary Germany, with some insightful comments about Munich's cultural and social scene].

Bauer, Reinhard, and Ernst Piper, *München: Die Geschichte Einer Stadt* (Piper 1993) [an excellent and detailed social history of the city].

Baumann, Angelika, ed., *Jüdisches Leben in München. Lesebuch zur Geschichte des Münchner Alltags* (Buchendorfer Verlag 1995) [Jewish life in Munich before and after World War II through the perspective of individual life histories].

Dumbach, Annette E., and Jud Newborn, *Shattering the German Night: The Story of the White Rose* (Little, Brown 1986).

Geipel, Robert, "Evangelische in München. Ein Indikator für Sozialräumliche Prozesse," *Bochumer Geographische Arbeiten* 50 (1989): 48–63 [a brief geographic history of Protestants in the Munich area].

Geipel, R., and G. Heinritz, eds., *München. Ein Sozialgeographischer Exkursionsfüher* (Lassleben 1987) [walking tours, with maps and photos, of Munich's *Altstadt* and districts, including their history, social character of their residents, and architecture; includes general chapters of Munich's socio-geographical development. A massive and excellent work].

Gordon, Herold J., *Hitler and the Beer Hall Putsch* (Princeton University Press 1972).

Gray, Jeremy, *Munich* (Lonely Planet Publications 2000) [one of the better travel guides to the city; includes good sections on history and the city's districts].

Herderer, Oswald, ed., *Bauten und Plätze in München: Ein Architekturführer* (Callwey 1985) [photos and ground plans of nearly 400 of Munich's more prominent buildings].

Kagermeier, Andreas, "Siedlungsentwicklung und Verkehrsmobilität im Verflechtungsraum München," *Geographische Rundschau* 50, no. 9 (1998): 494–500 [settlement growth and traffic in the Munich area].

Large, David C., *Where the Ghosts Walked: Munich's Road to the Third Reich* (Norton 1997) [analyzes the political and cultural factors in Munich and Bavaria that fostered the rise of the Nazi movement].

Laturell, Volker, D., *Volkskultur in München: Aufsätze zu Brauchtum, Musikalische Volkskultur, Volkstanz, Trachten und Volkstheater in einer Millionenstadt* (Buchendorfer Verlag 1997) [detailed description of folk traditions in past and present Munich (dance, dress, music, food), and attempts made to preserve them].

Marinescu, Marina, and Walter Kiefl, *Wir Werden Sehen . . . Das Leben der Griechen in und Zwischen Zwei Ländern. Eine Untersuchung über die Lebensweise der Griechischen Bevölkerungsgruppe in München* (R.G. Fischer 1990) [sensitive ethnography of the Greek community in Munich].

Rosenfeld, Gavriel D., *Munich and Memory: Architecture, Monuments, and the Legacy of the Third Reich* (University of California Press 2000) [partially pictorial account of how memories of the Nazi experience and World War II have influenced postwar reconstruction and new architectural works].

Seitz, Helmut, *Wie werde Ich ein Echter Münchner?* (Süddeutscher Verlag 1970) [humorous and perceptive account of what "real" Munich natives are culturally all about].

Useful Web Site

www.muenchen-tourist.de/englisch/index_e.htm [Landeshauptstadt München: the Web page of Munich, covers such topics as local government, recreation and sports, economic conditions, education, social services, urban planning, and tourism. Some of its content is available in English].

NORBERT DANNHAEUSER

Muscat
Oman

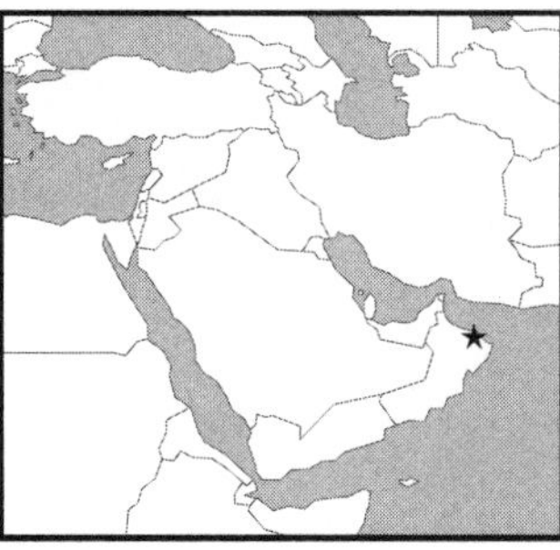

ORIENTATION

Name of City. Muscat is the capital of the Sultanate of Oman, which is the easternmost country of the Arabian Peninsula. The spelling *Muscat* is the most commonly used version of the city's name. English-language alternatives include *Musqat* and *Maskat;* however, these variations are rarely used at the present time. Modern transliteration systems that are taken from the Arabic language spell the name *Masqa. Muscat* is used invariably to mean both the larger metropolitan area and the old, small port of Muscat. Outside the city of Muscat, the term *Capital Area* is sometimes used. The name of traditional Muscat town's twin settlement is variously spelled *Matrah, Mutrah,* or *Muttrah,* and there are variant spellings in English for nearly every other location in the region.

Location. Muscat is located at 23°57′ north latitude and 58°36′ east longitude. It can be said to be situated in the (Arabian/Persian) Gulf, Middle East, and Southwest Asia regions.

Population. The 1993 census (Oman's first and only comprehensive census to date) enumerated a population of 622,506 for the Muscat Governorate (consisting of the capital city of Muscat and its surrounding areas). Of this number, 53% were Omani nationals.

Distinctive and Unique Features. Since 1970, the Muscat capital region has expanded greatly in population and size. While the name *Muscat* now applies to the entire metropolitan area, it also refers more specifically to the small town of Muscat. Muscat town, like its sister town of Matrah, was estab-

© ARTHUR THEVENART/CORBIS

Shadows create a pattern on the facade of an old house in Muscat, Oman.

lished as a seaport, but it is geographically constrained on all sides by abrupt, barren mountains. As a consequence, most government offices, businesses, and residences have moved out of Muscat town. Although the seafront al-'Alam Palace theoretically remains the seat of the sultan (the ruler of the country), the present sultan spends very little time in Muscat town. Only the ministry of national economy remains in the old town, and all embassies have been relocated in other nearby developments. Muscat town retains some features of its historical uniqueness, such as the walls that encircle the old part of the town and the two Portuguese forts built in the 16th–17th century, which perch on summits overlooking the harbor. Traditional architecture depended on thick walls and high ceilings to ameliorate the effects of the town's extremely hot and humid summer weather. Only a few older houses, dating to the early 19th century, still exist, and most of the town's mosques—like the palace and the town walls and gates—have been rebuilt in the last several decades. Other features, such as the old market area and a number of farms outside the walls, have disappeared as well. The presence of hills and mountains paralleling the coast has dictated a ribbonlike development whereby urban expansion has flowed into the immediate hinterland and especially along the seacoast to the west of Muscat town and Matrah.

Attractions of the City. Oman is a modest oil producer, although not a member of the Organization of the Petroleum Exporting Countries (OPEC), with crude-oil production scheduled to reach 900,000 barrels per day in 2002. This has given rise to a market-driven economy based largely on consumer imports, but the country's principal seaport, at Mina al-Sultan Qaboos in the Muscat area, faces stiff competition from the region's major entrepôt at Dubai in the adjacent United Arab Emirates. The country mined small amounts of copper until recently and continues to smelt imported copper ore. Recent economic developments have included completion of a terminus for the export of liquefied natural gas and the construction of a large container transshipment port. None of these activities are located in the Muscat area, however, which continues to depend on government spending as its economic engine. Oman was admitted to the World Trade Organization in October 2000. Once famously closed to the outside world, Oman has in recent years encouraged tourism. Attractions include good beaches, the exploration of mountains and sand deserts, the old town of Muscat, exotic shopping in the markets at Matrah and in the interior of the country, and visits to the magnificent forts scattered around the countryside.

Relationships Between the City and the Outside. Most of the metropolitan area of Muscat dates only from the last three decades of the 20th century and so exhibits a modern, cosmopolitan look. Much of its population has resulted from an inflow of Omanis from elsewhere in the country. But the overall cosmopolitan atmosphere is reflected by the city's other inhabitants. South Asia—particularly the southern Indian states of Kerala and Tamil; Sri Lanka; and Pakistan—produces the largest numbers of expatriates. There are also significant numbers of Arabs from nearly every Arab country but especially from Egypt, Lebanon, and Sudan. Most Western nations, as well as other Asian nations, such as Japan and the Philippines, are represented in Muscat's population, although the British influence is particularly noticeable. Oman's historical connection with Zanzibar and other parts of East Africa has resulted in a number of Omanis with African blood; many of these tend to be concentrated in the Muscat region.

Major Languages. Arabic is the official language of Oman and the spoken language of nearly all of its citizens. English, however, is widely spoken, especially by educated Omanis, and serves as the principal lingua franca of commerce, since Muscat's inhabitants speak a great number of languages. Urdu is the capital's second lingua franca. Some

Omanis of Muscat speak Baluchi or Swahili as their first language. Other languages often heard include Malayalam, Tamil, Hindi, Sinhalese, Pushtu, Baluchi, Persian, Dutch, French, and German.

HISTORY

The Origin of the City. Although Muscat appears to have been founded more than 2,000 years ago, very little of its history is known before the Portuguese conquest in 1507. When Portuguese fortunes in the Gulf region declined toward the end of that century, Muscat became their principal base in the region until Omanis regained control of the city in 1650. Still, Muscat remained on the sidelines of Omani history until made the country's capital for the first time by the present Al Bu Sa'id ruling dynasty in the early 19th century. The old town of Muscat possessed a superb natural harbor, but, because it lay open to the strong northern winter winds, most maritime trade relocated to nearby Matrah. The economic decline of Oman over the century prior to 1970 reduced Muscat's population considerably; it revived only with the discovery of oil in the country's interior and the accession of the present sultan in 1970.

Migration: Past and Present. Muscat's location on the Gulf of Oman and Oman's age-old maritime interests have meant that sailors and merchants from Oman and Muscat established ties throughout the Indian Ocean. Muscatis played their role in the spread of Islam in East Africa and South and Southeast Asia. During the country's economic decline, Omanis, including Muscatis, ranged throughout the Gulf and the African littoral in search of work. Since 1970, however, nearly all Omanis have returned home and the country has experienced a tremendous surge of labor in-migration. All expatriate workers need one- or two-year visas, their ownership of property is prohibited, and acquiring citizenship is nearly impossible.

INFRASTRUCTURE

Public Buildings, Public Works, and Residences. The official residence of Sultan Qaboos, al-'Alam Palace, is found in Muscat, although it tends to be used for state functions rather than as his main residence. A few former family homes have been turned into historic buildings open to the public, such as Bait al-Zubair. Because Bait Fransa served as the French consulate at the turn of the 20th century, it has been transformed into the Omani-French Museum. The town of Muscat is now dominated mainly by buildings of the Diwan of the Royal Court, the administrative organization that manages the sultan's affairs. Other museums and public buildings are found in Bait al-Falaj, the original military headquarters for the sultan's armed forces; in al-Qurm, where a popular children's interactive museum attracts large crowds of youngsters; in Madinat al-'Alam, where the ministry of information maintains a permanent exhibition of Omani culture and society; and in al-Khuwair, where a museum of natural history is housed. The Diwan of the Royal Court maintains a number of green areas in the metropolitan area. These include a park with children's rides along the corniche between Matrah and Muscat and a large family park on the western edge of the capital, al-Nissim, as well as the green islands at the major overpasses along the main arterial highway that runs from Muscat west to Seeb.

A number of small traditional villages have been swallowed up in the expansion of metropolitan Muscat, such as al-Qurm, Sidab, Bustan, Kalbuh, Riyam, Ruwi, al-Wutayyah, and Bawshar. Occasional touches of traditional life can be glimpsed in palm gardens and ruins of older houses. Surrounding them are modern—and in some cases "grid"-planned—housing units mainly of villas and bungalows. The latter are primary residences for the middle-class and wealthy Omani national and European expatriate.

Water and electricity are provided by the ministry of electricity and water. The first large project to furnish electricity to the Capital Area was the construction in 1976 of the al-Ghubrah power station and desalination plant. This has been expanded several times since, and both electricity and water (which is mainly desalinated) reach most residences in the Capital Area without interruption.

Muscat is linked by a network of roads, the most important of which is the four- to six-lane "dual carriageway" that extends from al-Bustan on the east, around Muscat town, to Seeb village 45 kilometers (28 miles) to the west. It is serviced by overpasses and traffic circles that allow access to side streets, all of which are paved. This is very much a "strip development," with the major shopping centers, parks, and open areas for the public easily accessible, if not actually visible, from the dual carriageway.

Politics and City Services. The metropolitan region of Greater Muscat falls under a governor of Muscat, who is appointed by the sultan and also

© NIK WHEELER/CORBIS

The buildings of Muscat, Oman, at dusk.

holds the rank of minister of state. His jurisdiction extends from the fishing port of Quriyat, some 80 kilometers (50 miles) southeast of Muscat town, to the area of Seeb on the west. This is the most densely populated part of Oman, and the governorate's realm of responsibility includes a multitude of government buildings scattered throughout the jurisdiction; foreign embassies; and the nation's commercial and banking hub, airport, seaport, military headquarters, and oil terminal and refinery, as well as more usual municipal concerns such as roads, parks, hotels, beaches, shopping centers, and far-flung residential developments. Services such as garbage collection, street sweeping, and beautification come under the administration of the ministry for regional municipalities and environment through a local municipality.

Educational System. Eradicating illiteracy has received high priority in each government five-year plan. As a result, Muscat has a large number of government-run coeducational primary schools and single-sex intermediate and high schools. In recent years a number of private schools have also been developed, and their curriculum is controlled by the ministry of education. The various expatriate communities also have schools that teach their national curriculum; these include British, American, French, Indian, Pakistani, and Sri Lankan schools. The Sultan Qaboos University was opened in 1986 and comprised a range of colleges, among them medicine, engineering, science, Islamic studies, and education. In the 1990s, several new colleges were added, including a faculty of commerce and economics and a faculty of Shari'ah (Islamic law) and law.

Transportation System. Public transport is not well developed in Muscat. The national bus company does operate a service linking Muscat town with the Batinah coastal area and the interior of the country. Moving around the metropolitan area can be managed with private taxicabs. Some popular routes are serviced by shared taxis and minibuses. Most residents prefer to navigate the city in private cars. Creation of a new highway parallel to the existing road is envisioned.

CULTURAL AND SOCIAL LIFE

Distinctive Features of the City's Cultures. Muscat is a city with a distinct cosmopolitan feel. Nearly 47% of its residents are expatriates, compared with only 26% of the residents in the rest of the country. Dress, in such circumstances, becomes a "badge," a marker of ethnic identity: European, Arab, Baluchi, Tamil, and Hindi ethnic associations are clearly expressed in dress. For Omani nationals, dress is more finely tuned, and the region of origin is clearly advertised in women's clothing and the way in which head and face covering is manipulated. Men wear long, ankle-length shirts (locally called thawb or dishdashah), the collars and sleeves of which are amenable to local variation. Head covering is required of men as well as women. In Muscat, the formal head covering for men is a turban, generally of cotton but occasionally of fine cashmere (*imamah*). This must be worn during working hours by all male government employees. A more informal head covering worn at informal occasions and at home and preferred by Omani males with cultural ties to East Africa is the embroidered cap (*qumah*).

Muscat is moreover a city marked by two overarching features: the separation of space into public and private spheres and the heterogeneous nature of its ethnic makeup. Among Omanis, men dominate the public spheres, although women are beginning to appear more often, engaging in public shopping or window gazing with their husbands, brothers, and sons. There is a "same sex" segregation in public, with men found in the marketplaces and women frequenting the health clinics and hospitals, where visiting patients is very much a female family duty. The private lives of the extended families are enacted behind high walls and not on general view. The city has few sidewalks. Those areas set out for strolling such as the public gardens and the oceanfront are dominated by expatriates, particularly from the Indian subcontinent.

Cuisine. Except in homes, there is no special indigenous cuisine in Muscat. What passes as local food actually owes much to the Indian subcontinent. Rice served with a souplike sauce, either of meat or of fish, is perhaps the most local of all dishes. Indian restaurants in all price ranges are very popular, as are a number of Western fast-food establishments, such as Pizza Hut, Burger King, and McDonald's. Muscat also boasts a variety of good French, Italian, Japanese, and Chinese restaurants, some housed in the city's five-star hotels.

Ethnic, Class, and Religious Diversity. A distinct ethnic composition is evident in Muscat. Omanis who have spent much of their lives in East Africa or have family there are labeled Zanzibaris by the rest of the population. They tend to speak Swahili and English at home and in private, and Arabic, when spoken, is not always completely mastered. The Omani communities with strong links to India, such as the Lawatiyah and Hindu families, tend to remain closely knit. They speak Sindi or Gujerati and English in private and marry among themselves or with Indian relatives. The Omanis of Baluchi origin are generally Sunni Muslims, while the Lawatiyah are Shi'ah Muslims. A small majority of Omanis are of the Ibadi sect, virtually unknown outside of Oman. Since 1970 Muscat's wealthy families have multiplied, and the trappings of wealth—large villas surrounded by walled gardens—have pushed them out of their traditional homes in the old quarters of Muscat, Matrah, and other settlements. The wealthy of the city are now found mainly in al-Qurm, Madinat al-Sultan Qaboos, and Shati' al-Qurm and on farms near al-Khawd and Seeb. At the same time, there are significant numbers of lower-income Omanis, some of whom live in public housing projects and makeshift homes in hidden areas of Muscat and Matrah.

Family and Other Social Support Systems. The extended family is particularly important to social and political life in Muscat. Although many nuclear-family units reside in single residences, individual family members keep in constant contact with each other either by daily visits or by regular telephone calls. In polygamous households (more prominently among the wealthy, but not restricted to them), the first wife tends to be a close cousin and the second wife a younger, less-close relative. The family and the kin group are the principal sources of support—social, political, and economic—for the very young, the old, and the ill. There are very few community organizations in the city. A few broad-based charitable organizations, primarily private family affairs, extend support to parents of handicapped and disabled children.

Work and Commerce. The government civil service is the single largest employer in Muscat. In recent years, the sultan has actively pressed for the expansion of private enterprise and employment. Government incentives and some financial assistance have been directed at getting Omanis, particularly the youth, to embark on business in the private sector. Most industry is concentrated in or near the Capital Area, as is most commercial activity. Although 25% of the total Omani population lives in Greater Muscat, a large number of those who work in the Capital Area commute to homes in the interior of the country for the Thursday/Friday weekend. It is at the beginning of these weekend trips that men are found shopping for fruits and vegetables in bulk from the large market stalls that are set up along the highway as it leaves the coast and begins its climb into the interior.

Arts and Recreation. The General Organization for Sport and Cultural Youth Activities, founded in 1990, is located in Muscat. It is an autonomous body that coordinates the activities of 52 sports clubs throughout the country. Soccer, tennis, hockey, and volleyball are among the most popular sports. Until 1994 women did not take part in sports, but now they participate in volleyball, basketball, squash, tennis, and table tennis. In 1985 the sultan commissioned the founding of the Oman Symphony Orchestra, and in 1987 it gave its first performance. It continues to perform on numerous occasions each year. In the evenings, men of all ages tend to congregate at the beaches and in grassy areas along the roads to talk, play cards, and occasionally play music.

QUALITY OF LIFE

Muscat is an affordable city for the middle-class expatriate or wealthy Omani. For those in low-paid jobs, several members of a family group need to work in order to support the whole unit. Lower-income Omani men who had migrated from the interior often share crowded accommodations to save money. It is a city with little pollution and an interest in being and keeping clean. Most contagious diseases have been controlled: no cases of poliomyelitis or diphtheria have been reported since 1995, and only 126 cases of malaria were reported in 1996, down from 32,000 in 1990. Infant mortality has likewise decreased from 110 per thousand in 1972 to 18 per thousand in 1996. Life expectancy has risen dramatically. Crimes are not regularly reported in the press, and in the Capital Area there seems to be no homelessness and poverty is not visible.

FUTURE OF THE CITY

Much of Muscat's infrastructure was put in place during the period of oil boom in the late 1970s and early 1980s. Rapid expansion is placing stress on such services as electricity and the traffic system, and the problem is likely to get worse as time goes on. The government's stated goal is to provide employment for young Omanis, especially by replacing expatriate workers, but demand remains greater for expatriates even as some Omanis resist taking low-prestige jobs. Although women in Oman have more freedom to move about and work than elsewhere in the Gulf, they are discouraged from taking up many occupations despite the fact that their doing so would reduce requirements for expatriate workers. The government actively seeks to spread economic and industrial development throughout the country, in part to mitigate migration to the capital. While Muscat can be expected to grow physically in the coming decades, its population growth will probably slow.

BIBLIOGRAPHY

Bhacker, M. Reda, *Trade and Empire in Muscat and Zanzibar: The Roots of British Domination* (Routledge 1992).

Costa, Paolo M., "Historical Interpretation of the Territory of Muscat," *Oman Studies: Papers on the Archaeology and History of Oman,* ed. by Paolo M. Costa and Maurizio Tosi, vol. 63 of *Serie Orientale Roma* (Instituto Italiano per il Medio ed Estremo Oriente 1989).

Hawley, Donald, *Oman and its Renaissance* (Stacey International 1995).

Peterson, J. E., *Oman in the Twentieth Century: Political Foundations of and Emerging State* (Barnes and Noble 1978).

Scholz, Fred, *Muscat—Sultanat Oman: Geographische Skizze einer einmaligen arabischen Stadt* (Das Arabische Buch 1990).

Skeet, Ian, *Oman: Politics and Development* (Macmillan 1992).

Wace, Barbara, "Master Plan for Muscat and Oman," *Geographical Magazine,* vol. 41, no. 12 (September 1969): 892–905.

Wilkinson, John C., *The Imamate Tradition of Oman* (Cambridge University Press 1987).

Wilkinson, J. C., "Maskat," *Encyclopedia of Islam,* 2d ed. (E. J. Brill 1989).

DAWN CHATTY *and* J. E. PETERSON

Nairobi

Kenya

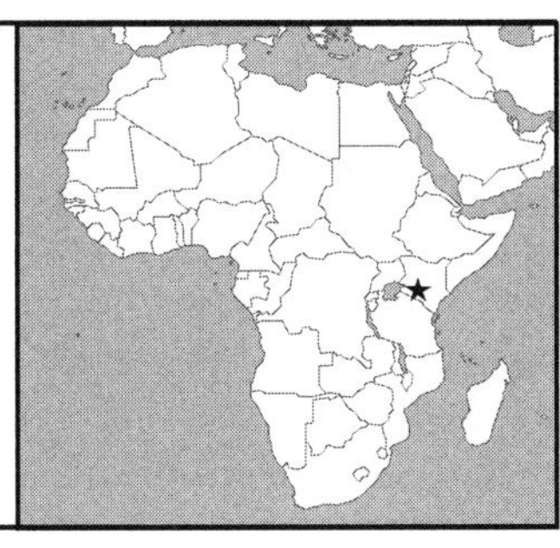

ORIENTATION

Situated in the temperate highland region of Kenya amid the rocky terrain of the Rift Valley and stretches of savanna on the Athi plains, Nairobi is one of East Africa's largest sprawling metropolises. With humble beginnings as a dismal railway camp, the city burgeoned into the colonial capital and continues as the bustling administrative center of the independent republic. Nairobi has attracted a variety of peoples with diverse backgrounds, languages, and customs, adding to the multifaceted character of the city.

Name of City. The city's name is derived from a term used by the Maasai (Masai), one of the area's indigenous inhabitants. These pastoralists once habitually watered their animals at a stream running through the region and thus dubbed the place, *Enkare Nairobi,* or "cold water."

Location. The Nairobi metropolis itself constitutes one of the country's eight provinces and lies in the scenic central highland area of Kenya at a latitude of 1°17′ south and a longitude of 36°48′ east. Positioned at an altitude of between 1,500 and 1,800 meters (5,000 and 6,000 feet), the city extends over an area of 689 square kilometers (266 square miles).

Population. The population of the city in 1989 was approximately 1,346,000, and it continues to grow as people are drawn to the urban center. Between 1948 and 1962 the urban population was growing at an annual rate of 7.9%. This figure dropped to 5.8% between 1962 and 1969, and then to 5% from 1969 to 1979. Since 1990, the population has reached over 2 million.

Distinctive and Unique Features. Called the "City in the Sun," Nairobi daily receives approximately 12 hours of sunlight year-round owing to its proximity to the equator. Its lofty altitude makes for pleasant temperatures and even chilly weather during its rainy seasons.

Nairobi encompasses part of the Athi-kapiti plains, which extend about 2,100 square kilometers (800 square miles) south and southeast of the city. This expansive river basin is home to a plethora of animals, including the black rhinoceros, zebras, hartebeest, lions, and gazelles, which can be seen among the acacia trees that dot the city's game park. To the north and west climbs the upward slope toward the Kikuyu upland area. The grassy hills and rises of this highland flank the Great Rift Valley, a gargantuan fissure in the earth that spans thousands of kilometers across the face of East Africa and contains some of the oldest known fossils of prehistory.

Attractions of the City. Many people migrate to the city of Nairobi in search of a means to earn a living. Motivated by employment and educational opportunities, in addition to the attraction of urban life, many young people from the countryside flock to the city in hopes of participating in the cash economy and procuring a formal education. Landlessness and destitution as well as the appeal of an urban lifestyle also spur many migrants to leave rural areas in order to eke out a living in the city.

Along with rural migrants, Nairobi also attracts tourists and researchers because it offers a fertile field of natural splendor to explore. Its abundant wildlife and the impressive scenery of the park reserves provide an interesting backdrop for a safari, while the dynamic National Museum houses an extensive collection of the region's fauna and important prehistoric fossils from the Rift Valley.

Relationships Between the City and the Outside. As Kenya's capital, Nairobi has a myriad of links to the international community. A number of foreign countries have diplomatic embassies and missions there, and Nairobi serves as the global headquarters of the United Nations Environmental Program as well as the United Nations Commitment for Human Settlement. The site of regional centers of the World Bank, the city also has media links to the rest of the world through various international news agencies and freelance journalists.

Major Languages. Although the official languages in Nairobi are Kiswahili and English, the number of languages spoken parallels the diversity of the population. English is commonly used for communication, yet some people might be heard speaking the language of their individual ethnic groups, such as Kikuyu, Kamba, Meru, Maasai, Luo, or Luhya. Another widely spoken tongue is called "Sheng," an urban variant of Swahili. This language arose to bridge the communication gap between the children of migrants to the city who had to interact with other children from various language groups. Thus many of these young people became multilingual and created Sheng, which comprises a mixture of English, Swahili, and other vernaculars. First frowned upon by language purists as a corruption of standard Swahili, the dialect has recently become more accepted.

HISTORY

The Origin of the City. The city of Nairobi emerged in the wake of a significant administrative and economic shift from the coast to the interior of the country. Much of the main commercial activity during precolonial times centered on the East African littoral, which fostered the growth of large port towns such as Mombasa. However, when European settlers and traders began to move toward the interior, they erected camps that served as administrative centers in the provinces that they encountered. On the banks of the Nairobi stream, caravans would stop to rest and obtain supplies after a long trek from the coast. This locality became one of the administrative posts of the Imperial British East Africa Company, which developed to oversee the flow of natural resources out of the country and the influx of manufactured products into the region. The Uganda railway, constructed to facilitate communication and transportation between the coast and the hinterland, reached Nairobi in 1899, and the chief engineer decided to make Nairobi its headquarters. After being located in Machakos, the administrative center of what was then known as Ukamba province moved to Nairobi the same year, and the settlement began to gain political and economic importance.

In the city's nascent years, the cold corrugated-iron workshops, marshaling, yards, and terminal facilities were its only edifices other than the railway workers' quarters. These residences were strewn along a swampy stretch of land near a river on the Athi plain. Thousands of Indian laborers referred to as "coolies" were brought over by the British to help work on the railroad and were packed into the

© WOLFGANG KAEHLER/CORBIS

The Nyayo Monument dominates a park in Nairobi, Kenya.

substandard housing provided by their employer. The Indian workers set up a bazaar and quickly started to build a commercial base in the area. Unfortunately, the overcrowded and unsanitary conditions, coupled with the wet land, attracted rats bearing bubonic plague. Striking several times between 1901 and 1913, the plague crippled the Indian population in the Bazaar area. These sections of the inchoate town were even burned to combat the disease, and at one point, officials considered burning the entire city and rebuilding it farther north. In contrast to the Indian and African settlements, railroad administrators located their homes away from the malarial, rat-infested swamp and built lavish estates on the well-drained areas on the opposite side of the tracks.

The incipient urban center flourished despite problems of disease, sanitation, and intergroup conflict as the area became more cosmopolitan. South of the river, commercial farms owned by Europeans began to emerge and different groups set up villages that dotted the surrounding countryside. Some rudimentary steps were taken toward organizing Nairobi as a town when the first municipal council met in 1901. A small number of streets were laid, new buildings were constructed according to health codes, police were hired, streetlights were installed, and some garbage collection was initiated. When the East African Townships ordinance was passed in 1903, Nairobi was accorded the status of a township and delineated by a circle with a diameter of approximately 5 kilometers (3 miles). When the British government took over the area from a folding Imperial British East Africa Company, it became the capital of the English colony in 1907. Nairobi's status as the capital of the East Africa Protectorate, as Kenya was then known, was secured when it served as a military base during hostilities between Tanganyika and Germany. Trains, banks, water purification, and permanent buildings of masonry appeared in the commercial European district by World War I, and Nairobi graduated to the status of a municipality in 1919. The population skyrocketed as rural migrants made their way to the town and settlers poured into the Rift Valley. Between 1901 and 1906, Nairobi's population rose from 8,000 to 13,500. By 1912 this figure had reached approximately 20,000. As the city's population increased, problems with accommodating the new residents and the development of an infrastructure arose. Housing, sanitation services, and transportation were major concerns for administrators. Although it could barely house 50,000 people sufficiently, the city had a population of roughly 67,000 in 1946.

Spreading from the railway center, the city expanded in a piecemeal fashion without reference to a structured plan during its first 30 years in existence. No formal residential area or public housing was provided for the rising tide of workers filtering into the city before 1919. As a result, a number of squatter communities began to spring up, especially in the Mathare River valley. This outcrop of squatter settlements perturbed officials, who eventually authorized the building of dormitory facilities for male migrants. In these ill-equipped living spaces, the migrants were subjected to overcrowding and insufficient restroom facilities. The unsanitary public rest area, which served hundreds of people, was little more than a large tin receptacle that was infrequently drained.

Although Nairobi's population remained high and dense in some areas, the colonial government sought to preserve the vacant land around the city. According to the 1948 plan of Nairobi's structure, the city consisted of the eight districts that had appeared by 1906: the railway center; the Indian Bazaar; the European commercial district; the administrative center; the railway workers' residences; the

© LIBA TAYLOR/CORBIS

Workers assemble ceramic necklaces in a factory in Nairobi, Kenya.

dhobi or washerfolk's section; the European suburbs; and the military barracks. The plan called for the augmentation of main roads into wide avenues with grassy medians, landscaped traffic circles on the order of British streets, and large parks and forest preserves. In south Nairobi and Eastleigh, the refurbished and expanded Indian areas were a degree above the African residential areas, but not as elaborate as the colonial homes. Often equipped with septic-tank systems, these colonial houses with terracotta roofs and terrazzo floors sat on large estates nestled in the midst of gardens, expansive lawns, and sporting clubs. Europeans were allotted a minimum of 0.2 hectare (0.5 acre) per home, while the African areas, such as Pumwani and Pangani, sustained 12 houses per acre. Since their construction, the population of these areas has more than tripled and squatter homes have come to fill the available space.

In 1948 Nairobi held 48% of the urban population in Kenya, and after the colonial period ended in the 1960s, the city continued to grow. By 1969, 56% of Kenyan urban dwellers resided in Nairobi and the city's boundaries expanded to encompass the Kibera and Dagoretti regions.

Migration: Past and Present. Movement between the city and the rural areas is complex in Kenya and is governed by a number of factors. In some cases, movement is dependent on the farmer's calendar. During the 1970s, males still considerably outnumbered females in migration to the city. Their total increased by 176,000 between 1969 and 1979, while females increased only by 142,000. Many people retain ties to the rural areas through family and ethnic affiliations. Some school-age children are sent to the city to obtain a higher-quality education, while others are sent to the rural areas to escape the influences of the city.

INFRASTRUCTURE

With skyscrapers grazing the horizon, congested boulevards, throngs of people, busy universities, and *matatus* (noisy private minibuses that serve as alternative transportation to the city bus system), Nairobi has all of the elements of a sprawling metropolis. The heart of the city abounds with public buildings, shops and businesses, hotels, and restaurants. High- and middle-income housing ranges from large elaborate estates to rows of four-story apartment buildings. Unlike the more affluent, many poor migrants cannot afford the highly sought-after public housing. Urban land values increased by 300% in Nairobi between 1964 and 1971, and a great percentage of families were unable to afford even the least expensive two-room housing units in 1972. The central government tightened its control of the city administration, and with little funding funneled into the city's infrastructure, the inadequacy of city services in some areas, such as garbage collection, plumbing, and clean water, has fostered the growth of large slum sections of the city. These squatter areas stand in stark contrast to the higher-income residential suburbs as well as the thriving business and official districts of the city.

Public Buildings, Public Works, and Residences. Many of the official and public buildings in Nairobi lie in the bustling central region of the city. Haile Selassie Avenue, one of the oldest streets in the city, borders the official district. On this broad boulevard stands the American embassy and the antiquated railway station that helped foster the birth of the town. The offices of the president and the treasury loom on Harambee Avenue, as well as the 28-story Kenyatta Conference Center. This massive edifice is a landmark in Nairobi, and its distinctive cylindrical shape and large circular roof, resembling a mushroom cap, stand out among the square buildings. When it was built in 1974, the circular conference hall was the second-largest in the world. Numerous flagpoles as well as a statute of the late first president, Jomo Kenyatta, precede the Parliament buildings and law courts. Other buildings in the area include the National Archives, which is open to the public, and City Hall.

Unlike its public buildings, housing in Nairobi remains scant in relation to its growing number of inhabitants. In 1971 an estimated one-third of the city's residents lived in squatter villages and others resided in dilapidated, overcrowded, and poorly serviced housing. Owing to a lack of resources, poor planning, and bureaucratic politics, previous plans to build low-income housing failed. Thus the city still grapples with providing housing for people inhabiting the substantial slums.

Politics and City Services. At its inception during the turn of the 20th century, Nairobi's government consisted of a township committee comprising two Europeans; two Asians, as Indians were called; and the subcommissioner of Ukamba province. To protect their interests, the European settlers established a Legislative Council in 1906, which had a persuasive influence on the colonial administration. A municipal council was formed in 1919, which by 1927 was predominantly European and based on the Johannesburg model of minority rule. By 1925, Africans had gained some political representation on the local level with the creation of Native Councils, which consisted of chiefs selected by the colonial administration. Nairobi was not officially recognized as a city until 1949, when it was granted a royal charter by Great Britain. The first African was appointed to the Legislative Council in 1944, and not until 1951 and 1957, respectively, did an African sit on the Executive Council and in the legislature. Much of the city's revenue derived from poll or hut taxes shouldered by the African population, who hardly received housing or city services. This group was still disproportionately taxed until independence in the early 1960s. When the government fell to African rule after independence, Kenya implemented a parliamentary government led by President Jomo Kenyatta, the famed former leader of the Kenya African Union. Although it was a multiparty state at the dawn of independence, Kenya was dominated by a single party, the Kenya African National Union, from 1969 to 1982, when it was made a one-party government, a circumstance that persisted until 1991.

Headed by a mayor, the elected city council governed Nairobi from 1963 to 1983, when, as the result of management problems, the council was suspended and replaced by an appointed commission. The transition from a settler-dominated city government to an African administration occurred rapidly but not without some problems. Nairobi's new administrators inherited the same task of remedying housing shortages and providing adequate services that had faced the colonial regime.

With funding from the World Bank and the central government, public housing projects were initiated to develop the city's large squatter areas. These projects failed, the victims of poor planning and management. Although the tourist areas and areas inhabited by the elite have adequate drainage and sewage systems, decent water supplies, and various other city services, slum sections occupied by a large proportion of the population lack these basic necessities.

Educational System. To many people in Nairobi, education is seen as an important avenue to improving their life situation. During the colonial era, however, Africans had little chance of obtaining a quality education in the city. The general policy of segregation implemented by the British administration promoted European, and to a lesser degree Asian and Arab, education over that of the African population. Each group attended separate schools, with the best facilities reserved for Europeans, who received the most rigorous curriculum. Much of the responsibility for educating African children was placed on missionary schools: less than 1% of African children attended government institutions in 1931. Compared with the expenditure for African education in 1955, the government spent 14 times as much for European children and 3.5 times as much for Asian children.

At independence the government adopted the British model of education in which students received seven years of elementary school, four years of secondary school, two years of advanced secondary school, and three years of university training. Primary school was customarily called standard 1–7, and secondary school was form 1–4 or "O level" for ordinary and form 5-6 or "A level" for advanced. Students were required to pass national exams to move to a different level.

The 7-4-2-3 system was changed to the 8-4-4 system, characteristic of that of the United States, in the 1980s. With the shortened length of secondary school, from six years to four, a larger number of students became eligible to go on to university. Among the main universities in Nairobi are the University of Nairobi, which opened in 1970, and Kenyatta University College, which was first intended as a teacher-training college in 1872. Education, however, can present an expensive, almost unbearable expense to poor Kenyan families. Students are required to purchase uniforms and books and to pay registration fees, which affords only some children in low-income families the opportunity to attend school.

Transportation System. In order to get to work, school, and other places of interest or necessity, a number of ways to travel exist in the city of Nairobi. The first two buses appeared on the streets in 1934 after people had to rely on automobiles and other forms of transportation to get about. Taxicabs can be found around the hotels and restaurants in tourist areas, and *matatus,* which operate independently and crowd people into the small seats as they speed through the streets, are commonly used by local people. Often heard blaring the latest pop music, with the vehicle's destination yelled out to pedestrians, the numerous *matatus* offer the cheapest—albeit most cacophonous—form of transportation in and around the city.

For international travel, the city has two major airports, Jomo Kenyatta International and Wilson.

A number of international airline companies use Jomo Kenyatta and Wilson service, as do many flying clubs and air charter companies.

CULTURAL AND SOCIAL LIFE

With its ethnically diverse population, Nairobi represents an amalgam of customs, languages, cuisines, and ideas. Historically a settler town, Nairobi reflects elements of the European influence from its colonial past as well as that of the expatriates who continue to reside in the region. The main ethnic groups that have historically made their homes in the region also add their own flavor to the cultural mélange, along with the substantial Indian population, and countless smaller ethnic groups from other parts of the country or other East African nations. All of these individuals attempt to hew out a living from the stone of life, whether through selling items at a street kiosk or teaching at a local university.

Distinctive Features of the City's Cultures. Nairobi's many ethnic groups contribute to the cosmopolitan nature of the city. The colorful streets offer a medley of dress, styles, and values. Among the variety, a Kikuyu man dressed in a Western shirt and pants may be standing next to a woman shrouded in a traditional *kanga* or *leso,* a length of brightly colored cloth often stenciled with a popular saying or Swahili proverb. This familiar and versatile piece of clothing can be worn as a skirt or a wrap, or even tied and used to carry children across one's back. It is commonly layered with other clothing or can be used as lingerie. A similar piece of clothing called a *kitenge* is also worn by many women. This stretch of cloth, often boldly patterned, is sold in standard lengths and can be used to make tailored clothing such as dresses, shirts, or whatever one might desire.

The influence of various cultures is apparent in the choice made by different individuals to don certain types of clothes. Western culture is apparent in the blue jeans, T-shirts, and baseball caps worn by many young men. Young women often opt for a conservative skirt that comes at least to the knee and a blouse. Dissimilarly, some groups such as the pastoral Maasai prefer to wear the traditional length of red fabric draped around their bodies and accentuated with brightly beaded necklaces, bracelets, and earrings and a hair caked with red ochre. In contrast, a graceful Somali woman may be simply wrapped in a thin sheath of cotton fabric.

Cuisine. Along with their distinctive modes of dress and other cultural traits, ethnic groups inhabiting Nairobi bring a multiplicity of savory comestibles. Restaurants in the city range from the Swahili cuisine of the coast to Japanese sushi bars. Spicy curries and *masalas* (a combination of spices) can be found at Indian eateries, while spaghetti and meatballs can be ordered in the Italian establishments about town. The city also has French and Ethiopian restaurants as well as places to get American hamburgers. Vendors on various street corners about town offer fresh corn off the grill, and ice cream parlors provide a cool dessert. A popular African dish is *nyama choma,* or grilled meat, and *ugali,* a grainy cake of thickened flour and water.

Ethnic, Class, and Religious Diversity. Originally, the region now considered part of metropolitan Nairobi was occupied by groups of Bantu Kikuyu farmers, Kamba farmers, and Maasai pastoralists. These groups intermarried, engaged in trade, and raided each other. When Europeans settled in the territory, established the administrative post that came to be Nairobi, and began to encourage Indian settlement to aid in constructing the railroad, they developed a rigid racial hierarchy. Although they never accounted for more than 10% of the population, Europeans viewed Nairobi as a "white" town, implementing segregation and other racial policies to restrict the movement of Africans and Asians. Since independence, Nairobi has increased in diversity through rapid urbanization. The Kikuyu remain the largest African group among other large groups such as the Kamba, Luo, and Luhya. Countless smaller groups have come to the city from various parts of the country and other East African nations. Many Europeans left the country after the political transition, and those who remained are largely dispersed throughout the high-income suburbs. Eastleigh has become the home of many Somalis and Ethiopians, and a lot of the more affluent Asian families have moved to the Parklands and Westlands. Large numbers of Kikuyu inhabit Mathare Valley and Kabete, whereas many Nubians from northern Uganda reside in Kibera.

The majority of the professionals and higher-income residents live in the growing estate areas of Nairobi South B and South C as well as in the plush suburbs historically reserved for Europeans, such as Langata, Muthaiga, and Karen. Nairobi's population primarily comprises of relatively affluent individuals and the very poor, with a small middle and working class. Middle-class neighborhoods include

Umoja and Buruburu. The sprawling slum areas of Mathare, Kibera, Mukuru, and Kawangare contain the overflow of the poor migrants to the city who are unable to find adequate or affordable housing.

Family and Other Support Systems. As in other parts of Africa, family ties are important in Nairobi and the sense of community is strong. Many city dwellers also have links to the rural areas through relatives. These links can foster migration to the city as family members already in the urban center can house their kin until they obtain a job and a place to live. Although kinship forms the basis for vital social networks in Nairobi, community also plays a key role for those living in the city. Men and women have created organizations, cooperatives, and rotating savings associations in order to help others improve their economic situations. Cooperative efforts such as buying communal property; manufacturing products such as baskets, pots, and other implements; and sharing the costs of materials are some of the activities of these organizations.

Work and Commerce. Individuals make their livings in Nairobi through a variety of creative means. In a context where the unemployment rate is very high, there are a considerable number of entrepreneurs called *jua kali,* or "hot sun," in Kiswahili, who attempt to sell their wares on the streets. Skilled craftsmen work scraps of metal into useful items such as buckets and charcoal-burning stoves, offering them at reduced prices. Kiosks and small stands made of old packing materials and other refuse line the streets around the shantytowns and sell traditional foods, fresh fruits and vegetables, and a variety of other products used in daily life. Purchasing items from these merchants usually involves a considerable amount of bargaining, since the seller typically sets an item at a slightly higher price than he or she expects to get for it. With the meager income obtained from *jua kali* activities and little hope of obtaining employment, many families find themselves relying on their rural backgrounds to grow some crops or keep some livestock in the city. Groups such as the Asian and Arab populations have prospered by opening a number of stores and shops in the commercial center of town.

Arts and Recreation. As a diversion from work, people can engage in a range of leisure activities around the city, including visiting museums, theaters, and cinemas, as well as attending sporting events and concerts. Most stage productions take place at the city's public theaters, the Kenyan National Theater and the Phoenix Players. In addition, the city has 12 cinemas, of which 2 are drive-ins. American, Indian, and English romance films are popular. Nairobi also has a thriving nightlife. Discotheques, beer gardens, and nightclubs abound, and people often linger in the streets until well after midnight in some areas. Music can be found everywhere in the city; whether blaring from a *matatu,* shop, or club, it mirrors the heterogeneity of the city. The rhythmically complex popular music of Congo (formerly Zaire) as well as ethnic tunes of the Swahili, Kamba, Kikuyu, and Luhya are prevalent. Hip-hop, soul, rhythm and blues, jazz, reggae, and rock are likewise very popular.

QUALITY OF LIFE

Although Nairobi's natural landscape offers a picturesque setting for the opulent homes of the elite, these rich enclaves stand in stark contrast to the city's overcrowded squatter areas littered with debris and makeshift housing. One of the largest slum areas in Africa, Mathare Valley, sustains a population of some 700,000, and many of these individuals are children. Unsanitary conditions lead to diseases such as cholera and hepatitis A, various types of infections, and other communicable scourges. The high fees related to education, the city's rapid urbanization, and the displacement of families in slum-removal efforts have resulted in 60,000 children living on the street. These "street children" resort to begging, prostitution, and scavenging garbage heaps to survive. Some programs have been implemented to help these destitute youth, and the government continues to search for solutions to the housing problems in the city. Also contributing to issues of sanitation are the close living quarters of many people who continue to lead a rural lifestyle. As vast numbers of its inhabitants make the transition from rural to urban life and city planners devise strategies for accommodating its population, Nairobi can improve the standard of living for its multitude of people. Despite its problems, this vibrant metropolis in temperate highlands of a scenic country remains one of the most elegant and culturally rich cities in Africa.

BIBLIOGRAPHY

Freeman, Donald B., *A City of Farmers* (McGill-Queens University Press 1991).

Morgan, W. T. W., *Nairobi: City and Region* (Oxford University Press 1967).

Ochieng, William R., ed., *Themes in Kenyan History* (James Curry 1990).

O'Connor, Anthony, *The African City* (Hutchinson & Co. 1983).

Robertson, Claire C., *Trouble Showed the Way* (University of Indiana Press 1997).

Watson, Mary Ann, *Modern Kenya: Social Issues and Perspectives* (University Press of America 2000).

Werlin, Herbert H., *Governing an African City: A Study of Nairobi* (Africana 1974).

TRAMAYNE M. BUTLER

Nanjing

China

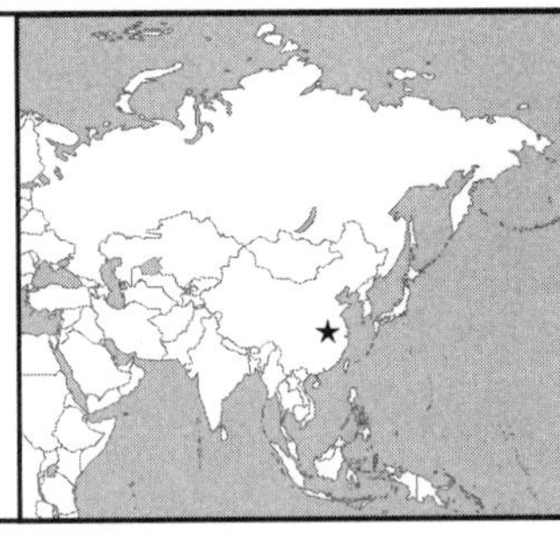

ORIENTATION

Name of City. Nanjing, formerly known in the West as Nanking, denotes the "Southern Capital." Throughout Chinese history Nanjing was known by various names, including Jinling, JianYe, Jiankang, Tianjing, and Shecheng. The city was first named Nanjing in 757 A.D., and renamed Nanjing again in 1368, 1421, and 1927. Nanjing is the capital of Jiangsu province.

Location. Nanjing is situated on the vast plain and the lower reaches of the Yangzi River in the eastern part of China, at 32°03′ north latitude and 118°47′ east longitude. Nanjing is 305 kilometers (190 miles) northwest of Shanghai and about 1,200 kilometers (745 miles) southeast of Beijing.

Population. According to the 1997 census, the total population in Nanjing was 5.3 million, with 1.85 million in its six urban districts, 900 thousand in the four suburban districts, and 2.6 million in the five agricultural counties.

Before 1949, like other cities in China, Nanjing suffered a great deal from political and social unrest, and it was not possible to obtain reliable population census data. According to estimates at the end of 1949, the total population in Nanjing was 2.5 million. By end of 1958, owing to the success of national economic recovery and development efforts, Nanjing's total population increased to 3.1 million, with an annual average growth rate of 2.26%. From the beginning of 1959 to the end of 1961, Nanjing experienced a significant decrease in the population growth rate and an increase in the mortality rate, resulting from the ineffectiveness of the state economic planning policy, specifically the disastrous effect of the Great Leap Forward campaign. During these three years, the annual growth rate in Nanjing was recorded at 0.66%. However, after 1961 Nanjing experienced another peak of population growth. By the end of 1972 the total population had reached 3.7 million, reflecting an annual growth rate of 2.48% since 1962. From 1973 to the end of 1993, owing to the implementation of national birth-control policy, Nanjing's population grew at an average annual rate of 0.93%, from 3.7 million to 5.1 million, a significant reduction from the previous period. A later population census also suggested that Nanjing's population was becoming older, with 13.23% of its residents over the age of 60.

Distinctive and Unique Features. Surrounded by mountains, with Niushou Mountain to the south, Zhongshan Mountain to the north, Tangshan Mountain to the east, and Shitou Mountain to the west, and with four major rivers and lakes crisscrossing the city, Nanjing historically has been described as a coiling dragon and crouching tiger. The Yangzi River, which is about 6,400 kilometers (4,000 miles) long and serves as the country's major commercial waterway, runs through the city from southwest to east, connecting Nanjing with the resource-rich and fertile Yangzi Delta to the east and the vast Jianghuai Plain to the north.

Nanjing lies in the north of the subtropical and torrential rain climate zone and it has cold winters, hot summers, and a short spring and autumn. The average temperature is 16°C (60°F); the average daily temperature in the hottest month is 28°C (83°F), and the average daily temperature in the coldest month is −2°C (32°F). Owing to the fact that during the hottest summer months the temperature in the city can reach above 35°C (95°F), with a frequent humidity rate of 90% and higher, Nanjing has earned (with Chongqing and Hankou) the reputation of being one of the "three furnace cities."

Nanjing is known throughout the country as a "green city," with 12% of the city area covered by forest, while trees or grassland covers 37% of the total area within the city. When walking on the main streets of the city, Chinese parasols and pine trees in orderly lines on both sides of the streets make pedestrians feel as if they are walking through green corridors.

Attractions of the City. Nanjing occupies a strategic site on the south bank of the Yangzi River, in the midst of a beautiful setting of lakes, rivers, wooded hills, and mountains. Since the 3d century A.D., Nanjing has been the capital city of ten dynasties and regimes. Because of its long history and its rich cultural resources and landscapes, Nanjing is regarded as one the "six ancient cities" (the others are Beijing, Xian, Luoyang, Kaifeng, and Hangzhou), and one of the seven cities in China most favorable to tourism.

The Nanjing city wall is one of the most well maintained ancient city walls in China. Built during the Ming dynasty (1368–1644), the original wall was more than 33 kilometers (20 miles) in circumference, 14 to 21 meters (46 to 79 feet) high, 14 meters (46 feet) wide at the bottom, and 4 to 9 meters (13 to 29 feet) wide at the top, making it the highest and longest city wall in the world at that time. About two-thirds of the old Ming city wall remains intact.

Besides the Nanjing city wall, there are more than 500 famous historical and scenic spots in Nanjing. The historical sites include the mausoleum of Sun Yat-sen (Su Zhongsan), the Ming tomb, the stone carvings of southern dynasties, the pagoda for Buddhist relics, Buddhist temples, tombs of the south Tang dynasty, the King Palace of Taiping Heavenly Kingdom, and the Rain Flower Terrace. Famous scenic spots include the Eastern Suburbs Scenic Area, the Qixia Mountain, the Xuanwu Lake, the Mochou Lake, and the Qinhuai River Scenic Belt. Sun Yat-Sen's mausoleum and the Qinhuai River Scenic Belt are among the 40 best scenic spots in China. In 1997 about 10 million people visited Nanjing, including 295,000 from abroad. By 2000, Nanjing was regarded as the second-largest tourist city (after Shanghai) in East China.

Relationships Between the City and the Outside. Because of its strategic location, its well-established infrastructure, its status as a capital of Jiangsu province, and its historic role as the capital city of ten dynasties and regimes, Nanjing has long been an important hub of transportation, economics, communications, education, and research in the eastern part of China. The importance of Nanjing in this region, as well as in the nation, is also the result of its ability to provide various natural and human resources to neighboring provinces and cities (including Zhejiang, Anhui, and Shandong provinces, and Shanghai), joining them to the rest of China. Historically, therefore, the social and economic developments in Nanjing have been intertwined with national social and economic development and have had a major impact on the region and its neighboring provinces and cities.

Major Languages. The Nanjing dialect and Putonghua (standard spoken Chinese, also known as Mandarin) are the two main spoken languages in Nanjing, with the Nanjing dialect the predominant language in everyday life. The Nanjing dialect, quite similar to Putonghua in sound, is based on the Wu dialect (Shanghai dialect) and the northern dialect. Because a significant number of people in Nanjing are migrants from all over China, people often have to rely on Putonghua to communicate. Putonghua has been recognized as the main dialect in all formal and public communications, including in schools, radio and television broadcasting, and formal public speaking.

HISTORY

The Origin of the City. In 1993 Chinese archaeologists discovered Homo erectus (Nanjing Man) skulls in Tangshan (now the eastern suburbs of Nanjing), suggesting that the area was inhabited by early humans as far back as perhaps 400,000 years ago. According to archaeological evidence, as early as 6,000 years ago there were villages in what is now Nanjing. However, according to written history, Nanjing was officially founded as a city in the 8th century B.C. For centuries thereafter, like many ancient cities in the world, Nanjing (along with its name) has been shaped and changed through wars, the rise and fall of dynasties, and social and cultural transformations.

In the early "Spring and Autumn" and "Warring States" periods (770 B.C.–221 B.C.) in Chinese history, the general area of Nanjing was divided and controlled by three states: Wu, Yue, and Chu. In 472

B.C., after Wu was defeated, the king of Yue began to build a city, naming it Yue City.

In 333 B.C., the king of Chu defeated Yue and took over the city. He built the "Jingling Castle" on Qingliang Hill, west of Nanjing city, and named the city "Jinling."

In 229 A.D., during the period of "Three Kingdoms," Sun Quan, the king of Wu, made Nanjing its capital and named the city Jianye, making the city the capital of the country for the first time. In 317 A.D., Si Marui established the Eastern Jin dynasty in China, and established his capital in Jiankang, later known as Nanjing.

During the so-called South dynasty (420–589 A.D.), which consisted of four dynasties—the Song (420–479 A.D.), the Qi (479–502 A.D.), the Liang (502–557 A.D.) and the Chen (557–589 A.D.)—Jiankang was the capital city. At the end of the South dynasty, Nanjing had become the economic, cultural, transportation, agricultural, trade, and industrial center of eastern China.

In 757 A.D. (Tang dynasty 618–907 A.D.), the city was named Nanjing. In 937 A.D. the dynasty of Southern Tang (also known as Later Tang) changed the city's name to Jinglin and made it the capital city until 975 A.D.

In 1368 Zhu Yuanzhang, emperor of the Ming dynasty, renamed the city Nanjing. In 1420 Yuanzhang's successor, Zhu Li, relocated the capital to Beijing, and left Nanjing as a "reserve capital." The Ming dynasty (1368–1644) marked another peak of economic and social development for Nanjing. With a population of over 400,000, the city of Nanjing became the most populous and developed in the nation. With Nanjing as his starting point, the sailor Zheng He visited countries in South Asia seven times, establishing close economic and trade relationships with many Asian counties that enhanced the economic development of the Ming dynasty.

In 1850 the largest and most successful popular uprising in Chinese history the Taipin Rebellion (also known as the Movement of Heavenly Kingdom led by Hong Xiuquan against the imperial government of the Qing dynasty) swept through much of China. Upon seizing Nanjing in 1853, the rebels renamed it Tianjing and made it the capital. In 1864 Qing troops, assisted by the western "Ever Victorious Army" (commanded first by American adventurer Frederick Ward and later by British soldier Charles Gordon) defeated the Taipin army and recaptured Nanjing.

In 1911 Sun Yat-sen led the first democratic revolution in Chinese history, overthrowing the Qing dynasty. On January 1, 1912, Sun Yat-sen took office as provisional president of the Republic of China and made Nanjing its provisional capital. On April 18, 1927, the Kuomintang government officially named Nanjing as the capital of the Republic of China.

© AFP/CORBIS

Soldiers carry wreaths at a memorial ceremony in Nanjing for Chinese killed there in 1937 by Japanese troops.

Nanjing was captured in 1937 by invading Japanese troops and victimized by one of the worst atrocities of World War II, the "Rape of Nanking." During the first few weeks following the Japanese invasion, more than 300,000 civilians were butchered by Japanese troops. Chiang Kaishek's government escaped the Japanese advance by moving west to Chongqing. In 1945, after Japan's surrender, Chiang's government returned to Nanjing and restored its status as the official capital of China. On April 23, 1949, Chinese Communist troops led by Mao Zedong defeated Chiang's army and captured Nanjing. Chiang Kaishek escaped to Taiwan, and the victorious Communists made Beijing the capital of the People's Republic of China.

Migration: Past and Present. Urban migration has been one of the most striking features in Nanjing's demographic development throughout its history. One of the most significant migrations occurred during the period of the Eastern Jin dynasty (317–420 A.D.), when hundreds and thousands of northerners migrated to Nanjing because of its leadership in the areas of agriculture, commerce, science, social development, and industry.

For centuries thereafter, Nanjing experienced large migration movements, especially when it became the capital city. After the Communist Party's victory in 1949, part of the government strategy included the influx of a large number of military personnel from all over the country, who remained in Nanjing to assist with the reconstruction of the city.

Nanjing experienced another migration wave toward the end of the 20th century that was a result of economic and social reform. Most of those migrants, however, were from neighboring rural provinces, and they migrated to Nanjing looking for employment opportunities.

INFRASTRUCTURE

Public Buildings, Public Works, and Residences. The urban structure of Nanjing reflects a set of distinct characteristics that come from over two thousand years of urbanization and development. During the Ming dynasty, urban construction reached its peak, and Nanjing was the most "modernized" city in the country. Many of the early buildings and constructions still remain, and they are major tourist attractions.

Before 1949 the majority of people in Nanjing resided in single-story brick buildings within or around the city. A century of wars and political and social chaos not only destroyed the ancient urban structure but also provided little incentive for the governments to improve the city's development. Like other major cities in China, Nanjing was crowded, and three or four generations lived under one roof, often in little more than 20 square meters (215 square feet). After 1949 the Communist government initiated some major reconstruction in the city, and living conditions improved significantly during the 1950s. However, following much social and political unrest, especially during the Cultural Revolution (1966–1976), urban development in Nanjing, as well as in the rest of the nation, came to a halt. In the middle of the 1970s, as a result of the expanding baby boomer population and a large migration from rural areas, residential conditions in Nanjing declined dramatically.

Since the 1980s, however, the city government has made a tremendous effort to reconstruct the city by attracting foreign investments and collaborating with major industrial companies in Nanjing. As a result, most inner-city roadways were built and expanded; over 80% of the old residential buildings were replaced by modern, high-rise apartment buildings; and the city's downtown areas were also renovated, with many modern skyscrapers housing banks, commercial centers, luxury hotels, and apartments.

The residential structure of Nanjing also has changed since the social and economic modernization began in the 1980s. Although many still live within the city area, an increasing number of Nanjing residents have moved to newly developed residential centers outside the city. To reduce the density of the urban residential population and to provide incentives for urban residents to relocate to suburban areas, these newly established residential centers feature shopping and commercial centers; convenient transportation systems, which often provide free services for residents to commute to and from the city; and, most important, these housing units are more spacious than those in the city.

Similar to other cities in China, the allocation of public housing in Nanjing comes from two major sources: the city housing department, and the work unit (owned by the city or the national government) in which a resident is an employee. However, many residents receive their housing assignments from the city government since only large companies can afford to provide housing for their employees. Most residents rent, not own, their apartments, and they have little or no choice about the size or the location of their homes: they feel lucky enough if they can get one. Especially for newly married couples, a public housing assignment often takes years. However, if one of the married couple (usually the man) works for a large company, the chance of getting an apartment is much better.

As a result of housing allocation reform, the city as well as companies are beginning to provide commercial housing. City government and businesses have encouraged existing tenants, as well as potential rental applicants, to purchase subsidized "home-ownership-scheme" apartments. At the same time, numerous luxury apartment and housing units are available for those who can afford to purchase.

At the turn of the century about 2 million square meters (21 million square feet) of residential housing is being constructed each year in Nanjing; these projects have been ongoing since the 1980s, with a significant increase in construction every year. Average living space has increased to 9 square meters (95 square feet) per person.

Politics and City Services. Nanjing covers an area of 6,515 square kilometers (2,516 square miles), including 976 square kilometers (377 square miles) of metropolitan area. The city has jurisdiction over six urban districts, four suburban districts, and five counties. The six urban districts are Xuan Wu, Bai Xia, Jianye, Gu lou, Qin Huai, and Xia Guan. The four suburban districts are Yu Huatai, Xi Xia, Pu Kou, and Da Chang. The five counties are Jiang Ning, Jiang Pu, Lu He, Li Shui, and Gao Chun, in which most people engage in agriculture.

Despite the magnitude of social development and economic expansion that Nanjing has experienced since the 1980s, the political structure of the city has remained essentially the same since 1949. The main branches of the city government include the Municipal Communist Party Committee, Municipal Administration, and the Municipal People's Congress, with the Communist Party Committee having more influence than the others. The main responsibilities of the Municipal Communist Party Committee are to carry out the policies made by the Central (National) Communist Party Committee (as well the Provincial Communist Party Committee) regarding national as well as regional political issues, and regional economic and social developments; and making and approving social, cultural, and economic development plans. The general secretary of the Municipal Communist Party Committee is nominated by the executive committee and approved by the Provincial Communist Party Committee.

The People's Congress is responsible for enacting laws and national economic, social, and political policies; approving city budgets and economic development plans; and debating social, cultural, political, and economic issues and policies. Another main function of the People's Congress is to approve nominations for various city government posts, including the mayor and the chief procurator.

The Municipal Administration, which is headed by the mayor, is responsible for reporting to the Municipal People's Congress and to the provincial administration, which is headed by the governor. The Municipal Administration carries out various social, cultural, and economic development plans that have been approved by the People's Congress and reinforces its laws and policies.

Educational System. The educational system in Nanjing, as in the rest of China, is run by the state and consists of universal basic education, higher education, and vocational and adult education. Universal basic education comprises preschool (including kindergarten), elementary, middle, and high school. By 2000 there were 746 kindergartens, 1,541 elementary schools, 228 middle schools, and 97 high schools in Nanjing. Although in theory the universal basic education is free, because of the great variation in quality among these schools and the high degree of competition to enter the best schools, many reputable schools, including kindergartens, often require a considerable amount of "donation" from the family.

Nanjing is also a leader in higher education in China. There are 48 colleges and universities that enroll well over 110,000 students. These include Nanjing University, Southeast University, Nanjing University of Traditional Chinese Medicine, Nanjing Medical University, Nanjing University of Sciences and Technology, Nanjing Normal University, and Nanjing University of Aeronautics and Astronautics.

Transportation System. Throughout China's history Nanjing has been an important transportation hub. The Yangzi River Bridge, which functions as both a railway and highway bridge, links the north and south banks, providing an important axis of transportation in eastern China.

The transportation system in Nanjing consists of railways, waterways, air transport, public bus lines, and taxicabs. Nanjing's railway system plays a very important role in national transportation and is still the major means of transportation for people traveling outside the city. Nanjing's two railroad stations receive and send more than 350 trains daily and carry more than 3 million passengers yearly.

Nanjing has one of the largest ports in Asia. Built on the banks of the Yangzi River and only 347 kilometers (216 miles) from the ocean, the port is important for both domestic and international transportation. The port is 98 kilometers (61 miles) in length and has over 200 docks, including 25 docks for ships of over 10,000 tons. In 1995 the port of Nanjing handled 50.40 million tons of freight.

Nanjing International Airport, located about 35 kilometers (22 miles) from downtown Nanjing, is about 10 square kilometers (4 square miles) in size. It handles more than 30 airlines leading to all major cities in China, and it receives and sends 17 direct flights to and from Hong Kong weekly.

Nanjing also has begun to establish a comprehensive and modern road system. There are four major national highways that go through Nanjing and nine interprovincial highways. More than 60 bus lines go in and out of the city daily, to all parts of the province as well as to neighboring provinces.

Since 1985 Nanjing's inner-city transportation system has been transformed significantly. Although inner-city bus lines and bicycles still remain important modes of transportation for the average city dweller, taxicabs are quickly becoming an alternative means of public transportation in the city. There are 42 state-run bus lines with 2,400 buses (excluding privately owned and run buses), and more than 8,000 taxicabs provide 24-hour service in the city. Although the number of privately owned automobiles increased in the late 20th century, the majority of Nanjing's residents still rely on public transportation and bicycles to commute.

CULTURAL AND SOCIAL LIFE

Distinctive Features of the City's Cultures. Nanjing is a city with a galaxy of talent and distinctive social and cultural characteristics. It is highly developed in the areas of science, technology, and education, and it is home to many talented scholars and personalities. There are 48 colleges and universities; 508 scientific research institutions; and more than 320,000 scientists, engineers, and technicians. As the provincial capital and one of China's top cities in higher education and scientific research, Nanjing leads China in social and economic development and modernization.

As one of China's six famous ancient cities, the landscapes and customs of Nanjing reflect thousands of years of social and cultural traditions. The people and the culture of Nanjing are considered to be "moderate"; residents of the city have a great sense of pride in its history and tend to preserve the traditional ways of life, while at the same time striving for modernization. To outsiders the people of Nanjing are progressive in their outlook, and moderately conservative in their social interactions. They are warm and frank, and yet sensitive to their social and cultural traditions. The people of Nanjing also place a great deal of importance on the values of family and the needs of kin and friends.

Cuisine. Nanjing, known as "a land of fish and rice," has a distinctive and reputable dining culture. The city offers not only a wide range of popular cuisines representing various traditions of China but also its own cuisine, which integrates the methods of northern and southern cuisines with local characteristics and is highly regarded in the region. Because of its rich water resource, one of the characteristics of Nanjing cuisine is the use of a number of aquatic vegetables that are locally produced, such as water celery, lotus root, water chestnut, wild rice stem, and arrowhead. It is known to the nation that Nanjing has a long history of making the finest snack foods, including various pastries, rice cakes, candies, and roasted seeds and nuts, and the city is particularly well known for its pressed salted duck.

For the people of Nanjing the culture of dining is very important in both family and social life. Collective dining not only serves as a way to maintain close relations with family members, relatives, and friends and a way to begin a new relationship or to resolve a conflict, it is also the proper way to begin a business relationship and to make a business deal. The culture of "eat first and talk later" encouraged the restaurant business to flourish throughout the city, creating intense competition for high-quality dining experiences, as well as high prices. At the end of the 20th century, as a result of the city's booming economy and the changing lifestyle, many families began to break away from traditional ways of dining; instead of preparing major meals at home, they often visit restaurants to celebrate holidays and to host important social events. During breakfast and dinner hours, hundreds of restaurants packed with people serve a full range of Chinese cuisines. Many small and privately operated restaurants and street food vendors serve food until three o'clock in the morning.

Ethnic, Class, and Religious Diversity. Similar to the ethnic composition of China's general population, Nanjing's ethnic makeup is predominately Han Chinese, with small distributions of other ethnic groups, mainly the Hui (Muslim), Manchu, Zhuang, Korean, and Bai. Most members of these ethnic groups are third and forth generation, and there are minimal differences between them and the Han.

Before the social and economic reform in 1980s, the economic structure in Nanjing, as well as in the country as a whole, was dominated by the state-planned economy, and a private sector practically did not exist in the economic structure. People's salaries were fixed, based on their years of working, the type of jobs they held, and their education backgrounds. Therefore, there was little economic class distinction within the population of Nanjing. It was one's political associations and position in the workplace that primarily determined social status.

Since the middle of the 1980s, the government has shifted its economic development policy from a state-planned economy to market economy, and it has begun to promote the development of private enterprise. The expansion and success of the private economy, which is to a large extent capitalistic, was instrumental in the late-20th-century social and economic modernizations. However, at the same time it began to polarize those who are economically well-to-do and those who are struggling to make ends meet.

Nanjing is the center for millions of Chinese Buddhists. There are dozens of well-known Buddhist temples located in and around the city, attracting vast numbers of Buddhists and tourists. Although ancestor worship and Buddhism are the most commonly practiced forms of religion, Christianity is also becoming popular in Nanjing.

Family and Other Social Support Systems. Family life is of great importance to people of Nanjing. Not only is family the primary source of educational, financial, spiritual, and emotional support but for most people in Nanjing family values and interests are the main considerations in their decision making. Filial piety, a thousand-year-old Confucian tradition, still is regarded as the essential social and cultural tradition and the key factor in intergenerational relations.

Although many young adults in the urban area, especially those who are married, live separately from their parents, they maintain very close relationships—especially since grandparents often provide child care. The extended family remains the dominant family structure for many Nanjing residents, particularly in rural areas where most families continue to follow patrilineal lines of descent and the patrilocal residential arrangement. In the urban area, however, adherence to these traditions is becoming less important. Many young and married adults choose where to live primarily based on housing availability rather than on physical proximity to their families.

Characteristic of Chinese culture, people of Nanjing are also very social-centered. Neighbors and friends, including coworkers, are the primary social contacts in people's daily lives. Such interactions not only provide individuals with social, emotional, educational, recreational, and sometimes financial support, they also play an important role in an individual's social and cultural confirmation. In addition, neighbors and friends frequently are the main consultants and mediators to whom individuals turn to help solve their social and familial conflicts.

Work and Commerce. The economic reform begun in 1980s drastically transformed Nanjing's economic infrastructure and development. With its unique advantages in industry, environment, science, and technology Nanjing has been listed 5th among the 50 most powerful cities in China in terms of its comprehensive strength, and one of the top 40 cities in the country with a favorable investment environment. According to the 1995 national index of sales value in manufactured goods, Nanjing was ranked one of the ten biggest cities. Nanjing is an economically progressive and important commercial and industrial center in the nation. It is also the second-largest international commercial center in the Yangzi River Delta area (Shanghai is the first) of eastern China.

The major industries in Nanjing include petroleum and refined chemicals; mining and metallurgy; manufacturing, including computers and communication equipment, electrical appliances, automobiles, and motorcycles; architecture and building materials; and such services as hotels, restaurants, recreation, and other tourism-related businesses. Many of these industries are supported by foreign investments or are joint ventures. Foreign businesses have played an increasingly important part in Nanjing's economic development. In 1995 the total value of imports and exports was $1.07 billion, with exports of $808 million.

Since the 1980s there have been some significant changes in Nanjing's economic development strategy in order to meet the increasing demands for consumer goods. As a result, much of the emphasis of the city's economic development has been placed on manufacturing and service industries. During the years from 1978 to 1993, the proportion of population engaged in the primary industries of mining and refining decreased from 42.5% to 29.4%, while the percentage of the population in the manufacturing industry increased from 37.8% to 44.5%; and that in the service industry increased from 19.7% to 26.1%. According to later statistics, in 1997 there were 0.77 million people employed in the mining and refining industries, 1.23 million in manufacturing, and 1.01 million in the service industries.

State industry prior to 1980 was the major source of employment for the vast majority of Nanjing's people. Economic reform and the growth of privately owned businesses have changed the employment structure. In 1997 there were 1.07 million people employed in state-owned industries, 1.54 million in collective (state and private) industries, 100,000 in privately owned industries, and 180,000 individual's were employed by foreign or jointly financed companies.

The average income per capita in Nanjing since 1980 has been multiplied dramatically. In 1980 the average per capita income was 500 yuan (U.S.$60) for urban workers and 200 yuan (U.S.$24) for farmers. In 1996, the average per capital income had increased to 8,000 yuan for urban workers and 3,000 yuan for farmers.

Arts and Recreation. Nanjing is considered to be a living museum of ancient architecture. Throughout the city there are hundreds of architectural sites, reflecting various historical and cultural eras and styles, that attract thousands of visitors each year. There are about 70 museums in Nanjing, presenting diverse forms of art and cultural history. The Nanjing Museum is one of the largest museums in China, with over 400,000 ancient artifacts.

The city's parks and other public spaces are heavily used. Especially during the early morning hours, many people of all ages gather in these public places to practice Tai Ji, Qi Gong, or to dance, sing, walk, and do martial arts and various other types of exercise. During the summer major parks in the city regularly provide outdoor musical concerts featuring local and national performing companies.

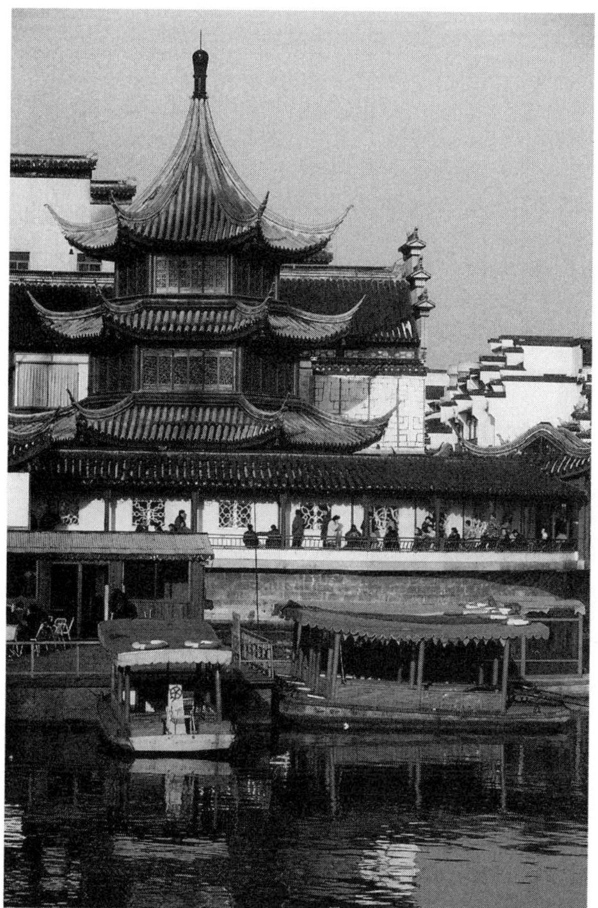

© KEREN SU/CORBIS

Traditional Chinese architecture may be seen along the waterfront at Nanjing, Jiangsu.

Nanjing supports over 30 local artistic companies representing a wide range of traditional and modern performing arts, from the Beijing Opera to modern dance. Some of these companies are popular not only in the city but also have gained reputations throughout the nation and abroad. Among them, Nanjing Acrobatic Company and Nanjing Youth Performing Company are the two most well known groups in the nation, and they often are invited for international tours.

Nanjing also hosts various professional and amateur sport clubs, including soccer, ping-pong, volleyball, basketball, martial arts, track and field, and gymnastics. Tournaments of these popular sports, organized by city and various community institutions, occur year-round and are among the most popular pastimes in the city.

During the year, Nanjing hosts various traditional and cultural festivals. Among them, the Yangzi Song and Dance festival, Temple Fair, and the Jingling Lantern festival are the most popular, attracting many visitors from both nearby and abroad.

Dining at restaurants and chatting at teahouses with friends and family are probably the most popular social and leisure activities in Nanjing. For the older generation, spending a couple of hours a day playing mah-jongg with friends and neighbors is considered not only recreational but also therapeutic. For younger generations, however, dancing at discotheques and surfing the Internet have become increasingly fashionable.

QUALITY OF LIFE

The quality of life in Nanjing has improved significantly as a result of the growth in the city's economy since the mid-1980s. The emphasis on a market economy, the privatization of previously state-owned businesses, and the increase in foreign investment have not only created a flourishing and competitive market, they have also changed people's consuming patterns from basic to luxurious. Personal computers, mobile phones, and other high-tech products are among the hottest items in the market. The average life expectancy of men and women in Nanjing is now 74 years old. The infant mortality rate is six per thousand births, lower than in most developed and developing countries.

Drastic social and cultural changes, however, especially with large numbers of workers laid off from state-owned industries and the influx of vast numbers of people from rural areas, have caused Nanjing to face a multitude of social and economic issues and challenges. The rapid industrialization, particularly the increasing number of automobiles filling the crowded city streets and the massive and sometimes out-of-control construction of office buildings and hotels, contribute to a very high level of air pollution in the city. Because of the decentralization of the health-care system, on which hospitals and health clinics must now rely to generate a large portion of their operating resources, many people (especially farmers, those who work for smaller companies that are unable to provide sufficient health insurance, and those who are self-employed, retired, and jobless) suffer from the increasingly high cost of medical care. Although the crime rate is rising, it is relatively low in comparison with other industrial cities of similar size in the world.

FUTURE OF THE CITY

According to Nanjing's development plan the city's objective for the first 15 years of the 21st century is to become a modern riverside city with a developed economy, combining the characteristics of an ancient culture with those of a modern, cosmopolitan city. However, to achieve these objectives Nanjing must depend on the continuation of economic development policies, and will also need to make greater efforts to develop adequate policies to deal with various social issues, including health care, care for the growing elderly population, housing, and political and economic corruption.

Nanjing will remain an important and attractive city in China, particularly in eastern China. Its primacy in natural resources, cultural traditions, education, technology, trade, and industrialization, and its strategic location, sizeable workforce and market will continue to help it flourish in all areas of social and cultural life.

BIBLIOGRAPHY

Chang, Iris, *The Rape of Nanking: The Forgotten Holocaust of World War II* (Putnam 1998).

Liu, Qinghao, "City Report: Nanjing City and Its Population Development," *The Newsletter of the Asian Urban Information of KOBE* (June 1998).

Peng, Peiyun, et al., *Encyclopedia of China Family Planning* (China Statistical Press 1997).

Rong, Bin, and Shidian Xu, et al., *Famous Cultural Cities in China* (Shangdong Friendship Publications 1996).

Ye, Zhaoyen, *Old Nanjing* (Jiangsu Artistic Publications 1999).

Yu, Yunxiao, *Nanjing: Past and Present* (Jiangsu Science and Technology Publications 1989).

ZIBIN GUO

Nassau

The Bahamas

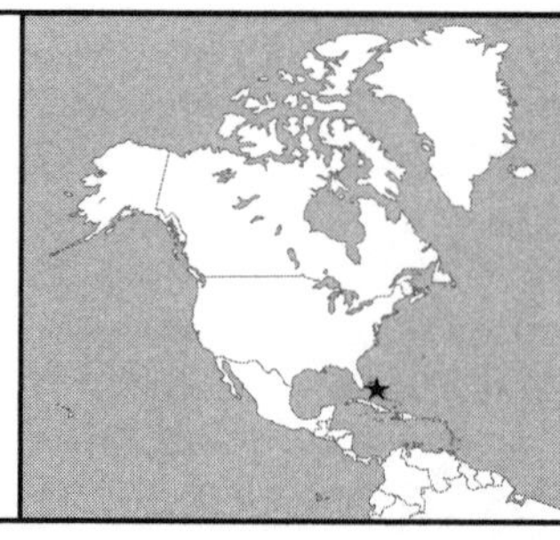

ORIENTATION

Name of City. Originally named Charles Town, in 1695 the city was renamed Nassau after King William III of Great Britain.

Location. Located in the Commonwealth of the Bahamas, an independent state made up of a chain of islands in the Atlantic Ocean, lying to the southeast of Florida and to the north of Cuba, Nassau is on the northeast coast of the island of New Providence at 24° north latitude and 76° west longitude. Although not technically within the Caribbean, the Bahamas is usually grouped with the other Caribbean islands, both culturally and politically.

Population. Nassau is coterminous with the island of New Providence, whose population in 2000 was 212,432. Although containing less than 2% of the country's total land mass, two-thirds of Bahamians live on New Providence. Most development is on the eastern and northern sides of the island; the south and west are more sparsely populated. Much of the interior is marsh and scrub forest. The island is made up of series of low ridges; its highest point is 37 meters (123 feet). Most of the population lives in the valley between two of these ridges—Prospect to the north and Blue Hill to the south. The population is diverse, 85% is of African ancestry, 12% is European, and 3% is Asian or Hispanic.

Distinctive and Unique Features. Nassau's most important feature is its harbor. Perhaps the best in the Caribbean, it features a deepwater port with a natural protective barrier—Paradise Island. The life of the harbor is tourism, not trade. Since the 1960s Nassau has been an important Caribbean cruise port, and as many as 10 ships can be in Nassau harbor on a Saturday. About 15 ships call on Nassau regularly with about 1.6 million cruise-ship tourists visiting annually.

Old Nassau, the central 20-block area along the wharf, still includes many colonial buildings, and Bay Street, the main thoroughfare, is lined with stores and restaurants catering to the tourist trade. While heavily influenced by the United States, Nassau retains a British atmosphere—cars drive on the left, the government is modeled on Westminster, and English is the official language. But Nassau also shows evidence of its role in the African slave trade, particularly during the annual festival of Junkanoo. With roots in the slave festivals held between Christmas and New Year, Junkanoo has become the premier cultural festival in the Bahamas. Nassau holds two parades, each composed of bands and dancers wearing elaborate costumes.

© PHILLIP GOULD/CORBIS

A resident of Nassau in the Bahamas participates in the colorful Junkanoo parade on Bay Street.

Attractions of the City. Although best known for its subtropical climate, duty-free shopping, gambling, and ocean beaches, Nassau's attractions are in fact much deeper. In central Nassau, many of late-18th- and early-19th-century buildings survive, including the legislative buildings on Parliament Square, the octagonal public library (originally a prison), and planter homes on Hill Street. Three 18th-century forts survive, including Fort Fincastle—accessed via the 66-step Queen's Staircase on the hill above downtown—and the much larger Fort Charlotte just west of the central settlement. Other 18th-century buildings open to the public include Vendue House, the original market and now the Pompey Museum of Slavery and Emancipation; and Balcony House, a Loyalist home. The new National Gallery of the Bahamas will be located in another restored mansion.

Nassau has few public parks. There is a small botanical garden near Fort Charlotte and the National Trust of the Bahamas runs a 4.5-hectare (11-acre) garden devoted to palms on the east side of the island. Ardastra Gardens Conservation Center has a small collection of native and imported animals with a daily flamingo show. Cable Beach and the beaches on Paradise Island are world famous and are now lined with resort hotels. Water sports—swimming, diving, snorkeling, jet-skiing, and fishing—are all available.

Tourism has made Nassau one of the major high-end shopping areas of the Caribbean. In addition to the duty-free shopping on Bay Street, handicraft vendors sell their wares at the Straw Market (temporarily relocated after a fire in September 2001). There are a wide variety of restaurants with seafood, particularly conch, a strong draw to the area. There is little nightlife in downtown, but the resort hotels offer a range of entertainment and dancing.

Relationships Between the City and the Outside. Nassau is dependent on the world outside the Bahamas; tourism and offshore banking are its two primary industries and together account for almost two-thirds of the gross domestic product of the Bahamas. More than 3.6 million tourists visited the Bahamas in 1999, 2.3 million of them (mostly from the United States) went to Nassau.

There are 415 institutions licensed to carry out banking or trust activities in the commonwealth; the vast majority are in Nassau. The Bahamian bank secrecy laws, and exemption from taxation, make the islands an attractive location for offshore banking, although the banking laws are undergoing reform owing to international pressure, especially from the United States, which is concerned about the Bahamas being used to funnel drug money.

The Bahamas depend on imports for most of their consumer items, agricultural goods, oil and petroleum products, and building materials. The Bahamas export some food products, chemicals (primarily salt), and some manufactured goods, but imports exceed exports by 6 to 1. The United States is the Bahamas' largest trading partner, accounting for 86% of imports and 75% of exports.

Major Languages. English is the official language of the Bahamas, and it is spoken by all except some Haitian immigrants who speak Creole. There is considerable variation in the dialects spoken, including Bahamian Standard English (which combines elements of British and American English), and a distinctive Afro-Bahamian dialect similar to that spoken in other Caribbean countries but not as pronounced. Most Bahamians can speak both dialects.

HISTORY

The Origin of the City. The Lucayan, the native peoples of the Bahamas, disappeared within two decades of the arrival of Christopher Columbus, owing to a combination of disease and enslavement. Puritans from Bermuda resettled the islands in 1647, and Nassau was settled in the 1660s. By the 1670s it was the largest settlement in the colony with about 900 people. Named Charles Town in the 17th century, the town was a disorganized affair of wooden houses and no public buildings except a church. The Spanish captured Charles Town in 1684 and burned it to the ground. The town was rebuilt, a fort established, and in 1695 it was renamed Nassau, after King William III. French and Spanish attacks in 1703 and 1706, respectively, led to the collapse of law and order. Blackbeard and other pirates filled the vacuum and made Nassau their base of Caribbean operations. In 1718 Britain appointed its first royal governor, Woodes Rogers, and suppressed piracy. The 18th-century city was more orderly, but included few public buildings. In 1731 the population of New Providence was 1,042, including 409 "Negroes," most of whom (but probably not all) were slaves. The community was becoming more settled, and most free inhabitants lived in family households. Periodic European wars helped to fuel Nassau's economy through privateering (legalized piracy), but otherwise the economic opportunities were limited.

The American Revolution led to dramatic changes in the city. After two brief American occupations, and one by the Spanish, the Bahamas were returned to the British at the end of the war. The settlement of the war also required that American Loyalists leave the newly independent United States for other British colonies. The influx of American Loyalists and their slaves probably doubled the population of New Providence. The Loyalists left their mark on the town itself. New legislative buildings, churches, forts, and planter homes were built in the central settlement, most copying British archetypes but adapted to local conditions through the use of indigenous materials. In 1834 Great Britain abolished slavery in the colonies, and by 1838 slavery ended in the Bahamas. Even before emancipation, however, there was a free black population in Nassau, but central Nassau became the home for white Nassauvians as blacks were pushed out and moved "Over the Hill" to the south. There they established new, predominantly black communities. These communities were augmented by "liberated Africans" who had been freed by the British Navy from slave ships after Britain's 1807 abolition of the slave trade. As the black population continued to increase, a number of new villages were established on the periphery of Nassau.

The American Civil War and the Union blockade of Southern ports led to Nassau's becoming the base of operations for the Confederate blockade-runners. Conveniently, the year before, the Bahamas had helped to underwrite the construction of Nassau's first major hotel, the Victoria. Although peace brought a period of recession, tourism increasingly tied the capital's fortunes to America. The Victoria offered seasonal accommodations, and wealthy tourists, mostly Americans, began to winter in the city. Henry M. Flagler, an American financier who developed resorts in Florida, bought the Victoria and constructed a second hotel, the Colonial, on the site of Fort Nassau on the waterfront in 1899. In 1873 a "library and literary institute" opened in the old public jail, and amateurs and visiting professionals presented concerts and plays during the winter season. By the turn of the century, tourism was becoming a mainstay for Nassau.

The population of Nassau grew slowly but steadily during the 19th century and by 1900 it totaled about 12,500 people. Although almost two-thirds of the population of the colony had lived in Nassau before the Loyalist arrival, only about one quarter of the population did so at the turn of the 20th century. The death rate in Nassau was higher than the colonial average, primarily the result of epidemic disease and poor living conditions. By the early 20th century Nassau had developed a complex social structure based, in part but not totally, on race. The lives of wealthy American and British tourists revolved around the two hotels, and Americans were hired to provide managerial and supervisory staff. Wealthy white Bahamians, nicknamed the "Bay Street Boys," for their control of businesses and homes along the main street of Nassau, controlled much of the commerce and government of the islands. Some "coloured" residents, those of mixed race, moved into professional positions and even held legislative seats and government posts. Although there was some interaction across race lines, the mass of black inhabitants continued to work in various menial occupations and lived in the Over the Hill communities of Baintown and Grant's Town. These communities created their own separate cultural activities, many of which were attended, nevertheless, by both whites and blacks. Racial tensions may have been most pronounced among poorer residents; poor whites had little beyond race to distinguish them from blacks. Both whites and coloureds held petty bourgeoisie positions, although one racial group often dominated certain occupations.

Prohibition during the 1920s revived Nassau's economy and the town became a center for bootlegging. The bootleggers not only occupied the hotels but also brought jobs on ships and docks and in construction trades and liquor storehouses. Sewage systems were installed in central Nassau, but the black neighborhoods continued to have access to city water only at central public standpipes. The harbor was dredged to accommodate cruise ships, and the Prince George docks were completed in 1928. Rum-running ended in 1933, and the Depression followed, but World War II brought a second influx of Americans, this time to build airbases and naval stations. The low pay for local workers led to a race riot in 1942; in response wages were increased. Local black laborers were hired for construction. The war years also saw the arrival of the Duke of Windsor to serve as royal governor; the duke and duchess brought Nassau to the attention of international society.

After the war tourism resumed, but the color barrier remained, primarily at the request of American tourists who expected racially segregated accommodations. Blacks were not admitted to most hotels, restaurants, and theaters until 1956. Blacks worked and performed in the tourist hotels and in Over the Hill nightclubs, which catered to white tourists. Junkanoo parades, organized and performed by black Bahamians, took over Bay Street on December 26 and January 1 each year. In the 1950s new resort hotels were built west of Nassau along Cable Beach. The Cuban Revolution in 1959 further increased Nassau's role as a Caribbean tourist destination. The old U.S. Air Force base became an international airport, and the harbor was dredged again for still larger cruise ships. Hog Island, across Nassau harbor, was developed as another major resort and renamed Paradise Island.

While the late 1950s and 1960s saw increased tourism, tensions between white and black Bahamians also increased. The Bahamas had continued to be controlled by a small white elite. Lynden Pindling founded the black Progressive Liberal Party (PLP) in 1953, and after a violent national strike in 1963, the PLP pushed for greater self-government for the colony. After winning elections in 1967 and 1972, Pindling's party solidified control, and in 1973 the Bahamas became an independent member of the British Commonwealth. The Pindling government kept up many of the previous government's economic policies, however, and the economy continued to focus on tourism and remaining a corporate and individual tax haven.

During the postwar period the country's population centralized in Nassau. Before the war less than one-third of Bahamians lived on New Providence, but by 1953 more than half of the population did, and by 1990 over two-thirds were living in the metropolis. Increasingly the Bahamas was equated with the capital, and the surrounding small settlements on New Providence were conjoined to the central settlement as a single conurbation. Unfortunately, the rise of Cable Beach and Paradise Island hurt the downtown as tourists left the older hotels, the Victoria and the Colonial, for new ones. The Victoria burned in 1971 and the Colonial lost much of its previous luster. Over the Hill suffered as well as middle-class blacks moved into new housing developments away from the central core, and shopping malls opened to serve these communities.

The new millennium showed signs of rebirth for the older sections of Nassau. Bay Street and the central settlement were no longer the territory only of cruise ships. Overnight tourists returned; the British Colonial was completely refurbished and opened as a Hilton Hotel. A new Holiday Inn opened in several refurbished 1950s hotels just to the west. The cultural life of Over the Hill blossomed with the expansion and reinvigoration of Junkanoo as a yearlong community-building activity.

Migration: Past and Present. English Bermudians and their slaves were the first modern settlers of Nassau in the 1660s. In the 1780s and 1790s, American Loyalists and their slaves joined this initial group, doubling the population. The black rebellion in Haiti in 1791 led to migrations of French slaveholders and slaves. The creation of new black neighborhoods in Over the Hill led to the increased segregation of the city, with the downtown increasingly inhabited by whites, and free blacks living in the valley to south. By the 1820s the failure of plantation agriculture led many white planters from the outer islands to move to Nassau. After Britain's abolition of the slave trade, the British Navy deposited in the Bahamas any surviving liberated Africans. These free blacks settled in Over the Hill and in specially created villages outside Nassau: Gambier, Carmichael, and Adelaide. With economic opportunities in the Bahamas limited, many black Bahamians left in the late 19th and early 20th century to work as stevedores on ships out of Haiti or in Florida. Beginning in the 1880s Greek sponge fishermen went to Nassau as middlemen in the expanding sponge industry. Lebanese traders and shop owners appeared in the early 20th century. In the 1920s Chinese immigrants established restaurants, laundries, and dry-goods stores. At the same time Jews began to settle in Nassau as merchants and storekeepers.

Relative prosperity in the postwar Bahamas, and increased poverty in Haiti, led to significant illegal migrations to the Bahamas since the 1950s. As many as 20% of the people living in the Bahamas, most on New Providence, were either legal or illegal Haitian immigrants. In addition, the Bahamas became a tax haven for an expatriate community of Americans, British, and other Europeans attracted by the warm climate and the lack of income taxes. New gated communities on the western end of New Providence became homes for the rich.

INFRASTRUCTURE

Public Buildings, Public Works, and Residences. Until the end of World War II, the government was housed in a handful of stone structures facing Rawson Square on Bay Street. In the 1960s and 1970s the government took over a number of older buildings in the area, and many departments were moved out of central Nassau and into modern office buildings in the newer outlying areas. The Bank of the Bahamas constructed a number of large modern buildings in Old Nassau.

Loyalist planters built large stone or tabby Georgian manor homes along the ridge that separated the central settlement from Over the Hill to the south. In black neighborhoods small one- or two-room wooden dwellings were the norm, usually constructed without permanent foundations so they could be moved if the family lost the lease on its property. As late as the 1960s only 37% of the households on New Providence had running water.

Following World War II building construction changed. Houses were more Floridian in style, often built out of cement block covered in stucco. New suburban communities for middle-class blacks began to dominate much of eastern New Providence; in style and design they replicated homes common to much of southern North America. Large estate homes in gated communities, such as Lyford Cay, attracted wealthy Americans and Europeans, along with a few wealthy Bahamians. The Pindling administration worked to improve the housing stock available to poorer residents and established public housing units in several Over the Hill neighborhoods.

Politics and City Services. Nassau technically does not exist as a separate municipality. The government of the Bahamas, until recently, was strongly centralized, and New Providence is one of 21 separate districts for the delivery of government services. Home to two-thirds of the country's population, in large measure the politics of Nassau are the politics of the Commonwealth. The British monarch rules the Bahamas, represented in the Commonwealth by the governor general, appointed on the recommendation of the Bahamian prime minister. The executive branch of the government is composed of a cabinet, headed by the prime minister, the leader of the majority party. The legislature includes two houses: the Lower House and the House of Assembly, which is the most powerful. There is an independent judiciary. All three branches of government are located in Nassau.

New Providence is slightly underrepresented in the House of Assembly with 24 of the 40 seats. There are two political parties. The PLP controlled the government from independence in 1973 until 1992. Traditionally the PLP drew its support from the underprivileged and was especially strong in the urban, Over the Hill neighborhoods. The moderate Free National Movement (FNM) controlled the government beginning in 1992. The government provides a wide range of city services including water, sewer, electricity, and telephones. Considerable controversy surrounded the government's attempt to privatize BaTelCo, the government owned phone company, with the long-term goal of improving communications services.

Educational System. The central government is responsible for Nassau's educational system. Public education, which expanded significantly beginning in the 1960s, is free throughout the Bahamas. Eighty-five percent of Bahamians are literate. There are 39 government-owned schools and 28 independent schools on New Providence. About three-fourths of the students in the Bahamas attend public school. Schools follow an amalgam of British and American models; primary school is from age 5 to 11 and secondary school from age 12 to about 16. At the end of secondary school students take Bahamian General Certificates of Secondary Education (BGCSE) in a wide range of subjects. There are four government-run institutions of higher education in Nassau, and a number of American universities also operate programs.

Transportation System. Nassau has an international airport with connections to North America and Europe, as well as to other parts of the Caribbean. Nassau's airport also serves as the central node of an interisland network of local flights. Mail boats provide interisland service on a weekly basis. New Providence has a paved highway circling the island and secondary roads crossing it. The main roads are in good condition. Privately owned, government-licensed jitney buses provide public transportation throughout the island on standard routes. All the routes begin or end in downtown Nassau.

CULTURAL AND SOCIAL LIFE

Distinctive Features of the City's Cultures. Nassau's culture combines American, British, and Afro-Caribbean elements. For many tourists staying in the large resorts on Cable Beach or Paradise Island, Nassau may simply replicate American culture in a warm, sunny climate of beautiful beaches. But, in fact, the culture of the city is much more complex. Nassau continues to be more formal—in dress, speech, and manners—than the United States. The quarterly opening of the supreme court and the changing of the guard at Government House, the home of the governor general, continue long-standing British traditions. And it is during Junkanoo, the country's largest celebration, that the distinctive elements of Afro-Bahamian culture are best captured. Junkanoo parades are held twice a year, on December 26 and January 1, from one o'clock to nine o'clock A.M. The highlight of the parade occurs when six or seven adult groups, each with as many as 500 performers, compete for prizes in a number of categories—costume, music, dance—as well as for an overall award. Each group picks a theme, and their costumes and choreography take an entire year to produce. In addition to the main groups, many smaller organizations, and even individuals—totaling thousands of participants—march in the parade.

Cuisine. Nassau offers a wide range of dining options, from high-end continental cuisine to hamburgers. Local Bahamian dishes, similar to those in other parts of the Caribbean (although not as spicy as Jamaican jerk), are still distinctive. Not surprisingly, seafood dominates the diet. Conch, a tough mollusk, is hand harvested and beaten before preparation. In salad conch is minced and served raw, like a ceviche. Cracked conch is lightly battered and fried. Steamed conch is served in a slightly spicy tomato-based sauce. Other popular seafoods include spiny lobster (actually a large crawfish), grouper (usually lightly battered and fried), and, in season, sea turtle (although the latter are now an endangered species). Both goat and lamb are popular, often served as barbecue. Peas and rice usually accompany entrees, or they can be a meal on their own. Rice is imported but peas (traditionally pigeon beans) are grown locally. The local dessert is guava duff, a steamed pudding that is sliced and served with a rum sauce. Tropical fruits, including guavas, mangos, papayas, soursops, and star apples, can be found as well. Souse is a standard breakfast dish. It is a broth with sheep's tongue, chicken or other meats, seasoned with lime juice and pepper.

Ethnic, Class, and Religious Diversity. Eighty-five percent of the population of the Bahamas is black, but this group is not homogeneous; it is differentiated by class and ethnic subgroups, such as Haitians. Moreover, many Bahamians are of mixed race and can trace their ancestry to both white and black Bahamians. White Bahamians, including descendents of the pre-Loyalist settlers, American Loyalists, and more recent British immigrants, make up about 12% of the population. Three percent of the population is Hispanic or Asian. The Greek and Asian communities are important, albeit small, subgroups. The class structure increasingly cuts across racial lines, although blacks, particularly Haitians, make up most of the underclass and whites continue to dominate the business class. Most Bahamians fall somewhere in between, but racial tensions do exist.

Religion is central to the lives of Bahamians, irrespective of their specific Christian denomination. Church leaders are important community leaders and appear frequently in the newspapers. Three denominations predominate: Baptist (32%), Anglican (20%), and Roman Catholic (18%). Obeah, based on native African religions, is practiced on some of the out islands and still infuses Bahamian spiritualism and folk practices.

Family and other Social Support Systems. Family is central to Bahamian culture. When either white or black Bahamians meet for the first time, one of the first discussions will be who each other's people are. Complex lineage and cousin relationships can be traced generations back. Although most Bahamians live in nuclear families, parents, siblings, aunts, and uncles all are important in the social support systems of the community. Traditionally the family played the primary role in social services, but increasingly the government has been called on to provide support to children whose families are unable or unwilling to do so. The department of welfare services employs 471 people and provides child welfare, disability services, family services, and senior citizen support. In addition, a wide range of nongovernmental organizations provides specialized support.

Work and Commerce. The Bahamas have a stable economy and the workforce is literate and well educated. Total gross domestic product (GDP) in 1999 was $4.5 billion. The Bahamas GDP per-capita income is one of the highest in the Caribbean, $15,000 in 1999. Work is focused on three business sectors: tourism, banking, and shipping. Although significant strides have been taken against illegal activities, drug trafficking still occurs. About half of the

© PHILIP GOULD/CORBIS

A woman examines straw bags on sale in an outdoor market in Nassau, Bahamas.

population is employed in tourism and 10% works in banking. The government employs one-third of Bahamians. Wealth is concentrated in Nassau (the banking sector is almost exclusively Nassau-based), and the better-paying tourist sector employment is also in Nassau and, to a lesser extent, Freeport.

Tourism is the most important business sector, generating 50% of the GDP and employing about 50,000 people. The banking and finance sector produces about 15% of the GDP and employs about 4,000 persons. Offshore banking for nonresidents and corporations is the predominate focus of the financial sector.

Arts and Recreation. Both Albert Bierstadt and Winslow Homer painted in the Bahamas in the 19th century, but an indigenous art circle has developed since the 1970s. Although the styles of the artists differ, most draw on Bahamian scenery or culture (Junkanoo, religion, or family life) for their inspiration. Amos Ferguson's intuitive paintings helped to bring Bahamian artists to the attention of the world in the 1980s. Later, Brent Malone and Stanley and Jackson Burnside all used Junkanoo as an inspiration for their work, giving Bahamian art a distinctive set of themes and styles. A new National Gallery of the Bahamas is being developed in Nassau in a converted 19th-century Loyalist mansion and is posed to provide an important focus for the visual arts.

The Bahamas offers a variety of musical experiences. Classical music groups exist alongside traditional Bahamian goombay and rake 'n' scrape. Goombay, famously heard at Junkanoo each year, combines horns, drums, and cowbells (the latter making the famous *kalik, kalik* sound that gives its name to the national beer). The music can be deafening, and its incessant beat is not simply heard but felt by the listener. Any song—contemporary, religious, or traditional—can be turned into goombay. Real goombay needs to be heard outdoors, but rake 'n' scrape is played indoors, often in bars, using guitars, accordions, shakers, and other instruments.

Because of the proximity of the ocean to all points in Nassau, water activities are one of the primary means of recreation. Swimming, snorkeling, and diving are all possible around Nassau, although the beaches and dive sites are not quite as good as on other islands. Deep-sea fishing is extremely popular and charter boats run from Nassau. Nassau has several golf courses and numerous tennis courts. The Bahamas made it to the world stage when four of its women won gold medals in track and field for the 4 × 100 women's relay at the Sydney, Australia, Olympics in 2000.

QUALITY OF LIFE

Nassau residents enjoy an excellent standard of living compared to many in the Caribbean: good employment prospects, a solid educational system, modern city services, and no income or sales tax. The country is politically stable and the economy is strong. The climate is excellent; temperatures are rarely below 15°C (60°F) or above 35°C (95°F).

The cost of living is high, however. Housing is expensive. Most consumer goods are imported and import duties can run as high as 100%. Many foodstuffs are also imported, so they are more expensive than they are in the United States. The telephone and Internet infrastructure is adequate but not as well developed as in the United States and Europe. Although there is good medical care in Nassau, for more serious conditions residents may need to go to the United States.

Nassau is, above all else, a tourist city and it is easy to miss its uniquely Bahamian qualities if one never leaves Bay Street or the resorts at Cable Beach or Paradise Island. The pace of life is slower and personal interactions are more important and valued than they might be on the mainland.

FUTURE OF THE CITY

Nassau will remain dependent on the tourist industry to fuel its economy. If the tourist market stays strong, Nassau's future looks bright, but if the economy stagnates, Nassau's economic prospects could dim and the overall gains in per-capita income over the last decades of the 20th century could be lost, leading to greater tensions within Bahamian society. Moreover, the ongoing development of the island—especially the new, gated communities for the wealthy—is leaving New Providence with less open space and fewer public beaches. There was considerable public protest over the development of the old Clifton Plantation on the southwest side of the island, which includes one of the last undeveloped coastlines on New Providence. Water is in short supply and has to be brought in daily from the neighboring island of Andros. Population increases and urban sprawl are creating traffic jams in a town where horse-drawn buggies were the norm as late as World War II.

After a period of neglect, during which the downtown area was left to the cruise ships and day-trippers from the resorts at Cable Beach and Paradise

Island, the central area of Old Nassau maybe experiencing a rebirth. The reopening of the British Colonial as a Hilton Hotel brought overnight guests back into the city, and new and renovated shops opened on Bay Street. The National Art Gallery provides an important cultural focus for the downtown area. There still are a number of historic properties that are in poor condition and at risk if they are not renovated. Nassau remains a hybrid city, a creative combination made up of its African, British, and American roots, but the economic boom also may lead to the further "americanization" of Nassau and a loss of cultural distinctiveness.

BIBLIOGRAPHY

Albury, Paul, *Paradise Island Story* (Macmillan 1984).

Baker, Christopher, *Bahamas Turks & Caicos* (Lonely Planet Publications 1998).

Collinwood, Dean Walter, *The Bahamas Between Worlds* (White Sound Press 1989).

Craton, Michael, and Gail Saunders, *Islanders in the Stream: A History of the Bahamian People,* 2 vols. (University of Georgia Press 1992; 1998).

Dahl, Anthony George, *Literature of the Bahamas, 1724–1992: The March Towards National Identity* (University Press of America 1995).

Eneas, Cleveland, *Baintown* (Cleveland and Muriel Eneas 1976).

Ferguson, Arlene Nash, *I Come to Get Me!: An Inside Look at the Junkanoo Festival* (Dongalik Studios 2000).

Glinton, Patricia, et al., *Bahamian Art: 1492–1992* (Finance Corporation of Bahamas Limited 1992).

Johnson, Howard, *The Bahamas In Slavery and Freedom* (Ian Randle Publishers 1991).

Johnson, Whittington Bernard, *Race Relations in the Bahamas, 1784–1834: The Nonviolent Transformation from a Slave to a Free Society* (University of Arkansas Press 2000).

Johnson, Howard, *The Bahamas from Slavery to Servitude, 1783–1933* (University Press of Florida 1996).

Saunders, Gail, and Donald Cartwright, *Historic Nassau* (Macmillan 1979).

Thomas, Sian, *Bahamas Handbook* (Entienne Dupuch Jr. Publications) [published annually, excellent source of government and national statistics].

JOHN D. BURTON

New York

United States

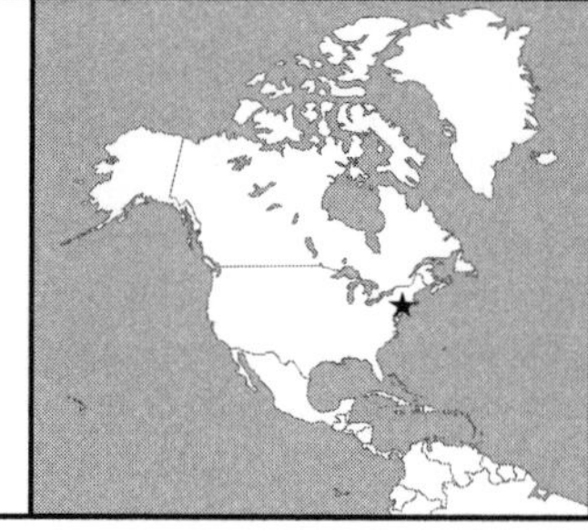

ORIENTATION

Name of City. New York, one of the oldest American cities, was originally settled by the Dutch West India Company (1624) and was first called New Amsterdam. On February 2, 1653, the settlement was granted legal autonomy. Conquered by an English fleet in 1664, it was renamed *New York* to honor its new proprietor, James, Duke of York, brother of King Charles II. Among many nicknames for the metropolis are *Gotham,* the *Big Apple,* and *Baghdad on the Hudson.*

Location. New York is located in North America, on the northeastern coast of the United States, in the state of New York. Situated at 40°4′ north latitude and 73°59′ west longitude, the city encompasses the islands of Manhattan and Staten Island, the western third of Long Island, and part of the United States mainland, and it is divided by two rivers. Five New York state counties—New York, Kings, Queens, Bronx, and Richmond; also called boroughs (Manhattan, Brooklyn, Queens, the Bronx, and Staten Island), respectively—located on these lands make up the present city. The Hudson River and the East River, which flow into New York Bay, are actually saltwater estuaries of the Atlantic Ocean, the latter for its full length and the former well beyond the city line. Together the rivers and bay give the metropolitan area almost 1,290 kilometers (800 miles) of waterfront to serve one of the world's foremost harbors.

Population. The 2000 U.S. census puts New York City's population at 8,008,000; it is the heart of a metropolitan area stretching over four states and taking in 21,199,865 persons. Owing to the city's density, mobile population, and large numbers of foreign-born residents, the city administration claims it has been consistently undercounted by census takers.

Distinctive and Unique Features. New York has been the largest and wealthiest American city for two centuries, a densely populated urban community whose most characteristic quality has been constant change. Throughout its history the city has maintained its close connection to the ocean and international trade, and its extensive waterfront has played a vital role in metropolitan development. With easy water access to New England, to the interior of the continent, and to southern markets, the harbor dominated both the import and export trade of the nation for over 150 years. Even today, New York remains the nation's prime importer.

The topography of the city was created some 12,000 years ago during the glacial recession that ended the Wisconsin Ice Age. The bedrock foundations (mica schist) of Manhattan Island make possible the concentration of skyscrapers for which New York is noted, and the world's most famous skyline displays a wide range of architectural motifs. But Manhattan's layout is easily comprehended by any visitor, since it largely follows a grid block pattern imposed in 1811. This utilitarian device was extended to other parts of New York when the city expanded in 1898.

Superlatives are inadequate when dealing with New York City's role in U.S. history. The city has reigned as the nation's largest commercial trader, premier manufacturing center, prime immigrant destination, and retailing heart since early in the 19th century. At the start of another millennium, it remains the financial, advertising, media, and cultural center of the United States.

Attractions of the City. New York quite simply has something for everyone. Preeminently a city of business, it has drawn the most ambitious and innovative American thinkers and manufacturers for over three centuries. The seal of the metropolis, adopted in 1686, displays both a beaver and a flour barrel, the first two of many industries centered in the city. Besides furs and milling, New York pioneered in such fields as transatlantic shipping, ship construction, and commercial banking; the clothing, piano, cigarette, and printing industries; legal and insurance services; and communication technology. Its economy is diversified enough to accommodate the needs of Tin Pan Alley (music and entertainment) and Silicon Alley (high technology, software), geographically dispersed in the city but concentrated in their economic impact. Business is what the city does best, but its hard-eyed insistence on performance sets a national standard of excellence.

The metropolis is an old city, and despite its tendency to reinvent itself every generation, it does boast an array of historical monuments. Its harbor contains the very symbols of America, the Statue of Liberty (1886), which promises freedom, and Ellis Island (1892), where millions entered the land of opportunity; an estimated 40% of Americans trace their origins to those who made that passage via Ellis Island. While most of the city's pre-1850 structures have fallen before bulldozers and construction crews, the modern city is an architectural textbook. Both scholars and tourists avidly trace the history of the skyscraper and marvel at the extraordinary system of bridges, tunnels, and transport that tie the five boroughs of the metropolis together. Although many Gilded Age mansions have been consumed by modern building projects, upper Fifth Avenue retains a goodly number that have been adapted for 21st-century uses. Central Park (Manhattan) and Prospect Park (Brooklyn) established models for urban park projects across the nation, while the Bronx Zoo and Bronx Botanical Gardens (Brooklyn and Queens have botanical gardens of their own) set the standard for such institutions elsewhere. In Queens and Staten Island, hints of the city's colonial past remain visible at the Bowne House and Richmondtown Restoration, respectively.

The terrorist attack that destroyed the World Trade Center (September 11, 2001) eliminated one of New York City's most recognizable landmarks, the "twin towers," which since 1973 had become a symbol of Manhattan's primacy in the global economy. But even as the city struggles to rebuild the devastated "Ground Zero," visitors to Manhattan can still view dozens of familiar sights and sites. "The Battery's down" at the tip of the island, where chapters of New York's colorful history can be experienced at Castle Clinton, Fraunces Tavern, and the Customs House (now the Museum of the American Indian, a branch of the Smithsonian Institution). North of the Bowling Green begin the "canyons" between skyscrapers where ticker-tape parades have greeted American heroes. Walkers pass Trinity Church and Wall Street before arriving at City Hall Park; from there they have a choice of "urban villages" to experience. South Street, Chinatown, Little Italy, Tribeca, Soho, and Greenwich Village all have their charms and are worth a visit. Ahead lie the spires of Midtown, the world's most expensive real estate. The glories of the Empire State, Chrysler, and

Citicorp buildings are readily apparent, and Rockefeller Center is a must-see stop, especially during the Christmas season. Beaux Arts monuments such as the New York Public Library on 42d Street and the recently renovated Grand Central Terminal beckon, and no visitor dares miss the United Nations building or the illuminated wonder of Times Square: If the United States has a single shared public area, it is almost certainly Times Square in Manhattan, where the annual New Year's Eve countdown draws a nation together. Fine restaurants are found everywhere, often scattered amid the apartment houses and brownstones of the East and West sides, areas of Manhattan separated not only by the magnificent Central Park but also by cultural perspectives. Above 100th Street are located Harlem and the "academic Acropolis" of Morningside Heights, as well as cultural attractions that even native New Yorkers may be less familiar with, such as the Jumel mansion, Grant's Tomb, the Cathedral of St. John the Divine, and the Cloisters (a branch of the Metropolitan Museum of Art housed in a re-created medieval monastery incorporating structures from European monastic sites). Manhattan offers virtually endless choices, and every visitor can create a personally satisfying itinerary.

New York ranks as the cultural capital of the United States. It has more museums than any other city, led by world-class institutions such as the Metropolitan Museum of Art (1874), the Brooklyn Museum (1823), the American Museum of Natural History (1868), the Guggenheim (1937), the Whitney (1931), and the Museum of Modern Art (1929). New York virtually invented the amusement park (Coney Island, 1897; Rockaway, 1901; and, in its northern suburb of Rye Beach in Westchester county, Play-

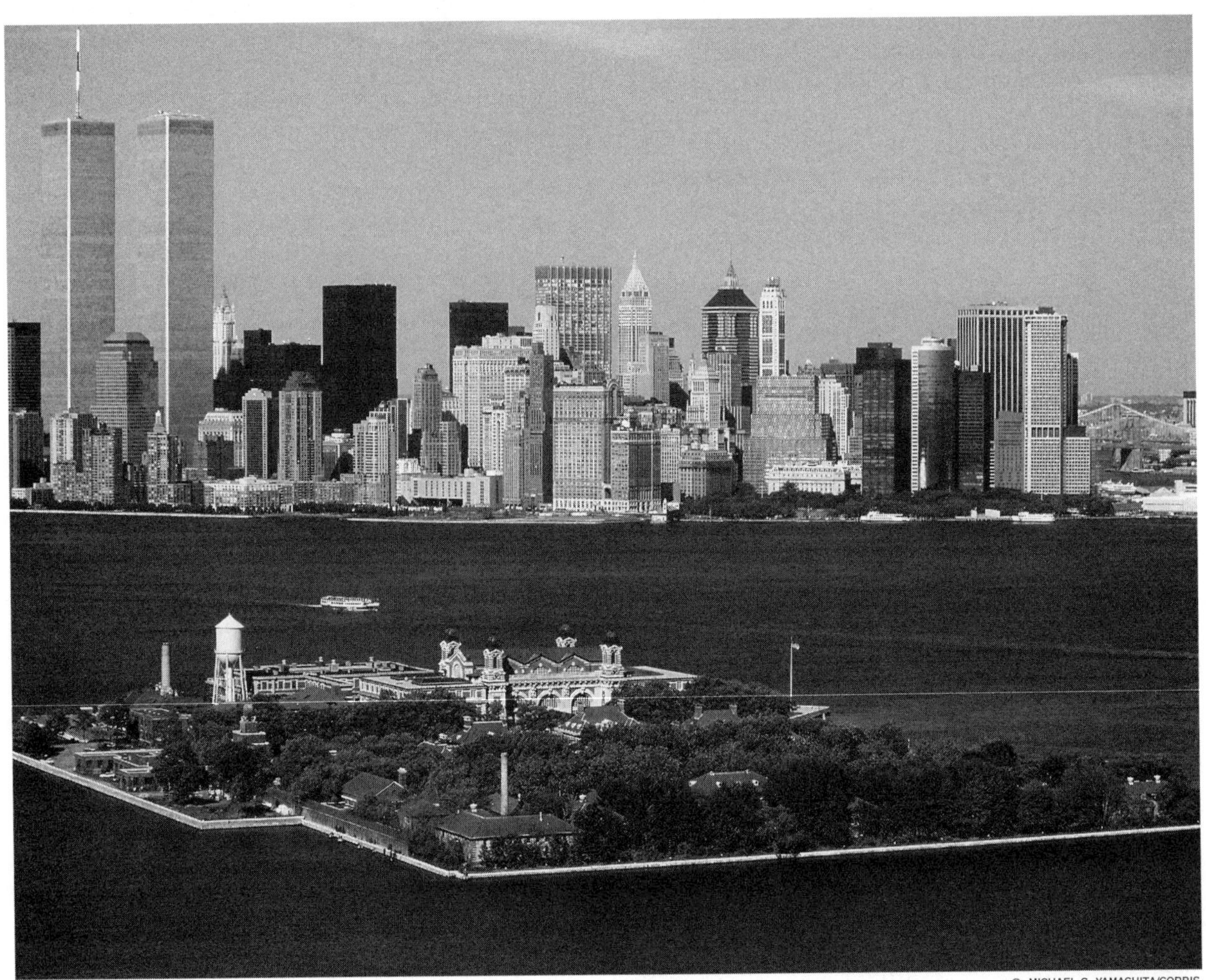

© MICHAEL S. YAMASHITA/CORBIS

This aerial view of Ellis Island, where millions of immigrants to the United States arrived, and the New York City skyline was taken in 1993. The twin towers of the World Trade Center, left, were destroyed in a terrorist attack on September 11, 2001.

land, 1928). Its professional sports teams have won championships in every area; the New York Yankees baseball franchise is the most valuable and successful of all sport dynasties. The mere mention of Broadway conjures theater, an art the city has dominated in all it many aspects since the mid-1800s. Brief paragraphs cannot convey the enormous variety of New York's attractions, but 38.5 million persons made it the most visited city in the United States in 2000.

Relationships Between the City and the Outside. Among its many roles Manhattan has starred both as the first capital of the United States and as capital of the "Empire State" of New York. Neither play enjoyed a long run. On April 30, 1789, George Washington was inaugurated as the first president of the United States on the steps of then–City Hall (Federal Hall), but within a year the national capital moved to Philadelphia. Alexander Hamilton, the Manhattan lawyer serving as first secretary of the Treasury, arranged a deal in which the capital would move from New York in return for congressional approval of a financial system that enhanced the authority and power of the national government. Manhattan's brief tenure as the state capital ended in 1797, when the "country members' dislike of the sophisticated metropolis" prompted the relocation of the legislature to Albany. Both the national and state capitals left New York not because the metropolis was inhospitable but because politics overruled judgment.

Thomas Jefferson believed New York was a "sore," a perversion of the "truer" American values found among the agrarian population. Despite his scorn, New York emerged as America's largest city and moneymaking center during his presidential administration. Its new role was as a national metropolis, "the place where the idea of America is created," the focus of half the nation's trade, and the stage where the epic of immigration would take place. New York became a world city. It transcended partisan politics to embody all the powerful forces creating the modern United States. As a result it became increasingly alien to the more established elements of the national consciousness; it was too vigorous, too commercial, too foreign. Since 1800 the city has been comfortably at odds with the prevailing mentality in both Washington, D.C., and Albany. Its tumultuous reality, while mistrusted by conservative domestic politicians, is appreciated abroad. The modern city constantly battles Albany over the bounds of "home rule"; despite its population it has rarely obtained adequate aid from the state, because upstate legislators established funding regulations that discriminated against the city and its minorities. City residents believe that Washington has not sufficiently rewarded New York with contracts or aid; for decades Senator Daniel Patrick Moynihan futilely protested federal funding formulas that did not return money to the state in proportion to its tax payments. Perhaps the greatest example of federal unconcern came in the 1970s, when the U.S. government appeared willing to accept bankruptcy for the city.

For 200 years New York has been more foreign, more ethnic, more dense, more noisy, and more successful than any other American city; its intense drive to succeed was resented and feared. Talented people fled into surrounding suburbs to obtain a different lifestyle, but they commuted daily to labor within the city's borders. If diversity is the glory of America, the metropolis recognizes this to a far greater degree than its political masters. It flaunts its separation from "sterile suburbs," Albany appleknockers, and Washington bureaucrats. Confident and proud of its differences, it relishes its status as "capital of the world."

Major Languages. As early as 1644 an observer verified 18 languages being spoken in New Amsterdam, and the city has remained true to that multicultural heritage; one scholar calls New York the "most heterogeneous of all North American cities in its social composition." For 350 years the city has welcomed "storm-tossed" ethnic groups, accepted their linguistic contributions to urban life, and acculturated them to the United States. Because of contemporary immigration patterns, Spanish has become de facto a second city language; it is the first language in 20% of New York City homes and the most frequently used in bilingual classes. In 1972 New York authorized an Office of Bilingual Education, and a dozen language groups now receive special instruction in the city's schools. In 1990 education officials found 28 languages spoken by at least 100 students and identified 196 ethnic groups. Every European language is heard on New York streets, as well as every dialect of Chinese and all other Asian languages; certain neighborhoods use Hebrew or Arabic, Italian or Greek, Haitian French or Russian, as their lingua franca. Experts found 140 languages being used in New York in 2000. Despite this Babel, the language of business and commerce remains English.

HISTORY

The Origin of the City. Before Europeans arrived, Indian tribes of the New York area used the island as a hunting ground and trading site they called Manna-hatta ("the land surrounded by hills"). No tribe claimed ownership, and when traders of the Dutch West India Company established a small settlement on the southeastern shore of the island, they were unconcerned. Commerce was from the start an essential part of New Amsterdam's value; the settlement played a vital role in the fur trade and acted as the prime shipping point for farm goods. Title to the land was therefore essential, and in 1626 Peter Minuet (1580–1638) concluded what has been regarded as the most advantageous real-estate transaction in history, purchasing the island for the equivalent of $24 (60 guilders) in trade goods. Subsequent purchases from other tribes secured other parts of the territory. Today, three places claim to be "the" site of Minuit's deal. Since the Indians never owned Manhattan, exactly who cheated whom has always been debated. Peter Stuyvesant (1610–1672) led the colony as director-general from 1647 to 1664, bringing order to a town already filled with "grog-shops," sailors from a dozen nations, and Dutch merchants eager for deals. His efforts to impose sobriety and religious uniformity failed, and the tolerance that still characterizes New York was established. In 1664 Stuyvesant discovered that city merchants preferred profits to fighting. He was forced to surrender the city to the British, and New Amsterdam became New York.

During a century of British rule, New York became an important trade center, reaching a population of 22,000 by 1775. Revolutionary attitudes seemed part of its heritage. It pioneered freedom of the press in the Zenger Case (1735), its assembly successfully limited the pay of royal governors, Manhattan hosted the Stamp Act Congress (1765), the "battle" of Golden Hill (1770) initiated violence against the British, and New Yorkers held their own "tea party" in 1774. General George Washington considered the city to be of "infinite importance" to the colonial cause, and its strategic value made it a target for British forces once revolution began. Washington desperately attempted to defend the city, but British forces defeated his army in Brooklyn (August 27, 1776). After peace negotiations on Staten Island failed, the British navy landed troops behind Washington's Manhattan defenses, and the American army was extricated by the slimmest of margins. At the Battle of Harlem Heights (September 16), Washington repulsed his pursuers, but Manhattan remained in British hands for the rest of the war, enduring the longest occupation of any American city. Many New Yorkers, Tory supporters of King George III, were quite happy with the situation and cooperated with the British. After the battle of Yorktown, many left along with the British. Washington reoccupied a city devastated by fire, the population of which had been halved. Nevertheless New York rapidly recovered in the 1780s, and in 1789 it was selected as the nation's first capital.

By 1800 Manhattan's population had quintupled to 60,000 and it was poised to became the national metropolis. Within another 20 years it had assumed commercial leadership and established scheduled transatlantic service. But full domination came only after De Witt Clinton (1769–1828) built the Erie Canal (1825) connecting the Hudson River to the Great Lakes, making the resources and markets of America's interior available to New Yorkers. By midcentury its port handled more goods than the rest of the nation combined, including the valuable cotton trade of the South. Despite those commercial ties, a quarter-million New Yorkers rallied for the Union in April 1861, and the city's contribution in the Civil War was unmatched. The city contributed its financial expertise, its manufacturing capacity, and more than its share of soldiers to the Union cause. Such services are, however, often overshadowed because the Draft Riots of 1863, directed at both conscription and Negro residents of Manhattan, represent (even today) the worst urban violence in U.S. history.

Wartime saw a fundamental change in the institutional life of New York as popular forces seized power from the merchant elite, which had long dominated city life. A "ring" of elected officials led by William Marcy Tweed (1823–1878), the first recognized "boss" of the Democratic Party, plundered the city. Reformers overthrew the corrupt ring in 1871, but a tradition of Democratic voting had been established. Tammany Hall, the headquarters building of the New York County Democratic Party, symbolized the power of the most important political organization in the city. Tammany americanized new immigrants and helped them get jobs—and asked only their votes in return. Occasionally ousted from power because of greed, corruption, or patronage excesses, Tammany always rebounded against "reform" because it could count on working-class votes. Only after the New York economy changed in the mid-20th century did this successful political formula fail.

By the 1890s New York had reigned as America's richest and most vibrant city for almost a century, but unlike other urban centers its physical expansion had been minimal. Although the Brooklyn Bridge (1883) established a connection to the nation's fourth-largest city, the two communities across the East River remained separate entities. Business leaders supported unification, and Andrew Haswell Green led the campaign for a referendum on consolidation. In November 1894 voters in New York, Kings, Queens, Richmond, and lower Westchester Counties—areas which became the five boroughs—approved the creation of a united metropolis. On January 1, 1898, Greater New York, a single city with 3.4 million citizens came into existence. Even Republicans supported the merger, believing that more conservative voters outside Manhattan would erode Tammany's power. (Their hopes proved futile; New York would provide reliable Democratic majorities for the entire 20th century).

Consolidation also assured the continued economic domination of New York. Residents of the "outer boroughs" persisted in calling Manhattan, "the city," but their skills and labor were vital in maintaining the city's position as America's leading commercial, financial, and manufacturing center. In 2000, with a population surpassing eight millions, New York had yielded supremacy only in manufacturing, and it had replaced that sector of its economy with thriving service industries. Commerce continued to flows through its port and air terminals, and it remained the world's leading financial marketplace.

Migration: Past and Present. New York, a city of unmatched opportunity and limitless possibilities, served as Europe's prime immigration site to the United States. No city matches its ability to accept new arrivals and acculturate them to American life. Racial variety was always apparent; in the colonial city of 1740, one of six persons was a slave, and the institution endured in New York until 1827. But the larger saga of European immigration began with a large German influx which established *Kleindeutschland* (Little Germany) in what was then the northeastern quarter of the city (extending as far north as 16th Street) during the 1830s. German craftsmen fled the effects of the Industrial Revolution, and German farmers fled declining agricultural prices. The promise of work drew additional thousands, and immigrant Irishmen labored to build the Erie Canal or found work on the city docks. Of the 1.5 million Irish who fled the potato blight of the 1840s, 1.1 million came to New York, and they soon filled the Five Points district in the "Bloody Sixth" war north of City Hall. Overcrowding gave the Bloody Sixth—a tenement district with a mixed population, predominantly Irish but also including free blacks and poor Germans and Italians—a reputation for violence that endured for decades. Known as the "cradle of gangs," it eventually vanished under the advancing courthouse complex of the modern Foley Square. Immigrants continued to arrive at the Castle Clinton reception center on the Battery from 1855 to 1890; some 7.5 million immigrants crossed a bridge from Castle Clinton to Manhattan. From 1890 to 1892, while Ellis Island was being prepared to receive immigrants, the U.S. Barge Office was the point of entry. (Castle Clinton reopened as the New York Aquarium in 1896.) Despite the nativism preached by Know-Nothings, by 1860 half of Manhattan's 800,000 residents were foreign born.

Temporarily halted by the Civil War, the flood of immigration from northern and western Europe continued into the 1870s. By the 1880s changed patterns of migration had become evident as "new" immigrants (Greeks, Italians, Poles, and Jews) arrived, primarily from southern and eastern Europe. Jews displaced the remnants of *Kleindeutschland* to create a totally ethnic neighborhood on the Lower East Side; Italians built a Little Italy around Mott Street. From 1892 to 1922 over 12 million newcomers arrived via the federal reception center at Ellis Island, a third of whom remained in the city. New York, which held only 39,951 Italians in 1890, had 390,832 by 1920; by 1910 the city was 40.8% foreign born. Adding to the dynamic mix, tens of thousands of blacks traveled north in the "Great Migration," which began in the late 1880s. Refugees from segregation and sharecropping, many of these newcomers, settled in Harlem, which by 1914 had 50,000 black residents and became America's "Black Metropolis."

During the 20th century the parade of new arrivals never ceased. The refugees of two world wars, persons displaced by communist governments and those who fled dictatorships elsewhere, found refuge in New York. In the 1950s another wave of new Americans, from Puerto Rico—the first migration by plane—came to New York seeking economic gain and established barrios in several locations. Although many succeeded, others lacked modern skills, and islanders soon constituted the largest number of city welfare clients. By 2000, Puerto Ricans New Yorkers represented only 36% of the city's Hispanic population. From the 1980s the Caribbean and the Far East provided the largest numbers of immigrants, with Dominicans (Washington Heights), Chinese (Flushing, Sunset Park), and Russians (Brighton Beach) dominating entire neighborhoods. In 2000 New York was once again 40% foreign born, and only its long tradition of tolerance made the social mix compatible.

INFRASTRUCTURE

Public Buildings, Public Works, and Residences. In 1812 New York dedicated a new City Hall, a structure then so far uptown that its northern side was left unfaced, since no one would ever see it. City Hall and the mayor's official residence, Gracie Mansion (1804), are prominent among the few 19th-century public buildings remaining in a modern city of skyscrapers. After consolidation, every borough constructed an administrative center where its "president," courts, and official agencies were to be found. The Croton-Catskill-Delaware water system provides the five boroughs with the purest drinking water in the nation, using a complex system of tunnels, aqueducts, and mains along with 18 storage reservoirs. The city's Third Water Tunnel, under construction for more than a decade, is the greatest public works project in New York's history. There are 1,162 kilometers (722 miles) of subway, and over 2000 bridges—76 of them over water. The Brooklyn Bridge (1883) still provides one of the most recognizable images of New York, although the facilities of the Port Authority (1921) and the Triborough Bridge and Tunnel Authority service half a million vehicles daily.

In the late 1920s Robert Moses began his career as the "Master Builder" of New York. For over 40 years, serving in a variety of city and state positions, he was responsible for the construction of $27 billion of public works, including such landmarks as the Triborough and Verrazano bridges, the Battery Tunnel, and the West Side Highway. As "housing czar," he built thousands of units of public apartments in 12- to 14-floor towers. From 1947 to 1949 Moses opened a project every month, but he was never able to solve the city's eternal housing problem. Yet neither the United Nations complex nor Lincoln Center would have succeeded without his leadership.

Manhattan has always been a rental market, and May 1 was its traditional "moving day," when annual leases expires. Families moved in a constant

© GAIL MOONEY/CORBIS

Bow Bridge in Central Park in New York City provides views of the park's natural beauty and the elegant residential buildings that surround it.

attempt to better their location, or sometimes because they could no longer maintain a lifestyle. Although the city enacted its first housing law in 1867, it was always difficult to house the growing population; brownstone homes for middle-class families and, for poor folk, tenements (4- to 6-story walkup residential buildings, with four apartments per floor) were part of the city response. New York is still chronically short of affordable housing. A "rent control" system (federal in 1942; state in 1947) was instituted in an attempt to prevent exorbitant rent increases yet guarantee owners a fair rate of return. It has never worked as envisioned and causes tremendous conflict and inequities. "Controls" benefit long-term residents, a compromise plan called "rent stabilization" has had ludicrous results, and the system has been so capricious that it caused the abandonment of buildings and "arson for profit" in the 1970s. Battles between landlords and tenant groups have remained an ongoing theme of New York City life, and apartments are handed down like heirlooms.

The New York Housing Authority was established to construct low-income housing (First Houses, Lower East Side, 1936), an effort that won state and federal support but never solved the shortage; Co-op City in the Bronx (1968–1970) included 15,550 middle-income apartments yet made little impact on demand. Shortages grew when abuses within low-income projects halted federal aid in the 1980s. But luxury construction continues to proliferate, and the powerful real-estate industry flourished during the lush 1990s.

Outside Manhattan, home ownership is far more common. One interesting contemporary development was the gentrification of older areas of the outer boroughs by Manhattan people with ample funds. Brooklyn areas have experienced tensions as a result of the influx, and even Harlem has white newcomers. Housing remains an absorbing topics for all New Yorkers.

Politics and City Services. New York had appointive mayors until 1834. Popular election ruled thereafter, but the prime responsibility of every chief administrative officer remained providing adequate services. Despite the city's one-party tradition, which might be deemed to reduce political incentive, this task has generally been done, if not always in the most efficient fashion. Currently mayors are elected to four-year terms and are eligible for reelection once; similar limitations bind the five borough presidents. Until 1990 these officials worked through a board of estimate to allocate funds, but a civil-rights suit abolished the board: the U.S. Supreme Court declared that the board violated the one-man, one-vote guarantee of the U.S. Constitution (*Board of Estimate* v. *Morris,* 1989). Voters then approved a system of electing city council representatives from 51 relatively equal population districts. The 51-member city council now approves annual budgets. Borough presidents continue to oversee local spending, appoint community planning boards, and name a member (one of seven) of the board of education.

New York is the "Land of Taxes," and residents pay a city income tax as well as state and federal levies; a wide range of licensing and nuisance fees exist in addition to city and state sales taxes. Outer borough leaders believe they are discriminated against in spending priorities, and each budgetary cycle brings new controversies. With a budget of over $39 billion, New York City outspends many states.

Educational System. Educating children from the various classes of the metropolis has always caused controversy. Private tutors dealt with the offspring of the elite until after 1800, when the Public School Society assumed control of primary education. Manhattan's growing Catholic population was alienated by what it perceived as Protestant indoctrination, and Archbishop John Hughes (1797–1864) initiated a rival parochial school system in the 1840s. That system continues to achieve better test results than the city's public schools. A Compulsory School Law (1874) was often ignored, and New York was one of the last cities to establish public high schools, there was little demand for education beyond the primary level until late in the 19th century. Public high schools authorized by the School Reform Law (1896) provided a means for the children of new immigrants to rise in the economic hierarchy, and more than natives, new immigrants insisted on publicly supported educational opportunity. Their children filled an expanding system in the 20th century. Jewish teachers helped to create the first union (1916) and became very influential within the civil service.

New York today has the largest educational establishment in the United States. But trouble engulfs a system of 1.1 million predominantly minority students, attending 1,000 schools and taught by 78,000 professionals. In the 1970s local groups battled teachers over control of school curricula and procedures, a "war" that led to decentralized administration. The initiative failed as 32 local community boards became patronage vehicles and student performance declined. Middle-class and elite parents responded by removing their children to private or parochial schools. In the 1990s the seven-member board of education was named by six different officials, while the school chancellor's office engaged in seemingly permanent battle with the mayor over authority. As the nation demands more accountability in school performance and the technology-driven "new economy" requires workers with ever-more-specialized skills, New York faces a severe problem in training its students for jobs.

In higher education, the story is different. New York City is home to some of the most prestigious colleges in the nation, and it administers America's most extensive urban university. Columbia University, formerly Kings College (1754); New York University (1831); and Fordham University, formerly St. John's College (1842) have always been educational leaders, and the Free Academy (1849) was the ancestor to the 19-unit City University of New York. A minimum of 65 institutions offer college degrees, and the city's range of medical and law facilities is unrivaled.

Transportation System. New York's traffic problems began in the 17th century and have never abated. Not too strangely, traversing the port by water has always been relatively efficient, since ferry lines ply the city's waters alongside the world's shipping. The Staten Island Ferry is probably the most famous ride in the nation, and recent success by private ferry operators has spurred plans for expanded municipal service. But the city's street traffic always stuns visitors. As the metropolis expanded after 1800 and became less a pedestrian city, it resorted to carriages, horsecars, and street railways as people-movers. Steam engines ran on city streets until elevated tracks and electric streetcars replaced them late in the 19th century. Pennsylvania Station (1911) and Grand Central Terminal (1913) were constructed to bring commuters into the city. The razing of "Penn Station" in 1964 was considered an architectural tragedy, and the loss fostered a landmark preservation movement that spread from New York across the nation.

The subway is the best means to get around in New York. Service began on October 27, 1904, with the inauguration of a four-track (local and express in both directions) system, which operates around the clock. In the "city that never sleeps," subways—originally built by private corporations but now municipally owned and operated—provide reliable transportation in all boroughs except Staten Island and carry over 1.2 billion passengers annually. Even isolated Staten Island has its own 23-kilometer (14-mile) light transit system. Subways and ferries are supplemented by extensive bus service, both municipally and privately operated, which runs into the suburbs. But none of this alleviates the crush of traffic. Pedestrians battle with buses, delivery trucks, vans, taxicabs, limousines, bicycles and the private car for right of way. Manhattan below 59th Street is inundated by 800,000 vehicles daily, and at peak travel times the city approaches gridlock with an average speed of 3 kilometers (2 miles) per hour. Manhattan pioneered the use of traffic lights, one-way avenues, and computerized signals, and it has 2,000 employees devoted to traffic enforcement—all to no avail. The person who can solve New York's traffic flow will merit a Nobel Prize.

Congestion is also a feature of the three airports, operated by the Port Authority, which currently serve the metropolis. Brooklyn's Floyd Bennett Field was the first municipal airport, but during the 1930s it averaged only one flight a day; after wartime service as naval base, it became part of the Gateway National Park. In 1939 La Guardia Airport opened, and the Port Authority took control of Idlewild (later renamed in honor of President John F. Kennedy) and Newark airports in 1948. Generations of air travelers have lamented the limited facilities, crowded conditions, and distance from Manhattan common to all three, but they continue to rank among the busiest in the nation. In recent years, helicopter service has eased the airport commute for the well-to-do. A rail link to Kennedy was promised for 2003.

CULTURAL AND SOCIAL LIFE

Distinctive Features of City Cultures. Essayist E. B. White wrote that New York "has to be tolerant, otherwise it would explode in a radioactive cloud of hate and bigotry." What else is feasible for a city that has more Irish than Dublin, more Jews than Tel Aviv, more Italians than Naples, and more Puerto Ricans than San Juan? It is a city where ethnic neighborhoods exist flush against each other, usually living in uneasy proximity, jockeying for additional space. Change, both in geographic boundaries and population mix, is the hallmark of the metropolis—as much as its crowding, inadequate housing, traffic, and noise. The environment imposes tolerance, but this virtue is often hidden behind brusque speech and a rapid stride. The pace of daily life often requires, seemingly, the sacrifice of cordiality to competence. New York is not innately rude or unfriendly; it is simply very busy and hence immensely hurried.

Cuisine. New Yorkers enjoy a more varied cuisine than is to be found on any place on earth. The city that invented the restaurant in 1831 (Delmonico's), now boasts more than 9,000 eating establishments, ranging from ubiquitous fast food to neighborhood ethnic cuisines, from singles bar to wine bar, from kosher to Cantonese. Whether one desires the cuisine of a specific Caribbean island or a Chinese province, Afro-American or Afghan, European or Ethiopian, New York can sate one's appetite. It is possible to spend $1,000 per person for a meal or to dine for a dollar. The restaurant business is cutthroat, attrition is high, and chefs from around the world compete to add new ideas and flavors to staple menus and to create taste sensations. From New York–cut steak to bagels, New York cheesecake to Bronx egg creams, the metropolis sets the dinner table of the nation.

Ethnic, Class, and Religious Diversity. Diversity is the essence of the New York experience. Its presence is most obvious in the network of ethnic neighborhoods that are stitched upon the metropolitan quilt. Contemporary Queens stands apart in its multi-peopled reality, containing over 100 recognized groups. In contrast, Staten Island is the most homogeneous of the boroughs. The city as a whole is "majority minority"; its 2000 population was 35% non-Hispanic white, 29% Hispanic, 26% black, and 10% Asian. Roman Catholics and Jews form the primary religious groups, but the city also contains Protestants of every variety, followers of Islam and of Santería, Mormons, and probably a few covens. As Voltaire noted long ago, a city with a hundred religions will learn to revere the virtue of tolerance. New York, since a bloody Irish-Jewish riot in 1902, has rarely experienced religious conflict in the streets. It is race far more than religion that causes modern confrontation.

More troubling is the huge gap between economic classes, for 24.3% of the population lives below the poverty line. Income extremes are most visible in Manhattan, where stock brokers receiving million-dollar bonuses may live in close proximity to minimum-wage earners. Most analysts consider economic factors, rather than ethnicity or religion, to be the primary cause of intergroup tensions.

Family and Other Social Support Systems. New York accepts the image of a cold, heartless town that "bestows the gift of loneliness and . . . privacy" on its residents. But the solitary single does not dominate the city. The outer boroughs are replete with nuclear families, and immigrant groups in particular enjoy extended family relationships, which are especially useful in child-care situations. Immigrant aid societies, some dating back to the 19th century, join with municipal workers to help stabilize families. In 2000 almost a quarter of the population earned income below the poverty level, but New York funds the nation's most extensive system of aid services—including a vast municipal hospital system. Welfare clients, numbering over a million during the 1970s, peaked at 1.2 million in 1990 before declining through the 1990s. During the administration of Mayor Rudolph Giuliani, funds obtained under the national welfare reform law permitted New York to construct the nation's largest "workfare" program. Some experts argued that the program did little to improve job skills and that a true test of its success would occur only after 2002, when the five-year limit on receiving aid would expire. Beyond the working poor, the city provides automatic shelter for some 25,000 residents (2001) made homeless by catastrophe, high rents, family disintegration, or any of the other vicissitudes of urban living. In addition to public programs, over 1,000 private soup kitchens to help the destitute are supported and staffed by "heartless" New Yorkers.

Work and Commerce. Since 1950 New York has changed from a city based on trade and manufacturing to one devoted to finance and services. The million manufacturing jobs existing at midcentury have fallen by three quarters, replaced by jobs created by the expansion of Wall Street and of accounting and consulting firms. In 1998, some 166,000 financial workers received 19% of all city pay. The stock-market boom of 1997–1999 created a large municipal budget surplus, an office-space shortage, and Silicon Alley's expansion to 144,000 workers. All these trends were reversed in the market downturn of 2000, and many believed the city had become too dependent on a stock market that had quadrupled its role in the economy since 1969. One segment of the work force that appears inviolate is the city's civil service, comprising over 300,000 employees who staff the agencies of government; police alone number over 35,000 and mobilize a fleet of 2,500 vehicles. A rebuilt Times Square area became the media center of the United States and once again functioned as a major tourist attraction. Traditional industries continued within the city; clothing sweatshops reminiscent of 1910 are still found in Queens and the Bronx. Some 1.8 million workers make less than poverty-level income in one of the world's richest cities. In stark contrast, the most expensive street for rental space in the world moved only from Fifth Avenue (1998) to Madison Avenue (1999) to East 57th Street (2000).

Arts and Recreation. Since 1850 New York has been the prime destination for those seeking to "make it" in the arts, whether in theater, literature, fashion, dance, painting, music, or film. The galaxy of artists who have called the city home is virtually endless, the roster of its museums and research facilities unparalleled, the variety and quality of its performing arts mind-boggling. Across the globe there is no more prestigious company than the Metropolitan Opera, and the "Great White Way" of Broadway means the finest in drama and musical theater. But New York also plays host to thousands of other performers whose efforts make Off Broadway and Off-Off Broadway productions a constant mother lode of talent. Carnegie Hall evokes musical excellence, while Madison Square Garden, Yankee Stadium (and the vanished venues of Ebbetts Field and the Polo Grounds) represent sports history, not only for New Yorkers but for the entire nation. Greenwich Village has represented countercultural trends for an entire century, whether realistic and naturalistic literature or the poetry of the "Beats," and the Manhattan art scene has spread to encompass Soho, Chelsea, Harlem, Queens, and Brooklyn. No American city is more recognizable, since the streets and neighborhoods of New York have been the subject of countless movies and television programs. This seems only just, since the movie industry began in New York and dozens of films are made in the city annually. In addition, the nation's television networks find it necessary to be located in the world's communication center. More than anything created by talented artists, however, the city itself is a work of art.

QUALITY OF LIFE

New York is *sui generis,* almost beyond ordinary classification. Over the first decade of the 21st century, it plans to complete construction projects that will only further confirm its domination. Port facilities are to expand to handle a predicted doubling of cargo; $350 million will be expended on public parkland; a new Pennsylvania Station is assured and transit plans contemplate a major expansion of subway service. The city will complete its third Water Tunnel, the most expensive project in municipal history. A minimum of $3 billion will refurbish the cultural citadels of the city. All this construction recalls the old saw, "New York will be a great place, if they ever finish it." It is the massive project, the grand gesture that characterizes New York and makes it the "capital of the world."

New Yorkers live with inconvenience, crowding, and intense competition within a city featuring "endless destruction and renewal." Four of its boroughs, if considered separately, would rank among the ten largest American cities. The metropolis is the world's greatest and longest-lasting experiment in multicultural living and is replete with the paradoxes created by its varied populations. It holds the world's highest-paid professionals and vast numbers of welfare recipients; it is the world's media center yet has the largest number of homes without telephones in the United States; it is the nation's most visited city, yet some residents of its outer boroughs have never been to Manhattan. Perennially short of housing, it added 3,000 hotel rooms in 2000, and the industry established national records for occupancy and cost. Its population drinks the best water, enjoys the finest system of municipal parks, rides the nation's best mass-transit system, has access to a cultural cornucopia, and lives in the safest large city in the nation. Yet New Yorkers constantly complain and are vilified by outsiders. Such are the pleasures and pains of the New York experience.

New York's preeminence is so undeniable, its style so aggressively unique, that the city generates a kind of fearful awe even among other Americans. It is different, foreign, busy, arrogant, and misunderstood. Enemies of the United States hate its wealth and power, its diversity, its capitalistic creed. On September 11, 2001, suicide terrorists destroyed the "twin towers" of the World Trade Center, causing some 3,000 deaths, they perhaps believed that a devastating bombing could break the spirit of the metropolis. The results were quite otherwise. The entire nation rallied behind New York, which—for perhaps the only time in its long history—was perceived as an "underdog" worthy of the affection of all citizens. The courage of New Yorkers, the heroism of its civil servants, and the leadership of Mayor Giuliani became the stuff of legend. Strangely, a wounded city became the stimulus for a patriotic explosion and a "war" against terrorism. In its tragedy, New York was recognized as the greatest example of national strength and power, the quintessence of the American spirit.

BIBLIOGRAPHY

Auletta, Ken, *The Streets Were Paved with Gold* (Random House 1975).

Bender, Thomas, *New York Intellect: A History of Intellectual Life in New York City* (Johns Hopkins University Press 1987).

Berrol, Selma, *The Empire City: New York and Its People, 1624–1996* (Praeger 1997).

Binder, Frederick M., and David M. Reimers, *All the Nations under Heaven: An Ethnic and Racial History of New York City* (Columbia University Press 1995).

Burrows, Edwin G., and Mike Wallace, *Gotham: A History of New York City to 1898* (Oxford 1998).

Caro, Robert A., *The Power Broker: Robert Moses and the Fall of New York* (Knopf 1974).

Douglas, Ann, *Terrible Honesty: Mongrel Manhattan in the 1920s* (Farrar, Straus 1995).

Ernst, Robert, *Immigrant Life in New York City, 1825–1863* (Columbia University Press 1949).

Goldberger, Paul, *The City Observed: New York* (Vintage 1979).

Hammack, David C., *Power and Society: Greater New York at the Turn of the Century* (Russell Sage Foundation 1982).

Howe, Irving, *World of Our Fathers* (Touchstone 1976).

Jackson, Kenneth T., ed., *The Encyclopedia of New York City* (Yale University Press 1995).

Kouwenhoven, John, *Columbia Portrait of New York City* (Doubleday 1951).

Lankevich, George J., *American Metropolis: A History of New York City* (New York University Press 1998).

Sayre, Wallace S., and Herbert Kaufman, *Governing New York City* (1956).

Silver, Nathan, *Lost New York* (Houghton Mifflin 1967).

Spann, Edward, *The New Metropolis, 1840–1857* (Columbia University Press 1981).

Still, Bayrd, *Mirror for Gotham: New York as Seen by Contemporaries from Dutch Days to the Present* (New York University Press 1956).

Willensky, Elliot, and Norvel White, eds., *The AIA Guide to New York City* (Macmillan 1988).

GEORGE J. LANKEVICH

Niamey

Niger

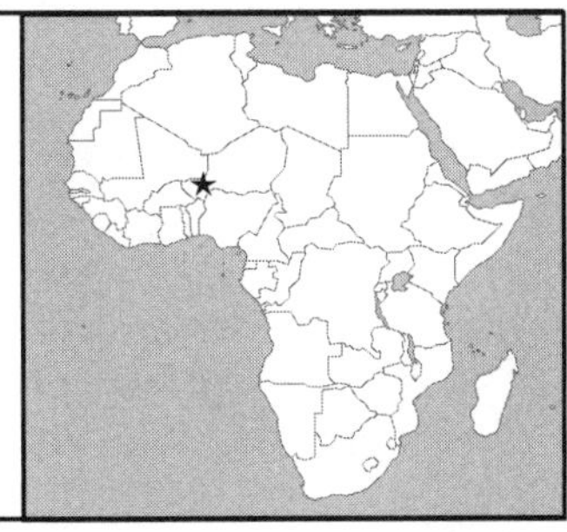

ORIENTATION

Niamey, the capital of the Republic of Niger, is an example of a rapidly growing urban agglomeration in the interior of West Africa. Since the mid-20th century it has grown from a sleepy village and administrative capital of the French colony of Niger to a major center of government and commerce.

Name of City. Niamey is the only name by which this city has ever been known.

Location. Niamey is located on both banks of the Niger River and situated only 160 kilometers (100 miles) from the southern edge of the Sahara desert, in a region known as the Sahel. Present-day Niamey is situated between 13°28′ and 13°35′ north latitude and between 2°30′ and 2°10′ east longitude. Its geographic location places it in a weather and rainfall zone typical of the western Sahel, with little more than 400 millimeters (15 inches) of rainfall annually in one season, normally extending from mid- to late May until late September or early October. Rainfall is often poorly distributed throughout this period and frequently comes in moderately intense but brief downpours preceded by strong winds from the south and east. During the hot dry season (March through May) the maximal temperature may reach 46°C (115°F), exacerbated by cloudless skies. During the cold dry season (November to mid-February) temperatures at night may fall to 7°C (45°F), with daytime temperatures hovering at 13° to 15°C (55° to 59°F). It is during this season that intertropical winds from the northeast produce the sandstorms and red haze known as the harmattan.

Population. Under colonial rule Niamey grew from a town of about 2,500 inhabitants in 1932 to a city of roughly 30,000 at independence in 1960. Since independence, Niamey has become the administrative, educational, and economic center of the country, with an accompanying explosion of population reaching approximately 175,000 people in 1975, 398,265 at the time of the 1988 census and an estimated 800,000 to 1 million inhabitants in 2000.

Geographic Extension. In addition to its growing population, the city has been spreading out geographically from an estimated 13.7 square kilometers (5.3 square miles) when the village became a temporary French administrative post in 1901 to nearly 100 square kilometer (38.6 square miles) in 1995. New neighborhoods spring up every few years, extending residential neighborhoods progressively farther from the city center and from municipal services. This runaway growth has been accompanied by increasingly severe problems of housing, transportation, health, education, and physical infrastructure.

Distinctive and Unique Features. Niamey's most distinctive feature is its geography. The city's development is closely tied to the form of the Niger River and to the elevation of the geographic features of the river valley. Over time the river has carved out the valley, leaving some mesas and outcroppings. On the right bank, as the river descends toward Nigeria, is an area of lowland that is easily flooded and is as a consequence only sparsely populated. The left bank is situated on a plateau rising high enough above that river valley to afford a series of advantages. The city proper is on the left bank and lies at an altitude varying between 180 and 250 meters (590 and 820 feet) above sea level. Even here the elevation is not consistently high enough to avoid flooding, since a seasonal tributary of the Niger River, known as the Gunti Yena, descends from the north and transects the city, resulting in a flood-prone valley dividing the town and emptying out into the Niger right behind the National Museum and Niamey's luxury hotel, the Gaweye. This area is inhabited only by the poorest citizens, as life here periodically becomes miserable. On the other hand, it is precisely this variation in elevation that enables some public infrastructure, such as water and sewers, to be available at least in some parts of the city through the use of low-cost gravity-fed canals.

Attractions of the City. The primary attraction of Niamey is the opportunity to experience an Islamic Sahelian city with all of its cultural differences and uniqueness. Standing on a main street of the city the visitor will see a string of camels carrying goods from the north, men pulling two-wheeled carts overladen with goods or construction materials, people carrying local crafts ranging from straw-hut roofs to woven mats to local pottery water pots, and Twareg (Tuareg) warriors in traditional garb—including their famous indigo turbans—now guarding residences and selling crafts. The setting for all this is a city whose architecture is a combination of colonial French and modern Sahelian-style office buildings, sprinkled among traditional adobe homes and courtyards. The overwhelming palette is ocher red.

Niamey has no traditional monuments or historical sites of importance. Visitors today come to see the vibrant life of the city; its extensive "Grand Marché," rebuilt in the 1980s after a fire destroyed the old market; and a remarkable museum that incorporates examples of home construction from Niger's various ethnic groups and the best crafts that the resident artisans can produce. Other visitors will want to see the central mosque, which was built with support from Saudi Arabia, and the Seyni Kountche Stadium, built by the People's Republic of China. It is possible to arrange to take a canoe (pirogue) ride on the Niger, to ride a horse, or even to play golf on the world's most unique course, carved out of the desert by European golf fanatics. But the tourist sector is poorly developed in Niamey itself. Most visitors attracted to the Sahel will want to leave the capital to see the Ténéré desert to the north or the ancient cities of Maradi and Zinder, or to visit the modest nearby national game park, the Parc du W.

Relationships Between the City and the Outside. At the heart of central Niamey is an old hotel known as the Hotel Terminus. It is all that remains of the dream that the French had to link Niamey to coastal West Africa by extending the railroad from Abidjan, Côte d'Ivoire, through Ouagadougou, Burkina Faso. Although that rail link was never realized, Niamey is intimately connected to all of the major cities of its region by trade and above all by the migratory patterns of its people. Each year an estimated 100,000 Nigeriens, mostly young men, leave the country in search of seasonal work. In times of drought this number can be much higher. These seasonal migrants come from all parts of the country, but especially from the regions of Tahoua and the Niamey Department, where agricultural incomes have always been low. Long distance trading of livestock, minerals (notably salt), weapons, religious ideas, and some agricultural commodities, along with the associated movement of people, date back at least five hundred years. In the past the movements and linkages were primarily in the direction of the Malian towns of Gao and Timbuktou to the northwest, and across the Sahara to North Africa. This trade and these linkages still exist but are overwhelmed today by the pull of the richer cities of the coastal South: Abidjan (Côte d'Ivoire), Accra

(Ghana), Lomé (Togo), Cotonou (Benin), and, of course, the big cities of Nigeria. Niamey's most important tie, however, has been and probably continues to be with Paris, given the ongoing dependence on French financial and technical assistance and on French markets. It is not just goods that bind these cities, though. It is also ideas, educational opportunities, and even military training and cooperation.

Major Languages. Today, Zarma remains the predominant language spoken in Niamey owing to the numeric superiority of Zarma and Maouri peoples. Now, however, Hausa is also widely spoken in the capital, representing a radical change from the situation 30 years ago owing to the importance of the Hausa people in the city's religious and commercial life. The spread of Hausa is no doubt due to the massive influx of people from outside the immediate area, including many Hausa speakers, and to the fact that Hausa has become the principal lingua franca for trade among both Hausa and non-Hausa peoples. Of course, Zarma is still widely spoken. There are also pockets of speakers of Fulfulde (Fulani) and Tamasheq (Twareg), as well as a small number of speakers of other Songhai dialects. Interestingly, the official language of the country and of the capital city is French. Given the very low level of literacy in French, however, probably not exceeding 35%, it is unlikely that the ordinary citizen and merchant on the streets of Niamey will know more than a few words of French.

HISTORY

Niamey is Niger's capital and leading city for reasons that are recent and have nothing to do with the long history of human habitation in central West Africa.

The Origin of the City. In 1901, prior to the colonization of Niger, Niamey became a temporary French administrative post. Some sources, including several published sources by foreign scholars, indicate that it was established initially by fishers from the Kallé subgroup of the Zarma ethnic group. Others, including numerous oral sources in Niamey, dispute this account, contending that the site was founded by people from the Maouri ethnic group. This dispute continues to color the struggle over the legitimacy of traditional titleholders to this day. In 1903 the village became the headquarters of the Third Military Territory, chosen by Captain Salaman for its favorable topography on a plateau above the Niger River. Niamey lost this distinction to the ancient city of Zinder (Damagaram) in the east-central part of the colony in 1911, and it regained it definitively in 1926 largely because of Niamey's adequate supply of water and its location in closer proximity to other French interests in Mali, Upper Volta (later, Burkina Faso) and Dahomey (later, Benin). The choice of Niamey, however, was also no doubt due to the fact that a series of French officials, including notably General Henri Gouraud and colonial governor Brevié, favored it for its beauty and strategic value. Following independence Niamey grew by leaps and bounds as it became the center not only of the Nigerien government and military but also of foreign presence in terms of diplomatic and commercial interests.

Migration: Past and Present. In precolonial times there was nothing to draw people to this site. Even under colonial rule the city grew very slowly, offering little to attract inhabitants, apart from the view of the river from the plateau on the left bank. This would change dramatically in the 1970s as a result of two important developments. First, the discovery of substantial quantities of uranium to the north at Arlit made it possible for the Nigerien regime to begin making major investments in the capital city and drew the attention, both sought after and unwanted, of a number of interested foreign powers. Second, the devastating droughts of 1973–1974 and of 1983—1984 that racked the Sahel brought an influx of people. Not only did the city attract refugees from rural farming areas, it also represented a haven for nomads from the desiccated pasturage lands to the north. Tens of thousands of Nigeriens, many settled initially in such notorious camps as Lazaret, poured into the capital region seeking food relief and work. In response to both developments, the presence of foreign donors and nongovernmental organizations increased exponentially, requiring whole new neighborhoods to house the foreigners in a lifestyle distinctly non-Nigerien. Since agriculture has repeatedly failed, at least in pockets, more villagers have moved to the capital in search of a way to make a living, populating the poorer refugee neighborhoods of the city and pushing it ever outward.

INFRASTRUCTURE

As might be anticipated for such a poor society, Niger has little in the way of impressive public facilities. What it has is largely a product of the French colonial design of the 1930s and the construction boom of the 1970s when uranium export revenues fueled interest and the modernization of the city's governmental and financial sectors.

Public Buildings and Public Works. Urban Niamey is the center of governmental life in Niger and this includes not only the government of Niger, but regional organizations and foreign legations as well. Together these buildings constitute the overwhelming majority of the modern structures in the city today.

Apart from the majestic Presidential Palace, located on the Plateau overlooking the river, and the nearby ministries (Foreign Affairs, Civil Service, Agriculture, Plan, and Higher Education), down the hill from the plateau is found the National Convention Center (Palais des Congrès) and Niamey's only modern tourist hotel, the Hotel Gaweye. On the right bank the only structures of note are the University of Niamey, renamed Abdou Moumouni University, built in the 1970s, and the Agro-Meteorological School (AGHRYMET). The University is a work of remarkable architecture in a neo-Sahelian style and classic ocher color. Today it is both run-down and seriously overcrowded after years of neglect of maintenance and failure to extend its dormitories, lecture hall, and labs to meet increasing demand. On the left bank are a series of high schools, each with its own tradition and role in the history of the student movement, but these are unimposing one-story affairs. The Seyni Kountche Stadium and Youth Complex on the northern edge of the city near the central mosque is a building remarkable for its scale and its role in contemporary Nigerien political history. It was here that the Sovereign National Conference sat for two and a half months in the summer of 1991 to overthrow the old regime. It was pressed into service when the roof of the ten-year-old National Convention Center collapsed just prior to the opening of the conference. Other government buildings are generally unattractive two- to four-story affairs, typically constructed of concrete with little style or adornment. Of some interest are the military and national police (Gendarmerie) facilities dominating the upper Plateau neighborhood above the Presidential Palace, and the region south of the commercial center along the river on the airport road, built of concrete block and adobe in a simple French colonial style. Other examples of this style are the old headquarters of the National Post Office in the city center, and the Municipal Hospital.

Notable on the skyline of Niamey now are the headquarters buildings of two major public banks, the Bank of the West African States (BCEAO) and the Rural Development Bank of Niger (BDRN). Both are impressive structures which sweep higher than any other public buildings in the city. None of the remaining banks, including the International Bank of Africa (BIA) is monumental or impressive in any way. There are some impressive diplomatic buildings in the city, mainly on the upper Plateau in the Yantala neighborhood. Chief among these are the French embassy; the Libyan embassy, which stood vacant for years; the residence of the U.S. ambassador, overlooking the river; and the American Compound, which houses the embassy, the Offices of the Agency for International Development, and the American School. The military coup of January 1996 led to a major reduction in U.S. official presence and the closing of much of the compound.

There are no major public works in Niamey. A single bridge, the John F. Kennedy Bridge, built with U.S. aid, spans the Niger River in central Niamey. The river that in the past always flowed year-round has now been so dramatically reduced in volume that a special interceptor canal, of "le seuil de Goudel," had to be constructed with Japanese aid to assure the population of adequate water supply. Plans to build a major dam upriver for irrigation and electricity generation never materialized but in mid-2000 were again being seriously considered by the World Bank. As a result, the city receives most of its electric power from transmission lines linking it to the Kandadji dam in Nigeria.

Politics and City Services. Since 1989 Niamey has been governed as an "urban community" with the same administrative status as one of Niger's major administrative divisions, the department. This broad governmental unit is divided into three communes: Niamey 1, Niamey 2, and Niamey 3, each with its own mayor. The mayor of each commune is still appointed by the national government, as is the préfet-président of the urban community. Until the implementation of Niger's decentralization plan and the election of local officials in the urban and rural communes, expected in 2001, the préfet holds all executive powers for the city of Niamey.

Niamey has two public hospitals, Lamordé and Central; two district-level referral hospitals; two maternity centers; and about 35 neighborhood-level health centers and maternity clinics. The quality of health care in these public facilities is not considered to be good, and a number of private medical clinics have emerged in recent years to meet the demand of those with more money. Medical insurance is almost unknown, and most of the city's inhabitants are forced to make use of the public facilities, to use traditional practitioners, or to treat themselves with products they can buy from street vendors or in the markets.

Educational System. There are more than 190 schools in Niamey, including primary schools, secondary schools (colleges and lycées), the university, and professional schools. In October 2000 nearly 93,000 students were expected to be enrolled, representing a rate of enrollment for the capital of over 75%. In recent years the number of private and religious schools (Islamic *mèdersas*) has grown significantly.

Transportation System. Niamey is linked to the world and the region by its international airport and by road transportation service entirely in the hands of private transporters and bus operators. The city's connection to the rest of the country has deteriorated considerably with the closing of the state carrier Air Niger, which used to serve regularly Maradi, Zinder, Tahoua, and Agades. Internal air service is now provided only by private aviation and small charter flights.

Within the city, transportation is poor. The majority of trips are taken by pedestrians, with another quarter via bicycles and motorbikes. Less than 10% of the trips are taken on public buses because service is poor and does not extend to many places in the city. Those who can afford it rely on a fleet of privately owned and operated taxicabs. These are shared taxicabs that can take quite indirect routes to get to one's destination, depending on where the other occupants are going. "Taximen," as they are called locally, are literally in the driver's seat. While taxicab rates are nominally controlled by the government, drivers may refuse to go to certain locations, notably across the Kennedy Bridge to the university, for the officially fixed fare. As of June 2000 fares were still reasonable by Western standards, at about $.30 a trip, but this represented a doubling in one step, working a considerable hardship on many of Niamey's citizens.

CULTURAL AND SOCIAL LIFE

The social life of Niamey is typical of that of a Sahelian city, with little to distinguish it from other cities in the same region such as Bamako, Mali's capital.

Cuisine. Daily fare for most of Niger's citizens follows a very traditional pattern heavy on cereals and bean flour with vegetable sauces. The evening meal typically will involve a pot of cooked cereal made from millet, sorghum, or maize flour and garnished with an okra or peanut sauce. Wealthier Nigeriens prefer a diet rich in animal products such as grilled chicken, beef, goat, or mutton on skewers; occasional portions of fish; and a breakfast drink of milk and millet. Increasingly, urban dwellers are consuming wheat-flour bread. In the capital region, fruit, vegetables, and salad are widely available depending on seasonal production, and they are readily consumed by those who can afford them. Rice and pasta are now more prevalent in the urban diet as well. A good deal of the food eaten during the day is purchased on the street from informal vendors or in local outdoor bars or restaurants, known as *maqui*. These meals may include bread, rice, and sauce, or fried bean-flour cakes and grilled meats. The normal cuisine is quite spicy, demonstrating a preference for hot pepper sauces and for ground red pepper mixed with peanut cake. Special occasions, including the Muslim holiday of Tabaski, are typically celebrated by the roasting of an entire sheep, and at other festive times stuffed, roasted sheep's head is eaten and considered a delicacy.

Social Stratification. The city of Niamey is divided into neighborhoods, or *quartiers*, that delineate not only the history of settlement but class and social-group differences as well. In terms of ethnic groups, the older neighborhoods are the principal domains of the Zarma, Maouri, and Kallé, while most of the commercial districts and built-up new areas are heavily populated by people from the Hausa ethnic group. No neighborhood today, however, is ethnically exclusive, particularly the areas built to house government workers, who are drawn from all of the country's ethnic groups.

© K.M. WESTERMANN/CORBIS

Children help their mother in Niamey, Niger.

Wealthy Neighborhoods. Initially, one neighborhood, the Plateau, was constructed by the colonial regime. It was exclusively the domain of administrative buildings, including the Presidential Palace, and residences for "whites." Today the Plateau, and its extension, the Issa-Beri neighborhood, continues to be the sphere of the rich, both African and foreign. Since the 1970s this has been an area of intensive construction of luxury housing destined mainly for rental to wealthy merchants and representatives of foreign governments and businesses. The Plateau is also home to most of the major secondary and professional schools in Niamey, as well as most of the headquarters of international organizations.

A second neighborhood, "Lower Niamey," was one of the initial sites of colonial construction of urban Niamey, but today it is primarily a commercial and administrative district with few residential buildings.

In recent years a number of new neighborhoods have grown up in Niamey that serve mixed functions, including as residences for the upper class of the capital's African population. Such is the case for villages of the Kouara Kano neighborhood, located on the land of the traditional villages of Yantala and Goudel beyond the Plateau to the west. Even this neighborhood, however, has its poor who live in shoddily built, temporary housing on lots that remain unimproved.

Middle-Class Neighborhoods. Most of Niamey's civil servants live in more modest neighborhoods that were initially constructed specifically to house them. These include Cité Fayçal and the Poudrière to the east and Cité Caisse and the area in the vicinity of the BCEAO to the north. Housing in these neighborhoods is either rented or purchased and was built on much smaller lots than in either the wealthy or traditional neighborhood, with the idea that these homes would lodge only nuclear families. The reality is clearly different, and as a result these residential neighborhoods are much more densely populated than was planned.

The Traditional Town. In the center of the city are located the neighborhoods inhabited principally by the original inhabitants of the town, mainly people from the Kallé and Maouri ethnic groups. These neighborhoods are known as Kalley/Lacouroussou, Zongo/Maourey, and West Grand-Marché. They were originally organized around the residences of village headmen, and over the years parcels have been subdivided among heirs and other people have moved in, creating a vast patchwork of tiny lots and small mud-brick constructions. What is unique about these neighborhoods is that, to a significant degree, families of Nigeriens who have become much more affluent through commerce and government employment continue to reside in their traditional homes in the old neighborhood.

Immigrant Neighborhoods. All of the remaining neighborhoods of the city are of recent origin, owing their settlement to the demographic pressure of people who are nonnative to Niamey coming into the city from the surrounding rural areas and even from the distant pasturelands of the north in search of work and the means of survival. This pattern began with the drought of 1968 and continues to this day. Some of these neighborhoods—notably Boukoki, Madina, Bandabari, North Couronne, Kouara Mé, Lazaret, Bani Fandou I and II, and the Filingué Road—were planned to accommodate the influx of migrants. Initially most were squatter settlements or refugee camps. Over time, however, they have been built up with very mixed usage, and some have become the sites of luxury homes, often constructed for rich merchants and foreign renters in the rush of real estate speculation in the uranium boom years of the late 1970s and early 1980s. Today these neighborhoods are still underequipped in terms of city services (water, sewers, and paved roads), but increasingly they are being electrified and are taking on a much more permanent appearance. Other neighborhoods—notably the Airport neighborhood, Talladjé, and the Pays Bas situated to the west of the city; Koubia to the east; Zarma Gandey; and Banga Bana, Kirkissoye, and Karadjé on the right bank of the Niger River—are purely unplanned "spontaneous" areas. These sectors have an almost entirely traditional look of small adobe homes, with no planning of roads or services. More and more, however, even these areas have attracted some "middle-class" workers who cannot afford to live elsewhere.

Family and Other Social Support Systems. Nearly everyone's security and livelihood depend on his or her integration into networks of support ranging from family ties to voluntary relationships of dependence on an employer in what are known as patron-client relationships. Family ties are based on relationships of kinship and affection and serve not only to buffer difficult times but also as sources of recruitment and advancement in all kinds of endeavors. Relationships with employers, on the other hand, derive almost exclusively from perceived mutual needs and rewards, and may not involve affection to any significant degree. Women in particular also rely on voluntary associations to mobilize savings and capital for emergency expenditures. Men's associations tend to be based more on friendships and common interests, such as going out together after work.

Work and Commerce. Niamey is the focus of all economic and administrative employment in the country. By far the largest source of wage and salary employment in the "formal sector" remains the public sector, which in 2000 employed about 40,000 workers. This represented more than one-third of all public formal-sector employees. Nearly a third of these are teachers.

The city is home to nearly all the private-sector firms and about 60% of all production facilities in the country. Industrial employment, however, is still very limited, and apart from the mining sector, it consists almost entirely of import-substitution firms that produce light consumer goods such as textiles, milk products, and beer. Nearly all employment in this sector is unskilled, and foreign managers and technicians still dominate positions requiring considerable training. In recent years, since the adoption of structural adjustment policies and the collapse of the uranium boom market, many of the import-substitution firms have shut down, heightening the problems of urban unemployment. In 2000 only 13% of the wage and salaried workforce worked in the modern industrial sector. Apart from this a small number of people are employed in commercial firms (CACI, CFAO, NIGER-AFRIQUE), in the modest hotel sector (Gaweye, Grand Hôtel, Terminus, Sahel, Ténéré, Ronier, Maoureye), and in the financial sector (Sonibank, BOA, BIA, Eco Bank, and Balinex).

The vast majority of Niamiens work in the informal sector, in more than 6,000 businesses em-

© NIK WHEELER/CORBIS

Umbrellas provide shade for vendors at this busy outdoor market in Niamey, Niger.

ploying two or more people. Many of these firms are involved in small-scale commerce and the provision of labor-intensive services. Although these businesses can be found in all the neighborhoods of the city, they are concentrated around the principal markets. Niamey has three primary daily outdoor markets (the Grand Marché, the Petit Marché, and Katako). These are linked to three secondary markets (Wadata, Yantala, and Haro Banda) and to a multitude of smaller markets and informal-sector shops in every neighborhood of the city.

Social Movements and Social Problems in Modern Niamey. Niamey, as a rapidly growing city in a very poor country, suffers from many contemporary problems that color the lives of its citizens. The most pressing are health and housing problems. Since the late 1970s the city has grown in a chaotic manner vastly outpacing the capacity of urban government to plan for and finance basic services. Problems of solid-waste disposal and sewer systems have reached critical proportions.

As a consequence of this unsanitary environment, and of seasonal climatic variations that intensify health problems, the population of the capital suffers from a number of serious illnesses that cause high morbidity and mortality rates. Chief among these is malaria, which is particularly virulent during the rainy season and which accounts for the highest percentage of deaths by illness. Meningitis is common during the hot dry season, and lung diseases are frequent during the cold dry season. Owing to the poor quality of drinking water, diarrheal diseases are epidemic year-round in the capital. These health problems have only intensified as the portion of the government's budget devoted to health has fallen since the mid-1980s.

In addition, Niamey increasingly suffers from high rates of poverty and unemployment and a number of phenomena that are associated with these economic conditions, notably rising levels of violent crime and robbery and of female prostitution. While these social problems were known in the past, they were considered fairly rare only a few decades ago.

Finally, alcohol addiction and, to a much lesser extent, drug use have become major urban social problems, particularly among the more educated and relatively affluent elites. This is true despite the fact that Niamey is an overwhelmingly Muslim city and that the use of these substances is prohibited to Muslims. The number of bars in Niamey, however, attests to how lightly these prohibitions are held.

Partially in reaction to these social trends, reformist Islamic movements have been growing rapidly in the capital, notably the movement known as "Izala." These movements preach strict adherence to Islamic prohibitions. They have created both modern Muslim schools (*mèdersas*) and health clinics and social centers. Some Nigeriens are concerned that they will also bring a brand of political Islam to the fore that may eventually challenge the secular state.

BIBLIOGRAPHY

Bernus, Suzanne, *Niamey, Population et habitat* (Etudes Nigerienne 1962).

Charlick, Robert B., *Niger: Personal Rule and Survival in the Sahel* (Westview Press 1991).

Decalo, Samuel, *Historical Dictionary of Niger,* 3d ed. (The Scarecrow Press 1997).

Delavignette, Robert, *Freedom and Authority in French West Africa* (Oxford University Press 1950).

Dudot, Bernard, *"Traditions sur les origins de la ville de niamey," Notes Africaines* 117 (January 1968): 19–20.

Fuglestad, Finn, *A History of Niger, 1850–1960* (Cambridge University Press 1983).

Miles, William F. S., *Hausaland Divided: Colonisation and Independence in Nigeria and Niger* (Cornell University Press 1994).

Poitou, Daniele, "Un example d'urbanisation sauvage: Le quartier Talladje a Niamey, Niger," *Actes du colloque international; Strategie urbaine dans les pays en voie de developpement,* ed. by N. Haumont and A. Maric (Harmattan 1987).

ROBERT B. CHARLICK *and* KOKOU HENRI MOTCHO

Nicosia
Cyprus

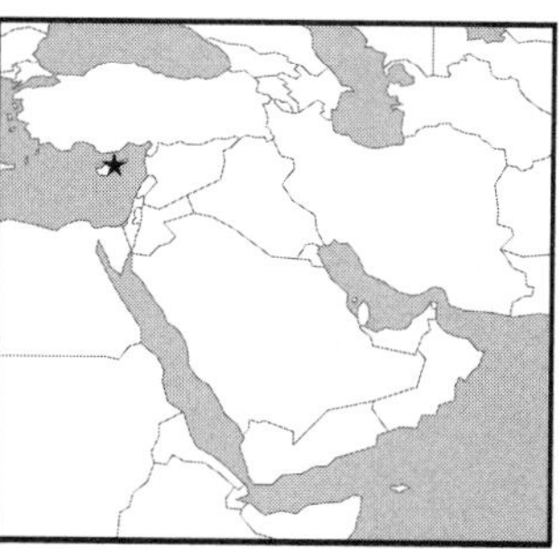

ORIENTATION

Name of City. Nicosia is the modern-day name of the capital of Cyprus and the name by which the city is known to the outside world. For the two major communities of the island—the Greek Cypriot majority and the Turkish Cypriot minority—Nicosia has its Greek and Turkish equivalents, Lefkosia and Lefkosha, respectively. Among Greek Cypriots it is sometimes referred to colloquially as *chora,* which literally means "city."

Location. Nicosia is the capital and major city of Cyprus, an island in the eastern Mediterranean. The city is located at 35°10′3″ north latitude and 33°21′4″ east longitude.

Population. According to the 1992 census, the municipality of Nicosia had a population of 46,990, the city's suburbs an additional 91,065, and the broader urban area another 39,355.

Distinctive and Unique Features. Nicosia is situated in the north-central part of Cyprus in what is known as the Mesaoria plain. It sits in a flat area about 150 meters (500 feet) above sea level that is made up of alluvium and Pliocene deposits. The island's two major mountain ranges, Pentadactylos in the north and Troodos in the south, face the city on each side. The Pedieos River, which used to pass through the center of the city, was diverted by the Venetians during the 16th century, and since then has passed through greater Nicosia before reaching Famagusta Bay. Although historically the river has played an important role for the city, in recent years, it has been mostly dry.

The old city is enclosed within the fortifications built by the Venetians in the 16th century A.D., and clearly reflects the multilayered history of the city itself and of the island more generally. The architecture within this core includes elements from the city's multiple conquerors—the Lusignans, the Venetians, and, later, the Ottomans and the British. Narrow and winding streets and two-story houses with balconies give the old center of the city its particular character. This contrasts sharply with the development outside the city walls—with wider streets, taller buildings, and modern architecture—that took place primarily during the second half of the 20th century.

Nicosia has grown from a small settlement in ancient times to a modern, highly developed city. Its de facto division, which resulted from the Turkish invasion of the island in 1974, remains its most distinctive feature today. The division line that separates the occupied north from the rest of the island also passes through Nicosia and divides it into two parts. This division line, referred to by natives as "the Green Line," is marked with barbed wire, sandbags, and guard posts, and the presence of soldiers from both sides and a United Nations (UN) peacekeeping force. For all practical purposes the Green Line stands as an obstacle to the free movement of Cypriots, not just in Nicosia but also on the entire island. Since the reunification of Germany, Nicosia remains the only divided European city.

Attractions of the City. Nicosia is clearly the business center of the island, the location of the biggest and most important companies. The city offers a variety of business services, and has in recent decades attracted a large number of offshore companies that are finding Cyprus, and Nicosia in particular, a very convenient place for their regional operations. Tax benefits offer additional incentives for foreign investment in the capital. Nicosia also features a variety of cultural events throughout the year, including theater, music, and an annual festival.

For the tourist Nicosia offers many attractions. The Cyprus Museum houses exhibits of artifacts dating back to the Neolithic era, including jewelry, coins, and terra-cotta. The Folk Art Museum focuses exclusively on traditional Cypriot life and art, exhibiting costumes, weaving, embroidery, carving, and pottery. The Leventis Municipal Museum concentrates more on the history of Nicosia through the centuries. The Laiki Yitonia is a renovated traditional neighborhood in the heart of the city, near Eleftherias Square, the main square of the city. Renovated houses, which have been supplemented with additional structures with the same architectural character, provide a tourist attraction. The neighborhood includes souvenir and antique shops, a number of workshops and art galleries, in addition to taverns offering traditional Cypriot cuisine. The Archbishop's Palace, where the head of the autonomous Cypriot church resides, adjoins St. John's cathedral, a small but interesting architectural structure. The church, which was built in the 17th century on the site of a Benedictine Abbey, exhibits an impressive array of wall paintings.

Also worth visiting are the several churches and the few mosques in the old part of the city enclosed within the Venetian walls, which themselves are interesting. Most notable among the religious shrines of the city is Agia Sofia, a church originally built by the Franks and later converted into a mosque later known as Selimiye.

Relationships Between the City and the Outside. Nicosia is today practically joined with its suburbs, constituting a larger urban unit. The city is clearly the administrative, political, economic, and cultural center of the island. Its importance as a center of activity more than makes up for its lack of a port and an airport. Similarly, Nicosia's reduced significance as a tourist destination compared with the coastal towns is more than compensated for by its centrality in the island's life.

The city is known in the international community for its Green Line. In a sense Nicosia is a microcosm of the island's troublesome history. The city's visitors can easily see the island's history over the centuries, and more recently the history of intercommunal conflict and the Turkish invasion and occupation of Cyprus in 1974.

Major Languages. Greek and Turkish are the official languages of the Republic of Cyprus. Following the Turkish occupation, the majority of Turkish Cypriots moved to the north, and the majority of Greek Cypriots moved to the south. So the language spoken in the south is primarily Greek, while in the north it is primarily Turkish. The two languages, however, as used in everyday speech, constitute dialects of Greek and Turkish, respectively. English is widely used in Nicosia and other major cities, given the island's recent colonial history. (Cyprus was under British rule from 1878 to 1960, and the British still retain military bases on the island.) Tourists and foreign visitors can count on being able to communicate in English—not only in restaurants, stores, and banks but also in most of their encounters with locals in the city.

© DAVID RUBINGER/CORBIS

United Nations forces patrolling the line between the Greek and Turkish sections of Nicosia, Cyprus, in 1991.

HISTORY

The Origin of the City. The origins of Nicosia date to the Bronze Age, about 5,000 years ago. The city was originally a small and insignificant settlement. By 700 B.C., the first reference to it is recorded under the name of Ledra, one of Cyprus's ten-city kingdoms. The fertile land from the Pedieos River, which passed through the city, might have been the initial motivation for establishing a settlement there. Ledra remained insignificant until the Byzantine period, when Arab raids forced the movement of the island's population from the coastal areas inland. As a result the city's population increased significantly.

There is evidence that other names—for example, Lefkothea and Lefkousia—were used simultaneously with Ledra. Although it is not clear how and why the name of the city changed from Ledra to Lefkosia, by the 10th century A.D., the latter name replaced the former. At that time the seat of the government was transferred to Nicosia, while in 1192 A.D., when Cyprus was passed on to the French crusader Guy the Lusignan, the city became the capital of the island. The Lusignans renamed the city Nicosia and fortified it. During this period a number of significant structures—mainly churches, monasteries, and palaces—were built in the city. During the Venetian period (1489–1571), the Lusignan fortifications were destroyed and replaced by the more compact walls that still survive today. The Venetian walls are an impressive structure about 5 kilometers (3 miles) in circumference, with 11 bastions and three gates. However, the walls ultimately failed to protect the city from the Ottomans, who conquered Nicosia in 1570. The siege, which lasted for seven weeks, destroyed much of the city. During the Ottoman period (1571–1878), Nicosia remained the capital of the island. For most of this time Nicosia was one of 17 administrative districts; in the 19th century the number of districts was reduced to 6, with Nicosia being the administrative center of one district. When Cyprus was ceded to Britain in 1878, Nicosia became an administrative center and the governor's place of residence. In 1925, when Cyprus officially became a Crown colony, Nicosia became the colonial capital of the island. This later history of the city is clearly reflected in the numerous colonial buildings that are found there, most notable among them the Presidential House. It was during this period that the city expanded outward and extensive road networks were built to connect it with other parts of the island.

When Cyprus gained its independence in 1960, Nicosia became the capital of the Republic of Cyprus. Following intercommunal conflicts between Greek and Turkish Cypriots in 1963 and the formation of a Turkish Cypriot enclave, Nicosia was partly divided. When, in 1974, Turkey invaded Cyprus, the city was completely divided. The biggest part of the city is currently under Turkish occupation. Since the 1974 war, development has been greater in the Greek Cypriot south compared to the occupied north. The expansion that has taken place since the 1970s resulted in the formation of a much larger urban center. Today, Nicosia is divided into seven municipalities, with the metropolitan area constituting the Municipality of Nicosia.

Migration: Past and Present. During the 20th century the population of Nicosia steadily increased. Part of this increase was the result of the natural growth of the city's population, but inward migration added significantly to this trend. During the second half of the 20th century, large numbers of people from rural areas moved to Nicosia in search of jobs, educational opportunities, and better living conditions. Following the 1974 war the city's population rose significantly as a result of the thousands of Greek Cypriot refugees who were forced by the occupying troops to move from the north to the south. Since then, several resettlement communities have been built in the broader urban area of Nicosia to house these refugees. In later years significant numbers of immigrants, mostly unskilled laborers and domestic workers, have also settled in the city. This type of migration is a fairly recent phenomenon for Nicosia and has brought about noticeable demographic changes in the ethnic composition of the city.

INFRASTRUCTURE

Public Buildings, Public Works, and Residences. Nicosia is the location of the island's most important public buildings: the House of Representatives, the Presidential Palace, the Archbishopric Palace, the Supreme Court, and the Municipal Office. Other important public buildings located in the city include the Famagusta Gate (one of the city's three gates, turned into a cultural center by the municipality), the Municipal Theatre, the Cyprus Museum, the Leventis Municipal Museum, the Folk Art Museum, the National Struggle Museum, the Byzantine Museum, and the State Gallery. The country's military and police headquarters are also located in Nicosia.

The most significant infrastructural program in the city is what is referred to as the Nicosia Master Plan. The plan, which is funded by the United Nations Development Program, aims to help the rational development of the city by treating it as one unified whole, despite its division. Since 1979, when the program was launched, the Greek Cypriot and the Turkish Cypriot municipalities have cooperated on several projects. One of the most important projects undertaken was the setting up and coordination of a joint sewerage system. Another significant project undertaken as part of this program has been the preservation and restoration of the city's historical quarters, the areas known as Arab Ahmet and Chrysaliniotissa. The purpose of the revitalization project is to attract new residents and more economic activity to these areas, to provide communal services, and to improve the residents' quality of life. To enhance the sense of tradition that exists in the area, a number of houses were declared as "protected" (*dhiatiritea*), expropriated, and renovated with public expenditure. These houses were then offered to young families who came from low- or middle-income groups, and who intended to reside in the area permanently. Parallel to this effort, there were initiatives by private individual owners to renovate their properties. To aid this effort the government offered attractive incentives through low-interest, long-term loans.

The historical quarters of the city reflect the multilayered history of Nicosia—including elements from the Byzantine, Venetian, Lusignan, and Ottoman architectures. The renovated residences stand in marked contrast to some of the houses that are closer to the buffer zone; these buildings are abandoned and falling apart.

Other major projects undertaken as part of the Nicosia Master Plan include the restoration of the Venetian walls that enclose the old city, and the "pedestrianization" and landscaping of the city's commercial center. The landscaping of the Pedieos River, which passes through Nicosia, and the improvement of traffic management and parking facilities are other ongoing municipal projects.

Politics and City Services. The municipality of Nicosia was first formed by the British in the 19th century. Today, it is governed by the mayor, who is helped by a council consisting of 26 members. Both the mayor and the municipal council are elected every five years by the eligible voters of the municipality. To be eligible to vote, one must be 18 years or over and must have resided in the city for the previous six months. To be eligible to stand for office, one must be at least 25 years old. The main task of the municipal council is to plan and approve budgets, and to enact, revise, and abolish regulations.

© EYE UBIQUITOUS/CORBIS

The northwestern section of Nicosia, Cyprus, has many attractive homes with red-tiled roofs.

The Nicosia municipality provides a number of programs and services to the city. These include, among others, road construction and maintenance, the development of public spaces and buildings, the restoration of historical buildings and other monuments, the design and implementation of environmental protection programs, traffic management and the provision of parking spaces, garbage disposal and the cleaning of public spaces, the protection of public health, and the control and regulation of recreational establishments. The municipality is supported mainly from taxes, fees, service charges, rents, and, to a lesser extent, from fines and national subsidies.

The city plays the most important role in the country's political system. This is where the seat of the government is and where all government offices are located. The president of the country resides in Nicosia, and all important political activity takes place there. Furthermore, all major political parties have their headquarters in Nicosia, and all embassies and foreign missions are found there.

Educational System. The public educational system of Cyprus is highly centralized. It consists of six years of primary and six years of secondary schooling provided free by the state. Primary education and the first three years of secondary education are compulsory. A technical/vocational track is also offered as an option at the secondary level. In addition to the city's public schools, a number of private schools, offering both primary and secondary education in English and other languages, are also found in the city.

Nicosia is the island's educational center. It is the location of the Ministry of Education, where all important decisions regarding public education are reached. The University of Cyprus is located in Nicosia, as are other institutions of tertiary education, including a number of private colleges offering courses in English. The city is also the venue for most of the educational symposia and conferences that take place on the island.

Transportation System. The most common means of transportation within Nicosia is by car or motorbike and secondarily by bus or taxicab. Regular bus service connects Nicosia with its suburbs, its district villages, and the other major towns on the island. However, as more and more people choose to use cars, the importance of buses as a mode of transportation has declined. Taxicabs also connect Nicosia with all other major cities on the island at regularly scheduled times.

Until 1974 Nicosia had its own international airport. However, since the Turkish invasion, the airport, which lies within the buffer zone, has been closed. An international airport in Larnaca—and another one in Paphos—currently serve the international transportation needs of the city and the island as a whole.

CULTURAL AND SOCIAL LIFE

Distinctive Features of the City's Cultures. Nicosia is a fully Westernized city; one may occasionally see an old widow with a black head scarf, but traditional dress has long been abandoned. It was during the British period that the city underwent major transitions in this respect and became modernized.

Cypriots value their tradition and pride in having *filotimo,* a sense of honor that may be expressed in one of its forms as hospitality in relation to outsiders. Though much has changed in recent decades, hospitality still remains a value in Cypriot society, even if not as pronounced as in the past.

What remains a living tradition in the old city are the two farmers' markets that take place on Wednesdays and Saturdays. In these markets, one may find fresh vegetables and fruit at better prices than in supermarkets.

The church and the coffee shop were traditionally the most important public social spaces—the former occupied primarily by women, the latter exclusively carved out for men. At the coffee shop (or *kafenion*), men gather to drink coffee, talk with one another, and play backgammon or cards. Today the importance of these spaces has greatly diminished, and they are more likely to be frequented by old people.

In later years a number of coffee bars and music clubs have made their appearance in the city core. These places have been particularly popular among younger crowds, mostly college students and young professionals who are fashion oriented and style conscious. As compared to previous decades, the city's center, both within and outside the walls, has experienced a remarkable popularity. The "pedestrianization" of some streets in the old part of the city has helped in this respect. Although there is more nightlife in the streets of the commercial center during the summer months, it is quite common to see people frequenting this area during the winter months as well. In fact, many cafés and bars have outdoor heaters that allow their customers to sit outside during the cooler winter months. This new cultural phenomenon is helping redefine the social spaces of the city, giving a new direction to the life of a very old and historical place.

Cuisine. Cypriots are very proud of their cuisine, and many of their social gatherings revolve around food feasts. Cypriot cuisine has been influenced primarily from Greece, Asia Minor, and the Middle East. Many of the dishes are rich, but vegetables are also widely used, either cooked or as salads. Similarly, fruit is also widely consumed, fresh or as preserves. While Cypriot beer is well known and the most widely consumed drink, Cypriot wines are of very high quality and have been famous since antiquity.

There is a wide variety of food in Nicosia, sold in places ranging from local taverns to fast-food chains such as McDonald's and Goody's. International cuisine is widely available in restaurants, and more recently a variety of ethnic cuisines (for example, Chinese, Indian, Lebanese, Italian, and French) is also accessible, although more limited. At a traditional *taverna,* one may try the local Cypriot *meze,* which usually includes a large number of appetizers and dishes from the local cuisine—such as *halloumi* (cheese), *souvlaki* (grilled kebabs), and *kleftiko* (usually lamb cooked in an earthenware pot).

Ethnic, Class, and Religious Diversity. During the 19th century and well into the 20th century, the old part of Nicosia was inhabited by different religious and ethnic groups. The majority of neighborhoods were either Muslim or Greek Orthodox, while a few were Latin (Roman Catholics) or Armenian. There were also a few mixed neighborhoods. During the 1930s and the 1940s, the area known as Chrysaliniotissa was one of the most aristocratic in the city and on the island as a whole. This is where many famous politicians, doctors, and lawyers resided. The area was ethnically mixed until the intercommunal conflicts of 1963. Following the violent events of that year, Turkish Cypriots moved to other areas that were inhabited predominantly by Turkish Cypriots. As a result, Chrysaliniotissa has become more ethnically homogeneous—with the exception of immigrant populations, which are scattered throughout the city in rented residences.

Today the Chrysaliniotissa area is inhabited mostly by older people and refugee families—that is, primarily individuals and families belonging to the lower-income groups. In later years the municipality's efforts to revitalize the area, mainly through the restoration of residences, have brought about a new image to the old part of the city. However, as a result of its proximity to the buffer zone, the area has lost much of its original prestige.

Family and Other Social Support Systems. The family is still one of the most important institutions in the life of Cypriots. Although the nuclear family is the primary unit of cooperation, the extended family is also important, and kinship ties usually imply a strong sense of solidarity. The Cypriot family also remains a patriarchal one in all important respects.

Much has changed in recent decades as a result of rapid modernization, especially in urban centers such as Nicosia. With the introduction of civil marriage, divorce, which was rare in the past, is more common today. The expectation that the bride brings dowry into the marriage is still quite common, although gradually declining in significance. Similarly, the code of honor and shame that influenced how males and females conducted themselves in the social domain has similarly declined in importance. Urbanization has also meant that the nuclear family today has had to depend more on itself and less on the cooperation and interdependence that characterized village life in the past.

Ceremonial kinship is a very well established institution in Cyprus. This kind of fictive kinship establishes a relationship of cooperation and reciprocity between the parties in the relationship. The so-called *koumbaroi* are expected to help each other when necessary, thus extending the support system beyond the mere biological relationships.

The centrality of the family as an institution has indirectly contributed to the underdevelopment of community organizations. However, in recent years, there has been a noticeable increase in the number of such organizations in Nicosia, including several nongovernmental organizations representing a variety of groups and interests dealing with issues such as the environment, the family and domestic violence, refugees, and immigrants.

Work and Commerce. Nicosia is the largest provider of services and the leading employer on the island. Most individuals are employed in the wholesale and retail trades and, to a lesser extent, in services and manufacturing. The majority of the working population drives to work from the city suburbs or the countryside.

The industrial activity of the city focuses, for the most part, on satisfying the local market. It includes the manufacturing of pharmaceuticals, cosmetics, textiles, clothing, and footwear, and the processing of canned fruits and vegetables, wine, and beer.

Nicosia is the commercial center of the island, with most major businesses and banks located there. Shopping activity is concentrated in a number of streets at the center of the city—for example, Ledra Street, Onasagorou Street, and Makarios Avenue. Some shopping streets in the old part of the city are pedestrian, allowing easy access to shops. Laiki Yitonia is a renovated pedestrian neighborhood near the center of the city, with many souvenir and handicraft stores. In recent years department stores have also made their appearance in the city, providing more convenience and selection.

Arts and Recreation. Art has been part of the Cypriot culture since antiquity. Pottery, an ancient art for Cypriots, is being further developed through the reproduction of traditional designs and the development of new, modern ones. Painting and sculpture are also common art forms. Theater and literature, while less developed, have been on the rise in recent years as a result of more individual and government support. Today the arts are developing rapidly on the island. Nicosia once again is playing a key role in this respect. There are numerous art galleries in the city, regular theatrical presentations, concerts and other musical events, and lectures.

Nicosia also provides the whole range of recreational activities offered by other European cities. There are numerous restaurants that cater to all tastes, pubs, discoteques, and music clubs. Cinemas and theatres provide additional outlets for entertainment in the city. Soccer is a very popular sport in Cyprus, and Nicosia has its own local teams. A new soccer stadium outside the urban center has recently been completed. In addition to recreation within the city, many residents often travel outside Nicosia on the weekends, primarily to the Troodos Mountains during the winter months, and to the beach during the summer.

QUALITY OF LIFE

Nicosia is a very affordable city compared to most western European cities. Health standards are quite high, with the incidence of infectious diseases being low. Diseases such as malaria and echinococcosis have been eliminated through persistent campaigns, and thalassemia has been greatly controlled as a result of preventive programs. Infant mortality rates are estimated at nine per thousand and life expectancy at 79.8 years for women and 75.3 years for men. The existence of piped water and sewage disposal early on has contributed to the high standards of health in the city. Both private and public health care are available to city residents, although there has been a move toward the privatization of health care in recent years. The general public hospital is located in Nicosia. A new, more modern building is currently under construction to meet the increasing demands for public health care. Free health care is provided to eligible citizens, mainly according to income and family size.

Pollution in the city is within the accepted limits set by the European Union and other international standards. The absence of heavy industry has meant lower pollution levels in general.

Similarly, crime levels in Nicosia are low, and it is very safe to walk in the city at any time. Pickpocketing and attacks on tourists, which might be common in other foreign cities, are almost totally absent in Nicosia.

Although poverty may characterize the lives of certain social groups in the city (primarily immigrant workers and retirees), homelessness is nonexistent. The strong support system provided by the institution of the family has until now prevented the development of homelessness on the island, and Nicosia is no exception.

BIBLIOGRAPHY

Keshishian, Kevork, *Nicosia: Capital of Cyprus Then and Now,* 2d ed. (Moufflon Book and Arts Center 1990).

Karouzis, George, and Christina Karouzis, *Touring Guide of Nicosia (Broader Urban Areas)* (SELAS, Center of Studies, Research and Publications 1994).

SPYROS SPYROU

Nouméa

New Caledonia

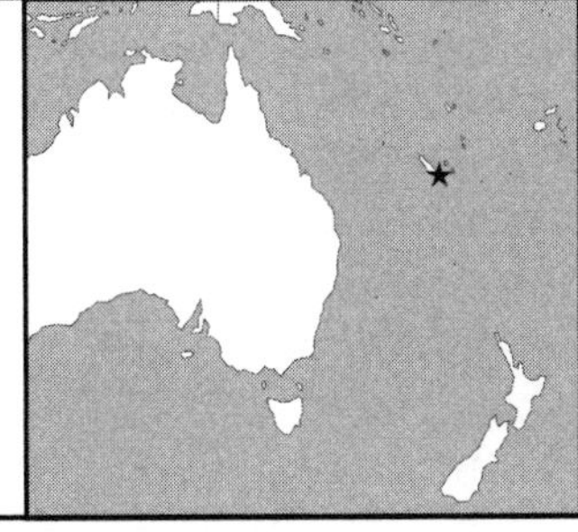

ORIENTATION

Name of City. The city was founded as Port-de-France in 1854. In 1866 the name was changed to Nouméa.

Location. The capital of the archipelago of New Caledonia, Nouméa is located at 22°6′ south latitude and 166°27′ east longitude. It is situated in the South Pacific, just south of the tropic of Capricorn.

Population. More than 60% of the nation's population lives in Nouméa. A total of 164,173 people live in New Caledonia (as of the 1989 census).

Distinctive and Unique Features. Nouméa is a city of many hills. It is located on a series of bays, two of which act as marinas for oceangoing yachts and smaller pleasure craft. The surrounding lagoon provides protection from the Pacific Ocean. One of the highest hills, Ouen Toro, offers views of the township and surrounding areas. The city has good beaches; a safe marina; and a bustling, French-flavored shopping area. It is situated on the main island (*la grande terre*) of the group. The main island is known more affectionately by its inhabitants as *notre caillou* (our small rock). The three islands of Maré, Lifou, and Ouvéa comprise the Loyalty Islands to the east, and the Isle of Pines (home to the Kunié people) lies to the south of the main island. There are numerous small, uninhabited islets that also form part of the archipelago.

Attractions of the City. The port is an established destination on South Pacific cruise routes, and is easily accessible from Sydney (2,200 kilometers; 1,366 miles) and Brisbane (1,500 kilometers; 932 miles) in Australia, Auckland (2,200 kilometers; 1,366 miles) in New Zealand, and Tahiti (5,000 kilometers; 3,105 miles). As a port, Nouméa is also the site for the export of large quantities of processed nickel, the industry upon which the local economy rests. Japanese vessels fish for tuna in the waters surrounding New Caledonia. The blend of Kanak (a political label devised in the 1960s to provide a sense of communal identity to the many Melanesian clans living in the archipelago), Polynesian, and French cultures offers a unique atmosphere for the tourist, together with Pacific-style entertainment, shopping for local and French goods, a variety of cuisines, and a casino. A small airport provides easy flights to the offshore Loyalty Islands and the Isle of Pines. As an avenue to understanding Melanesian ways of being and senses of political identity, the Centre Culturel Tjibaou should not be missed. Located on the Tina Peninsula, ten minutes from the town center, the new cultural center is a resolutely modern design inspired by the traditional architecture of the indigenous Kanak people and brought into being by Renzo Piano. It shows permanent and traveling exhibitions of contemporary and ancestral art, and hosts performances of works by indigenous peoples of the Pacific region. For students, the French University of the Pacific offers courses in anthropology that address issues of New Caledonian culture.

Relationships Between the City and the Outside. Nouméa is referred to as *la ville blanche* (the white town) by many Kanak people, because it is the township in which many of the local French (Caldoche) resettled after the troubling political events of the mid-1980s. As the main administrative site for the island group, Nouméa is also home to the metropolitan French bureaucrats who work in the public service on the island. Bourail, a township on the west coast, is a center for rural producers, and Koné—267 kilometers (166 miles) from Nouméa—is the administrative center for the northern province. Because New Caledonia is situated at the extreme south of the Melanesian arc formed by New Guinea, the Solomon Islands, Vanuatu, and Fiji, its indigenous politics are shaped by the independence politics of these and neighboring Pacific island states. However, many residents and most politicians in Nouméa prefer to retain strong links with France, owing to its economic support of New Caledonia's economy, its commercial links with Société Le Nickel (SNL)—a foundry on the outskirts of the city—and the long history of colonial control and modern power-brokering by France in the Pacific.

Major Languages. French is the official language, and there are 35 Kanak vernacular languages used in the archipelago by approximately 70,000 speakers. In rural areas, where children speak the language of their geographic location, multilingualism is the rule. There are also small but vibrant Tonkinese, Indonesian, and Tahitian communities making up about 14% of the population, as well as a Wallis and Futunan Islander population. In the northern province the majority of the population is Kanak, and local languages are, once again, being frequently practiced in families.

HISTORY

The Origin of the City. Although Lapita pottery remains have been carbon-dated to 1500 B.C., suggesting that Oceanic peoples used the islands from that time, stone and earth mounds containing gastropod shells have been located on the Isle of Pines and dated to 10,000 B.C.

Captain Cook astutely noted, when mapping parts of the archipelago's coastline in 1774, that the main island on which Nouméa is situated could have the potential for great mining riches. The main island currently accounts for 30% of world reserves of nickel, and has great deposits of cobalt, iron, manganese, and chrome.

Whalers, traders, and missionaries began the white settlement of New Caledonia in the 1700s, bringing with them new ways of thinking about objects, new beliefs and values, and importing the schism between Protestant and Catholic that reflected Anglo-French political relations of the time. It was on September 24, 1853, however, that France eventually "took possession" of New Caledonia, under the auspices of Napoleon's Second Empire. Thus began a relationship in which the political centers of Paris and Port-de-France were divided by a distance of 20,000 kilometers (12,420 miles). Contemporary New Caledonia was dramatically shaped by the French requirement for a new penal colony to receive those condemned to more than eight years of forced labor. Achieving the dual goal of ridding the native land of convicts and forcing them to contribute to the productivity of French territorial possessions, the penal colony was started in 1864 at present-day Nouville, an island close to Nouméa, with the arrival of the first boatloads of convicts. The territory is now designated an Overseas Territory (Territoire d'Outre-Mer—TOM) by the French.

John Higginson, after emigrating to Australia, reached New Caledonia to work with James Paddon in 1859. Paddon had settled on present-day Nouville and was working in the sandalwood trade that was a primary economic force in the Pacific at that time. Higginson made a quick fortune through his work with Paddon and, despite his English heritage, chose to cast his lot with New Caledonia, founding SLN in 1876.

The 1878 insurrection of the Kanak peoples in the north of the main island was precipitated by the increasing population of settlers and convicts who required land to survive, and the ensuing disputes with Kanak clans. The taking of land and the trampling of yam crops by cattle created extreme tensions between Kanak and French landholders. Following the deaths of police and settlers at La Foa, 120 kilometers (75 miles) north of Noumea, reinforcements were sent, and the leaders eventually were killed. The idea of Kanak people as "big children, sometimes sulky but always inoffensive" was forever changed. It is argued, however, that ultimately widespread revolt failed as enduring conflicts among Kanak peoples prevented broader alliances, and also because many could gain advantage from the colonizers' power.

After the violent political incidents that took place between Kanak peoples and French settlers from 1984–1988, two clear political forces emerged, then were manifest in the signing of the Matignon Accords in Paris on June 26, 1988: those who desired independence from France and who gathered in and around the Front de Libération Nationale Kanak et Socialiste (FLNKS), and those who wished to keep New Caledonia grouped within the French Republic via the Rassemblement pour la Calédonie dans la République (RPCR). Government is currently organized into three different provinces—the Northern, Southern, and Loyalty Islands. Each has a degree of autonomy and is administered by a provincial assembly. The congress is formed through a union of the provincial assemblies, with France responsible for law enforcement, the military, and other national interests.

Migration: Past and Present. Migration into Nouméa increased dramatically during the 1960s, when extra labor was required for SLN. From the 1950s Polynesians, Tahitians, and Wallis and Futunan islanders had flocked to Nouméa to participate in the important public works that were beginning, such as the construction of the Yaté Dam in the southern region of the main island. The new workers replaced the Indonesian and Vietnamese laborers who were choosing to return to their homelands. Wallis and Futunan islanders are today more numerous in New Caledonia than in Wallis and Futuna; most have settled in Nouméa. After the mid-1980s events, many Caldoche also moved to Nouméa, returning their land to Kanak clans as agreed by the Matignon Accords. Metropolitan French were able to settle freely until 1998, when Kanak leaders arranged that no new settlers would be allowed into New Caledonia without their agreement.

INFRASTRUCTURE

Public Buildings, Public Works, and Residences. St. Joseph's Cathedral is a Nouméan landmark, situated on a rise at the end of Rue de Verdun. Built by convict labor in 1888, it features lovely stained-glass windows that are illuminated on Wednesday evenings. The main library, the Bibliothèque Bernheim, was originally built as the New Caledonian pavilion for the Paris Universal Exposition in 1900. Louis Bernheim, a mining magnate, suggested that it be turned into a library, a project for which he donated the funds in 1901. It is a colonial building with beautiful wooden interior paneling, large rotating fans, and shuttered windows. The South Pacific Commission (Commission du Pacifique Sud) houses its headquarters in a large gathering of buildings opposite the Anse Vata waterfront. Here international and local conferences are hosted, meetings of the constituent island nations are held, and various administrators provide information, technical assistance, and advice about socioeconomic programs to ameliorate the living conditions of their member countries.

Cases, the thatched round huts supported by pillars around the circumference, are the Kanak peoples' traditional architecture. Examples can be seen in the New Caledonian Museum (Musée Néo-Calédonien) in Nouméa and are dotted around the countryside. Many villagers build cases as central meetinghouses, as examples of their architecture to be admired by passersby and villagers alike, and as popular tourist accommodations. Coconut fronds are usually used for thatching, vines for binding, and bark for wall coverings, but the local environment dictates what is used.

Politics and City Services. The Southern province headquarters is located on the southern edge of Port Moselle in Nouméa. Prior to the Matignon Accords, Nouméa was the base for the French administration and the receiving site of public funds forwarded by metropolitan France. Although some responsibilities and funding have been decentralized, the Southern province remains the most powerful and wealthy of the provinces, and it is from this building that most political and commercial decisions that shape Nouméa are made. In addition, the Town Hall (Mairie) manages projects to educate and assist women and families living in public housing on matters of health, budgeting, and children's schooling. It is in Nouméa that the foreign embassies are located, and where commercial activities can be assisted by government and private organizations.

Educational System. The French primary, secondary, and tertiary system is in place, with degrees being offered by the French University of the Pacific in Magenta and Nouville (both suburbs of Nouméa) to the end of the fourth year. Following the school boycott of the early 1980s, the Popular Kanak Schools (Écoles Populaires Kanaks; EPKs) were initiated in 1985. They were begun in order to counter the perception that "white schools" were training young Kanaks to enter the colonial order. However, over time it was argued that, other than offering a greater respect for Kanak customs, languages, and lifeways, they might not have an immediate impact on the direction of social and political change. Indeed, the EPKs have progressively closed in the face of continuing difficulties, except for one that continues to operate on the east coast of the main island at Canala. As agreed in the Matignon Accords, France has provided resources for construction and infrastructure in the Northern and Island provinces in an attempt to balance the provision of services and economic benefits toward Kanak people. A "fast-track" program in which 400 Kanak people were sent to France to be trained to enter the public service was initiated in the early 1990s. However, many argue that discrimination and exploitation against Kanak people still exist.

Transportation System. An efficient bus-shuttle system runs from the central bus station to various suburbs of Nouméa in a star shape, but the service stops toward 6:30 P.M. Buses also run daily to most townships or large villages on the main island, often starting with the early-morning mail buses. There is a regular coach service to Tontouta, the international airport 65 kilometers (40 miles) north of Nouméa. Taxicabs operate in the city of Nouméa and in some of the larger towns on the main island. Cars are available for hire from most international companies, and bicycles and mopeds can be hired from entrepreneurs in the city. As in France, driving is on the right-hand side of the road, and drivers must give way to the right. Aircraft are now the main mode of interisland travel, with connections available from Magenta Airport. An interisland ferry operates to the Isle of Pines every two weeks, but there are no organized boat services to the remote islands off the far-northern coast of the main island. It is possible to charter both yachts and speedboats in Nouméa.

CULTURAL AND SOCIAL LIFE

Distinctive Features of the City's Cultures. Owing to the warm climate, dress is light, bright, and casual for most tourists, although French residents still retain an urban sense of style. Kanak women have adopted the Mother Hubbard, a missionary-devised, shin-length, loose-fitting dress that is usually adorned with a strip of lace and worn without a belt. Despite the attempt to disguise the female form, many materials are diaphanous, a nice subversion of a regime of imposed decorum.

New Caledonians are a warm and welcoming people. When greeting French residents, it is usual to kiss them once on each side of the face. When being introduced to Kanak people, it is polite to shake their hand, but not to look directly into their eyes. When traveling in rural areas, it is polite to always greet a passerby; even when driving, a hand wave is necessary.

Public spaces are often used for resting, or just enjoying the warmth and sunshine. The Place des Cocotiers started its life as a vegetable garden for the French army in the 19th century. The square is now framed by flame trees and the old town hall, which was built in 1875 and is considered a fine example of colonial architecture.

Cuisine. Small cafés offer Chinese and Vietnamese dishes, tasty couscous, or daily menus. Restaurants offer similar fare, but it is presented with the flair demanded by lovers of fine food. The larger hotels offer a full range of French cuisine, as well as Polynesian floor shows and buffets. Fresh fish and seafood are primary ingredients of many dishes. As deer were imported by French settlers toward the end of the 19th century, venison is common. The Kanaks have a special dish called a *bougna*. It blends portions of yam, sweet potato, taro, and banana with small pieces of chicken, fish, lobster, or meat. The mixture is combined with coconut cream, wrapped in banana leaves, and tied with vine, then baked on hot coals in the ground or steamed. Its presentation as a single dish means that *bougna* is shared, usually on Sundays, for special meals or celebrations. To some European palates the mixture can be bland, so requests are sometimes made to Kanak chefs that extra spices be added prior to cooking.

Ethnic, Class, and Religious Diversity. Ethnic diversity in Nouméa is categorized primarily by "race." At 48% of the population, many Kanak people feel they have been made a minority in their own country. Polynesian people from Wallis and Futuna Island (9%), together with people of mixed heritage (métis) (22%), constitute a significant portion of the population (30+%), and tend not to align themselves with the political desires of Kanak independents. The small communities of Indonesians and Vietnamese are also present in restaurants, businesses, and the mining industry. In the 1980s more than 23% of the population was born outside the territory. The demographic increase brought by the new arrivals geographically benefited Nouméa and its neighboring communes of Mont-Dore, Dumbéa, and Païta. It has been argued that the migration may have separated the comfortable and wealthy south as a multiethnic space from the north and the offshore islands as monoethnic areas. Although Nouméa's communities have been described by residents as *cloisonnées* (partitions that make up a whole), members of the *métis* community and many Kanak peoples engage with processes of modernization in order to expand opportunities not offered by clan lifeways. Their actions suggest that Caledonians are now searching beyond ethnic divisions to create new modes of being and new social and political identities.

Class divisions are visible, however. The view from Ouen Toro across the wealthy beach suburbs also offers a contrasting view of the shanty homes surrounding the nickel smelter at Doniambo. Although some support from the French state is received by Kanak people (and the potential loss of such support is present in many people's discussions about independence), the divisions in wealth are dramatic. In the middle of the 1960s, a division appeared between the availability and demand for nickel. Consequently, in 1964–1965 SLN began an ambitious development program. From 1968 there was a severe shortage of labor. Société Le Nickel sent agents to recruit workers from neighboring states such as Wallis and Futuna, Polynesia, the New Hebrides (Vanuatu), Fiji, and Australia. While the new recruits helped, SLN needed to search in France also. At this time 15,000 metropolitans arrived in New Caledonia. The period known as the "boom" changed forever the constitution of New Caledonia's population and worked to change the values of its people. They learned to validate the need to *faire le 5.5*—a French term that describes the need to make the most money possible in the shortest amount of time (1 Caledonian franc equals 5.5 French centimes). But eventually the boom faded. At the end of 1970, supply and demand equalized so that the global price of nickel fell. In 1972 the recession started. Because many Kanaks were still horticulturalists and fishing folk, they had not profited from the boom. Those who were employed often lost their jobs and returned to their tribal lands (*en tribu*). Yet Nouméa had been the site for most of the important infrastructure such as roads, port, and airports, and retained most of the major investments and benefits of the boom.

In the past, Kanak religiosity focused on the veneration of ancestors and a wariness of spirits. There were no temples or constructed sites of worship at the time of exploration and colonization. When missionaries arrived, there was initial resistance and rivalry between proponents of the two major Christian belief systems. Contemporary religious diversity is polarized mainly between the Catholic and Protestant churches, with the Loyalty Islands being predominantly Protestant, and the main island and the Isle of Pines adopting Marist Catholicism. However, new creeds are offering alternatives, as the few people adopting the Baha'i faith in Nouméa and in Vao, the main village of the Isle of Pines, suggest. Different ways of thinking between Kanak and other New Caledonians can also be found regarding time (which is counted in terms of seasons—but not hours, minutes, and seconds), land (which is not bought), and social relations with others (a decision to not arrive for dinner with you, as arranged, because family have shown up at a Kanak person's home). Kanak people also explain that the sense of the individual is limited; rather, a sense of self is constructed through relations with other clan members.

Family and Other Social Support Systems. Among the metropolitan French, the nuclear family prevails. However, Caldoche and Kanak alike have learned the benefits of the extended family and the clan. Many Caldoche live in households that are home to older family members, siblings, and youngsters. As rural people who have moved to an urban environment, they retain many of the social customs of their parents' generation. Kanak people often live together in extended-kin units, with grandparents caring for younger offspring in village environments while the parents work in Nouméa. Children move freely by bus, car, and aircraft around the island group, and many board *en pension* at secondary and university levels, if parents live in the countryside.

In 1992 Marie-Claude Tjibaou, the wife of the assassinated independence-movement leader Jean-Marie Tjibaou, established SOS Violences Sexuelles. The crisis and counseling association was designed to ameliorate the sexual violence that was becoming acknowledged as a problem in New Caledonian communities.

Work and Commerce. Among the French settlers, many employ Kanak women as domestic labor, incorporating the women into their homes as nannies for younger children and as live-in help as the children age. Kanak men are often trained as carpenters and masons. They work on projects, and may then return *en tribu* when unemployment threatens. Some are entering commercial ventures as car and computer salesmen, clerks in the public service, car mechanics, and hotel staff. The administration and teaching services are dominated by metropolitan French people on contract, while many small businesses are owned and managed by, or employ, Caldoche who have moved to Nouméa from the countryside.

Most people who can afford to purchase a car on credit will drive to work. Consequently, the small Pacific island city experiences traffic snarls as dense as those found in many major European cities. Most Kanaks, particularly domestic workers who live away from the homes in which they work, travel by bus. This can be a time-consuming practice, since they need to return to the city center in order to travel to neighboring suburbs. The urban nature of Nouméa and the growth of the service industries that have developed to provide material and expertise for SLN and the burgeoning tourism market today offer a wider range of employment positions to people than in the 1960s.

The city center provides boutique and department-store shopping a short walk from the main bus station. The market operates early in the morning on the quay beside the Port Moselle marina, within easy access to the bus station.

Arts and Recreation. The Agency for the Development of Kanak Culture (l'Agednce pour le Développement de la Culture Kanak; ADCK) provides regular cultural events that portray Kanak songs, lifeways, and art. The agency has also supported street carnivals such as the Equinoxe festival, which began in 1995. Ballet and concerts featuring artists from France also appear regularly. Nautical sports such as yachting, sailing in an outrigger (pirogue), windsurfing, scuba diving, and snorkeling are popular pastimes for residents and tourists alike. Most coastal Kanak people also search for shellfish, fish, trap lobster, and crab. The men of the

© JACK FIELDS/CORBIS

Traditional dances are performed at a festival in Nouméa, New Caledonia.

tribes who dwell inland hunt deer and trap small animals. In the city, volleyball is a popular game among people of every ethnic heritage.

QUALITY OF LIFE

The quality of life for the wealthy in Nouméa is high. Suburbs are close to the beach, receive refreshing sea breezes, and are close enough to provide short commutes to work. Property is expensive, however, and life for those who live close to the nickel smelter in the poorer suburbs can be less attractive because of pollution, high-density apartment buildings, and limited facilities for activities.

Health is generally good. New Caledonians do not suffer from malaria, but high rates of tuberculosis are seen among the Kanak people. There is a major hospital at Magenta in Nouméa, and a large regional hospital at Koné. There is a medical dispensary on the Isle of Pines, but serious cases are helicoptered to Nouméa.

Crime is relatively low, but consumption of alcohol can cause dramatic road accidents, particularly in the countryside. Homelessness is not prevalent in the city, since people usually return to the extended-family members who populate the wooden shacks on the hillsides surrounding Nouméa, or revisit their clans in the rural areas until paid work becomes available again.

FUTURE OF THE CITY

Kanak peoples were already divided by geographic and linguistic differences, but European contact brought new divisions of religion, official and local languages, and culture. Customs have, since first contact, continued to change through the influence of missions and the administration. In contemporary New Caledonia, some Kanak people in Nouméa have been enculturated by Western education, are employed at high wages by French companies and the bureaucracy, and articulate a desire for the development of a harmonious, antiracial, and equal society. Other Kanak people perceive themselves to be permanent outsiders to the French administration, and yet others try to straddle the divide between clan and customary expectations and the powerful individualism of the Western economy. Nonetheless, some Kanak people have found a niche for themselves in a territory that is dominated by commercial enterprises and a region shaped by capitalist policies and endeavors, even though New Caledonia is situated at the edge of economic trading-bloc interactions, and French social and cultural institutions shape the details of daily life. In the rural areas coffee cultivation, raising animals, the installation of cooperatives, and wage earning have also introduced elements of capitalism that cannot be evaded.

Hence, it is hard to foresee the future for Nouméa without including an assessment of the social and political dynamics of a potentially decolonized, multifaceted, multiethnic people. Although New Caledonian peoples are invoking processes of modernity to create new ways of being, they continue to be shaped by a European power that wishes to retain its presence in the South Pacific as a strategic geopolitical arena.

BIBLIOGRAPHY

Bonnemaison, Joël, *The Tree and the Canoe: History and Ethnogeography of Tanna* (University of Hawaii Press 1994).

Connell, John, *New Caledonia or Kanaky?: The Political History of a French Colony,* tr. by Josée Pénot-Demetry (Australian National University 1987) [originally published in 1986 as *La dernière île*].

Dahlen, Jacqueline, *Nouvelle-Calédonie Pay Kanak: un récit, deux histoires* (L'Harmattan 1996).

Fraser, Helen, *New Caledonia: Anti-Colonialism in a Pacific Territory* (Department of the Parliamentary Library 1987).

Fullerton, Laurie, *New Caledonia–A Travel Survival Kit,* 3d ed. (Lonely Planet Publications 1994).

Johnson, Helen, "Interpreting 'Women' in New Caledonia," *Asian Journal of Women's Studies* 4, no. 2 (1998): 53–78.

Johnson, Helen, "The Right Kind of Women Things: Changing Compositions of Gendered Subjectivity in New Caledonia," *Australian Journal of Anthropology* 8, no. 2 (August 1997): 145–166.

Raluy, Antonio, *La Nouvelle-Calédonie* (Éditions Karthala 1990).

Spencer, Michael, et al., eds., *New Caledonia, Essays in Nationalism and Dependency* (University of Queensland Press 1981).

HELEN JOHNSON

Nuremberg
Germany

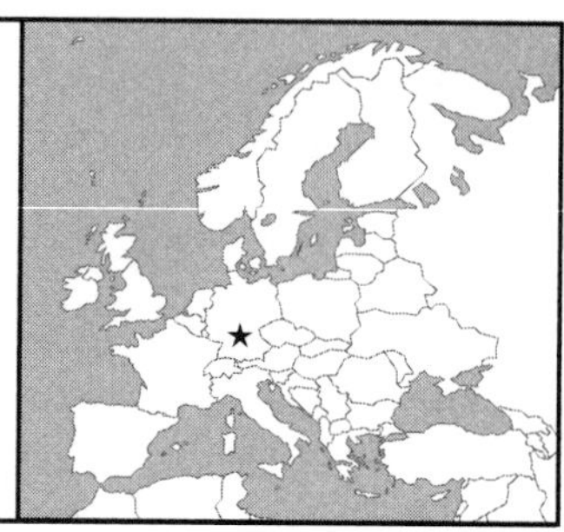

ORIENTATION

Name of City. The city is called Nürnberg in German, Nuremberg in English. The name has a geographic derivation. The Burg ("castle") under which the city eventually developed is located on a rocky cliff that used to be called in the local dialect, Nourenberc.

Location. The city is located 49°27′ north latitude and 11°5′ east longitude in the Franconian part of northern Bavaria (Germany) near the confluence of the Pegnitz and Regnitz rivers. It is 165 kilometers (102 miles) to the north of Munich, 432 kilometers (268 miles) south of Berlin, and 226 kilometers (140 miles) from Frankfurt. Just to the north are the cities of Erlangen (20 kilometers; 12 miles) and Fürth (7 kilometers; 4 miles); to the south is the town of Schwabach (15 kilometers; 9 miles).

Population. The population of the city in 1999 was 487,000 in an area of 186 square kilometers (72 square miles). The four sister cities of Fürth, Nuremberg, Erlangen, and Schwabach cover a region of 367 square kilometers (142 square miles) with a population of 738,000. The industrial region of Nuremberg (the four cities and three neighboring counties) had a population of 1.3 million in a 3,000 square kilometer (1,158 square mile) area.

Distinctive and Unique Features. Nuremberg is located in a 300-meter- (984-foot-) high, largely level basin between the Franconian Alps to the south and east, and the Franconian Terrace to the west. The sandy soil and continental climate support a combination of broadleaf and coniferous forests. These forests used to be a major resource, as were the water power of the Pegnitz River and the iron ore deposits in the Franconian Alps. The rock outcropping just to the north of the Pegnitz historically allowed for a defensive position, and the city's central location on a major transport route from Vienna and Munich northward enabled Nuremberg through its long history to serve as a transshipment point. Later, the completion of the Main-Donau Kanal (Euro-Kanal) and the reopening of the eastern European region resulted in new stimuli.

In 1806 the city territory covered 1.6 square kilometers (0.6 square mile). This had increased to 54.4 square kilometers (21 square miles) by 1899, and by 2000 the city area was 187 square kilometers (72 square miles). It is 23.5 kilometers (15 miles) long from north to south, and 21.4 kilometers (13 miles) from east to west. The center is formed by the 160-hectare (395-acre) Altstadt ("old city"). Shaped roughly like a parallelogram, this core is surrounded by still existing medieval walls, bordered on the northwestern edge by the Burg and bisected east to west by the Pegnitz River. Surrounding the Altstadt and within the *Ringstrasse* ("encircling highway") are found older residential and industrial settlements (the inner suburbs) and the main railroad station at the southern edge of the Altstadt. Toward the southeast is the large recreational lake area of Dutzendteich, and to the east are the pleasant *Wöhrder Wiese* and *Wöhrder See* ("meadows and lakes") along the Pegnitz. Beyond the *Ringstrasse*, the outer suburbs consist of later residential and commercial developments formed around once independent villages and towns. Intact villages and agricultural land (truck farming) are still encountered to the north in the Knoblauchsland ("garlic land"). A number of planned satellite towns exist to the south and east.

The Altstadt is dominated by the elevated Burg. This old center contains many east to west streets and alleyways, and a few north to south thoroughfares. Architecturally, the Gothic predominates in the churches and the residences, some of the latter half-timbered. Baroque influence has been very limited (some 17th- and 18th-century baroque gardens exist to the northeast of the Altstadt), while semblances of the Romanesque can be seen in some of the church doors and in the massive castle. After the destruction of World War II, some of the medieval ambiance of the center was recreated by the retention of the street layout and reconstruction of major historical buildings. Some streets are lined with three- to five-level burgher buildings, topped by steeply sloped roofs and with their narrow side facing the roadway. Modern architectural forms also exist (such as the renovated museums, several department stores, movie theaters). To the east of the Altstadt, impressive 19th-century mansions built by early industrialists and later villas on parklike grounds are found. Nuremberg has 65,000 residential buildings of which 65% are detached single- or two-family houses, mainly postwar in construction and located in the outer suburbs beyond the *Ring*. Most of the rest are inner suburban apartment buildings that range from 19th-century, ornate neo-Gothic style fronted by alcoves to modest and plain multistoried tenement rows. Post–World War II apartment blocks exhibit an emphatically functional design. High-rises—the first one was constructed in the 1950s immediately to the southwest of the Altstadt—are confined to the suburbs and do not define the skyline. This includes planned satellite towns that contain 6- to 16-story high-rise residential blocks. Glass paneled office buildings, some showing neobaroque and other contemporary features, are spreading in the commercial zones of the suburbs.

Attractions of the City. Industry is very important to Nuremberg's economy, with an emphasis on electronics, metal processing, printing and media technology, machine building, and heavy vehicle construction. This industrial presence, the long history of Nuremberg's excellence in technical fields, and its trained workforce make the city an attractive location for business. Other advantages include the presence of technical and research institutes that maintain cooperative programs with industry, the city trade fair complex (Messezentrum) used for regional and international meetings (such as the famous annual toy fair), assistance provided by the city administration and the IHK-Nümberg (chamber of industry and commerce) to new businesses in finding locations and financing, and good economic living conditions and recreational facilities. The presence of the nearby industrial city of Fürth helps, as does the proximity of Erlangen, the university town of the region. Nuremberg's connection to the global economy is indicated by the fact that about 40% of its industrial production is exported beyond Germany.

Nuremberg hosts one million visitors a year, many of them tourists and 25% of them foreign. Out of 50 European cities, Nuremberg is placed sixth by Germans as their "dream city." It is one of the largest cities in central Europe that has an intact medieval wall complex and turrets—including the imposing Burg—and its Altstadt has retained some of its old charm. Nuremberg houses the internationally known Germanisches Nationalmuseum, the largest museum of German art and culture in the country, and a number of other well-known museums, such as the Toy Museum and the Dürer Haus. Annually, the Chriskindlesmarkt (Christmas decorations and gifts) on the Altstadt's main market place ("Hauptmarkt") fronting the Frauenkirche is attended by thousands during the Christmas season. Mainly foreign tourists visit the somber site of the former NSDAP (Nazi Party) annual meetings near the Dutzendteich.

Relationships Between the City and the Outside. Suburban residents identify themselves strongly with Nuremberg's Altstadt, which they regard as the city's historic, cultural, and administrative core. Since Nuremberg has expanded, it has incorporated a large number of once independent towns and villages. Yet the city center is generally not considered to have undermined their position or exploited their economic resources. The situation is different with respect to neighboring Fürth, which gained its independence only in 1808 and has been guarding it ever since against encroachments from Nuremberg. As the largest industrial center in northern Bavaria, Nuremberg has a sensitive relationship with Munich, the domineering rival since the early 19th century. Local feelings are hurt when the importance of Nuremberg, according to southerners, lies mainly in the fact that it "happens to be on the way to Munich." Though intimately tied to the international scene through its economy, tourism, and its formal friendship ties with 13 sister cities, Nuremberg's international image is not helped by its strong Nazi past. Efforts are being made to improve this image by having a Street of Human Rights dedicated in the Altstadt and by initiating an international prize for human rights.

Major Languages. When, up to the mid-19th century, residents still lived only within the Altstadt walls, a local dialect existed, a mixture of Bavarian and of Eastern Franconian. A mild form of it is still encountered among working-class people. From the mid-1800s Eastern Franconian has become the language of daily speech for most residents, while High German is the official language of government, business, and formal education.

HISTORY

The Origin of the City. Nuremberg's role as the major urban and economic center of northern Bavaria (Franconia) can only be understood in terms of its near-millennium long history. The city was first mentioned in documents in 1050. Shortly before this, Henry III had constructed a *Burg* on the rock cliff to the north of the Pegnitz River. In 1062 the city received the right to hold markets, to coin money, and to tax. Until the 14th century the city was divided into two parts: the northern section under the *Burg* and around the St. Sebaldus-Kirche (church), and the section south of the river centered around the St. Lorenz-Kirche. Both were surrounded by walls, with the Pegnitz as the border between them. These sections were merged in the 14th century, a process that was accomplished after a pogrom of the Jews who were living near the new center where the Hauptmarkt and Frauenkirche then were built. After the completion in the 12th century of the Kaiserpfaltz (the imperial portion of the *Burg*), the city served until the 16th century as the location of a large number of imperial diets. In 1219 Nuremberg was pronounced a free imperial city. It was led by the patrician dominated Rat ("city council") in which merchants and especially craftsmen played only a minor role. From 1424 to 1796 (and again briefly during the Nazi period) the imperial insignia were kept in Nuremberg. In the 15th and 16th centuries the city reached the peak of its pre-19th-century cultural and commercial development. The first science university in Germany was established there in 1526. Peter Henlein, Veit Stoss, and Peter Visher excelled in watch making, sculpture, and bronze-casting, respectively. Painting was epitomized by renowned Albrecht Dürer; Hans Sachs (the Meistersinger) deepened German poetry and song; while the humanistic tradition was represented by Willibald Prickheimer. By the 17th century the city had 40,000 inhabitants. Nuremberg joined the Reformation in 1524 and has been a Protestant city ever since. Owing to the shift of trade routes westward as the result of the Age of Discovery, and also to the burden caused by the Thirty Year's War, Nuremberg entered a long period of stagnation in the 17th century. Also strict regulations of the craft industries reduced its competitiveness. By the early 19th century the population had declined to 20,000.

Nuremberg lost its imperial status in 1806 and was incorporated into the newly formed Kingdom of Bavaria. Governance passed out of the control of the city gentry into that of commercial interests, and a modernized administrative structure was introduced. From the 1820s, crafts and industries spread beyond the border of the Altstadt, which led the city (beginning in 1825) to incorporate outlying districts and their growing populations. The first railroad in continental Europe opened in 1835 between Nuremberg and Fürth, stimulating the initial industrial phase characterized by metal processing and the machine industry (1840s–1870s). Nuremberg had 100,000 residents in 1881, a growing proportion of whom were living in expanding tenement settlements beyond the city walls. The second phase of the city's industrialization (1880s–1890s) was characterized by the development of the electrical industry, and in 1906 the new, expansive Hauptbahnhof ("main railroad station") opened to the south of the Altstadt. In 1910 the population had reached 300,000, most of whom lived in the inner suburbs. The difficult times after World War I were partially alleviated with the establishment of a city welfare office and by a publicly subsidized residential building program in the periphery. There, the city also initiated the construction of the *Ringstrasse* and opened an airport. Winning 28% of the local vote in the March election, the National Socialists in 1933 took over power in the city. In memory of the imperial diets that historically took place in Nuremberg, Adolf Hitler chose the city as the location of the annual September party assembly (Reichsparteitag). It was in the city that the anti-Semitic "*Nürnberger Gesetze*" (laws on citizenship and race that established a legal basis for racial discrimination against the Jews) were proclaimed in 1935, and in 1938 the two existing synagogues were destroyed. Of the 8,266 Jewish residents living in Nuremberg in 1933, 6,635 had emigrated by 1941. Except for 72 survivors, the rest were transported to concentration camps and murdered. In 1939 Nuremberg's population stood at 420,000.

The city was subject to heavy bombing in January 1945, which destroyed 90% of the structures in the Altstadt. Between 1945 and 1949 the Nuremberg Trials of war criminals took place in the city's Justice Palace. By 1966 much of the city had been rebuilt, the *Ringstrasse* around the inner suburbs had been completed, and the city was fully connected to an expanded autobahn network. In 1962 Europe's first pedestrian street was inaugurated in the Altstadt, and in 1967 construction of a subway system was initiated. In 1972, when the population was approaching 500,000, the new *Staatshafen* ("harbor") was opened to service the Main-Donau Kanal (also known as the Euro-Kanal, completed in 1992). The first Nuremberg International Human Rights Prize was awarded in 1995, and in 2000 the city celebrated the 950-year anniversary of its existence.

Migration: Past and Present. Nuremberg's population originated largely from Franconia and northern Bavaria. Between 1806 and 1881 the population grew from 25,000 to 100,000, which partly was the result of incorporating neighboring communities whose populations had been swelling owing to immigration from rural and small towns in Middle and Upper Franconia, and from the Upper Palatine to the east. This process continued for the next 30 years, during which time the population tripled to 330,000, and at a slower pace to 1939. The city reached 480,000 in the 1970s with only slight net changes since then. Since 1990, 33,000 people have moved to Nuremberg, while 31,000 moved away, mainly to neighboring cities and rural communities. Annually 40,000 people change their residence within the city, often Germans moving away from the industrial belt to more outlying districts. Daily, 108,000 individuals commute to the city from surrounding communities to work, and 90,000 enter the Altstadt for the same reason. Beginning in the 1960s a wave of southern European guest workers entered the city for low-paying jobs; later they were joined by asylum seekers until the law was changed in 1992–1993, making it more difficult for them to become permanent residents. Since 1980, the number of foreigners in the city has increased by 38,000, so that by 2000 close to 18% of the city's population was classified as non-German.

INFRASTRUCTURE

Public Buildings, Public Works, and Residences. The medieval Altstadt is dominated by the 50-meter- (164-foot-) high Burg (including stables and a granary; part of them now used as a youth hostel), with its massive 220-meter- (722-foot-) long walls and towers. The three principal churches, all Gothic in style, are the dual-spired St. Sebaldus-Kirche (13th century), St. Lorenz-Kirche (14th century), and the Frauenkirche (14th century) headed by a single belfry fronting the Hauptmarkt with its tall, 14th-century *Schöner Brunnen* ("beautiful fountain") that represents a church spire. One of the most impressive historical structures is the 5-kilometer- (3-mile-) long double lined, red sandstone medieval wall, including defensive towers and five main gates, that surround the old city. Some large burgher residences with their massive roofs containing rows of dormers have been reconstructed. The upper parts of these structures are either half-timbered (the Dürer Haus) or made of stone (Fembohaus, which today houses the city museum). Noteworthy is the 14th-century city hall near the Hauptmarkt and its 17th-century reconstructed Italian Renaissance front. There are picturesque bridges over the Pegnitz, among them the oldest suspension bridge in Germany. The Altstadt also includes modern public buildings, most notably the renovated, partly glass-enclosed Germanisches Nationalmuseum at the southern edge and the university complex to northeast. As Nuremberg was an imperial free city, no residences for royalty (except for part of the Burg) or high religious representatives exist. Within the inner suburbs and to the northwest of the Altstadt is the large Klinikum Nürnberg Nord (city hospital complex). Also within this inner zone, but to the southeast of the Altstadt, is the 17-story tower-block of the Bundesanstalt für Arbeit (Federal Employment Office). Nearby is located the Meistersingerhalle (concert hall), not far from the long, copper-domed Hauptbahnhof at the southern edge of the Altstadt. In the outer suburbs notable public structures exist in the Dutzendteich (southeast), Nuremberg's old public recreational area. Here are found the neoclassical, expansive stone structures erected for the NSDAP's annual meetings between 1935 and 1938. The new Messezentrum is found nearby, as well as the Frankenhalle (used for concerts and meetings). Slightly farther south are the modern 1,000-bed Süd-Klinikum and the Frankenstadium (with its circular floating roof) for major sports events (1991). Toward the east are the extensive railroad shunting yard and, completed in 1980, the over 200-meter- (656-foot-) high Fernmeldeturm (television tower). Both are near the Main-Donau Kanal with its harbor. To the north of the city is the Flughafen Nürnberg (airport).

Politics and City Services. The city is governed by the Stadtrat (city council) and the Stadtverwaltung (city administration). The directly elected council (70 members) is the highest representative body within the city. It makes important political decisions and formulates the fundamental principles of city management. City administration is responsible for the daily operations of the city. Both are led by a directly elected *Oberbügermeister* (first mayor) who selects his or her own representatives (2d and 3d *Bürgermeister*) from the council. The city council, in turn, selects eight honorary professional councilors to oversee assigned administrative divisions, such as law and security, environment, culture and schools, youth and family, and city planning. The 71 city administrative offices are grouped according to functions under these professional councilors and are answerable to them. Finally, members of the city council form 18 committees (social welfare, health, education, and so on), which can make legislative suggestions. Since 1986 there has been a *Frauenbeauftragte* who makes sure that women are properly represented in the city administration. Nuremberg is divided into 18 citizen-assembly areas with 10,000–30,000 residents each. They serve as information and contact points between the city government and local residents. City income (DM 1.2 billion, or U.S. $1.12 billion, in 1998) is derived from business taxes (40%), from land taxes (12%), and from the city's share of the income tax (27%); the balance is received from the state and the federal governments. Of the income, 15% is apportioned to city districts for their local programs, and 30% is channeled into social services. In addition to the basic services offered, the city provides special assistance to the handicapped, needy families, seniors, and the young, and welfare relief to the poor and homeless.

As the second-largest city and the second-largest industrial zone in Bavaria (Munich and the region surrounding it being the first), Nuremberg plays an important role in the state's political structure. Some of this takes place by way of the Regireungsbezirk Mittelfranken, one of seven administrative districts of Bavaria, within which it is located. Even though *Mittelfranken* is headquartered in Ansbach to the west, Nuremberg's size assures it considerable influence on the district's relationship with the state. The city is also represented in the semipublic Deutscher Städtetag through its membership in the Bayerischer Städtetag, a voluntary association of 263 Bavarian cities and communities. Representatives in its general council are chosen from existing elected city and community councils. This body lobbies primarily for the financial well-being of its member communities on the state and federal levels.

Educational System. In 1998, 48,000 students attended primary and secondary educational institutions in Nuremberg. Secondary education is divided into *Hauptschulen* for entering industry and crafts, *Realschulen* for medium-level professional training, and *Gymnasium* leading to technical col-

© CHRISTIANE CUNNAR

Vendors in Nuremberg, Germany, set up booths along the Heilig-Geist-Spital Bridge at Christmastime.

leges and universities. Reflecting the industrial character of Nuremberg, 43% of the secondary student population attend *Hauptschulen,* while only 13% attend *Realschulen*. Forty-four percent are *Gymnasium* students. The city also supports 14 trade schools that are part of the secondary educational program. In 1997, 4% of the population (15 years and older) had not completed a secondary education, 47% had completed *Hauptschule,* 25% *Realschule,* and 24% *Gynmasium*. Higher education is represented by technical colleges such as the Georg-Simon Ohm Fachhochschule and the recently opened Hochschule für Musik Nürnberg-Augsburg. Erlangen to the north is the location of the Friedrich-Alexander-Universität Erlangen-Nürnberg, a regional university founded in 1743. With 23,000 students, it is the second largest university in Bavaria. Traditionally strong in the humanities, since the 1920s it has made considerable efforts in the scientific, technical, and medical fields. A branch of the university, specializing in the social sciences and economics, is located in Nuremberg and is attended by 6,000 students. Although many students live in or near the Altstadt, the city does not have a genuine student quarter. For general education the city maintains 4 centrally located libraries and 12 branches distributed in the residential suburbs. One of the oldest town archives in Germany (1370) is located there as a repository of the 950-year history of Nuremberg.

Transportation System. One of the advantages of Nuremberg is its central location between the east-to-west and the north-to-south transport systems in continental Europe. The interregional transport network passing through Nuremberg reflects this centricity. Three major freeway routes cross near Nuremberg, and it is also the location of one of Europe's main railroad junctions, which is connected to the Eurocity-Net and the high-speed InterCityExpress (ICE) network. The city's railroad container marshaling facility is one of the largest in southern Germany. With the completion of the Main-Donau Kanal, its 337-hectare (833-acre) harbor is growing in importance with an annual tonnage turnover of 8 million. The Nuremberg airport to the north has 20 nonstop flights to European cities and services nearly three million passengers and 50,000 tons of freight each year. Local public transport goes back nearly 150 years. By 2000, electric streetcars and bus service were supplemented by a growing subway system (begun in the 1960s) and the aboveground S-Bahn (fast or city train, 1980s). Altogether, 210,000 passenger cars were registered in the city. These, together with 30,000 trucks and thousands of commuter vehicles, were served by 123 kilometers (76 miles) of main highways and by 16 parking garages in or near the Altstadt.

CULTURAL AND SOCIAL LIFE

Distinctive Features of the City's Cultures. No distinctive or unique dress is commonly worn in Nuremberg. Up to the early 20th century traditional Franconian clothing could still be seen in surrounding villages and towns on special occasions—males wore tight jackets with tails and wide-brimmed hats, women wore colored ribbons, wide skirts, and conical hats. Very occasionally one can still encounter elderly *Kreeweibler* in their traditional garb coming to the Altstadt from the rural Knoblauchsland to the north, selling horseradish in jars house-to-house. Aside from the standard modern dress that the people of Nuremberg share with fellow Germans, Bavarian folk attire has made some inroads, especially among men (the so-called Low-Land Tirolers): knee-length leather pants, knee socks, green jackets with horn buttons, and a pointed hunting cap with an attached feather.

Nuremberg residents share their cultural orientation more with Franconians than Bavarians, although their gregarious and extroverted manner, and low regard for personal space in public, is shared with the people of the south. Franconians—and people in Nuremberg especially—are known for their mockery of others and of themselves. Outsiders often note a local proclivity to undervalue oneself and to take an underdog position, which translates into a tendency to complain. On the positive side, this leads to efforts to improve oneself, which is the foundation of the *"Nürnberger Witz"*; that is, a readiness to experiment, and to be good in organizational and technical detail. Though Nurembergers are problem solvers and innovators, they are careful, with a strong sense of conservative realism. Nuremberg residents have a reputation among others as open to the outside (free-thinkers) and adaptable, which in the political context has given them, at times, a reputation of duplicity. For many, the idyllic space is a place in nature that is one's own. It does not need to be much: a small rented garden (*"Schrebergarten"*), a flower pot in a courtyard. If the environment is grimy, it is ignored. Socially, Nuremberg residents tend to be traditional, and to them the home and relatives need careful tending.

Cuisine. The Nuremberg cuisine reflects the southern German preference for wholesome fare. It includes meat (especially pork), fish, dumplings and potatoes, and cabbage for the main meal at noon; bread, cheeses, and sliced sausages, for the evening meal; a great variety of sweet baked goods at coffee time in the afternoon (subject to change during working days). Nuremberg's culinary speciality includes the *rostbratwurst*: small, grilled pork sausage served on pewter platters, 6 to 12 of which are eaten at a time together with sauerkraut, potato salad, horseradish cream, and asparagus. Nuremberg residents share with Franconians a love for roast pig with dumplings (often preceded by potato soup) and *fränkische schlachtplatte* (potatoes and sauerkraut with a great variety of cold cuts, including blood sausage). The preferred fish is carp, either baked or poached in wine. Another Nuremberg specialty is *lebkuchen* ("honey bread"), which is consumed mainly during the Christmas season. A number of local breweries produce a large variety of beers. With Nuremberg's location at the edge of the Franconian Main River area, the white wine grown there—light and tart—is very popular. *Glühwein* ("mulled wine") is a favorite during the cold Christmas season in open markets. International foods (Italian, Greek, French, Chinese, and so on) are readily available in restaurants, and fast-food chains have spread in the Nuremberg area since the 1980s.

Ethnic, Class, and Religious Diversity. Since the early 1960s the proportion of foreigners living in Nuremberg had increased to nearly 18% of the population as of 1998—90,000 altogether. The largest groups were Turks (24,000), Yugoslavs (15,000), Greeks (11,000), and Italians (8,000). Of the 97 statistical districts of the city, 13 contained more than 30% foreigners. The proportions ranged from 25% to 50% in the Altstadt and the inner suburbs; beyond the *Ring* it was about 15%; and in the outlying areas in the south, north, and east of the city it was below 10%. Some tensions exist, especially between Turks and German worker families; many of the latter have tried to move when the proportion of foreigners in the neighborhood go above 30 or 40%. Foreigners tend to live in poorer districts and generally are less well-off than others. Thirty percent of all unemployed in Nuremberg were foreigners (1998), while 38% of all Nuremberg residents who received regular public assistance for subsistence were foreigners. Assimilation has taken place, but only slowly over the generations. The city maintains an office dealing with foreign residents, and efforts are made in public schools to integrate children of foreigners into the German mainstream.

On the two extreme ends, 12% of Nuremberg households brought in a monthly income of DM5,000 (U.S.$2,900) or more in 1997, whereas 6% had an income of DM1,000 (U.S.$590) a month or less. Thirty percent (the largest group) had an income of DM2,000–3,000 (U.S.$1,200–1,800) a month. Twenty percent of those employed are at the top of the occupational pyramid, consisting of the self-employed, executives, managers, and civil servants (2% of these make up the elite); 48% are middle-level white-collar workers, civil servants, and operators of small firms; 20% are craftspersons, forepersons, and skilled blue-collar workers; unskilled workers and those in training made up 10% of the work force. Income differences between the lowest and highest positions in industry were moderated by very progressive federal income taxes. Geographically, the wealthier population tended to live in the north and east, while the less well-off worker population was concentrated in the inner suburbs, especially in the west and south. Altogether, 71% of the 229,000 residential buildings in Nuremberg were occupied by renters, while the rest were inhabited by their usually wealthier owners (1997). Social mobility into the elite is very difficult. However, owing to broadened educational opportunities and the expansion of the service sector during the latter part of the 20th century, movement by the offspring of workers into white-collar positions was quite common. Also, foreigners experienced some upward mobility, indicated by the increasing number of self-employed among them and by residential moves by them into areas less dominated by foreigners.

Nuremberg has been a Protestant city since the Reformation. After the city was pronounced a religiously free city in the early 19th century, the proportion of Catholics increased steadily. In 1950, 34% of the population was Roman Catholic, 62% was Protestant, and 4% identified themselves as other or none. Since then, immigrants with different religious traditions have settled in the city. In 1998, 32% of the population was Catholic, 38% was Protestant, and 30% was "other" (mainly Muslim or Greek Orthodox) or declared no affiliation. A small Jewish community (about 300 members) reestablished itself in the city after World War II.

Family and Other Social Support Systems. In the last several decades of the 20th century, the structural variety of households increased in Nuremberg beyond the traditional male-dominated couple with unmarried children. In 1997 42% of Nuremberg households (out of 261,000) consisted of a single person, 3% were single-parent households with children, 16% were families (married parents) with children, and 39% were childless households with multiple adults (married, or unmarried life companions). Twenty-six percent of household heads had never been married, 48% were married, and 26% were either divorced, lived separately, or were widowed. The high proportion of residents living in single-person households is due to the large number of students and apprentices, foreigners, and elderly citizens living alone (18% of the population is over 65). Though Nuremberg's residents are family oriented, they rely less on extended kin networks for security than is practiced by Turks and other southern Europeans. Friendship networks are acted out in pubs, wine taverns, beer gardens or cellars, at outings, and while visiting movies and sports events. Private, religious, and city organizations offer social welfare services that cover the needs of the elderly, young people, families, the handicapped, and the economically needy and destitute. The city spends DM270 (U.S.$160) annually per resident on social services, more than other Bavarian cities, including Munich. Regular employment involves obligatory subsidized health and unemployment insurance and pension plans, which are, by international standards, quite generous. However, about 50,000 part-time workers were not covered.

Work and Commerce. Those in Nuremberg who are regularly employed, about 255,000, have ample annual vacations (about six weeks a year) and are subject to strictly enforced safety measures at work stations. Union and management-negotiated (and regionally enforced) pay scales prevail in Nuremberg, as well as set work hours (from 7 to 8 hours a day, five days a week are considered to be standard). Although there is a trend toward more individual work patterns, this still affects only a small minority of employed. Only 2% of employees work regularly on weekends.

A major restructuring of Nuremberg's economy has occurred since the 1980s. Whereas in 1975, 42% of the work force was employed in industry and crafts, in 1998 this figure was 26%; during the same period the proportion of service workers (other than trade, banking and finance, and public service) increased from 12% to 29%. White-collar workers make up 60% of the employed, blue-collar 40%. This transformation from an industrial to a service-based economy has not been without pain; 10% of the workforce is unemployed. Many factory workers live in districts near industrial sites and for them commuting is not a major problem, especially given the good public transport system. White-collar employees working in or near the Altstadt frequently live in the outer suburbs and tend to have a longer commute. Traffic jams and parking are a problem, although some of that was alleviated by limiting traffic in the Altstadt and with an aggressive program to offer public parking.

Employing some 43,000, trade is an important sector of the economy; in fact, Nuremberg's per capita retail sales volume is among the highest in Germany's large cities. The Altstadt remains the center of Nuremberg's retail trade, especially south of the Pegnitz River (St. Lorenz area) along the Königstrasse (north to south) and the Breite Gasse and Karolinstrasse (east to west). Department stores, specialty shops, antique shops, galleries, boutiques, and so on, of medium-to-high-quality are found here. Downtown malls and arcades have appeared in the Altstadt. The Altstadt also contains a number of public market places, most notably the Hauptmarkt (to the north of the Pegnitz River), which during the year is the location of a number of specialty open-air markets. Some of the outlying districts have retail centers that have a regional reach, such as near the satellite towns to the south and east. Most of the city's suburban districts have their own modest commercial streets with specialty stores, small supermarkets, and a few restaurants, cafés, and pubs to serve the neighborhood. Large malls and discount warehouses are found in greenfield locations near major transport nodes catering to the motorized public from Erlangen, Fürth, Nuremberg, and beyond.

Arts and Recreation. Toward the end of the 20th century, the eastern inner edge of the Altstadt was declared a Kulturmeile, the location of many of the city's theaters, museums, and other cultural facilities. The arts are well represented by the 15 museums, with about 300,000 visitors annually. The Nürnberger Philharmonic, the opera ensemble, and the city ballet attract an attendance of about 100,000 per year; the large Frankenhalle is the site of several rock concerts each year. The city's public theaters, Schauspielhaus and Kammerspiele (small theater), are complemented by nine private ones, such as the Nürnberger Bürgertheater and the popular Kleine Kommödie. The modern movie center, Cinecittà, in the Altstadt with its ten screens and a number of cafés and bistros is enjoyed mainly by the young. The city maintains 11 Kulturläden in the suburbs (about 280,000 visitors a year), which offer cultural presentations related to their neighborhoods.

Also attended mainly by residents are the *Stadtteil-feste*, of which 14 take place in different parts of the city each year, the largest of which is the Altstadtfest. Aside from these neighborhood festivals, every year Nuremberg offers a variety of popular events that are not exclusively tourist oriented. Among them are the Spring Festival at the Dutzendteich, Rock-im-Park (about 40,000 visitors), Fränkisches Weinfest (Hauptmarkt), Quelle Ironman Triathlon (approximately 100,000 participants and onlookers; biking, running, swimming), Sommer im Park (popular and Franconian folk music), Bardentreffen (songs for the young; Altstadt), Fall Festival (Dutzendteich area), Radkriterium (public bicycle race along the old city wall with around 100,000 watching), Nürnberger Fischtage (fish market and traditional water sports along the Pegnitz River), and the Christkindlesmarkt (Hauptmarkt); this is the most famous event in Nuremberg both among visitors and locals, attended by thousands each December.

Regular popular recreation consists of window-shopping in the Altstadt; visiting the cafés, taverns, and beer gardens and cellars; strolling along the banks of the Pegnitz River and on the *Wöhrder Wiese;* hiking and biking in the city parks to the north; and visiting the Tiergarten Zoo (900,000 annual visitors), which is one of the largest and most attractive of its kind in Europe. There is also the extensive public recreation area at the Dutzendteich for picnicking, water sports, roller-blading, visiting beer gardens, and more. Large state forests to the east of the city offer opportunities for hiking and jogging. The city has many public and private sports facilities, including 529 sports arenas and halls, 361 tennis courts, 187 bowling alleys, 21 horseback-riding facilities, and 8 golf and miniature golf courses. Twenty-six pools are also available. Spectator sports are dominated by the 1. FCN soccer club and international soccer events at the 52,000-capacity Frankenstadium. Ice hockey (Ice-Tigers) is very popular (the 2001 world championship took place in Nuremberg).

QUALITY OF LIFE

One of the more attractive features of Nuremberg and its environs is its affordable cost of living compared to such cities as Munich and Hamburg. Together with its considerable recreational amenities, this helps make the city a relatively comfortable place to live. The spacious pedestrian zone in the Altstadt solved the chronic traffic problem in the old city. Moreover, publicly subsidized urban renewal efforts in the inner suburbs is being extended to the Altstadt. This upgrading is being encouraged by Altstadtfreunde, a private association of concerned citizens that previously was instrumental in urging the reconstruction of historical buildings in the city center and the extension of the pedestrian zone.

Owing to public health insurance and high safety regulations in the workplace, health and disease are not a major problem in the city. Seventeen hospitals serve the area, including the largest communal hospital ("Klinikum") in Germany. The ratio of population to doctor has slowly declined over the years and stands at about 450 to 1.

FUTURE OF THE CITY

In 1997 Nürnberg Agenda 21 was established, a city office charged with implementing the goal of the 1992 Rio de Janeiro Conference on the Environment. Together with federal and state agencies, efforts were made to reduce industrial and vehicular emissions, and to slow the growth of per capita electric, gasoline, and water consumption. Into the 1990s air pollution was a problem because of high levels of sulfuric acid, especially from industrial plants in the former East Germany and Czechoslovakia. This abated during later years. Also the Pegnitz and Regnitz rivers, in the 1980s classified as "very polluted," are now close to being considered as only "moderately polluted." The banks along the Pegnitz in its western and eastern extensions are being re-naturalized. New traffic schemes and noise abatement measures have also been put into place to deal with one of the major complaints of residents: loud and heavy traffic affecting their neighborhoods. While land devoted to open-air recreation makes up only 3% of the city area, 25% of the area is used for agriculture (mainly in the north), and 17% is under forest (the state forests to the east are protected). Thirty-four percent of the city area is occupied by structures, while transport takes up 17% of the city land; the balance is under water or "other."

Crime is not a major concern in Nuremburg; with a crime rate of 8,900 per 100,000 people per annum and 66% of the cases solved, Nuremberg is one of the safest of Germany's large cities. If social background and economic class are taken into account, foreigners tend to be less involved in crime than the German majority. Experiments are taking place in some areas, such as to the west of the Altstadt, in which private citizens are designated as sponsors of five public spaces or buildings each and charged with reporting vandalism to the police. Aside from urban renewal efforts, public neighborhoods are being improved, such as around the Hauptbahnhof. The city has implemented a program based on the "broken window theory" to keep neighborhoods safe by repairing vandalism as soon as it takes place.

Earning less than half the monthly income of the average Nuremberg residents, about 6% of Nuremberg households can be considered poor. This group receives regular public welfare support (as of 1998 38% of these were under 18 years old, 38% were foreigners, and 33% were long-term jobless). Between 300 and 400 homeless adults are given assistance, and 7,232 public and private shelters are available for the elderly poor. Seven thousand children receive subsistence, shelter, and educational support because of poverty or lack of parental care. The social services provided by the city, state, and federal governments, both in finance and infrastructure, is second to none and help keep poverty and homelessness in the city at low levels.

BIBLIOGRAPHY

Benevolo, Leonardo, *The History of the City,* tr. by Geoffrey Culverwell (MIT Press 1980) [contains a section in which Nuremberg's urban and architectural development is traced into the post–World War II era].

Benton, Wilbourn T., and George Grimm, eds., *Nuremberg: German Views of the War Trials* (Southern Methodist University Press 1955).

Dastrup, Boyd L., *Crusade in Nuremberg: Military Occupation, 1945–1949* (Greenwood Press 1985).

Endres, Rudolf, and M. Fleishmann, *Nürnbergs Weg in die Moderne: Witschaft, Politik und Gesellschaft im 19. and 20. Jahrundert* (Nuremberg's passage into the modern. Economics, politics and society in the 19th and 20th centuries) (W. Tümmels 1996) [19th- and 20th-century development of Nuremberg; richly illustrated].

Glaser, Hermann, et al., eds., *Industriekultur in Nürnberg: Eine Deutsche Stadt im Maschinenzeitalter* (Industrial culture in Nuremberg: A German city in the industrial age) (Beck 1980).

Headlam, Cecil, *The Story of Nuremberg* (Dutton 1933) [historical and descriptive account of Nuremberg's pre–World War II city layout and architecture].

Henckle, Dietrich, et al., *Die Region Nürnberg im Strukturwandel (Deutsches Institut für Urbanistik, 1990)* (Technology, time and the domestic market. Structural change in the Nuremberg region) [includes research on reasons why industry and services locate in the Nuremberg region, problems they experience, and changes due to the opening of the European market].

Holtmann, Everhard, and Rainer Schäfer, *Wohnen und Wohnungspolitik in der Grossstadt: Eine Empirische Untersuchung über Wohnformen, Wohnwünsche und Kommunalpolitische Steuerung in Nürnberg* (Residents and residential politics in the metropolis: An empirical examination of residential types, wishes of residents and communal planning in Nuremberg) (Leske und Budrich 1996) [residential space and its uses in Nuremberg's communal planning].

Kusz, Fitzgerald, "Zim Dutzendteich mit Linie 4 (To the Dutzendteich with line 4)," *GEO Special Bayern* (1990): 47–60 [informal cultural description of today's Nuremberg public].

Maas, Herbert, *Geschichte und Geschichten für Jung und Alt* (Nuremberg: History and stories for young and old) (Hofmann 1988) [entertaining and informative vignettes taken from Nuremberg's history].

Monheim, Rolf, "Fussgängerbereiche in Deutschen Innenstädten (Pedestrian zones in German downtowns)," *Geographische Rundschau* 52, no. 7–8 (2000): 40–46 [Nuremberg's Alstadt as an example of effective pedestrian zones and traffic management].

Mulzer, Erich, *Der Wiederaufbau der Altstadt von Nürnberg: 1945 bis 1970* (The reconstruction of Nuremberg's old city center: 1945 to 1970) (Palm & Enke 1972) [post–World War II reconstruction of Nuremberg; many comparative photos].

Stadt Nurnberg, ed., *Juden in Nürnberg. Geschichte der Jüdischen Mitbürger vom Mittelalter bis zur Gegenwart* (Jews in Nuremberg. History of Jewish fellow-citizens from the middle ages to the present) (W. Tümmels Verlag 1995) [history of the Jewish community in Nuremberg up to the present].

Strauss, Gerald, *Nuremberg in the Sixteenth Century: City Politics and Life Between Middle Ages and Modern Times* (Indiana University Press 1976) [well-written and researched historical account; most aspects of social life in the 16th-century city are covered].

Wykes, Alan, *The Nuremberg Rallies* (Ballantine 1970).

Useful Web Site

www.nuernberg.de/english/index.html [Nürnberg Online: the official city Web page of Nuremberg containing a wide range of information, pictures, maps, and links about the city; parts of it are available in English].

NORBERT DANNHAEUSER

Odessa
Ukraine

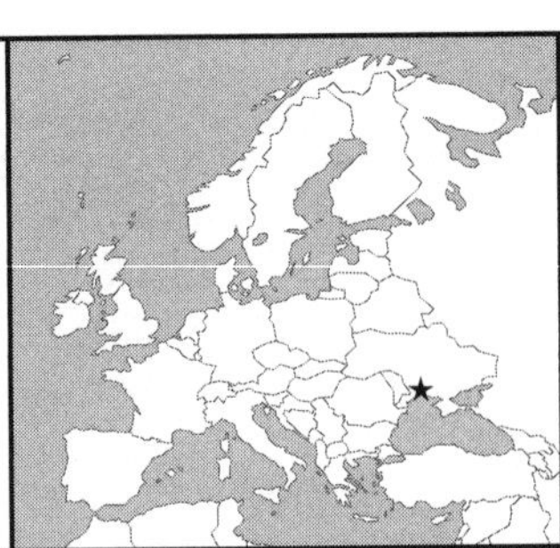

ORIENTATION

Name of City. The name *Odessa*—in Ukrainian spelling, *Odesa* derives from *Odessos,* the name of a Greek colony once located nearby. *Odessa* is the Russian spelling and was used throughout the Soviet period. *Odesa* became official in 1991.

Location. The administrative center of an oblast of the same name, the city of Odessa lies on the north shore of the Black Sea in southern Ukraine, at 46°28′ north latitude and 30°44′ east longitude. Its steppe climate, with hot summers and windy winters, is moderated by the sea. The average temperatures are −2°C (29°F) in January and 23°C (73°F) in July. Odessa is an important warm-water port leading to Ukraine's interior through the rivers Dnipro and Buh to the north and Dnister and Danube to the south.

Population. Odessa, with a population of approximately 1.1 million, is one of the largest cities in Ukraine. Over 2.5 million people live in its metropolitan area.

Distinctive and Unique Features. Odessa lies on a chalk and clay plateau rising at the seashore to above 46 meters (150 feet) and falling to sea level at the surrounding steppes. Several ravines divide the plateau, diversifying the city's topography. The mining of local chalk and stone produced a labyrinth of underground tunnels known as the Odessa catacombs. The northern part of the city, called Peresyp, is situated on the coastal lowlands, below sea level in places. This port warehouse area was protected by a levee to prevent flooding. There are two estuaries, Khadzhybei and Kuialnik, on the north of the city. Kuialnyky is a spa well known for its mineral water and therapeutic mud baths.

Odessa was designed as a seaport from its very beginning, with a downtown open to the sea. A steppe city built in the neoclassical period, Odessa represented the ideal city of the time, laid out in a wide grid. Its well-preserved old downtown and modern suburbs with tall apartment buildings feature spacious streets. Many well-preserved historical 18th- and 19th-century buildings are now used by public institutions.

Unlike most Ukrainian cities Odessa is not centered around a main square with public buildings. The latter are the nuclei of the city's various quarters. Odessa's boulevards are lined with acacia and chestnut trees that bloom in spring and early summer. Primorskii and Frantsuzkii boulevards are cultural landmarks. The 1828 Londonsky Hotel on the Primorskii Boulevard is an architectural landmark. The Potemkin Stairs are a famous Odessa landmark. Built between 1837 and 1842, they connect the port with the Primorskii Boulevard. They are topped by a plaza with a bronze statue, created in 1828 by the sculptor Ivan Martos, of the early-19th-century Odessa governor Armand du Plessis, Duke of Richelieu. Odessa's main artery, closed to vehicular traffic, is Derybasyvska Street, lined with fashionable shops, an arts-and-crafts market, and sidewalk cafes. The 1817 Richelieu Liceum, which became the basis for Odessa University in 1865, is located on Derybasyvska Street.

Financial centers were the Old Stock Exchange, built between 1829 and 1837 and remodeled in 1871 and again in 1946, and the New Stock Exchange, built in 1894 in a neo-Renaissance style. An eclectic mixture of classical, Renaissance, and even Romanesque styles is found in such Odessa landmarks as the Maritime Museum (1841), the Art Museum (1805), the Holy Trinity Church (1839), and St. Paul Church (1897). One of Odessa's most famous buildings is its 1887 Opera Theatre, which replaced an 1809 theater destroyed by fire. Its exterior is neo-Baroque, while the interior decor is rococo. It is topped by a statue of Melpomene (the Greek muse of tragedy). The main entrance is flanked by sculptures representing Tragedy and Comedy.

Attractions of the City. Historically Odessa has maintained international trade and cultural contacts. A member of the World Federation of Twinned

Cities, Odessa has economic and cultural links with 17 foreign cities, mostly seaports (among them Marseilles, Liverpool, Genoa, Baltimore, Vancouver, Haifa, Alexandria, and Calcutta). Trade flourishes among Ukraine and countries of the Black Sea and Mediterranean region: Romania, Bulgaria, Yugoslavia, Turkey, Greece, Italy, Israel, and Egypt. Odessa has branch offices of foreign companies and cultural and educational foundations from Greece, Israel, the United States, and Great Britain. Foreign consulates serve the needs of their citizens and foster international trade and educational exchanges. The city's multicultural character creates a good climate for international contacts. Thus, Odessa is a center of the developing Ukrainian tourist industry. Every year more than 100,000 foreign tourists visit the city and its seaside resorts. Odessa tourist companies provide ship cruises from Odessa to Crimea and on the Dnipro river to Kyiv (Kiev).

Relationships Between the City and the Outside. Odessa's growth affected more than its immediate metropolitan area. In 1957–1958 the port town of Illichivsk was built 23 kilometers (14 miles) southwest of Odessa to serve expanding commercial needs. Illichivsk became Odessa's satellite and it grew rapidly. Another important port, 105 kilometers (65 miles) south of Odessa, is Bilhorod-Dnistrovskii (*Akkerman* before 1944), at the mouth of the Dnister River. It is a gateway between southwestern Ukraine and Moldova, providing the latter with a maritime outlet. The port of Izmayil, at the mouth of the Danube River, is a similar trade gateway to Balkan and central European countries along the Danube, such as Austria, Hungary, Bulgaria, Romania, and Yugoslavia.

The seashore of the Odessa oblast has been a resort area since the mid-19th century. Many city dwellers buy or build *dachas* (cabins on plots of land surrounding the city) close to the sea; They grow fruits and vegetables in dacha gardens. The Odessa region is known for its vineyards. They were first developed in the early 19th century by Franco-Swiss settlers of the Shabo colony, near Akkerman. The coastal plains in Odessa produce large cash crops, mostly wheat and other grains. Immigration to Odessa and neighboring port cities developed an international community of tradespeople and merchants in the region during the 19th and early 20th century. After Ukrainian independence in 1991, this tendency reappeared, along with a traditional support of local cultural institutions and the arts.

In addition to the original Ukrainian population that settled in the area from the 16th to the 18th century, other ethnic minorities settled in the region throughout its history: Serbs came during the Russo-Turkish wars, and Russian Old Believers, Moldovians, Germans, and Jews were settled in colonies by Catherine II after she destroyed the Zaporozhian Sich in 1775. The Sich, headquarters of the military order of Ukrainian kozaks (Cossacks), was the last historic bastion of Ukrainian independence. Catherine II sought unsuccessfully to break Ukrainian hegemony in the steppes by colonizing them with foreigners. Bulgarian fugitives from the Ottoman Empire in the early 19th century, and Poles exiled into the southern steppes after the 1863 insurrection, settled in the area. The nomadic Roma (Rom, or gypsies) were forced by the Soviet government to settle on collective farms. Historically, Odessa proper had large Jewish and Greek populations. Odessa's Jewish culture developed to a high degree by the 20th century, with such literary exponents as the writers Sholom Aleikhem and Isaak Babel. These demographics enhance Odessa's multicultural-mosaic image.

The urban apartment-building courtyard in Odessa may be seen as a model of interpersonal communication at its most basic. Odessa's courtyards, traditional everyday meeting places in old, working-class neighborhoods such as Moldovanka, appeared during Soviet times in central areas when large buildings were subdivided into small communal residences (*komunalky*) with shared bathrooms and kitchens. This lifestyle, characterized by the smell of frying fish from balcony kitchens, is reflected in a distinctive Odessite sense of humor that survived the *komunalky* era.

Major Languages. The Ukrainian language is the official language in Odessa, although Russian is frequently used in everyday communication. Unlike other Ukrainian cities, Odessa has preserved its local slang. It combines Ukrainian, Russian, and Yiddish, and it has a distinctive syntax and intonation structure.

HISTORY

The Origin of the City. The first settlements in Odessa's territory date from the Bronze Age (2000 B.C.). From the 7th century B.C. the territory was occupied by Greeks. The Odessa harbor was used as a way station between the rich Greek colonies of Olvia in the confluence of Dnipro and Buh, and Tira in the Dnister delta. Later the area was populated by Scythians, Romans (the 2d century A.D.) and proto-Slavic tribes of the Chernyakhiv culture (3d to 5th centuries A.D.). Nomadic tribes in the area included Huns, Goths, Patzinaks, and Cumans. Tartars (Tatars) occupied the southernmost steppes from the 13th to the 18th century. The agricultural Slavic tribes Ulichi and Tivertsy and, later, Ukrainian kozaks, settled along the region's rivers.

From the end of 14th century, the territory was under the control of the Grand Duchy of Lithuania. The port town of Hadzhybei (Kachybei) was first mentioned in a 1415 chronicle. From the end of 15th century, Hadzhybei was under the control of the Ottoman Turks. In the second half of the 18th century, they built a fortress there, which fell to Ukrainian kozaks under the command of Anton Holovatyi during the Russian-Turkish war. By the treaty of 1791, the territory was ceded to the Russian Empire and became a part of the Novorossia vice royalty. In 1794 the city of Odessa was founded on the site of Hadzhybei. It was named after the ancient Greek colony Odessos by the Novorossia viceroy count, Grigorii Potemkin. He planned to expand the borders of the Russian Empire to the Balkans and Greece. Odessa was to be a window to the south. Although Potemkin's project failed, this particular function of the city became a reality. The Odessa port was built at the beginning of the 19th century by Joseph De Ribas (who was commemorated in the name of Deribasovska Street, the most fashionable venue in Odessa). The Odessa governor Armand du Plessis, Duke of Richelieu from 1802 to 1814, opened the city to free trade. This attracted merchants and traders as well as workers, craftsmen, and peasants who sought a freedom from serfdom in the new city.

The population of the city grew rapidly. It numbered 9,000 in 1803, 32,000 in 1827, 54,000 in 1836 and 104,000 in 1858. From 1819 to 1859 Odessa enjoyed the status of a Porto Franco, with tax free trade and warehousing. In the late 19th century, Odessa handled 25% of the Russian Empire's exports and 10% of its imports. Industry expanded from 16 plants and 23 flour mills in 1802 to 37 plants in 1837, and from 110 plants in 1896 to 486 plants in 1900. The development of capitalism from 1860 to the 1900s stimulated the growth of the port and transportation systems. In 1874 Odessa's shipping handled 97 vessels, compared to 41 in 1861. The trading volume of the port more than tripled between 1862 and 1893. In 1865 the first railroad in Ukraine connected Odessa with the city of Balta, in 1870 with Elisavetgrad (currently, Kirovograd), in 1876 with Kyiv, and then with Moscow and St. Petersburg.

In 1873 there were 3,000 merchants in Odessa. Among them were only 1,037 merchants of the first guild (guild categories in the Russian Empire were determined by the merchant's capital); the rest were small businesspeople. At the end of the 19th century, Odessa's multiethnic culture developed, paralleling the growth of trade and industry. Traditionally, ethnic groups found different occupational niches. Groups that became a part of Odessa's urban lore were Jewish teamsters (*byndiuzhnyky*), Greek sailors, and Ukrainian and Russian longshoremen. Each group had its own slang and folklore. The exchange and blending of elements between high and low cultural spheres were typical of the Odessa urban life in the 19th and 20th centuries: Odessa cabmen sang Italian opera arias at work, and local artists and writers skillfully portrayed Odessa's longshoremen and smugglers.

Odessa always had a rich cultural life supported by public and private funds. The first private newspaper in Ukraine, the *Odessa Herald* (*Odesskii vestnik*), was published in Odessa in French in 1820, becoming a daily in 1824. The Odessa Theater, founded in 1809, hosted many foreign opera companies and domestic theater companies, as well as the famous Russian and Ukrainian actors Mykhailo Shchepkin and Karpo Solenyk. In 1825 the first archeological museum in Ukraine opened in Odessa, and a public library opened in 1829. Both the Odessa Society of History and Antiquities and the Odessa Philharmonic Society were organized in 1839. The Odessa Conservatory opened in 1897 as a music school, becoming an institution of higher education in 1913. In 1899 the Odessa Art Museum was founded.

A series of Russian imperial decrees issued from 1870 to 1890 prohibited the use of the Ukrainian language in cultural and educational institutions of central and eastern Ukraine. Being less restricted because of its peripheral location, Odessa became a refuge of Ukrainian cultural life. Such prominent Ukrainian composers and scholars as Pavlo Sokalskii, Pavlo Nishchynskii, and Mykola Arkas lived and worked there. The famous Ukrainian playwright and actor Marko Kropyvnytskyi debuted there in 1871. The first professional Ukrainian drama company, led by Kropyvnytskyi, Mykhailo Starytskyi, and Panas Saksahanskyi, performed in Odessa very successfully. From 1828 to 1860 only one Ukrainian book was published in Odessa, but from 1883 to 1887 there were 44 books published. From 1900 to 1915 Odessa literary almanacs were published by Mykola Voronyj and Ivan Lypa, these played an important role in the development of Ukrainian nationhood.

At that time Ukrainian historians Mykhailo Slabchenko and Mykhailo Hryshevskii, the future president of the Ukrainian People's Republic (1917–1919) taught at Odessa University.

Odessa was a cradle of several national movements. In 1814 a secret Greek society was organized in Odessa to liberate Greece from the Turks. In the 1820s Odessa was home to a secret Russian revolutionary society, a branch of the Decembrists movement. Many Polish patriots were exiled there, including the poet Adam Mickiewicz. The Russian poet Alexander Pushkin was also exiled to Odessa in 1823–1824. Here he met the Decembrists and the Greek freedom fighters led by Constantine Liprandi.

The Russian government supported anti-Turkish movements in order to expand its influence to the Balkans and the Middle East. This involved Russia in an international crisis: a war with Turkey, Great Britain, and France in 1853–1855 (known in the West as the Crimean War). During this war British and French fleets tried to bomb Odessa but were driven away. From 1860 to 1870 Odessa became a center of the Bulgarian national movement. The Bulgarian poet and political leader Christo Botev studied in Odessa from 1863 to 1866. In 1877–1878 thousands of southern Ukrainian volunteers—many Odessites among them—fought in the Russian army that liberated Bulgaria from the Turks. In the 1880s the Orthodox Palestinian Society was organized in Odessa to support pilgrimages from Russia to the Holy Land. This movement organized many Ukrainian peasants from regions near Odessa and became truly religious, contrary to the political aims of the government. A passenger-ship line connected Odessa and Haifa. It was revived in the 1990s to provide a regularly scheduled service between Ukraine and Israel.

Before World War I socialist and communist movements appeared in Odessa. During the revolution of 1917, the period of the Ukrainian People's Republic (1917–1919), and the Civil War (1918–1920), the city changed hands repeatedly between the Ukrainian Revolutionary Committee; the Bolsheviks; German and Austrian armies; British, French, and Greek expeditionary forces; Otaman Hryhoriiv's rebels; Denikin's Russian White Army; the Ukrainian Galician Army; and the Bolsheviks again. In this period many Odessites emigrated either abroad or to the country's interior. From 1919 to 1925 Odessa was a gubernia (oblast, or state; a czarist-era term later revived) center; from 1925 to 1932 it became a district center, and then it became the capital of the newly formed oblast. In 1914, 669,000 people lived in Odessa. By 1920 the population of the city had decreased to 428,000. The militant communism of the Bolsheviks led to the first famine in Ukraine in 1921–1922, and many people died in villages and cities. By 1923 the population of Odessa had fallen to 324,000. In Soviet times, foreign trade was minimized and heavy industry was favored. In the 1930s a power station, a refinery, and an asphalt plant opened in the city, and old plants were retooled. A new population influx sought industrial jobs. By 1926 the population had grown to 420,900 people in Odessa, and by 1939 the population had climbed to over 600,000 people.

Beginning in the late 1920s, academic life in Odessa paralleled industrial development. Medical, technical, and agricultural research institutes were established, along with geodesic, seismic, and astronomic observatories such as the Odessa Meteorological Station, the Odessa Scientific Society of the All-Ukrainian Academy of Sciences, and the Odessa Regional Studies Committee. From 1926 until 1933

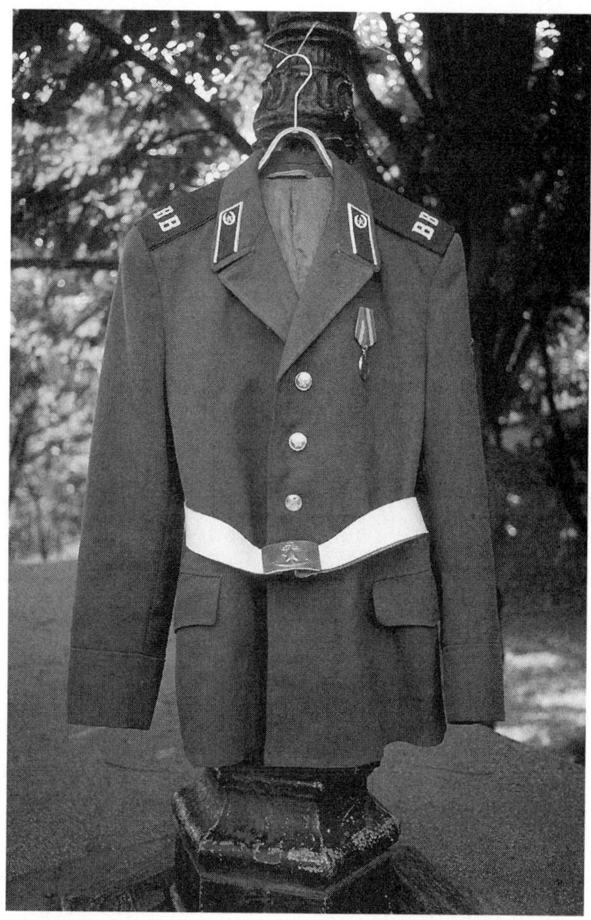

COPYRIGHT DAVE G. HOUSER/CORBIS

An army uniform is displayed for prospective buyers in Odessa, Ukraine.

the Communist Party of Ukraine successfully implemented a policy of "Ukrainization" that fostered the development of regional studies, Ukrainian history studies, literature, and arts. Established in 1919, the Odessa Artistic Film Studio pioneered the genre in Ukraine. The auteur filmmaker Oleksander Dovzhenko and the writer Yurii Yanovskii began their careers in the city. Between 1933 and 1941 Ukrainization was abruptly quashed by Stalin, who perceived it as separatism. Many talented Ukrainian artists, writers, and scholars were persecuted, jailed, exiled, or even executed by Stalin's regime. The artificial famine of 1932–1933 principally targeted the Ukrainian rural population, but it affected the cities as well. In the region people escaped from villages only to die on the streets of Odessa.

During World War II Odessa was besieged by German troops. The Odessa garrison defended the city tenaciously, making a stronghold of its catacombs. After the war a historical museum opened in the Nerubajsk catacombs. Many civilian Odessites were killed during the war. In 1926 there were 155,900 Jews in Odessa; by 1948 there were only 107,000. Not until 1956 did the city's population return to its prewar level.

By the 1970s new multistory apartment buildings surrounded Odessa's downtown. This did not alleviate the housing shortage, however, for the population reached 776,000 in 1967 and 1,115,000 in 1979. By the end of the 20th century, Odessa was a highly developed port and industrial city. One-third of its industries produced fabricated metal and machinery. The food and chemical industries were substantial as well. The Odessa and Illichevsk ports handled an expanding international trade. The Porto Franco concept reappeared in the 1990s as a part of market reform in independent Ukraine. The revival of the city's business and culture stimulated a renovation of Odessa's historical landmarks. Old street names were restored, and churches and historical buildings were returned to their traditional functions.

Migration: Past and Present. Odessa developed through the immigration of different groups. The 1795 population of 2,300 quickly increased. Soldiers and officers of the Russian army brought their families; Ukrainian kozaks moved into the city, escaping serfdom; Greek, Armenian, and Italian merchants settled on the north shore of the Black Sea. Aristocratic refugees from revolutionary France received land grants from the Russian imperial government in the Odessa region, and these new landlords preferred the city life. At the end of the 18th century, a ten-year tax exemption attracted new colonists to the Novorossia vice royalty. By Russian imperial design the southern steppes were to be populated by immigrants of diverse nationalities, the better to break the Ukrainian kozak hold on the land. Thus, Germans, Swiss, Jews, Greeks, Armenians, Bulgarians, Orthodox Albanians, and others came to settle in the area, but the steppes remained populated mostly by Ukrainian kozaks and peasants moving from the neighboring Ukrainian lands, especially from the Podolian gubernia. The settlers originally residing in villages and colonies nearest to Odessa—Ukrainians, Russians, Moldovians, Germans, and Jews—migrated into the city in search of better economic opportunities produced by Odessa's industrial growth in a process of a voluntary migrant resettlement. Since the mid-19th century thousands of seasonal workers have found employment in the city each summer.

Fluctuations and declines in Odessa's population correlated with the revolution, the Civil War, the famines of 1921 and 1932–1933, and with World War II. After Stalin's death in 1956, Odessa's population grew through migration from rural areas to the city. At that time the Soviet regime loosened its restrictions concerning the relocation of collective farm workers, who had been as attached to their agricultural workplaces just as the serfs had been under the czars. The establishment of educational and research institutions, along with the research needs of industry, generated an immigration of professionals academics from different parts of the former Soviet Union. In the 1980s, however, there was mass emigration of Odessites—mostly from the Jewish community—in search of the kind of freedom of worship that was not available under Soviet rule. These Odessa emigrants preserved very strong cultural links with their compatriots in Israel, the United States, and Canada.

INFRASTRUCTURE

Public Buildings, Public Works, and Residences. Odessa is among the few Ukrainian cities that house their municipal and administrative offices in their original historical buildings. In the 1990s many old buildings were restored to their original architectural splendor.

Public services in Odessa have not caught up with the needs of the steadily growing population. The city has difficulty providing enough drinking water. Some old residential areas still do not have municipal sewerage service, relying instead on antiquated septic collectors. Improving public utilities and services is a primary task of the 21st-century city government. The privatization of residences has allowed owners to restore and remodel houses and apartments and to invest profitably in real estate. The city's downtown has experienced a revival as a prestigious residential quarter.

Politics and City Services. Odessa is a city with an old tradition of self-governance. At the same time it is the administrative center of the Odessa oblast, which contains four sizable cities and a large rural area. Consequently there are frequent conflicts of interest and priorities between the city and oblast administrations.

Educational System. Odessa is an important educational center. Its institutions of higher learning include Odessa University, the Polytechnic Institute, the Medical Institute, the Merchant Marine Academy, the Pedagogical University, the Institute of Food, the Institute of Hydrometeorology, and the Conservatory of Music. In the 1990s several private colleges opened in the city, providing healthy competition to state institutions. Odessa's public educational institutions are open to private initiative and to international exchange programs. The center *Osvita* (Education) of the Renaissance/Soros Foundation, branches of the American Councils for International Education (formerly the American Council of Teachers of Russian/American Councils for Collaboration in Education and Language Study, or ACTR/ACCELS), and the British Councils and other international educational organizations work in the city. Elementary and secondary schooling is compulsory, and free-of-charge in public schools; it is universally available in Odessa as it is elsewhere in Ukraine. Odessa has schools for gifted children, and many private schools have been accredited.

Transportation System. Odessa connects by railroad, bus, ship, and airlines with other Ukrainian cities, including Mykolaiv, Sympheropol, Kherson, Vinnytsya, Kyiv, and Lviv, and with cities in Moldova, Russia, Romania, Poland, western European and Balkan countries, Greece, Turkey, and the Middle East. The adjacent ports of Odessa and Illichivsk make up the largest port area on the Azov and northern Black Sea. Odessa has international and domestic passenger ship terminals; Illichivsk handles mostly cargo. In the 1990s many domestic routes were curtailed because of the high cost of fuel but the volume of international passenger and cargo shipping actually increased.

Odessa's urban transportation lags behind its population growth. The privatization process has supplemented the overextended municipal system with new transportation companies. Private companies have refurbished old buses and trolleybuses, which compete successfully with municipal transit, providing transportation to all city points. Taxi service in Odessa was privatized as well. The large number of cars cause traffic jams during rush hours, particularly in the city's downtown area.

CULTURAL AND SOCIAL LIFE

Distinctive Features of the City's Cultures. Since its beginnings Odessa has been a cultural center of southern Ukraine. The average Odessite is an avid concert and theatergoer. One of Odessa's cultural phenomena is a local humor that pervades jokes, theatrical sketches, television programs, and festivals. The Humorina festival is held in the city annually, on April 1. Odessa humor owes its specific character to the mixture of diverse ethnic cultures in the area. At a grassroots level it is an original style of urban communication. People in the streets tell jokes to each other that may be whimsical, risqué, political, or all three. An example of typical Odessa humorous discourse is provided in the following anecdote: an Odessite runs into a well-known local television and radio personality and asks him: "Are you really [so-and-so] or are you just taking a walk?"

Cuisine. Odessa cuisine is very distinctive: it includes many ethnic culinary traditions. The Ukrainian borshch (borscht) and *varenyki* (pierogies), Jewish gefilte fish and strudel, Greek baklava, and Austrian-style tortes may all appear on a family's menu regardless of its ethnicity. Restaurants serve the same variety of Odessa dishes as well as the usual Ukrainian restaurant fare: chicken Kiev, veal cutlets, salade Olivier, meats, fowl, fish in aspic or variously prepared, or a well garnished rice pilaf with diced meat. Some restaurants specialize in diverse world cuisines. Odessa has Irish pubs, Italian pizzerias, and Chinese restaurants. Bistros and sidewalk cafes serve coffee, soft and alcoholic drinks, and sandwiches.

Ethnic, Class, and Religious Diversity. In contemporary Odessa, as in all the Ukraine, there is a renaissance of ethnic and religious traditions. The Ukrainian Orthodox church of the Kyevan Patriarchy, the Ukrainian Orthodox Church of the Moscow Patriarchy, the Ukrainian Autocephalous Orthodox Church, and the Ukrainian Catholic Church have large congregations in Odessa. Revived Roman Catholic and Lutheran churches of Odessa serve respectively the Polish and German communities. There is a Greek Orthodox church in the city as well. Jewish religious life is thriving in restored and new synagogues. Several Protestant denominations have established churches, prayer houses, and meeting places. Along with Ukrainian cultural organizations, there are Jewish, Bulgarian, and Greek cultural foundations. The gap between rich and poor is very marked in Odessa, but there is a growing middle class of small business- and tradespeople.

Family and Other Social Support Systems. Throughout Ukraine the extended family is the most basic social unit. The overpopulation of the city forced people to live in extremely close proximity. On the one hand, communal living—the *komunalka* phenomenon—generated gossip and conflicts caused by lack of privacy; but on the other hand, it created closely knit small communities within a shared living space. There are two trends in contemporary Odessa urban Life: one is to preserve such community relationships—amounting to an extended family—and the other is to strive for privacy. The younger and wealthier often choose a more private space, which has generated a construction boom in the city.

Work and Commerce. Historically Odessa's industry and commerce were the principal sources of employment at all levels of qualification, from mill workers to scientists and engineers, and from stock clerks to economists and lawyers. Under the Soviet regime industry remained a source of jobs, but commerce was replaced by bureaucracy . Hundreds of thousands of Odessites worked in plants and factories.

During the economic crisis in the late 1980–1990s the level of unemployment grew. In this situation small businesses became a creative force in the city life, just as they had been in the city's early history. Fashionable shops and department stores opened in downtown Odessa, but, owing to the economic crisis, they were patronized only by the rich few. Odessa's street markets became centers of private trade and goods exchange. An average Odessite buys food and consumer goods at street markets or bazaars. One of the most typical markets is the Pryvoz, active in the center of the city for over one hundred years. The largest bazaar is on the city's periphery and is accessible by bus. In Odessa's bazaars one can buy and sell anything. Small merchants called "shuttles" import and sell a lot of food and consumer goods from Turkey, Poland, Italy, Greece, and other countries.

Arts and Recreation. Leisure in Odessa is associated with its resorts and beaches. There are 14 year-round resorts on the oblast's sea coast. North of the metropolitan area are the sandy beaches of Lusanivka and Fontanka. To the northwest mineral-water and mud resorts line the Kuyalnik and Hadzhibej estuaries. The Lanzheron beach is the closest to the center of the city. South of the downtown are the Arcadia beach, a resort, an amusement park, and the beaches of Velykyi Fontan. The popular resort Chornomorka is situated between Odessa and Illichivsk.

Odessites are keenly aware of their rich urban cultural life. Drama theaters, operetta, opera, and concerts of classical music are very popular in the city. At the same time, pop and rock concerts attract ever-larger audiences. The immensely popular comedy talk shows pervade Odessa's cultural life. Some of the most popular humorists and performing groups began their careers in local university amateur theaters. Works by Odessa artists and craftspersons are shown both in private art galleries and in

© JANET WISHNETSKY/CORBIS

Sunbathers crowd the beach in Odessa, Ukraine.

street shows. Most representative of these is the arts and crafts show in a park near Deribasivska Street.

QUALITY OF LIFE

One of principal health problems in a large port city like Odessa was and is the control and prevention of epidemic diseases. Several times during its history, Odessa had epidemics of bubonic plague and typhus. Cholera is endemic in the Odessa area. This led to the establishment in Odessa of the first microbiological laboratory in the Russian Empire. In Soviet times it became the Research Institute of Microbiology. In the last decades of the 20th century cholera epidemics were eliminated, but some cases still appear sporadically. The poverty and lack of housing among significant segments of the urban population during the economic crisis facilitated the spread of tuberculosis. As a port with a large transient population, Odessa also has relatively numerous HIV (human immunodeficiency virus) and AIDS (acquired immune deficiency syndrome) cases. The city administration and state health institutions try to prevent epidemic diseases in the city through regular water and food testing, medical prophylaxis, and education. They cooperate actively with international health institutions and foundations. Atmospheric conditions in the region contribute to good air quality in Odessa.

FUTURE OF THE CITY

Odessa is one of the most promising centers of economic reform and business development in Ukraine. Its port is growing rapidly, and there are plans for future development of a modern oil terminal and refineries. Odessa's revival as a center of commerce and industry a promises a realization of its economic potential, which would exert a powerful and positive influence far beyond its geographic boundaries.

BIBLIOGRAPHY

Afanasiev-Chuzhbinskii, A., *Ocherki Dnestra* (Sketches of the Dniester), vol. 2 of *Poezdka v Yuzhnuyu Rossiyu* (Voyage to Southern Russia) (1891).

Druzhinina, E. I., *Severnoe Prichernomorje v 1775-1800 gg* (The Northern Black Sea Coast in 1775–1800) (AN SSSR 1959).

Herlihy, Patricia, *Odessa: A History 1794-1914* (Harvard University Press 1991).

Hodges, Linda, and George Chumak, *The Hippocrene Language and Travel Guide to Ukraine* (Hippocrene 1996).

Klaus, A., *Nashi kolonii* (Our Colonies) (Tipografiia vv T. Nusval't 1869).

Istoria mist I sil Ukrainskoi RSR. Odeska oblast (History of the Towns and Villages of the Ukrainian SSR; Odessa Oblast) (URSR 1969).

Panibudlaska, V. F., ed., *Natsional'ni procesy v Ukraini. Istoriya I suchasnist* (National Processes in Ukraine; History and Essence) *Dokumenty i materialy* (Documents and Materials), vol. 1, (Vyshcha shkola 1997).

Skalkovskii, A., *Opyt statisticheskogo opisaniya Novorossijskogo kraya* (Experience of the Statistical Survey of the New Russia Region) (1850).

Tayler, Jeffrey, "Flushing Out the Shlaki; The Surprising Consolidation of Formerly Soviet Medical Care," *The Atlantic Monthly* (January 2001): 23–26.

Trojnitskii, N. A., ed., *Pervaya vseobshchaya perepis naseleniya Rossijskoi imperii 1897 g* (First General Census of the Russian Empire, 1897), vol. 47, *Khersonskaya guberniya* (Kherson Gubernia) (1897).

Zinkewych, Osyp, and Volodymyr Hula, *Ukraine. A Tourist Guide,* tr. and ed. by Martha D. Olynyk (Smoloskyp 1993).

HANNA CHUMACHENKO

Oranjestad

Aruba

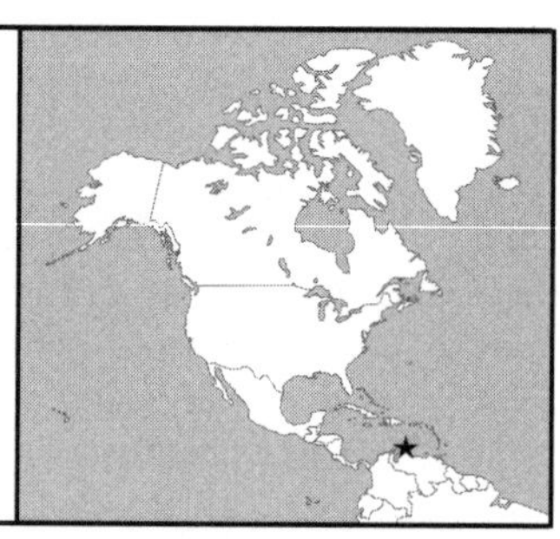

ORIENTATION

Name of City. In the early days of European settlement, Oranjestad was known as Playa ("beach"). Around 1800, when the Dutch lieutenant governor moved from Commandeursbaai (present-day Savaneta) to Oranjestad, the name *Playa* was still in use, but in 1824, shortly after the discovery of gold on Aruba's northern shore, the village's name was changed to *Oranjestad,* for the Dutch royal family.

Location. Oranjestad is situated at the Paardenbaai (Horse Bay) on the southern coast of Aruba. The island is an autonomous part of the Kingdom of the Netherlands. It is situated at the southwestern end of the Caribbean archipelago. Oranjestad is located at 12°30′ north latitude and 70°6′ west longitude.

Population. The population of Oranjestad is a mix of native Arubans and migrants from elsewhere in the Caribbean and from Latin America, North America, and Europe. In 1991, the year of the last census, Oranjestad had 20,045 inhabitants, of whom 6,542 were born abroad. For census purposes Oranjestad was deemed to consist of Oranjestad East and Oranjestad West, but both these regions extended beyond the actual borders of Oranjestad. When the areas outside the city limits were excluded, the population figure was 17,709. According to the Central Bureau for Statistics, in 1994 approximately one-third of the population of Oranjestad was foreign born.

Distinctive and Unique Features. Oranjestad is a typical Caribbean harbor town, wherein overnight and cruise-ship tourists spend their days shopping and swimming, and where native Arubans are employed as civil servants or salespersons. The harbor, the free zone, and an industrial area of small local industries (known as Eagle) are situated west of Oranjestad. The Reina Beatrix (Queen Beatrix) Airport is to the east. South of the Paardenbaai is a coral reef that protects the waterfront from the tide. The waterfront was reconstructed several times in the 20th century. It houses government buildings, hotels, restaurants, a small marketplace and a yacht basin.

Oranjestad's oldest building is Fort Zoutman, a small fort looking out over the Paardenbaai, which was first constructed in 1798. The Tower Willem III, named after the Dutch monarch, was finished in 1868. Renovation between 1973 and 1983 rescued the fort and the tower from collapse. The city's first Protestant church was built in 1846 and renovated in the 1980s. Other colonial buildings of interest are situated in and around the Wilhelminastraat and the Schelpstraat.

Attractions of the City. Oranjestad is the capital of Aruba and the national center for tourism, commerce, banking, and civil services. Approximately 300,000 tourists disembark at its harbor from cruise ships each year. Four luxury hotels and time-share complexes are situated in the center of town. Other luxurious hotels are located west of Oranjestad. Low-rise hotels can be found at Eagle Beach, while high-rise hotels are characteristic of Palm Beach. Tourists in Oranjestad spend their time shopping in malls on the bayside and on the main street. Together with several luxury hotels, casinos, and government buildings, the shops dominate the center of town. Restaurants, casinos, movie theaters, water-sports facilities, shopping malls, and a theater make Oranjestad an attractive location for tourists to spend their vacations.

The development of Oranjestad as a regional commercial and financial center was hampered by the fact that reformed international tax laws made the offshore financial industry less profitable; moreover, Panama and islands such as Curaçao and the Caymans have attractive competing tax laws. As a harbor for international transit trade, Oranjestad competes with, among other cities, Willemstad, on the island of Curaçao. The development of a free zone at the Barcadera harbor area will contribute to the diversification of the Aruban economy.

Relationships Between the City and the Outside. Following the closing of the Lago oil refinery (an Exxon affiliate) in eastern San Nicolas in 1985, tourism and the public sector became the major sources of employment on Aruba. Oranjestad provides job opportunities for people from all over the island. Most food products are imported from the United States, South America, and Europe.

Prevailing stereotypes in Oranjestad view the traditional Aruban elite as socially exclusive, with a tendency to marry close kin. Other stereotypes concern the political affiliation of particular neighborhoods; for example, inhabitants of Rancho are called "Wattys," after the popular politician Edgar "Watty" Vos (1937–2001), a typical Aruban charismatic, machine-style politician.

Major Languages. Papiamento is the native language spoken on Aruba. A Creole language, it developed in the 18th century on Curaçao out of a Portuguese-African-based dialect. Around 1800 Papiamento replaced the native Indian (Arowakken) language on the island, a consequence of increased colonization. Dutch is spoken in the educational and legal systems, but it is losing ground. Massive immigration in the 1920s from the Caribbean and elsewhere led to English becoming the predominant language in neighborhoods such as Dakota. Since 1988 another wave of migration brought migrant workers from the Spanish Caribbean and Latin America, who introduced Spanish especially to the poorer parts of western Oranjestad, known as Playa Pabao.

HISTORY

The Origin of the City. There were no Indian settlements on or near the site of Oranjestad. In the Spanish period (about 1500–1636) some settlement took place at Savaneta, 15 kilometers (9.5 miles) to the east. The Paardenbaai got its name because the Dutch West India Company (1621–1791) used the harbor in the 17th and 18th centuries for shipping horses bred on the island to Europe. The mangroves lining the bay were chopped for use on the more densely populated island of Curaçao. European settlement on the Paardenbaai was first permitted by the Dutch governor John Rudolph Lauffer around 1795, when the harbor became important to the trade between Curaçao and Venezuela and Colombia. After the discovery of gold in the early 1820s, colonists, slaves, and small numbers of native people moved to Oranjestad, which became the governmental, commercial, and trade center of Aruba. Roman Catholic priests from Venezuela undertook missionary activities on an irregular basis about 1762, visiting Aruba about twice a year. In the interim the Amerindian Catholic community was lead by laymen called *fiscalen* ("fiscals"). From 1816 the priests chose Oranjestad as their place of residence and traveled to the surrounding districts to pursue their missionary activities. A Spanish missionary named Manuel Lopez was the first Catholic priest to live in Oranjestad, and in 1813 he built the first Catholic church, which was dedicated to Saint Francis.

After the decline in commercial activities in the Paardenbaai in 1822 (following the gaining of independence by Venezuela and Columbia), and the end of the gold mining in 1829, the settlement's population declined. From 839 (including 315 slaves) in 1845, it dropped to 747 (including 297 slaves) in 1863. Impoverished white settlers moved to the outer districts, to make a living as farmers. Those remaining in Oranjestad were the elite, owners of most of the sailing ships, shops, and aloe plantations. Smuggling—of rum but also food, dry goods, and even cattle—to the South American mainland also contributed to the relative wealth of the elite.

Because of the absence of large-scale plantation slavery, many of the Aruban slaves (who were Catholics) lived and worked in Oranjestad, as house slaves, in shops, or as craftspeople. Most elite families had no more than five slaves. After the abolition of slavery in 1863, former slaves integrated rapidly into the free population. The remaining population of Oranjestad consisted of poor white Catholics who supported themselves by fishing or as craftspersons, sailors, and shopkeepers. Around 1850, east of Oranjestad, a small township called Rancho was formed by former slaves and poor whites; it served as a fishing town and was later incorporated into Oranjestad.

Migration: Past and Present. The establishment of the oil industry on Aruba in 1924 marked the beginning of the island's industrial age. Standard Oil (later Lago Oil and Refinery Company, an Exxon affiliate) was built in the eastern township of San Nicolas, which was Aruba's economic center until its closing in 1985. A smaller refinery, the Royal Dutch Shell Group–owned Eagle, was constructed west of Oranjestad, on Druif Beach, in 1929, in the area that is still called Eagle. The Oranjestad harbor was expanded between 1948 and 1952 and again in 1962. The growth of the oil industry resulted in the upheaval of the Aruban economy and population growth. The in-migration of thousands of Afro-Caribbean laborers; Jewish, Chinese, Madeirean, and Lebanese tradepersons; and Dutch and Antillean civil servants and teachers changed the face of Aruban society. San Nicolas became the Afro-Caribbean part of Aruba, since the oil industry attracted thousands of foreigners. East Oranjestad became the domicile of the local elite and trade migrants. As part of the country's social aid program, around 1949 the government started building houses for the lower-class population (*cas di pueblo*) in Dakota, east of Oranjestad, where foreign laborers who worked in the construction industry and lower-class Arubans intermixed. Urbanization resulted in the expansion of Oranjestad far beyond its original boundaries. By 1948 Oranjestad had approximately 12,000 inhabitants. Residential areas in the north and west of the old center, such as Madiki, Socotoro, and Companashi, expanded. Tarabana, on the east, and the former township of Rancho, on the west, were incorporated into Oranjestad.

The Eagle refinery stopped producing oil in 1950 and ceased all other operations in 1953; it was too small to compete in the international market. In the 1960s the former Eagle concession was reserved for small industries. After Eagle ceased its operations and Lago started automation, new sources of employment, including a bottling company and other small industries, were established. The harbor area was declared a free zone, where such commodities as coffee and rice from South America were imported, refined, and exported. Owing to the automation of the oil industry in San Nicolas, Oranjestad regained its position as the island's most important town. In 1969 the number of inhabitants was estimated to have grown to 14,000. Ponton, in the north became a residential area for the upper class. Dakota expanded westward in the 1960s. In Tarabana, west of Dakota, the government foundation Fundacion Cas pa Comunidad Arubano (FCCA) built another complex of homes for the poor. By 1985 the population of Oranjestad had grown to about 18,000.

In 1985 the Lago refinery, too, closed (owing to a worldwide overcapacity in oil refining, the cost of modernizing facilities, and contractual difficulties, among other problems) and the Aruban economy went into recession. To combat unemployment and the loss of government income, the tourism sector was successfully expanded. The number of hotel rooms was tripled. The need for extra labor resulted in a new wave of immigration. The Aruban population grew from approximately 60,000 in 1985 to an estimated 98,000 in 2000. Thousands of illegal immigrants live on Aruba, many of them in Oranjestad West. Legal and illegal immigration influenced the composition of the city's population, especially the western part. Between 1991 and 1994 the percentage of foreign-born residents of Oranjestad East grew from 32% to 39%. In Oranjestad West 34% of the inhabitants were born outside of Aruba.

INFRASTRUCTURE

Public Buildings, Public Works, and Residences. Aruba was poor and neglected during the 19th century, but the island began to be developed after the arrival of oil industry in 1924. By 1991 only 763 of the island's 6,031 existing housing units had been constructed before 1940. Nevertheless, some monumental buildings date from this period. The town hall, which holds several government offices, was a luxurious private residence (built in 1925); it was renovated and given its present functions in 1998. Many of the shops along the main street, Caya Betico Croes, date from the 1940s and 1950s. A number of historic buildings were renovated by private or public efforts. Monuments of political leaders and the former Dutch queen Wilhelmina are spread throughout the town. In 1988 polders were created from part of the Paardenbaai to make space for a hotel, casino, shopping mall, and a conference center.

Neighborhoods are loosely ordered around the center of town, marking the gradual expansion of Oranjestad. The city has few houses of multiple stories. The sizes of houses vary according to class: houses with an area of 60 square meters (646 square feet) are considered lower class. Houses of the upper class often measure over 400 square meters (4,306 square feet). A typical house of the middle class measures about 150 square meters (1,615 square feet) on a 450-square-meter (4,844-square-foot) lot. In 1991 Oranjestad had about 6,000 households. Most people lived in houses or in apartments or rented rooms. The number of rentals rose as a result of immigration at the end of the 20th century. Many new apartments and apartment buildings were built, within and between already existing neighborhoods.

Politics and City Services. Aruba has been an autonomous part (Status Aparte) of the Dutch kingdom since 1986. The governor of Aruba is the head of the Aruban government and the local representative of the Dutch monarch. The Netherlands' Council of Ministers consists of the Dutch cabinet and two ministers plenipotentiary, one representing

Aruba and the other the Netherlands Antilles. The council is in charge of joint foreign policy, defense, justice, and the safeguarding of fundamental rights and freedom.

Aruba is a parliamentary democracy with a multiparty system. Elections are held every four years. Since achieving the Status Aparte, the government has been dependent on coalitions between one of the two bigger parties and the smaller parties. The biggest parties are the Christian-democratic Arubaanse Volkspartij (AVP; Peoples' Party of Aruba), which traditionally has strong support in Oranjestad and the social-democratic Movimiento Electoral di Pueblo (MEP; Peoples' Electoral Movement), which is most popular in the townships outside Oranjestad. Democracy functions with a certain degree of patronage and nationalistic rhetoric. Political parties usually have one powerful leader who carefully selects candidates from different socioeconomic, regional, and ethnic backgrounds.

Politics on Aruba is strongly based on regional distinctions. Nationwide political participation is high; 89% of the population participated in the 1997 elections. In Oranjestad 84% of the population voted in 1997; Oranjestad made up 28% of the national electorate.

The AVP was led for three generations by members of the Eman family. The MEP was founded by Betico Croes, a teacher from the township of Santa Cruz. Between 1971 and 1985 Croes successfully advocated Aruba's separation from the Netherlands Antilles. In the 1997 elections, the AVP received 56% of the votes in Oranjestad; the MEP received 28%. The AVP, under the leadership of Henny Eman, held office between 1986 and 1989 and again in 1994. The AVP formed coalitions with the neoliberal Organisacion Liberal Arubano (OLA; Aruba Liberal Organization) in 1994.

Educational System. Aruba's educational system is based on that in the Netherlands. At the age of 4, children attend kindergarten (privately owned day-care centers), and after age 6 they attend primary school. At 12 years old they enroll in secondary or vocational schools. After secondary education many students leave for the Netherlands for further studies. In 1988 a large-scale renovation of the educational system at all levels was initiated, directed at modernizing and "arubanizing" the Dutch system.

Oranjestad has many private nursery schools, kindergartens, and primary schools. There is one school for special-needs education and one school for children with limited hearing. Most schools are Roman Catholic. After-school care is provided by the government-subsidized *Tras di Merdia* ("afternoon").

A lower vocational school is situated in Hato, northwest of Oranjestad. A middle vocational school, Educacion Profesional Intermedio, has a hospitality department, secretarial and business department, technical department, and social and health care department. Each of these departments has branches in Oranjestad. The University of Aruba has departments of law and business administration. Adult education is provided by Ensenanza pa Empleo (Education for Employment). The Aruban Teacher Training College, located in San Nicolas, also provides higher education.

Transportation System. Around the city are two beltways, connecting the surrounding villages and townships, San Nicolas, and the airport east of Oranjestad to the hotel area on the west coast. Oranjestad is located 3 kilometers (about 2 miles) from the newly expanded Queen Beatrix International Airport. In 1998 the number of passenger cars per 1,000 inhabitants on the island was 402. Nevertheless, public transportation is important for many workers in and around Oranjestad. Buses, taxicabs, and minibuses connect the city to the airport, hotel area, and residential areas surrounding Oranjestad and San Nicolas.

CULTURAL AND SOCIAL LIFE

Distinctive Features of the City's Cultures. Oranjestad's culture has been strongly influenced by globalization and the multicultural composition of its population. The rise of tourism, mass media, and the arrival of many immigrants from North America, Latin America, Europe, and elsewhere in the Caribbean have made Oranjestad both a Caribbean and a cosmopolitan town. Casinos and movie theaters are situated only a short distance away from traditional Aruban peasant houses. Columbian restaurants are situated next to pizzerias and French steak houses. Traditional Aruban architecture is juxtaposed with North American–style shopping malls.

Dress style reflects Caribbean and Latin American influences, with variations on European and North American trends noticeable as well. The traditional South American dress-shirt (*guajabera*) is worn by older men. Young men sport such hairstyles as Jamaican dreadlocks and wear North American baseball caps. The island's dress code tends to be formal on special occasions. People dress with care when they are going to be in public, but at home the dress style is informal. Dress codes also define the life cycle of traditional Arubans. During the mourning period women wear mostly black. For celebrations, such as a fifteenth of fiftieth birthday, white is the preferred color.

Younger generations shun traditional culture in favor of North American styles. Soft rock, hip-hop, and reggae are popular musical styles, next to salsa and meringue. The mass media strongly threatens the traditional Aruban ways.

Cuisine. Traditional Aruban cuisine features maize dishes (*funchi, pan bati*), goat meat, fish, and *stoba* (a stew often featuring local vegetables, such as peas and beans). Rice, chicken, beef, and fish are eaten most often. A favorite snack is the *pastechi,* a small pie filled with cheese, chicken, or beef. International fast food chains and French, Argentine, Japanese, Chinese, Italian, and other ethnic restaurants have gained in popularity. Tourists and Arubans meet in the many restaurants of Oranjestad.

Ethnic, Class, and Religious Diversity. As mentioned earlier the population of Oranjestad consists of traditional elite and nonelite native Aruban families, English-speaking families descended from the oil immigrants of the 1920s, and of later arrivals (mostly Spanish-speaking immigrants). Although class lines are loosely drawn, strong differences exist between the poor and the rich. Socioeconomic stratification and ethnicity go together. The local upper class and wealthy immigrants who hold better positions in trade and tourism live in neighborhoods such as Klip and Mon Plaisir. Middle-class Arubans and immigrants can be found in Socotoro and Companashi. Lower-class Arubans and Afro-Caribbean immigrants live in Dakota and Madiki. Lower-class Arubans and poor immigrants from Latin America (Venezuela, Columbia, Peru) and the Caribbean (Dominican Republic, Haiti, Jamaica) live in such older neighborhoods as Rancho and Madiki. These neighborhoods face problems with illegal aliens, drug addiction, and prostitution. Upper-, middle-, and lower-class neighborhoods are often situated next to each other.

The educational system fosters the acceptance of social and cultural diversity. Protestant and Roman

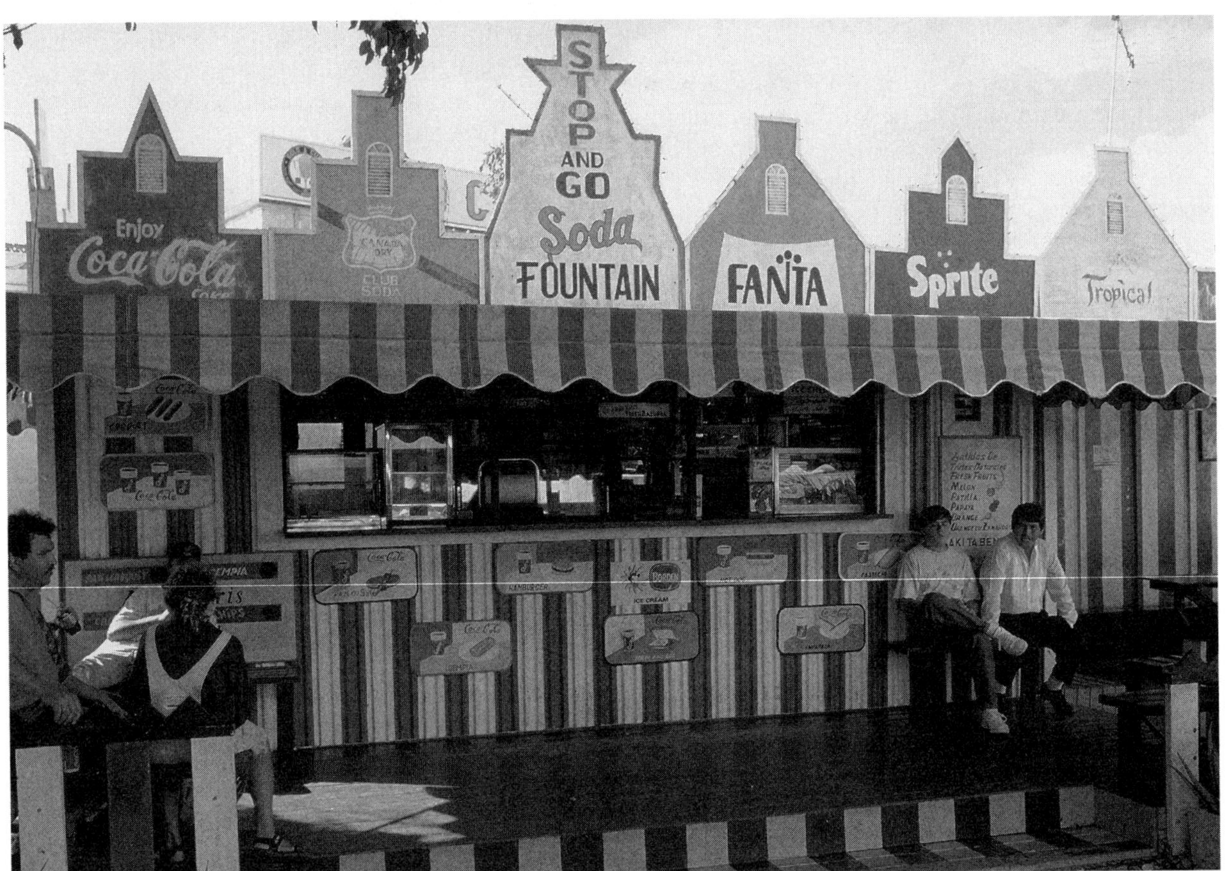

© DAVE G. HOUSER/CORBIS

A snack bar in Oranjestad, Aruba, offers a wide variety of soft drinks.

Catholic private schools have a better reputation but are far from exclusive. Especially in Catholic and public schools, children from different classes and ethnic backgrounds interact.

The Aruban Protestant Community was founded in 1822, when Dutch Reformed and Lutherans congregations joined in one religious community. Formal recognition took place in 1859. In contrast to the population outside of town, Oranjestad's residents remained predominantly Protestant. The traditional elite is Dutch Reformed and Lutheran. Most Afro-Caribbean immigrants belong to other Protestant denominations. Most middle-class Arubans and Latin American immigrants are Roman Catholic. As elsewhere, there are trends toward secularization, and an interest in religious sects and the New Age movement.

Family and Other Social Support Systems. On Aruba monogamy and legal marriage are the norm, but extramarital and premarital relations are common. The conjugal nuclear family is the typical domestic unit. Within the traditional household, the daily authority lies with the mother, but the ultimate authority lies with the father. In colonial times the local elite had a tendency to marry within the kinship group (often with first cousins), but this type of marriage lost popularity in the 20th century. On Aruba the family is an important aspect of social interaction.

Some groups attracted by the oil industry in the 1920s, such as the Lebanese, have integrated with the traditional elite by means of intermarriage. Other groups, such as the Chinese, Jews, and Portuguese, have hewn to more isolated positions. Well-to-do families send their children to the Netherlands or the United States for studies, where they might also find marriage partners. Despite some interethnic tensions, the number of interethnic marriages is high. The 1991 census showed that in 1990 and 1991, 45% of Aruba-born men married foreign spouses. Oranjestad is no exception to this pattern.

Social organizations are important for social interaction. Oranjestad has several community centers and many sports and service clubs. In the past, ethnic organizations were of great importance, but they lost their impact on later generations. Frequently immigrants socialize together in ethnic restaurants.

Work and Commerce. In 1994 approximately 74% of the male population and 56% of the female population were economically active. The unemployment rate was just over 5%. In 1999 Aruba had 3,716 civil servants, most of whom worked in Oranjestad. Hotels, restaurants, and shopping malls offered work to thousands of Arubans and immigrants. In the Eagle area, small industries such as bottling companies, import and export companies, and manufacturers of local crafts, were established. Eagle has six large supermarkets almost next to each other. The harbor is used almost exclusively as a cruise terminal. Other facilities and the free zone are relocating to the area of Barcadera, southeast of Oranjestad.

Arts and Recreation. The Cas di Cultura ("House of Culture") provides accommodations for the national school of music and the national theater. Every two years international dance and theater festivals take place. Oranjestad has several museums: the Archaeological Museum exhibits much of Aruba's pre-Colombian history from both the preceramic (4000–1500 B.C.) and the ceramic (*caquetio,* 1500 B.C.–500 A.D.) periods. The Historical Museum is situated in Aruba's oldest building, Fort Zoutman (1798). Fort Zoutman is also the home of the weekly Bon Bini festival ("welcome festival"), a cultural show for tourists. Next to Fort Zoutman is the smaller Numismatic Museum. Arts expositions take place in such venues as the Cas di Cultura, Centro Bolivariano, National Library or Cultural Institute, or in local banks and privately owned galleries. Literary life is centered on the National Library of Aruba. Aruba has few professional authors or publishers. Denis Henriques, an Aruban writer living and working in the Netherlands, portrayed lower-class life in his native Oranjestad in the 1940s and 1950s in his much-praised novel *Zuidstraat* (*Southern Street*).

Popular music festivals usually take place in one of the several sports parks. Movie theaters and nightclubs are visited by locals and tourists alike. Oranjestad has several community centers, but many of them lack financial and professional support and are in need of repair. Oranjestad has several play gardens and numerous sports facilities, although some of these also are in need of repair.

Aruba's largest cultural festival is held on the streets of Oranjestad during the carnival weekends. The Aruba Tivoli Club—a formerly elite club—organizes the yearly Lightning Parade, which takes place on the Friday night one week before the final Carnival weekend, which is highlighted by the Great Parade. During the evening—between approximately 9:00 and 12:00 P.M.—the Tivoli Club parades through the streets of Oranjestad with much splendor. Carnival costumes and floats are illuminated by thousands of lights. In recent years other Carnival groups have participated in the Lightning Parade. The Children's Parade takes place the Sunday afternoon before the Great Parade. It features the children's Carnival queen and the prince and his pancho (court jester). The winners of the children's musical contests perform during the parade. The Great Parade is the climax of the Aruban Carnival season. It is the biggest parade on the island and also the most luxurious. Carnival groups from all over the island participate. Dresses and costumes of many colors, often with feathers, make Aruba's carnival one of the most beautiful in the world and worthy of comparison with those of Port of Spain, Trinidad, or Brazil.

QUALITY OF LIFE

The cost of living in Oranjestad roughly resembles that in the United States. The quality of life it offers varies according to personal social status and income. Oranjestad is a relatively safe city. Its population reflects the national variations in welfare. Some drug addicts, called "chollers," live on the streets, in shacks, or in abandoned, dilapidated houses. The number of homeless is unknown. Wealthy neighborhoods, such as Klip, tend to be clean and have very little crime. Western parts of town, toward Playa Pabao, have more crime and more apparent drug abuse and prostitution. However, these areas are not unsafe and do not threaten tourism or the safety on the streets.

Public health is generally good, and the incidence of contagious tropical diseases is negligible. Travelers to Aruba do not have to take any medical precautions. Oranjestad has a geriatric home; the Horacio Oduber Hospital is situated west of Oranjestad. Oranjestad has Catholic, Protestant, Jewish, and Free Masonry cemeteries next to one another.

Because Oranjestad has no major heavy industries, it has little air pollution. Household trash is burned and dumped at Parkietenbosch, not far from the airport. In the southeast part of town, airplane traffic can cause something of a noise nuisance.

FUTURE OF THE CITY

Owing to a lack of city planning, the future of Oranjestad is not very clear. Most likely the city center will lose its function as a residential area, while its position as a center of government, commerce, finance, and tourism may expand. Renovation of older houses in the center of town may contribute to the improvement of Oranjestad. In the western part of town, dilapidation and decay are a serious threat, and government intervention is needed. It is likely that the eastern part of town will remain a residential area for well-to-do foreigners and older, elite Aruban families. The process of urbanization of the districts immediately adjoining Oranjestad will probably continue. The relocation of the semi-industrial free zone to Barcadera and the expansion of cruise tourism will contribute to increased commercial activities in Oranjestad.

BIBLIOGRAPHY

Alofs, Luc, "Indian Aruba: An Anthropological Perspective," *Publication of the Archaeological Museum of Aruba* (forthcoming).

Alofs, Luc, and Leontine Merkies, "Ken ta Arubiano?: Sociale integratie en natievorming op Aruba (Who's an Aruban? Social Integration and Nation Building on Aruba, 1924–2001)," (VAD/De Wit Stores 2001).

Censo 2000 (Fourth population and housing census, October 2000) (Central Bureau of Statistics 2001).

Green, Vera, "Migrants in Aruba," *Assen* (Van Gorcum 1974).

"Labor Force Survey 1997" (Central Bureau of Statistics 1997).

Razak, V. M., "Carnival in Aruba: History and Meaning in Aruba's Bacchanal," (Cenda Publications 1997).

Versteeg, A., et al., eds., *The Archaeology of Aruba: The Tanki Flip Site* (Publications of the Archaeological Museum of Aruba 8/Publications of the Foundation for Scientific Research in the Caribbean 141 (n.d.).

Luc Alofs

Osaka
Japan

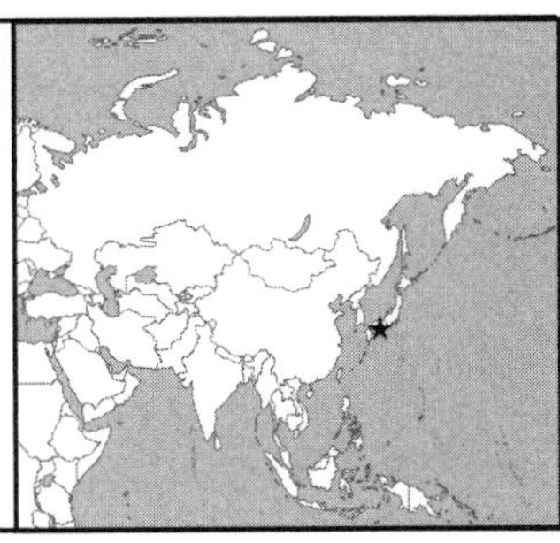

ORIENTATION

Location. Osaka lies on the main Japanese island of Honshu at the head of Osaka Bay. Located at 34°40′ north latitude and 135°30′ east longitude, Osaka is in a temperate climate zone.

Population. Osaka, often described as Japan's second city, is currently third in population to Tokyo and Yokohama, with a 1993 population within the city of 2,588,989 persons. The population of the Osaka urban agglomeration is given as 10.6 million by the United Nations, second to that of the Tokyo metropolitan area, which includes nearby Yokohama. In 1995 Osaka contained 8.5% of the Japanese population, compared with Tokyo's 21.6%. In a country where 78% of the population lived in urban areas in 1995, Osaka is a major urban-industrial center.

Distinctive and Unique Features. Known historically as Naniwa, Osaka has been a center of habitation since ancient times and is located on a low deltaic site formed by the Yodo River at the head of shallow Osaka Bay. Distinctive features of the city include its central location in the Keihanshin urban-industrial area, which encompasses Kyoto, Osaka, and Kobe. Osaka has served as a center for commercial activity, industrial or handicraft-industrial production, and cultural life since the 17th century and has functioned as a port from ancient times. Whereas Kobe is now the port for the largest oceangoing vessels, Osaka port is active for smaller ships, and Osaka International Airport and Kansai International Airport, located on an artificial island off the coast, are air-transport hubs for both domestic and international flights.

Osaka is a city with many canals and waterways and once contained more than 1,300 bridges. Many of the canals are no longer in use, but several, such as the great Doton Canal, are focal points for festivals and the site of waterfront restaurants. While Osaka provides extensive opportunities for entertainment, some visitors have described it as a grimy industrial city or a smoky, dirty Venice. One author has suggested that "Osaka is not Japan's easiest city to love." Despite this reputation, Osaka is a vibrant, dynamic center of culture as well as of business and industry.

Attractions of the City. Among the city's attractions are extensive underground shopping malls in the Umeda and Shinsaibashi districts. These malls link major railway and subway stations and department stores as well as other commercial buildings. The arcades provide restaurants, food shops, Japanese regional specialties, and a wide range of other consumer goods. Osaka also boasts many fine restaurants, bars, and nightclubs along with several main entertainment districts featuring movies; music; traditional Bunraku, Kabuki, and modern theater; and most other forms of modern entertainment.

The city's principal tourist attractions include Osaka Castle, originally built in the 1580s and rebuilt in concrete in 1931; the Shitennōji Buddhist Temple, founded in 593; the Sumiyoshi Taisha Shinto Shrine; and many museums and surviving historical buildings. Among the important museums in the city are the Osaka City Museum, the Osaka Municipal Museum of Art, the Osaka National Museum of Art, the Osaka Science Museum, the Open-air Museum of Japanese Farm Houses, and the Museum at the Osaka Mint. Other attractions of interest are the Idemitsu and Itsuō Art Museums, the Kubosō Memorial Museum of Arts, the Manno Art Museum, the Yayoi Museum on prehistoric cultures, and the Yoshimura residence, a fine example of a Tokugawa farmhouse built in about 1620. While many of Osaka's historic buildings were destroyed in the bombing of the city during World War II or in urban-renewal efforts since, some good examples survive at the Osaka Mint, the Osaka Castle compound, and elsewhere in the city. Additional attractions are the Tennōji Zoo; the new aquarium known as the Kaiyukan; the centrally located Convention Center; city parks, including those at Nakanoshima, Hamadera,

Tennōji, Sumiyoshi, and Osaka Castle; and the Twin Towers and their rooftop observation platform.

Relationships Between the City and the Outside. Osaka is a city surrounded by suburban bedroom communities from which commuters flock to the city for work and play. The daytime and nighttime populations of the central city vary dramatically, with more and more of the former residential property converted to commercial use since the end of the World War II. By 1975, if the population of the four central wards of Osaka were given a value of 100 at night, on workdays it exceeded 600, and the variance has continued to increase as the result of the construction of major office buildings, shopping arcades, subway and rail lines, and highway networks. Commuters come to the city not only from outlying areas of Osaka prefecture but also from cities and towns in Wakayama, Nara, Kyoto, and Hyogo prefectures. Because of the excellent private and public transportation systems in the Keihanshin region, long commutes are not uncommon.

Major Languages. Standard Tokyo-dialect Japanese is the primary language of Osaka. In addition, many Osaka residents speak Osaka-ben, the local dialect characteristic of the region and often called Kansai-ben (western Japan dialect). While the population of foreign residents has increased in recent decades, Japanese is still the language for everyday interactions, with many residents also having some knowledge of English. English words are widely used on signs and in advertisements, but most Japanese, despite the six years of training in middle and high school, tend to have better reading than speaking skills in English. Although there are communities of Koreans, Chinese, Europeans, North Americans, and residents from elsewhere within Osaka prefecture, effective communication works best in standard Japanese.

HISTORY

The Origin of the City. Osaka has been a site for human habitation since prehistoric times. Both the Jomon and Yayoi cultures are represented in artifacts found in and near Osaka, known initially as Naniwa. From the 5th century Osaka was a leading political center as well as a port for communication with China, Korea, and other coastal areas of Japan. The many large tombs located south of the city near Sakai indicate that Osaka was important in the formation of the early Japanese imperial state.

© ROGER RESSMEYER/CORBIS

Osaka Castle and a modern skyscraper stand side-by-side in heavily industrialized Osaka, Japan.

Ancient and Medieval History. In the 7th century Osaka, as Naniwakyo, was the imperial capital, which was built on the Uemachi Plateau along the Yodo River. While the capital was relocated inland by the 690s, Osaka remained an important port and religious center, the site of the Shitennōji Buddhist Temple and the Sumiyoshi Shinto Shrine. Pilgrims came from Heian (Kyoto) and elsewhere by the 10th and 11th centuries. Thereafter a market town developed to service pilgrims and the religious communities. By the 15th century a permanent market existed at Tennōji along the sea. By the late 15th century, the Uemachi Plateau in central Osaka became the site of a True Pure Land Sect (Jōdo Shinshū) Buddhist Temple at Ishiyama. By 1538, this site—later the home of Osaka Castle—would be the main temple of the sect known as the Ishiyama Honganji, and a temple town grew up within the temple precincts to service the needs of the clerics and lay adherents. The True Pure Land Sect controlled much of the Osaka region until challenged in the 1570s, and in 1580 Oda Nobunaga, the first of the great unifiers of Japan, took over the site and the temple moved elsewhere.

Early Modern Osaka. Nobunaga was assassinated in 1582 and was replaced by Toyotomi Hideyoshi. Hideyoshi completed the process of national reunification. He claimed the Osaka region in 1583 and quickly began the construction of a massive castle on the site of the former Ishiyama Honganji. Osaka Castle became the largest, most heavily fortified castle/residence in Japan. Measuring 12 kilometers (7 miles) in circumference and surrounded by immense stone walls and watch towers, it symbolized Hideyoshi's power and wealth as national military hegemony. Osaka Castle became the focus of a new castle town as Hideyoshi's vassals built residences around the castle and merchants and artisans settled in designated sections of Osaka to service the needs of the military residents and their families and retinues. Many regional military leaders constructed residences in Osaka and left their wives and children there as hostages to symbolize their loyalty and subordination to Hideyoshi. Major Buddhist temples were encouraged to establish branches in designated areas of Osaka. By the time Hideyoshi died in 1598, Osaka had extensive neighborhoods of merchants, artisans, and warriors as well as many temples and was probably Japan's second-largest city, after Kyoto.

Following Hideyoshi's death, control of Osaka was passed to his son and heir, Toyotomi Hideyori. The most powerful regional military leaders competed to succeed to his position of national hegemonic leadership. In a great battle at Sekigahara in 1600, Tokugawa Ieyasu emerged as Hideyoshi's successor. In 1603 Ieyasu accepted the title of shogun, or military hegemony. He and 14 generations of his male heirs would control that office for the next 264 years.

While Tokugawa Ieyasu was national leader, Toyotomi Hideyori still retained the loyalty of many of his father's former vassals as well as Osaka Castle, the most formidable castle in the land. The Tokugawa garrisoned nearby Fushimi, and they placed a military governor in Kyoto at Nijo Castle to assert Tokugawa authority in western Japan. Ieyasu passed the title of shogun to his son Hidetada in 1605, establishing a precedent for a Tokugawa monopoly over the office of shogun. While the Tokugawa controlled eastern Japan from their castle town of Edo (modern Tokyo), Hideyori commanded strong loyalties in the Osaka area. In 1614, using the pretext of a slight to Ieyasu, the Tokugawa attacked Osaka Castle with 200,000 troops in the so-called Winter Campaign. Hideyori and his supporters held them off for more than 40 days, and Ieyasu arranged a favorable truce that required Hideyori to fill in the outer moats surrounding the castle. In 1615 the Tokugawa broke the truce and attacked again in the Summer Campaign, which proved successful. The castle walls were breached and Hideyori and his mother committed suicide, ending the Toyotomi challenge to Tokugawa dominance. The winter and summer campaigns destroyed the castle and much of the city. Most of the merchants and artisans fled from Osaka as their shops and residences were laid to ruin. As Nobunaga had leveled much of the city in his campaign against the Ishiyama Honganji in the 1570s, in 1614–1615 the Tokugawa did so once again.

Osaka Under the Tokugawa. Once the Tokugawa assumed control of the city, they encouraged its reconstruction. They attracted merchants and artisans to the city, supervised the construction of new residential and business quarters, and promoted the digging of canals to assist the movement of goods and people throughout the city. Osaka emerged as a major trade and population center and the Higashiyoko, Nishiyoko, and Awa canals were constructed. While Matsudaira Tadaaki, Ieyasu's grandson, controlled the city from 1615 to 1619, thereafter it was directly ruled by the Tokugawa government. Tadaaki began the rebuilding process, but the Tokugawa intensified the effort after 1619, making Osaka and its rebuilt castle the symbol of Tokugawa authority in western Japan. Between 1620 and 1629 Osaka Castle was rebuilt and enlarged under the supervision of Tōdō Takatora with assistance from 64 of the regional military houses (daimyo) who were required to participate in the project. Daimyo were assigned specific portions of the castle walls, watch towers, and gateways, with contributions scaled to the income received from their domains. The Tokugawa house also shared in taking responsibility for the central castle keep, the family residence within the walls, and various gates. Tokugawa Hidetada, the second Tokugawa shogun, visited Osaka in 1619, discussed the rebuilding project, and inspected progress during a subsequent trip in 1623. Tokugawa Iemitsu, the third shogun, also visited later in 1623 and again in 1626 and 1634 to inspect the castle and other facilities in the area as well as to enjoy the cities of Osaka and Kyoto. The completed castle and the multiple shogunal visits between 1619 and 1634 reflect the importance assigned to an Osaka presence for Tokugawa military authority in western Japan.

Construction of Osaka Castle accomplished a series of goals for the Tokugawa bakufu (shogunate). First, it demonstrated the ability of the bakufu to levy service obligations on the western daimyo, the area where Hideyoshi and the imperial court exercised their authority. Second, it forced the western daimyo to help build the stronghold that would be the major barrier to any challenge to Tokugawa authority in the Kansai region and over the imperial house in Kyoto. Third, it consolidated bakufu control over the imperial house and the city of Kyoto. The repeated visits by Hidetada and Iemitsu were demonstrations of this control. Fourth, by building a castle even larger than Hideyoshi's it showed that the Tokugawa had not merely replaced him but had surpassed his power as the holder of central authority and military supremacy.

During Iemitsu's 1634 visit to the city, he granted the merchants and artisans of Osaka an exemption from land taxes. This encouraged expansion of the city and its commercial life. Despite the impressive castle, Osaka was never fully garrisoned. While representing Tokugawa authority in western Japan, the city became more important as a center of commerce and handicraft-industrial production. While Edo included as many as 500,000 warriors among its 1 million peak residents, Osaka warriors were limited to the tens of thousands, a much smaller proportion of the city's population peak of around 400,000. To ease the transportation in the city, an extensive network of canals was created, reducing shipping costs and encouraging economic activity. Merchant communities were moved wholesale into Osaka from Fushimi in 1619 to spur the recovery of its commercial life. They were joined by the many artisans working on the castle reconstruction and populated the Semba district west of the castle.

Initially under Hideyoshi, and then under the Tokugawa, Osaka became the leading market for rice collected as taxes by daimyo in western Japan in the late 16th and the early 17th century. Daimyo built warehouses in the city on Dōjima and Nakanoshima islands, and the many rivers and canals eased the movement of bulk cargoes. By 1626, Osaka had 111 daimyo rice warehouses. The rice was consumed in the city, used for sake brewing and bean-paste production, or sold to other cities in the region. The shipping routes for rice provided a network for conveying other goods, and Osaka became a major market for cash crops purchased by Osaka merchants and distributed locally or processed in the city. Seed cotton, ginned cotton, rapeseed, and other goods came in large quantities. They were processed by Osaka artisans for sale in the city, the region, and elsewhere throughout Japan. Osaka's access to good waterborne transportation made it a center for regional trade as well as a primary source of goods for Edo.

Osaka was also the center of the Tokugawa-era banking system. Revenues from rice sales were transferred to Edo, and bills of credit and deposit emerged to ease monetary exchanges across long distances. Osaka bankers provided loans to daimyo as well as merchants, and many daimyo became deeply in debt to Osaka bankers. Although the city was under Tokugawa administrative control and was supervised by warriors at the top, the administrative control of the three districts of the city was in the hands of townsmen. Warriors held legal authority, but actual authority was exercised by commoners who were responsible for local control. Townsmen conducted inquiries, transmitted messages, and mediated between the warrior elite and the residents of the city. They also collected taxes and service levies; regulated commerce and handicraft production through guilds; recorded land transfers, population, and religious affiliation; and kept records on imports and exports, prices, and so forth. Warriors issued major policies, but their implementation was in the hands of ordinary citizens.

Construction of the city, aside from the castle, was also left to commoners. Neighborhoods, canals, and markets were assigned to prominent townsmen who were often given administrative control over new parts of the city. Property owners were placed in charge of the block units into which the city's three districts were divided. Warriors provided oversight and planning assistance, but the work was left to the merchants and artisans of the city. During the Tokugawa period many new areas were added to the city as merchants and artisans migrated to Osaka and more sectors for residential and business activity were needed to accommodate them.

Osaka commerce and handicraft production were oriented toward commoners, not the military or aristocratic elite. The processed foodstuffs, cotton textiles, books, art, utensils, medicines, cosmetics, and sundries made in the city served the consumption needs of townspeople in Osaka and other cities and towns in western Japan and elsewhere. While Osaka was known as the "kitchen of Japan," most of its exports were processed goods, not unprocessed food or raw materials. Osaka served urban consumers with lamp oil, bedding, inexpensive textiles, metal tools, and other goods. By the late 17th century it had a wide range of merchants and artisans specializing in specific types of goods. Expansion of Osaka business continued well into the 18th century. Data from 1736 indicate imports to Osaka from 45 out of the 66 provinces of Japan. It also had well-organized guilds supporting the interests of its merchants and artisans. As competition from rural areas near the city increased in the late 18th century, the guilds expanded and tried to preserve the position of the Osaka business community.

The importance of the Osaka market increased into the early 19th century, but by 1840 it was in decline. Imports to the city fell, the monopoly positions of the Osaka guilds were challenged, and the status of Osaka as a center of processing industries and trade was gradually undermined. The population of the city decreased from the 1760s and 1770s as fewer residents from other areas migrated to Osaka in search of work. After 1779 the population dropped more rapidly, from about 400,000 in 1759 to under 270,00 by the Meiji Restoration in 1868.

Although notable as a center of commerce and industry, Osaka played an important cultural role as well, particularly in the late 17th and the early 18th century. Ihara Saikaku, the preeminent 17th-century writer, wrote in Osaka, as did Chikamatsu Monzaemon, Japan's most famous playwright. The Bunraku or Jōruri puppet theater was famous in Osaka, as was Kabuki. Takemoto Gidayū's puppet troupe defined a new form of theater combining chanted narratives, music, and large puppets. It is still popular in Osaka today. Aside from its literary and theatrical heritage, Osaka was also a center for scholarship. Ogata Kōan encouraged Dutch studies, studied European science and medicine, and advocated international trade. His school, the Tekijuku, was the forerunner of Osaka University.

Modern Osaka. Osaka went into a steep decline after the Meiji Restoration of 1868. The new imperial government was located in Tokyo (the former Edo), and political, cultural, and economic life was centered in eastern Japan. The transition from a directly controlled Tokugawa city to a modern metropolis required fundamental shifts in objectives, concepts, and institutional structures. Between 1868 and 1889, the contours of a modern city administration were created. The first issue was defining Osaka's relations to the modern state. Second was how Osaka city fit into Osaka prefecture as an urban district. Third was how the boundaries of the city and the prefecture should be created along with their internal units of administration. Finally, how would the central government redefine local control?

Migration: Past and Present. As a port and market center, Osaka has attracted migrants from other areas since ancient times. Local farmers and traders came to the city to sell their wares since Osaka was ideally situated astride both waterborne and land routes linking western Japan to the Kyoto region, site of the imperial capital until 1868.

During the period of unification in the late 16th century, Osaka was badly damaged in warfare and then rebuilt, first under Toyotomi Hideyoshi after 1583 and then under the Tokugawa shogunate after 1619. The construction of the castle attracted many artisans and laborers to the city as well as the merchants and service providers who helped to feed, clothe, entertain, and house them. This greatly expanded Osaka's population. Many stayed after the castle was completed and worked on building the more common parts of the city, digging canals, and providing for the needs of the growing community. As the city expanded in size, new immigrants were needed to augment the labor force, and migrants came from nearby areas as well as from more distant parts of western Japan. The population of the city continued to expand well into the mid-18th century, after which it began to dwindle.

One reason for this decline was the spread of both trade and processing industries to the Osaka hinterland in the 18th century. Jobs previously available only within the city were now to be found in towns and villages outside its borders, where fewer regulations impeded access to specific forms of employment. Migrants could now find work outside the city and compete with those within Osaka. New trade routes linking areas of western Japan directly to the large markets in Edo and eastern Japan also bypassed Osaka, reducing the monopoly power of the Osaka merchants and traders. This gradual slump in the city's population and status increased dramatically after the Meiji Restoration of 1868, when both business and government were concentrated in the new imperial capital of Tokyo.

With the expansion of industry in the 1880s and 1890s, Osaka again attracted migrants from other areas of western Japan. Osaka offered jobs, better education facilities, and opportunities for advancement, so migrants came from areas in western Japan to help fill the needs of the growing city. This process has continued ever since, with much of the migration coming not only to Osaka but also to the cities and smaller communities in the immediate Keihanshin area.

INFRASTRUCTURE

Public Buildings, Public Works, and Residences. As the center of both the Osaka prefectural government and the Osaka city government, the municipality includes not only government buildings but also the prefectural library, major educational facilities, hospitals, and the central post office and is the hub of the local transportation network. While Osaka has many residential neighborhoods, many middle-class residents have moved to outlying suburban communities and live in multistoried apartment buildings. With much of the housing stock in

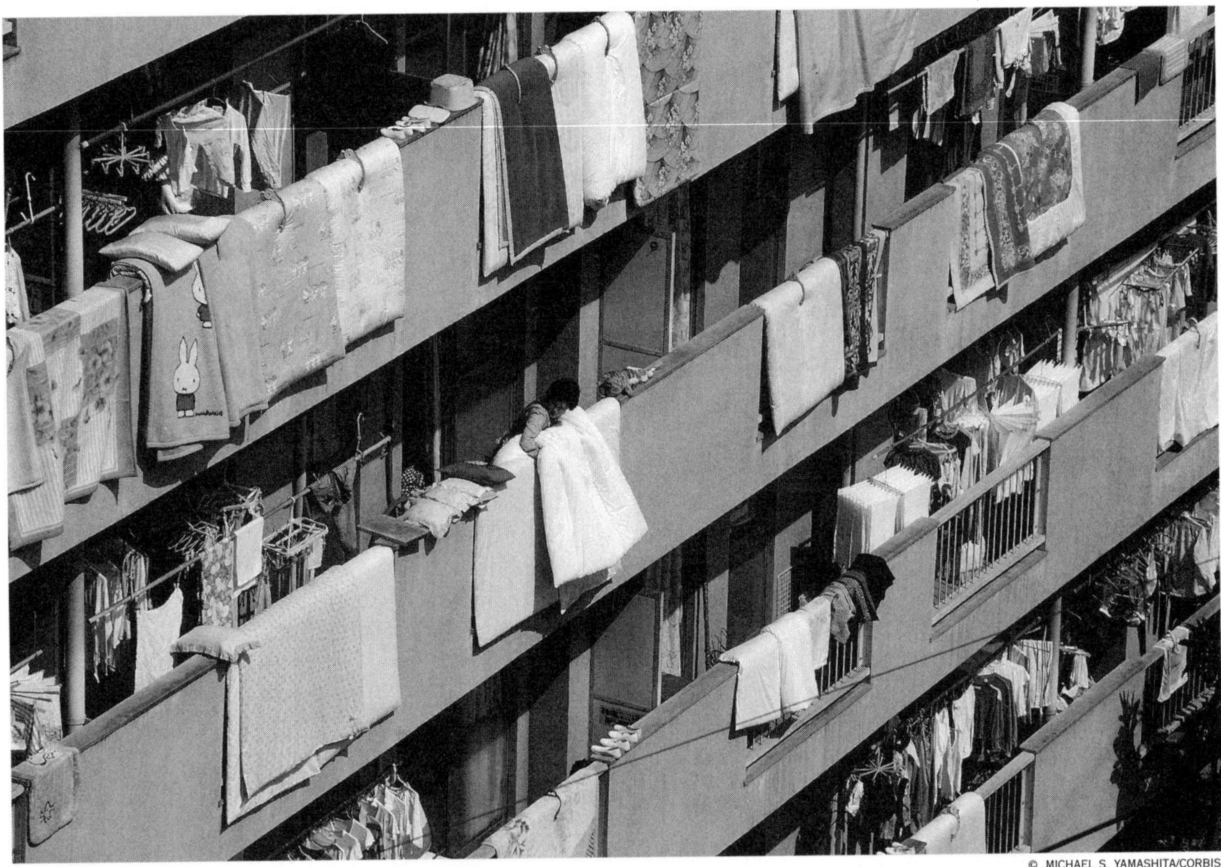

© MICHAEL S. YAMASHITA/CORBIS

One of the many apartment buildings in Osaka, Japan.

the city destroyed during World War II, blocks of five-story apartments were built to house residents in the 1950s. Since that time, most have been replaced with more modern apartments or displaced by commercial or industrial facilities, and those residents who can have moved to bedroom communities that are near the city and easily accessible by rail, bus, or automobile.

Politics and City Services. From 1619 to 1868, Osaka was directly administered by Tokugawa bakufu authorities. When the Tokugawa garrison left the castle in early 1868, mobs sacked and burned the fortress until new Meiji government forces occupied the city. With the new government in charge, the old system of city magistrates and their samurai and civilian subordinates was no longer appropriate. A new system was needed for management of the lands and waterways, temples and shrines, commercial activity, police matters, and the like. In 1868 the city was still divided into three districts and 620 block units. Initially the old governing officials were asked to continue as before, restore the city to a normal condition, and reestablish peace and tranquillity.

From 1868 to 1889 administration was redefined in cities, towns, and villages across Japan. During the first stage, through trial and error, new systems were defined. Between 1879 and 1889, they were perfected. All Tokugawa lands were confiscated by the government in January 1868, whereas private lands were unchallenged. Later in that year the new urban prefecture of Osaka was created, and its boundaries shifted several times in 1868, 1869, 1871, and 1874. A new prefectural government building was constructed in Osaka, and the city became one part of the redefined Osaka prefecture. The emperor was brought to Osaka from Kyoto for the first time in centuries to add his prestige to the changes in local and national governance. Internal units of the city were redefined in 1869, and in 1871 a new system of family registration was extended to the entire country. Internal divisions of the city were changed in 1872, and officials were told to serve the interests of the government and the people. While popular assemblies were tried, more and more of the city administration came under prefectural administrative control as systems were created and modified throughout the 1870s. Not until 1879 would a consistent organizational structure be implemented. All units of local government were tied to the national government in Tokyo. A law for local assemblies was issued in 1880 and revised in 1884. All regulations that those bodies instituted needed the approval of the prefectural governor, appointed from Tokyo.

City administration was changed in 1889 with a new system that rationalized and consolidated authority, extending the arm of city government further into the neighborhoods. The role of citizens was greatly reduced from Tokugawa-era practices, and the remnants of townsmen authority in Osaka disappeared. Bureaucratic authority extended to all levels of city government. Until 1898 Osaka was not allowed to elect its own mayor; the Tokyo-appointed prefectural governor was the chief executive. In 1922, large cities nationwide were allowed more administrative autonomy, and Osaka got additional local authority. Yet substantial centralized control would persist until eliminated by the Allied occupation of Japan in 1947.

The Allied occupation of Japan from 1945 to 1952 was designed to democratize Japanese government and society. An attempt was made to loosen national controls and enhance local autonomy. Local government laws were revised in 1946, and a Local Autonomy law was issued in 1947. While much amended since, it is the cornerstone of local government structures in Japan. Yet in 1950, the Osaka municipal office stated:

> Apart from the epoch-making decentralization of police, fire, and education services . . . the old state of affairs still remains and almost all the other administrative functions are treated as national functions.

In 1956, large cities were given additional authority over municipal functions, including welfare; health; city planning and land readjustment; and regulation of hotels, entertainment places, bathhouses, outdoor advertising, and building standards. Cities such as Osaka were exempted from prefectural control and subjected instead to direct control from Tokyo.

Economic Development. Although the economic decline of Osaka was severe after 1868, the city regained its importance by the 1880s as a center of the cotton spinning industry. Public telegraph and postal services linked major Japanese cities in the 1870s, and telephone service was initiated in the 1890s. As commerce and industry expanded in Osaka, so too did the population. From a population of 750,000 in 1897, Osaka had grown to 1.76 million by 1920. The lack of urban planning meant that factories and residential areas were mixed. Overcrowding and pollution led many wealthier residents to move from the central city to residential enclaves in the suburbs. Efforts toward city and regional planning failed until after World War II.

Wartime bombing severely damaged the city. Some 57% of its residences were destroyed, along with much of its infrastructure. In 1944 conditions were so bad that police estimated that 46% of crimes involved food. Conditions immediately following the surrender in August 1945 were no better. Food was limited, vacant lots were used for growing vegetables, and privation was the norm. Many residents sold off their possessions to purchase food on the black market, as government food distribution was inadequate. Yet despite the hardships of the late 1940s, the city was rebuilt and became a center of the metal, shipbuilding, machinery, chemical, food-processing, printing, and textile industries in the 1950s and 1960s. In 1965 the Meishin Expressway linked Osaka by road to Nagoya, and the Tōmei Expressway connected Nagoya and Tokyo in 1968, expanding truck transport along the heavily urbanized and industrialized Tokaido Belt. Improved roadways, high-speed rail lines, and expanded port facilities in Osaka and nearby Kobe all contributed to a rapid increase in industrial expansion and urban growth. New industries such as electrical appliances and electronics brought new jobs. The World Exposition of 1970 focused attention on the city and the surrounding area. Large-scale regional projects such as the Osaka World Trade Center, Kansai International Airport (opened 1994), the growing Kansai Science City on the Osaka-Kyoto-Nara border, and the Osaka International Convention Center (2000) all illustrate the dynamic energy of Osaka and the surrounding region, despite the economic slowdown of the 1990s.

Educational System. Education is compulsory through nine years of school. In addition to its system of free public elementary, middle, and high schools, Osaka also has many private schools. Universities include Osaka University, Osaka University of Foreign Studies, Osaka University of Education, City University, Prefectural University, and many private colleges. Noted for its private academies in the Tokugawa period, particularly the Tekijuku, Osaka is a center for scientific research and medical education.

Transportation System. The Umeda section of the city is the focal point of many of the rail lines in Osaka, including Japan Railways and the Hankyu and Hanshin networks. Osaka Station was built in Umeda in 1874 and continues to be the major Japan Rail hub in the city, except for the Shinkansen Bullet Trains, which use Shin-Osaka Station. Three subway lines also have stations in Umeda, and all are linked to the rail lines by underground shopping malls in underground Umeda. Japan Rail provides a Loop Line for surface commutes around the core of the city. Other rail networks are run by the Keihan, Kintetsu, and Nankai railways, and additional subway lines run both east-west and north-south under the city. The web of interlocking rail networks provides excellent transportation within Osaka and between Osaka and other cities in the Kansai region and elsewhere in Japan. Surface transport is served by buses, taxicabs, and private automobiles. While roads were widened in the postwar rebuilding of the city, the volume of traffic has overwhelmed them.

Osaka is served not only by the port of Osaka but also by the larger, deepwater port of Kobe. Raw materials as well as finished goods are brought to and shipped from Osaka via Kobe, the primary port in the Keihanshin region. As a wholesale and retail center, an industrial center, and a center for technical and scientific research and education, Osaka is linked with other parts of the metropolitan prefecture and surrounding areas. Although less important than Kyoto and Nara as a tourist destination, Osaka is a focus of commercial, financial, pharmaceutical, and industrial activity.

CULTURAL AND SOCIAL LIFE

Distinctive Features of the City's Cultures. Osaka has a vibrant nightlife, with many bars and restaurants, movie theaters, theatrical productions, and both Japanese and Western musical performances. Most forms of entertainment can be found in the Umeda and Shinsaibashi areas of the city, and other parts of the city offer entertainment venues on a smaller scale.

Osaka is also home to many art galleries, bookstores, and museums as well as attractive parks. Tour boats provide excursions along the many surviving waterways, and many bus tours are also available.

Cuisine. Osaka has a well-deserved reputation for excellent food. Seafood specialties have a long tradition in the city, and there are a number of fine restaurants, many with regional styles of Japanese cuisine. Pressed sushi made with mackerel, fish stews, crabmeat, and blowfish as well as other foods are among the Osaka delicacies. During the Tokugawa era many Osaka commoners were known as *kuidaore* (food enthusiasts), who engaged in extravagant eating. Chinese, Korean, Indian, American, and European foods are among the varieties of cuisine offered by restaurants in the city.

Ethnic, Class, and Religious Diversity. Most residents of Osaka are Japanese, although many are migrants to the city from other areas. Osaka also has a large Korean population, descendants of workers brought to Japan from Korea during the period of Japanese colonial control from 1910 to 1945. They have long been treated as second-class citizens, together with the ethnically Japanese "Burakumin," a group of hereditary outcasts traditionally viewed as subhuman because of their involvement with animal slaughtering, leather tanning, and burial. While Burakumin have legal equality with other Japanese, they often face discrimination, and the Buraku Liberation League has lobbied for and won special housing, schools, and employment opportunities in the areas of the city where they have been traditionally concentrated.

There are also residents of Chinese, South and Southeast Asian, American, and European backgrounds in the city, but in far fewer numbers than the Korean and Burakumin inhabitants of Osaka. Traditionally Japanese were suspicious of non-Japanese residents, although this has changed dramatically as Japan has become a world economic power and more Japanese have traveled abroad. With its many universities, Osaka also hosts a large number of foreign students studying in Japan on a study-abroad or long-term basis.

Most Japanese claim some affiliation with Buddhism or Shinto, and many use both religions for different rites of passage. There are quite a few different sects of Buddhism represented in the city and numerous Buddhist temples and Shinto shrines. Most Japanese are not actively religious, with the exception of many adherents of the so-called new religions such as Soka Gakkai, or Tenriky. There are also a number of Japanese Christians, but they represent less than 3% of the population.

Family and Other Social Support Systems. Traditional families in Japan were closely linked and subordinated to the head of the main house. Many Osaka business houses were based on family affiliation with a main house and branch families linked together in the same enterprise and all subject to family rules and control by the main house. Until 1945, family law in Japan placed the male head of the household in a strong position of control, able to arrange marriages, determine inheritance, and make important decisions for other members of the corporate family structure.

Women who married into Osaka merchant families generally cut their ties to their natal families and were subordinated to their mothers-in-law until their husbands either were appointed head of the household or were established as the head of a branch family. When sons were unavailable to succeed the house head, husbands could be adopted for daughters, or other relatives, employees, or sons from other households could be adopted as the successor. In Tokugawa Osaka, women were allowed to serve as house heads for up to three years, but only a male proxy could sign all contracts and could formally represent the household in many instances. When a couple divorced, the husband usually kept their sons while the wife would often be allowed to keep their daughters.

Family law since 1945 considers individual interests rather than corporate family interests. Consequently, men and women can make their own marital arrangements based on love, rather than on the interests of their households or family businesses. Arranged marriage is still possible for those who fail to find a spouse independently, and typically a go-between is used even for love marriages to mediate between the families and to help the couple in times of marital conflict. Employers, dating services, and friends of the family are frequently used to help find a marital partner for those too shy or socially inept to find someone on their own.

Traditionally, social welfare was provided by the family, and often wives were expected to help care for their husband's aging parents. Three-generation households were not uncommon, but the increase in nuclear families, smaller residences, and social and spatial mobility have all helped break down the ability and willingness of families to carry the social-welfare burdens of aging or ill family members. The national government now provides some assistance, as do municipal governments. Child-care facilities have expanded, as has day care for aging parents. National and corporate pensions help support those too old to work, but personal savings and family resources are still important for elderly Japanese. With a burgeoning older population, Japanese are struggling to develop mechanisms to both provide sufficient labor power to the workforce and employ older workers and women in jobs previously serviced by young men. Immigrants from elsewhere in Asia or from overseas Japanese communities are filling many of the dirty, dangerous, or demeaning jobs, but demographic change and an aging population will require more types of social-welfare expenditures in the future.

Work and Commerce. Osaka is a bustling commercial, industrial, and service center. Trains, buses, and cars crowd into the city bringing commuters to the many small and large employers. High-tech industries, traditional manufacturing, banking, pharmaceuticals, brewing, trading companies, printing, and a wide range of service industries provide a variety of employment opportunities. In the past, many jobs were filled by middle-school graduates. Increasingly, high school and college backgrounds are required by most employers owing to the technical skills required for many jobs. While on-the-job training is common, educational credentials are viewed as extremely important in Japan and can determine access to employment and one's future in the labor market. This has led to strenuous competition to get into the best schools.

Arts and Recreation. While Tokyo is the center of Japan's art and music communities, Osaka also has many artists, musicians, and galleries. A number of modern architects have built impressive structures in the city. Galleries and department-store exhibitions provide access to both modern and traditional art and craft goods. Kyoto has a larger representation of traditional artists and craft producers, but Osaka has a vibrant cultural life and many educational institutions. Traditional Bunraku puppet theater and dance as well as music are taught and performed in the city, along with more modern Japanese and European forms. The city also has many public festivals that show off its cultural heritage.

All forms of recreation are available in the Osaka area. One special attraction is the National High School Baseball tournament held annually in nearby Koshien Stadium in Nishinomiya. There are also professional baseball, cycle racing, horse racing, and sumo wrestling tournaments. Schools for martial arts, tennis, and other forms of physical activity are likewise available, as are those for traditional and modern forms of cultural expression. Nearby in Takarazuka is a unique form of all-female theatrical productions, another special feature of the Osaka area.

QUALITY OF LIFE

Osaka is a crowded urban metropolis with excellent rail transportation but very expensive housing and congested roads. Since it is no longer a center of heavy industry, however, water and air pollution has been substantially reduced, enhancing the quality of the environment. Although good facilities exist for most forms of recreational activity, costs can be high and access limited to those who can afford it or have access to business expense accounts. Entertainment facilities exist for many different budget levels, with inexpensive neighborhood bars and restaurants for public use and prohibitively expensive restaurants and nightclubs catering to business clients on expense accounts. While a very modern city, Osaka has a well-deserved reputation for hard work and play. It is Japan's second city and possesses many features that distinguish it from Tokyo, which is the center of government, business, education, and the arts.

FUTURE OF THE CITY

As the Japanese economy recovers, Osaka's future looks bright. The business community is energetic and focused on both domestic and overseas demand for Japanese goods, particularly in Asia. Research endeavors in biotechnology, pharmaceuticals, electronics, lasers, and other scientific and technical fields make Osaka and the Keihanshin region a major focal point for continued economic growth. With good access to land, air, and waterborne transportation, Osaka should retain its position at the core of the urban-industrial Kansai area.

BIBLIOGRAPHY

Association of Japanese Geographers, eds., *Geography of Japan* (Teikoku Shoin 1980).

Dunfield, David M., *Exploring Osaka: Japan's Second City* (Weatherhill 1993) [an excellent guide to places of interest].

Fujimoto Atsushi, *Osaka-fu no rekishi* (The History of Osaka Prefecture; Yamakawa Shuppansha 1969).

Hauser, William B., *Economic Institutional Change in Tokugawa Japan: Osaka and the Kinai Cotton Trade* (Cambridge University Press 1974).

Hauser, William B., "Osaka: A Commercial City in Tokugawa Japan," *Urbanism Past & Present,* no. 5 (Winter 1977–78).

Hauser, William B., "Osaka Castle and Tokugawa Authority in Western Japan," *The Bakufu in Japanese History,* ed. by Jeffrey P. Mass and William B. Hauser (Stanford University Press 1985).

Kyoto-Osaka: A Bilingual Atlas (Iris Co. 1992).

McClain, James L., and Wakita Osamu, eds., *Osaka: The Merchants' Capital of Early Modern Japan* (Cornell University Press 1999).

Miyamoto Mataji, *Osaka* (Ibundo 1962).

Trewartha, Glenn T., *Japan: A Geography* (University of Wisconsin Press 1965).

United Nations, *World Population Prospects* (1998).

United Nations, *World Urbanization Prospects* (1998).

WILLIAM B. HAUSER

Oslo

Norway

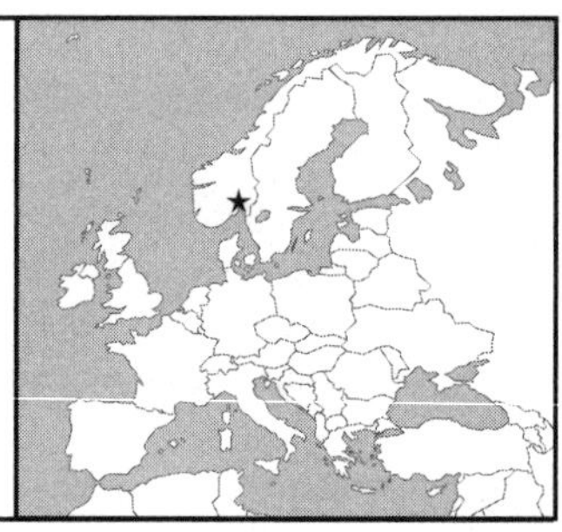

ORIENTATION

Name of City. From the time the town first appeared around the year 1000, its name (in Old Norse) was spelled *Áslo.* From around 1350 it was commonly spelled *Óslo;* in low German, *Auslo* or *Anslo;* in Latin, *Asloia* or *Ansloia.* After a devastating fire in 1624 the town was moved westward 2 kilometers (1.2 miles) across the Bay of Bjørvika and named *Christiania* after its founder, King Christian IV of Denmark-Norway. In the late 1870s the municipality modernized the name to *Kristiania,* although many institutions continued spelling the name with *Ch.* In 1925 the city was renamed *Oslo,* a decision that must be seen in the light of Norwegian national identity: Norway was in political unions with Denmark or Sweden, under foreign kings, from 1380 until 1905. The Norwegians pronounce the *o* of the name like a Continental *u* and the *s* like a thin *s* or a broader *sh*.

Location. Oslo is located at 59°55′ north latitude and 10°45′ east longitude. The city constitutes one of Norway's 19 counties and is situated (southeast) in southern Norway. Norway is the northernmost country in Europe.

Population. On January 1, 1999, the population of the municipality of Oslo was 502,867. Including the contiguous built-up area, the population was just over 750,000. Including the preponderately urbanized surrounding county of Akershus, the population was 963,431. With the addition of the 10 municipalities in adjoining counties with a considerable commuting population, the metropolitan population stands at about 1,050,000.

Distinctive and Unique Features. Despite its far-north location, Oslo has a temperate, semicontinental climate. The average daily high temperature in the summer months of June, July, and August is between 20° and 25°C (68° to 77°F). The corresponding figure for December, January, and February is between –5° and 0°C (23° to 32°F). The annual precipitation is 760 centimeters (30 inches), rather evenly distributed throughout the year. The central parts of the city have snow covering the ground from December to March, whereas the hills are snow-clad from November until April. Oslo belongs to an organization of world winter cities. Being sheltered by hills on most sides, the city has little wind. The hills rise from 150 to 530 meters (492 to 1,739 feet). The highest point in the municipality, farther north, stands 629 meters (2,064 feet) above sea level. The trough where the city is situated is locally referred to as *Oslo-gryta,* the "Oslo pot," and contributes to air pollution, especially in the winter.

The municipality of Oslo covers an area of 454 square kilometers (175 square miles), of which only 25% is built-up area. On all sides, but especially to the north, Oslo is surrounded (inside and outside the city limits) by large tracts of hilly, forested land with hundreds of lakes, providing a unique recreation area for the more than 1 million people in the metropolitan area. Oslo is located at the bottom of the 150-kilometer- (93-mile-) long Oslo Fjord, with its numerous islands and inlets. The forests are in the main protected from urban development, meaning that Oslo grows in beams or vectors outward from the center in all directions (except north), or by building more densely in the existing urban area. Even if we leave out the protected areas, one can safely say that Oslo, compared with most European cities, is characterized by a lavish use of space.

Quite uniquely for a large city, Oslo has a particularly interesting and internationally renowned geology of both volcanic and sedimentary origin. Its temperate climate allows 45 species of wild mammals, 113 species of birds, and 1,200 wild-plant species to live within the town borders.

Architecturally, there are three main elements in Oslo. There is, first, what may be labeled the 19th-century city, triangular in shape, covering roughly the 16 square kilometers (6 square miles) that made up the municipality before the incorporation in 1948 of the surrounding municipality of Aker. This 19th-century city includes a few 17th- and 18th-century buildings, some areas with small wooden houses from the first two-thirds of the 19th century (in the suburbs outside older city limits; inside, you had to build in stone or timber-frame), and a few 19th-century villas and scattered areas with 20th-century apartment houses. The area's dominant feature, however, is tenement and apartment blocks from the last three decades of the 19th century, three to five floors high. Built on a German pattern, they are the basis of the saying that since World War II, Oslo is the largest 19th-century "German" city. Beyond this densely built triangle, now housing 150,000 people although its population was once double this figure, are large areas of once-suburban settlement, consisting partly of blocks of apartments and partly of villas or semidetached houses. Modern suburban development in the form of villas and other small houses began about 1880 as a result of the advent of railways and trams. The present pattern is partly a result of development by local landowners and private organizations, and partly of public—that is, municipal—planning. Almost all houses with fewer than half a dozen apartments are built of wood. There are, finally, the blocks of apartments—built partly as individual buildings or groups of buildings and partly as satellite towns, planned as urban units with their own educational and social institutions and commercial services. The heyday of such satellites was the period from the 1950s to the 1980s.

Attractions of the City. Oslo has a double attraction for visitors. First, the city is the gateway to much of what tourists find attractive outside Oslo: the western fjords, the mountains and valleys, the

© JOHN HESELTINE/CORBIS

Statues by Gustav Vigeland line a staircase in Vigeland Park in Oslo, Norway.

picturesque small towns, stave churches, and so on. This is because Oslo is Norway's undisputed communication center, particularly with respect to air and rail traffic. The second draw is Oslo itself. The city's attractions include the fortress and castle of Akershus, the oldest parts of which date from the 14th century; the ruins of the medieval town, a 19th-century royal castle; a Viking-ship museum; an outdoor-folk museum; museums displaying the polar ship *Fram* and the raft *Kon-Tiki,* and the Vigeland sculpture park. There is a world-famous ski jump and a ski museum. Among a host of art and historical museums, the Edvard Munch Museum stands out as particularly interesting.

These attractions point to several general features of interest. The closeness of the Norwegians to nature, sports, and outdoor life is evident not only in the city's forests, lakes, and coastal area and also in the parks and arenas. Also, of prime importance is Oslo's global relations. There is a strong Norwegian seafaring tradition: the country has one of the world's largest merchant fleets, and Oslo is one of the major ports of the world (measured in the number and size of ships, with a 5.6 million tonnage in 1995). However, most of the ships never visit the city, and the Oslo of 2000 was better known for its major shipping establishments (ship brokers) than for its shipping fleet. Oslo's relation to the global economy rests mainly on its role as the country's undisputed financial and administrative center. Although the oil industry, Norway's biggest export industry, is located on the west coast and in some respects is managed from Stavanger, its real headquarters is in Oslo.

Relationships Between the City and the Outside. Unlike from most other Norwegian towns and cities, Oslo has not had its municipal borders extended for more than 50 years (since 1948). The metropolitan population is therefore double that of the city proper. There is a certain cooperation between Oslo and the surrounding county of Akershus and the various municipalities concerning matters such as transportation. In several respects—for example, with regard to housing—most administrative units follow their own policy, with the result that there are few cooperative arrangements that might contribute to making Oslo function better as a metropolitan area.

Since it became a capital in 1814, Oslo has grown from a small town to a large city, and it has often been perceived from outside as the cuckoo in the country's nest. The centralizing forces have been very strong, giving rise to political and ideological countermovements. There is thus a certain animosity toward Oslo and its inhabitants on the part of the rest of the country, stemming from the perception of Oslo as a parasite (as a center of bureaucracy) and the place where decisions are made for the rest of the country. One might argue, however, that the periphery has always had a strong position in Norwegian politics and culture. Therefore, while Norway is ruled *from* Oslo, one might say it is ruled *on behalf of* the periphery—or "the districts" (*distriktene*), as they are commonly called. It has for many decades been governmental policy to decentralize the government by relocating governmental agencies to various parts of the country.

Major Languages. The Norwegian language has many dialects but two official written languages, mutually understandable. These are *bokmål* (literally, "book-language"), rather close to Danish, and *nynorsk* (new Norwegian), which developed from Old Norse. In Oslo, the former is more common. On occasion, one might hear the Sami (Lappish) language. Since Oslo is a city of in-migrants, all Norwegian dialects are heard. Nowadays, as opposed to more than a generation ago, people are encouraged to retain their spoken dialects. There are "sociolects" as well. One can easily spot the difference between a westender and an eastender, the latter sociolect being closer to the rural new Norwegian. The difference, however, may now be slighter than before.

Owing to the considerable immigration in the most recent generation, a number of languages from all over the world can be heard in the streets. In 1998, 28% of the pupils in elementary school (age 6 to 16) had a foreign mother tongue, the most common being Urdu, Arabic, Turkish, Somalian, Vietnamese, English, Spanish, Punjabi, Albanian, Persian, and Serbo-Croat, in that order. All Norwegians in Oslo master English; mastery of German and French is not uncommon.

HISTORY

The Origin of the City. The sagas of Snorre Sturlasson (Sturluson) tell that King Harald Hardråde ("hard-ruler") founded Oslo, probably around 1050. Archaeologists, however, maintain that Oslo appeared around the year 1000 at the end of the Oslo Fjord, at the outlet of two small rivers in a fertile agricultural area. Its site and situation were both favorable—located at a point where goods were reloaded for shipping, it early became a small trade center, one of the few small towns in a thinly settled country. A major impetus to growth was its role as a religious center; Oslo had as many as seven churches and two monasteries in the High Middle Ages. Although there was a small royal castle in the town, the medieval kings spent more time in Trondheim or Bergen than in Oslo. From around 1300, with the erection of the Akershus fortress and castle, Oslo had some functions as a "capital."

At its medieval zenith, around 1300, the population stood at no more than 3,000. At that time, Bergen already had 7,000 inhabitants, and it remained the country's most populous town until the 1830s. The demographic and economic crisis in the Late Middle Ages reduced Oslo's population to about 2,000 in the 16th century. From then on, more-favorable economic conditions—namely, the lumber trade—made the city grow. *Christiania,* the renamed and slightly relocated city, reached 4,000 inhabitants by the end of the 17th century and 12,000 (suburbs included) by the beginning of the 19th. During the last two centuries of the union with Denmark, ending in 1814, the town had gained an additional impetus to growth through its role as a provincial capital.

© CHARLES & JOSETTE LENARS/CORBIS

An ocean liner sails past an oil drilling platform in a shipyard in Oslo.

Oslo's new role as capital in the semi-independent kingdom of Norway (from 1814) is perhaps the most important fact in the history of the city. Norway governed itself in all respects except foreign policy, meaning that an array of institutions had to be founded in the newly appointed capital. This, by the way, is a somewhat misleading expression, since Oslo is the capital of Norway not by appointment, but by virtue of the fact that the governing bodies are located in the city. This is to say that "capital" (*hovedstad*) is not a legal concept.

From 1814 Oslo (Christiania) grew very fast, first by simply building the capital and thereafter owing to the secondary effects stemming from its capital status. The town became a major trade center, a transport hub, and the country's major export and import (especially) port. From the 1840s on, the town industrialized and soon became the major industrial center in the country. Other secondary effects included the city's rise as a center for public and private organizations, higher education, and cultural institutions. Norway's major newspapers are published in Oslo, and one may therefore safely say that Oslo in the two last centuries was the country's center of attention. At the end of the 20th century, nine daily newspapers were published in Oslo, with a total sale of 1.2 million copies. In the last third of the 20th century, much of the manufacturing industry left the city, leaving, however, most of the other central functions intact. The population of Oslo increased from around 13,000 in 1814 to 250,000 in 1900, and slightly above 500,000 in 1950, suburbs included.

Migration: Past and Present. Although the mass emigration to North America in the 19th and early 20th centuries is the best-known migratory movement, Oslo has, conversely, received immigrants (foreign) and in-migrants (domestic) through all its 1,100 years. Through most of its history, immigrants to Oslo have come mainly from the nearest hinterland, particularly from the northeast. In the 20th century in-migration to the capital has come from most of the country.

Before the 19th century, immigrants to Oslo came mainly for career reasons. They were German Hansa merchants during the High and Late Middle Ages, and, during the long union, Danish (and through Denmark, German) civil servants and some noblemen, Dutch merchants, and artisans from several northern European countries. The 19th century, in particular its last third, saw a mass immigration of Swedes, principally common people heading for the nearest larger city. Smaller but still quite visible foreign groups in the 19th century included German and Danish craftspeople and workers and English skilled workers in the manufacturing industry, as well as French, Italians, Poles, and Russian Jews. In 1900, 6% of Oslo's population was Swedish-born; between 1% and 2% were born in other foreign places. In the 20th century immigration became more restricted: the century could be labeled the century of refugee immigration. The exceptions were passport union and a common labor market among the Nordic countries since the 1950s and the importation of laborers from developing nations in the 1960s and early 1970s. After 1975 immigration from outside the Nordic countries has taken the shape of reuniting families (including fetching brides and grooms from the country of origin), granting asylum, and receiving refugees or specialist workers from the West. In 1999, 18% of Oslo's population was classified as immigrants, being born abroad or in Norway of two foreign-born parents; 76% of the immigrants were non-Western, the major places of origin being Pakistan, Morocco, Somalia, Eritrea, Turkey, the former Yugoslavia, Iran, Sri Lanka, and Vietnam.

INFRASTRUCTURE

Public Buildings, Public Works, and Residences. As the Norwegian capital, Oslo has quite a few noticeable national institutions. The royal castle, finished in 1848, is, of course, one of them. There is the *stortingsbygningen* (or Stortinget, the Parliament building), erected in 1866, and a number of other governmental buildings, built mainly from the 20th century. There used to be two railway stations. The western is closed down, and the eastern has been transformed into a central station. Fornebu Airport, to the west of the city, was closed down in 1998 and was replaced by the larger Gardermoen, 48 kilometers (30 miles) northeast of the center, but connected with Oslo by a fast train (20 minutes). Oslo's major source of energy is hydroelectric power, transported from the mountains of the interior to power stations at the outskirts of the city.

In preindustrial Oslo, until past the middle of the 19th century, the upper classes (meaning the burghers or the bourgeoisie, since there was virtually no aristocracy after the 17th century) clustered in the central parts of the town. In the warmer season, however, many lived in their summer residences on the outskirts of town; many of these mansions can still be seen. The workers partly populated the attics and cellars of the central town but huddled mainly in poor suburbs, some of which remain, now partly gentrified. In the second half of the 19th century, the leading classes increasingly moved out of the center, and a social division of the city into a west end (*vestkant*) and an east end (*østkant*) appeared. The concepts of *vestkant* and *østkant* have for generations loomed prominently in the minds of Oslo's inhabitants. The tendency for the lower (working) class to live on the eastern side and the middle classes to settle on the western side to a certain degree continues in the areas beyond the 19th-century city and even into the neighboring suburban municipalities. Bearing this fundamental geographic cleavage in mind, we nevertheless find mixed housing and a mixing of social strata everywhere.

Politics and City Services. Local democratic self-government was introduced in Norwegian municipalities in 1837, through the election of a council that, in turn, elected a mayor. This system is still in use. However, Oslo adopted a municipal parliamentary system in 1986 whereby a city government was formed on the basis of the political majority in the city council. (Oslo is the only city in Norway with this governmental structure.) Throughout the whole of the 20th century, the Conservative and Labor parties have been alternately in power; as of 2000 the city was governed by the Conservatives.

Oslo has a history as a pioneer city in social services, and used to advertise itself in the 1950s and 1960s as no less than "the welfare capital of the world." Notable among the government services were support for single mothers (beginning in 1920), *oslotrygden* (the Oslo security), and a free health breakfast to all schoolchildren (the Oslo breakfast), programs emulated by many other countries. From the 1970s on, harder economic times made Oslo's social welfare programs far less conspicuous.

The most noticeable trait at the turn of the century was perhaps, the decentralized system of social services. Fully effective since 1988, Oslo is divided into 25 wards or townships (*bydeler*), dealing with health services, social security, and benefits (the services for the elderly being by far the most expensive), children's welfare, and daycare centers. There is room for 75% (1999) of the under-six-year-olds at the daycare centers, corresponding to the demand. Resources are distributed to the wards according to need, as measured demographically or according to the observed need—for example, cases of child negligence. This system means a colossal redistribution of means from wealthy western wards to less-well-off eastern wards.

Educational System. In the late 1990s Norway introduced compulsory schooling from the age of 6. There is compulsory attendance for 10 years, until the age of 16. Almost all schools are public and thereby free of cost. These primary/secondary schools (through age 16) are municipal, while high schools (for ages 16–19) are administered by the counties. In the case of Oslo, this makes no difference, since the city is both a municipality and a county. High schools are not compulsory, but all have the right to attend, an opportunity taken by almost everybody. Students can chose between theoretical or more-practically oriented courses. Since 1994, however, the theoretical element has been high in all courses, which is probably one of the major causes of a rising dropout rate.

Oslo is the home of the University of Oslo, the oldest and largest of Norway's four universities, founded in 1811. By the turn of the century, there were 35,000 students at the campus. The Oslo College, the result of a merger of a number of smaller colleges and schools, has about 10,000 students, most of whom are pursuing professional careers as nurses, primary-school teachers, journalists, physiotherapists, and so on. There are also colleges and academies for the study of architecture, sports, war, business, and the arts, making Oslo by far the national center for higher education. The total number of university and college students is 56,000, of whom 59% are women (1997).

Transportation System. Oslo's internal transport system is based on an underground railway, a tram system, and a number of bus lines, in addition to the national rail and a few boat lines. The subway carries the most passengers. The tram dates back to 1875. In 1894 Oslo became the fourth city in Europe to introduce electric trams (hence its popular name, *trikken,* "the electric"). By 2000 only a few tram routes were still running. The first suburban railway was opened in 1898, and the first subway in 1928. In 1966, four eastern and four western suburban lines were connected underground in the center of the city.

CULTURAL AND SOCIAL LIFE

Distinctive Features of the City's Cultures. The social atmosphere of Oslo is an informal one. In practically all social situations, people use the informal you (*du*) instead of the more formal *De* (corresponding to German *Sie* or French *vous*) that was so much more common 30 or 40 years ago. There is little formal etiquette except on certain formal occasions, particularly those connected with bourgeois business or social activities. As concerns body language, Norwegians are known to be rather reserved. A popular ad on TV shows a black man using beer to cure the Norwegian "stiffness." The beer is a low-alcoholic beer, to be sure, since advertising for alcohol or cigarettes is forbidden. The pietistism of Norwegian urban culture is about to disappear in Oslo. Only a handful of restaurants existed 30 years ago, but there are now more than a thousand pubs, bars, and restaurants where alcohol can be bought within the borders of Oslo.

Cuisine. There is no outstanding Norwegian (or Oslo) cuisine, just a few well-known dishes, although there are chefs and restaurants in Oslo with Michelin stars and international reputations. The most recent generation, however, has witnessed the opening of hundreds of restaurants of non-Norwegian ethnicity. In the Yellow Pages of Oslo's phone book, restaurants are now arranged by ethnicity (31 in all at the turn of the century). There has been a marked gentrification of several parts of inner Oslo, such as the former working-class district of Grünerløkka. Trendy pubs, restaurants, galleries, shops, and residential areas pop up here and elsewhere. The quayside entertainment district of Aker brygge (wharf), a former shipyard, was rebuilt in the 1980s.

Ethnic, Class, and Religious Diversity. More than 100 ethnic minorities are now resident in Oslo, with 18% of the city's inhabitants counted as immigrants in the sense of being born abroad or in Norway of two foreign-born parents. Only half of these, however, are foreign citizens. Ethnic diversity also entails growing religious diversity. The great majority of Oslo's inhabitants belong to the Norwegian Lutheran state church, but there is a growing number of (especially) Muslims (there are several mosques), Roman Catholics, and people of no declared religion or denomination. The ethnic minorities are particularly numerous in the inner east side of the city ("Little Karachi"), without, according to researchers, approaching ghettolike conditions.

Family and Other Social Support Systems. Norwegian families are small, particularly in a big city such as Oslo. The most common household is the one-person household. Only one-quarter of the households contain children under 18 years of age. Immigrants tend to have larger families and, even to some degree, three-generation families, but they are increasingly approaching the native pattern. Despite the pattern of single and childless households, Norwegian fertility has grown since the early 1980s, and its rate is now one of the highest in Europe. Oslo is no exception. Most men and women have children sooner or (rather) later. The reasons for the relatively high fertility rate might be a good daycare system (most mothers have paid work), good social benefits (one-year maternity leave with pay), and a fair amount of gender equality. Still, single mothers are among the groups with the most difficult living conditions, along with the unemployed (2%–3% in 2000).

Work and Commerce. Until the 1970s Oslo was an important manufacturing center. At a pace faster than the rest of the country, Oslo has become rather deindustrialized, leaving only some consumer-oriented industries. In 2000 only about one in seven people in the city earned their living from manufacturing or crafts. Oslo is more than ever the national center of trade, finance, public and private administration, and other services. Some 90,000 people commute daily into the municipality, but an almost equal number go in the opposite direction. Manufacturing industries and wholesale firms are located in certain areas at a distance from the city center, while more-service-oriented business tends to be more centrally located. Much of the retail trade is now concentrated in large centers throughout the metropolitan area. The downtown retail business seems to survive, however, partly thanks to the great revival of downtown in the past 20 or 30 years—in entertainment, restaurants, cultural institutions, and so forth.

Arts and Recreation. Oslo has experienced an enormous vitalization of urban cultural life over the past generation. The availability and variety of food and drink have already been mentioned. The art galleries are too numerous to enumerate. Oslo also has a number of theaters and 14 cinemas with 33 auditoriums. There is one opera, with plans for its own building. There are three or four large concert halls, together with a large number of smaller concert facilities and clubs. Oslo has been characterized as the best city for all kinds of music in the Nordic countries. The vitalization is no doubt connected to the city's new multicultural life.

QUALITY OF LIFE

Immigration and in-migration have led to a rise in the price of housing, making it difficult for young people to establish themselves. The market for rented dwellings is unstable and insufficiently regulated by law (perhaps paradoxically for a social democratic society). Norway is an owner's society—81% of Oslo's inhabitants (the share is higher elsewhere in the country) own their own residences, individually or collectively (as a joint owner of a building society). Houses and apartments are, on average higher in cost than in Stockholm or Copenhagen. There are almost two rooms per person, counting only living rooms and bedrooms, albeit unevenly distributed. According to the 1990 census, about 1,500 people had no regular residence.

Although electricity is the major source of energy and is also used for heating, pollution is noticeable, especially during the winter. This pollution results from a combination of the need for heating oil during the cold winter, the exhaust from the cars, and the dust stemming from studded tires in winter, usually in dry weather conditions. The crime rate is on the rise, particularly drug-related crimes. There were seven homicides in 1996.

The benevolent combination of nature and culture—of beautiful surroundings and good recreation facilities accompanied by a plentiful labor market and a varied urban culture—makes Oslo an attractive place to live for most of its residents. However, the city offers not only the best living conditions in the country, but also some of the worst. There are areas with bad housing, a high crime rate, and severe drug problems. The influx of immigrants from developing nations has created some social tensions and has given rise to racist manifestations. The challenge to Oslo in the future will be to balance integration and tolerance culturally, ethnically, class-wise, and in terms of religion.

BIBLIOGRAPHY

Benum, Edgeir, *Byråkratienes by: Oslo bys historie, Bind 5, 1948–1986* (Cappelen 1994) [five-volume history published 1990–1994].

Benum, Edgeir, "The City of the Bureaucracies: Oslo's Expanding Role as a Capital in the Postwar Period," *Scandinavian Journal of History* 3 (1990): 207–236.

Blom, S., "Residential Concentration Among Immigrants in Oslo," *International Migration* 37, no. 3 (1999): 617–641.

Brevik, Ivar, "Income Inequalities and Socio-economic Segregation in Oslo—Governance by the Market," *Governing Cities: Social Exclusion, Social Fragmentation and Urban Governance,* ed. by Hans Thor Andersen and Ronald van Kempen (Ashgate 2000).

Hjorthol, Randi, "Reurbanization and Its Potential for the Reduction of Car Use: Analysis of Preferences of Residence, Activity and Travel Patterns in the Oslo Area," *Scandinavian Housing and Planning Research* 15, no. 4 (1998): 211–226.

Myhre, Jan Eivind, "Middle Classes and Suburban Lives," *The Nordic Middle Classes, 1840–1940,* ed. by Geoffrey Crossick, et al. (Berghahn 2000).

Myhre, Jan Eivind, "'Soon Christiania will be all Norway': The Growth of the Norwegian Capital Since 1814," *Capital Cities and Cultural Identities,* ed. by Lars Nilsson (Institute of Urban History 2000).

Myhre, Jan Eivind, "Wanted and Unwanted Suburbs: Annexations and Urban Identity: The Case of Christiania (Oslo) in the Nineteenth Century," *Scandinavian Economic History Review,* XLIV, no. 2 (1996): 124–139.

Myhre, Jan Eivind, and Erik Lorange, "Planning and Urbanization in Norway," *Urban Planning in the Nordic Countries,* ed. by Thomas Hall (Spon 1991) [a useful overview of all the Nordic countries].

Oslo Byleksikon, 4. Utg. (The Oslo Encyclopedia of Oslo, 4th Edition) (Oslo 2000) [invaluable for both details and overviews].

Statistisk Årbok for Oslo (Statistical Yearbook of Oslo) [published annually since 1899, with forerunners from 1883—a treasury of information].

Wessel, Terje, "Social Polarisation and Socio-economic Segregation in a Welfare State: The Case of Oslo," *Urban Studies* 37, no. 11 (2000): 1947–1967 [Wessel argues that the level of spatial segregation has remained stable despite increasing income inequality, owing to a more flexible design in city planning and policy].

JAN EIVIND MYHRE

Ottawa

Canada

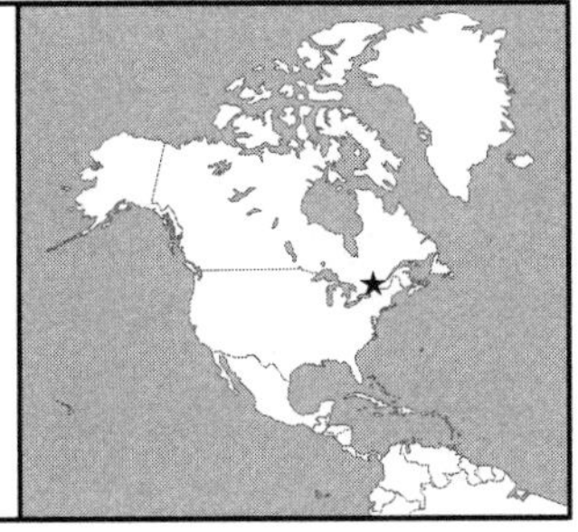

ORIENTATION

Ottawa, the Canadian capital, is the lynchpin of the National Capital Region. This region, measuring 4,715 square kilometers (1,820 square miles), comprises the city of Ottawa and the surrounding area and includes 28 municipalities in the provinces of Ontario and Quebec. The population of the National Capital Region is 1.3 million.

As of January 2001, a new and much larger city of Ottawa came into being. Ontario provincial legislation passed in 1999 provided for the amalgamation of the former city of Ottawa and 11 adjacent Ontario municipalities. The newly enlarged city of Ottawa is now Canada's fourth-largest city.

Name of City. The toponym *Ottawa* is the anglicized version of the name of an aboriginal nation that has been variously referred to as the Outauac, Outaouais, or Otaouit. In fact, in French the region is still referred to as the Outaouais. For over 6,000 years aboriginal peoples used the Ottawa River to travel between the Great Lakes and the St. Lawrence River.

Location. Ottawa is situated at 45°25′ north latitude and 75°43′ west longitude, just below the Canadian Shield, which is visible from Ottawa in the form of the Gatineau Hills, just to the north of the city. The Canadian Shield, a very prominent and distinct geological feature in North America, occupies almost half of Canada's total area and extends in a semicircle from Hudson Bay to the Great Lakes and northeastern New York State. The retreat of the last Ice Age left behind a myriad of lakes and rivers of all shapes and sizes. Ottawa benefits from these geological features and from the abundant forests of pine and hardwoods characteristic of the southern part of the shield. It was these timber resources that initially gave rise to the settlement of the Ottawa region as an urban area.

Population. In 2001 the population of Ottawa was approximately 800,000 and it is estimated that this will increase to over 1 million by 2010. Exact statistics cannot be extrapolated from the 1996 census; owing to the recent reorganization of the city, these statistics no longer reflect the population of the city alone, but to the region as a whole.

Distinctive and Unique Features. Despite its northern location, the short summers in Ottawa can be surprisingly hot and humid—swimming, boating, canoeing, and other water sports can be pursued at a level of quality and enjoyability comparable to anywhere in the world. The very cold and lengthy winters, with their short hours of daylight, are perceived by the local population as opportunities to turn their attention to indoor activities, which are facilitated by access to a very well developed communications infrastructure. Ottawa has the highest rate of computer access and internet connectivity in the country—four out of five households own a computer. There are also boundless opportunities for outdoor winter activities such as skating, hockey, skiing, snowboarding, sledding, icefishing, and snowmobiling. The ambiance for outdoor winter activities is sufficiently pleasant to attract large numbers of tourists, particularly from the adjacent United States; New York state is a one-hour drive by car.

Attractions of the City. Until recently Ottawa, unlike many capitals, was not one of the country's largest cities—certainly not on the scale of Toronto, Montreal, or Vancouver. Ottawa throughout much of its history was a medium-sized urban area with many parks and an abundance of waterways, such as the Ottawa, Rideau, and Gatineau rivers and the Rideau Canal, all of which are widely used for recreational purposes in both summer and winter.

Relationships Between the City and the Outside. Ottawa has begun to offer the atmosphere of a large city. It is the seat of the federal government of Canada. This means that it is a city of politicians, civil servants, diplomats, and other foreign representatives. In fact, this deeply marks the central core of the National Capital Region. Ottawa is a center for diplomacy and foreign relations with many and varied official links to the rest of the world. The diplomatic corps is one of the largest in the world; it includes more than 4,000 diplomats and over 100 foreign missions.

Since the 1980s the region has witnessed the emergence of what has been called "Silicon Valley North." Large high-tech companies, such as Nortel Networks and Corel Corporation, originated in the Ottawa region, and, as was the case with Compagnie Financiére Alcatel (Alcatel), they established themselves there through acquisitions. Many middle-sized and smaller entrepreneurial firms are active in telecommunications, information technology, and other high-tech businesses and research, attracted to the city by its excellent network of schools, community colleges, and universities in both English and French; world class medical facilities; low crime rates; very low pollution levels; well-preserved natural setting; and very well-developed communications and transportation networks.

Major Languages. English and French are the official languages for all purposes of the federal government in the National Capital Region. Approximately one in five Ottawa residents is French-speaking, and rates of bilingualism in English and French, which have been rising in the younger age groups, are quite high.

HISTORY

The Origin of the City. Historical documents name Étienne Brulé as the first European to explore the region. He arrived in 1610 and was followed three years later by Samuel de Champlain, who drew up detailed maps of the area. At that time people belonging to the Algonquian nation hunted and trapped in winter and fished, hunted, and gathered in the summer and fall, and engaged in slash-and-burn horticulture. To travel around, they used birch bark canoes and snowshoes. This reflects the influence of centuries of trade and travel and communication in the region. These transportation technologies, well suited to the local environment, were adopted by the Europeans.

Following the arrival of the Europeans, the Outaouais region became an important waterway for the fur trade and, subsequently, the scene of continuous conflict related to this trade between the Huron and the Iroquois confederacies. The local Algonquins, whose territories geographically overlapped those of the belligerents, suffered greatly. As if this were not enough, they also became the victims of smallpox, which was introduced among them from contact with the French. Not surprisingly, the Algonquians moved further north in the mid-1600s, well away from the Ottawa River.

The Ottawa River was of increasing strategic importance during the 17th, 18th, and 19th centuries. Travel by water was the only way to access the interior of the American continent. Coming from the east,

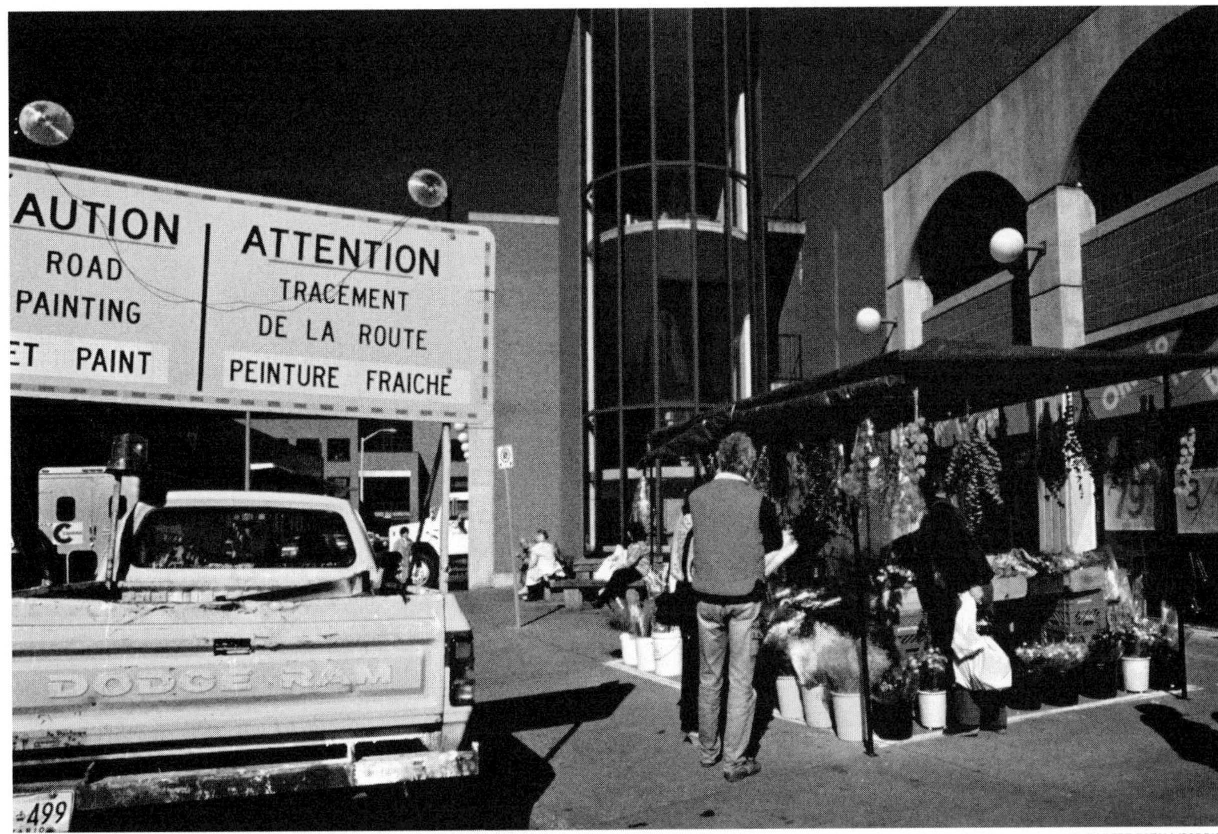

© ROBERT ESTALL/CORBIS

Signs in both English and French in the officially bilingual National Capital Region.

traders and colonizers would navigate the St. Lawrence River and then the Ottawa River to reach further west. All who used the Ottawa River (aboriginals, traders, missionaries, or adventurers) were obliged to stop in the Ottawa area because of several sets of dangerous rapids and the Chaudière Falls. These obstacles could only be circumvented by lengthy portages.

By the first decades of the 19th century, the fur trade was in relative decline. There were still no permanent settlements in the Ottawa region and only a few temporary encampments. What was later the city of Hull on the north bank of the river was settled by a group of American colonists from Massachusetts, who built a mill, houses, and other buildings. The attraction was the plentiful supply of white pine. By 1806 the colonists found a way to float rafts of timber down the Ottawa River to Quebec City and hence to markets abroad. This proved that logging in the region was commercially viable and the expansion of the timber trade began. The Napoleonic Wars brought great demand for Ottawa valley timber. Agricultural activity remained marginal. Winters were spent cutting timber and hauling it to waterways; springs and summers were spent building large rafts of timber and floating these to the St. Lawrence and then to Quebec City.

Despite the development of the timber trade, what is now Ottawa was still virtually uninhabited as late as the 1820s. Change came only when Britain decided to build a navigable waterway from where the Rideau and Ottawa rivers meet, and hence to the St. Lawrence River at Kingston, adjacent to Lake Ontario. The purpose was to provide a secure supply route in the event of military conflict with the United States. The construction of the Rideau Canal was an immense engineering project that required skilled workers and laborers from the British Isles, as well as English and French Canada. Many of those involved in the construction of the canal remained in what was then called Bytown, after Lieutenant Colonel By, the British army officer in charge. Bytown was incorporated as the city of Ottawa in 1855, by which time lumber was being sawn into boards locally for shipment to the American market. This led to extensive wealth accumulation by regional entrepreneurs.

Ottawa was easily reached by water, in a military secure location, had publicly owned land available for government use (acquired during the construction of the Rideau Canal), and was on the borders of Ontario and Quebec. These factors are believed to have been important in the choice of Ottawa as the capital of the Province of Canada by Queen Victoria in 1857. The hill at the intersection of the Rideau Canal with the Ottawa River, where British soldiers had been housed during the building of the canal, became the site of the Canadian Parliament buildings. Fortuitously, the Parliament buildings were completed the year before the Canadian Confederation came into being in 1867. Ottawa was confirmed as the capital of the new country, in part, because the necessary buildings were in place.

Many additional government buildings were constructed in Ottawa following confederation. Although these reflected British architectural traditions, Ottawa was never considered to be impressive in its appearance. An Ottawa Improvement Commission was established in 1899 by Prime Minister Wilfred Laurier. Of greater and more immediate impact, was the Great Fire of 1900, which started in Hull and spread through the lumber mills and across the Ottawa River. Almost 2,000 buildings were destroyed including Parliament, with the exception of the library. Parliament and the cities of Ottawa and Hull were subsequently rebuilt. The Ottawa Improvement Commission was replaced by the Federal District Commission in 1927, and its mandate was extended into the province of Quebec. Following World War II, Jacques Gréber, a French architect, was brought in to design a master plan for the Federal District. This resulted in the removal of railway lines from the city center and the creation of scenic driveways, parks, and boulevards, which remain at the core of the form and layout of Ottawa. The old downtown railway station, next to the Rideau Canal locks at the Ottawa River, became the main Federal Government Conference Centre, adjacent to which the modern Congress Centre was later constructed. By 1958 the Federal District Commission was superseded by the National Capital Commission, a Crown Corporation, with the mandate to plan and assist in the development, construction, and improvement of the National Capital Region. The National Capital Commission, which pays grants in lieu of taxes to the municipalities in which it owns properties, has the mandate to present the capital to visitors, domestic and foreign, as a place in which the Canadian cultural heritage and achievements can be experienced. In addition, it is responsible for capital parks, parkways, and recreational pathways, not to mention Canada Day celebrations, the Parliament Hill sound and light shows, and Winterlude events.

INFRASTRUCTURE

Public Buildings, Public Works, and Residences. The most prominent feature of the Ottawa Region is undoubtedly the Parliament buildings complex located on a promontory overlooking the Ottawa River and the city of Hull. Adjacent to Parliament, to the east is the historic Chateau Laurier Hotel, the Ottawa Congress Centre, the new American Embassy, the National Arts Centre, the National Gallery, the War Museum, the bilingual University of Ottawa, and the Roman Catholic Cathedral. Within walking distance are the official residences of the governor-general and prime minister, next to the Ottawa River. Immediately to the rear is Rockcliffe Park Village, an established upscale residential area in which many embassies are located as well as the residences of many active and retired diplomats, politicians, and leading entrepreneurs.

Yet another prominent feature of Ottawa is the parkways along the Ottawa River to the east and to the west, and the parkways leading south along both banks of the Rideau Canal. In the summer the Rideau Canal is full of boats of all kinds and in winter it becomes the world's longest skating rink. By following the Queen Elizabeth Parkway on the west side of the Canal, one arrives in just a few minutes by car at Agriculture Canada's Experimental Farm and Museum. In both summer and winter there are free horse-drawn carriage rides around the farm on wagons or sleighs, to the delight of young and old. There is a clear view of Carleton University on the other side of the canal from the farm. The Rideau River and the canal are crossed by dozens of structures, most notably the Pretoria and Plaza bridges in the downtown area.

To the west of Parliament are the Supreme Court, the National Library and Archives, and the Anglican Cathedral. Across the Ottawa River from Parliament is the modern Canadian Museum of Civilization, a cluster of modern federal government highrise office buildings, and a spectacular view in the background of the forest-covered Gatineau Hills.

Politics and City Services. Partly in response to the infrastructural problems accompanying economic and demographic growth and urban sprawl in all directions, and partly to increase the efficiency of local government while containing or reducing costs, the old city of Ottawa was, in 2001, amalgamated with 11 surrounding municipalities. This greatly expanded the geographical perimeters of the city, in addition to boosting the population. From east to west the city boundaries extend 110 kilometers (68 miles) and the urban core is surrounded by 532 square kilometers (205 square miles) of greenbelt. There is an extensive area to the east in which French speakers comprise from 25% to 45% of neighborhood populations, and an extensive area to the west in which nine out of ten residents are English speaking. Also, a higher proportion of the population in the eastern part of the city commutes downtown to work in government and related activities. In contrast, the western part is characterized by high technology and local job availability and a lower proportion of commuters to the city center. A transition period of a good number of years may be needed in order to make this new municipal system fully operational in terms of acceptable modes of delivery of services in both official languages and for a consensus to emerge on policy and program priorities. Making citizens feel welcome is therefore a priority, and the civic bureaucracy, the council chamber, and the committee rooms of the new city government are located in a modern open structure featuring a wide promenade. Ottawa is the first Canadian municipality to offer transactional services on the Internet—in addition to paying property taxes and obtaining building permits online, the system will provide citizens the means to exert influence on legislators between elections.

Educational System. Ottawa has more than 400 English and French elementary and secondary schools, both public and private. The public school system, a provincial responsibility with local school boards, includes a Roman Catholic school sector run separately from other public schools. There are English and French schools in all sectors of the public school system. In addition, bilingual (English and French) immersion programs are offered in both public and private schools. There are eight colleges and universities, and these programs are also available in English or French.

Transportation System. The main forms of transportation in Ottawa are by private car or city bus. A Light Rail Pilot Project was introduced in 2001 to provide convenient connections with the existing city bus routes. For much of the year the numerous bicycle paths are used not only for recreational purposes but also for commuting to work. Traffic congestion is increasing, particularly during rush hours, owing to suburban sprawl, which spills across the Ottawa River and into the neighboring province of Quebec. From east to west, the main bridges across the Ottawa River are the Macdonald-Cartier, adjacent to External Affairs; the Alexandra, next to the National Gallery; the Portage, leading to a massive federal government complex in Hull; the Chaudière, which runs by the sites of the old lumber and paper mills; and the Champlain, much farther west, which provides a link to suburban communities. Regional economic and population growth is putting increasing pressure on infrastructure—not only on the transportation network but also on housing and office space. Prime location office space has been declining in availability for a number years, and a shortage of housing is appearing—rental vacancy rates are the lowest in the country.

CULTURAL AND SOCIAL LIFE

Distinctive Features of the City's Cultures. Given its location on the border with the predominantly French-speaking province of Quebec, Ottawa has been, since its inception, an area of extensive intercultural contact for both of Canada's official language groups. The city of Ottawa is in the officially bilingual National Capital Region, in which federal services to the public must, by law, be available in both English and French. Within the federal administration, both of these languages have equal status as languages of work and government services. This has resulted in rising rates of bilingualism in the region, which is reflected in daily life in both the government and private sectors of the economy and in leisure activities.

Ottawa has long had a reputation as being one of the duller world capitals. Younger people tend to prefer the excitement of Montreal or Toronto to life in a city in which, until recently, the sidewalks were rolled up at five o'clock in the evening. Traditionally, local youth used to flock across the Ottawa River in large numbers to Hull where the bars ("boites de nuit") and bistros were open until three o'clock in the morning, if not beyond. This is changing as Ottawa becomes larger, more cosmopolitan, and more multicultural. But the city, in 2001, implemented the strictest nonsmoking laws of any city in Canada. Smoking is banned in bars, restaurants, bingo halls, bowling alleys and, in effect, in almost all public places. Once again there is a parade of Ottawans to the restaurants and bars across the river to Hull-Gatineau where smoking laws are among the most liberal in the country. This tendency may become even more pronounced given the plans announced by the government of Quebec to create a large-scale urban resort adjoining the existing Hull Casino with the addition of a 23-story Hilton hotel with a theater showroom, European-style spa, conference center, and five-star restaurant.

Cuisine. Increasing social and economic diversity has been accompanied by the growth of a rich and varied spectrum of high quality dining and entertainment, which is quite moderately priced by both European and American standards and remains within reach of a significant majority of the population. The diverse nightlife extends late into the morning hours, despite the fact that Ottawa's population has the second-largest percentage of senior citizens of any city in Canada.

Ethnic, Class, and Religious Diversity. The main ethnic groups in the Ottawa and National Capital Region are, by size, those with origins in the British Isles, the French, and the Irish. In addition to the importance of language as an ethnic boundary, those with origins in the British Isles are predominantly Protestant, whereas the French and the Irish are predominantly Roman Catholic. These language and religious divisions are still reflected in the way elementary and secondary schooling is organized in the province of Ontario. The rate of intermarriage between these groups is high as the salience of religious differences has decreased and as diversity in occupations, incomes, and lifestyles has increased within each group. Though the language boundary is still apparent in work and leisure activities, it has become much more permeable as rates of bilingualism have increased; even language has declined as a barrier to ethnic intermarriage. In recent decades visible minority immigrant groups have been growing in numbers and importance. In order of size, the Chinese, those of Arab or West Asian descent, South Asians, and Africans are the largest of the "new" ethnocultural groupings in Ottawa, and these groups are likely to grow more rapidly than the older ethnicities in the region.

In terms of class structure, Ottawa has one of the highest median incomes of any Canadian city. This reflects the facts that almost half of Ottawa's residents hold a university degree or postsecondary certificate or diploma, and government-related activities and the high-tech sector are the major sources of direct and indirect employment. Although Ottawa remains a city in which the middle class is predominant, this may change in the decades ahead to the extent that it becomes more differentiated in terms of economic activities and occupational structure.

Family and Other Social Support Systems. Ottawa and the National Capital Region provide a very congenial environment for family living. In Ottawa, as in most Canadian cities, families are becoming smaller as birthrates decline. Typically, families are nuclear and there are one or two children per household. Young people are remaining with their families longer and marrying later, rates of cohabitation have been increasing, and common-law families, along with single-parent households are the fastest-growing family type in the region. As in most Canadian cities, downtown living involves apartment lodging. Most families who wish to live in townhouses or single, detached dwellings must commute to the suburbs. Vacancy rates for apartments and other types of rental housing are usually very low and prices can be higher than those in larger Canadian metropolises. Most forms of family support emanate from the provincial and/or federal governments reflecting the Canadian welfare-state framework.

Work and Commerce. The federal government was for many decades the leading employer in the region, accounting for as many as one-third of total jobs. In addition many people worked for the provincial and municipal governments in the city as well as for government supported elementary, secondary, and postsecondary levels of the educational system, making it clear that Ottawa was for many decades a civil service town. The proportion of the labor force working for the federal government has declined since the last quarter of the 20th century, in part because of federal government cutbacks and hiring freezes, but mostly because of the spectacular growth of the high technology sector that now accounts for the same proportion of workers as the federal government. The infrastructure in telecommunications and high technology is such that it is no longer as necessary or as attractive for businesses to keep their organizational activities in the center of the city. Even so, the vacancy rate of prime office space in the city center has fallen because of the strong local economy.

Tourism is a thriving part of the local economy, particularly in summer. Main attractions include the Tulip Festival in spring, the Parliament buildings, Canada Day celebrations, the National Gallery and other museums, the Christmas lights displays, and Winterlude. Many hundreds of thousands visit the city as tourists every year. In recent years, the lower value of the Canadian dollar and the more secure and serene environment of Ottawa have attracted older Americans from adjacent and nearby American states in significant numbers.

Arts and Recreation. The National Arts Centre, right across from Parliament Hill, offers musical, theatrical, dance, and variety performances in both official languages. As in any capital, there is a large number of museums and cultural institutions, including the National Library, National Gallery, and the National Arts Centre. Other museums are particularly appealing to families and children—notably, the Museum of Science and Technology and, just across the river in Hull, the Museum of Civilization with its IMAX theaters. These institutions often serve as the venues for all kinds of cultural events that link the diplomatic, political, and administrative communities. In addition to these types of cultural activities, residents also enjoy the National Hockey League games starring the Ottawa Senators.

QUALITY OF LIFE

In addition to a thriving economy, a well-developed urban infrastructure, and a greenbelt surrounding the urban core, there are more than 500 kilometers (310 miles) of major and minor bicycle routes and, in winter, a 7.8-kilometer (5-mile) skating rink on the Rideau Canal between the locks at the Ottawa River and Hartwell's Locks at Carleton University. Sensitivity to environmental issues is increasing. For instance, the main channel of the Ottawa River, formed some 12,000 years ago during the retreat of the post-glacial seas, was recognized in 1995 as an internationally significant wetland under the United Nations Ramsar Convention. Federal protection has been extended to most of this area, known as the *Mer Bleue* ("Blue Sea"), and which is located in the Ottawa green belt, to conserve the many rare species of plants, birds, and animals that inhabit this immense bog. Ecotourism to the region in general is on the increase as concern with environmental quality has become more widespread.

In summer, both residents and tourists mingle by the thousands in the Byward Market, some hundred yards from Parliament, with its tightly concentrated nexus of boutiques, delicatessens, and vegetable and flower stalls by day, and in its busy and popular restaurants, bars, and outdoor terraces by night. This area has been described as the heart and soul of the city, and many are attracted to it by the opportunity for shared experience, atmosphere, and just plain people watching.

© THE PURCELL TEAM/CORBIS

Ice-skaters crowd Ottawa's Rideau Canal each winter.

FUTURE OF THE CITY

The Ottawa economy, driven in large part by technology, is the least diversified of all major Canadian cities. It remains to be seen whether, in historical terms, the high technology boom will prove to be a modern equivalent of the lumber trade boom and bust of the past. The development of high technology industries occurred in Ottawa over a period of several decades, resulting directly from federal government support of the public sector laboratories of the National Research Council (NRC) and the Communications Research Centre. The NRC was set up during World War I but expanded tremendously during World War II, during which time a great number of scientists went to Canada to work on radar, nuclear power, and chemical engineering. By the end of World War II, there were many thousands of scientists working in the region. Spinoffs of the NRC, such as Computing Devices of Canada, provided a foundation for the future electronics and telecommunications industries. In the private sector, Nortel Networks hired thousands of scientists and engineers in its research laboratories in Ottawa in the 1960s. As was the case with the NRC, a significant number of these workers left to set up their own firms. The high technology sector in Ottawa comprises some 1,000 firms, which focus mainly on telecommunications and software. There is particular strength in fiber optics, in which Nortel Networks and JDS Uniphase, for instance, are world leaders. It is the presence of this highly sophisticated, high technology industry and workforce that has resulted in an entrepreneurial business climate, which had not been present in the region since the lumber trade boom. At the end of the twentieth century, venture capital from all over the world was invested in dozens of companies, and huge multinationals such as Alcatel, which bought Newbridge Networks, set up shop in town through such purchases of successful local companies. These developments resulted in the region being called "Silicon Valley North."

There was also considerable growth in lower-level high-tech jobs. The number of call centers reportedly increased considerably in the recent past, attracted by the high technology infrastructure and industry of the region. There was some apprehension concerning call centers—which can involve, on the one hand, income tax processing, computer help desks, airline reservations, or on the other hand, telemarketing in which workers call potential customers to sell newspaper and magazine subscriptions, and other products and services. The latter kind of activity may be associated with highly stressful, poorly paid, temporary and part-time work without any future for the workers involved.

Whatever uncertainties may surround the future of the high technology sector, a demographic uncertainty confronts the federal government, local government, and the educational system in the region at all levels. A significant proportion of public- and parapublic-sector employees, from civil servants to engineers and professors, will begin retiring at the start of the 21st century. In the federal government alone, it was estimated that between 10,000 to 12,000 employees would need to be hired annually over ten years, simply to replace those who will be retiring. The population of Ottawa and the National Capital Region is an aging one. The region is likely to become increasingly multicultural as a substantial percentage of the next generation of employees will have to be hired from elsewhere and will no doubt reflect the growing ethnic and cultural diversity of Canada.

BIBLIOGRAPHY

Andrew, Caroline, "Ottawa-Hull," *City Politics in Canada,* ed. by Warren Magnusson and Andrew Sancton (University of Toronto Press 1983).

Holzman, Jacquelin, *An Economic Profile, Ottawa* (Office of the Mayor, Ottawa 1994).

Holzman, Jacquelin, and Rosalind Tosh, *Ottawa: Then and Now* (Magic Light Publishing 1999).

Taylor, Charles, et al., eds., *Capital Cities: International Perspectives* (Carleton University Press 1993).

Taylor, John H., *Ottawa: An Illustrated History* (James Lorimer & Company 1986).

Van de Wetering, Marion, *An Ottawa Album: Glimpses of the Way We Were* (Hounslow Press 1997).

Woods, Shirley E., *Ottawa: The Capital of Canada* (Doubleday Canada 1980).

VICTOR DA ROSA *and* PAUL LAMY

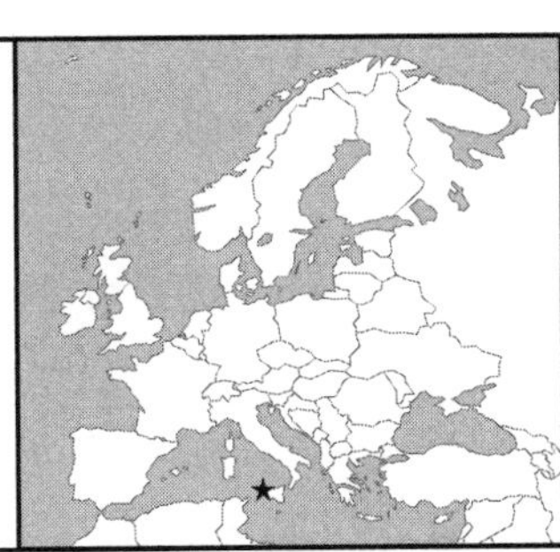

Palermo

Italy

ORIENTATION

Name of City. The inhabitants of the capital of Sicily call their city Palieimmú. In Italian, the official language of Italy, the name is *Palermo*. About the 4th century B.C., the Greeks gave the settlement the name *Panhormos*.

Location. Palermo is located at 36°7′ north latitude and 13°22′ east longitude, on the northern coast of Sicily, on the Bay of Palermo. With an area of 25,426 square kilometers (9,814 square miles), Sicily is the largest island in the Mediterranean and of southern Europe. Sicily is also the largest region in Italy. The province of Palermo covers an area of 5,016 square kilometers (1,936 square miles).

The island consists of 60% hilly terrain, 24% mountains, and 16% plains. The plains are located mainly along the coastal areas. The city of Palermo is situated on a plain called Conca d'Oro ("Golden Shell"). The Conca d'Oro got its name because of its fertile ground, in which citrus, orange, almond, and olive trees grow, and because it is surrounded by a mountainous fringe that serves as a natural city wall around Palermo. On the north the city borders the Tyrrhenian Sea. On the west the dividing line is the 607-meter (1,990-foot) Monte Pellegrino and the lower Monte Gallo. On the east Monte Catalfano and Capo Zofferano form the boundary.

The pleasant climate in Palermo invites the traveler to visit the city during the whole year. Winter brings mild temperatures that seldom drop below 8° to 10°C (46° to 50°F), while the summers are hot and dry, with the average temperatures ranging from 25° to 30°C (77° to 86°F). The Sirocco, a hot, sandy wind that blows in from the Sahara desert in North Africa, brings especially hot and humid weather. It reaches Palermo five to six times a year and usually lasts for two to three days. The Mediterranean climate is responsible for the water scarcity in Sicily, since the annual precipitation is only 1,000 millimeters (39 inches) per year.

Population. The official estimate of the number of inhabitants is 760,000, excluding nonregistered newcomers and refugees.

Distinctive and Unique Features. With its fine harbor, Palermo was, and still is, the gateway to Sicily. Until 40 years ago, one could get a good view of old Palermo from the sea. Now the old town is surrounded by modern concrete apartment blocks. The reason for this is the desolation of Palermo that took place in the 1950s and 1960s in two regards: on one hand, there was no reconstruction of the old part of Palermo after World War II, so the buildings fell into ruin; on the other hand, the total population of Palermo had doubled by the 1970s, while the population of the old part of the town dropped to one-third its former number (from a little more than 125,000 to 40,000). New apartments were provided in the form of concrete apartment blocks, which not only fronted for the shadow business of the Mafia, which earned its money until 1970 especially in the building and construction industry and the real-estate business, but also gave evidence of the city's climate of deceit. Owing to a lack of quality in construction and materials, the new buildings, together with the old parts of Palermo, decayed shortly after they were built. With its ruins and squalid dwellings, Palermo for the most part looks like the backyard of the European Union.

Attractions of the City. Today Palermo is in a time of new departures. In contrast to the stagnation of recent decades in the economic, political, and cultural sectors (also due to the activities of the Mafia), the city is now opening up to the global market. Industry is expanding both in terms of employment and net output. Building construction is still responsible for 50% of industrial employment, but the industrial base is also changing; manufacturing now generates some 77% of income. The beverage and food industry is growing, and metalwork has returned to the fore. Also, agriculture and the fishing industry are developing. The service sector has resurrected the economy of Palermo, accounting for 70% of the city's total employment. Recent service-sector output was valued at more than four times that of industry. The revolution in business services is most important; advanced tertiary initiatives are growing fastest, with information technology and the Internet providing a formidable stimulus to Sicilian economic innovation.

For Palermo, as for all of Sicily, tourism serves as an important social and economic factor, having increased steadily in recent years. Palermo has a number of historical sites of interest to visitors. The Palazzo dei Normanni (Norman Palace), currently the seat of the Sicilian parliament, was erected on Punic and Roman remains and was at its most splendid during Sicily's Norman period (1072–1250). The church of San Giovanni degli Eremiti (1072), despite its Christian purpose, displays features typical of Islamic art, with its red domes on cubic structures and its orange blossoms, the latter drifting up from the garden that surrounds the magnificent cloisters. The cathedral is a witness to various contrasting epochs and styles (1185–1801). The catacombs inside the Capuccini Conventare are horrifying. There are 8,000 mummified bodies of aristocrats and ecclesiastics exhibited in period (16th- to 19th-century) costume.

To get a feeling of the cultural and social diversity of Palermo, one should visit the traditional bazaars. The bazaar Bocceria Vecchia (called Vucciria in the dialect) became well known thanks to a painting (1974) by Renato Guttuso (1912–1987). The traditional fish market, with its different smells and crowded stands, served as location for the movie *Tano da Morire* (1997), made by the Milanese Roberta Torre. The movie was the first official satire on the Mafia played by the inhabitants of the quarter themselves. Another market worth seeing is the Ballaro bazaar, which captivates with its great variety. Arabic traders live and work in this market, and African women who do their laundry at the wells contribute to the Oriental atmosphere.

Relationships Between the City and the Outside. Palermo is the capital of the Italian island and autonomous region of Sicily as well as of the province of Palermo. As a political, economic, and cultural center of the island, it is identified with all of Sicily. While Palermo was a nodal point for the international drug business in the 1980s, the city tried to fight back against organized crime with the start of the so-called "Maxi trials" (1985–1987), in which leading mafiosi were taken to court. A turning point was reached in 1992, when the two judges who were working on the trial case, Giovanni Falcone and Paolo Borsellino, were killed by the Mafia. Since then, Palermo has received international and national support in its assertive actions against the Mafia, crime, and the drug trade. The Italian government developed programs to protect trial witnesses (although these have now been modified, to the disadvantage of the witnesses), and made a special police force available. After that, Rome played the alma mater, considering the positive changes in Palermo and in Sicily as a whole as its personal contribution. Yet in fact the political and economic stagnation of the Mezzogiorno ("midday" in Italian, the regions of Abruzzi, Compania, Molise, Puglia, Basilicata, and Calabria as well as the islands of Sicily and Sardinia) was created partly by the Italian government.

In order to gain admission to the European Union, Rome reduced important support programs for the south or cut them completely. The gap between south and north gets bigger, poverty and illiteracy increase, and the water supply in the south deteriorates. Although the south tries to improve its standards, some elements in the north act politically secessionistic. The Lega-North Party wants Italy to split off from the Mezzogiorno using radical means.

Major Languages. The lingua franca in Palermo is Italian. In everyday life people speak a Palermitan dialect that is difficult for non-Italians to understand. It is problematic that children of underprivileged families as well as illiterate people often speak only dialect.

HISTORY

The Origin of the City. Palermo, and Sicily as a whole, has a colonial history that is more than 2,500 years old. The first settlers of Sicily were the Siculi, who evidently arrived in the 3d millennium B.C. Palermo was founded in the 7th and 6th centuries B.C. as a Phoenician town. The Punic name *ziz* ("flower") stands for the fertility of the country. The Greeks, who tried to invade the harbor of the Carthaginians between 408 and 391 B.C., gave Palermo the name *Panhormos* ("the whole harbor"). Between 254 B.C. and 491 A.D., Palermo was under the rule of the Romans. The city then was characterized by its mixed population, with the people speaking Greek, Latin, and Punic.

In the middle of the 5th century, the Vandals invaded Palermo and destroyed it. When the Byzantines conquered the city in 535 A.D., only a small part of the Roman settlement was left, and the

Roman buildings fell into disrepair. In 831 A.D. the Saracens took over the city and in 948 gave Palermo the status of a capital. At this time the Muslim city Balerm, with its cultural and linguistic diversity and its 300,000 inhabitants—including Greeks, Lombards, Jews, Persians, and Tartars as well as descendants of the Siculi, Romans, and Carthaginians—was a cultural center of the Arab world. Balerm at this time was a match for Islamic metropolises such as Cairo, Baghdad, and Córdoba.

In 1072 Sicily was conquered by the Normans, who delighted in Palermo and did not destroy anything. After 1194 Palermo was under the reign of the Hohenstaufens and Frederick II, who was crowned king in Sicily. Palermo became a European center because Frederick managed to promote the academic life and the arts. He also established a flourishing trade between the Islamic and Christian European worlds.

In 1266 the French house of Anjou took over the rule of Sicily. The national uprising of the Sicilian Vespers, which was started during the ringing of the vespers bells on Easter Monday, 1282, in front of the Church of Santo Spirito, gave evidence of the discontent of the Palermitans with the exploitative maladministration of the French. Screaming "Death to the French," the Palermitans massacred their rulers or chased them away from the island. The war against authority lasted until 1302. A hundred years later (1409), rule passed to the House of Aragon. While the island was degenerating politically to the status of a province, the Spanish viceroys who ruled during the 16th and 17th centuries, were busy competing against each other in terms of pomp and circumstance.

From 1713 onward Sicily was ruled by a succession of powers. First there was the House of Savoyen; then, until 1720, the Habsburgs; and from 1730, the Bourbons. The Sicilians reacted toward feudalism with revolts, but only Garibaldi with his "Company of a Thousand" managed, in May 1860, to put an end to the rule of the Bourbons, after four days of battle on the streets of Palermo. Sicily was then affiliated with the Kingdom of Italy. During World War II, especially from January until July 1943, Palermo was hit hard by bombing raids. That same year, the Allies landed on Sicily. In 1946 the head office in Rome took steps to counter separatist trends that were again evolving by giving Sicily the status of an autonomous region with its own parliament.

Migration: Past and Present. The shift in the economic and political focus within Italy following the integration of the Mezzogiorno into the newly founded Kingdom of Italy (1861) caused structural damage from which the south never recovered. In the beginning of the 20th century, much was done to support the economic progress of the north. In the industrial triangle of Turin, Genoa, and Milan, the government created protectionist tax cuts. The south suffered from the economic upturn of the north, especially when the prices of oil, wine, and cotton sank, confronting the Mezzogiorno with an economic crisis. Through all of these years, the Mezzogiorno had to pay higher taxes than the north, although it received fewer subsidies and investment aid. Between 1901 and 1910 almost 1,750,000 people emigrated from the Mezzogiorno, seeking work in South America and North America in order to attain a minimal living income for their families. In the beginning of the 1920s, Benito Mussolini put a stop to emigration and tried to develop a self-sufficient economy. In this way he planned to evade the political and economic isolation Italy was facing because of the sanctions of the League of Nations.

After the war many southern Italians moved to the northern part of the country seeking employment. Between 1946 and 1957 the number of Italian emigrants outnumbered the number of those returning home by 1 million. Three-quarters of the emigrants came from the south. Between 1951 and 1971 the Mezzogiorno lost more than 4 million inhabitants (of a total population of a little more than 18 million) due to migration within Italy and abroad. Sicily was hit hardest, losing 850,000 of its inhabitants.

Thereafter the number of emigrants from Mezzogiorno sank owing not only to the betterment of economic and political standards in the south but also to an international economic crisis that took place in industrial countries. Although Palermo has an unemployment rate of 30%, it is nowadays a shelter for refugees and migrants from Africa, Asia, Latin America, and eastern Europe.

INFRASTRUCTURE

Public Buildings, Public Works, and Residences. The headquarters of the regional government is located in the Palazzo dei Normmani. The provincial administration has its seat on the Palazzo Comitini. Next to the cathedral, one can find the Palazzo Arcivescovile, the seat of the Parlermitan archbishop. Palermo has a university, an academy for scientific literature and art (founded in 1568), a musical academy, and many museums (one of

© ENZO & PAOLO RAGAZZINI/CORBIS

Many of the old houses in Palermo, Italy, open onto courtyards. The owner of this house has filled the courtyard with pots of flowers.

them—the Archaeological Museum—is world famous), galleries, and archives. Especially notable are the Palazzo Asmundo, an aristocratic palace, sometimes opened to the public, and the Palazzo Abatellis, which houses the Sicilian Regional Gallery. Palermo has a district court and a main prison (the Ucciardone).

Politics and City Services. In 1993 Leoluca Orlando won the post of mayor with 76% of the vote. He is also the official representative in Palermo for La Rete (The Net), a movement formed in 1991, recruiting its members from different organizations that want to fight the Mafia and political corruption. Since the parliamentary elections in 1992, La Rete has also been engaged on the national level. The city government, together with the people, has tried to establish a "new Palermo" under the motto "Palermo opens its gates," in order to bring a good quality of life back to the old part of the city. One example is the Project of the 99 Churches, through which unemployed people—often highly qualified—take care of churches and palaces. They print brochures and organize sight-seeing tours, helping to finance the projects.

The government supports anti-Mafia campaigns and organizations such as the "Foundation Giovanni and Francesca Falcone." This foundation came into being through the initiative of youth and gets support from private sponsors. One of its aims is to reduce the high unemployment rate through aid programs and grants. In addition, there exist organizations that function without a bureaucratic superstructure—for example, Donne contro la Mafia (Mothers Against Drugs)—through which widows, sisters, and daughters of victims of the Mafia act together against crime. Political groups such as the independent left-wing organizations Città per l'oumo and Centro Impasato are involved in reducing the crime rate. The Centro Sociale Santo Francesco Saverio, located in the neighborhood of Albergheria, participates in the intellectual and political movement against the Mafia and official corruption in Palermo. Since the state often neglects social work and does not support it financially, the Roman Catholic Church jumps in, establishing language programs in monasteries and helping refugees and asylum seekers to find a place to live in Palermo.

Besides those sociopolitical changes, the municipal promotion of culture plays an important role. For example, the Teatro Massimo, the neoclassical opera house that is, after the Milan Skala (La Scala), considered the most famous and important opera house in Italy, was restored by the urban government. It had been closed since 1974 because the substantial sum of money that was to have been used for the restoration disappeared. The new opening in 1997 was a victory for the "new Palermo."

In addition to the many concerts and art exhibitions held in the city, the yearly festival of Santa Rosalia, Palermo's patron saint, has become another symbol of new departures in Palermo. Santa Rosalia is regarded as the saint who freed the city from the plague in 1624. Since then, the U Fistinu processions have taken place every year from July 10–15 in honor of Santa Rosalia. In 1996, for the first time, artists from around the Mediterranean turned the old town into a huge open-air theater. In recent years more than 400,000 pilgrims have taken part in the procession each year. Mayor Leoluca Orlando uses this event to strengthen the feeling of community in order to reinforce resistance to the Mafia. Other cultural programs include the Sicily Rally in March, the Rally Conca d'Oro in May, and the Coppa degli Assi horse show in October.

Educational System. Palermo has the same educational system as Italy. Before the first day of school, parents put their children either in the *Asilo nido* (day care; up to age 3), *Asilo* (nursery school), or in the *cuola materna* (nursery school; ages 3–6). Children start the *scuola elementare* (elementary school) at the age of 6. When they are 11, they attend the *scuola media unica* for three years. School attendance is compulsory for eight years, from age 6 until age 14. After that, one can attend the *scuola superiore* (university and college) or a technical school, vocational school, grammar school, or language school.

Transportation System. The most popular means of locomotion in Palermo is still, unfortunately, the car. The lack of parking spaces and the daily traffic jams do not seem to be able to change the situation. The best way to get around the city is by walking. Palermo has an excellent bus system within and going out of the city, and there is also a metro. By train, every other substantial city in Sicily can be reached, and connections to the north and to central Italy are available. It is also possible to cross over to Naples by ferry. Besides offering passenger service, the port also ships manufactures and produce to northern Italy and to Europe. Falcone-Borsellino Airport is, according to specialists, one of the most dangerous in Europe because of 910-meter (2,986-foot) Monte Pecoraro, situated right at the foot of the runway.

CULTURAL AND SOCIAL LIFE

Distinctive Features of the City's Cultures. Palermo presents itself in such a complex, mystical, and often paradoxical way that it is impossible to categorize the city. The *sicilianità* might be a key to the understanding of Palermo. Living conditions are hard, and it is not *dolce vita* that dominates. Southern Italian culture has many faces; clothing and etiquette vary according to the social stratum, although everyone is dressed very elegantly and stylishly. Three basic commodities have high status in Palermo: the car, the television, and the cell phone. In addition to those material appurtenances, gestures play an important role. Sicily and Palermo, respectively, have their own code of body language. Until ten years ago, people avoided public life because of the Mafia. Today, public places are crowded with young people out on their motorbikes or in their cars.

Cuisine. One of the remarkable features of Palermitan cuisine is its variety, owing to different geographic origins. African, Arab, and Spanish elements contribute to the local tradition. Palermo's restaurants are famous for their fish dishes, especially *pasta con sarda* (pasta with sardines), often transformed into *pasta che sardi a mari* (pasta with sardines in the sea). Sweet and sour triumphs in Palermo—for example, *vruoccoli arriminati* (hashed broccoli) and tomato sauce served over miniature pasta rings, or pasta with walnut cream. Besides the pasta dishes, *frutti di mare,* sweets, cheese, ice cream, coffee, and wine play important roles in Palermitan cuisine.

Ethnic, Class, and Religious Diversity. The old town is divided into four quarters: la Kalsa, il Ballaro, il Capo, and la Vucciria. The quarters are characterized by their ethnic heterogenity, since Sicily has always been a place of immigration. Officially, the immigrants form the lowest social class, wherein the unemployment rate and illiteracy are constantly very high. The small middle class lives at the borders of the old town. The border to the richer district is fluid, although the rich avoid the city and have their houses in the suburbs of Palermo or on the coastline. While homogenity is predominant in the suburbs, the old part of the town enjoys a multicultural atmosphere. Officially, 98% of the people living in Sicily are Roman Catholic. But Palermo also has a Presbyterian church and one Greek Orthodox church of the Albanian minority. Some monasteries provide the Muslim population with a place to pray.

Family and Other Social Support Systems. One can't speak of the Sicilian family as a distinct social type, but all forms of living together can be characterized by the will to come to grips with life together. Despite structural changes, set off by emigration, the destruction of the family by the Mafia, the introduction of the law of divorce (1972), the legalization of abortion (1975), and the increasing popularity of living as a single person or as a couple living together without getting married, the family can still be considered the central social unit. The network of each individual family functions through the mechanisms of friendship, the exchange of favors, and clientelism. These are the only social strategies that are able to compensate for the failure of the Italian state, which, apart from awarding families legal protection for expectant and nursing mothers and a child allowance, leaves the families to their own devices.

Work and Commerce. The onus of the Mafia still attaches to Palermo. The main field for Mafia investments is still the *lavori pubblici,* the expenses out of the public budgetary funds that make up almost 70% of Sicily's overall investments. Compared with Italy's other provincial capitals, Palermo has the lowest income per person and the highest illiteracy rate. The black market, as well as illegal economic activities, dominates in many branches. Children from socially disadvantaged backgrounds work on the black market, often starting at a very early age. The survival strategies of the poor consist of *mille mestieri* ("thousand trades") and *l'arrangiarsi* ("the art of getting by"). In almost all cases it is the patronage system—the asymmetrical relationship between patron and client—that helps people to acquire jobs and distribute their resources.

Palermo invests in the chemical, automobile, furniture, and food industries. The annual Fiera del Meditteraneo is the most important economic and industrial fair. It serves as a bridge to the other Mediterranean states and supports economic development in southern Italy.

Arts and Recreation. Cultural resources are manifold and very avant-garde in Palermo. There are workshops, art nouveau, and contemporary-art exhibitions, avant-garde theater productions, and cultural debates widely available. For recreation, one might visit one of the city's museums or its botanical gardens, or make use of the facilities for sports activities such as sailing, tennis, bodybuilding, or swimming.

QUALITY OF LIFE

According to the 1999 survey on the quality of life in Italian provinces conducted by the authoritative newspaper *Sole 24 Ore,* in Palermo you live badly. The negative factors are income, wealth, unemployment, pensions, bank deposits, public water, bureaucratic procedure, the justice system, and crime. The old part of the town is full of wastes, its air polluted with fumes, and the city is loud and hectic. Poverty forces especially the youth into the business of trading drugs or consuming them, thus supporting criminality. Surprisingly, fewer than five deaths a year are due to the activities of the Mafia.

FUTURE OF THE CITY

History demonstrates that efforts to overcome repression, corruption, and apathy were, and still are, difficult for the Palermitans. Right now, it is not possible to make any kind of prognosis about the development of civil society in Palermo. The "silence" of the Mafia does not mean that their public crime of violence has stopped. Instead, they work "peacefully." Although all of the Mafia's known important bosses are locked up behind bars, and despite the anti-Mafia campaigns, the Mafia's structure is still a formidable factor in the life of this city.

BIBLIOGRAPHY

Alongi, Nino, *Palermo, Gli anni dell'utopia* (The Years of Utopia) (Rubbettino Editore 1997).

Bonavita, Petra, *Donna Sicilia* (Lady Sicily) (Centaurus-Verlagsgesellschaft 1993).

Cole, Jeffey, *The New Racism in Europe: A Sicilian Ethnography* (Cambridge University Press 1997).

Delle Donne, Vincenzo, "Palermo palcoscenico d'Italia? ("Palermo, Stage of Italy"?)," *Adesso* (October 1999): 41.

Dolci, Danielo, *Report from Palermo* (Orion Press 1956).

Finley, Moses F., et al., *A History of Sicily* (Chatto & Windus 1986).

Gaetano, Basile, *Palermo é . . . viaggio intrigante tra luoghi e miti tavolo e personaggi* ("Palermo . . . Enigmatic Voyage amid Places and Myths . . . ") (Dario Flaccovio Editore 1998).

Quilici, Vieri, ed., *Palermo centro storico* ("Palermo Historical Center") (Officina Edizioni 1980).

Robb, Peter, *Midnight in Sicily* (Duffy & Snellgrove 1996).

Valentini, Maurizio, "La città che lavora ('The City that Works')," *Arrividerci-Palermo-Allitalia* (May 2000): 38–45.

Useful Web Site

www.europa.eu.int/comm/regional_policy/urban2/urban/audit/results/palermo.htm

ANNEMARIE GRONOVER

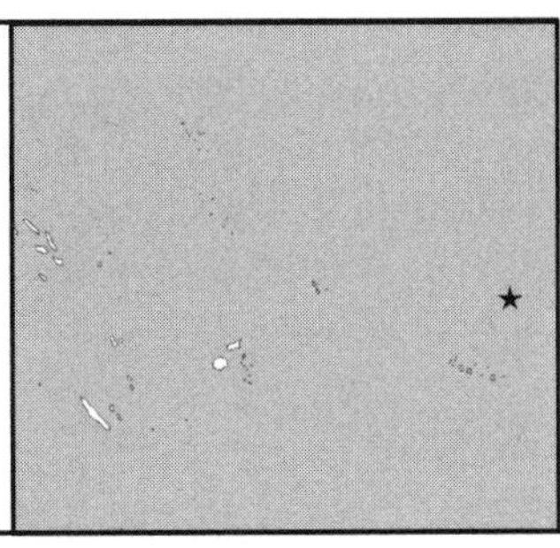

Papeete

French Polynesia

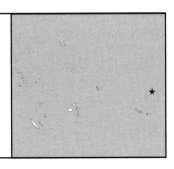

ORIENTATION

Name of City. Papeete translates from the Tahitian language as "basket of water," a reference to the many streams that flow from the mountains above the city through its valleys and across the coastal plain to the sea. Papeete is the capital city of French Polynesia, an overseas territory of the Republic of France.

Location. Papeete is located on the northern coast of the island of Tahiti, in the eastern, or windward, Society Islands in the South Pacific Ocean. Its orientation is 17°37′ south latitude and 149°27′ west longitude.

Population. While French Polynesia contains 118 inhabited islands, nearly 70% of the population resides in the urban zone centered on Papeete. In 1998 the population of the Papeete metropolitan area was approximately 150,000.

Distinctive and Unique Features. Papeete is the only urban area in the enormous territory of French Polynesia (which encompasses 3,266 square kilometers, or 1,261 square miles, covering an area from 7° to 29° south latitude and 132° to 156° west longitude) and is its commercial, employment, and government center. Papeete enjoys a beautiful geographic setting: the city sits at the base of a scenic volcanic mountain and is centered on its port, looking out through the pass in the reef to the neighboring island of Moorea. The waterfront is separated from the commercial heart of the city by a wide, tree-lined boulevard, and a series of parks linked by a promenade allow wide views of the port with its yachts, cruise liners, and cargo ships.

Inland from this remarkable waterfront, the luxurious vegetation of the tropics shades the streets, buildings, and homes of the city. At the commercial heart of Papeete, there are a few blocks of multistory modern office and commercial buildings but most of the city is characterized by single- or two-story structures nearly hidden from view by lush tropical trees and gardens.

Relationships Between the City and the Outside. Papeete is the destination for many thousands of workers who commute daily from the suburban areas that fringe the northern and western sides of Tahiti. The agricultural districts of the southern half of the island send truckloads of produce, meat, and other products to the markets and processing factories in the city. Most of the island is served by a single coastal road, and automobile and truck traffic can be extremely congested.

Papeete is the commercial and government center of French Polynesia, and people and goods move frequently from the outer islands to and from the harbor at Papeete on interisland ferries and freighters. The residents of surrounding islands visit Papeete for medical services and access to higher education, as well as to purchase consumer goods that are not easily available on the smaller islands. Nearly every citizen of French Polynesia has close relatives who have migrated to live and work in the urban zone of Papeete, and visitors from the outer islands are warmly welcomed by their families when they arrive. Papeete's residents also make frequent vacation visits to their home islands or to the neighboring resort islands of Moorea, Raiatea, and Huahine.

The port of Papeete is a destination for many international cargo ships, crossing from Australia, New Zealand, or Chile to northern Pacific Ocean ports. A modest number of international tourists (about 189,000 in 1998) pass through Papeete on their way to the more rustic charms of the outer islands, including tourist destinations such as Moorea, Borabora, and Rangiroa. Papeete's residents also enjoy international travel, and voyage from the airport in nearby Faaa to France, New Zealand, Chile, New Caledonia, and the United States for vacation and business.

Major Languages. The most commonly heard language in the urban zone of Papeete is French, with the native Tahitian language a close second. French Polynesia is officially bilingual, and while French is the language of school instruction and of commerce, Tahitian is widely spoken and dominates political and religious discourse. Secondary languages include Chinese (Hakka dialect) and English.

HISTORY

The Origin of the City. When the island of Tahiti was first visited by European explorers in the late 1700s (the first European ship was the British vessel the Dolphin in 1767), Papeete was a small village surrounding the residence of a sacred chief. With the assistance of European allies, the family of the chief, who ruled this district of the island, became the royal family of Tahiti, known as the Pomare family. While there are more sheltered deepwater harbors on the island, the political influence of the Pomare family insured that government, missionary, and trading relationships would center on their home village and its harbor.

In the 1800s Papeete became a lively little town whose economy was based on providing provisions for whaling ships and on exports of copra and vanilla. Famous for its beauty and hospitality, the island was also a popular destination for writers and artists, including Paul Gauguin, Robert Louis Stevenson, and Herman Melville.

The town of Papeete remained a small Pacific port town until the late 1950s, when the Republic of France constructed a nuclear weapons testing facility in French Polynesia, on the island of Moruroa in the Tuamotu archipelago. The French government expanded the port and its military bases in Papeete and constructed the international airport in Faaa as support facilities for the Centre d'Experimentation nuclear du Pacifique (CEP). This massive construction boom continued throughout the 1960s and 1970s, drawing tens of thousands of workers and military personnel into the Papeete area. The CEP was the impetus for the emergence of Papeete as a truly urban port city. The CEP was officially closed in 1992, ending the controversial nuclear testing in the territory, creating a climate of economic uncertainty in a city long dominated by military and government spending.

Migration: Past and Present. In its early years as a small port town, Papeete was inhabited largely by Tahitian relatives and dependents of the ruling Pomare family and a host of foreign missionaries, traders, and adventurers, as well as by the transient population of whalers and adventurers. Many of these (largely British and American) European visitors married Tahitian women and became permanent residents. In 1842, at the height of the whaling period, France declared Tahiti to be a protectorate of France and expelled British and American citizens and missionaries. Queen Pomare fled the island, and with her supporters she launched a war of resistance against French occupation that lasted until 1847, when the Tahitian forces were finally defeated.

The beginning of the French colonial period saw an influx of French administrators and military personnel. Following the war trade resumed, and during the American Civil War, several ambitious attempts to develop a plantation economy growing sugar cane and cotton were launched. Because the local Tahitian population was in decline owing to the effects of introduced diseases and the war, laborers were brought in from China to work on the plantations. Many of these Chinese labor migrants settled permanently in Papeete and married Tahitian women, or brought Chinese brides to join them. Chinese labor migrations continued from the 1860s until the early 1900s.

© OWEN FRANKEN/CORBIS

Women and children sit in front of a copy of a Gauguin painting at a cultural center in Papeete, Tahiti, French Polynesia.

During the rapid urbanization of the 1960s, migration from outer islands to Papeete was the major source of population growth, as was the arrival of French military personnel. In later years population growth was largely attributed to local births, and in fact there was a decline in the number of foreign-born residents following the closure of the nuclear testing facilities. In 2001 the government of French Polynesia actively recruited affluent French retirees to settle in the islands in order to bolster a weakening economy.

INFRASTRUCTURE

Public Buildings, Public Works, and Residences. Papeete has a dense concentration of public buildings in the area that originally housed the palace of the Pomare family, where the Territorial Assembly building, the French high commissioner's office, and a more recently constructed presidential palace are now located. Surrounding this center is a score of government office buildings housing the various government ministries and services. A secondary concentration of government offices is found in the port area. Public buildings are either revivals of high colonial architectural style, such as the Presidential Palace or the Papeete Town Hall, or fairly typical examples of modern Pacific and international style architecture: a hybrid of indigenous decorative elements and modern concrete office building construction that can be seen from Honolulu to Suva to Manila.

Major public works include the water supply and the hydroelectric system, which have exploited the energy of Tahiti's most powerful rivers to support the needs of Papeete. Waste disposal continues to be a challenge as the population grows and the urban zone moves up into deep valleys that traditionally hosted landfills. Major public works projects that were underway at the start of the 21st century included roadway improvements in Papeete and the surrounding suburbs to address traffic congestion, and expansion of airport construction on outer islands.

Residential areas of Papeete are fairly dense with small, single-story houses on tiny lots, apartments above retail shops, and a few multistory apartment buildings. In surrounding suburbs, middle- and upper-class residents build modern houses along the coast and on the mountains, while the poor crowd into slums that extend up into the narrow river valleys. Land is scarce and many families have built second and third houses in what were once spacious gardens.

Politics and City Services. Within the French-designed political system, Papeete is a commune managed by a mayor. In this system a politician may hold more than one elected office simultaneously and the mayor may also be elected to the Territorial Assembly, may be president, vice president, or a minister in the territorial government, or even a delegate to the National Assembly in Paris. The mayor of Papeete is a very powerful political figure and almost without exception has held additional elected or appointed offices.

The local political system supports a number of rival political parties, many of which are closely allied to political parties in metropolitan France. One of the key strategies mayors use to maintain and increase their political support base in this highly contested political arena is the creation of patronage relationships through the distribution of government jobs, services, and contracts. The city's financial resources are largely received thorough grants from the Territorial or National government, which may be under the control of politicians from rival parties acting as a check on the ambitions of the mayor. The city of Papeete provides its residents with the range of urban services, including refuse collection, police and fire protection, and modest recreational facilities (an Olympic swimming pool, a soccer field, and a theater).

Educational System. Public education modeled on the French system is free and available to all residents. Attendance through the age of 14 is mandatory. Among native Polynesians, more than 60% stop at this level. Papeete also has a number of private and religious schools, as well as a university (Universite Française de la Pacifique) founded in the neighboring suburb of Punaauia in the late 1990s. The quality of education is generally very good, particularly at the secondary-school level where preparation for the French national baccalaureate examinations is quite intense and rigorous.

Transportation System. Within Papeete there are basically two transportation systems: private automobiles and public "trucks." The "truck" system involves licensed drivers who own their own vehicles: picturesque flatbed trucks with benches in the back and wooden half-walls, a roof, and sliding plexiglass windows. These trucks follow mapped routes throughout the city, the suburbs, and even out to the farthest end of the island from designated hubs on various street corners of central Papeete. Trucks are used by working-class Tahitians, children, and an occasional tourist. Anyone who can afford to drives a car or small truck.

CULTURAL AND SOCIAL LIFE

Distinctive Features of the City's Cultures. Papeete's population includes a number of subgroups. The majority of its residents are native Polynesians, who combine traditional domestic life with modern educational and occupational activities. These residents often live in extended family residential compounds, with traditional communal sleeping rooms and separate outdoor cooking houses. These houses are generally constructed of concrete, although in the poorer neighborhoods plywood shacks are also present, surrounded by a fenced yard to keep small children, chickens, and dogs from running into the street. Surfboards, outrigger racing canoes, and bicycles crowd the yards, which also contain breadfruit, papaya, and banana trees among the flowering hibiscus and frangipani blossoms.

Within the city's retail and commercial center, a number of Chinese families still live above the businesses founded by their grandparents and great grandparents. These urban neighborhoods are the most densely populated in Papeete and are centered on hidden interior courtyards, balconies, and rooftop gardens.

Along the waterfront and in the government center there are a number of modern apartment buildings occupied almost exclusively by French civil servants and contract employees. These residents frequent the restaurants and cafes of Papeete, where they mingle with tourists and yacht sailors in a truly cosmopolitan international scene.

Cuisine. Papeete has three major cuisines: Tahitian or Polynesian, French, and Chinese. The city has dozens of restaurants, a host of snack bars and cafes, and a thriving mobile kitchen *"roulotte"* scene on the waterfront. Residents spend a great deal of time preparing and enjoying meals, usually in the company of friends and family.

Tahitian cuisine has two facets: a very traditional set of dishes generally prepared only on Sundays and for weddings, and a more evolved local cuisine. Traditional foods include breadfruit, taro and manioc roots, fish, pork, and local fruits typically prepared in an earth oven and served with coconut milk sauces. On weekdays most Polynesian residents make and eat a less time-consuming variation of this cuisine, with some imported foodstuffs as well: for example boiled taro, fried or marinated fish, breadfruit with corned beef, or chicken with greens. Polynesian residents also enjoy the occasional night out at a Chinese restaurant, or pizza, chow mein, or *steak frites* (steak and french fries) at a waterfront *roulotte*.

Chinese cuisine in Papeete includes the familiar range of Chinese vegetables and sauces, with an emphasis on seafood and some incorporation of local Polynesian specialities such as roast pork, marinated fish, coconut milk, and taro root. Dishes served in Papeete's Chinese restaurants are nearly identical to those served in local Chinese homes, and a thriving garden market economy provides abundant supplies of Chinese produce.

French restaurants in Papeete are generally quite expensive, however the quality of the food is also very high. French cuisine ranges from metropolitan style, with heavy sauces, large portions of meat, and a great deal of wine to a lighter, seafood-based local variant. The cooks in French restaurants in Papeete come from France, as does the wine, but most of the other ingredients are gathered from the local markets or imported from New Zealand.

Ethnic, Class, and Religious Diversity. There are four major ethnic divisions: Tahitian or Polynesian, Chinese, European, and mixed race ("demi"). Nearly 70% of the population is Polynesian, with the remaining 30% equally divided among the three other groups. Papeete is the only true city in French Polynesia and has the region's most diverse population, with much higher representations of non-Polynesian ethnic groups than the rural districts and outer islands.

Unfortunately, these ethnic differences have a class dimension as well, with the ethnic minority groups generally enjoying a higher standard of education, income, and living conditions than the indigenous majority. Children from European, Chinese, or mixed-race families are nearly twice as likely to finish secondary school as children from Polynesian families. French, Chinese, and mixed-race residents dominate the highly paid, salaried senior government service and management positions in the tourism industry, while Polynesians are strongly represented in clerical positions in government offices.

In general, urban Polynesians are employed in labor or service occupations such as dockworkers, construction workers, hotel service work, child care, or in the fishing fleet. Unemployment is fairly high, and with a growing population of young, under-educated Polynesians entering an economy in transition, ethnic tensions occasionally erupt into violence. So far the occasional demonstration has been limited to the destruction of property; interpersonal ethnic attacks are rare.

There is considerable religious diversity in Papeete, with particularly strong representation by Evangelical Protestant, Roman Catholic, and Seventh Day Adventist communities. There are, however, large congregations of Mormons, Jehovah's Witnesses, and Pentecostal Church members in Papeete as well. Missionary activity accounts for this diversity and active missionary efforts are still underway through the city and indeed throughout all the islands of French Polynesia. In central Papeete the Catholic Church and Evangelical Protestant Church are both major landowners and in addition to historic landmark churches, they provide schools, medical clinics, and social services to their members.

Family and Other Social Support Systems. For Papeete's Polynesian residents, family networks are a complex web of generosity and obligations. Food, shelter, and financial assistance are obligatory between close relatives in this community. Those Polynesian families who migrate from rural districts or outer islands to work in the city are obliged to offer shelter to visiting relatives, sometimes for extended periods of time. The advantage of maintaining these relationships for the urban Polynesian, however, is the ability to return home to the rural district and maintain their inherited land rights. Many Polynesians return to their natal districts when they retire or become unemployed, and access to land for a house and garden is essential. The inability to use land as a financial asset and the difficulty in accumulating savings in the face of requests for assistance from family members has hindered the economic development within the Polynesian community, where hospitality and generosity are more highly valued than competitiveness or thrift. A generous French-funded social benefit system has provided free medical care, and education and welfare payments, which make the standard of living among the highest in the Pacific.

The Chinese community also has strong networks of family and business ties, with family members often working in the same business and a tradition of extended family residential organization. These family and business networks in the Chinese community extend overseas to Chinese relatives in Hong Kong, Taiwan, New Caledonia, New Zealand, Australia, and the People's Republic of China. The Chinese community has used cheap family labor and low-interest loans from cooperative associations to bolster Chinese businesses in Papeete.

The community of Europeans in Papeete is dominated by fixed-term contract civil servants, who rely greatly on each other for social support, and make frequent visits home to France. They may socialize with business associates from the Chinese or "demi" community, and in some cases they form lasting friendships.

Work and Commerce. The urban economy is dominated by government, commerce, service, and transport jobs related to Papeete's status as a major regional port, government capital, and tourist hub. Many jobs involve unloading, inspecting, and distributing cargo from the port. Papeete's center also hosts the territory's biggest concentration of retail shops, where islanders go to shop for imported goods at competitive prices, in contrast to the situation in rural areas, where often there is poor selection and little price competition for consumers. In addition to the significant number of government sector employees, there is a service sector of insurance and travel agencies, salons, and restaurants catering to affluent salaried workers in the city.

There is some light industry in the city, including bottling plants for soft drinks, beer, juice, and water, and small artisanal furniture, boatmaking, and clothing factories. The port hosts a fishing fleet and an active yacht and sportfishing charter sector. While the focus of the tourist industry is elsewhere, Papeete is the starting point for cruise lines and has a handful of hotels for business visitors and tourists in transit. The retail shops facing the cruise ship dock have developed to serve tourists and include postcard and souvenir stands as well as exclusive black pearl jewelry shops and boutiques of imported resort clothing.

Arts and Recreation. Papeete enjoys a very lively arts scene, including several theaters, art galleries, and flourishing traditional Polynesian dance, music, and craft cultures. Locally produced art—from wood carvings to watercolor paintings to handmade Tahitian appliquéd quilts—decorate every public space. Local music, from traditional drumming and a cappella hymn singing to ukulele ballads and modern rock and reggae, dominates the radio waves in Papeete. In July the annual Tiurai festival takes place in Papeete and brings people from all over the Territory to compete in singing, dancing, canoe racing, bareback horseracing, javelin throwing, and other traditional contests. Visitors sometimes mistakenly conclude that these events are staged for tourists, but in fact local residents train year-round to compete in these events.

In addition to these traditional Polynesian activities, residents enjoy active football (soccer) and rugby leagues, and passionately follow school contests in basketball and volleyball as well. Water sports of all kinds—canoe paddling, fishing, jet skis, sailing, scuba diving—are, of course, extremely popular. With the exception of canoe paddling (every lunchtime and every evening the racing canoes train in the port of Papeete), residents travel to beaches outside the city or on neighboring islands on weekends to enjoy the water.

QUALITY OF LIFE

The quality of life in Papeete is generally very high for an isolated island community with limited exportable natural resources. This is the result of two major factors: a local economy that has been inflated by French government assistance for more than 40 years and, secondly, by the enduring beauty of Papeete with its magnificent geographical setting, lush tropical climate, and friendly local culture. In comparison to other Polynesian island cities, ethnic Polynesians continue to control the government and most of the real estate, if not the commercial sector. However, there is a significant problem with urban unemployment and a number of neighborhoods where, while hunger is unknown, the material standard of living and sanitation is unacceptably low. Per-capita income in French Polynesia is more than U.S.$1,500, among the highest in the Pacific.

FUTURE OF THE CITY

Papeete's future, in its long-delayed, postcolonial period, is uncertain. There are major efforts underway to replace French government subsidies with other sources of investment and income, most notably development of the tourist industry and the recruitment of European retirees. The export sector is also attempting to expand in the areas of fisheries, perliculture, and specialized agricultural production (such as vanilla, flowers, and tropical fruit).

With the loss of jobs directly related to the nuclear testing efforts, and a decrease in government sector employment in general, some Polynesians are returning to their home districts and islands. This return migration eases overcrowding in urban neighborhoods, which may alleviate social discontent if it offsets the rise in unemployment. There is also return migration of French civil servants and military personnel, and in 1998 the population of Papeete actually experienced a modest decline.

Papeete is a city in transition. The coming years will be a test of the creativity and fortitude of its vigorous and diverse population.

BIBLIOGRAPHY

Atlas de Tahiti et de la Polynesie Francaise, 3d ed. (Les Editions de Pacifique 1996).

Bresson, Louis, *Tourism: L'anti-crise, La voie royal pour l'economie de l'apres nucleaire* (Pacific Promotion Tahiti 1993).

Crocombe, Ron, and Pat Hereniko, *Tahiti: The Other Side* (Editions Haere Po No Tahiti 1985).

Danielsson, Bengt, and Marie-Therese, *Papeete 1818–1990* (Mairie de Papeete 1990).

Danielsson, Bengt, and Marie-Therese, *Poisoned Reign* (Penguin Books 1986).

Newbury, Colin, *Tahiti Nui: Change and Survival in French Polynesia 1767–1945* (University of Hawaii Press 1980).

Robineau, Claude, "Reciprocity, Redistribution and Prestige Among the Polynesians of the Society Islands," *French Polynesia: A Book of Selected Readings,* ed. by N. J. Pollock and R. Crocombe (University of the South Pacific 1988).

LAURA JONES

Paris

France

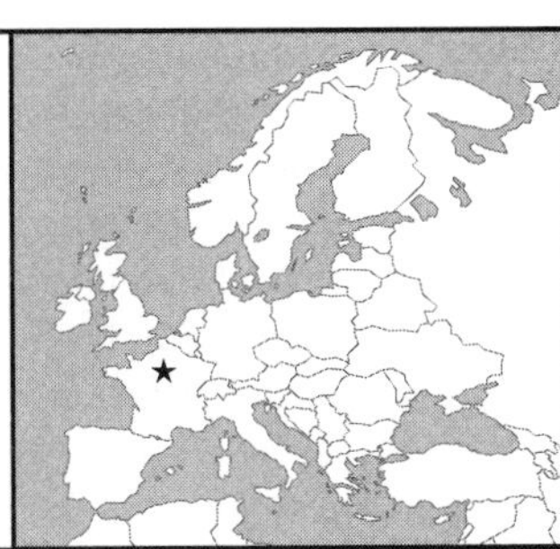

ORIENTATION

Paris is a city that captures imaginations, evokes history and romance, inspires writers and artists, and attracts millions of tourists. It is one of Europe's largest cities and metropolitan areas and has long been a center for finance and industry. The home of the European Enlightenment and perhaps the capital of modernism, Paris has been the object of vast experiments in urban and social planning. It is the political, economic, and cultural capital of France. At the same time, it is a city of neighborhoods, each marked by shifting social arrangements over the city's long history. Varied architecture, neighborhood parks, boulevards, and local cafés make the city visually interesting, while the Parisians themselves, in all their variety, create a particular urban culture.

Name of City. Although the city's first inhabitants were the Gallic Parisii (who lived on the Île de la Cité as early as the 3d century B.C.), it was the Romans who gave the city its first recorded name, *Lutetia* (*Lutèce*), in the early part of the 1st century A.D. The name *Paris* became common in the 4th century A.D. While the city is generally referred to as Paris, the name *Lutetia* is an occasional, usually literary, synonym. During the 18th century Enlightenment, Paris's reputation as a center for intellectual life and higher education earned it the nickname City of Light, (*Ville Lumière*), which is also a common literary reference.

Location. Paris is located in western Europe, in the north of France, at 48°52′ north latitude and 02°20′ east longitude, at the center of the largely agricultural Paris basin and the rapidly urbanizing Île-de-France administrative region. The region consists of eight *départements* (regions and *départements* are local administrative and political units in France). The city (which is itself one *département*) is surrounded most immediately by the *départements* of Seine-Saint-Denis, Val-de-Marne, and Hauts-de-Seine, which form the inner ring of suburbs. These in turn are surrounded by the Val-d'Oise, Seine-et-Marne, Essonne, and Yvelines *départements.*

Population. As of 1999 the population of Paris proper was about 2.1 million, the population of the official Paris metropolitan area (which exists only for statistical purposes) was about 9.6 million, and the population of the Île-de-France region was about 10.9 million. With nearly 19% of the country's total population, Paris is by far the largest city in France and one of the largest in Europe. A population density of 912 inhabitants per square kilometer (352 per square mile) also makes it one of the most densely populated (the population density of Paris proper is 20,164 inhabitants per square kilometer, or 7,783 per square mile).

Distinctive and Unique Features. Paris is centered on and cut in two by the Seine river, which curves east to west through the city. The historic core of the city is the Île de la Cité, one of three islands in the Seine within Paris (the Île St. Louis lies just to the east of the Île de la Cité, and the Île aux Cygnes is downriver, at the point where the Seine flows out of Paris). Paris is bounded by the Boulevard Périphérique, a ring highway 36 kilometers (22 miles) long. From east to west, the city is about 18 kilometers (11 miles) wide, and from north to south the distance is about 9.5 kilometers (6 miles).

The layout of Paris reflects the transformation of the city during the Second Empire, under the rule of Napoleon III and the administration of Baron Georges-Eugène Haussmann as prefect of the Seine. As prefect, Haussmann was responsible for modernizing Paris, giving it the look it has today. His work included the development of many of the wide boulevards that form Paris's main traffic arteries. These include the north to south dividing line formed by the Boulevard Strasbourg and Boulevard Sébastopol on the Right Bank and the Boulevard St. Michel on the Left Bank, as well as the widening of the Rue de Rivoli, which forms Paris's east-to-west axis. The Rue de Rivoli ends at the Place de la Concorde, where it connects with the Champs-Élysées and, further on, the Place Charles-de-Gaulle (also known as l'Étoile; it surrounds the Arc de Triomphe). In the 20th century this sweeping vista, which begins in central Paris, was extended to include the Grande Arche de la Défense in the western suburbs. Twelve wide boulevards radiate from the Place Charles-de-Gaulle (seven of which were added under Haussmann), making it the traffic center for western Paris. The system of boulevards, connecting traffic circles and squares, provides a network for traffic and a variety of architectural vistas characteristic of modern Paris.

Attractions of the City. Divided broadly into the Rive Gauche and Rive Droite (Left Bank and Right Bank, designations that reflect the point of view of a person facing downstream), the city is organized into 20 districts (arrondissements), that spiral out from the Île de la Cité. Paris is notable for its vistas and monuments designed by successive governments, and for local neighborhoods, with their markets, parks, schools, and churches.

Islands and the River. The Île de la Cité lies at the historic center of Paris. It is the site of the original city settled by the Parisii in the 3d century B.C. Notre-Dame Cathedral, located at the upstream end of the island, is surrounded by gardens, except at the front, where it faces the Place du Parvis, a public square that was cleared of buildings in the 19th century. In addition to the cathedral, the central police headquarters (Préfecture de Police), the law courts (Palais de Justice), the Conciergerie (a medieval prison, parts of which are used today to hold prisoners awaiting trial in the adjacent courts), the Hôtel-Dieu hospital, and the Sainte-Chapelle church are the principal points of interest there.

The Pont St. Louis connects the Île de la Cité with the Île St. Louis. Primarily residential, the Île today is inhabited by Paris's elites and is known for its luxurious *hôtels particuliers,* mansions whose unassuming street-side facades often hide elaborate courtyards and gardens.

Thirty-six bridges connect the Right and Left banks of the Seine. Of these, 30 carry automotive traffic, 3 are pedestrian bridges, and 2 carry rail traffic. The oldest bridge still in its original form and site is the Pont Neuf (ironically, "New Bridge"), constructed between 1578 and 1607. Completed in 1996, the Pont Charles de Gaulle is Paris's newest bridge.

Barges use the river and the city's canals to carry goods from throughout France and Europe, making Paris one of the busiest river ports on the continent. The river is also home to dozens of large, glass-enclosed tourist boats that provide visitors with a unique perspective on the city's monuments. In central Paris quays along both banks are lined with the wooden display boxes of the *bouquinistes,* who sell used books, engravings, and greeting cards. The banks of the Seine within Paris were classified as a World Heritage Site by the United Nations Educational, Scientific and Cultural Organization (UNESCO) in 1991.

The Seine connects with the city's canal system via the Bassin de l'Arsenal. Renovated in the 1980s as a marina for private craft, the waterway runs under the Place de la Bastille and surfaces 1.5 kilometers (0.9 miles) to the north, near the Place de la République, where it joins the Canal St. Martin and the Bassin de la Villette and finally exits Paris by splitting into the Canal St. Denis and the Canal de l'Ourcq in the northeast corner of the city.

Right Bank. Near the center of the city, Paris's city hall (Hôtel de Ville) has long played an important role in both municipal and national political life. City Hall is located on the Place de l'Hôtel de Ville, known until 1830 as the Place de Grève, which was long the city's central port. The Place de Grève was also the main location for public executions in Old Regime Paris. Since the French Revolution, City Hall and its surrounding space have been one of the central gathering points for popular revolts and insurrections. Control of the Paris city hall has signified, at least in the minds of Parisians, control of France itself.

The Marais neighborhood, immediately to the east of City Hall, has been known over the centuries for the *hôtels particuliers* of the aristocracy, the shops of artisans, light industry, and a small Jewish community. The aristocracy built mansions in the area following the lead of Henri IV, who built the royal residence around the Place Royale (the present-day Place des Vosges) in 1605. Today the Place des Vosges is a pleasant park, and the neighborhood is known for its many elegant buildings, several of which have become museums.

The Bastille neighborhood, just to the east of the Marais, is best known for the famous prison, torn down by the people of Paris on July 14, 1789. The Place de la Bastille now centers on the Colonne de Juillet (July Column), which commemorates the revolutions of 1830 and 1848. The Opéra-Bastille, built on the site of a former train station, was inaugurated in 1989 and is now the home of Paris's opera company. While the area around the Bastille, as well as the adjacent Faubourg St. Antoine neighborhood have gentrified in recent years, they have long been the symbolic heart of working-class Paris.

Two other areas that have played important roles in Paris working-class uprisings are Belleville and Montmartre. Both are built on hills that overlook the rest of Paris. Belleville grew rapidly in the 19th century as thousands of peasants migrated to Paris in search of work. Popular with artists until the 1920s, Montmartre has long had a reputation for a bohemian lifestyle. Montmartre played a fundamental role in the 1871 Paris Commune. One consequence of this was the construction, promoted by right-wing Catholics, of the Église du Sacré-Coeur in Montmartre, to atone for the city's sins. Built of white stone, its striking dome is now an important part of the Paris skyline.

Père-Lachaise cemetery, located east of the Bastille neighborhood and bordering on Belleville, is one of the city's best-known landmarks. Many famous people are buried there, as well as the last insurgents of the Paris Commune, who were executed in 1871 in the southeast corner of the cemetery and buried where they fell. The cemetery is an important pilgrimage site for many visitors to Paris.

Located to the west of City Hall, the Place du Châtelet was once the site of a major defensive fortress. Today it is notable for its fountain and two theaters (on the surface), and for Paris's largest métro and regional rapid transit system (RER) station underground. The Gothic St. Jacques tower, which stands near the Place du Châtelet, is all that remains of the 16th century church St. Jacques-la-Boucherie.

The Centre National d'Art et de Culture Georges-Pompidou, known locally as Beaubourg, is just to the north of the Place du Châtelet. Constructed in the 1970s, the building is notable for its futuristic architecture, with brightly colored pipes, ducts, and escalators all built outside the walls. While the design, unusually modern for Paris, has been controversial, Beaubourg has become one of the most-visited cultural sites in the world. It houses the Musée national d'art moderne (French National Museum for Modern Art), a large public library, and a research center for 20th-century music.

The former central markets, Les Halles, are just to the west of Beaubourg. While Paris's main food markets were moved to Rungis, in the suburbs, in the 1960s, the site has been redeveloped as a sunken shopping center. The surrounding neighborhoods,

© BUDDY MAYS/CORBIS

Artists display their work at stands along the Seine River in Paris, France.

known historically for textiles, prostitution, and poverty—as well as for the market—have become gentrified in recent years.

The Rue de Rivoli, which begins at Châtelet, leads to some of the city's most well-known buildings. The first of these is the Louvre, one of the largest art museums in the world. Begun in the 1200s under the reign of Philippe Auguste, the Louvre was often the residence of French kings, as well as a residence and gathering place for artists. The current building extends nearly 750 meters (2,460 feet) along the Rue de Rivoli and the Seine. At the east end, the Cour Carrée (Square Courtyard) contains part of the original castle, although extensively renovated and developed in later centuries. Two wings extend to the west. While the southern Denon wing has long contained galleries devoted to the display of art, until the early 1990s the northern Richelieu wing was occupied by the Ministry of Finance. The most recent renovation entailed moving the ministry to Bercy and building a glass pyramid in the courtyard, between the two wings; this has become the main entrance to the museum.

The Louvre pyramid is the first point in a vista that extends westward to the Grande Arche de La Défense, through the Arc de Triomphe du Carrousel (just west of the pyramid), the Place de la Concorde, up the Champs-Élysées to the Arc de Triomphe, and from there down the Avenue de la Grande Armée into the western suburbs and up to La Défense. This vista first passes through the Tuileries gardens, which begin just west of the Louvre and extends westward along the Seine to the Place de la Concorde. The Palais Royal, also on the Rue de Rivoli, was originally built as a home for Cardinal Richelieu in 1632 and has served as home to kings and other aristocracy. Today it houses the Ministry of Culture, the Council of State, and a quiet park. The Palais Royal adjoins the Comédie Française, the French national theater.

Located at the western end of the Rue de Rivoli and the Tuileries gardens, the Place de la Concorde is a vast open space centered on two fountains and an Egyptian obelisk. The Avenue des Champs-Élysées begins on the western side of the Concorde and the Rue Royale, flanked by two enormous mansions, and leads north to the Church of La Madeleine and the Faubourg St. Honoré neighborhood, the location of the Palais de l'Élysée, the official residence of the president of the French Republic.

The area known as the Grands Boulevards begins north and northeast of La Madeleine and runs across the city, east to the Place de la République. Long known for its popular theaters and dance halls, this area may have also given birth to modern consumerism in the 19th century with the development of covered pedestrian shopping arcades linking the boulevards. Built of iron, covered with glass roofs, and lit by gaslight, these passages provided Parisians with a new experience of commerce. Several, including the Passage Jouffroy and the Passage de Panoramas, still exist.

The development of these shopping arcades led to the rise of the department store, which many believe was invented in Paris early in the 19th century. The first of these temples of consumerism, Au Bon Marché, is on the Left Bank, but two of the more famous Parisian department stores, the Galeries Lafayette and Printemps, are located near the western end of the Grands Boulevards. The area surrounding the Galeries Lafayette and Printemps is one of Paris's main commercial and banking districts. It is also home to the Opéra-Garnier, built in the 19th century to be the home of the Paris opera company, where it remained until the opening of the Opéra-Bastille in 1989.

World expositions and fairs have left several architectural marks on Paris's Right Bank. These include the Grand Palais and Petit Palais museums, at the eastern end of the Champs-Élysées, built for the 1900 World Exposition, and the Palais de Chaillot, constructed for the 1937 World's Fair. The latter houses several museums, including the ethnographic Musée de l'Homme and the Cinémathèque film library.

Left Bank. The Eiffel Tower is situated on the Left Bank of the Seine, at one end of the Champs de Mars, a large public park that originally served as a parade ground for the École Militaire (Military Academy), located at the other end. Completed in 1889 for the World Exposition, the Eiffel Tower is probably the most well-known landmark in Paris. At the time it was built, it was the tallest structure in the world. The 300-meter (984-foot) metal tower (321 meters, or 1,053 feet, with radio and television aerials) remains a prime tourist attraction, with three viewing platforms that provide spectacular views of the city.

The neighborhoods surrounding the Eiffel Tower and École Militaire are home to both wealthier members of the French upper classes and to several government ministries. Located to the east of these landmarks, the Hôtel des Invalides was built under Louis

XIV in the late 1600s to house retired troops. Napoleon's tomb is located there, as are two military museums.

The Faubourg St. Germain is an elegant neighborhood between the Invalides and the Latin Quarter. Elegant mansions and hidden gardens characterize the area, which is also home to a number of government ministries, embassies and the prime minister's residence (the Hôtel Matignon). Other notable landmarks in this area include the building housing the French National Assembly, which is the lower house of parliament, and the former Orsay railway station, located along the Seine on the Quai d'Orsay. The Musée d'Orsay was opened in 1986 as a museum devoted to the 19th century.

Just to the east of the Faubourg St. Germain, the neighborhood surrounding the Church of St. Germain des Près is often considered to be the heart of literary and intellectual Paris. The church, founded in 542, is the oldest in Paris. The St. Germain des Près neighborhood is also the home of several universities and schools, as well as of Institut de France, which houses the Académie Française, whose 40 members are responsible for the development of the French language.

The Quartier Latin (Latin Quarter) begins in St. Germain des Près and continues eastward through most of the university district. The name of the neighborhood refers to the requirement that students and professors speak only Latin, a rule that was followed until 1793. The neighborhood is centered on the Boulevard St. Michel and, near the Seine, the Place St. Michel. The area just to the east of the Place St. Michel is one of the oldest neighborhoods in Paris. Its narrow, winding streets are lined with restaurants and art cinemas. The Luxembourg Gardens connect the Latin Quarter with St. Germain des Près. Along with immaculate formal gardens and fountains, they contain the French Senate building.

Located south and west of the Latin Quarter, the Montparnasse neighborhood replaced Montmartre as the center of the Paris avant-garde early in the 20th century. Although it was long a working-class area known for its artisans, the development of the Tour Montparnasse, its shopping center, and the later renovation of the Montparnasse train station all have contributed to the neighborhood's transformation into an important business center. The Tour Montparnasse is, at 209 meters (686 feet), by far the tallest office building in Paris proper.

Along with monuments and buildings, Paris is a city of parks and green spaces. The Bois de Boulogne and the Bois de Vincennes are two vast parks that frame the city, the former in the west and the latter in the east. The Bois de Boulogne is an extensive expanse of woods and gardens that contains museums, horse racing facilities, and restaurants. Vincennes is built around a medieval castle and royal forest. The Parc de la Villette, in the northeast corner of Paris, is a vast complex devoted to science, industry, and music. There are many other small parks throughout the city.

Relationships Between the City and the Outside. Over 80% of the population of Paris actually lives in the suburbs. In many ways the characteristics of the suburbs reflect the historic growth of the city itself. The western sections of the city have long been inhabited by the upper classes and are also home to service industries that cater to those classes. In contrast to this, the northern and eastern sections of the city are historically associated with the French working class. To a certain extent, the city's suburbs are an extension of this division, with service industries and upper-class residential suburbs in the west and manufacturing and working-class housing in the north and east.

While the city is the region's economic motor, the suburbs also make a significant and distinctive contribution to the regional and national economies. About 70% of the regional labor force works in the city itself and in the inner ring of suburbs (known as the petite couronne), while the remaining 30% work in the outer ring of suburbs (the grande couronne). Yet since the late decades of the 20th century, most of the regional job and population growth has been in the outer ring, which draws workers from the city and inner ring as well as from surrounding regions outside of Île-de-France. In addition, residents of the suburbs are more likely to include working- and middle-class families with children, while residents of the central city tend to be wealthier professionals as well as young single people.

For many Parisians the suburbs have become synonymous with vast blocks of public housing (often in disrepair), unemployment, and discontented (often immigrant) youth. This common stereotype contrasts sharply with the growing economic and social importance of the Parisian suburbs. While Paris itself is home to many government ministries, international organizations, and corporations, manufacturing and research are increasingly located in the suburbs. Paris's influence now extends well into the *départements* of the Paris basin that surround the Île-de-France region (these are the Aisne, Aube, Eure,

Eure-et-Loire, Loiret, Marne, Oise, and Yonne *départements*). A growing number of people of all social classes are choosing to live and work in the suburbs or in this surrounding region.

The Paris region also plays an important role within the European Union. The Île-de-France region is at the center of a network of highways and high-speed rail lines connecting northern and southern Europe. Paris's reputation as a center for the arts, culture, and intellectual life continues to attract millions of tourists from all over the world each year. It has a reputation among urban planners as a well-managed and livable city.

Major Languages. All official communications in Paris are conducted in French. While it is possible to speak and hear Arabic, Vietnamese, Spanish, Creole, or many other languages associated with immigrants or regions of France, French remains the language used in most official and unofficial communications.

HISTORY

The Origin of the City. The first evidence of settlement in Paris, by the Gallic Parisii tribe, dates to the 3d century B.C., on what is now the Île de la Cité. Conquered in 52 B.C., the city was developed by the Romans during the 1st century A.D. By the 4th century the city became known as Paris. The Roman baths at Cluny and the Arènes de Lutèce are the only public monuments from the Roman period.

Christianity spread to Paris around this time as well. Its arrival, around 250 A.D., is attributed to St. Denis, who was the first bishop of Paris. According to legend, St. Denis was tortured on the Île de la Cité, then beheaded at the Temple of Mercury, located in what was later Montmartre. He then carried his head to the site of the current Basilica of St. Denis, several kilometers away, where he was finally buried.

St. Geneviève, the patron saint of Paris, is said to have led the Parisians in resistance to Attila and his Huns in 451 and to have broken the blockade imposed on the city by the Franks in 470. The Franks, under the leadership of Clovis, made Paris their capital in 486. Under the Merovingians and subsequent Carolingians, Paris developed as a center for commerce and religion.

Paris regained its political importance only with the election to the throne in 987 of Hughes Capet, count of Paris. Population and commerce increased under the Capetian kings, and the framework for city governance was established. Philippe II, known in France as Philippe-Auguste (reigned 1179–1223), oversaw extensive development of the city, including street paving, the initial construction of the Louvre, the development of the city's first guilds, and the enclosure of parts of both the Right and Left banks within fortifications. Originally governed through a representative of the king, the *prévôt du roi,* responsibility for taxation and related issues were transferred to a representative of the river merchant's guild, the *prévôt des marchands*. Philippe II also recognized the University of Paris in 1200. In addition to effectively establishing the division of Paris into commercial (the Right Bank) and university (the Left Bank) sections, the university was given autonomy from governance by both royal and church authorities. This autonomy marked the birth of the Latin Quarter as a student zone. By the 13th century the city's population had reached 100,000.

Urban development slowed considerably in the 14th and 15th centuries. The Black Death (1348–49), cold winters, famines, and war all contributed to a sharp decline in Paris's population by the middle of the 15th century. Uprisings against royal power during the Hundred Years' War (1337–1456) durably marked the political organization of the city. In 1356 Etienne Marcel, the *prévôt des marchands*, took control of the city, establishing a city council outside of royal supervision, leading to the suspension of municipal self-governance and the removal of the monarchy to Touraine.

The monarchy returned to Paris under François I, in 1528. As the seat of government, the city grew significantly during the 16th and 17th centuries. Paris expanded to the west, with the development of the Tuileries, and on the Left Bank, with the construction of the Luxembourg Palace and of new colleges. Successive kings made Paris the showplace of the French monarchy, building churches, public places, boulevards, fountains, and hospitals. Royal influence in design drew on Renaissance perspectives on urban planning, designing new residential places that allowed more light and created a greater sense of space. Building in Paris began to reflect legislated notions of taste and, especially, the power of the state.

Paris also played a central role in the French Wars of Religion which, between 1562 and 1598, transformed the character of the monarchy. Protestantism had been severely repressed in Paris beginning with François I, although a community of Protestants continued to live there until the Saint Bartholomew's Day massacre in 1572. Attempts to mediate between Roman Catholics and Protestants resulted in uprisings against the monarchy by the Catholic League in Paris in 1588. Henri of Navarre, a Protestant, unsuccessfully laid siege to Paris for five years and later converted to Catholicism (commenting, famously, that "Paris is worth a mass") to become Henri IV. His conversion and ascension to the throne ended the Wars of Religion.

Population growth during the 17th and 18th centuries was fueled by immigrants from northern France, seeking upward mobility or fleeing conflicts elsewhere. While many churches and other buildings for religious orders were built during this period, the aristocracy and well-to-do merchants contributed to the development of new residential areas. The Marais, for instance, became popular among the aristocracy following the development of the Place Royale there by Henri IV (completed in 1612, it was Paris's first square and is now known as the Place des Vosges). Spectacular mansions (*hôtels particuliers*) were built in the Marais and on the nearby Île St. Louis, which had been made by connecting two islands (the Île aux Vaches and the Île Notre Dame). Begun in 1614 by Christophe Marie, the island was the subject of a great deal of real estate speculation over the course of the 17th century. More construction occurred in the area just to the west of the Palais-Cardinal, built for Cardinal Richelieu (now the Palais Royal).

Although Louis XIV made Versailles his personal residence, he continued the tradition of monumental building in Paris. Tree-lined boulevards were developed to replace the city walls, which had been removed to symbolize France's sense of military superiority within Europe. Many of Paris's better-known architectural vistas, including the view from the Louvre up the Champs-Élysées, were initially developed in this period. This expansion continued under the rule of Louis XV and Louis XVI. By the end of the 18th century, Paris's population had grown to nearly 700,000 and the city had become a center for the arts, fashion, and intellectual life. At the same time, the division between wealthy neighborhoods in the west of the city and the more popular neighborhoods in the east (the Faubourg St. Marceau and the Faubourg St. Antoine, for instance) was accentuated.

Paris played a central role in the events of the French Revolution. The people of Paris provided the mass pressure and movement behind many of the revolution's key events. These included the taking of the Bastille, the return of King Louis XVI from Versailles to Paris, and the insurrection that led to the arrest and execution of the king. The Place de la Révolution (now the Place de la Concorde) was the site of many executions, including that of the king and, later, of many of the revolutionaries as well. The pattern of popular uprisings and insurrections set by the revolution of 1789 would be repeated several times over the course of the following century.

The 19th century was pivotal for Paris. The city's centrality for French political, economic, and cultural life was reinforced by every regime, from Napoleon to the Third Republic. Any semblance of local self-government was ended by Napoleon, who controlled the city through the prefect of the Seine and the prefect of police. New monuments, including the Arc de Triomphe, were built, and a wide range of initiatives were taken to improve the quality of urban life. Paris also began to industrialize under the Empire and, along with the growth of the banking industry, developed an important stock market. Subsequent regimes added gaslighting and the city's first railroads.

The government of France coincided during the 19th century with the government of Paris, so much so that successive rebellions against the state made the takeover of the Paris city hall their first objective. This was the case in both 1830 and 1848. Neither of these revolutions slowed the city's dramatic growth. At the end of the revolution of 1789, Paris's population had dropped to less than 600,000. By 1846 it had grown to 1,053,000, and by 1901 it had reached 2,715,000. This growth was, in part, the result of a flow of immigrants from the provinces, but it was also a result of the city's changing boundaries. With the fall of Napoleon and the occupation of the city by foreign troops, the principle of an open city was rejected in favor of new fortifications. Built in the 1840s, these new walls brought surrounding villages into Paris's jurisdiction, including Belleville, La Villette, Montmartre, La Chapelle, Charonne, and Bercy.

By midcentury much of Paris still resembled a medieval city. Crowded, cramped neighborhoods; poor housing conditions; open sewers; and undrinkable water all contributed to a public health disaster, and, indeed, cholera swept the city at least five times over the course of the century. The narrow streets and dense neighborhoods also made the city nearly impossible to navigate. Politicians and social reformers linked these conditions to the Parisian working-class uprisings that regularly occurred. As prefect of the Seine, Baron Haussmann, working under Napoleon III, made profound transformations to the medieval city, shaping it in ways that are still recognizable today. The Île de la Cité and other elements of the medieval core of Paris were essentially cleared and replaced with broader streets and more modern buildings. New boulevards were driven through the old city, alleviating traffic problems and allowing for better crowd control. The medieval market was modernized, new parks were developed, and the sewer and water systems were improved.

The Second Empire ended with the French defeat in the Franco-Prussian war of 1870. The Paris revolution of 1871 (the Paris Commune) began as resistance to the German siege and ended as a working-class uprising against the social segregation in Haussmann's city. The repression of the commune by the French government resulted in over 20,000 deaths and the destruction of many buildings and monuments, and it reinforced Paris's social and political separation from the rest of France. At the same time, the Paris Commune's brief existence provided a revolutionary mythology for activists in Paris and elsewhere.

The Third Republic continued many of the modernization projects begun under Haussmann, improving transportation with the Métro, annexing suburban residential districts, and constructing new monuments, including the Eiffel Tower and the Trocadéro. The population of Paris proper reached its apogee in 1931, with 2.9 million inhabitants. Moderate-income housing projects were developed in the outer arrondissements to accommodate this population, along with projects to eliminate slums in other parts of the city. By the end of the 1930s, most of the city's housing was electrified. Substantial immigration during the 1920s, from both rural France and other countries (especially from eastern and southern Europe), contributed to population growth in Paris.

Paris suffered little physical damage during either of the world wars, but the city and French national politics were marked by the political struggles of the interwar years and by the German occupation during the World War II. Demonstrations and riots were especially common during the 1930s, as the struggle for political control of France played itself out in the streets of Paris. The German occupation isolated Paris from the rest of the country. For the first time in centuries, Paris was not the country's capital.

While Paris continued to dominate the French political, economic, and cultural scenes following the end of World War II, the city also changed in important ways. Its population declined significantly until reaching a plateau in the 1990s, while the population of the Paris region continued to grow. This growth led to a chronic housing shortage, which, in the decades after the war, was addressed with the construction of massive low- and moderate-income housing projects on the city's periphery and in the suburbs.

French political life was, from the end of the war, marked by Parisian street politics. Demonstrations, strikes, and riots contributed to changes in French colonial policy in the 1950s and 1960s. The student uprising in Paris in 1968 sparked a national general strike that paralyzed the country for a month. Yet fear of Paris's threat to state authority dissipated in the late 20th century. In 1975 the National Assembly passed a law permitting the city to have its own mayor, and in 1977 Jacques Chirac became the first mayor of Paris since the Paris Commune.

Paris remained a showplace for the French state in the 20th century. Successive governments used the city to demonstrate France's commitment to its history and its engagement with modernity. This was especially true under President François Mitterrand, who oversaw several large construction projects, including the new National Library and Ministry of Finance, the renovation of the Louvre, the Grande Arche de la Défense, the Musée d'Orsay, and the Opéra-Bastille.

Migration: Past and Present. Paris has attracted immigrants from its earliest days as a Roman settlement. Early industrialization in the 17th and 18th centuries brought migrants from the north of France to work in the city. Paris continued to draw millions of migrants from rural France throughout much of the 19th and 20th centuries. In fact, until the late 20th century the majority of Parisians were born outside the city. Immigrants from rural France formed associations based on their origins and used ties to their home villages and regions to succeed in business and politics. For instance, for much of the 20th century, people from Auvergne dominated the café trade in Paris.

France has been an important destination for immigrants from other countries since the 19th century, and many of those immigrants settled in the Paris region. Industrialization in Paris was accompanied by the arrival of immigrants from southern Europe and, before and during the World War I, from French colonies in Africa and Asia. In the 1920s millions of migrants from eastern and southern Europe moved to Paris to work in industry. From the end of World War II until the 1990s, immigration continued from southern Europe, especially Portugal, from former French colonies in North and sub-Saharan Africa, and from the French Caribbean.

INFRASTRUCTURE

Public Buildings, Public Works, and Residences. Along with 20 arrondissements, Paris is made up of at least 80 neighborhoods, identified with parishes, historic events, or local monuments. There are thousands of notable buildings, parks, and landmarks (see above, "Attractions of the City"). The city's character is marked by the presence of 370 newspaper kiosks, close to 800 Morris columns carrying advertising for theaters, and hundreds of electronic panels used by the municipality to announce traffic delays, public events, and news.

Since the late 19th century, municipal and state authorities have worked to create architectural coherence among the city's public buildings, monuments, and residences. While Paris's neighborhoods feature a wide variety of architectural styles, the city is perhaps best known for long rows of large apartment buildings with characteristic mansard roofs. The uniform facades of these buildings often hide gardens and courtyards in the rear. In many neighborhoods, they house small shops on the ground floors.

Paris streets were illuminated with gaslights beginning in the 19th century. Electricity and gas, distributed by the public utilities, have been available to residential customers since early in the 20th century, although electrification of the city was not completed until the end of World War II.

As in all major cities, the availability of potable water and the disposal of waste water have long been a concern in Paris. Until the 18th century the city depended on a combination of a few public aqueducts and fountains, as well as private wells, to provide water for its residents, while waste was mostly disposed of in open sewers that ran down the middle of the streets. The resulting odors were significant—as were the epidemics of cholera and dysentery that occurred with regularity, since the city's water sources were largely polluted with the city's waste. The discovery of the links between health and water quality contributed, over the course of the 19th century, to motivate the construction of networks of sewers. Under the administration of Haussmann as prefect of the Seine, the city's water system acquired its modern structure. Today the city receives potable water from both underground springs (25%) and rivers (75%), all of which is treated in 14 plants before delivery to the population. Drinking water in Paris is produced and delivered by the City of Paris, which has formed a semipublic corporation with two private companies, the Générale des Eaux and the Compagnie des Eaux de Paris. Water from local canals is used to clean waste from the streets, while human waste products are treated in a series of plants outside the city. Paris's water infrastructure has a capacity to produce 4,730,000 cubic meters of water per day through a system of 21,500 kilometers (13,350 miles) of pipes. An additional 19,500 kilometers (12,100 miles) of sewers carry waste water in a system that is distinct from the system that carries rain water. Parisians currently consume approximately 670 million liters (180 million gallons) of water per day, or about 300 liters (80 gallons) per person, up from 7 liters (2 gallons) per person per day in the middle of the 19th century.

Solid waste has also long been a concern in Paris. The modern system for collecting residential waste was established at the end of the 19th century, under the direction of the prefect of Paris, Eugène Poubelle, who required landlords to provide covered garbage containers for renters (*poubelle* has subsequently become the French word for garbage can) and organized the regular collection of solid waste. Municipal waste is collected daily by the city and transported to sites outside of the city for incineration or recycling in cooperation with regional authorities. Many of the city's streets are swept daily, often by hand. Since the late 1980s, the municipal authorities have increasingly emphasized recycling and required residents to separate their waste for

© VINCE STREANO/CORBIS

Street cleaners wash the famous boulevards of Paris, France.

that purpose. Paris is also known for the approximately 10 tons of dog droppings left by pets on streets and sidewalks each day. The municipality has tried a variety of strategies to clean up after the dogs, including the use of motorcycles equipped with brooms and vacuum cleaners, driven by sanitation workers.

Politics and City Services. The mayor of Paris is elected to a six-year term by the Municipal Council (Conseil de Paris), which itself is elected every six years in proportional elections by arrondissement. The 163 members of the Municipal Council are selected from the 517 members of the arrondissement councils. Socialist Bertrand Delanoë was elected mayor in March 2001, succeeding two conservative mayors, Jacques Chirac (1977–1995) and Jean Tiberi (1995–2001).

There are 1,200 separate municipalities (communes) in the suburbs of Paris and, at least on the level of municipal councils, there is very little regional coordination. The region is made up of eight *départements* (Paris, Seine-Saint-Denis, Val-de-Marne, Hauts-de-Seine, Val-d'Oise, Seine-et-Marne, Essonne, and Yvelines), each with its own elected council. These *départements* are, in turn, part of the Île-de-France region, which also has an elected council and president.

The city's budget (some 33 billion francs [U.S.$4.4 billion] in 2000) is mostly derived from municipal taxes and fees and from French government subsidies. Because Paris is both a municipality and *département,* the mayor is responsible for the services provided by both jurisdictions. These include managing traffic and road repairs, public housing, public health, day-care centers, school buildings, public recreation, and parks. At the same time, certain powers that are often controlled by mayors are administered by the state, region, or another jurisdiction in Paris. Both police and fire services are provided by the central government, and the mass-transit system is managed by a regional administration.

Educational System. Education in France is organized under the direction of the French Ministry of Education. While the ministry is responsible for pedagogy and teaching personnel, the city is responsible for maintenance and construction of preschool, elementary, and junior high schools (*collèges*). The regional government is responsible for high schools (*lycèes*); the state maintains and builds universities.

Paris has long been the intellectual center of France and is home to many of France's more famous institutions. These include some of the most prestigious public high schools in France, as well as many of the universities and *Grandes Écoles* (specialized universities) that have produced France's most prominent thinkers and its business and political elites. There are eight public universities within Paris proper and seventeen in the Île-de-France region. Prestigious *Grandes Écoles* in the region include the Institut d'Études Politiques de Paris (Institute for Political Studies), the École Normale Supérieure (a school that specializes in preparing teachers and philosophers), the Institut des Langues et Civilisations Orientales (a language institute), and the École Polytechnique (an engineering school).

Transportation System. The subway (the Métropolitain, or Métro) is at the heart of Paris's transit system, and its design plays an essential role in defining the city's character. The first line, connecting the Porte de Vincennes and the Porte Maillot, opened on July 19, 1900. The fourteenth line, running between the Madeleine and the François Mitterrand Library, was inaugurated on October 15, 1998. The system runs on 211 kilometers (131 miles) of track, with 297 stations. The Métro is quite dense—no point within Paris proper is more than 500 meters (1,640 feet) from a station—and very popular, serving over 3.5 million passengers every day. Some lines extend into the suburbs, but many suburban commuters access the city via the high-speed Réseau Express Régional (RER), several of the five lines of which connect to the national railway system. There are also six passenger train stations that link Paris to the rest of France and to Europe, and to the two main airports, Charles de Gaulle and Orly.

The system of wide boulevards and traffic circles designed by Haussmann in the 19th century has been supplemented with a few expressways underground or along the Seine, and by a 36-kilometer (22-mile) ring highway, the Boulevard Périphérique, which links the city to the national expressway system. In addition, the Seine and the canals continue to be used for both commerce and tourism in Paris.

CULTURAL AND SOCIAL LIFE

Distinctive Features of the City's Cultures. Paris is known throughout the world as a capital of fashion and taste. Dress and public behavior are self-consciously manipulated by Parisians of all social classes in order to assert group identity and define public space. While members of the Parisian bourgeoisie may be identified by a particular designer scarf or a brand of overcoat, members of the working class are often associated with "working blues." The identification of certain spaces or parts of the city with social classes becomes especially evident during demonstrations. Left-wing groups, associated with working-class ideologies, march from the Place de la République or the Place de la Nation in the east of the city, while conservative and bourgeois groups often occupy spaces near the Champs-Élysées in the west of Paris.

Cuisine. With more than 11,000 restaurants and 20,000 cafés, Paris makes eating well a central cultural concern in Paris. Cafés play an important role in Parisian social life as a place for friends or business associates to gather on an almost daily basis. More elaborate meals are taken at restaurants and in the more famous establishments can often last several hours. While relaxed meals might be eaten in a neighborhood bistro, late night meals and large parties often gravitate to the large *brasseries* found around the city, or to one of the many wine bars.

Paris cuisine reflects the food of France, but Paris's domination of France has made the city's own specialties synonymous with French food itself. These include particular ways of serving herring and seafood, specific cuts of steak, and desserts, such as *mousse au chocolat.* With a strong tradition of culinary innovation, French cuisine is by far the dominant type of food found in Paris restaurants. Nevertheless, North African, Chinese, Vietnamese, and other cuisines are increasingly available in Paris. Fast food, whether American-style hamburgers, French sandwiches, or other types of cuisine from around the world, is increasingly popular as well.

Even in Paris, however, most meals are taken at home. Parisians are somewhat less likely to shop at supermarkets and hypermarkets than other French people, preferring neighborhood specialty stores and daily street markets. This is especially true for bread, which Parisians purchase daily in the city's over 1,500 bakeries.

Ethnic, Class, and Religious Diversity. Social class provides the most significant form of cultural distinction in Paris. Divisions between working-class and bourgeois Parisians are marked by neighborhood, clothing, and leisure, as well as by income. Inequality between classes is especially notable in admissions to the elite *Grandes Écoles,* where children of working-class origin are much less likely to be admitted.

Class distinctions are often linked to ethnic differences in Paris. About 12% of the population of Île-de-France is foreign born and many more are descendants of immigrants who arrived after World War II. People from Portugal, Algeria, Morocco, Tunisia, sub-Saharan Africa, the French Antilles, Spain, Vietnam, and eastern Europe are among the most common groups in Paris. Some neighborhoods have historically become associated with specific groups, including the Marais (associated with Jews) and Barbès-Rochechouart (associated with North Africans), although there are actually no neighborhoods that are overwhelmingly populated by a single non-French ethnic group in Paris or its region. The substantial presence of working-class people of foreign descent (most often French citizens themselves) in the suburbs means that references to the suburbs in France are often invocations of both class and ethnic difference.

Family and Other Social Support Systems. In the late decades of the 20th century, the number of individuals living alone in the Île-de-France region increased significantly, especially in Paris proper, but households with two parents and one or more children remain common. Kinship networks, especially those involving close family (parents, siblings, children, grandparents, and close cousins), are important for many people, both for affective reasons and for the cultural and social capital they can provide. However, since many Parisians now come from elsewhere, these networks are less often based in neighborhoods than they were in the past, and they may often involve kin who reside in other regions or even in other countries.

Parisians, like other French people, benefit from the existence of an extensive set of government assistance programs and subsidies that can supplement family support networks. These include nearly universal health insurance, generous paid leave policies for women with children, subsidies to families with children, a wide range of public day-care options, free public preschool starting at age 3, generous paid vacations for all workers, and other programs designed to make having and raising children affordable.

In Paris kin networks and government assistance are often combined with active participation in community organizations. Nearly half of all Parisians belong to one kind of association or another, including organizations of property owners or renters, parent-teacher associations, child-care collectives, sports clubs, and alumni associations. Such groups often receive subsidies from the city and state, as well as access to facilities (buildings, fields) for their activities.

Work and Commerce. Eighty percent of Parisians who work, do so in the tertiary (service) sector. The public sector is one of the largest employers in Paris, including government agencies, transportation workers, museum workers, and many health-care professionals. Teachers, university professors and researchers also represent an important segment of the Parisian workforce. The headquarters of most of France's large corporations, in industries as varied as chemicals, telecommunications, finance, and insurance, are located in Paris. Media, in the form of television, radio, and print, is well represented in Paris, and most French publishers are based there as well. Restaurants, cafés, hotels, and other elements of the hospitality industry are also major employers in Paris.

Manufacturing still represents a significant part of regional economy. The production of luxury products, including fashion and jewelry, is concentrated in the city itself. The suburbs are home to France's printing industry, automobile manufacturing, and other forms of large-scale manufacturing. The region has become a center for research and development in electronics, computers, and biotechnology.

Arts and Recreation. The arts, including music, cinema, painting, theater, and dance, are important to Parisians as both a form of entertainment and as a sign of their city's cultural significance in the world. Government cultural policy is the object of intense media discussion and public debate. Parisians would like to believe that their city and its culture set the pace for the world.

There are two major opera houses, along with several other venues, where opera is performed regularly. Other forms of classical music are performed in concert halls and churches, and there are countless venues for the performance of popular music, ranging from jazz to hip-hop. There are over 150 theaters in Paris, offering productions of everything from the classics of French drama to the works of the avant-garde theater. Cinema remains one of the primary cultural activities for all Parisians; there are still over 350 movies presented in cinemas in Paris on any given day. Paris is home to hundreds of museums, galleries, and monuments. There are also several large street festivals in Paris and its suburbs each year. These include the Fête de la Musique (Festival of Music), with musicians performing in public squares all around Paris annually on June 21 (the summer solstice); the annual Bastille Day celebrations, with dozens of street parties all over the city on the night of July 13, followed by parades and fireworks on the 14th; and the annual Fête de l'Humanité, organized in the suburbs in September by the Communist Party.

Professional sports are very popular with Parisians. One first-division soccer team, the Paris-St. Germain, is based in Paris, and a new stadium was built for the soccer World Cup, which was held in Paris in 1996. The French Open tennis tournament is held annually in Paris. Thousands of spectators line up each year to watch the last leg of the Tour de France bicycle race on the Champs-Élysées. Horse racing, hockey, basketball, handball, and rugby are among the many other professional sports played in Paris.

QUALITY OF LIFE

The quality and quantity of cultural activities, universities, and government and career opportunities make Paris an exciting and attractive place. For many French people the only way to advance in their careers is to move to Paris, where the headquarters of most large French firms are located, as are the most prestigious universities and schools.

At the same time, while Parisians enjoy slightly higher salaries, the cost of living in Paris is often substantially higher than elsewhere in France. Housing can be expensive and cramped. One consequence of this is that Paris is especially attractive to younger people without children. Easy access to Paris via high-speed train from medium-size provincial cities has permitted many French people to enjoy a lower cost of life in other cities yet go to Paris for work or leisure activities.

FUTURE OF THE CITY

Paris remains by far the largest metropolitan area in France as well as its political, economic, and cultural capital. Since Paris is the showcase for French government, there is a great deal at stake in cultural and political terms in its continued growth and success. The French government can be expected to continue to make large investments in the Paris region, improving its transportation systems, modernizing housing, and building new monuments and public facilities.

BIBLIOGRAPHY

Benjamin, Walter, *The Arcades Project,* tr. by Howard Eiland and Kevin McLaughlin (Belknap Press 1999) [originally published in 1982 as Passagen-Werk as edited by Tiedemann].

Berlanstein, Lenard R., *The Working People of Paris, 1871–1914* (Johns Hopkins University Press 1984).

Chevalier, Louis, *Laboring Classes and Dangerous Classes in Paris During the First Half of the Nineteenth Century,* tr. by Frank Jellinek (Princeton University Press 1973) [originally published in 1958 as *Classes Laborieuses et Classes Dangereuses à Paris pendant la première moitié du XIXe Siècle*].

Combeau, Yvan, *Histoire de Paris* (Presses Universitaires de France 1999).

Fierro, Alfred, *Historical Dictionary of Paris,* tr. by Jon Woronoff (Scarecrow Press 1998) [originally published in 1996 as *Histoire et Dictionnaire de Paris*].

Garrioch, David, *The Formation of the Parisian Bourgeoisie* (Harvard University Press 1996).

Harvey, David, *Consciousness and the Urban Experience* (Johns Hopkins University Press 1985).

Hemingway, Ernest, *A Moveable Feast* (Scribner 1964).

Marchand, Bernard, *Paris, Histoire d'une Ville XIXe-XXe Siècle* (Ed. du Seuil 1993).

Michelin Tyre PLC, *Michelin Guide Paris* (Michelin et Cie 1996).

Pinkney, David, *Napoleon III and the Rebuilding of Paris* (Princeton University Press 1958).

Radula-Scott, Caroline, ed., *Insight Guide: Paris* (APA Publications 1998).

Ranum, Orest, *Paris in the Age of Absolutism* (Wiley 1968).

Shattuck, Roger, *The Banquet Years: the Origins of the Avant Garde in France, 1885 to World War I* (Vintage Books 1968).

Stovall, Tyler, *The Rise of the Paris Red Belt* (University of California Press 1990).

Useful Web Sites

www.paris-france.org/VR/anglais/ [City of Paris official site].

www.cr-ile-de-france.fr/english/english.asp [Île-de-France regional council site].

www.louvre.fr/louvrea.htm [site of the Louvre Museum].

www.cnac-gp.fr/english/infos/infos_pratiques.htm [site of the Centre Pompidou].

David Beriss

Perth

Australia

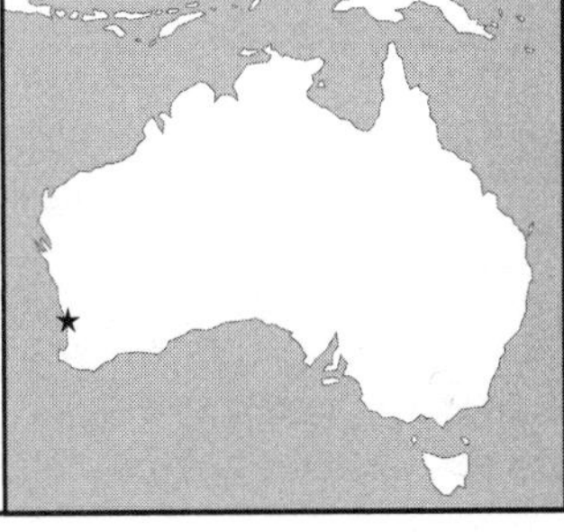

ORIENTATION

Name of City. Perth, which is the capital and urban center of Western Australia, was originally a British colony. It was named in 1829 on the instruction of Sir George Murray, the British Secretary of State to the Colonies. The city was named in honor of his birthplace in Scotland. The establishment of Perth displaced the local Aboriginal groups whose descendants refer to themselves as Nyungar. While Aboriginal people had (and still have) their own names for many places within the Perth region, many English names were imposed through the process of colonization.

The term *City of Perth* refers formally to a local council administrative region that covers only the Central Business District (CBD) and its immediate surrounding area; however, the *city of Perth* is popularly understood to also comprise a vast surrounding area of suburbs.

Location. Perth is often described as the most isolated capital city in the world. It is located on the southern west coast of Australia, at 31°57′ south latitude and 115°51′ east longitude. It is the fourth-largest capital city in Australia and the most remote. While it is surrounded by many small towns, the closest capital city is Adelaide, approximately 2,000 kilometers (1,242 miles) to the east.

The city center is on the banks of the Swan River, 16 kilometers (10 miles) upstream from the port of Fremantle. The suburbs are laid out around the Swan and Canning rivers, and stretch for approximately 110 kilometers (68 miles) from north to south and about 60 kilometers (37 miles) from west to east.

Perth is situated, for the most part, on a sandy coastal plain, which earned its residents the nickname of *Sand-gropers* during the first decades of settlement. It has a Mediterranean type climate with average temperatures ranging from 8° to 18°C (46° to 64°) in winter, and 17° to 30°C (63° to 86°) in summer. The average annual rainfall is 879 millimeters (34 inches), most of which falls in winter.

Population. In 1998 the estimated Australian population was almost 19 million; nearly 2 million lived in Western Australia, and over 1 million were residents of Perth. According to the 1996 census, approximately 30% of Perth's population was born overseas, and almost half of these were from Ireland and the United Kingdom. Approximately 1.4% of Perth residents claimed Aboriginal or Torres Strait Islander heritage.

Distinctive and Unique Features. One of Perth's most distinctive features is the Swan River, which is a popular recreation area for fishing and boating activities. The Barrack Street Jetty links the CBD with ferries to South Perth, Rottnest Island, and Fremantle. It is also the departure point for river cruises to local vineyards upstream. In the Swan Valley to the east of Perth, there are more than 30 wineries ranging from small family-run businesses to larger producers.

Kings Park is another of the city's unique features. Situated on Mount Eliza, it offers panoramic views of the city center, the river and surrounding suburbs. The park consists of approximately 400 hectares (988 acres) of natural bushland, botanic gardens, walking trails, children's playgrounds, barbecues, and picnic lawns. It includes educational and research facilities and is home to over 300 plant and animal species. It is also host to many public events.

Perth's buildings exhibit an eclectic mixture of colonial and modern architectural styles. Many public buildings were constructed by convict laborers in the 1850s, but the earliest surviving structure is the Old Courthouse, built in 1836. This is situated alongside the current Supreme Court complex in Stirling Gardens, the city's oldest parklands.

Perth's main street, St. George's Terrace, is the primary financial and business strip in the city center. The Barracks Arch, originally positioned in 1863 at the top of St. George's Terrace, is now dwarfed by high-rise office blocks. Also on the central terrace is the Gothic-style Government House, completed in 1864. The Perth Town Hall was completed

© DAVID BATTERBURY, EYE UBIQUITOUS/CORBIS

A Chinese arch frames a view of the business district of Perth, Australia.

in 1870 and Parliament House was built in 1903. St. Mary's Roman Catholic Cathedral was completed in 1865 and St. George's Anglican Cathedral in 1888. Perth's first mosque was built in 1905, an indication of the early multicultural nature of the city's population. On the south side of the river is the Old Mill Museum, housed in Perth's first flour mill.

Another of Perth's landmarks is London Court, a Tudor-style arcade connecting the Hay Street Mall and St. George's Terrace, which was built in 1937. Much of the city center has been reconstructed since World War II, and the skyline began to change dramatically in the late 1960s when the first high-rise buildings appeared. The city's tallest building, built in 1993, is Central Park Tower with 52 stories. The Perth Cultural Centre, which incorporates the state's library, museum, and art gallery, functions as a pedestrian corridor connecting the city center with the restaurant and entertainment zone of Northbridge. The Hay Street and Murray Street pedestrian malls constitute the main shopping areas in the CBD. Forrest Place, part of the Murray Street Mall, is a restored city square contained by the grand General Post Office on one side and a large shopping complex on the other. It is the venue for many public events, from political rallies to theatrical performances.

Attractions of the City. In addition to being the state's major educational, commercial, service, and retail center, Perth is the administrative center for Western Australia's mining and agricultural industries. The major industrial complex is smaller than that of most other Australian capital cities and is south of the city at Kwinana. While there are some manufacturing businesses, the economy continues to rely heavily on the natural resources sector. Some of Western Australia's main exports are wheat, wool, iron ore, gold, and natural gas.

A popular tourist attraction is the Perth Zoo, opened in 1898, which is a world leader in the preservation of threatened species and has the only numbat display in the world. Other attractions include historical buildings, museums, markets, beaches, wildlife parks, and the casino. Perth is home to Australia's oldest operating mint, established in the city center in 1899. Fremantle is Perth's historic port and has over 4,000 heritage sites listed on the municipal heritage inventory. It is a major tourist destination of considerable commercial value, and was the home base for the 1987 America's Cup yacht race.

Rottnest Island, half an hour from the Perth coastline by ferry, was initially settled by farmers in 1830. In 1838 it became a prison for Aboriginal people. The gaol (jail) was closed in 1903 and the island later became a nature reserve and holiday destination. Penguin Island, part of the Shoalwater Islands Marine Park just south of Perth, is home to Western Australia's largest fairy penguin colony. The nearby Seal Island accommodates a group of rare and protected Australian sealions.

Relationships Between the City and the Outside. Perth is well known for its urban sprawl. In both 1997 and 1998 the population grew by approximately 1.8%, exceeding the national growth rate by 0.6%. Almost 60% of this growth happened in outer suburbs. The outward expansion and division of land into small residential units impinges on land available for agricultural production, and produces a sense of the constant encroachment of urban lifestyles into previously rural settings.

Perth-based policymakers and residents are often viewed by people living in country towns as being disinterested and uninformed about rural issues. Many country people believe that Perth is more focused on developing its connections outside of the state, in spite of the urban reliance on Western Australia's primary industries.

© PAUL A. SOUDERS/CORBIS

The skyline of Perth, Australia, can be seen from this flower garden.

The city of Perth has six sister cities—Kagoshima (Japan), Houston and San Diego (United States), Rhodes and Megisti (Greece), and Vasto (Italy)—as well as charters of mutual friendship with Grenoble (France), Nanjing (China), and Taipei (Taiwan). Perth is becoming a "global city" as investors and others involved in the global economy show increasing interest in locating their businesses and homes there. It is well positioned geographically to develop stronger economic links with Asia, Africa, and the Middle East in investment, trade, migration, and tourism.

Perth is a popular holiday destination, attracting approximately 50,000 overseas visitors in 1997. Some travel guides have characterized the city as "boring" and lacking in charisma, but Perth officials describe it as a growing, vibrant city with "clear sky, clean air, yachts on the river, and beautiful beaches." Perth is known for its sunshine, open spaces, relaxed lifestyle, and friendly people, and for its easy access to a variety of natural environments. It has been described as one of the most livable cities in the world, and some residents claim that it has a strong community spirit and is a good place to raise a family or retire. More critical perceptions allege a growing crime rate, limited trading hours, poor public transport, underutilization of the river, and the lack of a vibrant arts scene. In 1962 astronaut John Glenn christened Perth the "City of Lights" because it was visible from space when he passed overhead, the result of Perth's residents leaving all their lights on in recognition of the journey.

Major Languages. English is the major language spoken in Perth. According to the 1996 census, approximately 72% of residents spoke English as their only language; 2.5% spoke Italian; and 2% spoke Cantonese, Mandarin, or another Chinese language. Many other languages also spoken include Vietnamese, Lebanese, Indonesian, and Greek, but only by comparatively small numbers of people. In 1996, only 0.04% of people claimed to speak Australian Aboriginal languages.

HISTORY

The Origin of the City. The colony that later became the city of Perth was founded on the Swan River by Captain James Stirling in August 1829. The decision to establish a British colony on the western coast of Australia was made partly in response to rumored threats of the French government's ambitions to colonize the land. The British government was unwilling to invest significant capital in the new colony. Instead, it was agreed that all settlers who arrived before 1831 would be allocated land according to the quantity of capital and labor they could provide at their own expense. This encouraged an initial migration of some 25 ships carrying settlers, their families, laborers, livestock, seed, and plants.

Frequent interactions between the new settlers and the local Aboriginal population were largely to the detriment of the indigenous people. Although Aboriginal people were initially nonconfrontational towards the settlers, very different attitudes to property ownership became a major source of conflict. Aboriginal people were often accused of thefts or injury to settlers, resulting in repeated "punitive expeditions" against them. The combination of these and the diseases introduced by the settlers had the effect of reducing the local Aboriginal population by an estimated two-thirds within the first 35 years of settlement.

The Perth colony faced many difficulties in its first years. The main problem was that, contrary to expectations, the land was not well suited to agriculture. Also, the land allocation process was highly disorganized. There was insufficient labor available to clear the land at a rate suitable for establishing self-sufficiency, and the reliance on imported supplies meant that local stores of cash quickly diminished. British convicts were first transported to the colony in 1850, attracting financial assistance from the British government as well as increasing the number of available laborers.

Queen Victoria proclaimed Perth a city in 1856 and the Perth City Council was established in 1858. The last convict was sent to Fremantle in 1868, and shortly afterwards more Chinese laborers were transported from Singapore to maintain the market gardens along the banks of the Swan River. However, as with the Aboriginal people, Chinese immigrants were not readily integrated into the white settler community.

The first substantial period of growth for the city occurred in the 1890s, with the discovery of the Western Australian goldfields. During this period of increasing wealth and population, housing began to spread outward into surrounding suburban settlements. Central Perth began to lose its residents to these surrounding suburbs, and became primarily a business and shopping district.

Migration: Past and Present. Migration has always been a significant source of population growth for Perth. There have been four major waves of inward migration to date. The first was the arrival in 1829–1830 of approximately 1,554 British settlers, attracted by the promise of free land. The second was the arrival of British convicts from 1850 to 1868, accompanied by an equal number of free settlers, primarily women, who were selected to balance the influx of a male convict population. The third, which quadrupled Perth's population, was the 1890s gold rush that attracted many migrants from other Australian colonies. The fourth wave was also significant in terms of population growth, but arguably more so in terms of economic growth and social and cultural change. This was the arrival of European migrants following World War II.

Perth has usually experienced a net increase in population from both interstate and intrastate migration in recent decades. The interstate migration to Western Australia has been attributed to the perceived high levels of economic activity in the state and the high standard of living available. The intrastate migration into Perth has been attributed to the relative lack of opportunities for employment outside of the metropolitan area, particularly following the drought and economic recession of the 1980s.

INFRASTRUCTURE

Public Buildings, Public Works, and Residences. Until recently, many services were the responsibility of either state or local government authorities. Privatization of a number of public organizations and assets, such as the metropolitan bus service, the state bank, and the gas utility, has meant that a number of formerly public buildings are now either partially or completely owned by private companies. Ongoing commitment to privatization means that many buildings currently designated as "public" will likely become private property in the future.

While local governments have control over municipal buildings, libraries, and facilities situated in city parks, state authorities have jurisdiction over other significant public amenities such as hospitals, train stations, law courts, government schools, and publicly owned utilities.

Later public works projects include the development of housing estates, a new industrial park, and the expansion of the public transport system and the metropolitan freeway and highway networks. Development for tourism purposes is extensively funded by the state government, an example of which is the belltower on the Swan River foreshore.

An average Perth house has three or four bedrooms and one or two bathrooms, a kitchen, a dining room, and a lounge area, a laundry room, and a carport or garage. Many homes also have outdoor entertaining areas. For a time the ideal residential property was a quarter-acre block with a single story brick and tile house and a large garden. However, population expansion threatens this ideal, and more people are now living in smaller, inner-city units and apartments. For example, the residential population of the CBD quadrupled between 1996 and 2000. In 1996 just over 70% of residential dwellings in Perth were either owned, or being purchased, by their occupants. Approximately 21% of dwellings were being rented from private owners, and 5% were being rented from the state government.

Politics and City Services. Western Australia's state government operates out of Perth. The parliament consists of representatives from 57 electorates. There are 31 local government areas in the Perth metropolitan region. Local government elections take place irregularly and councillors can be appointed for 1 or 3 year terms. Unlike federal, state, and territory elections, voting at the local government level is voluntary. Local government responsibilities include pest control, vehicle and dog licensing, garbage collection, and the maintenance of streets and parks.

Educational System. Education in Western Australia is compulsory for children aged 5 to 15 years. Kindergarten and informal playgroups are available for children under 5, and at 5 years they go to preprimary for 30 hours a week (full time). From ages 6 to 12 children attend primary school full-time, and from 13 to 17, full-time secondary school. Tertiary education is optional. Some high school graduates take on apprenticeships, while others undertake further study and training at universities or Technical And Further Education (TAFE) institutions.

In 1996, close to 20,000 children attended preschool in Perth, approximately 123,000 attended primary school, and just over 82,000 attended high school. Over half of these children attended government schools, nearly 20% attended privately run Catholic schools, and the remainder attended other nongovernment schools, which are subsidized by government funding. Approximately 56,000 people were attending a university in Perth in 1996, and just under 36,500 were attending TAFE.

Perth has five universities. The oldest is The University of Western Australia, established in 1913. The Western Australian Institute of Technology became Curtin University of Technology in 1987, and Murdoch University was established in 1974. In 1990 Notre Dame, a private Catholic university, was established, and in 1991 The Western Australian College of Advanced Education became Edith Cowan University. All these institutions have home campuses in the metropolitan area.

Transportation System. Western Australia has the world's highest rate of automobile ownership. In 1991 Perth had more than 515 cars per thousand people, and 76% of personal travel was in cars. Increases in population, pollution levels, and traffic congestion suggest that Perth's reliance on cars, vans, and trucks for transport is not sustainable in the long term. Perth's Metropolitan Transport Strategy (1995–2029) seeks to reduce the predominance of automobiles by improving public transport, encouraging cycling and walking as alternatives, and promoting car pooling.

Across Perth there are over 300 scheduled bus routes, 4 suburban train lines, and a ferry link across the Swan River. These are provided on a contract basis to the Western Australian Government Department of Transport. Although Perth's public transport system is generally recognized as being of a high quality, the urban sprawl and lack of demand make it difficult to maintain. Perth's government-regulated taxicab industry consists of around 900 private vehicles and operates on a 24-hour basis.

Heavy freight vehicles play an important role in transporting goods within and outside the Perth region. Although they only constitute 1% of road travel they carry 44% of the total urban freight load. Rail freight is also important for the export of natural resources. There are two major rail freight lines into Perth. The East-West line carries wheat, coal, and minerals interstate while the North-South line carries ores, minerals, and coal from the South West region of Western Australia.

Bulk commodities such as petroleum, grains, livestock, and motor vehicles pass through Fremantle Port. In 1993–1994 the port handled 80% of the state's imports (by value) and 40% of its exports. Its inner harbor also provides facilities for visiting passenger and naval vessels. Air travel provides a crucial link with the rest of the world. In addition to transporting thousands of passengers to and from Perth daily, planes flying in and out of the city air freight around 600 tons of high-value perishable exports interstate and overseas every week. Perth's domestic and international airports are located about 20 minutes from the city center. Four smaller airfields also operate around the metropolitan area.

CULTURAL AND SOCIAL LIFE

Distinctive Features of the City's Cultures. The people of Perth dress predominantly in Western styles, with an emphasis on casual attire except when conducting business or attending formal events. Modes of dress appropriate to particular ethnic communities are also visible. Owing to the warm climate in summer, most people wear lightweight clothing during that season. The threat of skin cancer has led to public announcements encouraging people to wear hats and more clothing that covers greater areas of the body, although many people still choose to disregard this advice.

Australians emphasize equality in their social relations. For example, service people (such as waiters and taxicab drivers) expect to be treated with the same level of respect as professionals (such as accountants and school teachers). Laws exist prohibiting drunkenness, use of indecent language, and indecent behavior in public spaces. Spitting in public is also unacceptable.

The urban environment of Perth is very spacious. There is limited high-rise development outside of the city center, the streets tend to be wide, and pedestrians are less evident than cars in suburban areas. The streetscapes are generally flat and open in appearance. Most suburbs have large shopping centers, containing various shops under a single roof that are surrounded by parking lots. Adolescents often use the shopping centers as meeting places, particularly those who are not old enough to attend the nightclubs and public bars where many young adults spend their recreation time. While some of these bars and nightclubs are located in suburban areas such as Fremantle and coastal suburbs, Northbridge is a popular central location for those going to restaurants and clubs.

Some suburbs, such as Northbridge, Subiaco, and Fremantle, have become inscribed with the histories and biographies of particular migrant communities. The cultural meanings of some places in Perth are also subject to conflicting interpretations by Aboriginal people and others. One public conflict centered on the old Swan Brewery site at the base of Mount Eliza. According to some Nyungar groups, this is an important area and is associated with the Waugal, a creator spirit in the form of a giant snake, believed to reside in and beneath the river. Efforts to develop this site for tourism met with resistance from some local Aboriginal people and their supporters. Aboriginal meanings for the site of the East Perth urban renewal project have been better acknowledged with the incorporation of Nyungar symbols in its design.

Public monuments throughout Perth tend to pay tribute to British pioneers, early officials of the colony, and those who have participated in wars overseas. One monument that recognizes Aboriginal history is a bronze statue of Yagan, a Nyungar leader who was murdered by a young white settler in 1833. The monument is situated on Herisson Island in the Swan River.

Significant emphasis is placed on the outdoor lifestyle available in Perth, and many of the city's parks and public waterways are heavily used by families for barbecues or picnics, joggers, cyclists, swimmers, rowers, and wedding parties. The annual Australia Day Sky Show, a fireworks display held on the evening of January 16, attracts many thousands of Perth residents. People gather early in the morning to claim prime viewing spots along the Swan River.

Cuisine. Eating habits in private homes have not been researched. However, it is fair to assume that they are in line with the rest of Australia. Some of the trends in food consumption in the Australian diet include decreased consumption of meat, increased consumption of seafood, fruits, vegetables, and dairy products, decreased consumption of oils and sugars, increased consumption of coffee, wine, and carbonated drinks, and decreased consumption of beer and tea.

Perth has a large number of restaurants and public eating places. The range of cuisines available reflects the variety of migrant communities. They include Greek, Italian, Irish, Vietnamese, Indonesian, Thai, Malaysian, Korean, Japanese, Chinese, and Ethiopian. Tourism guides advertise fresh seafood as a specialty, particularly in Fremantle, and there has been an increase in the availability of native Australian foods, such as kangaroo, emu, and crocodile in restaurants and stores. In Perth, smoking is illegal in most eating establishments owing to legislation.

Particularly in the summer months, outdoor eating becomes a popular option in Perth's restaurants and parklands. In many parks, free electric barbecues are provided by local councils.

Ethnic, Class, and Religious Diversity. At the time of the 1996 census, approximately 30% of the Perth population had been born overseas and most of these overseas-born residents were from the United Kingdom and Ireland (about 44%), Southeast Asia (about 14%), and southern Europe (about 11%). Aboriginal and Torres Strait Islanders accounted for 1.4% of the population. Class diversity, as indicated by income levels, is limited. For example, the income levels recorded in 1996 indicated that a fifth of Perth households had a weekly income of A$300 or less, the median household income was A$500–699, and a fifth of the population had a weekly income of A$1,200 or more. The majority of Perth residents belonged to Christian religions, with Catholics and Anglicans the most common. Less than 3% were members of non-Christian religions, and a fifth belong to no religion.

There is evidence of class and ethnic segregation. The western suburbs have high percentages of people with high income levels, tertiary education, and employment in the managerial, administrative, and professional sectors. The eastern suburbs, in contrast, have high percentages of people with low incomes, no postsecondary qualifications, and high unemployment. Migrants tend to settle in distinctive patterns: those from southern Europe who arrived in the 1950s and 1960s tended to settle in suburbs where land was available for market gardening and in suburbs close to the city center that supported manufacturing industries. Later immigrants from England and Ireland, on the other hand, tended to settle in the emerging suburbs on the fringes of the Perth metropolitan area in the northern coastal region. This is also the most common location for first-home-buying families with young children. Religious communities are not recorded as occupying particular areas of the Perth suburbs, and are dispersed throughout the metropolitan region.

Family and Other Social Support Systems. The dominant family form is nuclear, comprised of a male and female adult and their dependent children. Other common family forms include the couple with no dependent children and the single parent with dependent children. According to the 1996 Census, most households in Perth contained one family, with only 1% of households having more than one family. However, 8% of households with Aboriginal inhabitants include more than one family.

Government and community organizations provide a range of social support systems. Many migrant communities have established clubs that offer support and the opportunity to share interests and cultural activities. Some Perth suburban councils provide community centers and clubs for specific groups such as local youth or new mothers. Another community-based program is Neighborhood Watch, in which members watch over each other's property as a means of combating crime and improving the local sense of security. Several means of income support and housing assistance are available from the state government, and food, clothing, furnishings, and personal assistance are among the items distributed by volunteer and religious organizations.

Work and Commerce. The most common occupational category of employees in Perth is professionals, which includes engineers, scientists, information specialists, and medical practitioners; and intermediate clerical, sales and services workers (receptionists, bank workers, child care givers, and sales representatives). The industries that employ the most people are retail, property, and business services; manufacturing; and health and community services. The industries that employ the most women are health and community services, and the industry that employs the most men is manufacturing.

Arts and Recreation. The government sponsors many artistic and cultural activities in Perth, including a number of arts festivals. The most prominent of these festivals is the Perth International Arts Festival, which is held each year in January and February and features local, national, and international performances, visual arts, and music events. Other prominent festivals include the annual Awesome Children's Arts Festival, the Alternative Artrage Festival, the Fremantle Festival, and the annual Spring in the Valley Festival. Northbridge is also host to many street parades, one of the most visible and controversial being the annual Gay Pride parade.

Over 12% of the Western Australian population over the age of 15 contributed to the arts and culture industry in 1996, and more than half of these were unpaid. More than 30% of people participate in organized sport or physical activities, which constitute a distinctive part of Perth's urban popular culture. Australian rules football and national and international cricket matches, for example, attract large numbers of spectators, and there are high participation rates in sports such as aerobics, golf, netball, and Australian rules football. Soccer is increasing in popularity as a participant and spectator sport, and the state team is gathering a strong following. The central city foreshore is also host to an annual motor rally, a popular spectator event.

QUALITY OF LIFE

The most commonly used indicator of cost of living in Australia is the cost of housing. The 1991 Housing Affordability paper concluded that Australians had comparatively better access to home ownership than those in New Zealand and the United Kingdom, but were disadvantaged compared to those in the United States. Housing costs in Perth are comparatively lower than in several other Australian cities, especially Sydney, but people on low incomes still have limited access to adequate housing. Single parents and single elderly people, in particular, were required to spend 30–40% of their incomes on housing costs, according to the 1991 figures. There are an estimated 15,000 homeless people in Western Australia. An annual event in Perth encourages people to sleep outdoors in selected public venues for one night in winter to raise funds and awareness for homelessness issues.

Perth residents have a life expectancy at birth of 81.3 years for women and 75.4 years for men. The most common cause of death is heart disease, followed by cancer. Infectious and parasitic diseases account for only 1% of deaths in Western Australia, compared to 2.2% of deaths resulting from road traffic accidents. Health care, as elsewhere in Australia, is available free or heavily subsidized by a national Medicare system paid for with taxes, as well as through private health insurance schemes. There is a heavy public emphasis on prevention of disease, for example by advertising the dangers of skin cancer, a diet high in fats and sugars, and cigarette smoking.

Western Australia has a high rate of crime compared to other Australian states. The most common crime in Western Australia is theft. Assault and murder rates remain comparatively low.

The primary environmental problems are water use and air pollution. Sprinkler bans are placed on gardens during the summer months to conserve limited freshwater supplies. The Swan River has good water quality considering it flows through a large city. However, algal blooms in some sections of the river suggest that this is under threat. Air pollution is a constant concern, particularly because Perth is a car dominated city. During the 1990s records showed acceptable and declining levels of air pollutants, with the exception of ozone, which occasionally reached unacceptable levels.

The city of Perth is one of only a few local municipalities in Western Australia to have a City Environment Plan. It is also a member of the international Cities for Climate Protection Program, and runs a series of Greening the City projects, which emphasize tree planting and landscaping.

Salinity is a major environmental threat to the agricultural districts of Western Australia. Predictions estimate that up to 30% of the state's agricultural land could be rendered nonproductive as a result of increasing salinity levels. The impact of reduced agricultural production on Perth's economy is potentially very significant in the long term.

FUTURE OF THE CITY

The Australian Bureau of Statistics predicts that by 2029, Perth's bicentenary year, the city's population will be around 2 million. The government's vision for Perth's future includes increasing international economic and tourism connections, improving housing and education, developing more effective use of information technologies, and making it a more "livable" city by planning further development in the metropolitan region around urban villages. As its population continues to grow, urban containment and inner-city urban renewal and revitalization, along with a greater emphasis on environmental protection and efficient use of natural resources, are important priorities for Perth if it is to become a sustainable city.

BIBLIOGRAPHY

Appleyard, R. T., and Toby Manford, *The Beginning: European Discovery and Early Settlement of Swan River Western Australia* (University of Western Australia Press 1979).

Driesen, I. H. Vanden, *Essays on Immigration Policy and Population in Western Australia 1850–1901* (University of Western Australia Press 1986).

Horton, D., ed., *Encyclopedia of Aboriginal Australia* (Aboriginal Studies Press 1994).

Seddon, George, *Swan Song: Reflections of Perth and Western Australia 1856–1995* (Centre for Studies in Australian Literature 1995).

Seddon, George, and David Ravine, *A City and Its Setting: Images of Perth, Western Australia* (Fremantle Arts Press 1986).

Stannage, C. T., *The People of Perth: A Social History of Western Australia's Capital City* (Perth City Council 1979).

Useful Web Sites

www.abs.gov.au/ausstats [Australian Bureau of Statistics].

www.wa.gov.au [the official website of the government of Western Australia].

David Trigger *and* Raelene Wilding *and* Jane Mulcock

Philadelphia

United States

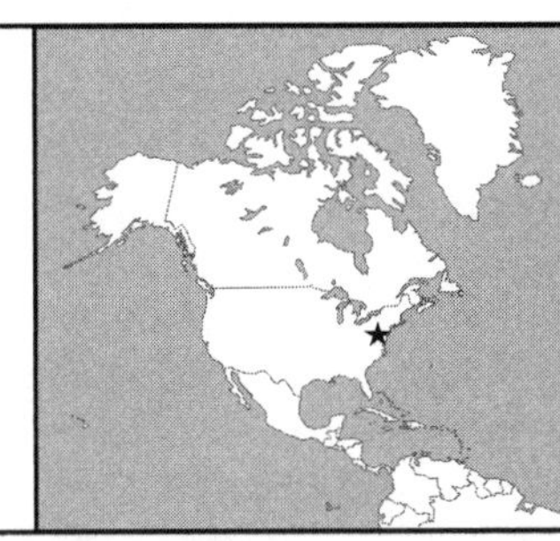

ORIENTATION

Name of City. *Philadelphia,* derived from Latin roots to signify "city of brotherly love," was the name given by William Penn in 1683 to the new settlement he founded as leader of a dissenting religious group, the Society of Friends, or Quakers. Penn carefully planned the layout of a "green country town" within the colony of Pennsylvania, or Penn's Wood, which later became one of the original states within the United States of America. Residents often refer to the city by the sobriquet *Philly.*

Location. Located at 39° north latitude and 75° west longitude, at the convergence of the Delaware and Schuylkill rivers, Philadelphia is a port linked to the mid-Atlantic coast via the Delaware.

Population. The city of Philadelphia had a population of 1.5 million according to the 2000 U.S. census, and it ranked fifth in the nation. The city is located in a growing Metropolitan Statistical Area comprised of 4.9 million people including the central city, four counties in Pennsylvania, and three in New Jersey. While the central city increased in population size and density until the 1960s, it has subsequently lost population to the suburbs. Secondary business districts have grown up in the suburbs as new residential home, industrial park, and shopping mall construction have produced suburban sprawl.

Distinctive and Unique Features. Philadelphia's site was selected because of its potential as a seaport with access to the Atlantic Ocean via the Delaware River. The city served as a major port link to England during the colonial period in the 18th century. At the same time, the central location of the city within the colonies made it the site of major political events, including production of the U.S. Declaration of Independence and the Constitution. Independence National Park contains several icons of this period, such as the Liberty Bell and Independence Hall. In the 19th century Philadelphia became the largest industrial city on the Atlantic rim, and it served as a gateway for several waves of labor immigration from various European nations.

The city, in spite of its former economic and political centrality, is generally low in density and has predominantly low-rise housing. Residents and media often refer to Philadelphia as a "city of neighborhoods," referring to the small-town nature of localities, which tend to be marked as ethnic communities. The city had no notable skyline until the last quarter of the 20th century. An informal "gentlemen's agreement" prevailed, which prohibited skyscrapers by restricting buildings to the height of William Penn's hat atop the dome over the center of City Hall. Furthermore, Penn's original plan incorporated many green squares, which still remain today. The Fairmount Park system is the largest in-city park system in the United States. The city has a high proportion of individual homeowners, as opposed to renters, and the residential housing stock, even in the city's center, are predominantly row homes.

In the 20th century the city declined as the result of deindustrialization, which kept density low. In the last quarter of the 20th century, however, when economic restructuring increased the importance of service industries providing professional education, financial, legal, and business services as well as real estate development, there was pressure to develop a new image as a dynamic and cosmopolitan center with many new skyscrapers forming a recognizable cityscape.

Relationships Between the City and the Outside. Philadelphia's former positions as a major port in the colonial period and as a major center of industry and export in the 19th century made it the largest city in the United States until the construction of the Erie Canal enhanced the position of New York City. Philadelphia produced both regionally oriented consumer goods, such as textiles, and larger capital goods, such as heavy machinery and transportation equipment for the national economy.

The city, like other rustbelt northeastern cities in the second half of the 20th century, lost much of its industrial base to the new industrial areas of the southwestern United States and to offshore production in the rest of the world. At the same time, many of the new professional and managerial workplaces and their workers moved to the suburbs. As a restructuring service economy, Philadelphia has a restricted regional hinterland competing with nearby New York, Baltimore, and Washington, D.C., to provide financial and business services. It houses a small number of corporate headquarters. Since the construction of a major convention center and the related increase in hotel capacity, increasingly sophisticated restaurants, and such recreational venues as the Avenue of the Arts, the city has increased its marketing to international, national, and local tourists. Higher education and medical education and health care are the other major industries that draw consumers from a regional, national, and international base.

Major languages. English is the official language in Philadelphia. Although there are many immigrant groups in the city, Spanish is the only alternative language for which translations are available on some commercial and public documents. Commercial signs in Spanish, Korean, Vietnamese, and other immigrant languages are found in some neighborhoods.

HISTORY

The Origin of the City. Philadelphia, a city 5 square kilometers (2 square miles) in size, was founded and developed by members of the Society of Friends under the leadership of William Penn. The planned city, which stretched from the Delaware River port in the east to the Schuylkill in the west, had a grid pattern for selling lots and included many green spaces, squares, and gardens. The surrounding county of Philadelphia consisted of agricultural land and small towns. Population and activities in colonial Philadelphia was highly concentrated. Walking was the major mode of human transportation and workplaces (the docks, mercantile warehouses, and artisan shops), zones of leisure activities, and homes for all classes were crowded together along the Delaware. Servants, porters, and other laborers lived in alleyways near their employers.

By the second half of the 19th century, the city had become a major industrial site. Towns along the rivers, such as Kensington and Manayunk, became mill towns, attracting new Irish immigrants to work in expanding factory production. The working classes lived in small row homes built for workers within walking distance of the factories. They built a community life around nationality based churches and extended families. New but costly fixed-route transportation produced a system that allowed the expanding managerial classes to move to larger new houses on big lots in "streetcar suburbs" in the north and west. In 1854 the city annexed the entire Philadelphia County, moving from 5 square kilometers (2 square miles) to 260 square kilometers (100 square miles). The city now incorporated the mill towns and new suburbs and created new metropolitan transportation, regulation, taxation, policing, and firefighting systems.

Migration: Past and Present. While the original Pennsylvania colony was settled primarily by English speaking Protestants, there are place-name reminders of small Swedish and German settlements. During industrialization in the 19th century, the city experienced several European immigration waves, including, in midcentury, Irish and German laborers. The largest wave of immigration occurred between 1880 and 1920, when European ships often came directly to Philadelphia and not via New York. This wave included southern and eastern Europeans. The former came from the southern regions of Italy and from Slavic speaking Russia, Poland, and the Baltic and Balkan regions. Eastern European Jewish immigration was significant as well. The entry settlement for most immigrants was South Philadelphia, which teemed with varied languages and food outlets.

The city was also a major destination for African Americans. There were small numbers of free blacks in Philadelphia during the colonial period and others arrived from the South before and after the Civil War. African Americans were clustered with Irish laborers in the south of the colonial city. The most significant wave of black in-migration occurred during and between the two world wars, as the city became an important point of new settlement for rural Southern blacks. African Americans, settling in Philadelphia in increasing numbers during the 1950s and 1960s, entered a declining and segregated economy.

Postwar black in-migration occurred along with suburbanization, producing white flight and racial segregation. Like most older industrial cities in the Northeast, Philadelphia was strongly affected by the flight of middle-class populations to the newly built residential suburbs in the surrounding counties. The new suburbanites were the children of turn-of-the-century immigrants who moved into the mainstream through government-sponsored college educations and mortgage subsidies. Soon, workplaces began to relocate to suburban industrial parks and malls that were located near strategic highway intersections. The new communities were established in over 300 local municipalities in which suddenly there was a need to provide schooling, policing, and transportation for local residents. There was little regional or cross-municipal cooperation between these fragmented political entities.

The downturn in the local economy at the start of the 21st century has reduced the role of the city as an immigrant destination. Philadelphia ranked 16th as a destination for the wave of Latin American, Caribbean, and Asian immigrants. However, owing to the overall population loss in the city, new immigrants (entering a racially divided city) totaled about 10% of Philadelphia's population.

INFRASTRUCTURE

Public Buildings, Public Works, and Residences. From a crowded warren of colonial buildings clustered along the Delaware River, Philadelphia's central business district has continued to move westward. City Hall, an ornate multiblock French Second Empire–style structure in the center of the city, was built in the late 19th century just west of the new department store pioneered by John Wanamaker. The early 20th century art deco city grew nearby. Development plans of the mid-20th century moved the expanding business, legal, and financial center even further west of city hall to modernist office towers. A skyscraper building boom occurred in the 1980s after a successful campaign against the height restriction.

In the 1970s an attempt was made to reclaim the decaying commercial zone east of City Hall to compete with suburban malls. This failed to stem the area's decline until the construction of the Convention Center in the early 1990s, which spurred investment in a zone of tourist consumption: hotels, restaurants, and upscale shopping. While the city marketed itself as a tourist destination, upscale zones locations such as Rittenhouse Row and the Avenue of the Arts were packaged as sites for investment.

New investment in the downtown spurred gentrification and a "return to the city" residential movement for young urban professionals. Most of the housing stock in Philadelphia was built before World War II. High-rise homes are relatively rare in the city. Upscale examples are located predominantly to take advantage of views along the rivers, along the 19th-century Benjamin Franklin Parkway (reminiscent of European boulevards), and around the squares.

Gentrified neighborhoods focus on rehabilitating or fitting in new construction that blends with the older artisan and worker row homes. These were tall and narrow three-story homes consisting of small rooms stacked one above the other; they were clustered together on narrow streets and in alleys near what was later Independence National Park. Nearby, Elfreth's Alley is described as the oldest continuously inhabited block in the United States. Gentrification began in the original colonial city, later called Society Hill, in the 1970s and continued in other older housing areas on the margins of center city, such as Queen Village (southeast), the Art Museum area (northwest), and Olde City (northeast); an old warehouse district was converted to lofts for artists and designers. These investments dislocated poor and working-class people and shrank the pool of available affordable housing.

Larger homes on landscaped lots in several late-19th and early-20th-century streetcar suburbs were also restored and maintained, including Victorian Powelton Village (west of the Schuykill River) and West Mount Airy–Chestnut Hill. Other areas, such as much of west Philadelphia and Strawberry Mansion, were subdivided by landlords into high-density, multifamily apartments.

Postwar suburban housing responded to the automobile by expanding in the surrounding suburban counties. For example, two of the three Levittowns, emblems of U.S. middle-class suburban housing, were built outside of Philadelphia. The Great Northeast, inside the city, remained farmland until after the war. There new communities of homes range from modern attached row houses to twins to substantial single houses on larger lots.

Along with displacement caused by gentrification, the demolition of most postwar high-rise public housing for the poor created a housing crisis. Much of the old housing for workers lies outside zones of investment in blighted areas with high rates of vacant homes and substandard housing. Seven thousand city blocks have at least one abandoned house, and 62% of these blocks have more than one vacant structure. The blight issue is a major focus of city policy. Many sealed homes are subject to squatting and drug activities. Local community-based organizations are involved in antiblight activities through federal housing programs. These include attempts to rehabilitate structures or to demolish them. Empty lots are used to construct limited amounts of new suburban type housing. Other less costly programs emphasize such nonresidential uses as parks, play areas, and community gardens. Beautification programs attempt to remove graffiti from local walls and to replace it with community sponsored murals. Today, Philadelphia claims to have among the most mural walls in the United States.

Politics and City Services. After Philadelphia's early political importance to the nation, historians described local politics as increasingly subordinate to private interests. Civic ventures depended on the whims of private philanthropy rather than on public responsibility.

The city is chartered by Pennsylvania state government, which controls taxation and the Home Rule

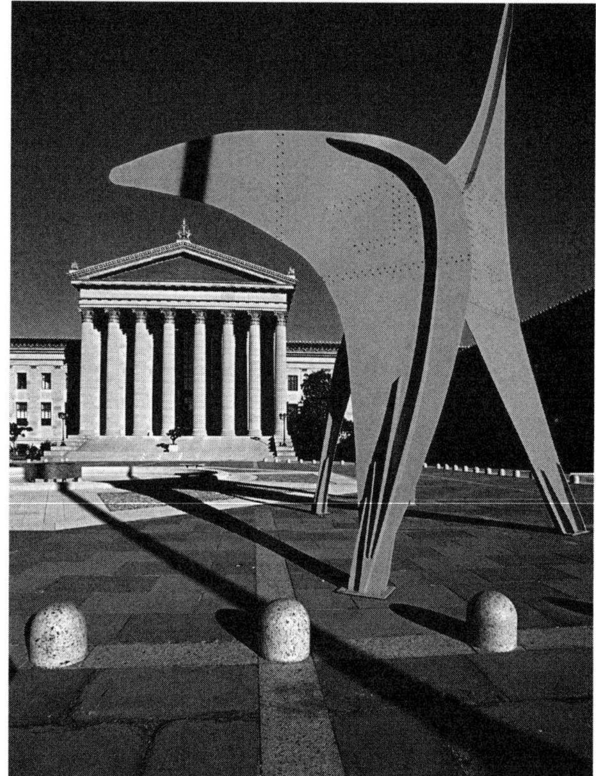

© DAVE G. HOUSER/CORBIS

An Alexander Calder sculpture, *Eagle*, stands in front of the Philadelphia Museum of Art.

Charter. The state, heavily rural in its center and increasingly suburban, has long been dominated by anti-Philadelphia interests. In the 19th century the state constructed a transportation infrastructure of canals and highways linking parts of the state to other Atlantic ports, bypassing the city. Now the fragmented suburban municipalities turn their backs on initiatives for regional cooperation. Governance of the regional transportation system is fraught with conflict over local interests. Attempts to equalize school funding bases are similarly problematic.

The city of Philadelphia, where the remaining residents are poorer, older, and sicker than those who left for the suburbs, relies on a shrinking real-estate tax base. The city also relies on a wage tax as a major source of income, levying the tax on all residents whether they work in the city or not as well as on nonresidents who work in the city (the latter are taxed at a lower rate). The city sales tax is also 1% higher than in the rest of the state. The paradox of these taxes is under constant debate. The income tax, while necessary, also discourages businesses from locating in the city, and residents from living or consuming there.

Philadelphia is governed by a mayor and a city council, each with strong powers. Until the 1950s local government was dominated by manufacturing and banking interests through the Republican party political machine. In the 1950s a newly ascendant Democratic reform movement took over. It was based on a coalition of the city's strong labor movement, emerging African American political leaders representing the growing number of minority voters, and the new professional and managerial elite representing the expanding service industries of center city: finance, insurance, legal and business services, and real estate development. The reformers put their faith in technocratic planning and expertise to revitalize the downtown. This led to a series of projects, such as expressway links, commuter rail links, the convention center, and the Avenue of the Arts. These projects favored downtown economic interests and the needs of new professional and managerial residents, suburbanites, and long-distance tourists as consumers of arts and leisure.

In the 1970s and 1980s a neighborhoods movement responded to these projects, which had diverted tax money and private capital away from poor and working class neighborhoods. As industrial job loss weakened the political strength of labor unions, the working class expressed their political demands through neighborhood-based campaigns for bank mortgage lending to their neighborhoods and better schools and against neighborhood-destroying expressway locations and gentrification.

Since the late 1960s African Americans with increasing demographic strength have ascended politically and were significantly represented in the mayoralty and on the city council. New immigrant groups with much smaller numbers seek political power through alliances with African Americans. Between 1990 and the turn of the century, Latinos became more visible and effective in political life.

Educational System. Schools in Philadelphia are funded through real estate taxes, which have declined with the suburbanization of the middle class and the closing and relocation of businesses. At the same time, federal support for urban schools has declined and the state legislature has stood firmly against increasing aid to Philadelphia schools. Teachers' salaries are relatively low, and older school buildings are overcrowded and in bad repair.

Among cities in the United States, Philadelphia always has had one of the highest proportions of students attending private schools. These schools include a large number of Catholic schools that were built for the predominantly Catholic labor immigrants, and a system of Quaker schools as well as other elite private schools. The demand for private schools increased with the growing perception that public schools were diminished in quality. This resulted in declining political support for the public schools.

Attempts to improve public education included strengthening the mayor's control over the formerly autonomous school board, decentralization of control over local schools, the increase of specialized magnet schools with enhanced programs, and the creation of 34 publicly funded but relatively autonomous charter schools.

Transportation System. The Southeastern Pennsylvania Transportation Authority, or SEPTA, runs a system of subway lines and bus routes in the city and a commuter rail line that connects the city and the suburbs. Public transportation suffered severely as a result of suburbanization and growing dependence on the automobile. The cost of public transportation is expensive relative to other cities, and its low ridership means routes are not served frequently, which in turn further lowers ridership.

The likelihood of improved public transportation is limited because there are no penalties for using cars. A study released in 2000 showed that people in Greater Philadelphia spent less time stalled in traffic over the year than people in most other large cities; eventually the cost and availability of parking in the city became a real disincentive.

The regional rail line is costly to ride, and while it effectively brings middle-class, suburban workers and shoppers into the city, it does not connect the suburbs to each other. It also fails to serve the newly agglomerated areas where industrial parks and shopping malls are located at highway intersections. Consequently, a crisis developed in which the growing unskilled job market of janitorial, retail, and data-input work located at these sites could not connect with the unskilled workers who lived mostly in the city.

Philadelphia was relatively late in completing a ring of expressways around the city. The Blue Route, the final link, was completed in 1992. This alleviated some of the traffic congestion on the roads between city and the suburbs and between the suburbs. On the other hand, as urban sprawl moved housing farther away from the city, the road capacities were not upgraded, creating several zones of heavy congestion, especially between suburban areas.

CULTURE AND SOCIAL LIFE

Distinctive Features of the City's Cultures. People refer to particular locales within Philadelphia in ethnic terms, such as Chinatown, South Philly (Italian American), and Port Richmond (Polish American). These links reflect the past locations of ethnic institutions (nationality parishes, markets and mutual aid societies) more than present residential populations. By the 21st century, the city was more clearly demarcated by race and class than by ethnic origin. Olney, in North Philadelphia, is the most multicultural section of the city, with over 50 nationalities represented. It features stores purveying foods and items from all over the world, each marked by signs in different languages. The old Chinatown near the center of the city later became the site of businesses owned by more recent Asian immigrants, such as Chinese from Hong Kong and Taiwan as well as Southeast Asians.

Cuisine. Since 1990 Philadelphia has become known for its restaurants, both ethnic and high cuisine. In the 1970s center city experienced a restaurant renaissance. Once seen as a culinary wasteland, many small storefronts with creative chef owners "fused" such cuisines as French and Thai. A restaurant school emerged to teach culinary arts and management. Upscale French restaurants developed national reputations. Today there is stiff competition between restaurants that serve Asian fusion, Latino fusion, and other experimental cuisines in highly styled ambience. The city runs an annual Cook and Book event at which visiting celebrity chefs partner with local restaurants to produce new menus.

One well known example of Italian street food, formerly available only in Philadelphia, the Philly cheese-steak sandwich has now spread across the nation and is even found on menus outside of the United States. The city also claims to have originated the submarine sandwich, which is locally called a hoagie. South Philadelphia is full of classic and nouveau Italian food outlets. New immigrant groups and rural Southern soul foods also contribute to an ethnic cuisine variety that has become popular with the city's young, urban professionals.

Ethnic, Class, and Religious Diversity. By 2000, the city proper was 6% Hispanic and 3% Asian, with the remaining 90% or so divided relatively equally between whites and blacks. The suburban areas, on the other hand, were predominantly white with fewer than 10% African Americans and small numbers of Asians and Latinos.

Significant shifts in ethnic identity occurred after World War II when many descendants of turn-of-the-century immigrants married across ethnic boundaries or left ethnic enclaves for the suburbs. As increasing numbers of blacks moved into the city from the rural South, a pattern of segregation developed with white-dominated areas in the east and black areas in the west. Since 1960 the color lines have continued to shift as integration develops on the boundaries. One exception to this pattern is the generation-old successful and deliberately integrated middle-class neighborhood of West Mount Airy in the northwest of the city.

Philadelphia is spatially divided by income as well. Households in the center, the surrounding zones of gentrification, and the northeast and northwest city borders have the highest income. The poorest households are in North, West and Southwest Philadelphia.

New demographic clusters of cultural diversity are developing from the post-1965 new immigration. Spanish speakers from Puerto Rico, the Dominican Republic, and Colombia, as well as several other Central American and South American nations are clustered in 14 contiguous census tracts in a narrow north to south corridor in North Philadelphia, between white neighborhoods in the east and black neighborhoods in the west. Southeast Asian refugees, predominantly Vietnamese, placed by state

© APRIL SAUL/CORBIS

Street musicians, hoping to receive money from passers-by, play in front of an Italian market in Philadelphia, Pennsylvania.

refugee resettlement agencies, are clustered in two locations: one near South Philadelphia, where they took over many businesses in the "Italian Market." Koreans, Asian Indians, and Pakistanis frequently settle in Olney or the suburbs. African immigrant settlements are found in West Philadelphia.

Early Philadelphia was dominated by white Protestants. Irish and German immigration brought in the first wave of Catholics, prompting anti-Catholic riots in the mid-19th century. Philadelphia became an increasingly Catholic city with the turn-of-the-century Italian and Slavic migrations. It was also the second-largest U.S. destination for eastern European Jews. Later immigration further increased diversity. The Islamic community is estimated at between 25,000 and 30,000, and it includes Black Muslims, Palestinians, Albanians, Sudanese, and Pakistanis. Hindu and Buddhist congregations also formed.

Family and Other Support Systems. The professional and managerial middle classes are less inclined to spend time with, or to depend for economic assistance on kin. Other segments of the citizenry, such as poor and working-class white ethnics who are descendants of turn-of-the-century immigrants and African Americans who moved from the rural South in the 20th century, are both heavily embedded in webs of obligation to their extended or fictive kin. Much of the latter groups' leisure time is spent with relatives, and significant exchanges of food, child-care services, and goods and cash flow between households. Moreover, the immigrants of all classes from Latin America, Asia, the Caribbean, and Africa tend to rely on networks of kin as initial hosts, and to help locate work and housing; entrepreneurs depend on family labor, and they borrow capital through formal and informal loan groups.

Community life in the early 20th century was based on the church, ethnic clubs, sports teams, and men's and women's service organizations, which were loosely connected to political parties. Today, while churches are still important, community life is often structured by state agencies for the purposes of self-help economic development, such as housing rehabilitation, local entrepreneurship, clean up and beautification, and town watch.

Work and Commerce. In the service economy Philadelphia no longer exported manufactured goods but instead provided health care, education, and hospitality for regional, national, and international consumers. Philadelphia's biggest employers include universities and health-care institutions, as well as services for businesses, such as accounting and law. A growing hospitality industry of hotels and restaurants emerged as part of the city's development strategy. The city once was dominated by skilled and semiskilled unionized factory jobs earning a family wage. A two-tier labor market emerged with an expanding number of high-end skilled workers and increased numbers of low-end unskilled workers in insecure jobs in sanitary services, food services, data input and health care. Limited manufacturing work remained in small, flexible, nonunion sewing and metalworking shops, which subcontract to larger firms. Many workers produced luxury goods for upscale consumers, such as fresh and new varieties of produce, handmade prepared foods, and baked goods.

At the same time, the shopping strips of mom-and-pop stores in the older neighborhoods were initially hurt by the increase in centralized suburban shopping malls featuring national chain stores. To some extent, these strips were revived by immigrant entrepreneurs.

Arts and Recreation. As part of economic development oriented toward tourists and suburban customers, the city launched a project to develop an Avenue of the Arts near its center. This entertainment space contains two concert halls, theaters, and an arts-oriented university and high school. These venues, along with two significant fine arts museums and a gallery zone in Olde City—as well as a dozen repertory theater companies—produce predominantly "high culture" events aimed at the upscale market of tourists and suburbanites. An international film festival and a festival of fringe performances became annual events. The city is a major center for popular music and is important in the history of jazz, rock and roll, and rap, as well as to the recording industry. The Avenue of the Arts features stars embedded in the sidewalk inscribed with the names of great local musicians.

The city fields major teams in baseball, football, basketball, hockey, and soccer. Sports generate tax revenue and also will require major public investment, since the professional teams are pressuring the city to build and maintain a large stadium complex. The many area college sports teams help to make the city very sports conscious, and Philadelphia fans have a reputation for being hard to please.

QUALITY OF LIFE

Philadelphia is a city divided between wealth and poverty and contains many stark contrasts between them, from the new downtown cityscape to the war-zone appearance of blocks of abandoned homes and factories. In general the housing market is relatively affordable, especially compared to other major Atlantic coast cities. The proliferation of teaching hospitals provides a high standard of medical care, although health care is not evenly distributed. The public health system, restructured in the 1960s, does not serve the poor well. The city suffers from high rates of AIDS (acquired immune deficiency syndrome), substance abuse, infant mortality, and homelessness. The crime rate in the city, like most other major American cities, rose with the increased drug trade in the 1980s and fell in the 1990s; crime is unevenly distributed in the city with poor neighborhoods most vulnerable. The image of a city of neighborhoods competes with North Philadelphia's reputation as "the badlands," a drug supermarket often mentioned in bestselling books, national newspapers, films, and television programs.

FUTURE OF THE CITY

There are two imagined scenarios for the future of Philadelphia. In one, the city recoups its former position as a major urban center by finding a way to compete successfully with other cities to market itself as an international city, a major tourist destination, or a new site for high-technology innovation. In the other scenario, the city continues to lose population but takes advantage of its new, smaller scale to become a more livable, green place. Neither of these scenarios includes a place for the increasing numbers of poor people who live in substandard housing and receive substandard education and health care. Any plan for the future must find a way to deal with the needs of these people in an environment with little political will to publicly support social services. The future is unclear in an economic environment in which the "rustbelt" cities of the Northeast are pitted against each other in attempts to capture the newer industries of the high-tech economy and the high-income consumers of the postindustrial landscape.

BIBLIOGRAPHY

The following agencies produce periodic forecasts and planning documents for the city and region: Delaware Valley Regional Planning Commission; Pennsylvania

Economy League, Eastern Division; Philadelphia City Planning Commission.

Adams, Carolyn, et al., *Philadelphia: Neighborhoods, Division and Conflict in a Postindustrial City* (Temple University Press 1991).

Anderson, Elijah, *Streetwise: Race, Class and Change in an Urban Community* (University of Chicago Press 1990).

Baltzell, Digby, *Philadelphia Gentlemen: The Making of a National Upper Class* (Free Press 1958).

Bissinger, Buzz, *A Prayer for the City* (Random House 1997).

Davis, Allen F., and Mark Haller, *The Peoples of Philadelphia: A History of Ethnic Groups and Lower Class Life, 1790–1940* (Temple University Press 1970).

Du Bois, W. E. B., *The Philadelphia Negro* (1899; reprint, University of Pennsylvania Press 1996).

Ershkowitz, Miriam, and Joseph Zikmund, eds., *Black Politics in Philadelphia* (Basic Books 1973).

Golab, Carolyn, *Immigrant Destinations* (Temple University Press 1977).

Goode, Judith, and Jo Anne Schneider, *Reshaping Ethnic and Racial Relations in Philadelphia: Immigrants in a Divided City* (Temple University Press 1994).

Goode, Judith, "The Contingent Construction of Local Identities: Koreans and Puerto Ricans in Philadelphia," *Identities*, 5, vol. 1 (1998): 33–64.

Hershberg, Theodore, ed., *Philadelphia: Work, Space, Family and Group Experience in the Nineteenth Century* (Oxford 1981).

Luce, Thomas, and Anita Summers, *Local Fiscal Issues in the Philadelphia Metropolitan Area* (University of Pennsylvania Press 1987).

Scranton, Philip, *Proprietary Capitalism: The Textile Manufacture at Philadelphia, 1800–1885* (Temple University Press 1983).

Smith, Neil, "Society Hill," *The New Urban Frontier: The Revanchist City* (Routledge 1996).

Summers, Anita, and Thomas F. Luce, *Economic Development Within the Philadelphia Metropolitan Area* (University of Pennsylvania Press 1987).

Warner, Sam Bass, *The Private City: Philadelphia in Three Periods of Growth*, 2d ed. (University of Pennsylvania Press 1987).

Yancey, William, and Eugene Ericksen, "The Antecedents of Community: The Economic and Institutional Structure of Urban Neighborhoods," *American Sociological Review* 44 (1979): 253–62.

JUDITH GOODE

Phnom Penh

Cambodia

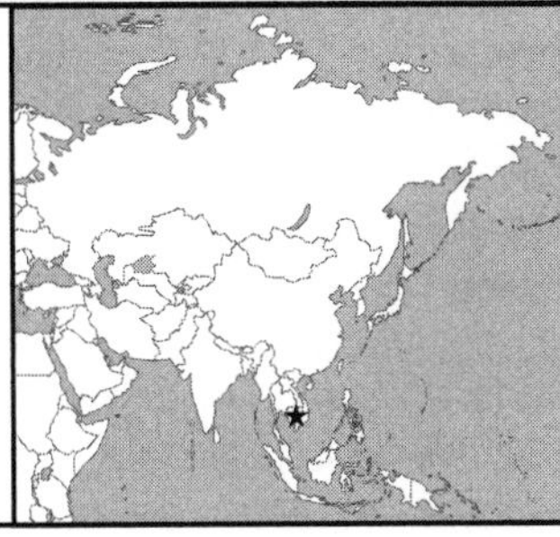

ORIENTATION

Name of City. Phnom Penh derives its name from a small artificial hill (*phnom*) in the north of the city. Legend holds that a major flood struck the area in the 14th century. When the flood subsided, a wealthy local woman by the name of Penh found four Buddha images wedged in a hole in a tree. She instructed the local people to build a hill there as the site of a Buddhist sanctuary. This became known as the hill of Penh (*Phnom Penh*). The site remains a major landmark in the city to this day.

Location. Phnom Penh is located at the confluence of the Mekong, Bassac, and Tonle Sap rivers in central Cambodia, 290 kilometers (180 miles) from the Gulf of Thailand. It is located at 11°35′ north latitude and 104°55′ east longitude.

Population. Phnom Penh's population is estimated at 1 million people residing on 290 square kilometers (112 square miles) of land. In addition, as many as 200,000 to 300,000 temporary migrants may enter the city following the rice planting period or during other slack periods in agricultural labor. These migrants work in construction, drive pedicabs, and engage in other types of labor until farming work picks up. The city consists of four densely settled urban districts, known as Khand in Khmer, and three sparsely populated rural districts, known as Srok. The latter remain largely agricultural, although recent years have seen significant residential development in these areas.

Distinctive and Unique Features. An estimated 85% of Khmer live in rural areas, and Phnom Penh is by far the largest city in the country. It has more than ten times the population of the next largest city, Battambang, and is unchallenged as the economic, political, and educational heart of Cambodia. It gained this status owing to its location at the confluence of three major rivers, which has made it a strategic point in the exchange of goods between the Cambodian hinterland and the outside world. However, access by river to the South China Sea is via southern Vietnam, and since Cambodia gained independence from French colonial rule in 1953, the constraints this places on the country's economic independence have become a matter of concern. The government has plans to develop Sihanoukville, a southern city on the Gulf of Thailand, as an alternative port.

Prior to the 1970s Phnom Penh was renowned for its tree-lined boulevards and French colonial architecture. However, it suffered considerable damage and decay during the Khmer Rouge revolution of the early 1970s, and their subsequent rule between 1975 and late 1978. The Khmer Rouge (French for *Red Khmer,* a term applied to them by King Norodom Sihanouk) adopted a bizarre model of Marxism-Leninism that stressed the need to build economic power through agricultural collectivization and the construction of large infrastructure projects using forced labor. Extremely poor planning, lack of technical skills, and the paranoid xenophobia and cruelty of the Khmer Rouge leaders during their rule resulted in massive deaths among the population from execution, starvation, and exhaustion. After the Vietnamese ouster of the Khmer Rouge regime in late 1978, the United States backed an international embargo of Cambodia that impeded efforts at reconstruction until the embargo was lifted a decade later. During the 1990s the country has gradually reintegrated into the global economy. Phnom Penh has consequently undergone a dramatic economic, social, and cultural transition as a flood of foreign aid and investment in tourism, manufacturing, and real estate brought rapid growth and development.

Attractions of the City. While the stresses of its recent history have left Phnom Penh somewhat frayed, the city nonetheless retains much of the beauty and charm that earned its reputation as one of the most endearing cities in Southeast Asia. The combination of French colonial buildings, Chinese shophouses, Buddhist temples in traditional Khmer style, and villas lend the city a distinct atmosphere. The city's main attractions are located along the riverfront, which is lined by a park that is a popular place for evening strolls. The Royal Palace, built in 1866 by King Norodom, is closed to the public. Adjacent to the Royal Palace is the Silver Pagoda, famed for its floor, which consists of 5,000 silver tiles, and its Buddha images. Nearby is the National Museum, which houses a magnificent collection of Khmer art from the 4th century onward, including a large number of pieces from the Angkor period (10th to 14th centuries). Among the more impressive structures left from the colonial era is the New Market (Psar Thmei), a large dome in the center of the city that houses a market containing stalls selling consumer goods and fresh meats and produce.

Relationships Between the City and the Outside. Apart from its close ties to China during the Khmer Rouge period and to Vietnam during the 1980s, Cambodia's economic links to the outside world were quite limited from the mid-1970s until the early 1990s. However, since 1989 the country has moved from a socialist to a market-based economic system and the government has encouraged foreign investment. In 1991 the Paris Agreement on a Comprehensive Political Settlement of the Cambodian Conflict was signed, resulting in United Nations–monitored elections and the end of the United States–backed embargo of Cambodia. As a result, the country has reintegrated into the global and regional economies and has experienced a flood of foreign aid and investment. This trend was further encouraged by the country's admission to the Association of Southeast Asian Nations (ASEAN) in 1999. Donors committed $880 million to Cambodia's reconstruction in 1992, and aid has continued to constitute a large part of its government budgets. Foreign investment has focused on tourism services, logging, textile manufacturing, and real estate and has come primarily from elsewhere in Asia, most notably Malaysia, Thailand, Singapore, Hong Kong, and the Republic of Korea.

Cambodia's trade is primarily with other Southeast Asian countries—trade with ASEAN countries accounted for 59% of total exports and 69% of imports from 1993 to 1995. Until the mid-1990s exports were mainly of primary goods, such as timber, rubber, kapok, and soybeans, but in later years garment manufacturing increased dramatically, accounting for almost two-thirds of exports by 1998. The lure of the Angkor temples of Siem Reap in the north led to a growth in tourism. There were 260,489 arrivals in Cambodia in 1996, about three-quarters of whom were tourists, and the vast majority of these came through Phnom Penh.

Major Languages. Khmer is Cambodia's official language. Various Chinese dialects and Vietnamese, respectively, are spoken by the city's two largest ethnic minority groups. English is a favored language of study, while French speakers are few and declining in number.

HISTORY

The Origin of the City. Phnom Penh was founded following the fall of the capital at Angkor in 1431. The king, Ponhea Yat, settled in the area in 1434 and ordered the filling of the land immediately surrounding the Phnom, which was flooded for much of the year. Flooding has always been a major constraint on the city's growth. The city has only gradually expanded as a series of concentric dikes have been constructed and land within these dykes has been reclaimed. Urbanization has proceeded, however, because the city's location at the confluence of three rivers allows it relatively easy access to the Cambodian hinterland and to the South China Sea, making it economically strategic. In addition, most low-lying areas along rivers are similarly flood-prone.

Between the 15th and 19th centuries, Phnom Penh existed as an administrative center, and a center for trade with the outside world. During this period the Cambodian capital relocated several times, with Phnom Penh occasionally receiving that designation. When the French arrived in the middle of the 19th century, they found Indian, Chinese, and Malay traders bartering metals, pottery, tobacco, and a variety of agricultural products. The population at the time stood at about 10,000. In 1863 Cambodia became a protectorate of France, and the colonial government established Phnom Penh as the country's capital. The French ruled Phnom Penh as an entrepôt of secondary significance to Saigon in neighboring Vietnam. The colonial government produced a series of plans that established separate districts for the European, Khmer, Chinese, and Vietnamese inhabitants. In 1953 Cambodia gained its independence, and Phnom Penh embarked on a period of expansion that included the completion of the outermost dyke, the reclamation of large amounts of land from the Bassac River in the eastern part of the city, and the urbanization of many previously semirural parts of the city. However, this expansion ground to a halt in the 1970s as the Vietnam War spilled across the border into Cambodia and the Khmer Rouge revolution grew in intensity. As noted above, significant government investment in urban development did not resume until the Paris peace accords in 1991.

Migration: Past and Present. Until the 1970s Phnom Penh's population followed the trajectory of rapid growth common to cities in developing countries—the population grew from 354,000 in 1950 to about 600,000 in 1970. Thereafter, however, the city experienced perhaps more population fluctuation than any other city in the world, owing to the ravages of war, the vehemently antiurban policies of the Khmer Rouge, and dramatic social change.

During the early 1970s the intensification of war in the countryside and a bombing campaign carried out by the United States drove large numbers of people, including peasants and residents of provincial towns, to seek refuge in the capital. By early 1975 the population had swelled to approximately 2 million, with many living in "refugee villages" established by the government and in sprawling informal settlements. Crowded informal settlements emerged wherever space was available, including in public parks, on sidewalks, on rooftops, and elsewhere. On April 17, 1975, the Khmer Rouge prevailed and established a socialist government, renaming the country *Democratic Kampuchea.* They considered the country's urban intellectual class a threat to their regime and consequently decided to forcibly evacuate all cities. Residents of Phnom Penh were instructed to abandon the city for their ancestral villages, where they were assigned to work for agricultural cooperatives. Thus, until the fall of Democratic Kampuchea at the end of 1978, Phnom Penh was almost completely abandoned, with only a few thousand Khmer Rouge troops and government officials and a handful of factory workers and foreign diplomats residing in the city. In the countryside intellectuals faced severe repression. Many were executed, but many more died of starvation and exhaustion, or escaped the country by crossing the borders into Thailand or Vietnam. Thus a fraction of Phnom Penh's original population remained when the Khmer Rouge were overthrown.

Since 1979 Phnom Penh has gradually repopulated as people have trickled back into the city, and by 1989 the city had recovered its prewar population of about 600,000. Since the peace agreement of 1991 growth has been steady, as industrial and commercial development have brought new economic opportunities in Phnom Penh. In addition, the resettlement of 750,000 people, including returned refugees, internally displaced people, and demobilized soldiers, has added to the flow of migrants to Phnom Penh.

INFRASTRUCTURE

Public Buildings, Public Works, and Residences. Phnom Penh's development in recent years has been shaped by its unique historical circumstance. During the 1970s the city's infrastructure, and particularly sewage and drainage systems, suffered catastrophic damage as a result of the war and of neglect, and it has been estimated that some 67% of the housing stock in the city was destroyed or damaged during this time. During the 1980s, as the city gradually repopulated, the government (which formally owned all property) simply accorded usership rights to abandoned residential properties on a first-come, first-served basis. Early arrivals to the city had a choice of housing options available to them, including large, colonial-style villas and flats in three- to four-story apartment buildings, which had constituted the main source of housing for the middle class during the 1950s and 1960s. In some cases people built houses of wood and thatch in areas around Buddhist temples, possibly in imitation of traditional Cambodian village settings. In 1989 the government privatized the housing stock by simply providing existing residents with full private ownership rights to the units they occupied. In some cases, however, several families occupied a single unit, and considerable displacement occurred as families were bought or forced out by their fellow residents. With rising housing prices low-income people have found legal housing increasingly unaffordable and have been forced to settle in informal settlements. Such settlements were estimated to house about 15% of the city's population by the mid-1990s. The housing stock in these settlements is generally of bamboo and wood, and infrastructure and services are often not available.

Politics and City Services. The Municipality of Phnom Penh is subdivided into districts (Khand and Srok, discussed earlier) and subdistricts (Sangkat). It is governed by four vice-governors who are appointed by the central government. The municipality is responsible for water, sewage, and solid-waste disposal, while the central government administers the electricity network through the Ministry of Energy. International organizations such as the World Bank and the Asian Development Bank have invested considerable sums in rehabilitating the city's infrastructure in recent years, but progress has been limited. Private generators are still widely used owing to the frequent power outages, and water pressure is often too low to reach beyond the first few stories of buildings. Furthermore, the growth of informal settlements means that an increasing number of people are not reached by municipal services, and they must access vital services through other means.

Educational System. Cambodia's educational system has been in a continual process of rehabilitation since 1979. The deaths and out-migration of educated people during and immediately after the Khmer Rouge period left the country with a severe dearth of potential teachers. While the state provides free primary and secondary education, the quality is often quite poor. The low wages of government workers has exacerbated this problem—many teachers supplement their incomes by providing important after-school lessons to students for a fee. This makes it difficult for students from low-income families to be competitive on exams for high school and university admission. Currently primary education is compulsory for six years between 6 and 12 years of age, and in 1996 nationwide enrollment in primary schools was 97%. Enrollment at the secondary level was only 24%, and tertiary education enrollment was 1.4%, although enrollment in Phnom Penh was presumably much higher than the national average. Tertiary institutions in Phnom Penh include the University of Phnom Penh, the Royal University of Fine Arts, the Institute of Technology, the Faculty of Economic Sciences and Law, the University of Health Sciences, and the Royal University of Agriculture. Males have better access to education than females, as indicated by the fact that 36.7% of females in Phnom Penh are illiterate as compared with only 8.1% of males.

Transportation System. The main modes of transportation in Phnom Penh are motorbikes and walking. The public transit system is extremely limited, with infrequent bus service along a few of the main thoroughfares. Private cars and taxicabs are relatively rare, although they are growing in number. The city is also known for its pedicabs, referred to as cyclos, which are popular with tourists.

Travel overland to other parts of Cambodia has become increasingly easy as a result of the improvement of roads and, more important, the improved security situation in rural areas as the civil conflict has wound down. Private buses connect Phnom Penh to other major Cambodian towns, and Siem Riep in the north is accessible by high-speed ferry. Rail service is also available to Thailand via Poipet

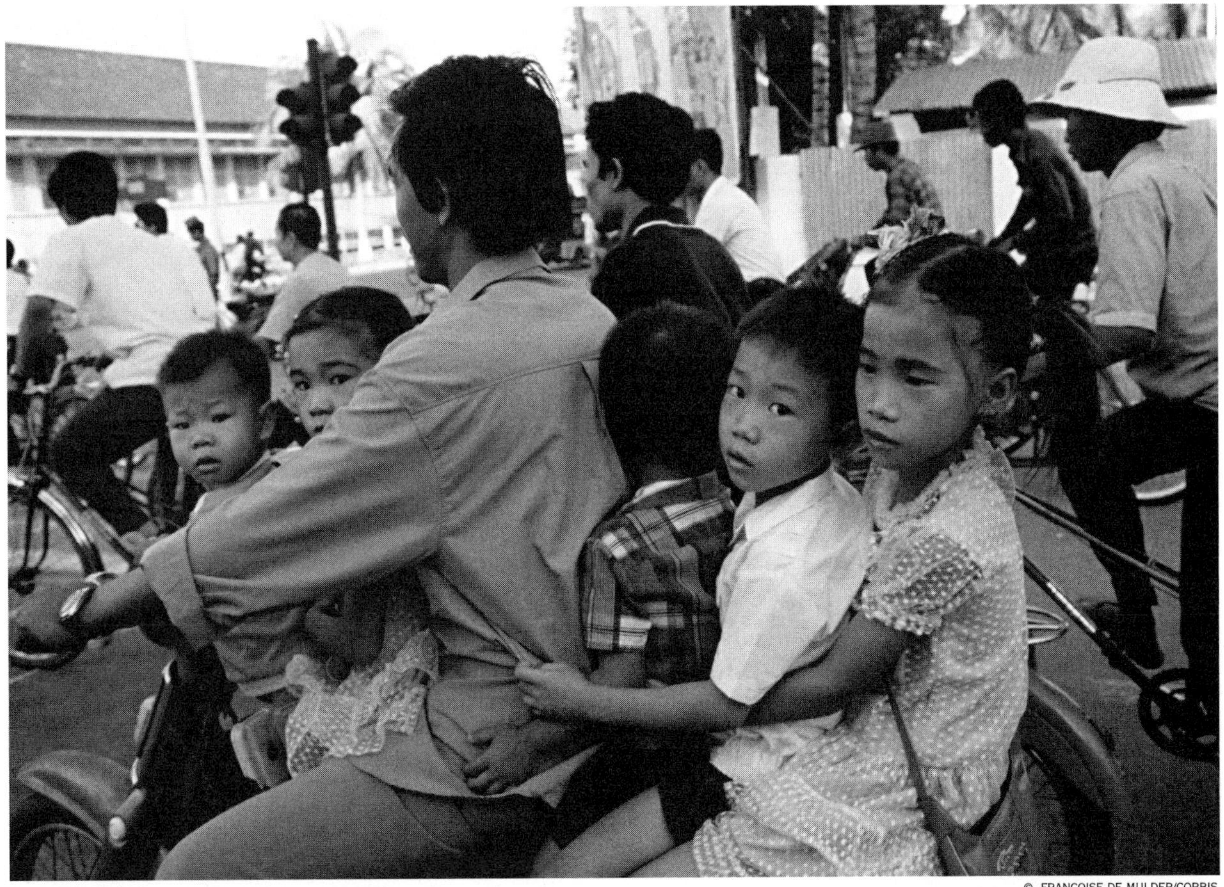

© FRANCOISE DE MULDER/CORBIS

A Cambodian man and his five children ride on one moped in Phnom Penh in 1989.

in the west and to Sihanoukville in the south. Pochentong Airport has been expanded and modernized, and air transport is currently available from Phnom Penh to eight foreign and eight domestic destinations.

CULTURAL AND SOCIAL LIFE

Distinctive Features of the City's Cultures. Phnom Penh residents have gradually rewoven the fabric of social life in the city in the years since 1979. An estimated one-quarter of Cambodians died during the war and United States bombing of the early 1970s and during the Khmer Rouge rule of 1975 to 1978; most families lost at least one member. In the early 1980s Phnom Penh was nearly empty, and early migrants, out of a fear of crime or simply loneliness, often asked relatives and friends in the countryside to come share their houses and apartments in the city. Thus, families reconstructed their social networks in their new environment, and life has gradually returned to normal. However, many continue to bear the psychological scars of 30 years of civil conflict. Weapon ownership is common, and rates of armed robbery and other forms of violent crime are quite high.

Because of its relative isolation, Phnom Penh has not seen the dramatic social and cultural changes that have affected many other Southeast Asian cities. While many Phnom Penh residents wear Western-style clothing , many women still wear sarongs and other types of traditional dress, particularly during religious holidays. The influx of foreign investment in the tourism industry has brought changes to the cultural life of the city, and foreign cultural influences have become more apparent.

Cuisine. The staples of Cambodian cuisine are rice and fish, although poultry, beef, and pork are also eaten, particularly by wealthier families. A central feature of many Khmer dishes is *prahok,* or fermented fish, a pungent concoction that comes in a multitude of varieties. It may be eaten alone with rice or added to other dishes for flavoring. Noodle dishes are also common. A wide variety of fruits are available, including bananas, rambutan, and mangoes.

Restaurants were a rarity in Phnom Penh until the early 1990s, but a large number have opened since then to cater both to expatriates and to the growing number of wealthier Khmer. Chinese and Vietnamese dishes have long been available in Cambodia and are enjoyed by the Khmer as well as by their Chinese and Vietnamese neighbors. As the number of expatriates has grown, so has the market for non-Cambodian food, and consequently foreign entrepreneurs have opened restaurants serving Thai, Indian, European, Malaysian, and a variety of other cuisines.

Ethnic, Class, and Religious Diversity. The vast majority of Phnom Penh's residents are Khmer, an ethnic group that is concentrated in Cambodia, with smaller populations in Thailand, Vietnam, and Laos. The Khmer were among the first people in Southeast Asia to develop centralized kingdoms, and the golden age of the Buddhist and Hindu kings of Angkor from the 10th to the 14th century continues to captivate the imaginations of many Khmer to this day. Other major groups include the Vietnamese, Chinese, and Cham Muslims. While these groups are each estimated to constitute less than 5% of the Cambodian population, they are disproportionately concentrated in Phnom Penh. The Khmer are predominantly Theravada Buddhist, while the Vietnamese and Chinese are generally Mahayana Buddhist. The Cham are a Muslim minority group, partly made up of immigrants from the Malay archipelago who settled in Cambodia centuries ago. In addition, there are a considerable number of expatriates from various parts of the world who have come to Cambodia on business or to work for international aid organizations.

The economic change that began in the last decade of the 20th century has brought widening socioeconomic disparities. This is particularly evident in the growth of the informal settlements. These settlements are characterized by highly congested conditions, the rural style of housing construction, and the lack of basic services. In contrast, a growing upper class has increased access to amenities such as private cars that were virtually unheard of prior to the mid-1990s.

Family and Other Social Support Systems. In rural areas of Cambodia the extended family plays an important economic role, as family members are often called on to assist in agricultural labor. This is less characteristic of urban areas, but the extended family nonetheless plays an important social and economic role, and extended family members often live together. The Khmer kinship system is organized bilaterally, and a man is traditionally expected to live with his wife's family after marriage. However, this custom is frequently broken where it is deemed impractical. While marriages were traditionally arranged, this is changing, especially in Phnom Penh and other urban areas.

Because of the impacts of war, female-headed households are quite common, particularly in Phnom Penh, where they constitute almost 30% of households. Female-headed households face special difficulties owing to the limited employment opportunities and lower pay for women. These problems are exacerbated by the fact that female heads of household in Phnom Penh are less likely than their rural counterparts to live with or close to extended family members, and they therefore have difficulty in accessing childcare.

Work and Commerce. In 1994 Phnom Penh's economy was dominated by service industries—74% of employees worked in the service sector, while 14% worked in industry, and the remaining 12% in agriculture. Almost half of employed women were in retail trade. Many of these women ran small streetside stalls selling cigarettes, gasoline, or sweets. However, in the late 1990s employment patterns began to change owing to investment in the textile industry from Malaysia, Hong Kong, Taiwan, and the Republic of Korea. By 1998 there were 110 garment factories in Cambodia employing 72,000 workers, and most of these were in Phnom Penh. Manufacturing employment is likely to continue to increase in coming years.

Much of the city's commerce takes place in markets in various parts of the city, or in Chinese shophouses in the central districts of Khand 7 Makara and Khand Daun Penh. Recent years have seen a limited development of Western-style shopping centers.

Arts and Recreation. Traditional arts suffered during the troubled years of the 1970s but are experiencing a revival. Cambodian classical dance (related to the dance of Thailand) is the most famed contemporary Cambodian art form. It is taught at the Royal University of Fine Arts in Phnom Penh, and occasional public performances are held. Recent years have seen the development of a large number of bars and discos that cater both to foreigners and wealthy Khmer. The Naga, a floating casino, attracts high-stakes gamblers from elsewhere in Asia.

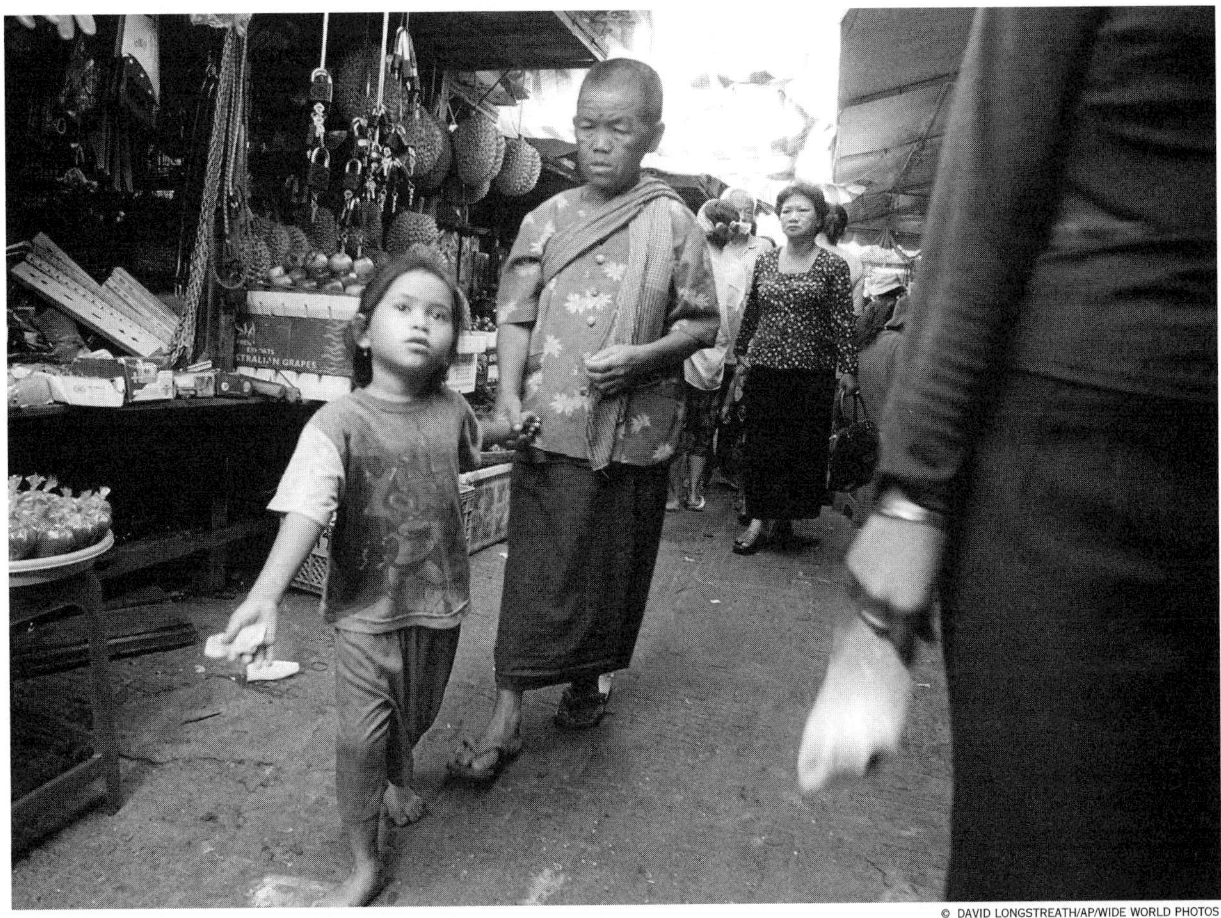

© DAVID LONGSTREATH/AP/WIDE WORLD PHOTOS

A young girl leads a blind woman through the central market in Phnom Penh.

Forms of recreation more affordable to most Khmer include streetside karaoke and video parlors, and evening motorcycle cruises and strolls along the river. Occasional football and kickboxing matches are held at the National Stadium.

QUALITY OF LIFE

By most measures the quality for life of Phnom Penh residents is quite poor. Overall, Cambodia ranks 140th among 174 countries on the United Nations Development Program's human development index, and the country has a life expectancy of 54 to 56 years for men and 58 years for women. Many parts of the city continue to lack piped water, and an estimated 17% of households have no toilet. Owing to poor drainage heavy monsoon rains cause flooding in large parts of the city, and open sewers make such floods a considerable public-health risk. The public health-care and educational systems are inadequate, and private systems are only accessible to the relatively wealthy. One factor that substantially improves the quality of life of many low-income families is their housing situation. The government's policy of allowing in-migrants during the 1980s to settle in abandoned housing units of their choice has left many with good-quality housing that has, since the privatization of housing, turned into substantial financial assets. However, for new migrants to the city the housing market is quite tight, and conditions in the informal settlements are generally deplorable.

FUTURE OF THE CITY

Phnom Penh's future development is largely dependent on two factors: future political developments in Cambodia, and the economic situation elsewhere in Asia. The trend in the 1990s was one of rapid economic growth and development, and rising inequalities. Toward the turn of the 21st century, there was a rapid influx of investment in textile manufacturing from other Asian countries, and the trend towards further industrialization and consequent rapid urbanization seems likely to continue. Likewise, visitor arrivals have increased dramatically, resulting in the rapid development of hotels and recreational facilities for tourists, and the lure of the monuments of Angkor is likely to lead to future tourism growth. However, political turmoil and the Asian financial crisis have both slowed investment. Prior to 1997 post–Khmer Rouge Cambodian politics had been characterized by a power struggle between the country's two prime ministers, Hun Sen of the Cambodian People's Party and Prince Norodom Ranarridh of the United National Front for an Independent, Neutral, Peaceful, and Cooperative Cambodia (FUNCINPEC). In July of 1997 the conflict between the two came to a head, and Hun Sen eventually prevailed as the country's sole leader following days of fierce fighting in Phnom Penh. Thereafter the political situation remained relatively peaceful, but many investors remained wary of the potential for future instability.

Nevertheless, there is little indication that Cambodia will reverse its integration into the global economy. The continued lack of investment in rural infrastructure and services means that rural poverty will continue to be a major issue; rural people will continue to stream to the city in search of opportunity, thus contributing to population growth and increasing pressure on the city's infrastructure and service-delivery systems.

BIBLIOGRAPHY

An Introduction to the Urban Poor in Phnom Penh, Cambodia (Asian Coalition for Housing Rights, New Initiatives Programme 1993).

Blancot, Christiane, "Phnom Penh: Defying Man and Nature," *Cultural Identity and Urban Change in Southeast Asia: Interpretive Essays,* ed. by M. Askew and W. Logan (Deakin University Press 1994).

Chandler, David, *A History of Cambodia* (Westview Press 1991).

Ebihara, May C., et al., eds., *Cambodian Culture Since 1975* (Cornell University Press 1994).

Igout, Michael, *Phnom Penh: Then and Now* (White Lotus 1993).

Kusakabe, Kyoko, "Women Retail Traders in Cambodia," *Gender, Technology and Development* 3, 3 (1999): 411–27.

Oxley, Michael, *Comprehensive Report on the Kop Sreou Resettlement Project* (Municipality of Phnom Penh: State of Cambodia, September 1992).

Shatkin, Gavin, "'Fourth World' Cities in the Global Economy: The Case of Phnom Penh, Cambodia," *International Journal of Urban and Regional Research,* 22:3 (1998): 378–93.

Utting, Peter, *Between Hope and Insecurity: The Social Consequences of the Cambodian Peace Process* (UNRISD 1994).

GAVIN SHATKIN

Port Moresby

Papua New Guinea

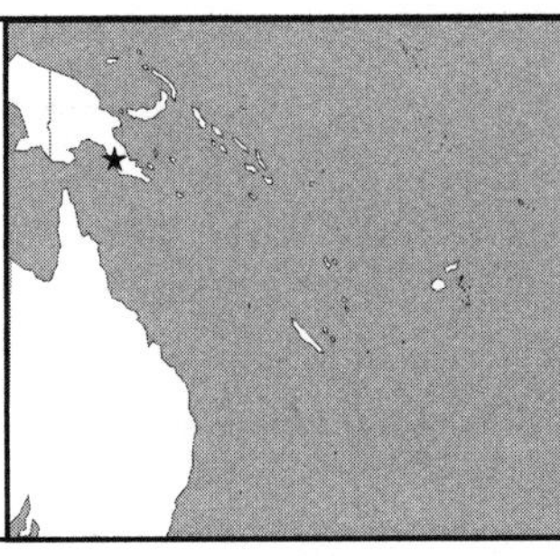

ORIENTATION

Name of City. Port Moresby is the capital of Papua New Guinea. Its name derives from the circumstances of its sighting by Captain John Moresby in 1873. Nigel Oram provides a summary of the events leading up to the naming of Port Moresby:

> In February 1873, Captain John Moresby, R.N., in H.M.S. *Basilisk,* anchored in Redscar Bay. . . . Accompanied by his navigating officer and boats' crews, he set off with a cutter and galley to the south-east. Standing on Pyramid Point, he saw the deep passage through the reef which he called the Basilisk Passage. On 20 February, *Basilisk* entered a large landlocked harbour. Captain Moresby's father was Admiral Sir Fairfax Moresby, R.N., and he named the inner harbour Fairfax, and the outer harbour Moresby, in his father's honour.

Location. The city is located on the southern coast of Papua New Guinea about 9°29′ south of the equator.

Population. The population of the city in 1990 was 188,089; the 2000 estimated population was 282,588.

Distinctive and Unique Features. The natural landscape of Port Moresby is very untypical of the lush vegetation usually associated with the tropics, as the city occupies a thin belt of predominantly savanna grassland scattered with eucalyptus trees over the undulating hills. In fact, its typically hot and dry (sometimes humid) climate is very similar to that of the northern parts of Australia.

Attractions of the City. Apart from sporting events, and as elsewhere in the Pacific, Port Moresby's main attractions are the various cultural events that occur annually. Additionally, about 50 minutes' drive inland are the Rouna Waterfalls, Variarata National Parks, and the Kokoda Trail, where visitors can enjoy bush walks and explore the natural habitats of birds and other animals. The islet resort of Loloata, some 30 minutes' drive from the city and 10 minutes by boat, is popular for its snorkeling and scuba-diving facilities. Parliament House is another attraction, the unique design of which derives from the traditional Sepik *haus tambaran* (a traditionally male-only house). The botanical garden on the campus of the University of Papua New Guinea, located in the city, holds some of world's unique orchids as well as reptiles and birds, including the most colorful bird of paradise. The local Motuan women are renowned for their fine pottery and shell beads, which commonly line the main shop arcades for sale.

Relationships Between the City and the Outside. As the nation's capital, Port Moresby houses the primary administrative offices of the national government. Therefore the bulk of the country's activities related to commerce, foreign affairs, trade, and industry are concentrated in Port Moresby. That includes embassies of various countries. Within Papua New Guinea (PNG), the city remains the political and economic center for the National Capital District and the nation's other 19 provinces.

Major Languages. There are three main languages spoken in the city: Motu (a local lingua franca), Tok Pisin (a creole comprising vocabularies borrowed from many of the indigenous languages as well as German and English), and English. English is the language of instruction in all schools throughout the country, while Tok Pisin is spoken by at least two-thirds of the population. Motu is, however, spoken by the local people of the villages surrounding the city and those who have married into these villages. In addition, several Asian and European languages are also heard in the city, making Port Moresby perhaps the most linguistically diverse city in the world today.

HISTORY

The Origin of the City. The Motu people were among the first to originally settle the present site of the city, which now includes the villages of Manumanu, Boera, Porebada, Kouderika, Baruni, Elevala, and Poreporena (Hanuabada) to the west and Kourabada, Akarogo, Kirakira, Pari, Taurama, Dogura, Motupore (Motuhanua), Tubusereia, Barakau, Gaire, and Gabagaba to the east. The Koitabu people, on the other hand, occupy the inland portions of Port Moresby and are arguably the original owners of much of the region's land.

The town itself was settled by members of the London Missionary Society toward the latter part of the 19th century and was gradually occupied by

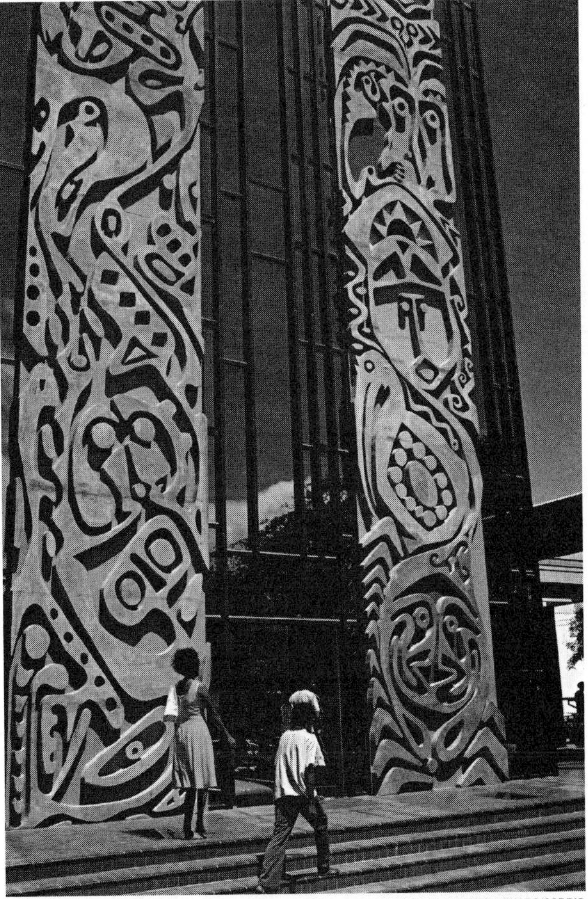

© CHARLES & JOSETTE LENARS/CORBIS

The facade of a bank in Port Moresby, Papua New Guinea, is decorated in traditional style.

the British government as an administrative center. After World War I, the British passed the administrative functions to Australia, which continued to develop Port Moresby into another Australian town until 1975, when Papua New Guinea became a fully independent country within the Commonwealth of Nations. Much of the city lacked proper planning for a full integration of the indigenous population until very recently.

Since the missionaries' and later the colonial administration's occupation of Port Moresby's land, the issue of landownership, lack of it, and land deprivation has grouped the Motuans and the Koitabuans together as a political entity on an ad hoc basis. They are now called the Motukoita people, a name created by using a blend of their original names.

Migration: Past and Present. Around the time of British administration, other immigrants came from the distinct ethnic groups of Aroma as well as Hula, situated to the east of Port Moresby within the central province of Papua New Guinea. The rest of the squatters coming from the western Gulf of Papua and other parts of the highlands region have been there only since the 1950s or so. The Tatana and Vabukori are more recent settlers whose specialization lies in the production of shell beads and the like. Presently, many of the people move freely between the rural towns/villages and the city of Port Moresby.

INFRASTRUCTURE

Public Buildings, Public Works, and Residences. Port Moresby is among the many cities in developing nations that were poorly planned for a metropolitan lifestyle, affording few buildings for cultural gatherings. In fact, major rallies and national celebrations are normally held at sports fields and stadiums. The only public places that allow free intermingling of people are chapels, vegetable marketplaces, sports fields, and a handful of community halls within the Motuan-Koitabuan villages along the coast. Residences sprawl all over the city, even overlapping with government and industrial areas. Generally, the most desirable residential areas are restricted to the small expatriate population, embassies, and well-to-do Papua New Guineans. These are distinctly characterized by high barbed-wire fences along the slopes and hilltops, especially adjacent to Port Moresby's harbor. On the other hand, the majority of the indigenous population live in one- or two-bedroom, boxlike structures constructed on stilts, which are found all over the suburbs.

Politics and City Services. The city's own municipal authority, called the National Capital District Commission (NCDC), administers the city. Politically, it is divided into three constituencies: the northwest open, the northeast open, and the south, with an additional seat for the regional member representing the entire city in the National Parliament. The NCDC provides most of the basic services, such as water supply, sewerage and garbage services, road maintenance, and city beautification and related parks. Very recently the functions of water services were transferred to a separate statutory body. Similarly, the supply of electricity services is administered by the Electricity Commission of Papua New Guinea.

Educational System. The PNG government is the major provider of the city's educational services through its national system. These consist of preparatory schools, primary or community schools, high schools, national higher schools, technical schools, and colleges and universities. In addition to the University of Papua New Guinea, other institutions located in the city include vocational centers and religious centers. Some colleges also provide the option for correspondence courses.

Transportation System. Port Moresby is the main business center for the country and perhaps within the South Pacific region as well. Air services constitute the principal form of transportation between the city and the provinces. Apart from cargo ships, air services are also the primary form of travel into and out of the nation; limited sea transport is available for trips to nearby towns and islands. Within the city, privately owned buses and taxicabs provide public transportation, and hotels offer airport shuttle services. Private cars, vans, and motorbikes also operate within the city. Trucks function as public transport to villages within two to eight hours' drive of the city.

CULTURAL AND SOCIAL LIFE

Distinctive Features of the City's Cultures. The city of Port Moresby is a melting pot for the nation's 800 different ethnic groups. Cultural performances occur almost monthly at hotels, schools, and night spots. The chewing of betel nut—a mild tropical narcotic—is a common activity among the average citizen in the city, so much so that concrete walls and pavements are characteristically stained red with spat-out betel nut juice or paste. The majority of the youth are very fond of local music, which evinces an undeniable influence from Jamaican reggae beats blended with traditional tunes. The vegetable markets are a feast to eye and palate, offering a host of delicious tropical fruits, nuts, and root crops. Largely as a result of the prior British and Australian presence, soccer and rugby are the most popular games played throughout the city, although other sports are also popular at various times of the year.

The beautiful Ela beach is a frequent destination for the majority of the people on the weekend, while the numerous nightclubs within the city afford an exciting nightlife. Barking dogs at night and barbed-wire fences surrounding most residences are a blight on the Port Moresby landscape, a fair indication of the prevalence of petty crimes in the city. Private security firms do a thriving business in the city, so much so that even guard dogs rate higher fees than do other professional services that may be provided by humans.

Cuisine. Indian, Asian, Italian, French, Mediterranean, Australian, Pacific—one can easily find much of the world's renowned cuisine in the city. Most local dishes typically incorporate the tasty coconut cream. The local way of preparing food is either using the earth oven with heated stones (for example, the more popular Tolai *aigil*, a traditional dish combining vegetables; chicken, meat, or fish; bananas; taros; and sweet potatoes, all mixed with coconut cream), roasted over fire, or boiled in clay pots. Most Papua New Guineans' have a "soft palate," such that spices were never part of traditional recipes until very recently. Nowadays, fresh local spices, coconut cream, and other, imported ingredients make up much of the average dish.

Lamb and chicken are the most common meats, although fresh pork is preferred, particularly when these are cooked in the earth oven with taros and sweet potatoes. Tropical fruits such as mangoes, pineapples, watermelons, and papaya abound, especially at the height of the fruit season in September. The ubiquitous fast-food outlets often referred to as "tucker boxes" sell baked vegetables along with lamb flaps, chicken, and other chunks of meat that most Papua New Guineans love; however, poor handling renders the service a health risk at times. Big Rooster and Tasty Fried Chicken are both Australian versions of America's Kentucky Fried Chicken franchise, and both have been very well received by the city's population. Although most hotels provide pizzas and other international dishes, the majority of the population prefer to settle for a blend of traditional and modern foods at relatively cheaper costs.

Ethnic, Class, and Religious Diversity. Over 800 different languages and more than 1,000 different ethnic groups are found in Papua New Guinea. There is no clear-cut class differentiation in Port Moresby, but by economic factors alone, it is fair to say that a large bracket of the city's population are very low income and are probably squatting. Of the city's total population, perhaps only 40% are employed.

Christianity is the dominant religion in the city, comprising countless fundamentalist sects in addition to the mainstream Uniting Church (a Christian church that originated with the Wesleyan church and the London Missionary Society), Seventh Day Adventists, Catholics, and Jehovah's Witnesses. Only a handful of Muslims and some expatriate Hindus are found in the city. There are also a number of Papua New Guineans who do not belong to any formal religion but choose to remain followers of tradition and local customs. Church activities occur daily during the evenings and culminate on Sundays. Many of the sects are evangelistic in their approaches.

Family and Other Social Support Systems. The social organization of Papua New Guinea's ethnic groups provides one of the strongest social bonds between persons in the Pacific or even the world. The western region of the Pacific is in fact notorious in its stubbornness to adhere to what is called the *wantok* system, a network of extended-family relationships. Notwithstanding, this support system is both a "safety net" and a liability depending on how one views it and when. Most residents live together in units comprising two to four nuclear families who have allied along kinship lines. In principle, all should contribute toward the daily maintenance of the household's needs. This can work perfectly for all, but the capitalist system is not so sympathetic to the sentimental and traditional *wantok* system: although the *wantok* system helps all who are linked by social relations, it certainly strains the resources in urban cities such as Port Moresby. For instance, a household made up of ten people might have only one "breadwinner." *Wantoks* and relatives constantly move between village and city. Some come in search of jobs, others to ask for financial assistance, and still others want to take a break from the predominantly traditional and rural lifestyles. In a country like Papua New Guinea, where the government pays only lip service to some idealized wel-

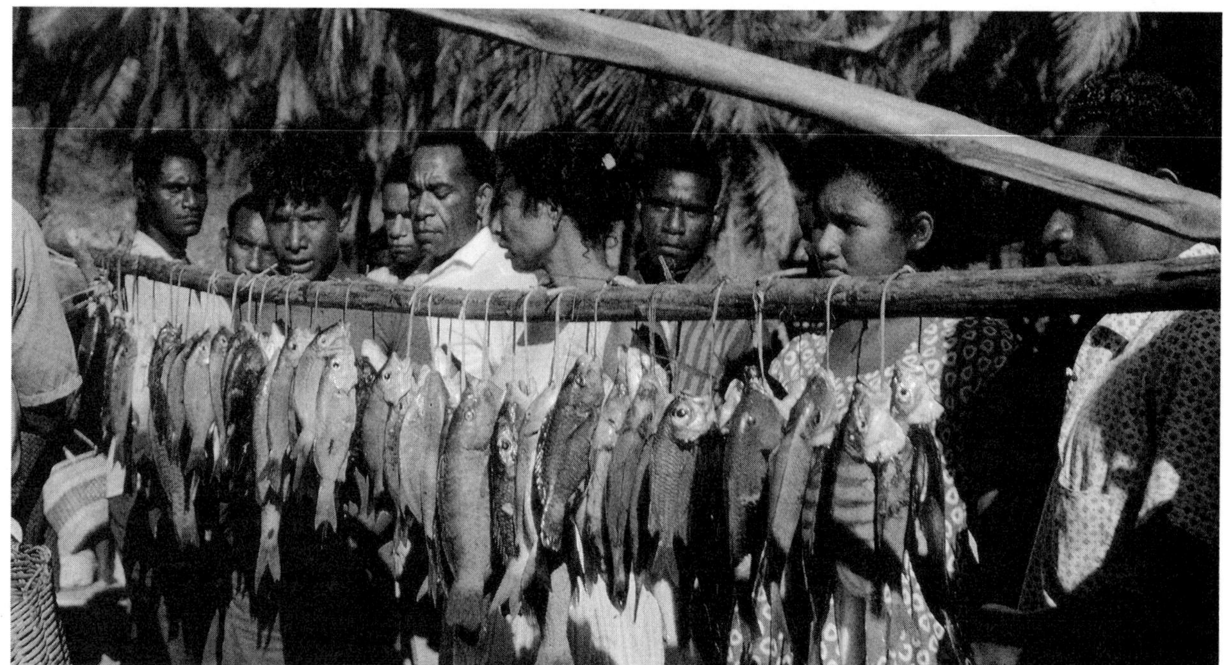

© CHARLES & JOSETTE LENARS/CORBIS

Freshly caught fish are displayed for sale at an open-air market in Port Moresby, Papua New Guinea.

fare system, kinship ties, manifested in the convoluted term *wantok,* nevertheless provide some tangible form of social security and support when needed.

Work and Commerce. Although Port Moresby is comparatively small in area and can be covered by car in about an hour, it has a varied economy. Sectors include public service, hotels, department stores, tucker shops, security firms, street vending of vegetables and handicrafts, motor sales and motor mechanics, factories, sale of cash crops, stevedoring, and export of mineral resources. These have been the avenues for employment, work activities, commerce, and social intermingling as well. Nearby villagers commute daily to the city for work. Drunkards and unemployed youths are just as common a sight as is gambling in hotels and in "open-air casinos" at the squatter settlements.

Arts and Recreation. There are technical schools and colleges that offer programs for all forms of artistic disciplines—music, painting, textiles, wood carvings, printing, and so forth. Most works are displayed during the annual cultural shows mentioned earlier. Institutions such as the Papua New Guinea National Museum and Art Gallery and the national cultural commission, together with local artifact dealers, not only promote the nation's cultural heritage but also run activities that conserve it. Freelance artists hawk their artworks along the streets or in stalls during major cultural events.

QUALITY OF LIFE

The present social and physical character of the city was very much shaped by the attitude and degree of attention given by the British and, later, Australian administrators in the last century. The city had no proper infrastructural plans in the first place, nor was there any real effort to build it as a capital city. In a sense, Port Moresby evolved rather spontaneously, perhaps urged along only by population pressure. The recent major road networks in the city, which are being widened, expanded, resealed, and extended, are testimony to the need for proper planning in the early days. The government, through the city authority, is now, however, laying out foundation road networks for a rapidly developing city.

For as long as the Australian government continues to exert a direct influence on the PNG government to maintain a subtle but systematic segregation and suppression of the indigenous population toward the lower echelons of society, the people of Papua New Guinea will never have the full freedom of a quality life. The evolution of the city to its present status clearly makes many indigenous residents look poor—for example the assorted imported foodstuffs sold in the supermarkets (both fresh and overdue), the way Australian aid to Papua New

Guinea is granted and administered, and the double standards of education (children of the rich go to Australia or New Zealand for high school studies). On the other hand, while the foreign expatriates may appear to have the material wealth, the average citizen appears to have the social wealth: most of the people are happy to share what little they have with their own *wantoks.*

Unfortunately, while many of the city's residents work hard to earn a living, a lot of the well-to-do foreigners and PNG businesspeople and public servants live a very luxurious life in Port Moresby. It is very common to see a rich politician with a load of villagers in the car providing personal security. Papua New Guinea is rich with resources that are currently underutilized, especially for food to feed the population. Presently, timber and mineral deposits are being harvested heavily, much of the profits from which are spent or invested in Port Moresby and offshore.

FUTURE OF THE CITY

Around 1990 there was a very strong debate on the possible relocation of the capital city into the highlands of Papua New Guinea. The colonialists had in the previous century decided to settle in Port Moresby because they thought it posed the least threat to their health, especially from malaria, as the missionaries had been living there for years. So good health, along with a good harbor, was the prime reason in choosing Port Moresby as the site.

But conditions have deteriorated markedly over the last century. With population figures reaching hundreds of thousands by the late 20th century, suddenly there was pressure to expand the area and to improve and intensify services such as water, sewerage, and electricity. Granted, business activities also picked up, as did foreign investment; many of the rich and highly educated indigenous professionals began to set up base in Port Moresby; and the government started to establish more hospitals and schools for the burgeoning young population that is mostly unemployed. Nevertheless, quality of life is degenerating rather rapidly.

Given such a scenario, the city is facing significant social pressures in the 21st century. The challenge is to plan well and for the majority of its citizens. Social problems will continue to increase for as long as culturally unsuitable planning leading to endemic unemployment prevails. The city now requires brave Papua New Guinean planners to both socially and physically realign the development path of the entire city. So far it seems that such initiatives are lacking.

BIBLIOGRAPHY

Biskup, P., et al., *A Short History of New Guinea* (Angus and Robertson Ltd. 1968).

Kirkland, D., *Impressions of Papua New Guinea* (Frontier Publications Pty. Ltd. 1991).

Monsell-Davis, M., "Safety Net or Disincentive?: Wantoks and Relatives in the Urban Pacific," *National Research Institute* Discussion Paper no. 72, 1993.

Office of National Planning and Implementation, *PNG Provincial Population Data Sheet* (2000).

Oram, N. D., *Colonial Town to Melanesian City: Port Moresby 1884–1974* (Australian National University Press 1976).

Sinclair, J., et al., *Papua New Guinea,* rev. ed. (Crawford House Publishing Pty. Ltd. 1999).

LINUS S. DIGIM'RINA

Port-au-Prince

Haiti

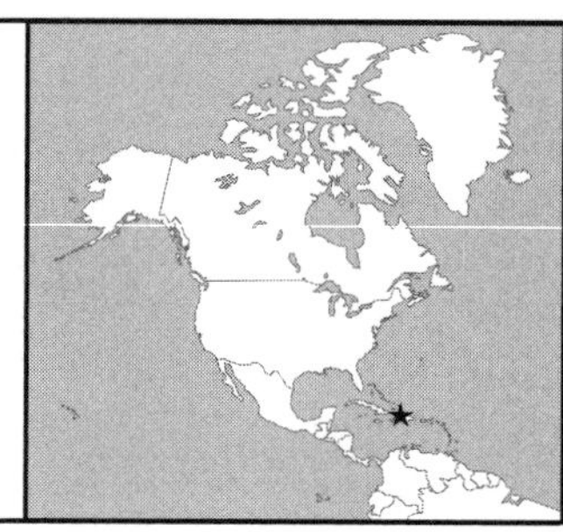

ORIENTATION

Name of City. Port-au-Prince is the capital of the Republic of Haiti. It is also known in Haitian Creole, the nation's dominant official language, as Pòtoprens.

Location. Port-au-Prince is located at 18°33′ north latitude and 72°20′ west longitude. It is situated on the Bay of Port-au-Prince at the juncture of the two major peninsulas that make up Haiti. The Republic of Haiti covers the western third of Hispaniola, an island that is shared by the Dominican Republic. It sits at the boundary line between the Atlantic Ocean and the Caribbean Sea, about 950 kilometers (600 miles) from Florida. The Mona Passage separates Haiti from Puerto Rico, and the Windward Passage lies between Haiti and the island nations of Jamaica and Cuba.

Population. As of the 1990 Haitian census, the population of Port-au-Prince was 846,247. The larger metropolitan area was estimated to have 2 million inhabitants. This estimate may be low owing to the large number of squatters and new immigrants into the city. Since the 1960s, Haiti has been considered one of the most densely populated countries in the world. Recent migration from the provinces to urban areas has only exacerbated the problem.

Distinctive and Unique Features. Port-au-Prince is a typical Caribbean city in many respects, but aspects of Haitian geography and topography have created an interesting nook for the city. The Bay of Port-au-Prince bounds the city on the east, and mountain ranges border it on the west. Port-au-Prince's land area is situated on the sea-level plain called the Cul-de-Sac. The Chaine de Mateaux and the Massif de la Selle bound the Cul-de-Sac to the north and south, respectively. The Bay of Port-au-Prince hosts the largest port in Haiti and thus is too disturbed for large-scale fishing. There are few mineral resources, but sand and bauxite are mined in nearby areas.

The historic district of Port-au-Prince is arranged on a grid system, similar to that found in most colonial cities in the Caribbean. This grid system deteriorates into a maze of short streets, alleys, and unpaved roads farther away from the central squares. The heart of the city, where the majority of the historical and political offices are located, is bisected by the Avenue Jean-Jacque Dessalines and by the Rue Pavée. Moving out from this heart are the business and residential sectors of the city. The most central neighborhoods are Morne à Tuf, Bois Verna, Poste Marchand, Bel-Air, and Croix de Bossales. Farther out are the neighborhoods of Bolosse, Carrefour Feuille, Turgeau, Cité St. Martin, Bourdon, Canapé Vert, Bois Patate, Babiole, and La Saline. Because of the growth of the city, areas even farther from the center of the city are now considered part of the larger metropolitan area. The neighborhoods of Cité Simone, Village Lamothe, Cité St. George, Delmas, Bois Caradeux, Musseau, and even Petion-Ville (Pétionville) and Thomassin are included in the city's activities.

Most of the historical sights are located in the central district, as are nearly all of the city squares. Business and banking are generally concentrated in the neighborhoods of Delmas, and Petion-Ville. Owing to the migration of large numbers of Haitian peasants into the city's urban areas, most of the mulatto elite have moved into the suburbs. Many businesses have followed, leaving the heart of Port-au-Prince relatively deserted. Only government offices, a few businesses, the poor, and the homeless remain.

The homeless fill the major neighborhoods of the city and have begun building on land previously considered too dangerous for construction. Whole neighborhoods have been built in the ravines leading down into Port-au-Prince, on land that is susceptible to natural disturbances. The houses, constructed predominantly from cinder blocks and tin, are massed together in such density that it would seem impossible for the inhabitants to live with any comfort. These areas are called bidonvilles (shantytowns) or *cités carton* (cardboard cities). The houses here have no services and residents survive by tapping water lines and stealing electricity.

Attractions of the City. There are few business opportunities in Port-au-Prince, aside from participation in the market economy that has existed since Haiti was a French colony. Light industry and telecommunications activities may soon bring more employment to Haiti, but little business growth has been seen in the Port-au-Prince area. Haiti was the first country to accept the Caribbean Basin Initiatives and build an economic production zone near the airport. Unfortunately, this zone has not led to any appreciable economic growth, and Haiti's position in the world economy has declined: in 1998 the country had a trade deficit of $197 million, signifying an imbalance of imports and exports. Port-au-Prince's few exports are agricultural, brought from the provinces for shipment to France and the United States, Haiti's chief purchasers of exports. Haiti receives millions of dollars in international aid as a result of the declining economy. In addition, food commodities are provided for the many poor and homeless in the capital and throughout Haiti.

For tourists, the principal attractions are the National Palace and the surrounding squares and monuments. The immaculate white National Palace is encircled by a wrought-iron fence and stands as a symbol of political power. It is also now seen as a symbol of Haiti's developing democracy, a theme repeated in many statues in the nearby squares. Statues commemorating the Marron Inconnu, the unknown Maroon who fought for Haiti's independence from French colonial rule, and honoring Jean-Bertrand Aristide, who fought for Haiti's independence from the rule of military dictators, are visible from the front of the National Palace. Haiti's historical museum of national heroes is also noteworthy. Built primarily underground, the museum houses national treasures, including important works of art, photography, and historical artifacts. The National Cathedral, completed in 1914 and renovated in 1966, is in the area as well.

There are many examples of Victorian colonial architecture, both great and small, to be seen in Port-au-Prince. The Victorian style, called "gingerbread" in Haiti, is characterized by extreme attention to detail and embellishment in trim. Bright, pastel colors are often used to accentuate the woodwork. Unfortunately, many of these houses are in disrepair. Perhaps the best example of Caribbean Victorian architecture is the Hôtel Olaffson. Hotels in the Port-au-Prince area also support Haitian artists and craftspeople. For example, the intricately carved doors to the casino at the Hotel Montana in Petion-Ville are entirely handmade by local artisans.

Tourists may see other Haitian art at one of the many galleries scattered throughout Petion-Ville, a wealthy suburb of Port-au-Prince. These galleries specialize in all types of Haitian art, from the abstract expressionism of painter Yves Meus to the intricate, folk beadwork of Haitian Vodou (Voodoo) flags. Many of the galleries purchase particularly important works for resale at higher values to collectors in Haiti and abroad.

Relationships Between the City and the Outside. Port-au-Prince has always been a stratified city. It was once divided along lines of color and class, corresponding to the dividing lines of the major metropolitan neighborhoods. This division is still evident as one moves from place to place in Port-au-Prince. The influx of Haitian peasants from the provinces increased the heterogeneity of these neighborhoods, as the result mainly of squatting and the rapid construction of poor housing in alleys and in largely deserted commercial areas. Now the city is the home of the poor, while the wealthy live in the suburbs higher up in the mountains, particularly in Petion-Ville, Thomassin, and Fermathe. Interestingly, the Haitian poor refer to their places of residence in the city as "down here" and the places of residence of the more well-to-do as "up there," a phraseology that reinforces the strict class separation that has been named "class apartheid."

Because Port-au-Prince is bordered on the west by the ocean and on the east by steep mountains, its physical growth is limited and it is thus increasingly unable to accommodate its mushrooming population. The massive surge in population density has led to a decline in the provision of services by the municipal government.

As the capital of Haiti, Port-au-Prince is the center of all domestic and international activities. It is the largest city in Haiti, followed by Cap Haitien. It is the seat of all governmental and diplomatic operations, as well as the locus of most nongovernmental and missionary endeavors in the country. In effect, Port-au-Prince mediates the majority of formal, informal, and development activities that occur. The largest airport in Haiti is on the outskirts of Port-au-Prince, making the city the first and last location that many travelers see. The airport has been on and off the U.S. Department of State's list of dangerous travel locations for many years, owing to poor security and concerns over air safety. At the turn of the 21st century, the airport was not on that list, but its ominous reputation has remained.

The notoriety of the Port-au-Prince airport is only one facet of the largely negative opinion that many people have about the city itself. As a result of Haiti's bad press, most individuals who have never visited Port-au-Prince expect a near-military state filled with homeless, extremely poor individuals infected with HIV (human immunodeficiency virus). Most Americans, even members of the American military, consider Port-au-Prince to be a dangerous city. Inhabitants of the city also recognize the extreme perils it presents, scrambling to be away from the downtown areas before dark falls and safety becomes harder to ensure. As time progresses, if the municipal government is unable to maintain infrastructure and security, the reality will soon meet the reputation. Ironically, most residents are fiercely loyal to their neighborhoods: while characterizing their own city as a dangerous place where crime and violence are common, each neighborhood is considered safe and protective of its inhabitants.

Major Languages. Haiti's major languages are French, Haitian Creole, and, increasingly, English. French and Creole share the title of official national language, as specified in the 1987 constitution. In the past, French was used as the official language for political and formal interactions. But since 7% or less of the population spoke French, this seriously restricted access to activities in the formal sector. Jean-Bertrand Aristide changed the constitution after becoming president in 1991, making Creole the second official language of state. English is increasingly spoken in Port-au-Prince because of the presence of American dignitaries and military. Trade and migration have also encouraged the use of English in the city.

HISTORY

The Origin of the City. Port-au-Prince was founded in 1749 to provide protection for the central part of the French colony of St. Domingue and to secure colonial interests in the port on the bay. Construction began in 1750, and as soon as possible the capital was transferred from Leogane to Port-au-Prince. After the French Revolution, the city served as a central location for the royal government, for international trade, and for commerce of all types. Port-au-Prince has remained at the hub of all activities pertaining to Haiti, its supremacy growing through the years.

During the American occupation of 1915–1934, U.S. military forces linked the capital with the provinces and with other urban areas, strengthening its position as the dominant urban area. Because both political power and commercial activities are concentrated in the city, Port-au-Prince has been the locus for most major political, economic, and social upheavals. The distress caused by countless uprisings has created an intensely charged atmosphere in Port-au-Prince; every action seems liable to catalyze an insurgence.

The Duvalier family came to power in 1957. Interest in the development of Port-au-Prince began to wane because of the Duvaliers' increasingly dictatorial and repressive government. Infrastructural development projects were abandoned, and few improvements were made to accommodate the numbers of migrants moving into the city. Municipal services started to decline, and the elite of the city began migrating out. Urban planners assert that there have been no major urban improvement projects since the 1950s, although Port-au-Prince's urban needs have grown drastically.

Migration: Past and Present. Port-au-Prince has been a nexus for migration since the early 1900s. Traditionally, poor peasants seeking the promise of urban success moved into the lower-income neighborhoods of the city. The American occupation of Haiti reestablished Port-au-Prince as the center of all political, economic, and social activity, and most Haitians yearning for change were drawn to the capital. In more recent times, beginning in the 1980s, migration has swelled from a trickle to a flood. New immigrants occupy all available space in Port-au-Prince and have contributed to broadening the class heterogeneity of its neighborhoods. In effect, the poor have appropriated Port-au-Prince, in the process making the already deficient provision of services even worse and sparking an increase in crime, disease, and economic distress.

Many of the rural poor use Port-au-Prince as an intermediary destination in a migration pattern that leads out of Haiti altogether. Haitians move to Port-au-Prince, amass enough resources to pay for boat transportation, and then leave for the United States, the Bahamas, or Jamaica. The motivation for most of the movements is economic: the promise of greater success and the availability of resources drives the migration. Economic distress also prompts many of the migrants to send badly needed cash remittances to poorer family members remaining in Port-au-Prince. While patterns of migration have not changed much over time, the rate of migration has increased markedly.

INFRASTRUCTURE

The infrastructure of Port-au-Prince is considered by many to be nonexistent. The municipal and state presence that should be evident in such a large political center is almost invisible. Economic researchers suggest that municipal services and urban management in Port-au-Prince have failed, owing to the burgeoning ranks of rural migrants. Many of these migrants have no knowledge of municipal institutions that should be providing services, much less which services are being provided. Infrastructural changes, particularly improvement of service delivery, public health, and security, have been recommended to improve the conditions of life in Haiti's capital city. Unfortunately, new municipal structures have not replaced the deteriorating structures that can no longer support contemporary Port-au-Prince.

Public Buildings, Public Works, and Residences. All offices for the government of Port-au-Prince and of Haiti are located within the boundaries of the city. Of primary importance are the National Palace, the Legislative Palace, and the Judicial Palace, which house the major national offices. The national magistrates, the national prison, and the remaining national offices are also located downtown. The offices of the city government of Port-au-Prince are situated in the same area, housed mostly in the Hôtel de Ville. The bureaus of tourism and commerce are in the historic district, as are the headquarters of the National Bank of Haiti and of the public services. Port-au-Prince boasts several large parks; the most important of these is the Champs de Mars, flanked by the principal national offices. Diplomatic offices, bureaus, and ministries are scattered throughout the city, usually occupying large homes.

Homes in the city vary in style and in level of comfort. Some houses, particularly in the older areas, are large Victorian-style residences made of wood. Others are more modern, built of concrete, brick, and stone. Walls and gates surround most homes for privacy and protection; many of the fences are topped with razor wire or with shards of broken glass embedded in cement. In poorer neighborhoods, most dwellings are constructed from concrete blocks or tin. In the poorest neighborhoods the houses may even be fashioned from plywood or cardboard. Because of the rapid growth of the city, dwellings that were originally temporary have become permanent, lending the city the appearance of a slum. Nearly all neighborhoods have a local boutique, where water and basic supplies are sold. Street merchants provide for the remainder of most citizens' needs.

Politics and City Services. Haiti is divided into nine departments, which are subdivided into arrondissements and communes. Port-au-Prince lies in the department of the West, and in the arrondissement and the commune of Port-au-Prince. The offices of the mayor govern the city, but if the opinions of the citizens are correct, there is very little activity associated with the offices of the municipal government. The post office, library, courthouse, Chamber of Commerce, and most other municipal agencies are located in downtown Port-au-Prince. Because of problems with delivery of services at a national level, most service providers are now private; telephone and electricity services have been privatized, with little improvement.

Educational System. The educational system of Port-au-Prince is based on the system of Catholic education that has been in place since the colonial era. There are both public and private institutions, with the latter using French as the language of instruction. There are some private schools that provide English-language education, attended mainly by the children of dignitaries or by Haitian-American children whose parents prefer that they be taught in English. Although schooling is free, books, supplies, and uniforms are not and must be

© TONY ARRUZA/CORBIS

Cité Soleil is a slum area in Port-au-Prince, Haiti.

provided for each child. Because Haitians hold education with high regard, parents shoulder the expense of sending their children to school for as long as possible. There is massive overcrowding in the schools of Port-au-Prince. In the afternoon, as students are released from school, their brightly colored uniforms fill the streets. Traffic that arises from the rush of children at three o'clock leads most Haitians who transact business in the city to finish their affairs before they get caught in the crush.

Public schools in Haiti now teach in Haitian Creole, the native language of all Haitians, but this was not always the case. Because of the French colonial influence, classes were in French and covered topics ranging from French history to matrix algebra. The structure of the school system is similar to that of the French system, with several years in lower school and then in intermediate school and finally five years in upper school. At the end of the school program each year students take exit exams, which stress memorization and rote repetition over problem-solving and critical-thinking skills.

Evaluations of the educational system suggest that it is lacking in the provision of most skills. High rates of attrition and poor attendance lead to low academic performance in Port-au-Prince schools. Particularly for schools that service children of the lower socioeconomic groups, educational opportunities may be affected by the need to work to meet a family's daily needs.

The only university in Haiti is located in Port-au-Prince. The State University of Haiti and its accompanying medical, dental and law schools are situated near the National Palace. Experts who have assessed the university system have concluded that improvements should be made in course content and in administrative structure to make the university a successful institution again.

Transportation System. Port-au-Prince's transportation system is almost nonexistent. The roads that do exist are riddled with potholes or open sewer grates. Most of the streets are significantly narrowed by the presence of street merchants selling fruits and vegetables, other foodstuffs, local crafts, water, charcoal, or other necessities of daily life in the city. In addition, many roads in the municipality become impassable after rainstorms, when water and mud fill the streets.

Public transportation exists in the form of *taptaps,* converted pickup trucks or minibuses that run regular routes for a small fare. *Taptaps* are usually very colorfully painted trucks whose beds have been converted into covered seating. Most of these vehicles are named, and citizens of Port-au-Prince often have preferences for which they choose to take from one destination to another. *Taptaps* connect all of the major neighborhoods with each other, tie in the suburbs with the rest of the city, and link the city with the rest of Haiti to some degree. They are an informal-sector response to a municipal need, serving as the primary mode of transportation for many Haitians. In addition, they carry agricultural and other goods to the markets in Port-au-Prince, thus supporting the largest and most important economic activity in the country.

CULTURAL AND SOCIAL LIFE

Distinctive Features of the City's Cultures. Despite its many political, economic, and social problems, Port-au-Prince maintains a vibrant culture. First and foremost, this vibrancy begins with the citizens of Port-au-Prince. Men and women alike are known for their animated speech, their enjoyment of life, and their hospitality. It is common practice throughout Haiti to provide for the needs of guests, whether or not a host has the means. Women are generally renowned for their beauty—according to folktales, the women of yesteryear's Port-au-Prince had an almost supernatural ability to captivate men and create romance merely by tying their head kerchiefs in a particular way. Even now, the women of Port-au-Prince are noted for wearing these brightly colored scarves.

Many women in Port-au-Prince work in street markets throughout the city. These women often transport their goods on their heads, balancing 45-kilogram (100-pound) bags of rice while carrying two other large bundles in their hands. Market days are usually twice a week, but many street merchants remain throughout the rest of the week to sell their goods. Some of the markets are located in designated squares or market buildings, but as a result of the growth of Port-au-Prince, many have spilled over into the surrounding streets. The market buildings in Port-au-Prince are important gathering places for Haitians, becoming the locus for all types of interaction. In one of the larger markets, one can buy everything from the latest designer clothes to a single dose of antibiotic. The streets teem with activity, and the stalls are packed full of goods for resale. In addition, water sellers move through the throng hawking their goods, and *fresca* carts sally forth stopping every few feet for the driver to shave ice into a paper cup and pour over the flavored syrup that the customer has chosen.

Port-au-Prince also has a number of public squares that have become centers of activity. Often artists set up along the sidewalks of the squares to sell their works. All types of people mingle on the grassy lawns. It is not unusual to see students memorizing their lessons, children playing, the homeless sleeping, and the health-conscious exercising.

The citizens of Port-au-Prince, and Haitians in general, enjoy relaxing. Most major Catholic holidays are celebrated with festivals, and each city in Haiti, including Port-au-Prince, has a city festival at some time during the year. These events are accompanied by roaming bands of musicians, dancing, and drinking. The most important of these festivals is Carnivale. In Port-au-Prince, parades wrap through the city, passing each of the main squares and ending up at the Champs de Mars. Usually, popular musical groups write songs and perform them during the parade, staging elaborate shows from the floats. Carnivale is a time for religious celebration as well as for political expression. Many songs have political themes and call attention to popular sentiment about topics ranging from governmental corruption to mulatto elitism.

Another distinguishing facet of the culture of Port-au-Prince is Vodou. Port-au-Prince is host to one of the largest expressions of the Vodou faith each All Saints' Day. In the morning after Allhallows Eve, Vodou participants, still dressed in finery from ceremonies the night before, parade to the National Cemetery, where they celebrate the day in honor of their ancestors. The National Cemetery is filled with aboveground crypts, maintained by each family member's survivors. Often the crypts are colorfully painted and adorned with flowers, trinkets, and gifts for the ancestors who are housed within. During the All Saints' Day festivities, these crypts become the center of the celebration, and family members pay their respects to the dead.

Cuisine. The cuisine of Port-au-Prince is fundamentally the same as the cuisine in the rest of Haiti, based primarily on the staple foods rice and beans. Plantains also play a large part in the diet of most Haitians, whether boiled (*bannan bouyi*) or fried (*bannan peze*). Haiti's tropical climate and mountainous topography support the cultivation of many kinds of fruits and vegetables, from lettuces and onions to mango and avocado. These fruits and vegetables are often included in the Haitian diet, as are papaya, passion fruit, and limes. At higher elevations, root vegetables such as beets and carrots are grown, and they are transported to the city for resale in the street markets.

Animal-protein sources are limited on the island and consist mainly of pork, goat, chicken, and fish. In general, meat is too expensive for the average Haitian to eat every day. The most famous of meat dishes are *taso* and *griyo,* pork dishes that involve both boiling and frying pork. Fresh meats are supplemented with dried and salted herring imported from the United States. The fish is washed, cut into small pieces, and cooked into a sauce that is served over boiled plantains to make one of Haiti's characteristic dishes.

Two other distinctive Haitian dishes are made of cornmeal, but of two very different types. The first is a breakfast beverage consisting of cornmeal flour that is boiled with milk, sugar, and vanilla. This drink, called *akasan,* is known throughout Haiti. A larger grind of cornmeal is boiled with dried Haitian mushrooms, called *djondjon,* to make a dish very similar to Italian polenta or American grits. The mushrooms lend a purplish black color to the cornmeal and give the dish an earthy flavor.

There are several other Haitian foodstuffs that deserve mention in a discussion of Haitian cuisine. Millet used to be the principal staple food of most Haitians, but with the influx of American rice, Haitians are eating rice to the exclusion of most other carbohydrate sources. Besides millet, cassava is grown, dried, ground, washed, and baked into flat cakes similar to large crackers. Haitians drink very sweet, very strong, low-acidity coffee grown in the region (particularly in the region of St. Mark) each morning for breakfast. Local rums, from aged Barbancourt to *kleren,* are drunk throughout Haiti.

The chief flavoring agents in Haitian food are thyme and garlic, which most Haitians grow in kitchen gardens. Peppermint and lemongrass grow readily in most areas of Haiti and are often present in kitchen gardens as well.

Ethnic, Class, and Religious Diversity. Since Haiti's independence in 1804, persistent classism and color hierarchy have plagued Haitian citizens. First, the Francophile mulatto elite maintained control of most political and economic activities. This re-created the plantation economy for the remainder of uneducated black Haitians, who had no possibility for participation in the governmental and private sectors of the economy. These class divisions, nearly synonymous with color divisions, have remained in Haitian society until the present. Port-au-

Prince provides a particularly stark example of this strict casteism. As mentioned earlier, the neighborhoods of Port-au-Prince were divided along class lines. Now most upper-class Haitians have left the city for the suburbs, making the class distinctions more glaring.

Within the bounds of Port-au-Prince proper, it is estimated that between 95% to 99% of the inhabitants are of African descent. The remaining inhabitants are of European or Middle Eastern descent, but the cultural diversity of Port-au-Prince remains low. In the metropolitan area, including the suburbs, this is not the case. Many of the elite suburbs are culturally heterogeneous, with class becoming more important than culture or color in housing choice and neighborhood demography.

Religious diversity is increasing in Port-au-Prince. Although it was once considered entirely Roman Catholic, there is a growing presence of Protestant and Evangelical religious organizations in the metropolitan area. In addition, Vodou practitioners abound, but it is not considered sacrilege to practice both Roman Catholicism and Vodou. More Catholic Haitians are participating in the Haitian Catholic Church, which conducts Mass in Haitian Creole rather than in French and incorporates drums and chanting into the Catholic liturgy.

Family and Other Social Support Systems. The family is very important in Haiti and often comprises an extended set of relatives who cooperate to meet the collective needs of the group. Because many inhabitants of Haiti live at a subsistence level, the cooperation of all family members is expected and necessary for survival. Members of a family typically live in close proximity to each other, share responsibilities, and support each other in times of need. This has led to the concept of the *lakou,* a courtyard area surrounded by houses inhabited by members of one family. Members of a *lakou* are expected to work together and share resources. An individual's loyalty to his or her *lakou* is customarily stronger than his or her loyalty to the neighborhood in which the *lakou* is located.

In addition to immediate family ties, Haitian individuals are tied to each other through informal bonds. Each Haitian child has godparents, who are frequently called upon to help with school expenses, First Communions, family festivals, and medical expenses. If resources are limited, children are sent to live with other families, where they trade work for room and board. This system, called *restavek,* has been considered both a form of child slavery and a form of resource sharing. In the worst case, the children are used for labor only. In most cases, the children cook, clean, and care for younger members of the household in exchange for access to school, uniforms, medical care, and other necessities of life.

Although marriage rites are performed both as religious and civil ceremonies, many Haitian couples live in common-law marriages, a system called *plaçage.* It is understood that such couples will live together and share the responsibilities of the household. It is also common for men in Haiti to have more than one wife in separate neighborhoods or cities, although the prevalence of these types of marital arrangements in Port-au-Prince is difficult to determine.

Work and Commerce. The majority of Port-au-Prince's inhabitants participate to some degree in the market economy that has developed there. Many individuals sell agricultural products, dry goods, or clothing. Others are tradespeople, working as mechanics, welders, carpenters, masons, or plumbers. Artisans abound and make furniture, coffins, metalwork, paintings, or wooden toys to sell on the street or in the markets. There is very limited industrial development, but what little there is occurs in the industrial park on the edge of the city near the airport. Unemployment is high, estimated at around 60% in 1999. This figure does not take into account employment in the informal economy, seasonal employment, or occasional service employment.

Work places are undeveloped and may consist of a few wooden beams covered with tin. Often work is done on the side of the road, in the shade of a tree, allowing passersby to view products for sale. As a result, travel to places of work is limited. Those who do travel to offices for governmental, medical, or commercial jobs often drive their own cars or travel via *taptap.* Most of the urban commercial area at the heart of Port-au-Prince lies abandoned, the owners having left for the suburbs or even for America.

Arts and Recreation. Traveling the streets of Port-au-Prince, one is barraged with the sounds of radios playing. Radio is and has been the major medium of mass communication for most of Haiti's history. Stations are usually mixed format, presenting news, current events, and music. In Port-au-Prince, there are several dominant popular musical forms. *Konpa* is a popular type of dance music related to *merenge,* as is *rara.* In addition, traditional forms of music are supported throughout the city. This type of music is called *mizik racin,* or roots music, and is related to the drum cadences of Vodou. Other popular music borrows from the reggae sounds of Jamaica and the hip-hop sounds of American rap.

Artisans crowd the streets of Port-au-Prince, making everything from wooden models of *taptaps* to mahogany beds. Carpenters, metalworkers, painters, and seamstresses sell their wares in the street markets of Haiti. Most important of these artisanal works are woodcarving and metalworking. Carvers create all types of works, and stain and varnish them in a variety of ways for resale to tourists or visitors to the city. Metalworkers transform scrap sheet metal into works of art that commonly depict scenes from Haiti's folkloric past or from Vodou. These works sometimes sell for thousands of dollars when transported to the United States by gallery owners or art speculators.

Some sports are important as recreational activities for citizens of Port-au-Prince. Most important is soccer, played professionally in the National Stadium and recreationally throughout the city. Cockfighting and gambling are also leading pastimes of the inhabitants of Port-au-Prince.

QUALITY OF LIFE

The quality of life for most residents of Port-au-Prince has been steadily declining since the end of the Duvalier reign in 1986. During the Duvalier era, the Haitian gourde was linked to the U.S. dollar and the currency was stable. Now the Haitian gourde is unstable and inflation is rampant. Prices have risen markedly, and many residents of Port-au-Prince rely on food aid. The presence of international development and governmental interests has driven housing prices up, making it difficult for Haitians to afford appropriate housing in Port-au-Prince. As a result, many individuals and families are homeless or must live in substandard housing.

Most substandard housing has no municipal services at all, and the remaining housing has very limited services. Houses rely on cisterns that gather rainwater for most of their water needs, and the sewer system is ineffective. Most newly constructed, modern houses are equipped with septic tanks for the

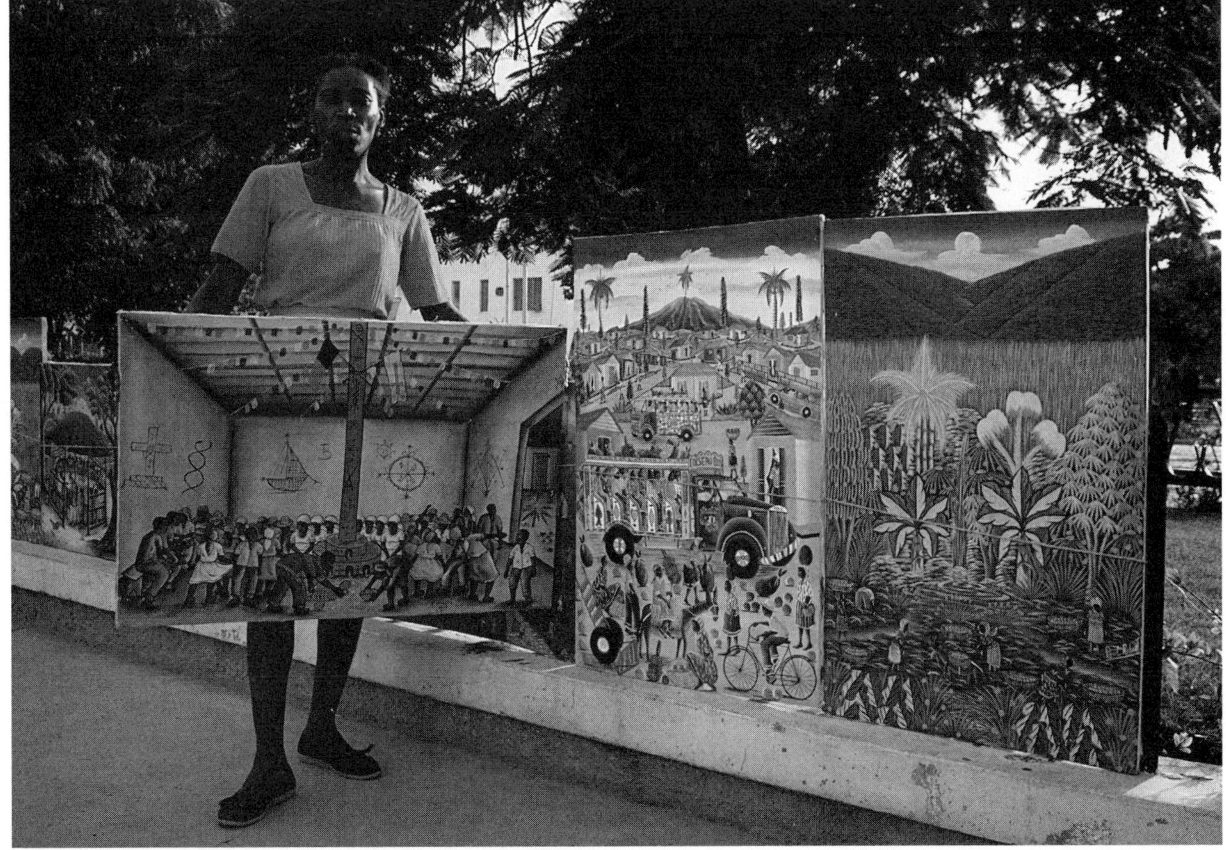

© OWEN FRANKEN/CORBIS

A Haitian woman sells paintings on a street in Port-au-Prince.

elimination of household wastes. Garbage is often burned rather than collected and taken to the city dump. Electrical service is restricted to a few hours a day. Many individuals rely on inverters, which gather and store electricity during periods of service and act as batteries during other times, to ensure that their appliances function. Telephone service is difficult to obtain and expensive to use. Because many residents of Port-au-Prince tap the phone lines, many individuals choose not to have accounts at their homes, fearing that they will incur expenses stemming from service theft.

The unstable economy has led to high unemployment, a lack of capital for investing, and high interest rates. Because resources are very limited, crime is on the rise. Roaming bands of *zenglendos,* or bandits, imitate police officers and rob those traveling at night. It is not unusual to hear of or see bodies lying in the street after a night filled with gunfire. The national police, whose headquarters are in Port-au-Prince, are unable to curb the escalating crime wave. Those criminals who are caught languish in the national prison, where they typically wait for months for a hearing.

The crowded conditions in Port-au-Prince make communicable diseases a very real threat in the city, and the U.S. State Department's International Travel Bulletins warn that Haiti harbors a number of infectious diseases. Mosquito-transmitted malaria, typhoid, and dengue fever are widespread in Haiti, particularly in Port-au-Prince. In addition, tuberculosis; hepatitis A, B, and C; and HIV (human immunodeficiency virus) infection rates are estimated to be very high.

Deforestation, burning wood for charcoal, diesel fuels, and other volatile chemicals have increased air pollution. The expanding use of chemical fertilizers has led to contaminated soil and water. Leaching of chemicals from garbage dumps into the soil has also affected the areas surrounding Port-au-Prince. Reports suggest that Haiti has depleted most of its available natural resources and that this is doubly true for the areas around Port-au-Prince. The density of humanity has led to the exploitation of all possible resources.

FUTURE OF THE CITY

At the moment, with little municipal activity and with few services provided, most residents of Port-au-Prince cannot meet their basic needs. International development funds frozen during the parliamentary and prime ministerial impasse in the late 1990s were released following the elections in 2000. These funds, while not all earmarked for Port-au-Prince, will have a drastic effect on the quality of life for inhabitants of the city. Infrastructural revamping within the city paid for with the money will, of course, lead to direct improvements. But improvements in the provinces financed by international donors will have a major impact on the city as well: if the quality of life for the peasants in Haiti is improved, then the constant migration into the city will be slowed, which will somewhat alleviate the problems of health, sanitation, overcrowding, and provision of material goods throughout the metropolitan area.

BIBLIOGRAPHY

Bazabas, Dingan, *Du Marché de Rue en Haïti* (L'Harmattan Villes et Enterprises 1997).

The Economist Intelligence Unit, *Country Profile: Haiti* (1999).

The Economist Intelligence Unit, "Country Report: Haiti," *The Economist Intelligence Unit Quarterly Reports* (First Quarter 2000): 20–27.

Etienne, Sauver-Pierre, *Haiti: L'Invasion Des ONG* (L'Imprimerie Natal, S.A. 1997).

Farmer, Paul, *Aids and Accusation: Haiti and the Geography of Blame* (University of California Press 1992).

Farmer, Paul, *The Uses of Haiti* (Common Courage Press 1994).

Fick, Carolyn E., *The Making of Haiti: The St. Domingue Revolution from Below* (University of Tennessee Press 1990).

Fondation Friedrich Ebert et Centre Pétion Bolivar, eds., "Port-Au-Prince: Peut-Il Etre Sauve?," *Forum Libre* (Presses des Ateliers Mitspa 1994).

James, C. L. R., *The Black Jacobins: Toussaint L'Ouverture and the San Domingo Revolution* (Vintage Books 1963).

Lawless, Robert, *Haiti's Bad Press* (Schenkman Books, Inc. 1992).

Manigat, Sabine, "Haiti: The Popular Sectors and the Crisis in Port-Au-Prince," *The Urban Caribbean: Transition to the New Economy,* ed. by Alejandro Portes, et al. (Johns Hopkins University Press 1997): 87–123.

Nicholls, David, *From Dessalines to Duvalier* (Rutgers University Press 1996).

North American Congress on Latin America, *Haiti: Dangerous Crossroads* (South End Press 1995).

Ridgeway, James, *The Haiti Files: Decoding the Crisis* (Essential Books/Azul Editions 1994).

Stepick, Alex, *Pride Against Prejudice: Haitians in the United States* (Allyn and Bacon 1998).

Weil, Thomas, et al., *Haiti: A Country Study* (U.S. Department of the Army 1982).

Willentz, Amy, *The Rainy Season: Haiti Since Duvalier* (Touchstone Books 1989).

HAROLD D. GREEN, JR.

Port-of-Spain
Trinidad and Tobago

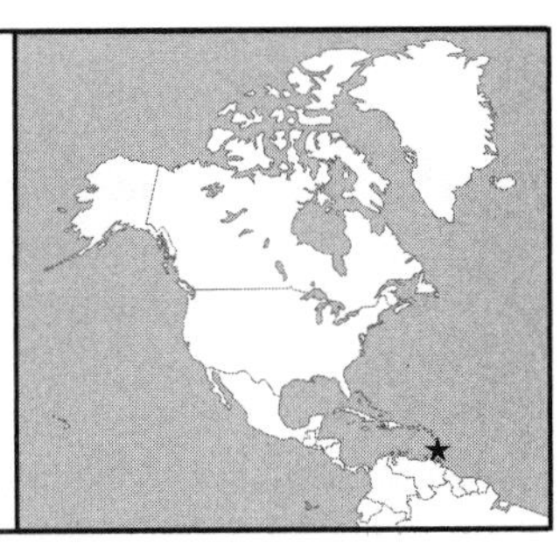

ORIENTATION

Name of City. Port-of-Spain (abbreviated PoS), lovingly called "town" in native Trinidadian, is the capital city of the island of Trinidad; Scarborough is the capital city of the island of Tobago. The two islands constitute what is known as the Republic of Trinidad and Tobago within the Commonwealth nations. The islands were unified by British colonizers in 1889 with a single governor, judiciary, and code of law; but the islands have very distinct historical trajectories.

Location. Trinidad and Tobago are the most southerly islands of the Caribbean archipelago. Trinidad is situated north of and opposite the mouth of the Orinoco River and is separated by the straits of the Gulf of Paria. The actual physical area of this rectangular-shaped island is 80 kilometers (37 miles) by 60 kilometers (50 miles), a total area of 4,828 square kilometers (1,864 square miles). It is half-forested with a range of low mountains on the north coast.

Port-of-Spain, a commercial and cultural center, is a seaport. It is located between the mountains of the Northern Range and extends eastward from the Gulf of Paria at 10°39′ north latitude and 61°31′ west longitude along the northwest coast.

Population. The population of Trinidad and Tobago was estimated at about 1.1 million (Census Report 1997). Port-of-Spain is the largest metropolitan area with a population of 58,400, almost one-third of Trinidad's total population. Other major cities are San Fernando (population 30,100) in the south and Arima (population 29,700) in the east.

Distinctive and Unique Features. Port-of-Spain is one of the liveliest and most fascinating cities of the Caribbean. It is a city of opposites, encompassing the most urban and the least developed parts of the island. For purposes of orientation, one can start with the Queen's Park Savannah, a glorious landmark that was donated to the city in 1820 by a colonial governor. To the north of Port-of-Spain are the Northern Range hills. To the south is the downtown area. To the east are the residential suburbs of St. Anns and Cascade; the Hilton Hotel perched on a ridge (originally the abode of the colonial governors); Belmont, the city's oldest suburb and the origin of many facets of Trinidad's carnival; and Laventille, the city's poorest suburb, where the first freed slaves squatted in the 1840s, and the birthplace of the first steel pans, or drums). To the southwest of the savannah is Maraval, a modest residential area with small businesses and many restaurants; St. Clair, the city's most affluent suburb, home of the German and American embassies, as well as one of the most picturesque cricket grounds in the Caribbean; and St. James, perhaps the liveliest suburb, famous for its Hosay celebrations, a feature of its strong Indian heritage, as well as its steel-band orchestras' pan yards. Hindu temples jostle for space alongside carnival mas camps, consolidating the city's heterogeneous nature. The Western Main Road runs for almost two kilometers (a mile) through the middle of St. James, lined with fast-food outlets, Chinese restaurants, bars, betting shops, and entertainment bars.

Despite the dazzle of urban life, farther to the west one can still experience the island's rural rhythms. The Chaguaramas area is covered with ancient rainforest, beyond which there is a series of rocky islands (including Gaspar Grande and Chacachacare) home to fishers and yachting enthusiasts.

One unique feature of Port-of-Spain is the custom called "liming" or "ole blagging" in Trinidadian English. A lime is an occasion, at any time and any place, when people congregate and chatter pleasantly about everything and nothing. Chattering embodies behaviors ranging from "ole talk" (idle chatter), to "sweet talk" (courtship and love chatter), to *mamaguy* (deceptive talk normally intended to fool the listener into believing or doing something). Liming is quite common in downtown Port-of-Spain, especially on Friday evenings after work.

Attractions of the City. Port-of-Spain's major attraction is its carnival (the national celebration of Trinidad and Tobago), a massive festival of freedom and renewal for Trinidad's multiethnic population. Carnival spawned the music of calypso, Soca, and the steel band. Port-of-Spain is the most popular venue for carnival celebrations, although other smaller carnivals are celebrated in other cities on the island. Around carnival time the entire city is converted into a theatrical stage, with thousands of masqueraders dressed in costumes parading in and around the streets vying for prizes. The city also becomes alive with music from calypso tents, pan yards, and massive, organized calypso and steelband shows, which demonstrate the nation's creativity. Calypso and steel bands are primary tourist attractions. Many small clubs, hotels, and practice yards provide forums for favorite musicians to perform alongside newer talents.

Relationships Between the City and the Outside. As a global city Port-of-Spain enjoys one of the most diversified economies in the Anglophone Caribbean. Its petroleum, chemical, food-processing, textile, and beverage industries attracted high levels of foreign investments from international markets. It is the world's second-largest producer of methanol and a major exporter of steel, ammonia, and oil.

Tourism is an underdeveloped revenue source, particularly on the island of Trinidad. However, with Port-of-Spain, as the major center for carnival, increasing numbers of tourists are drawn to the islands. Europe accounts for 50% of all tourist arrivals, with tourists from North America taking second place.

Trinidad and Tobago is also a signatory to the Lomé Convention. This facilitates duty-free access to the European Economic Community countries for industrial and agricultural products. A quota system is also in place for rum, sugar, and other items.

Major Languages. English is the major language spoken on Trinidad and Tobago. However, Spanish, Hindi, French, and English-based Creoles are also spoken.

HISTORY

The Origin of the City. Port-of-Spain became the capital city of Trinidad almost by accident. This provided the city with a sort of frontier characteristic, since peoples of different races and cultures flocked to the city seeking new horizons. Three important historical movements contributed to Port-of-Spain's genesis as a capital and also explain the waves of migration thereafter to the city.

The first movement dates to 1757 and the Spanish colonizers' Puerto de Los Hispanoles (a port next to the Amerindian village, Cu-Mucurapo, later Mucurapo—Amerindian for "the place of the Silk Cotton trees"). This was a little fishing village with mud huts and a few wooden thatched-roof houses, surrounded by hills and swamps, where the Spaniards lived and visited for approximately two centuries. The population of about 60 inhabitants included mainly Amerindians and persons of mixed Spanish descent, who earned a living through fishing and trade with the Venezuelan mainland. At that time the Spanish governor, Don Pedro de la Moneda, established residence in Port-of-Spain after deciding that the governor's residence in St. Joseph, the country's then capital, was neither habitable nor befitting a governor's status. The neglected outpost had two streets and was constantly plagued by floods.

In 1787 the immigration policy of King Carlos IV of Spain was to change the city's sleepy character. He issued a decree, *La Cédula de Población* (the Cédula of Population, which invited non-Spanish, Roman Catholic allies to take up offers of land). His intention was to accelerate the development of sugar and cocoa production. The only condition was that the planters had to be Catholic. The size of the parcel of land they were given was determined by the number of slaves they brought with them. Thousand of immigrants—mostly French—from the neighboring islands of Grenada, Martinique, and St. Dominique poured into Port-of-Spain to take advantage of the offer. French-speaking "coloureds" also migrated converting Port-of-Spain's population into a multicultural mishmash.

With this steady flow of immigrants, Port-of-Spain became overcrowded, but its economy grew owing to the newly developing agrarian enterprise. The city needed to expand and consolidate its resources. Don Maria José Chacon, the Spanish governor, supported urban expansion in the city. He reclaimed land from the sea, giving orders to construct streets over the surrounding mangrove swamps and woods. He was also responsible for diverting the Rio Santa Ana (St. Ann River) to the outskirts of the town, which solved the flooding problem.

The city's booming economy set the stage for the next set of colonial actors in Port-of-Spain's checkered history—the invasion of the British in 1797, giving Port-of-Spain its English name and its status as a capital city. After a devastating fire in 1808, the British governor, Sir Ralph Woodford, developed the city by establishing the Queen's Park Savannah and Woodford Square. The British also constructed two Forts, George and Picton, to safeguard the city's defenses.

Migration: Past and Present. With the abolition of slavery and the emancipation of the slaves in 1838, massive migrations to the city occurred. The freed slaves flocked to Port-of-Spain seeking jobs. They squatted on the eastern side of the city, later known as Laventille and Belmont, causing the city to spread towards the former Maraval and St. Ann's plantations. The colonial population remained divided into competing interest groups: the British controlled politics but the French influenced the culture, both in numbers and language.

Diverse populations continued to arrive in Port-of-Spain during the 19th century. The largest group, South Asian indentured laborers, appeared between 1845 and 1917 and settled in St. James. There were also *peones* (a Spanish-speaking peasant class from nearby South America); Chinese indentured workers and Portuguese shopkeepers; French royalists and republicans; and economic refugees from the Middle East known as Syrians, seeking better fortunes on the island. Because of the city's booming economy and employment prospects, immigrants from other neighboring islands such as Barbados, St. Vincent, and Grenada came, eventually making Port-of-Spain the hub of the southern Caribbean. This constant wave of migrations created one of the most heterogeneous, creolized cities in the region.

INFRASTRUCTURE

Public Buildings, Public Works, and Residences. Many of Port-of-Spain's public buildings are relics from its varied colonial past, providing the city with very stark contrasts. The city can be divided into two parts: "downtown," its oldest part, and "uptown," its fashionable, affluent area. Downtown stretches from King's Wharf Docks and the Cruise Ship Complex at the south end to Independence Square, Woodford Square, and the Queen's Park Savannah in the north. King's Wharf is the seat of Trinidad's burgeoning import and export trade. After the dredging of the deepwater harbor in the 1930s, deep-draught ships could be accommodated, visibly boosting the nation's economy and providing the capital city with the most important port in the southern Caribbean. In the port boats arrive and depart from St. Vincent, Barbados, St. Lucia, and Venezuela.

From the port one crosses Wrightson Road, leading into Independence Square (later renamed Brian Lara Promenade after Trinidad's record-holding cricketer), the main focus of business life in the city. On the square there is a bronze statue of Arthur Cipriani, the city's only mayor (1920s) who defended workers' rights. Opposite the statue is the Drag Brothers Mall, "the Drag" consisting of small shops run by Rastafarians, specializing in handmade leather crafts and souvenirs. From the Drag, one crosses Chacon to Frederick Street, the main shopping boulevard in Port-of-Spain. This street is lined with department stores selling merchandise from all over the world.

Along the southern side of Independence Square are some of the most important buildings in the country. These include the Financial Complex, with the Central Bank twin towers (the tallest buildings in Trinidad, rising 92 meters [302 feet] high) home of the ministry of finance and the prime minister's office. On the north side is the Treasury Building, the former residence of the Central Bank and the head office of Customs and Excise.

The Roman Catholic Church Cathedral of the Immaculate Conception lies on the eastern end of Independence Square, a twin-towered Gothic construction. Of interest are the stained-glass windows: one set depicts the apparition of the Blessed Virgin at Lourdes. The other windows depict the children of Trinidad and Tobago, in all their ethnic diversity. Immediately behind the cathedral is Columbus Square, with a statue of Christopher Columbus, who landed on the island in 1498, beyond which is Piccadilly Street, where Port-of-Spain originally began as a city. The Riverside Plaza houses government ministries and other departments. Fort San Andres, built in 1787, was Port-of-Spain's defense when the British invaded the island in 1797. It is the best example of a wooden Spanish fort, and it is the oldest colonial relic in the city; it houses the traffic police.

Woodford Square, lovingly called "The People's Parliament," was named after Governor Ralph Woodford, who was responsible for laying out the square in the heart of the city a few blocks up on Frederick Street. The square has a colonial-style bandstand and an elegant 18th-century cast-iron fountain supported by mermaids. The Square has been the scene of much political activity: in 1956 it was unofficially renamed the University of Woodford Square because of the variety of political lectures delivered there at the dawning of the People's

National Movement Party under the leadership of Eric Williams, who became the first prime minister of Trinidad and Tobago.

On the southern side of Woodford Square is the late-Gothic-style, Anglican Trinity Cathedral, constructed in 1816–1826. The roof of Trinity is a replica of Westminster Hall in London. There are six stained-glass windows and a life-sized marble statue of Sir Ralph Woodford.

To the west of the Trinity cathedral is the neo-Renaissance-style Red House, the seat of Parliament. The building inherited its name from a former building on the site that was painted red in honor of Queen Victoria's Diamond Jubilee in 1897. The present structure was burned in the 1902 water riots, and was also stormed during a 1990 coup attack. There is an eternal flame outside the front entrance, commemorating government and security officers who died in the coup.

© RICHARD T. NOWITZ/CORBIS

This young woman is a security guard in Port-of-Spain, Trinidad and Tobago.

On the northwest side of Woodford Square is the Trinidad Public Library, built in 1901. To the left is the Hall of Justice, built in 1979, which houses the Supreme Court of Trinidad and Tobago; and to the right of the library lies City Hall, the mayor's office and home of Port-of-Spain's City Council.

Another prominent building is the National Museum and Art Gallery built in 1892 as the Science and Art Museum to commemorate Queen Victoria's Jubilee. The Museum houses Amerindian artifacts, lithographs, and some works by Trinidadian artists. Worthy of mention is Memorial Park with its cenotaph in memory of those who died in the two world wars.

Frederick Street ends in the north, however, at the most beautiful and famous park in the city, namely the Queen's Park Savannah, Port-of-Spain's largest space. Traffic circles the Savannah clockwise, making it perhaps the largest roundabout in the world. The Savannah is the scene of joggers, corn and coconut vendors, and other hucksters who constantly circle its "pitch walk." In addition to cricket, football matches, and international musical events, the Savannah comes alive annually for the nation's carnival, where, according to the natives, the city becomes a stage at the "Big Yard."

Some of the city's best architectural structures overlook the Savannah: on Queen's Park West there are several examples of "gingerbread" architecture (distinctive fretted woodwork on the buildings). There is also a row of mansions—the Magnificent Seven—on the Savannah's west side. They consist of colonial houses built in the 1900s, in various European styles that run the gamut from German Renaissance to neo-Romanesque. These include Queen's Royal College, a prestigious boys' school; Hayes Court, the Anglican Bishop's Residence; Archbishop's House, the Roman Catholic Bishop's residences; Mille Fleurs, offices of the National Security Council; and Roomor, a private residence in French baroque style. There is also White Hall, the prime minister's offices; and Stollmeyer Castle, Killarney, which are government offices. Also of architectural interest are Knowsley, the Ministry of Foreign Affairs, and the George Brown house on the Savannah's south side. To the north is the Emperor Valley Zoo, next door to which lies the Botanical Gardens, containing a large collection of international tress and plants. The President's House is situated behind the Botanical Gardens, which originally housed the British Governors in the late 1880s.

Politics and City Services. Port-of-Spain is the seat of the government of Trinidad and Tobago, keeping the city very much in the public sphere. Politics date to 1888 when the two islands were officially merged to form a single colony. Trinidad and Tobago achieved independence from Britain in 1962, becoming a republic within the commonwealth in 1976 with a fully democratic government that has held elections regularly since 1956. Under the Constitution of Trinidad and Tobago Act of 1976, the president is the head of state and commander-in-chief of the country's armed forces. The president is generally elected by an electoral college comprising parliamentarians, and all members of both the house of representatives and the senate.

Parliament is fashioned after Britain's Westminster, with a bicameral type of legislature consisting of a 36-member house of representatives, and the lower house elected by the populace every five years. There is also a 31-member senate (the Upper House), whose members are appointed by the president: 16 members are recommended by the prime minister, six on the advice of the opposition leader, and nine independent senators are named at the president's discretion. The prime minister is appointed by the president and the cabinet.

Port-of-Spain, as the nation's capital, has witnessed both the nation's political unrest (including the 1970s Black Power Revolution and the bloody coup attempt by Abu Baku in 1990) and the increased prosperity of the 20th century. Traditionally, as early as the 1970s, petroleum has been the government's largest source of revenue, contributing to one-third of all revenue and two-thirds of the country's foreign exchange. From this source the city developed its sophisticated financial district identified by the imposing twin towers of the Central Bank. Oil prices dropped in the 1980s and 1990s following the decline in world oil prices. At the end of the 20th century the nation experienced a financial recovery from its exports of other products such as methanol, urea, and ammonia.

Educational Systems. Education is compulsory, and free, for all children between the ages of 6 and 12. Entry to secondary school is competitive, since students are required to pass the Common Entrance Examination held annually for pupils aged from 10 to 12 years. Approximately 70% of this group attends secondary school; the remainder pursue vocational and technical forms of training. Several schools function under the "dual system," in which the government and religious organizations—or other recognized bodies—cooperate as partners. The government sponsors a Youth Training and Employment Partnership Programme (YTEPP), whose nine-month courses produce on an average 8,000 graduates per year. There are also schools that offer programs for the hotel, catering, and management industries.

Tertiary education is also available at the University of the West Indies (UWI), an institution of higher learning that serves the entire Caribbean region. One of its campuses is located at St. Augustine, Trinidad, offering undergraduate and postgraduate programs in engineering, agriculture, business administration, humanities, languages, and the natural and social sciences. The other two campuses are at Mona, Jamaica, and Cave Hill, Barbados. UWI also has an Institute of Business, offering post-graduate business courses where one can earn the Executive Masters of Business Administration (EMBA) and the International Masters in Business Administration (IMBA).

In 1999 the National Carnival Institute was inaugurated to address the need to easily disseminate information on carnival's evolution and organization management, as well as to develop and deliver training courses in all the carnival arts including mask making, calypso competitions, music literacy, and musicology for persons (local and foreign) with diverse educational backgrounds.

Port-of-Spain also houses the National Institute of Higher Education, Research and Technology (NIHERST). It has a wide variety of offerings including health science, nursing, information technology colleges, and the institute of languages. A new project is in the pipeline to develop software writing skills. The Eric Williams Medical Complex, with its dual teaching and medical science facilities, is one of the leading medical facilities in the Caribbean.

Transportation Systems. Port-of-Spain is 20 kilometers (12 miles) Northwest of Piarco, Trinidad's international airport. Its compact city center operates on a grid system. Transportation is diverse, with three types of taxicabs: hire, route, and maxi-taxis.

Hire taxicabs are privately run, taking passengers to any destination. They are similar to the yellow cabs in New York City, although not metered, with some fixed fares for specific routes.

Route, or shared, taxicabs are more like buses. They drive along specific routes, picking up passengers along the way. They start at various points in the city and serve routes towards the west and north.

There are also those that circle the Queen's Park Savannah.

Maxi-taxis are small minibuses that operate like route-taxis, generally painted in bright colored stripes to indicate their routes. Yellow-band maxis operate around Port-of-Spain and have four different taxicab stands allocated to them.

There is also a bus service owned by the Public Transport Service Corporation (PTSC), which provides one of the cheapest modes of transport in and around the city. The main bus terminal is located at Citygate (South Quay, Port-of-Spain) in an old Victorian building—the former train station which was demolished in 1960. It is the hub of transportation to and from Port-of-Spain and other cities throughout the island.

CULTURE AND SOCIAL LIFE

Distinctive Features of the City's Cultures. Although Trinidad and Tobago is a patriarchal society, women set the pace for city life. They are self-confident and quietly assertive, particularly with men. Women are also fashion trend setters, many traveling to other global centers to shop. It is quite normal to see impeccably dressed women sporting the latest British or American fashions on the streets of Port-of-Spain.

People are extremely friendly and uninhibited; it is considered impolite not to acknowledge other people as they pass along on the street. A simple nod of the head or a friendly glance suffices. Before starting a conversation, one is expected to greet another with "good morning" or "good evening" depending on the time of day. Life operates at a slower pace, so that it is not unusual for a person to arrive at an appointment minutes later than the arranged time; that is called Trinidad time.

Religion is very much a part of everyday life. Although overt sexual dancing can be seen at parties, and especially in the streets during carnival time, this should not be misconstrued in any way. Uninhibited dancing belongs entirely to the carnival or party atmosphere. When the party is over the dancing is over, too. Obscene language is illegal, but the law is not generally enforced.

Cuisine. Cuisine in Port-of-Spain owes its distinctive flavors and rich variety to a number of ethnic influences: European, African, Indian, Chinese, Middle Eastern, and Mediterranean. "Trinis" like to eat, and food reflects this characteristic in its variety of spices, seasonings, and the many available choices. Food ranges from international to Creole cuisine and fast foods.

Traditional Creole is an African legacy, although other ethnic groups have also contributed to the major ingredients used: a blend of fresh, local vegetables, spices, and pepper marinades. The more popular dishes include *pelau,* the Trinidadian version of pilaf (rice and peas cooked with pepper and marinated meat) and callalloo (a somewhat slippery green soup made with okra, dasheen leaves, seasonings of hot pepper, and crab meat). There is also *souse* (a French legacy of pigs' feet boiled and served cold with lime, cucumber, pepper, and onions). *Buljol* is a Portuguese shredded saltfish, which is served with tomatoes, onions, watercress, pepper, and olive oil.

Trinidad in general, and Port-of-Spain in particular, boast of a diverse blend of fast foods unique to the island. Fast foods does not translate into hamburgers, fried chicken, french fries, or pizza (even though the city is flooded with the international fast-food chains). The most popular fast foods in Trinidad are *roti* and *doubles,* originally foods brought by Indians to the island. *Roti* is basically curried meat or vegetables folded in a *roti skin* (a soft, rounded, dough wrapping). There are several types of roti skins, the most popular of which are *dhalpouri* (dough layered with seasoned ground split peas) and *buss-up-shot* (a thin, shredded roti skin, used like a spoon for eating curries). Popular roti shops can be found along the West Main Road, in St. James, and in Port-of-Spain.

Doubles refers to two pieces of fried *bara* (sandwich-type bread), filled with curried *channa* (chick peas) and spiced with pepper sauce and *kucheela* (mango chutney). Other lighter Indian delicacies include *aloo* pies (curried potatoes folded into pie-shaped loaves of bread) and *phulouri* (deep-fried balls of dough served hot in paper bags with pepper, hot mango, or bitter sweet tamarind). The best thirst-quenching drink for these "pepper hot" delicacies is ice-cold fresh coconut water, bought and served from the back of a vendor's pick-up truck.

Many of the Creole fast foods can be bought around the Savannah. These include corn soup, a thick split-pea broth with chunks of sweet corn and small dumplings; *accra,* a hot pepper saltfish cake; and oysters, sold by vendors recognized by their flaming flambeaux. Other Creole soups include *san coche* (made with lentils and flavoured with pigs' tails); *cow heel soup* (thickened with split peas and meat that is slowly cooked so that it falls off the bone); and *fish tea* (a delicious broth boiled with pieces of fish, green bananas, and small dumplings). Last but by no means least there is *pacro* or *Man water*, similar to fish tea but *pacro* or *chip-chips* (a small shellfish found in Trinidad) is used instead of fish. It is reputed to be a very strong aphrodisiac.

Ethnic and Class Diversity. Ethnic diversity today, like two centuries ago, is still shaped by the traumatizing experience of slavery, which stratified the society along racial lines. Various ethnic groups in Trinidad and Tobago contributed to the cosmopolitan nature of Port-of-Spain. The people are chiefly West Indians of African descent (50%) and East Indians (40%). However, another 18.4% are of mixed ethnicities—0.4% Chinese; 0.6%, European; 0.2%, other; and 0.4% include those of Mediterranean Middle Eastern descent. Some Trinidadians boast of this diversity, laying claim to family roots in Africa, India, Scotland, France, Lebanon, and Spain, hence the term *callallo* (potpourri) to describe this diversified interethnic mixing. Callallo is an indigenous delicacy, typically eaten on Sundays, but the term has come to refer to a blending of unlikely ingredients.

Cultural and ethnic diversity are mirrored in the city's calendar of public holidays. There are holidays celebrated by Hindus, Muslims, Baptists, Roman Catholics, and so on. Others are recognized by trade unions and those of African, Indian, Chinese, or Hispanic descent. Other holidays, such as Carnival, involve the entire multicultural populace.

Family and Other Social Support Systems. Because of Trinidad's ethnically diverse population, family patterns vary. Traditionally, African family patterns did not adhere to the typical Western family system of marriage and the nuclear family. Common-law unions were prevalent, and women exercised great authority in this area since many households were headed by women (35% of all families listed women as the head of the household). Today, however, with the large, educated middle class, and upward social mobility, family structures, both among the Africans and Indians, have facilitated but not necessarily copied Western patterns.

Extended family networks prevail, with grandmothers indispensable to care for children, since many mothers spend long hours working away from home. Urban living, with its high costs has helped to strengthen kinship ties and coping strategies.

Work and Commerce. Prior to the 20th century the majority of Trinidad's population was primarily concerned with agricultural production: plantations of sugar, cocoa, coffee, and coconuts. This was replaced by oil in the 20th century. At the turn of the 21st century, the oil sector provided 76% of all available jobs, with the sugar and construction industries supplying another 24%. Unemployment decreased from 16% to 14%, and this trend is predicted to continue. After a period of radical economic adjustment, there is a good deal of construction work taking place across the country, helping to keep supermarkets well stocked. Other industries—manufacturing, service, music, and fashion—are busy. This augers well for commercial and industrial opportunities in the city.

Arts and Recreation. Trinidadians are reputed to enjoy life, celebrating anything from public holidays to "liming" after work. There is no shortage of night life in the city—bars, pubs, discotheques, and American-style nightclubs cater to every taste. This spirit also favors partying in private homes, community centers, and sporting complexes with live-music bands playing until the patrons choose to leave. The city also has a number of home-grown theater companies. The best known is the Trinidad Theatre Workshop (founded in 1959 by the Nobel-laureate playwright and poet Derek Walcott), which puts on most of his work as well as other international dramas. Other companies such as Bagasse Company, Raymond Choo Kong, and Ragoo Productions feature light-hearted comedy and other local productions.

Shopping, eating, and beach "limes" on Sundays are other forms of leisure. Sports also occupy a central place in the nation's psyche, with cricket, football (soccer) and basketball the major activities. (Many international cricket test match and international football matches have taken place in Port-of-Spain). There is also good golf at the St. Andrew's course, north of the capital, as well as tennis and horseback riding.

A unique artistic feature in the city is "Under the Trees." These are evening performances that feature local artists whose repertoires include anything from solo shows and local plays to calypso and steel-band performances—literally performed under the shady trees at the Normandie Hotel.

QUALITY OF LIFE

As a young, rapidly developing global city, Port-of-Spain's quality of life is quite good. Its natural reserves of oil and gas, coupled with its powerful manufacturing industry, have ensured economic growth, and the city has not been tarnished by a massive tourist trade. It is a good place for business offering rich investment opportunities. The cost-of-living in the city has remained relatively inexpensive. There are some drug-related crimes, robberies, and muggings. Nonetheless, Trinidad and Tobago enjoy a long-standing reputation of democratic stability, with a highly educated, skilled workforce, and a strategically located capital, forming a hub of the Americas. That totals a healthy, profitable place to live.

FUTURE OF THE CITY

As Port-of-Spain enters the 21st century it is confronted with the urgent challenge of charting the course of its own destiny. This can be seen in the dynamic interplay between the political and economic forces that influence the city in different ways.

While Port-of-Spain boasts of multicultural diversity in the realm of artistic creativity, it needs to address the issue of political leadership in the interest of maintaining democratic governance and in upholding the rights and interests of the various ethnic groups that live in the city. Lack of strong leadership also has an impact on the economic sphere, fostering other problems of unemployment and urban growth. The city must devise and implement feasible strategies to stimulate and maintain higher levels of economic growth and employment geared toward the social betterment and empowerment of its diverse population. In this sense the city is faced with the challenge of formulating and implementing new sociopolitical and economic strategies to deal effectively with these problems in the 21st century.

BIBLIOGRAPHY

Anthony, Michael, *The Making of Port-of-Spain,* vol. 1, 1757–1939 (National Cultural Council of Trinidad and Tobago 1978).

Borde, Pierre Gustav, *History of the Island of Trinidad Under the Spanish Government,* vols. 1 & 2 (Paria Publishing Company 1982).

Braithwaite, Lloyd, *Social Stratification in Trinidad* (Institute of Social and Economic Research 1975).

Brereton, Bridget, *A History of Modern Trinidad: 1783–1962* (Heinemann 1981).

Brereton, Bridget, *Race Relations in Colonial Trinidad, 1870–1900* (Cambridge University Press 1979).

Cowley, John, *Carnival, Canboulay and Calypso: Caribbean Traditions in the Making* (University of Cambridge Press 1996).

De-Light, Dominique, and Polly Thomas, *Trinidad and Tobago: The Rough Guide* (Penguin Books Ltd. 1998).

Dyde, B., *Caribbean Companion: The A–Z Reference* (Macmillan 1992).

Hill, Errol, *The Trinidad Carnival: Mandate for a National Theatre* (University of Texas Press 1972).

Knight, F. W., and C. A. Palmer, eds., *The Modern Caribbean* (University of North Carolina Press 1989).

Lewis, Gordon K., *The Growth of the Modern West Indies* (Monthly Review Press 1968).

Lewis, W. A., *Labour in the West Indies* (New Beacon Books 1977).

Majid, A., *Urban Nationalism: A Study of Political Development in Trinidad* (University of Florida Press 1988).

Manuel, Peter, *Caribbean Currents* (Latin American Bureau 1995).

Mendes, John, *Cote ce Cote la: Trinidad and Tobago Dictionary* (College Press 1986).

Ryan, Selwyn, *Race and Nationalism in Trinidad and Tobago: A Study of Decolonization in a Multiracial Society* (University of Toronto Press 1972).

Ryan, Selwyn, ed., *Trinidad and Tobago: The Independence Experience, 1962–1987* (Institute for Social and Economic Research 1988).

Stuempfle, Stephen, *The Steelband Movement: The Forging of a National Art in Trinidad and Tobago* (University of Pennsylvania Press 1996).

Taylor, Jeremy, *Trinidad and Tobago: An Introduction and Guide* (Macmillan 1992).

Warner, Keith, *The Trinidad Calypso* (Heinemann 1982).

Williams, Eric, *Capitalism and Slavery* (Andre Deutsch 1964).

Wood, Donald, *Trinidad in Transition: The Years After Slavery* (Oxford University Press 1968).

Yelvington, Kevin, *Trinidad Ethnicity* (Macmillan; Warwick University Caribbean Studies 1993).

PATRICIA T. ALLEYNE-DETTMERS

Prague

Czech Republic

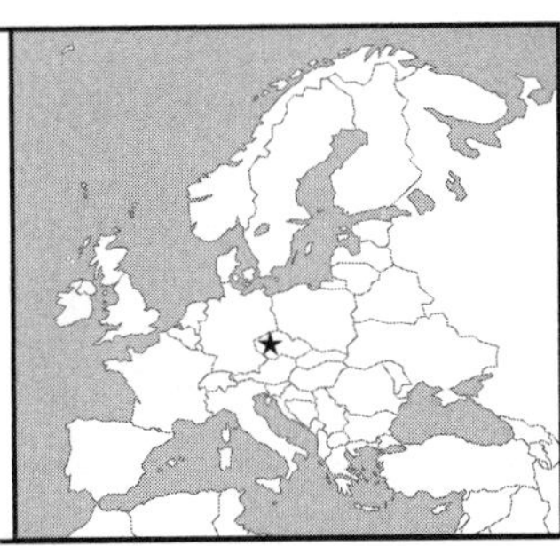

ORIENTATION

Name of City. Prague (Praha) is the capital of the Czech Republic. Legend has it that the city was founded by the legendary Princess Libuše and her husband, Přemysl.

Location. Prague is located at 49°56′ north latitude and 50°10′ east longitude in the middle of Bohemia, which is the western half of the Czech Republic. It is in central Europe, strategically placed at the crossroads of western and eastern Europe amid Germany, Austria, Slovakia, and Poland. The city has a mild climate with an average temperature of about 10°C (50°F) and annual precipitation around 450 millimeters (18 inches).

Population. According to the March 1991 census, Prague had a population of 1.21 million inhabitants with permanent residency in the city. The city population steadily declined during the 1990s, and by the end of 1999 it was 1.18 million living in an area of 496 square kilometers (191 square miles). However, at the same time a population of foreigners was steadily increasing, estimated at between 120,000 to 150,000. There is no exact definition of the Prague metropolitan area. Two districts surrounding the city of Prague—Prague-East and Prague-West—have almost 200,000 inhabitants living within 1,171 square kilometers (452 square miles).

Distinctive and Unique Features. The most distinctive and unique feature of Prague is its large historic core, which presents 800 years of architecture untouched by any major devastation caused by natural disasters or wars. In 1971 Prague was declared by the Czechoslovak government as a Historic Monument Conservation Area, and in 1992 it was included on the United Nations Educational, Scientific, and Cultural Organization's (UNESCO's) list of World Heritage sites. The succession of building styles within the medieval street network created an exceptional array of urban architecture. Although the basic street layout from Romanesque and Gothic times was not altered, the townscape was transformed by the incorporation of baroque and Renaissance buildings, and later enriched by classicist, art nouveau, cubist, modern, and contemporary architecture.

Avant Guide Prague (1998) presents a popular view of the town, which symbolizes the picture of Prague in the minds of many visitors. "The very heart of Prague is what enraptures the aesthetes, one historical square mile that is the most beautiful little city on earth. Prague is storybook beautiful; made of cobblestone streets, frilly baroque buildings, a castle on a hill, and a river that runs through it. Strolling along the center's narrow lanes, past magically sculpted buildings garnished with golden spires is like wandering through a giant jewel box. With poetic harmony, Gothic cathedrals rub shoulders with Renaissance mansions, baroque churches, cubist office buildings and art nouveau houses. The smorgasbord of evolutionary architecture is a miracle of contrasts and colors that exists nowhere else."

Although Prague is well known for the beauty of its medieval center, most of the city is formed by neighborhoods that have emerged since 1850. The spatial structure consists of five concentric zones: 1) the historical core; 2) the inner city with blocks of apartment houses; 3) the belt of villa neighborhoods and garden towns; 4) the ring of communist housing, prefabricated high rise buildings; and 5) the zone of rural landscape with small towns and villages. Prague is unique by its compactness, well developed and functioning public transport, and accessibility for walking.

The historic core concentrates business, government, and tourist functions and facilities. During the 20th century, it gradually lost its residential function, through the modernization of housing stock and the incorporation of new government and commercial buildings. The historical core accounts for a bare 2% of the city's administrative area and contains only 5% of the total population. A thick belt of inner-city neighborhoods, built from the mid-19th century to World War II, encircles the city core. The inner city is characterized by blocks of four- to five-story apartment houses, which form a regular street pattern, and by scattered old industrial districts. About two-fifths of Prague's population live in this zone, which can be accurately described as "urban." This area is a symbol of periods of rapid urban growth, concentration, and density. It also reflects urban decline associated with later population shifts to suburban living, and, under communism, the neglect of urban rehabilitation in favor of investments in the construction of prefabricated high-rise housing complexes. Around the compact inner city, villa neighborhoods and garden towns emerged in the interwar period. They are exclusively residential areas consisting of low-rise detached, semidetached, or terraced single- or two-family houses. During communism a ring of massive housing estates encircled Prague's inner city and sharply demarcated the outermost boundary of the urbanized area. This zone consists of prefabricated high-rises, usually four- to twelve-story buildings concentrated in resi-

© ANNETTE FOURNET/CORBIS

Old houses line a narrow street in Prague, Czech Republic.

dential districts with large industrial zones at the eastern edge of the city. Over two-fifths of Prague's population live in such areas. Beyond the housing estates, but still within the administrative boundary of Prague, there is a rural landscape with small towns and villages. This zone, along with areas beyond the city boundary, is subject to both commercial and residential suburbanization.

Attractions of the City. The post-1989 reforms, which established a pluralist democracy, a market economy, and liberalized foreign trade, integrated the Czech Republic into the international economy, political institutions, and cultural life. Prague plays the role of a gateway into the Czech Republic. It is the primary place for businesses, labor, and tourists.

After the "Velvet Revolution of 1989," Prague attracted thousands of young Westerners, especially Americans, who settled in the city as artists, consultants, and entrepreneurs. In the mid-1990s there were up to 50,000 young Westerners living in this "Paris of the 1990s."

However, the most important force behind the internationalization of postcommunist Prague was capital investments by foreign companies that extended their operation's into postcommunist Europe. With increasing political and economic stability, there was a growing inflow of direct foreign investments into the Czech Republic. In Prague foreign activities were particularly important in trade and producer services, such as finance, accounting, law, consultancy, real estate development, marketing, public relations, and media. Foreign companies demanded space for their operations and foreign investors and developers supplied prime office and retail space for lease or sale. Foreign investors dominated property development and were the major force changing Prague's urban landscape.

Internationalization also had an important influence on the labor market. On the one hand there was an inflow of Western managers and employees and on the other hand international economic migration brought workers from eastern Europe, especially Ukraine, and small traders and vendors from Vietnam and China. Expatriate workers contributed to labor market polarization.

The historical, architectural, and cultural heritage of Prague attract more than two million foreign tourists annually, especially from Germany, Italy, the United Kingdom, the United States, Spain, France, and the Netherlands. On average visitors stay for four days.

Relationships Between the City and the Outside. Prague is the capital city, and with a population of 1.2 million it is also the largest urban center in the Czech Republic; it also dominates the country's settlement system. The second-largest city, Brno, has a population of only 400,000. Prague accounts for 12% of the country's population, 15% of all jobs, and 21% of the gross domestic product (GDP). All of the major banks and more than one-third of the nation's companies are headquartered in Prague. Salaries in Prague are one-third higher than the average in the Czech Republic. Prague has one of the lowest unemployment rates (approximately 4%) in the country and the highest share of jobs in the tertiary sector (75%), namely in finance and other business services.

Prague is the wealthiest region not only in the Czech Republic but also in all of postcommunist central and eastern Europe. In 1995 the Czech Republic became the first former Eastern bloc country to be accepted by the Organization for Economic Cooperation and Development (OECD) and in March 1999 it became a member of the North Atlantic Treaty Organization (NATO).

Major Languages. The official language is Czech, a western Slavic tongue. A minority of Slovaks residing in Prague speak Slovak, which is very close to Czech. Increasing numbers of foreigners working and living in Prague speak their native language. Westerners working in large international firms generally speak English or German. Members of Chinese and Vietnamese communities rarely speak fluent Czech. There is also a growing population of Russians and Croatians, who often master Czech. A large number of blue-collar workers from Ukraine can understand Czech; however, they do not speak it actively. For Czechs the most common second languages are English, German, and Russian. Older generations understand German and later generations understand Russian. The English-speaking population is steadily increasing, especially among the younger generation and within the business community. German is often spoken in tourist-oriented facilities.

HISTORY

The Origin of the City. The founding of Prague coincided with the arrival of Slavic tribes into the Bohemian Basin in the 6th century. At the end of the 9th century, Prague Castle (Hradčany) was founded in a strategic position to control a merchant path on the Vltava River. Prague's second castle, Vyšehrad, was built in the 10th century, and an extensive settlement grew up between Prague's castles on both riverbanks.

The medieval development of Prague culminated with the planned foundation of New Town (Nové Město) by king Charles IV in 1348. Prague's four historic towns (Hradčany, Malá Strana, Staré Město, and Nové Město) were encircled by new fortification. A university and an archbishop were established, and Charles Bridge, later a popular tourist attraction, was constructed of stone. The city covered a total area of more than 800 hectares (1,977 acres), and with an estimated 40,000 to 50,000 inhabitants it ranked among the largest European cities of that time. The area of the New Town accommodated urban development until the beginning of the 19th century.

From the 15th to the 19th century, periods of decline alternated with times of economic expansion, cultural revival, and population growth in the city. In the second half of the 16th century there was a recurrence of economic and cultural expansion with a considerable immigration of foreigners (Germans, Italians, and Jews) engaged in art, science, and diplomacy. Prague, a royal and imperial residence of the Habsburgs, gained the status of an important Renaissance European cultural center. After the Thirty Years' War in the first half of the 17th century, Prague become a provincial town. It regained some of its importance during the 18th century, when many new buildings were erected and old buildings were transformed into the baroque style.

The Industrial Revolution, abolishment of serfdom, and migration influenced the city's development in the 19th century. Manufacturing plants emerged beyond the city fortification, followed by expanding residential suburbs. While the population of the historic core stagnated, suburban areas developed quickly, ultimately becoming independent towns. At the end of the 19th century, these towns had double the number of inhabitants as the historic district. However, the suburbs and the core, in morphological terms, formed one urban unit with a total population of more than half a million. At the turn of century a part of the historic core was transformed by an urban sanitation and clearance project, which replaced the tortuous streets and tiny, dilapidated houses of the medieval Jewish ghetto with wide streets and large buildings of a new art nouveau district.

After World War I and the proclamation of the independent Czechoslovak Republic in 1918, Prague became the capital city. Its new geopolitical position brought rapid development to the urban area. In 1922 Greater Prague was formed by the amalgamation of 37 surrounding municipalities. The city area expanded more than eight times to 198 square kilometers (76 square miles), with 677,000 inhabitants. New public buildings were erected in the inner city, serving especially the needs of newly formed government ministries. Urban growth was concentrated in outer areas of low-rise housing in the form of villa neighborhoods, garden towns, and more distant commuting suburbs. Suburbanization processes became clearly visible in the wider metropolitan area. The population of the city rose to nearly one million in 1940; but after World War II, the prewar population size was not reestablished until 1957.

The Communist takeover in 1948 started a new historical epoch of building a socialist city. Urban land was nationalized and a large proportion of housing (with the exception of single-family houses) was transferred to state ownership. The state took over responsibilities for the management of housing as well as for new construction. The construction of state housing was predominantly based on industrialized, prefabricated technology. Standardized design led to uniformity in new residential areas. Smaller districts of prefabricated housing for a few thousand inhabitants constructed in the early 1960s evolved into huge "New Towns" built in the 1970s and the 1980s, each for up to 100,000 people. These housing developments created a characteristic picture of the communist city. The residents of communist housing were on average younger and better educated than the rest of the city population. It was the "middle class of communism." The planned city growth required land for new construction; this was solved by the expansion of the city territory in 1968 and 1974 to 496 square kilometers (191 square miles), when 51 surrounding municipalities were amalgamated. One of the important achievements was the construction of an underground rail system, which formed the backbone of the city transport system. With the economic recession of Communist Czechoslovakia, public investments and city growth declined after 1975.

After 40 years of communism and a centrally planned economy, a democratic political regime, and a market economy were quickly established during the first half of the 1990s. The government especially pursued privatization of state assets and liberalization of prices. The establishment of a market and growing exposure to the global economy brought internationalization, economic restructuring in terms of deindustrialization, and the growth of producer services and increasing social polarization. The most important processes of urban change in post-Communist Prague were the reinvention, commercialization, and expansion of the city center, the radical transformation of outer-city areas and urban hinterlands through commercial and residential suburbanization, the islands of dynamic revitalization and gentrification within the overall stagnation in inner-city neighborhoods, and the differentiation between communist housing estates.

Migration: Past and Present. The decisive factor for the population growth of Prague in the 19th and 20th centuries was migration. The highest migration gains were reached during the 1920s and the 1930s. After World War II, Prague's migration gains were negatively influenced by stagnation in new housing construction. The annual net-migration has slowly increased since the 1960s, when the construction of large-scale housing projects started. It reached its peak in the second half of the 1980s with an annual net-migration of about 9,000 people. At the beginning of the 1990s, migration gains rapidly declined, and since 1994 Prague has lost population compared to the rest of the Czech Republic. A large portion of migration out of the city is from wealthier households moving to suburban settlements behind Prague's administrative boundary. In such cases migration is realized within the metropolitan area, which as a whole does not lose its population.

Prague attracts young, well-educated people at the peak of their productive lives. On the other hand, families with children and older people are leaving the city for a healthier environment and a lower cost of living. The crucial factor that positively influences the migration balance of Prague is the supply of well-paid jobs. For young people, this outweighs such unfavorable conditions as the housing shortage or pollution. The city also attracts migrants because of the availability of good training and education opportunities.

While Prague has negative net migration compared to the rest of the Czech Republic, it has gained population through foreign immigration. In 1996 there were over 60,000 foreigners with permanent or long-term residential status in Prague. Many citizens of Slovakia, Russia, Poland, and the United States had permanent residential status. Ukrainians, Slovaks, and Chinese most often held long-term residency permits. According to estimates, approximately 75,000 to 90,000 foreigners lived in the city without legal permits. Ukrainians make up the largest group of foreigners. Typically, they are males working in the construction industry. Western foreigners (most often citizens of the United States, Germany, France, and the United Kingdom) work as managers or professionals in local headquarters of foreign companies or in financial and business services. The Chinese and Vietnamese operate predominantly in small retail or catering businesses.

INFRASTRUCTURE

Public Buildings, Public Works, and Residences. Most renowned public buildings in Prague are historic monuments, government offices, cultural centers, and some specific landmarks. The primary historic monuments are Prague's castle, which is the seat of the president, and Charles Bridge. The historic core is a dense net of historic monuments; about one-third of all buildings are protected. Parliament and the Senate use some of the prime historic buildings. Other buildings serve as galleries, museums, theaters, concert halls, and churches. The best known cultural centers are Municipal House, Žofín, Vinohrady National House, and the Prague Exhibition Grounds. Many historic buildings have been acquired by private property investors and converted into offices, shops, entertainment centers, and hotels.

Clusters of historic landmarks and open public spaces characterize the cultural landscape of the city center. Squares, such as Old Town Square, and Wenceslas Square; pedestrian zones, such as Na Príkop or Celetná; and numerous passageways and arcades create a dense network of interconnected public spaces.

The most important public work is the underground rail system, called the Metro, which extends throughout most of the city. Prague is well equipped with a basic technical infrastructure. Virtually all homes are supplied with electricity and water from public systems, and connected to public sewerage. Four-fifths of the city's homes are linked to the gas supply network, and a large share of homes use centralized long-distance heating.

In 1991 there were 495,804 dwellings in 78,977 houses. Only 12% of the dwellings were in family houses (which accounted for 60% of all houses). About 88% of all dwellings were in apartment houses. During the 1990s new dwelling construction declined to the lowest levels in the past 100 years (annually between 2,000 and 5,000 dwellings). The loss of housing through demolition and conversion to nonresidential uses was higher than new construction and the city lost some residential stock.

Politics and City Services. The Czech Republic consists of about 6,200 municipalities and 14 regions. Both levels have elected representatives. Prague has the status of both municipality and region and municipal government also serves as regional government. Prague is further subdivided into 57 boroughs with elected local governments. However, the crucial power is at the municipal level, which determines the decentralization of responsibilities to the borough level. For instance, Prague as a municipality owns the real estate; however, it decentralizes the management of public housing to boroughs.

Municipalities in the Czech Republic have a right to manage municipal property, adopt municipal budgets, establish legal entities, adopt a municipal development program, approve local physical plans, and issue municipal ordinances. Therefore, municipalities enjoy independence in the spheres of management of their property and financial resources and in the fields of local strategic development and physical planning.

In 1999 and 2000 the General Assembly of the Capital City of Prague approved two important documents governing urban development: a new Master Plan and a Strategic Plan. Major public investments are planned for extending the underground system, continuing construction of new sections in inner and outer express ring roads, and modernizing the technical infrastructure in the inner city. Concerning spatial development, the city government would prefer to maintain a compact urban structure and would like to decentralize some commercial operations from the city center, expanding the central business district to selected neighborhoods in the outer city (in other words, to transform the city from a monocentric to a polycentric urban structure).

Educational System. In the Czech Republic there is 9-year compulsory education. A majority of pupils and students attend public schools where education is free of charge. However, private and religious schools, especially on the secondary level, provide an increasing share of education. According to 1991 census data, about 30% of men and 24% of women from age 30 to 34 had a university education.

Prague is the major educational center in the Czech Republic. In 1998 and 1999 there were 366 kindergartens attended by about 30,000 children under 6 years old, and 241 primary schools for over 100,000 pupils from ages 6 to 15. Most primary schools are public. One percent of pupils attend private and religious primary schools. Secondary education is represented by 61 grammar schools with 20,000 students and 165 vocational schools with 43,000 students. About three-quarters of students attend public secondary schools and the rest attend private and religious schools. Prague's 8 universities were, in 1998 and 1999, attended by 70,000 students of whom 2,000 were foreigners. The best known, largest, and oldest is Charles University, which was established in 1348.

Transportation System. Prague has a well-developed public transportation system. Its backbone is formed by three lines of underground train called the Metro, with a total length of 50 kilometers (31 miles), serving 49 stations. The Metro links the city center with major residential areas in the inner city and outer housing estates. In the central and inner city, the Metro is combined with tram (streetcar) lines, with a total length of 136 kilometers (84 miles). The outer city is predominantly served by buses, which connect outer-city and suburban residential areas with Metro and tram lines. The Metro carries 39% of public-transport passengers, trams carry 31%, and buses carry 30%. Public transportation carries on average 3.4 million passengers a day. In 1992 an integrated regional public transportation system was developed. In 1998 it served 83 municipalities in the metropolitan region using 48 bus lines and 181 railway stations.

The 1990s were characterized by a rapid growth in car ownership and an increase in private car traffic. Public transportation in Prague lost about one-third of its passengers, and its share of total trips declined from 75% to 60%. The number of private cars in Prague increased from 336,037 in 1990 to 612,128 in 1998, and there were 513 cars per 1,000 inhabitants by the end of 1998. The total distance traveled by car increased even faster than car ownership, greatly exacerbating congestion on Prague's streets.

The construction of the Metro continued with the extension of some existing lines. The major investments in the city road network focused on the construction of inner-city and outer-city ring roads. The reconstruction and extension of the international Prague-Ruzyně airport doubled its capacity to 4.8 million passengers. Prague has rail links to 25 different European cities.

CULTURAL AND SOCIAL LIFE

Distinctive Features of the City's Cultures. Czechs have been at the forefront of European culture for much of the modern era. In fact, the European Union's Council of Ministers awarded Prague the prestigious title of the "European City of Culture" for the year 2000. Prague is known not only for medieval architecture but also for modern architecture. Before World War I, Prague boasted a strong cubist architecture movement; between the wars emerged a modernist, avant-garde style of architecture. Some buildings, such as the postmodern *Dancing Building* on the banks of the Vltava River, add new architectural jewels to the cultural landscape of Prague.

Prague is sometimes called *musicopolis Europae* or even *regina musicae.* It has several major orchestras and grand operas that perform in the city. There is some type of music performance every night. In addition to well-known concert halls, such as Rudolfinum or Smetana Hall in the Municipal House, orchestras also perform in smaller pleasant places such as Bertramka (the Mozart museum), and in numerous churches. Prague also has a long indigenous tradition of clubs where one can hear live jazz, and younger people enjoy several rock clubs and discotheques.

Prague has many theaters. The most prestigious performances are held in the National Theatre, the Estates Theatre, and the State Opera. In addition to drama, opera, and ballet, Prague also has a tradition of pantomime, black-light theater, and puppetry. Musicals, motion picture, and multimedia performances also enrich the cultural scene.

© OWEN FRANKEN/CORBIS

Handmade marionettes are sold on a street in Prague.

Cuisine. Czech cuisine is typically central European, with German, Austrian, and Hungarian influences. The food is a simple, filling, and unhealthy. Dishes are overwhelmingly based on roasted or boiled meat, usually pork, beef, or poultry, accompanied by dumplings, potatoes, or rice, and topped with a heavy cream or fatty sauce and served with a mix of pickled and fresh vegetables. Roasted or smoked pork, boiled semisweet cabbage or sauerkraut, and dumplings are considered the most typical Czech dish. Other local specialities include dumplings, smoked meat, and potato pancakes. Dumplings are made from dough formed into the shape of a small baguette, steamed or boiled, and then sliced into patties. There are several varieties of dumplings, with flour and potato the most common. Smoked meats are a very common part of Czech cuisine used in warm as well as cold dishes at any time of day. Wild game, roast duck, and goose are other tasty local specialties. Czech cuisine does not feature many fresh vegetables, but their availability is increasing. Vegetarian food was virtually nonexistent at the beginning of the 1990s (fried cheese and egg omelets were the typical options offered in restaurants), but it has become more prevalent.

Alcohol consumption has always been high in the Czech Republic, with beer as the favorite drink. Beer (*pivo* in the vernacular) is an intrinsic part of Czech culture. There are two traditional kinds of beer: pale and dark lager. The most famous brands include Pilsner Urquell, Gambrinus, Budvar, and from Prague's largest brewery, Staropramen. There are several microbreweries in the city. The most famous, U Flek, originated in 1499; it offers a dark caramel beer and has become a favorite tourist destination. There are special local spirits, such as Becherovka (sweet and spicy), Fernet (bitter), and Slivovice (plum brandy). Czechs traditionally drink so-called Turkish coffee (hot water poured over ground coffee in a cup) and Viennese coffee with a head of cream on top.

Czechs have distinct eating habits; they eat early in comparison with Western nations. The main meal of the day is at lunchtime, between noon and two o'clock P.M., and it starts with soup followed by a main dish. A typical breakfast consists of bread or a roll with butter, cheese, ham, eggs, jam, yogurt, and tea or coffee. Dinner, in the evening, can be similar to breakfast or a full lunch.

Prague's restaurant scene changed radically during the 1990s, with increasing numbers of places and improved choices. It started with pizzerias and Western-style fast-food outlets. Now Prague offers a variety of ethnic restaurants ranging from Japanese and Lebanese to Balkan and French. There are also many stand-up buffets that offer meat sausages, fried cheese, and gyros, and local fast-food facilities with cakes and open sandwiches. Prague is a "publand." Typical local pubs are smoky, male-dominated places, where most customers just drink beer and the food menu is short and simple. Pubs, where customers sit around tables and are served by a waitperson, are traditional, but Western-style bars began to emerge in the 1990s. Tea houses, often nonsmoking places, emerged as an alternative to pubs. Internet cafés are another later phenomenon.

Ethnic, Class, and Religious Diversity. Prague is quite ethnically homogeneous. The 1991 census showed that 96.4% of the population was Czech; about 2% was Slovak, and the rest were Romany (Gypsy), Hungarian, Polish, and German. Before World War II, Prague had large German and Jewish communities. They were concentrated in the historic district, where (in 1921) 10% of the inhabitants were Jewish and 6% were German-speaking (non-Jewish). By the start of the 21st century, the Jewish community had 1,500 members. The ethnic composition rapidly changed from around 1991, owing to the immigration of foreigners. In 2000 eastern Europeans were represented by Ukrainians, Slovaks, Russians, Poles, and Croatians; Westerners, by citizens of the United States, Germany, France, and the United Kingdom; and Asians, especially by Vietnamese and Chinese.

Prague is not a religious place. In the 1991 census, 34% of Prague's inhabitants claimed to be religious. However, this did not mean that they belonged to a church. About 28% was Roman Catholic, 5% was Protestant, and the remaining 1% claimed to be Orthodox and other.

The socioeconomic status of Prague's population was homogeneous during the socialist period. However, a modest sociospatial differentiation existed, and since the introduction of a market economy in 1991, social and economic disparities have increased and have started to influence neighborhood change, producing a more segregated residential pattern. The traditional pattern of declining social status as distance from the city center increases, however, has changed with the suburbanization of the wealthy population.

Family and Other Social Support Systems. The nuclear family is considered to be a basic building block of Czech society. The most common family model is two working adults. There is limited cooperation among kin. The most common scenario finds family members sharing housing, usually two flats in a two-family house or one apartment. However, this does not mean that parents and their children's families will have a common budget. In 1991 only 1.6% of households cooperated in economic terms. In 1991 over 90% of nuclear families had their own dwellings. Housing is shared not only among relatives but often by divorced partners who have difficulty affording separate apartments. In 1991 about half of all families consisted of both partners (26% with children), 16% were incomplete families (10% with children), and 34% were single-person households. One-child families are more common than families with two or more children. The most important trends in the 1990s were the increasing percentage of single-person households, postponing marriage (28 years old for men and 25 years old for women in 1997), and a sharp decrease in the birthrate.

Work and Commerce. The service sector accounts for three-quarters of employment in the city. Economic restructuring in the 1990s brought deindustrialization and tertiarization. While employment in industry declined by 36% between 1992 and 1996, the number of employees in financial businesses more than doubled. Prague is the region in the country with the lowest rate of unemployment and the highest average salaries (132% of the national average in 1997).

Shopping is the area that best illustrates Prague's radical turn toward a consumer society. In the mid-1990s there were no hypermarkets in Prague. By 2000, hypermarkets were the primary shopping venues for 28% of consumers; supermarkets, for 64%; and smaller shops, for only 8% of the population. While in 1989 about half of the retail turnover was realized in the city center, most shopping was later concentrated in suburban locations. A decline in the frequency of trips, the high volume of purchased goods, the use of a car, and the ability to visit many shops that were open 24 hours a day became an integral part of the shopping culture.

Arts and Recreation. Prague has 22 museums and 11 major galleries, whose collections are seen annually by 3 million visitors. Besides the most prestigious facilities with permanent collections, such as the National Gallery, there are numerous smaller commercial galleries. The city has over 100 libraries serving 180,000 registered readers.

The first cinema in Prague opened in 1907; by the end of the 1960s there were 135 cinemas. In 1989, 57 cinemas were operated by the city (private theaters did not exist). By 2000, the city operated 3 cinemas, and there were about 30 private cinemas including a handful of multiscreen complexes.

Czechs are big fans of ice hockey, soccer, and tennis. Many people actively participate in sports, and urban green spaces offer opportunities for recreation. One-third of Prague households own a second home in the countryside or the wilderness, which are used extensively on the weekends and during vacations.

QUALITY OF LIFE

Czechs are inclined towards pragmatism in daily life and passivity in public life. They are quite ironic about politics done "out there"; however, major disputes can send them to the streets to show their opinions. The centuries of foreign domination have made Czechs somewhat xenophobic and suspicious of outsiders. However, they quickly learned to live in a postmodern culture of plurality.

Emissions from stationary air polluters radically declined during the 1990s, the result of tight environmental legislation on major producers, and also a program through which the city supported the replacement of coal with gas heating in residential houses. However, the emissions from transportation remained at the same level. While individual cars emit lower levels of pollutants, the growth in the number of cars and the frequency of their use keep emissions at high levels.

The crime rate increased steadily during the 1990s, with 114,000 crimes reported in 1998. A growing problem is drug abuse by young people. Despite a well-established social welfare system, there are people living in poverty, including an increasing number of homeless. Numerous voluntary organizations attempt to help those with the greatest need and to assist them in reintegrating into mainstream society.

BIBLIOGRAPHY

A Cultural Guide to Prague (Praha-Evropské město kultury 2000).

Avant Guide Prague (Empire Press 1998).

Barlow, Max, et al., eds., *Development and Administration of Prague* (Universiteit van Amsterdam 1994).

Carter, Frank W., "Prague and Sofia: An Analysis of their Changing Internal City Structure," *The Socialist City: Spatial Structure and Urban Policy,* ed. by R.A. French and F. E. I. Hamilton (Wiley 1979).

Drbohlav, Dušan, and Zdeněk Čermák, "International Migrants in Central European Cities," *Social Change and Urban Restructuring in Central Europe,* ed. by G. Enyedi (Akadémiai Kiadó 1998).

Drbohlav, Dušan, and Luděk Sýkora, "Gateway Cities in the Process of Regional Integration in Central and Eastern Europe: The Case of Prague," *Migration, Free Trade and Regional Integration in Central and Eastern Europe* (Verlag 1997).

Eskinasi, Martijn, "Changing Housing Policy and its Consequences: The Prague Case," *Housing Studies* 10, no. 4 (1995): 533–48.

Hammersley, Richard, and Tim Westlake, "Planning In the Prague Region: Past, Present and Future," *Cities* 13, no. 4 (1996): 247–56.

Hoffman, Lilly M., and Jií Musil, "Culture Meets Commerce: Tourism In Postcommunist Prague," *The Tourist City,* ed. by S. S. Fainstein and D. R., Judd (Yale University Press 1997).

Maier, Karel, et al., *Urban Development of Prague: History and Present Issues* (CVUT 1998).

Moscheles, Julie, "The Demographic, Social, and Economic Regions of Greater Prague: A Contribution to Social Geography," *Geographical Review* 27 (1937): 414–29.

Musil, Jií, "The Development of Prague's Ecological Structure," *Readings in Urban Sociology,* ed. by R. E. Pahl (Oxford 1968).

Musil, Jií, "Housing Policy and the Sociospatial Structure of Cities in a Socialist Country: The Example of Prague," *International Journal of Urban and Regional Research* 11, no. 1 (1987): 27–36.

Norberg-Schulz, Christian, *Genius Loci* (Academy Editions 1979).

Pucher, John, "The Transformation of Urban Transport in the Czech Republic, 1988–1998," *Transport Policy* no. 6 (1999): 225–36.

Simpson, Fiona, "Tourist Impact in the Historic Center of Prague: Resident and Visitor Perceptions of the Historic Built Environment," *Geographical Journal* 165, no. 2 (1999): 173–83.

Sýkora, Luděk, "Prague," *European Cities, Planning Systems and Property Markets,* ed. by J. Berry and S. McGreal (E & FN Spon 1995).

Sýkora, Luděk, "Processes of Socio-Spatial Differentiation in Post-Communist Prague," *Housing Studies* 14, no.5 (1999): 679–701.

Sýkora, Luděk, and Vít Štěpánek, "Prague," *Cities* 9, no. 2 (1992): 91–100.

LUDĚK SÝKORA

Pretoria

South Africa

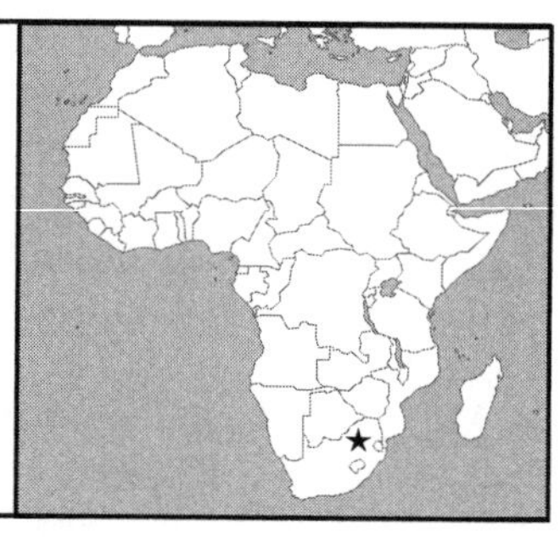

ORIENTATION

Name of City. Pretoria was first called Pretoria-Philadelphia (named after the voortrekker, or pioneer, leader Andries W. J. Pretorius, 1798–1853) to commemorate the brotherhood of the first trekkers who settled in the northern territory known as the Zuid-Afrikaansche Republiek (ZAR, the South African Republic). In 2000 Pretoria became part of the unicity Tshwane, an indigenous name for the area, and the name of a chief who was associated with the area during the 19th century.

Location. Pretoria is situated 1,370 meters (4,495 feet) above sea level. The city is located at 25°45′ south latitude, and 28°12′ east longitude. Pretoria enjoys a mild climate, with temperatures ranging from an average of 15° to 28°C (59° to 82°F) in summer and 6° to 23°C (43° to 73°F) in winter, with a summer rainfall of 700 millimeters (27 inches).

Population. While the population of Pretoria proper is about 1.5 million, that of the unicity Tshwane is 2.4 million.

Distinctive and Unique Features. The town was established on the banks of the Apies ("monkeys") River, in a fertile valley between the ridges known as the Magaliesberg (indigenous name: Thaba tsa Mogale), running east-west. Today Pretoria is spread out among the valleys and hills that form the eastern spurs of the Magaliesberg Range and that give the city its distinctive urban landscape. The climate favors luxuriant growth of plants and trees; during the 19th century the town was known as "City of Roses."

The first suburbs (1890–1910) were laid out on the typical colonial grid plan, while later extensions took the contours of the hilly landscape into consideration. Radial plans were applied in some cases, with parks forming focal points. In town, many of the hills are fully built-up, creating a variety of human-made skylines that compete with the high-rise buildings in the city center.

From the 1880s separate areas were set aside by whites for blacks. The first official black area was Marabastad in 1888, named after a chief who resided there in early years. In time, small pockets of black communities developed throughout Pretoria, sometimes with freehold tenure. During the 1930s and 1940s some were removed on grounds of health (and "aesthetic") hazards, but after the victory of the National Party in 1948, separate development was legalized by the apartheid paradigm. Such black communities as Mamelodi and Soshanguve still owe their distance from the city center to the segregationist policies of the apartheid era. A comparison between the spacious properties and comprehensive amenities of the historically white suburbs and the tiny sites and rudimentary services of the historically black townships recalls the original purpose of the black townships as dormitory labor reservoirs; they were meant to have a limited lifetime.

Historically, growth of the town gravitated toward the southeast. This part of Pretoria has an attractive, undulating cityscape, away from the industries in the west. In addition, the location of the black townships, Atteridgeville in the west and Mamelodi in the east, also had negative influence on the white development axis. After the country's first democratic election in 1994, new urban-development frameworks were created that took the huge black residential areas to the north, such as Mabopane and Winterveld, into consideration. The unicity has an area of 3,200 square kilometers (1,235 square miles). The Centurion-Mabopane Development Corridor runs north-south, while Pretoria also serves as a hub in the transnational Maputo Corridor that runs east-west from Mozambique.

Attractions of the City. Apart from the mild, sunny climate and lush plant growth, Pretoria offers a host of attractions. As the administrative capital of the country, the largest employment sector in the city is the national government with its various departments. As a consequence, one may find the corporate headquarters of major organizations in the city, such as the South African Reserve Bank, the South African Bureau of Standards, the South African Tourism Board, State Archives, and the regional offices of international agencies. There are more than 100 embassies and overseas missions in the city.

Pretoria is also called the City of Knowledge, with its four universities (the University of Pretoria, University of South Africa, Medical University of South Africa, and Vista University Mamelodi Campus) and 11 general and teacher-training colleges. In addition, the city boasts scientific institutions, including seven research councils, military and police headquarters, botanical and zoological parks, a national library, and about 30 museums.

Although Pretoria is not an industrial city, it has benefited from large industries such as the South African Iron and Steel Corporation (ISCOR) in the west, and automobile industries in the northwest (Nissan at Rosslyn) and east (Samcor/Ford at Waltloo). The Johannesburg International Airport is a 30-minute drive along a freeway, while access to the harbors in Durban and Maputo are largely by rail and freeways. To the north, a rail and freeway connect Pretoria to the rest of Africa.

During the month of October, Pretoria is covered in a magical mauve haze of thousands of jacaranda trees (*Jacaranda mimosifolia*) blooming along the streets and in gardens, heralding the arrival of summer. The city is affectionately called the "Jacaranda City," after its famous trees.

© ADIL BRADLOW/AP/WIDE WORLD PHOTOS

South African president Nelson Mandela, left, congratulates Archbishop Desmond Tutu, chairperson of the Truth and Reconciliation Commission, at a ceremony in Pretoria in 1998.

Main tourist attractions in the city reflect its rich natural and cultural assets. Close to the city center are the Fountains Valley (source of pure water for the city for nearly 150 years and oldest nature reserve in Africa [1895]), the National Zoological Gardens, National Botanical Gardens, and the Wonderboom ("wonder tree"), while various dams and game reserves can be found in the district. North of the city, the Tswaing Meteorite Crater is a reminder of the long geologic history of the region.

Other key tourist attractions are the impressive Union Buildings (overlooking central Pretoria in a sweeping panorama, originally the seat of government in 1913); the Kruger House (residence of President Paul Kruger, built in 1884); the Voortrekker Monument (built in 1949); Melrose House (where a peace treaty was signed in 1902, ending the Anglo-Boer War); Church Square (laid out in 1910, surrounded by several historical buildings dating from the days of Paul Kruger); the Staatsmodelschool (government school of 1897, from which Winston Churchill, then a British war correspondent captured by the Boers, made a daring escape in December 1899); various mansions in large gardens; decorative parks; and a site to commemorate the struggle for liberation during the second half of the 20th century.

Relationships Between the City and the Outside. As administrative capital of South Africa, Pretoria has gained world-city status, first for being the center of apartheid for 40 years, and during the 1990s for becoming the seat of the first democratic government of the country. Half an hour's drive from Johannesburg, Pretoria is situated in the Gauteng province. Whereas Johannesburg is the financial and commercial hub in southern Africa, Pretoria is the institutional and knowledge center, containing the headquarters of the government, corporations and embassies, and numerous centers of research and learning.

Major Languages. Afrikaans and English are the main languages spoken by whites, while Tswana and Northern Sotho are the languages spoken most often by blacks. However, the wide array of overseas missions that have arrived since 1994 have introduced a cosmopolitan element—and a variety of languages—into the city.

HISTORY

The Origin of the City. Centuries before the establishment of Pretoria, people of the middle and late Stone Age lived in the area, making their stone tools from the quartzite found in the mountains. The earliest evidence of African communities who grew crops, kept domesticated animals, made pots, and smelted iron to make tools and weapons dates from about 1200 A.D.

About 1825 or 1826 the Matabele tribe conquered the Bakwena tribe, and, under the powerful leadership of Mzilikazi, settled along the Magaliesberg. A few years later the Matabele moved on to the western territories.

The first voortrekkers arrived on the fertile plains between the Magaliesberg Ranges during the late 1830s. The earliest white settlers were the two Bronkhorst brothers and the Van der Walt family. Attracted by the good water and safe environment, more Boers converged to establish a congregation of the Dutch Reformed Church in 1854.

Marthinus Wessel Pretorius, son of Andries Pretorius and state president of the ZAR, founded the city on November 16, 1855. The first *landdrost* (magistrate), A. F. du Toit, gave Pretoria its spacious grid plan. Five years later the town was proclaimed the seat of government of the ZAR. For decades central government administered the town.

Two wars had an effect on the city—the First War of Independence (1881) and the Anglo-Boer War (1899–1902)—with forts and blockhouses built on the surrounding hills and mountains. Only after the discovery of gold on the Witwatersrand (Johannesburg) in 1886 did the government collect revenue to build a modern civil administration. Professionals were attracted from Europe, and some became leading politicians in later years. Electricity was introduced in 1892. Pretoria's ZAR architecture—such as the Old Raadsaal, Palace of Justice, and Netherlands Bank Building—dates from the 1890s.

With the proclamation of union, when the four provinces that made up South Africa from 1910 to 1994 were consolidated into one country, a new wave of building activity hit the city. Landmarks of this period are the Union Buildings, Railway Station, Transvaal Museum, and Post Office. At the same time, municipal services such as sewerage, water provision, and transport were brought into line with the needs of the time.

On October 14, 1931, Pretoria was awarded city status. This was celebrated in a series of new buildings such as the Town Hall and various theaters. Industries were introduced to Pretoria during the 1930s when the government-subsidized iron and steel works, ISCOR, was established on the western outskirts of the city. During the 1940s various research institutions were established, all with their headquarters in Pretoria. In 1940 a model township, Atteridgeville, was established in the west to accommodate the native Africans, Coloured (mixed race), and Indian people who were removed from sites in the suburbs. After the promulgation of the infamous Group Areas Act in 1950, which established apartheid in towns and cities, yet another township, Vlakfontein (later named Mamelodi), was established in 1953.

In 1964 the residential neighborhoods spread out around the center of Pretoria were incorporated into the area of jurisdiction, thereby increasing the size of the city by three—one of the largest municipalities in the world at that time. As part of the transformation process, Pretoria became a substructure of the Greater Pretoria Metropolitan Council in 1994, and in 2000 it became part of the unicity Tshwane.

Migration: Past and Present. Work opportunities in and associated with the civil service attracted white workers to Pretoria since the end of the 19th century. Today it is predominantly blacks who converge on the city for job opportunities in this sector. However, with the city's industrial development since the 1940s, blacks from as far afield as Dennilton in Mpumalanga province—150 kilometers (93 miles)—commuted daily to and from Pretoria. This was the result of the Grand Apartheid policies of the government of the time. The process of commuting still continues today.

INFRASTRUCTURE

Public Buildings, Public Works, and Residences. Most public buildings, such as the Union Buildings, were mentioned earlier in the text. Other landmark structures are university buildings, especially the University of South Africa (from the early 1970s) on the slope of Lukasrand, the Armscor Building (1980s) at Erasmuskloof, and the Human Sciences Research Council Building (1987) in the city center.

Roads make up the most important public-works projects of the city. Pretoria is situated on the north-south axis from Cape Town to Beit Bridge (border of Zimbabwe) and the east-west axis from Maputo (Mozambique) to Windhoek (Namibia). Wonderboom Municipal Aerodrome serves the city and its district. Huge water reservoirs and radio and telephone towers and masts have been built on the tops of the hills in and around the city.

Politics and City Services. Pretoria has been governed by a city council since 1902. Up to 1994 it consisted of white politicians only, but since that date an integrated, nonracial council has governed the city. The transformation process since 1994 has not been completed at the time of writing. Pretoria was scheduled to become a substructure of a large unicity during 2000, including a number of black communities to the north that had previously been rural.

Educational System. Most schools in Pretoria are run by the Gauteng Provincial Department of Education. In addition, there are a number of private schools active in the area, each with its own school board. The Bantu Education system of the apartheid government has been replaced with an integrated, nonracial system across the country. However, owing to backlogs in providing schools in the townships with educational resources, many black parents send their children to schools in historically white areas. Tertiary education is also split in two—namely, government-subsidized colleges and universities on the one hand, and private colleges and offices of overseas colleges and universities on the other hand

Transportation System. Because of the sprawling nature of urban growth of Pretoria, public transport has always been very expensive, and never developed to the comfort levels that can be found in western European cities. During apartheid days whites enjoyed privileged transportation arrangements by municipal buses. Since urban resources have been more democratically spread since 1994, usage of bus transport declined in favor of minibus taxis (carrying up to 14 passengers). The minibus-taxi industry has grown exponentially all over the country since the early 1980s as a means of freedom from government-subsidized long-, medium-, and short-distance train and bus transport and as an expression of black economic empowerment. Today minibus taxis are still owned and used mainly by blacks.

Private motorcars still dominate the roads of the city. Pretoria is connected to the main cities in the southern African region by freeways (largely toll roads) or other first-class roads. In 1893 Pretoria became connected by rail to Cape Town and Durban harbors, and in 1894 to Maputo.

CULTURAL AND SOCIAL LIFE

Distinctive Features of the City's Cultures. Apart from a huge deposit site with stone implements dating from the Stone Age and some disturbed wall sections of natural packed stone dating from the 18th and 19th centuries, little has remained of human habitation before the arrival of whites during the 1840s. Most Africans, Coloureds, and Indians still live in the townships created during apartheid years. These areas have developed their own local cultures, with specific music and dance, architecture, and fine arts. The Indian community living in Laudium has a higher standard of living and a much more colorful public and residential environment than do the blacks and the Coloureds. In all these communities various societies (especially religious) act as conduits for cultural expression. Historically, institutions such as libraries and museums abounded in the white community. This is set to change with the imperative to spread resources more evenly throughout society.

Cuisine. Pretoria's cuisine is typically South African, a mix of white traditions such as *braaivleis* (barbecue) and African (mealies) and Indian (curry dishes) traditions. Meat is a favorite in most dishes (also relatively cheap), regardless of cultural origin.

Ethnic, Class, and Religious Diversity. The picture of Pretoria as a predominantly white city changed after 1994 to a city with an equal proportion of black and white residents. With the creation of Tshwane unicity in 2000, the region changed to a predominantly black population.

With the political and social changes after 1994 came a new class structure. Whereas whites enjoyed most privileges in the past and were able to acquire good education and fixed property, this situation has drastically been equalized. Today the class differences are drawn more between rich and poor. Race plays an increasingly lesser role in society. However, there is a large gap between the wealthy (white and black) and the poor. There is a disturbing increase in the number of homeless people on the streets of Pretoria.

The majority of whites belong to Protestant churches, especially the Dutch Reformed Church of South Africa, and to an extent also to charismatic and Roman Catholic churches. In black communities there is a legion of independent African churches. Indian devotees are either Islamic or Hindu.

Family and Other Social Support Systems. In urbanized families, the rights of the individual are paramount, with these rights declining in more-rural value systems where the interest of the group reigns supreme. In general, the first approach is identified with white families, and the latter with black families.

Work and Commerce. Pretoria is a city of administration, science, and education; commerce plays a minor role. Civil servants and military staff make up a significant part of the residents of the city. Most head offices of departments and military units are in central Pretoria, but there is a tendency to move such offices to the tranquillity of the suburbs. Huge shopping centers can be found in the wealthy white suburbs since the center of town became the shopping district for blacks from the townships. In the latter no chain store has yet opened its doors.

The country knows no wintertime or summertime, as is the case in Europe. People go to work early, and after work enjoy the last part of the afternoon in their garden during summer.

Arts and Recreation. With abundant sunshine, outdoor life and sports compete with the arts. There are a number of music and art schools at tertiary institutions and secondary schools, but by and large the inhabitants of South Africa are not known for their exceptional achievements in the art world.

Sports such as rugby and cricket are very popular in white society, while soccer is the game in the black townships. Throughout Pretoria there are large sports complexes, such as Loftus Minolta, with a collection of athletic fields and other facilities.

QUALITY OF LIFE

Compared to the rest of Africa, residents of Pretoria enjoy a high standard of living. However, compared to Europe and North America, it is visibly lower. This pattern will likely be retained in the future even with the incorporation of far-outlying (poor) areas to the north into the unicity Tshwane. A prerequisite for maintaining a relatively high standard of living will be sustained economic growth.

FUTURE OF THE CITY

Much reference has already been made to the extension of urban boundaries to the north to include areas such as New Eersterust, Dilopye, and Stinkwater during 2000. In addition, a new urban complex, also named Tshwane, will be formed. Much of the future of Pretoria, which will become one of many components of the unicity, will depend on balanced and cohesive urban management.

BIBLIOGRAPHY

Allen, Vivien, *Kruger's Pretoria* (Balkema 1971).

Engelbrecht, S. P., et al., *Centenary Album: Pretoria's First Century in Illustration* (City Council of Pretoria 1955).

Greyling, P. J., *Pretoria and the Anglo-Boer War: A Guide of Buildings, Terrains, Graves and Monuments* (Protea Book House 2000).

Krige, L., ed., *Fountains Valley* (City Council of Pretoria 1992).

Krige, S. du T., and G.-M. van der Waal, eds., *Church Street: Pretoria's Artery of Life* (City Council of Pretoria 1994).

Krige, S. du T., and G.-M. van der Waal, eds., *Cultural Resources: The Environment of Pretoria* (City Council of Pretoria 1994).

Krige, S. du T., and G.-M. van der Waal, eds., *Musuem Park: Yours to Discover* (City Council of Pretoria 1995).

Krige, S. du T., and G.-M. van der Waal, eds., *Religious Landmarks: Religious Diversity as Cultural Resource* (City Council of Pretoria 1996).

Meiring, Hannes, *Pretoria 125* (Human & Rousseau 1980).

Ploeger, Jan, and Tom Andrews, *Street and Place Names of Old Pretoria* (J. L. van Schaik 1989).

Reinold, W. U., et al., *Tswaing Meteorite Crater: An Introduction to the Natural and Cultural History of the Tswaing Region Including a Description of the Hiking Trail* (Council for Geoscience 1999).

G.-M. VAN DER WAAL

Puebla

Mexico

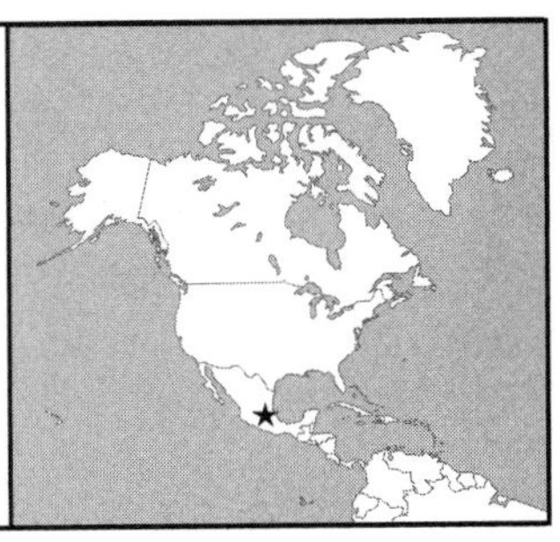

ORIENTATION

Name of City. Puebla's official name is *Heroica Puebla de Zaragoza* ("Heroic City of Zaragoza"), which replaced the original name, *Puebla de los Ángeles* ("City of Angels"), in the 19th century.

Location. The city covers an area of nearly 200 square kilometers (77 square miles). It is a municipal seat and the capital of the state, which shares its name. Puebla is situated in the southeastern part of the Mexican Plateau at 19°02′ north latitude and 98°15′ west longitude, with an altitude of 2,209 meters (7,248 feet) above sea level. The climate is temperate, with a summer rainy season. Average annual temperatures range from 16°C to 18°C (61°F to 64°F). The warmest months are April and May, with average temperatures between 18°C and 20°C (68°F) and highs of 30°C to 32°C (86°F to 90°F). Soils, vegetation, and wildlife in the urban area have been profoundly altered by prolonged human activity, which has noticeably changed the natural landscape.

Population. The municipality of Puebla has over 1.3 million residents according to preliminary figures from the 2000 population census. The gender ratio is about 91 males per 100 females, and the growth rate is 2.6%. The population is relatively young, with 28% 15 years old and younger. This group, together with that of people 65 years and older (13.2%), make for a rather large economically dependent portion of the population (41.2%). Of the total population, 54% is economically active.

Distinctive and Unique Features. The city is situated in a valley surrounded by four volcanoes: Pico de Orizaba, or Citlaltépetl (5,610 meters; 18,400 feet); Popocatépetl (5,465 meters; 17,930 feet); Iztaccíhuatl (5,230 meters; 17,159 feet); and La Malinche (4,461 meters; 14,636 feet)—the first three are the highest peaks in Mexico.

Puebla is undoubtedly the best-preserved colonial city in Mexico. The brick, plaster, and tile buildings give the city a unique polychromatic quality, and its numerous churches and monasteries, with their baroque and neoclassical altarpieces and gilt walls and vaults, lend it an air of distinction. Puebla's architectural character (seen in its triangular balconies and the beauty of its houses and streets) reflects the city's singular past and traditions; it is the result of the labor and artistry of the indigenous people of the region as well as of the Spaniards who settled there. In 1987 the United Nations Educational, Scientific, and Cultural Organization (UNESCO) declared the historic center of the city a World Heritage Site.

At the end of the 19th century, the trend in architecture shifted to Romanticism and French eclecticism. In the *Zócalo* (main square), gardens were planted, a Moorish gazebo was constructed, and cast-iron benches were installed. The atrium of the cathedral was enclosed by an iron and bronze gate. To illuminate the city, turpentine street lamps were installed and later replaced by arc lamps.

Other distinctive features of the city include its cuisine, considered the best in the country; the typical, old-fashioned attire—worn by women known as *chinas poblanas,* (or Chinese woman of Puebla, so-called because of an ancient legend), which has come to be equated with the national costume; its blue Talavera ceramics; its textile industry; and its automobile industry. The latter is dominated by Volkswagen, which has its only Mexican operations in Puebla.

Attractions of the City. Sightseeing in Puebla is tantamount to a journey through the past. The historic center contains the Zócalo, or main square; the cathedral (construction began 1539); the Palafoxiana Library (1773); the Casa del Deán ("dean's house" museum, 1580); the Casa del Alfeñique (circa 1790), which houses the State Museum and the Museum of Ceramics; the Casa de los Muñecos ("house of the figures," 1792), which houses the University Museum; the early *colonia* Casa del que Mató al Animal ("house of he who killed the animal"), which houses the newspaper *El Sol de Puebla;* the Casa de los Hermanos Serdán ("Serdan brothers' house"), which houses the Museum of the Mexican Revolution; the Chapel of the Rosary at Santo Domingo church (1690); San Francisco church (circa 1585); Soledad church (1731); San Cristóbal church (1676); the church and former convent of El Carmen; the Parish of San José (17th century); the former convent of Santa Mónica (circa 1606), which houses the Museum of Religious Art; the former convent of Santa Rosa (circa 1697), which houses the Museum of Pueblan Popular Art; San Pedro Hospital (1647), which houses the Museum of Viceregal Art; the Amparo Museum; the Jose Luis Bello y González Art Museum; the Jose Luis Bello y Zetina Museum; the Regional Museum of Puebla; the National Museum of Railroads, housed in the old train station (1869); the Puebla Cultural Institute (formerly the state penitentiary); El Parián artisans' market; Plazuela de los Sapos antiques market; the artists' quarter; the Main Theater (circa 1760); Santa Clara Street; and the Municipal Palace (17th century). Outside of the historic city center are such attractions as the Loreto and Guadalupe forts, the Planetarium, the Valsequillo Dam, and the African Safari Zoo, which has re-created diverse natural habitats.

Less than 30 minutes from the city are the churches of San Francisco Acatepec and Santa María Tonantzintla, jewels of Mexican baroque; the archaeological site of Cholula; and part of a chain of 16th-century Franciscan monasteries.

Relationships Between the City and the Outside. Puebla is the most important economic center in southeastern Mexico, and it has medical and educational facilities that serve not only the local population but the rest of the region and other parts of the country as well.

Modern highways connect the city with the port at Veracruz, the city of Oaxaca, and Mexico City. Puebla also enjoys the services of an airport located near the town of Huejotzingo, 30 minutes from the city center.

Major Languages. The majority of the inhabitants speak Spanish. However, 3.2% of the population aged five years and older speak some indig-

© NIK WHEELER/CORBIS

Houses of many colors line this street in Puebla, Mexico.

enous language, principally Nahuatl, Mixtec, or Totonaco.

HISTORY

The Origin of the City. La Puebla de los Ángeles was founded in 1531 by decree of the second Royal Audiencia (colonial court) and was settled by Spanish conquistadors, civilians, and clergymen and indigenous groups that were relocated from the nearby villages of Tlaxcala, Tepeaca, Calpan, Heujotzingo, and Cholula to build the new city. The Franciscan Agustín de Betancourt claimed that the settlement was established through the initiative of the Franciscan brothers, who believed that it was important to found a city where Spaniards could apply themselves to cultivating the land, thereby putting an end to the royal grants of land and Indian labor to which those who had participated in the conquest aspired. Thus Puebla was, unlike other centers in New Spain, envisioned as a city for Spaniards without tributary-labor rights and thus willing to work the land for themselves. Each of the original 33 settlers was given a plot of land. The settlement also drew tradesmen who later would organize into guilds.

The municipal government was rooted in the *Cabildo,* or city council, consisting of 2 ordinary mayors and 12 councilmen, in addition to the offices of chief ensign, high constable, general trustee, and judge of minors. The indigenous population was not allowed to reside in the Spanish settlement and therefore built their huts at the town's margin. It was not until 1550 that their settlement was given legal status through the formation of "Indian commonwealths," which had their own governments, supervised by the city council. The commonwealths emerged in response to the need for a free labor pool to build the city and cultivate the fields. The early mestizo population was prohibited from living in the Indian commonwealths and thus always lived among the Europeans. This prohibition was extended to apply also to blacks and mulattos, who began to arrive in the 16th century as domestic slaves.

During the early colonial period the cathedral and main square were built at the city's center, surrounded by government buildings and the homes of affluent families. From there the city expanded outward through an ordered pattern of rectangular blocks of equal size (each block had two rows of four lots running from east to west).

Puebla occupied a central position within New Spain between the capital of the Viceroyalty and the port of Veracruz, where people and products from Spain entered the colony. With the passing years Puebla became the second-largest city in New Spain. The most important settlement was Mexico City, the seat of viceregal political power.

From the end of the 16th century through the 17th century, Puebla was a significant commercial and industrial center. It was most prominent for trade in cochineal, a coloring agent produced in what was later the state of Oaxaca, and for controlling the production of grains harvested in the valleys surrounding the city, particularly in Atlixco. The flour, bread, and biscuits produced in Puebla supplied Mexico City, Veracruz, Antequera, Yucatán, the Antilles, the San Agustín garrison in Florida, and the Barlovento Royal Armada.

Most articles imported from Europe passed through Puebla, where they were redistributed to the rest of New Spain. The city was likewise a gathering point for merchandise produced in New Spain and destined for export. Puebla was thus an essential supplier for the merchant fleets anchored at Veracruz.

It was not, however, only a trading center; its own varied production sustained the city and partially supplied ships and other centers in New Spain. Some of Puebla's most sought-after goods for export and for the internal market were ham, bacon, butter, biscuits, soaps, cloth, silk, mantas, hats, earthenware, glass, leather products, forged-iron products, farming equipment, and its renowned Talavera ceramics, which were exported to the Caribbean, Florida, Central America, Venezuela, Colombia, and Peru.

In 1625 the English traveler Thomas Gage calculated that 10,000 people lived in Puebla, attributing the opulence that he saw there to commercial activity and manufacturing. In 1679 the bishop Manuel Fernández de Santa Cruz described the city as populous, with handsome squares and streets that accommodated approximately 3,800 houses—the majority of which were new and of considerable size—and monasteries and hospitals under the auspices of different religious orders. The bishop considered the cathedral to be one of the best in the Viceroyalty, owing to its beauty and lavishness. At the end of the 16th and beginning of the 17th century, the first architects, stonecutters, sculptors, gypsum workers, engravers, joiners, lathe-makers, cabinetmakers, marquetry workers, painters, upholsterers, lapidaries, and textile weavers established themselves in Puebla, helping to diversify and lend splendor to urban life. Beyond the well-ordered Spanish city extended the Indians' settlements, with their houses of adobe and straw ranging around hermitages and small churches. The bishop estimated that about 40% of the population was Spanish (whether born in Spain or the New World), while the remainder were Indians, blacks, mestizos, and mulattos. In addition, there were more than 1,000 members of the clergy. Based on the figures provided by the prelate, it is estimated that the total population was approximately 70,000.

Puebla was unique within New Spain for being a cultural and religious center. The first printing press arrived in 1640. Travelers and chroniclers who visited the city commented on its prosperity and the great number of churches, monasteries, and colleges. Owing to such resources, Puebla produced many figures of great renown. Furthermore, the city had been a diocese since 1550. People congregated either in the city center, or in the surrounding neighborhoods, towns, mills, ranches, or plantations. By the end of the 17th century, Puebla had six parishes (Sagrario de la Santa Iglesia Catedral, Señor San José, San Marcos, San Sebastián, Santo Ángel Custodio, and Santa Cruz).

The boom that the city enjoyed during the reign of the Habsburg declined in the last quarter of the 17th century. The decadence of the following century coincided with and, in some cases, was caused or aggravated by new economic and fiscal policies instituted by the Bourbon government. By order of the Bourbons, trade between New Spain and Peru was suspended, which caused a decline in Puebla's manufacturing, since the city was closely tied to overseas trade. Moreover, there emerged other textile production centers, such as Querétaro. Grain production also declined owing to internal competition with the Toluca valley and the Bajío region, thereby decreasing the flour trade and taking work from Puebla's millers and bakers. The expansion of hog farming in the capital and surrounding areas affected local production and trade in pork products, but trade was hardest hit when, in the early 1720s, a commercial fair was approved for Jalapa, which meant that many products would no longer make it to Puebla's markets. The 18th century saw the greatest mining boom of the colonial period. Puebla, however, was located far from the silver route and, as a consequence, the towns and cities of Bajío and those of northern New Spain benefited from the flourishing mines. The economic crisis occasioned by declining production and trade, combined with the ravages wrought by epidemics and famine throughout the 18th century, caused the city's population to fall by 50,000 toward the end of the century.

At the end of the 18th century, however, Puebla still enjoyed prestige for its manufactured goods, the prosperity of its monasteries, and the refinement of its inhabitants. The city's appearance was already distinctive, especially with respect to the cathedral, finished in 1649 by the bishop Juan de Palafox y Mendoza; the peculiar coloring that was the result of profuse application of brick, plaster, and polychrome tile to building facades; and the use of finials and pinnacles.

Beginning in the 19th century Puebla was both witness to and participant in the processes that led to the formation of the nation: the War of Independence, internal struggles between federalists and centralists, North American intervention, the War of Reform, French intervention, the empire of Maximillian of Habsburg, the restoration of the Republic, and the protracted dictatorship of Porfirio Díaz. Throughout the century the city suffered numerous sieges that further harmed its precarious economy and caused great material loss. Many Pueblans became important actors in these momentous 19th-century conflicts.

During this period, however, there was a resurgence of the textile industry. Esteban de Antuñano established the textile factory La Constancia Mexicana, considered the first of its type to use hydraulic energy and Arkwright's automatic spindles.

The unrest occasioned by constant military conflict did not interrupt the city's intellectual life. With the promulgation of the Reform Laws, the properties formerly controlled by monasteries were parceled and sold to private individuals, which led to new neoclassical construction, thus radically changing the appearance of the city.

The reparation for losses occasioned by the War of Reform was slow but effective, by virtue of the agricultural potential of the region, the protectionist measures granted to the textile industry, and the new markets that were opened to local manufactured goods by the construction of railroads.

At the end of the 19th century, cultural life continued to flourish. Among the city's institutions of higher education, the most important was the Colegio del Estado (State College). There were also musical and literary institutes; Spanish and Pueblan social clubs; the Guerrero Theater, the Miranda Theater, and the Main Theater (also known as the old Coliseum of Comedy); a racetrack; and a bullring.

During the last decade of Porfirio Díaz's dictatorship Puebla underwent significant changes in its appearance owing to the economic prosperity of particular social groups and the initiative of some of its mayors. The principal streets were covered with asphalt, and the sidewalks were edged and paved with quarried stone. The cobblestones and boardwalks were removed, and the old colonial drainage canals were stopped up. The city's borders began to extend beyond the limits of the old colonial plan.

The Mexican Revolution, which began in 1910, halted the city's growth. A few important city works were completed, however, such as La Victoria market and the State General Hospital. When the "Constitutional" troops occupied the city, they expropriated buildings that belonged to the church, thus closing almost all religious educational institutions. New construction at the city's periphery followed the same grid pattern of the older sections of the city.

The quadricentennial of the founding of Puebla in 1931 sparked a number of public-works projects to beautify the city. A rapid process of expansion began, tied to the establishment of the high-tech industry and an increase in commercial activity.

The central part of the city, called the Historic Center—which is the traditional hub of almost all social, political, administrative, commercial, and religious activity—is coextensive with the colonial plan and enjoys all public services, but this old part of town has deteriorated as commercial establishments have displaced residential properties. The Historic Center contains a number of civil and religious buildings from the 16th through the 19th century that possess great artistic and historic value, but there are serious obstacles to their conservation owing to overexploitation of the land and inadequate procedures for restoration and conservation.

Migration: Past and Present. Puebla originated as a village constructed by Indians to give shelter to "a commonwealth of Spanish planters," who became the first inhabitants of Puebla de los Ángeles. The Spanish immigrants who settled in the city came principally from Andalucia and Extremadura.

Three years after the founding of the city, in 1534, 61 families and 24 individuals lived in Puebla. A little more than half of the families were those of conquistadors, of which seven were married to native women.

As time passed, many immigrants made their way to Puebla, and although the Spanish population was numerically smaller than the rest of the inhabitants, the immigrants retained economic control of agriculture, trade, and industry, as well as of political power by occupying the most important positions in the municipal government throughout the colonial period.

In the 17th century the colonists from Andalusia and Extremadura were joined by waves of immigrants from Brihuega (in the Spanish province of Guadalajara), who gave the local textile industry its impetus. Throughout the colonial period, as well as in the 19th and early 20th century, more immigrants came from Old Castile, New Castile, the Basque Country, Galicia, León, Asturias, Santander, Aragon, and Catalonia. The last important wave of Spanish immigration was that of 200 Republicans who were political refugees from the Spanish Civil War. Although Spanish immigration tapered off as the centuries progressed, there are still cultural features of contemporary Pueblan society that hark back to the influence exerted by Spain over a period of 400 years.

At the beginning of the 20th century, the city also became home to Lebanese and, later, German immigrant communities. Both groups have had an impact on the economy and educational activities, despite their relatively small numbers.

According to later figures, 90% of the city's population was born in the state of Puebla; the remaining 10% came from other states. With respect to immigration in the state of Puebla, 84% of the people are nonimmigrants, 16% are immigrants, and 0.03% are unspecified. Only 4% of persons born in Puebla reside in other states. During the period from 1990 to 1995, 84% of foreign immigrants to Puebla remained and 16% returned to their place of origin.

INFRASTRUCTURE

Public Buildings, Public Works, and Residences. Puebla's most important public buildings are City Hall, seat of the municipal government, and the Government Palace, seat of the state government. Other principal buildings include the Superior Court of Justice, the State Legislature, buildings housing the representatives of other state governments, a Convention Center, and the Casa Puebla, the governor's private residence.

Politics and City Services. Puebla has all of the advantages of a modern city: potable water; drainage and sewage systems; electricity; postal, telephone, and telegraph services; radio and television stations; police and fire departments; parks; banks and exchange houses; car-rental and travel agencies; museums, libraries, theaters, and movie houses; restaurants, malls, markets, and stores; sports arenas; hospitals; and public and private schools.

Public spending has targeted urban development, housing, and the environment; communications and transportation; education, culture, sports, and recreation; public administration; public health; and industrial, agricultural, and forest development.

Educational System. Puebla's literacy rate is about 95%. The educational system consists of both public and private institutions at all levels: preschool, primary, secondary, vocational and technical, teacher training, and university (with both undergraduate and graduate programs). Puebla's institutions of higher learning include the Benemerita Autonomous University of Puebla, the University of the Americas, the Plantel Golfo-Centro Ibero-American University, Madero University, Puebla State People's Autonomous University, a branch of the National Pedagogical University, the Regional Technical Institute, the Free Law School, the Conservatory of Music and Oratory, and the School of Arts and Trades, as well as a dozen smaller, private universities.

Transportation System. Motor vehicles are the predominant form of transportation in Mexico. One can reach even the most outlying areas of Puebla using buses, microbuses, and *combis* (10- to 20-seat vans). There are numerous taxicabs as well. There are also passenger and cargo transport services that connect the city with the rest of the state and other regions of the country. At the Central de Autobuses de Puebla (CAPU; Central Bus Station of Puebla) many different companies have offices to service a constant flow of passengers traveling to destinations throughout the state and the country. Puebla also enjoys the services of the Hermanos Serdán Airport, which offers flights to the major cities and most popular vacation destinations in Mexico, as well as some U.S. cities. Rail service to and from Puebla was recently suspended.

CULTURAL AND SOCIAL LIFE

Distinctive Features of the City's Cultures. Puebla's culture is a relevant piece of the vast cultural diversity of Mexico. Its people are extremely proud of their city, its colonial monuments, and above all its famous cuisine.

Cuisine. Puebla's renowned cuisine grew out of the conjunction of two culinary traditions: the pre-Columbian and the Spanish. Among the most representative dishes that enjoy national fame are *mole poblano* (a hodgepodge sauce served over meat, traditionally turkey) and *chiles en nogada* (peppers in walnut sauce). Within Mexican cooking the distinctly Pueblan mode of seasoning a dish consists of mixing in strips of poblano peppers. Other dishes worth mentioning include *chalupas* (deep-fried flat tortillas topped with meat, chili sauce, and cheese), *molotes* (deep-fried cornmeal shells filled with pork, tomato sauce, raisins, almonds, and sweetmeat), *pipián verde* (sauce made with green tomatoes, serrano peppers, pumpkin seeds, and cilantro), *chanclas* (meat and avocado stuffed rolls covered with salsa), *guajolotes* (enchilada sandwiches), *tinga* (poached pork loin prepared with sausage, tomatoes, potatoes, and chipotle), *gusanos de maguey* (maguey worms, fried and served with sauce), *escamoles* (ant roe), and many other delicious dishes. Puebla's cuisine also includes an assortment of sweets, sold in Santa Clara street, such as *camote* (sweet potato candy); *tortitas* (pumpkinseed tarts); milk, pumpkinseed, and pinenut *jamoncillos* (confection made with condensed milk); candied fruit; *gaznates* (glazed meringue-filled cones); macaroons; and more.

Ethnic, Class, and Religious Diversity. Puebla's inhabitants are, like those in the rest of Mexico, primarily *mestizo,* although Spanish, Lebanese, and German communities are also present and play an important economic and educational role in the life of the city. Social class is determined by income, and thus coexisting within the city are the bourgeoisie, the middle class, and numerous popular classes.

Although the Constitution of the United Mexican States provides for freedom of religion, Roman Catholicism is, for historical reasons, the predominant religion in Puebla. There are smaller numbers of Protestants and members of other religions. The city offers religious services for Catholics, Protestants, Mormons, and other sects.

Family and Other Social Support Systems. The average family size in Puebla is 4.4 persons. Most families are the result of civil and religious marriage. About one-third of all families live in multigenerational households. The incidence of three or more generations living together diminished significantly at the end of the 20th century.

In 80% of families the father is the head of the household. In households with preschool age children in which the woman works outside the home the children are typically sent to daycare. In general, less well-off women who work rely on relatives for child care.

Organizations at the national, state, and local levels provide social support to the population. These include Whole Family Development (DIF), the National Institute of Aging (INSEN), the Puebla Women's Institute (IPM), the CARITAS Foundation, and many hospices and retirement homes.

Work and Commerce. The economic sectors in which Puebla's workforce is employed are the following: agriculture, cattle raising, forestry, and fishing; mining; tourism; manufacturing, which includes food processing, beverages, tobacco, textiles, and clothing; leather, lumber and wood products, and paper and paper products; printing and publishing; chemicals, petroleum-derived products, and rubber and plastics; nonmetallic mineral products (except petroleum and carbon derivatives), metals, machinery and equipment, and automobiles; construction and utilities; commerce, restaurants, and hotels; transportation, storage, and communications; financial services, insurance, real estate, and rental properties; public administration and finance; and community, social, and personal services.

Puebla is the state's principal commercial center. Its commerce includes foodstuffs and beverages; music, toys, and gifts; clothing and shoes; furniture; industrial materials; motor vehicles and automotive parts; pharmaceuticals and medical and laboratory supplies and instruments; books and paper products; petroleum, its derivatives, and fuels; industrial chemicals; lumber; construction materials; electrical equipment for industrial and home use; industrial metals; garbage, recycling, and packaging; agricultural raw materials, farm provisions, and veterinary medicines; machinery for use in industry, commerce, and services; hardware and paint; gas and gasoline; department stores, and supermarket and convenience stores.

Arts and Recreation. Among the city's many cultural and recreational facilities are the Instituto Cultural Poblano (Puebla Cultural Institute), the Casa de Cultura (House of Culture), the Barrio del Artista (Artists' Quarter), theaters, museums, a few art galleries, temporary exhibits, numerous movie theaters, libraries, parks, sports complexes, shopping centers, discotheques, nightclubs, bars, and restaurants. The latter offer a variety of cuisine choices, including Pueblan, Mexican, international, seafood, vegetarian, Spanish, Italian, Chinese, Japanese, German, Argentine, and Middle Eastern. Of course there are also fast-food restaurants, taco stands, and sandwich shops.

Residents of Puebla have access to tennis and basketball courts in local public parks, where they also run, walk, and ride bicycles. Puebla is home to a professional soccer team, Club de Futbol Puebla, and a baseball team, Pericos.

QUALITY OF LIFE

Puebla's residents enjoy a temperate climate throughout the year and are therefore free from the ups and downs of drastic weather changes. Moreover, the city is favored with a cultural heritage that promotes development and improvement of the quality of life of its inhabitants.

With respect to the socioeconomic status of the population, quality of life varies considerably. The wealthiest classes have access to all of the services available in highly developed countries with the advantage of paying developing-world prices for them. Nearly 100% of the population have electricity, 99% have running water, and 93% have sewers.

FUTURE OF THE CITY

Like most Mexican cities, Puebla has not escaped the consequences of disorderly urban growth. In the future, authorities and citizens alike must fight to protect the environment, improve public services, expand educational and cultural resources, attend to the needs of the most vulnerable social groups, and support the diverse economic enterprises that are at the foundation of civic life.

Likewise, one of the tasks that the people of Puebla have before them is the preservation of the richness, both tangible and intangible, of the city's cultural and historic heritage. In the new millennium it must remain a place for forging community identity and bringing together all of its potential—as the center of economic activity; citizens' rights; social relations; and public, social, and private institutions.

BIBLIOGRAPHY

Garavaglia, Juan Carlos, and Juan Carlos Grosso, "La región de Puebla-Tlaxcala y la economía novohispana, 1680–1810," *Puebla de la Colonia a la Revolución* (Centro de Estudios Históricos y Sociales 1987).

Gerhard, Peter, "Un censo de la diócesis de Puebla en 1681," *Historia Mexicana* 30, vol. 4 (El Colegio de México 1981).

Grajales Porras, and Lilián Agustín e Illades Aguiar, *Presencia española en Puebla, siglos XVI–XX* (Instituto de Ciencias Sociales y Humanidades-UAP 2001).

Ibarra Mazari, Ignacio, *Crónica de la Puebla de los Ángeles según testimonios de algunos viajeros que la visitaron entre los años 1540–1910* (Gobierno del Estado de Puebla 1990).

Leicht, Hugo, *Las Calles de Puebla* (Junta de Mejoramiento Mora, Cívico y Material del Municipio de Puebla 1992).

Veytia, Mariano, *Historia de la Fundación de la Ciudad de la Puebla de los Ángeles en la Neuva España, su Descripción y Presente Estado* (1931; Ediciones Altiplano 1963).

LILIÁN ILLADES AGUIAR

Pusan

South Korea

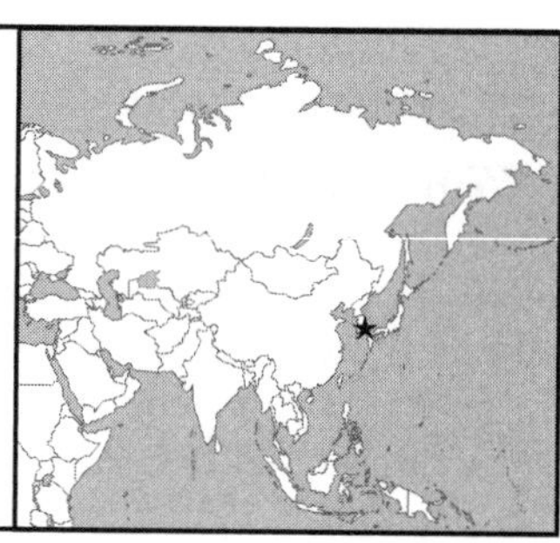

ORIENTATION

Name of City. Pusan (Busan) is the second-largest city in South Korea, after Seoul, and the nation's largest port city. The name *Pusan* means "Cauldron Mountain," referring to the ring of peaks that rise behind the city.

Location. Situated at 35°6′ north latitude and 129°2′ east longitude, Pusan lies in the southeasternmost corner of Korea. Once a part of South Kyongsang province, it is now a separate entity, an independent city no longer a part of the province or subject to provincial administrative authority.

Population. In 1998 the population of the city was approximately 3,879,000. The land area of Pusan encompasses nearly 760 square kilometers (295 square miles).

Distinctive and Unique Features. Pusan is a sprawling city stretched thinly in places because of its location between the ocean and mountains on one side (to the south and east) and a large river estuary, that of the Naktong River, on another (to the west). Its large, deepwater harbor—the largest in South Korea—is the fifth-largest international port in the world, handling 95% of the country's container cargo. There is a great variety of landscape to be found, from broad beautiful beaches and hot-spring resorts (the Haeundae area), to mountain fortresses and Buddhist temples, to skyscrapers, to the vast harbor area.

Attractions of the City. The attractions of Pusan include a large and active fish market, where all kinds of fish and seafood are auctioned off in the early morning hours, and a bustling old-fashioned market area (the International Market). A wetland within the estuary of the Naktong, South Korea's largest river, also serves as a vast migratory bird refuge. Other sites of interest include the UN Memorial Cemetery, the only cemetery in the world managed by the United Nations, and Yongdusan Park, where a 118-meter (387-foot) tower offers a panoramic view of the harbor.

Relationships Between the City and the Outside. Pusan affords many of the advantages of Seoul, the nation's capital, but because it is located farther to the south, snow seldom falls in Pusan, whereas one often sees snowfall in Seoul in the winter. Much of the traffic through the port of Pusan makes its way to Seoul or to the factories throughout the country. And many of the manufactured goods from all over South Korea are exported through the port of Pusan. In this way, the city is the lifeblood of South Korea's modern economy.

Major Languages. Korean is the only official language of South Korea, but in the hotels and shops of Pusan, signs are frequently posted in English and at times in Japanese, Chinese, and/or Russian.

HISTORY

The Origin of the City. There are numerous archaeological excavations from many areas of the city that reveal the fact that prehistoric humans lived in the region. Shell mounds showing that the people relied on the ocean for food have been found all along the coast of this expansive city. It is mentioned in the history of the Shilla dynasty (from early historic times to 935), the Koryo dynasty (to the 1300s), and the Choson or Yi dynasty (to 1910).

The port was first opened, according to the historical records, in July 1407. In 1490 a fortress was built around the city to help protect it from invasions by sea. Unfortunately for the residents of Pusan, and the remainder of the country as well, the Japanese under the direction of the warlord shogun Hideyoshi invaded in overwhelming numbers in May 1592. The Japanese soldiers and sailors, experienced in war from a generation of combat in Japan between the Ashikaga and Tokugawa shogunates, were able to quickly overrun the outnumbered and ill-prepared Korean population. In September

1592, Yi Sunshin, the famous naval hero of the war, led his ships to victory in the battle for Pusan harbor.

Prior to the war, and reestablished after the war, Pusan was designated as one of three port cities that were authorized to trade with Japanese merchants. The Japanese were allowed to visit the port city and engage in trade with Korean merchants. In the meantime, the fortresses around the Pusan area were rebuilt and fortified.

Today's Pusan, a vast city, includes the area that was once the separate town of Tongnae. In traditional times, society was dominated by a social and political system inspired by Confucianism. In Confucianism, the scholar and the official were honored and respected at the top of the social hierarchy. Farmers were in the middle, but fishers and seafarers were looked down upon. Therefore the scholars and the officials lived in a place inland from the port of Pusan. The administrative center for the region was located in Tongnae, about 16 kilometers (10 miles) from the coast and from the port. There, the magistrate who was assigned from Seoul and the local aristocracy would meet.

Much of Korea's early contact with foreign countries took place in Pusan. The British battleship *Shyvoia* entered Pusan harbor in 1855, and in 1859 a British merchant ship tried to enter the harbor to engage in trade. Then in 1875 the Japanese, inspired by the forced opening that they had suffered at the hands of Commodore Matthew Perry, attempted to forcibly open Pusan to modern ships and trade. They were successful the following year in coercing the reluctant Korean court to sign a trade treaty, but the site of the treaty was Kanghwa Island, nearer Seoul. As part of the pact, however, Japanese presence increased in Pusan.

Americans first appeared in Pusan in 1880, before they entered into a treaty for trade and amity in 1882. Other foreign powers soon had ships steaming in and out of Pusan harbor.

In the early 20th century, under great pressure and influence from the Japanese, many changes began to take place in Pusan. In 1901 rail service between Seoul and Pusan was instituted, and soon thereafter the port was expanded and the sea was reclaimed to create more docks and to deepen the harbor. Eventually, Pusan, with its railhead, was to be a key staging area for the expanding Japanese empire. The first ferry service to Japan was inaugurated in 1905, the same year that Japan declared Korea its protectorate.

Pusan expanded its role as a commercial port, a fishing port, and a port for passenger vessels throughout the Japanese period. Japan made Korea its colony in 1910, and economic advances that suited the Japanese were allowed in Korea. By the time the colonial period ended, in 1945, Pusan was an important modern port and the city had grown to match its harbor.

When the Korean War broke out on June 25, 1950, Pusan became a major gateway for U.S. and UN soldiers and supplies entering Korea. More notably, in the war, the North Korean Army pushed the South Koreans and a small group of American advisers to the southeast corner of Korea—an area around Pusan called the Pusan Perimeter. When General Douglas MacArthur landed forces near Inchon and cut off the advancing North Korean Army, much of the leadership of South Korea was in Pusan under refugee status.

One of the more interesting features of Pusan's history was what occurred during the Korean War. With many of the people from the institutions of Seoul in exile in Pusan, schools, libraries, churches, and many other social organs from Seoul were reconstituted in Pusan. Seoul high schools and universities reconvened in tents and temporary quarters in Pusan during the war years. The Seoul National University library's holdings from the Royal Library of the Choson dynasty, for example, were moved to Pusan by train, protected, preserved, and eventually returned to Seoul at the end of the war.

After the war, South Korea began rebuilding, and Pusan, although not hit by bombs or war's destruction as was the rest of the country, still needed to modernize and build. And that is what it did by revamping its harbor to accommodate container vessels and other modern, large ships. Preceding normalization of diplomatic ties with Japan in 1965, in the early 1960s regular ferry service was opened between Pusan and the Japanese port cities of Shimonoseki and Osaka.

In recent years, waterborne traffic has continued to increase and the harbor has continued to be enlarged. To augment the Pusan-Seoul rail line, in the early 1970s the Seoul-Pusan Expressway was opened for vehicular traffic. Pusan became the harbor through which raw materials for factories up and down the peninsula passed, and manufactured goods, ready for export, were sent by rail or expressway to Pusan for export to North America, Asia, and Europe.

In the 1980s, Pusan developed as a center for the manufacture of shoes, especially sports shoes. Then

© BOHEMIAN NOMAD PICTUREMAKERS/CORBIS

A woman leans from her boat to wash a container in the harbor at Pusan, South Korea.

as that industry began to move to Malaysia and China in the 1990s, Pusan looked for other industries and started to attract some high-tech industries, including automobile manufacturing. The Kimhae airport, on the west side of Pusan, took over air traffic, and the small airport on the east side of Pusan was replaced in the early 1980s. The east side, with the beautiful Haeundae Beach as its centerpiece, became a tourist site, and world-class hotels were built along the beach.

Thereafter upscale apartment complexes were built in the area and beyond the beach up the hill to the east. In the meantime, to the west, the city limits of Pusan were extended beyond the Naktong River, and many new industrial complexes were built along the shores of the river. Yet, to the credit of the city planners, the Naktong River delta, a broad, expansive wetland and home to numerous species of waterfowl and migratory birds, has been undisturbed.

Migration: Past and Present. During the 1950–1953 Korean War, Pusan's population swelled from 300,000 to over 1 million. In recent years the general trend in South Korea has leaned toward city living: the percentage of the population living in cities of 1 million or more inhabitants increased from 17.3% in 1965 to 50% in 1990. The number of South Koreans emigrating in 2001 jumped 21% over 2000 levels. Many of these migrants are moving abroad for better opportunities and better education for their children. The South Korean government is very methodical and careful about monitoring and controlling large city populations and overcrowding owing to land restraints in such cities. To channel internal migration, it has established commercial centers in rural, less populated areas.

INFRASTRUCTURE

Public Buildings, Public Works, and Residences. Office buildings for private businesses and buildings for government administration can be found in the downtown area and several regional areas as well. City Hall, for example, recently moved from a relatively small facility downtown to a new complex of tall buildings in the northern section of town. Many buildings in the downtown and harbor areas house offices for the government and private sectors that deal with the shipping industry. The skyline of tall buildings is beautiful and modern.

The city government administers to the basic needs of the citizens. Electricity, water, and sewer lines are connected to every house and office in the city. Police services for safety and traffic control are efficient and visible. In addition to the main police station, there are smaller police stations scattered throughout the city. Fire departments have modern equipment and are ready to respond quickly to emergencies.

South Koreans typically live in apartment or small houses with only a few rooms used for living, eating, and sleeping. One advantage that Pusan residents have is that their city has less than half the population that Seoul contains, with more land area (square kilometers). Traditional single-family homes built before the 1970s can easily be found in some of the city's neighborhoods, but newer neighborhoods most often consist of tall, high-rise apartment complexes (some as tall as 30 stories). Koreans like to own their own homes and the percentage of homes that are rented, even in high-rise building complexes, is relatively low. In the minds of many Koreans, owning an apartment is more prestigious than owning a single-family home. In some neighborhoods, there are townhouses, homes that are two or three stories tall, arranged in a complex with common parking and security—a cross between older single-family homes and high-rise apartment complexes.

Politics and City Services. Pusan contains 16 general districts. Fifty-five members from 55 electoral districts make up the council of Pusan Metropolitan City, which is run by a mayor, who serves anywhere from one to three years on average. City programs include helping those in need to become more self-sustaining, along with various counseling and guidance services for troubled individuals. Disabled persons are also ensured government support under Pusan laws.

Educational System. South Koreans see education as the keys to their future. They are determined to give every child the best possible schooling. Education is free and compulsory for the first 11 years. The standard for education in South Korea is six years of primary school, three years of middle school, and three years of high school, followed by postsecondary education, which can be college or university, or a two-year junior college or trade school. The most prestigious university in the city is Pusan National University, located in the foothills north of the city, near one of the hot spring resort areas. Other prominent schools include Donga University, Dongui University, and Pusan Teachers' College. Postsecondary education is expanding in South Korea, including in Pusan, and new schools have opened in recent years.

Transportation System. In addition to ships, trains, trucks, cars, buses, and all variety of street traffic, there is also a subway line to quickly shuttle passengers from the northern limits of the city to downtown and around the southern point and out to the northwest. The subway is an efficient way to get around the city, as the streets are often crowded with bumper-to-bumper traffic.

© BOHEMIAN NOMAD PICTUREMAKERS/CORBIS

A bus rider reads a newspaper on his way to work in Pusan, South Korea.

CULTURAL AND SOCIAL LIFE

Distinctive Features of the City's Cultures. For businesspeople, general attire in Pusan is much the same as it is in the United States: jacket and tie for men and conservative attire for women. Lightweight clothing is generally worn in the hot and humid summer season. Although it is not customary to tip in South Korea, in some Western-style restaurants it is not unheard of if one's meal was enjoyable and the service particularly accommodating. South Koreans base their business relationships on personal ones. The heavy drinking of the Korean alcohol (*soju*), beer, or other liquor is commonplace in establishing a personal business relationship.

Cuisine. As Pusan is a port city, seafood is abundant in its inhabitants' diet. Other typical entrées and side dishes include traditional kimchi, tea, an assortment of barbecued meats, and a wide variety of vegetables (usually pickled or seasoned). A majority of entrées are prepared in the traditional spicy Korean manner, incorporating hot chili paste, garlic, and Korean green and red peppers.

Ethnic, Class, and Religious Diversity. Ethnically Pusan is very homogeneous in nature, the general populace being mostly Korean. There is a large middle class in Pusan, as well as an upper class. Only a small percentage of the population lives below the poverty line, such as homeless individuals. Religious affiliations include Buddhism, Protestantism, Catholicism, Confucianist groups, and other Christian sects.

Family and Other Social Support Systems. The average family in Pusan comprises 3 to 5 individuals (3.3 in 1995). The family unit is of great importance throughout South Korea, which is reflected in family-oriented customs and traditions. Most Koreans emphasize honoring deceased relatives through various traditions. Children and adolescents usually form strong ties with their classmates, most likely owing to the amount of time put in to schooling (which can average more than 10 hours a day).

Work and Commerce. The import/export business is quite large in Pusan. Commerce is carried on in both large-scale department stores and traditional markets. Farming and fish farms account for a decent amount of the city's commerce as well. The average workweek is approximately 44 hours, although many Pusan natives work overtime hours.

Arts and Recreation. Pusan hosts a number of annual festivals, including film, contemporary and traditional art, and sea festivals celebrated on boats in the harbor and on shore to provide recreation for its citizens and to celebrate and recall ancient traditions and cultural heritage.

QUALITY OF LIFE

In a 1999 survey of Asia's best cities, *Asia Now* magazine ranked Pusan 15th among more than 50 cities. Some of the contributing factors for such a rating were the low level of pollution in the city, its burgeoning economy, generous educational spending, excellent ratio of hospital to citizenry, low commute time, and a good life expectancy (74.4 years). Pusan offers a nice mix of urban living with a thriving economy in a scenic, almost rural atmosphere.

FUTURE OF THE CITY

The most exciting recent news concerning Pusan is the construction of a new high-speed rail system. The Seoul-Pusan Korean High-Speed Rail is the largest transportation infrastructure project in the world, involving the engineering and construction of 412 kilometers (256 miles) of track bed, with over 47% of the alignment through 83 tunnels and 27% over bridges and viaducts. Built to accommodate trains running at a maximum speed of 300 kilometers per hour (over 185 miles per hour), it is slated to open for commercial operations in December 2003. The Republic of Korea will field 46 trains sets, each capable of carrying 1,000 passengers from Seoul to Pusan in 1 hour and 56 minutes. (Currently it takes 5 hours to make this commute by regular train.) The project is characterized by the exploitation of leading-edge technologies in high-speed rails systems, communications, and construction methods.

BIBLIOGRAPHY

Eckert, Carter, and Ki-Baik Lee, *Korea Old and New: A History* (Harvard University Press 1991).

English, Alexander, *Lonely Planet: Korea 2001* (Lonely Planet Publications 2001).

The Korean War: Pusan to Chosin: An Oral History (Harvest Books 1987).

Le Bas, Tom, *Insight Guide Korea* (Langenscheidt Publishers 2001).

Oberdorfer, Don, *The Two Koreas: A Contemporary History* (Basic Books 1999).

Nilsen, Robert, *Moon Handbooks: South Korea* (Moon Publications 1997).

Saccone, Richard, *Travel Korea Your Way* (Pelican 1997).

Yup, Paik Sun, *From Pusan to Panmunjom: Wartime Memoirs of the Republic of Korea's First Four-Star General* (Books International 1999).

Useful Web Sites

www.atheism.about.com/library/world/KZ/bl_SKoreaReligion.htm [pages on religion sponsored by about.com].

www.southkorea.asiaco.com/english/ [sponsored by the United States Commercial Service].

www.iclei.org/mia98-99/pusan.htm [sponsored by the city government of Pusan].

www.metro.pusan.kr/english/overview/overview.htm [sponsored by the city of Pusan].

MARK PETERSON

P'yŏngyang

North Korea

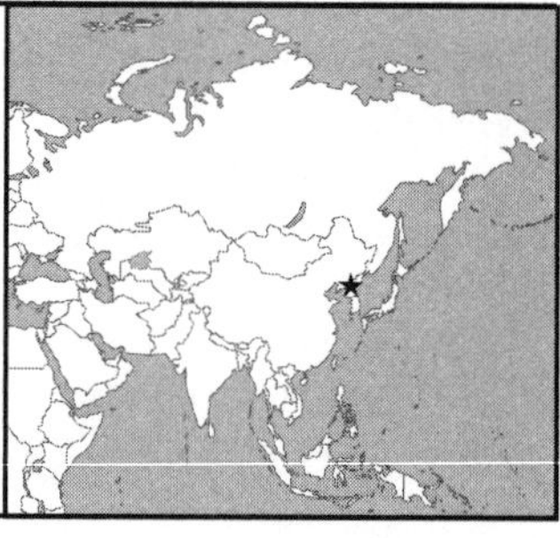

ORIENTATION

Name of City. P'yŏngyang si (P'yŏngyang City) is the capital of the Democratic People's Republic of Korea (DPRK, or North Korea). The name *P'yŏngyang* means "city on level land" in Chinese characters. This name dates from the early 5th century A.D., when the state of Koguryŏ moved its capital to the large plain surrounding the city. Poetically the city is sometimes called Ryugyŏng, or "Willow Capital," from the willows that line the banks of its rivers, and there are numerous other poetic and historic names for the city.

Location. P'yŏngyang is situated along both banks of the Taedong River in the northwestern part of the Korean peninsula at 39°03′ north latitude, and 125°48′ east longitude. It is approximately 800 kilometers (497 miles) due east of Beijing, China, 1,250 kilometers (776 miles) west northwest of Tokyo, Japan, and 200 kilometers (124 miles) north northwest of Seoul, Korea.

Population. Administered as a "direct rule city" (*chikhalsi*), equivalent to a province in the administrative hierarchy, P'yŏngyang City includes a good deal of agricultural land as well as the built-up area of the city proper. The official 1987 population figure released to the United Nations and noted by Nicholas Eberstadt and Judith Banister (*The Population of North Korea*, 1992) was 2.4 million inhabitants. Of these, 157,000 were considered agricultural. Government tour guides in the early 1990s estimated that the population of the built-up area of the city was approximately 1.2 million.

Distinctive and Unique Features. P'yŏngyang is the oldest continuously inhabited city on the Korean peninsula. It has a superb situation on both banks of the Taedong River at a point where cliffs on the west bank recede to a broad terrace directly accessible from the river. The main entrance to the old city was Taedong Gate, an arched stone gate topped by a two-story tower that was the east entrance through the city wall from the Taedong River ferry crossing. Just north of this, on a small cliff known as Tŏgam Rock, was Refined Brightness Pavilion (Yŏn'gwang Chŏng), which provided a famous vista of the eastern plains and mountains across the river. Both have been rebuilt. The cliffs of Peony Hill (Moran pong) contain gates and pavilions from the old city fortress with fine vistas overlooking the Taedong River. The Central District (Chung kuyŏk) covers the area of the walled city proper that stretched some 3 kilometers (1.8 miles) south of Peony Hill along the west bank of the Taedong River. On the western edge of the Central District, the Pot'ong River flows south to meet the Taedong River just downstream from the historic city center. An oxbow of the Pot'ong River squeezes the center of town into a wasp waist less than a kilometer wide, and provides a parklike ambience to the district of the same name. Located some 75 kilometers (47 miles) upstream from the mouth of the Taedong River at Namp'o, P'yŏngyang was long the farthest point inland navigable on the river by seagoing craft. Today, since Namp'o can be reached in less than an hour by railway or divided highway, little boat traffic reaches the city.

Attractions of the City. The contemporary city has a modern, clean, and attractive downtown of broad boulevards, parks and monuments, transportation, and underground utilities. It has excellent sports facilities and other cultural amenities. In the Central District the streets follow the grid of the old city. The axis of the modern city was moved somewhat south of Taedong Gate to the area between the two main east-to-west bridges that cross the Taedong River: Ongnyu Bridge on the north and Taedong Bridge on the south. Kim Il-sŏng Square opens to the river between these two bridges providing a vista across to the east bank and the 170-meter- (558-foot-) high Tower of the Juche Idea that was built to commemorate the 70th birthday of the late Kim Il-sŏng, leader of the DPRK from 1948 until his death in 1994. Visitors can ascend to a parapet just below the sculpted flame to view the entire city. The Taedong River has been tamed by barrages upstream and is graced with fountains in the center channel there. Farther north on Victory Street is the massive Arch of Triumph (Kaesŏn mun) built to commemorate Kim Il-sŏng's return from exile to P'yŏngyang in 1945. The numerous monuments, parks, broad avenues, and squares provide an appropriate backdrop for the mass mobilization parades favored by the government regime. These and numerous other monuments together relate a story of P'yŏngyang as the heroic city of the Korean revolution and heir to the martial kingdom of Koguryŏ that covered North Korea and Manchuria from the 4th through the 6th century.

Relationships Between the City and the Outside. P'yŏngyang has been the capital of the DPRK since the state's founding in 1948. The built-up part of the city contains the major ministries and agencies of the central government of the DPRK, the Korean Worker's Party, and the mass media. The city is home to more than a dozen national universities. A few textile and electronics assembly plants are located in P'yŏngyang, but most heavy and polluting industries are located in satellite cities or entirely outside the administrative area of P'yŏngyang. The city thus functions primarily as the residential and service center for government cadres and intelligentsia. Persons from other parts of the DPRK can visit P'yŏngyang only with a travel permit. About two dozen countries maintain embassies in P'yŏngyang (the Russian and Chinese are the largest), and there is a small number of foreign technicians, but the total number of foreign residents is no more than a few thousand.

Major Languages. Korean (Chosŏn ŏ) is the universal language of communication. The standard language of North Korea, known as cultured language (*munhwa ŏ*), is based on P'yŏngyang speech. It is similar to the standard speech of South Korea with the chief difference that the initial *r* is both pronounced and spelled. North Korea also emphasizes vocabulary of native origin rather than Chinese or other foreign words. The script is alphabetic with no admixture of Chinese characters. English and Russian are the most widely studied foreign languages. Persons competent in Japanese can be found at major hotels and stores.

HISTORY

The Origin of the City. Some legends associate P'yŏngyang with the city founded by Tan'gun, Korea's heavenly ancestor, in 2333 B.C. Other legends say that Kija, an advisor to the last Chinese emperor of Shang, took over the kingdom of Old Chosŏn centered at P'yŏngyang in 1122 B.C. The exact historical founding date of the city is not known, but by 195 B.C., when the historical figure Wiman arrived from Manchuria to usurp the throne, Wanggŏm Sŏng, as the city was then known, was the capital of the Old Chosŏn state. The word *wanggŏm* is thought to be a rendering with Chinese characters of a native word that meant "king" or "great man." *Sŏng* means "fortress." The kingdom ruled by Wiman and his descendents was conquered by Han China in 108 B.C.

After conquering Old Chosŏn, Han China set up a military commandery known as Lèlàng (Nangnang in Korean). The Japanese archaeologist Sekino identified the earthen fortress of T'osŏng-ni, 8 kilometers (5 miles) from P'yŏngyang, as the site of Lèlàng because the seal of the governor of Lèlàng was excavated there along with other Han Chinese artifacts. Lèlàng prospered during the former and later Han (to 220 A.D.) with the population reaching 2.5 million persons. Only the residents of the city and closely surrounding areas were probably ethnic Chinese. The Chinese governors of the city gave titles to indigenous chieftains in outlying areas. The city was taken over by the northern Korean state of Koguryŏ in 313 A.D. The population of the Chinese-controlled area by then was a mere 15,000 people. (North Korean historiography does not recognize P'yŏngyang as the site of Lèlàng, and considers the city to have an unbroken line of Korean rule from Old Chosŏn through Koguryŏ to the present DPRK.)

Koguryŏ expanded rapidly from the 4th century A.D. to take control of most of northern Korea and Manchuria. King Changsu named the city P'yŏngyang when he moved the capital there in 427. There are more than 1,000 Koguryŏ tombs at the foot of Mount Taesŏng on the northeast edge of what is now P'yŏngyang, as well as the remains of the Peaceful Crane Palace (Anhak Kung). Koguryŏ was destroyed in 668 by a combined invasion of Tang China and the southern Korean kingdom of Silla. The Chinese at first left 20,000 troops in P'yŏngyang, calling the city "Prefecture for Protecting the Pacified East" (Andong Tohobu), but they gradually withdrew and the area became part of Silla, the first Korean kingdom to unite the Korean peninsula. P'yŏngyang was far from the Silla capital in the southeast, however, so the area languished as a neglected periphery under Silla.

Migration: Past and Present. When the kingdom of Koryŏ replaced Silla in 918, the Koryŏ king sent Korean settlers to repopulate the P'yŏngyang area, calling it "Prefecture for Protecting the Great Capital" (Taedo Hodobu) at first, but later Sŏgyŏng, or "Western Capital." The city grew under royal patronage, and because of favorable geomancy the royal court considered moving the capital there. Under Chosŏn, which succeed Koryŏ in 1392, the name *P'yŏngyang* was restored and the city continued as one of the most important walled cities in the kingdom, famous for its historical associations. Just outside the northwest wall was the tomb of Kija, which was maintained by the Sŏnu clan who claimed to be his descendants. By the late 19th century it had a population of about 80,000.

During the Japanese colonial period (1910–1945), the old city wall was torn down leaving just the larger gates. Railways were brought in, and a modernized urban district developed between the railway station and South Gate (today's P'yŏngch'ŏn District). By 1940 about 10% of the city's 250,000 residents were ethnic Japanese, who lived predominantly in the modern city and dominated government and commerce. P'yŏngyang was also an important center of Protestant Christianity, (some observers estimated that one-third of the population was Christian). The Northern Presbyterian Mission from the United States maintained one of the largest missionary compounds in the world and, with the Northern Methodists, ran a hospital and numerous schools.

Liberation in 1945 brought occupation by the Soviet Union. The People's Committee that ran the city was headed by the Korean Christian Cho Man-sik at first, but by February 1946, with the establishment of the North Korean Provisional People's Committee, Kim Il-sŏng was in charge, and the political fates of North and South Korea diverged. Land reform in March was followed by the nationalization of industry in August. The unbridgeable differences between the administration of People's Committees in the north backed by the Soviet Union and the American Military Government in the south led to the creation of separate states in the two parts of the peninsula. The Democratic People's Republic of Korea (DPRK, or North Korea) was established on September 9, 1948, with its capital at P'yŏngyang, three weeks after the establishment of the United Nations- (UN-) sanctioned Republic of Korea in the south with its capital at Seoul.

North Korea invaded the south on June 25, 1950, in order to reunify the country. By early September the north had almost succeeded, but intervention by United Nations forces (largely from the United States) reversed this. P'yŏngyang was captured in mid-October, and UN forces advanced almost to the Chinese border. In late November the People's Republic of China entered the war on the North Korean side and once more the tides turned. P'yŏngyang was quickly recaptured. Much of P'yŏngyang's Christian community and upper classes had fled south by this time. A stalemate developed near the 38th parallel, while negotiations to end the war dragged on for two more years. P'yŏngyang, which had already been heavily damaged, suffered bomb and napalm raids, which, according to Jon Halliday and Bruce Cumings (*Korea: The Unknown War*), probably killed more than 10% of the remaining population and left few buildings standing intact. Life went on for governing cadres in underground bunkers. North Koreans are proud that the contemporary city was rebuilt from the ground up after the 1953 armistice, and they recall the UN bombing with bitterness.

P'yŏngyang was reconstructed after the armistice with aid from the socialist countries. Undesirable people were periodically deported to the countryside, but the population grew quickly owing to large numbers of migrants from all over the DPRK. Growth slowed in the 1970s, but P'yŏngyang continued to attract educational and governmental elites from throughout the country. Residence in P'yŏngyang is by permit only. Except on a few major holidays, interregional travel and hotel stays are possible only by obtaining travel passes (*yŏhaeng chŭngmyŏngsŏ*). By this means P'yŏngyang is kept largely free from illegal internal migrants.

INFRASTRUCTURE

Public Buildings, Public Works, and Residences. Impressive public buildings are a feature of P'yŏngyang. The Grand People's Study Hall, a multistory building capped with terraces and immense green-tiled roofs in the traditional style, rises on a hill on the west side of Kim Il-sŏng Square. The Korean-style P'yŏngyang Grand Theater sits at the junction of Victory and Glory streets. To the north of Kim Il-sŏng Square, Victory Street leads past P'yŏngyang Student and Children's Palace and the Supreme People's Assembly to the immense Korean Revolution Museum that sits atop Mansu Hill to the west of the street. The museum is approached by a monumental set of terraces leading up from the Taedong River to a 60-meter- (197-foot-) high bronze statue of Kim Il-sŏng. The statue is flanked by 108 smaller heroic bronze statues of revolutionary masses; behind them is a gigantic mosaic mural of Mt. Paektu that decorates the front of the museum building. The opulent Mansudae Art Theater (used mostly for official performances) is located nearby.

The city was rebuilt in a planned way after the Korean War so that the term *kŏri* ("street") refers to large integrated developments as well as the roads themselves. Each *kŏri* has been built in a different and distinctive style. Glory Street (Yŏnggwang kŏri), one of the older developments in the city, is lined with six-story yellow brick buildings decorated with terra-cotta, reminiscent of Russia. Although neighborhoods of small, single-story houses still exist in out-of-the-way parts of town, the government has tried to plan the central parts of town with tree-lined streets and modern high-rise apartments. Restoration Street (Kwangbok kŏri), a development in the Mangyŏngdae District west of the Pot'ong River, contains ultramodern apartments of 305- to 605-square-meters (1,000- to 2,000-square-feet), housing some 30,000 families; several restaurants; a department store; movie theaters; and even a circus, all lining a 100-meter- (382-foot-) wide boulevard. It was completed in 1989 for the thirteenth World Youth Conference and has both subway and tram connections to the rest of P'yŏngyang. Unification Street (T'ongil kŏri), located in Nangnang District just south of the Taedong River, is a similar development completed in 1994 for some 40,000 families. The oxbow of the Pot'ong River, just northwest of the Central District, forms a pleasant, willow-lined park in the center of town in summer and a natural skating rink in winter.

Politics and City Services. The P'yŏngyang City Committee of the Korean Workers Party and the Municipal People's Committee govern the city. The former sets policy while the latter serves administrative functions. The city is divided into districts (*kuyŏk*), streets (*kŏri*), precincts (*tong*), and people's teams (*inminban*). There are about 14 districts in the built-up area and in some 30 of the integrated developments known as *kŏri*. The city is provided with underground utilities, modern streetlights, and sewage and garbage service (some of the single-story residential districts lack these), but public telephones are rare. The brightest of the public lights are turned off at 10:00 P.M. Government ministries and most other buildings are unmarked.

Educational System. Eleven years of education are compulsory: one year of kindergarten (*yuch'iwŏn*), four years of people's school (*inmin hakkyo*), and six years of higher middle school (*kodŭng chunghakkyo*). Students are assigned to schools according to where they reside in the city, but magnet and special foreign-language schools also exist. After completing compulsory education students take the government service exam (chŏngmuwŏn sihŏm), which determines whether they will be assigned directly to work, to the army, or will be given a certificate that would allow them to take a university entrance exam.

In P'yŏngyang's better schools the majority of the students go on to higher education consisting of two- to four-year technical high schools, or four- to six-year universities. Students do not pick their schools, but are assigned to them by county, provincial, and central university assignment offices. The best students go to national universities that recruit from the entire country. Most reports claim that advancement to university is based mainly on exams, but social background (*sŏngbun*) will affect opportunities for preparation and the course of study to which one is assigned. Kim Il-sŏng Consolidated University, located north of Peony Hill (also known as Kimdae), is the most famous university in the DPRK with the stiffest admissions requirements. Kim Ch'aek University of Technology, located on Glory Street, is also well known.

© JEREMY HORNER/CORBIS

North Korean children enjoy picture books in this nursery school in P'yŏngyang.

Transportation System. P'yŏngyang is served by an airport capable of handling international jets at Sunan, 20 kilometers (12 miles) west of P'yŏngyang. It has scheduled service to China and Russia. The city is a rail hub with lines radiating in all directions that connect to Chinese and Russian rail service at the border in the north (there are no train connections to South Korea). The majority of the trains are electric, but not many routes are double tracked. Superhighways link P'yŏngyang with Namp'o, Wŏnsan, Kaesŏng, and other major cities. Owing to shortages of fuel and vehicles, traffic is light both within P'yŏngyang and on the major highways.

Transportation within the city is by foot, subway, electric tram, bus, and a small number of Mercedes Benz taxicabs. The two subway lines cross in the Central District. The typically elaborate Kwangbok subway station is decorated with crystal chandeliers and a huge mosaic of Mt. Paektu. High-level cadres and delegations are provided with cars and drivers. World-class athletes are also provided with automobiles; however, private automobiles are so few in number, air pollution is practically absent in the city. Work units sometimes transport employees in the backs of trucks. Smartly uniformed young women on wooden stands direct cars and pedestrians at major intersections. Some P'yŏngyang residents have bicycles although they are not a major form of transportation.

Considering the population of the city and the density of its high-rise housing, visitors to P'yŏngyang have frequently been struck by the lightness of both pedestrian and vehicular traffic even in the center of town. This partly reflects city planning, in which each integrated development has local shopping and entertainment facilities, and partly reflects people's busy schedules. Political study sessions often follow the workday, so that streets are often teeming with people coming home between 10:00 and 11:00 at night, after the city lights have been turned off.

CULTURAL AND SOCIAL LIFE

Distinctive Features of the City's Cultures. Political and other forms of expression are tightly controlled by government agencies, with only approved domestic media freely available. The government tends to regard almost all information about the outside world as threatening to the regime and harmful to their ideology of self-reliance and ethnic purity. For this reason, although some approved foreign movies (especially from the former Soviet bloc) are shown, access to foreign publications, broadcasts, and other media is granted only to trusted high-level cadres. Enthusiasm for the regime is maintained through techniques of social mobilization: education; small group political sessions; patriotic celebrations complete with propaganda workers exhorting the masses with exalted, trembling voices; and large billboards with slogans like *uri siktaero salja* ("Let's live in our own fashion"), *purŏun iri ŏpta* ("We have nothing to envy in the world"), or *tang kwa kuji tangyŏlhayŏ ap 'ŭro kaja* ("Let's go forward firmly united around the party").

Western-style dress similar to that worn in eastern Europe is the norm for both men and women. Male factory workers and laborers wear cotton trousers with jackets and a cloth cap, while their female counterparts wear midcalf skirts with blouses, or colorful print dresses, and a scarf. White-collar workers wear slacks and shirts with ties, or Western-style suits. Fashion trends in Japan and the West are known, but people gravitate to the more conservative styles. Men almost never wear Korean national costume in P'yŏngyang, but a small number of women, especially for family celebrations and holidays, wear traditional *hanbok*—a colorful skirt with an empire waist, topped with a short vest in a contrasting color covering the shoulders, arms, and breasts.

Cuisine. People's ordinary diet at home is a simple one of steamed rice, noodles, soup, and *kimch'i*, a spicy Korean pickled cabbage. This is livened up with eggs, meat, fish, and vegetables in season. Each district of P'yŏngyang has restaurants specializing in various types of food, such as Chinese. Some eating establishments serve liquor, but P'yŏngyang does not have separate bars, cafes, or tearooms. P'yŏngyang noodle dishes are well known. The Ongnyu-gwan restaurant, situated in a large traditional-style building along the west bank of the Taedong River just north of Ongnyu Bridge, is particularly famous for its cold noodles, or *P'yŏngyang naengmyŏn*. Taedong River mullet (*sungŏ*), served steamed or in soup, is a beloved local dish. *Tan'gogi*, or "sweet meat" (that is, dog meat) restaurants also exist. Western food and coffee can be obtained at major hotels such as the Koryŏ Hotel, which has a revolving restaurant atop its 46 stories.

Ethnic, Class, and Religious Diversity. Christianity, the major source of organized opposition to the establishment of the communist regime, was quickly branded a tool of imperialism by the DPRK, and both Catholics and Protestants were harshly repressed at the beginning of the regime. Buddhism was considered a superstition and also suppressed. Only the syncretic, indigenous Ch'ŏndogyo faith was allowed, with a central church located in P'yŏngyang. Repressions of religion has eased greatly since the late 1980s, however. A number of historical temples have been restores, and a small number of monks and nuns have been allowed in to worship on traditional Buddhist holidays. In P'yŏngyang, Pongsu Church for Protestants and Changch'ung Cathedral for Catholics have services. There are a number of active Protestant ministers, although no Catholic priests. House churches are tolerated, but propagation of religion is not allowed, so most Christians have inherited their faith from before 1945. Individual citizens often continue the tradition of ancestor memorial ceremonies (*chesa*) in their homes, and of visits to tombs on major lunar holidays. Traditional fortune-tellers are also still active.

Most of the industries creating pollution in the P'yŏngyang area are located outside the city proper, although electronics, textile, machine tool, and transportation equipment manufacturers are found in the city. In addition to the workers in these industries the residents consist mostly of cadres (*kanbu*, those who rank high enough to have decision-making authority in the Korean Workers Party), the state bureaucracy, the armed forces, state-owned businesses, and state social organizations. Cadres are selected from among those who have good social and political background (*sŏngbun*), good education, and excellent scores on the civil service exams. Lower level white-collar workers, affluent ethnic Koreans repatriated from Japan, the intelligentsia of the major universities, research institutes, art groups, and publishing houses are also well-represented in the P'yŏngyang population. P'yŏngyang receives preference in the provision of necessities and luxuries, and cadres and intelligentsia typically earn three to seven times the monthly salary of a worker. This, combined with the fact that authorization for residence in P'yŏngyang is strictly controlled, limits the amount of poverty visible in the city. Ordinary citizens receive gifts of meat or candies from President Kim Chŏng-il on holidays (such as "birthday of the leader" and New Years), but high-ranking persons might receive a watch, fountain pen, or even a television or a refrigerator. Those of higher rank get more generous and varied ration coupons, access to special stores and clinics, and other perks (including cars for the highest-ranking cadres). There are thus greater differences in consumption than nominal differences in salary would imply. Laborers can easily be distinguished from higher-level workers by the cut, style, and quality of their clothes and accessories.

Apartments are state-owned, but dwelling rights can be inherited. Rents for modern apartments are cheap in relation to income, but the size, location, and amenities of assigned housing vary with a person's status. For this reason many districts of town have a specialized character. Youth Street, which is in the An'gok Sports Village—an integrated development where world-class athletes live—includes several gymnasiums, stadiums, and other sports-related facilities. East P'yŏngyang is less elaborately appointed than other parts of the city. Ch'anggwang Street in the Central District houses high-level cadres and functionaries, with excellent health-care facilities located nearby. Nonresidents are denied access to this street by sentries. The part of the Peony Hill District facing Pot'ong River Park is said to be home to many Koreans who have returned from Japan with access to hard currency, or who have relatives with such access. Several stores and clinics in the area cater to this relatively affluent group. The laborers who live in P'yŏngyang tend to live on the outskirts of town.

Family and Other Social Support Systems. From 1946 on, North Korean authorities promoted the equality of the sexes and worked to abolish such institutions as dowry, concubinage, and indentured female service. With the socialization of the economy, the family is no longer a unit of production in urban or rural areas, and transmission of productive property between the generations—and concern with maintaining the family line—is thus no longer important. The authorities occasionally decry traditional Korean familism, but families remain strong and are officially deemed a basic unit of society. Filial piety and respect for parents is promoted by the state. Both husbands and wives normally work outside the home with young children attending daycare or school, but women typically bear the double burden of work and housework. Men are encouraged to "love" their wives and wives to "respect" their husbands, but observers say patriarchal attitudes remain entrenched. Children live at home until they have finished their education. Newly married couples establish neolocal residence as soon as the husband's work unit is able to provide a housing assignment. Apartments for more prosperous families in P'yŏngyang accommodate traditional stem families, in which the eldest son brings his bride to live with him and his parents. Three-room apartments, for example, have a living room (*kŏsil*), a bedroom (*sallimbang*), and an old people's room (*noinbang*).

Men tend to marry around the age of 27, and women somewhat younger. In recent years people have been marrying at younger ages. Love matches are common, particularly among university students, but many people's social networks are limited to their immediate neighbors and coworkers, so modified arranged marriages or "introduction matches" are also common. Prospective spouses are introduced to each other by matchmaking friends, relatives, or coworkers and will date if they decide to marry. Dates may consist of strolls in the parks along the Taedong or Pot'ong rivers. Public displays of affection between the sexes is taboo, however, and sexual liaisons outside marriage are punishable if discovered. Wedding ceremonies tend to be simple family affairs followed by a small reception.

Medical care is provided through one's work unit. Ultramodern facilities such as the Changwon Health Complex along the Pot'ong River are available to treat high-level cadres in central state organs. P'yŏngyang Maternity Hospital near P'yŏngyang Station is another modern facility that treats a wider section of the population. Recent visitors to North Korea have reported seeing serious shortages of medical supplies in most North Korean hospitals, although the situation is undoubtedly better in P'yŏngyang than other North Korean locations.

Work and Commerce. People are assigned to their work units based on their performance in the State Service Examination taken at about the age of 17. P'yŏngyang residents generally do well in these exams, achieving access to higher education in large numbers. In addition to education, assignment to occupations is affected by membership in the Korean Workers Party, political performance, and social background (*sŏngbun*). Most people start work at eight o'clock A.M., rest at work between one o'clock and four o'clock P.M., and then finish at eight o'clock P.M.

As in China, much of peoples' lives are organized around their work units—the ministry, state-owned factory or business at which one works, or the school that one attends. Cooperative work units, such as small restaurants and craft and service enterprises also exist. In addition to work, political study sessions, Korean Workers Party activity, and volunteer community work is organized at the level of the work unit. Tickets to sporting and theatrical events are difficult to get, so excursions to these events are most often organized on the basis of work units. Because husbands, wives, and children most typically involved with different units, P'yŏngyang families frequently have little time to spend together.

P'yŏngyang residents are able to purchase their inexpensive rationed allocation of basic goods at state stores. During the *kimch'i*-making season in the fall, people receive large amounts of cabbage, radishes, and peppers (some large apartment houses collectively process this). Fancier consumer items can be purchased with ration coupons at special state stores, such as First Department Store. Stores are based on a socialist system: one orders an item from a clerk by presenting a ration coupon, pays another clerk, and then receives the item by presenting the receipt to the first clerk. Long lines are not a regular feature of this system, but can form when items in short supply become available. Higher-ranking individuals have access to unmarked special stores supplied with goods not available to the general public. There are two types of money: regular and foreign exchange certificates (so-called blue money). Rare and imported goods can be purchased with foreign exchange certificates at hard currency stores. Anybody with the proper kind of money (for example those who receive remittances from relatives abroad) can purchase items, but only the elite receive part of their salary in blue money. Goods outside the state distribution system can be purchased, when available, at the factory direct sales outlets that exist in P'yŏngyang. The city also has a number of walled farmers' markets where farmers sell goods produced in their kitchen gardens at market prices.

Arts and Recreation. P'yŏngyang has theaters, several circuses, and many sports facilities. Soccer is popular, and matches at Nŭngna Island Stadium are well attended. Movie theaters are also widespread, showing mostly DPRK films but occasionally also films from Russia or other countries. The opulent Mansudae Art Theater gives performances mostly for official delegations, but other theaters offer musical performances for the larger public. Recreational life is highly organized, and access to cultural and sporting events tends to be based on school or work-unit outings. Most people in P'yŏngyang have televisions and watch evening and weekend broadcasts at home. On Sundays families may stroll in some of P'yŏngyang's many parks and visit monuments, such as Kaesŏn Youth Park, Peony Hill Park, or Pot'ong River Park. Outdoor ice-skating is popular in the winter. The Central Zoo and Botanical Gardens, as well as an amusement park with rides, are located just northeast at Taesŏng Mountain, the old Korguryŏ fortress. Several other amusement parks exist on the edge of town. Outings to Mangyŏngdae, the village where Kim Il-sŏng was born, are popular.

Art in North Korea is supposed to express socialist values, be accessible to the people, and to embody the national ideology of *chuch'e*—to creatively and progressively express the Korean spirit while eschewing bourgeois self-expression. In both art and music socialist realism is generally deemed the most appropriate style, but this general style must be creatively adapted to the actual conditions in North Korea. Artists are organized into the General Association of Korean Writers and Artists (Chosŏn munhak yesulga ch'ong tongmaeng) headquartered in P'yŏngyang, with sections for writers, artists, and performing artists. Painters provide large murals for public buildings, as well as smaller works. Comprehensive companies of musicians, singers, and dancers are maintained by the Mansudae Art Theater and the P'yŏngyang Grand Theater. These companies provide variety performances of popular and folk song and dance as well as full-length narrative ballets and revolutionary operas such as *Sea of Blood* (*P'i pada*). In North Korean musical culture there is a deliberate mixing of Western and native instruments (many of the latter improved so as to be able to handle the 12-tone diatonic scale, rather than the traditional pentatonic scale only), as strictly traditional performance practices are associated with the old upper classes. Smaller-scale troops are often maintained by work units.

QUALITY OF LIFE

P'yŏngyang provides the highest quality of life available in North Korea. The residents of the city are, in general, individuals and the families of those who plan and run the country and have the proper social background (*sŏngbun*) and political loyalty. The city, with its parks and monuments, modern transportation, and high-rise apartment buildings, was designed to display the achievements of the revolution to foreigners and residents alike. Some residents enjoy access to the finest cultural and educational facilities and have access to the best commodities available in North Korea. At the same time life in P'yŏngyang (as in the DPRK as a whole) is highly controlled. Children spend most of their time in organized activities at school or with Young Pioneers. Adults spend 12 hours a day at their places of work, and may also engage in political study or organized leisure activities through their work units, so people have little time for unstructured social gatherings. Shopping is not a recreational activity. P'yŏngyang, while beautiful, thus lacks the lively street life and entertainment districts found in many other cities.

FUTURE OF THE CITY

The North Korean economy has suffered severe difficulties since the disintegration of the socialist block in 1989 and the consequent elimination of state-to-state trade with socialist countries. Declining production due to shortages of fuel and foreign exchange was exacerbated by severe weather, ecological destruction, and other difficulties. In 1998 food shortages reached even P'yŏngyang. Full recovery of the North Korean economy will require adjustments to promote a greater degree of engagement in the global trading system. If the DPRK initiates more foreign contacts and allows direct foreign investment, P'yŏngyang may see more foreign visitors and residents.

The relatively high standard of living in P'yŏngyang has been sustained by favorable central state allocation of resources, combined with limited migration to P'yŏngyang from poorer, less favored parts of the DPRK. Opening the economy and lifting restrictions on movement, as has happened in the People's Republic of China and Russia, would lead to a movement of poor rural migrants into the city. This would lead to a more unequal, disorderly P'yŏngyang, but perhaps a more equal DPRK.

BIBLIOGRAPHY

Hunter, Helen-Louise, *Kim Il-song's North Korea* (Praeger 1999).

Kim, C. I., Eugene Koh, and B. C. Koh, eds., *Journey to North Korea: Personal Perceptions* (University of California Press 1983).

Marker, Chris, *Coréennes* (Aux éditions du Seuil 1959).

Salisbury, Harrison E., *To Peking and Beyond: A Report on the New Asia* (New York Times 1973).

CLARK W. SORENSEN

Quebec City

Canada

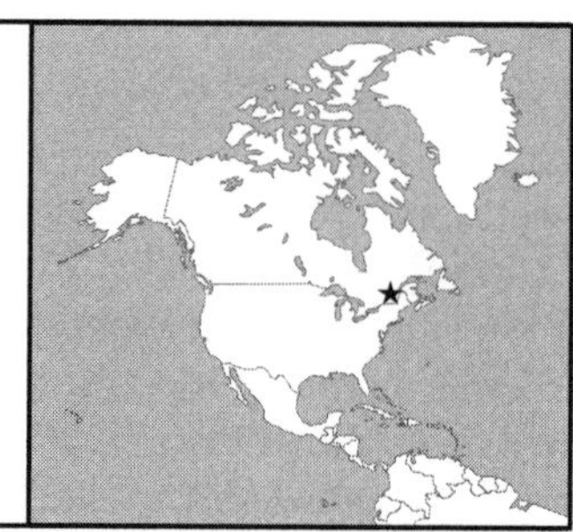

ORIENTATION

Name of City. Quebec City, capital of the province bearing the same name, is also known as "La Vieille Capitale" ("The Old Capital") or "Old Wonderful Quebec," mainly in brochures designated for tourists. These nicknames refer directly to the historicity of this town.

Location. The Old Capital is located at 46°47′ north latitude and 71°13′ west longitude, in the lower part of the huge province of Quebec—1,667,926 square kilometers (643,819 square miles)—the only one of the ten Canadian provinces where French is the official language, although Canada is officially bilingual.

Population. The Urban Community of Quebec (CUQ) comprises 14 cities and the Amerindian reserve of Wendake (Hurons-Wendat). As shown in the table on the following page, Quebec City is suffering a gradual decrease of its population, whereas the population of the CUQ is constantly expanding. This decrease is due partly to a general drop in the birthrate that is affecting all industrialized countries. On the other hand, the accelerated growth of suburban cities has drained away a large number of families from the city proper since the end of the 1960s.

Distinctive and Unique Features. Physically, the city may be divided into three distinct and parallel areas. The first area is a narrow strip of land—less than 1.6 kilometers (1 mile) deep—bordering the St. Lawrence River. The second area is a hill starting at the southeast by the Cap Diamant. This hill, an old, eroded volcano, is buried under an almost-flat surface and supports two other cities, Sillery and Ste. Foy. A large and fertile plain, ending at the foot of the Laurentian Mountains, makes up the third area. The St. Charles River crosses it roughly 3 kilometers (2 miles) from the hill.

Initially founded at the St. Lawrence's level, near the St. Charles estuary on the southeast side, the city grew simultaneously on top of the promontory and between the latter and the St. Charles River. Later on, the restricted space within the walls forced the city to expand to other sectors. First to appear was the suburb of St. Jean Baptiste, which implanted itself on the north side of Cap Diamant, facing Porte St. Jean (St. John's Gate), the main entrance to the fortifications. The location of this suburb was well chosen, for that side of the hill is definitely more accessible than the southern one, which ends in a steep cliff. From the river's edge, the transportation of supplies uphill from the port and the market was made much easier. Because of the proximity of the St. Lawrence and the founding of other towns nearby, the expansion potential of the city is quite limited.

Attractions of the City. The oldest city in Canada and one of its most picturesque, Quebec City is seen by a great number of visitors, as an adequate representation of many medieval cities from the Old World. The Citadel, a fortress started under the French regime and finished under the British one, crowns the Cap Diamant. Built for defensive purposes, it enclosed the "Quartier Latin" ("Latin Quarter"). It is one of Quebec's unique features, awarding it the title "The only fortified town in North America." Somewhat exaggerated, this does not take into account other cities, such as Campeche (Mexico), that also enjoy fortifications. However, the obvious presence of these formidable walls is a constant reminder that this old part of Quebec is in a class of its own. The entire fortification complex includes a large concentration of buildings erected under the French regime, most of which are still in excellent shape.

Three types of architecture cohabit harmoniously inside the walls. Buildings dating back to the French regime are in greater number and integrate themselves perfectly with those built during the English one, also in fair quantities. Somewhat in the background, the fewer and more recent (post-1800) structures were implanted on the rare vacant lots available at that time or on sites liberated by fires or the demolition of irretrievable buildings. However, the entire enclosed area has been declared a historical site, and further destructions are forbidden.

Relationships Between the City and the Outside. Certain tensions are dividing factors in the CUQ. These tensions are due essentially to the special characteristics of the town itself. In a city such as Quebec, with a weak economy, where government jobs and tourism are the denominating factors, the local population must be ready and willing to absorb the larger share of regional infrastructure operating expenses. All concerned parties do not regard the adequate sharing of implicated costs with the same eye. To test their respective populations, all cities and towns concerned have already held a referendum on a potential union. Looked at as a foregone conclusion, it was massively rejected. In spite of these results, the minister concerned has already announced her intention to pursue and achieve this goal.

On the provincial scene, Montreal and Quebec are engaged in a fierce rivalry dating from the very beginning of the colony. In all truthfulness, Quebec has no demographic or economic weight in this "fight." Its only prestige comes from being the provincial capital. Mockingly, Montrealers call it "the Big Village," which is more than a metaphor. From time to time, attempts to move Parliament to Montreal resurface, a scornful idea that causes the local

POPULATION AND SURFACE

	C.U.Q.			Quebec		
Years	1991	1996	Variation	1991	1996	Variation
Population	645,550	671,889	+ 4.1%	167,264	167,517	−0.2%
Surface	3,150 square kilometers (1,216 square miles)			89 square kilometers (34 square miles)		

Source: Statistiques Canada, *1991 Census* and *1996 Census*

© PAUL A. SOUDERS/CORBIS

Signs in English and French testify to the freshness of fruits and vegetables for sale in Quebec City, Quebec.

population to wince with indignation whenever it comes up.

On the International scene, aggressiveness is on the leaders' agenda. Cases of twinning with other cities are numerous, especially with French ones. Quebec's biggest asset is its tourist industry. As a northern town, summer has always been the busiest tourist season. However, in recent years, marketing has been aimed at showing Quebec, with its large ski resorts and the vast Laurentian wildlife reserve, as an ideal year-round destination.

Because of its aura of Old Europe and its fortified old city, Quebec has been included on the United Nations Educational, Scientific and Cultural Organization's (UNESCO's) list of World Heritage cities. As a matter of fact, the headquarters of this organization are located in the Old Capital.

Major Languages. Another subject of dissension between Montreal and Quebec is the title "the Greatest Francophone City in America." In sheer numbers, Montreal is well ahead, with its 1,016,376 inhabitants. However, that figure doesn't take into account the great number of Anglophones who live there. Quebec, on the other hand, is almost 100% Francophone. The rather small number of Anglophones is concentrated in the city of Sillery and north of Quebec, in Tewksbury, Shannon, and Stoneham. It is indisputable that the Old Capital is clearly French speaking.

Except for the British migratory waves at the beginning of the English regime and those at the beginning of the 19th century (many of which were Irish), immigration has never been a true population-expansion factor. The two main reasons are the language barrier and the few opportunities of employment for unspecialized workers. In Montreal, however, the use of English is widespread, and opportunities for work there are multifold; it has thus attracted far more immigrants over the years.

Despite the low percentage of English-speaking residents, almost all services are available in English throughout Quebec City. This reflects the impact of tourism, with Americans historically forming the larger percentage of visitors. Therefore, a minimum knowledge of English is required around the historical sites in order to access employment. Nonetheless, French remains the official language and the only one in daily use, as visitors can testify when they venture outside the historical grounds.

HISTORY

Jacques Cartier (or Quartier), the "official" discoverer of Canada in 1534, was commissioned by François I. In 1535 Cartier sailed up the St. Lawrence and reached the site that was later to become Montreal. He then sailed back and spent the winter in Stadaconné, a Huron village on the north shore of the St. Croix River (today the St. Charles), which was then navigable. He reached a point where Quebec would later be founded.

Ill-prepared to face the harsh Canadian winter, 25 crew members fell victim to scurvy. Had it not been for the Amerindians' knowledge of the environment, no one would have survived. In the spring, Cartier was forced to abandon one of his ships (the *Emerillon*) for lack of crew.

Fifty-four years later, in 1608, Samuel de Champlain founded Quebec. He chose to do so at the foot of Cap Diamant (then Cap-aux-Diamants), to plant the settlement's roots on the banks of the St. Lawrence. The chosen name for his city originates from the Algonquian, and means approximately "the spot where the river narrows." It is quite an appropriate name, since the very wide St. Lawrence almost closes itself at that point. From a military perspective, it was a highly strategic choice of location.

The Origin of the City. Champlain built the Abitation, a small fort comprising a fur-trading center and living quarters. Soon after, the growing city developed in two distinct axes, a choice imposed by its topography. The colonists first chose to settle at the top of the cape, where Champlain built Fort St. Louis, later to become the Château St. Louis, official residence of the governor-general. However, the site was rather cramped and hard to get to from the southeast. Expansion was made along an east/northeast line, revolving around the hill, but south of the river bordering the entire city. A third, much smaller area, a narrow strip of land south of the cape and bordering the St. Lawrence, soon found its vocation: shipbuilding.

The major conflicts between European empires had important impacts on the city. Already in 1629 Sir David Kirke, leading British forces, captured Quebec City. However, they were obliged to give it back to the French, since peace had been signed between England and France prior to their conquest. Again the city was threatened in 1690, by English forces, but without success.

In 1759 the city was once again besieged, this time by the British general James Wolfe. Fearing the rapidly approaching winter, he decided to make a suicidal move. The target was well protected by the walls erected by the French between 1690 and 1745. However, the defenses at the southeast of the hill were not without flaws. The negligence in failing to prevent a possible attack from that point was first and foremost due to the defenders' blind faith in the high and steep cliff, a formidable barrier seen as being insurmountable. But overnight Wolfe succeeded in lifting 4,000 men over the cliff. Dawn found the British army poised for battle in tight ranks, only a few hundreds yards from the city's walls. To Wolfe's amazement, Governor Frontenac left his impregnable entrenchments to fight an open battle.

The English forces were made up of career soldiers, experienced in combat. Such was not the advantage of the arrogant Frontenac, whose professional soldiers were few. The core of his troops were militiamen of Canadian roots, whom he openly scorned. The battle was an unequal one, and in a mere 30 minutes it was all over; the English victory was complete. Wolfe died on the battlefield, and Frontenac succumbed to his wounds the next day. The city was ransacked. The Treaty of Paris handed the country over to England.

Finally, Quebec was attacked by Benedict Arnold's American army in 1775, in the course of the American war for independence, but the British defenders pushed back the invaders. The English quickly realized the immediate need to fortify the city. In 1778 they began to build a series of defensive works. The Citadel was the last undertaking of those fortifications, achieved between 1829 and 1832. The entire project had two precise objectives: protection against potential American or European invaders and against the possible uprising of the Canadian population.

Relations between the conquerors and the vanquished were strained. The crown's solution was to favor a massive flow of English immigrants in order to accelerate a quick assimilation of Francophones. Nevertheless, the British plans had little or no success, for most of the immigrants lost no time in moving west toward Montreal and Toronto; only a very small number remained in Quebec.

Migration: Past and Present. The first French immigrants were almost exclusively manual workers, hunters, and colonists, headed by a few learned and cultivated leaders. The loss of Canada by France caused the immigration of rich and shrewd English business people. With local government and crown support, they quickly made their own commercial and industrial regulations that reduced the French-Canadians to the rank of third-rate workers.

This new wave of immigrants implanted itself in Montreal, where the profits were for the taking. As a result, Quebec was relegated to a position of secondary importance. However, it remained the nerve center of naval construction. A good number of Irishmen took up residence in the vicinity of the shipbuilding yards toward the end of the 19th century. They may be looked upon as the first ethnic group settling in Quebec. On the other hand, the pulp and paper jobs remained in the hands of Quebecers of old stock, even if the leaders were English.

Some industrialization emerged, mainly around the St. Charles. The two world wars contributed enormously toward the area's development. Consequently, a noticeable slackening of activity was felt at the end of the hostilities. From the end of the 1950s, the flow of imported goods caused the shutdown of the few medium-size enterprises that up to that point had survived.

The city had to wait for the middle of the 1960s to really see immigrants taking solid roots. In fact, during that period, Quebec witnessed the arrival of a considerable number of refugees from Vietnam and Central and South America, escaping political pressures in their respective countries. A very small number of African refugees also immigrated around the 1980s.

The almost nonexistent infatuation of immigrants for Quebec was above all linked to the acute shortage of employment opportunities. The attraction of the French language was the primary incentive for the groups mentioned above.

INFRASTRUCTURE

Public Buildings, Public Works, and Residences. As its provincial-capital title implies, Quebec is first of all an administrative city. It shelters the province's Parliament, but also many provincial and federal government buildings. In spite of this, the real center of decision making remains Montreal, where the province's economic and industrial structures are concentrated. Curiously, the prime ministers have no official residence in their own capital. During parliamentary sessions, they lodge in an administrative building, erected during the extensive Parliament Hill building period at the end of the 1960s. Typical of the modern architecture of this era, the residence is called "The Bunker," a well-deserved nickname. This is due not only to the building's forbidding aspect, but also because of the extremely tight and restrictive security measures that filter all visitors.

Public buildings may be divided into two categories. First, there are the historical buildings, often restored and renovated in conformity with the actual specifications. We must emphasize the Baillargé family's role in the construction of the Parliament, the seat of government. Second are the modern buildings, erected during a period of economic growth around the 1970s. Since the end of that era, construction has been almost at a standstill. Whatever development has been undertaken has taken place in surrounding municipalities.

The residential zones are concentrated mostly on the northern slope of the hill. Available land is extremely scarce, which explains why most of the residential districts have been developed in the suburbs.

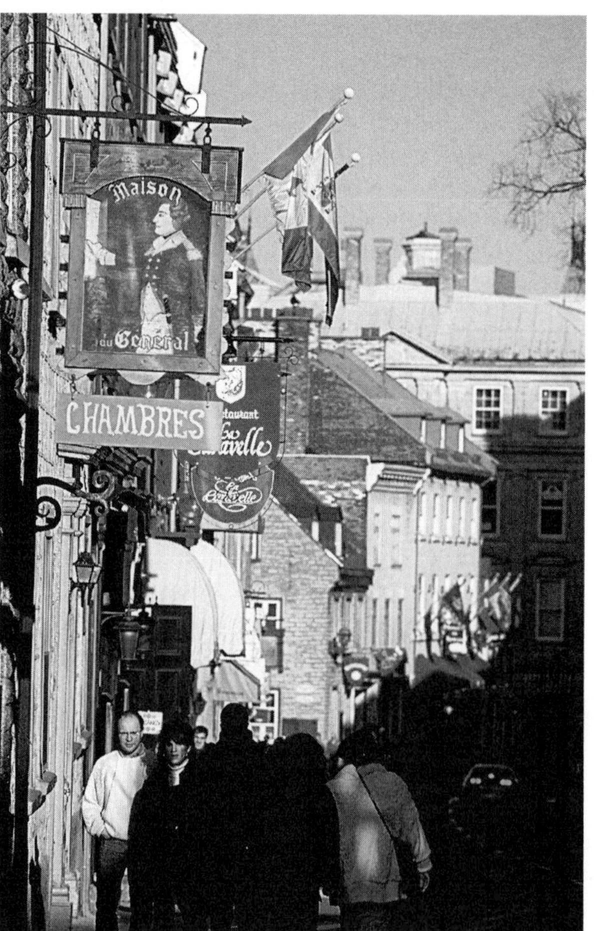

© PAUL A. SOUDERS/CORBIS

Pedestrians walk by an inn on a busy street in Quebec City, Canada.

Up until the 1990s, the city was mostly the home of workers. However, a strong will to revive the lower town and the historical zones has initiated the development of superior-quality condominiums. The average income of these new residents is climbing rapidly, changing the very soul of those districts, once at a visible disadvantage.

Politics and City Services. On the provincial scene, Quebec City is clearly disadvantaged by its weak economy. As such, the city is foremost a big service center, profiting the eastern part of the province. Its role as provincial capital has no real impact—the true power center is Montreal. In a way, Quebec remains a ceremonial city, not much more.

Educational System. The educational system is well structured and widespread, whether public or private. Laval University, Canada's first university, originated from the Quebec Seminary. Monsignor de Laval, the first bishop of New France, established the latter in 1663. It was given its actual statute by a royal decree issued by Queen Victoria in 1852.

At the beginning of the 1960s, the demographic explosion forced the opening of many district schools. However, when the birthrate fell dramatically only 20 years later, many of them were forced to close down. It therefore became necessary to redistribute the students beyond their districts' natural borders. This reorganization forced the creation of an adequate school-transport system. Education is free and compulsory to age 16.

While most schools are French language, it must be noted that two English school boards are operative in Greater Quebec. This underlines the relative importance of the English-speaking community, which, however, remains discreet in daily life. The Ministry of Education has decided that access to English education should be restricted to children whose parents are Anglophones. Other parents, who are aware of the usefulness of the English language in the modern world, strongly oppose this decision.

The average level of education is rather high in the region. In fact, 43.7% have reached college level or have graduated from a professional course, and 21.4% have completed college.

Transportation System. Four urban freeways, permitting quick access to any point within the limits of Quebec City or its suburbs, serve the area. They symbolize the automobile's glorious days before became a collective problem. Some 15 years ago, public transportation began to make a difference. Its expansion has a lot to do with the restrictive measures aimed at cutting down on individual transportation, for instance by raising parking costs considerably. Reserved bus routes have given birth to the metrobus concept: quick circuits with limited stops and routes in two main directions, north-south and east-west.

Transit authorities are currently studying the use of propane-gas vehicles, at least within the walled part of the city, where pollution levels related to transportation are high. In that respect, the great number of tourist buses crisscrossing the Old Quebec district is a major problem and does not lend itself to any easy solution. Understandably, a project to banish them from this area has not been welcomed by all parties.

CULTURAL AND SOCIAL LIFE

Distinctive Features of the City's Cultures. The main employer remains the provincial government. Most of the civil servants live in the suburbs. The average income in Quebec City is well in line with the national average. This can easily be observed by the care given to clothing of good taste, a standard. As a whole, the population is well mannered. Many tourists underline the friendly and warm reception felt at all times.

Two main sites are used for large public gatherings: the Plains of Abraham (officially designated as Parks of the Battlefields) and d'Youville Square, facing Porte St. Jean. These two sites hold the festivities on Quebec's national day, St. Jean-Baptiste Day (June 24). They are also the sites of the impressive Quebec Summer Festival (900,000 participants in ten days in 2000) and also the New France Festival. The latter is still at a modest stage, being rather a newcomer to the entertainment scene. However, it generates a growing interest from year to year, infiltrating within the walls down to the Place Royale in the lower part of the city, where Champlain built his Abitation. This spot is often referred to as the "Cradle of French Civilization in America."

Cuisine. The fast-growing tourist industry has led to the introduction of new, prestigious restaurants. Many of them are set in buildings dating back to colonization. Others are situated in renowned hotels outside the walls but close to Old Quebec. Many Europeans share the strong opinion that Quebec is one of the rare cities in North America where superior-quality cuisine may be enjoyed. Needless to say, American fast food has quickly slipped in since the middle of the 1960s. All the big names have dozens of restaurants throughout the region.

The immigrant phenomenon at the end of the 1960s has given birth to other restaurants, offering more and more international cuisine. It has led to the opening of many specialized food stores, mainly Asian, and the introduction of exotic foods to hardcore Quebecers.

Ethnic, Class, and Religious Diversity. One of the dominating characteristics of the city is the near absence of any ethnic ghettos; the city is almost totally Francophone. Here and there, however, there are very small strongholds of ethnic lineage. For instance, the Irish descendants have moved away from the old naval district to take up residence about 20 miles to the north, in Tewksbury and Shannon. The city of Sillery and the western end of the city also shelter a small concentration of wealthy Anglophones.

The embryo of a typical Chinatown, dating back from the early 19th century, was destroyed by the construction of a direct-access highway to Parliament Hill. Following this, the Chinese did not regroup again. However, the arrival of Vietnamese has set up a modest concentration in the ancient working quarters, between the St. Charles and the hill. The same applies to Hispanic refugees, mostly from El Salvador, although many of them returned to their country following a calm spell in Latin American politics.

In any event, all these small groups go about their business almost unnoticed. In the past, their small numbers never presented the threat of racism, but today, some racism may be perceived, as many refugees in the 1970s may have lit a spark. There may in fact be a link between the increase in racism and the rise of the nationalist movement.

People work and play in Quebec; few live there. It is an administrative city with little or no industrialization. Therefore, it is not surprising to notice the absence of large commercial and industrial fortunes. In fact, the well-to-do are top civil servants or senior administrators, and most of them live outside the city limits.

The stampede toward the suburbs has created a situation in which the actual city's residents are the less-educated workers and people on social welfare. A very small minority can afford the luxury condominiums mentioned before or the prestigious homes north of the Plains of Abraham. There is no real middle class represented within the city limits. The sharp differences between the classes are clearly indicated and quite visible. The rich are on top of the hill, the poor at its feet.

The city, along with the entire province, has long adhered to the Catholic faith. In fact, many high administrative posts were under religious authority, particularly in education. The Catholic grip was unshakable until Prime Minister Jean Lesage shattered it in the early 1960s. This radical change was called the "Quiet Revolution," since it was achieved without violence in spite of the forces involved. One of the main results was that education fell under nonreligious control, and the Catholic church had no choice but to relinquish its control. The population welcomed the change by embracing religious freedom. However, baptism, performed soon after birth, introduces the newborn to the Roman Catholic religion; it is still practiced as are the great rites of marriage and funerals.

The British conquest introduced the Anglican religion to the city. Irish immigrants brought a new language to Quebec's Catholicism. At first, the Irish were invited to use accommodations that were graciously provided by their church's French counterparts. In 1832, however, they built their own church in the Old City. In 1885 the parish of St. Patrick was established, adjacent to the city of Sillery—a rational decision, considering the Anglophone concentration there.

There were no noticeable changes for a long time. But the progressive abandonment of traditional religion, started with the Quiet Revolution, opened the doors to many evangelistic movements. However, their growth has been laborious. Quebecers are reluctant to accept a related faith, remembering the religious yoke from which they only recently freed themselves. All together, these new approaches to Christian faith remain marginal.

Family and Other Social Support Systems. The actual provincial government follows the social-democrat ideology. In the 1980s, important measures caused the expansion of the health, education, and social-services systems. However, internal as well as external crises have eaten away at the systems' structures. They still function rather well, but suffer from a lack of material and manpower. Related to these crises, food banks and various mutual-help centers have also appeared.

The Catholic indoctrination had played a determining role in the concept of family values in Quebec. Families of ten children and more were common. The bonds uniting families were strong. The Quiet Revolution has introduced the people to birth-control methods, a practice forbidden by Catholicism. As a result, the birthrate has gone down dramatically, and most couples now have two children at most. As an associated phenomenon, the bonds of family relations have considerably slackened, with a sharp increase in individualism. Quick and easy relations between unrelated people have replaced the once-flourishing family life of days forever gone.

Work and Commerce. The original commercial importance of fur trading at the founding of the colony slowly disappeared, and Montreal, which is more strategically located, took over. Gradually, shipbuilding and the pulp and paper industry replaced fur trading. Yet, as evolution would have it, there remains today only one very large pulp and paper mill (which was established by Canadian-Anglo Pulp and later taken over by Japanese interests). This is the sole reminder of this highly specialized industrial era.

Naval yards, once in large numbers, also have disappeared. Consequently, Quebec is far from an industrial center and few jobs originate from industry. However, real efforts are being made to attract large companies to ultramodern facilities, freshly implanted in many of the CUQ's adjacent cities and towns. To date, such undertakings have yet to bear fruit. Quebec's economic growth is therefore centered on services and tourism, both huge.

The overwhelming importance in employment of the three levels of government (federal, provincial, municipal) surpasses all else, with other possibilities of employment found in services, tourism, and entertainment.

Shopping centers are plentiful, one of which, Place Laurier, is one of the largest in America. Certain streets have attracted many shops, art galleries, and boutiques of imported goods, particularly St. Jean, Cartier, and Grande-Allée, where bars, sidewalk cafés, and restaurants are lined up. Antique shops are concentrated near Place Royale.

Arts and Recreation. Quebec is somewhat outside the larger artistic circuits, and shows from high-caliber groups are rather scarce. In spite of this flaw, the cultural and artistic life remains intense, if mostly on a local basis. Small and medium-size halls and a number of museums are spread throughout the city, one of which is the Museum of Civilization, located close to Place Royale. The network of municipal libraries is quite important. Two marinas are the remainders of the city's maritime vocation. One is the starting point of the prestigious Quebec–St. Malo (France) race.

Quebec's strongest appeal is its smallness. Of human dimensions, it can be visited on foot. Sports and recreational facilities are everywhere to be discovered. Skiing, fishing, hunting, camping, rafting, and other activities are only minutes away by car from the city's center.

QUALITY OF LIFE

The near absence of polluting industries gives Quebec a clean environment. In addition to the large battlefields, green space is plentiful and easy to get to. The only dark spot is the St. Lawrence. It carries the remnants of factories located upriver. A serious attempt to clean it up is now being made, and the effort is starting to show promising signs.

The cost of living is generally acceptable, and the average family income for the city was somewhat higher than the official figure for the whole of Canada for 2000. Almost 67% of families live in rented apartments, which is 54,615 out of 61,010 available dwellings. At the time of the last census in 1996, unemployment had reached 12.8%. This high rate was due partly to the restrictive employment measures at the provincial government level. However, this rate has fallen to around 10%, owing mainly to the state's improved financial health. It must be noted that men are less favored than women (13.5% unemployed versus 12.%). This may be explained by the very nature of work opportunities. In fact, a great number of jobs held by civil servants are administrative support and have traditionally been filled by women.

The escape from rural centers so prevalent elsewhere did not really affect Quebec. Knowing that work opportunities are scarce in Quebec City, those who emigrate choose mainly Montreal. As proof, the responsible ministry reports that the primary sector employs a mere 0.7% of the market. The secondary sector is a meager 11.1% (7.3% manufacturing and 3.8% construction). The tertiary sector tops it with 88.2%.

The decrease in birthrate is the direct cause of the aging population. In 1996, only 13.4% of the city's population consisted of children 14 and under, compared to 15.9% who were senior citizens (65 and over).

On the crime scene, Quebec City compares favorably with Montreal. Violent crimes account for 4.26 per 1,000 (11.26 per 1,000 for Montreal); crimes against property, 33.57 per 1,000 (55.36 per 1,000 for Montreal); and other crimes, 16 per 1,000 compared to 32 per 1,000 in Montreal. Traffic offenses are also lower in Quebec: 16 infractions per 600 miles versus 32 for Montreal.

FUTURE OF THE CITY

Much is happening in today's Quebec City. Important investments in the city's infrastructure are taking place. There is a will to restore the old commercial zone, which was adversely affected by the coming of large shopping centers to the suburbs and by the construction of Dufferin-Montmorency Highway, leading to Parliamentary Hill. This has caused many people to move west, to what formerly had been working quarters, while the original residents moved to the then quickly mushrooming dormitory suburbs.

Speculation is well under way in the sector touched by revitalization. High-class businesses have already implanted themselves or are about to. Timeworn buildings are bought cheap, renovated, and then rented at prohibitive prices. This speculation is the cause of a second migration, again toward the west. It seems that the St. Charles River is an impassable psychological barrier; even though the region was annexed a long time ago, the culture of the city on either side of the river already differs.

Recently street gangs have emerged on the crime scene. The precarious employment market is at the mercy of government fiscal policies and the doubtful setting of new industries. All in all, the main source of revenue remains tourism. Will the future of Quebec City lie in its past?

BIBLIOGRAPHY

Bailey, A. G., *A Reply to the Report of the Earl of Durham: Thomas Chandler Haliburton* (Golden Dog Press 1976).

Desloges, Yvon, *A Tenant's Town: Québec in the 18th Century* (Environment Canada 1991).

Donnelly, Joseph P., *A Tentative Bibliography for the Colonial Fur Trade in the American Colonies, 1608–1800* (Saint Louis University Press 1947).

Grace, Robert J., "The Irish in Mid-Nineteenth-Century Canada and the Case of Quebec: Immigration and Settlement in a Catholic City," Doctoral thesis, Laval University, Quebec 1999.

Guitard, Michelle, *Jacques Cartier in Canada* (National Library of Canada 1984).

Lacoursiére, Jacques, et al., *Canada-Quebec Historic Synthesis* (Editions du Renouveau Pédagogique 1973).

Mathieu, Jacques, *The Plains of Abraham: The Search for the Ideal,* tr. by Käthe Roth (Éditions du Septentrion 1993).

Nish, James Cameron, *The French Canadians, 1759–1766: Conquered? Half-Conquered? Liberated?,* tr. by Cameron Nish (Copp Clark Publishing 1966).

Paulette, Claude, *Place-Royale, Birthplace of a City,* tr. by Direction de la traduction Ministère des communications (Ministère des affaires culturelles, Direction régionale de Quebec 1986).

Roy, Pierre Georges, *La ville de Québec sous le régime français,* 2 vols. (Service des archives du gouvernement de la province de Québec 1930).

Thornton, Patricia A., and Sherry Olson, *The Tidal Wave of Irish Immigration to Montreal and Its Demographic Consequences* (Department of Geography 1993).

Useful Web Sites

www.archives.ca/08/08_e.html [National Archives of Canada].

www.parcscanada.gc.ca/parks/quebec/fortifications/en/index.html [Parks Canada, the Fortifications of Quebec].

www.statcan.ca/start.html [Statistics Canada (Statistical Profile of Canadian Communities].

Yvon Poirier

Rabat

Morocco

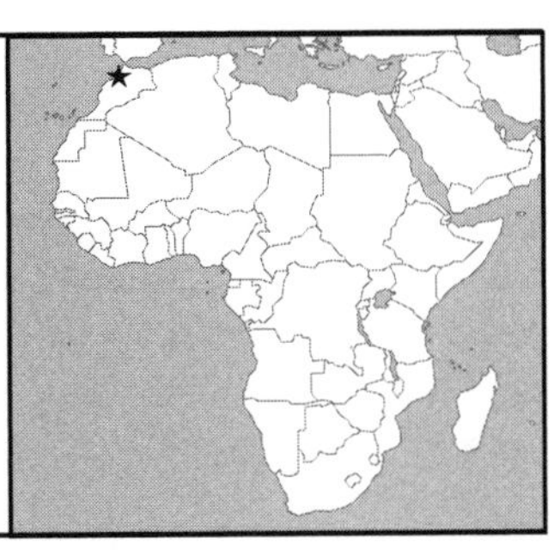

ORIENTATION

Name of City. The name *Rabat* is a shortened and corrupted form of Ribāṭ al-Fatḥ, the "fortress of the conquest." In the 10th century a fortress was established there by devout Sunnī Muslims to guard against heretic forces.

Location. Rabat, the capital of the kingdom of Morocco and the king's residence, is situated on the Atlantic coast in the northwestern corner of Africa. The city is located at 34°03′ north latitude, 6°51′ west longitude.

Population. The city's population, as of the last census in 1994, was 1,385,872.

Distinctive and Unique Features. The city has a beautiful location on the southern bank of the Oued Bou Regreg. At the city's highest point, the Kasbah des Oudayas overlooks the Atlantic Ocean to the west, the estuary and the medina inland, and its historic rival and twin city, Salé, on the north bank of the river. The old medina stands in vivid contrast to the early-20th-century city center.

Attractions of the City. Rabat's attractions include the old medina, the Bab er Rouah city gate; Kasbah des Oudayas, Tour Hassan (the unfinished mosque), and its many 20th-century neo-Moorish-style official buildings.

Relationships Between the City and the Outside. Rabat is the political and administrative capital of Morocco. The economic center of Morocco is Casablanca.

Major Languages. The city's major languages are Arabic, Berber (Tachelhit, Tamazight, and Ta'rifit), and French.

HISTORY

The Origin of the City. Rabat comes into written history as Colonia Sala Junonia, a prosperous Roman settlement. Sala gave way to the Berber city of Chellah, and then, in the 11th century, came the Almohads, who made Rabat a key city in their empire, which extended over northwest Africa and Andalusia. In the 17th century, Rabat, rebuilt by Andalusian refugees, became the capital of a pirate republic for a short but vivid period. In the early 20th century, during the French protectorate over Morocco, the land between the sultan's palace and the medina was developed as a pleasant city of wide avenues and gardens.

Rabat, capital since 1913, is Morocco's second-largest city after Casablanca. The ambitiously extensive city walls, which were laid out in the 12th century by the third Almohad sultan, Abu Yusuf Ya'qoub el Mansour, now enclose, with the river and the sea on the remaining sides, the Casbah, the old medina, and the core of the *ville nouvelle*—placing the old and the new directly alongside each other. In the second half of the 20th century, the city developed rapidly eastward on agricultural and grazing land.

The first major human settlement in the area was probably established outside the present city walls, on the site of the later Merinid mausoleum of Chellah. The Phoenicians may well have operated a trading post here. Rabat's proven urban history begins with the Roman Sala Colonia. Accorded municipal privileges, Sala Colonia was the most southwesterly town of the Roman Empire for more than two centuries. It was important as a trading post and fort on the Oued Bou Regreg (a river, which has since changed course), located close to a line of frontier outposts.

In the late 7th century, the Arabs brought their new monotheistic religion, Islam, to northwest Africa. From the 8th to the 10th century, Sala Colonia was a Berber settlement. However, their heretic Kharijite beliefs represented a challenge to orthodox Islam. In the 10th century, the Zenata tribe built a fort, or *ribat*, on the site of the current Kasbah des Oudayas, as a base from which to challenge the Kharijite heretics and their supporters, the powerful Berghouata tribe. Sala Colonia was gradually abandoned.

The *ribat* was used by the Almoravid dynasty, but it was the Almohad sultan Abd el Mu'min who redeveloped the settlement in 1150, transforming it into a permanent fortress town with palaces, the main mosque—which still stands—reservoirs, and houses for followers, and using it as an assembly point for the large Almohad army. From 1184 his grandson, Ya'qoub el Mansour, carried out an ambitious development program, creating a vast walled area for a future imperial capital. The walls were probably completed by 1197 and ran along two sides of the city, broken by four gates. A grid of broad streets, residential quarters, a covered market, public baths, hotels, workshops, and fountains were built, along with a new gateway to the medina. A bridge over the river to Salé, home to a fine mosque, was also constructed.

Yet the most impressive monument from this period, the Tour Hassan mosque, was never completed. Ya'qoub el Mansour's death in 1199 led to the project being abandoned. Rabat then fell into decline, some of it destroyed in the fighting between the Almohads and Merinids, so that Leo Africanus, visiting in 1500, found only 100 or so houses, two or three inhabited quarters, and very few shops. As Rabat declined under the Merinids, Salé prospered. It is impossible to know today to what extent the area within the Almohad walls—basically the core of the *ville nouvelle*—was actually built-up.

Rabat's fortunes revived in the 17th century, when the Atlantic Ocean became important to international trade, and piracy boomed. For a time, Rabat was a center of corsair activity. Rabat also benefited from the flow of Muslims leaving Spain during the Inquisition in the early 17th century. The town they settled in was considerably smaller than the city Ya'qoub el Mansour had envisaged, as indicated by the 17th-century rampart, which, when built, demarcated the extent of the settlement, and now runs between the medina and the *ville nouvelle*. The area beyond this rampart was used for agricultural purposes, and most of it remained undeveloped until the arrival of the French.

A fierce rivalry existed between different Andalusian immigrant communities. The period 1610 to 1666 was marked by intermittent strife among the three towns of the Bou Regreg estuary (Rabat, Salé, and the Casbah). By 1627 these were united under

© NIK WHEELER/CORBIS

Rabat, the capital of Morocco, was protected by a wall around the city dating from the late 12th century.

the control of the Hornachero group, and were known as the republic of the Bou Regreg, against which the main Andalusian group frequently rebelled, most notably in 1636. The republic lost its independence in 1638. In 1641 the three cities were united, and in 1666 were brought under the authority of the Alaouite sultanate when Moulay Rachid captured the estuary.

The principal background to these conflicts was the struggle for control over the gains from piracy, a profitable activity. Piracy was a form of trade, but also fed off trade. The legal, illegal, and governmental aspects were often closely linked.

In the 18th century, the port declined, replaced by Mogador (Essaouira), farther down the coast. The second Alaouite sultan, Moulay Ismail, finally broke the power of the corsairs. Since the late 18th century, the Alaouite sultans have maintained a palace in Rabat, making the city one of their capitals. Increased trade with Europe in the 19th century temporarily revitalized Rabat's role as a port. Ultimately, the shallow Bou Regreg estuary proved inadequate for larger boats. Casablanca, more open to European influence, became the main Atlantic port.

In 1912, after intense diplomatic activity, Morocco was split into two protectorates, with a large French central region and small Spanish zones in the north and the Sahara. The Moroccan sultanate had no fixed capital, the power center being where the sultan happened to be. For the new French protectorate, a capital was necessary, and Rabat was chosen in 1913. Efficiency and beauty were French planners' watchwords as they created the new Rabat on expropriated land. The first European neighborhoods were laid out in an area between the medina, on the coast, and the *mechouar,* or sultan's palace complex, to the south east. The tree-lined street between the medina and *ville nouvelle,* today's Boulevard Hassan II, became a meeting place for Muslim and foreign communities, with municipal markets, bus and taxicab stations, and cafés. Medina streets were paved; drinking water and sewers were put in. Works were financed by the profits generated by the sale of building land.

After Morocco gained its independence from France in 1956, Rabat continued to expand, its population swelled by the large number of civil servants required for the newly independent kingdom. Rabat's economy today is based primarily on its role as Morocco's capital, with massive numbers on the government payroll. The city has attracted large numbers of migrants from the countryside, and the formal-housing market has been unable to keep up with the demand for accommodation, leading to the development of new, self-built neighborhoods on the edge of the city. Out toward Casablanca, the new planned residential area of Hay Riad is larger than the whole colonial city center, while at Médinat el Irfane ("city of knowledge"), Rabat has the country's largest concentration of faculties and university institutes. Neither Almohad sultans nor Lyautey could have imagined that a city could grow so fast in just a couple of decades. This growth has not been without its negative consequences, however. The once-fine gardens and tree-lined avenues have become distinctly scruffy; the sidewalks are in a poor state of repair. Municipal management is clearly not keeping up with the pace of change. Morocco's capital, with its historic medina and one of the finest examples of 20th-century city planning, certainly merits proper upkeep. After all, Rabat is very much a showcase for modern Morocco.

Migration: Past and Present. Rabat is a city of immigrants. Muslim immigrants from Spain gave the old city its reputation for fine urban living. Rejected by Salé, the Hornacheros, a Muslim group from Estremadura with a strong military tradition, settled in the Rabat Casbah in 1609. Morisco Andalusians—that is, those who had opted for Christianity to avoid persecution—settled in the Rabat medina (then known as New Salé) in 1610. Both groups were looked down upon by the long-established Muslim community north of the river. The 17th century was a cosmopolitan time, with a small but significant group of European pirate renegades, many of Mediterranean origin, joining the city's population. In 1832 the rebellious Oudaya tribe settled in the abandoned Casbah, giving it its current name.

In the early 20th century, there was an influx of French working in the protectoral administration. They were joined by Spaniards and Italians fleeing the totalitarian regimes of their homelands. Almost all this population, along with the local Jewish community, left in the late 1950s. Rabat became a city of opportunity for Moroccans, with plenty of jobs in the burgeoning civil service. Students now come from all over the kingdom to train at the city's universities. After graduating, some stay on, acquiring some work experience before putting in for an emigration permit to move to Canada or to France to acquire a postgraduate degree. Many young educated people are seeking to emigrate, to the point that the local press has frequent articles on the national brain drain.

From the early days of the city's 20th-century expansion, the formal-housing market proved totally unable to cater to large numbers of poorly skilled rural people. Rural migrants thus built themselves simple homes in shantytowns (bidonvilles) on the city edge. The first of these (Douar Doum and Douar Debbagh) date back to the early 1920s. The shantytown problem continued to worsen, however. Early-20th-century planners did not foresee the sharp fall in the Moroccan mortality rate in the 1940s that helped swell the urban population. In 1948 work started on the Cité Yacoub el Mansour, the first of numerous developments designed to rehouse shantytown dwellers. The basic housing unit was the courtyard home. State investment was never really able to keep pace with demand for low-cost housing, however. Close to the middle-class Aviation neighborhood, Youssoufia was built to re-house bidonville inhabitants, but to no avail, since a whole series of new, "informal" settlements joined Douar Doum on the southern periphery of the city. New arrivals simply fitted into an ever-growing network of kinship solidarity. Eventually, the state was forced to provide them with urban services. Corrugated iron gave way to simple permanent homes in concrete blocks as the rural migrants became permanent city residents. In the 1990s much of Morocco's countryside still had what one commentator has called "Fourth World" levels of poverty, and the country people continued to flow to the city.

INFRASTRUCTURE

Public Buildings, Public Works, and Residences. Rabat has an interesting combination of monumental religious architecture, medieval defensive walls, and residential and official buildings from the first half of the 20th century. The most imposing example of monumental building is the 12th-century Tour Hassan, the unfinished, yet still impressive, stump of what would have been a huge minaret overlooking the Oued Bou Regreg. Apart from a few pillars and this unfinished minaret, little remains of what was projected to be the largest mosque in western Islam. The late-medieval Merinid dynasty contributed a funeral quarter on the walled Chellah site. In the 17th century, Moulay el Rachid took over the Casbah and built the Qishla fortification to overlook and control the medina. As it stands today, the old town displays marked Iberian influence, especially in its mosques and architectural detailing.

Central Rabat took on its present shape in the early 20th century, when French planner Henri Prost laid out a pleasant new town for the incoming European population. The first "résident-général," Maréchal Lyautey, took the line that France was in Morocco to protect and assist its people in their development. This attitude to Moroccan culture was given shape even in urban planning. City walls were reconstructed, and Chellah was preserved. The two main avenues of the new Rabat—Boulevard Dar el Makhzen, today's Avenue Mohamed V, and the Avenue de Casablanca, today's Avenue de la Victoire—lead to Moroccan monumental buildings, the former leading up to the Sunna Mosque, the latter from the Agdal neighborhood to Bab er Rouah, perhaps the city's finest Almohad gate. It would have been possible, given the freedom to act that Lyautey had, to build the Residency General at a focal point on a new avenue, somewhat like Lutyen's House of the Viceroy in New Delhi. Rather, the new administrative buildings were built in a discreet garden-city area close to the palace. The buildings, despite their importance to French rule, have simple whitewashed walls and green-tile roofs, and are linked by pergola walkways. They were deliberately kept unmonumental in scale (even the entrance to the Residency General had no obvious feature), hidden in lush vegetation. French policy was thus to use architectural devices to emphasize local culture, while keeping the seats of power hidden in a mini-garden suburb.

Monumental buildings were only rarely used as a symbol of power. Today's Parliament Building, on the Avenue Mohamed V, started life as the Palais de Justice. Strongly symmetrical, with a massive colonnade, the building was probably designed to symbolize the equity and reason of French justice. Today, it is the center of national political life.

Housing in Rabat varies hugely in quality. In the original medina, the courtyard house was the rule, some of them very splendid indeed by the early 20th century. By the 1950s old Rabati families were moving into villa-type housing introduced by the French. Another recent southern European import, the urban apartment, is a widespread form of housing. "Traditional" extended families go for three-level apartment houses, where the ground floor is garage/utility space, the first floor a vast Moroccan-style reception room for guests and special occasions, and the top floor(s) reserved for family accommodation. Tin-roofed huts with breeze-block walls are the main housing for low-income groups, at constant risk from fire caused by paraffin lanterns and candles. Though the poor are aware of the inside appearance of prosperous homes (from television), it is doubtful whether many of the comfortable classes know what goes on in a bidonville, partly concealed as it is by a wall put up by the local authorities.

Politics and City Services. To the outside observer, Moroccan city government appears complex and arcane. However, the distribution of responsibilities is unclear to many Moroccans, too. Basically, there are two hierarchies of local government (three if one includes the Regional Council as well). Rabat is part of the *wilaya* (governorate) of Rabat-Salé. The *wali* (governor), representative of the crown, is responsible for urban security and, in principle, for coordinating everything going on in the city. Each *wilaya* is divided into prefectures (Arabic: *'amala*). Rabat is a prefecture in itself, subdivided into *da'irat*. Parallel to this system, which is the direct responsibility of the minister of the interior, is the elected municipal city government, or *baladiya*. In this hierarchy, the city is divided into arrondissements (Arabic: *muqata'a*), each headed by a *qa'id*, a powerful figure in local politics. Although there are municipal elections, local government comes under heavy criticism in everyday conversation and in the Moroccan press for corruption and gross mismanagement. Cordial contacts with the local administration are essential for citizens, however. Morocco is a bureaucratic sort of place, and the *wali*'s local representative is the only one who can provide vital documents such as the *certificat de résidence*, essential for undertaking other paperwork.

In Rabat's case, there was felt to have been a distinct improvement in urban management in the late 1990s. Water services are now provided by a private company, the REDAL, which buys water from the National Water Corporation (ONE). Sewage disposal, once the responsibility of the municipality, is now dealt with by the REDAL. Enormous investment will be necessary to extend sewage lines to all areas. The dumping of raw sewage into the ocean makes sea bathing near the city a health risk. In low-income areas such as Taqadum and Youssoufia, poor services (and jobs) create a feeling of discontent. It is in such neighborhoods that the Islamic fundamentalist groups find the majority of their supporters.

Central government and paragovernmental bodies have considerable weight in shaping the physical form of Moroccan cities such as Rabat. Municipal government generally lacks adequate technical expertise, hence the importance of bodies such as the Ministry of Public Works, the CGI (Compagnie Générale Immobilière), and the ANHI (Agence Nationale pour la Lutte contre l'Habitat Insalubre), a national agency working to improve the housing conditions of low-income groups. Mixed public-private development companies, the ERACs, build and sell low- and medium-cost homes. Over the river from Rabat, Salé el Jadida (New Salé) was planned by the central government but constructed by French construction-industry leader Bouygues. For historic parts of the city, the National Inspectorate of Historic Monuments has a say on new projects.

Educational System. The vast majority of boys and girls attend primary school in Rabat—in stark contrast to isolated mountain areas, where illiteracy remains extremely high, especially among girls. State education is available to all—provided that parents can cover the cost of books and basic school supplies. Schools vary greatly in quality. Rabat is well covered by state primary and secondary schools, some of the latter being quite prestigious. The city also has two main university areas, in the Agdal neighborhood and Médinat el 'Irfane. The latter area is home to the Hassan II School of Agronomy and Veterinary Medicine and the École d'Architecture. Also located in Rabat is Morocco's top engineering school, the École Mohamedia des Ingénieurs.

Private schools are increasingly popular in Rabat. As the French elementary schools and the elite Lycée Descartes are heavily oversubscribed, the Spanish school and an increasing number of Moroccan private schools satisfy middle-class requirements for quality education; the American school is the most expensive. High student-teacher ratio, badly maintained buildings, and in particular the curricula, taught overwhelmingly in Arabic, are the main reasons for growing disaffection for state education. Compared with those coming from private schools, many students who have come up through the state system, where the sciences are taught in Arabic, are at a major disadvantage when they enter higher education, where technical subjects, business, and commercial law are all taught in French.

The late 1980s saw the creation of a number of private tertiary-level education establishments, many of them twinned with universities in France and Canada. These tend to offer training and qualifications directly related to the needs of the job market, including business administration and marketing, information technology, and graphic design.

Transportation System. Rabat is linked to the rest of Morocco by rail, road, and air. There are adequate but rather slow (by European standards) train services to the country's main cities. Fast shuttle trains link Rabat to downtown Casablanca. The intercity autoroute system is being expanded, and twin-lane toll highways now link Rabat to Casablanca to the southwest, Meknes and Fez to the east, and Larache to the north. Work on the remaining northern section to Tangier is well under way. Eventually, the toll highway will go all the way to Marrakech. Intercity trains remain popular owing to Morocco's appallingly high road-accident rate. Rabat is also an important center for intercity bus and taxicab routes. Passengers from the east of the country can find direct connections in Rabat for all major destinations on the north-south Atlantic coast axis, some southern destinations, and France and Spain. Rabat also has a small international airport with frequent flights to France and to some destinations within Morocco.

In contrast to this network of international and national connections, public transport within the city is increasingly inadequate. Alongside the city bus company, a range of private companies operate local services. *Petits taxis* are plentiful, handy for medium-length trips across the city, but too expensive for most people except for occasional use. Large taxis link Rabat to the neighboring cities of Kenitra, Salé, Temara, Mohammedia, and Casablanca. Walking can be hazardous owing to sidewalks being broken up by street works. The growing level of diesel pollution makes walking unpleasant in the city center, especially at the end of the working day. As people move out to new housing areas with inadequate public transport, even families on small incomes are purchasing cars, helped in this by the ready availability of consumer credit at low interest rates. The result is vehicle-packed streets in the central area at rush hour.

CULTURAL AND SOCIAL LIFE

The pace of life in Rabat is slow by European or North American standards. If Moroccan cities could be personified, Casablanca would be a golden boy, Fès a solemn imam, and Rabat a comfortable civil servant. Though the city center is packed in the early evening with vehicles and office workers heading home, there are plenty of places in the city for relaxation and enjoyment.

In social terms, visiting members of the extended family for major life-span events is of great importance. These occasions (weddings, births, circumcisions of baby boys, funerals) and the preparations for them require time, effort, and, depending on the family, significant expenditure. They allow family members and friends to see each other, if not always to talk. And thus, the social pecking order is maintained.

Rabat, like other North African cities, has many other places where people can meet and socialize. Most are heavily gender-segregated. Attendance at the local mosque on Friday is largely a male affair, as is spending time chatting in city-center cafés. Any average Rabati neighborhood will have a selection of gendered places where the individual can care for appearance and the body: the *hammam,* or public baths (important in low-income areas where few have hot running water at home); barbershops and hairdressers (*salons de beauté*); and small gymnasiums devoted to bodybuilding and the Japanese martial arts. In poor neighborhoods, boys and young men spend much free time out-of-doors, playing cards on an upturned cardboard box, or football (soccer) on any patch of wasteland. Thus, pressure on space in overcrowded homes is reduced, and the male-female divide of traditional Muslim Moroccan society is maintained.

Away from their home neighborhoods, Rabat's people are involved in various forms of social activity. Well-heeled women attend exhibition openings, see their caftan seamstress, or do charity work. Wealthy men play golf, while others watch the city football team, the FAR (Forces Armées Royales). Consumed in bars and restaurants, alcohol is moderately popular across the social classes, as is hashish, bought discreetly from "someone reliable." Kef, the dried cannabis plant, is the poor person's drug: much spare time is necessary for the careful sorting and chopping of leaves and flowers. Both hashish and kef are generally smoked at home. Children's free-time activities outside the home reflect parental finances. The children of the wealthy may take tennis and horseback-riding lessons; others go to video-game clubs. A world away from the ideal Muslim home, street children cadge enough centimes to watch a Hindi film. Or sometimes they just sniff glue and fall further out of mainstream social life.

In the late 1990s, as the political climate of Morocco became more liberal, intellectual life began to free up. At the start of the 21st century, political activists hold meetings of various kinds; unemployed graduates plan their next campaign of sit-ins; AMDH (League of Human Rights) supporters meet to plan their next publications. Islamists organize free Koran-study classes. And a long-established round of cultural activities continues: comic plays at the Théâtre Mohamed V, film festivals organized by the European Uníon embassies, literary readings at a bookshop.

The annual cycle is important to city cultural life as well. During Ramadan, the Muslim month of fasting, office hours are shorter, and torpor descends in the early afternoon. In the evening, normally quiet downtown Rabat is busy until well after midnight with strollers out shopping or on their way to visit friends. In summer, the rhythm of city life changes, too. Families with money go north to the Mediterranean resorts near Tangier or to Spain; others take time to stay with family in other cities.

Distinctive Features of the City's Cultures. Rabat experienced huge changes in the 20th century. In 1900 it was a small, largely Muslim community living in an old walled town. A significant Jewish community lived within the walls in the *mellah,* or Jewish quarter. The Rabatis, similar in physical appearance to southern Spaniards, were known for their deep-rooted Andalusian heritage and urban *art de vivre.* By 1950 a well-planned European town peopled largely by French civil servants and their families had grown up alongside the medina. After independence in 1956, a new Moroccan political and administrative elite moved into property left by the departing Europeans. The French social infrastructure of schools, restaurants, cafés, cinemas, and sports clubs was taken over by the Moroccans. Offering jobs in the civil service and education, Rabat became a magnet for people from all over the kingdom. The rural poor settled in a ring of bidonvilles on the city edge.

Today's Rabatis are increasingly mixed in terms of their origins. Ethnic or regional origins remain important to many. Having parents or grandparents from one of the old inland cities such as Fès is a marker of social status, while the Berbers are taking increasing pride in their identity. Most striking perhaps to the outsider is the combination of tradition and modernity so much in evidence in Rabat. While an educated male may have a mobile phone, information-technology skills, and a master's degree in business administration, his mother will still be choosing his future wife. Discussions in families with a couple of generations of European higher education may still revolve around the finer points of Rabati cooking. Others may regret their insufficient knowledge of traditional choral music while being up-to-date on the latest trends in Gnawa jazz.

In common with other North African cities, the gender divide is the other major feature of Rabati culture. Although the workplace is increasingly mixed, public space and the main spectator sports are male affairs. Respectable women of lower- and middle-income groups do not on the whole go out at night in the central areas of the city. Upper-income women may go to restaurants, out-of-town cinemas, and nightclubs if accompanied by men. Whether this cultural characteristic will change as more women gain economic status remains to be seen. After all, in 1956, very few Moroccan women had any formal education at all. A sign of the future, perhaps: young people of both sexes meet at cafés in the Agdal neighborhood, an area where housing is largely in the form of small apartments, and where the population is young, professional, and relatively affluent.

Cuisine. Food is plentiful and varied for the vast majority of city residents. Although there are two large hypermarkets (Marjane and Salam), on the whole, people buy basic products in neighborhood shops. Fruit and vegetables are impressively fresh, with fruit availability subject to seasonal variations. Meat and fish are bought from small family businesses with whom the client will have developed a friendly relationship. Men rarely cook, although they may be expected to be able to shop effectively (and within the family budget) for quality foodstuffs. Women take considerable pride in their ability to turn out good meals and to combine produce and spices to create the expected nuance of taste. In poorer neighborhoods, breads (and certain dishes) made at home are taken to the neighborhood oven to bake. On Fridays, the family gathers for lunch, and cooking skills are under close scrutiny.

Many Moroccans consider their cooking to be one of the four great cuisines of the world (the others being Chinese, French, and Indian, in this view). Staples include salads, couscous, and *tajines,* stews cooked on a low heat for several hours. Combinations of sweet and sour ingredients are popular, and Moroccan cooking also makes use of a variety of Mediterranean greens largely ignored elsewhere. Meals at home are accompanied by water (tap water is drinkable) and main-brand sodas. Postprandial digestion is assisted by *ettay,* sweet green tea flavored with mint. When women gather at home, this tea will be served along with Moroccan pastries made with almonds and walnuts, honey, and orange-flower water.

Ethnic, Class, and Religious Diversity. In 1956, although Rabat had a large Catholic population and a significant Jewish community, it was 90% Muslim. Today, it is an even more homogenous city in religious terms, with the overwhelming majority of inhabitants belonging to Sunni Islam of the conservative Malikite rite. The king of Morocco, the young Mohamed VI, styled "prince of the faithful" (*amir al mu'minin*), is leader of the national community of believers and has his main residence in Rabat. However, over the river in the neighboring town of Salé, there is a challenge to the legitimacy of this official state Islam. Sheikh Yassine, aging leader of the Islamist movement Al Adl wal Ihsan, has in the past rejected the Moroccan monarch's claim to the title *amir al mu'minin*. The movement is highly active in the poorest reaches of Moroccan society.

In terms of ethnic diversity, the situation is rather interesting at the turn of the century. To the foreigner, there is little physical difference between the city's residents. There is no color bar at all—most residents have Mediterranean/Middle Eastern looks. Certain faces are typically Berber, however. The main ethnic differentiating factor is language. Berbers are essentially recent migrants. They learn a Moroccan form of spoken Arabic, the language of everyday interaction, and often intermarry with Arabic-speaking Moroccans. It is extremely rare, however, for an urban Moroccan to learn anything of the three major Berber languages (Tachelhit, Tamazight, and Ta'rifit). In the late 1990s Berber cultural movements gained considerable ground, in particular those with roots in the Agadir/Souss region. Publications such as *Tafoukt* (Sun), a Berber weekly newspaper, can be found in the news kiosks of Rabat. Cheap video technology now allows amateur filmmakers to produce documentaries and dramas in Berber languages, thus compensating for the exclusion of Berbers from national television. Films circulate rapidly via video clubs. Whether the Berber movement is to become more political remains to be seen.

For outsiders traveling beyond the central neighborhoods, class markers are far more obvious than any ethnic division. In many ways, Rabat is a place of extremes, with streets of fine villas not far from crowded slums. In the year 2000, on Avenue Mohamed V, witness the drama of the city's socioeconomic contrasts on an average workday morning. Outside the Parliament, the ministerial Mercedes half block the sidewalks; on the lawns down the middle of the street, unemployed graduates are staging a sit-in under their hand-painted banners. Under the arcades, a wealthy bourgeoise and her daughter are looking at rings at Azuelos the jewelers (they will pause for coffee at *Le Délice*). The Méditel shop is doing a roaring trade in mobile phones, at 400 dirhams (U.S.$40) for the cheapest model, well within the reach of all but the poorest. Files on the table, functionaries take their mid-morning break at the Café des Ambassadeurs. Tourists with backpacks head toward the medina in search of a cheap hotel. An urchin sells packets of facial tissue. Around the corner, in an alley behind the Hotel Balima, his brother sells cigarettes, an upended carton on the sidewalk the symbol of his trade. (Maybe he has a small stipend from the police to keep an eye out.) Two tall males in ankle-revealing robes go by. Their beards and black kohl eyeliner indicate they are members of the Tablighi Jama movement, exponents of a gentle, outreach version of revivalist Islam. Yet despite the deprivation and the wealth, Rabat is hardly a dangerous city. Although there may be desperation, street crime is still rare.

Family and Other Social Support Systems. How do the deprived get by? In the absence of a reliable social-security system, the family unit is vital—but not always sufficient. Migration and urban poverty have allowed other bodies to emerge to help the poor find homes and food. Islamic groups often provide basic services to people in need, as do charitable associations focusing on groups such as single mothers or street children. For those who work, there are some guarantees of health insurance and retirement benefits. Many businesses and individuals invest in supplementary health plans, however.

The family network is in fact vital to all. A *piston* ("personal contact") is often crucial to getting a job, a contract, or a document. Individuals develop and maintain their contacts, asking for and performing favors as time and circumstances require. This is the unseen (but essential) lubricant that keeps the machinery of Rabati society turning.

Work and Commerce. In Rabat, the state remains the largest employer. Other large employers include the REDAL (city water company) and agrofood companies. There is some light industry, including garment factories working on contract for major European companies. Factories are located south of the city center in areas such as the Youssoufia Industrial Zone and over the river in Salé. Traditional crafts, including tailoring and woodworking, survive. Rabat also has a huge informal sector. Recent rural migrants eke out a living buying and selling from sidewalk stalls.

In terms of monthly incomes, there are huge differences between the top and bottom of the wage pyramid. There is a tiny rentier class. A highly qualified graduate in, say, a financial institution can command 10,000 dirhams (U.S.$1,000) a month in salary plus benefits. An experienced primary-school teacher may make up to 4,000 dirhams a month; a newly recruited graduate in a sales position cannot hope for much more than 2,000 dirhams. As rents for apartments in a good neighborhood start at around 2,000 dirhams a month, setting up an independent home can remain a dream for many years. Though there is a national minimum wage, it is often ignored by employers who prefer to recruit workers as *stagiaires* (trainees) or for short-term contracts. Women are particularly vulnerable to this sort of exploitation. Craft workshops also often employ children as unpaid apprentices, thereby reducing costs—and the availability of work for adults.

Many of Rabat's inhabitants have no work at all. In fact, nationwide, it is estimated that fully one-third of university graduates are unemployed. Although middle-class women are moving into salaried employment, many still prefer household work after marriage, provided the family income is sufficient.

Arts and Recreation. In terms of activity in the modern cultural sector, Rabat occupies the number-three slot in Morocco, coming after Casablanca and Marrakech. The city has a large theater and several cinemas, including a multiplex belonging to the national Dawliz chain. Art exhibitions are held in private galleries and the great vaulted guardrooms of two Almohad gates: Bab er Rouah and the main gate to the Kasbah des Oudayas. Cultural centers funded by European countries—in particular, France, Germany, Italy, and Spain—organize exhibitions and film festivals and bring over theater and dance troops. Seminars and conferences are regularly held at the universities. There are a number of libraries and research centers, including the Centre Jacques Berque and La Source.

Rabat does not have highly developed public sports facilities. There are a couple of large stadiums for spectator sports, but no large public swimming pools. For the wealthy, private tennis, golf, and riding clubs are available. The eucalyptus woods near the Hotel Hyatt are a pleasant place to run, and surfing is popular on the coast below the Kasbah des Oudayas. The ocean off the city beaches tends to be polluted, however, and those with cars head north to Plage des Nations or Mahdia. Courting couples meet to stroll in Agdal or one of the hypermarkets, or perhaps go out to the Jardins Exotiques at Bou Knadel. Again, Agdal and the city center have a handful of nightclubs and piano bars, although nothing like the number in a European city of similar size. For the moment, most people's incomes are too limited for more than the cheapest activities: cards, football, and the café for men; the hairdresser's, shopping, and visiting at home for women.

QUALITY OF LIFE

Rabat offers a reasonable quality of life to those with stable incomes, although there is a feeling that state salaries have not kept pace with the rising cost of living—and the increased availability of consumer goods. The onetime jewel of French colonial urban planning, Rabat has become a city of great socioeconomic segregation. Family network and a good range of personal contacts must be maintained to get on in the city. Unlike Morocco's economic capital, Casablanca, and unlike Marrakech, center of a booming tourist industry, Rabat does not offer much scope for those with great career ambitions. It is a city where many are able to carve out a pleasant niche for themselves in civil service or education. People in the professions, business, and the upper reaches of the state apparatus are able to acquire large villas in pleasant neighborhoods such as Souissi, Hayy al Nahda, and Hay Riad. Domestic help is readily available, and in comparison with Casablanca and European capitals, journey times to work are short. There is access to good education, as well as plenty of leisure facilities for the children of the middle classes. For those with low qualifications, there are opportunities to pick up bits of work here and there in the city's informal sector.

FUTURE OF THE CITY

Rabat looks set to expand rapidly in the first decade of the 21st century. An extension of upscale Hayy Riad is now planned. Severe droughts in 1998, 1999, and 2000 hit the rural areas of Morocco hard. Rabat, with its large pool of citizens in salaried government jobs and self-built housing areas on the periphery, will doubtless continue to attract people fleeing the poverty of the countryside. Whether central government action to improve living conditions in *al-'alam al-qarawi* ("the rural world," as it is called in Moroccan political jargon) will reduce this flow of migrants remains to be seen. The reform of local government before Parliament in early 2001 may give the city a *conseil de ville* capable of implementing long-term projects such as the creation of a light-metro system. It is hoped that the contracting out of water- and sewage-system management will improve service in these utilities. Effective, professional urban management is essential for Rabat's people, increasingly under pressure from vehicle noise and pollution and the complex logistics of traveling growing distances for work and education. On a positive note, Rabat still has a great heritage of Muslim monuments and early-20th-century architecture. As Morocco's travel industry becomes more sophisticated, urban tourism may develop to make Rabat more than just a one-night stopover. The recent restoration of houses in the medina is a promising new trend. After all, Rabat has a magnificent site, a pleasant year-round climate, and is within a few hours' drive of the other great historic cities of Morocco.

BIBLIOGRAPHY

Abu-Lughod, Janet, *Rabat: Urban Apartheid in Morocco* (Princeton University Press 1980).

Abun-Nasr, Jamil M., *A History of the Maghrib* (Cambridge University Press 1971).

Rivet, Daniel, *Le Maroc de Lyautey à Mohammed V, le Double Visage du Protectorat* (Denoël 1999).

Wright, Gwendolyn, *The Politics of Design in French Colonial Urbanism* (University of Chicago Press 1991).

JUSTIN MCGUINNESS

Rangoon

Myanmar

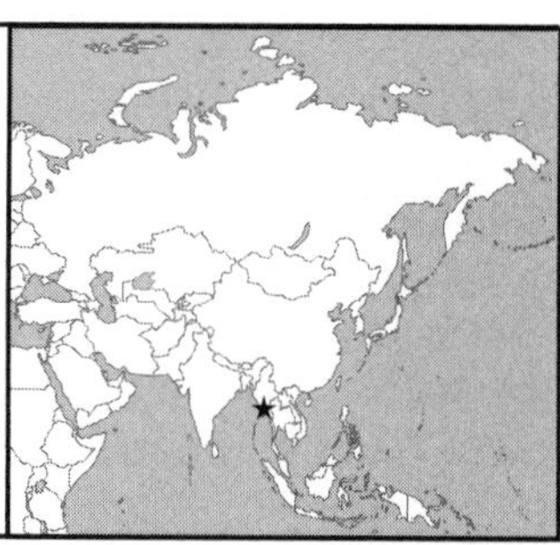

ORIENTATION

Name of City. The site where the city is now located was originally occupied by a village named Dagon. A new town was established on the site in 1755 and named Yangon (meaning "end of strife") by King Alaung-hpaya. After assuming control of the town in 1852, the British changed its name to Rangoon (an English transliteration of Yangon). After the State Law and Order Restoration Council under General Saw Maung assumed power in September 1988, the regime in 1989 changed the name back to Yangôn. However, because of the lack of legitimacy of the regime, it remains common practice internationally to continue to refer to the city as Rangoon. [Note: The current regime changed the names of many locations and geographic features in Burma (now known as Myanmar). Throughout the text, the common spelling will be used, followed, in parentheses, by the spelling adopted by the regime.]

Location. Rangoon is the capital of Myanmar and is located about 30 kilometers (19 miles) from the coast in the Irrawaddy (Ayeyarwady) delta region within Rangoon division (Yangon division), or *tain* in Burmese. It lies adjacent to the Yangon (Rangoon) River, which flows into the Gulf of Martaban (Mottana) and is navigable by seagoing vessels. Rangoon is located at 16°47′ north latitude, and 96°10′ east longitude. The city is bounded on the south and west by the Yangon River (which becomes the Hlaing River farther north). While relatively flat, the terrain of the city includes a number of low-lying hills. The metropolitan area of Rangoon covers 578 square kilometers (223 square miles), while Rangoon division occupies 35,949 square kilometers (13,880 square miles).

Population. There are no reliable recent census figures for Rangoon. The current population of the city is probably a little over 4 million (some estimates place the figure as high as 5 million).

Distinctive and Unique Features. While it has changed a great deal over the past few years, Rangoon remains one of the least modern and least crowded large cities of Asia. The city retains much of its colonial architecture, even though many of the buildings are in poor repair. In sharp contrast to many modern Asian cities, there is also a great deal of greenery in Rangoon, including large trees and a good deal of open space covered with vegetation. The city also boasts two good-sized lakes: Kandawgyi (Royal) Lake near the center of the city, and the much larger Inya Lake in the northern part of the city.

The skyline of Rangoon is dominated by the golden dome of the Buddhist temple (*paya*) Shwedagon Paya, whose stupa rises some 98 meters (322 feet) above its base situated on Singuttara Hill.

The complex surrounding the pagoda covers about 6 hectares (15 acres) and includes an incredible array of smaller religious structures and statuary. Scattered throughout the city are a number of other Buddhist temples, including Sule Paya in the center of the city, and Chaukhtatgyi Paya with its huge reclining Buddha figure.

Attractions of the City. Shwedagon Paya is by far Rangoon's most prominent attraction. On any day, it will be crowded with local residents and visitors from throughout Burma, as well as by foreign tourists. There are other Buddhist temples in the city that are less spectacular and less frequently visited by foreigners but that are noteworthy nevertheless. Sule Paya is of particular religious significance since its central stupa is said to contain a hair of Buddha. Other attractions in Rangoon include a number of public markets, a relatively large zoological garden, and several museums. The latter include the National Museum (which contains numerous displays relating to the kings of Burma as well as archaeological and ethnographic displays) and Myanmar Gems Museum (highlighting one of the country's best-known industries).

Relationships Between the City and the Outside. Legitimate international commerce between Myanmar and the outside world is relatively limited. What there is, however, is centered largely in Rangoon. The port of Rangoon continues to handle most shipping in and out of the country. Those foreign enterprises that operate in Myanmar generally have offices in the city as well. There was a burst of foreign investment in the country in the early 1990s, but by the end of the decade, this had slowed considerably, and many companies began pulling out of the country.

Historically, most tourists visiting the country have entered through Rangoon. Prior to World War

© WOLFGANG KAEHLER/CORBIS

Worshipers carry offerings to the Shwedagon Paya in Rangoon, Myanmar.

II, they came mainly by ship, although some came by air as KLM Royal Dutch Airlines began flights to Rangoon in the 1930s. After World War II, Rangoon became an important international hub for European airlines, and tourist visits to Rangoon increased during the 1950s. After the 1962 coup, Burma was effectively closed to tourists, and most international flights ceased. Later, the regime began issuing seven-day visas, and a small tourist industry began to grow once again. Following the political upheavals of 1988, the country was closed again for a brief period. It was reopened the following year, but there were relatively few tourists. As the political situation stabilized and visa requirements for tourists were eased in the early 1990s, the number of tourists grew to around 180,000 in the mid-1990s. Since then, the regional economic crisis has seen numbers decline once again. At present, all international flights to Myanmar land at Rangoon's international airport, located on the northern edge of the city in Mingaladon township. Air traffic is relatively limited. There are daily flights between Rangoon and Bangkok and Singapore, and less-frequent flights each week to and from other Asian cities (such as Chiang Mai, Thailand; Calcutta, India; Dhaka, Bangladesh; and Hong Kong and Kunming, China).

Major Languages. Burmese is the national language and is spoken by virtually everyone living in Rangoon. Under British rule, Rangoon had a large South Asian population. As a legacy of British colonial rule and reflecting the relatively high level of education among urban dwellers, many people in Rangoon also speak English as a second language. While many South Asians left the country after independence, there is still a significant South Asian population in Rangoon, and most of the Indians, Pakistanis, and Bengalis speak their own native tongues as well as Burmese and English. There is also a Chinese minority in the city.

HISTORY

The Origin of the City. The site of the present city of Rangoon was originally a Mon village named Dagon, located on the eastern bank of the Yangon River. It served as an important place of pilgrimage because of its *zedi* (*cedi*), or shrine, known as Shwe-Dagon Paya, which was believed to contain a number of Buddha relics. As Burma became increasingly involved in the Indian Ocean trade from the late 16th century, the main trading port was located at Syriam (Thanlyin), on the eastern bank of the Yangon River. In 1599, the kingdom of Arakan (which occupied a portion of southwestern Burma) placed Syriam in the hands of a Portuguese mercenary named Felipe de Brito y Nicote, who served as their trade representative. He allied himself with the Mon (whose kingdom occupied a large portion of southeastern Burma) in their war with the Burmese (who ruled central Burma), and was killed by the Burmese in 1613. Syriam remained the Irrawaddy delta's main port until it was destroyed by the Burmese king Alaung-hpaya in 1756, as part of his conquest of southern Burma. Earlier, the Burmese had built a large temple complex over the original Shwe-Dagon shrine across the river from Syriam. In 1755 King Alaung-hpaya built a new town at Dagon, which he named Yangon. With the destruction of Syriam, Yangon assumed the role as the primary port and international trading center in the delta.

Yangon was the scene of intense fighting during the First Anglo-Burmese War. The British occupied the town in 1824, but returned it to Burmese hands in 1826. Much of Yangon was destroyed by fire in 1841. It was rebuilt, but suffered considerable damage during the Second Anglo-Burmese War in 1852. After the war, Yangon and the surrounding area became British territory. Yangon was renamed Rangoon by the British. The city was rebuilt along plans designed by a member of the British engineering corps, Lieutenant Fraser. The new city was laid out in a chessboard fashion, with wide roads running in north-south and east-west directions. Norman Lewis, writing in the early 1950s, perhaps a little unkindly described the city as "imperial and rectilinear . . . built by a people who refused to compromise with the East [with] wide, straight, shadeless streets, with much solid bank-architecture of vaguely Grecian inspiration." The city was the administrative and economic center of British-controlled territory in Burma. In 1862 southern Burma officially became a British colony, with Rangoon serving as its administrative center. Rangoon remained the capital of a now-unified Burma following the British conquest of Upper Burma in 1886.

Under British rule, Burma was transformed into an export-oriented state, with Rangoon serving as the commercial and trading center for the colony. Thus, in addition to various government buildings, the city was home to numerous commercial enterprises and boasted a busy port. One early-20th-century visitor described the port thus: "Moored to the wharves or, anchored in midstream, are a surprisingly large number of ocean steamers . . . . Other ships, steam tugs, and lighters, and a multitude of sampans and small sailing craft add to the general effect of bustling commerce." The primary items being exported were rice and teak. Rangoon was badly damaged by an earthquake in 1930, but was soon rebuilt once more. It suffered damage once again during World War II, when Burma was occupied by the Japanese.

Upon gaining independence from Britain in 1948, the national government of Burma retained Rangoon as the capital. Postwar instability, however, meant that the character of the city remained distinctly colonial, with relatively little new construction taking place. Norma Bixler provides a description of the city in the early 1960s: "Rangoon, with its 800,000 people, may be smaller and less cosmopolitan than the capital cities of its neighbors in India and Thailand, but it is nevertheless a large city and a capital and has about it the air of being the center of things, which a capital possesses . . . . The center of the city was not only a city of shops and public buildings, but of residences. Three- or four-story buildings had shops on the first floor and apartments on the floors above; people liked living in the heart of things."

Following General Ne Win's coup in 1962, Burma was largely closed to the outside world, and private commerce was suppressed by the new Revolutionary Council. The character of Rangoon changed as a result, with a decline in port traffic and the overall sharp drop in commercial activity. This situation changed little until the 1990s, when, starting in 1992, a degree of economic liberalization allowed for the reemergence of private enterprise. The result has been a growth in the construction of new buildings (modest by Asian standards, but significant for Myanmar) and in the amount of vehicular traffic on the roads.

Migration: Past and Present. The village of Dagon and its vicinity was originally inhabited by Mon, a Mon-Khmer-speaking people who settled in this area prior to the Burmese. After the area was conquered by the Burmese and the new town of Yangon was founded in 1755, Burmese came to make up most of inhabitants. The coming of British rule in 1852 changed the character of the growing city dramatically. It quickly lost most of ists Burmese character and assumed more of a British-Indian atmosphere. Talbot Kelly's observations are fairly typical: "On landing, the first impression received is the *Indian* character of the place . . . . The Burman seems crowded out here." The other group that Kelly mentions are the Chinese. As Kelly himself notes, there were in fact many Burmese living in the city, but they were little in evidence "on the bustling quayside and business streets."

Census figures from the British period bear out Kelly's observations. The 1931 census reported that more than half of the population of Rangoon were Indian. This so-called Indian population, however, was itself a very heterogeneous one, both ethnically and in terms of class. This ethnic category included people from all over South Asia, including not only a wide variety of Hindus, but also Sikhs, Tamils, Bengalis, and so forth. At the top were the Chettiars, a class of bankers originally from Madras. The Indians (and Chinese) also constituted an important middle class of merchants, traders, and landowners. In fact, much of Rangoon was owned by Indians (in addition, they paid more than half of the municipal taxes). When the British administration sought to raise money to rebuild Rangoon after 1852, it did so largely by selling land, and the main buyers were Indians. Even much of the city's lower classes consisted of Indians. Most Indian laborers entered Burma via Rangoon's port. Some remained in the city, while others moved out into the countryside to work.

Besides the Indians, the other most significant groups living in Rangoon were Europeans, Eurasians, and Chinese. The number of Europeans (mainly English) was quite small, but they included most of the colony's administrative and managerial elite. Close to this group was a small Eurasian population that also held posts in the colonial government and in British firms. The Chinese were especially important around the waterfront, and much of the river trade was in their hands. The Burmese population included a white-collar middle class. This group consisted of Burmese who from the 1870s onward had taken advantage of British colonial rule to leave their villages to attend school and move into many of the newly created salaried and professional positions available in Rangoon and other large towns. For the most part, each of these ethnic groups lived in residentially distinct areas.

An estimated half of Burma's Indian population fled the country in 1942 when it was invaded by Japan (about 500,000 out of just over 1 million). Immediately after the war, there was some migration of Indians to Burma once again, but both the governments of India and Burma discouraged the flow of immigrants (especially unskilled laborers). Thus, the 1953 census revealed that there were only 40,396 Indians and Pakistanis (that is, Bengalis) out of a total population of 737,079. The European and Eurasian population of Rangoon had also declined as a result of the war and national independence after the war. Architecturally, the city retained an Anglo-Indian look, but by the 1950s its population was largely Burmese. This became even more the case after 1962, when most remaining Europeans left, as did more of the remaining Indians.

INFRASTRUCTURE

Public Buildings, Public Works, and Residences. Most of the city's public buildings date from the British period. There are also numerous other buildings throughout the city dating from the colonial period, including the Strand Hotel, which was originally built in 1896 and renovated in the 1990s. There are a number of important public markets in Rangoon. The largest of these is the Theingyi Zei (*zei* meaning market in Burmese). Another large market is the Bogyoke Aung San Market (formerly known as the Scott Market), which was originally built in the early 20th century.

Many of the residences in the inner city date from the colonial era and include crowded apartments and shop-houses, especially in the commercial areas, as well as rambling colonial mansions, some on relatively large plots of land. There are also more or less traditional wood and bamboo houses toward the outskirts of the city, as well as more modern looking brick houses of various size.

Politics and City Services. Rangoon is the national capital and the center of national politics. This has meant that the city has experienced a great deal of politically generated turmoil over the years. Among the most dramatic disturbances in recent years were antigovernment riots that took place in 1988 and left around 3,000 people dead. Rangoon is home to Nobel laureate and leader of the political opposition Aung San Suu Kyi, who has been under house arrest since 1989.

The city itself is administered by an appointed city committee that has between 7 and 15 members. Its chair also serves as mayor. The city is divided into townships. It has been the custom for neighborhoods to function somewhat along village lines, with a recognized headman and communal responsibility for many local affairs.

Educational System. Primary education is free in Myanmar, although the system of education has deteriorated badly since 1962. There is a shortage of trained teachers, and many families cannot afford to send their children to school. Nationally less than 30% of children complete primary school, although the percentage is higher in urban areas such as Rangoon. In recent years United Nations agencies have initiated programs aimed at improving primary education standards, but progress has been limited. Primary education is also available through monasteries. Most of the country's higher-education institutions are in Rangoon. Many of these were closed by the regime in 1996, although Yangon University (formerly Rangoon University) and Yangon Institute of Technology (formerly Rangoon Institute of Technology) have been allowed to operate a few programs of a largely technical nature. There are a number of small private schools offering training in business, computer operations, and foreign languages. There is also a Buddhist university that is allowed to operate.

Transportation System. The city has a public bus system that covers most of the metropolitan area, although the buses tend to be decades old and are often overcrowded. There are also numerous trishas, known locally as *saiq-ka,* as well as licensed taxicabs. The townships to the north of the city can be reached by train from the central train station. Ferries cross the Yangon River to Dala and small flat-bottomed boats (sampans) carry passengers along the river.

CULTURAL AND SOCIAL LIFE

Distinctive Features of the City's Cultures. Rangoon exhibits much less evidence of globalization than do many other cities in Asia. This is changing, but much less than elsewhere in Asia. Rangoon continues to exhibit some of the cultural features that developed during the colonial era. There are far fewer Indians and Chinese in the city today than there were in former times, and they no longer live in distinct quarters of Rangoon, yet they continue to form somewhat distinct communities within the city. Taking the Chinese community, for example, Rangoon still has a Chinatown that is located near the riverfront. The city's so-called iron bazaar is located in this area, along with an active night market. Nearby, many Chinese can be seen carrying out tai chi exercises in the morning in Mahabandoola Gardens. There are a variety of Chinese temples, such as the Hokkien Association's Kheng Hock Keong Temple, which serve as important gathering places for Chinese residents of the city who come to worship and socialize.

But the dominant culture of the city is Burmese. Urban Burmese culture in some ways is surprisingly cosmopolitan given the relative isolation of the country since 1962. Nevertheless, contact with the outside world remains relatively restricted, and it is largely an inward-looking society. For members of Rangoon's lower classes in particular, life still bears many characteristics of the village. Beyond activities necessary to make a living, family, neighbors, friends, and Buddhism remain the focal points of most people's lives. Almost all ethnic Burmese are Buddhists (albeit a Buddhism with many local folk elements), and Buddhist beliefs and practices play an important role in people's lives. Even in Rangoon, most young males reside in monasteries for a time, and many men and women eventually become monks (*pongyi* in Burmese) or nuns (*dasasila* or *thilashin* in Burmese). Sgwedagon Paya in Rangoon is considered to be the most sacred site in Burma by the country's Buddhists, and virtually all Burmese hope to visit the temple complex at least once in their life.

Cuisine. The dominant cuisines of Rangoon are those of its Burmese, Chinese, and Indian inhabitants. In terms of restaurants, the highest class of restaurants tend to be Chinese. These range from the Palace, which is the oldest Chinese restaurant in the city, to a number of Chinese restaurants in Rangoon's newer upscale hotels. While Cantonese cuisine dominates, the city also has restaurants featuring a variety of regional Chinese cuisines (for example, Hokkien and Sichuan). While the Indian population of the city has declined in number since World War II, there are still many Indian restaurants in Rangoon, ranging from relatively fancy ones to very modest establishments. These also feature various regional cuisines from India, with North Indian and South Indian styles being especially popular. In the past, Burmese cuisine was found mainly in people's homes or in modest food stalls, but in recent years there have been a growing number of restaurants in the city featuring Burmese food. The city also has a few restaurants serving food of some of the country's ethnic minorities, especially the Shan. In the past, Western-style food was found mainly in a handful of the hotels that catered to foreign visitors, such as the Strand Grill in the Strand Hotel. The relative opening of Burma to the outside world in the 1990s is reflected in the appearance of a variety of Western-style restaurants around the city—ranging from relatively fancy French restaurants to such establishments as Charlie Fried Chicken, Rodeo Bar & Grill, Burger Buster, Pizza Corner, and J' Donuts—as well as restaurants serving styles of food from neighboring countries such as Thailand and Vietnam.

Ethnic, Class, and Religious Diversity. Today, the vast majority of Rangoon's inhabitants are ethnic Burmese. Nevertheless, there is still a visible Indian and Chinese population (including a section of the city still known as Chinatown). The class structure of the city reflects political conditions in Myanmar. The elite consists largely of those who run the regime, and members of their families. Economic reforms since the early 1990s have allowed the emergence of a small commercial elite that is not so directly a part of the regime, such as sometime city resident and prominent drug lord Khun Sa, who, along with others who have profited from the narcotics trade, has invested heavily in commercial property in the city. There is also a relatively small professional and commercial middle class. The professions are largely in the hands of Burmese, while a good deal of private commerce is still run by Indians and Chinese, although an increasing number of Burmese are seeking to take advantage of the more liberal economic atmosphere and can be seen engaging in business as well.

The vast majority of ethnic Burmese are Buddhists. As a result, the population of Rangoon is mainly Buddhist. The city's minorities, however, tend to follow other religions. Many Indians in Rangoon are Hindu, but some are Christian and Sikh. The Church of England is now called the Church of Myanmar, and its followers are served by a large cathedral in Rangoon. There are also Catholic and other Protestant churches in the city with small congregations. The country's Moslem minority lives mainly elsewhere in the country, but there are some Moslems in Rangoon. The Chinese population includes Buddhists and Taoists. The largest Chinese temple is the Kheng Hock Temple, which is supported by the Hokkien Association. At one time, there were more than 2,000 Jews in Rangoon (from a variety of backgrounds), but at present there are only a few dozen, who continue to maintain a synagogue and a cemetery.

Family and Other Social Support Systems. Family is very important to the Burmese, including those living in Rangoon, and is the most important institution that provides social support. The Burmese reckon descent bilaterally. Upon marriage, a newly wed couple may reside with the parents of one partner for a time (often with the parents of the wife), but usually they soon establish their own household. The nuclear family is the core of the domestic unit, but it is common for it to include extended-family members as well. This may include unmarried siblings, widowed parents, or a variety of more-distant unmarried or widowed male and female relatives. The husband is the nominal head of the household, but the wife retains considerable authority as well.

Beyond the family, for most people the most important source of social support comes from religious institutions. Throughout Rangoon, religious centers are popular gathering places—not only for worship, but also for socializing, seeking advice, and seeking assistance in time of need. Especially for those closely associated with the regime, the government also provides many forms of support. This is particularly evident in the case of the military, and families of those in the military have access to many special services and facilities.

Work and Commerce. The government is by far the single largest employer in Rangoon. The city is home to all of the country's 30 ministries. The military is also a large employer in the city. Myanmar has relatively little industry. Processing and manufacturing account for only a little over 9% of gross domestic product, and employ only about 8% of the labor force. Much of this is concentrated in and around Rangoon.

Private enterprise was suppressed for decades, but since the early 1990s has been allowed to grow. This is evident in Rangoon, in its public markets, its numerous street vendors, and private shops and offices selling a wide range of items and offering many services that before were under government control or rarely available to the public. Evidence of the change can be seen in gem trading. In 1969 the regime banned private exploration and mining for gems and sought to control gem trading. The centerpiece of the latter was the gems, jade, and pearls emporium held three times a year in Rangoon, which was attended by a select group of foreign gem buyers. The government allowed some licensed dealers to sell gems to foreigners, but much of the gem trade went underground, and the bulk of gems were smuggled out of the country. In 1995 the regime once again allowed private citizens to trade in gems. Gems are now widely sold in public in Rangoon, and the need for a black market has declined.

The tourist industry has become a much more important part of Rangoon's economy over the past decade. In the past, all government hotels catering to foreigners were government-owned. There were few such hotels, and services were minimal. By 1999 there were only 28 state-owned hotels in the country out of a total of 492. In contrast, there were 439 hotels that were owned by private nationals. The growth of such hotels has been highly concentrated in Rangoon and Mandalay—136 of the new private hotels are located in Rangoon. In addition to hotels, there are many new related businesses, such as travel agencies, tour companies, and restaurants catering to tourists.

Arts and Recreation. The most popular art form in Rangoon is the *pwe*, or show. The *pwe* commonly combine various types of music, dance, and drama. They take place at night and can last for the entire night. They are held at fairs, religious festivals, weddings, funerals, sporting events, and just about any other type of public event. They typically include performances based on legends and Buddhist epics, comedy skits, singing, dancing, music performances, and sometimes a puppet show.

Tea shops play an important role in Rangoon's social life. Young Burmese in particular commonly congregate for hours at tea shops. The large zoological garden (which includes a playground and miniature train), the National Aquarium, and the grounds around the city's two large lakes (Kandawgyi and Inya) are popular spots for city residents on weekends.

Rangoon is an important center for classical arts in Myanmar. The National Theatre in Rangoon stages traditional, Thai-derived dance-dramas that tend to be based on stories from the Indian epic *Ramayana.* Short versions of these dance-dramas are also staged at some of the city's hotels. Rangoon also boasts a small but active community of artists, whose works can be seen in a number of galleries.

QUALITY OF LIFE

Myanmar is one of the world's poorest countries, and it is ruled by one of the most oppressive regimes. The standard of living of Rangoon's inhabitants is in many respects better than that of people living elsewhere in the country, but on the whole, they are certainly poor by comparison with urban dwellers in many other cities around the world. There is, of course, an elite that lives very comfortably, and a small middle class that in some ways has seen its standard of living improve a little in recent years.

With the exception of those working with the regime or benefiting from its policies, most residents of Rangoon obviously care little for their government. But rather than risk brutal treatment at the hands of the regime, most people try to get on with their lives as best they can. Economic liberalization has made this a little easier in some respects, but many uncertainties remain. Residents of Rangoon, along with their fellow citizens, must endure the regime's oppressive policies. People are subject to arbitrary arrest, and detainees are often tortured. Residents on occasion have been forcibly relocated at the whim of government authorities. Periodically, they may also be pressed into service as laborers for civic projects.

FUTURE OF THE CITY

The future of Rangoon will depend in part on relations between the Myanmar regime and the outside world, and in part on whether or not there are further internal political and economic reforms. Reforms initiated in 1992 led to an initial miniboom in building and a spurt of growth in the commercial sector, but since this initial impetus, further change has come slowly. This in part reflects the economic downturn in the region as a whole that began in the late 1990s, but also the impact of serious economic deterioration of the national economy as a whole over the past few years, and indecision on the part of the regime about what steps to take in the face of ongoing economic and political problems.

BIBLIOGRAPHY

Andrew, E. J. L., *Indian Labour in Rangoon* (Oxford University Press 1933).

Bixler, Norma, *Burmese Journey* (Antioch Press 1967).

Chakravarti, N. R., *The Indian Minority in Burma: The Rise and Decline of an Immigrant Community* (Oxford University Press 1971).

Kelly, Talbot, *Burma: The Land and the People* (J. B. Millet 1910).

Lewis, Norman, *Golden Earth: Travels in Burma* (Charles Scribner's Sons 1952).

Pearn, B. R., *History of Rangoon* (ABM Press 1939).

MICHAEL C. HOWARD